❧ Praise for *1,000 Italian Recipes* by Michele Scicolone ❧

"Michele Scicolone has written the best all-encompassing Italian cookbook to hit the shelves in years. Her recipes are accessible and beautifully written and the result is a masterpiece of traditional and nontraditional Italian cookery. This tome is pure inspiration for me, and its mouth-watering infinity is the crowning jewel of Michele's already brilliant output."

—**Mario Batali,** *chef-owner of Babbo, Lupa, Esca, Otto, and Casa Mono (New York City) and host of the Food Network's "Molto Mario"*

"For the past year I had not seen much of Michele around town, and then a two-inch-thick manuscript landed on my desk. It was *1,000 Italian Recipes* by Michele Scicolone, and what a great collection of recipes it is. Italy is an endless resource for recipes and Michele in *1,000 Italian Recipes* has captured some of the best with detailed instructions and informative prose. A must-have for any serious Italian cook. Brava, Michele!"

—**Lidia Matticchio Bastianich,** *chef, restaurateur, cookbook author, host of public television's "Lidia's Italian-American Kitchen"*

"The wide range of recipes and wealth of information on Italian food in *1,000 Italian Recipes* confirms why Michele Scicolone was the only chef we would go to when we wanted to do our *Sopranos Family Cookbook*."

—**David Chase,** *creator and executive producer, HBO's "The Sopranos"*

"Michele Scicolone leaves nothing behind in this one-stop luscious library of Italian recipes. All your favorites in one book!"

—**Mary Ann Esposito,** *host of public television's "Ciao Italia" and author of* Ciao Italia in Tuscany

"In the day and age of single subject cookbooks, it's refreshing to see the amazing compilation that Michele has put together. Real Italian Food with Real Flavor from Real Italian Places. I look forward to making good use of this book in my kitchen for years to come. I'm sure you will enjoy it too. Salute."

—**Michael Chiarello,** *chef, author, founder of NapaStyle, and host for Fine Living and the Food Network*

"Nowhere else will you find such a depth and wealth of traditional and contemporary dishes, all written in Michele's concise and crystal-clear style...If you can have only one Italian cookbook on your shelf, this should be it. If you think you have too many Italian cookbooks, you haven't flipped through this one yet."

—**Arthur Schwartz,** *host of radio's "Food Talk" and author of* Naples At Table

"Everyone who knows me knows I love to eat. Show me recipes this good, and easy, and I can't hold back. I've already planned 1,000 lunches, 1,000 dinners, and 1,000 midnight snacks."

—**Steven R. Schirripa,** *author of* A Goomba's Guide to Life *and Bobby Bacala on HBO's "The Sopranos"*

"I have always considered Michele Scicolone a great cook and an outstanding food writer. Now, with her amazing new book, she shares with the reader the simplicity and authenticity of 1,000 splendid Italian dishes. Her recipes, which use wholesome, fresh ingredients, are straightforward and easy to follow. This book will be an asset to anyone who loves Italian food."

—**Biba Caggiano,** *author of seven best-selling cookbooks and chef-owner of BIBA restaurant, Sacramento*

❧ Dedication ❧

To my mother, Louise Balsamo Scotto,
and my father, Michael Scotto,
who introduced me to the importance and
pleasure of eating well and set me on my path.

1,000 ITALIAN
Recipes

MICHELE SCICOLONE

WILEY

Wiley Publishing, Inc.

For general information on our other products and services or to obtain technical support please contact our Customer Care Department within the U.S. at 800-762-2974, outside the U.S. at 317-572-3993 or fax 317-572-4002.

Wiley also publishes its books in a variety of electronic formats. Some content that appears in print may not be available in electronic books.

ISBN 0-7645-6676-8

Publisher: Natalie Chapman

Editor: Linda Ingroia

Assistant Editor: Adam Kowit

Production Editor: David Sassian

Production Assistant: Ava Wilder

Cover Design: Jeff Faust

Interior Design and Layout: Holly Wittenberg

Manufacturing Buyer: Kevin Watt

Cover Illustration: Elizabeth Traynor

Manufactured in the United States of America

10 9 8 7 6 5 4 3 2 1
First Edition

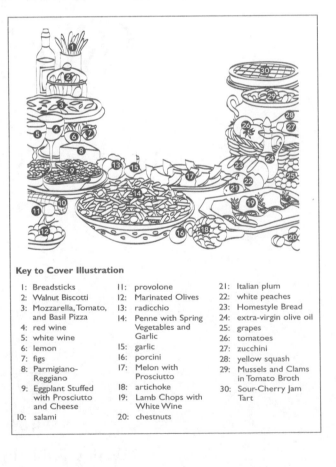

Key to Cover Illustration

1: Breadsticks
2: Walnut Biscotti
3: Mozzarella, Tomato, and Basil Pizza
4: red wine
5: white wine
6: lemon
7: figs
8: Parmigiano-Reggiano
9: Eggplant Stuffed with Prosciutto and Cheese
10: salami
11: provolone
12: Marinated Olives
13: radicchio
14: Penne with Spring Vegetables and Garlic
15: garlic
16: porcini
17: Melon with Prosciutto
18: artichoke
19: Lamb Chops with White Wine
20: chestnuts
21: Italian plum
22: white peaches
23: Homestyle Bread
24: extra-virgin olive oil
25: grapes
26: tomatoes
27: zucchini
28: yellow squash
29: Mussels and Clams in Tomato Broth
30: Sour-Cherry Jam Tart

Contents

(continues)

Acknowledgments

Tante grazie, "many thanks," to the friends, family members, cooking-school students, and acquaintances who helped me with this book, either by supplying me with information or recipes, giving me ideas, correcting my Italian, sampling my experiments, or offering encouragement or professional advice.

Anne Amendolara Nurse, Loretta Balsamo, and Millie Castagliola are my culinary muses, and I love to talk with them about traditional foods. Thanks to Diane Darrow and Tom Maresca for sharing great wines, great meals, and their Italian cookbook library with me; Arthur Schwartz for his vast knowledge of Italian food; and friends in Italy for their hospitality and generosity, including Anna Tasca Lanza, Marina Thompson, Daniele Cernili, Livia Colantonio, Paolo Nodari, Paola di Mauro, and many others. In the United States, thank you to Mauro Mafrici, Nicola Marzovilla, Dora Marzovilla, Domenica Marzovilla Frankland, Tony May and the Gruppo Ristoratori Italiani, Augusto Marchini and the Italian Trade Commission, Tony Mazzola, Phil and Jackie Cicconi, Maurizio De Rosa, Donatella Arpaia, Francesco Rabellino, Luciano Castiello, Russell Bellanca of Alfredo the Original of Rome, Peggy Tagliarino, Lars Leicht, and Pauline Wasserman. Judith Weber is not only my agent but also a dear friend and adviser and a wonderful cook with clear insights.

At Wiley, a big thank you to my editor, Linda Ingroia, for suggesting this book in the first place and for her careful editing. A book as large as this requires a lot of help to pull together. Thank you to Adam Kowit for thoughtful queries, David Sassian for shepherding the book through its many stages, Holly Wittenberg for an elegant book design, Jeff Faust for his art direction, and Elizabeth Kurtzman for a beautiful cover illustration.

As always, thank you to Charles Scicolone, my husband, for his encouragement, enthusiasm, wisdom, and support.

Introduction

I grew up in an Italian-American home. Most of the time we were like any other family in our neighborhood, but at mealtimes our Italian side took over.

We ate aged cheeses, wrinkled oil-cured black olives, spicy salami, and prosciutto. Fresh ingredients were essential, and we consumed lots of vegetables—stuffed, fried, and in soups and pastas. The bread was bought fresh daily from an Italian bakery, and it was crisp and chewy. Dessert meant perfect seasonal fresh fruit. Our coffee was espresso made in a little silver stove-top pot called a *machinetta*. Everyone in the family cooked, and I learned about combining flavors and cooking techniques by watching and helping my parents and other relatives. I learned that cooking was fun and sharing food with others one of life's great pleasures.

Holidays and special occasions meant a house full of friends and family. Preparations began days in advance, and we all participated. Guests would bring special desserts from prized bakeries or their favorite homemade dishes, such as Struffoli (Honey Balls, pages 610–611), Cannoli (page 616–617), or a grand Zuppa Inglese (Italian Trifle, page 521), and wines that were more distinctive than the jug wines we drank every day.

When I married in 1970, my husband and I took our first trip to Italy. We marveled at the architecture of Rome, the awesome beauty of Venice, and the magnificent art of Florence. We also discovered that there was far more to Italian food and wine than we had experienced back home. My grandparents were from the Naples area, and my husband's were from Sicily. Until we began to travel, our Italian culinary experience was pretty much limited to the foods of those southern regions, often reinterpreted over the years and filtered through the availability of ingredients in America.

When we traveled in Italy, we ate risotto in Milan, white truffles in Piedmont, and fresh egg pasta in Emilia-Romagna. We boldly sampled horsemeat in the Veneto and learned to eat sea urchins in Puglia. We experienced the German-accented dishes of northeastern Trentino–Alto Adige and the Middle Eastern–spiced cooking of Sicily.

When we returned home, we added these foods to our family favorites and enhanced the experience with great Italian wines.

I became fascinated by the different regions of Italy and why and how their culinary traditions differed. Until the 1860s, what is now Italy had been a group of separate kingdoms, each with its own history, geography, and cultural influences. Language and monetary systems were different, too.

Sicily, for example, had been invaded countless times and ruled by the Greeks, Arabs, Normans, and Romans, all of whom left their traces on its culinary traditions. *Cassata*, a very sweet layered ricotta and sponge cake (page 578) that is the pride of Sicily, is a vestige of Arab domination. Its name comes from the Arabic word *qas'ah*, for a deep terra cotta mold used to make the cake. The Arabs also introduced Sicily to cane sugar. While the rest of Italy used honey or cooked grape must—which have distinctive flavors of their own—for sweetening, Sicilian bakers had neutral-tasting sugar, which revolutionized pastry making.

Naples was originally a Greek settlement that was later ruled by Spain and France. The city was originally called Neopolis by the Greeks, and it is said that they introduced a flatbread called *pitta* seasoned with herbs and oil that was a forerunner of the modern pizza. Portions of Trentino–Alto Adige and Friuli–Venezia Giulia were once part of the Austro-Hungarian Empire. German is the common language in Trentino, and popular recipes there and in Friuli include *gulasch*, made in many different ways. Geography and climate also helped to determine how people in the different regions ate. With its long, narrow shape, Italy has a variety of climates from cold and wet in the north to sunny, hot, and dry in the south. Though the Alps border the northernmost regions, there are wide, fertile plains and plenty of water across northern Italy for growing crops such as rice and corn and for raising cattle. Risotto and polenta are eaten more frequently than pasta in the north, and veal, butter, cow's milk cheeses, and cream are plentiful.

The south has stony, mountainous terrain that supports only a limited range of crops. Sheep graze on the rocky hillsides, and small plots of vegetables grow on every bit of arable soil. Pasta is made with flour and water. Olive, fig, and almond trees thrive in the hot sun. Lamb, goat, and pork are the most commonly eaten meats.

As if these physical, cultural, and historical differences were not enough to divide the regions, there were also the people themselves, who were reluctant to surrender their local customs as the country merged politically. Italy was finally united in 1864, though it took many, many years for the separate regions to begin to function together as one country. There are times when they still do not.

Today, improvements in transportation, education, and communication have blurred some of the regional characteristics. Though there are efforts to keep the old dialects alive, Italian children study the same curriculum and learn to speak standard Italian. Food customs are changing, too. Health- and fashion-conscious Italians are concerned about making a good appearance, and low-fat, low-calorie foods are becoming more available. Olive oil has replaced lard as one of the principal cooking fats.

Chain restaurants are everywhere, and young people in particular are attracted to them. In Rome, fast food eateries feature *insalata caprese,* the classic Italian tomato and mozzarella salad, as well as *macedonia*, Italian fruit salad, alongside the french fries and hamburgers on the menu, though the burgers seem to be gaining in popularity. Lunch hours are shorter, and many people make do with a sandwich or salad rather than the full meal at midday. Supermarkets are replacing open air markets, and the European Economic and Monetary Union has brought bureaucracy to the food supply, resulting in conformity, rules, and regulations that often are more concerned with efficiency than quality. Most women work, and few spend as much time cooking as they once did. Family-run restaurants with home cooking are disappearing as smaller families mean fewer people to work and maintain them.

Many Italians have been alarmed by these negative changes, and they are determined to reverse the trends. The government has taken steps to protect the good names of regional specialties such as cheeses and wines by passing laws that specify how and where they can be produced. In the past few years, several professional schools have opened to train chefs in classic Italian cooking. Organizations such as Slow Food publish scholarly papers, support research projects, and organize conferences so that the public can become involved. They are making good progress in holding back the trend toward globalization of foods like Parmigiano-Reggiano and balsamic vinegar, and hopefully a balance can be struck between tradition and change.

Fashions in cooking change and evolve as with anything else. On a recent trip, I noticed that rather than typical *aperitivi* such as Campari and soda or

Aperol, young Italians were enjoying predinner wine coolers made with fruit juices. Chinese and Japanese restaurants have proliferated in Italy, and Asian ingredients are turning up more frequently in many creative Italian restaurants. Sushi and raw fish dishes are very popular, especially in Milan. And more restaurants seem to be foregoing fresh fruit desserts in favor of cakes, ice cream, and other rich sweets. Rome, Florence, and many other cities are seeing a boom in wine bars that serve cheeses, *salumi*, and perhaps a few hot dishes along with wines by the glass.

Any collection of recipes is a reflection of the taste and experience of the writer and how he or she likes to cook and what he or she likes to eat. I have compiled the recipes in this book from a number of different sources. Many are old family recipes. Though I first learned to cook like my grandmothers and mother—with a handful of this, a pinch of that, and my own judgement—I have adapted these recipes to today's cooking style by giving specific information on ingredients, measurments, pan sizes, and cooking times. Others are recipes I have collected in my travels, either from friends who are good home cooks or from restaurants where I have eaten. Still others are recipes I have come across in Italian regional cookbooks and magazines. I've chosen and adapted recipes that would appeal to today's home cooks who are interested not only in authenticity but also in flavor, ease of preparation, variety, and health.

I have tried to create a balance between old favorites and contemporary recipes. Many traditional recipes are rich in fat. Where possible, I have reduced the fat without sacrificing flavor. Overall, I have tried to keep the recipes as close as possible to their Italian roots by using techniques I have observed in Italy. For example, most of the Italian cooks I know begin many cooking operations by adding olive oil to a cold pan, along with aromatics like onion and garlic. When the heat is turned on, the pan, oil, and aromatics warm up together so that the vegetables can slowly release their flavors into the oil. Adding oil and aromatics to a preheated pan increases the danger of burning the flavoring ingredients and decreases the time alotted for the vegetables to soften and flavor the oil. Pasta cooked al dente, firm to the bite—the way the Italians like it—is much more interesting to eat than the mushy overcooked pasta often served in the United States. On the other hand, I often serve meat, fish, and vegetables less well cooked than they do in Italy, because it better suits the ingredients we have in the United States. No recipe can compensate for differences in how animals are raised and butchered, varieties of fruits and vegetables, and availability of some ingredients.

As an old Italian adage declares, *A tavola si sta sempre in allegria* ("At the table, one is always happy"). I hope that you find joy and satisfaction in cooking and eating the Italian way.

The Italian Pantry

More than any other factor, Italian cooking relies on the quality of the ingredients to achieve its flavors. Making an effort to locate the right ingredients will pay off in the end result. Fortunately, most of the ingredients used in this book, such as the staples that follow, are now widely available. Look for stores in your area that sell an array of Italian foods, or check out the mail order sources listed in the back of this book (pages 625–626).

Amaretti

Crisp almond macaroons from Lombardy that have a pronounced bitter almond flavor. Serve them after a meal with coffee or crush them for use in desserts.

Anchovies

Although it is hard to convince anyone unfortunate enough to have only eaten dried out, salty anchovies on a pizza, good-quality anchovies add marvelous subtle flavor to many Italian dishes. These flavorful little fish are sold either packed in oil or in salt. Do not substitute anchovy paste, and avoid anchovies packed with capers.

Oil-packed anchovies filleted and ready to use are widely available in small tins or glass jars. Jarred anchovies are preferable, so that you can see that they are firm and plump and not crumbled because they are too old. Leftover anchovies can be refrigerated, topped off with additional oil in a small jar. Keeping leftovers covered in oil is important, as the anchovies dry out and lose flavor when exposed to air.

Salt-packed anchovies are not as widely available, and they do require cleaning. Their flavor is very good, though, and they are firm and plump. They come in large cans, and you can sometimes buy them by weight in Italian markets. Most often, though, you will need to buy the whole can.

To clean salted anchovies, rinse them well under cool water. Slit them open and separate the two fillets. Scrape off the skin and rinse out the bones and innards. The prepared fillets can be used in salads, stuffings, pasta, or marinated with garlic, parsley, oil, and vinegar as an antipasto.

Also available in many specialty markets are white anchovy fillets packed in vinegar. These have a delicate flavor and texture and are best rinsed and added to salads or eaten as the Italians do on slices of buttered bread.

Bread Crumbs

Leftover bread has many uses in the Italian kitchen, and one of the most important is bread crumbs. They should be made from day-old Italian or French bread. Cut them into chunks and grind them in a food processor or blender until fine. Spread the crumbs in a baking pan and bake, stirring occasionally, until lightly toasted, about 10 minutes.

Let cool completely and store in the refrigerator or freezer in an airtight container. Never substitute canned, ready-flavored bread crumbs.

Capers

These little green berries are actually the unopened flowers of a plant that grows wild around the Mediterranean. Some of the best capers come from the island of Pantelleria off the coast of Sicily. Fresh capers have a delicate flavor and a short season. They are rarely seen in stores in this country.

Most capers are imported preserved in salt or vinegar. Soak salted capers in warm water for several minutes. Rinse thoroughly and pat dry before using. Vinegared capers need just a quick rinse to remove some of the vinegar. Large capers are more flavorful and less costly than tiny capers. Capers add a tangy flavor to sauces, salads, and pastas.

Chiles

In parts of central and southern Italy, fresh and dried chiles are used for seasoning. Any variety of chile can be used. Italians use both the seeds and flesh of the chile, often passing the whole chiles around the table to be sliced as a garnish onto soup or pasta.

In the absence of fresh chiles, substitute tiny red dried chiles, which you can crush for extra spice or leave whole and remove before serving if you prefer less. Dried chiles sold in jars as crushed red pepper can also be used.

Keep in mind that the chiles, whether fresh or dried, are meant as an accent and should not overwhelm the flavors of the dish. They are used primarily in quick cooking dishes or as a garnish.

Garlic

Fresh garlic is an important flavoring in many Italian dishes, but not every dish should contain garlic. When it comes to garlic, more is not necessarily better. Except for a few dishes, Italian cooks use garlic in moderation.

Fresh garlic can be white, pink, or purple, depending on the variety. Look for cloves that are plump and free of mold. As garlic ages, the skin becomes yellowish, dry, and papery and the flavor intensifies. Store garlic in a cool, dry place.

Garlic should always be freshly prepared for a recipe. Do not use harsh dried garlic flakes or granules, or stale-tasting jarred garlic, either whole or prechopped.

To prepare garlic for cooking, break off as many cloves as you will need for the recipe. Lay the cloves on a cutting board and lay a large chef's knife on its side over the garlic. Smack the knife with the heel of your hand to crack open the skin. If you are chopping or slicing the garlic, cut off the stem end of the clove, which can be hard. The green shoot inside the garlic is fine to use. I do not remove it.

For maximum garlic flavor, chop it very fine. For a more subtle flavor, slice the garlic cloves. For just a hint of garlic, leave the cloves whole (or crush them slightly with the side of the knife) for cooking, then remove them from the pot before serving.

Garlic should be cooked until it is a light gold or deep gold, depending on the intensity of the flavor you want. Never allow garlic to turn dark brown, as the flavor becomes bitter.

Grating Cheeses

Various types of cheeses are used for grating in Italy, depending on the region and the dish. These cheeses are collectively known as *grana,* meaning "grainy." The three most popular varieties are Parmigiano-Reggiano, Grana Padano, and Pecorino Romano.

Though many cheeses are called "Parmesan," *Parmigiano-Reggiano* is the name of the genuine article, an aged cow's milk cheese made exclusively in Italy around the cities of Parma and Reggio Emilia. Genuine Parmigiano-Reggiano is rich and nutty and perfect for eating as an hors d'oeuvre or snack as well as grating on soups and pasta.

Always buy whole chunks of Parmigiano-Reggiano, never grated pieces, so that you can be sure of what you are buying. Also, grated cheese dries out quickly and loses its flavor. The rind of the cheese has the name impressed into it so that it is easily recognizable. The cheese should be a creamy golden color and the rind slightly darker.

Grana Padano is also made from cow's milk. The flavor is slightly milder than Parmigiano and the color is lighter. Otherwise it can be used in similar ways.

Pecorino Romano is the preferred grating cheese of southern Italy. *Pecora* is Italian for "sheep," and this cheese is made from sheep's milk. Pecorino

Romano is very white in color and has no discernible rind. It is sharper and saltier than Parmigiano and is particularly good with vegetables, lamb, and pasta dressed with vegetables or southern Italian ragùs.

Other cheeses that are used for grating are *ricotta salata* (aged salted ricotta), Asiago, and *caciocavallo*. Sicilians have a caramel-colored, smoked pressed ricotta that is very distinctive, though I have never seen it sold in the United States.

Cheese should always be grated at the last moment. A hand-cranked mill known as a Mouli grater does an excellent job, as does an old-fashioned box grater. Rasp-type graters are good, though they grate the cheese a little too fine for my taste. Large quantities of cheese can be ground in a food processor with a steel blade, but the texture is more like little pellets than grated cheese.

Note that Italians sprinkle grated cheese on foods sparingly. They rarely use it in dishes made with fish or seafood, where it might mask the delicate flavor, though there are exceptions.

Herbs

Parsley is the essential herb in Italian cooking. It is used in every region of Italy in a wide range of dishes, from fish to meatballs, stews, sauces, and vegetables. The preferred variety has dark green flat leaves and is sometimes sold here as Italian parsley. Its fresh color and taste lifts the flavor of dishes that it is added to without overwhelming them.

Parsley should always be fresh. Dried parsley has little flavor, and what flavor it has is unpleasant. Fortunately, parsley keeps very well in the refrigerator. Look for a very fresh bunch with no yellow or wilted leaves. Trim 3/4-inch from the base of the stems and insert the bunch in a jar with a couple of inches of warm water. Invert a plastic bag over the leaves and place the jar in the refrigerator. Change the water in the jar every day or two and the parsley should last at least a week.

Basil is another staple herb in Italian cooking. Like parsley, it should only be used in its fresh state

and not dried. Fresh basil is widely available in supermarkets all year round, and it is easy to grow in most areas in a pot on a window sill. Basil is a very tender plant and does not keep as long as parsley or herbs with woody stems like rosemary and sage. I wrap fresh basil in paper towels, place them in a plastic bag and store them in the refrigerator. They last for two to three days. If you have a large bunch to use up, puree it with olive oil and store it in the freezer in small containers, or toss the leaves in a salad. As a last resort, I rinse and pat dry the basil leaves, wrap them in plastic, and store them in the freezer. When I need a few fresh leaves for a sauce, I toss them in still frozen. The leaves blacken and become limp, but they are good in a pinch, adding close to fresh flavor to cooked dishes. I usually prefer to add basil at the end of the cooking time to better capture its fresh essence, but I sometimes add it as the food is cooking for another level of flavor.

Rosemary and *sage* are important herbs for cooking roasts, game, stews, and beans. Sage leaves and melted sweet butter make one of the quickest and best sauces for fresh pasta. Both herbs are best when fresh, and they keep well in the refrigerator if kept in a container that allows air to circulate around the leaves so that they do not get wet and moldy. Both also freeze well tightly wrapped. Dried rosemary and sage are good for backups, though once the jar is open, their flavor is good for only six months.

Oregano and *marjoram* have a similar flavor and appearance, though you are more likely to find oregano used in southern Italy and marjoram in the north, especially in Liguria. Oregano is the stronger of the two, useful for tomato sauces and with fish. It is almost always used in its dried state.

Marjoram is less assertive than oregano, with a floral and slightly lemony flavor. Fresh marjoram is preferable, though not so easy to find, unless you grow it yourself. Use marjoram for fish and seafood, vegetables, pasta stuffing, and sauces.

Thyme, tarragon, and *mint* are also used in Italian cooking, mostly in regional recipes.

Olive Oil

Olive trees grow in Italy as far north as Liguria and the Veneto all the way south through Sicily. Not so long ago, it was easy to divide Italian kitchens into the butter-using north and olive oil south, but today cooks all over Italy use olive oil both for reasons of health and good flavor.

Olive oils are classified by the way they are processed and the amount of oleic acid they contain. Oil extracted without the use of solvents and with less than 1 percent oleic acid is the best quality and is classified as "extra virgin." The flavor of the oil will vary according to where the olives were grown, the types of olives used, and their quality and ripeness. Some oils have fruity flavors, while others are more vegetal or herbal. To find one that you like, buy small bottles of a few brands and sample them before you commit to a larger container. Olive oil should be used within a year of the time it was produced. The flavor fades as it ages, so look for brands marked with the year they were produced.

I use extra-virgin olive oil for most cooking and for salad dressings and usually have more than one variety open at a time so that I can match it to the flavor of the dish I am preparing. At one time, the standard advice was not to cook with extra-virgin olive oil, because its flavor was compromised by heating. But I find that extra-virgin olive oil enhances most foods, whether cooked or uncooked, and contributes authentic Italian flavor.

Olive oil should be kept in a dark container in a cool place. If you buy it in a large container, transfer it to a small jar or can to minimize exposure to oxygen, which will eventually cause the oil to turn rancid.

It is not necessary to refrigerate olive oil, unless you have a large quantity that you will not be able to use in a short amount of time. Chilled, the oil will become cloudy and semi-solid. It will liquefy and turn clear again after a few minutes at room temperature.

Olive Paste

This is a bottled product that is made up simply of finely chopped olives and olive oil. It is convenient for sauces or as a spread for crostini. There are both black and green versions, and some can be rather strong. Olive paste keeps well for a long time in the refrigerator if covered with a layer of olive oil.

Olives

Both black and green cured olives are eaten in Italy, and they are frequently used in cooking. Green Sicilian olives are cracked before curing and are often flavored with garlic, fennel, or chile. Black olives are either brine- or oil-cured. Gaeta olives are brownish black, round, and meaty. Wrinkled, glossy black oil-cured olives have a chocolaty, bitter flavor. Ligurian olives are small and black. Large green or black Cerignola olives come from Puglia and are rather bland.

It is not always easy to tell where olives originate, so just be sure to use a flavorful olive. Olives should be whole (assuming they are not the type that are cracked open in processing), firm, and meaty, without discolorations. Store them in the refrigerator for up to two weeks.

An easy way to pit olives is to place them on a flat surface, lay the side of a large knife blade on top facing away from you, and smack the blade with the heel of your hand. The olives will break open and the pits can be removed.

Pancetta

This is the cured but not smoked Italian version of bacon. The meat comes from the belly, or *pancia,* of the pig; it is cured with salt and spices, rolled up pinwheel fashion, and wrapped in a casing. Sliced pancetta can be eaten as is or used to wrap small birds or other foods to keep them moist as they cook. Chopped pancetta is used to flavor soups, sauces, stews, and many other dishes. Sliced pancetta freezes well and in fact is easier to chop when it is partially frozen.

Tomatoes

There is nothing quite like the flavor of vine-ripened fresh tomatoes at the height of the summer, but since their season is short, we must rely on canned tomatoes for stews and sauces much of the year. Good canned tomatoes are far better than out-of-season fresh for cooking. Italians use canned tomatoes all the time. Try several brands of plum or pear-shaped tomatoes. Avoid those that are packed in thick, sweetened puree or that are hard and greenish, indicating that they are underripe.

At one time the designation San Marzano was an indication that the tomatoes were of high quality and grown and packed in the small town of that name near Naples. The laws have been changed, and this is no longer a reliable indicator.

When I want a fresh tomato flavor and texture outside of the summer season, I often use grape or cherry tomatoes, which can be quite good even in the dead of winter.

Tomato paste is useful for bolstering tomato flavors in sauces, soups, and stews. I use the kind sold in tubes like toothpaste. Not only does it have a sweet and less metallic flavor than do some canned tomato pastes, it is also easy to use in small amounts and then recapped and stored.

Vinegar

Red and white wine vinegars and balsamic vinegar are the varieties typically used in Italy. Though very popular, balsamic vinegar should not be used as an all-purpose substitute for wine vinegar, since it is quite sweet.

The finest-quality *balsamico*, made in Modena, is labelled "tradizionale" and comes in a unique round bottle with a square base. It bears a sticker that certifies it as genuine, aged balsamico made in the traditional way. The production involves many years of aging in various types of wood barrels. Costly and rare, fine balsamico is meant to be used as a condiment. A drop or two may be dribbled on cheese or grilled meat. It lifts the flavor of berries and is so thick and luscious it can even be drizzled on ice cream.

Less aged, and less costly, balsamic vinegar does exist. Find a store in your area that will let you sample some before you buy it.

Supermarket balsamic ranges from harsh and artificial-tasting to perfectly acceptable for salads, marinades, and everyday use. One brand I like is Lucini, which is widely available.

Wine for Cooking

Wine is frequently used for cooking in the Italian kitchen. I have often read that one should use the same wine she or he will serve with the meal to cook with, but I do not necessarily agree. Fine wines are too delicate to pour into the pot. An ordinary table wine is ideal for most cooking purposes. Look for a wine that will not overwhelm the other ingredients and that you find enjoyable to drink. Avoid cooking with wine that has pronounced oak or fruit flavors. Try to use an Italian wine for the most authentic flavor.

Bottles labeled "cooking wine" should never be used, as these are poor-quality wines adulterated with sugar and salt to make them salable in food stores.

Kitchen Equipment

The recipes in this book do not require a lot of special equipment. My best advice is to buy the highest quality that you can afford. Fine equipment does a better job and lasts longer, so in the end, it is more economical.

Start with a few basic pots and pans made from heavy-gauge stainless steel, such as a 6-quart pot for cooking pasta, soup, and vegetables. You will need small, medium, and large saucepans, and a heavy Dutch oven for stews and braises. Nonstick skillets are good for frying and sautéing. Be sure to get one 12 inches wide—large enough to hold a pound of pasta and its sauce.

There are many excellent brands of cookware made nowadays, but be careful about buying restaurant-grade equipment unless you have a restaurant range. The average household stove does not have burners large enough or heat output strong enough for some restaurant pots and pans, and while they are durable, they can be bulky and cumbersome.

You will also need small and large roasting pans, and baking dishes. The two sizes I find most useful are 13 × 9 × 2 inches and 9 inches square.

For baking cakes, tarts, and cookies, get a sturdy springform pan, two layer cake pans, a tart pan with a removable base, and at least two large heavy cookie sheets, as well as large racks for cooling baked foods.

Good knives are essential for anyone who spends time in the kitchen. They will make most of your chores easier and more enjoyable and are actually safer to use. Fine knives are not inexpensive, but they are a good investment. The three knives that I use the most are my large heavy chef's knife, a boning knife, and paring knives. A long sharp carving knife and fork are useful for slicing roasts and the like. Get a sharpening steel to keep them honed and learn how to use it. A serrated bread knife does a good job on crisp breads and cakes.

Electric Mixer

A portable hand-held mixer is useful for whipping eggs and heavy cream and for mixing most cakes. However, if you bake a lot and make pasta and bread, a heavy-duty stand mixer is invaluable. My large Kitchen Aid mixer is more than twenty years old and despite a few dings in the enamel is as good as new. The pasta-making attachment makes quick work of a batch of pasta dough. An extra bowl and beaters makes it easy to prepare cake batter in one bowl and whip egg whites in another without stopping to wash out the bowl.

Food Mill

No Italian kitchen would be complete without a food mill, a hand-cranked device used to puree foods while straining out hard seeds, tough skins, or other debris. While a processor or blender can be used for many of the same functions, neither one will separate out unwanted bits. Use a food mill to make light, fluffy mashed potatoes, smooth tomato puree, fruit sauces, vegetable soups, and baby food. A food mill is inexpensive and easy to maintain. Look for one made of stainless steel with removable disks.

Food Processor

A food processor is handy for chopping large quantites, shredding, grating, and making sauces and creamy soups. With the blade attachment, I can slice foods paper-thin for salads. It also does a good job of kneading bread and pasta dough.

Pasta Machine

You don't need a machine to make fresh pasta, but it is helpful. The best kind to buy is imported from Italy, made of metal and either hand-cranked or electrified. It consists of two rollers that adjust from wide apart to close together, kneading and thinning the dough. Other than the fettuccine cutter, you probably won't use the various cutting attachments, so don't bother to buy them.

Never wash a pasta machine, as residual moisture can damage the works or cause the dough to stick. When you are finished using it, just wipe it with a dry cloth and remove any particles of pasta dough. Store it in a dry place (loosely covered—to prevent it from getting dusty).

Pizza Cutter

A pizza cutter is useful not only for cutting up pizza, but also for cutting out pasta dough, pastry, and cookies. Look for a heavy cutter with a large wheel.

Rolling Pin

A long rolling pin is ideal for rolling out pasta dough as well as pastry. Look for a long wooden pin that does not taper at the ends. The slight graininess of the wood helps to grip the dough and gives it a subtle texture. A plain straight pin is better than the roller type pin with ball bearings because you have more control.

Menus

Quick Meals

Tomato Toasts
Sliced Steak with Arugula
"Drowned" Ice Cream

Figs and Melon with Prosciutto
Linguine with Sun-Dried Tomatoes
Zabaglione

Avocado and Tomato Salad
Sole Rolls with Basil and Almonds
Peas with Prosciutto and Green Onions
Mascarpone and Peaches

Zucchini Carpaccio
Skewered Tuna with Orange
Strawberries with Balsamic Vinegar

Meatless Meal

Melted Cheese, Silversmith's Style
Fava Bean Puree with Seven Salads
Polenta and Pear Cake

Traditional Southern Italian Sunday Dinner

Veal-Stuffed Mushrooms or other
  antipasto
Baked Ziti
Meat from Ragù
Mixed Green Salad
Italian Bread
Cannoli

Sunday Family Dinner

Winter Squash Soup
Roast Pork with Potatoes and
  Rosemary
Broccoli Rabe with Garlic and
  Hot Pepper
Lemon–Olive Oil Cake

Hearty Winter Meal

Creamy Bean Soup
Pork Ribs and Cabbage
Polenta
Oranges in Orange Syrup

(continues)

Elegant Spring Menu

Venetian Risotto with Peas

Veal Cutlets with Truffles

Spinach or Other Greens with Butter and Garlic

Poached Pears with Gorgonzola

Taste of Summer

Bow Ties with Cherry Tomatoes and Bread Crumbs

Grilled Tuna and Peppers, Molise Style

Watermelon Granita

Supper for a Fall Day

Cannelloni with Tarragon and Pecorino

Lamb and Pepper Stew

Tricolor Salad

Autumn Fruit Torte

Antipasto Buffet for a Crowd

Roasted Olives

Asparagus and Prosciutto Rolls

Crostini, three ways:

Chickpea, Broccoli, and Eggplant and Tomato

Sweet-and-Sour Eggplant

Spinach Frittata

Russian Salad

Bow Ties with Uncooked Puttanesca Sauce

Cream Puffs with assorted fillings

Easter Dinner

Asparagus and Egg Salad

Bow Ties with Artichokes and Peas

Leg of Lamb with Lemon, Herbs, and Garlic

Roasted Potatoes with Mushrooms

Spinach with Butter

Easter Wheat-Berry Cake

Christmas Eve Dinner with Seven Fishes

Seafood Salad

Pasta with Sardines and Fennel

Fried Salt Cod

Baked Fish with Olives and Potatoes

Clams and Mussels Posillipo

Escarole with Garlic

Prosecco Lemon Slush

Sicilian Ricotta Cake

Christmas Day Dinner

Egg Crepes in Broth

Stuffed Roasted Capon

Roasted Brussels Sprouts

Mushrooms in Marsala

Neapolitan Potato Croquettes

Italian Trifle

Assorted Biscotti

Brunch all'Italiana

Omelet Strips in Tomato Sauce

Roasted Asparagus

Baked Polenta with Cheese

Red Onion Flatbread

Almond and Peach Tart

Antipasti

An Antipasto Platter

Cheese Antipasti

Goat Cheese with Herbs
Goat Cheese, Valle d'Aosta Style
Gorgonzola-Stuffed Endive
Warm Ricotta in Fresh Tomato Sauce
Provolone in Pizza Sauce
Grilled Mozzarella
Grilled Cheese and Prosciutto Skewers
Montasio Cheese Crisps
Melted Cheese, Silversmith's Style
Mozzarella in a Carriage
Roman Skewered Mozzarella Sandwiches
Parmesan Custards
Walnut Cheese Wafers
Gorgonzola Biscuits

Vegetable Antipasti

Marinated Olives
Black Olives with Citrus
Spicy Olives in the Pan
Roasted Olives

Zucchini Fritters
Marinated Mushrooms
Mushroom Pâté of the Two Sicilies
Veal-Stuffed Mushrooms
Mushrooms Stuffed with Mozzarella and
Prosciutto
Peppers Piedmontese
Roasted Pepper Rolls
Tuna-Stuffed Peppers
Sweet-and-Sour Eggplant
Asparagus and Egg Salad
Roasted Radicchio with Mozzarella and
Anchovies

Egg Antipasti

Stuffed Eggs
Tuna-Stuffed Eggs

Meat Antipasti

Figs and Melon with Prosciutto
Asparagus and Prosciutto Rolls
Roasted Figs in Prosciutto
Lemon Meatballs
Chicken and Olive Pâté

Seafood Antipasti

❧

Scallops al Gratin
Baked Scallops with Marsala and Almonds
Seafood Salad
Salt Cod Puree

Dips and Spreads

❧

Olive Oil Dip
Poor Man's Caviar
Sun-Dried Tomato Spread
Piedmontese Hot Bath
Tuna Spread
Eggplant Caviar

Bruschetta and Crostini

❧

Garlic Bruschetta
Tomato Bruschetta
Tomato and Avocado Bruschetta
Beans and Greens Toasts
Chicken Liver Toasts
Zucchini and Cheese Toasts
Chickpea Toasts
Broccoli Toasts
Eggplant and Tomato Toasts

Fried Antipasti

❧

"Little Orange" Rice Balls
"Telephone-Wire" Rice Balls
Sicilian Chickpea Flour Fritters
Basil Fritters
Fried Sage Leaves

The word *antipasto* comes from Latin and means "before the meal." In the strictest sense, an antipasto is a little something extra as a starter. It is a small snack meant to awaken the appetite, not to satisfy it.

In Italy, unless it is a special occasion, home-cooked meals rarely start with an antipasto, though restaurant meals often do. Antipasto dishes also vary a lot by region. In the north, especially in the Piedmont, a long succession of antipasto dishes are served one at a time at formal dinners. The classic antipasto in Tuscany is *crostini* (toasted bread) with chicken livers and a few slices of salami such as *finocchiona*, a regional specialty made with ground pork and flavored with fennel seeds. In southern Italy, antipasti are simpler, often just a few slices of dried sausage or prosciutto, pickled vegetables, and olives.

When I have company, I often serve an antipasto. Olives, sliced *salumi* (a collective word for cold cuts), and cut up raw vegetables are the easiest antipasto, and a nice way to welcome guests as they gather. More elaborate dishes can serve as a first course, and a group of antipasti can form the basis for a buffet meal.

Antipasto dishes can be served hot, room temperature, or cold. With the exception of dried sausages and cured meats like *salame*, prosciutto, or mortadella, meat is used sparingly, usually ground or chopped as a vegetable stuffing. Though shellfish is often offered as an antipasto, whole fish is usually not, except for tiny fish such as anchovies or whitebait.

Many other dishes throughout this book can be served as antipasti. From the vegetable chapters, fried artichokes or cauliflower, any of the stuffed or grilled vegetables, and salads are always good choices. Many of the sautéed vegetable dishes are good as starters, served warm or at room temperature.

Slices of focaccia or olive- or cheese-flavored breads are good companions for vegetable antipasti. Pasta salads are rarely seen in Italy, but Italians do serve rice salads frequently as part of an antipasto assortment. Cold seafood salads are popular, as are stuffed shellfish, such as clams, mussels, and oysters.

An Antipasto Platter

An assortment of antipasti is a great way to start a casual meal or a special dinner. Platters of sliced meats, cheeses, and preserved vegetables decoratively arranged are great for parties. Use your imagination to place the ingredients so that the colors and shapes complement one another. For best flavor, the ingredients should be at room temperature or just slightly chilled.

Here are some suggestions for a typical antipasto assortment. Serve accompanied by crunchy breadsticks and crusty Italian bread or focaccia.

Salumi

Serve one or two slices per person of three of the following meats. Fold or roll up the slices for easier serving.

mortadella: a specialty of Emilia-Romagna; large, mildly spiced smooth-textured pork sausage, with chunks of fat and sometimes pistachios.

prosciutto: from all over Italy (the best-known here is from Parma or San Daniele in Friuli–Venezia Giulia); a whole pork leg cured with salt.

capocollo: from all over Italy; cured pork shoulder, can be either mild or spiced with hot pepper.

salami: from all over Italy; usually ground pork, though other meats may be used, with various spices and seasonings including black peppercorns, fennel seeds, crushed red pepper, wine. There are many different varieties.

sopressata: from all over Italy; a large, wide salame made of coarsely ground lean pork and pork fat, flavored with black peppercorns, or crushed red pepper, salt, and red wine.

pepperoni: in North America, a long, thin dried sausage made of coarsely ground pork with either black peppercorns or crushed red pepper. In Italy, the word *peperoni* means bell peppers, not a dried hot sausage.

Cheeses

Serve one wedge of one variety of cheese. Buy cheeses in large chunks and cut them into wedges for serving. Look for aged cheeses imported from Italy.

provolone: from all over Italy. Do not use the bland, sliced variety. Imported provolone is sharp and slightly smoky-flavored.

young pecorino: mostly from central and southern Italy; semifirm and mild to sharp in flavor, depending on the variety and origin.

fresh or smoked mozzarella: mild, soft and creamy; can be either salted or unsalted. Fresh mozzarella should be very moist and eaten the same day that it is made. Smoked mozzarella is drier, with smoky flavor and firmer texture.

ricotta salata: a pressed and salted version of ricotta, mild, firm, and crumbly.

Pickles and vegetables

One or two varieties of the following preserved vegetables should be sufficient.

marinated artichokes, mushrooms, or dried tomatoes.

hot or mild vinegar peppers or peperoncini.

giardiniera: mixed pickled vegetables (page 45).

Garnishes

Decorate the platter with anchovy fillets, sliced tomatoes, cherry tomatoes, lettuce or radicchio, and carrot and celery sticks.

Cheese Antipasti

Goat Cheese with Herbs

Caprino alle Erbe

MAKES 6 SERVINGS

Capra *is Italian for "goat," and* caprino *is the name given to Italian goat cheese. Look for a mild, fresh goat cheese for this recipe. If Italian goat cheese is not available, use an American or French goat cheese. Their flavors are very similar.*

8 ounces fresh mild goat cheese
2 tablespoons chopped fresh herbs, such as chives, rosemary, parsley, basil, thyme
1/4 teaspoon coarsely ground black pepper
2 tablespoons extra-virgin olive oil
Fresh herbs for garnish
Thin slices of toasted Italian bread

1 Mash the cheese in a medium bowl with a fork or spoon. Stir in the herbs and pepper.

2 Spoon the cheese mixture onto the center of a piece of plastic wrap. Bring one end of the plastic over the cheese to meet the other end. Tuck the plastic around the cheese and shape the cheese into a log. Roll the log to secure the shape. Refrigerate one hour up to overnight.

3 Unwrap the cheese and place it on a serving plate. Drizzle with the oil. Garnish with sprigs of fresh herbs. Serve with toasted Italian bread.

Goat Cheese, Valle d'Aosta Style

Tomini di Courmayeur

MAKES 6 SERVINGS

Courmayeur, a popular ski resort in the Valle d'Aosta, is just across the border from France through the Mont Blanc tunnel. The local dialect sounds more French than Italian. Though the region is best known for its cow's milk cheeses, such as Fontina Valle d'Aosta, small goat cheeses, known locally as tomini, *are eaten with the local dark rye bread, or drizzled with honey for dessert. I enjoyed goat cheese with a crunchy, flavorful topping at La Maison de Filippo, a rustic country inn that serves hearty meals in a charming setting.*

1/4 cup extra-virgin olive oil
2 tablespoons wine vinegar
1 garlic clove, minced
1 teaspoon chopped fresh thyme
Pinch of crushed red pepper
Salt and freshly ground black pepper
1 cup finely chopped tender celery
2 tablespoons chopped fresh flat-leaf parsley
2 sage leaves, chopped
8 ounces fresh mild goat cheese
Thin slices toasted Italian or French bread

1 In a medium bowl, whisk together the oil, vinegar, garlic, thyme, red pepper, and salt and black pepper to taste. Stir in the celery, parsley, and sage.

2 Place the cheese on a serving plate. Pour the sauce over the cheese. Cover and let stand 1 hour at room temperature. Serve with toasted bread.

Gorgonzola-Stuffed Endive

Indivia Ripiene

MAKES 6 SERVINGS

The large endive family of vegetables includes many that are used in Italian kitchens, including several kinds of chicory, escarole, and radicchio. Belgian endive grows in small pointed heads that are kept covered as they mature. The covering prevents photosynthesis, so that the endive remains white with yellowish tips instead of turning green as it would if allowed to develop naturally. It also keeps the leaves tender and the flavor delicate. Their long spear shape makes Belgian endive leaves perfect containers for stuffing or dipping. Here the filling is a classic flavor combination of creamy gorgonzola and crunchy toasted walnuts.

8 ounces gorgonzola cheese, rind removed
4 ounces mascarpone
2 to 4 tablespoons milk
4 medium Belgian endive, separated into leaves
1/4 cup coarsely chopped toasted walnuts

1 In a medium bowl, mash the two cheeses together with a fork. Stir in just enough of the milk to make the mixture soft and spreadable.

2 Arrange the endive leaves on a platter. Spoon the cheese mixture into the leaves. Sprinkle with the walnuts and serve immediately.

Warm Ricotta in Fresh Tomato Sauce

Ricotta Calda in Salsa di Pomodori Freschi

MAKES 4 SERVINGS

Warm creamy ricotta in a pool of fresh tomato sauce is a heavenly starter that I first encountered at Remi, one of my favorite Italian restaurants in New York. Tangy sheep's milk ricotta is preferred, though cow's milk ricotta works well too. Serve with fresh Italian bread.

8 ripe plum tomatoes, peeled, seeded, and chopped
4 tablespoons extra-virgin olive oil
Salt
Pinch of crushed red pepper
6 fresh basil leaves, torn into bits
I cup whole- or part-skim ricotta

1 In a medium saucepan, combine the tomatoes, oil, salt, and red pepper. Bring to a simmer. Cook until the tomatoes are just softened, about 5 minutes. Remove from the heat. Add half the basil leaves.

2 In a medium bowl, whisk the ricotta with the remaining basil, and salt and pepper to taste.

3 Spread the tomato sauce on 4 small plates or shallow bowls. With an ice cream scoop, shape the ricotta mixture into 4 balls and place them on top of the sauce. Serve warm.

Provolone in Pizza Sauce

Provolone alla Pizzaiola

MAKES 4 SERVINGS

In a pizzeria in Naples, I had provolone cheese heated until it was just barely melted, in a spicy tomato sauce. It makes a good lunch, accompanied by bread and a green salad.

2 1/2 cups Pizzaiola Sauce (page 91)
8 ounces aged provolone, rind removed and cut into
    1/4-inch slices
Pinch of dried oregano

1 Prepare the sauce, if necessary.

2 In a medium skillet, bring the sauce to a simmer over medium heat. Add the cheese slices and sprinkle with the oregano. Remove from the heat and let stand 3 to 4 minutes or until the cheese begins to melt. Serve immediately.

Grilled Mozzarella
Mozzarella ai Ferri

MAKES 4 SERVINGS

One summer in Rome, my favorite luncheon dish was fresh mozzarella grilled until it had a golden crust outside and was warm and melty inside. Most days I ate it with a salad of arugula, tomatoes, and sweet onions.

A nonstick skillet or griddle is essential here, and for best results, the cheese, which can be very moist when freshly made, must be quite dry.

1 pound fresh mozzarella, cut into 1/2-inch-thick slices

1 If the mozzarella is very moist, lay the slices on paper towels to drain the excess moisture. Refrigerate one hour, turning the slices once.

2 Place a nonstick skillet over medium heat. When a drop of water flicked onto the skillet bounces and evaporates quickly, the pan is ready.

3 Place a slice of the mozzarella in the skillet. When it begins to turn brown around the edge, turn it over with a spatula. Cook 1 minute more. Repeat with the remaining slices. Serve hot.

Grilled Cheese and Prosciutto Skewers
Spiedini di Formaggio e Prosciutto

MAKES 6 TO 8 SERVINGS

Tuscan friends Anna and Lucio Trebino prepared dinner on the barbecue one summer night. I loved the appetizers that Anna served: balls of goat cheese wrapped in crisped prosciutto. The skewers can be assembled several hours ahead of time and stored covered in the refrigerator until ready to cook. Anna says this works well with cubes of semifirm cheeses like mozzarella in place of the goat cheese.

6 to 8 ounces fresh goat cheese
1/2 teaspoon coarsely ground black pepper
8 thin slices imported Italian prosciutto, cut in half crosswise

1 In a small bowl, mash the cheese with the pepper. Divide the cheese into 16 pieces. Shape the pieces into balls. Spear the cheese balls on short bamboo skewers. Tightly wind a piece of the prosciutto around each ball of cheese.

2 Preheat the broiler. Broil the skewers 2 to 3 minutes, turning often until the prosciutto is lightly browned. Serve hot.

Montasio Cheese Crisps
Frico

MAKES ABOUT 2 DOZEN

In Friuli–Venezia Giulia, montasio, a cow's milk cheese, is used to make frico, *thin crispy cheese wafers. If montasio is not available, use Parmigiano-Reggiano or Grana Padano. Though frico is often made in a skillet on the stovetop, I find the results are more reliable in the oven.*

The fragile crisps are good with a glass of sparkling prosecco, or serve them as an accompaniment to soup.

4 ounces freshly grated montasio
2 ounces freshly grated Parmigiano-Reggiano

1 Preheat the oven to 350°F. In a small bowl, mix the two cheeses together. On a large heavy ungreased baking sheet, sprinkle about 1 tablespoon of the cheese in a thin layer in the form of a disk about 2 inches in diameter. Make as many additional disks as will fit comfortably about 1 inch apart.

2 Bake in the center of the oven 8 minutes or until the cheese is melted and lightly golden.

3 Place several overturned juice glasses on a countertop. When the cheese crisps are done, remove the baking sheet from the oven. Working quickly (because they firm up rapidly as they cool), remove the cheese wafers from the baking sheet one by one with a thin metal spatula, then gently mold the disks over the glasses. Let cool until firm. Carefully remove the cheese crisps from the glasses. Repeat baking and molding the remaining cheese.

4 Store in an airtight container up to 1 week.

Melted Cheese, Silversmith's Style

Formaggio all'Argentiera

MAKES 4 SERVINGS

According to Mary Taylor Simeti's book Pomp and Sustenance: Twenty-Five Centuries of Sicilian Food, *this recipe gets its name from an unknown, and perhaps mythical, silversmith who invented it to disguise the fact that he had fallen on hard times. The aroma of the cheese, garlic, vinegar, and oregano cooking is said to be similar to rabbit, and the silversmith wanted his neighbors to believe that he could still afford meat. Serve with crisp bread and a bottle of red wine.*

Provolone in Italy is not the same as the bland cheese of that name we often see in the United States. Imported Italian provolone is aromatic and slightly smoky, mild when young and sharp when aged. Many cheese shops sell imported provolone, or you can substitute caciocavallo, *which is similar in flavor and texture to provolone, though it comes in a different shape. Asiago is a cheese from northern Italy that takes very well to this treatment.*

6 to 8 ounces imported provolone, caciocavallo, or Asiago cheese

2 tablespoons olive oil

2 large garlic cloves, thinly sliced

2 tablespoons white wine vinegar

1/2 teaspoon dried oregano

1 Remove the rind from the cheese and cut the cheese into 1/2-inch-thick slices.

2 In a large heavy skillet, heat the oil over medium heat. Add the garlic and cook until just beginning to turn golden, 1 to 2 minutes.

3 Place the cheese slices in a single layer on top of the garlic. Raise the heat and add the vinegar. Cook 1 to 2 minutes or until the cheese just begins to melt.

4 With a metal spatula, quickly turn the slices and sprinkle with the oregano. Cook 1 to 2 minutes more or until the cheese is slightly melted and bubbling around the edges. Transfer to serving dishes and serve hot.

Mozzarella in a Carriage

Mozzarella in Carrozza

MAKES 4 TO 8 SERVINGS

I love the whimsical name of this Neapolitan version of a toasted cheese sandwich. It makes me think of royalty, though in this case, it is a slice of mozzarella, not a king and queen, riding in a coach made of sliced bread. This was a favorite lunchtime sandwich when I was growing up. Cut into pieces, it also makes a nice appetizer.

1 cup milk

3 large eggs

1/2 teaspoon salt

Freshly ground black pepper

3/4 cup all-purpose flour

12 ounces fresh mozzarella, cut into slices to fit the bread

12 to 16 slices Italian bread

3 tablespoons unsalted butter

1 In a medium bowl, whisk together the milk, eggs, and salt and pepper to taste. Spread the flour on a sheet of wax paper.

2 Sandwich the cheese between two slices of bread. Dip the sandwiches in the milk mixture, then turn them in the flour.

3 Melt two tablespoons of the butter in a large skillet over medium heat. Add the sandwiches and cook, flattening them with a metal spatula, until browned on both sides, about 3 minutes per side. Serve hot.

Roman Skewered Mozzarella Sandwiches
Spiedini alla Romana

MAKES 4 TO 8 SERVINGS

If you don't want to use the anchovies in the sauce, leave them out and just drizzle the sandwiches with the garlic butter.

12 (¹/₂-inch-thick) slices Italian or French bread
8 ounces fresh mozzarella, cut into 8 slices
4 tablespoons unsalted butter
1 tablespoon olive oil
1 garlic clove, peeled and finely chopped
6 anchovy fillets
Freshly ground black pepper

1 Preheat the oven to 450°F. Brush a baking sheet with oil.

2 On each of 4 short skewers, thread 3 slices of the bread alternately with 2 slices of mozzarella, beginning and ending with the bread. Place on the prepared baking sheet. Bake in the center of the oven 20 minutes or until the bread is toasted and the cheese is slightly melted.

3 Meanwhile, in a small skillet, melt the butter with the oil and garlic over medium heat. Add the anchovies and pepper to taste and stir until the anchovies dissolve.

4 Transfer the skewers to a warm serving platter, sliding the bread and cheese off the skewers. Pour the sauce over the sandwiches and serve immediately.

Parmesan Custards
Tartra

MAKES 4 SERVINGS

Individual baked custards flavored with cheese or vegetables are favorite appetizers in the Piedmont region of northern Italy. I like to serve these as an elegant appetizer or brunch dish with spinach, mushrooms, cherry tomatoes, or other vegetables braised in a little butter.

1 cup heavy cream
¹/₄ cup milk
2 fresh sage leaves
2-inch sprig fresh rosemary
2 tablespoons unsalted butter
¹/₄ cup finely chopped onion
2 large eggs
2 tablespoons freshly grated Parmigiano-Reggiano
Pinch of freshly grated nutmeg
¹/₂ teaspoon salt
¹/₄ teaspoon freshly ground black pepper
Salt

1 In a bowl, combine the cream, milk, sage, and rosemary. Cover and refrigerate 2 hours up to overnight.

2 Melt the butter in a small skillet over medium heat. Add the onion and cook until tender, about 5 minutes.

3 Place a rack in the center of the oven. Preheat the oven to 350°F. Butter four 6-ounce custard cups.

4 In a large bowl, beat the eggs until well blended. Pour the cream mixture through a fine-mesh strainer into the eggs. Stir in the onion, cheese, nutmeg, salt, and pepper. Pour mixture into the prepared cups.

5 Place a roasting pan in the oven. Pour ¹/₂ inch hot water into the pan. Place the custard cups in the pan. Bake for 55 minutes or until the tops are lightly golden and the custards are just set. Remove the custards from the pan and let stand 15 minutes.

6 Run a small knife around the inside of the cups and invert them onto serving plates. Serve warm.

Walnut Cheese Wafers
Biscotti al Parmigiano

MAKES 48

Though they may look like dessert cookies, these buttery biscuits belong to the category of foods Italians call salatini, *literally little salted things. Salatini are perfect with drinks or a glass of wine. You can serve them as an appetizer with olives and salame or with a bowl of soup or a salad for lunch.*

1¼ cups unbleached all-purpose flour
4 ounces freshly grated Parmigiano-Reggiano
¼ teaspoon salt
½ cup (1 stick) unsalted butter, cut into bits
½ cup walnuts, toasted and finely chopped
About 2 tablespoons milk
1 large egg

1 In a medium bowl, stir together the flour, cheese, and salt. With a pastry blender or a fork, blend in the butter until the mixture resembles coarse crumbs. Stir in the nuts.

2 In a small bowl, beat together the milk and egg. Pour the mixture over the dry ingredients and stir just until moistened. Add more milk, a teaspoon or so at a time, if needed to moisten the dough. Squeeze the dough together and form it into a ball.

3 Cut the dough into two equal pieces. Shape each piece into a 7-inch log and place each on a sheet of plastic wrap. Wrap tightly and refrigerate until firm, 4 hours up to overnight.

4 Place a rack in the center of the oven. Preheat the oven to 400°F. Butter two large baking sheets.

5 Cut the logs into ¼-inch slices and arrange the slices 1 inch apart on the prepared baking sheets. Bake until the biscuits are lightly browned around the edges, 10 to 12 minutes. Transfer to wire racks to cool. Serve at room temperature. Store in an airtight container up to 2 weeks.

Gorgonzola Biscuits
Biscotti di Gorgonzola

MAKES 2 DOZEN

Gorgonzola, a blue cheese made from cow's milk in the Lombardy region of Italy, comes in two forms. Dolce is the milder, younger variety; stagionato *or* piccante, *sometimes called mountain gorgonzola, is older and sharper, with more of the blue-green mold that gives the cheese its distinct flavor. For these biscuits, I prefer the younger form of the cheese.*

1 stick (4 ounces) unsalted butter, softened
8 ounces imported Italian gorgonzola dolce, rind removed
2 egg yolks
¼ teaspoon freshly grated nutmeg
¼ teaspoon freshly ground black pepper
2½ cups all-purpose flour
1 egg white, beaten
2 teaspoons sesame seeds

1 In a large mixing bowl, beat the butter until it is fluffy. Add the cheese a little at a time, beating until well blended. Beat in the egg yolks, nutmeg, and pepper.

2 Add the flour and stir until smooth. Shape the dough into a disk and wrap in plastic wrap. Refrigerate 30 minutes up to overnight.

3 Place a rack in the center of the oven. Preheat the oven to 450°F. Butter and flour a large baking sheet.

4 Roll out the dough between two sheets of plastic wrap to a ¼-inch thickness. With a 2-inch round cookie cutter, cut out the biscuits. Place the biscuits on the prepared baking sheet. Gather the scraps together and, handling them as little as possible, roll out and cut the dough scraps in the same way. Brush the tops with the beaten egg white. Sprinkle with the sesame seeds.

5 Bake 12 to 14 minutes or until lightly browned around the edges. Transfer to a wire rack to cool. Serve at room temperature. Store in an airtight container for up to 2 weeks.

❧ Vegetable Antipasti

Marinated Olives
Olive Marinate

MAKES 6 TO 8 SERVINGS

For many Italians, a bowl of good olives and chewy bread can be a whole meal. Brine- or oil-cured olives are full of flavor. Most come from Italy, France, or Greece, and you can usually find them sold by weight in the deli section of the grocery store. Avoid the bland, mushy black olives sold in cans.

Olives take well to a variety of marinades. You can vary these by adding hot pepper, herbs, celery leaves, or strips of sun-dried tomatoes. Try a mix of several types of both green and black varieties, if you like.

8 ounces Gaeta or other mild black olives
1 lemon
1/2 cup extra-virgin olive oil
2 garlic cloves, lightly crushed
1 teaspoon fennel seeds

1 Rinse the olives under cold running water. Drain well and pat dry with paper towels.

2 With a swivel-blade vegetable peeler, remove two 2-inch strips of the yellow zest of the lemon. Avoid digging into the white pith, or remove the pith with a knife.

3 Combine all of the ingredients in a container and stir well. Cover and refrigerate, shaking the container occasionally, for 1 week. Serve at room temperature.

Black Olives with Citrus
Olive Nere Condite

MAKES 6 TO 8 SERVINGS

Sometimes I add very thin slices of celery, fennel, or carrots to these olives and serve them as a salad with sandwiches. Use a swivel-blade vegetable peeler to remove just the thin colored portion of the citrus skin, known as the zest, without digging into the bitter white pith below the surface.

8 ounces Gaeta or other mild black olives
1 (1-inch strip) orange zest
1 (1-inch strip) lemon zest
1/4 cup extra-virgin olive oil
2 tablespoons fresh lemon juice
1 tablespoon coarsely chopped fresh marjoram or thyme
1 small dried chile or a pinch of crushed red pepper

1 Place the olives in a bowl. Stack the zests and cut them into very thin slivers with a large heavy chef's knife.

2 Combine all of the ingredients in a container and stir well. Cover and refrigerate, shaking the container occasionally, for 1 week. Serve at room temperature.

Spicy Olives in the Pan
Olive in Padella

MAKES 8 SERVINGS

For this easy appetizer, choose a mildly flavored olive that is not too salty, such as Gaeta.

2 garlic cloves, lightly crushed
1/4 cup olive oil
8 ounces mild black olives
1 fresh green chile, seeded and chopped,
    or 1/4 teaspoon crushed red pepper
1/2 teaspoon dried oregano
1 cup cherry tomatoes, quartered
2 tablespoons chopped fresh flat-leaf parsley

1 In a small skillet, cook the garlic in the olive oil over medium heat, pressing it with the back of a wooden spoon until the garlic is lightly golden around the edges, about 2 minutes.

2 Add the olives, chile, and oregano. Cook, stirring often, for 5 minutes.

3 Stir in the tomatoes and cook 2 to 3 minutes more. Stir in the parsley. Let cool, then serve at room temperature.

Roasted Olives
Olive al Forno

MAKES 6 TO 8 SERVINGS

Moist, meaty olives that are not too salty or strongly flavored are best for roasting. The oven heat concentrates their flavors, so look for olives that are mild to begin with. Serve these olives with bread to dip in the flavorful oil that surrounds them.

8 ounces mild black olives, such as Gaeta or Alfonso
4 ounces cured green olives, rinsed and drained
6 garlic cloves, peeled
1/2 lemon, thinly sliced
1/3 cup olive oil
1 teaspoon fennel seeds
Pinch of crushed red pepper
2 tablespoons chopped fresh flat-leaf parsley

1 Preheat the oven to 350°F. In a small baking pan, stir together all of the ingredients. Bake 45 minutes, stirring 2 or 3 times.

2 Transfer the olives to a bowl and serve warm.

Zucchini Fritters
Frittelle di Zucchine

MAKES 6 SERVINGS

Little silver-dollar size pancakes of zucchini and herbs make a tasty appetizer, whether served warm or at room temperature. I also serve them with fish as a side dish.

1 pound small zucchini or yellow squash,
    scrubbed and trimmed
1 medium onion, trimmed and quartered
2 large eggs, beaten
1/2 cup unbleached all-purpose flour
1/2 cup freshly grated Parmigiano-Reggiano
2 tablespoons chopped fresh parsley
2 tablespoons chopped fresh oregano or mint
Salt and freshly ground pepper to taste
About 3 tablespoons olive oil

1 In a food processor or with the large holes of a box grater, grate the zucchini and onion into a bowl. Add in the remaining ingredients except for the oil and stir briefly to combine.

2 In a large skillet, heat the oil over medium heat until a bit of the zucchini mixture sizzles when placed in the pan. Add the batter by tablespoonfuls, flattening it slightly to a 1/4-inch thickness. Cook 2 minutes or until browned around the edges. Turn the rounds with a slotted spatula and cook 2 minutes more or until browned.

3 Drain on paper towels. Serve hot or at room temperature.

Marinated Mushrooms
Funghi Marinati

MAKES 1 QUART

Marinated mushrooms are ideal for an antipasto platter, or use them in sandwiches or as a side dish with a frittata. This recipe comes from my aunt Loretta Balsamo. She is an excellent cook, and when she approves of one of my recipes, I know it is just right.

1 cup white vinegar
1 cup water
1 1/2 pounds white mushrooms, halved or quartered if large
4 garlic cloves
1 teaspoon salt
1/2 teaspoon dried oregano
Pinch of crushed red pepper
Extra-virgin olive oil (optional)

1 In a large saucepan, bring the vinegar and water to a boil. Add the mushrooms and return the liquid to boiling. Cook 5 minutes. Drain the mushrooms, reserving the liquid.

2 Place the mushrooms in a quart-size glass jar, pressing them down with the back of a spoon. Add the garlic, salt, oregano, and crushed red pepper. Add enough of the reserved liquid to cover the mushrooms. Let cool slightly, then cover and refrigerate at least 24 hours before serving.

3 Serve the mushrooms drizzled with the oil, if desired. The mushrooms keep well in the refrigerator up to 2 weeks.

Mushroom Pâté of the Two Sicilies
Pâté delle Due Sicilie

MAKES 6 TO 8 SERVINGS

In Jeanne Carola Francesconi's La Cucina Napoletana, this recipe is attributed to one of the highly regarded French-trained chefs who worked for aristocratic families in southern Italy in the eighteenth and nineteenth centuries. Such a chef was known as a monzu, *a corruption of the French* monsieur.

2 tablespoons unsalted butter
12 ounces mushrooms, trimmed and sliced
1/2 teaspoon chopped fresh thyme
Salt and freshly ground black pepper
1/4 cup dry Marsala
2 tablespoons black olive paste or chopped mild black olives, such as Gaeta
1 tablespoon capers, rinsed and drained
2/3 cup heavy cream
Toasted thin-sliced Italian or French bread

1 In a large skillet, melt the butter over medium heat. Add the mushrooms, thyme, and salt and pepper to taste. Cook, stirring frequently, until the mushrooms release their juices. Raise the heat and cook until the liquid has evaporated, about 10 minutes.

2 Add the Marsala and simmer until evaporated. Stir in the olives and capers. Cook 5 minutes more. Stir in the cream and cook until evaporated. Let cool.

3 Scrape the mixture into a food processor or blender. Process until smooth. Pack the mixture into a small bowl. Serve at room temperature with toasted or grilled bread.

Veal-Stuffed Mushrooms
Funghi Ripieni di Vitello

MAKES 8 TO 12 SERVINGS

Mushrooms stuffed with ground meat, bread crumbs, vegetables, or cheese are a perfect addition to a hot antipasto assortment and also make a good side dish for roasts or steaks. White or button mushrooms with a 1- to 2-inch diameter cap are the right size for appetizers, since they can be eaten in one or two bites.

24 medium white mushrooms, lightly rinsed and patted dry
2 tablespoons unsalted butter
1/4 cup shallots, peeled and finely chopped
1/2 teaspoon chopped fresh thyme
8 ounces ground veal
I large egg
1/2 cup plain bread crumbs
1/4 cup freshly grated Parmigiano-Reggiano
2 tablespoons chopped fresh flat-leaf parsley
Salt and freshly ground black pepper

1 Place a rack in the center of the oven. Preheat the oven to 400°F. Oil a 13 × 9 × 2–inch baking pan.

2 Snap off the mushroom stems and chop them.

3 In a medium skillet, heat the butter over medium heat. Add the shallots and cook, stirring, until tender, about 4 minutes. Add the chopped mushroom stems and thyme. Cook until the mushrooms are tender and lightly browned, about 10 minutes.

4 In a large bowl, combine the meat, egg, bread crumbs, cheese, parsley, and salt and pepper. Mix in the cooked mushroom stem mixture. Fill the mushroom caps, mounding the stuffing slightly.

5 Place the mushrooms in the prepared pan. Bake for 30 minutes or until the mushroom caps are tender and the stuffing is browned. Serve warm.

Mushrooms Stuffed with Mozzarella and Prosciutto
Funghi Ripieni

MAKES 4 SERVINGS

In Torino in Piedmont, I ate big mushroom caps filled with chopped mushrooms, prosciutto, and a creamy sauce. Here is a much simpler stuffed mushroom that has some of the same flavor characteristics from the creamy, fresh cheese and salty prosciutto. Serve one per person as a hot appetizer or cut them into quarters for guests to share.

4 large shiitake or portobello mushrooms, lightly rinsed and patted dry, stems removed
Olive oil
4 thin slices imported Italian prosciutto or cooked ham
4 slices fresh mozzarella
4 fresh basil leaves, torn

1 Place a barbecue grill or broiler rack about 5 inches away from the heat source. Preheat the grill or broiler.

2 Brush the mushroom caps on both sides with olive oil. Broil with the top side up until slightly browned, about 5 minutes. Turn the caps and broil the other side until tender, about 3 minutes more.

3 Place a slice each of the prosciutto and cheese inside each cap, folding the pieces to fit. Broil 1 minute or until the cheese is slightly melted.

4 Sprinkle with basil and serve immediately.

Peppers Piedmontese
Peperoni Piemontese

MAKES 6 SERVINGS

Piedmont is famous for excellent wines, sweet hazelnuts, and big bell peppers. Called quadrati *because of their large, squarish shape, the peppers are quite a sight when piled high in a market stall as I first saw them in Asti, with their orange, green, red, and golden colors brilliant in the morning sun. Piedmontese cooks often pair bell peppers with garlic, capers, and anchovies for a sweet, salty, and sharp symphony of flavors.*

4 large red or yellow peppers

3 tablespoons olive oil

8 anchovy fillets, chopped

2 tablespoons chopped fresh flat-leaf parsley

2 tablespoons chopped basil

I garlic clove, minced

I tablespoon capers

Salt and freshly ground black pepper to taste

2 tablespoons red wine vinegar

I Cut out the cores and seeds from the peppers. Cut peppers into 1/2-inch strips and trim away the white membranes.

2 Heat the oil over medium heat in a large skillet. Add the pepper strips and cook 20 to 25 minutes or until tender, stirring frequently.

3 Add the remaining ingredients. Raise the heat and cook, stirring occasionally, until most of the liquid evaporates. Let cool. Serve at room temperature.

Roasted Pepper Rolls
Involtini di Peperoni

MAKES 8 SERVINGS

I had peppers prepared this way in Sorrento. The mozzarella there is made fresh daily from the milk of water buffaloes. The milk is exceptionally creamy and rich, and the cheese made from it is very tender, with a slight tanginess. It melts beautifully, so it is ideal for this dish. Fresh cow's milk mozzarella is very good, too, and widely available here, but try to avoid the hard, yellowish packaged mozzarella. It lacks the flavor and texture of the real thing.

4 large red or yellow bell peppers

2 large ripe tomatoes, peeled, seeded, and chopped

1/4 cup freshly grated Pecorino Romano

2 tablespoons chopped fresh basil

2 tablespoons olive oil

Salt and freshly ground black pepper

8 ounces fresh mozzarella

I Place a rack in the center of the oven. Preheat the oven to 450°F. Cut the peppers in half lengthwise and cut away the cores, stems, and white membranes. Place the peppers cut side down on a roasting pan. Bake 25 minutes, or until the skins are wrinkled and the peppers are tender when pierced with a knife. Place the peppers in a bowl and cover with plastic wrap. Let cool. Remove the skin.

2 When ready to bake the peppers, reheat the oven to 450°F. Oil a large baking dish.

3 Stir together the tomatoes, pecorino, basil, oil, salt, and pepper to taste. Set aside 1/2 cup. Stir the mozzarella into the remaining tomatoes.

4 Divide the mozzarella and tomato filling among the pepper halves. Fold over the ends to enclose the filling. Place the rolls in the prepared pan. Spoon on the reserved tomato mixture.

5 Bake for 15 minutes or until the cheese is melted. Serve hot.

Tuna-Stuffed Peppers

Peperoni Ripieni

MAKES 8 SERVINGS

My mother used to make this recipe often, using whatever ingredients she had on hand. Sometimes the peppers were stuffed with tuna, sometimes with anchovies, and sometimes olives were added to the mix. Bread crumbs, salt, and pepper were about the only things that were constant. No matter; it always tasted great.

2 large red bell peppers
2 large yellow bell peppers
1 (6¹/₂-ounce) can tuna packed in olive oil
1 large tomato, finely chopped
¹/₂ cup plain bread crumbs
2 tablespoons capers, rinsed and chopped
2 tablespoons chopped fresh flat-leaf parsley
Salt and freshly ground black pepper
¹/₂ cup dry white wine
2 tablespoons olive oil

1 Place a rack in the center of the oven. Preheat the oven to 400°F. Oil a 13 × 9 × 2–inch baking dish.

2 Cut the peppers lengthwise into quarters and remove the seeds, stems, and white membranes. Place the wedges cut side up in the pan.

3 Put the tuna and its oil in a bowl. Stir in the tomato, bread crumbs, capers, parsley, and salt and pepper to taste. Spoon the mixture into the peppers. Pour the wine around the peppers. Drizzle with the remaining oil.

4 Bake the peppers for 40 minutes or until tender. Serve at room temperature.

Sweet-and-Sour Eggplant

Caponata

MAKES 8 SERVINGS

Caponata is one of the classic dishes of Sicilian cooking, and there are many variations, including one with seafood and another with raisins and pine nuts. At Christmas time, many Sicilians make a special caponata with celery, almonds, capers, and olives. This recipe is caponata the way I like it, based on the variations I have tasted. Caponata tastes best if it is allowed to mellow at least a few hours or overnight. It keeps well in the refrigerator for several days but should be served at room temperature.

2 medium eggplants, about 12 ounces each, cut into 1-inch dice
Salt
1 large onion, chopped
¹/₄ cup olive oil
1¹/₂ cups tomato puree
2 tender celery ribs, chopped
1 cup chopped green olives
¹/₄ cup capers, rinsed and drained
3 tablespoons sugar
¹/₃ cup red wine vinegar
Vegetable oil for frying
2 medium red bell peppers, cut into bite-size pieces

1 Layer the eggplant pieces in a colander, sprinkling each layer with salt. Place the colander over a plate and let stand 1 hour.

2 In a large saucepan, cook the onion in the olive oil over medium heat until tender, about 5 minutes. Add the tomato, celery, olives, capers, sugar, and vinegar and stir well. Bring to a simmer and cook 15 minutes.

3 In a large heavy skillet, heat ¹/₂ inch of the vegetable oil over medium heat. Add a piece of pepper. If it sizzles rapidly, the oil is hot enough. Carefully add the remaining peppers. Cook until the peppers are tender and beginning to brown, about 10 minutes. Remove the peppers with a slotted spoon and add them to the tomato sauce.

4 Rinse the eggplant pieces and pat them dry with paper towels. Add more oil to the skillet if necessary. Fry the eggplant in batches until tender and browned, about 5 minutes. Transfer the eggplant to paper towels to drain.

5 Stir the eggplant into the tomato sauce and simmer 10 minutes. Serve at room temperature.

Asparagus and Egg Salad
Insalata di Asparagi

MAKES 4 SERVINGS

Asparagus and eggs seem to have a special affinity for one another, perhaps because they are both at their best in the spring. I had this lovely salad in Bassano del Grappa, in the Veneto region, a town known for its outstanding white asparagus. To make them white and keep the flavor delicate, the asparagus are covered as they grow. As they require a lot more care than ordinary asparagus, they are considerably more expensive. Green asparagus can be used, if you prefer.

3 large eggs
1 pound asparagus (white preferred), trimmed
Salt
2 tablespoons chopped fresh flat-leaf parsley
1 tablespoon chopped fresh chives
2 tablespoons extra-virgin olive oil
1 to 2 tablespoons fresh lemon juice
Freshly ground black pepper

1 Place the eggs in a medium saucepan with cold water to cover. Cover the pan and bring the water to a simmer. Cook 12 minutes. Drain and cool the eggs under running water.

2 Bring about 2 inches of water to a boil in a large skillet. Add the asparagus and salt to taste. Cook until the asparagus are tender, about 5 to 8 minutes, according to the thickness of the spears. Cool the asparagus under cold running water. Drain and pat dry.

3 Cut the asparagus and eggs into bite-size pieces. Place them in a medium bowl with the parsley and chives.

4 In a small bowl, beat together the oil, lemon juice, and salt and pepper to taste. Pour the dressing over the asparagus and eggs in the bowl and gently toss. Serve immediately.

Roasted Radicchio with Mozzarella and Anchovies
Radicchio al Forno con la Mozzarella

MAKES 6 SERVINGS

I find the bittersweet flavor of cooked radicchio very appealing, especially when paired with smooth, creamy mozzarella and salty anchovies. This is my version of a dish I have tasted often in Italian restaurants in the United States.

2 medium heads radicchio, trimmed
1/3 cup olive oil
Salt and freshly ground black pepper
8 ounces fresh mozzarella, cut into 16 slices
1 (2- to 3-ounce) jar anchovy fillets, drained

1 Place a rack in the center of the oven. Preheat the oven to 425°F. Oil a 13 × 9 × 2–inch baking dish.

2 Cut each radicchio head through the core into 8 wedges. Arrange the wedges in the baking dish. Brush the wedges with the oil and sprinkle with salt and pepper. Bake the radicchio for 20 minutes or until tender when pierced with a knife and lightly browned. Remove the dish from the oven, but leave the oven on.

3 Place a piece of mozzarella, an anchovy fillet, and a sprinkle of parsley on each wedge. Return the pan to the oven and bake 2 minutes more, or until the cheese begins to melt. Serve hot.

❧ Egg Antipasti

Stuffed Eggs
Uova Ripiene

MAKES 8 SERVINGS

When I was growing up, Easter dinner would always begin with an appetizer of stuffed hard-boiled eggs, salame from the local pork store, celery, and olives. It was my job to make the eggs. Here is one of my favorite ways to make them.

8 large eggs
Lettuce leaves
4 anchovy fillets, rinsed and chopped
1 tablespoon capers, rinsed and drained
1 tablespoon finely chopped fresh flat-leaf parsley
2 tablespoons mayonnaise
1 tablespoon olive oil
Salt and freshly ground black pepper
Fresh parsley leaves, for garnish

1 Place the eggs in a medium saucepan with cold water to cover. Cover the pan and bring the water to a simmer. Cook 12 minutes. Drain and cool the eggs under running water.

2 Line a plate with lettuce leaves. Peel the eggs and cut them in half lengthwise. Scoop out the yolks and place them in a bowl. Arrange the egg white halves on the bed of lettuce.

3 In a medium bowl, mash the egg yolks with the anchovies, capers, parsley, mayonnaise, and olive oil until blended. Add salt and pepper to taste.

4 Spoon the yolk mixture into the whites. Garnish with parsley leaves. Serve immediately.

Tuna-Stuffed Eggs
Uova Ripiene di Tonno

MAKES 4 TO 8 SERVINGS

Recipes are some of my favorite souvenirs of memorable dining experiences. Whenever I make these eggs, for example, I am reminded of the first time I ate them at Belvedere, a favorite restaurant in La Morra in Piedmont. The owner told me what was in them, and at home I experimented with the proportions of the ingredients to get the flavor I remembered.

4 large eggs
2 tablespoons unsalted butter, softened
¼ cup drained oil-packed tuna, mashed
1 tablespoon grated Parmigiano-Reggiano
Salt and freshly ground black pepper
Lettuce leaves
Finely chopped fresh parsley, for garnish

1 Place the eggs in a medium saucepan with cold water to cover. Cover the pan and bring the water to a simmer. Cook 12 minutes. Drain and cool the eggs under running water.

2 Peel the eggs in half lengthwise and remove the yolks. In a medium bowl, mash the yolks with the butter. Stir in the tuna, cheese, and salt and pepper to taste.

2 Place the egg whites on a plate lined with lettuce leaves. Stuff the whites with the yolk mixture. Garnish with chopped parsley. Serve immediately.

ꕥ Meat Antipasti

Figs and Melon with Prosciutto
Fichi e Melone al Prosciutto

MAKES 4 SERVINGS

For summer, ripe figs and juicy wedges of melon with prosciutto are a classic antipasto. Either brown or green figs will do, and you can use honeydew, cantaloupe, or other sweet, ripe melon, except watermelon. Figs do not ripen after they are picked, so buy them when they are soft, with a drop of nectar visible in the opening at the flower end. If figs are not available, wedges of ripe pear, pineapple, or persimmon are good complements for the prosciutto.

Use the very best prosciutto for this simple antipasto, such as Prosciutto di Parma. Make sure the prosciutto is moist, not dried out, and that the slicer cuts the meat paper-thin and lays it out flat on wax paper. If stacked, the slices will stick together and be very hard to separate.

4 ripe fresh figs
8 (1-inch-thick) slices honeydew, cantaloupe, or other melon
12 thin slices imported Italian prosciutto

With a small sharp knife, peel the figs. Arrange the figs and melon slices on serving plates. Drape the prosciutto on top. Serve immediately.

Asparagus and Prosciutto Rolls
Involtini di Prosciutto e Asparagi

MAKES 4 TO 8 SERVINGS

Thin slices of tender prosciutto wrapped around asparagus spears make attractive appetizers. There are many variations on this theme. For example, substitute smoked salmon or salami for the prosciutto and breadsticks for the asparagus.

1 pound medium asparagus
Salt
1/4 pound thinly sliced imported Italian prosciutto

1 Snap or cut off the base of the asparagus where the color changes from green to white. In a large skillet, bring about 2 inches of water to a boil. Add salt to taste. Add the asparagus. Cook until an asparagus spear bends gently when lifted by the stem end, about 4 to 8 minutes, according to the thickness of the asparagus. They should be tender yet crisp. Drain the asparagus and cool under running water. Blot dry.

2 Cut the prosciutto slices in half crosswise. Leaving the tips uncovered, wind a piece of prosciutto around the length of each asparagus spear. Arrange the asparagus on a serving platter.

3 Serve immediately or cover with plastic wrap and refrigerate up to 3 hours.

Roasted Figs
in Prosciutto
Fichi in Prosciutto

MAKES 4 TO 8 SERVINGS

In Italy, fig trees grow everywhere. They are widely cultivated, of course, but you also find the trees growing randomly along the roadside, sprouting out of stone walls and even from cracks in the pavement.

Fresh figs are increasingly popular and available in the United States. They are good for dessert, but also with cheese or prosciutto for a first course. The Italians say the best figs have "a teardrop in the eye," una lacrima nell'occhio, that is, a drop of juice oozing out of the flower end at the base of the fruit, which indicates that they are perfectly ripe.

If you don't have a thick, rich, aged balsamico tradizionale, serve the figs plain. Any other kind just won't do.

8 large fresh brown figs
**8 slices of imported Italian prosciutto,
    halved crosswise**
Best quality balsamic vinegar (optional)

1 Preheat the oven to 350°F. Cut the figs in half lengthwise. Wrap a piece of prosciutto completely around each fig half. Place the figs on a baking sheet. Bake 10 minutes or until heated through.

3 Transfer the figs to a serving plate. Dribble each half with a drop or two of balsamic vinegar, if using. Serve immediately.

Lemon Meatballs
Polpettine al Limone

MAKES 6 SERVINGS

Everybody loves when I make these tasty little meatballs, which I first ate on Capri. I usually make a double recipe, to be sure that everyone gets enough. They are also good served with a light, fresh tomato sauce.

1/2 cup dry crustless bread, cut into bite-size pieces
1/2 cup cold water
1/2 pound lean ground beef
1/4 cup freshly grated Parmigiano-Reggiano
2 tablespoons finely chopped pine nuts
2 tablespoons finely chopped fresh flat-leaf parsley
Salt and freshly ground black pepper
1/2 teaspoon grated lemon zest
1 tablespoon fresh lemon juice
1 large egg, beaten
3 tablespoons olive oil
Lemon wedges

1 Soak the bread in the water for 10 minutes. Squeeze out the excess liquid.

2 In a large bowl, mix together all the ingredients except the oil and lemon wedges. Knead the mixture with clean hands until it is thoroughly blended.

2 Rinse your hands in cool water. Form the meat mixture into 1-inch balls.

3 Heat the oil in a large skillet. Add just enough of the meatballs as will fit comfortably without crowding. Cook, turning the balls occasionally, until browned on all sides, about 8 minutes.

4 Serve hot with lemon wedges.

Chicken and Olive Pâté
Pâté di Pollo

MAKES 8 SERVINGS

Game, pork, and veal are the typical meats used for pâté, but this easy Piedmontese version is appealing because it is made with chicken. It can be shaped in a bowl or mold and makes an attractive appearance on a buffet, garnished with pickled onions, cornichons, cherry tomatoes, or marinated sun-dried tomatoes.

1 medium onion, chopped
1 medium carrot, chopped
1 celery rib, chopped
6 boneless, skinless chicken thighs
Salt
$^1/_2$ cup (1 stick) unsalted butter, softened
1 teaspoon grated lemon zest
$^1/_2$ teaspoon ground nutmeg
1 garlic clove, minced
Freshly ground black pepper
$^1/_2$ cup imported mild black olives, such as Gaeta, pitted and coarsely chopped
Tender salad greens
Toasted Italian or French bread

1 Place the onion, carrot, celery, and chicken in a large saucepan. Add cold water to cover and salt to taste. Bring to a simmer and cook until the chicken is tender, about 30 minutes. Let the chicken cool slightly in the broth.

2 Transfer the chicken to a food processor fitted with a steel blade, or to a cutting board. Chop very finely. Transfer it to a large bowl and mix in the butter, lemon zest, nutmeg, garlic, and salt and pepper to taste. Stir in the chopped olives.

3 Line a small bowl with plastic wrap. Add the chicken mixture and pack it in firmly. Cover and chill several hours or overnight.

4 To serve, cut the pâté into 8 slices. Serve on a bed of salad greens with toasted bread.

❧ Seafood Antipasti

Scallops al Gratin
Capesante al Gratin

MAKES 4 SERVINGS

In Italy, scallops are sold live in their shells with the crescent-shaped, coral-colored roe still attached. The roe can be cooked along with the scallop, and the flavor is excellent. You may not have much luck outside Italy, though; most scallops sold in the United States have been removed from their shells, and the roe, which is highly perishable, is discarded so that the seafood will keep longer.

Large, reuseable scallop shells are sold in many kitchen equipment stores. The shells make pretty bake-and-serve dishes for these scallops, or for serving nuts, olives, or other small foods.

16 large sea scallops
1 teaspoon chopped fresh tarragon
1 teaspoon chopped fresh basil
1 teaspoon chopped fresh flat-leaf parsley
2 tablespoons fresh lemon juice
2 tablespoons unsalted butter, melted and cooled
Salt and freshly ground black pepper to taste
2 tablespoons fine dry bread crumbs
Lemon wedges

1 Preheat the broiler. Butter a small flame-proof baking dish or 4 scallop shells.

2 Arrange the scallops in the dish or divide them among the shells. Sprinkle each of the herbs over them. In a small bowl, mix together the butter and lemon juice and season with a pinch of salt and some pepper. Pour the mixture over the scallops. Sprinkle them with the breadcrumbs.

3 Place the scallops under the broiler for 2 to 3 minutes or until the crumbs are toasted and the scallops are just slightly opaque in the center. Serve hot, with lemon wedges.

Baked Scallops with Marsala and Almonds

Capesante al Marsala

MAKES 4 SERVINGS

My husband and I ate scallops prepared this way at a popular trattoria in Venice. Baking them in individual scallop shells, available in cookware stores, offers a pretty presentation.

1 pound large sea scallops
6 tablespoons unsalted butter, melted
2 tablespoon very finely chopped shallots
2 tablespoons dry Marsala
1 to 2 teaspoons fresh lemon juice
Salt and freshly ground black pepper
2 tablespoons sliced almonds
Lemon wedges

1 Place a rack in the center of the oven. Preheat the oven to 375°F. Butter a 9-inch baking dish. Or, if using scallop shells, butter 4 shells, then place them on a baking sheet.

2 Cut the scallops in half crosswise. Sprinkle them with salt and pepper and place them in the dish or shells.

3 Melt the butter in a small skillet. Add the shallots and cook 2 minutes or until tender. Stir in the Marsala and bring to a simmer. Stir in the lemon juice, and salt and pepper to taste.

4 Pour the butter mixture over the scallops. Scatter the almonds on top. Bake 12 minutes or until the scallops are opaque and the almonds are lightly browned. Serve immediately with lemon wedges.

Seafood Salad

Insalata di Mare

MAKES 8 SERVINGS

When I was growing up, no Christmas Eve dinner in our house ever began without this Neapolitan-style seafood salad. Now I serve it all year round as a starter for a seafood dinner. Scallops, clams, and mussels can also be used in addition to or instead of the seafood listed below.

2 pounds octopus, thawed if frozen
Salt
1 pound cleaned calamari (squid)
1 pound medium shrimp, shelled and deveined
3 tender celery ribs, thinly sliced
1/2 cup imported mild black olives, such as Gaeta,
    pitted and coarsely chopped
1/3 cup extra-virgin olive oil
3 tablespoons fresh lemon juice, or to taste
1/4 cup chopped flat-leaf parsley
2 garlic cloves, minced
1/2 teaspoon freshly grated lemon zest
Pinch of crushed red pepper
1 whole lemon, cut into wedges

1 In a large pot, bring 2 quarts of water to a simmer. Add the octopus and 1 tablespoon salt. Cook, covered, until the octopus is tender when pierced with a fork, 45 to 60 minutes. Drain the octopus and let cool slightly. Scrape away the loose skin. Cut the flesh into bite-size pieces.

2 Cut the calamari bodies into 1-inch rings. Cut each set of tentacles in half lengthwise through the base.

3 Bring a large saucepan of water to a boil. Add salt and the shrimp. Cook until the shrimp turn pink and are just cooked through, 2 to 3 minutes. Scoop out the shrimp and cool them under cold running water. Let the water return to a boil in the pot. Drain the shrimp well.

4 Drop the calamari into the boiling water and cook until opaque, about 1 minute. Drain thoroughly and cool under running water.

5 Cut the shrimp into bite-size pieces. Combine the seafood, celery, and olives on a large serving platter.

6 Whisk together the oil, lemon juice, parsley, garlic, lemon zest, crushed red pepper, and salt to taste. Pour the dressing over the salad mixture and toss well. (If you are making the salad ahead of time, toss with only half of the dressing. Cover and refrigerate the salad up to 2 hours. Toss with the remaining dressing just before serving.) Taste for seasoning. Garnish with lemon wedges.

Salt Cod Puree
Brandacujun or Baccala Mantecato

MAKES 8 SERVINGS

If you have never tried salt cod or stockfish before, start with this recipe. (For more information about these two types of fish, see page 264.) It makes an excellent appetizer or first course and is typically served with toasted bread or slices of grilled polenta.

Ligurians make it with stockfish and call it brandacujun, *though a similar recipe made with salt cod in the Veneto is called* baccala mantecato. *In Liguria, the fish and potatoes are cooked together, then shaken vigorously in their pot until they form a slightly chunky puree. Venetians whip the cooked fish with olive oil using only a wooden spoon. I prefer to puree the fish in a mixer or food processor, then blend in the mashed potatoes by hand so they stay light and fluffy.*

Leftovers can be reheated in a bowl set over simmering water (or a double boiler), or you can shape it into small patties, roll them in egg and bread crumbs, and fry them in oil.

1 pound soaked boneless salt cod or stockfish (see page 265)
3 medium potatoes, peeled and cut into chunks
2 garlic cloves, peeled
Salt
1/2 cup extra-virgin olive oil
1/4 cup finely chopped fresh flat-leaf parsley
Toasted Italian or French bread

1 Prepare the fish, if necessary. Then bring 2 quarts of water to a simmer. Add the fish and cover the pan. Cook 20 to 30 minutes or until the fish is very tender. Remove the fish with a slotted spoon and place it on a plate.

2 Place the potatoes, garlic, and salt to taste in a medium saucepan with cold water to cover. Cover and bring to a simmer over medium heat. Cook until the potatoes are very tender when pierced with a knife. Drain the potatoes, reserving the cooking water.

3 With a small knife and your fingers, remove and discard any bones and skin from the fish. Place the fish in a food processor or heavy duty mixer and beat until very smooth.

4 Mash the potatoes and garlic with a ricer or in a food mill or potato masher.

5 In a large bowl, combine the fish and potatoes. Beat in the oil and salt to taste. Add some of the potato water and beat until light and fluffy. Stir in the parsley.

6 Scrape the mixture into a serving bowl and drizzle with additional oil. Serve warm with toast.

🌿 Dips and Spreads

Olive Oil Dip
Pinzimonio

MAKES 4 SERVINGS

The custom of using olive oil as a dip for bread at mealtimes is an American invention, not an Italian one (even though now you occasionally may see it in Italy, too). However, Italians do serve full-flavored extra-virgin olive oil with an assortment of fresh vegetables as an appetizer. They call it pinzimonio, *from the word for pincers—what your fingers resemble as they dip a piece of vegetable in the oil. In Italy, you can even buy special* pinzimonio *serving dishes consisting of a large bowl for the vegetables and smaller bowls for individual servings of oil.*

1 cup extra-virgin olive oil
Fine sea salt and freshly ground black pepper
Assorted raw vegetables cut into strips, such as carrots, celery, green onions, peppers, zucchini, radishes

Divide the olive oil among four small cups. Each diner should add salt and pepper to taste. Serve with the raw vegetables.

Poor Man's Caviar
Caviale di Povero Uomo

MAKES 1 CUP

I first sampled this tasty olive spread in Bergamo, on crisp slices of fried polenta. It is also good on toasted bread or sticks of raw vegetables.

1 garlic clove
2 anchovy fillets
1 cup chopped pitted imported black olives
2 tablespoons chopped fresh flat-leaf parsley
Extra-virgin olive oil

In a food processor or blender, finely chop the garlic and anchovies. Add the olives and chop them coarsely. Blend in the parsley and enough oil to moisten the mixture. Serve.

Sun-Dried Tomato Spread
Salsa di Pomodori Secchi

MAKES 1 CUP

Serve this spread with toasted bread or bread sticks, or try spooning it over a soft cheese, such as robiola, *a mild creamy cheese from Piedmont, or goat cheese.*

1 cup sun-dried tomato halves
1 garlic clove
1 tablespoon capers
2 tablespoons extra-virgin olive oil
1 tablespoon balsamic vinegar
Salt

1 Place the tomato halves in a medium bowl with warm water to cover. Let stand 10 minutes. Drain and pat dry.

2 In a food processor or blender, combine the tomatoes, garlic, and capers and process until chopped fine. Stir in the oil, vinegar, and a little salt. Taste and adjust seasoning.

3 Scrape the mixture into a bowl. Cover and let stand 1 hour before serving.

Piedmontese Hot Bath
Bagna Cauda

MAKES 6 SERVINGS

In Piedmont, this butter-oil "hot bath" flavored with anchovies and garlic is served as a dip for fresh vegetables and chunks of good bread. Use a chafing dish or fondue pot to keep the sauce warm. Be sure to provide small plates and plenty of napkins, as the sauce is drippy.

1/2 cup unsalted butter
1/3 cup extra-virgin olive oil
6 garlic cloves, finely chopped
2 (2-ounce) cans anchovy fillets with their oil
Assorted cooked and raw vegetables, cut up, such as carrots, peppers, green onions, celery, broccoli, cauliflower, and potatoes
Italian or French bread, cut into bite-size pieces

1 In a small saucepan, combine the butter, oil, garlic, and anchovies. Cook over medium heat for 5 minutes, mashing the anchovies with a wooden spoon.

2 Pour the sauce into a small chafing dish or fondue pot set over a warming device. Serve with the vegetables and bread.

Tuna Spread
Salsa Tonnata

MAKES 1½ CUPS

Everyone needs reliable recipes that can be put together in a flash. This tuna dip is high on my list. I always have the ingredients in the pantry, and it's a true crowd pleaser. The sauce is also good on hard-cooked eggs, asparagus, cherry tomatoes, or toast. Tuna packed in oil is important here for best flavor and texture.

1 (6½-ounce) can tuna packed in olive oil
4 anchovy fillets
½ cup mayonnaise
2 tablespoons capers, drained
1 small garlic clove, peeled
½ teaspoon grated lemon zest
1½ to 2 tablespoons fresh lemon juice
Belgian endive leaves, carrot or celery sticks, or other raw vegetables

1 In a food processor or blender, combine the tuna with its oil, anchovies, mayonnaise, capers, garlic, and lemon zest. Process until smooth, about 3 minutes, stopping to scrape the mixture down as necessary. Add lemon juice to taste.

2 Scrape the tuna mixture into a small bowl. Serve with the vegetables.

Eggplant Caviar
Caviale di Melanzana

MAKES ABOUT 2 CUPS

Many dips for vegetables or toasts are made with butter, mayonnaise, or other high-fat ingredients. This dip gets its creamy texture from roasted eggplant and good flavor from the mushroom, pine nuts, and garlic with just a small amount of extra-virgin olive oil.

1 large portobello mushroom, wiped or lightly rinsed and stemmed
1 large eggplant, about 1 pound
2 tablespoons chopped fresh flat-leaf parsley
2 tablespoons toasted pine nuts
1 small garlic clove, minced
2 tablespoons olive oil
Salt and freshly ground black pepper
Toasted Italian or French bread or raw vegetables

1 Place a rack in the center of the oven. Preheat the oven to 450°F. Line a small baking pan with foil.

2 Brush the mushroom lightly with oil. Place the mushroom and the eggplant in the pan. Pierce the eggplant skin in several places with a fork. Bake 20 minutes or until the mushroom is tender when pierced with a fork. Remove the mushroom. Turn the eggplant and cook 20 minutes more or until tender when pierced with a knife.

3 Remove the eggplant from the oven. Let cool a little, then remove the eggplant stem and cut the eggplant in half lengthwise. Place it in a colander to drain and cool completely.

4 Scoop out the eggplant flesh and discard the skin. Chop the eggplant and mushroom and place them in a large bowl. Stir in the parsley, pine nuts, garlic, oil, and salt and pepper to taste.

5 Scrape the mixture into a serving bowl. Serve with toasted bread or raw vegetables.

❧ Bruschetta and Crostini

Garlic Bruschetta
Bruschetta

MAKES 8

In the Castelli Romani district outside of Rome, I was served thick slices of crusty bread, toasted and rubbed with fresh garlic cloves and dripping with rich green extra-virgin olive oil. Little chunks of young grana cheese accompanied it, and we washed it down with a fruity local wine. It was so simple, yet so perfect; it was a meal I will never forget.

In Umbria and Tuscany, this antipasto originated as a way to sample freshly pressed olive oil. The pressing is typically done in autumn when it is quite chilly. While the olive growers waited for their freshly picked olives to be pressed, they would toast some bread and drizzle it with the oil directly from the mill. The warmth of the bread brings out the essence of the oil. The garlic is optional, especially when the oil is really fine.

8 (¹/₂-inch-thick) slices chewy Italian bread
4 large garlic cloves, peeled
Extra-virgin olive oil
Fine sea salt or kosher salt (optional)

1 Place a barbecue grill or broiler rack about 5 inches away from the heat source. Preheat the grill or broiler. Toast the bread on one side until golden brown, about 2 minutes. Turn the bread and toast the other side, about 2 minutes.

2 Immediately rub the bread with a garlic clove. Drizzle generously with oil. Sprinkle with salt, if desired. Serve immediately.

Bruschetta and Crostini

Bruschetta and *crostini* are slices of toasted Italian bread served with a topping. Though the two words are sometimes used interchangeably, bruschetta, from *bruscare*, "to toast," usually applies to the simplest form—a generous slice of chewy bread toasted or, better yet, grilled over a fire, rubbed with garlic and drizzled with extra-virgin olive oil. When tomatoes are ripe, bruschetta is often topped with a chopped tomato salad.

Crostini, meaning "little crusts," usually have more complex toppings, which can be anything from a cooked vegetable to liver pâté to cheese spreads.

The most important ingredient for bruschetta and crostini is the bread. It should be crusty and chewy and firm enough so that it will not collapse under the weight of the topping. The bread is typically toasted under a broiler, on a grill, or on top of the stove in a grill pan or *tostapane*, a thin, perforated metal sheet topped with a rack for making toast. The device is sold in many Italian kitchenware stores. The bread quickly browns on the surface, yet the inside of the slice stays soft and does not dry out as it would if toasted in an electric toaster. Day-old bread is fine and sometimes preferable if the bread is not as chewy as it should be.

Crostini and bruschetta taste best when they are freshly made, though many of the toppings can be made ahead and kept warm, then applied to the bread just before serving.

Many other recipes in this book can be used to top crostini, such as caponata (Sweet-and-Sour Eggplant, page 16), peperonata (Sweet Peppers with Tomatoes and Onions, page 449), or Mushroom Pâté (see page 13).

Tomato Bruschetta
Bruschetta di Pomodori

MAKES 8

Toasted country bread topped with tomatoes has become so popular it is almost a cliché. But when it is made properly with good, chewy bread and ripe tomatoes in season, there really is nothing better. Save this one for the summer tomato season. Here is the basic formula, plus some variations.

2 to 3 medium ripe tomatoes
3 tablespoons extra-virgin olive oil
3 fresh basil leaves or 1/2 teaspoon dried oregano
Salt and freshly ground black pepper
8 1/2-inch slices Italian bread
1 garlic clove

1 Cut the tomatoes in half through the stem end. Cut away the cores. Squeeze out the seeds and juice. Chop the tomatoes into 1/2-inch pieces.

2 In a medium bowl toss the tomatoes with the oil and salt and pepper to taste. If using fresh basil, stack the leaves and cut them crosswise into thin ribbons. Add the basil or the oregano to the tomatoes and stir well.

3 Place a barbecue grill or broiler rack about 5 inches away from the heat source. Preheat the grill or broiler.

4 Toast the bread on one side until golden brown, about 2 minutes. Turn the bread and toast the other side, about 2 minutes. Rub it on one side with the garlic clove. Pile on the tomatoes and serve immediately.

Ten Ways to Vary Tomato Bruschetta

1 Add finely minced garlic or red or green onion.
2 Add parsley, mint, or thyme instead of basil.
3 Add chopped fresh arugula or watercress.
4 Add diced mozzarella or ricotta salata cheese.
5 Add pitted chopped black or green olives or capers.
6 Top with a slice of mozzarella and run the toasts under the broiler.
7 Top with one or two anchovy fillets.
8 Drizzle with balsamic vinegar.
9 Add olive oil–packed tuna.
10 Top with shavings of Parmigiano-Reggiano.

Tomato and Avocado Bruschetta
Bruschetta di Pomodori e Avocado

MAKES 8

Avocados are not common in Italy. But because they go so well with tomatoes and good olive oil, I often use them as a topping for bruschetta.

2 medium ripe tomatoes
3 tablespoons extra-virgin olive oil
1 tablespoon chopped red onion
Salt and freshly ground black pepper
1/2 medium ripe Hass avocado, diced
1 to 2 tablespoons fresh lemon juice
4 to 8 (1/2-inch-thick) slices Italian bread

1 Cut the tomato in half through the stem end. Cut away the core. Squeeze out the seeds and juice. Chop the tomato into 1/2-inch pieces.

2 In a medium bowl toss the tomatoes with the oil, onion, and salt and pepper to taste. Stir in the avocado and lemon juice.

3 Place a barbecue grill or broiler rack about 5 inches away from the heat source. Preheat the grill or broiler.

4 Toast the bread on one side until golden brown, about 2 minutes. Turn the bread and toast the other side, about 2 minutes. Top with the tomato mixture. Serve immediately.

Beans and Greens Toasts
Crostini di Fagioli e Verdura

MAKES 8

Creamy beans are often served with cooked greens such as broccoli rabe, chicory, or escarole in southern Italy. Often, the beans and greens are served over bread. I adapted the combination for these crostini, which should be eaten with a knife and fork.

5 tablespoons olive oil
2 large garlic cloves, peeled and chopped fine
1 small dried chile (peperoncino preferred), crushed, or a pinch of crushed red pepper flakes
1 pound broccoli rabe, chicory, or escarole, washed, trimmed, and cut into bite-size pieces
1/4 cup water
Salt to taste
2 cups cooked dried or canned cranberry or cannellini beans, drained
8 (1/2-inch-thick) slices Italian bread, toasted

1 In a large saucepan, put 3 tablespoons of the oil, half the garlic, and all of the red pepper. Cook over medium heat until sizzling, about 1 minute.

2 Add the greens, 1/4 cup water, and salt to taste. Cover and lower the heat. Cook until the greens are tender, about 10 minutes for broccoli rabe or dandelion greens and 5 minutes for spinach.

3 Meanwhile, in a medium saucepan, heat the remaining 2 tablespoons oil and garlic 1 minute. Stir in the beans, cover, and cook over low heat until heated through, about 4 minutes. Coarsely mash the beans. Season to taste.

4 Place a barbecue grill or broiler rack about 5 inches away from the heat source. Preheat the grill or broiler.

5 Toast the bread on one side until golden brown, about 2 minutes. Turn the bread and toast the other side, about 2 minutes. Spread the toast with the beans. Top with the greens and a spoonful of their cooking liquid. Serve immediately.

Chicken Liver Toasts
Crostini di Fegato di Pollo

MAKES 8

Tuscan cooks serve these crostini accompanied by slices of locally made salumi (cured meat), made with pork or wild boar. One of my favorites is finocchiona, *salame made with ground pork and fennel seeds.*

8 chicken livers
3 tablespoons olive oil
I medium red onion, sliced and separated into rings
2 sage leaves, chopped
I teaspoon balsamic vinegar
Salt and freshly ground black pepper
8 (¹/₂-inch-thick) slices Italian bread, toasted

1 Trim the chicken livers, cutting away the connecting fibers with a sharp knife. Cut each liver into 2 or 3 pieces. Rinse the livers and pat dry.

2 Pour the oil into a medium skillet. Add the onion and sage leaves and cook over medium heat until softened, about 5 minutes.

3 Add the chicken livers and cook, mashing the livers with the back of a spoon, until just slightly pink, about 2 minutes. Add the vinegar and salt and pepper to taste.

4 Place a barbecue grill or broiler rack about 5 inches away from the heat source. Preheat the grill or broiler. Toast the bread on one side until golden brown, about 2 minutes. Turn the bread and toast the other side, about 2 minutes.

5 Top the bread with the liver mixture. Serve immediately.

Zucchini and Cheese Toasts
Crostini di Zucchine

MAKES 8

Crostini and bruschetta are favorite appetizers at Roman wine bars. For lunch one day, I had an assortment of hot crostini including this one topped with zucchini and melted Fontina Valle d'Aosta, a flavorful cow's milk cheese. Substitute swiss, Asiago, or another semifirm cheese if Fontina Valle d'Aosta is not available.

4 small zucchini (about I pound), scrubbed
4 tablespoons olive oil
I garlic clove, minced
I tablespoon chopped fresh flat-leaf parsley
I tablespoon chopped fresh basil
¹/₂ teaspoon dried oregano
Salt and freshly ground black pepper, to taste
8 (¹/₂-inch-thick) slices Italian bread
2 ounces Fontina Valle d'Aosta or swiss cheese, cut into thin slices

1 Trim the ends from the zucchini and cut into ¹/4–inch sticks, 2 inches in length. Pat the sticks dry with paper towels.

2 Heat the oil in a large skillet over medium heat. Add the zucchini and cook, stirring occasionally, until lightly browned, about 10 minutes.

3 Stir in the garlic, all the herbs, and the salt and pepper. Cook 2 minutes more.

4 Place a barbecue grill or broiler rack about 5 inches away from the heat source. Preheat the grill or broiler. Toast the bread on one side until golden brown, about 2 minutes. Turn the bread and toast the other side, about 2 minutes. Remove the toast but leave the oven turned on.

5 Place the toast on a baking sheet. Pile the zucchini on the toast and top with the cheese. Run the crostini under the broiler for 2 minutes or until the cheese is melted. Serve immediately.

Chickpea Toasts
Crostini di Ceci

MAKES 8

Chickpeas, sometimes called garbanzo beans, take a long time to cook from the dried state, so I usually buy them in cans. They are good with pasta, in soups, or coarsely mashed as a topping for crostini. This recipe is my version of the crostini I tasted at Babbo restaurant in New York.

1/2 cup chopped shallots or onions
1/2 teaspoon snipped fresh rosemary leaves
2 tablespoons extra-virgin olive oil, plus more
  for drizzling
1 (16-ounce) can chickpeas, drained
2 tablespoons water
1 tablespoon balsamic vinegar
Salt and freshly ground black pepper to taste
8 slices Italian bread, about 1/2-inch thick

1 In a small saucepan, combine the shallots, rosemary, and the 2 tablespoons of oil over medium-low heat. Cook 2 to 3 minutes or until the shallots are tender.

2 Add the chickpeas, water, and salt and pepper to taste. Cook 3 to 4 minutes more or until heated through, stirring frequently and coarsely mashing the chickpeas with the back of a spoon. Add a little more water if the mixture seems dry. Stir in the vinegar and taste for seasoning.

3 Place a barbecue grill or broiler rack about 5 inches away from the heat source. Preheat the grill or broiler. Toast the bread on one side until golden brown, about 2 minutes. Turn the bread and toast the other side, about 2 minutes.

4 Spread with the chickpea mixture. Drizzle with additional oil and serve immediately.

Broccoli Toasts
Crostini con Crema di Broccoli

MAKES 8

Roman broccoli, known as broccoli romanesco, *is pale green with a beautiful shape that resembles an exotic seashell. I can find it in the fall at my local farmers' market and occasionally at gourmet groceries. The flavor is more delicate than dark green broccoli, more like a cross between broccoli and cauliflower. Ordinary broccoli works fine for this recipe. The cooked vegetable is pureed with garlic and olive oil and makes a delicious spread for crostini.*

1 pound broccoli
Salt
1/4 cup extra-virgin olive oil
1 whole garlic clove
Freshly ground black pepper
8 (1/2-inch-thick) slices Italian bread

1 Trim the broccoli, reserving some of the stems. Bring a large saucepan of water to boiling. Add the broccoli and salt to taste. Cook until the broccoli is tender, about 10 minutes. Drain well, reserving some of the water.

2 Transfer the broccoli to a food processor. Add the garlic and process until chopped fine. With the motor running, add the oil through the tube and process until smooth and spreadable. Add a tablespoon or two of the broccoli water if the mixture is too thick. Season with salt and pepper to taste.

3 Place a barbecue grill or broiler rack about 5 inches away from the heat source. Preheat the grill or broiler. Toast the bread on one side until golden brown, about 2 minutes. Turn the bread and toast the other side, about 2 minutes. Spread with the warm broccoli puree. Serve immediately.

Eggplant and Tomato Toasts

Crostini alla Melanzane

MAKES 8

Eggplant, tomato, garlic, and cheese are a classic flavor combination throughout southern Italy— think of eggplant parmesan or the Sicilian pasta alla Norma. Here the same flavors team up as a topping for crostini.

1 medium eggplant, about 12 ounces
Salt and freshly ground black pepper to taste
2 or 3 large garlic cloves
1 large ripe tomato, cored and chopped
¹/₄ cup chopped fresh basil
2 tablespoons extra-virgin olive oil
8 (¹/₂-inch-thick) slices Italian bread
¹/₂ cup (about 3 ounces) ricotta salata cheese, crumbled

1 Place a rack in the center of the oven. Preheat the oven to 375° F. Place the eggplant on a baking sheet and pierce the skin with a fork two or three times to allow steam to escape. Bake 60 minutes or until soft. Let cool slightly.

2 Remove the eggplant from the oven. Let cool a little, then remove the eggplant stem and cut the eggplant in half lengthwise. Place it in a colander to drain and cool completely.

3 Scoop out the eggplant flesh and discard the skin. Mash it to a paste with a fork or masher or puree it in a food processor. Add salt and pepper to taste.

4 Combine the tomato with the basil and oil, and add a little salt and pepper.

5 Place a barbecue grill or broiler rack about 5 inches away from the heat source. Preheat the grill or broiler. Toast the bread on one side until golden brown, about 2 minutes. Turn the bread and toast the other side, about 2 minutes. Rub the slices with the garlic. Spread the toast with the eggplant puree. Top with the chopped tomato mixture and the ricotta salata. Serve immediately.

Ten Quick Crostini

1 Robiola or other soft cheese and slivers of sun-dried tomato
2 Chopped marinated sun-dried tomatoes and smoked mozzarella
3 Sweet butter, chives, and smoked salmon
4 Mascarpone and smoked salmon
5 Mashed ripe figs and a slice of prosciutto
6 Mashed gorgonzola cheese and toasted walnuts
7 Black olive paste and mozzarella— run under the broiler
8 Fresh mozzarella and anchovies— run under the broiler
9 Tomato sauce, mozzarella slices— run under the broiler
10 Sautéed mushrooms, fontina cheese— run under the broiler

❧ Fried Antipasti

"Little Orange" Rice Balls
Arancine

MAKES 18

Golden fried rice balls are a classic Sicilian snack. The Italian name—arancine—comes from their resemblance to oranges. Two versions are popular: one with the meat ragu filling that follows and the other with ham and béchamel.

FILLING

2 tablespoons olive oil
1/2 cup very finely chopped onion
1 garlic clove, finely chopped
8 ounces ground beef chuck
1 1/2 cups chopped canned Italian peeled tomatoes
Salt and freshly ground black pepper
1/2 cup fresh or frozen peas

RICE

5 cups chicken broth
1/2 teaspoon saffron threads, crumbled
2 cups (1 pound) medium-grain rice, such as Arborio, Carnaroli, or Vialone Nano
2 tablespoons unsalted butter
Salt to taste
4 large egg yolks
1/2 cup grated Parmigiano-Reggiano plus 1/2 cup grated Pecorino Romano

TO ASSEMBLE

5 large egg whites
2 cups plain dry bread crumbs
1 cup all-purpose flour
4 ounces imported provolone, cut into small dice
Vegetable oil for frying

1 To make the filling, put the oil, onion, and garlic in a medium skillet. Turn on the heat to medium and cook until the onion is soft, about 5 minutes.

2 Add the beef to the skillet and cook, stirring to break up the lumps, until lightly browned, about 10 minutes. Stir in the tomatoes, and salt and pepper to taste. Bring the sauce to a simmer and reduce the heat to low. Cook, stirring occasionally, until thick, about 30 minutes.

3 Add the peas and cook 5 minutes more. Let cool.

4 Bring the broth and the saffron to a boil in a large pot. Stir in the rice, butter, and salt. Cover and reduce the heat to low. Cook about 18 minutes, or until the rice is tender.

5 Remove the rice from the heat. Let cool slightly, then stir in the egg yolks and grated cheese.

6 To assemble, beat the egg whites in a shallow plate until foamy. Spread the bread crumbs on one sheet of wax paper and the flour on another. Place a cake rack over a baking sheet.

7 Dip your hands in cool water to prevent the rice from sticking. Scoop up about 1/3 cup of the rice mixture and place it in the palm of one hand. Poke a shallow hole in the center of the rice. Press a scant tablespoon of the meat sauce into the hole and top it with a piece of provolone. Cup your hand slightly, molding the rice over the filling to enclose it completely. Add a little more rice if necessary to cover the filling completely. Very gently squeeze the rice to compact it and form a ball.

8 Carefully roll the rice ball in the flour, then in the egg whites to coat it completely. Roll the ball in the bread crumbs, being sure not to leave any spots uncovered. Place the rice ball on a rack to dry.

9 Continue making rice balls with the remaining ingredients. Let the rice balls dry on the rack for 30 minutes.

10 Line a tray with paper towels; set the oven at the lowest temperature. Pour about 3 inches of oil into an electric deep fryer or a deep heavy saucepan. Heat the oil until the temperature reaches 375°F on a deep-frying thermometer or when a drop of egg white sizzles when it is added to the oil.

11 Carefully place the rice balls a few at a time in the hot oil. Do not crowd the pan. Cook until golden brown and crisp all over, 3 to 4 minutes. With a slotted spoon or strainer, transfer the rice balls to the paper towels to drain. Repeat with the remaining rice balls. Keep the cooked rice balls in the warm oven while you fry the remainder. Serve hot or warm.

"Telephone-Wire" Rice Balls
Suppli' di Riso

MAKES 24

Romans make rice balls filled with cheese. When you pull the rice ball apart, the melted cheese in the center stretches into strings like telephone wires, which gives the rice balls their name. Suppli' are served all over Rome; Italians love to stop in after school or work to have a suppli' snack before dinner.

5 cups chicken broth

2 cups medium-grain rice, such as Arborio, Carnaroli, or Vialone Nano

4 tablespoons unsalted butter

Salt to taste

3 large eggs, beaten

1 cup freshly grated Parmigiano-Reggiano

2 tablespoons chopped fresh flat-leaf parsley

Pinch of freshly grated nutmeg

6 ounces mozzarella, cut into small dice

TO ASSEMBLE

3 large eggs, beaten

2 cups plain dried bread crumbs

1 cup all-purpose flour

Vegetable oil for frying

1 Bring the broth to a boil in a large pot. Stir in the rice, butter, and salt. Cover and reduce the heat to low. Cook until the rice is tender, about 18 minutes.

2 Remove the rice from the heat. Let cool slightly, then stir in the three beaten eggs, grated cheese, parsley, and nutmeg.

3 To assemble, beat the other three eggs in a shallow plate until foamy. Spread the bread crumbs on one sheet of wax paper and the flour on another. Place a cake rack over a baking sheet.

4 Dip your hands in cool water to prevent the rice from sticking. Scoop up about 1/4 cup of the rice mixture and place it in the palm of one hand. Poke a shallow hole in the center of the rice. Press a bit of the mozzarella in the hole. Cup your hand slightly, molding the rice over the filling to enclose it completely. Add a little more rice if necessary to cover the filling completely. Very gently squeeze the rice to compact it and form a ball.

5 Carefully roll the rice ball in the flour, then in the eggs to coat it completely. Roll the ball in the bread crumbs, being sure not to leave any spots uncovered. Place the rice ball on a rack to dry.

6 Continue making rice balls with the remaining ingredients. Let the rice balls dry on the rack for 30 minutes.

7 Line a tray with paper towels; set the oven at the lowest temperature. Pour about 3 inches of oil into an electric deep fryer or a deep heavy saucepan. Heat the oil until the temperature reaches 375°F on a deep-frying thermometer or when a drop of egg white sizzles when it is added to the oil.

8 Carefully place the rice balls a few at a time in the hot oil. Do not crowd the pan. Cook until golden brown and crisp all over, 3 to 4 minutes. With a slotted spoon or strainer, transfer the rice balls to the paper towels to drain. Repeat with the remaining rice balls. Keep the cooked rice balls in the warm oven while you fry the remainder. Serve hot or warm.

Sicilian Chickpea Flour Fritters
Panelle

MAKES 4 TO 6 SERVINGS

Chickpea flour (see shopping sources on page 626) is available in many Italian and Middle Eastern markets and natural foods stores. Some stores offer a choice of roasted and unroasted chickpea flour. The latter is closer to the Italian kind.

In Palermo, these panelle are served as an appetizer, often accompanied by some caponata (see Sweet-and-Sour Eggplant, page 16), or they are piled up in a sesame seed roll, topped with ricotta and grated pecorino and eaten as a sandwich.

1³/4 cups cold water
1 cup chickpea flour
1 teaspoon salt
Freshly ground black pepper
Vegetable or peanut oil for frying

1 Pour the water into a medium saucepan. Slowly whisk the chickpea flour into the water. Stir in the salt.

2 Place the saucepan over medium heat and cook, stirring constantly, until the mixture comes to a simmer. Reduce the heat to low and cook, stirring constantly, until very thick, about 5 minutes.

3 Pour the mixture onto a baking sheet. With a spatula, spread it evenly to about a ¹/4-inch thickness. Let cool one hour or until firm. For longer storage, cover with plastic wrap and refrigerate.

4 Just before serving, heat about 1 inch of the oil in a deep heavy saucepan. Line a tray with paper towels. Cut the dough into 2-inch squares. To test if the oil is hot enough, drop a small piece of the dough into the oil. The oil should sizzle rapidly. Add enough of the dough as will fit without crowding. Fry the pieces, turning once, until puffed and golden brown, about 4 minutes. Transfer the fritters with a slotted spoon to the paper towels to drain. Keep warm while frying the remainder.

5 Sprinkle with salt and pepper and serve hot.

Basil Fritters
Foglie di Basilico Fritte

MAKES 6 SERVINGS

Basil leaves in a crisp batter are irresistible appetizers. Try sage and parsley, too.

¹/2 cup all-purpose flour
¹/4 cup cornstarch
1 teaspoon salt
About ¹/2 cup club soda or sparkling mineral water
Vegetable oil
24 large basil leaves

1 In a small bowl, whisk together the flour, cornstarch, and salt. Stir in enough of the club soda to make a thick, smooth batter. Let stand 1 hour.

2 Pour the oil to a ¹/2-inch depth in a small heavy saucepan. Heat over medium heat until a small drop of the batter sizzles and swims around the pan when added to the hot oil.

3 Line a tray with paper towels. Wipe the basil leaves with a damp paper towel. Dip the leaves in the batter. Remove the leaves a few at a time and slip them into the hot oil. Fry 2 minutes or until golden on both sides. Transfer to the paper towels to drain.

4 Fry the remaining leaves in the same way. Serve hot.

Fried Sage Leaves
Salvia Fritta

MAKES 4 TO 6 SERVINGS

*At a large banquet organized by the restaurateurs'
association of the Marches region, these crisp fried
sage leaves were passed as an accompaniment to
prosecco, a dry sparkling wine. The leaves are as
addictive as potato chips.*

¹/₃ cup fine dry bread crumbs
24 large fresh sage leaves
2 tablespoons all-purpose flour
Salt
1 large egg yolk, beaten
2 tablespoons olive oil
1 tablespoon unsalted butter
Lemon wedges

1 Spread the bread crumbs on a sheet of wax
paper. In a small bowl, toss the sage leaves with
the flour and 1 teaspoon salt.

2 One at a time, dip the sage leaves in the egg
yolk, then roll them in the bread crumbs. Place
the leaves on a cake rack to dry 30 minutes.

3 Line a tray with paper towels. Just before serving, heat the oil and butter in a small skillet.
When the butter foam subsides, arrange the sage
leaves in the pan in a single layer. Fry, turning the
leaves once, until browned and crisp on both
sides, about 4 minutes. Transfer to paper towels to
drain. Sprinkle with salt and serve hot with lemon
wedges.

Salads

Green Salads

Mixed Green Salad

Tricolor Salad

Green Salad with Lemon and Pine Nuts

Spinach and Egg Salad

Arugula and Parmigiano Salad

Roman Spring Salad

Green Salad with Gorgonzola and Walnuts

Tomato Salads

Tomato, Mozzarella, and Basil Salad

Neapolitan Tomato and Bread Salad

Tuscan Bread Salad

Tomato, Arugula, and Ricotta Salata Salad

Tomato and Egg Salad

Avocado and Tomato Salad

Vegetable Salads

Riviera Salad

Pickled Vegetables

Russian Salad

Mushroom and Parmigiano Salad

Fennel and Parmigiano Salad

Fennel and Olive Salad

Spicy Carrot Salad

Potato and Watercress Salad

Artusi's Potato Salad

Green Bean, Potato, and Red Onion Salad

Green Bean, Celery, and Olive Salad

Warm Lentil Salad

Fava Bean Puree with Seven Salads

Summer Rice Salad

Salads with Fruit

"Crunchy" Salad

Pear and Pecorino Salad

Orange and Fennel Salad

Beet and Orange Salad

Fish Salads

Shrimp and Rice Salad

Shrimp, Orange, and Anchovy Salad

Sardine and Arugula Salad

Grilled Scallop Salad

Venetian Crab Salad

Calamari Salad with Arugula and Tomatoes

Lobster Salad

Tuscan Tuna and Bean Salad

Couscous Tuna Salad

Tuna Salad with Beans and Arugula

Friday-Night Tuna Salad

Dressings

Gorgonzola and Hazelnut Dressing

Lemon Cream Dressing

Orange-Honey Dressing

To me, there is nothing like a salad to demonstrate the brilliant simplicity of Italian cooking at its best. Perfectly fresh vegetables, locally grown and full of flavor, rich extra-virgin olive oil, and good wine vinegar or fresh lemon juice are the basic ingredients. A simple salad is usually eaten with the main course in Italy (or sometimes after, as a light finish or palate cleanser). With the addition of cheese, canned tuna, cooked chicken, or eggs, the salad may be served as a first or main course.

Italian salad dressing is always very simple, so as to let the quality of the ingredients shine through. Like the sauce on pasta, there should be just enough dressing to coat the salad, and never so much that there is a pool of it left at the bottom of the bowl.

Dried herbs, bottled lemon juice, flavored vinegars, or poor-quality oil do not make a good salad, so don't even think about it. The so-called Italian dressing sold in bottles has nothing to do with the real thing.

Italian salad greens include all the familiar varieties, such as romaine, Boston, and leaf lettuce, as well as less well known kinds, such as *soncino,* known here by its French name, mâche, or sometimes as lamb's lettuce. The silver-dollar size leaves are dark green and tender and have a mild flavor and soft texture. *Misticanza* is a mix of wild baby greens and herbs, preferred in central Italy, especially Rome and Abruzzo. The flavor depends on the type of herbs gathered. In the springtime, Romans eat *puntarella*, Catalan chicory. Trimmed and soaked in cold water, the greens curl up, resembling pale green ribbons. Puntarella is crisp and chewy and has a slightly bitter flavor.

To keep them fresh as long as possible, it is best not to trim or wash salad greens until shortly before you plan to use them. Tear off the stems and discard any bruised or discolored portions and tough outer leaves. Wash the greens in a large basin or bowl of lukewarm water. Slightly warm water removes soil better and helps to perk up greens that are a little wilted. Allow the greens to stay in the water briefly to allow any grit to sink to the bottom while the greens float to the surface. Lift the greens out of the water with your hands and drain them. Repeat, washing the greens until there is no grit in the bottom of the basin.

An important key to a good-tasting salad is to dry the greens thoroughly. A salad spinner does the job best. Once dried, the greens can be wrapped in paper towels and stored in a plastic bag in the refrigerator for up to 6 hours, though the sooner they are used the better. Many greens turn brown when cut with a knife, so just before assembling the salad, tear the leaves into bite-size pieces.

❧ Green Salads

Mixed Green Salad
Insalata Mista

MAKES 4 SERVINGS

When I first went to Italy more than thirty years ago, I remember that whenever someone ordered a salad in a restaurant, the waiter would make the dressing and toss the salad to the diner's specifications. First, he would pour a little oil over the greens and toss them until lightly coated. Then he would pour a little wine vinegar into a large serving spoon, add salt and, with a fork, whisk the mixture briefly in the spoon to dissolve the salt before dribbling it over the salad. Then he would toss the whole thing until the greens were evenly coated.

The basic Italian salad dressing is simply extra-virgin olive oil, red or white wine vinegar, and salt. If it is a fish meal, fresh lemon juice is sometimes substituted for the vinegar. The dressing does not contain herbs or spices, not even pepper. Balsamic vinegar, which has become so popular, was until recently little known outside of Emilia-Romagna.

Nowadays, in most restaurants, the oil and vinegar are placed on the table in cruets for you to mix your own dressing.

1 head romaine, Boston, iceberg, or other lettuce, or a combination
About 3 tablespoons extra-virgin olive oil
1 tablespoon wine vinegar
Salt to taste

1 Trim the lettuce, discarding the outer leaves and any that are bruised. Wash them in several changes of cool water. Dry very well. Tear the lettuce into bite-size pieces. There should be about 6 cups.

2 Place the lettuce in a large salad bowl. Drizzle with the oil and toss well. In a small bowl, whisk together the vinegar and salt until the salt is dissolved. Pour the vinegar over the salad and toss again. Taste a piece of lettuce and add more oil, vinegar, or salt if needed. Serve immediately.

> **Variation:** For added color and substance, add 1 cup shredded carrots or torn radicchio, and 1 or 2 tomatoes, cut into wedges.

Tricolor Salad
Insalata Tricolore

MAKES 4 SERVINGS

The Italian flag has three bold stripes of red, white, and green, so it is called familiarly the tricolore. *These same colors appear frequently in Italian cooking. A number of dishes that have the colors are associated with the flag and patriotic pride, such as pizza Margherita, made with basil, tomato, and mozzarella, said to have been invented in honor of a queen, or the Pugliese pasta with tomatoes, potatoes, and arugula, known as* la bandiera, *meaning the flag. This pretty salad with its red radicchio, white endive, and green arugula is often called* insalata tricolore.

2 Belgian endive, separated into leaves
1 small head radicchio
1 small bunch arugula
3 tablespoons extra-virgin olive oil
1 to 2 tablespoons red wine vinegar
Salt

1 Trim the vegetables, discarding the outer leaves and any that are bruised. Wash them in several changes of cool water. Dry very well. Cut the endive crosswise into 3 or 4 pieces. Tear the radicchio into bite-size pieces. Trim off the tough stems of the arugula and tear the leaves into bite-size pieces. Place the vegetables in a large salad bowl.

2 Drizzle the vegetables with the oil and toss well. In a small bowl, whisk together the vinegar and salt until the salt is dissolved. Pour the vinegar over the salad and toss again. Taste the salad and add more oil, vinegar, or salt if needed. Serve immediately.

Green Salad with Lemon and Pine Nuts

Insalata Verde al Pinoli

MAKES 4 SERVINGS

This salad is a modern recipe that I had in Florence. I use tiny mixed greens often sold as mesclun, but baby spinach would be good too. A little bit of lemon zest gives it extra flavor and the pine nuts add crunch. They are easy to toast in a dry skillet.

1/4 cup pine nuts
6 cups mixed baby greens
1/4 cup extra-virgin olive oil
2 tablespoons fresh lemon juice
Pinch of grated lemon zest
Salt and freshly ground black pepper

1 Place the pine nuts in a small skillet. Turn the heat to medium and cook the nuts, shaking the pan occasionally, until they are fragrant and lightly toasted, about 5 minutes. Let cool.

2 Wash the greens in several changes of cold water. Dry very well. Tear the greens into bite-size pieces.

3 In a large salad bowl, whisk together the oil, lemon juice, zest, and salt and pepper to taste. Add the greens and toss well. Add the pine nuts and toss again. Serve immediately.

Spinach and Egg Salad

Insalata di Spinaci

MAKES 4 SERVINGS

Leaves of baby spinach are perfect for salads. They are tender and mild tasting, and, because they don't need trimming and usually are free of sand, they are very easy to prepare.

4 large eggs
6 ounces baby spinach leaves 3 tablespoons extra-virgin olive oil
1 tablespoon balsamic vinegar
Salt and freshly ground black pepper
1 tablespoon chopped capers

1 Place the eggs in a small saucepan with cold water to cover. Bring the water to a simmer. Cook for 12 minutes. Let the eggs cool under cold running water. Drain and peel.

2 Trim the spinach, discarding any bruised leaves and tough stems. Wash them in several changes of cool water. Dry very well. Tear into bite-size pieces.

3 Separate the cooked egg whites and yolks. Place the yolks in a bowl and mash them. Stir in the oil, vinegar, and salt and pepper to taste. Chop the egg whites and set aside.

4 In a large bowl, toss together the spinach leaves and capers. Add the egg yolk mixture and toss well. Add half the egg whites and toss again.

5 Mound the salad on 4 plates and sprinkle with the remaining egg white. Serve immediately

Arugula and Parmigiano Salad

Insalata di Rughetta e Parmigiano

MAKES 4 SERVINGS

The variety of arugula used to make this salad in Italy is crisp, peppery, and nutty, with small pointy leaves. Arugula here is a slightly different variety, with rounded leaves that are not quite as crisp in texture or as nutty in flavor, so I buy arugula seeds in Italy and grow them in a big windowbox. From spring through fall, I enjoy my home-grown Italian rughetta, *though the rest of the year, I still serve this salad with the domestic arugula.*

For a change, top this salad with toasted walnuts.

3 tablespoons extra-virgin olive oil
2 teaspoons balsamic vinegar
Salt and freshly ground black pepper
2 bunches arugula
2-ounce piece Parmigiano-Reggiano cheese

1 Trim the tough stems of the arugula and discard any yellowed or bruised leaves. Wash the arugula in several changes of cool water. Dry very well. Tear the arugula into bite-size pieces.

2 In a large bowl, drizzle the arugula with the oil and toss well. In a small bowl, whisk together the vinegar and salt and pepper until the salt is dissolved. Pour the vinegar over the salad and toss again. Taste for seasoning. Pile the salad onto serving plates.

3 With a vegetable peeler, shave the cheese over the salad. Serve immediately.

Roman Spring Salad
Insalata di Puntarella

MAKES 4 SERVINGS

In spring, Roman greengrocers sell a pale greenish white vegetable known as puntarella. *A member of the endive family, it is known as Catalan chicory in English. Because it is not widely available in the United States, I substitute either frisée or Belgian endive. They are members of the same large chicory family and have a similar pleasantly bitter flavor that goes well with the zesty anchovy and garlic dressing. Romans consider this salad a harbinger of spring.*

8 cups frisée or 4 medium Belgian endive
6 anchovy fillets, chopped
1 small garlic clove, very finely chopped
Salt
1/4 cup extra-virgin olive oil
1 to 2 tablespoons red wine vinegar
Freshly ground black pepper

1 Trim the frisée or endive, discarding the outer leaves and any that are bruised. Wash the vegetable in several changes of cool water. Dry very well. Tear the frisée, if using, into bite-size pieces. Cut the endive crosswise into narrow strips.

2 In a large salad bowl, mash the anchovy fillets, garlic, and a pinch of salt with a fork to form a smooth paste. Whisk in the oil and vinegar.

3 Add the vegetable and toss well. Add pepper to taste. Season to taste. Serve immediately.

Green Salad with Gorgonzola and Walnuts
Insalata con Gorgonzola

MAKES 6 SERVINGS

The flavors of walnuts and gorgonzola fit together perfectly. Here they are tossed with tender Boston lettuce leaves and a simple oil and vinegar dressing. I often have this salad as a light meal, or to follow a bowl of soup.

2 small heads Boston lettuce
1/4 cup extra-virgin olive oil
1 to 2 tablespoons red or white wine vinegar
Salt and freshly ground black pepper
4 ounces gorgonzola, rind removed and crumbled
1/2 cup walnuts, toasted and chopped

1 Wash the lettuce in several changes of cold water. Dry very well. Tear the greens into bite-size pieces.

2 Whisk together the oil, vinegar, and salt and pepper to taste. Pour the dressing over the salad and toss until well coated. Taste for seasoning.

3 Add the cheese and walnuts. Toss again. Serve immediately.

Tomato, Mozzarella, and Basil Salad
Insalata Caprese

MAKES 4 SERVINGS

This salad is sheer perfection when made with summer ripe tomatoes, fresh mozzarella, top-quality extra-virgin olive oil, and fresh basil. Don't even think of using anything less. It is best to assemble and serve the salad just before serving. Chilling would destroy its delicate flavor.

4 medium ripe tomatoes, cut into 1/4-inch slices
12 ounces fresh mozzarella, cut into 1/4-inch slices
Salt and freshly ground black pepper
8 fresh basil leaves
1/4 cup extra-virgin olive oil

1 Alternate the tomato and mozzarella slices on a serving platter. Sprinkle with salt and pepper.

2 Stack the basil leaves and cut them crosswise into thin strips. Scatter the strips over the salad. Drizzle with the oil and serve immediately.

Variation: If you have a good supply of fresh basil, add a basil leaf for every row of tomato and mozzarella.

Neapolitan Tomato and Bread Salad
La Caponata

MAKES 4 SERVINGS

Hard biscuits known as freselle *(found in Italian food stores) are used for this salad in Naples, but toasted bread can be used too. My grandmother always added ice cubes to this salad, a clever Italian trick. The ice cools the ingredients slightly, and as the ice melts, the cold water extends the vegetable juices so that they can soak into the bread.*

Don't confuse this salad, known as caponata *in Naples, with the Sicilian caponata (Sweet-and-Sour Eggplant, page 16), made with cooked eggplant, tomatoes, and capers.*

4 freselle or 1-inch-thick slices of Italian or French
    bread, toasted
2 large ripe tomatoes
2 small kirby cucumbers, sliced
3 or 4 slices of red onion, chopped
4 fresh basil leaves, torn into small pieces
1/4 cup extra-virgin olive oil
About 2 tablespoons white vinegar
Salt and freshly ground black pepper
8 ice cubes

1 Break the freselle or bread into bite-size pieces and place them in a bowl. Sprinkle with about 1/4 cup cool water or enough to slightly soften the bread.

2 Add the tomatoes, cucumbers, onion, and basil to the bowl. Drizzle with oil and vinegar and season to taste with salt and pepper. Toss well.

3 Add the ice cubes to the salad and let stand 15 minutes. Toss again and taste for seasoning, adding more vinegar if needed. Serve immediately.

Variation: You can make the Pugliese version of this salad, called *cialedda*. They use a round variety of cucumber (but use what is available), plus radishes, arugula, and celery.

Tuscan Bread Salad

Panzanella

MAKES 4 TO 6 SERVINGS

The most important ingredient in this salad is the bread, which needs to be crusty and chewy. Soft mushy bread would melt when soaked, instead of crumbling. Cucumbers and radishes can also be added.

6 to 8 slices day-old country-style Italian bread
1/2 cup water
2 ripe tomatoes, cut into bite-size pieces
2 tender celery ribs, thinly sliced
I medium red onion, thinly sliced
1/2 cup fresh basil leaves, torn into bits
1/2 cup extra-virgin olive oil
3 to 4 tablespoons red wine vinegar
Salt and freshly ground black pepper

I Place the bread in a large serving bowl and sprinkle with the water. Let stand 1 hour. Squeeze out the excess water, and wipe out the bowl. Tear the bread into bits, returning them to the bowl.

2 Add the tomatoes, celery, onion, and basil. Toss well. In a small bowl, whisk together the oil, vinegar, and salt and pepper to taste. Pour the dressing over the salad and toss again. Cover and let stand in a cool place 1 hour.

3 Toss the salad, and taste and adjust the seasoning. Serve immediately.

Tomato, Arugula, and Ricotta Salata Salad

Insalata di Pomodori e Ricotta Salata

MAKES 4 SERVINGS

This is a lovely, simple composed salad. Ricotta salata is pressed salted ricotta, which is semifirm and resembles feta. It nicely complements the sweet tomatoes and slightly bitter arugula. Substitute feta or crumbled gorgonzola if ricotta salata is not available.

I bunch arugula
2 large ripe tomatoes, cored and thinly sliced
2 thin slices red onion, separated into rings
1/4 cup extra-virgin olive
Salt and freshly ground black pepper
4 ounces ricotta salata, coarsely grated

I Trim the tough stems of the arugula and discard any yellowed or bruised leaves. Wash the arugula in several changes of cool water. Dry very well. Tear the arugula into bite-size pieces.

2 Arrange the tomatoes on a platter. Top with the arugula and onion rings. Drizzle with olive oil and sprinkle with salt and pepper to taste.

3 Sprinkle the ricotta salata over the salad. Serve immediately.

Tomato and Egg Salad

Insalata di Pomodori e Uova

MAKES 2 TO 4 SERVINGS

I make this Sicilian salad for lunch at least once a week in the summertime. It's great in a sandwich, too.

4 large eggs
2 large ripe tomatoes, cut into wedges
4 green onions, thinly sliced
6 fresh basil leaves, stacked and cut into thin ribbons
2 tablespoons extra-virgin olive oil
I tablespoon red wine vinegar
Salt and freshly ground black pepper

I Place the eggs in a small saucepan with cold water to cover. Bring the water to a simmer. Cook for 12 minutes. Let the eggs cool under cold running water. Drain and peel. Cut the eggs into quarters.

2 In a large bowl, combine the eggs, tomatoes, green onions, and basil.

3 In a small bowl, whisk together the oil, vinegar, and salt and pepper to taste. Pour the dressing over the salad and toss gently. Serve immediately.

Avocado and Tomato Salad
Avocado in Insalata

MAKES 6 SERVINGS

*With luscious ripe tomatoes and rich, flavorful avo-
cados alone this would be a great salad. It is a contemporary recipe, inspired by a salad I ate in Milan.
Imported provolone has a sharp, slightly smoky flavor and a drier texture than the sliced domestic
cheese. Tarragon is not used very much in Italy, but
here it adds something a little different. If you prefer not to use it, just leave it out or substitute
another herb such as basil or parsley.*

I medium head Boston or leaf lettuce
^{1}/4 cup olive oil
2 tablespoons lemon juice
I teaspoon Dijon mustard
Salt and freshly ground black pepper to taste
6 basil leaves, torn into bits
I tablespoon chopped fresh tarragon
2 small ripe avocados, peeled and sliced
4 ounces imported provolone, sliced
2 medium tomatoes, sliced

I Trim the lettuce, discarding the outer leaves
and any that are bruised. Wash it in several changes
of cool water. Dry very well. Tear the lettuce into
bite-size pieces. There should be about 8 cups.

2 In a small bowl, whisk together the oil, lemon
juice, mustard, and salt and pepper to taste.

3 In a deep platter, toss together the lettuce, basil,
and tarragon. Add half of the dressing and toss well.

4 Arrange the avocado, provolone, and tomato
slices alternately on top. Drizzle with the remaining dressing and serve immediately.

❧ Vegetable Salads

Riviera Salad
Condion

MAKES 4 SERVINGS

*This salad is popular all along the Riviera from
Italy to France. Other versions I have seen include
celery, artichokes, and white and green onions, so
feel free to improvise.*

2 medium boiling potatoes
Salt
4 large eggs
2 tomatoes, halved and sliced
I small cucumber, peeled and sliced ^{1}/4 inch thick
I small red or yellow bell pepper, cut into
    narrow strips
6 anchovy fillets, cut into 5 or 6 pieces
^{1}/2 cup pitted green olives, rinsed and drained and
    coarsely chopped
6 basil leaves, torn into bits
3 tablespoons extra-virgin olive oil
I tablespoon wine vinegar
Freshly ground black pepper

I Place the potatoes in a saucepan with cold water
to cover and salt to taste. Bring to a simmer and
cook until tender, about 20 minutes. Drain and peel
the potatoes. Cut them into ^{1}/4-inch-thick slices.

2 Meanwhile, place the eggs in a small saucepan
with cold water to cover. Bring the water to a simmer. Cook for 12 minutes. Let the eggs cool under
cold running water. Drain and peel. Cut the eggs
into quarters.

3 In a large serving bowl, combine the potatoes,
tomatoes, cucumber, bell pepper, anchovies, and
olives. Scatter the basil leaves on top.

4 In a small bowl, whisk together the oil, vinegar,
and salt and pepper to taste. Pour the dressing
over the salad and toss gently. Garnish with the
eggs. Serve immediately.

Pickled Vegetables
Giardiniera

MAKES 2 PINTS

Pickled vegetables are a nice accompaniment to antipasti, cold meats, or sandwiches. Vary the vegetables according to what is in season or available. Button mushrooms, green beans, small turnips or radishes, cucumbers, and many others can be prepared this way. Be sure to cut them into bite-size pieces. Packed in a pretty glass jar, these colorful vegetables make great gifts.

1 cup white wine vinegar

2 cups water

2 tablespoons sugar

2 teaspoons salt

1 bay leaf

3 medium carrots, quartered lengthwise and cut into 1 1/2-inch lengths

2 tender celery ribs, halved lengthwise and cut into 1 1/2-inch lengths

1 red bell pepper, cut into 1-inch squares

1 cup small cauliflower florets

6 small pearl onions, peeled

2 garlic cloves

1 In a large saucepan, bring the vinegar and water to a boil. Add the sugar, salt, and bay leaf and cook, stirring, until the sugar and salt are dissolved, about 1 minute.

2 Add the vegetables and bring the liquid back to boiling. Cook until the vegetables are tender yet still crisp, about 5 minutes. Drain the vegetables, reserving the liquid.

3 Divide the vegetables between two sterilized pint jars. Add the vinegar mixture. Let cool, then cover and refrigerate 24 hours before using. These keep well for at least 2 weeks in the refrigerator.

Russian Salad
Insalata Russa

MAKES 8 SERVINGS

I don't know how this colorful salad became so popular in Italy, but it is ubiquitous for buffet dinners or as an antipasto. I also like to serve it for a summer meal with cold shrimp, lobster, poached or smoked fish, or hard-cooked eggs. For a party, it looks great garnished with anchovy fillets, lemon slices, tomatoes, or herbs.

Vary the vegetables according to the season. Cauliflower, broccoli, and zucchini are all good to use.

3 medium boiling potatoes, peeled and cut into 1/2-inch cubes

Salt

8 ounces green beans, trimmed and cut into 1/2-inch lengths

3 medium carrots, trimmed and cut into 1/2-inch cubes

1 cup fresh or frozen peas

2 tablespoons extra-virgin olive oil

2 tablespoons white wine vinegar

3 or 4 sour pickles, cut into 1/2-inch pieces (about 1 cup)

2 tablespoons capers, rinsed and drained

Freshly ground pepper

1 cup mayonnaise

2 tablespoons chopped fresh flat-leaf parsley

1 Place the potatoes in a saucepan with cold water to cover and salt to taste. Bring to a simmer and cook until tender, about 5 minutes. Let cool under running water. Drain.

2 Bring about 2 quarts of water to boil in a medium saucepan. Add the green beans, carrots, and peas, and salt to taste. Cook until tender, about 5 minutes. Let cool under running water. Drain.

3 In a large bowl, whisk the oil, vinegar, and salt to taste. Pat the vegetables dry. Add all of the cooked vegetables, the pickles, and the capers to the dressing and stir well. Add pepper to taste.

4 Stir in the mayonnaise. Taste and adjust seasoning. Mound the salad in a serving bowl. Cover and chill at least 1 or up to 4 hours before serving. Garnish with parsley and serve immediately.

Mushroom and Parmigiano Salad
Insalata di Funghi e Parmigiano

MAKES 6 SERVINGS

For an all-year-round salad, you can't beat this one made with mushrooms, celery, and carrots. White mushrooms can be used, or you can substitute a wild mushroom such as porcini. In Bologna, I had this salad with ovoli, *beautiful white and orange mushrooms with an egg-shaped cap. Though I usually top the salad with Parmigiano-Reggiano, Grana Padano, a mild pecorino, or even a nutty Emmenthal can be used.*

Be sure to slice the vegetables paper-thin. Use a food processor with the narrowest cutting blade or a mandoline slicer for best results.

12 ounces white mushrooms, sliced paper-thin
2 tender celery ribs, sliced paper-thin
2 medium carrots, sliced paper-thin
2/3 cup extra-virgin olive oil
2 to 3 tablespoons fresh lemon juice
Salt and freshly ground black pepper
A small wedge of Parmigiano-Reggiano

1 On a large platter, toss together the mushrooms, celery, and carrots.

2 Whisk together the oil, lemon juice, and salt and pepper to taste. Pour the dressing over the salad and toss well. Taste and adjust seasoning.

3 With a swivel-blade vegetable peeler, shave the cheese over the salad. Serve immediately.

Fennel and Parmigiano Salad
Insalata di Finocchio e Parmigiano

MAKES 4 SERVINGS

The mild licorice flavor of the fennel, the tang of the lemon, and the fresh taste of the parsley balance wonderfully in this salad. It would be a perfect first course for a seafood meal, or serve it for a buffet dinner. The crisp fennel holds up well without wilting. For really thinly sliced fennel, use a mandoline slicer or food processor.

2 medium fennel bulbs, trimmed
2 tablespoons chopped fresh flat-leaf parsley
3 tablespoons olive oil
1 to 2 tablespoons fresh lemon juice
A small wedge of Parmigiano-Reggiano

1 Cut the fennel in half lengthwise and remove the core. With a mandoline slicer or a food processor fitted with narrowest blade, cut the halves crosswise into very thin slices.

2 In a bowl, toss the fennel with the parsley, oil, lemon juice, and salt and pepper to taste. Taste and adjust seasoning. Pile the salad onto 4 plates.

3 With a swivel-blade vegetable peeler, shave the Parmigiano into thin flakes and scatter them over the salad. Serve immediately.

Fennel and Olive Salad
Insalata di Finocchio e Oliva

MAKES 4 SERVINGS

Large green olives are cured in brine in Sicily and have a tart, tangy flavor and crisp texture. To help the curing liquid penetrate the olive flesh more rapidly, the olives are often cracked open by the manufacturer. The pits are usually easy to remove, but if needed, the olives can be crushed lightly with the side of a knife so that they release the pit. Don't press too hard, though, or the pit may crack.

This is a good crunchy side salad or a great addition to a sandwich made with cheese or cold cuts.

1 small red onion, thinly sliced
8 ounces Sicilian green olives
1 small fennel bulb, trimmed, cored, and thinly sliced
2 tablespoons chopped fresh flat-leaf parsley
1/2 teaspoon dried oregano
1/4 teaspoon crushed red pepper
1/4 cup extra-virgin olive oil
2 tablespoons white wine vinegar

1 Soak the onion slices in a medium bowl of ice water for 15 minutes. Drain the onion and pat dry.

2 To pit the olives, place them on a cutting board. Lay a large chef's knife on its side on top of an olive and smack it firmly but gently with the heel of your hand. The olive should break open. Remove the pit. Repeat with the remaining olives. Add the pitted olives to the bowl.

3 Add the fennel, parsley, oregano, red pepper, oil, and vinegar to the bowl. Toss very well. Chill slightly before serving.

Spicy Carrot Salad
Insalata di Carote Piccante

MAKES 4 TO 6 SERVINGS

I used to make this salad with cooked carrots, but I like the dressing on shredded raw carrots, too. This is a colorful side dish to go with an antipasto assortment or a frittata.

1 pound carrots
3 tablespoons extra-virgin olive oil
2 tablespoons white wine vinegar
1 garlic clove, very finely chopped
1 teaspoon sugar
Pinch of crushed red pepper
Salt and freshly ground black pepper
2 tablespoons chopped fresh mint or parsley

1 Peel the carrots. In a food processor fitted with the shredding blade, or on a box grater, shred the carrots. Place them in a bowl.

2 In a small bowl, whisk together the oil, vinegar, garlic, sugar, crushed red pepper, and salt and pepper to taste. Whisk until the sugar is dissolved.

3 Pour the dressing over the salad and toss. Add mint and toss again. Serve immediately, or chill up to one hour.

Potato and Watercress Salad
Insalata di Patate e Crescione

MAKES 4 SERVINGS

Horseradish is commonly used in the Trentino–Alto Adige region of northern Italy. This recipe was given to me a number of years ago by a chef from that region. The unusual dressing is made with yogurt and olive oil, a surprisingly tasty combination. It makes sense when you think about it. The oil is blended with a high-acid ingredient, though instead of the usual vinegar or lemon juice, here the acid tang comes from yogurt.

1 1/2 pounds Yukon gold or other waxy boiling potatoes
Salt
3/4 cup unflavored yogurt
1/4 cup extra-virgin olive oil
2 tablespoons peeled and minced fresh horseradish or drained bottled horseradish
Freshly ground black pepper to taste
1 large bunch watercress, tough stems removed (about 4 cups)

1 Place the potatoes in a medium saucepan with cold water to cover and salt to taste. Bring to a simmer and cook until the potatoes are tender when pierced with a knife, about 20 minutes. Drain and let cool slightly. Peel the potatoes and cut into 1/4-inch-thick slices.

2 In a medium bowl, whisk together the yogurt, oil, horseradish, and salt and pepper to taste until smooth and well blended.

3 Add the potatoes and watercress to the bowl and mix well. Taste and adjust seasoning. Serve immediately or cover and chill in the refrigerator up to 3 hours.

Artusi's Potato Salad

Insalata di Patate al'Artusi

MAKES 6 TO 8 SERVINGS

I adapted this potato salad recipe from Pellegrino Artusi's classic Italian cookbook, Scienza in Cucina e l'Arte di Mangiar Bene *(published in English as* Science in the Kitchen and the Art of Eating Well*). Few households in Italy are without a copy of L'Artusi, as it is familiarly called, and millions have been sold since it was first printed in 1891.*

2 pounds Yukon gold or other waxy potatoes
Salt
1/3 cup extra-virgin olive oil
3 tablespoons white wine vinegar
1/2 teaspoon dried oregano
Freshly ground black pepper
1 (2-ounce) can anchovy fillets, drained and chopped
1 small red bell pepper, chopped
1 cup chopped celery
1/4 cup chopped red onion
3 tablespoons capers, drained and chopped

1 Place the potatoes in a medium saucepan and add cold water to cover and salt to taste. Bring to a simmer over medium heat. Cook until the potatoes are tender when pierced with a knife, about 20 minutes. Drain and let cool slightly. Peel the potatoes and cut into bite-size pieces.

2 In a large bowl, whisk together the olive oil, vinegar, oregano, and salt and pepper to taste. Add the potatoes, anchovies, bell pepper, celery, onion, and capers. Stir gently. Taste and adjust seasoning. Cover and chill at 1 to 3 hours before serving.

Green Bean, Potato, and Red Onion Salad

Insalata di Fagiolini

MAKES 4 SERVINGS

My mother often made this salad as a summertime alternative to a salad made with leafy greens. It is popular all over southern Italy. Fresh parsley, basil, or mint can be used.

4 medium boiling potatoes
Salt
1 pound green beans, trimmed
1 small red onion, chopped
1/3 cup extra-virgin olive oil
3 tablespoons red wine vinegar
2 tablespoons chopped fresh basil, mint, or parsley,
    or 1/2 teaspoon dried oregano
Freshly ground black pepper

1 Place the potatoes in a medium saucepan and add cold water to cover and salt to taste. Cover and bring to a simmer over medium heat. Cook until the potatoes are tender when pierced with a knife, about 20 minutes. Drain well. Let cool slightly. Peel the potatoes and cut into 1/4-inch slices.

2 Bring another large saucepan of water to a boil. Add the green beans and salt to taste. Cook the beans until they are tender, about 8 minutes. Drain the beans and cool them under running water. Drain and pat dry. Cut the beans into bite-size pieces.

3 In a large bowl, whisk together the oil, vinegar, herbs, and salt and pepper to taste. Add the potatoes, beans, and onion and toss well. Taste and adjust seasoning. Serve immediately.

Green Bean, Celery, and Olive Salad
Insalta di Fagioli, Sedano, e Olive

MAKES 6 SERVINGS

This salad gets better with time, so it's good to make in advance, for picnics or other gatherings. After it has been refrigerated, let it warm up slightly at room temperature. Taste the salad before serving, because the vinegar and salt flavors diminish as the salad stands. It may need a splash more vinegar or a sprinkle of salt before serving to brighten the flavor, as is true of any marinated salad.

I pound green beans, trimmed
Salt
¼ cup extra-virgin olive oil
2 tablespoons red wine vinegar
I small garlic clove, minced
A pinch of crushed red pepper
I tender celery rib, trimmed and chopped
½ cup pitted green olives, chopped

1 Bring 2 quarts of water to a boil in large saucepan. Add the beans and salt to taste. Cook uncovered, until the beans are tender, about 8 minutes. Drain the beans and cool them under cold running water. Pat the beans dry.

2 In a large serving bowl, whisk together the oil, vinegar, salt to taste, garlic, and red pepper. Add the beans and toss well. Add the remaining ingredients and stir until well coated with the dressing. Taste and adjust seasoning. Serve immediately or chill in the refrigerator up to 3 hours.

Warm Lentil Salad
Insalata di Lenticchie

MAKES 8 SERVINGS

Serve this earthy salad with cotechino or other sausage, or, for something completely different, serve it with grilled salmon. If you can find them, use the tiny green lentils from Umbria known as lenticchie di Castelluccio, or French le Puy lentils. These tasty lentil varieties keep their shape better than the typical brown lentils sold here.

I pound lentils, rinsed and picked over
2 unpeeled garlic cloves
3 sprigs fresh thyme
I bay leaf
Salt
⅓ cup extra-virgin olive oil
3 tablespoons red wine vinegar
I teaspoon Dijon mustard
Freshly ground black pepper
I small red onion, finely chopped
¼ cup chopped fresh flat-leaf parsley

1 Place the lentils in a large pot with cold water to cover by 1 inch. Add the garlic and herbs. Bring the liquid to a simmer and cook 35 minutes. Add salt to taste and cook until the lentils are tender, about 10 minutes more.

2 Drain the lentils and discard the herbs and garlic.

3 In a small bowl, whisk together the oil, vinegar, mustard, and salt and pepper to taste. Add the lentils, onion, and parsley. Mix well. Serve warm or at room temperature.

Fava Bean Puree with Seven Salads

Fave con Sette Insalate

MAKES 6 SERVINGS

As peeled, dried fava beans cook, they lose their shape and are easy to mash into a smooth paste. A favorite dish in southern Italy is mashed fava beans topped with sautéed greens. Cooks in Puglia take this idea further and top the favas with a combination of cooked, raw, and pickled vegetables. Because the toppings are cold, or at least room temperature, they are called salads. Typically, seven different toppings are used, but you can use as few as you want. This makes a fine appetizer or meatless main dish.

8 ounces dried peeled fava beans, rinsed and drained

Salt to taste

4 tablespoons extra-virgin olive oil

1 pound fresh spinach, escarole, or broccoli rabe, trimmed and cut into bite-size pieces

1 large ripe tomato, seeded and chopped

1 cup mild black olives, such as Gaeta, pitted and coarsely chopped

1 cup arugula, tough stems removed

1/2 cup hot or sweet pickled peppers, drained and sliced

1/2 cup thinly sliced cucumbers or radishes

2 green onions, thinly sliced

1 Place the beans in a large pot with fresh cold water to cover by 1 inch and 1 teaspoon salt. Bring the water to a simmer and cook over low heat until very soft and all of the liquid has been absorbed, about 1 hour. If necessary, add a little more water to prevent the beans from drying out.

2 Put the greens in a large pot with 1/4 cup water over medium heat. Add salt to taste. Cover and cook 5 minutes or until wilted and tender. Drain well.

3 In the pot, mash the beans until smooth. Taste for salt. Stir in the oil.

4 Spread the fava beans on a warm serving platter. Drizzle with a little olive oil. Place piles of the vegetables around the edge. Serve immediately.

Summer Rice Salad

Insalata di Riso

MAKES 4 SERVINGS

When the weather is warm, rather than serve salads made with pasta, which can get mushy, Italians make salads with rice. Long-grain rice is used to help the grains remain separate in the salad. The rice will harden in the refrigerator, so it is best to serve this salad at room temperature.

This salad goes well with grilled swordfish or tuna, or serve it with chicken or steak. I sometimes add a can of tuna to the salad and serve it as a whole meal.

1 1/2 cups long-grain rice

Salt

2 roasted red or yellow bell peppers, chopped

1 cup cherry or grape tomatoes, halved or quartered if large

1 (2-ounce) can anchovies, drained and chopped

3/4 cup flavorful black olives, such as Gaeta, pitted and chopped

1/4 cup chopped fresh basil

1 garlic clove, very finely chopped

1/4 cup extra-virgin olive oil

2 to 3 tablespoons fresh lemon juice

1 In a large saucepan over medium heat, bring 3 1/2 cups water to a boil. Add the rice and salt to taste. When the rice returns to a boil, reduce the heat to low and cover the pan. Cook until the water is absorbed and the rice is tender, about 18 minutes. Let cool slightly.

2 In a large serving bowl, combine the peppers, tomatoes, anchovies, olives, basil, and garlic. Toss well. Add the rice and toss again.

3 In a small bowl, whisk together the oil and lemon juice. Pour the dressing over the ingredients in the bowl. Taste and adjust seasoning. Serve warm or at room temperature.

❧ Salads with Fruit

"Crunchy" Salad
Insalata Croccante

MAKES 4 SERVINGS

In winter, when there is a dearth of fresh vegetables, I like to make this tasty salad. The name says it all—it is croccante, or crunchy, with apples, nuts, and crisp vegetables tossed with a hint of creamy gorgonzola. To peel or not peel the apple is up to you. I generally leave them unpeeled, unless the apple is waxed.

3 to 4 Belgian endive, separated into leaves
2 tablespoons olive oil
1 to 2 tablespoons fresh lemon juice
Salt and freshly ground black pepper
1 medium apple, such as gala, Fuji, or Braeburn, cored and thinly sliced
1 small fennel, trimmed and thinly sliced
2 green onions, thinly sliced
4 ounces gorgonzola, crumbled
1/2 cup toasted walnuts

1 Fan the endive leaves out on 4 serving plates.

2 In a medium bowl, whisk together the oil, lemon juice, and salt and pepper to taste.

3 Add the apple, fennel, and green onions and toss well. Add the gorgonzola and toss again.

4 Scoop the salad mixture onto the base of the endive. Sprinkle with the nuts and serve immediately.

Pear and Pecorino Salad
Insalata di Pere e Pecorino

MAKES 4 SERVINGS

Ripe pears and pecorino are a classic combination often served after a meal in Rome and Tuscany. This salad extends the concept a little further with the addition of peppery watercress or arugula and a simple lemon dressing. The sweet, soft pear is a nice counterpoint to the salty cheese and peppery greens. Substitute apples for the pears, if you prefer.

About 6 cups watercress or arugula, tough stems removed
2 to 3 teaspoons fresh lemon juice
3 tablespoons extra-virgin olive oil
Salt and freshly ground black pepper
2 firm ripe pears, thinly sliced
Small wedge Pecorino Romano or Parmigiano-Reggiano

1 Trim the tough stems from the watercress or arugula and discard any yellowed or bruised leaves. Wash the greens in several changes of cool water. Dry very well. Tear the greens into bite-size pieces. Divide the greens among four salad plates.

2 In a medium bowl, whisk together the lemon juice, oil, and salt and pepper to taste. Add the pears, and toss gently with the dressing.

3 Place the pears on top of the greens. With a small paring knife or a swivel-blade vegetable peeler, shave thin flakes of the cheese over each salad. Serve immediately.

Orange and Fennel Salad

Insalata di Arancia e Finocchio

MAKES 4 SERVINGS

The flavor combination in this popular Sicilian salad is sensational. Sweet, juicy oranges, crunchy fennel and red onions, fresh mint, and intense black olives not only taste great together, but they look great too.

**2 large navel oranges, peeled, pith removed,
      and cut into crosswise slices**
1 medium fennel bulb, trimmed and sliced very thin
1/2 red onion, very thinly sliced
12 imported black olives, such as oil-cured
3 tablespoons extra-virgin olive oil
Salt to taste
2 tablespoons chopped fresh mint

Arrange the orange slices alternately on a platter with the fennel. Scatter the onion and black olives over the top. Drizzle with olive oil and salt. Sprinkle with the mint. Serve immediately.

Beet and Orange Salad

Insalata di Barbabietole e Arancia

MAKES 4 SERVINGS

This is an especially pretty salad with the contrasting colors of red beets, orange slices, and mint. To make it more substantial, serve it with some goat cheese or crumbled gorgonzola.

4 roasted beets (see page 125), peeled
2 navel oranges, peeled and sliced
2 tablespoons extra-virgin olive oil
1 teaspoon fresh lemon juice
Salt and freshly ground black pepper
2 tablespoons chopped fresh mint

1 Cut the beets into 1/4-inch slices. Alternate the beet and orange slices on a platter.

2 Whisk the oil and lemon juice with salt and pepper to taste. Pour the dressing over the beets and oranges. Scatter the mint on top. Serve immediately.

❧ Fish Salads

Shrimp and Rice Salad

Insalata di Riso con Gamberi

MAKES 4 SERVINGS

Fiumicino, outside of Rome, is best known as the location of one of Italy's largest airports, named for the artist Leonardo Da Vinci. But Fiumicino is also a seaport, where Romans like to go in the summer to enjoy the cool breezes and eat at one of the great seafood restaurants along the shore. At Bastianelli al Molo, we sat on the terrace under a big white umbrella and watched the sea. I had a multicourse meal that included this simple shrimp and rice salad.

Cooked long-grain rice hardens when it is refrigerated, so make this salad shortly before you plan to serve it.

2 cups long-grain rice
1/3 cup extra-virgin olive oil
3 tablespoons fresh lemon juice
1 pound medium shrimp, shelled and deveined
1 bunch arugula
2 medium tomatoes, cut into wedges

1 Bring 4 cups of water to a boil in a large saucepan. Add the rice and 1 teaspoon salt. Stir well. Reduce the heat to low, cover the pan, and cook until the rice is tender, 16 to 18 minutes. Pour the rice into a large serving bowl.

2 In a small bowl, whisk together the oil, lemon juice, and salt and pepper to taste. Stir half the dressing into the rice and let cool.

3 Trim the tough stems of the arugula and discard any yellowed or bruised leaves. Wash the arugula in several changes of cool water. Dry very well. Tear the arugula into bite-size pieces.

4 Bring 2 quarts of water to a boil in a medium saucepan. Add the shrimp and salt to taste. Bring to a simmer and cook until the shrimp are pink and just cooked through, about 2 minutes. Drain and cool under running water.

5 Cut the shrimp into bite-size pieces. Stir the shrimp and arugula into the rice. Add the rest of the dressing and stir well. Taste and adjust seasoning. Garnish with the tomatoes. Serve immediately.

Shrimp, Orange, and Anchovy Salad
Insalata di Gamberi, Arancia, e Acciughe

MAKES 4 SERVINGS

One of my favorite Venetian restaurants is La Corte Sconta, "the hidden courtyard." Despite its name, it is not too difficult to find, as it is a very popular trattoria, serving a set menu of all seafood dishes. This salad, zesty with Dijon mustard, is inspired by one I ate there.

1 small red onion, thinly sliced
2 teaspoons Dijon mustard
1 garlic clove, lightly crushed
4 teaspoons fresh lemon juice
1/4 cup extra-virgin olive oil
1 teaspoon chopped fresh rosemary
Salt and freshly ground black pepper
24 large shrimp, shelled and deveined
4 navel oranges, peeled, white pith removed and sliced
1 (2-ounce) can anchovy fillets, drained

1 Place the onion in a medium bowl with very cold water to cover. Let stand 10 minutes. Drain the onion and cover it again with very cold water and let stand 10 minutes more. (This will make the onion flavor less sharp.) Pat the onion dry.

2 In a large bowl, whisk together the mustard, garlic, lemon juice, oil, and rosemary with salt and freshly ground black pepper to taste.

3 Bring a medium saucepan of water to a boil over medium heat. Add the shrimp and salt to taste. Cook until the shrimp turn pink and are just cooked through, about 2 minutes, depending on their size. Drain and cool under running water.

4 Add the shrimp to the bowl with the dressing and toss well. Arrange the watercress on serving plates. Top with the orange slices. Spoon the shrimp and dressing over the oranges. Scatter the onion slices on top. Serve immediately.

Sardine and Arugula Salad
Insalata con le Sarde

MAKES 2 SERVINGS

This salad is based on one I tasted in Rome that was served on top of a thick slice of toasted bread and served as bruschetta. Though I liked the combination, it was hard to eat. I prefer to serve the bread as an accompaniment. Canned sardines packed in olive oil have a delicious smoky flavor that adds a lot to this simple salad.

1 large bunch arugula
2 tablespoons olive oil
1 tablespoon fresh lemon juice
Salt and freshly ground black pepper
1/2 cup black cured olives, pitted and cut into 2 or 3 pieces
1 (3-ounce) can sardines in olive oil
2 green onions, cut into thin slices
4 slices Italian bread, toasted

1 Trim the tough stems of the arugula and discard any yellowed or bruised leaves. Wash the arugula in several changes of cool water. Dry very well. Tear the arugula into bite-size pieces.

2 In a large bowl, whisk together the oil, lemon juice, and salt and pepper to taste. Add the arugula, olives, sardines, and green onions and toss well. Taste and adjust seasoning.

3 Serve immediately with the toasted bread.

Grilled Scallop Salad
Insalata di Capesante alla Griglia

MAKES 3 TO 4 SERVINGS.

Large, plump sea scallops are delicious grilled and served on a bed of tender salad greens and tomatoes. The scallops can be cooked on an outside grill, but I make this salad all year round, so I cook the scallops most often on a grill pan. This salad is inspired by one I have enjoyed often at I Trulli Restaurant and Enoteca in New York.

Olive oil
1 pound large sea scallops, rinsed
2 tablespoons fresh lemon juice
Salt and freshly ground black pepper
2 tablespoons chopped fresh basil
1 tablespoon chopped fresh mint
2 large ripe tomatoes, cut into bite-size pieces
6 cups tender salad greens, torn into bite-size pieces

1 Heat a grill pan over medium-high heat until a drop of water sizzles when dropped on the surface. Brush the pan lightly with oil.

2 Pat the scallops dry and place them on the grill pan. Cook until the scallops are lightly browned, about 2 minutes. Turn the scallops and cook until browned and slightly translucent in the center, 1 to 2 minutes more.

3 In a large bowl, whisk together the lemon juice with 3 tablespoons oil. Add the scallops and toss well. Let stand 5 minutes, stirring once or twice.

4 Add the herbs and tomatoes to the scallops and stir gently.

5 Arrange the lettuce on serving plates. Top with the scallop mixture and serve immediately.

Venetian Crab Salad
Insalata di Granseola

MAKES 6 SERVINGS

Venice has many wine bars, called bacari, *where people gather to meet friends and sample a glass of wine and small plates of food. This delicate salad made from large crabs called* granseole *is often served as a topping for crostini. In more formal restaurants, you will find it served elegantly in radicchio cups. It makes a nice starter for a summer meal.*

2 tablespoons chopped fresh flat-leaf parsley
1/4 cup extra-virgin olive oil
2 tablespoons fresh lemon juice
Salt and freshly ground black pepper to taste
1 pound fresh crab meat, picked over
Radicchio leaves

1 In a medium bowl, whisk together the parsley, oil, lemon juice, and salt and pepper to taste. Add the crab meat and stir well. Taste for seasoning.

2 Arrange the radicchio leaves on serving plates. Scoop the salad onto the leaves. Serve immediately.

Calamari Salad with Arugula and Tomatoes
Insalata di Calamari

MAKES 6 SERVINGS

The crisscross cuts on the surface of the calamari (squid) cause the pieces to curl up tightly as they cook. This not only tenderizes the calamari, but also makes it very attractive.

For best flavor, allow for good marinating time. You can prepare the calamari up to three hours ahead.

1 1/2 pounds cleaned calamari (squid)
2 garlic cloves, minced
2 tablespoons chopped fresh flat-leaf parsley
5 tablespoons olive oil
2 tablespoons fresh lemon juice
Salt and freshly ground black pepper
1 large bunch arugula
1 tablespoon balsamic vinegar
1 cup cherry or grape tomatoes, halved

1 Slit the calamari lengthwise and open them flat. With a sharp knife, score the bodies, making diagonal lines about 1/4-inch apart. Turn the knife and make diagonal lines in the opposite direction, forming a crisscross pattern. Cut each squid into 2-inch squares. Cut the base of each group of tentacles in half. Rinse and drain the pieces and put them in a bowl.

2 Add the garlic, parsley, 2 tablespoons of the olive oil, the lemon juice, and salt and pepper to taste, and toss well. Cover and marinate up to 3 hours ahead of cooking.

3 Transfer the squid and marinade into a large skillet. Cook over medium-high heat, stirring frequently, just until the squid are opaque, about 5 minutes.

4 Trim the tough stems of the arugula and discard any yellowed or bruised leaves. Wash the arugula in several changes of cool water. Dry very well. Tear the arugula into bite-size pieces. Arrange the arugula on a platter.

5 In a small bowl, whisk together the remaining 3 tablespoons oil and the vinegar, and salt and pepper to taste. Pour over the arugula and toss well. Spoon the squid over the arugula. Scatter the tomatoes on top and serve immediately.

Lobster Salad
Insalata di Aragosta

MAKES 4 TO 6 SERVINGS

Sardinia is famous for its shellfish, especially spiny lobsters, known as astice, *and sweet shrimp. My husband and I ate this fresh-tasting salad at a little seaside trattoria in Alghero as we watched the fishermen repairing their nets for the next day's work. One sat on the dock barefoot. With his toes, he clutched one end of the net and held it taut so that both of his hands were free for sewing.*

This salad could be a whole meal or a first course. A bottle of chilled Sardinian vernaccia would be the perfect accompaniment.

Some fish markets will steam the lobsters for you, saving you a step.

4 lobsters (about 1¼ pounds each)
1 medium red onion, halved and thinly sliced
6 basil leaves
4 tender celery ribs, thinly sliced
About ½ cup extra-virgin olive oil
2 to 3 tablespoons fresh lemon juice
Salt and freshly ground black pepper
Lettuce leaves
8 thin slices crusty Italian bread
1 garlic clove
3 large ripe tomatoes, cut into wedges

1 Place a rack or steamer basket in the bottom of a pot large enough to hold all four lobsters. (An 8- or 10-quart pot should work.) Add water to come just below the rack. Bring the water to a boil. Add the lobsters and cover the pot. When the water returns to a boil and steam escapes from the pot, cook the lobsters 10 minutes or longer, depending on their size. Transfer the lobsters to a platter and let cool.

2 Place the onion in a small bowl and cover with ice water. Let stand 15 minutes. Replace the water and let stand 15 minutes more. Drain and pat dry.

3 Meanwhile, remove the lobster meat from the shells. Break off the lobster tails. With poultry shears, remove the thin shell that covers the tail meat. Smack the claws with the blunt side of the knife to crack them. Break the claws open. Remove the meat with your fingers. Cut the meat into thin slices and place it in a large bowl.

4 Stack the basil leaves and cut them crosswise into thin ribbons. Add the basil, celery, and onion to the bowl with the lobster. Drizzle with ¼ cup of the oil and the lemon juice, and sprinkle with salt and pepper to taste. Toss well. Arrange the lobster mixture on four plates lined with lettuce leaves.

5 Toast the bread, then rub it with a cut garlic clove. Drizzle the toast with the remaining oil and sprinkle with salt. Garnish the platter with the toast and tomato wedges. Serve immediately.

Tuscan Tuna and Bean Salad

Insalata di Tonno alla Toscana

MAKES 6 SERVINGS

Tuscan cooks are famous for their ability to cook beans just right. Tender, creamy, and full of flavor, the beans elevate an ordinary dish into something special, such as this classic salad. If you can find it, buy ventresca di tonno, *tuna belly, canned in good olive oil. The belly is considered the finest part of the tuna. It is more expensive, but full of flavor, with a meaty texture.*

3 tablespoons extra-virgin olive oil

1 to 2 tablespoons fresh lemon juice

Salt and freshly ground black pepper

3 cups cooked or canned cannellini beans, drained

2 tender celery ribs, thinly sliced

1 small red onion, very thinly sliced

2 (7-ounce) cans Italian tuna packed in olive oil

2 or 3 Belgian endive, trimmed and separated
    into spears

1 In a medium bowl, whisk together the oil, lemon juice, and salt to taste and a generous grinding of pepper.

2 Add the beans, celery, onion, and tuna. Stir well.

3 Arrange the endive spears on a platter. Top with the salad. Serve immediately.

Couscous Tuna Salad

Insalata di Tonno e Cuscusu

MAKES 4 SERVINGS

Couscous is eaten in several Italian regions, including parts of Sicily and Tuscany. Every year, the Sicilian town of San Vito lo Capo hosts a couscous festival that attracts hundreds of thousands of visitors from around the world. Traditionally, the couscous is cooked with a variety of seafood, meats, or vegetables and served hot. This quick tuna and couscous salad is a satisfying, modern dish.

1 cup quick-cooking couscous

Salt

2 tablespoons chopped fresh basil

3 tablespoons olive oil

2 tablespoons lemon juice

Freshly ground black pepper

1 (7-ounce) can Italian tuna packed in olive oil

2 tender celery ribs, chopped

1 tomato, chopped

1 small cucumber, peeled, seeded, and chopped

1 Cook the couscous with salt to taste, according to the package directions.

2 In a small bowl, whisk together the basil, oil, lemon juice, and salt and pepper to taste. Stir in the warm couscous. Mix well. Taste and adjust seasoning. Drain the tuna and place it in the bowl with the celery, tomato, and cucumber.

3 Stir well. Taste and adjust seasoning. Serve at room temperature or chill in the refrigerator briefly.

Tuna Salad with Beans and Arugula
Insalata di Tonno, Fagioli, e Rucola

MAKES 2 TO 4 SERVINGS

I think I could write a whole book about my favorite tuna salads. This is one I make often for a quick lunch or dinner.

1 large bunch arugula or watercress
2 cups cooked or canned cannellini or cranberry beans, drained
1 (7-ounce) can Italian tuna packed in olive oil
1/4 cup chopped red onion
2 tablespoons capers, rinsed and drained
1 tablespoon fresh lemon juice
Salt and freshly ground black pepper
Lemon slices for garnish

1 Trim the tough stems of the arugula or watercress and discard any yellowed or bruised leaves. Wash the arugula in several changes of cool water. Dry very well. Tear the greens into bite-size pieces.

2 In a large salad bowl, stir together the beans, tuna and its oil, red onion, capers, and lemon juice. Toss well.

3 Stir in the greens and serve garnished with lemon slices.

Friday-Night Tuna Salad
Insalata di Venerdi Sera

MAKES 4 SERVINGS

At one time, Fridays were meatless days in Catholic homes. Dinner at our house usually consisted of pasta and beans and this easy salad.

1 (7-ounce) can Italian tuna packed in olive oil
2 ribs celery with leaves, trimmed and sliced
2 medium tomatoes, cut into bite-size pieces
2 hard-cooked eggs, peeled and quartered
3 or 4 slices red onion, thinly sliced and quartered
Pinch of dried oregano
2 tablespoons extra-virgin olive oil
1/2 of a medium head of romaine lettuce, rinsed and dried
Lemon wedges

1 Place the tuna with its oil in a large bowl. Break the tuna into pieces with a fork.

2 Add the celery, tomatoes, eggs, and onion to the tuna. Sprinkle with the oregano and olive oil and toss lightly.

3 Arrange the lettuce leaves on a platter. Top with the tuna salad. Garnish with lemon wedges and serve immediately.

❦ Dressings

Gorgonzola and Hazelnut Dressing
Salsa di Gorgonzola e Nocciole

MAKES ABOUT 2/3 CUP

I had this dressing in Piedmont, where it was served on endive leaves, but it is good on any number of chewy greens, such as frisée, escarole, or spinach.

4 tablespoons extra-virgin olive oil
1 tablespoon red wine vinegar
Salt and freshly ground black pepper
2 tablespoons crumbled gorgonzola
1/4 cup chopped toasted hazelnuts (see How to Toast and Skin Nuts, page 559)

In a small bowl, whisk together the oil, vinegar, and salt and pepper to taste. Stir in the gorgonzola and hazelnuts. Serve immediately.

Lemon Cream Dressing
Salsa di Limone alla Panna

MAKES ABOUT 1/3 CUP

A little bit of cream takes the edge off a lemony dressing. I like this on tender lettuce leaves.

3 tablespoons extra-virgin olive oil
1 tablespoon fresh lemon juice
1 tablespoon heavy cream
Salt and freshly ground black pepper

In a small bowl, whisk together all of the ingredients. Serve immediately.

Orange-Honey Dressing
Citronette al'Arancia

MAKES ABOUT 1/3 CUP

The sweetness of this dressing makes it a perfect match for mixed greens like mesclun. Or try it on a combination of watercress, red onions, and black olives.

3 tablespoons extra-virgin olive oil
1 teaspoon honey
2 tablespoons fresh orange juice
Salt and freshly ground black pepper

In a small bowl, whisk together all of the ingredients. Serve immediately.

Soups

Broths

Meat Broth

Chicken Broth

Bean, Grain, and Legume Soups

Antonietta's Bean Soup

Pasta and Beans

Creamy Bean Soup

Friulian Barley and Bean Soup

Bean and Mushroom Soup

Milan-Style Pasta and Beans

Lentil and Fennel Soup

Spinach, Lentil, and Rice Soup

Lentil and Greens Soup

Pureed Lentil Soup with Croutons

Chickpea Soup from Puglia

Chickpea and Pasta Soup

Ligurian Chickpea and Porcini Soup

Vegetable Soups

Tuscan Bread and Vegetable Soup

Winter Squash Soup

"Cooked Water" Soup

Zucchini Pesto Soup

Leek, Tomato, and Bread Soup

Zucchini and Tomato Soup

Zucchini and Potato Soup

Creamy Fennel Soup

Mushroom and Potato Soup

Creamy Cauliflower Soup

Sicilian Tomato Barley Soup

Red Pepper Soup

Fontina, Bread, and Cabbage Soup

Creamy Mushroom Soup

Vegetable Soup with Pesto

Egg Soups

Egg Soup from Pavia

Roman Egg Drop Soup

Egg Crepes in Broth

Semolina Fritters in Broth

Bread Noodles in Broth

Tyrolean Bread Dumplings

Meat and Fish Soups

Green Bean and Sausage Soup

Escarole and Little Meatballs Soup

"Married" Soup

Tuscan Fish Soup

Chunky Fish Soup

Seafood, Pasta, and Bean Soup

Mussels and Clams in Tomato Broth

Italians have many ways of referring to soup. According to the dictionary *Il Nuovo Zingarelli* (1989), *zuppa* refers to a soup of either meat, fish, or vegetables thickened with bread. *Minestra*, on the other hand, is a soup that contains pasta or rice in addition to the other ingredients. *Minestrina* is a light soup or clear broth, often made for babies or invalids. *Minestrone*, of course, is a big soup, thick with vegetables and legumes as well as pasta or rice. The basis for any of these soups is either water or *brodo* ("broth"), which can be made from vegetables, meat, poultry, or fish.

In everyday usage, the terminology is often confused, open to individual interpretation, and varies according to region, so don't be surprised to find a minestra called a zuppa and vice versa. As an old saying goes, *Se non e' zuppa, e' pane bagnato*, meaning it is all the same thing. (Literally, "If it is not soup, it is soaked bread.")

Soup generally takes the place of pasta or rice as a first course of a meal, or it can be the main course of a light meal. Of all Italians, Tuscans probably eat the most soup, and they are said to prefer soup to pasta.

Contrary to what you might expect, Italian minestre and zuppe are often served warm or at room temperature rather than hot or chilled. Italians feel that extreme hot or cold temperatures mask the flavor, as anyone who has ever burned their tongue on hot food or chilled their tastebuds with too much ice cream can attest.

Regional differences are very apparent when it comes to soup. In Tuscany, bread and beans are the typical soup ingredients, while southern Italians use a lot of vegetables. Neapolitans like leafy greens especially. Every region seems to have its own particular bean soup, and many Italians will insist that their region's soup is the most authentic. Northerners use more meat and meat broth and cheese in their soups, while every coastal region has its fish soup made with local varieties.

Soup toppings vary from region to region and depend on the kind of soup being eaten. Thick bean or vegetable soups often get a drizzle of extra-virgin olive oil as a topping, while grated cheese is the topping for soups made with butter and those containing vegetables.

❧ Broths

Homemade broth, known as *brodo*, is the foundation of many soups in Italy. It is easy to make and well worth having on hand. I try to keep some in the freezer so I can make soup quickly. I freeze the broth in small plastic containers for sauces and in larger containers for soups and risotto. If I run out of homemade, I sometimes substitute canned or boxed broth. Unfortunately, not all commercially prepared broths taste good, and many are high in sodium. Try several brands to find one with real flavor and dilute it with water if it seems too strong. Bouillon cubes tend to be extremely salty and artificial tasting and are best avoided.

Meat Broth
Brodo di Carne

MAKES ABOUT 4 QUARTS

Here is a basic broth made from different kinds of meat to use for soups, risotti, and stews. A good broth should be full of flavor but not so aggressive that it takes over the flavor of the dish. Beef, veal, and poultry can be used, but avoid pork or lamb. Their flavor is strong and can overwhelm the broth. Vary the proportions of the meats for this broth to your own taste or according to the ingredients you have on hand.

2 pounds meaty beef bones
2 pounds veal shoulder with bones
2 pounds chicken or turkey parts
2 carrots, trimmed and cut into 3 or 4 pieces
2 celery ribs with leaves, cut into 3 or 4 pieces
2 medium onions, peeled but left whole
I large tomato or I cup chopped canned tomatoes
I garlic clove
3 or 4 sprigs fresh flat-leaf parsley with stems

I In a large stockpot, combine the meat, bones, and chicken parts. Add 6 quarts cold water and bring to a simmer over medium heat.

2 Adjust the heat so that the water is barely simmering. Skim off the foam and fat that rises to the surface of the broth.

3 When the foam stops rising, add the remaining ingredients. Cook 3 hours, regulating the heat so that the liquid bubbles gently.

4 Let the broth cool briefly, then strain it into plastic storage containers. The broth can be used right away, or let it cool completely, then cover and store it in the refrigerator up to 3 days or in the freezer up to 3 months.

Chicken Broth
Brodo di Pollo

MAKES ABOUT 4 QUARTS

An old chicken, known as a fowl, gives broth a fuller, richer flavor than a younger bird. If you can't find a fowl, try adding turkey wings or necks to the broth, but don't use too much turkey or the flavor will overwhelm the chicken.

After cooking, much of the flavor will be boiled out of the meat, but thrifty Italian cooks use it to make a salad or chop it up for a pasta or vegetable stuffing.

I 4-pound whole fowl or chicken

2 pounds chicken or turkey parts

2 celery ribs with leaves, cut up

2 carrots, cut up

2 medium onions, peeled and left whole

I large tomato or I cup chopped canned tomatoes

I garlic clove

3 or 4 sprigs fresh parsley

I Place the fowl and chicken or turkey parts in a large stockpot. Add 5 quarts cold water and bring to a simmer over medium heat.

2 Adjust the heat so that the water is barely simmering. Skim off the foam and fat that rises to the surface of the broth.

3 Once the foam stops rising, add the remaining ingredients. Cook 2 hours, regulating the heat so that the liquid bubbles gently.

4 Let the broth cool briefly, then strain it into plastic storage containers. The broth can be used right away, or let it cool completely, then cover and store it in the refrigerator up to 3 days or in the freezer up to 3 months.

❧ Bean, Grain, and Legume Soups

Antonietta's Bean Soup
Zuppa di Fagioli

MAKES 8 SERVINGS

When I visited the Pasetti family's winery in Abruzzo, their cook, Antonietta, prepared this bean soup for lunch. It is based on the classic Abruzzo-Style Ragù (page 93), but you can use another tomato sauce with or without meat.

A food mill is used to smooth the beans and eliminate the skins. The soup can also be pureed in a food processor or blender. Antonietta served the soup with freshly grated Parmigiano-Reggiano, though she told us that it is traditional for diners in that region to season the soup with the seeds of a fresh green chile. Alongside the grated cheese, she passed around a plate with chiles and a knife, so that each diner could chop and add his or her own.

2 cups Abruzzo-Style Ragù (page 93), or another meat or tomato sauce

3 cups water

4 cups drained cooked dried or canned cranberry or cannellini beans

Salt and freshly ground black pepper to taste

4 ounces spaghetti, cut or broken into 2-inch pieces

Freshly grated Parmigiano-Reggiano

I or 2 fresh green chiles, such as jalapeno (optional)

I Prepare the ragù, if necessary. Then, in a large pot, combine the ragù and water. Pass the beans through a food mill into the pot. Cook over low heat, stirring occasionally, until the soup is hot. Add salt and pepper to taste.

2 Add the pasta and stir well. Cook, stirring often, until the pasta is soft. Add a little more water if the soup becomes too thick.

3 Serve hot or warm. Pass the cheese and fresh chiles, if using, separately.

Pasta and Beans
Pasta e Fagioli

MAKES 8 SERVINGS

This Neapolitan version of bean and pasta soup (known by its dialect name as "pasta fazool") is typically served very thick, but it should still be eaten with a spoon.

1/4 cup olive oil

2 celery ribs, chopped (about 1 cup)

2 garlic cloves, finely chopped

1 cup peeled, seeded, and chopped fresh tomatoes, or canned tomatoes

Pinch of crushed red pepper

Salt

3 cups drained cooked dried or canned cannellini or Great Northern beans

8 ounces ditalini or broken spaghetti

1 Pour the oil into a large saucepan. Add the celery and garlic. Cook, stirring frequently, over medium heat until the vegetables are tender and golden, about 10 minutes. Add the tomatoes, crushed red pepper, and salt to taste. Simmer until slightly thickened, about 10 minutes.

2 Add the beans to the tomato sauce. Bring the mixture to a simmer. Mash some of the beans with the back of a large spoon.

3 Bring a large pot of water to a boil. Add the salt to taste, then the pasta. Stir well. Cook over high heat, stirring frequently, until the pasta is tender, but slightly underdone. Drain the pasta, reserving some of the cooking water.

4 Stir the pasta into the bean mixture. Add a little of the cooking water, if needed, but the mixture should remain very thick. Turn off the heat and let stand about 10 minutes before serving.

Creamy Bean Soup
Crema di Fagioli

MAKES 4 TO 6 SERVINGS

I came upon a version of this recipe in A Tavola ("At the table"), an Italian cooking magazine. Creamy and smooth, this soup is pure, soothing comfort food.

3 cups drained cooked dried or canned cannellini or Great Northern beans

About 2 cups homemade Meat Broth (page 62) or a mix of half store-bought beef broth and half water

1/2 cup milk

2 egg yolks

1/2 cup freshly grated Parmigiano-Reggiano, plus more for serving

Salt and freshly ground black pepper

1 Puree the beans in a food processor, blender, or food mill.

2 In a medium saucepan, bring the broth to a simmer over medium heat. Stir in the bean puree and return to a simmer.

3 In a small bowl, beat together the milk and egg yolks. Pour about a cup of the soup into the bowl and whisk until smooth. Pour the mixture into the pot. Cook, stirring, until very hot but not boiling.

4 Stir in the Parmigiano-Reggiano and salt and pepper to taste. Serve hot with a sprinkle of additional cheese.

Friulian Barley and Bean Soup
Zuppa di Orzo e Fagioli

MAKES 6 SERVINGS

Though it is better known in the United States as a small pasta shape, orzo in Italian is the name for barley, one of the first grains ever cultivated. The region that is now Friuli in Italy was once part of Austria. The presence of barley reveals the Austrian roots of this soup.

If using already cooked or canned beans, substitute 3 cups or two 16-ounce cans of drained beans, reduce the water to 4 cups, and cook the soup only 30 minutes in step 2. Then proceed as indicated.

2 tablespoons olive oil
2 ounces finely chopped pancetta
2 celery ribs, chopped
2 carrots, chopped
I medium onion, chopped
I garlic clove, finely chopped
I cup (about 8 ounces) dried cannellini or Great Northern beans, soaked and drained (page 406)
$^1/_2$ cup pearl barley, rinsed and drained
Salt and freshly ground black pepper

I Pour the oil into a large pot. Add the pancetta. Cook, stirring frequently, over medium heat until the pancetta is lightly browned, about 10 minutes. Add the celery, carrots, onion, and garlic. Cook, stirring frequently, until the vegetables are golden, about 10 minutes.

2 Add the beans and 8 cups water. Bring to a simmer. Cover and cook over low heat for $1^1/_2$ to 2 hours or until the beans are very tender.

3 Mash some of the beans with the back of a large spoon. Add the barley, and salt and pepper to taste. Cook 30 minutes or until the barley is tender. Stir the soup frequently so that the barley does not stick to the bottom of the pot. Add water if the soup is too thick. Serve hot or warm.

Bean and Mushroom Soup
Minestra di Fagioli e Funghi

MAKES 8 SERVINGS

A chilly fall day in Tuscany had me craving a hearty bowl of soup and led me to a simple but memorable meal. At Il Prato, a restaurant in Pienza, the waiter announced that the kitchen had prepared a special bean soup that day. The soup was delicious, with an earthy, smoky flavor that I later learned came from the addition of dried porcini mushrooms. After the soup, I ordered some of the excellent pecorino cheese for which Pienza is famous.

$^1/_2$ ounce dried porcini mushrooms
I cup warm water
2 medium carrots, chopped
I celery rib, chopped
I medium onion, chopped
I cup peeled, seeded, and chopped fresh tomatoes or canned tomatoes
$^1/_4$ cup chopped fresh flat-leaf parsley
6 cups homemade Meat (page 62) or Chicken Broth (page 63) or a mix of half store-bought broth and half water
3 cups drained cooked dried or canned cannellini or great northern beans
$^1/_2$ cup medium-grain rice, such as Arborio
Salt and freshly ground black pepper to taste

I Soak the mushrooms in the water for 30 minutes. Remove the mushrooms and reserve the liquid. Rinse the mushrooms under cold running water to remove any grit, paying special attention to the stems, where soil collects. Chop the mushrooms coarsely. Strain the mushroom liquid through a paper coffee filter into a bowl and reserve.

2 In a large pot, combine the mushrooms and their liquid, the carrots, celery, onion, tomato, parsley, and broth. Bring it to a simmer. Cook until the vegetables are tender, about 20 minutes.

3 Add the beans and rice and salt and pepper to taste. Cook until the rice is tender, 20 minutes, stirring occasionally. Serve hot or warm.

Milan-Style Pasta and Beans

Pasta e Fagioli alla Milanese

MAKES 8 SERVINGS

Scraps of leftover fresh pasta, called maltagliati *("badly cut"), are typically used for this soup, or you could use fresh fettuccine cut into bite-size pieces.*

2 tablespoons unsalted butter

2 tablespoons olive oil

6 fresh sage leaves

1 tablespoon chopped fresh rosemary

4 carrots, chopped

4 celery ribs, chopped

3 medium boiling potatoes, chopped

2 onions, chopped

4 tomatoes, peeled, seeded, and chopped, or 2 cups chopped canned tomatoes

1 pound (about 2 cups) dried cranberry or cannellini beans, cooked as directed on pages 406–407, or 4 16-ounce cans

About 8 cups homemade Meat Broth (page 62) or a mix of half store-bought beef or vegetable broth and half water

Salt and freshly ground black pepper

8 ounces fresh maltagliati, or fresh fettuccine cut into 1-inch pieces

Extra-virgin olive oil

1 In a large pot, melt the butter with the oil over medium heat. Stir in the sage and rosemary. Add the carrots, celery, potatoes, and onions. Cook, stirring often, until softened, about 10 minutes.

2 Stir in the tomatoes and beans. Add the broth and salt and pepper to taste. Bring the mixture to a simmer. Cook over low heat until all of the ingredients are very tender, about 1 hour.

3 Remove half of the soup from the pot and pass it through a food mill or puree it in a blender. Pour the puree back into the pot. Stir well and add the pasta. Bring the soup to a simmer, then turn off the heat.

4 Let the soup cool slightly before serving. Serve hot, with a drizzle of extra-virgin olive oil and a generous grinding of pepper.

Lentil and Fennel Soup

Zuppa di Lenticchie e Finocchio

MAKES 8 SERVINGS

Lentils are one of the oldest legumes. They can be brown, green, red, or black, but in Italy the finest lentils are the tiny green ones from Castelluccio in Umbria. Unlike beans, lentils do not need to be soaked before cooking.

Save the feathery tops of the fennel to garnish the soup.

1 pound brown or green lentils, picked over and rinsed

2 medium onions, chopped

2 carrots, chopped

1 medium boiling potato, peeled and chopped

1 cup chopped fennel

1 cup fresh or canned tomatoes, chopped

1/4 cup olive oil

Salt and freshly ground black pepper

1 cup tubetti, ditalini, or small shells

Fresh fennel tops, optional

Extra-virgin olive oil

1 In a large pot, combine the lentils, onions, carrots, potato, and fennel. Add cold water to cover by 1 inch. Bring the liquid to a simmer and cook over low heat 30 minutes.

2 Stir in the tomatoes and olive oil. Add salt and pepper to taste. Cook until the lentils are tender, about 20 minutes more. Add a little water as needed so that the lentils are just covered with the liquid.

3 Stir in the pasta and cook until the pasta is tender, 15 minutes more. Taste and adjust seasoning. Garnish with the chopped fennel tops, if available. Serve hot or warm, with a drizzle of extra-virgin olive oil.

Spinach, Lentil, and Rice Soup
Minestra di Lenticchie e Spinaci

MAKES 8 SERVINGS

If less water is added and the rice is omitted, this soup becomes a side dish to serve with grilled fish fillets or pork. Escarole, kale, cabbage, Swiss chard, or other leafy greens can be used instead of the spinach.

1 pound lentils, picked over and rinsed
6 cups water
3 large garlic cloves, chopped
1/4 cup extra-virgin olive oil
8 ounces spinach, stemmed and torn into bite-size
    pieces
Salt and freshly ground black pepper
1 cup cooked rice

1 In a large pot, combine the lentils, water, garlic, and oil. Bring to a simmer and cook over low heat 40 minutes. Add a little water as needed so that the lentils are just covered.

2 Stir in the spinach and the salt and pepper to taste. Cook until the lentils are tender, about 10 minutes more.

3 Add the rice and cook until heated through. Serve hot, with a drizzle of extra-virgin olive oil.

Lentil and Greens Soup
Minestra di Lenticchie e Verdura

MAKES 6 SERVINGS

Look the lentils over before cooking them to eliminate any small stones or debris. For a heartier soup, add a cup or two of cooked ditalini or broken spaghetti.

1/4 cup olive oil
1 medium onion, chopped
1 celery rib, chopped
1 medium carrot, chopped
2 garlic cloves, finely chopped
1/2 cup chopped canned Italian tomatoes
8 ounces lentils (about 1 cup), picked over and rinsed
Salt and freshly ground black pepper
1 pound escarole, spinach, or other leafy greens,
    trimmed and cut into bite-size pieces
1/2 cup freshly grated Pecorino Romano
    or Parmigiano-Reggiano

1 Pour the oil into a large pot. Add the onion, celery, carrot, and garlic and cook over medium heat for 10 minutes or until the vegetables are tender and golden. Stir in the tomatoes and cook 5 minutes more.

2 Add the lentils, salt and pepper, and 4 cups water. Bring the soup to a simmer and cook 45 minutes or until the lentils are tender.

3 Stir in the greens. Cover and cook 10 minutes, or until the greens are tender. Taste for seasoning.

4 Just before serving, stir in the cheese. Serve hot.

Pureed Lentil Soup with Croutons

Purèa di Lenticchie

MAKES 6 TO 8 SERVINGS

Crunchy slices of bread top this smooth lentil puree from Umbria. For added flavor, rub the croutons with a raw garlic clove while they are still warm.

I pound lentils, picked over and rinsed
I celery rib, chopped
I carrot, chopped
I large onion, chopped
I large boiling potato, chopped
2 tablespoons tomato paste
Salt and freshly ground black pepper
2 tablespoons extra-virgin olive oil, plus more
     for serving
8 slices Italian or French bread

1 Place the lentils, vegetables, and tomato paste in a large pot. Add cold water to cover by 2 inches. Bring to a simmer. Cook 20 minutes. Add salt to taste and more water if needed to keep the ingredients covered. Cook 20 minutes more or until the lentils are very soft.

2 Drain the contents of the pot, reserving the liquid. Put the lentils and vegetables in a processor or blender and puree, in batches if necessary, until smooth. Pour the lentils back into the pot. Season to taste with salt and pepper. Reheat gently, adding some of the cooking liquid if needed.

3 In a large skillet, heat the 2 tablespoons olive oil over medium heat. Add the bread in a single layer. Cook until toasted and brown on the bottom, 3 to 4 minutes. Turn the bread pieces over and brown about 3 minutes more.

4 Remove the soup from the heat. Spoon into bowls. Top each bowl with a slice of toast. Serve hot, with a drizzle of olive oil

Chickpea Soup from Puglia

Minestra di Ceci

MAKES 6 SERVINGS

In Puglia, this thick soup is made with short strips of fresh pasta known as lagane. *Fresh fettuccine cut into 3-inch strips can be substituted, as can small dried pasta shapes or broken spaghetti. Instead of a broth, anchovies are used to flavor this soup, with water as the cooking liquid. The anchovies melt into the soup and add a lot of character without being obvious.*

¹⁄₃ cup olive oil
3 garlic cloves, slightly crushed
2 2-inch sprigs fresh rosemary
4 anchovy fillets, chopped
3¹⁄₂ cups cooked chickpeas or 2 16-ounce cans,
     drained and liquid reserved
4 ounces fresh fettuccine, cut into 3-inch lengths
Freshly ground black pepper

1 Pour the oil into a large pot. Add the garlic and rosemary and cook over medium heat, pressing the garlic cloves with the back of a large spoon, until the garlic is golden, about 2 minutes. Remove and discard the garlic and rosemary. Add the anchovy fillets and cook, stirring, until the anchovy dissolves, about 3 minutes.

2 Add the chickpeas to the pot and stir well. Coarsely mash half of the chickpeas with the back of a spoon or a potato masher. Add just enough water or chickpea cooking liquid to cover the chickpeas. Bring the liquid to a simmer.

3 Stir in the pasta. Season to taste with a generous grind of black pepper. Cook until the pasta is tender yet firm to the bite. Remove from the heat and let stand 5 minutes. Serve hot, with a drizzle of extra-virgin olive oil.

Chickpea and Pasta Soup
Minestra di Ceci

MAKES 6 TO 8 SERVINGS

In the Marches region in central Italy, this soup sometimes is made with quadrucci, *small squares of fresh egg pasta. To make quadrucci, cut fresh fettuccine into short lengths to form small squares. Let each person drizzle his or her soup with a little extra-virgin olive oil.*

Of all legumes, I find chickpeas to be the trickiest to cook. Sometimes they take far longer to become tender than I expect. It is a good idea to prepare this soup in advance through step 2 and then reheat and finish it when ready to serve, to be sure the chickpeas have sufficient time to become tender.

I pound dried chickpeas, soaked overnight
   (see pages 406–407)
1/4 cup olive oil
I medium onion, chopped
2 celery ribs, chopped
2 cups canned tomatoes, chopped
Salt
8 ounces ditalini or small elbows or shells
Freshly ground black pepper
Extra-virgin olive oil

I Pour the oil into a large pot. Add the onion and celery and cook, stirring frequently, over medium heat for 10 minutes or until the vegetables are tender and golden. Add the tomatoes and bring to a simmer. Cook 10 minutes more.

2 Drain the chickpeas and add them to the pot. Add 1 teaspoon salt and cold water to cover by 1 inch. Bring to a simmer. Cook 1 1/2 to 2 hours or until the chickpeas are very tender. Add water if necessary to keep the chickpeas covered.

3 About 20 minutes before the chickpeas are done, bring a large pot of water to a boil. Add salt, then the pasta. Cook until the pasta is tender. Drain and add to the soup. Season to taste with salt and pepper. Serve hot, with a drizzle of extra-virgin olive oil.

Ligurian Chickpea and Porcini Soup
Pasta e Ceci con Porcini

MAKES 4 SERVINGS

This is my version of a soup that is made in Liguria. Some cooks make it without the Swiss chard, while others include cardoons in the ingredients.

1/2 ounce dried porcini mushrooms
I cup warm water
1/4 cup olive oil
2 ounces pancetta, chopped
I medium onion, finely chopped
I medium carrot, finely chopped
I medium celery rib, finely chopped
I garlic clove, finely chopped
3 cups cooked dried or drained canned chickpeas
8 ounces Swiss chard, cut crosswise into narrow strips
I medium boiling potato, peeled and chopped
I cup peeled, seeded, and chopped fresh or canned
   tomatoes
Salt and freshly ground black pepper
I cup ditalini, tubetti, or other small pasta

I Soak the mushrooms in the water for 30 minutes. Remove them and reserve the liquid. Rinse the mushrooms under cold running water to remove any grit. Chop them coarsely. Strain the liquid through a paper coffee filter into a bowl.

2 Pour the oil into a large pot. Add the pancetta, onion, carrot, celery, and garlic. Cook, stirring frequently, over medium heat until the onion and other aromatics are golden, about 10 minutes.

3 Stir in the chickpeas, Swiss chard, potato, tomatoes, and mushrooms with their liquid. Add water to just cover the ingredients, and salt and pepper to taste. Bring to a simmer and cook until the vegetables are tender and the soup is thickened, about 1 hour. Add water if the soup becomes too thick.

4 Stir in the pasta and 2 more cups water. Cook, stirring often, about 15 minutes, or until the pasta is tender. Let cool slightly before serving.

❧ Vegetable Soups

Tuscan Bread and Vegetable Soup
Ribollita

MAKES 8 SERVINGS

One summer in Tuscany, I was served this soup wherever I went, sometimes twice a day. I never tired of it, because every cook used her own combination of ingredients, and it was always good. This is really two recipes in one. The first is a mixed vegetable soup. The next day, the leftovers are reheated and mixed with day-old bread. The reheating gives the soup its Italian name, which means reboiled. This is typically done in the morning, and the soup is allowed to rest until lunchtime. Ribollita is typically served warm or at room temperature, never steaming hot.

Be sure to use a good-quality chewy Italian or country-style bread for the right texture.

4 cups homemade Chicken Broth (page 63) or Meat Broth (page 62) or a mix of half store-bought broth and half water

¹/₄ cup olive oil

2 tender celery ribs, chopped

2 medium carrots, chopped

2 garlic cloves, finely chopped

I small red onion, chopped

¹/₄ cup chopped fresh flat-leaf parsley

I tablespoon chopped fresh sage

I tablespoon chopped fresh rosemary

1¹/₂ pounds peeled, seeded, and chopped fresh tomatoes or 1¹/₂ cups canned Italian peeled tomatoes with their juice, chopped

3 cups drained cooked dried or canned cannellini beans

2 medium boiling potatoes, peeled and diced

2 medium zucchini, chopped

I pound cabbage or kale, thinly sliced (about 4 cups)

8 ounces green beans, trimmed and cut into bite-size pieces

Salt and freshly ground pepper to taste

About 8 ounces day-old Italian bread, thinly sliced

Extra-virgin olive oil

Very thin slices red onion (optional)

I Prepare the broth, if necessary. Then, pour the olive oil into a large pot. Add the celery, carrots, garlic, onion, and herbs. Cook, stirring frequently, over medium heat until the celery and other aromatics are tender and golden, about 20 minutes. Add the tomatoes and cook 10 minutes.

2 Stir in the beans, remaining vegetables, and salt and pepper to taste. Add the broth and water to just cover. Bring to a simmer. Cook gently, over very low heat, until the vegetables are tender, about 2 hours. Let cool slightly, then if not using right away, store in the refrigerator overnight or up to 2 days.

3 When ready to serve, pour about 4 cups of the soup into a blender or food processor. Puree the soup, then transfer it to a pot along with the remaining soup. Reheat gently.

4 Choose a soup tureen or pot large enough to hold the bread and soup. Place a layer of bread slices on the bottom. Spoon on enough of the soup to cover the bread completely. Repeat the layering until all of soup is used and the bread is soaked. Let stand at least 20 minutes. It should be very thick.

5 Stir the soup to break up the bread. Drizzle with extra-virgin olive oil and sprinkle with the red onion. Serve warm or at room temperature.

Winter Squash Soup
Zuppa di Zucca

MAKES 4 SERVINGS

At the fruttivendolo, *the fruit and vegetable market, Italian cooks can buy hunks of large pumpkins and other winter squashes to make this delicious soup. I generally use butternut or acorn squash. The crushed red pepper called* peperoncino *adds an unexpected piquancy.*

4 cups homemade Chicken Broth (page 63) or a mix
　　of half store-bought broth and half water
2 pounds winter squash, such as butternut or acorn
1/2 cup olive oil
2 garlic cloves, finely chopped
Pinch of crushed red pepper
Salt
1/4 cup chopped fresh flat-leaf parsley

1 Prepare the broth if necessary. Then, peel the squash and remove the seeds. Cut into 1-inch pieces.

2 Pour the oil into a large pot. Add the garlic and crushed red pepper. Cook, stirring frequently, over medium heat until the garlic is lightly golden, about 2 minutes. Stir in the squash and salt to taste.

3 Add the broth and bring to a simmer. Cover and cook 35 minutes or until the squash is very soft.

4 With a slotted spoon, transfer the squash to a food processor or blender and puree until smooth. Return the puree to the pot with the broth. Bring the soup back to a simmer and cook 5 minutes. Add a little water if the soup is too thick.

5 Add salt to taste. Stir in the parsley. Serve hot.

"Cooked Water" Soup
Acquacotta

MAKES 6 SERVINGS

Just a few vegetables, eggs, and leftover bread are needed to make this tasty Tuscan soup, so Italians jokingly call it "cooked water." Use whatever mushrooms are available.

1/4 cup olive oil
2 celery ribs, thinly sliced
2 garlic cloves, chopped
I pound assorted mushrooms, such as button, shiitake
　　and cremini, trimmed and sliced
I pound fresh plum tomatoes, peeled, seeded,
　　and chopped, or 2 cups canned tomatoes
Pinch of crushed red pepper
6 eggs
6 slices Italian or French bread, toasted
4 to 6 tablespoons freshly grated pecorino cheese

1 Pour the oil into a medium pot. Add the celery and garlic. Cook, stirring frequently, over medium heat until softened, about 5 minutes.

2 Add the mushrooms and cook, stirring occasionally, until the mushroom juices evaporate. Add the tomatoes and the crushed red pepper and cook 20 minutes.

3 Add 4 cups water and salt to taste. Bring to a simmer. Cook 20 minutes more.

4 Just before serving, break one of the eggs into a cup. Carefully slip the egg into the hot soup. Repeat with the remaining eggs. Cover and cook over very low heat 3 minutes or until the eggs are done to taste.

5 Place a slice of toast in each serving bowl. Carefully ladle an egg on top and spoon on the hot soup. Sprinkle with the cheese and serve immediately.

Zucchini Pesto Soup
Zuppa di Zucchine al Pesto

MAKES 4 TO 6 SERVINGS

The aroma of the pesto when it is stirred into the hot soup is irresistible.

2 cups homemade Chicken Broth (page 63) or a mix
    of half store-bought broth and half water

3 tablespoons olive oil

2 medium onions, chopped

4 small zucchini (about 1¼ pounds), scrubbed and
    chopped

3 medium boiling potatoes, peeled and chopped

Salt and freshly ground black pepper, to taste

1 cup broken spaghetti

PESTO

2 to 3 large garlic cloves

½ cup fresh basil

¼ cup fresh Italian flat-leaf parsley

½ cup grated Parmigiano-Reggiano, plus more
    for sprinkling

2 to 3 tablespoons extra-virgin olive oil

Salt and freshly ground black pepper

1 Prepare the broth, if necessary. Then, pour the oil into a medium pot. Add the onions. Cook, stirring often, over medium heat until the onions are tender and golden, about 10 minutes. Add the zucchini and potatoes and cook, stirring occasionally, 10 minutes. Add the chicken broth and 4 cups water. Bring the liquid to a simmer and cook 30 minutes. Add salt and pepper to taste.

2 Stir in the pasta. Simmer 15 minutes more.

3 Prepare the pesto: In a food processor, chop the garlic, basil, and parsley until very fine. Add the cheese and gradually drizzle in the olive oil to make a thick paste. Season to taste with salt and pepper.

4 Transfer the pesto to a medium bowl; with a whisk, beat about 1 cup of the hot soup into the pesto. Stir the mixture into the pot with the remaining soup. Let rest 5 minutes. Taste and adjust seasoning. Serve with additional cheese.

Leek, Tomato, and Bread Soup
Pappa al Pomodoro

MAKES 4 TO SERVINGS

Tuscans eat a lot of soup and make many of them with bread instead of pasta or rice. This is one that is a favorite in the early fall when there are plenty of ripe tomatoes and fresh leeks around. It is also good in the winter, made with canned tomatoes.

6 cups homemade Chicken Broth (page 63) or a mix
    of half store-bought broth and half water

3 tablespoons olive oil, plus more for drizzling

2 medium leeks

3 large garlic cloves

Pinch of crushed red pepper

2 cups peeled, seeded, and chopped fresh tomatoes,
    or canned tomatoes

Salt

½ loaf day-old Italian whole-wheat bread,
    cut into 1-inch cubes (about 4 cups)

½ cup torn fresh basil

Extra-virgin olive oil

1 Prepare the broth, if necessary. Then, trim off the roots and dark green portion of the leeks. Cut the leeks in half lengthwise and rinse thoroughly under cool running water. Chop fine.

2 Pour the oil into a large pot. Add the leeks and cook, stirring frequently, over medium-low heat until softened, about 5 minutes. Stir in the garlic and crushed red pepper.

3 Add the tomatoes and broth and bring to a simmer. Cook 15 minutes, stirring occasionally. Add salt to taste.

4 Stir the bread into the soup and cook 20 minutes, stirring occasionally. The soup should be thick. Add more bread if necessary.

5 Remove from the heat. Stir in the basil and let stand 10 minutes. Serve hot, with a drizzle of extra-virgin olive oil.

Zucchini and Tomato Soup
Zuppa di Zucchine e Pomodori

MAKES 6 SERVINGS

Though small zucchini have better flavor, even larger vegetables are good in this soup, because their wateriness and lack of flavor are not noticeable with all of the other flavorful ingredients.

5 cups homemade Chicken Broth (page 63) or a mix of half store-bought broth and half water

3 tablespoons olive oil

1 medium onion, finely chopped

1 garlic clove, chopped

1 teaspooon chopped fresh rosemary

1 teaspoon chopped fresh sage

1 1/2 cups peeled, seeded, and chopped tomatoes

1 1/2 pounds zucchini, chopped

Salt and freshly ground black pepper

3 cups day-old Italian or French bread cubes

Freshly grated Parmigiano-Reggiano

1 Prepare the broth, if necessary. Then, pour the oil into a large pot. Add the onion, garlic, rosemary, and sage. Cook over medium heat, stirring frequently, until the onion is golden, about 10 minutes.

2 Add the tomatoes and stir well. Add the broth and bring to a simmer. Stir in the zucchini and cook 30 minutes or until tender. Season to taste with salt and pepper.

3 Stir in the bread cubes. Cook until the bread is soft, about 10 minutes. Let rest 10 minutes more before serving. Serve with grated Parmigiano-Reggiano.

Zucchini and Potato Soup
Minestra di Zucchine e Patate

MAKES 4 SERVINGS

This soup is typical of what you might be served in summertime at homes throughout southern Italy. Feel free to change it as an Italian cook would, switching the zucchini for another vegetable such as green beans, tomatoes, or spinach and substituting basil or mint for the parsley.

6 cups homemade Chicken Broth (page 63) or a mix of half store-bought broth and half water

2 tablespoons olive oil

1 medium onion, finely chopped

1 pound boiling potatoes (about 3 medium), peeled and chopped

1 pound zucchini (about 4 small), scrubbed and chopped

Salt and freshly ground black pepper

2 tablespoons chopped flat-leaf parsley

Freshly grated Parmigiano-Reggiano or Pecorino Romano

1 Prepare the broth, if necessary. Then, pour the oil into a medium pot. Add the onion and cook, stirring frequently, over medium heat until tender and golden, about 10 minutes.

2 Stir in the potatoes and zucchini. Add the broth and salt and pepper to taste. Bring to a simmer and cook until the vegetables are tender, about 30 minutes.

3 Add salt and pepper to taste. Stir in the parsley. Serve with the grated cheese.

Creamy Fennel Soup
Zuppa di Finocchio

MAKES 6 SERVINGS

Potatoes and fennel have an affinity for each other. Serve this soup garnished with chopped fennel leaves and a drizzle of extra-virgin olive oil.

6 cups homemade Chicken Broth (page 63) or a mix of half store-bought broth and half water

2 large leeks, trimmed

3 medium fennel bulbs (about 2 1/2 pounds)

2 tablespoons unsalted butter

I tablespoon olive oil

5 boiling potatoes, peeled and sliced

Salt and freshly ground black pepper

Extra-virgin olive oil

1 Prepare the broth, if necessary. Then, cut the leeks in half lengthwise and rinse them well to eliminate all traces of sand between the layers. Chop coarsely.

2 Trim the fennel stalks even with the bulbs, reserving some of the feathery green leaves for a garnish. Trim away the base and any brown spots. Cut the bulbs into thin slices.

3 In a large pot, melt the butter with the oil over medium heat. Add the leeks and cook until soft, about 10 minutes. Add the fennel, potatoes, broth, and salt and pepper to taste. Bring to a simmer and cook until the vegetables are very soft, about 1 hour.

4 With a slotted spoon, transfer the vegetables to a food processor or blender. Process or blend until smooth.

5 Return the vegetables to the pot and reheat gently. Spoon into soup bowls, sprinkle with the reserved fennel tops, and drizzle with olive oil. Serve hot.

Mushroom and Potato Soup
Minestra di Funghi e Patate

MAKES 6 SERVINGS

Here is another soup from Friuli-Venezia Giulia, a region renowned for excellent mushrooms. Fresh porcini mushrooms would be used there, but because they are hard to find, I substitute a combination of wild and cultivated mushrooms. Both potatoes and barley are added as thickeners.

8 cups homemade Meat Broth (page 62) or a mix of half store-bought broth and half water

2 tablespoons olive oil

2 ounces sliced pancetta, finely chopped

I medium onion, finely chopped

2 celery ribs, finely chopped

I pound assorted mushrooms, such as white, cremini, and portabello

4 tablespoons chopped fresh flat-leaf parsley

2 garlic cloves, finely chopped

3 medium boiling potatoes, peeled and chopped

Salt and freshly ground black pepper

1/2 cup pearl barley

1 Prepare the broth, if necessary. Pour the oil into a large pot. Add the pancetta. Cook, stirring frequently, over medium heat until golden, about 10 minutes. Add the onion and celery and cook, stirring occasionally, until softened, about 5 minutes.

2 Add the mushrooms, 2 tablespoons of the parsley, and the garlic. Cook, stirring often, until the mushroom juices evaporate, about 10 minutes.

3 Stir in the potatoes, salt, and pepper. Add the broth and bring to a simmer. Add the barley and cook, uncovered, over low heat for 1 hour or until the barley is tender and the soup is thickened.

4 Sprinkle with the remaining parsley and serve hot.

Creamy Cauliflower Soup
Vellutata di Cavolfiore

MAKES 6 SERVINGS

An elegant soup to serve at the start of a special dinner. If you have some truffle oil or paste, try adding a little to the soup just before serving, leaving out the cheese.

1 medium cauliflower, trimmed and cut into
    1-inch florets
Salt
3 tablespoons unsalted butter
1/4 cup all-purpose flour
About 2 cups milk
Freshly grated nutmeg
1/2 cup heavy cream
1/4 cup freshly grated Parmigiano-Reggiano

1 Bring a large pot of water to a boil. Add the cauliflower and salt to taste. Cook until the cauliflower is very tender, about 10 minutes. Drain well.

2 In a medium saucepan, melt the butter over medium heat. Add the flour and stir well for 2 minutes. Very slowly stir in 2 cups milk and salt to taste. Bring to a simmer and cook 1 minute, stirring constantly, until thickened and smooth. Remove from the heat. Stir in the nutmeg and cream.

3 Transfer the cauliflower to a food processor or blender. Puree, adding a little of the sauce, if necessary, to make the puree smooth. Transfer the puree to the pan with the remaining sauce. Stir well. Heat gently, adding more milk if necessary to make a thick soup.

4 Remove from the heat. Taste and adjust seasoning. Stir in the cheese and serve.

Sicilian Tomato Barley Soup
Minestra d'Orzo alla Siciliana

MAKES 4 TO 6 SERVINGS

Rather than grate the cheese, Sicilians often serve soup with cheese chopped into small bits. It never fully melts into the soup, and you can taste some of the cheese in each bite.

8 cups homemade Chicken Broth (page 63) or Meat
    Broth (page 62) or a mix of half store-bought
    broth and half water
8 ounces pearl barley, picked over and rinsed
2 medium tomatoes, peeled, seeded, and chopped,
    or 1 cup chopped canned tomatoes
1 celery rib, finely chopped
1 medium onion, finely chopped
Salt and freshly ground black pepper
1 cup diced Pecorino Romano

1 Prepare the broth, if necessary. In a large pot, combine the broth, barley, and vegetables and bring to a simmer. Cook until the barley is tender, about 1 hour. Add water if the soup becomes too thick.

2 Season with salt and pepper to taste. Spoon the soup into bowls, scattering the cheese over the top.

Red Pepper Soup
Zuppa di Peperoni Rossi

MAKES 6 SERVINGS

The vibrant red-orange color of this soup is an appealing and appropriate cue to the refreshing, delicious flavor. It is inspired by a soup I tasted at Il Cibreo, a popular trattoria in Florence. I like to serve it with warm focaccia.

6 cups homemade Chicken Broth (page 63) or a mix of half store-bought broth and half water

2 tablespoons olive oil

I medium onion, chopped

I celery rib, chopped

I carrot, chopped

5 large red bell peppers, seeded and chopped

5 medium boiling potatoes, peeled and chopped

2 tomatoes, cored and chopped

Salt and freshly ground black pepper

I cup milk

Freshly grated Parmigiano-Reggiano

1 Prepare the broth, if necessary. Then, pour the oil into a large pot. Add the onion, celery, and carrot. Cook, stirring frequently, over medium heat until the vegetables are tender and golden, about 10 minutes.

2 Add the peppers, potatoes, and tomatoes and stir well. Add the broth and bring to a simmer. Lower the heat and cook 30 minutes or until the vegetables are very tender.

3 With a slotted spoon, transfer the vegetables to a food processor or blender. Puree until smooth.

4 Pour the vegetable puree into the pot. Heat the soup gently and stir in the milk. Do not allow the soup to boil. Add salt and pepper to taste. Serve hot, sprinkled with cheese.

Fontina, Bread, and Cabbage Soup
Zuppa alla Valpelline

MAKES 6 SERVINGS

One of my fondest memories of the Valle d'Aosta is the aromatic fontina cheese and flavorful whole grain bread of the region. The cheese is made from cows' milk and aged in mountain caves. Look for a cheese with a natural rind and the silhouette of a mountain pressed into the top to be sure you are getting the real fontina. Use a good, chewy bread for this hearty soup. Crinkly Savoy cabbage is milder tasting than the smooth-leaf variety.

8 cups homemade Meat Broth (page 62) or a mix of half store-bought beef broth and half water

2 tablespoons unsalted butter

I small Savoy cabbage, thinly shredded

Salt

¼ teaspoon freshly ground nutmeg

¼ teaspoon ground cinnamon

Freshly ground black pepper

12 ounces Fontina Valle d'Aosta

12 slices crusty seedless rye, pumpernickel, or whole-wheat bread, toasted

1 Prepare the broth, if necessary. Then, melt the butter in a large pot. Add the cabbage and salt to taste. Cover and cook on low heat for 30 minutes, stirring occasionally, until the cabbage is tender.

2 Preheat the oven to 350°F. Put the broth, nutmeg, cinnamon, salt, and pepper in a large pot and bring to a simmer over medium heat.

3 Place 4 slices of bread in the bottom of a deep 3-quart ovenproof Dutch oven or deep, heavy pot or baking dish. Cover with half of the cabbage and one third of the cheese. Repeat with another layer of bread, cabbage, and cheese. Top with the remaining bread. Carefully pour on the hot broth. Tear the reserved cheese into bits and scatter it on top of the soup.

5 Bake the casserole until browned and bubbling, about 45 minutes. Let rest 5 minutes before serving.

Creamy Mushroom Soup
Zuppa di Funghi

MAKES 8 SERVINGS

Thanksgiving is not a holiday celebrated in Italy, but I often serve this creamy fresh and dried mushroom soup from northern Italy as part of my holiday menu.

8 cups homemade Meat Broth (page 62) or a mix of half store-bought beef broth and half water
I ounce dried porcini mushrooms
2 cups hot water
2 tablespoons unsalted butter
I medium onion, finely chopped
I garlic clove, finely chopped
I pound white mushrooms, thinly sliced
¹/₂ cup dry white wine
I tablespoon tomato paste
¹/₂ cup heavy cream
Chopped fresh flat-leaf parsley, for garnish
Salt and freshly ground black pepper

I Prepare the broth, if necessary. Then, put the porcini mushrooms in the water and let soak 30 minutes. Remove the mushrooms from the bowl and reserve the liquid. Rinse the mushrooms under cold running water to removing any grit, paying special attention to the ends of the stems where soil collects. Chop the mushrooms coarsely. Strain the mushroom liquid through a paper coffee filter into a bowl.

2 In a large pot, melt the butter over medium heat. Add the onion and garlic and cook 5 minutes. Stir in all of the mushrooms and cook, stirring occasionally, until the mushrooms turn lightly golden, about 10 minutes. Add salt and pepper to taste.

3 Add the wine and bring to a simmer. Stir in the broth, mushroom liquid, and tomato paste. Lower the heat and simmer 30 minutes.

4 Stir in the cream. Sprinkle with parsley and serve immediately.

Vegetable Soup with Pesto
Minestrone al Pesto

MAKES 6 TO 8 SERVINGS

In Liguria, a dollop of fragrant pesto sauce is added to bowls of minestrone. It is not essential, but it really lifts the flavor of the soup.

¹/₄ cup olive oil
I medium onion, chopped
2 carrots, chopped
2 celery ribs, chopped
4 ripe tomatoes, peeled, seeded, and chopped
I pound Swiss chard or spinach, chopped
3 medium boiling potatoes, peeled and chopped
3 small zucchini, chopped
8 ounces green beans, cut into ¹/₂-inch pieces
8 ounces shelled fresh cannellini or borlotti beans or 2 cups drained cooked dried or canned beans
Salt and freshly ground black pepper
I recipe Pesto (page 72)
4 ounces small pasta shapes such as tubetti or elbows

I Pour the oil into a large pot. Add the onions, carrots, and celery. Cook, stirring frequently, over medium heat until the vegetables are tender and golden, about 10 minutes.

2 Stir in the tomatoes, chard, potatoes, zucchini, and beans. Add enough water to just cover the vegetables. Add salt and pepper to taste. Cook, stirring from time to time, until the soup is thickened and the vegetables are soft, about 1 hour. Add a little water if it becomes too thick.

3 Meanwhile, prepare the pesto, if necessary. When the soup has thickened, add the pasta. Cook, stirring, until the pasta is tender, about 10 minutes. Let cool slightly. Serve hot, passing a bowl of the pesto, to be added at the table, or ladle the soup into bowls and dollop some pesto in the center of each.

🌱 Egg Soups

Egg Soup from Pavia
Zuppa alla Pavese

MAKES 4 SERVINGS

Eggs poached in broth are a quick and delicious meal. The soup is ready to serve when the whites are just set and the yolks are still soft.

2 quarts homemade Meat Broth (page 62) or a mix of half store-bought broth and half water
4 slices country bread, lightly toasted
4 large eggs, at room temperature
4 to 6 tablespoons freshly grated Parmigiano-Reggiano
Salt and freshly ground black pepper

1 Prepare the broth, if necessary. If not freshly made, heat the broth to a simmer. Season to taste with salt and pepper.

2 Have ready 4 heated soup bowls. Place a slice of toast in each bowl, then crack an egg over each slice of toast.

3 Pour the hot broth over the eggs to cover by a few inches. Sprinkle with the cheese. Let stand until the egg white is cooked to taste. Serve hot.

Roman Egg Drop Soup
Stracciatella

MAKES 4 SERVINGS

Stracciatella means "little rags," a reference to the appearance of the eggs in the soup. To enhance the flavor of the broth, you can add a little lemon juice or ground nutmeg.

8 cups homemade Chicken Broth (page 63) or a mix of half store-bought broth and half water
3 large eggs
1/4 cup freshly grated Parmigiano-Reggiano
Salt and freshly ground black pepper
1 tablespoon very finely chopped fresh flat-leaf parsley

1 Prepare the broth, if necessary. If not freshly made, heat the broth until it is simmering.

2 In a small bowl, beat the eggs, cheese, salt, and pepper until well blended. Slowly pour the mixture into the broth, stirring constantly with a fork, just until the eggs are set and form ribbons. Stir in the parsley and serve immediately.

Egg Crepes in Broth
Scrippelle 'mbusse

MAKES 6 SERVINGS

Scrippele is Abruzzese dialect for crespelle, or crepes. These are the same crepes that are layered with cheese, mushrooms, and tomato sauce on page 198. Here, they are filled with grated cheese and served in broth.

8 cups homemade Chicken Broth (page 63) or a mix of half store-bought broth and half water
12 Crepes (pages 198–199)
1/2 cup freshly grated Parmigiano-Reggiano
2 tablespoons finely chopped fresh Italian flat-leaf parsley

1 Prepare the broth, if necessary. Then, prepare the crepes, if necessary. Sprinkle each crepe with some of the cheese and parsley. Roll up the crepes to form tubes. Have ready 6 heated soup bowls. Place 2 tubes in each bowl.

2 If not hot, heat the broth until simmering. Spoon the hot broth onto the crepe tubes and serve immediately.

Semolina Fritters in Broth
Frittatine di Semola in Brodo

MAKES 6 SERVINGS

At a formal dinner party at an elegant New York Italian restaurant, I got to talking with my friend Tony Mazzola about the foods we enjoyed as children. Tony told me about the simple soup his mother, Lydia, who came from Sicily, used to serve. As we ate our guinea hen and risotto covered in rare and expensive white truffles matched with fine wines, he described this comforting soup of tasty little semolina and cheese fritters in chicken broth. His mother only served it around Christmas and the New Year because, she said, its simplicity was good for you after all the rich food eaten during the holidays. A few days later, the fancy meal was all but forgotten, but I couldn't wait to try Tony's soup. This is the recipe as he and his sister Emilia were able to recreate it.

Note that the skillet is brushed very lightly with olive oil before the fritters are fried. There is no need to use more. The fritters brown and hold their shape better with less oil.

6 cups homemade Chicken Broth (page 63) or a mix of half store-bought broth and half water

2¹/₂ cups water

1 teaspoon salt

1 cup fine ground semolina

1 large egg, beaten

1 cup freshly grated Parmigiano-Reggiano

2 tablespoons chopped fresh flat-leaf parsley

Freshly ground black pepper

Olive oil

1 Prepare the broth, if necessary. Then, in a medium saucepan over medium heat, bring the water to a simmer. Whisk in the semolina and salt. Reduce the heat to low and cook, stirring, until the semolina is thickened, about 2 minutes.

2 Remove the pot from the heat. Whisk in the egg, cheese, parsley, and pepper to taste.

3 Line a tray with a piece of plastic wrap. Scrape the semolina mixture onto the plastic and spread it out to a ¹/₂-inch thickness. Let cool to room temperature, at least 30 minutes. Use immediately or cover with plastic wrap and store in the refrigerator up to 24 hours.

4 Just before serving the soup, cut the semolina mixture into bite-size pieces. Brush a large nonstick skillet with olive oil and heat the skillet over medium heat. Add enough of the semolina pieces as will fit comfortably in one layer without crowding. Cook until golden brown, about 4 to 5 minutes.

Turn the pieces and brown the other side, about 4 to 5 minutes more. Remove the pieces to a plate. Cover with foil and keep warm. Brown the remaining semolina pieces in the same way.

5 Meanwhile, bring the broth to a simmer. Divide the semolina fritters among 4 bowls. Spoon on the broth. Serve immediately.

Bread Noodles in Broth
Passatelli in Brodo

MAKES 6 SERVINGS

Passatelli are noodlelike strands of dough made with dry bread crumbs and grated cheese bound together with beaten eggs. The dough is passed through a device similar to a potato ricer or food mill directly into simmering broth. Some cooks add a little freshly grated lemon zest to the dough. Passatelli in broth was at one time a traditional Sunday dish in Emilia-Romagna, followed by a roast.

8 cups homemade Meat Broth (page 62) or Chicken Broth (page 63) or a mix of half store-bought broth and half water

3 large eggs

1 cup freshly grated Parmigiano-Reggiano, plus more for serving

2 tablespoons very finely chopped fresh flat-leaf parsley

¹/₄ teaspoon grated nutmeg

About ³/₄ cup plain dry bread crumbs

1 Prepare the broth, if necessary. Then, in a large bowl, beat the eggs until blended. Stir in the cheese, parsley, and nutmeg until smooth. Add enough bread crumbs to form a smooth, thick paste.

2 If not freshly made, bring the broth to a simmer in a large pot. Taste the broth and adjust the seasoning, if necessary.

3 Place a food mill fitted with the large-hole blade, a potato ricer, or a colander with large holes over the pot. Push the cheese mixture through the food mill or colander into the simmering broth. Cook over low heat for 2 minutes. Remove from the heat and let stand 2 minutes before serving. Serve hot with additional cheese.

Tyrolean Bread Dumplings
Canederli

MAKES 4 SERVINGS

Cooks in northern Italy close to the Austrian border make bread dumplings that are completely different from the passatelli dumplings made in Emilia Romagna. Similar to the Austrian knödel, canederli are made with whole-wheat or rye bread, flavored with salame (a dried sausage made from coarsely ground pork) or mortadella (a delicate sausage made from very finely ground pork flavored with nutmeg and often whole pistachios). They are simmered in a liquid, then served in the broth, though they are also good with tomato sauce or butter sauce.

8 cups homemade Meat Broth (page 62) or Chicken Broth (page 63) or a mix of half store-bought broth and half water

4 cups day-old seedless rye bread or whole-wheat bread

1 cup milk

2 tablespoons unsalted butter

1/2 cup minced onion

3 ounces salame, mortadella, or smoked ham, very finely chopped

2 large eggs, beaten

2 tablespoons chopped fresh chives or fresh flat-leaf parsley

Salt and freshly ground black pepper

About 1 cup all-purpose flour

1/2 cup freshly grated Parmigiano-Reggiano

1 Prepare the broth, if necessary. Then, in a large bowl, soak the bread in the milk for 30 minutes, stirring occasionally. The bread should begin to crumble.

2 In a small skillet, melt the butter over medium heat. Add the onion and cook, stirring often, until golden, about 10 minutes.

3 Scrape the contents of the skillet onto the bread. Add the meat, eggs, chives or parsley, and salt and pepper to taste. Stir in enough of the flour, a little bit at a time, so that the mixture just holds its shape. Let stand 10 minutes.

4 Moisten your hands with cool water. Scoop up about 1/4 cup of the mixture and shape it into a ball. Roll the ball in flour. Place the dumpling on a piece of wax paper. Repeat with the remaining mixture.

5 Bring a large pot of water to a boil. Reduce the heat so that the water is just simmering. Carefully drop in half of the dumplings, or just enough so that the pot is not crowded. Cook 10 to 15 minutes or until the dumplings are cooked through. With a slotted spoon, transfer the dumplings to a plate. Cook the remaining dumplings in the same way.

6 When ready to serve the soup, heat the broth to simmering. Add the dumplings and cook gently for 5 minutes or until heated through. Serve the dumplings in the broth with the grated cheese.

🌿 Meat and Fish Soups

Green Bean and Sausage Soup
Zuppa di Fagiolini

MAKES 4 SERVINGS

One summer when I was little, I visited a great aunt who had a marvelous old Victorian home on the Long Island shore in New York. Every day she would cook elaborate lunches and dinners for her husband, who seemed to expect nothing less than three courses. This was one of the soups she would prepare.

I use medium-grain rice for this soup—the kind I use for risotto—because that is what I tend to have at home, but long-grain rice would work too.

2 tablespoons olive oil
1 medium onion, chopped
1 red or yellow bell pepper, chopped
3 Italian-style pork sausages
2 large tomatoes, peeled, seeded, and chopped, or 1 cup canned tomatoes, chopped
8 ounces green beans, trimmed and cut into bite-size pieces
Pinch of crushed red pepper
Salt
3 cups water
1/4 cup medium-grain rice, such as Arborio

1 Pour the oil into a medium pot. Add the onion, pepper, and sausages and cook, stirring occasionally, until the vegetables are tender and the sausages are lightly browned, about 10 minutes.

2 Add the tomatoes, green beans, crushed red pepper, and salt to taste. Add 3 cups cool water and bring to a simmer. Lower the heat and cook 15 minutes.

3 Transfer the sausages to a plate. Thinly slice the sausages and return them to the pot.

4 Stir in the rice and cook until the rice is tender, 15 to 20 minutes more. Serve hot.

Escarole and Little Meatballs Soup
Zuppa di Scarola e Polpettini

MAKES 6 TO 8 SERVINGS

This was my favorite soup when I was growing up, though we only ate it on holidays and special occasions. I still can't resist it, and I make it often.

4 quarts homemade Chicken Broth (page 63) or a mix of half store-bought broth and half water
1 medium head of escarole (about 1 pound)
3 large carrots, chopped

MEATBALLS

1 pound ground veal or beef
2 large eggs, beaten
1/2 cup very finely minced onion
1 cup plain bread crumbs
1 cup freshly grated Pecorino Romano, plus more for serving
1 teaspoon salt
Freshly ground black pepper, to taste

1 Prepare the broth, if necessary. Then, trim the escarole and discard any bruised leaves. Cut off the stem ends. Separate the leaves and wash well in cool water, especially in the center of the leaves where soil collects. Stack the leaves and cut them crosswise into 1-inch strips.

2 In a large pot, combine the broth, escarole, and carrots. Bring to a simmer and cook 30 minutes.

3 Meanwhile, prepare the meatballs: Mix all of the meatball ingredients in a large bowl. With your hands (or a small scoop dispenser), shape the mixture into tiny balls, about the size of small grapes, and place them on a plate or tray.

4 When the vegetables are ready, gently drop the meatballs one at a time into the soup. Cook over low heat, until the meatballs are cooked through, about 20 minutes. Taste and adjust seasoning. Serve hot, sprinkled with grated Pecorino Romano.

"Married" Soup
Minestra Maritata

MAKES 10 TO 12 SERVINGS

Many people assume that this Neapolitan soup got its name by being served at wedding banquets, but in fact "married" refers to the wedding of the flavors of the assorted meats and vegetables that are the principal ingredients. It is a very old recipe—at one time a dish that people would eat on a daily basis, adding whatever scraps of meat and vegetables they could find. Today it is considered somewhat old-fashioned, though I can't imagine a more satisfying meal on a cold day.

Chard, chicory, kale, or cabbage can be used instead of the vegetables below. Try Genoa or other Italian-style salami in place of the soppressata, or a ham bone for the prosciutto bone. For best flavor, make the soup a day before serving it.

1 pound meaty pork ribs (country-style pork ribs)

1 prosciutto bone (optional)

2 medium carrots, trimmed

2 celery ribs with leaves

1 medium onion

1 pound Italian-style pork sausage

1 thick slice imported Italian prosciutto (about 4 ounces)

1 4-ounce chunk of soppressata

Pinch of crushed red pepper

1 1/2 pounds (1 small head) escarole, trimmed

1 pound (1 medium bunch) broccoli rabe, trimmed

1 pound (about half of a small head) savoy cabbage, cut into strips

8 ounces broccoli, cut into florets (about 2 cups)

Freshly grated Parmigiano-Reggiano

1 In a large pot, bring 5 quarts water to a boil. Add the pork ribs, prosciutto bone if using, carrots, celery, and onion. Lower the heat to a simmer and cook 30 minutes over medium heat.

2 Skim off the foam that rises to the surface. Add the sausage, prosciutto, soppressata, and crushed red pepper. Cook until the pork ribs are tender, about 2 hours.

3 Meanwhile, wash and trim all of the vegetables. Bring a large pot of water to a boil. Add half the greens. Bring to a simmer and cook 10 minutes. With a slotted spoon, transfer the greens to a colander set over a large bowl. Cook the remaining greens the same way. Drain well and let cool. When cool, chop the greens into bite-size pieces.

4 After 2 hours cooking time, remove the meats and sausage from the broth. Discard the bones and cut the meats and sausage into bite-size pieces.

5 Let the broth cool slightly. Skim the fat from the broth. Strain the broth through a fine-mesh strainer into a large clean pot. Return the meats to the broth. Add the greens. Return to a simmer and cook 30 minutes.

6 Serve hot, sprinkled with grated Parmigiano-Reggiano.

Tuscan Fish Soup
Cacciucco

MAKES 6 SERVINGS

The more varieties of fish you add to the pot for this Tuscan specialty, the better the soup will taste.

1/4 cup olive oil

1 medium onion

1 celery rib, chopped

1 carrot, chopped

1 garlic clove, chopped

2 tablespoons chopped fresh flat-leaf parsley

Pinch of crushed red pepper

1 bay leaf

1 live lobster (1- to 2-pound)

2 whole fish (about 1 1/2 pounds each) such as porgy, stripped bass, red snapper, or sea bass, cleaned and cut into chunks (remove and reserve the heads)

1/2 cup dry white wine

1 pound tomatoes, peeled, seeded, and chopped

1 pound calamari (squid), cleaned and cut into 1-inch rings

Slices of Italian bread, toasted

1 Pour the oil into a large pot. Add the onion, celery, carrot, garlic, parsley, pepper, and bay leaf. Cook over medium heat, stirring frequently, until the vegetables are tender and golden, about 10 minutes.

2 Place the lobster on a cutting board with the cavity facing up. Do not remove the bands that keep the claws shut. Protect your hand with a heavy towel or pot holder and hold the lobster above the tail. Plunge the tip of a heavy chef's knife into the body where the tail joins the chest. Use poultry shears to remove the thin shell that covers the tail meat. Remove the dark vein in the tail, but leave the green tomalley and red coral, if any. Set the tail aside. Cut the lobster body and claws at the joints into 1- to 2-inch chunks. Smack the claws with the blunt side of the knife to crack them.

3 Add the lobster chest cavity and the reserved fish heads and trimmings to the pot. Cook 10 minutes. Add the wine and simmer 2 minutes. Stir in the tomatoes and 4 cups water. Bring to a simmer and cook 30 minutes.

4 With a slotted spoon, remove the lobster cavity and fish heads and bay leaf from the pot and discard. Pass the remaining ingredients through a food mill into a large bowl.

5 Rinse out the pot and pour in the soup. Bring the liquid to a simmer. Add the seafood that needs the longest cooking, such as the calamari. Cook until almost tender, about 20 minutes. Stir in the lobster tail and claws and fish chunks. Cook until the lobster and fish are opaque inside, about 10 minutes more.

6 Place slices of toasted bread in each soup bowl. Ladle the soup over the bread and serve hot.

Chunky Fish Soup
Ciuppin

MAKES 6 SERVINGS

You can use one type of fish or several varieties for this soup. For a more garlicky flavor, rub the slices of toasted bread with a raw garlic clove before adding the soup to the bowls. Sailors from Genoa introduced this classic soup to San Francisco, where many of them settled. San Franciscans call their version cioppino.

2 1/2 pounds assorted firm white-fleshed fish fillets, such as halibut, sea bass, or mahi mahi
1/4 cup olive oil
1 medium carrot, finely chopped
1 tender celery rib, finely chopped
1 medium onion, chopped
2 garlic cloves, finely chopped
1 cup dry white wine
1 cup peeled, seeded, and chopped fresh tomatoes or canned tomatoes
Salt and freshly ground black pepper
2 tablespoons chopped fresh flat-leaf parsley
6 slices Italian or French bread, toasted

1 Rinse the fish pieces and pat them dry. Cut the fish into 2-inch chunks, discarding any bones.

2 Pour the oil into a large pot. Add the carrot, celery, onion, and garlic. Cook, stirring frequently, over medium heat until tender and golden, about 10 minutes. Add the fish and cook, stirring the pieces occasionally, 10 minutes more.

3 Pour in the wine and bring to a simmer. Add the tomatoes, and the salt and pepper to taste. Add cold water to cover. Bring to a simmer and cook 20 minutes.

4 Stir in the parsley. Place a slice of toast in each soup bowl. Ladle the soup over the bread and serve hot.

Seafood, Pasta, and Bean Soup

Pasta e Fagioli ai Frutti di Mare

MAKES 4 TO 6 SERVINGS

Soups combining pasta and beans with seafood are popular throughout southern Italy. This is my version of one I tasted at Alberto Ciarla, a famous seafood restaurant in Rome.

1 pound small mussels

1 pound small clams

2 tablespoons olive oil

2 ounces pancetta, finely chopped

1 medium onion, finely chopped

2 garlic cloves, finely chopped

3 cups drained cooked dried or canned
     cannellini beans

1 cup chopped tomatoes

1/2 pound calamari (squid), cut into 1-inch rings

Salt and freshly ground black pepper

8 ounces spaghetti, broken into 1-inch pieces

2 tablespoons chopped fresh flat-leaf parsley

Extra-virgin olive oil

1 Place the mussels in cold water to cover for 30 minutes. Scrub them with a stiff brush and scrape off any barnacles or seaweed. Remove the beards by pulling them toward the narrow end of the shells. Discard any mussels with cracked shells or that do not shut tightly when tapped. Place the mussels in a large pot with 1/2 cup cold water. Cover the pot and bring to a simmer. Cook until the mussels open, about 5 minutes. With a slotted spoon, transfer the mussels to a bowl.

2 Place the clams in the pot and cover the pan. Cook until the clams open, about 5 minutes. Remove the clams from the pot. Strain the liquid in the pot through a paper coffee filter into a bowl and reserve.

3 With your fingers, remove the clams and mussels from the shells and place them in a bowl.

4 Pour the oil into a large pot. Add the pancetta, onion, and garlic. Cook, stirring frequently, over medium heat, until tender and golden, about 10 minutes.

5 Add the beans, tomatoes, and calamari. Add the reserved juices from the shellfish. Bring to a simmer and cook 20 minutes.

6 Stir in the seafood and cook until just cooked through, about 5 minutes.

7 Meanwhile, bring a large pot of water to a boil. Add the pasta and salt to taste. Cook until tender. Drain the pasta and add it to the soup. Add a little of the pasta liquid if the soup seems too thick.

8 Stir in the parsley. Serve hot, drizzled with extra-virgin olive oil.

Mussels and Clams in Tomato Broth
Zuppa di Cozze

MAKES 4 SERVINGS

You can make this with all mussels or all clams, if you like.

2 pounds mussels

¹/₃ cup olive oil

4 garlic cloves, very finely chopped

2 tablespoons chopped fresh flat-leaf parsley

Pinch of crushed red pepper.

1 cup dry white wine

3 pounds ripe tomatoes, peeled, seeded, and chopped
   or 2 (28- to 35-ounce) cans imported Italian
   peeled tomatoes, chopped

Salt

2 pounds small clams

8 slices Italian or French bread, toasted

1 whole garlic clove

1 Place the mussels in cold water to cover for 30 minutes. Scrub them with a stiff brush and scrape off any barnacles or seaweed. Remove the beards by pulling them toward the narrow end of the shells. Discard any mussels with cracked shells or that do not shut tightly when tapped.

2 In a large saucepan, heat the oil over medium heat. Add the chopped garlic, parsley, and crushed red pepper and cook over low heat until the garlic is golden, about 2 minutes. Stir in the wine and bring to a simmer. Add the tomatoes and a pinch of salt. Cook over medium heat, stirring occasionally, until slightly thickened, about 20 minutes.

3 Gently stir in the mussels and the clams. Cover the pot. Cook 5 to 10 minutes, until the mussels and clams open. Discard any that do not open.

4 Rub the toast with the cut garlic clove. Place a piece of bread in each soup bowl. Top with the mussels and clams and their liquid. Serve hot.

Sauces

Tomato Sauces

Marinara Sauce

Fresh Tomato Sauce

Tomato Sauce, Sicilian Style

Tomato Sauce, Tuscan Style

Pizzaiola Sauce

"Fake" Meat Sauce

Pink Sauce

Tomato Sauce with Onion

Roasted Tomato Sauce

Meat Sauces (Ragù)

Abruzzo-Style Ragù

Neapolitan Ragù

Sausage Ragù

Marches-Style Ragù

Tuscan Meat Sauce

Bologna-Style Ragù

Duck Ragù

Rabbit or Chicken Ragù

Porcini and Meat Ragù

Pork Ragù with Fresh Herbs

Truffled Meat Ragù

Other Pasta Sauces

Butter and Sage Sauce

Holy Oil

Fontina Cheese Sauce

Béchamel Sauce

Sauces for Meat and Fish

Garlic Sauce

Green Sauce

Sicilian Garlic and Caper Sauce

Parsley and Egg Sauce

Red Pepper and Tomato Sauce

Olive Sauce

Sun-Dried Tomato Sauce

Molise-Style Pepper Sauce

Olive Oil Mayonnaise

Orange Mayonnaise Sauce

Some people have the idea that making tomato sauce for pasta is a difficult, time consuming production. They think you need a host of ingredients and hours to cook it. How else to explain all of the ready-made tomato sauces available, even from famous restaurants and movie stars? Most of these products are over-sweetened, pastelike (due to the starchy thickeners), and overspiced, as well as overpriced. In fact, a delicious, heathful tomato sauce can be made with just a few ingredients in less than 30 minutes, no more than it takes to boil water and cook pasta.

The most important ingredient is the tomatoes. It would be nice if we all had access to fresh, ripe tomatoes all year round, but many of the fresh tomatoes available through the seasons are disappointing.

I rely on canned tomatoes, as cooks in Italy do for much of the year. Brands imported from Italy are generally the best, for the variety of tomatoes used and their ripeness. Canned tomatoes from other places are sometimes underripe when packed—sour tasting, hard and greenish at the ends, the juices thin and watery. Some packers try to compensate by adding thick tomato puree to the cans, but this does not disguise the lack of flavor and hard, astringent taste or the unyielding texture of the tomatoes. One of my criteria for a good canned tomato is whether or not it is tender enough to be chopped with a cooking spoon. Some cooks add sugar to their tomato sauce to counteract the acidity, but this is unnecessary if the tomatoes are ripe.

I also avoid prechopped or pureed tomatoes in cans. They are either too thin or too thick, and the texture masks the quality of the tomato. Buy several cans of tomatoes and taste them until you find a brand you like. It is hard to recommend any particular brand, since most imported brands are distributed in limited areas.

Many of the sauces, as well as other recipes in this book, are made with a food mill. This old-fashioned cooking tool consists of a metal strainer fitted with a hand-cranked paddle that pushes the food through the holes of the strainer. The strainer has retractable legs so that it can be set securely over a bowl or pot. The pureed foods pass through while the seeds, skins, and other hard objects are kept back. A blender or food processor can puree foods, but both pulverize the seeds and skins so that they cannot be separated out.

The little seeds in tomatoes can be annoying, sometimes bitter, and interfere with the texture of sauces that you want to be perfectly smooth. If you don't have a food mill, you can simply cut the tomatoes in half and scrape the seeds out with a spoon or your finger, before pureeing them in a food processor or blender. Or, if the seeds don't bother you, you can just leave them in. A little extra fiber is probably good for you.

When ripe fresh tomatoes are in season, their sweet, delicate flavor is incomparable. Plum or Roma tomatoes are meatier and best for sauces. To peel fresh tomatoes, bring a saucepan of water to a boil. Drop in the tomatoes a few at a time. When the water returns to the boil, cook the tomatoes 1 minute, then remove them with a slotted spoon and drop them into a bowl of cold water. With your fingers, peel off the skins. Cut the tomatoes in half through the stem and cut out the core. Squeeze the tomatoes over a bowl to extract the seeds.

Unlike a simple tomato sauce, a meat sauce, known in Italy as a ragù, is time-consuming. The meat needs long, slow simmering to become tender and to marry with the other ingredients. Though not particularly difficult to make, it takes time, but a meat ragù can easily be made ahead and refrigerated or even frozen until needed.

Exact proportions are difficult to give when it comes to pairing pasta and sauce. Italians like a minimal amount of sauce, and they use just enough to coat the pasta. Americans generally prefer more sauce, to coat their pasta heavily. The pasta sauce and ragù recipes in this chapter make at least enough for one pound of pasta. Some of the ragùs make more than enough for one pound, but because of the number and type of ingredients involved, it makes more sense to cook a large batch. Leftover sauces freeze well and can be used for another meal.

White sauce, often called by its French name, béchamel, or in Italian *salsa balsamella* or *besciamèlla*, is another Italian staple. It is used so often by Italian home cooks that there is even a ready-made version that can be bought in Italian supermarkets. Béchamel is typically mixed with grated cheese or other ingredients and served with pasta or vegetables. Many baked pasta dishes call for salsa balsamella.

Butter sauce is a classic Italian favorite, often served with fresh pasta, especially ravioli or other stuffed pastas. Usually it is flavored with fresh sage, but other herbs may be used. Holy oil is not really a sauce but a condiment made from whole or crushed dried chili peppers and olive oil that is used on pasta, vegetables, and other foods.

Beyond these sauces, there are many others made with herbs, olive oil, and other ingredients that are eaten with meats, fish, eggs, or vegetables. Mayonnaise made with olive oil is sensational with poached fish or ripe tomatoes as well as on salads. Green sauce, made with olive oil, parsley, garlic, and other ingredients is often served at room temperature with boiled meat or roasted fish. Throughout this book, you will find many other sauces that are meant to accompany particular dishes but can also be adapted for use with other foods.

❧ Tomato Sauces

Marinara Sauce
Salsa Marinara

MAKES 2¹/₂ CUPS

Garlic gives this southern Italian–style quick-cooking sauce its characteristic flavor. Neapolitans lightly crush the cloves with the side of a large knife. This makes it easy to remove the skin and opens the cloves to release their flavor. Remove whole garlic cloves before serving.

I add the basil at the end of the cooking time for the freshest flavor. Dried basil is a poor substitute for fresh, but you can substitute fresh parsley or mint. This sauce is ideal for spaghetti or other dried pastas.

¹/₄ cup olive oil
2 large garlic cloves, crushed
Pinch of crushed red pepper
3 pounds fresh plum tomatoes, peeled, seeded, and chopped, or 1 (28-ounce) can imported Italian peeled tomatoes with their juice, passed through a food mill
Salt to taste
4 fresh basil leaves, torn into bits

1 Pour the oil into a medium saucepan. Add the garlic and red pepper. Cook over medium heat, turning the garlic once or twice until it is golden, about 5 minutes. Remove the garlic from the pan.

2 Add the tomatoes and salt to taste. Cook 20 minutes, stirring occasionally, or until the sauce is thickened.

3 Turn off the heat and stir in the basil. Serve hot. Can be made ahead and stored in a tightly sealed container in the refrigerator up to 5 days or in the freezer up to 2 months.

Fresh Tomato Sauce
Salsa Leggero

MAKES 3 CUPS

This sauce is unusual because it does not begin with the usual onion or garlic cooked in olive oil or butter. Instead, the aromatics are simmered along with the tomatoes so the sauce has a delicate vegetable flavor. Serve it with any of the fresh pastas or as a sauce for a frittata or other omelet.

4 pounds ripe plum tomatoes, peeled, seeded, and chopped
1 medium carrot, chopped
1 medium onion, chopped
1 small celery rib, chopped
Salt to taste
6 fresh basil leaves, torn into small pieces
¹/₄ cup extra-virgin olive oil

1 In a large, heavy saucepan, combine the tomatoes, carrot, onion, celery, a pinch of salt, and basil. Cover the pot and cook over medium heat until the mixture comes to a simmer. Uncover and cook, stirring occasionally, 20 minutes or until the sauce is thickened.

2 Let cool slightly. Pass the sauce through a food mill or puree it in a food processor or blender. Reheat gently and taste for seasoning. Stir in the oil. Serve hot. Can be made ahead and stored in a tightly sealed container in the refrigerator up to 5 days or in the freezer up to 2 months.

Tomato Sauce, Sicilian Style

Salsa di Pomodoro alla Siciliana

MAKES ABOUT 3 CUPS

I watched Anna Tasca Lanza, who has a cooking school at her family's Regaleali wine estate in Sicily, make tomato sauce this way. Everything goes into the pot, then when it has simmered long enough, the sauce is pureed in a food mill to eliminate the tomato seeds. Butter and olive oil, added at the end of the cooking time, enrich and sweeten the sauce. Serve it with potato gnocchi or fresh fettuccine.

3 pounds ripe tomatoes
1 medium onion, thinly sliced
1 garlic clove, finely chopped
2 tablespoons chopped fresh basil
Pinch of crushed red pepper
1/4 cup olive oil
1 tablespoon unsalted butter

1 If using a food mill to puree the tomatoes, cut them into quarters lengthwise and go to step 2. If using a food processor or blender, first peel the tomatoes: Bring a medium saucepan of water to boiling. Add the tomatoes a few at a time and cook 1 minute. With a slotted spoon, remove them and place in a bowl of cool water. Repeat with the remaining tomatoes. Peel the tomatoes, then core them and scrape out the seeds.

2 In a large pot, combine the tomatoes, onion, garlic, basil, and crushed red pepper. Cover and bring to a simmer. Cook over low heat 20 minutes or until the onion is tender. Let cool slightly.

3 Pass the mixture through a food mill, if using, or puree it in a blender or food processor. Return the puree to the pot. Add the basil, red pepper, and salt to taste.

4 Just before serving, reheat the sauce. Remove from the heat and stir in the olive oil and butter.

Serve hot. Can be made ahead and stored in a tightly sealed container in the refrigerator up to 5 days or in the freezer up to 2 months.

Tomato Sauce, Tuscan Style

Salsa di Pomodoro alla Toscana

MAKES 3 CUPS

A soffritto is a mix of chopped aromatic vegetables, usually onion, carrot, and celery, cooked in butter or oil until tender and lightly golden. It is the flavoring base for many sauces, soups, and braises and an essential technique in Italian cooking. Many Italian cooks put all of the soffritto ingredients into a cold pan together, then turn on the heat. This way all of the ingredients cook gently and nothing gets too brown or overcooked. With the alternative method of heating the oil first, then adding the chopped ingredients, there is a danger of the oil becoming overheated. Vegetables can brown and become overcooked and bitter. This Tuscan-style tomato sauce starts with a soffritto of the usual vegetables plus garlic cooked with olive oil.

4 tablespoons olive oil
1 medium onion, finely chopped
1/2 cup chopped carrot
1/4 cup chopped celery
1 small garlic clove, minced
3 pounds fresh ripe plum tomatoes, peeled, seeded, and finely chopped, or 1 (28-ounce) can imported Italian peeled tomatoes with their juice, passed through a food mill
1/2 cup chicken broth
Pinch of crushed red pepper
Salt
2 or 3 basil leaves, torn

1 Pour the oil into a medium saucepan. Add the onion, carrot, celery, and garlic. Cook over medium heat, stirring occasionally, until the vegetables are tender and golden, about 15 minutes.

2 Stir in the tomatoes, broth, red pepper, and salt to taste. Bring to a simmer. Partially cover the pan and cook over low heat, stirring occasionally, until thickened, about 30 minutes.

3 Stir in the basil. Serve hot. Can be made ahead and stored in a tightly sealed container in the refrigerator up to 5 days or in the freezer up to 2 months.

Pizzaiola Sauce
Salsa Pizzaiola

MAKES ABOUT 2¹/₂ CUPS

Neapolitans use this tasty sauce to cook small steaks or chops (see page 317), or they serve it over spaghetti. It is not usually used on pizza, though, since the extreme heat of wood-fired Neapolitan pizza ovens would overcook an already cooked sauce. It gets its name from the tomatoes, garlic, and oregano—the same ingredients a pizzamaker typically uses on pizza.

Chop the garlic until it is very fine, so that there are no large pieces it in the sauce.

2 large garlic cloves, very finely chopped
¹/₄ cup olive oil
Pinch of crushed red pepper
1 (28-ounce) can imported Italian peeled tomatoes with their juice, chopped
1 teaspoon dried oregano, crumbled
Salt

1 In a large skillet, cook the garlic in the oil over medium heat until golden, about 2 minutes. Stir in the crushed red pepper.

2 Add the tomatoes, oregano, and salt to taste. Bring the sauce to a simmer. Cook, stirring occasionally, 20 minutes or until the sauce is thickened. Serve hot. Can be made ahead and stored in a tightly sealed container in the refrigerator up to 5 days or in the freezer up to 2 months.

"Fake" Meat Sauce
Sugo Finto

MAKES ABOUT 6 CUPS

Sugo finto means "fake sauce," a strange name for such a delicious, useful sauce, and one that is used frequently in central Italy, according to my friend Lars Leicht. This recipe comes from his aunt, who lives outside of Rome. It is so full of flavor you might be fooled into thinking there was some meat in it. The sauce is perfect for those times when you want something more complex than a plain tomato sauce, but do not want to add meat. This recipe makes a lot, but it can easily be halved, if you prefer.

¹/₄ cup olive oil
1 medium-size yellow onion, finely chopped
2 small carrots, peeled and finely chopped
2 garlic cloves, finely chopped
4 fresh basil leaves, chopped
1 small dried chili pepper, crushed, or a pinch of crushed red pepper
1 cup dry white wine
2 cans (28 to 35 ounces each) imported Italian peeled tomatoes with their juice or 6 pounds fresh plum tomatoes, peeled, seeded, and chopped

1 In a large saucepan, combine the oil, onion, carrots, garlic, basil, and chili. Cook over medium heat, stirring occasionally, until the vegetables are tender and golden, about 10 minutes.

2 Add the wine and bring to a simmer. Cook 1 minute.

3 Pass the tomatoes through a food mill into the pot or puree them in a blender or food processor. Bring to a simmer and turn the heat to low. Season to taste with salt. Cook, stirring occasionally, for 30 minutes or until the sauce is thickened. Serve hot. Can be made ahead and stored in a tightly sealed container in the refrigerator up to 5 days or in the freezer up to 2 months.

Pink Sauce
Salsa di Pomodoro alla Panna

MAKES ABOUT 3 CUPS

Heavy cream smooths out this lovely pink sauce. Serve it with ravioli or green gnocchi.

1/4 cup unsalted butter
1/4 cup chopped fresh shallots
3 pounds fresh tomatoes, peeled, seeded, and chopped, or 1 (28-ounce) can imported Italian peeled tomatoes with their juice
Salt and freshly ground black pepper
1/2 cup heavy cream

1 In a large saucepan, melt the butter over medium-low heat. Add the shallots and cook until golden, about 3 minutes. Add the tomatoes and salt and pepper and cook, stirring, until the sauce comes to a simmer. If using canned tomatoes, chop them with a spoon. Cook, stirring occasionally, until the sauce is slightly thickened, about 20 minutes. Let cool slightly.

2 Pass the tomato mixture through a food mill. Return the sauce to the pot and heat it over medium heat. Add the cream and cook 1 minute or until slightly thickened. Serve hot.

Tomato Sauce with Onion
Salsa di Pomodoro con Cipolla

MAKES 2 1/2 CUPS

The natural sugar in the onion complements the sweetness of the butter in this sauce. This sauce is also good made with shallots in place of the onion.

3 tablespoons unsalted butter
1 tablespoon olive oil
1 small onion, very finely chopped
3 pounds plum tomatoes, peeled, seeded, and chopped, or 1 (28-ounce) can imported Italian peeled tomatoes with their juice, passed through a food mill
Salt and freshly ground black pepper to taste

1 In a medium, heavy saucepan, melt the butter with the oil over medium heat. Add the onion and cook, stirring once or twice, until the onion is tender and golden, about 7 minutes.

2 Add the tomatoes and salt and pepper. Bring the sauce to a simmer and cook 20 minutes or until thickened.

Roasted Tomato Sauce
Salsa di Pomodoro Arrostito

MAKES ENOUGH FOR 1 POUND OF PASTA

Even less-than-perfect fresh tomatoes can be cooked this way. You can use just one variety of tomatoes, or several types. A combination of red and yellow tomatoes is particularly nice. Basil or parsley are the obvious choices for the herbs, but you can also use a mixture including chives, rosemary, mint, or whatever you have on hand.

I like to do the roasting ahead of time, then toss the room-temperature sauce with hot pasta such as penne or fusilli. My friend Suzie O'Rourke tells me that her favorite way to serve it is as an appetizer slathered on slices of toasted Italian bread.

2 1/2 pounds round, plum, cherry, or grape tomatoes
4 garlic cloves, very finely chopped
Salt
Pinch of crushed red pepper
1/2 cup olive oil
1/2 cup chopped fresh basil, parsley, or other herbs

1 Place a rack in the center of the oven. Preheat the oven to 400° F. Oil a 13 × 9 × 2–inch nonreactive baking pan.

2 Coarsely chop round or plum tomatoes into 1/2-inch pieces. Cut cherry or grape tomatoes into halves or quarters.

3 Spread the tomatoes in the pan. Sprinkle with the garlic, salt, and crushed red pepper. Drizzle with the oil and stir gently.

4 Roast 30 to 45 minutes or until the tomatoes are lightly browned. Remove the tomatoes from the oven and stir in the herbs. Serve hot or at room temperature.

❧ Meat Sauces (Ragù)

A sauce made with meat in Italy is called a ragù, from the French word *ragoûter*, "to restore or stimulate the appetite." The mouth-watering aroma of a simmering ragù will stimulate anyone's appetite.

Meat ragù is made everywhere in Italy, from the very famous Ragù Bolognese, made with ground meat, to the equally famous though very different Neapolitan-style, made with chunky pieces of various meats. Some are made with vegetables, others with spices, some add poultry, others use lamb. Some feature tomatoes, while others rely on tomato paste or concentrate. Every region has its own style, and, of course, every cook has his or her own favorite combination and technique.

The recipes that follow are just a small sample of the possibilities you will find in Italy.

Abruzzo-Style Ragù
Ragù Abruzzese

MAKES ABOUT 7 CUPS

The vegetables for this ragù are left whole, and some of the meats are cooked on the bone. At the end of the cooking time, the vegetables and loose bones are removed. The meats are typically removed from the sauce and served as a second course. Serve this sauce with chunky pasta shapes like rigatoni.

3 tablespoons olive oil
1 pound pork shoulder with some bones, cut into 2-inch pieces
1 pound lamb neck or shoulder with bones, cut into 2-inch pieces
1 pound boneless veal stew meat, cut into 1-inch pieces
1/2 cup dry red wine
2 tablespoons tomato paste
4 pounds fresh tomatoes, peeled, seeded, and chopped, or 2 (28-ounce) cans imported Italian peeled tomatoes with their juice, passed through a food mill
2 cups water
Salt and freshly ground black pepper
1 medium onion
1 rib celery
1 medium carrot

1 In a large heavy pot, heat the oil over medium heat. Add the meats and cook, stirring occasionally, until lightly browned.

2 Add the wine and cook until most of the liquid evaporates. Stir in the tomato paste. Add the tomatoes, water, and salt and pepper to taste.

3 Add the vegetables and bring to a simmer. Cover the pot and cook, stirring occasionally, until the meat is very tender, about 3 hours. If the sauce seems thin, uncover and cook until slightly reduced.

4 Let cool. Remove any loose bones and the vegetables.

5 Reheat before serving or cover and store in the refrigerator up to 3 days or in the freezer up to 3 months.

Neapolitan Ragù
Ragù alla Napolitana

MAKES ABOUT 8 CUPS

This hearty ragù, made with different cuts of beef and pork, is what many Italian-Americans call "gravy," which is made for the Sunday midday meal or dinner. It is ideal for tossing with substantial pasta shapes like shells or rigatoni and for using in baked pasta dishes, such as Neapolitan Lasagne, pages 174–175.

The meatballs are added to the sauce toward the end of the cooking time, so you can prepare them while the sauce simmers.

2 tablespoons olive oil

1 pound meaty pork neck bones or spare ribs

1 pound beef chuck in one piece

1 pound Italian-style plain or fennel pork sausages

4 garlic cloves, lightly crushed

¼ cup tomato paste

3 (28- to 35-ounce) can imported Italian peeled tomatoes

Salt and freshly ground black pepper to taste

6 fresh basil leaves, torn into small pieces

1 recipe Neapolitan-Style Meatballs (page 327), the larger size

2 cups water

1 In a large heavy pot, heat the oil over medium heat. Pat the pork dry and put the pieces in the pot. Cook, turning occasionally, about 15 minutes or until nicely browned on all sides. Remove the pork to a plate. Brown the beef in the same way and remove it from the pot.

2 Place the sausages in the pot and brown on all sides. Set the sausages aside with the other meats.

3 Drain off most of the fat. Add the garlic and cook 2 minutes or until golden. Discard the garlic. Stir in the tomato paste; cook 1 minute.

4 With a food mill, puree the tomatoes and their juice into the pot. Or, for a chunkier sauce, just chop up the tomatoes. Add 2 cups water and salt and pepper. Add the pork, beef, sausages, and basil. Bring the sauce to a simmer. Partially cover the pot and cook over low heat, stirring occasionally, for

2 hours. If the sauce becomes too thick, add a little more water.

5 Meanwhile, prepare the meatballs. When the sauce is almost done, add the meatballs to the sauce. Cook 30 minutes or until the sauce is thick and the meats are very tender. Remove the meats from the sauce and serve as a second course or separate meal. Serve the sauce hot. Cover and store in an airtight container in the refrigerator up to 3 days or in the freezer up to 2 months.

Sausage Ragù
Ragù di Salsiccia

MAKES 4½ CUPS

Little bits of Italian-style pork sausage meat stud this sauce from southern Italy. If you like it spicy, use hot sausages. Serve this sauce on Potato Tortelli (pages 188–189) or chunky pasta, like shells or rigatoni.

1 pound plain Italian pork sausages

2 tablespoons olive oil

2 garlic cloves, finely chopped

½ cup dry white wine

3 pounds fresh plum tomatoes, peeled, seeded, and chopped, or 1 (28-ounce) can imported Italian peeled tomatoes with their juice, passed through a food mill

Salt and freshly ground black pepper

3 to 4 fresh basil leaves, torn into bits

1 Remove the sausage from the casings. Chop the meat finely.

2 In a large pot, heat the oil over medium heat. Add the sausage meat and the garlic. Cook, stirring frequently, until the pork is lightly browned, about 10 minutes. Add the wine and bring to a simmer. Cook until most of the wine evaporates.

3 Stir in the tomatoes and salt to taste. Bring to a simmer. Reduce the heat to low. Cook, stirring occasionally, until the sauce is thickened, about 1 hour and 30 minutes. Stir in the basil just before serving. Serve hot. Can be made ahead and stored in a tightly sealed container in the refrigerator up to 3 days or in the freezer up to 2 months.

Marches-Style Ragù
Ragù di Carne alla Marchigiana

MAKES ABOUT 5 CUPS

The town of Campofilone in the Marches of central Italy hosts an annual pasta festival that attracts visitors from all over. The highlight of the feast is maccheroncini, *hand-rolled egg pasta that is served with this flavorful meat sauce. A mix of herbs and a pinch of cloves give this ragù a special flavor. A little milk added at the end of the cooking time gives it a smooth finish. If you are making this sauce ahead of time, add the milk just before serving it. Serve with fettuccine.*

I cup homemade Meat Broth (page 62)
    or store-bought beef broth
¼ cup olive oil
I small onion, finely chopped
I celery rib, chopped
I carrot, chopped
I tablespoon chopped fresh flat-leaf parsley
2 teaspoons chopped fresh rosemary
I teaspoon chopped fresh thyme
I bay leaf
I pound boneless beef chuck, cut into 2-inch chunks
I (28-ounce) can imported Italian peeled tomatoes,
    drained and passed through a food mill
Pinch of ground cloves
Salt and freshly ground black pepper
½ cup milk

1 Prepare the broth, if necessary. Pour the oil into a large saucepan. Add the vegetables and herbs and cook over medium heat, stirring occasionally, for 15 minutes or until the vegetables are tender and golden.

2 Add the beef and cook, stirring often, until the meat is browned. Sprinkle with salt and pepper. Add the tomato puree, broth, and cloves. Bring to a simmer. Partly cover the pan and cook, stirring occasionally, until the meat is tender and the sauce is thick, about 2 hours.

3 Remove the meat, drain it, and chop it finely. Stir the chopped meat back into the sauce.

4 Add the milk and heat 5 minutes before serving. Serve hot. Can be made ahead and stored in an airtight container in the refrigerator up to 3 days or in the freezer up to 2 months.

Tuscan Meat Sauce
Ragù alla Toscana

MAKES 8 CUPS

Spices and lemon zest give this beef and pork ragù a sweet flavor. Serve it with pici *(page 199).*

4 tablespoons unsalted butter
¼ cup olive oil
4 ounces imported Italian prosciutto, chopped
2 medium carrots
2 medium red onions
I large celery rib, chopped
¼ cup chopped fresh flat-leaf parsley
I pound boneless beef chuck, cut into 2-inch pieces
8 ounces Italian sweet sausages or ground pork
2 pounds fresh tomatoes or I (28-ounce) can
    imported Italian peeled tomatoes, chopped
2 cups homemade Meat Broth (page 62)
    or store-bought beef broth
½ cup dry red wine
½ teaspoon grated lemon zest
Pinch of cinnamon
Pinch of nutmeg
Salt and freshly ground black pepper to taste

1 In a large saucepan, melt the butter with the olive oil over medium heat. Add the prosciutto and chopped vegetables and cook, stirring frequently, for 15 minutes.

2 Stir in the meats and cook, stirring frequently, until browned, about 20 minutes.

3 Add the tomatoes, broth, wine, lemon zest, cinnamon, nutmeg, and salt and pepper to taste. Bring the mixture to a simmer. Cook, stirring occasionally, until the sauce is thickened, about 2 hours.

4 Remove the beef chunks from the pot. Place them on a cutting board and chop into small pieces. Stir the chopped meat into the sauce. Serve hot. Can be made ahead and stored in an airtight container in the refrigerator up to 3 days or in the freezer up to 2 months.

Bologna-Style Ragù

Ragù Bolognese

MAKES ABOUT 5 CUPS

At Tamburini, Bologna's finest gourmet food and takeout shop, you can buy many types of fresh egg pasta. The most famous are tortellini, nickel-sized pasta rings filled with mortadella, a finely spiced pork sausage. The tortellini are served either in brodo, "broth," alla panna, in a heavy cream sauce, or, best of all, al ragù, with a rich meat sauce. Long, slow cooking of the soffritto—aromatic vegetables and pancetta—gives Bolognese-style ragù a deep, rich flavor.

2 cups homemade Meat Broth (page 62)
    or store-bought beef broth
2 tablespoons unsalted butter
2 tablespoons olive oil
2 ounces pancetta, finely chopped
2 small carrots, peeled and finely chopped
1 onion, finely chopped
1 tender celery rib, finely chopped
8 ounces ground veal
8 ounces ground pork
8 ounces ground beef
1/2 cup dry red wine
3 tablespoons tomato paste
1/4 teaspoon grated nutmeg
Salt and freshly ground black pepper
1 cup milk

1 Prepare the broth, if necessary. In a large pot, melt the butter with the oil over medium-low heat. Add the pancetta, carrots, onion, and celery. Cook the mixture over low heat, stirring occasionally, until all the flavorings are very tender and a rich golden color, about 30 minutes. If the ingredients are beginning to brown too much, stir in a little warm water.

2 Add the meats and stir well. Cook, stirring often to break up the lumps, until the meats lose their pink color, but do not brown, about 15 minutes.

3 Add the wine and simmer until the liquid evaporates, about 2 minutes. Stir in the tomato paste, broth, nutmeg, and add salt and pepper to taste. Bring the mixture to a simmer. Cook on low heat, stirring occasionally, until the sauce is thick, about 2 1/2 to 3 hours. If the sauce becomes too thick, add a little more broth or water.

4 Stir in the milk and cook 15 minutes more. Serve hot. Can be made ahead and stored in an airtight container in the refrigerator up to 3 days or in the freezer up to 2 months.

Duck Ragù

Ragù di Anatra

MAKES ABOUT 5 CUPS

Wild ducks thrive in the lagoons and marshes of the Veneto, and local cooks make wonderful dishes with them. They are roasted, braised, or prepared like this, in ragù. The rich, gamy sauce is eaten with bigoli, thick whole-wheat spaghetti prepared with a torchio, a hand-cranked pasta press. Fresh domesticated ducks, while not as flavorful as the wild variety, are a good substitute. I serve the sauce with fettuccine and the duck pieces as a second course.

Have the butcher cut the duck into quarters for you, or do it yourself using poultry shears or a large chef's knife. If you prefer not to use it, just leave out the liver.

1 duckling (about 5 1/2 pounds)
2 tablespoons olive oil
Salt and freshly ground black pepper, to taste
2 ounces pancetta, chopped
2 medium onions, chopped
2 medium carrots, chopped
2 celery ribs, chopped
6 fresh sage leaves
Pinch of freshly grated nutmeg
1 cup dry white wine
2 1/2 cups peeled, seeded, and chopped fresh tomatoes

1 Rinse the duck inside and out and remove any loose fat from the cavity. Using poultry shears,

cut the duck into 8 pieces. First cut the duck along the backbone. Open the duck like a book. With a heavy knife, cut the duck in half lengthwise between the two sides of the breast. Cut the thigh away from breast. Separate the leg and thigh at the joint. Separate the wing and breast at the joint. If using the liver, cut it into dice and set aside.

2 In a large heavy saucepan, heat the oil over medium heat. Pat the duck pieces dry with paper towels. Add the duck pieces and cook, stirring occasionally, until browned on all sides. Sprinkle with salt and pepper. Remove the duck to a platter. Spoon off all but 2 tablespoons of the fat.

3 Add the pancetta, onions, carrots, celery, and sage to the pan. Cook for 10 minutes, stirring occasionally, until the vegetables are tender and golden. Add the wine and simmer for 1 minute.

4 Return the duck to the pot and add the tomatoes and water. Bring the liquid to a simmer. Partially cover the pot and cook, stirring occasionally, for 2 hours, or until the duck is very tender when pierced with a fork. Stir in the duck liver, if using. Remove the pan from the heat. Let cool slightly, then skim the fat from the surface. Remove the pieces of meat from the sauce with a slotted spoon and transfer to a platter. Cover to keep warm.

5 Serve the sauce with hot cooked fettuccine, followed by the duck meat as a second course. The entire dish can be cooked ahead of time up to 2 days in advance, stored in an airtight container and refrigerated.

Rabbit or Chicken Ragù
Ragù di Coniglio o Pollo

MAKES 3 CUPS

For Easter dinner it was traditional at our house to begin with pasta in a rabbit ragù. For those in the family averse to eating rabbit, my mother would make the same sauce with chicken. Given the blandness of rabbit meat, I always found the chicken ragù much tastier. Have the butcher cut up the rabbit or chicken for you.

I small rabbit or chicken, cut into 8 pieces
2 tablespoons olive oil
I (28-ounce) can imported Italian peeled tomatoes with their juice, chopped
I medium onion, finely chopped
I medium carrot, finely chopped
I garlic clove, finely chopped
¹/₂ cup dry white wine
I teaspoon chopped fresh rosemary
Salt and freshly ground black pepper

I In a large skillet, heat the oil over medium heat. Pat the rabbit or chicken pieces dry and sprinkle them with salt and pepper. Place them in the pan and brown well on all sides, about 20 minutes.

2 Remove the pieces to a plate. Spoon off all but two tablespoons of the fat in the pan.

3 Add the onion, carrot, garlic, and rosemary to the pan. Cook, stirring often, until the vegetables are tender and lightly golden. Add the wine and simmer for 1 minute. Pass the tomatoes with their juices through a food mill, or puree them in a blender or food processor, and add them to the pot. Add salt and pepper to taste. Reduce the heat to low and partially cover the pan. Simmer for 15 minutes, stirring occasionally.

4 Return the meat to the pan. Cook 20 minutes, stirring occasionally, until the meat is tender and falling off or easily pulls away from the bone. Remove the pieces of meat from the sauce with a slotted spoon and transfer to a platter. Cover to keep warm.

5 Serve the sauce over hot, cooked fettuccine, followed by the rabbit or chicken as a second course. Can be made ahead and stored in an airtight container in the refrigerator up to 3 days or in the freezer up to 2 months.

Porcini and Meat Ragù
Ragù di Funghi e Carne

MAKES ABOUT 6 CUPS

Though much has been written about the great white truffles of Piedmont, porcini mushrooms, called cèpes by the French, are as great a treasure of the region. Abundant after the rain, the thick brown caps of porcini are supported by short, creamy white stems, giving them a chubby look. Their name means little pigs. Grilled or roasted with olive oil and herbs, the mushroom flavor is sweet and nutty. Because fresh porcini are only available in the spring and fall, cooks in this region rely on dried porcini the rest of the year to give sauces and braises a rich, woodsy flavor.

Dried porcini are usually sold in clear plastic or cellophane packages. Look for large whole slices with a minimum of crumbs and debris in the bottom of the bag. The "sell by" date should be within the year. The flavor fades as the mushrooms get older. Store dried porcini in a tightly sealed container.

1 1/2 cups homemade **Meat Broth** (see page 62) or store-bought beef broth

I ounce dried porcini mushrooms

2 cups warm water

2 tablespoons olive oil

2 ounces chopped pancetta

I carrot, chopped

I medium onion, chopped

I celery rib, chopped

I garlic clove, very finely chopped

1 1/2 pounds ground veal

1/2 cup dry white wine

Salt and freshly ground black pepper

I cup chopped fresh or canned imported Italian tomatoes

1/4 teaspoon freshly grated nutmeg

I Prepare the broth, if necessary. In a medium bowl, soak the mushrooms in the water for 30 minutes. Lift the mushrooms out of the soaking liquid.

Strain the liquid through a paper coffee filter or a piece of dampened cheesecloth into a clean bowl and set aside. Rinse the mushrooms under running water, paying special attention to the base where soil collects. Finely chop the mushrooms.

2 Pour the oil into a large saucepan. Add the pancetta and cook over medium heat about 5 minutes. Add the carrot, onion, celery, and garlic and cook, stirring frequently, until tender and golden, about 10 minutes more. Add the veal and cook until lightly browned, stirring frequently to break up the lumps. Add the wine and cook 1 minute. Season to taste with salt and pepper.

3 Add the tomatoes, mushrooms, nutmeg, and reserved mushroom liquid. Bring to a simmer. Cook 1 hour or until the sauce is thickened. Serve hot. Can be made ahead and stored in an airtight container in the refrigerator up to 3 days or in the freezer up to 2 months.

Pork Ragù with Fresh Herbs
Ragù di Maiale

MAKES 6 CUPS

At the home of Natale Liberale in Puglia, my husband and I ate this ground pork ragù on troccoli, fresh square-cut spaghetti similar to the pasta alla chitarra of Abruzzo. It was made by his mother Enza, who showed me how she cut sheets of homemade egg pasta using a special ridged wooden rolling pin. The ragù is also good on orecchiette or fresh fettuccine.

The variety of herbs makes Enza's ragù distinctive. They deepen the flavor of the sauce as they simmer. Fresh herbs are ideal, but frozen or dried herbs can be substituted, though I avoid dried basil, which is unpleasant. Substitute fresh parsley if basil is not available.

4 tablespoons olive oil

1 medium onion, finely chopped

1/2 cup chopped fresh basil or flat-leaf parsley

1/4 cup chopped fresh mint leaves or 1 teaspoon dried

1 tablespoon chopped fresh sage or 1 teaspoon dried

1 teaspoon chopped fresh rosemary or 1/2 teaspoon dried

1/2 teaspoon fennel seeds

1 pound ground pork

Salt and freshly ground black pepper

1/2 cup dry red wine

1 (28-ounce) can imported Italian peeled tomatoes with their juice, chopped

1 Put the oil, onion, all the herbs, and the fennel seeds in a large saucepan and turn the heat to medium. Cook, stirring occasionally, until the onion is tender and golden, about 10 minutes.

2 Stir in the pork, then the salt and pepper to taste. Cook, stirring frequently to break up the lumps, until the pork loses its pink color, about 10 minutes. Add the wine and simmer 5 minutes. Stir in the tomatoes and cook 1 hour or until the sauce is thickened. Serve hot. Can be made ahead and stored in an airtight container in the refrigerator up to 3 days or in the freezer up to 2 months.

Truffled Meat Ragù
Ragù Tartufato

MAKES 5 CUPS

In Umbria, black truffles grown in the region are added to the ragù at the very end of the cooking time. They give the sauce a special woodsy flavor.

You can leave out the truffle or use a jarred truffle, readily available in specialty stores. Another alternative is to use a tiny bit of truffle oil. Use just a scant amount, as its flavor can be overwhelming. Serve this sauce with fresh fettuccine. The sauce is so rich, grated cheese is not needed.

1 ounce dried porcini mushrooms

2 cups hot water

2 tablespoons unsalted butter

8 ounces ground pork

8 ounces ground veal

2 ounces sliced pancetta, chopped fine

1 celery rib, cut in half

1 medium carrot, cut in half

1 small onion, peeled but left whole

2 medium-size fresh tomatoes, peeled, seeded, and chopped, or 1 cup imported Italian canned tomatoes, drained and chopped

1 tablespoon tomato paste

1/4 cup heavy cream

1 small black fresh or jarred truffle, thinly sliced, or a few drops of truffle oil

Pinch of freshly grated nutmeg

1 Place the porcini mushrooms in a bowl with the water. Let soak 30 minutes. Lift the mushrooms out of the liquid. Strain the liquid through a coffee filter or dampened cheesecloth into a clean bowl and set aside. Wash the mushrooms well under cool water, paying special attention to the base of the stems where soil collects. Finely chop the mushrooms.

2 In a large saucepan, melt the butter over medium heat. Add the meats and cook, stirring to break up lumps, until the meat loses its pink color but does not brown. It should remain soft.

3 Add the wine and simmer 1 minute. Add the celery, carrot, onion, and mushrooms and 1 cup of their liquid, the tomatoes, and tomato paste and stir well. Let cook over very low heat for 1 hour. If the sauce becomes too dry, add a little of the mushroom liquid.

4 When the ragù has cooked for 1 hour, remove the celery, carrot, and onion. The sauce can be prepared ahead to this point. Let it cool, then store in an airtight container and refrigerate up to 3 days or store in the freezer up to 2 months. Reheat the sauce before proceeding.

5 Just before serving, add the cream, truffle, and nutmeg to the hot sauce. Stir gently but do not cook, to preserve the flavor of the truffle. Serve hot.

❧ Other Pasta Sauces

These sauces are used with pasta, with vegetables, and in whatever other ways creative cooks devise.

Butter and Sage Sauce
Salsa al Burro e Salvia

MAKES ¹/₂ CUP

This is so basic, I hesitated whether to include it, but it is the classic sauce for fresh egg pasta, especially stuffed pasta like ravioli. Use fresh butter and sprinkle the finished dish with freshly grated Parmigiano-Reggiano cheese.

1 stick unsalted butter
6 sage leaves
Salt and freshly ground black pepper
Parmigiano-Reggiano

Melt the butter with the sage over low heat. Simmer 1 minute. Season to taste with salt and pepper. Serve with hot, cooked pasta and top with Parmigiano-Reggiano cheese.

> **Variation:** *Brown Butter Sauce:* Cook the butter for a few minutes until it browns lightly. Leave out the sage. *Hazelnut Sauce:* Add ¹/₄ cup chopped toasted hazelnuts to the butter. Leave out the sage.

Holy Oil
Olio Santo

MAKES 1 CUP

Italians in Tuscany, Abruzzo, and other regions of central Italy call this holy oil because it is used to "anoint" many soups and pastas, just as blessed oil is used in certain sacraments. Dribble this oil into soups or toss into pasta. Be careful—it is hot!

You can use dried chiles that you find in your supermarket. If you are in an Italian market, look for peperoncino or "hot peppers" sold in packages.

1 tablespoon crushed dried chiles or crushed red pepper
1 cup extra-virgin olive oil

In a small glass bottle, combine the peppers and oil. Cover and shake well. Let stand 1 week before using. Store in a cool, dark place up to 3 months.

Fontina Cheese Sauce
Fonduta

MAKES 1³/₄ CUPS

At the Locanda di Felicin in Monforte d'Alba in Piedmont, owner Giorgio Rocca serves this rich, delicious sauce in shallow plates, topped with shaved truffles as an appetizer, or over vegetables like broccoli or asparagus. Try it on Potato Gnocchi (pages 189–190), too.

2 large egg yolks
1 cup heavy cream
¹/₂ pound Fontina Valle d'Aosta, cut into ¹/₂-inch cubes

In a small saucepan, whisk together the egg yolks and cream. Add the cheese and cook over medium heat, stirring constantly, until the cheese is melted and the sauce is smooth, about 2 minutes. Serve hot.

Béchamel Sauce
Salsa Balsamella

MAKES ABOUT 4 CUPS

This basic white sauce is usually combined with cheese and used on baked pasta or vegetables. The recipe can easily be halved.

1 quart milk
6 tablespoons unsalted butter
5 tablespoons flour
Salt and freshly ground black pepper to taste
Pinch of freshly grated nutmeg

1 Heat the milk in a medium saucepan until small bubbles form around the edge.

2 Melt the butter in a large saucepan over medium-low heat. Add the flour and stir well. Cook 2 minutes.

3 Slowly begin adding the milk in a thin stream, stirring it in with a wire whisk. At first the sauce will become thick and lumpy, but it will gradually loosen up and become smooth as you stir in the remainder.

4 When all of the milk has been added, stir in the salt, pepper, and nutmeg. Raise the heat to medium and stir constantly until the mixture comes to a simmer. Cook 2 minutes more. Remove from the heat. This sauce can be made up to 2 days before using. Pour it into a container, place a piece of plastic wrap directly against the surface and seal tightly to prevent a skin from forming, then refrigerate. Reheat over low heat before using adding a little more milk if it is too thick.

❧ Sauces for Meat and Fish

Boiled, roasted, and grilled meat and fish are often served with one or more of the following sauces.

Garlic Sauce
Agliata

MAKES 1 1/2 CUPS

Garlic sauce can be served with boiled or grilled meats, chicken, or fish. I have even tossed it with hot cooked pasta for a quick meal. This version is from Piedmont, though I have also eaten agliata made without nuts in Sicily. I like the flavor that the toasted walnuts give it.

2 garlic cloves
2 or 3 slices Italian bread, crusts removed
1/2 cup toasted walnuts
1 cup extra-virgin olive oil
Salt and freshly ground black pepper

1 In a food processor or blender, combine the garlic, bread, walnuts, and salt and pepper to taste. Process until finely chopped.

2 With the machine running, gradually blend in the oil. Process until the sauce is thick and smooth.

3 Let stand at room temperature 1 hour before serving.

Green Sauce
Salsa Verde

MAKES 1½ CUPS

Though I have eaten green sauce in one form or another throughout Italy, this version is my favorite, because the bread gives it a creamy texture and helps to keep the parsley suspended in the liquid. Otherwise the parsley and other solids tend to sink to the bottom. Serve green sauce with the classic boiled meat dish Bollito Misto *(Mixed Boiled Meats, pages 333–334), with grilled or roasted fish, or over sliced tomatoes, boiled eggs, or steamed vegetables. The possibilities are endless.*

3 cups loosely packed fresh flat-leaf parsley
1 garlic clove
¼ cup crustless Italian or French bread, cubed
6 anchovy fillets
3 tablespoons drained capers
1 cup extra-virgin olive oil
2 tablespoons red or white wine vinegar
Salt

1 In a food processor, finely chop the parsley and garlic. Add the bread cubes, anchovies, and capers and process until finely chopped.

2 With the machine running, add the oil and vinegar and a pinch of salt. Once blended, taste for seasoning; adjust as needed. Cover and store at room temperature up to two hours or in the refrigerator for longer storage.

Sicilian Garlic and Caper Sauce
Ammoghiu

MAKES ABOUT 2 CUPS

The island of Pantelleria off the coast of Sicily is well known for both its aromatic dessert wine moscato di Pantelleria *and its excellent capers. The capers thrive and grow wild all over the island. In the spring the plants are covered with beautiful pink and white flowers. The unopened buds of the flowers are the capers, which are harvested and preserved in coarse sea salt, another local specialty. The Sicilians feel that the salt preserves the fresh flavor of the capers better than vinegar.*

This uncooked sauce of capers, tomatoes, and lots of garlic is a Sicilian favorite for fish or pasta. One way to serve it is with crispy fried fish or calamari.

8 garlic cloves, peeled
1 cup basil leaves, rinsed and dried
½ cup fresh parsley leaves
A few celery leaves
6 fresh plum tomatoes, peeled and seeded
2 tablespoons capers, rinsed and drained
½ cup extra-virgin olive oil
Salt and freshly ground black pepper

1 In a food processor, finely chop together the garlic, basil, parsley, and celery leaves. Add the tomatoes and capers and process until smooth.

2 With the machine running, gradually add the olive oil and salt and pepper to taste. Process until smooth and well blended. Let stand 1 hour before serving. Serve at room temperature.

Parsley and Egg Sauce
Salsa di Prezzemolo e Uova

MAKES 2 CUPS

In Trentino–Alto Adige, this sauce is served with fresh spring asparagus. Hard-cooked eggs give it a rich flavor and creamy texture. It goes well with poached chicken, salmon, or vegetables such as green beans and asparagus.

4 large eggs
1 cup lightly packed fresh flat-leaf parsley
2 tablespoons capers, rinsed, drained, and chopped
1 garlic clove
1 teaspoon grated lemon zest
1 cup extra-virgin olive oil
1 tablespoon fresh lemon juice
Salt and freshly ground black pepper

1 Place the eggs in a small saucepan with cold water to cover. Bring the water to a simmer. Cook for 12 minutes. Let the eggs cool under cold running water. Drain and peel. Chop the eggs and place them in a bowl.

2 In a food processor or by hand, very finely chop together the parsley, capers, and garlic. Transfer them to the bowl with the eggs.

3 Stir in lemon zest. With a whisk, beat in the oil, lemon juice, and salt and pepper to taste. Scrape into a sauce boat. Cover and chill 1 hour or overnight.

3 Remove the sauce from the refrigerator at least 1/2 hour before serving. Stir well and taste for seasoning.

Variation: Stir in 1 tablespoon chopped fresh chives.

Red Pepper and Tomato Sauce
Bagnetto Rosso

MAKES ABOUT 2 PINTS

In Piedmont in northern Italy, this sauce is made in big batches during the summer months when vegetables are plentiful. The name means "red bath," because the sauce is used for boiled meat or with chicken, pasta, omelets, or raw vegetables.

4 large red bell peppers, chopped
1 cup peeled, seeded, and chopped fresh tomatoes
1 medium onion, chopped
2 tablespoons olive oil
1 tablespoon wine vinegar
1 teaspoon sugar
Pinch of crushed red pepper
Pinch of ground cinnamon

1 In a large pot, combine all of the ingredients. Cover the pot and cook over low heat. Bring to a simmer. (Watch carefully that it does not scorch. Add a little water if there is not enough liquid.) Cook 1 hour, stirring occasionally, until the peppers are very tender.

2 Let cool slightly. Pass the ingredients through a food mill or process until smooth in a blender or food processor. Taste for seasoning. Transfer the sauce to tightly sealed containers and refrigerate up to 1 week or freeze up to three months. Serve at room temperature.

Olive Sauce
Salsa di Olive

MAKES ABOUT 1 CUP

Jarred olive paste is convenient to have on hand for a quick topping for crostini or this easy sauce for grilled meats. Finely chopped olives can be substituted. This is marvelous on roast beef tenderloin or as a dip for bread or focaccia.

1/2 cup black olive paste
1 garlic clove, peeled and flattened with the side of a knife
1 tablespoon snipped fresh rosemary
1/2 cup extra-virgin olive oil
1 to 2 tablespoons balsamic vinegar

In a medium bowl, whisk together the olive paste, garlic, rosemary, oil, and vinegar. If the sauce is too thick, thin it with a little more oil. Let stand at room temperature at least 1 hour. Remove the garlic before serving.

Sun-Dried Tomato Sauce
Salsa di Pomodori Secchi

MAKES ABOUT ¾ CUP

Drizzle this sauce over steaks, cold roast beef or pork, or, for an antipasto, over a log of mild goat cheese.

½ cup drained marinated sun-dried tomatoes, very finely chopped
2 tablespoons chopped fresh parsley
1 tablespoon chopped capers
½ cup extra-virgin olive oil
1 tablespoon balsamic vinegar
Freshly ground black pepper

In a medium bowl, whisk together all of the ingredients. Let stand 1 hour at room temperature before serving. Serve at room temperature. Store in an airtight container in the refrigerator up to 2 days.

Molise-Style Pepper Sauce
Salsa di Peperoni

MAKES ABOUT 1 CUP

Molise is one of Italy's smallest and poorest regions, but the food is full of flavor. Try this zesty pepper sauce—called jevezarola *in dialect—as a condiment with grilled or roasted meats or chicken. I even like it on grilled tuna. You can use your own Pickled Peppers (page 446) or the store-bought variety. If you like your food spicy, add some hot red pickled peppers.*

1 cup red pickled peppers, drained
1 medium onion, chopped
1 tablespoon sugar
4 tablespoons olive oil

1 Place the peppers, onion, and sugar in a food processor or blender. Blend until smooth. Add the oil and blend well.

2 Scrape the mixture into a small heavy saucepan. Cook, stirring often, until very thick, about

45 minutes. Remove from the heat and let cool before serving. Serve at room temperature. Store in an airtight container in the refrigerator up to 1 month.

Olive Oil Mayonnaise
Maionese

MAKES 1 CUP

Homemade mayonnaise makes all the difference when served simply, for example, slathered on ripe tomatoes, hard-cooked eggs, poached fish, sliced chicken, or sandwiches. To make it, I like to use a mild-flavored extra-virgin olive oil or blend a full-flavored oil together with vegetable oil. Make the mayonnaise by hand with a wire whisk or use an electric mixer.

Salmonella in raw eggs has been greatly reduced in recent years, but if you have any doubts, you can make a reasonable substitute by enhancing jarred mayonnaise with drops of olive oil and fresh lemon juice to taste.

2 large egg yolks, at room temperature
2 tablespoons fresh lemon juice
¼ teaspoon salt
1 cup extra-virgin olive oil or ½ cup vegetable oil plus ½ cup extra-virgin olive oil

1 In a medium bowl, whisk together the egg yolks, lemon juice, and salt until pale yellow and thick.

2 Continue whisking while very gradually adding the oil by drops until the mixture begins to stiffen. As it turns thick, whisk in the remaining oil more steadily, making sure that it is absorbed before adding more. If at any time the oil stops being absorbed, stop adding the oil and whisk rapidly until the sauce is smooth again.

3 Taste and adjust seasoning. Serve immediately or cover and refrigerate up to 2 days.

Variations: *Herb Mayonnaise:* Stir in 2 tablespoons very finely chopped fresh basil or parsley. *Lemon Mayonnaise:* Stir in ½ teaspoon grated fresh lemon zest.

Orange Mayonnaise Sauce

Salsa Maionese all'Arancia

MAKES 1 1/4 CUPS

Sweet red shrimp are a specialty in Sardinia. While staying at the Hotel Cala di Volpe on the Costa Smeralda, we were served shrimp on a bed of tender green lettuce with a delicate orange-tinged sauce. The shrimp were excellent on their own, but I could not stop eating the sauce. I knew it was based on mayonnaise, but somehow it seemed lighter. Finally, I asked the waiter, who told me the secret: The chef had added yogurt to the mayonnaise, which adds creaminess while cutting through the richness of the mayonnaise. This easy dressing is very good on poached salmon or eggs.

1/2 cup mayonnaise (homemade or store-bought)
1/2 cup plain yogurt
2 tablespoons fresh orange juice
1/2 teaspoon grated orange zest
2 teaspoons chopped chives
Salt and freshly ground black pepper to taste

In a bowl, stir together all of the ingredients. Taste and adjust seasoning. Refrigerate until serving time.

Pasta

Dried Pasta with Vegetables

Linguine with Garlic, Oil, and Hot Pepper

Spaghetti with Garlic and Olives

Linguine with Pesto

Thin Spaghetti with Walnuts

Linguine with Sun-Dried Tomatoes

Spaghetti with Peppers, Pecorino, and Basil

Penne with Zucchini, Basil, and Eggs

Pasta with Peas and Eggs

Linguine with Green Beans, Tomatoes, and Basil

Little Ears with Potato Cream and Arugula

Pasta and Potatoes

Shells with Cauliflower and Cheese

Pasta with Cauliflower, Saffron, and Currants

Bow Ties with Artichokes and Peas

Fettuccine with Artichokes and Porcini

Rigatoni with Eggplant Ragù

Sicilian Spaghetti with Eggplant

Bow Ties with Broccoli, Tomatoes, Pine Nuts, and Raisins

Cavatelli with Garlicky Greens and Potatoes

Linguine with Zucchini

Penne with Grilled Vegetables

Penne with Mushrooms, Garlic, and Rosemary

Linguine with Beets and Garlic

Bow Ties with Beets and Greens

Pasta with Salad

Fusilli with Roasted Tomatoes

Elbows with Potatoes, Tomatoes, and Arugula

Roman Country-Style Linguine

Penne with Spring Vegetables and Garlic

"Dragged" Pasta with Cream and Mushrooms

Dried Pasta with Tomatoes

Roman Tomato and Mozzarella Pasta

Fusilli with Tuna and Tomatoes

Linguine with Sicilian Pesto

Spaghetti with "Crazy" Pesto

Bow Ties with Uncooked Puttanesca Sauce

Pasta with Raw Vegetables

"Hurry Up" Spaghetti

"Angry" Penne

Rigatoni with Ricotta and Tomato Sauce

Bow Ties with Cherry Tomatoes and Bread Crumbs

Stuffed Shells

Dried Pasta with Cheese and Eggs

Spaghetti with Pecorino and Pepper

Linguine with Lemon

Linguine with Ricotta and Herbs

Ziti with Spinach and Ricotta

Rigatoni with Four Cheeses

Linguine with Creamy Nut Sauce

Bow Ties with Amaretti

Spaghetti with Fried Eggs, Salerno Style

Tagliarini Soufflé

Dried Pasta with Meat

Spaghetti Charcoal Burner's Style

Bucatini with Tomatoes, Pancetta, and Hot Pepper

Penne with Pancetta, Pecorino, and Black Pepper

Penne with Pork and Cauliflower

Spaghetti with Vodka Sauce

Bow Ties with Asparagus, Cream, and Prosciutto

"Dragged" Penne with Meat Sauce

Spaghetti, Caruso Style

Penne with Beans and Pancetta

Pasta with Chickpeas

Rigatoni Rigoletto

Anna's Fried Spaghetti

Eggplant Pasta Timbale

Baked Ziti

Sicilian Baked Pasta

Sophia Loren's Baked Pasta

Dried Pasta with Seafood

Linguine with Clam Sauce

Tuscan Spaghetti with Clams

Linguine with Anchovies and Spicy Tomato Sauce

Linguine with Crab and Little Tomatoes

Linguine with Mixed Seafood Sauce

Thin Spaghetti with Bottarga

Venetian Whole-Wheat Spaghetti in Anchovy Sauce

Capri-Style Spaghetti

Linguine with Shrimp, Venetian Style

Pasta with Sardines and Fennel

Penne with Zucchini, Swordfish, and Herbs

Christmas Eve Spaghetti with Baccala

Linguine with Tuna Pesto

Cold Pasta with Vegetable Confetti and Seafood

Fresh Pasta

Fresh Egg Pasta

Fettuccine with Butter and Parmigiano

Fettuccine with Butter and Cheese

"Triple-Butter" Fettuccine

Fettuccine with Spring Vegetables

Fettuccine with Gorgonzola Cream

Tagliarini with Pesto, Genoa Style

Fettuccine with Artichokes

Fettuccine with Tomato Fillets

Fettuccine with a Thousand Herbs

Fettuccine with Sausage and Cream

Green and White Pasta
with Sausage and Cream

Fettuccine with Leeks and Fontina

Fettuccine with Mushrooms and Prosciutto

Summer Tagliatelle

Fettuccine with Mushroom
and Anchovy Sauce

Fettuccine with Scallops

Tagliarini with Shrimp and Caviar

Crisp Pasta with Chickpeas, Puglia Style

Tagliarini with Abruzzese Chocolate Ragù

Lasagne

Bologna-Style Lasagne

Neapolitan Lasagne

Spinach and Mushroom Lasagne

Green Lasagne

Green Lasagne with Ricotta, Basil,
and Tomato Sauce

Eggplant Lasagne

Stuffed Fresh Pasta

Ricotta and Ham Cannelloni

Veal and Spinach Cannelloni

Green and White Cannelloni

Cannelloni with Tarragon and Pecorino

Cheese Ravioli with Fresh Tomato Sauce

Parma-Style Spinach and Cheese Ravioli

Winter Squash Ravioli with Butter
and Almonds

Meat Ravioli in Tomato Sauce

Tuscan Sausage Ravioli

Spiced Ravioli, Marches Style

Mushroom Ravioli in Butter and Sage Sauce

Giant Ravioli with Truffle Butter

Beet Ravioli with Poppy Seeds

Meat-Filled Pasta Rings in Cream Sauce

Potato Tortelli with Sausage Ragù

Fresh Gnocchi

Potato Gnocchi

Potato Gnocchi with Lamb Ragù

Gratinéed Potato Gnocchi

Sorrento-Style Potato Gnocchi

Winter Squash Gnocchi

Spinach and Potato Gnocchi

Seafood Gnocchi with Tomato
and Olive Sauce

Green Gnocchi in Pink Sauce

Semolina Gnocchi

Abruzzese Bread Dumplings

Other Fresh Pasta Dishes

Ricotta-Filled Crepes

Abruzzese Crepe and Mushroom Timbale

Tuscan Handmade Spaghetti
with Meat Sauce

Pici with Garlic and Bread Crumbs

Semolina Pasta Dough

Cavatelli with Ragù

Cavatelli with Calamari and Saffron

Cavatelli with Arugula and Tomato

Orecchiette with Pork Ragù

Orecchiette with Broccoli Rabe

Orecchiette with Cauliflower and Tomatoes

Orecchiette with Sausage and Cabbage

Orecchiette with Swordfish

othing says *la cucina Italiana* more eloquently than pasta. Whether homemade or store-bought, fresh or dried, pasta is the glory of Italian cooking. Fresh egg pasta is delicate and delicious, but for versatility nothing is better than dried pasta. It is inexpensive, easy to cook, and always available.

Making fresh pasta is an art and skill worth learning. I used to love to watch my grandmother making pasta. My sister and I knew it was time to make pasta when she began spreading clean white sheets over all the flat surfaces in her dining room. Then she would pour a mound of flour onto her old wooden kitchen table. With her fingers, she would make what she called *la fontana*, the fountain or well, a depression in the center of the flour that made it look like a volcano. Into the well would go fresh eggs and just a few drops of olive oil. Then she would begin, slowly at first, to mix the eggs with her hands, incorporating the flour a little at a time. Soon she would have a messy mass of dough that I always doubted could be saved. But grandma never disappointed us. Kneading slowly and deliberately, she would turn the mass into a moist, golden dough.

With her extra-long rolling pin that my grandfather had made from a sturdy broom handle, she would swiftly roll out the dough into sheer eggy sheets. Sometimes she cut them into ribbons for fettuccine, but more often she made ravioli. She would dab the dough with bits of cheese or meat filling, then cover the filling with a second layer of dough. An inverted juice glass was all she needed to punch the round ravioli out of the dough.

Finally the ravioli, or other pasta, would be laid out on the clean sheets in the dining room. No one, or I should say no child, was allowed to enter the room where the pasta was resting. Instead, she gave us scraps of dough to play with, and we fashioned our own creative pasta shapes.

Though we are inclined to assume that fresh anything is better than a dried product, that is not the case with pasta. Dried pasta is as good as fresh, but different. At one time dried pasta was eaten mostly in southern Italy, where it was preserved by drying in the hot sun. Today it is eaten all over the country.

Italians have some informal rules about combining pastas and sauces. Some dishes are traditionally made with fresh pasta, while others are typically made with dried, and I have suggested the variety accordingly. While some pasta and sauce pairings are better than others, few dishes will suffer from substitutions. Use your own good judgment about substituting dried pasta for fresh, or vice versa, just as Italian cooks do today. Lasagne, for example, is often made with dried pasta in southern Italy, and if you prefer, don't hestitate to make it that way.

In Italy, pasta is typically served in small portions as a first course, followed by an equally small meat, fish, or vegetable main course. Depending on several variables—the ingredients used for the pasta, the rest of your menu, whether you are serving the pasta as a first or main course, and, of course, the appetites of those who will be eating—one pound of pasta makes between 4 large and 8 small servings. I usually calculate between 4 and 6 servings per pound, because everyone loves pasta, and I would rather have a little left over (which rarely happens) than run short.

Dried Pasta

In general, long dried pasta strands like spaghetti or linguine are matched with thin sauces, such as those made with fish. Thicker pasta tubes and chunky shells are paired with heavier meat sauces or those with vegetable pieces. This is not an arbitrary rule; it is based on which cut or shape will hold or mix best with the sauce. This is why in Italy you would never find spaghetti topped with meatballs—a purely American invention. A sauce or ragu made with meat or tiny meatballs no larger than a grape would be served on a thick cut such as rigatoni, and large meatballs and other chunks of meat would be served as a second course or at a separate meal altogether.

How To Cook Dried Pasta

Pasta will cook perfectly without sticking if you follow these simple instructions. This is a more detailed master method than you'll find described in the recipes that follow. Refer back here if you need a refresher on cooking pasta, or on the simple, efficient way to heat the serving bowl.

Be sure to use pasta made from hard durum wheat, usually found in imported brands. The hard wheat helps the pasta keep its shape when cooked; pasta made from soft wheat becomes mushy as it stands.

1 Use a large pot with a 6-quart capacity for 1 pound of pasta. Fill with at least 4 quarts of cold water and cover. Over high heat, bring the water to a rolling boil. If you are cooking more than 1 pound of pasta, use two pots instead of one large one.

2 Add at least 2 tablespoons of salt to the pot. This may seem like a lot, but most of it gets drained off with the water when the pasta is done. It is difficult to salt pasta properly after it is cooked.

3 Add the pasta all at once. Stir it immediately. Stir often until the water comes back to a boil. Long, thin pasta may not fit completely under the water level. Gently push it down until it becomes pliable enough to be completely immersed.

4 Do not cover the pot, or the water will boil over when it returns to the boiling point. To speed things up, you can partially cover until the water is again boiling. Watch the pot carefully. Continue to stir the pasta occasionally as it cooks.

5 Have ready a large colander or mesh strainer. Place a heatproof serving bowl in the sink. Place the colander in the bowl.

6 Cooking time varies with the type of pasta. Ideally, the pasta should cook until it is tender, but still keeps its shape firmly. The best way to judge is by tasting a piece. The cooking times on the package are just guidelines. When you bite the pasta, the pieces should be cooked through and not chalky white in the center. The pasta should be firm, not mushy, perhaps a little firmer than you want it, as the residual heat will continue to soften the pasta before it is served. The Italians call this *al dente*, meaning to the tooth.

7 When the pasta is done, scoop out a little of the water with a cup and set it aside to thin the sauce if needed. Bring the pot to the sink and pour it into the colander. Lift the colander and allow the water to drain off into the serving bowl. (This also heats the bowl.) Set aside the colander with the pasta. If you forgot to save some of the cooking water, you have another opportunity to do so here. Set it aside. Carefully tip the bowl to remove the remaining cooking water.

(continues)

8 Add the pasta and sauce to the warmed bowl and toss well. Add a little of the cooking water if it is needed and toss again. Serve immediately.

Dried Pasta Tips

- Do not add oil to the water. It will not help to prevent it from sticking. The only way to prevent the pasta from sticking is to use a large amount of water, stir it frequently, and sauce the pasta immediately after it is drained.
- Do not rinse cooked pasta. This cools it and removes the surface starch, and as a result sauces will not adhere.
- Heat a serving bowl as described above, or place a bowl in the oven on low to heat. Some cooks place the serving bowl over the pasta pot, but this is tricky, as the pot can boil over.
- Heat the serving dishes.
- Immediately toss the pasta and sauce together. The longer the pasta stands without the sauce, the more likely that it will stick together.
- Many pastas are finished in the skillet in which the sauce is cooked, so be sure to have a 10- to 12-inch skillet for this purpose. After the pasta is drained, it is added to the skillet where the sauce is ready and waiting. The two are then tossed together for a minute or so, so that the pasta can absorb the flavor of the sauce. A little of the pasta water can help to liquify dry sauces.
- Many Italian cooks like to drizzle a finished pasta made with an oil-based sauce with a stream of extra-virgin olive oil just before serving. It adds smoothness and good flavor.

❧ Dried Pasta with Vegetables

Linguine with Garlic, Oil, and Hot Pepper
Linguine Aglio, Olio, e Peperoncino

MAKES 4 TO 6 SERVINGS

Garlic, fruity extra-virgin olive oil, parsley, and hot pepper are the simple seasonings for this tastiest of pastas. A full-flavored olive oil is essential, as is fresh garlic and parsley. Cook the garlic slowly so that the oil becomes saturated with its potent flavor. Don't let the garlic turn more than a golden color, or it will become bitter and acrid tasting. Some cooks leave out the parsley, but I love the fresh flavor it adds.

¹/₂ cup extra-virgin olive oil
4 to 6 large garlic cloves, thinly sliced
¹/₂ teaspoon crushed red pepper
¹/₃ cup chopped fresh flat-leaf parsley
Salt
I pound linguine or spaghetti

I Pour the oil into a skillet large enough to hold the cooked pasta. Add the garlic and crushed red pepper. Cook over medium heat, stirring often, until the garlic is a deep gold, about 4 to 5 minutes. Stir in the parsley and turn off the heat.

2 Bring at least 4 quarts of cold water to a boil. Add 2 tablespoons of salt, then the pasta, pushing it down until the pasta is completely covered with water. Cook over high heat, stirring frequently, until the pasta is al dente, tender yet still firm to the bite. Set aside some of the cooking water. Drain the pasta and add it to the skillet with the sauce.

3 Cook over medium heat, tossing until the pasta is well coated with the sauce. Add a little of the reserved cooking water if the pasta seems dry. Serve immediately.

Variations: Add chopped black or green olives, capers, or anchovies along with the garlic. Serve sprinkled with bread crumbs toasted in olive oil or grated cheese.

Spaghetti with Garlic and Olives
Spaghetti al Aglio e Olive

MAKES 4 TO 6 SERVINGS

This quick pasta sauce can be made with olives that you pit and chop yourself, but prepared olive paste is more convenient. Because the olive paste and olives can be salty, do not add grated cheese to this dish.

¹/₄ cup olive oil
3 garlic cloves, sliced thin
Pinch of crushed red pepper
¹/₄ cup green olive paste, or to taste, or I cup chopped pitted green olives
2 tablespoons chopped fresh flat-leaf parsley
Salt
I pound spaghetti or linguine

I Pour the oil into a skillet large enough to hold the cooked pasta. Add the garlic and crushed red pepper. Cook over medium heat until the garlic is a deep gold, about 4 to 5 minutes. Stir in the olive paste or the olives and parsley and remove the skillet from the heat.

2 Bring 4 quarts of water to boiling in a large pot. Add 2 tablespoons of salt, then the pasta, gently pushing it down until the pasta is completely covered with water. Cook over high heat, stirring frequently, until the pasta is al dente, tender yet still firm to the bite. Set aside some of the cooking water. Drain the pasta and add it to the skillet with the sauce.

3 Cook over medium heat, tossing until the pasta is well coated with the sauce. Add a little of the hot cooking water if the pasta seems dry. Serve immediately.

Linguine with Pesto
Linguine al Pesto

MAKES 4 TO 6 SERVINGS

In Liguria, pesto is made by pounding the garlic and herbs in a mortar until a thick paste forms. A variety of basil with a mild flavor and tiny leaves no more than half an inch long is used there. The pesto that it makes is much more subtle than that made with the basil we have in the United States. To approximate the flavor of Ligurian pesto, I add some flat-leaf parsley. Parsley keeps its color better than basil, which tends to blacken when chopped, so the pesto remains a velvety green. If you are traveling in Liguria and like to garden, buy a package of tiny basil seeds and cultivate them in your home garden. There is no prohibition on bringing home packaged seeds from Italy.

1 cup tightly packed basil leaves, rinsed and dried
1/4 cup tightly packed fresh flat-leaf parsley, rinsed and dried
2 tablespoons pine nuts or blanched almonds
1 garlic clove
Coarse salt
1/3 cup extra-virgin olive oil
1 pound linguine
1/2 cup freshly grated Parmigiano-Reggiano
2 tablespoons unsalted butter, softened

1 In a food processor, chop the basil and parsley leaves with the pine nuts, garlic, and a pinch of salt until very fine. Gradually add the olive oil in a thin stream and blend until smooth. Taste for seasoning.

2 Bring 4 quarts of water to a boil in a large pot. Add 2 tablespoons of salt, then the pasta, gently pushing it down until the pasta is completely covered with water. Stir well. Cook, stirring frequently, until the pasta is al dente, tender yet still firm to the bite. Set aside some of the cooking water. Drain the pasta.

3 Place the pasta in a large heated serving bowl. Add the pesto, the cheese, and the butter. Toss well, adding a little of the reserved pasta water to thin the pesto if needed. Serve immediately.

Thin Spaghetti with Walnuts
Spaghettini con le Noci

MAKES 4 TO 6 SERVINGS

This is a Neapolitan recipe that is often eaten at meatless Friday meals. The walnuts should be very finely chopped for this pasta sauce, so that the pieces will cling to the pasta as it is twirled. Chop them with a knife, or use a food processor if you prefer, but don't overprocess into a paste.

1/4 cup olive oil
3 large garlic cloves, lightly crushed
1 cup walnuts, finely chopped
Salt
1 pound spaghettini, fine linguine, or vermicelli
1/2 cup freshly grated Pecorino Romano
Freshly ground black pepper
2 tablespoons chopped fresh flat-leaf parsley

1 Pour the oil into a skillet large enough to hold the pasta. Add the garlic and cook over medium heat pressing the garlic occasionally with the back of a spoon until it turns deep gold, about 3 to 4 minutes. Remove the garlic from the pan. Stir in the walnuts and cook until lightly toasted, about 5 minutes.

2 Bring at least 4 quarts of water to a boil in a large pot. Add 2 tablespoons of salt, then the pasta. Stir well. Cook over high heat, stirring frequently, until the pasta is al dente, tender yet still firm to the bite. Drain the pasta, reserving some of the cooking water.

3 Toss the pasta with the nut sauce and just enough of the cooking water to keep it moist. Add the cheese and a generous grinding of black pepper. Toss well. Add the parsley and serve immediately.

Linguine with Sun-Dried Tomatoes

Linguine con Pomodori Secchi

MAKES 4 TO 6 SERVINGS

A jar of marinated sun-dried tomatoes in the pantry and unexpected guests inspired this quick pasta dish. The oil most marinated sun-dried tomatoes are packed in is generally not of the highest quality, so I prefer to drain it off and add my own extra-virgin olive oil to this easy sauce.

1 jar (about 6 ounces) marinated sun-dried tomatoes, drained

1 small garlic clove

1/4 cup extra-virgin olive oil

1 tablespoon balsamic vinegar

Salt

1 pound linguine

6 fresh basil leaves, stacked and cut into thin ribbons

1 In a food processor or blender, combine the tomatoes and garlic and process until chopped very fine. Slowly add the oil and vinegar and blend until smooth. Taste for seasoning.

2 Bring at least 4 quarts of water to a boil in a large pot. Add 2 tablespoons of salt, then the pasta, gently pushing it down until the pasta is completely covered with water. Stir well. Cook over high heat, stirring frequently, until the pasta is al dente, tender yet still firm to the bite. Set aside some of the cooking water. Drain the pasta.

3 In a large bowl, toss the pasta with the tomato sauce and fresh basil, adding a little of the reserved pasta water if needed. Serve immediately.

Variations: Add a can of drained olive oil–packed tuna to the pasta and sauce. Or add some chopped black olives or anchovies.

Spaghetti with Peppers, Pecorino, and Basil

Spaghetti con Peperoni

MAKES 4 TO 6 SERVINGS

Eating spaghetti, linguine, or other long pasta with a spoon and fork is not considered good manners in Italy, nor is cutting the strands into short pieces. Children are taught from a very young age to twirl a few strands of pasta around a fork and eat it neatly without slurping.

According to one story, the three-tined fork was invented for this purpose in the mid-nineteenth century. Up until that time, pasta was always eaten with the hands, and forks had only two tines because they were used primarily for spearing meat. King Ferdinand II of Naples asked his chamberlain, Cesare Spadaccini, to invent a way to serve long pasta at court banquets. Spadaccini came up with a fork with three tines, and the rest is history.

Fresh hot chiles are typical of Calabrian cooking. Here they are paired with bell peppers and served with spaghetti. The grated pecorino is a nice, salty counterpoint to the sweetness of the bell peppers and basil.

1/4 cup olive oil

4 large red bell peppers, cut into thin strips

1 or 2 small fresh chiles, seeded and chopped, or a pinch of crushed red pepper

Salt

2 garlic cloves, thinly sliced

12 fresh basil leaves, cut into thin ribbons

1/3 cup freshly grated Pecorino Romano

1 pound spaghetti

1 In a skillet large enough to hold the cooked pasta, heat the oil over medium heat. Add the peppers, chiles, and salt. Cook, stirring occasionally, 10 minutes.

2 Stir in the garlic. Cover and cook 10 minutes more or until the peppers are very tender. Remove from the heat and stir in the basil.

(continues)

3 Bring at least 4 quarts of water to a boil in a large pot. Add 2 tablespoons of salt, then the pasta, gently pushing it down until the pasta is completely covered with water. Stir well. Cook, stirring often, until the spaghetti is al dente, tender yet still firm to the bite. Set aside some of the cooking water. Drain the pasta and add it to the skillet with the sauce.

4 Cook over medium heat, stirring constantly, for 1 minute. Toss well, adding a little of the reserved pasta water. Add the cheese and toss again. Serve immediately.

Penne with Zucchini, Basil, and Eggs
Penne con Zucchine e Uova

MAKES 4 TO 6 SERVINGS

The myth that pasta was "invented" in China and brought to Italy by Marco Polo is a persistent one. While noodles may have been eaten in China when Polo visited, pasta was well known in Italy long before his return to Venice in 1279. Archeologists have found drawings and cooking implements that resemble modern-day pasta-making tools, such as a rolling pin and cutting wheel, in a fourth-century BC Etruscan tomb just north of Rome. The legend can probably be attributed to Hollywood's depiction of the Venetian explorer in a 1930s movie starring Gary Cooper.

In this Neapolitan recipe, the heat of the pasta and vegetables cooks the eggs until they are just creamy and lightly set.

4 medium zucchini (about 1 1/4 pounds), scrubbed
1/3 cup olive oil
1 small onion, finely chopped
Salt and freshly ground black pepper
3 large eggs
**1/2 cup freshly grated Pecorino Romano
     or Parmigiano-Reggiano**
1 pound penne
1/2 cup torn fresh basil or parsley

1 Cut the zucchini into 1/4-inch-thick sticks about 1 1/2 inches in length. Pat the pieces dry.

2 Pour the oil into a skillet large enough to hold the cooked pasta. Add the onion and cook over medium heat, stirring occasionally, until softened, about 5 minutes. Add the zucchini and cook, stirring frequently, until lightly browned, about 10 minutes. Season to taste with salt and pepper.

3 In a medium bowl, beat the eggs with the cheese and salt and pepper to taste.

4 While the zucchini cook, bring about 4 quarts of water to a boil in a large pot. Add 2 tablespoons of salt and the pasta. Stir well. Cook over high heat, stirring frequently, until the pasta is al dente, tender yet still firm to the bite. Set aside some of the cooking water. Drain the pasta and add it to the skillet with the sauce.

5 Toss the pasta with the egg mixture. Add the basil and toss well. Stir in a little of the cooking water if the pasta seems dry. Add a generous grinding of pepper and serve immediately.

Pasta with Peas and Eggs
Pasta con Piselli

MAKES 4 SERVINGS

My mother used to make this old-fashioned dish often when I was a child. She used canned peas, but I like to use frozen ones because they taste fresher and have a firmer texture. It may seem contrary to tradition to break the spaghetti into small pieces, but that is a clue to this recipe's origins. When people were poor and there were many mouths to feed, the ingredients could easily be stretched by adding extra water and making it into a soup.

This is one of those standby dishes I can put together at any time, since I am rarely without a package of peas in the freezer, pasta in the pantry, and a couple of eggs in the refrigerator. Because the peas, eggs, and pasta are rather filling, I generally make this amount for 4 servings. Add a full pound of pasta if you want 6 to 8 servings.

¹/4 cup olive oil
I large onion, thinly sliced
I (10-ounce) package frozen tiny peas, partially thawed
Salt and freshly ground black pepper
2 large eggs
¹/2 cup freshly grated Parmigiano-Reggiano
¹/2 pound spaghetti or linguine, broken into 2-inch lengths

I Pour the oil into a skillet large enough to hold the pasta. Add the onion and cook over medium heat, stirring occasionally, until the onion is tender and lightly browned, about 12 minutes. Stir in the peas and cook for about 5 minutes more, until the peas are tender. Season with salt and pepper.

2 In a medium bowl, beat the eggs with the cheese and salt and pepper to taste.

3 Bring at least 4 quarts of water to a boil in a large pot. Add 2 tablespoons of salt, then the pasta. Stir well. Cook over high heat, stirring frequently, until the pasta is tender but slightly underdone. Drain the pasta, reserving some of the cooking water.

4 Stir the pasta into the skillet with the peas. Add the egg mixture and cook over low heat, stirring constantly, about 2 minutes, until the eggs are lightly set. Add a little of the cooking water if the pasta seems dry. Serve immediately.

Linguine with Green Beans, Tomatoes, and Basil
Lingiune con Fagiolini

MAKES 4 TO 6 SERVINGS

Ricotta salata is a salted and pressed form of ricotta. If you can't find it, substitute a mild, unsalty feta cheese or fresh ricotta and grated pecorino. This pasta is typical of Puglia.

12 ounces green beans, trimmed
Salt
¹/4 cup olive oil
I garlic clove, finely chopped
5 medium tomatoes, peeled, seeded, and chopped (about 3 cups)
Freshly ground black pepper
I pound linguine
¹/2 cup chopped fresh basil
I cup grated ricotta salata, mild feta, or fresh ricotta

I Bring about 4 quarts of water to a boil. Add the green beans and salt to taste. Cook 5 minutes or until crisp-tender. Scoop out the green beans with a slotted spoon or strainer, reserving the water. Pat the beans dry. Cut the beans into 1-inch lengths.

2 Pour the oil into a skillet large enough to hold the cooked pasta. Add the garlic and cook over medium-low heat until lightly golden, about 2 minutes.

3 Add the tomatoes and salt and pepper to taste. Cook, stirring occasionally, until the tomatoes thicken and the juices evaporate. Stir in the beans. Simmer 5 minutes more.

4 Meanwhile, bring the pot of water back to a boil. Add 2 tablespoons of salt, then the linguine, gently pushing it down until the pasta is completely covered with water. Cook over high heat, stirring frequently, until the pasta is al dente, tender yet still firm to the bite. Set aside some of the cooking water. Drain the pasta and add it to the skillet with the sauce.

5 Toss the linguine with the sauce in the skillet. Add the basil and cheese and toss again over medium heat until the cheese is creamy. Serve immediately.

Little Ears with Potato Cream and Arugula

Orecchiette con Crema di Patate

MAKES 4 TO 6 SERVINGS

Wild arugula grows all over Puglia. It is crisp, with a narrow, saw-toothed leaf and an appealing nutty flavor. The leaves are eaten both raw and cooked, often with pastas. Potatoes are starchy, but they are viewed as just another vegetable in Italy, so there are no qualms about serving them with pasta, especially in Puglia. The potatoes are cooked until tender, then mashed with the cooking water until creamy.

2 medium boiling potatoes, about 12 ounces

Salt

1/4 cup olive oil

1 garlic clove, finely chopped

1 pound orecchiette or shells

2 bunches arugula (about 8 ounces), tough stems removed, rinsed and drained

Salt and freshly ground black pepper

1 Peel the potatoes and place them in a small pot with salt to taste and cold water to cover. Bring the water to a simmer and cook the potatoes until tender when pierced with a sharp knife, about 20 minutes. Drain the potatoes, reserving the water.

2 Pour the oil into a medium saucepan. Add the garlic and cook over medium heat until the garlic is golden, about 2 minutes. Remove from the heat. Add the potatoes and mash well with a masher or fork, stirring in about a cup of the reserved water to make a thin "cream." Season with salt and pepper.

3 Bring 4 quarts of water to a boil. Add 2 tablespoons of salt, then the pasta. Stir well. Cook over high heat, stirring frequently, until the pasta is al dente, tender yet firm to the bite. Add the arugula and stir once. Drain the pasta and arugula.

4 Return the pasta and arugula to the pot and add the potato sauce. Cook and stir over low heat, adding a little more of the potato water if needed. Serve immediately.

Pasta and Potatoes

Pasta e Patate

MAKES 6 SERVINGS

Like pasta with beans or lentils, pasta and potatoes is a fine example of la cucina povera, *the southern Italian way of taking a few humble ingredients and turning them into delicious fare. When times were really lean and there were a lot of mouths to feed, the custom was to add extra water, usually the liquid left from cooking vegetables or boiling pasta, stretching these dishes from a pasta to a soup to make them go further.*

1/4 cup olive oil

1 medium carrot, chopped

1 medium celery rib, chopped

1 medium onion, chopped

2 garlic cloves, finely chopped

2 tablespoons chopped fresh flat-leaf parsley

3 tablespoons tomato paste

Salt and freshly ground black pepper

1 1/2 pounds boiling potatoes, peeled and chopped

1 pound tubetti or small shells

1/2 cup freshly grated Pecorino Romano or Parmigiano-Reggiano

1 Pour the oil into a large saucepan and add the chopped ingredients except the potatoes. Cook over medium heat, stirring occasionally, until tender and golden, about 15 to 20 minutes.

2 Stir in the tomato paste and salt and pepper to taste. Add the potatoes and 4 cups of water. Bring to a simmer and cook until the potatoes are very tender, about 30 minutes. Crush some of the potatoes with the back of a spoon.

3 Bring about 4 quarts of water to a boil in a large pot. Add 2 tablespoons of the salt, then the pasta. Stir well. Cook, stirring often, until the pasta is al dente, tender yet still firm to the bite. Set aside some of the cooking water. Stir the pasta into the potato mixture. Add some of the reserved cooking water if necessary, but the mixture should remain quite thick. Stir in the cheese and serve immediately.

Shells with Cauliflower and Cheese
Conchiglie al Cavolfiore

MAKES 6 SERVING

Versatile cauliflower is the star of many pasta dishes in southern Italy. In Sicily, we had this simple dish made with the local purple-tinged cauliflower.

¹/₂ cup olive oil
1 medium onion, finely chopped
1 medium cauliflower, trimmed and cut into bite-size florets
Salt
2 tablespoons chopped fresh flat-leaf parsley
Freshly ground black pepper
1 pound shells
³/₄ cup freshly grated Pecorino Romano

1 Pour the oil into a skillet large enough to hold the cooked pasta. Add the onion and cook over medium heat 5 minutes. Add the cauliflower and salt to taste. Cover and cook 15 minutes or until the cauliflower is tender. Stir in the parsley and black pepper to taste.

2 Bring at least 4 quarts of water to a boil in a large pot. Add 2 tablespoons of salt, then the pasta. Stir well. Cook over high heat, stirring frequently, until the pasta is al dente, tender but still firm to the bite. Drain the pasta, reserving some of the cooking water.

3 Add the pasta to the skillet with the cauliflower and stir well over medium heat. Add some of the cooking water if needed. Add the cheese and toss again with a generous grinding of black pepper. Serve immediately.

Pasta with Cauliflower, Saffron, and Currants
Pasta Arriminati

MAKES 6 SERVINGS

Sicilian cauliflower varieties range from purple-white to pea green and have a marvelous flavor in the autumn and winter when they are freshly harvested. This is one of several Sicilian pasta and cauliflower combinations. The saffron adds a golden yellow color and subtle flavor while the currants and anchovies add sweetness and saltiness. Toasted bread crumbs provide a gentle crunch as a finishing touch.

1 teaspoon saffron threads
²/₃ cup currants or dark raisins
Salt
1 large cauliflower (about 2 pounds), trimmed and cut into florets
¹/₃ cup olive oil
1 medium onion, finely chopped
6 anchovy fillets, drained and chopped
Freshly ground black pepper
¹/₃ cup pine nuts, lightly toasted
1 pound penne or shells
¹/₄ cup toasted plain bread crumbs

1 In a small bowl, sprinkle the saffron threads with 2 tablespoons of hot water. Place the currants in another bowl with hot water to cover. Let both stand about 10 minutes.

2 Bring at least 4 quarts of water to a boil in a large pot. Add 2 tablespoons of salt and the cauliflower. Cook, stirring frequently, until the cauliflower is very tender when pierced with a knife, about 10 minutes. Remove the cauliflower with a slotted spoon, reserving the water to cook the pasta.

3 Pour the oil into a skillet large enough to hold the cooked pasta. Add the onion and cook over medium heat 10 minutes. Add the anchovies and cook 2 minutes more, stirring frequently until they dissolve. Stir in the saffron and soaking liquid. Drain the currants and add them to the skillet.

(continues)

4 Stir in the cooked cauliflower. Scoop up some of the cooking water and add it to the skillet with the cauliflower. Cook 10 minutes, breaking up the cauliflower with the back of a spoon, until it is in small pieces. Add salt and pepper to taste. Stir in the pine nuts.

5 While the cauliflower cooks, bring the cooking water back to a boil. Add the pasta and stir well. Cook over high heat, stirring frequently, until the pasta is al dente, tender yet still firm to the bite. Set aside some of the cooking water. Drain the pasta, then add it to the skillet with the cauliflower mixture. Stir well, adding some of the cooking water if the pasta seems dry.

6 Serve the pasta sprinkled with the toasted bread crumbs.

Bow Ties with Artichokes and Peas
Farfalle con Carciofi

MAKES 4 TO 6 SERVINGS

Though many Italian resorts close for the winter months, most reopen for Easter. Such was the case in Portofino one year when I was there, though the weather was rainy and chilly. At last the sky cleared and the sun came out, and my husband and I were able to enjoy lunch on the terrace of our hotel overlooking the sea.

We began with this pasta, followed by a whole fish, roasted with olives. Dessert was a lemon tart. It was a perfect Easter dinner.

If baby artichokes are not available, substitute larger artichokes, cut into wedges.

1 pound baby artichokes
2 tablespoons olive oil
1 small onion, finely chopped
1 garlic clove, finely chopped
Salt and freshly ground black pepper
2 cups fresh peas or 1 (10-ounce) package frozen
1/2 cup chopped fresh basil or flat-leaf parsley
1 pound farfalle
1/2 cup freshly grated Parmigiano-Reggiano

1 With a large knife, trim off the top 1 inch of the artichokes. Rinse them well under cold water. Bend back and snap off the small leaves around the base. With scissors, trim the pointed tops off the remaining leaves. Peel off the tough outer skin of the stems and around the base. Cut the artichokes in half. Use a small knife with a rounded tip to scrape out the fuzzy leaves in the center. Thinly slice the artichokes.

2 Pour the olive oil into a skillet large enough to hold the cooked pasta. Add the onion and garlic and cook, stirring occasionally, over medium heat 10 minutes. Add the artichokes and 2 tablespoons water. Add salt and pepper to taste. Cook 10 minutes or until the artichokes are tender.

3 Stir in the peas. Cook 5 minutes or until the peas are tender. Remove from the heat and stir in the basil.

4 Bring at least 4 quarts of water to a boil. Add 2 tablespoons of salt, then the pasta. Stir well. Cook, stirring often, until the pasta is al dente, tender yet still firm to the bite. Set aside some of the cooking water. Drain the pasta.

5 Toss the pasta with the artichoke sauce and a little of the cooking water if needed. Add a drizzle of extra-virgin olive oil and toss again. Toss with the cheese and serve immediately.

Fettuccine with Artichokes and Porcini
Fettuccine con Carciofi e Porcini

MAKES 4 TO 6 SERVINGS

Artichokes and porcini may sound like an unusual combination, but not in Liguria, where I ate this pasta. Beacause this dish is so flavorful, grated cheese is not necessary, especially if you finish it with some good extra-virgin olive oil.

I ounce dried porcini mushrooms

I cup warm water

I pound artichokes

1/4 cup olive oil

I small onion, chopped

I garlic clove, very finely chopped

2 tablespoons chopped fresh flat-leaf parsley

I cup peeled, seeded, and chopped fresh tomatoes
    or drained and chopped canned imported Italian
    tomatoes

Salt and freshly ground black pepper

I pound dried fettuccine

Extra-virgin olive oil

1 Put the mushrooms in the water and let soak 30 minutes. Lift the mushrooms from the water, reserving the liquid. Rinse the mushrooms under cold running water to remove any grit, paying special attention to the ends of the stems where soil collects. Chop the mushrooms coarsely. Strain the mushroom liquid into a bowl. Set aside.

2 With a large knife, trim off the top 1 inch of the artichokes. Rinse them well under cold water. Bend back and snap off the small leaves around the base. With scissors, trim the pointed tops off the remaining leaves. Peel off the tough outer skin of the stems and around the base. Cut the artichokes in half. Use a small knife to scrape out the fuzzy leaves in the center. Thinly slice the artichokes.

3 Pour the oil into a skillet large enough to hold the cooked pasta. Add the onion, mushrooms, parsley, and garlic and cook over medium heat for 10 minutes. Stir in the artichokes, tomatoes, and salt and pepper to taste. Cook 10 minutes. Add the mushroom liquid and cook 10 minutes more or until the artichokes are tender when tested with a knife.

4 Bring 4 quarts of water to a boil in a large pot. Add 2 tablespoons of salt, then the pasta. Stir well. Cook over high heat, stirring frequently, until the pasta is al dente, tender yet still firm to the bite. Set aside some of the cooking water. Drain the pasta.

5 Toss the pasta with the sauce and a little of the cooking water if needed. Drizzle with extra-virgin olive oil and serve immediately.

Rigatoni with Eggplant Ragù

Rigatoni with Ragù di Melanzane

MAKES 4 TO 6 SERVINGS

Meat is usually added to tomato sauce to make a ragù, but this vegetarian version from Basilicata uses eggplant because it is similarly rich and flavorful.

Riga in the name of a pasta shape, such as rigatoni *or* penne rigate, *indicates that it has ridges that act as grippers for the sauce. Rigatoni are large, grooved pasta tubes. Their thickness and large shape complement hearty ragùs with chunky ingredients.*

1/4 cup olive oil

1/4 cup chopped shallots

4 cups chopped eggplant

1/2 cup chopped red bell pepper

1/2 cup dry white wine

1 1/2 pounds plum tomatoes, peeled, seeded, and chopped,
    or 2 cups canned imported Italian tomatoes with
    their juice

A sprig of fresh thyme

Salt

Freshly ground black pepper

I pound rigatoni, penne, or farfalle

Extra-virgin olive oil, for drizzling

1 Pour the oil into a large, heavy skillet. Add the shallots and cook 1 minute over medium heat. Add the eggplant and red pepper. Cook, stirring frequently, until the vegetables are wilted, about 10 minutes.

2 Add the wine and cook 1 minute until evaporated.

3 Add the tomatoes, thyme, salt, and pepper to taste. Reduce the heat to low. Cook, stirring occasionally, 40 minutes or until the sauce is thick and the vegetables are very tender. If the mixture becomes too dry, stir in some water. Remove the thyme.

4 Bring at least 4 quarts of water to a boil in a large pot. Add 2 tablespoons of salt, then the pasta. Stir well. Cook over high heat, stirring frequently, until the pasta is al dente, tender yet still firm to the

(continues)

bite. Set aside some of the cooking water. Drain the pasta and transfer it to a warm serving bowl.

5 Spoon on the sauce and toss well, adding a little of the cooking water if needed. Drizzle with some extra-virgin olive oil, and toss again. Serve immediately.

Sicilian Spaghetti with Eggplant
Spaghetti alla Norma

MAKES 4 TO 6 SERVINGS

Norma is the name of a beautiful opera composed by the Sicilian Vincenzo Bellini. This pasta, made with eggplant—a beloved vegetable in Sicily—was named in honor of the opera.

Ricotta salata is a pressed form of ricotta that is good sliced as an eating cheese or grated over pasta. There is also a smoked version that is particularly delicious, though I have never seen it outside of Sicily. If you cannot find ricotta salata, substitute feta, which is very similar, or use Pecorino Romano.

I medium eggplant, trimmed and cut into 1/4-inch thick slices

Salt

Olive oil for frying

2 garlic cloves, lightly crushed

Pinch of crushed red pepper

3 pounds ripe plum tomatoes, peeled, seeded, and chopped, or 1 (28-ounce) can imported Italian peeled tomatoes, drained and chopped

6 fresh basil leaves

I pound spaghetti

I cup grated ricotta salata or Pecorino Romano

I Layer the eggplant slices in a colander set over a plate, sprinkling each layer with salt. Let stand 30 to 60 minutes. Rinse the eggplant and pat very dry with paper towels.

2 Pour about 1/2 inch of oil into a deep, heavy skillet. Heat the oil over medium heat until a small piece of the eggplant sizzles when placed in the pan. Fry the eggplant slices a few at a time until golden brown on both sides. Drain on paper towels.

3 Pour 3 tablespoons of the oil into a medium saucepan. Add the garlic and crushed red pepper and cook over medium heat until the garlic is deep golden, about 4 minutes. Remove the garlic. Add the tomatoes and salt to taste. Reduce the heat to low and simmer 20 to 30 minutes or until the sauce is thickened. Stir in the basil and turn off the heat.

4 Bring at least 4 quarts of water to a boil in a large pot. Add 2 tablespoons of salt, then the pasta. Stir well. Cook over high heat, stirring frequently, until the pasta is al dente, tender but still firm to the bite. Set aside some of the cooking water. Drain the pasta.

5 Toss the pasta with the sauce in a warm serving bowl, adding a little of the cooking water if needed. Add the cheese and toss again. Top with the eggplant slices and serve immediately.

Bow Ties with Broccoli, Tomatoes, Pine Nuts, and Raisins
Farfalle alla Siciliana

MAKES 4 TO 6 SERVINGS

Pine nuts add a pleasant crunch and raisins bring sweetness to this delicious Sicilian pasta. The broccoli is cooked in the same pot as the pasta, so their flavors really come together. If you find yourself with large round tomatoes instead of the plum variety, you can substitute them, though the sauce will be thinner and may need slightly longer cooking.

1/3 cup olive oil

2 garlic cloves, finely chopped

Pinch of crushed red pepper

2 1/2 pounds fresh plum tomatoes (about 15), peeled, seeded, and chopped

Salt and freshly ground black pepper

2 tablespoons raisins

1 pound farfalle

1 medium bunch of broccoli, stems removed and cut into small florets

2 tablespoons toasted pine nuts

1 Pour the oil into a skillet large enough to hold the pasta. Add the garlic and crushed red pepper. Cook over medium heat until the garlic is golden, about 2 minutes. Add the tomatoes and salt and pepper to taste. Bring to a simmer and cook until the sauce is thickened, 15 to 20 minutes. Stir in the raisins and remove from the heat.

2 Bring at least 4 quarts of water to a boil in a large pot. Add 2 tablespoons of salt, then the pasta. Stir well. Cook, stirring frequently, until the water returns to the boil.

3 Add the broccoli to the pasta. Cook, stirring frequently, until the pasta is al dente, tender yet still firm to the bite. Set aside some of the cooking water.

4 Drain the pasta and broccoli. Add them to the pan with the tomatoes, adding a little of the cooking water if needed. Toss well. Sprinkle with pine nuts and serve immediately.

Cavatelli with Garlicky Greens and Potatoes
Cavatelli con Verdure e Patate

MAKES 4 TO 6 SERVINGS

Washing greens may not be my favorite task, but finding grit in my food is even worse, so I wash them at least three times. It is worth the trouble. You can use only one variety in this recipe, but a mix of two or three different greens adds an interesting texture and flavor to the dish.

The potatoes in this recipe should be cut into small pieces so that they cook along with the pasta. In the end, they are somewhat overcooked and crumbly and add a creamy smoothness to the pasta.

1 1/2 pounds assorted greens, such as broccoli rabe, mizuna, mustard, kale, or dandelions, trimmed

Salt

1/3 cup olive oil

4 garlic cloves, thinly sliced

Pinch of crushed red pepper

Salt and freshly ground black pepper

1 pound cavatelli

1 pound boiling potatoes, peeled and chopped into 1/2-inch pieces

1 Fill a sink or large bowl with cool water. Add the greens and swirl them in the water. Transfer the greens to a colander, change the water, then repeat at least two more times to eliminate all traces of sand.

2 Bring a large pot of water to a boil. Add the greens and salt to taste. Cook until the greens are tender, 5 to 10 minutes, depending on the varieties you use. Drain the greens and let them cool slightly under cold running water. Chop the greens into bite-size pieces.

3 Pour the oil into a skillet large enough to hold the cooked pasta. Add the garlic and crushed red pepper. Cook over medium heat until the garlic is golden, 2 minutes. Add the greens and a pinch of salt. Cook, stirring, until the vegetables are coated with oil, about 5 minutes.

4 Bring at least 4 quarts of water to a boil in a large pot. Add 2 tablespoons of salt, then the pasta. Cook, stirring frequently, until the water returns to a boil. Add the potatoes and cook until the pasta is al dente, tender yet firm to the bite. Set aside some of the cooking water. Drain the pasta.

5 Add the pasta and potatoes to the greens and toss well. Add a little of the reserved cooking water if the pasta seems dry. Serve immediately.

Linguine with Zucchini
Linguine con Zucchine

MAKES 4 TO 6 SERVINGS

Resist the urge to buy any but small to medium zucchini, and say no thanks to gardener friends who desperately offer dachshund-size squashes. Giant zucchini are watery, seedy, and tasteless, but those the length of a hot dog, and no thicker than a knockwurst, are tender and delicious.

I particularly like Pecorino Romano—a sharp and tangy sheep's milk cheese from southern Italy—in this recipe.

6 small green or yellow zucchini (about 2 pounds)
1/3 cup olive oil
3 garlic cloves, finely chopped
Salt and freshly ground black pepper
1/4 cup chopped fresh basil
2 tablespoons chopped fresh flat-leaf parsley
1 tablespoon chopped fresh thyme
1 pound linguine
1/2 cup freshly grated Pecorino Romano

1 Scrub the zucchini under cold water. Trim the ends. Cut into quarters lengthwise, then into slices.

2 In a skillet large enough to hold the pasta, heat the oil over medium heat. Add the zucchini and cook, stirring occasionally, until lightly browned and tender, about 10 minutes. Push the zucchini to the side of the pan and add the garlic, salt, and pepper. Cook for 2 minutes. Add the herbs, stir the zucchini back into the seasonings, and then remove from the heat.

3 While the zucchini is cooking, bring 4 quarts of water to a boil in a large pot. Add 2 tablespoons of salt, then the pasta. Stir well. Cook over high heat, stirring frequently, until the pasta is al dente, tender yet firm to the bite. Set aside some of the cooking water.

4 Drain the pasta. Place the pasta in the skillet with the zucchini. Toss well, adding some of the cooking water if needed. Add the cheese and toss again. Serve immediately.

Penne with Grilled Vegetables
Pasta con Verdure alla Griglia

MAKES 4 TO 6 SERVINGS

Though I normally leave the skin on eggplants, grilling tends to make the skin tough, so I peel it off before firing up the grill. Also, if your eggplants are not fresh off the farm, you may want to salt them before cooking to reduce any bitterness, which increases as the vegetable matures. To do this, peel and slice the eggplant, then layer the slices in a colander, sprinkling each layer with coarse salt. Let stand 30 to 60 minutes to eliminate liquid. Rinse the salt off, pat dry, and cook as directed.

2 pounds plum tomatoes (about 12)
Olive oil
1 medium eggplant, peeled and cut into thick slices
2 medium red or white sweet onions, thickly sliced
Salt and freshly ground black pepper
2 garlic cloves, very finely chopped
12 leaves fresh basil, torn into little pieces
1 pound penne
1/2 cup freshly grated Pecorino Romano

1 Place a barbecue grill or broiler rack about 4 inches from the source of the heat. Preheat the grill or broiler. Place the tomatoes on the grill. Cook, turning frequently with tongs, until the tomatoes are softened and the skin is lightly charred and loosened. Remove the tomatoes. Brush the eggplant and onion slices with oil and sprinkle them with salt and pepper. Grill until the vegetables are tender and browned but not blackened, about 5 minutes on each side.

2 Slip off the tomato skins and cut out the stem ends. Place the tomatoes in a large serving bowl and mash them well with a fork. Stir in the garlic, basil, 1/4 cup oil, and salt and pepper to taste.

3 Cut the eggplant and onions into thin strips and add them to the tomatoes.

4 Bring at least 4 quarts of water to a boil in a large pot. Add 2 tablespoons of salt, then the pasta. Stir well. Cook over high heat, stirring frequently, until the pasta is al dente, tender yet firm to the bite. Set aside some of the cooking liquid.

5 Drain the pasta. In a large serving bowl, toss the pasta with the vegetables. Add some of the cooking water if the pasta seems dry. Add the cheese and serve immediately.

Penne with Mushrooms, Garlic, and Rosemary
Penne con Funghi

MAKES 4 TO 6 SERVINGS

You can use any kind of mushroom you like in this recipe, such as oyster, shiitake, cremini, or the standard white variety. A combination is especially good. If you have some truly wild mushrooms, such as morels, be sure to clean them very well, as they can be very gritty.

¹/₄ cup olive oil
I pound mushrooms, thinly sliced
2 large garlic cloves, finely chopped
2 teaspoons very finely chopped fresh rosemary
Salt and freshly ground black pepper
I pound penne or farfalle
2 tablespoons unsalted butter
2 tablespoons chopped fresh parsley

I In a skillet large enough to hold the pasta, heat the oil over medium heat. Add the mushrooms, garlic, and rosemary. Cook, stirring frequently, until the mushrooms begin to release their liquid, about 10 minutes. Add salt and pepper to taste. Cook, stirring often, until the mushrooms are lightly browned, about 5 minutes more.

2 Bring at least 4 quarts of water to a boil in a large pot. Add 2 tablepoons of salt, then the pasta. Stir well. Cook over high heat, stirring frequently, until the pasta is al dente, tender yet firm to the bite. Set aside some of the cooking water.

3 Drain the pasta. Toss the pasta in the skillet with the mushrooms, butter, and parsley. Add a little of the cooking water if the pasta seems dry. Serve immediately.

Linguine with Beets and Garlic
Linguine con Barbabietole

MAKES 4 TO 6 SERVINGS

Pasta and beets may sound like an unusual combination, but ever since I tasted it in a little town on the coast of Emilia-Romagna, it has been a favorite of mine. Not only is it delicious, but it is also one of the prettiest pasta dishes I know. Everyone will be amazed at its stunning color. Make this in the late summer and early fall when fresh red beets are at their sweetest.

8 medium red beets, trimmed
¹/₃ cup olive oil
3 garlic cloves, finely chopped
Pinch of crushed red pepper, or to taste
Salt
I pound linguine

I Place a rack in the center of the oven. Preheat the oven to 450°F. Scrub the beets and wrap them in a large sheet of aluminum foil, sealing tightly. Place the package on a baking sheet. Bake for 45 to 75 minutes, depending on size, or until the beets feel tender when pierced through the foil with a sharp knife. Let the beets cool in the foil. Peel and chop the beets.

2 Pour the oil into a skillet large enough to hold the cooked pasta. Add the garlic and crushed red pepper. Cook over medium heat until the garlic is golden, about 2 minutes. Add the beets and stir them in the oil mixture until just heated through.

3 Bring at least 4 quarts of water to a boil in a large pot. Add 2 tablespoons of salt, then the pasta. Stir well. Cook over high heat, stirring frequently, until the pasta is al dente, tender yet firm to the bite.

(continues)

4 Drain the pasta, reserving some of the cooking water. Pour the linguine into the skillet with the beets. Add some of the cooking water and cook over medium heat, turning the pasta with a fork and spoon until evenly colored, about 2 minutes. Serve immediately.

Bow Ties with Beets and Greens
Farfalle con Barbabietole

MAKES 4 TO 6 SERVINGS

This is a variation of the previous recipe, using both the beets and the beet greens. If the tops on the beets look limp or brown, substitute a pound or so of fresh spinach, swiss chard, or other greens.

1 bunch fresh red beets with tops (4 to 5 beets)
1/3 cup olive oil
2 large garlic cloves, finely chopped
Salt and freshly ground black pepper
1 pound farfalle
4 ounces ricotta salata, shredded

1 Place a rack in the center of the oven. Preheat the oven to 450°F. Trim off the beet greens and set aside. Scrub the beets and wrap them in a large sheet of aluminum foil, sealing tightly. Place the package on a baking sheet. Bake for 45 to 75 minutes, depending on size, or until the beets feel tender when pierced through the foil with a sharp knife. Let the beets cool in the foil. Unwrap the foil, then peel and chop the beets.

2 Wash the greens well and remove the tough stems. Bring a large pot of water to a boil. Add the greens and salt to taste. Cook 5 minutes or until the greens are almost tender. Drain the greens and cool them under running water. Coarsely chop the greens.

3 Pour the oil into a skillet large enough to hold all of the pasta and vegetables. Add the garlic.

Cook over medium heat until the garlic is golden, about 2 minutes. Add the beets and greens and a pinch of salt and pepper. Cook, stirring, about 5 minutes or until the vegetables are heated through.

4 Bring at least 4 quarts of water to a boil in a large pot. Add 2 tablespoons of salt, then the pasta. Stir well. Cook over high heat, stirring frequently, until the pasta is al dente, tender yet firm to the bite.

5 Drain the pasta, reserving some of the cooking water. Add the pasta to the skillet with the beets. Add some of the cooking water and cook, stirring the pasta constantly, until it is evenly colored, about 1 minute. Add the cheese and stir again. Serve immediately with a generous sprinkling of freshly ground black pepper.

Pasta with Salad
Pasta al Insalata

MAKES 4 TO 6 SERVINGS

Pasta tossed with a fresh vegetable salad is a lovely light summer dish. I had this while visiting friends in Piedmont. Don't let it sit too long or the vegetables will lose their bright flavor and appearance.

2 medium tomatoes, chopped
1 medium fennel bulb, trimmed and cut into bite-size pieces
1 small red onion, chopped
1/4 cup extra-virgin olive oil
2 tablespoons basil cut into thin ribbons
Salt and freshly ground black pepper
2 cups trimmed arugula, torn into bite-size pieces
1 pound elbows

1 In a large serving bowl, combine the tomatoes, fennel, onion, olive oil, basil, and salt and pepper to taste. Stir well. Top with arugula.

2 Bring at least 4 quarts of water to a boil in a large pot. Add 2 tablespoons of salt, then the pasta. Cook over high heat, stirring frequently, until the pasta is al dente, tender yet firm to the bite. Set aside some of the cooking water. Drain the pasta.

3 Toss the pasta with the salad mixture. Add a little of the cooking water if the pasta seems dry. Serve immediately.

Fusilli with Roasted Tomatoes
Fusilli con Pomodori al Forno

MAKES 4 TO 6 SERVINGS

Roasted tomatoes are a favorite side dish in my house, something I serve with fish, veal chops, or steak. One day I had prepared a big pan full, but I had nothing to serve them with except some dried pasta. I tossed the roasted tomatoes and their juices with freshly cooked fusilli. Now I make it all the time.

2 pounds ripe plum tomatoes (about 12 to 14), cut into 1/4-inch-thick slices
3 large garlic cloves, finely chopped
1/2 teaspoon dried oregano
Salt and freshly ground black pepper
1/3 cup olive oil
1 pound fusilli
1/2 cup chopped fresh basil or flat-leaf parsley

1 Place a rack in the center of the oven. Preheat the oven to 400°F. Oil a 13 × 9 × 2–inch baking dish or roasting pan.

2 Spread half of the tomato slices in the prepared dish. Sprinkle with the garlic, oregano, and salt and pepper to taste. Top with the remaining tomatoes. Drizzle with the oil.

3 Bake until the tomatoes are very soft, 30 to 40 minutes. Remove the dish from the oven.

4 Bring at least 4 quarts of water to a boil in a large pot. Add 2 tablespoons of salt, then the pasta. Stir well. Cook over high heat, stirring frequently, until the pasta is al dente, tender yet firm to the bite. Drain the pasta, reserving some of the cooking water.

5 Place the pasta on the baked tomatoes and toss well. Add the basil or parsley and toss again, adding some of the reserved cooking water if the pasta seems dry. Serve immediately.

Elbows with Potatoes, Tomatoes, and Arugula
La Bandiera

MAKES 6 TO 8 SERVINGS

In Puglia, this pasta is called "the flag," because it has the red, white, and green of the Italian flag. Some cooks make it with more liquid and serve it as a soup.

1/4 cup olive oil
2 large garlic cloves, finely chopped
Pinch of crushed red pepper
1 1/2 pounds ripe plum tomatoes, peeled, seeded, and chopped (about 3 cups)
2 tablespoons chopped fresh basil
Salt and freshly ground black pepper
1 pound elbows
3 medium boiling potatoes (1 pound), peeled and cut into 1/2-inch pieces
2 bunches arugula, trimmed and cut into 1-inch lengths (about 4 cups)
1/3 cup freshly grated Pecorino Romano

1 Pour the oil into a skillet large enough to hold the pasta. Add the garlic and crushed red pepper. Cook over medium heat until the garlic is golden, 2 minutes.

2 Add the tomatoes, basil, and salt and pepper to taste. Bring to a simmer and cook, stirring occasionally, until the sauce is thickened slightly, about 10 minutes.

3 Bring at least 4 quarts of water to a boil in a large pot. Add 2 tablespoons of salt, then the pasta. Stir well. When the water returns to the boil, stir in the potatoes. Cook, stirring frequently, until the pasta is al dente, tender yet firm to the bite.

(continues)

4 Drain the pasta and potatoes, reserving some of the cooking water. Stir the pasta, potatoes, and arugula into the simmering tomato sauce. Cook, stirring, 1 to 2 minutes or until the pasta and vegetables are well coated with the sauce. Add some of the reserved cooking water if the pasta seems dry.

5 Stir in the cheese and serve immediately.

Roman Country-Style Linguine
Linguine alla Ciociara

MAKES 4 TO 6 SERVINGS

My friends Diane Darrow and Tom Maresca, who write about Italian wine and food, introduced me to this Roman pasta. The name means "peasant-woman's style" in the local dialect. The fresh, grassy flavor of green bell pepper makes this simple pasta unusual.

I medium green bell pepper

¹/2 cup olive oil

2 cups peeled, seeded, and chopped fresh tomatoes or drained and chopped canned imported Italian tomatoes

¹/2 cup coarsely chopped Gaeta or other mild oil-cured black olives

Salt

Pinch of crushed red pepper

I pound linguine or spaghetti

¹/2 cup freshly grated Pecorino Romano

I Cut the pepper in half and remove the stem and seeds. Cut the pepper into very thin lengthwise slices, then cut the slices crosswise into thirds.

2 In a skillet large enough to hold the cooked spaghetti, heat the oil over medium heat. Add the tomatoes, pepper, olives, salt to taste, and crushed red pepper. Bring to a simmer and cook, stirring occasionally, until the sauce is slightly thickened, about 20 minutes.

3 Bring at least 4 quarts of water to a boil in a large pot. Add 2 tablespoons of salt, then the pasta. Stir well. Cook over high heat, stirring frequently, until the pasta is al dente, tender yet still firm to the bite. Drain the pasta, reserving some of the cooking water.

4 Add the pasta to the skillet with the sauce. Cook and toss over medium heat for 1 minute, adding some of the reserved cooking water if the pasta seems dry. Add the cheese and toss again. Serve immediately.

Penne with Spring Vegetables and Garlic
Penne alla Primavera

MAKES 4 TO 6 SERVINGS

Though the classic way to make a primavera sauce is with heavy cream and butter, this method based on olive oil flavored with garlic is good too.

¹/4 cup olive oil

4 garlic cloves, finely chopped

8 asparagus, cut into bite-size lengths

4 green onions, cut into ¹/4-inch slices

3 very small zucchini (about 12 ounces), cut into ¹/4-inch slices

2 medium carrots, cut into ¹/4-inch slices

2 tablespoons water

Salt and freshly ground black pepper

2 cups small cherry or grape tomatoes, halved

3 tablespoons chopped fresh flat-leaf parsley

¹/2 cup freshly grated Pecorino Romano

I Pour the oil into a skillet large enough to hold the pasta. Add the garlic and cook over medium heat for 2 minutes. Stir in the asparagus, green onions, zucchini, carrots, water, and salt and pepper to taste. Cover the pan and lower the heat. Cook until the carrots are almost tender, 5 to 10 minutes.

2 Bring at least 4 quarts of water to a boil in a large pot. Add 2 tablespoons of salt, then the pasta. Stir well. Cook over high heat, stirring frequently, until the pasta is al dente, tender yet still firm to the bite. Drain the pasta, reserving some of the cooking water.

3 Stir the tomatoes and parsley into the skillet with the vegetables and toss well. Add the pasta and cheese and toss again, adding some of the reserved cooking water if the pasta seems dry. Serve immediately.

"Dragged" Pasta with Cream and Mushrooms

Pasta Strascinata

MAKES 4 TO 6 SERVINGS

The main reason to visit Torgiano in Umbria is to stay at Le Tre Vaselle, a beautiful country inn with a fine restaurant. My husband and I ate this unusual "dragged" pasta there some years ago. Short, pointed pasta tubes known as pennette *were cooked right in the sauce, in the style of risotto. I have never seen pasta cooked this way anywhere else.*

Because the technique is quite different, be sure to read through the recipe before beginning and have the broth heated and all of the ingredients at hand before you begin.

The Lungarotti family of winemakers owns Le Tre Vaselle, and one of their excellent red wines, such as Rubesco, would be ideal with this pasta.

1 medium onion, finely chopped

6 tablespoons olive oil

1 pound pennette, ditalini, or tubetti

2 tablespoons Cognac

5 cups hot homemade Meat Broth (page 62)
     or Chicken Broth (page 63) or 2 cups canned
     broth mixed with 3 cups water

8 ounces sliced white mushrooms

Salt and freshly ground black pepper

3/4 cup heavy cream

1 cup fresly grated Parmigiano-Reggiano

1 tablespoon chopped fresh flat-leaf parsley

1 In a skillet large enough to hold all of the pasta, cook the onion in 2 tablespoons of the oil over medium heat until tender and golden, about 10 minutes. Scrape the onion into a dish and wipe out the pan.

2 Pour the remaining 4 tablespoons of the oil into the pan and heat over medium heat. Add the pasta and cook, stirring often, until the pasta begins to brown, about 5 minutes. Add the Cognac and cook until it evaporates.

3 Return the onion to the pan and stir in 2 cups of the hot broth. Turn the heat to medium-high and cook, stirring often, until most of the broth is absorbed. Stir in 2 more cups of the broth. When most of the liquid is absorbed, stir in the mushrooms. As you continue stirring, add the remaining broth a little at a time as needed to keep the pasta moist. Season to taste with salt and pepper.

4 After about 12 minutes from when you began adding the broth, the pasta should be almost al dente, tender yet firm to the bite. Stir in the cream and simmer until slightly thickened, about 1 minute.

5 Remove the pan from the heat and stir in the cheese. Stir in the parsley and serve immediately.

❧ Dried Pasta with Tomatoes

Roman Tomato and Mozzarella Pasta
Pasta alla Checca

MAKES 4 TO 6 SERVINGS

When my husband first tasted this pasta in Rome, he liked it so much he ate it practically every day of our stay. Be sure to use a creamy fresh mozzarella and really ripe tomatoes. It's the perfect summer day pasta.

3 medium size ripe tomatoes
1/4 cup extra-virgin olive oil
I small garlic clove, finely chopped
Salt and freshly ground black pepper
20 basil leaves
I pound tubetti or ditalini
8 ounces fresh mozzarella, cut into small dice

1 Cut the tomatoes in half and remove the cores. Squeeze out the tomato seeds. Chop the tomatoes and place them in a bowl large enough to hold all of the ingredients.

2 Stir in the oil, garlic, and salt and pepper to taste. Stack the basil leaves and cut them into thin ribbons. Stir the basil into the tomatoes. This sauce can be made ahead of time and kept at room temperature up to 2 hours.

3 Bring at least 4 quarts of water to a boil in a large pot. Add 2 tablespoons of salt, then the pasta. Stir well. Cook over high heat, stirring frequently, until the pasta is al dente, tender yet still firm to the bite. Drain the pasta and toss it with the sauce. Add the mozzarella and toss again. Serve immediately.

Fusilli with Tuna and Tomatoes
Fusilli al Tonno

MAKES 4 TO 6 SERVINGS

As much as I enjoy good fresh tuna steaks grilled rare, I think I probably like canned tuna even more. It makes great sandwiches and salads, of course, but Italians have a number of other uses for it, such as in classic Vitello Tonnato (Veal in Tuna Sauce, pages 350–351) for veal, or formed into a pâté, or paired with pasta, as cooks often make in Sicily. Don't use water-packed tuna for this sauce. The flavor is too bland and the texture too soggy. For best flavor and texture, use a good brand of olive oil–packed tuna from Italy or Spain.

3 medium tomatoes, chopped
I (7-ounce) can imported Italian or Spanish tuna packed in olive oil
10 fresh basil leaves, chopped
1/2 teaspoon dried oregano, crumbled
Pinch of crushed red pepper
Salt
I pound fusilli or rotelle

1 In a large serving bowl, combine the tomatoes, tuna with its oil, basil, oregano, red pepper, and salt to taste.

2 Bring at least 4 quarts of water to a boil in a large pot. Add 2 tablespoons of salt, then the pasta. Stir well. Cook over high heat, stirring frequently, until the pasta is al dente, tender yet still firm to the bite. Set aside some of the cooking water. Drain the pasta.

3 Toss the pasta with the sauce. Add a little of the cooking water if the pasta seems dry. Serve immediately.

Linguine with Sicilian Pesto

Linguine al Pesto Trapanese

MAKES 4 TO 6 SERVINGS

Pesto sauce is usually associated with Liguria, but that pertains mostly to the basil and garlic kind. Pesto in Italian refers to anything that is pounded, chopped, or mashed, which is how this sauce is typically made in Trapani, a seaside town in western Sicily.

There is a lot of flavor in this dish; no cheese is needed.

1/2 cup blanched almonds
2 large garlic cloves
1/2 cup packed fresh basil leaves
Salt and freshly ground black pepper
1 pound fresh tomatoes, peeled, seeded, and chopped
1/3 cup extra-virgin olive oil
1 pound linguine

1 In a food processor or blender, combine the almonds, garlic, basil, and salt and pepper to taste. Chop the ingredients fine. Add the tomatoes and oil and process until smooth.

2 Bring at least 4 quarts of water to a boil in a large pot. Add 2 tablespoons of salt, then the pasta, gently pushing it down until the pasta is completely covered with water. Stir well. Cook over high heat, stirring frequently, until the pasta is al dente, tender yet still firm to the bite. Set aside some of the cooking water. Drain the pasta.

3 Pour the pasta into a large warm serving bowl. Add the sauce and toss well. Add a little of the reserved pasta water if the pasta seems dry. Serve immediately.

Spaghetti with "Crazy" Pesto

Spaghetti al Pesto Matto

MAKES 4 TO 6 SERVINGS

This recipe is adapted from a booklet "The Pleasures of Cooking Pasta," published by the Agnesi pasta company in Italy. The recipes were submitted by home cooks, and the author of this recipe probably improvised this untraditional pesto (hence its name).

2 medium ripe tomatoes, peeled, seeded, and chopped
1/2 cup chopped black olives
6 basil leaves, stacked and cut into thin ribbons
1 tablespoon chopped fresh thyme
1/4 cup olive oil
Salt and freshly ground black pepper
1 pound spaghetti or linguine
4 ounces soft fresh goat cheese

1 In a large serving bowl, mix together the tomatoes, olives, basil, thyme, oil, and salt and pepper to taste.

2 Bring at least 4 quarts of water to a boil in a large pot. Add 2 tablespoons of salt, then the pasta, gently pushing it down until the pasta is completely covered with water. Stir well. Cook over high heat, stirring frequently, until the pasta is tender. Drain the pasta.

3 Add the pasta to the bowl with the tomatoes and toss well. Add the goat cheese and toss again. Serve immediately.

Bow Ties with Uncooked Puttanesca Sauce
Farfalle alla Puttanesca

MAKES 4 TO 6 SERVINGS

The ingredients in this pasta sauce are similar to those for Linguine with Anchovies and Spicy Tomato Sauce (page 153), but the flavor is quite different, as this sauce requires no cooking.

1 pint cherry or grape tomatoes, halved
6 to 8 anchovy fillets, chopped
1 large garlic clove, very finely chopped
1/2 cup pitted and chopped Gaeta or other mild black olives
1/4 cup finely chopped fresh flat-leaf parsley
2 tablespoons capers, rinsed and chopped
1/2 teaspoon dried oregano
1/4 cup extra-virgin olive oil
Salt to taste
Pinch of crushed red pepper
1 pound farfalle or dried fettuccine

1 In a large serving bowl, combine the tomatoes, anchovies, garlic, olives, parsley, capers, oregano, oil, salt, and red pepper. Let stand 1 hour at room temperature.

2 Bring at least 4 quarts of water to a boil in a large pot. Add 2 tablespoons of salt, then the pasta. Stir well. Cook over high heat, stirring frequently, until the pasta is tender. Set aside some of the cooking water. Drain the pasta.

3 Toss the pasta with the sauce. Add a little of the cooking water if the pasta seems dry. Serve immediately.

Pasta with Raw Vegetables
Pasta alla Crudaiola

MAKES 4 TO 6 SERVINGS

Celery adds crunch and lemon juice a clean, light flavor to this easy summer pasta.

2 pounds ripe tomatoes, peeled, seeded, and chopped
1 garlic clove, very finely chopped
1 cup tender celery ribs, thinly sliced
1/2 cup basil leaves, stacked and cut into thin ribbons
1/2 cup Gaeta or other mild black olives, pitted and chopped
1/4 cup extra-virgin olive oil
1 tablespoon lemon juice
Salt and freshly ground black pepper
1 pound fusilli or gemelli

1 Place the tomatoes in a large bowl with the garlic, celery, basil, and olives and toss well. Stir in the oil, lemon juice, and salt and pepper to taste.

2 Bring at least 4 quarts of water to a boil in a large pot. Add 2 tablespoons of salt, then the pasta. Stir well. Cook over high heat, stirring frequently, until the pasta is tender. Drain the pasta, then quickly toss it well with the sauce. Serve immediately.

"Hurry Up" Spaghetti
Spaghetti Sciue' Sciue'

MAKES 4 TO 6 SERVINGS

Little grape tomatoes have a big tomato flavor and are in season all year round. Cherry tomatoes work well in this recipe too. The Neapolitan phrase sciue' sciue' *(pronounced shoo-ay, shoo-ay) means something like "hurry up," and this sauce is quick to make.*

1/4 cup olive oil
3 garlic cloves, thinly sliced
Pinch of crushed red pepper
3 cups grape tomatoes or cherry tomatoes, halved
Salt
Pinch of dried oregano, crumbled
1 pound spaghetti

1 Pour the oil into a skillet large enough to hold the cooked pasta. Add the garlic and red pepper. Cook over medium heat until the garlic is lightly golden, about 2 minutes. Add the tomatoes, salt to taste, and the oregano. Cook, stirring once or twice, 10 minutes or until the tomatoes are tender and the juices slightly thickened. Turn off the heat.

2 Bring at least 4 quarts of water to a boil in a large pot. Add 2 tablespoons of salt, then the pasta, gently pushing it down until the pasta is completely covered with water. Stir well. Cook over high heat, stirring frequently, until the pasta is al dente, tender yet still firm to the bite. Drain the pasta, reserving some of the cooking water.

3 Place the pasta in the skillet with the tomato sauce. Turn the heat to high and cook, stirring for 1 minute. Add a little of the cooking water if the pasta seems dry. Serve immediately.

"Angry" Penne
Penne all'Arrabbiata

MAKES 4 TO 6 SERVINGS

These Roman-style penne are called "angry" because of the red-hot flavor of the tomato sauce. Use as much, or as little, crushed red pepper as you like. This pasta is usually served without cheese.

¼ cup olive oil

4 garlic cloves, lightly crushed

Crushed red pepper to taste

2 pounds fresh tomatoes, peeled, seeded, and chopped, or 1 (28-ounce) can imported Italian peeled tomatoes, drained and chopped

2 fresh basil leaves

Salt

1 pound penne

1 Pour the oil into a skillet large enough to hold all of the pasta. Add the garlic and pepper and cook until the garlic is deeply golden, about 5 minutes. Remove the garlic.

2 Add the tomatoes, basil, and salt to taste. Cook 15 to 20 minutes or until the sauce is thick.

3 Bring at least 4 quarts of water to a boil in a large pot. Add 2 tablespoons of salt, then the pasta.

Stir well. Cook over high heat, stirring frequently, until the pasta is al dente, tender yet still firm to the bite. Set aside some of the cooking water. Drain the pasta.

4 Transfer the penne to the skillet and toss well over high heat. Add a little of the cooking water if the pasta seems dry. Serve immediately.

Eleven Pastas with Uncooked Sauces

When it's hot out, you're in a hurry, or you just don't want to cook, you can still prepare simple and delicious pastas, such as the following dishes.

1   Roman Tomato and Mozzarella Pasta, page 130
2   Fusilli with Tuna and Tomatoes, page 130
3   Linguine with Sicilian Pesto, page 131
4   Bow Ties with Uncooked Puttanesca Sauce, page 132
5   Pasta with Salad, page 126
6   Spaghetti with "Crazy" Pesto, page 131
7   Linguine with Pesto, page 114
8   Linguine with Sun-Dried Tomatoes, page 115
9   Pasta with Raw Vegetables, page 132
10   Linguine with Ricotta and Herbs, page 136
11   Spaghetti with Pecorino and Pepper, page 135

Rigatoni with Ricotta and Tomato Sauce

Rigatoni con Ricotta e Salsa di Pomodoro

MAKES 4 TO 6 SERVINGS

This is an old-fashioned southern Italian way of serving pasta that is quite irresistible. Some cooks like to dress the pasta just with the tomato sauce, then pass the ricotta separately, while others like to mix it all up before serving. The choice is up to you.

2¹/₂ cups tomato sauce, such as **Marinara Sauce (page 89)** or **Tuscan Tomato Sauce (pages 90–91)**
I pound rigatoni, shells, or cavatelli
Salt
I cup whole or part-skim ricotta, at room temperature
Freshly grated Pecorino Romano or Parmigiano-Reggiano, to taste

1 Prepare the sauce, if neccessary. Bring at least 4 quarts of water to a boil in a large pot. Add 2 tablespoons of salt, then the pasta. Stir well. Cook over high heat, stirring frequently, until the pasta is al dente, tender yet still firm to the bite.

2 While the pasta is cooking, bring the sauce to a simmer, if needed.

3 Spoon a little of the hot sauce into a heated serving bowl. Drain the pasta and place it in the bowl. Toss immediately, adding more sauce to taste. Add the ricotta and stir well. Pass the grated cheese separately. Serve immediately.

Bow Ties with Cherry Tomatoes and Bread Crumbs

Farfalle al Pomodorini e Briciole

MAKES 4 TO 6 SERVINGS

This pasta is currently very much in vogue in Italy. Serve it with a drizzle of extra-virgin olive oil.

6 tablespoons olive oil
I pound cherry or grape tomatoes, halved lengthwise
¹/₂ cup plain dry bread crumbs
¹/₄ cup freshly grated Pecorino Romano
2 tablespoons chopped fresh flat-leaf parsley
Salt and freshly ground black pepper
I pound farfalle
Extra-virgin olive oil

1 Place a rack in the center of the oven. Preheat the oven to 350°F. Drizzle 4 tablespoons of the oil in a 13 × 9 × 2-inch baking dish. Spread the tomatoes cut-side up in the pan.

2 In a small bowl, combine the crumbs, cheese, parsley, remaining 2 tablespoons olive oil, and salt and pepper to taste. Scatter the crumbs over the tomatoes. Bake 30 minutes or until the tomatoes are tender and the crumbs are lightly toasted.

3 Bring at least 4 quarts of water to a boil in a large pot. Add 2 tablespoons of salt, then the pasta. Stir well. Cook over high heat, stirring frequently, until the pasta is tender but slightly underdone. Drain the pasta and toss it in the pan with the tomatoes and a drizzle of extra-virgin olive oil. Serve immediately.

Stuffed Shells

Conchiglie Ripiene

MAKES 6 TO 8 SERVINGS

Jumbo pasta shells look like boats sailing in a sea of tomato sauce. Because of the rich filling, this recipe will make 6 to 8 servings. These shells are nice for a party.

About 4 cups of your favorite tomato sauce or ragù, such as "Fake" Meat Sauce (page 91) or Marches-Style Ragù (page 95)

Salt

1 package (12 ounces) jumbo shells

2 pounds whole or part-skim ricotta

8 ounces fresh mozzarella, shredded

1 cup freshly grated Parmigiano-Reggiano

2 tablespoons chopped fresh flat-leaf parsley

1 egg, lightly beaten

Freshly ground black pepper

1 Prepare the sauce, if neccessary. Bring at least 4 quarts of water to a boil in a large pot. Add 2 tablespoons of salt, then the pasta. Stir well. Cook over high heat, stirring frequently, until the pasta is about half-cooked, flexible but still very firm. Drain the pasta and drop it into a large bowl of cold water.

2 Mix together the ricotta, mozzarella, 1/2 cup of the Parmigiano, the parsley, egg, and salt and pepper to taste.

3 Place a rack in the center of the oven. Preheat the oven to 350°F. Spoon a thin layer of the sauce into a baking dish large enough to hold the shells in a single layer. Drain the pasta shells well and pat dry. Stuff the shells with the cheese mixture and place them side by side in the dish. Spoon on the remaining sauce. Sprinkle with the remaining 1/2 cup cheese.

4 Bake the shells 25 to 30 minutes or until the sauce is bubbling and the shells are heated through.

❧ Dried Pasta with Cheese and Eggs

Spaghetti with Pecorino and Pepper

Spaghetti Cacio e Pepe

MAKES 4 TO 6 SERVINGS

Dried pasta began to be made commercially in the fourteenth century in Naples. A pasta maker was known as a vermicellaio, *and pasta was called by the generic name* vermicelli, *meaning "little worms," because most pasta was made into long strands.*

Romans make this quick pasta with lots of black pepper and Pecorino Romano. In this dish with so few ingredients, use good-quality fresh pecorino and grate it just before you are ready to use it, for best flavor.

Salt

1 pound spaghetti or linguine

2 tablespoons extra-virgin olive oil

1 tablespoon coarsely ground black pepper

1 cup freshly grated Pecorino Romano

1 Bring at least 4 quarts of water to a boil in a large pot. Add 2 tablespoons of salt, then the pasta, gently pushing it down until the pasta is completely covered with water. Stir well. Cook over high heat, stirring frequently, until the pasta is al dente, tender but still firm to the bite. Drain the pasta, reserving some of the cooking water.

2 In a large serving bowl, toss the pasta with the oil, pepper, half of the cheese, and a little of the cooking water until the cheese is melted. Toss the pasta again with the remaining cheese. Serve immediately.

Linguine with Lemon
Linguine al Limone

MAKES 4 TO 6 SERVINGS

The ingredients for this recipe—pasta, butter, a lemon, and cheese—could be an Italian still life. This is so easy to do; you can make the sauce while the pasta cooks. As a variation, add chopped basil or parsley to the pasta just before serving.

1 stick (4 ounces) unsalted butter
Grated zest of one lemon
2 tablespoons fresh lemon juice
Salt
Freshly ground black pepper
1 pound linguine
3/4 cup freshly grated Parmigiano-Reggiano

1 In a skillet large enough to hold all of the pasta, melt the butter over medium heat. Remove from the heat and stir in the lemon zest and juice, a pinch of salt, and pepper to taste.

2 Bring at least 4 quarts of water to a boil in a large pot. Add 2 tablespoons of salt, then the pasta, gently pushing it down until the pasta is completely covered with water. Stir well. Cook over high heat, stirring frequently, until the pasta is al dente, tender but still firm to the bite. Drain the pasta, reserving some of the cooking water.

3 Add the pasta to the sauce and toss well. Add the cheese and toss again. Stir in a tablespoon or two of the cooking water if the pasta seems dry. Serve immediately.

Linguine with Ricotta and Herbs
Linguine con Ricotta e le Erbe Fini

MAKES 4 TO 6 SERVINGS

This is one of the quickest pastas I know, and a delicious summer dish. Serve it followed by a fresh tomato and red onion salad.

1 pound linguine
Salt
1/4 cup extra-virgin olive oil
2 tablespoons snipped fresh chives
2 tablespoons finely chopped fresh flat-leaf parsley
1 tablespoon chopped fresh thyme
1 teaspoon chopped fresh rosemary leaves
1 cup whole or part-skim ricotta
Freshly ground black pepper

1 Bring at least 4 quarts of water to a boil in a large pot. Add 2 tablespoons of salt, then the pasta, gently pushing it down until the pasta is completely covered with water. Stir well. Cook over high heat, stirring frequently, until the pasta is al dente, tender yet still firm to the bite. Drain the pasta, reserving some of the cooking water.

2 In a large serving bowl, toss the pasta with the oil and herbs. Add the ricotta and a generous grind of black pepper and toss again. Add a little of the cooking water if the pasta seems dry. Serve immediately.

Ziti with Spinach and Ricotta
Ziti con Spinaci e Ricotta

MAKES 4 TO 6 SERVINGS

Spinach, ricotta, and Parmigiano-Reggiano are a typical stuffing for ravioli in Emilia-Romagna and many other regions. In this recipe, the filling for fresh pasta becomes the sauce for dried pasta. The flavors are similar, but the method is much easier for every day. Chopped cooked broccoli can stand in for the spinach if you like.

1 1/2 pounds spinach, tough stems removed
4 tablespoons unsalted butter
1 medium onion, finely chopped
Salt
1 pound ziti or penne
1 cup whole or part-skim ricotta, at room temperature
1/2 cup freshly grated Parmigiano-Reggiano
Freshly ground black pepper

1 Put the spinach in a large pot over medium heat with 1/4 cup water. Cover and cook for 2 to 3 minutes or until wilted and tender. Drain and cool. Wrap the spinach in a lint-free cloth and squeeze out as much water as possible. Finely chop the spinach.

2 In a large saucepan, melt the butter over medium-low heat. Add the onion and cook until tender and golden, about 10 minutes. Add the chopped spinach and cook, stirring, until the spinach is heated through, 3 to 4 minutes. Add salt to taste

3 Bring at least 4 quarts of water to a boil in a large pot. Add 2 tablespoons of salt, then the pasta. Stir well. Cook over high heat, stirring frequently, until the pasta is al dente, tender yet still firm to the bite. Drain the pasta, reserving some of the cooking water.

4 In a large heated serving bowl, toss the pasta with the spinach, ricotta, and cheese. Add a little of the cooking water if the pasta seems dry. Sprinkle with freshly ground black pepper and serve immediately.

Rigatoni with Four Cheeses
Rigatoni ai Quattro Formaggi

MAKES 4 TO 6 SERVINGS

The four cheeses suggested below are just a suggestion. Use whatever you have on hand, even pieces that are a little dried out are fine when grated. I can't think of any cheese that does not go well with pasta. I have eaten versions of this pasta in Rome, Tuscany, and Naples, and I suspect it is the kind of thing that cooks throw together whenever they have small amounts of a variety of cheeses.

1 pound rigatoni, ziti, or fusilli
Salt
6 tablespoons unsalted butter, melted
1/2 cup shredded Fontina Valle d'Aosta
1/2 cup shredded fresh mozzarella
1/2 cup shredded Gruyere or Emmenthal
3/4 cup freshly grated Parmigiano-Reggiano
Freshly ground black pepper

1 Bring at least 4 quarts of water to a boil in a large pot. Add 2 tablespoons of salt, then the pasta. Stir well. Cook over high heat, stirring frequently, until the pasta is al dente, tender but still firm to the bite. Drain the pasta, reserving some of the cooking water.

2 In a large heated serving bowl, toss the pasta with the butter. Add the cheeses and a couple of tablespoons of the pasta water. Toss until the cheese is melted. Sprinkle with black pepper and serve immediately.

Linguine with Creamy Nut Sauce
Linguine con Salsa di Noci

MAKES 4 TO 6 SERVINGS

My friend Pauline Wasserman came across this recipe while traveling in Piedmont and gave it to me some years ago. The nuts give the pasta a rich flavor, while the ricotta keeps it creamy and moist. I serve it with dolcetto, a light, dry red wine from Piedmont.

1/2 cup walnuts
2 tablespoons pine nuts
4 tablespoons unsalted butter
I small garlic clove, very finely chopped
I tablespoon chopped fresh flat-leaf parsley
1/4 cup whole or part-skim ricotta, mascarpone, or heavy cream
Salt
I pound linguine
1/2 cup freshly grated Parmigiano-Reggiano

I Place the walnuts and pine nuts in a food processor or blender. Grind the nuts just until fine. (Don't overprocess into a paste.)

2 In a medium skillet, melt the butter over medium heat. Add the garlic and parsley and cook 1 minute. Stir in the ground nuts and ricotta. Stir to blend and heat through.

3 Meanwhile, bring about 4 quarts of water to a boil in a large pot. Add 2 tablespoons of salt, then the pasta, gently pushing it down until the pasta is completely covered with water. Stir well. Cook, stirring often, until the pasta is al dente, tender yet still firm to the bite. Set aside some of the cooking water. Drain the pasta.

4 In a large heated serving bowl, toss the pasta with the sauce and grated cheese. Add a little of the cooking water if the pasta seems dry. Serve immediately.

Bow Ties with Amaretti
Farfalle con gli Amaretti

MAKES 4 TO 6 SERVINGS

One of the specialties of Lombardy is fresh egg pasta stuffed with winter squash and crushed amaretti, crunchy almond cookies (Winter Squash Ravioli with Butter and Almonds, page 184). *Bathed in melted butter and sprinkled with salty and nutty Parmigiano, the combination of flavors is most unusual and unforgettable. The waiter at a little trattoria in Cremona told me that this simple recipe made with dried pasta was inspired by that elaborate dish.*

If your raisins are on the dry side, plump them by dropping them into the boiling pasta water just before draining.

Salt
I pound farfalle
I stick unsalted butter, melted
12 to 16 amaretti cookies, crushed (about 1/2 cup crumbs)
1/3 cup golden raisins
I cup grated Parmigiano-Reggiano

I Bring at least 4 quarts of water to a boil in a large pot. Add 2 tablespoons of salt, then the pasta. Stir well. Cook over high heat, stirring frequently, until the pasta is al dente, tender yet still firm to the bite. Set aside some of the cooking water. Drain the pasta.

2 Place the butter in a large warm serving bowl. Add the pasta and toss it with the cookie crumbs and raisins. Add the cheese and toss again. Add a little of the cooking water if the pasta seems dry. Serve hot.

Grating Cheese for Pasta

All firm cheeses for grating are in the category known as *grana*, meaning grainy. The most common are Parmigiano-Reggiano, Grana Padano, and Pecorino Romano, though there are also regional favorites for grating, such as *ricotta salata* in Puglia, Asiago in the Veneto, and *caciocavallo* in Sicily. Parmigiano-Reggiano and Grana Padano, which are both produced in northern Italy, are used throughout Italy. Pecorino is used mostly in southern and central regions.

Not every pasta needs cheese, though. Most Italian cooks will tell you that pasta dressed with shellfish sauces, like spaghetti with clams or lobster, are never tossed with cheese, because the cheese flavor would overwhelm the flavor of the seafood.

But as with everything else in Italian cooking, there are exceptions to this rule. Recently in Rome in a very good restaurant, I was served *bucatini* pasta with octopus in tomato sauce topped with pecorino cheese. To be on the safe side, though, avoid adding cheese to anything but pasta with meat, tomato, and vegetable sauces.

When purchasing cheese, it is best to buy it in one piece and grate it yourself as close as possible to serving time. Tiny flakes of grated cheese dry out quickly and lose flavor when they are exposed to air, so the less time between grating and eating, the more flavorful the cheese will be. I like to place a chunk of cheese and a small grater on the table and let everyone grate his or her own.

How To Grate Cheese

An old-fashioned box grater is still perfect for grating cheese for pasta. The medium-size holes give the cheese good texture, which enhances its ability to blend with the pasta and sauce and improves the flavor. Another grater I like is the Mouli grater, which has a perforated rotary drum. You put a piece of cheese in the hopper, crank the handle, the drum grates against the cheese and out it comes in fine shreds.

A microplane grater, which was originally a tool used by woodworkers, also does a good job, but it grates the cheese so fine it may throw off your measuring when using the cheese for recipes.

If I have a large quantity of cheese to grate, I use the food processor with a steel blade, though it is not ideal. Grana cheeses are too hard for the shredding blade, and the solid steel blade grinds the cheese into little pellets. It is not as desirable as cheese that has been grated, but it does not make a difference in cooked dishes because the cheese melts.

Spaghetti with Fried Eggs, Salerno Style
Spaghetti con l'Uuovo Fritto alla Salernitana

MAKES 2 SERVINGS

Though I had heard about this recipe from the Naples area, I never tried making it until one day when I thought I had nothing in the house to cook for myself and my husband. It is simple and comforting and could even be served for brunch. The eggs should be cooked until the whites are set but the yolks are still soft. The ingredients for this recipe will serve two, but you can double or triple them as needed.

4 ounces spaghetti or linguine
Salt
2 tablespoons olive oil
4 eggs
1/2 cup freshly grated Pecorino Romano
Freshly ground black pepper

1 Bring at least 4 quarts of water to a boil in a large pot. Add 2 tablespoons of the salt, then the pasta, gently pushing it down until the pasta is completely covered with water. Stir well. Cook over high heat, stirring frequently.

2 Heat the oil in a large skillet over medium heat. Add the eggs, sprinkling them with salt and pepper. Cook until the whites are just set and the yolks are still soft.

3 Drain the pasta, reserving some of the cooking water. Toss the pasta with the cheese and 2 to 3 tablespoons of the water.

4 Divide the pasta between 2 serving dishes. Top each with two eggs and serve immediately.

Tagliarini Soufflé
Soufflé di Tagliarini

MAKES 6 SERVINGS

Some recipes reach my kitchen in a roundabout way. My friend Arthur Schwartz shared this unusual one with me. He learned it from his cooking school partner, Baronessa Cecilia Bellelli Baratta, who in turn learned it from her mother, Elvira. The Baratta family lives in Battipaglia, in the province of Salerno, where Cecilia's father was in the tomato packing business. But for the duration of World War II, the family lived in Parma, where it was much safer.

Elvira (at age 91) still cooks many dishes from Parma and claims to have created the idea of a pasta soufflé while living in that region, though in fact other versions do exist. Cecilia points out that northern Italians hardly have a monopoly on egg pasta and cream sauces, no matter what the rest of us think.

What is different about this recipe is that it is made with dried egg pasta rather than fresh. Look for tagliarini, cappellini, or cappelli di angelo, though ordinary thin egg noodles would work as well. The lemon flavor makes the dish seem even lighter than it is.

BÉCHAMEL SAUCE

4 tablespoons unsalted butter
4 tablespoons all-purpose flour
2 cups milk
3/4 cup grated Parmigiano-Reggiano
1/8 teaspoon freshly grated nutmeg
1 1/2 teaspoons salt
1/2 teaspoon freshly ground black pepper
Finely grated zest of 1 lemon
Juice of 1 lemon
4 large eggs, separated
Salt

8 ounces dried tagliarini, or another fine dried egg pasta, broken into 3-inch lengths
4 tablespoons unsalted butter
1 egg white
1/4 cup plus 2 tablespoons plain dry bread crumbs

1 Prepare the sauce: Melt the butter in a small saucepan over medium heat. Stir in the flour using a whisk and let cook for 2 minutes.

2 Whisking constantly, add the milk. Bring to a simmer, stirring frequently. Remove from the heat and stir in the cheese. Allow to cool slightly before stirring in the nutmeg, salt, pepper, lemon zest, and juice.

3 Scrape the mixture into a large mixing bowl and let cool to room temperature. (Or, if you are in a hurry, cool the mixture by placing the bowl in another bowl filled with ice water.) Stir in the egg yolks, mixing thoroughly.

4 Bring about 3 quarts of water to a boil. Add 2 tablespoons of salt, then the pasta. Boil it until it is only half done. The pasta will be flexible but still hard in the center. Drain well. Transfer the pasta back to the pot it was cooked in and toss with 2 tablespoons of the remaining butter. Let the pasta cool slightly.

5 Place a rack in the center of the oven. Preheat the oven to 375°F. Using 1 tablespoon of the remaining butter, grease a 9 × 9 × 2–inch baking dish. Sprinkle with about 1/4 cup of the bread crumbs, coating the dish well.

6 In a large bowl with an electric mixer on medium speed, beat the egg whites with a pinch of salt until soft peaks form. Gently fold the whites into the béchamel sauce. With a rubber spatula, fold the sauce into the pasta a little at a time. Work carefully so as not to deflate the whites too much. Scrape the mixture into the prepared baking dish.

7 Sprinkle with the remaining 2 tablespoons bread crumbs. Dot with the remaining 1 tablespoon of butter.

8 Bake for 30 minutes or until the soufflé is puffed and lightly golden.

9 For maximum lightness, cut into squares and serve immediately. The soufflé will sink slightly as it cools.

❧ Dried Pasta with Meat

Spaghetti, Charcoal Burner's Style
Spaghetti alla Carbonara

MAKES 6 TO 8 SERVINGS

Romans credit the hard-working charcoal delivery man as the inspiration for this quickly made pasta. They say the generous grinding of black pepper resembles specks of coal dust!

Some cooks in the United States add cream to the sauce, but this is the way it is made in Rome.

4 ounces pancetta, cut into thick slices
1 tablespoon olive oil
3 large eggs
Salt and freshly ground black pepper
1 pound spaghetti or linguine
3/4 cup freshly grated Pecorino Romano
**   or Parmigiano-Reggiano**

1 Cut the pancetta into 1/4-inch pieces. Pour the oil into a skillet large enough to hold all of the cooked pasta. Add the pancetta. Cook over medium heat, until the pancetta is golden around the edges, about 10 minutes. Turn off the heat.

2 In a medium bowl, beat the eggs with a generous amount of salt and pepper.

3 Bring at least 4 quarts of water to a boil in a large pot. Add 2 tablespoons of salt, then the pasta, gently pushing it down until the pasta is completely covered with water. Stir well. Cook over high heat, stirring frequently, until the pasta is al dente, tender yet still firm to the bite. Drain the pasta, reserving some of the cooking water.

4 Place the cooked pasta in the pan with the pancetta and toss well over medium heat. Add the eggs and a little of the cooking water. Toss gently until the pasta looks creamy. Sprinkle with cheese and more pepper. Toss well and serve immediately.

Bucatini with Tomatoes, Pancetta, and Hot Pepper
Bucatini all'Amatriciana

MAKES 4 TO 6 SERVINGS

Amatrice is the name of a town in the Abruzzo region. Many people from that area settled in Rome, and this recipe became one of the city's signature dishes. As with all traditions, everyone argues about the right way to uphold it. I once listened to a Roman call-in radio program on the subject that went on for an hour discussing the pros and cons of adding onion.

I have tried numerous versions, and this is the way I like it best. Bucatini, a very thick spaghetti shape with a hole in the center, is traditional but hard to eat. Unlike spaghetti, linguine, and other long pasta strands, it does not twirl neatly around the fork, especially if it is cooked firm the way the Romans like it. A short thin pasta tube like penne is also good and a lot neater to eat.

2 tablespoons olive oil

2 ounces sliced pancetta, about 1/8 inch thick, chopped into tiny bits

1 medium onion, finely chopped

Pinch of crushed red pepper

1/2 cup dry white wine

1 (28-ounce) can imported Italian peeled tomatoes, drained and chopped

Salt

1 pound bucatini, perciatelli, or penne

1/2 cup freshly grated Pecorino Romano

1 Pour the oil into a skillet large enough to hold all of the cooked pasta. Add the pancetta, onion, and crushed red pepper. Cook, stirring occasionally, over medium heat, until the pancetta and onion are golden, about 12 minutes.

2 Add the wine and bring to a simmer.

3 Stir in the tomatoes and salt to taste. Bring the sauce to a simmer and cook, stirring occasionally, until the sauce is thickened, about 25 minutes.

4 Bring at least 4 quarts of water to a boil in a large pot. Add 2 tablespoons of salt, then the pasta. Stir well. Cook over high heat, stirring frequently, until the pasta is al dente, tender yet still firm to the bite. Set aside some of the cooking water. Drain the pasta.

5 Pour the pasta into the pan with the sauce. Toss the pasta and sauce together over high heat about 1 minute, or until the pasta is coated. Add a little cooking water if the pasta seems dry. Remove from the heat. Add the cheese and toss well. Serve immediately.

Penne with Pancetta, Pecorino, and Black Pepper
Penne alla Gricia

MAKES 4 TO 6 SERVINGS

I was reminded of how good this pasta can be at New York's San Domenico Restaurant, where it was prepared for a luncheon celebrating the cooking of Rome. I had to include it in this collection.

Penne alla Gricia is a close relative, and quite possibly the forerunner, of the Bucatini all'Amatriciana at left. Traditional recipes for both have the same ingredients—salted meat, lard, and grated sheep's cheese, which were the typical flavorings for pasta before tomatoes arrived from the New World and were accepted in Italy. Pork lard adds a very good flavor, but olive oil can be substituted if you prefer.

In Rome, this is made with guanciale, *cured pork cheek. Unless you live near an Italian specialty butcher, guanciale is hard to find, but pancetta is very similar. Have the slices cut about 1/8-inch thick, if you can. To make the slices easier to chop, try freezing them briefly on a piece of wax paper.*

2 tablespoons pork lard or olive oil

4 ounces sliced guanciale or pancetta, about 1/8 inch thick, chopped into tiny bits

Salt

1 pound spaghetti

1/2 cup freshly grated Pecorino Romano

1/2 teaspoon freshly ground black pepper or more to taste

1 In a skillet large enough to hold all of the cooked pasta, heat the lard or olive oil over medium heat. Add the guanciale or pancetta, and cook, stirring frequently, 10 minutes or until crisp and golden brown.

2 Bring at least 4 quarts of water to a boil in a large pot. Add 2 tablespoons of salt, then the pasta. Stir well. Cook over high heat, stirring frequently, until the pasta is al dente, tender yet still firm to the bite. Set aside some of the cooking water. Drain the pasta.

3 Pour the pasta into the skillet and toss it with the cheese, pepper, and a couple of tablespoons of the water until the pasta is well coated. Serve immediately with more pepper, if desired.

Penne with Pork and Cauliflower

Pasta Incaciata

MAKES 4 TO 6 SERVINGS

My friend Carmella Ragusa showed me how to make this recipe, which she learned when visiting her family in Sicily.

2 tablespoons olive oil
2 garlic cloves, finely chopped
8 ounces ground pork
1 teaspoon fennel seeds
1/2 cup dry red wine
1 pound fresh plum tomatoes, peeled, seeded, and chopped, or 2 cups canned imported Italian tomatoes, drained and chopped
Salt and freshly ground black pepper
3 cups cauliflower florets
1 pound penne
About 1 cup freshly grated Pecorino Romano

1 Pour the oil into a large skillet. Add the the garlic and cook over medium heat until golden, about 2 minutes. Add the pork and fennel seeds and stir well. Cook, stirring occasionally, until the meat is browned, about 15 minutes.

2 Add the wine and simmer 3 minutes, or until most of the liquid evaporates.

3 Add the tomatoes and salt and pepper to taste. Simmer 15 minutes or until the sauce is slightly reduced.

4 Bring at least 4 quarts of water to a boil in a large pot. Add the cauliflower and 2 tablespoons of salt. Cook until the cauliflower is tender, about 10 minutes. With a slotted spoon, scoop out the cauliflower and drain well. Do not discard the water.

5 Add the cauliflower to the sauce and cook, stirring frequently and breaking up the pieces with a spoon, until the sauce is thick, about 10 minutes more.

6 Bring the water back to a boil and add the pasta. Cook, stirring frequently, until the pasta is al dente, tender yet still firm to the bite. Set aside some of the cooking water. Drain the pasta.

7 Transfer the pasta to a heated serving bowl. Toss the pasta with the sauce, thinning it if necessary with the cooking water. Add the cheese and toss well. Serve immediately.

Spaghetti with Vodka Sauce

Spaghetti alla Vodka

MAKES 4 TO 6 SERVINGS

According to my friend Arthur Schwartz, a cookbook author and food authority, this pasta was invented in the 1970s in Italy as part of an advertising campaign for a major vodka company. I first had it in Rome, but it seems to be more popular now in the United States than it is in Italy.

¼ cup unsalted butter
¼ cup finely chopped shallots
2 ounces sliced imported Italian prosciutto, cut into thin strips
1 (28-ounce) can imported Italian peeled tomatoes, drained and coarsely chopped
½ teaspoon crushed red pepper
Salt
½ cup heavy cream
¼ cup vodka
1 pound spaghetti or linguine
½ cup freshly grated Parmigiano-Reggiano

1 In a skillet large enough to hold all of the cooked pasta, melt the butter over medium heat. Add the shallots and cook until golden, about 2 minutes. Stir in the prosciutto and cook 1 minute.

2 Add the tomatoes, crushed red pepper, and salt to taste. Simmer 5 minutes. Stir in the cream and cook, stirring well, for 1 minute more. Add the vodka and cook 2 minutes.

3 Bring 4 quarts of water to a boil in a large pot. Add 2 tablespoons of salt, then the pasta, gently pushing it down until the pasta is completely covered with water. Cook over high heat, stirring frequently, until al dente, tender yet still firm to the bite. Set aside some of the cooking water. Drain the pasta.

4 Add the pasta to the skillet with the sauce. Toss the pasta in the sauce over high heat until it is well coated. Add a little cooking water if the sauce seems too thick. Stir in the cheese and toss again. Serve immediately.

Bow Ties with Asparagus, Cream, and Prosciutto

Farfalle con Asparagi

MAKES 6 TO 8 SERVINGS

This combination is perfect for a spring menu. I find the cream makes it very rich, so I tend to serve this pasta in small portions as a first course before something simple like grilled veal or chicken. I have added chopped roasted peppers to this pasta and like the combination very much.

1 pound fresh asparagus, trimmed
Salt
1 cup heavy cream
1 pound farfalle
½ cup freshly grated Parmigiano-Reggiano
2 ounces sliced imported Italian prosciutto, cut crosswise into thin strips

1 In a large skillet, bring about 2 inches of water to a boil. Add the asparagus and salt to taste. Cook until the asparagus are just tender and bend slightly when lifted from the water. The cooking time will depend on the thickness of the asparagus. Pat the asparagus dry. Cut them into bite-size pieces.

2 Bring the cream to a simmer in a small saucepan. Cook 5 minutes or until slightly thickened.

3 Bring a large pot of water to a boil. Add 2 tablespoons of salt, then the pasta. Stir well. Cook over high heat, stirring frequently, until the pasta is al dente, tender yet still firm to the bite. Set aside some of the cooking water. Drain the pasta.

4 Pour the pasta, cream, and cheese into a large serving bowl and toss well. Add a little cooking water if the sauce seems too thick. Add the asparagus and prosciutto and toss again. Serve immediately.

"Dragged" Penne with Meat Sauce

Penne Strascinate

MAKES 6 SERVINGS

I first had this pasta at a little country restaurant in Tuscany, a region in which every cook has her or his own way of making it. It is called "dragged" penne because the pasta finishes cooking as it is stirred in the sauce. This infuses the pasta with the flavor of the sauce.

1/4 cup olive oil

1 medium onion, finely chopped

1 medium carrot, finely chopped

1 tender celery rib, finely chopped

1 garlic clove, very finely chopped

2 tablespoons chopped fresh basil

12 ounces ground veal

1/2 cup dry red wine

2 cups peeled, seeded, and chopped fresh tomatoes or canned imported Italian peeled tomatoes, drained and chopped

1 cup homemade Meat Broth (page 62) or Chicken Broth (page 63) or store-bought beef or chicken broth

Salt and freshly ground black pepper

1 pound penne

1/2 cup freshly grated Pecorino Romano

1/2 cup freshly grated Parmigiano-Reggiano

1 Pour the oil into a skillet large enough to hold all of the cooked pasta. Add the onion, carrot, celery, garlic, and basil. Cook over medium heat until the vegetables are tender, about 10 minutes.

2 Add the veal and cook, stirring frequently to break up any lumps, about 10 minutes. Add the wine and bring to a simmer. Cook 1 minute.

3 Stir in the tomatoes, the broth, and salt and pepper to taste. Simmer on low heat 45 minutes, stirring occasionally.

4 Bring 4 quarts of water to a boil in a large pot. Add 2 tablespoons of salt, then the pasta. Stir well. Cook over high heat, stirring frequently, until the pasta is almost tender but slightly underdone. Set aside some cooking water. Drain the pasta.

5 Add the pasta to the skillet and raise the heat to medium. Cook, stirring the pasta well, for 2 minutes, adding some of the water if necessary. Stir in the cheeses and serve immediately.

Spaghetti, Caruso Style

Spaghetti Enrico Caruso

MAKES 6 SERVINGS

Enrico Caruso, the great Neapolitan tenor, loved to cook and eat. Pasta was his specialty, and this is said to have been one of his favorites.

1/4 cup olive oil

1/4 cup finely chopped shallots or onions

8 ounces chicken livers, trimmed and cut into bite-size pieces

1 teaspoon finely chopped rosemary

Salt and freshly ground black pepper

2 cups peeled, seeded, and chopped fresh tomatoes, or canned imported Italian peeled tomatoes, drained and chopped

1 pound spaghetti or linguine

2 tablespoons unsalted butter

1/2 cup freshly grated Parmigiano-Reggiano

1 Pour the oil into a skillet large enough to hold all of the pasta. Add the shallots. Cook over medium heat until tender, about 3 minutes. Add the livers, rosemary, and salt and pepper to taste. Cook 2 minutes or until the livers are no longer pink.

2 Stir in the tomatoes and bring to a simmer. Cook 20 minutes or until slightly thickened.

3 Bring 4 quarts of water to a boil in a large pot. Add 2 tablespoons of salt, then the pasta, gently pushing it down until the pasta is completely covered with water. Stir well. Cook over high heat, stirring frequently, until the pasta is al dente, tender yet still firm to the bite. Set aside some of the cooking water. Drain the pasta.

4 Add the spaghetti to the sauce and toss together 1 minute over high heat. Add a little cooking water if the sauce seems too thick. Add the butter and cheese and toss again. Serve immediately.

Penne with Beans and Pancetta

Penne e Fagioli

MAKES 4 TO 6 SERVINGS

Some pasta and bean recipes are thick and souplike, with equal parts beans and pasta. This Tuscan version is really pasta with a bean and tomato sauce.

2 tablespoons olive oil

2¹/2 ounces pancetta, finely chopped

I medium onion, finely chopped

I large garlic clove, peeled and finely chopped

2 cups drained cooked or canned cranberry
    or cannellini beans

1¹/2 pounds plum tomatoes, peeled, seeded, and
    chopped, or 3 cups canned imported Italian
    tomatoes, drained and chopped

Salt to taste

I pound penne

Freshly ground black pepper

¹/2 cup chopped flat-leaf parsley

¹/2 cup freshly grated Parmigiano-Reggiano

1 Pour the oil into a large saucepan. Add the pancetta. Cook over medium heat, stirring occasionally, 10 minutes or until lightly browned. Add the onion and cook until it is tender and golden, about 10 minutes.

2 Stir in the garlic and cook 1 minute more. Add the beans, tomatoes, and salt and pepper. Cook 5 minutes.

3 Bring about 4 quarts of water to a boil in a large pot. Add 2 tablespoons of salt, then the pasta. Stir well. Cook over high heat, stirring frequently, until the pasta is al dente, tender yet still firm to the bite. Set aside some of the cooking water. Drain the pasta.

4 In a large warm serving bowl, toss the pasta with the sauce and parsley. Add a little of the cooking water, if needed. Add the cheese and toss again. Serve with freshly grated Parmigiano-Reggiano.

Pasta with Chickpeas

Pasta e Ceci

MAKES 4 SERVINGS

A drizzle of extra-virgin olive oil is the perfect finishing touch for pasta with chickpeas. If you want to make it spicy, try it with some of the Holy Oil on page 100.

2 tablespoons olive oil

2 ounces thick-sliced pancetta, finely chopped

I medium onion, chopped

I pound tomatoes, peeled, seeded, and chopped

I tablespoon chopped fresh sage

Pinch of crushed red pepper

Salt

2 cups drained cooked or canned chickpeas

8 ounces small pasta, such as elbow or ditali

Extra-virgin olive oil

1 Pour the oil into a large saucepan. Add the pancetta and onion and cook, stirring occasionally, over medium heat, about 10 minutes or until tender and golden.

2 Add the tomatoes, ¹/2 cup water, sage, red pepper, and salt to taste. Bring to a simmer and cook 15 minutes. Add the chickpeas and cook 10 minutes more.

3 Bring about 4 quarts of water to a boil in a large pot. Stir in 2 tablespoons of salt, then the pasta. Stir well. Cook, stirring frequently, until the pasta is tender yet firm to the bite. Set aside some of the cooking water. Drain the pasta.

4 Add the pasta to the pan with the sauce. Stir well and bring to a simmer, adding some of the cooking water if needed. Serve immediately.

Rigatoni Rigoletto
Pasta al Rigoletto

MAKES 6 SERVINGS

This pasta is named for Rigoletto, the tragic hero of Verdi's glorious opera. The story is set in Mantua, where this pasta is well known.

2 or 3 Italian-style pork sausages (about 12 ounces)

2 tablespoons olive oil

1 medium onion, finely chopped

2 garlic cloves, finely chopped

4 tablespoons tomato paste

2 cups water

2 cups cooked dried cranberry or cannellini beans, lightly drained

Salt and freshly ground black pepper

1 pound rigatoni

1 tablespoon unsalted butter

1/4 cup finely chopped fresh basil

1/2 cup freshly grated Parmigiano-Reggiano

1 Remove the casings from the sausages and finely chop the meat.

2 Pour the oil into a saucepan large enough to hold all of the ingredients. Add the onion, sausage meat, and garlic. Cook over medium heat, stirring frequently, until the onions are tender and the sausage is lightly browned, about 15 minutes.

3 Add the tomato paste and water. Bring to a simmer and cook 20 minutes or until slightly thickened.

4 Add the beans and salt and pepper to taste. Cook 10 minutes, mashing some of the beans with the back of a spoon to make the sauce creamy.

5 Bring at least 4 quarts of water to a boil in a large pot. Add 2 tablespoons of salt, then the pasta. Stir well. Cook over high heat, stirring frequently, until the pasta is al dente, tender yet still firm to the bite. Set aside some of the cooking water. Drain the pasta.

6 Add the pasta to the pan with the sauce, toss together, and cook 1 minute, adding a little of the water if needed. Stir in the butter and basil. Add the cheese and toss again. Serve immediately.

Anna's Fried Spaghetti
Spaghetti Fritti alla Anna

MAKES 4 SERVINGS

When my husband and I and a group of friends visited cooking school owner and teacher Anna Tasca Lanza at her family's farm and wine estate at Regaleali, Sicily, we shared numerous meals. Toward the end of our stay, we decided to make a casual lunch with whatever was in the refrigerator. While the rest of us were busy slicing bread and cheese, pouring wine, and making a salad, Anna took out some leftover spaghetti and poured it into a heavy skillet. In a few minutes, the pasta had turned into a crunchy golden cake that everyone devoured. Anna seemed surprised that we had enjoyed it so much and said it was just something that you can do with leftover pasta. My friend Judith Weber eventually got more information about how she had made it and passed the recipe along to me. This is great for a midnight supper, and it can be made with just about any type of leftover pasta, though long strands are best because they will stick together.

4 to 8 ounces cold leftover spaghetti with Sicilian Tomato Sauce (page 90) or Marinara Sauce (page 89)

3 tablespoons olive oil

2 tablespoons grated Pecorino Romano

1 Prepare the spaghetti with tomato sauce if necessary. Chill at least 1 hour or overnight.

2 In a large nonstick skillet, heat 2 tablespoons of the oil over medium heat. Sprinkle the oil with 1 tablespoon of the cheese and immediately add the pasta to the pan, pressing it flat with the back of a spoon. The pasta should be no more than 3/4 inch deep.

(continues)

3 Cook the pasta, flattening it occasionally against the pan, until golden brown and crisp on the bottom, about 20 minutes. Slide a thin spatula underneath the pasta occasionally to make sure that it is not sticking.

4 When the pasta is nicely browned, remove the skillet from heat. Slide a spatula under the pasta to be sure that the it is not stuck. Place a large inverted plate on top of the skillet. Protecting your hands with oven mitts, invert the skillet and plate so that the pasta cake falls out of the skillet onto the plate.

5 Add the remaining oil and cheese to the skillet. Slide the pasta cake with the crisp side up back into the pan. Cook the same way as the first side until browned and crisp, about 15 minutes more. Cut into wedges and serve hot.

Eggplant Pasta Timbale
Pasta al Timballo

MAKES 6 SERVINGS

Pasta, cheeses, and meats encased in a dome of eggplant slices make a spectacular dish for a party or any special occasion. It is not difficult to make, but be very careful when unmolding the heavy timbale hot from the oven.

In Sicily, this is made with caciocavallo, *semifirm cow's milk cheese sold in a pear-shaped casing. The name means horse cheese, and why it is called that has been debated for centuries. Some historians think the cheese was originally made with mare's milk, while others say that it was once transported on horseback suspended from poles. Caciocavallo is similar to provolone, which can be substituted, or use Pecorino Romano.*

2 medium eggplants (about 1 pound each)
Salt
Olive oil
1 medium onion, chopped
1 garlic clove, finely chopped
8 ounces ground beef
8 ounces Italian pork sausages, skinned and chopped
2 pounds fresh tomatoes, peeled, seeded, and chopped, or 1 (28-ounce) can imported Italian peeled tomatoes, chopped
1 cup fresh or frozen peas
Freshly ground black pepper
1 pound perciatelli or bucatini
12 ounces mozzarella, chopped
1 cup freshly grated caciocavallo or Pecorino Romano
3 ounces salami, chopped
2 tablespoons chopped fresh basil
2 hard cooked eggs, sliced

1 Cut the eggplant lengthwise into 1/4-inch thick slices. Sprinkle the slices generously with salt and place them in a colander to drain at least 30 minutes. Rinse the slices and blot dry.

2 Heat 1/4-inch of oil in a large skillet over medium heat. Fry the slices a few at a time until lightly browned on both sides, about 5 minutes per side. Drain on paper towels.

3 Pour the oil into a large saucepan. Add the onion and garlic and cook over medium heat, stirring frequently, until the onion is softened, about 5 minutes. Add the beef and sausage meat. Cook, stirring often, until lightly browned, about 10 minutes.

4 Add the tomatoes and salt and pepper to taste. Cook on low heat 20 minutes. Add the peas and cook 10 minutes more or until the sauce is thickened.

5 Bring at least 4 quarts of water to a boil in a large pot. Add 2 tablespoons of salt, then the pasta. Stir well. Cook over high heat, stirring frequently, until the pasta is tender but still very firm. Drain the pasta and return it to the pot. Toss the pasta with the sauce. Let cool 5 minutes.

6 Line a 4-quart ovenproof bowl or baking dish with foil, pressing it smoothly against the sides. Brush the foil with olive oil. Starting in the center of the bowl, arrange half the eggplant slices, overlapping slightly against the inside and reserving a few slices for the top.

7 Add the mozzarella, grated cheese, salami, and basil to the pan with the pasta and toss well. Add half the pasta to the prepared bowl, being careful not to disturb the eggplant. Arrange the egg slices over the pasta. Top with the remaining pasta and the reserved eggplant slices. Press down lightly.

8 Place a rack in the center of the oven. Preheat the oven to 400°F. Bake 45 to 60 minutes, or until hot in the center, 140°F measured on an instant-read thermometer. (Exact baking time will depend on the diameter of the bowl.)

9 Let the timbale stand 15 minutes. Invert the bowl onto a serving plate. Remove the bowl and gently peel off the foil. Serve immediately.

Baked Ziti
Ziti al Forno

MAKES 8 TO 12 SERVINGS

Baked pasta dishes like this one are popular all over southern Italy. At a time when few homes had ovens, the pans of pasta would be brought to the local bakery to be cooked after the baker had finished making the day's bread.

4 cups Neapolitan Ragù (page 94)
Salt
I pound ziti, penne, or rigatoni
I pound whole or part-skim ricotta
I cup freshly grated Pecorino Romano
    or Parmigiano-Reggiano cheese
12 ounces fresh mozzarella, chopped or shredded

I Prepare the ragù, if necessary. Then, bring 4 quarts of water to a boil in a large pot. Add 2 tablespoons of salt, then the pasta. Stir well. Cook over high heat, stirring frequently, until almost tender. Drain the pasta.

2 In a large bowl, toss the pasta with 2 cups of the ragù, 1 cup of the ricotta, and half the grated cheese. Slice some of the meatballs and sausages from the ragù and stir them into the pasta. (The remaining meats can be served as a second course.)

3 Place a rack in the center of the oven. Preheat the oven to 350°F. Spread half the ziti in a 13 × 9 × 2–inch baking dish. Spread the remaining ricotta on top. Sprinkle with the mozzarella. Pour on 1 cup of the sauce. Top with the remaining ziti and another cup of sauce. Sprinkle with the remaining 1/2 cup grated cheese. Cover the dish securely with foil.

4 Bake the ziti 45 minutes. Uncover and bake 15 to 30 minutes more, or until the blade of a thin knife inserted into the center feels hot and the sauce is bubbling around the edges. Cool 15 minutes on a wire rack. Serve hot.

Sicilian Baked Pasta
Pasta al Forno alla Siciliana

MAKES 12 SERVINGS

My husband's Sicilian family looked forward to eating this pasta on special occasions like Christmas and Easter. It was a specialty of his grandmother, Adele Amico, who came from Palermo.

Anellini, "little rings," are the typical pasta shape used, but they can be hard to find. Fusilli lunghi, "long fusilli," or bucatini, thick spaghetti with a hole in the center, are good substitutes. This is a perfect party dish, as it can be made in stages or completely assembled a day ahead of time, and it serves a crowd.

If you don't feel comfortable unmolding the pasta, it can be cut into squares and served directly from the pan. A 20- to 30-minute rest after baking helps the pasta to hold its shape.

SAUCE

¼ cup olive oil
1 medium onion, finely chopped
2 garlic cloves, finely chopped
¼ cup tomato paste
4 (28-ounce) cans imported Italian peeled tomatoes
Salt and freshly ground black pepper
¼ cup chopped fresh basil

FILLING

2 tablespoons olive oil
½ pound ground beef
½ pound ground pork
1 garlic clove, very finely chopped
Salt and freshly ground black pepper
1 cup fresh or frozen peas
2 tablespoons unsalted butter, softened
1 cup plain dry bread crumbs
2 pounds anellini or perciatelli
Salt
½ cup freshly grated Parmigiano-Reggiano
½ cup freshly grated Pecorino Romano
1 cup imported provolone, diced

1 Prepare the sauce: Pour the oil into a large saucepan. Add the onion and garlic. Cook over medium heat 10 minutes or until the onion and garlic are tender and golden. Stir in the tomato paste and cook 2 minutes.

2 Add the tomatoes and bring to a simmer. Add salt and pepper to taste and cook 1 hour or until the sauce is thickened, stirring occasionally. Stir in the basil.

3 Prepare the filling: Heat the oil in a large skillet over medium heat. Add the meats, garlic, and salt and pepper to taste. Cook 10 minutes, stirring to break up the lumps. When the meat is browned, add two cups of the prepared tomato sauce. Bring to a simmer and cook until thickened, about 20 minutes. Stir in the peas. Let cool slightly.

4 Smear the butter over the bottom and sides of a 13 × 9 × 2–inch baking pan. Coat the pan with the bread crumbs, patting them so that they adhere.

5 Place a rack in the center of the oven. Preheat the oven to 375°F. Bring at least 4 quarts of water to a boil in each of two large pots. Add 3 tablespoons of salt to each pot, then the pasta. Stir well. Cook over high heat, stirring frequently, until the pasta is tender but slightly underdone. Drain the pasta and return it to the pot. Toss the pasta with 3 cups of the plain tomato sauce and the grated cheeses.

6 Carefully spoon half the pasta into the prepared pan, trying not to disturb the bread crumbs. Spoon the meat filling evenly over the pasta. Scatter the cheese cubes on top. Spoon the remaining pasta over all. Flatten the contents of the pan with a spoon.

7 Have ready a cooling rack and a large tray or cutting board the size of the pan. Bake 60 to 90 minutes or until the pasta is heated through and crusty on top. Let the pasta cool in the pan on the rack 30 minutes. Slide a small knife around the edges of the pan. Protecting your hands with oven mitts, invert the pasta onto the tray or cutting board. Cut into squares and serve warm with the remaining tomato sauce.

Sophia Loren's Baked Pasta

Pasta al Forno alla Loren

MAKES 8 TO 10 SERVINGS

The actress Sophia Loren loves to cook and has even written cookbooks. Her real last name is Scicolone, the same as mine, though my name comes from my husband and his Sicilian family. Sophia is from Naples, like my grandparents, though my maiden name was Scotto. I am often asked if we are related. We are not, though I do admire Sophia's beauty and talent, both as an actress and a cook.

This is my interpretation of a baked pasta recipe I once heard her describe as a favorite dish for company. If you have prepared the dish ahead and stored it in the refrigerator, be sure to add at least a half hour to the baking time.

4 cups Bologna-Style Sauce (page 96) or other meat
    and tomato sauce
4 cups Béchamel Sauce (page 101)
Salt
1 1/2 pounds penne, ziti, or mostaccioli
1 cup freshly grated Parmigiano-Reggiano

1 Prepare the two sauces, if necessary. Then, butter a 13 × 9 × 2–inch baking pan.

2 Bring at least 4 quarts of water to a boil in a large pot. Add 2 tablespoons of salt, then the pasta. Stir well. Cook over high heat, stirring frequently, until the pasta is almost tender. Drain the pasta.

3 Place a rack in the center of the oven. Preheat the oven to 400°F. Set aside 1/4 cup of the cheese. Toss the pasta with half of the Bolognese sauce. Spread about 1/3 of the pasta in the pan. Spoon on about 1/3 of the Béchamel sauce and cheese. Dot with additional Bolognese sauce.

4 Repeat, adding two more layers, using all of the ingredients. Sprinkle with the reserved cheese.

5 Cover the pan with foil. Bake until bubbling around the edges and the blade of a thin knife inserted into the center feels hot, about 45 minutes. Uncover and bake 15 minutes more. Remove the pasta from the oven. Cool 15 minutes on a wire rack. Serve hot.

❧ Dried Pasta with Seafood

Linguine with Clam Sauce

Linguine alle Vongole

MAKES 4 TO 6 SERVINGS

Use the smallest clams you can find, such as Manila clams or littlenecks. New Zealand cockles have become widely available in my area and may have in your area, too. These work well also. Italians use dime-size vongole, *tender, hard-shell clams with beautiful zigzag markings. Either these clams are not very sandy, or they are well cleaned before they are cooked, because Italians do not bother to remove the clams from their shells before making the sauce.*

Linguine with clam sauce should not be served with grated cheese.

3 pounds small hard-shell clams or New Zealand
    cockles, well scrubbed
1/3 cup extra-virgin olive oil, plus more for drizzling
4 garlic cloves, finely chopped
2 tablespoon chopped fresh flat-leaf parsley
Pinch of crushed red pepper
1 pound linguine
Salt

1 Place the clams in a large pot with 1/4 cup water over medium-high heat. Cover the pot and cook until the liquid is boiling and the clams begin to open. Remove the opened clams with a slotted spoon and transfer to a bowl. Continue cooking the unopened clams. Discard any that refuse to open. Reserve the clam juices.

2 Working over a small bowl to catch the juices, scrape the clams from the shells, placing them in another bowl. Pour all of the liquid from the pot into the bowl with the juices. If the clams are sandy, rinse them one at a time in the clam juices. Pass

(continues)

the liquid through a fine-mesh strainer lined with cheesecloth.

3 Pour the oil into a skillet large enough to hold the cooked pasta. Add the garlic, parsley, and crushed red pepper. Cook over medium heat until the garlic is golden, about 2 minutes. Add the clam juices. Cook until the liquid is reduced by half. Stir in the clams. Cook 1 minute more.

4 Meanwhile, bring at least 4 quarts of water to a boil in a large pot. Add 2 tablespoons of salt, then the linguine, gently pushing it down until the pasta is completely covered with water. Stir well. Cook, stirring frequently, until the linguine is al dente, tender yet still firm to the bite. Drain the pasta.

5 Transfer the pasta to the skillet with the sauce and toss well over high heat. Add a drizzle of extra-virgin olive oil and toss again. Serve immediately.

Tuscan Spaghetti with Clams
Spaghetti alla Viareggina

MAKES 4 TO 6 SERVINGS

Here is another version of spaghetti with clams as it is made in Viareggio, on the coast of Tuscany. Onion, wine, and tomatoes give the sauce a more complex flavor.

3 pounds small hard-shell clams or New Zealand cockles, well scrubbed

Salt

1/3 cup olive oil

1 small onion, finely chopped

2 garlic cloves, finely chopped

Pinch of crushed red pepper

1 1/2 cups peeled, seeded, and chopped fresh tomatoes or drained and chopped canned imported Italian tomatoes

1/2 cup dry white wine

2 tablespoons chopped fresh flat-leaf parsley

1 pound spaghetti or linguine

1 Place the clams in a large pot with 1/4 cup water over medium-high heat. Cover the pot and cook until the liquid is boiling and the clams begin to open. Remove the opened clams with a slotted spoon and transfer to a bowl. Continue cooking the unopened clams. Discard any that do not open.

2 Working over a small bowl to catch the juices, scrape the clams from the shells, placing them in another bowl. Pour all of the liquid from the pot into the bowl with the juices. If the clams are sandy, rinse them one at a time in the clam juices. Pass the liquid through a fine-mesh strainer lined with cheesecloth.

3 Pour the oil into a large saucepan. Add the onion and cook, stirring frequently, over medium heat until the onion is golden, about 10 minutes. Add the garlic and crushed red pepper and cook 2 minutes more.

4 Stir in the tomatoes, wine, and strained clam juice. Simmer 20 minutes or until the sauce is reduced and thickened.

5 Bring at least 4 quarts of water to a boil in a large pot. Add 2 tablespoons of salt, then the pasta, gently pushing it down until the pasta is completely covered with water. Stir well. Cook over high heat, stirring frequently, until the pasta is al dente, tender yet still firm to the bite. Set aside some of the cooking water. Drain the pasta.

6 Stir the clams and parsley into the sauce. Add some of the water if needed. In a heated serving bowl, toss the sauce and pasta together. Serve immediately.

Linguine with Anchovies and Spicy Tomato Sauce
Linguine alla Puttanesca

MAKES 4 TO 6 SERVINGS

The usual explanation for the Italian name for this tasty sauce is that it was invented by either Roman or Neapolitan streetwalkers who had little time for cooking but wanted a hot, tasty meal.

1/4 cup olive oil

3 garlic cloves, very finely chopped

Pinch of crushed red pepper

1 (28-ounce) can imported Italian peeled tomatoes, drained and chopped

Salt

6 anchovy fillets, chopped

1/2 cup chopped Gaeta or other mild black olives

2 tablespoons chopped rinsed capers

2 tablespoons chopped fresh flat-leaf parsley

1 pound linguine or spaghetti

1 Pour the oil into a skillet large enough to hold all of the cooked pasta. Add the garlic and the crushed red pepper. Cook until the garlic is golden, about 2 minutes.

2 Add the tomatoes and a pinch of salt. Bring to a simmer and cook 15 to 20 minutes or until the sauce is thickened.

3 Add the anchovies, olives, and capers and simmer 2 to 3 minutes more. Stir in the parsley.

4 Bring at least 4 quarts of water to a boil in a large pot. Add the linguine and salt to taste. Gently push the pasta down until it is completely covered with water. Cook, stirring frequently, until the pasta is al dente, tender yet still firm to the bite. Set aside some of the cooking water. Drain the pasta.

5 Add the pasta to the skillet with the sauce. Toss 1 minute over high heat, adding a little of the cooking water if needed. Serve immediately.

Linguine with Crab and Little Tomatoes
Linguine al Granchio

MAKES 4 TO 6 SERVINGS

In Naples, tiny dried chiles add flavor to many seafood sauces, but use any hot red pepper sparingly, as it can overwhelm the delicacy of the crab meat. The same goes for the garlic, which in this recipe is used just to flavor the cooking oil, then removed before the tomatoes and crab are added.

1/3 cup olive oil

3 large garlic cloves, crushed

Pinch of crushed red pepper

2 pints cherry or grape tomatoes, halved or quartered if large

Salt and freshly ground black pepper

8 ounces fresh lump crabmeat, picked over to remove bits of shell, or chopped cooked lobster

8 fresh basil leaves, torn into bits

1 pound linguine

1 Pour the oil into a large skillet. Add the garlic cloves and red pepper and cook over medium heat, pressing down on the garlic once or twice with the back of a spoon, until the garlic is deep golden, about 4 minutes. Remove the garlic with a slotted spoon.

2 Add the tomatoes and salt and pepper to taste. Cook, stirring frequently, until the tomatoes are softened and have released their juices, about 10 minutes.

3 Gently stir in the crab and basil. Remove from the heat.

4 Bring at least 4 quarts of water to a boil in a large pot. Add 2 tablespoons of salt, then the pasta, gently pushing it down until the pasta is completely covered with water. Stir well. Cook over high heat, stirring frequently, until the linguine is al dente, tender yet still firm to the bite.

5 Drain the pasta, reserving a little of the cooking water. Add the pasta to the pan with the sauce, adding a little of the water if it seems dry. Toss over high heat 1 minute. Serve immediately.

Linguine with Mixed Seafood Sauce
Linguine ai Frutti di Mare

MAKES 4 TO 6 SERVINGS

Sweet little grape tomatoes are full of flavor like the pomodorini della collina, *little hillside tomatoes, grown around Naples. If grape tomatoes are not available, use cherry tomatoes or chopped fresh plum tomatoes instead.*

This sauce can be prepared in the brief time it takes to cook the pasta. To be sure that nothing gets overcooked, have all of the ingredients and needed equipment ready before starting. To save time and effort, you can use precut calamari (squid) rings.

1 pound cleaned calamari (squid)
6 tablespoons extra-virgin olive oil,
    plus more for drizzling
Salt
1 pound medium shrimp, shelled and deveined
2 large garlic cloves, very finely chopped
1/4 cup chopped fresh flat-leaf parsley
Pinch of crushed red pepper
1 pint grape or cherry tomatoes, halved
1 pound small hard-shell clams or mussels, cleaned and
    shelled as directed in steps 1 and 2 of Linguine
    with Clam Sauce (pages 151–152), including juice
1 pound linguine or thin spaghetti

1 Cut the calamari bodies into 1/2-inch rings and the base of the tentacles in half crosswise. Cut the shrimp into 1/2-inch pieces. Pat the seafood dry.

2 In a skillet large enough to hold all of the ingredients, heat 4 tablespoons of the oil over medium-high heat. Add the calamari and salt to taste. Cook, stirring often, until the calamari are just opaque, about 2 minutes. Scoop the calamari out with a slotted spoon and transfer to a plate. Add the shrimp and salt, to taste, to the pan. Cook, stirring, until the shrimp are just pink, about 1 minute. Transfer the shrimp to the plate with the calamari.

4 Add the remaining 2 tablespoons of the oil, and the garlic, parsley, and red pepper to the pan.

Cook, stirring, until the garlic is golden, about 2 minutes. Add the tomatoes and clam juice. Cook 5 minutes or until the tomatoes are tender. Stir in the calamari, shrimp and clams.

5 Bring at least 4 quarts of water to a boil in a large pot. Add 2 tablespoons of salt, then the pasta, gently pushing it down until the pasta is completely covered with water. Stir well. Cook over high heat, stirring frequently, until the pasta is al dente, tender yet still firm to the bite. Drain the pasta, reserving some of the cooking water.

6 Add the pasta to the pan with the seafood. Cook over high heat, tossing the pasta with the sauce, for 30 seconds. Add a little cooking water if needed. Drizzle with extra-virgin olive oil and toss again. Serve hot.

Thin Spaghetti with Bottarga
Spaghettini con Bottarga

MAKES 4 TO 6 SERVINGS

Bottarga *is the dried salted roe of mullet, tuna, or other fish. Most of it comes from Sardinia or Sicily. It is sold in a whole piece in the refrigerator case of many seafood markets and gourmet shops and shaved or grated with a vegetable peeler or cheese grater. There is also a dried, powdered type that is sold in jars. It is convenient, but I prefer the refrigerated variety. The flavor of bottarga is somewhere between that of caviar and top-quality anchovies.*

1/3 cup extra-virgin olive oil
2 garlic cloves, finely chopped
2 tablespoons chopped fresh flat-leaf parsley
Pinch of crushed red pepper
Salt
1 pound thin spaghetti
3 to 4 tablespoons shaved or grated bottarga

1 Pour the oil into a skillet large enough to hold all of the pasta. Add the garlic, parsley, and pepper. Cook over medium heat until the garlic is golden, about 2 minutes.

2 Bring at least 4 quarts of water to a boil in a large pot. Add 2 tablespoons of salt, then the pasta. Stir well, gently pushing the pasta down until it is completely covered with water. Cook over high heat, stirring frequently, until the pasta is al dente, tender yet still firm to the bite. Drain the pasta, reserving some of the cooking water.

3 Add the pasta to the skillet and toss well 1 minute over high heat Add some of the cooking water if needed. Sprinkle with the bottarga and toss again. Serve immediately.

Venetian Whole-Wheat Spaghetti in Anchovy Sauce
Bigoli in Salsa

MAKES 4 TO 6 SERVINGS

In Venice, thick whole-wheat spaghetti is handmade with a special device called a torchio that works something like a meat grinder. The dough is forced through small holes in the torchio and emerges as long strands. For this recipe, which is a Venetian classic, I use dried whole-wheat spaghetti.

¼ cup olive oil
2 medium red onions, halved and thinly sliced
½ cup dry white wine
1 (3-ounce) jar anchovy fillets
Salt
1 pound whole-wheat spaghetti
Freshly ground black pepper

1 Pour the oil into a skillet large enough to hold all of the pasta. Add the onions and cook over medium heat until the onions are golden, about 10 minutes. Add the wine and cook, stirring frequently, until the onions are soft but not browned, about 15 minutes more.

2 Drain the anchovies, reserving the oil. Add the anchovies to the skillet and stir. Cook 10 minutes more, stirring often, until the anchovies dissolve.

3 Bring at least 4 quarts of water to a boil in a large pot. Add 2 tablespoons of salt, then the pasta. Stir well, gently pushing the pasta down until it is completely covered with water. Cook over high heat, stirring frequently, until the pasta is al dente, tender yet still firm to the bite. Set aside some of the cooking water. Drain the pasta.

4 Add the pasta to the pan with the sauce, and toss together 1 minute over high heat, adding a little of the water if needed. Drizzle with some of the reserved anchovy oil if desired, and top with freshly ground pepper. Serve immediately.

Capri-Style Spaghetti
Spaghetti alla Caprese

MAKES 4 TO 6 SERVINGS

Fish and cheese are rarely combined in Italy, because the sharpness of the cheese may overwhelm the delicacy of the fish. But for every rule, there is an exception. Here is a pasta from the island of Capri that combines two types of fish with mozzarella. The flavors work because the cheese is mild and rich, yet easily dominated by the anchovies and tuna.

⅓ cup olive oil
2 cups peeled, seeded, and chopped fresh tomatoes or drained and chopped canned imported Italian tomatoes
Salt
4 anchovy fillets, chopped
1 (7-ounce) can tuna in olive oil, drained and chopped
12 Gaeta or other mild black olives, pitted and chopped
Freshly ground black pepper
1 pound spaghetti
Salt
4 ounces fresh mozzarella, diced

1 In a skillet large enough to hold the cooked pasta, heat the olive oil over medium heat. Add the tomatoes and salt to taste. Cook, stirring occasionally, 10 to 15 minutes or until the tomato juices have evaporated. Turn off the heat.

(continues)

2 Stir the chopped ingredients into the tomato sauce. Add pepper to taste.

3 Bring at least 4 quarts of water to a boil in a large pot. Add 2 tablespoons of salt, then the pasta. Stir well, gently pushing the pasta down until it is completely covered with water. Cook over high heat, stirring frequently, until the pasta is al dente, tender yet still firm to the bite. Drain the pasta, reserving some of the cooking water.

4 Add the pasta to the pan with the sauce and toss well 1 minute over medium heat. Add a little water if the pasta seems dry. Add the mozzarella and toss again. Serve immediately.

Linguine with Shrimp, Venetian Style
Linguine al Gamberi alla Veneta

MAKES 6 SERVINGS

Perhaps because their city was once a major trading port with the East, Venetian cooks have always been open to experimentation. This linguine, for example, is flavored with a slice of fresh ginger, which is not often used in Italian cooking but works wonderfully with shrimp.

1¹/₂ pounds large shrimp, shelled and deveined
¹/₂ cup olive oil
3 garlic cloves, finely chopped
¹/₄-inch thick piece fresh ginger, peeled
Pinch of crushed red pepper
Salt to taste
1 tablespoon fresh lemon juice
1 cup dry white wine
2 tablespoons chopped fresh flat-leaf parsley
1 pound linguine

1 Rinse the shrimp and pat them dry. Cut each shrimp into ¹/₂-inch pieces.

2 Pour the oil into a skillet large enough to hold all of the cooked pasta. Add the garlic, ginger,

and crushed red pepper. Cook over medium heat until the garlic is golden, about 2 minutes. Add the shrimp and a big pinch of salt. Cook, stirring, until the shrimp are cooked through, about 2 minutes. Add the lemon juice and wine and bring to a simmer. Cook 2 minutes. Stir in the parsley. Remove from the heat.

3 Bring at least 4 quarts of water to a boil in a large pot. Add 2 tablespoons of salt, then the pasta. Stir well, gently pushing the pasta down until it is completely covered with water. Cook over high heat, stirring frequently, until the pasta is al dente, tender yet still firm to the bite. Drain the pasta, reserving some of the cooking water.

4 Add the pasta to the skillet and toss over high heat 1 minute until well mixed. Add a little of the cooking water if needed. Remove the ginger. Serve immediately.

Pasta with Sardines and Fennel
Pasta con le Sarde

MAKES 6 SERVINGS

Sicilians are passionate about this dish, and every cook claims to have the best and most authentic recipe. Some add tomatoes, and some stew the sardines along with the fennel, but I prefer this method of cooking the sardines separately and layering them with the pasta and saving the tomatoes for another recipe.

Fennel grows wild all over Sicily, and the green fronds are used to make this pasta. Cultivated fennel does not have the same flavor, but the wild fennel is not widely available here. I use a combination of fresh dill and cultivated fennel to approximate the flavor of this classic Sicilian dish. Toasted bread crumbs, not cheese, are the appropriate topping.

2 medium fennel bulbs, trimmed and sliced

1 cup chopped fresh dill

$1/2$ teaspoon saffron threads

$1/2$ cup plus 1 tablespoon olive oil

$1/4$ cup plain dry bread crumbs

1 pound fresh sardines, cleaned and filleted
   (see Note)

Salt and freshly ground black pepper

1 large onion, chopped

6 anchovy fillets

$1/2$ cup dried currants

$1/2$ cup pine nuts

1 pound perciatelli or bucatini

1 Bring at least 4 quarts of water to a boil in a large pot. Add the fennel and dill and cook until tender when pierced with a fork, about 10 minutes. Scoop out the fennel and dill with a slotted spoon, reserving the cooking water. Let the fennel and dill cool, then finely chop them. In a small bowl, soak the saffron threads in 2 tablespoons of the fennel water.

2 In a small skillet, heat 1 tablespoon of the oil over medium heat and cook the bread crumbs, stirring constantly, until toasted, about 5 minutes.

3 In a large skillet, heat $1/4$ cup of the oil. Fry the sardines cut-side down first in the oil until cooked through, about 1 minute on each side. Sprinkle with salt and pepper. Transfer the sardines to a plate.

4 Wipe out the skillet. Pour the remaining $1/4$ cup of the oil into the skillet. Add the onion and cook over medium heat until golden, about 10 minutes. Add the anchovies, currants, pine nuts, saffron, and salt and pepper to taste. Cook, stirring often, 10 minutes.

5 Add the fennel and dill to the onion with one cup of the cooking water. Cook, stirring, 10 minutes.

6 Add more water to the pot to equal 4 quarts of water for cooking the pasta. Bring the water to a boil. Add 2 tablespoons of salt, then the pasta. Stir well, gently pushing the pasta down until it is completely covered with water. Cook over high heat, stirring frequently, until the pasta is al dente, tender yet still firm to the bite. Drain the pasta.

7 Transfer the pasta to the skillet with the fennel mixture and toss well. Spoon half the pasta into a warm serving bowl. Layer with half of the sardines. Add the remaining pasta. Sprinkle with the bread crumbs and top with the sardines. Serve immediately.

Note: *To clean sardines:* With a large heavy chef's knife or kitchen shears, cut off the heads. Slit the fish open along the belly and remove the innards. Pull out the backbone. Snip off the fins. Rinse and drain.

Penne with Zucchini, Swordfish, and Herbs
Penne con Zucchine e Pesce Spada

MAKES 4 TO 6 SERVINGS

This pasta is inspired by one I saw in a favorite Italian cooking magazine, A Tavola ("at the table"), in a story about cooking at a beach house. The zest and herbs make the dish light and fresh. It is perfect on a summer day—even if you're not at the beach—followed by a tomato salad.

$1/4$ cup olive oil

12 ounces swordfish, trimmed and cut into
   $1/2$-inch cubes

Salt and freshly ground black pepper

4 to 6 small zucchini, about 1 pound, cut into
   $1/2$-inch pieces

4 green onions, chopped

2 tablespoons chopped fresh rosemary

2 tablespoons chopped fresh chives

1 tablespoon chopped fresh mint

$1/2$ teaspoon dried oregano, crumbled

$1/2$ teaspoon grated lemon zest

1 pound penne

1 In a large skillet, heat 1 tablespoon oil over medium heat. Add the swordfish and cook until the fish loses its pink color, about 5 minutes. Remove the swordfish and transfer to a plate. Sprinkle with salt and pepper.

(continues)

2 Add the remaining 3 tablespoons oil to the pan and heat over medium heat. Add the zucchini, green onions, and salt to taste. Cook, stirring often, until the zucchini are just tender, about 10 minutes.

3 Return the swordfish to the pan. Stir in the herbs and lemon zest and remove from the heat.

4 Bring at least 4 quarts of water to a boil in a large pot. Add 2 tablespoons of salt, then the pasta. Stir well. Cook over high heat, stirring frequently, until the pasta is al dente, tender yet still firm to the bite. Drain the pasta, reserving some of the cooking water.

5 Add the pasta to the skillet and toss over high heat 1 minute to combine. Add some of the reserved pasta water, if needed. Serve immediately.

Christmas Eve Spaghetti with Baccala
Spaghetti con la Baccala

MAKES 6 SERVINGS

Baccala is an important part of the all-fish menu served in most southern Italian homes on Christmas Eve. This recipe was given to me by my aunt, Millie Castagliola, whose family came from Sicily. Aunt Millie makes this same sauce as a filling for a double-crust pizza.

I pound stockfish or baccala, soaked as described on page 265, cut into I-inch pieces
Salt
¼ cup olive oil
2 medium onions, thinly sliced
2 celery ribs, thinly sliced
2 garlic cloves, finely chopped
2 cups chopped canned imported Italian tomatoes with their juice
Pinch of crushed red pepper
½ cup sliced green olives
2 tablespoons capers, rinsed and drained
I pound spaghetti or linguine
Extra-virgin olive oil

I Bring about 1 quart of water to a boil in a wide saucepan. Add the fish and salt to taste. Reduce the heat to low. Simmer the fish until very tender, about 10 minutes. Remove the fish with a slotted spoon. Let cool slightly. With your fingers, remove any skin and bones. Cut the fish into bite-size pieces.

2 Pour the oil into a large saucepan. Add the onions and celery and cook over medium heat until the vegetables are golden, about 15 minutes. Stir in the garlic and cook 2 minutes more.

3 Add the tomatoes and red pepper. Cook, stirring occasionally, until the sauce is thick, 20 to 30 minutes.

4 Add the fish, olives, and capers and cook 10 minutes. Taste for salt.

5 Bring at least 4 quarts of water to a boil in a large pot. Add 2 tablespoons of salt, then the pasta. Stir well, gently pushing the pasta down until it is completely covered with water. Cook, stirring frequently, until the pasta is al dente, tender yet still firm to the bite. Drain the pasta, reserving a little of the cooking water.

6 Add the pasta to the pan with the sauce. Toss well over medium heat, adding a little of the cooking water if needed. Drizzle with a little extra–virgin olive oil and serve immediately.

Linguine with Tuna Pesto
Linguine al Tonno

MAKES 4 TO 6 SERVINGS

The uncooked sauce for this Sicilian pasta is similar to pesto, but flavored with anchovies. Just before serving, the sauce and pasta are tossed with canned tuna.

1 cup tightly packed fresh basil leaves

3/4 cup tightly packed fresh parsley leaves

1/3 cup pine nuts

2 medium garlic cloves

1 (2-ounce) can anchovy fillets, drained

1/3 cup extra-virgin olive oil

2 tablespoons fresh lemon juice

1 (7-ounce) can tuna in oil (preferably imported Italian or Spanish tuna in olive oil)

Salt

1 pound linguine

1 In a food processor fitted with the steel blade, chop the basil, parsley, pine nuts, and garlic until fine. Add the anchovy fillets, oil, and lemon juice and process until smooth.

2 Bring at least 4 quarts of water to a boil in a large pot. Meanwhile, in a large serving bowl, mash the tuna with a fork. Stir in the sauce.

3 Add 2 tablespoons of salt, then the pasta, to the boiling water. Stir well, gently pushing the pasta down until it is completely covered with water. Cook the pasta, stirring frequently, until al dente, tender yet still firm to the bite. Drain the pasta, reserving some of the cooking water.

4 Transfer the pasta to the bowl with the sauce. Add some of the cooking water and toss well. Serve immediately.

Cold Pasta with Vegetable Confetti and Seafood

Pasta Fredda con Verdure e Crostacei

MAKES 6 TO 8 SERVINGS

On one trip to Italy, the main reason I visited Argenta, a small town in Emilia-Romagna, was to dine at a fine restaurant called Il Trigabolo. The restaurant is closed now, but I still remember my delight when they served me this refreshing cold pasta, crunchy with bits of chopped vegetables and seafood. Most of the vegetables are blanched—that is, they are dropped into the boiling water, then immediately placed under cold water to stop the cooking and cool them. The cool water sets their bright color, and the vegetables keep some of their crunchy texture.

Pasta should be rinsed in cool water only in a preparation like this—when you want to stop the cooking and serve the pasta cold.

1 large firm ripe tomato, cored and diced

1/2 pound cooked small shrimp, cut into 1/4-inch pieces

1 cup chopped cooked lobster or 1/4 pound cooked crabmeat, picked over

1/4 cup snipped fresh chives

1/4 cup chopped fresh basil

1/4 cup extra-virgin olive oil, plus more for drizzling

Coarse salt and freshly ground black pepper

1 pound thin spaghetti

3/4 cup very finely chopped red bell pepper

3/4 cup very finely chopped yellow bell pepper

3/4 cup very finely chopped zucchini

2 small carrots, cut into matchstick strips

1 In a large serving bowl, combine the tomato with the shrimp, lobster, herbs, and olive oil. Season with salt and pepper.

2 Bring at least 4 quarts of water to a boil in a large pot. Add 2 tablespoons of salt, then the spaghetti. Stir well, gently pushing the pasta down until it is completely covered with water. Cook over high heat, stirring frequently. About 30 seconds before the pasta is ready, add the peppers, zucchini, and carrots. Stir well. As soon as the pasta is al dente, tender yet still firm to the bite, drain it and the vegetables into a large colander placed in the sink. The vegetables will be just slightly wilted.

3 Rinse the pasta and vegetables under cool running water. Drain well.

4 Add the pasta to the tomato and seafood mixture. Toss well. Drizzle with additional oil and toss again. Serve immediately.

🌿 Fresh Pasta

In the United States, we make pasta dishes with whatever pasta—fresh or dried—is available or preferred. In Italy, distinctions are made as to which dishes can be made with dried and which with fresh pasta.

Homemade fresh pasta can be a supreme pleasure. The directions below will help you master it for yourself.

You can also prepare most of the recipes in this section with store-bought fresh pasta. Look for a store that sells good-quality fresh pasta sheets that you can cut to the size you prefer and stuff and shape yourself.

Fresh Egg Pasta
Pasta al Uovo

MAKES ABOUT 1 POUND

Here is a basic all-purpose pasta dough that I use for fettuccine, lasagne, and ravioli. The dough can be assembled by hand, in a food processor, or in a heavy-duty mixer, and it can be rolled out on a board with a rolling pin or in a pasta rolling machine. If you have never made pasta before, read the recipe through before beginning. The most important thing is to get the balance of flour and eggs right so that the dough is neither sticky nor dry. Because the freshness and size of the eggs and the type and humidity level of the flour vary slightly, it is not possible to give exact proportions.

Making fresh pasta is as easy as making any other dough, but it does take some patience. Make it ahead of time, if you like. It keeps well at cool room temperature up to a week, or it can be refrigerated or frozen. A small amount of olive oil helps to keep the dough moist as you work.

About 2¹/₂ cups unbleached all-purpose flour

4 large eggs, beaten

1 teaspoon olive oil (optional, but a good idea, especially for stuffed pastas)

Preparing the Dough by Hand

1 Pour the flour into a mound on a countertop or large pasta board. A rough surface such as wood or plastic is better than a smooth one such as marble or granite. With a fork, make a wide hole in the center of the mound. Pour the eggs and olive oil into the hole and begin stirring with one hand, gradually incorporating some of the flour from the inside of the hole. Use your other hand to support the wall of flour surrounding the eggs, so they don't spill out.

2 When the dough forms a ball and becomes too firm to stir, in about 1 minute, sweep the remaining flour to one side. Lightly flour your hands and begin kneading. Push the dough away with the heels of your hands and pull it back toward you with your fingertips. Turn the dough as you are doing this for even kneading. Continue kneading, gradually incorporating some of the remaining flour until the ball becomes somewhat smooth, feels moist, and is only slightly sticky, about 3 minutes. Add only enough flour to create a firm ball of dough, or it may become too dry.

3 Put the dough aside for a moment and cover it with an inverted bowl. Wash and dry your hands to remove hardened scraps of dough. Scrape the kneading surface clean with a plastic or metal dough scraper or spatula to remove any hardened pieces of dough and excess flour that might later cause lumps. Throw out the scraps.

4 Lightly dust your hands with flour. Resume kneading the dough until it is smooth and elastic, moist yet not sticky, about 8 to 10 minutes. Add more flour if necessary. There should be no streaks of flour on the dough, and the color should be evenly yellow. The more the dough is kneaded, the lighter and more resilient the pasta will be, so do not skimp on kneading. Work quickly so that the dough does not dry out.

Making the Dough with a Food Processor or Heavy-Duty Mixer

1 Pour the eggs and olive oil into a food processor fitted with the steel blade, or into the bowl of a heavy-duty electric mixer fitted with the flat beater. With the machine running, begin adding the flour a tablespoon at a time. Mix until the dough forms a ball and cleans the inside of the bowl, about 1 minute. Pinch the dough. It should feel moist but not sticky and should be fairly smooth. If not, add more flour as needed.

2 Place the dough on a lightly floured surface and knead it for 1 minute, adding more flour if necessary, until it is firm, smooth without streaks of flour, and moist but not sticky.

> **Spinach Pasta:** Pasta made with fresh spinach has not only a bright green color but also a good flavor. To make fresh spinach pasta, use 3 cups flour, 3 large eggs, and 1 pound of fresh spinach, cooked, squeezed dry, and very finely chopped (about 3/4 cup cooked spinach). Combine the ingredients as for Fresh Egg Pasta at left. Makes about 1 1/4 pounds of pasta.

Letting the Dough Rest

Whether you have made it by hand or machine, cover the dough with an inverted bowl and let it rest for 30 minutes or up to 2 hours at room temperature.

Rolling Out the Dough By Hand

1 Lightly dust a countertop or large board with flour. Be sure that the surface is perfectly flat and not warped.

2 Cut the dough into 2 pieces. It may feel moister after it rests because the eggs have absorbed the flour. While you work with one piece, keep the remainder covered. With your hands, shape one piece of dough into a disk. Choose a wooden rolling pin at least 24 inches long and 1 1/2 to 2 inches wide and dust it lightly with flour. Place the pin in

the center and push it away from you toward the edge of the dough. Rotate the dough a quarter turn, center the pin on it and push it toward the edge once more. Repeat, rotating the dough and rolling it out from the center, keeping the shape round and the thickness even, until the dough reaches the desired thinness. Flip the dough over from time to time to be sure it is not sticking. If necessary, dust lightly with flour.

3 Work quickly so that the dough does not dry out. If it should tear, pinch it together or patch it with a small piece of dough from the edge. The dough is ready when it is very thin and you can easily see your hand through it when it is held up to the light. Roll out the remaining dough in the same way. Be sure to make all of the dough pieces of equal thickness. Turn the pieces often so that they do not stick. If the dough will be used to make stuffed pasta such as ravioli, it should be kept covered so that it remains pliable. Use it as soon as possible.

4 Cut the dough into the desired size and shape while it is still soft and pliable. See pasta recipes on pages 164–189 for instructions on cutting and shaping the dough.

Rolling Out the Dough with a Pasta Machine

1 Following the manufacturer's instructions, clamp the pasta machine to one end of a large countertop or sturdy table. Set the rollers at the widest opening and dust them lightly with flour.

2 Cut the dough into 4 to 6 pieces. It may feel moister after it rests because the eggs have absorbed the flour. While you work with one piece, keep the remainder covered. Flatten one piece of dough into an oval disk. Turn the handle of the pasta machine with one hand while the other guides the piece of dough through the rollers. If the dough sticks or tears, dust it lightly with flour.

(continues)

3 Remove the dough from the machine and fold it lengthwise into thirds. Pass the dough through the machine again, flouring it if necessary.

4 Close the rollers slightly by moving the dial to the next notch. Pass the dough through the rollers. As the dough emerges, lift it straight out so that it stays flat without wrinkling. Do not fold it.

5 Continue to pass the dough through the machine, moving the dial up one notch each time until the desired thinness is reached. This will vary according to the machine, but I usually stop at the second-to-last setting for fettuccine and flat pasta and the last notch for stuffed pasta. The pasta should be thin enough that you can see your hand through it without tearing. Don't be tempted to re-roll scraps of dough. Hardened edges can stick in the machine and tear the pasta.

6 Lay the strip of dough on a lightly floured kitchen towel. Roll out the remaining dough in the same way. Be sure to make all of the strips of equal thickness. Turn the pieces often so that they do not stick. If the dough will be used to make stuffed pasta such as ravioli, it should be kept covered so that it remains pliable. Use it as soon as possible.

7 Cut the dough into the desired size and shape while it is still soft and pliable. See pasta recipes on pages 164–189 for instructions on cutting and shaping the dough.

Making Pasta Noodles

Lasagne, papardelle, fettuccine, tagliatelle, and *tagliarini* are all flat ribbons of pasta. Their use depends on the type of sauce you are making and regional preferences. Generally, the lighter the sauce, the narrower the pasta.

1 Make the pasta as described on pages 160–162.

2 Let the dough dry until it is slightly leathery but still pliable, about 20 minutes.

3 If using your pasta machine's cutting attachment, follow the manufacturer's instructions. Turn the crank with one hand, passing the sheet of dough through the cutters. As the dough emerges, lift it straight out with your other hand so that the strands do not collect on the countertop and become wrinkled.

4 If working by hand, first cut the dough into 5-inch lengths for pappardelle and 10-inch lengths for the other pastas. Loosely roll up a strip of dough. With a large heavy chef's knife, cut the rolled up pasta crosswise into strips 3 inches wide for lasagne, 3/4 inches wide for papardelle, 1/3 inch wide for fettuccine, 1/4 inch for tagliatelle, and 1/8 inch for tagliarini. Separate the strips and place them flat on a floured surface to dry about 1 hour at room temperature.

Storing Fresh Egg Pasta

Fresh pasta may be used immediately, frozen, or allowed to dry completely. To freeze the pasta, place the strips on baking sheets lightly dusted with flour so that they do not touch. Place the baking sheets in the freezer. When the pasta is firm, gently gather it into a bundle and wrap it well in layers of plastic wrap or foil. Store in the freezer up to one month.

To dry, place the pasta strips, not touching, on baking sheets. Cover each sheet with lightweight cloth kitchen towels. Do not cover them with plastic or foil or they will turn moldy. Leave the strips at room temperature for several days until the pieces are completely dry and snap when broken. Store in plastic bags in the pantry until ready to use.

Tips For Making Fresh Pasta

It takes practice to get the knack of making pasta, but once you have the feel for it, it is not difficult. Make pasta when you have plenty of time, and don't be disappointed if the first batch doesn't come out right.

- If possible, make pasta on a dry day. However, avoid making fresh pasta near a hot stove or radiator or near a fan. The heat and breeze may dry the pasta out too quickly.
- A pasta machine is very helpful if you enjoy making fresh pasta and want to do it frequently. The most familiar machine is hand-cranked. It kneads, stretches, and cuts pasta dough perfectly. Most machines come with a variety of cutting attachments, but all you need are a fettuccine and tagliarini cutter. Buy a wide machine that feels heavy for its size. Smaller machines are flimsy and hard to handle. If you have a heavy-duty mixer, you may be able to purchase a pasta attachment for the mixer. I have one for my heavy-duty Kitchen Aid mixer that works very well.

- Avoid the type of pasta maker that combines all the ingredients and extrudes them through a die (metal cutting mold). It makes poor-quality pasta.
- Flour quality varies according to the weather and how, where, and how long it has been stored. Be prepared to adjust the amount of flour needed.
- Eggs vary in moisture content and lose moisture through their shells as they age. If they have been stored for a while, they may be slightly drier than fresh eggs. I have used large eggs for all of the recipes in this book. If you use another size egg for making pasta, you may need to adjust the amount of flour accordingly.
- When saucing fresh pasta, use just enough sauce to coat the pasta without leaving a pool of sauce in the bottom of the bowl. I have given quantities with each recipe, but consider these suggestions. The amount really depends on the type of sauce, how thick it is, and other factors.

Fettuccine with Butter and Parmigiano

Fettuccine al Burro

MAKES 4 TO 6 SERVINGS

Even the pickiest children love fresh egg pasta tossed with butter and cheese. Keep in mind that fresh pasta cooks quickly; it will get mushy fast if you walk away.

6 tablespoons unsalted butter
I pound fresh fettuccine
Salt
I cup freshly grated Parmigiano-Reggiano
Freshly ground black pepper

1 Melt the butter in a small saucepan and keep warm.

2 Bring at least 4 quarts of water to a boil. Add the pasta and salt to taste. Stir well. Cook over high heat, stirring frequently, until the pasta is al dente, tender yet firm to the bite. Drain the pasta, reserving some of the cooking water.

3 Pour the pasta into a warm serving bowl. Add half the cheese and toss well. Add the butter and a little of the cooking water if the pasta seems dry. Sprinkle with the remaining cheese and toss again. Sprinkle with freshly ground pepper if desired.

Fettuccine with Butter and Cheese

Fettuccine all'Alfredo

MAKES 6 TO 8 SERVINGS

In the early 1910s Alfredo Di Lelio, whose family owned a trattoria in Rome, created this rich pasta dish of fresh fettuccine, butter, and Parmigiano. The dish became so popular that Alfredo was soon running a bigger, fancier restaurant under his own name, where he would prepare the pasta at tableside, serving it up to diners with great fanfare and a gold fork and spoon. Silent movie stars Douglas Fairbanks, Sr., and his wife, Mary Pickford, were said to have been among the restaurant's many famous patrons.

This recipe was given to me by Russell Bellanca, owner of the Alfredo The Original of Rome Restaurants in New York City and Epcot Center, Florida. According to Russell, this is the recipe as developed by Alfredo Di Lelio. His son, Alfredo II, gave it to Russell's dad, who was a business partner many years ago. At Alfredo The Original, the pasta is handmade from a mix of three different flours and organic egg yolks, though I use my own homemade pasta.

Serve the pasta in small portions. It is very rich.

I¹/₂ sticks (³/₄ cup) unsalted butter, at room temperature for at least 30 minutes
I cup freshly grated Parmigiano-Reggiano, plus more for serving (optional)
I pound fresh fettuccine
Salt

1 In a large bowl with an electric mixer, beat the butter with the cheese until it forms a smooth cream, about 2 minutes.

2 Bring at least 4 quarts of water to a boil. Add the pasta and salt to taste. Stir well. Cook over high heat, stirring frequently, until the pasta is al dente, tender yet still firm to the bite. Drain the pasta, reserving a little of the cooking water. Toss the pasta with the butter and cheese and a few tablespoons of the cooking water.

3 Serve immediately with additional cheese, if desired.

"Triple-Butter" Fettuccine
Fettuccine al Triplo Burro

MAKES 4 TO 6 SERVINGS

Cream, butter, and cheese are the three "butters" of this Roman pasta. It is quite possibly a variation of Fettucine with Butter and Cheese (above) , which is sometimes called fettuccine al doppio burro, *or "double-butter fettuccine." Some cooks use Gruyere instead of the Parmigiano, but I like it this way better.*

1 pound fresh fettuccine
Salt
1 stick (¹/2 cup) unsalted butter
1 cup heavy cream
³/4 cup freshly grated Parmigiano-Reggiano
Freshly ground black pepper

1 Bring at least 4 quarts of water to a boil. Add 2 tablespoons of salt and the pasta. Stir well. Cook over high heat, stirring frequently, until the pasta is al dente, tender yet still firm to the bite. Drain the pasta, reserving some of the cooking water.

2 Meanwhile, in a skillet large enough to hold all of the pasta, melt the butter over medium-low heat. Add the pasta, cream, ¹/2 cup of the cheese, and a pinch of salt, tossing until well coated. Add some of the cooking water if the pasta seems dry. Sprinkle with pepper.

3 Serve immediately with the remaining cheese.

Fettuccine with Spring Vegetables
Fettuccine Primavera

MAKES 4 TO 6 SERVINGS

This recipe was reportedly invented at Le Cirque Restaurant in New York. Though it has never been on the menu there, regular patrons know that they can request it at any time. Other vegetables can be used, such as peppers, green beans, or zucchini, so feel free to improvise according to what you have on hand.

4 tablespoons unsalted butter
¹/4 cup chopped shallots
1 cup chopped carrots
1 cup broccoli florets, cut into bite-size pieces
4 asparagus, trimmed and cut into bite-size pieces
¹/2 cup fresh or frozen peas
1 cup heavy or whipping cream
Salt and freshly ground black pepper
1 pound fresh fettuccine
³/4 cup freshly grated Parmigiano-Reggiano
10 basil leaves, stacked and cut into thin ribbons

1 In a skillet large enough to hold the fettuccine, melt the butter over medium heat. Add the shallots and carrots and cook, stirring occasionally, five minutes or until softened.

2 Bring at least 4 quarts of water to a boil in a large pot. Add salt to taste. Add the broccoli and asparagus and cook for 1 minute. With a slotted spoon, scoop out the vegetables and drain them well, leaving the water boiling in the pot.

3 Put the broccoli and asparagus in the skillet along with the peas and cream. Bring to a simmer. Season to taste with salt and pepper. Remove from the heat.

4 Put the fettuccine into the boiling water and cook, stirring frequently, until the pasta is al dente, tender yet still firm to the bite. Drain the fettuccine and add it to the skillet. Add the cheese and toss well. Sprinkle with basil and serve immediately.

Fettuccine with Gorgonzola Cream

Fettuccine con Crema di Gorgonzola

MAKES 4 TO 6 SERVINGS

Of all the blue cheeses produced around the world, gorgonzola is my favorite. To make it, cow's milk is innoculated with penicillin spores, which gives the cheese its color and distinct flavor. It is not too sharp and melts beautifully, so it is ideal for sauces. Use a mild type of gorgonzola for this recipe.

2 tablespoons unsalted butter
8 ounces gorgonzola dolce, rind removed
1 cup heavy or whipping cream
Salt
1 pound fresh fettuccine
Freshly ground black pepper
1/2 cup freshly grated Parmigiano-Reggiano

1 In a medium saucepan, melt the butter and add the gorgonzola. Stir over low heat until the cheese is melted. Stir in the cream. Bring the sauce to a simmer and cook 5 minutes or until the sauce is slightly thickened.

2 Bring at least 4 quarts of water to a boil. Add the pasta and salt to taste. Stir well. Cook over high heat, stirring frequently, until the pasta is al dente, tender yet still firm to the bite. Drain the pasta, reserving some of the cooking water.

3 In a large warm serving bowl, toss the pasta with the sauce. Add the Parmigiano and toss again. Add a little of the cooking water, if needed, to thin the pasta. Serve immediately.

Tagliarini with Pesto, Genoa Style

Tagliarini al Pesto

MAKES 4 TO 6 SERVINGS

In Liguria in the springtime, thin strands of fresh pasta are served with pesto tossed with slender green beans and sliced new potatoes. The vegetables carry the flavor of the pesto, cut some of the richness, and add texture.

The word pesto *means pounded, and there are several other types of pesto sauces, though this is the best known.*

1 cup packed fresh basil leaves
1/2 cup packed fresh flat-leaf parsley
1/4 cup pine nuts
1 garlic clove
Salt and freshly ground black pepper to taste
1/3 cup extra-virgin olive oil
1 cup freshly grated Parmigiano-Reggiano
     or Pecorino Romano
4 medium waxy potatoes, peeled and thinly sliced
8 ounces thin green beans, cut into 1-inch lengths
1 pound fresh tagliarini or fettuccine
2 tablespoons unsalted butter, at room temperature

1 In a food processor or blender, combine the basil, parsley, pine nuts, garlic, and a pinch of salt. Chop fine. With the machine running, add the oil in a steady stream and process until smooth. Stir in the cheese.

2 Bring at least 4 quarts of water to a boil. Add the potatoes and green beans. Cook just until tender, about 8 minutes. Scoop out the vegetables with a slotted spoon. Place them in a warmed serving bowl. Cover and keep warm.

3 Add the pasta to the boiling water and stir well. Cook over high heat, stirring frequently, until the pasta is al dente, tender yet still firm to the bite. Drain the pasta, reserving some of the cooking water.

4 Add the pasta, pesto, and butter to the serving bowl with the vegetables. Toss very well, adding a little of the cooking water if the pasta seems dry. Serve immediately.

Fettuccine with Artichokes
Fettuccine con Carciofi

MAKES 4 TO 6 SERVINGS

Carts loaded with artichokes appear at the outdoor markets all over Rome in springtime. Their long stems and leaves are still attached, which helps to keep them from drying out. Roman cooks know that the stems are as tasty as the artichoke hearts. They only need peeling and can be cooked right alongside the artichokes or chopped for a stuffing.

3 medium artichokes
1/4 cup olive oil
I small onion, finely chopped
1/4 cup chopped fresh flat-leaf parsley
I garlic clove, finely chopped
Salt and freshly ground black pepper to taste
1/2 cup dry white wine
I pound fresh fettuccine
Extra-virgin olive oil

I Cut off the top 1/2 to 3/4 inch of the artichokes with a large, sharp knife. Rinse artichokes under cold water, spreading the leaves open. Avoid the little thorns on the remaining tips of the leaves. Bend back and snap off all of the dark green leaves until you reach the pale yellowish cone of tender leaves at the center of the artichoke. Peel the tough outer skin around the base and stems. Leave stems attached to the base; trim the ends of stems. Cut artichokes in half lengthwise and scoop out the fuzzy chokes with a spoon. Cut artichokes into thin lengthwise slices.

2 Pour oil into a saucepan large enough to hold the cooked pasta. Add onion, parsley, and garlic and cook over medium heat until the onion is golden, about 15 minutes.

3 Add artichoke slices, wine, and salt and pepper to taste. Cover and cook until artichokes are tender when pierced with a fork, about 10 minutes.

4 Bring at least 4 quarts of water to a boil. Add 2 tablespoons of salt, then the pasta. Stir well. Cook over high heat, stirring frequently, until the pasta is al dente, tender yet still firm to the bite. Drain the pasta, reserving some of the cooking water. Add the pasta to the pan with the artichokes.

5 Add a drizzle of extra-virgin olive oil and a little of the reserved cooking water if the pasta seems dry. Toss well. Serve immediately.

Fettuccine with Tomato Fillets
Fettuccine al Filetto di Pomodoro

MAKES 4 TO 6 SERVINGS

Strips of ripe peeled tomatoes cooked until barely tender are wonderful with fresh fettuccine. The tomatoes retain all of their sweet fresh flavor in this mild sauce.

4 tablespoons unsalted butter
1/4 cup finely chopped onion
I pound plum tomatoes, peeled and seeded and cut into 1/2-inch strips
6 fresh basil leaves
Salt to taste
I pound fresh fettuccine
Freshly grated Parmigiano-Reggiano

I In a large skillet, heat 3 tablespoons of the butter over medium-low heat until melted. Add the onion and cook until golden, about 10 minutes.

2 Stir in the tomato fillets, basil leaves, and a couple of pinches of salt. Cook until the tomatoes are tender, about 5 to 10 minutes.

3 Bring at least 4 quarts of water to a boil. Add 2 tablespoons of salt, then the pasta. Stir well. Cook over high heat, stirring frequently, until the pasta is al dente, tender yet still firm to the bite. Drain the pasta, reserving some of the cooking water.

4 Add the fettuccine to the skillet along with the remaining 1 tablespoon of butter. Toss well. Add a little of the cooking water if the pasta seems dry. Serve immediately with the cheese.

Fettuccine with a Thousand Herbs

Fettuccine alle Mille Erbe

MAKES 4 TO 6 SERVINGS

This is one of my favorite summer pastas, one that I love to make when the herbs in my garden are in full bloom and the tomatoes are perfectly ripe. The recipe comes from the Locanda dell'Amorosa, a restaurant and inn located in Sinalunga in Tuscany. There they used stracci, *meaning "raggedy," a shape of pasta similar to pappardelle cut with a fluted pastry wheel so that the edges are jagged. Fettuccine are a good substitute.*

There is a lot of chopping involved in making this sauce, but it can be done well in advance of serving. Do not substitute dried herbs for the fresh. Their flavor would be too aggressive in this pasta. The more varieties of herbs that you use, the more complex the flavor will be, but even if you don't use all of the varieties listed, it will still be delicious.

¹/4 cup chopped Italian parsley
¹/4 cup chopped fresh basil
¹/4 cup chopped fresh tarragon
2 tablespoons chopped fresh mint
2 tablespoons chopped fresh marjoram
2 tablespoons chopped fresh thyme
8 fresh sage leaves, finely chopped
1 sprig fresh rosemary, finely chopped
¹/3 cup extra-virgin olive oil
Salt and freshly ground black pepper
1 pound fresh fettuccine
¹/2 cup freshly grated Pecorino Romano
2 medium ripe tomatoes, peeled, seeded, and chopped

1 In a bowl large enough to contain all of the ingredients, combine the herbs, olive oil, and salt and pepper to taste. Set aside.

2 Bring at least 4 quarts of water to a boil. Add 2 tablespoons of salt, then the pasta Stir well. Cook over high heat, stirring frequently, until the pasta is al dente, tender yet still firm to the bite. Drain the pasta, reserving some of the cooking water.

3 Add the pasta to the bowl with the herb mixture and toss well. Add the cheese and toss again. Scatter the tomatoes over the pasta and serve immediately.

Fettuccine with Sausage and Cream

Fettuccine con Salsiccia

MAKES 4 TO 6 SERVINGS

Roasted red peppers, bits of sausage, and green peas get tangled among the creamy fettuccine for great flavor in every bite in this recipe from Emilia-Romagna. Try to find meaty pork sausages without a lot of spices for this recipe.

8 ounces plain Italian pork sausages, casings removed
1 cup heavy or whipping cream
¹/2 cup diced drained roasted red peppers
¹/2 cup fresh or frozen tiny peas
1 tablespoon chopped fresh flat-leaf parsley
Salt and freshly ground black pepper
1 pound fresh fettuccine
¹/2 cup freshly grated Parmigiano-Reggiano

1 Heat a large skillet over medium heat. Add the sausage and cook, stirring often to break up any lumps, until no longer pink, about 5 minutes. Remove the meat to a cutting board, let cool a little, then chop finely.

2 Wipe out the skillet. Pour the cream and the chopped sausage into the pan and bring it to a simmer. Stir in the roasted peppers, peas, parsley, and salt and pepper to taste. Cook 3 minutes or until the peas are tender. Turn off the heat.

3 Bring at least 4 quarts of water to a boil. Add 2 tablespoons of salt, then the pasta. Stir well. Cook over high heat, stirring frequently, until the pasta is al dente, tender yet still firm to the bite. Drain the pasta, reserving some of the cooking water.

4 Toss the pasta in the pan with the sauce. Add the cheese and toss again. Stir in a little of the cooking water, if necessary. Serve immediately.

Green and White Pasta with Sausage and Cream
Paglia e Fieno

MAKES 4 TO 6 SERVINGS

Paglia e Fieno literally translates as "straw and hay," the whimsical name in Emilia-Romagna for this dish of thin green and white noodles cooked together. They are typically dressed with a creamy sausage sauce.

2 tablespoons unsalted butter
8 ounces plain Italian pork sausage, casings removed and chopped fine
I cup heavy cream
1/2 cup fresh or frozen tiny peas
Salt
1/2 pound fresh egg tagliarini
1/2 pound fresh spinach tagliarini
Freshly ground black pepper
1/2 cup freshly grated Parmigiano-Reggiano

1 In a skillet large enough to hold the cooked pasta, melt the butter over medium heat. Add the sausage meat and cook, stirring frequently, just until the meat is no longer pink, about 5 minutes. Do not brown.

2 Stir in the cream and peas and bring to a simmer. Cook 5 minutes or until the cream is slightly thickened. Remove from the heat.

3 Bring at least 4 quarts of water to a boil. Add 2 tablespoons of salt, then the pasta. Stir well. Cook over high heat, stirring frequently, until the pasta is al dente, tender yet still firm to the bite. Drain the pasta, reserving some of the cooking water.

4 Stir the pasta into the sausage mixture. Add a generous grind of black pepper and the cheese and toss thoroughly. Serve immediately.

Fettuccine with Leeks and Fontina
Fettuccine con Porri e Fontina

MAKES 4 TO 6 SERVINGS

The finest fontina cheese comes from the Valle d'Aosta in northwestern Italy. It has a creamy texture and an earthy flavor reminiscent of truffles. It is a perfect eating cheese, and it melts well.

4 medium leeks
1/2 cup water
2 tablespoons unsalted butter
Salt
3/4 cup heavy cream
4 ounces sliced imported Italian prosciutto, cut crosswise into thin strips
Freshly ground black pepper
I pound fresh fettuccine
I cup grated Fontina Valle d'Aosta or Asiago

1 Trim away the green tops and root ends of the leeks. Cut them in half lengthwise and rinse well under cold running water, getting any grit out from between the layers. Drain the leeks and cut them into thin crosswise slices. There should be about 3 1/2 cups of sliced leeks.

2 In a skillet large enough to hold the pasta, combine the leeks, water, butter, and salt to taste. Bring the water to a simmer and cook over low heat until the leeks are tender and slightly translucent and most of the liquid has evaporated, about 30 minutes.

3 Add the cream and simmer 2 minutes more or until slightly thickened. Stir in the prosciutto and some pepper. Remove the sauce from the heat.

4 Bring at least 4 quarts of water to a boil. Add 2 tablespoons of salt, then the pasta. Stir well. Cook over high heat, stirring frequently, until the pasta is al dente, tender yet still firm to the bite. Drain the pasta, reserving some of the cooking water.

5 Add the pasta to the skillet with the sauce and toss well. Add a little cooking water if the pasta seems dry. Add the fontina, toss again, and serve.

Fettuccine with Mushrooms and Prosciutto

Fettuccine con Funghi e Prosciutto

MAKES 4 TO 6 SERVINGS

Prosciutto is normally sliced paper-thin, but when adding it to a cooked dish, I often prefer to have the meat cut into a single thick slice, which I then cut into narrow strips. It holds its shape better and doesn't overcook when exposed to heat.

4 tablespoons unsalted butter

1 package (10 ounces) mushrooms, thinly sliced

1 cup frozen peas, partly thawed

Salt and freshly ground black pepper

4 ounces imported Italian prosciutto, in one slice about 1/4 inch thick, cut crosswise into thin strips

1 pound fresh fettuccine

1/2 cup heavy cream

1/2 cup freshly grated Parmigiano-Reggiano

1 In a skillet large enough to hold all of the ingredients, melt the butter over medium heat. Add the mushrooms and cook, stirring occasionally, until the mushroom juices evaporate and the mushrooms begin to brown, about 10 minutes.

2 Stir in the peas. Sprinkle with salt and pepper and cook 2 minutes. Stir in the prosciutto and turn off the heat. Cover to keep warm.

3 Bring at least 4 quarts of water to a boil. Add 2 tablespoons of salt, then the pasta. Stir well. Cook over high heat, stirring frequently, until the pasta is al dente, tender yet still firm to the bite. Drain the pasta, reserving some of the cooking water.

4 Transfer the pasta to the skillet with the vegetables and prosciutto. Turn the heat to high. Add the cream and cheese and toss again. Add some of the cooking water if the pasta seems dry. Serve immediately.

Summer Tagliatelle

Tagliatelle Estiva

MAKES 4 TO 6 SERVINGS

Everything about this pasta is sweet and fresh, from the disks of small, fresh zucchini, to the sunny ripe flavor of the tomatoes, to the creamy mild flavor of the ricotta salata cheese. This pressed, firm, dry form of ricotta is used both as a table cheese and for grating. Substitute a mild pecorino or Parmigiano-Reggiano if you cannot find this kind of ricotta.

1 small onion, chopped

1/4 cup olive oil

3 very small zucchini, cut into 1/4-inch disks

Salt

2 cups grape tomatoes, halved lengthwise

1 cup torn basil leaves

1 pound fresh spinach fettuccine

1/2 cup grated ricotta salata

1 In a large skillet, cook the onion in the oil over medium heat 5 minutes. Add the zucchini and salt to taste. Cook 5 minutes or until softened. Stir in the tomatoes and cook 5 minutes more or until the zucchini are tender. Stir in half of the basil and turn off the heat.

2 Meanwhile, bring at least 4 quarts of water to a boil. Add 2 tablespoons of salt, then the pasta. Stir well. Cook, stirring often, until the pasta is al dente, tender yet still firm to the bite.

3 Drain the pasta and toss it with the sauce. Add the cheese and remaining 1/2 cup of the basil and toss again. Serve immediately.

Fettuccine with Mushroom and Anchovy Sauce

Fettuccine al Funghi

MAKES 4 TO 6 SERVINGS

Even those who don't ordinarily enjoy anchovies will appreciate the flavor boost they give to this sauce. Their presence isn't obvious; the anchovies melt into the sauce.

2 large garlic cloves, finely chopped

1/3 cup olive oil

12 ounces white or brown-white mushrooms, very thinly sliced

Salt and freshly ground black pepper

1/2 cup dry white wine

6 anchovy fillets, chopped

2 large fresh tomatoes, peeled, seeded, and chopped, or 1 1/2 cups chopped canned imported Italian tomatoes, with their juice

1 pound fresh fettuccine

1/4 cup chopped fresh flat-leaf parsley

2 tablespoons unsalted butter

1 In a skillet large enough to hold all of the pasta, cook the garlic in the oil over medium heat for 1 minute.

2 Add the mushrooms and cook, stirring often, until the liquid evaporates and the mushrooms begin to brown, about 10 minutes. Stir in the wine and bring to a simmer.

3 Add the anchovies and tomatoes. Reduce the heat to low and cook 10 minutes.

4 Bring at least 4 quarts of water to a boil. Add 2 tablespoons of salt, then the pasta. Stir well. Cook over high heat, stirring frequently, until the pasta is al dente, tender yet still firm to the bite. Drain the pasta, reserving some of the cooking water.

5 Transfer the pasta to the skillet with the sauce and toss well with the parsley. Add the butter and toss again, adding a little of the cooking water if needed. Serve immediately.

Fettuccine with Scallops

Fettuccine con Canestrelli

MAKES 4 TO 6 SERVINGS

I usually make this pasta with large sea scallops. They are plump and sweet and available all year round. Smaller bay scallops, available primarily in the northeast in the summer time, are excellent too. Do not confuse them with the tasteless calico scallops that come from warm waters. They are sometimes passed off as bay scallops, though they are generally much smaller and lacking in flavor. Bay scallops are about a half-inch in diameter, with a creamy white color, while the calicos are about a quarter of an inch in size and very white.

4 large garlic cloves, finely chopped

1/4 cup olive oil

1 pound sea scallops, cut into 1/2-inch pieces, or bay scallops, left whole

Pinch of crushed red pepper

Salt

1 large ripe tomato, seeded and diced

2 cups fresh basil leaves, torn into 2 or 3 pieces

1 pound fresh fettuccine

1 In a skillet large enough to hold all the pasta, cook the garlic in the oil over medium heat until the garlic is lightly golden, about 2 minutes. Stir in the scallops, pepper, and salt to taste. Cook just until the scallops are opaque, about 1 minute.

2 Stir in the tomato and basil. Cook 1 minute until the basil is slightly wilted. Remove the skillet from the heat.

3 Bring at least 4 quarts of water to a boil. Add 2 tablespoons of salt, then the pasta. Stir well. Cook over high heat, stirring frequently, until the pasta is al dente, tender yet still firm to the bite. Drain the pasta, reserving some of the cooking water.

4 Add the pasta to the skillet. Toss well, adding some of the cooking water if needed. Serve immediately.

Tagliarini with Shrimp and Caviar
Tagliarini al Gamberi e Caviale

MAKES 4 TO 6 SERVINGS

Coral-colored salmon caviar is a delicious counter-point to the sweetness of the shrimp and creamy sauce on this pasta. I came up with this recipe several years ago for an Italian New Year's Eve feast for the Washington Post.

12 ounces medium shrimp, peeled and deveined, cut into 1/2-inch pieces

1 tablespoon unsalted butter

2 tablespoons vodka or gin

1 cup heavy cream

Salt and freshly ground white pepper

2 tablespoons very finely chopped green onion

1/2 teaspoon fresh lemon zest

1 pound fresh tagliarini

3 ounces salmon caviar

1 In a skillet large enough to hold all of the pasta, melt the butter over medium heat. Add the shrimp and cook, stirring, until pink and almost cooked through, about 2 minutes. With a slotted spoon, remove the shrimp to a plate.

2 Add the vodka to the skillet. Cook, stirring, until the liquid evaporates, about 1 minute. Add the cream and bring to a simmer. Cook until the cream thickens slightly, about one minute more. Stir in the shrimp and a pinch of salt and pepper. Add the green onion and lemon zest. Remove from the heat.

3 Bring at least 4 quarts of water to a boil. Add 2 tablespoons of salt, then the pasta. Cook, stirring frequently, until the pasta is al dente, tender yet still firm to the bite. Drain the pasta, reserving a little of the cooking water.

4 Pour the pasta into the skillet with the sauce and toss well over medium heat. Add a little of the cooking water if the pasta seems dry. Divide the pasta among the plates. Top each portion with a spoonful of caviar and serve immediately.

Crisp Pasta with Chickpeas, Puglia Style
Ceci e Tria

MAKES 4 SERVINGS

Short strips of fresh pasta are sometimes called tria *in Puglia and elsewhere in southern Italy. In the tenth century, the Norman ruler of Sicily, Roger II, had an Arabic geographer prepare a survey of his kingdom. The geographer, al-Idrisi, wrote that he saw people making food from flour in the form of threads that they called by the Arabic word for string,* itriyah. *The shortened form,* tria, *is still used.*

Tria are about as wide as fettuccine, but they are cut into 3-inch lengths. The pasta in this recipe is given an unusual treatment: Half is boiled in the normal way, but the other half is fried until it becomes crisp, like the noodles you find in Chinese restaurants. The two are combined in a tasty chickpea sauce. This is a traditional recipe from the southern part of Puglia, near Lecce. It is unlike any other pasta recipe I have tried in Italy.

3 tablespoons plus 1/2 cup olive oil

1 small onion, chopped

1 celery rib, chopped

1 garlic clove, finely chopped

1 1/2 cups cooked or canned chickpeas, drained

1 cup peeled, seeded, and chopped tomato

2 tablespoons finely chopped fresh flat-leaf parsley

2 cups water

Salt and freshly ground black pepper

12 ounces fresh fettuccine, cut into 3-inch lengths

1 In a large saucepan combine the 3 tablespoons olive oil and the onion, celery, and garlic. Cook over medium heat until softened, about 5 minutes. Add the chickpeas, tomato, parsley, and water. Season to taste with salt and pepper. Bring to a simmer and cook 30 minutes.

2 Set out a tray covered with paper towels. In a large skillet, heat the remaining 1/2 cup oil over medium heat. Add one fourth of the pasta and cook, stirring, until it blisters and begins to brown lightly, about 4 minutes. Remove the pasta with a slotted spoon and drain it on the tray. Repeat with another quarter of the pasta.

3 Bring at least 4 quarts of water to a boil. Add 2 tablespoons of salt, then the rest of the pasta. Stir well. Cook over high heat, stirring frequently, until the pasta is al dente, tender yet still firm to the bite. Drain the pasta, reserving some of the cooking water.

4 Stir the boiled pasta into the simmering sauce. Stir in some of the cooking water if the pasta seems dry. It should resemble a thick soup.

5 Add the fried pasta to the pan and stir. Serve immediately.

Tagliarini with Abruzzese Chocolate Ragù
Pasta Abruzzese al Cioccolato Amaro

MAKES 4 TO 6 SERVINGS

I adapted this recipe from one that my friend Al Bassano told me he had gotten from an Italian language website. I was intrigued because I had never seen or tasted anything like it before. I couldn't wait to try it, and I was not disappointed. A small amount of chocolate and cinnamon adds a subtle richness to the sauce.

The original recipe called for serving the ragù with chitarrina, *a typically Abruzzese-style egg pasta made on a device known as a* chitarra, *or "guitar." The guitar in this case is a simple wooden frame strung with a row of guitar strings. A sheet of fresh pasta dough is laid across the strings and a rolling pin is rolled over the dough. The taut strings cut the dough into square spaghetti-like strands. Tagliarini are a good substitute for the chitarrina.*

1 medium onion, finely chopped
1/4 cup olive oil
8 ounces ground pork
Salt and freshly ground black pepper
1/2 cup dry red wine
1 cup tomato puree
1/4 cup tomato paste
1 cup water
1 tablespoon chopped bittersweet chocolate
1/2 teaspoon sugar
Pinch of ground cinnamon
1 pound fresh tagliarini

1 In a medium saucepan, cook the onion in the oil over medium heat until the onion is tender and golden, about 10 minutes. Add the pork and cook, crumbling the meat with the back of a spoon, until lightly browned. Season with salt and pepper to taste.

2 Add the wine and bring to a simmer. Cook until most of the wine has evaporated.

3 Stir in the tomato puree, tomato paste, and water. Turn the heat to low and cook 1 hour, stirring occasionally, until the sauce is thick.

4 Stir in the chocolate, sugar, and cinnamon until the chocolate is melted. Taste for seasoning.

5 Bring at least 4 quarts of water to a boil. Add 2 tablespoons of salt, then the pasta. Stir well. Cook over high heat, stirring frequently, until the pasta is al dente, tender yet still firm to the bite. Drain the pasta, reserving some of the cooking water.

6 In a large warm serving bowl, toss the pasta with the sauce. Add a little of the reserved cooking water if needed. Serve immediately.

❧ Lasagne

Bologna-Style Lasagne
Lasagne Bolognese

MAKES 8 TO 10 SERVINGS

This lasagne from Bologna in northern Italy is alto-gether different from the southern Italian version that follows this recipe, though both are classics. The Bolognese verison is made with green-tinted spinach lasagne rather than egg lasagne, and the only cheese used is Parmigiano-Reggiano, while the southern version has mozzarella, ricotta, and Pecorino Romano. Creamy white béchamel sauce is a standard ingredi-ent in the northern variety, while the southern ver-sion contains much more meat. Try them both—they're equally delicious.

3 to 4 cups Bologna-Style Ragù (page 96)
3 cups Béchamel Sauce (page 101)
I pound fresh spinach lasagne
Salt
1 1/2 cups freshly grated Parmigiano-Reggiano
2 tablespoons unsalted butter

I Prepare the two sauces. Bring at least 4 quarts of water to a boil. Have ready a large bowl of cold water. Add to the boiling water half the lasagne and 2 tablespoons of salt. Cook until the pasta is tender but slightly underdone. Remove the pasta with a slotted spoon and place it in the cold water. Cook the remaining lasagne strips the same way. Lay the cooled lasagne sheets out flat on lint free towels.

2 Butter a 13 × 10 × 2–inch pan. Set aside the 2 best-looking pasta strips for the top layer. Set aside 1/2 cup of the béchamel and 1/4 cup of the cheese. Make a layer of pasta, overlapping the pieces. Spread with thin layers of the béchamel, then the ragu, then the cheese. Repeat the layering, ending with the pasta. Spread the top layer with

the reserved 1/2 cup of béchamel. Sprinkle with the reserved 1/4 cup cheese. Dot with the butter. (If you are making the lasagne ahead of time, cover tightly with plastic wrap and refrigerate overnight.)

3 Place a rack in the center of the oven. Preheat the oven to 375°F. Bake the lasagne 45 minutes. If the lasagne is browning too much, cover it loosely with foil. Bake 15 minutes more or until the sauce is bubbling and a knife inserted in the center comes out warm. Let stand 15 minutes before serving.

Neapolitan Lasagne
Lasagne Napolitana

MAKES 8 TO 10 SERVINGS

Whenever I make lasagne, I can't help but think of my favorite Italian children's fable, Pentolin delle Lasagne, *written by A. Rubino and published in the children's section of the newspaper* Corriere della Sera *in 1932. It is the story of a man who always wore on his head a pentolino di terracotta, a clay pot for cooking lasagne. He felt that it protected him from the elements, and he was always ready to make lasagne on a moment's notice. Not surpris-ingly, he was the best lasagne maker in his country of Pastacotta ("cooked pasta"), though people laughed at him because of his silly headgear. Thanks to his lasagne pot and a bit of magic, he saved the citizens of Pastacotta from a famine, became king, and lived happily ever after, making lasagne every Sunday for everyone in his kingdom.*

This is lasagne the way my mother made it, and my grandmother before her. It is incredibly rich, but absolutely irresistible.

About 8 cups Neapolitan Ragù, made with tiny meatballs (page 94)
Salt
I pound fresh lasagne
2 pounds whole or part-skim ricotta
1 1/4 cups freshly grated Pecorino-Romano
I pound fresh mozzarella, thinly sliced

1 Prepare the ragù. Remove the meat pieces, meatballs, and sausages from the sauce. Set aside the pork and veal for another meal. Cut the sausages into thin slices and set them aside with the meatballs for the lasagne.

2 Lay out some lint-free kitchen towels on a flat surface. Have ready a large bowl of cold water.

3 Bring about 4 quarts of water to a boil. Add 2 tablespoons of salt. Add the lasagne a few pieces at a time. Cook the lasagne until tender but slightly underdone. Scoop the pasta out of the water. Place the cooked pasta in the cold water. When cool enough to handle, lay the pasta sheets out flat on the towels. The towels can be stacked one on top of the other. Continue cooking and cooling the remaining lasagne in the same way.

4 In a 13 × 9 × 2–inch pan, spread a thin layer of the sauce. Make a layer of pasta, overlapping the pieces slightly. Spread with 2 cups of the ricotta, then the tiny meatballs and sliced sausages, then the mozzarella. Spoon on about 1 cup more of the sauce and sprinkle with 1/4 cup of the grated cheese.

5 Repeat the layers, ending with pasta, sauce, and grated cheese. (If you are making the lasagne ahead of time, cover tightly with plastic wrap and refrigerate overnight.)

6 Place a rack in the center of the oven. Preheat the oven to 375°F. Bake the lasagne 45 minutes. If the lasagne is browning too much, cover it loosely with foil. Bake 15 minutes more or until the top is browned and the sauce is bubbling around the edges.

7 Remove the lasagne from the oven and let set 15 minutes. Cut the lasagne into squares and serve.

Spinach and Mushroom Lasagne
Lasagne di Funghi e Spinaci

MAKES 8 TO 10 SERVINGS

Parma is heaven for pasta lovers. Wrapped around tasty fillings, tossed with sauces, or layered with different ingredients, the pasta there seems light as air and always delicious. This dish is based on my recollection of a heavenly creamy lasagne I ate in Parma many years ago.

3 cups Béchamel Sauce (page 100)
1 pound fresh spinach, trimmed
Salt
5 tablespoons unsalted butter
1 small onion, finely chopped
1 1/2 pounds button mushrooms, chopped
1 pound fresh lasagne
1 1/2 cups freshly grated Parmigiano-Reggiano

1 Prepare the béchamel sauce. Then, place the spinach in a large pot with 1/2 cup of water. Add a pinch of salt. Cover and cook over medium heat until the spinach is tender, about 5 minutes. Drain the spinach well. Let cool. Wrap the spinach in a towel and squeeze it to extract as much of the juice as possible. Chop the spinach and set it aside.

2 In a large skillet, melt four tablespoons of the butter over medium heat. Add the onion and cook, stirring occasionally, until softened, about 5 minutes.

3 Stir in the mushrooms and salt and pepper to taste. Cook, stirring frequently, until all of the liquid evaporates and the mushrooms are tender. Stir in the chopped cooked spinach.

4 Set aside 1/2 cup of the béchamel sauce. Stir the remainder into the vegetable mixture.

5 Have ready a large bowl of cold water. Lay out some lint-free kitchen towels on a work surface.

6 Bring a large pot of water to a boil. Add 2 tablespoons of salt. Add the lasagne a few pieces at a time. Cook the lasagne until tender but slightly

(continues)

underdone. Scoop the pasta out of the water. Place the cooked pasta in the cold water. When cool enough to handle, lay the pasta sheets out flat on the towels, which can be stacked one on top of the other. Continue cooking and cooling the remaining lasagne in the same way.

7 Butter a 13 × 9 × 2–inch pan. Set aside the 2 best-looking pasta strips for the top layer. Make a layer of pasta in the prepared pan, overlapping the pieces. Spread with a thin layer of the vegetables and a sprinkle of cheese. Repeat the layering, ending with the pasta. Spread with reserved béchamel. Sprinkle with the remaining cheese. Dot with the remaining butter.

8 Preheat the oven to 375°F. Bake 45 minutes. If the lasagne is browning too much, cover it loosely with foil. Bake 15 minutes more or until the top is browned and the sauce is bubbling around the edge. Remove from the oven and let stand 15 minutes before serving. Cut into squares to serve.

Green Lasagne
Lasagne Verde

MAKES 8 TO 10 SERVINGS

Green lasagne noodles are layered with ham, mushrooms, tomatoes, and béchamel sauce. To make this meatless, just eliminate the ham.

3 cups Béchamel Sauce (page 100)
1 ounce dried porcini mushrooms
2 cups hot water
4 tablespoons unsalted butter
1 tablespoon olive oil
1 garlic clove, finely chopped
12 ounces white mushrooms, chopped
1/2 teaspoon dried marjoram or thyme
Salt and freshly ground black pepper
1 cup peeled, seeded, and chopped fresh tomatoes
    or canned imported Italian tomatoes, drained
    and chopped
8 ounces sliced boiled ham, chopped
1 1/4 cups freshly grated Parmigiano-Reggiano
1 1/4 pounds green lasagne

1 Prepare the béchamel sauce. Put the dried mushrooms in the water and let soak 30 minutes. Remove the mushrooms from the bowl and reserve the liquid. Rinse the mushrooms under cold running water to remove any grit, paying special attention to the ends of the stems where soil collects. Chop the mushrooms coarsely. Strain the mushroom liquid through a paper coffee filter into a bowl.

2 In a large skillet, melt two tablespoons of the butter with the oil over medium heat. Add the garlic and cook one minute. Add the fresh and dried mushrooms, marjoram, and salt and pepper to taste. Cook, stirring occasionally, for 5 minutes. Add the tomatoes and reserved mushroom liquid and cook until thickened, about 10 minutes more.

3 Have ready a large bowl of cold water. Lay out some lint-free kitchen towels on a work surface.

4 Bring at least 4 quarts of water to a boil. Add 2 tablespoons of salt. Add the lasagne a few pieces at a time. Cook the lasagne until tender but slightly underdone. Scoop the pasta out of the water. Place the cooked pasta in the cold water. When cool enough to handle, lay the pasta sheets out flat on the towels, which can be stacked one on top of the other. Continue cooking and cooling the remaining lasagne in the same way.

5 Butter a 13 × 9 × 2–inch pan. Set aside the 2 best-looking pasta strips for the top layer. Set aside 1/2 cup of the béchamel and 1/4 cup of the cheese. Make a layer of pasta, overlapping the pieces. Spread with a thin layer of the béchamel, mushroom sauce, ham, and cheese. Repeat the layering, ending with the pasta. Spread with reserved béchamel. Sprinkle with the remaining cheese. Dot with the remaining butter.

6 Place a rack in the center of the oven. Preheat the oven to 375°F. Bake the lasagne 45 minutes. If the lasagne is browning too much, cover it loosely with foil. Uncover and bake 15 minutes more or until the top is browned and the sauce is bubbling around the edges. Let stand 15 minutes before serving. Cut into squares to serve.

Green Lasagne with Ricotta, Basil, and Tomato Sauce

Lasagne Verde con Ricotta, Basilico, e Marinara

MAKES 8 TO 10 SERVINGS

My grandmother always made the Neapolitan-style lasagne, but once in a while she would surprise us with this meatless version, especially in the summer when a typical meat ragù seemed too heavy.

Just thinking about this lasagne makes me hungry. The fragrance of the basil, the richness of the cheese, and the sweetness of the tomato sauce is a combination that I find tantalizing. It is a beautiful dish, too, with its layers of red, green, and white.

5 to 6 cups Marinara Sauce (page 89) or Fresh
    Tomato Sauce (page 89)
Salt and freshly ground black pepper
1 1/4 pounds fresh green lasagne
2 pounds fresh part-skim ricotta
1 egg, slightly beaten
1 cup freshly grated Parmigiano-Reggiano
    or Pecorino Romano
8 ounces fresh mozzarella cheese, thinly sliced
1 large bunch basil, stacked and cut into
    narrow ribbons

1 Prepare the sauce, if necessary. Then, have ready a large bowl of cold water. Lay out some lint-free kitchen towels on a work surface.

2 Bring at least 4 quarts of water to a boil. Add 2 tablespoons of salt. Add the lasagne a few pieces at a time. Cook the lasagne until tender but slightly underdone. Scoop the pasta out of the water. Place the cooked pasta in the cold water. When cool enough to handle, lay the pasta sheets out flat on the towels, which can be stacked one on top of the other. Continue cooking and cooling the remaining lasagne in the same way.

3 In a bowl, beat the ricotta, egg, and salt and pepper to taste.

4 In a 13 × 9 × 2–inch pan, spread a thin layer of the sauce. Place two of the lasagne in the pan in a single layer, overlapping slightly. Spread evenly with half of the ricotta mixture, and sprinkle with 2 tablespoons of the grated cheese. Arrange one third of the mozzarella slices on top.

5 Make a second layer of lasagne and spread it with sauce. Scatter the basil on top. Layer with the cheeses as described above. Repeat for a third layer. Make a final layer of lasagne, sauce, mozzarella, and grated cheese. (Can be made ahead to this point. Cover with plastic wrap and refrigerate several hours or overnight.)

6 Place a rack in the center of the oven. Preheat the oven to 375°F. Bake the lasagne for 45 minutes. If the lasagne is browning too much, cover it loosely with foil. Bake 15 minutes more or until the top is browned and the sauce is bubbling around the edges. Let stand 15 minutes. Cut into squares and serve.

Eggplant Lasagne
Lasagne con la Parmigiana

MAKES 8 TO 10 SERVINGS

My friend Donatella Arpaia, who spent childhood summers with her family in Italy, remembers a favorite aunt who would make lasagne with fresh vegetables early in the morning to bring to the beach for lunch later in the day. The pan was carefully wrapped in towels, and the contents would still be warm when they sat down to eat.

This version resembles eggplant Parmesan, with the addition of fresh lasagne noodles. It is perfect for a summer buffet or to serve vegetarians.

2 medium eggplants (about 1 pound each)
Salt
Olive oil
1 medium onion, finely chopped
5 pounds fresh plum tomatoes, peeled, seeded, and
   chopped, or 2 (28-ounce) cans imported Italian
   peeled tomatoes, drained and chopped
Freshly ground black pepper
2 tablespoons chopped fresh flat-leaf parsley
2 tablespoons chopped fresh basil
1 pound fresh lasagne
1 pound fresh mozzarella, quartered and cut into
   thin slices
1 cup freshly grated Parmigiano-Reggiano

1 Trim the eggplants and cut them into thin slices. Sprinkle the slices with salt and layer them in a colander set over a plate. Let stand at least 30 minutes. Rinse the eggplant in cold water and pat dry.

2 Place a rack in the center of the oven. Preheat the oven to 400°F. Generously brush the eggplant slices on both sides with oil. Arrange the slices on large baking sheets. Bake the eggplants 30 minutes, or until tender and lightly browned.

3 In a large saucepan, cook the onion in 1/3 cup of olive oil over medium heat, stirring, until tender but not browned, about 10 minutes. Add the tomatoes and salt and pepper to taste. Bring to a simmer and cook until slightly thickened, about 15 to 20 minutes. Stir in the basil and parsley.

4 Lay out some lint-free kitchen towels on a work surface. Have ready a large bowl of cold water. Bring at least 4 quarts of water to a boil. Add 2 tablespoons of salt. Cook the lasagne strips a couple of pieces at a time. Remove the strips after one minute, or when they are still firm. Place them in the bowl of water to cool. Then lay them out flat on the towels. Repeat, cooking and cooling the remaining pasta in the same way; the towels can be stacked one on top of the other.

5 Lightly oil a 13 × 9 × 2–inch lasagne pan. Spread a thin layer of the sauce in the pan.

6 Make a layer of pasta, slightly overlapping the pieces. Spread with a thin layer of sauce, then eggplant slices, mozzarella, and grated cheese. Repeat the layering, ending with pasta, tomato sauce, and grated cheese. (Can be made up to 24 hours in advance. Cover with plastic wrap and refrigerate. Remove from the refrigerator about 1 hour before baking.)

7 Preheat the oven to 375°F. Bake 45 minutes. If the lasagne is browning too much, cover it loosely with foil. Bake 15 minutes more or until the top is browned and the sauce is bubbling around the edges. Remove from the oven and let stand 15 minutes before serving. Cut into squares to serve.

❧ Stuffed Fresh Pasta

Ricotta and Ham Cannelloni
Cannelloni al Prosciutto

MAKES 8 SERVINGS

Ricotta means "recooked." This fresh cheese is made in Italy from either cow's or sheep's milk whey, the watery liquid left after making a firm cheese, such as pecorino. When the whey is heated, the residual solids coagulate. After draining, the curds are transformed into the soft cheese we know as ricotta. Italians eat it as a breakfast or dessert cheese and in many pasta dishes. This is a southern Italian style cannelloni filled with ricotta and slivers of prosciutto. Any of the tomato sauces can be used with this pasta, but if you prefer a richer dish, you can substitute a meat ragù.

I recipe Fresh Egg Pasta, cut into 4-inch squares for cannelloni (pages 160–162)
I recipe (about 3 cups) Fresh Tomato Sauce (page 89) or Tuscan Tomato Sauce (pages 90–91)
Salt
I pound fresh mozzarella
I (16-ounce) container whole or part-skim ricotta
1/2 cup chopped imported Italian prosciutto (about 2 ounces)
I large egg, beaten
3/4 cup freshly grated Parmigiano-Reggiano
Freshly ground black pepper

I Prepare the pasta and sauce. Lay out some lint-free kitchen towels on a flat surface. Have ready a large bowl of cold water. Bring about 4 quarts of water to a boil. Add salt to taste. Add the pasta squares a few pieces at a time. Cook the pasta until tender but slightly underdone. Scoop the pasta out of the water and place it in the cold water. When cool enough to handle, lay the pasta sheets out flat on the towels, which can be stacked one on top of the other. Continue cooking and cooling the remaining pasta in the same way.

2 In a large bowl, combine the mozzarella, ricotta, prosciutto, egg, and 1/2 cup of the Parmigiano. Mix well and add salt and pepper to taste.

2 Spoon a thin layer of sauce in the bottom of a large baking dish. Spread about 2 tablespoons of the filling on one end of each pasta square. Roll up the pasta, starting with the filled end, and place the rolls seamside down in the prepared pan.

3 Spoon a thin layer of sauce over the pasta. Sprinkle with the remaining Parmigiano.

4 Place a rack in the center of the oven. Preheat the oven to 375°F. Bake 30 minutes or until the sauce is bubbling and the cheeses are melted. Serve hot.

Veal and Spinach Cannelloni
Cannelloni di Vitello e Spinaci

MAKES 8 SERVINGS

Cannelloni always seem so elegant, yet they are one of the easiest stuffed pastas to make at home. This classic version from Piedmont is typically made with leftover roasted or stewed veal. This is my version of a recipe from Giorgio Rocca, proprietor of Il Giardino da Felicin, a cozy inn and restaurant in Monforte d'Alba.

3 to 4 cups Béchamel Sauce (page 101)
I pound fresh spinach
2 tablespoons unsalted butter
2 pounds boneless veal, cut into 2-inch pieces
2 medium carrots, chopped
I tender celery rib, chopped
I medium onion, chopped
I garlic clove, finely chopped
Salt and freshly ground black pepper
Pinch of freshly ground nutmeg
1 1/2 cups freshly grated Parmigiano-Reggiano
1 1/2 pounds Fresh Egg Pasta, cut into 4-inch squares for cannelloni (pages 160–162)

(continues)

1 Prepare the béchamel sauce.

2 Put the spinach in a large pot over medium heat with 1/4 cup of water. Cover and cook 2 to 3 minutes or until wilted and tender. Drain and cool. Wrap the spinach in a lint-free cloth and squeeze out as much water as possible. Finely chop the spinach.

3 In a large skillet, melt the butter over medium-low heat. Add the veal, carrots, celery, onion, and garlic. Season to taste with salt and pepper and a pinch of nutmeg. Cover and cook, stirring occasionally, until the meat is very tender, about 1 hour. If the meat becomes dry, add a little water. Let cool. On a cutting board with a large knife, or in a food processor, chop the mixture very fine. Scrape the meat and spinach into a bowl and add 1 cup of the béchamel and 1 cup of the Parmigiano. Mix well and taste for seasoning.

4 Meanwhile, prepare the pasta. Lay out some lint-free kitchen towels on a flat surface. Have ready a large bowl of cold water. Bring about 4 quarts of water to a boil. Add 2 tablespoons of salt. Add the pasta squares a few pieces at a time. Cook the pasta until tender but slightly underdone. Scoop the pasta out of the water and place it in the cold water. When cool enough to handle, lay the pasta sheets out flat on the towels, which can be stacked one on top of the other. Continue cooking and cooling the remaining pasta in the same way.

5 Spoon half of the remaining béchamel in a thin layer in a large baking pan. Spread about two tablespoons of the filling on one end of each pasta square and roll up, starting from the filled end. Place the pasta roll seam-side down in the prepared pan. Repeat with the remaining pasta and filling, arranging the rolls close together in the pan. Spoon on the remaining sauce and sprinkle with the remaining 1/2 cup of Parmigiano. (Can be made up to 24 hours in advance. Cover with plastic wrap and refrigerate. Remove from the refrigerator about 1 hour before baking.)

6 Place a rack in the center of the oven. Preheat oven to 375°F. Bake 30 minutes or until the cannelloni are heated through and lightly golden. Serve hot.

Green and White Cannelloni
Cannelloni alla Parmigiana

MAKES 8 SERVINGS

If you visit the Emilia-Romagna region, be sure to stop in Parma. This elegant little city, the birthplace of the great conductor Arturo Toscanini, is renowned for its fine cooking. Many of the city's buildings are painted a sunny yellow color, known as Parma gold. Parma has many fine restaurants where you can taste superb hand-rolled pasta, aged Parmigiano-Reggiano, and the finest balsamic vinegar. I ate these cannelloni at Angiol d'Or, a classic Parma restaurant.

1 pound Fresh Spinach Pasta, cut into 4-inch squares for cannelloni (page 161)
2 cups Béchamel Sauce (page 101)
8 ounces fresh spinach, trimmed
Salt
1 pound whole or part-skim ricotta
2 large eggs, lightly beaten
1 1/2 cups freshly grated Parmigiano-Reggiano
1/4 teaspoon freshly grated nutmeg
Freshly ground black pepper
4 ounces Fontina Valle d'Aosta, coarsely grated

1 Prepare pasta and béchamel sauce. Put the spinach in a large pot over medium heat with 1/4 cup of water. Cover and cook 2 to 3 minutes or until wilted and tender. Drain and cool. Wrap the spinach in a lint-free cloth and squeeze out as much water as possible. Finely chop the spinach.

2 Lay out some lint-free kitchen towels on a flat surface. Have ready a large bowl of cold water. Bring about 4 quarts of water to a boil. Add 2 tablespoons salt. Add the pasta squares a few pieces at a time. Cook the pasta until tender but slightly underdone. Scoop the pasta out of the water and place it in the cold water. When cool enough to handle, lay the pasta sheets out flat on the towels, which can be stacked one on top of the other. Continue cooking and cooling the remaining pasta in the same way.

3 Stir together the spinach, ricotta, eggs, 1/2 cup of the Parmigiano, the nutmeg, and salt and pepper to taste. Stir in the fontina.

4 Place a rack in the center of the oven. Preheat the oven to 375°F. Butter a 13 × 9 × 2–inch baking dish.

5 Spread about 1/4 cup of the filling at one end of each pasta square. Roll up the pasta, starting with the filled end. Place the cannelloni seamside down in the pan.

6 Spread the sauce over the pasta. Sprinkle with the remaining 1 cup of Parmigiano. Bake 20 minutes or until lightly browned.

Cannelloni

Cannelloni comes from the Italian word *cannello*, a hollow tube or pipe. These big pasta tubes are rolled around a filling, placed side by side in a pan, covered with a sauce, and then baked. Cannelloni are especially popular in Emilia-Romagna, though I have eaten them in Piedmont, Tuscany, and as far south as Sicily. Easy to make, cannelloni can be stuffed with a variety of fillings, though meat or cheese is the most typical.

Cannelloni are sometimes made from crepes, rather than pasta dough, rolled around a filling. In southern Italy, both the crepe and pasta versions are sometimes called *manicotti*, cooked hands—a joking reference to the handling of the hot pasta or crepe.

To make cannelloni, roll out the pasta as directed on page 162, as for lasagne. Cut the strips into 4-inch squares.

Cannelloni with Tarragon and Pecorino
Cannelloni di Ricotta al Dragoncello

MAKES 6 SERVINGS

Tarragon, with its mild licorice flavor, is not used much in Italy, except occasionally in Umbria and Tuscany. Fresh tarragon is essential for this recipe, since dried tarragon would be too assertive. If you cannot find the fresh tarragon, substitute fresh basil or parsley.

These Umbrian-style cannelloni are made with a sheep's milk cheese, such as Pecorino Romano, but Parmigiano-Reggiano can be substituted. Despite the cheese, nuts, and pasta, these cannelloni seem light as air.

1/2 recipe (about 8 ounces) Fresh Egg Pasta, cut into 4-inch squares for cannelloni (pages 160–162)
Salt
1 pound whole or part-skim ricotta
1/2 cup freshly ground Pecorino Romano, or substitute Parmigiano-Reggiano
1 egg, beaten
1 tablespoon chopped fresh tarragon or basil
1/4 teaspoon ground nutmeg
2 tablespoons unsalted butter
1/4 cup extra-virgin olive oil
1/4 cup pine nuts
1 tablespoon tarragon or basil
Freshly ground black pepper
2 tablespoons freshly grated Pecorino Romano

1 Prepare the pasta. Bring at least 4 quarts of water to a boil. Add half the pasta and salt to taste. Stir gently. Cook over high heat, stirring frequently, until the pasta is tender but slightly underdone. Use a slotted spoon to remove the pasta. Transfer the pasta to a bowl of cold water. Cook the remaining pasta in the same way.

2 In a large bowl, stir together the cheeses, egg, tarragon, and nutmeg.

(continues)

3 Place a rack in the center of the oven. Preheat the oven to 350° F. Butter a large baking dish.

4 Drain a few of the pasta squares on lint-free towels. Spread about 2 tablespoons of the filling in a line at one at one end of each pasta square. Roll up the pasta, starting with the filled end, and place it seam-side down in the pan. Repeat with the remaining pasta and filling.

5 In a small saucepan over medium heat, melt the butter with the olive oil. Stir in the pine nuts, tarragon, and pepper. Spoon the sauce over the cannelloni. Sprinkle with the cheese.

6 Bake the cannelloni 20 to 25 minutes or until the sauce is bubbling. Let rest 5 minutes before serving.

Cheese Ravioli with Fresh Tomato Sauce
Ravioli alla Ricotta

MAKES 8 SERVINGS

Cookware stores sell all kinds of ravioli-making equipment. I have a metal traylike contraption that impresses pasta sheets with a series of bellies to hold the filling, then flips over to seal and cut out the perfect ravioli in two sizes. I have handsome brass and wood stamps that I bought in Parma to cut out squares and circles. Then there is the clever wooden rolling pin that cuts out ravioli if you press down on it with the strength of Hercules, and the ravioli cutter that came with my hand-cranked pasta machine. Though I have tried them all, I never use any of them. The simplest way to make ravioli is by hand with minimal equipment. A wavy-edge pastry wheel gives them a pretty border, though you can also cut them with a sharp knife or pizza wheel. They may not be perfect in appearance, but that is part of their homemade charm, and no one has ever complained about their flavor.

This is a basic recipe for cheese-filled ravioli the way it is made in many regions of Italy.

I pound whole or part-skim ricotta
4 ounces fresh mozzarella, coarsely grated or very finely chopped
I large egg, beaten
I cup freshly grated Parmigiano-Reggiano or Pecorino Romano
2 tablespoons chopped fresh parsley
Salt and freshly ground black pepper to taste
4 cups Fresh Tomato Sauce (page 89)
I pound Fresh Egg Pasta, rolled out and cut into 4-inch strips (pages 160–162)

I Mix together the ricotta, mozzarella, egg, $1/2$ cup of the Parmigiano, the parsley, and the salt and pepper to taste. Cover and refrigerate.

2 Prepare the sauce and pasta. Dust 2 or 3 large baking sheets with flour. Set out a small bowl filled with cool water.

3 Lay a strip of the dough on a lightly floured surface. Fold it lengthwise in half to mark the center, then unfold it. Beginning about 1 inch from one of the short ends, place teaspoonfuls of the filling about 1 inch apart in a straight row down one side of the fold. Lightly brush around the filling with the cool water. Fold the dough over the side with filling. Press out any air bubbles and seal the edges. Use a fluted pastry wheel or a sharp knife to cut between the dough-covered mounds of filling. Separate the ravioli and press the edges firmly with the back of a fork to seal. Place the ravioli in a single layer on a baking sheet.

4 Repeat with the remaining dough and filling. Cover with a towel and refrigerate until ready to cook, or up to 3 hours, turning the pieces several times so that they do not stick to the pan. (To store them longer, freeze the ravioli on the baking sheets until firm. Place them in a heavy-duty plastic bag and seal tightly. Store in the freezer up to one month. Do not thaw before cooking.)

5 Just before serving, bring about 4 quarts of water to a boil in a large pot. Meanwhile, in a medium pot, heat the sauce over low heat. Pour some of the sauce into a heated serving bowl.

6 Lower the heat under the pasta pot so that the water boils gently. Add the ravioli and cook until tender, 2 to 5 minutes depending on the thickness of the ravioli and whether or not they were frozen. Scoop the ravioli out of the pot with a slotted spoon. Drain well.

7 Place the ravioli in the serving bowl. Pour on the remaining sauce. Sprinkle with the remaining 1/2 cup cheese and serve immediately.

Ravioli and Other Stuffed Pasta

A pillow of fresh pasta enclosing a cheese, vegetable, fish, or meat filling is made in practically every region of Italy. The shape varies, and the name changes, too, according to the region and the filling. *Anolini* from Emilia-Romagna are round and filled with meat. *Marubini* from Lombardy and *pansotti* from Liguria are triangular, though the first has a meat filling while the other is filled with cheese. *Cappelletti* from Emilia-Romagna resemble little hats. *Tortelli* from Emilia-Romagna and Tuscany can be either round, half-moon, or ring-shaped.

Depending on the filling, ravioli can be made up to a few hours ahead and refrigerated or frozen. Moist fillings may soak through the pasta and cause it to become sticky, so it is best to cook ravioli with this kind of filling as soon as possible. If refrigerated, keep the ravioli pieces from touching one another and turn them occasionally so that they do not stick to the surface. For longer storage, spread them on floured baking sheets and freeze until firm. Then place them in a heavy-duty plastic bag and seal tightly. Store in the freezer up to one month. Do not thaw the ravioli or other stuffed pasta before cooking.

Parma-Style Spinach and Cheese Ravioli
Tortelli alla Parmigiana

MAKES 8 SERVINGS

While ricotta-filled ravioli are probably the most popular in Italy, a similar version with cooked greens is a favorite also. Spinach or Swiss chard are the most commonly used greens, but escarole, dandelion, beet greens, and borage are also used, depending on the region.

In this recipe from Parma, mascarpone is substituted for some of the ricotta, and Swiss chard is the typical green. At one time, it was traditional to serve these for Saint John's Day, June 21st. Note that the Parmigiani call these tortelli.

I pound fresh spinach or Swiss chard, stems removed
Salt
I cup whole or part-skim ricotta
I cup mascarpone (or an additional cup of ricotta)
I large egg, beaten
I cup freshly grated Parmigiano-Reggiano
Pinch of freshly ground nutmeg
Freshly ground black pepper
I recipe Fresh Egg Pasta, rolled out and cut into 4-inch strips (pages 160–162)
8 tablespoons (I stick) unsalted butter

1 Place the greens in a large pot with 1/2 cup water and salt to taste. Cover and cook over medium-low heat until the vegetable is wilted and tender, about 5 minutes. Drain and let cool. Wrap the greens in a lint-free kitchen towel or a piece of cheesecloth and squeeze it with your hands to extract all of the juice. Finely chop the greens.

2 In a large bowl, stir together the chopped greens, ricotta, mascarpone if using, the egg, 1/2 cup of the grated cheese, nutmeg, and salt and pepper to taste.

3 Prepare the pasta. Make and cook the ravioli as described in the recipe for Cheese Ravioli (pages 182–183), steps 2 to 6.

4 While the ravioli are cooking, melt the butter over medium heat. Pour half of the butter into a

(continues)

serving bowl. Add the ravioli and the remaining melted butter.

5 Sprinkle with the remaining ¹/₂ cup Parmigiano and serve immediately.

Winter Squash Ravioli with Butter and Almonds
Tortelli di Zucca al Burro e Mandorle

MAKES 8 SERVINGS

In the fall and winter when winter squashes are plentiful in the market, cooks in Lombardy and Emilia-Romagna make these slightly sweet ravioli accented with the almond flavor of amaretti cookies. The recipe is very old, probably dating back to the Renaissance, when sweet foods often appeared during a meal on aristocratic tables as a sign of wealth.

Some recipes call for adding a spoonful of drained, finely chopped mostarda—*fruits preserved in a tangy mustard syrup—to the squash mixture. Toasted almonds add a nice crunch to the topping.*

About 2 pounds butternut or Hubbard squash
1¹/₄ cup freshly grated Parmigiano-Reggiano
¹/₄ cup finely crushed amaretti cookies
1 large egg
¹/₄ teaspoon ground nutmeg
Salt to taste
1 pound Fresh Egg Pasta, rolled out and cut into 4-inch strips (pages 160–162)
1 stick (4 ounces) unsalted butter
2 tablespoons chopped toasted almonds

1 Place a rack in the center of the oven. Preheat the oven to 400°F. Oil a small baking pan. Cut the squash in half and scoop out the seeds and fibers. Place the halves cut-side down in the pan. Bake 1 hour or until tender when pierced with a knife. Let cool.

2 Scrape the flesh away from the skin. Pass the flesh through a food mill fitted with the fine blade or puree it in a food processor or blender. Stir in ³/₄ cup of the cheese, the amaretti, egg, nutmeg, and salt. Taste for seasoning.

3 Prepare the pasta. Make and cook the ravioli as described in the recipe for Cheese Ravioli (pages 182–183), steps 2 to 6.

4 While the ravioli are cooking, melt the butter over medium heat. Pour half of the butter into a warm serving bowl. Add the ravioli and the remaining melted butter. Toss them with almonds. Sprinkle with the remaining ¹/₂ cup cheese. Serve immediately.

Meat Ravioli with Tomato Sauce
Agnolotti in Salsa di Pomodoro

MAKES 8 TO 10 SERVINGS

Italian cooks rarely start from scratch when making a meat filling for fresh pasta. Typically, leftovers from a stew or roast are chopped up and moistened with the meat juices. Cheese, cooked vegetables, or breadcrumbs may be added to extend the filling, and the mixture is bound together with beaten eggs. Because I don't always have leftovers available for ravioli filling, I make this easy stew as a filling for ravioli.

3 cups Tuscan Tomato Sauce (pages 90–91)
2 tablespoons unsalted butter
1 pound ground veal or beef
1 boneless skinless chicken breast, cut into 1-inch pieces
1 medium onion, chopped
1 medium carrot, chopped
1 small celery rib, chopped
1 garlic clove, finely chopped
Salt and freshly ground black pepper
¹/₂ cup dry white wine
1 cup Parmigiano-Reggiano or Pecorino Romano
2 large egg yolks
1 pound Fresh Egg Pasta, rolled out and cut into 4-inch strips (pages 160–162)

1 Prepare the sauce. Then, melt the butter in a large skillet over medium heat. Add the meat and chicken and cook until the meat loses its pink color, breaking up the lumps of ground meat with a spoon.

2 Add the onion, carrot, celery, and garlic. Cook 10 minutes, stirring often, or until the vegetables are softened. Season to taste with salt and pepper.

3 Add the wine and simmer 1 minute. Cover the pan and reduce the heat to low. Cook 1 1/2 hours or until the meat is very tender. Add a little water to the pan if the mixture becomes too dry. Remove from the heat and let cool.

4 Scrape the meat mixture into a food processor or a food grinder. Chop or grind the meat until it is finely ground, but not pasty. Transfer the meat mixture to a bowl.

5 Add 1/2 cup of the grated cheese to the meat mixture and mix well. Taste for seasoning. Stir in the egg yolks.

6 Prepare the pasta. Make and cook the ravioli as described in the recipe for Cheese Ravioli (pages 182–183), steps 2 to 6. Serve hot with the sauce and sprinkle with remaining 1/2 cup of the cheese.

Tuscan Sausage Ravioli
Tortelli Casentinese

MAKES 8 SERVINGS

Tortelli is another name for ravioli that is used frequently in Tuscany and Emilia-Romagna. These tortelli, stuffed with pork sausage, are made in the style of the Casentino section of Tuscany, a region that is also known for its beautiful wool products.

3 cups Tuscan Tomato Sauce (pages 90–91)
1 garlic clove, very finely chopped
2 tablespoons olive oil
1 pound plain Italian pork sausage, skinned
2 large eggs
2 tablespoons tomato paste
1 cup freshly grated Pecorino Romano
1/4 cup plain dry bread crumbs
2 tablespoons chopped fresh flat-leaf parsley
Pinch of freshly grated nutmeg
Salt and freshly ground black pepper
1 pound Fresh Egg Pasta, rolled out and cut into 4-inch strips (pages 160–162)

1 Prepare the sauce. Then, in a large skillet, cook the garlic in the oil over medium heat for 1 minute. Add the sausage meat and cook, stirring frequently, until the meat is just cooked through. Transfer the sausage meat to a cutting board and chop fine.

2 In a large bowl, beat the eggs until blended. Beat in the tomato paste. Stir in the sausage meat, 1/2 cup of the cheese, bread crumbs, nutmeg, and salt and pepper to taste.

3 Prepare the pasta. Make and cook the ravioli as described in the recipe for Cheese Ravioli (pages 182–183), steps 2 to 6. Spoon on the sauce and serve immediately with the remaining 1/2 cup grated cheese.

Spiced Ravioli, Marches Style
Ravioli Marchegiana

MAKES 8 SERVINGS

Cooks in the Marches region on the Adriatic coast, are known for their deft use of spices in savory dishes. These ravioli, for example, made with a variety of vegetables and cheese, are flavored with lemon zest, cinnamon, and nutmeg. Serve them with Marches-Style Ragù (page 95) or a simple Butter and Sage Sauce (page 100).

About 4 cups Marches-Style Ragù (page 95)
12 ounces assorted greens such as spinach, Swiss chard, chicory, or dandelion
1 cup whole or part-skim ricotta
1 large egg, beaten
1 cup grated Parmigiano-Reggiano
1 teaspoon grated lemon zest
Pinch of grated nutmeg
Pinch of ground cinnamon
Salt and freshly ground black pepper
1 pound Fresh Egg Pasta, rolled out and cut into 4-inch strips (pages 160–162)

1 Prepare the ragù. Then, put the spinach in a large pot over medium heat with 1/4 cup of water. Cover

(continues)

and cook for 2 to 3 minutes or until wilted and tender. Drain and cool. Wrap the spinach in a lint-free cloth and squeeze out as much water as possible. Finely chop the spinach.

2 In a large bowl, mix together the ricotta, egg, 1/2 cup of the cheese, the lemon zest, nutmeg, cinnamon, and salt and pepper to taste.

3 Prepare the pasta. Make and cook the ravioli as described in the recipe for Cheese Ravioli (pages 182–183), steps 2 to 6. Transfer ravioli to a serving bowl. Spoon on the sauce and serve immediately with the remaining 1/2 cup of cheese.

Mushroom Ravioli in Butter and Sage Sauce
Agnolotti ai Funghi

MAKES 8 SERVINGS

The combination of mushrooms and marjoram is typical of Liguria, where this recipe originates. White button mushrooms are fine as the stuffing for these ravioli, but for extra-special flavor add some wild mushrooms to the filling.

3 tablespoons unsalted butter
1 tablespoon olive oil
1 pound fresh mushrooms, sliced thin
1 teaspoon fresh marjoram or thyme or a pinch of dried
Salt and freshly ground black pepper
1/2 cup whole or part-skim ricotta
1 cup freshly grated Parmigiano-Reggiano
1 egg yolk
1 pound Fresh Egg Pasta, rolled out and cut into 4-inch strips (pages 160–162)
1/2 cup Butter and Sage Sauce (page 100)

1 In a large skillet, melt the butter with the oil over medium heat. Add the mushrooms, marjoram, and salt and pepper to taste. Cook, stirring occasionally, until the mushrooms are tender and the juices have evaporated. Let cool.

2 Scrape the mushrooms into a food processor and chop finely. Add the ricotta and 1/2 cup of the Parmigiano and taste for seasoning. Stir in the egg yolk.

3 Prepare the pasta. Make and cook the ravioli as described in the recipe for Cheese Ravioli (pages 182–183), steps 2 to 6.

4 Meanwhile, make the sauce. Pour half the sauce into a warm serving bowl. Add the cooked ravioli. Spoon on the remaining sauce, and sprinkle with the remaining 1/2 cup of Parmigiano-Reggiano. Serve immediately.

Giant Ravioli with Truffle Butter
Ravioloni al Tuorlo d'Uovo

MAKES 4 SERVINGS

One of these extra-large and extra-rich ravioli is sufficient for a first course serving. I first had these years ago at San Domenico Restaurant in Imola, founded by the great chef Nino Bergese, known for his creative approach to classic Italian cooking.

This is a most unusual recipe. The fresh egg pasta is filled with a ring of ricotta piped around an egg yolk. When the raviolo is cut, the lightly cooked yolk oozes out and blends with the butter sauce. At San Domenico, the ravioloni were topped with thinly shaved fresh white truffles. The heat of the pasta and sauce brought out their flavor and aroma. The effect was extraordinary, and I will always remember it as one of the most delicious things I have ever eaten.

Though they may seem a little tricky, these ravioli really are quite simple to make and very impressive to serve. For best results, assemble the ravioli just before cooking. You can substitute freshly shaved flakes of Parmigiano-Reggiano for the truffle. Most truffle oils have an artificial flavor, so I avoid them.

1 pound Fresh Egg Pasta, rolled out and cut into four
   8 × 4–inch strips (pages 160–162)
1 cup whole or part-skim ricotta
2 tablespoons freshly grated Parmigiano-Reggiano
Pinch of ground nutmeg
Salt and freshly ground black pepper
4 large eggs
1/2 cup unsalted butter, melted
Fresh white or black truffle or a large piece
   of Parmigiano-Reggiano

1 Prepare the pasta. Then, mix together the ricotta and grated cheese, nutmeg, and salt and pepper to taste. Scrape the filling into a pastry bag fitted with a 1/2-inch tip or a heavy-duty plastic bag, cutting off one corner to create a 1/2-inch opening.

2 Keeping the remaining pasta covered, lay out one strip on a countertop. Fold the strip in half crosswise, then unfold to crease the center. Leaving a 1/2-inch border all around, pipe a circle of the cheese mixture on the pasta to one side of the crease. Separate one egg, setting the white aside for another use. Carefully drop the yolk into the center of the circle. Lightly brush around the cheese with cool water. Fold the other half of the pasta over the filling. With a fork, press the edges of the pasta together to seal. Repeat with the remaining pasta and filling.

3 Bring at least 2 quarts of water to a boil. Lower the heat until the water is simmering. Add salt to taste. Carefully place the ravioli in the water and cook just until the pasta is tender, about 3 minutes.

4 Spoon a little of the butter into each of 4 warm serving dishes. Remove the ravioli one at a time with a slotted spoon. Place a raviolo in each dish and spoon on the remaining butter. With a swivel-blade vegetable peeler, shave thin slices of the truffle, if using, or flakes of Parmigiano over the top. Serve immediately.

Beet Ravioli with Poppy Seeds
Casunziei di Barbabietole Rosse

MAKES 8 SERVINGS

In the Veneto, it is traditional to serve these beautiful ravioli at Christmas. I love the way the red beet filling shows through the pasta like a delicate blush. These ravioli are typical of Cortina d'Ampezzo, a world famous ski resort in the Alpine northern part of the region. The poppy seeds in the sauce reflect the influence of nearby Austria. Poppy seeds lose their freshness quickly at warm room temperatures, so smell them to be sure they have not turned rancid. Store poppy seeds in a tightly sealed container in the refrigerator or freezer.

4 medium beets, trimmed and scrubbed
1/2 cup whole or part-skim ricotta
1 cup freshly grated Parmigiano-Reggiano
2 tablespoons plain dry bread crumbs
Salt and freshly ground black pepper
1 pound Fresh Egg Pasta, rolled out and cut into
   4-inch strips (pages 160–162)
8 tablespoons (1 stick) unsalted butter
1 tablespoon poppy seeds

1 Place the beets in a medium saucepan with cold water to cover. Bring to a simmer and cook until tender when pierced with a knife, about 30 minutes. Drain and let cool.

2 Peel the beets and cut them into chunks. Place them in a food processor and chop finely. Add the ricotta, 1/2 cup of the Parmigiano-Reggiano, bread crumbs, and salt and pepper to taste. Process just until blended but still slightly coarse.

3 Prepare the pasta. Make and cook the ravioli as described in the recipe for Cheese Ravioli (page 182), Steps 2 to 6.

4 Meanwhile, melt the butter with the poppy seeds and a pinch of salt. Pour half the butter into a warm serving bowl. Transfer the ravioli to the bowl. Spoon the remaining sauce over the ravioli and sprinkle with the remaining 1/2 cup of Parmigiano-Reggiano. Serve immediately.

Meat-Filled Pasta Rings in Cream Sauce
Tortellini alla Panna

MAKES 8 SERVINGS

According to a romantic legend, these ring-shaped pasta pockets were invented by a cook who spied on the goddess Venus in her bath. Inspired by her beauty, he created a pasta in the shape of her navel. Other versions of the story say that the beauty was Caterina di Medici. Whatever the inspiration behind them, these are wonderful served swimming in a rich meat or chicken broth or a simple cream or butter sauce. Anything more than that would be overkill.

4 tablespoons unsalted butter
4 ounces boneless pork loin, cut into 1-inch cubes
4 ounces imported Italian prosciutto
4 ounces mortadella
1 1/2 cups freshly grated Parmigiano-Reggiano
1 large egg
1/4 teaspoon freshly ground nutmeg
1 pound Fresh Egg Pasta (pages 160–162), rolled out and cut into 4-inch strips
1 1/2 cups heavy or whipping cream
Salt

1 Melt 2 tablespoons of the butter in a small skillet over medium heat. Add the pork and cook, stirring occasionally, until cooked through, about 20 minutes. Let cool.

2 In a food processor or meat grinder, grind the pork, prosciutto, and mortadella until very fine. Transfer the meats to a bowl. Stir in 1 cup of the Parmigiano-Reggiano, egg, and nutmeg.

3 Line 2 or 3 large baking sheets with lint-free towels. Dust the towels with flour.

4 Prepare the pasta. Working with one piece at a time, keep the remainder covered.

5 Cut the pasta into 2-inch squares. Place about 1/2 teaspoon of the filling on each square. Fold the dough over the filling to form a triangle. Press the

edges together firmly to seal. Work quickly so that the dough does not dry out.

6 Bring the two opposite points of the triangle together to form a circle. Pinch the ends to seal. Place the formed tortellino on a baking sheet while you prepare the remaining dough and filling in the same way.

7 Refrigerate the tortellini up to several hours or overnight, turning the pieces occasionally. (For longer storage, freeze them on the baking sheet 1 hour or until firm, then transfer them to heavy-duty plastic bags and store in the freezer up to one month. Do not thaw before cooking.)

8 To make the sauce, melt the remaining 2 tablespoons of the butter with the cream and a pinch of salt in a skillet large enough to hold all of the pasta. Bring to a simmer and cook 1 minute or until lightly thickened.

9 Bring at least 4 quarts of water to a boil in a large pot. Add the tortellini and salt to taste. Stir occasionally until the water returns to a boil. Reduce the heat so that the water is boiling gently. Cook 3 minutes or until slightly underdone. Drain well.

10 Pour the tortellini into the skillet with the cream and stir gently. Add the remaining 1/2 cup of Parmigiano-Reggiano and stir again. Serve immediately.

Potato Tortelli with Sausage Ragù
Tortelli di Patate al Ragù di Salsiccia

MAKES 6 TO 8 SERVINGS

Mashed potatoes flavored with Parmigiano-Reggiano fill fresh pasta rings in southern Emilia-Romagna and northern Tuscany. Instead of squares, as in the previous recipe, these start out as circles of dough and are then shaped into rings. Serve them with a rich Sausage Ragù (page 94), or simply enjoy them with Butter and Sage Sauce (page 100).

4 1/2 cups Sausage Ragù (page 94)

3 medium boiling potatoes

2 tablespoons unsalted butter, at room temperature

1 cup freshly grated Parmigiano-Reggiano

1/8 teaspoon freshly grated nutmeg

Salt and freshly ground black pepper

1 pound Fresh Egg Pasta, rolled out and cut into
    4-inch strips (pages 160–162)

1 Prepare the ragù. Then, place the whole potatoes in a pot with cold water to cover. Bring to a simmer and cook until the potatoes are tender when pierced with a knife, about 20 minutes. Drain and let cool.

2 Peel the potatoes and mash them with a ricer or food mill until smooth. Stir in the butter, 1/2 cup of the cheese, the nutmeg, and salt and pepper to taste.

3 Sprinkle two baking sheets with flour.

4 Prepare the pasta. With a 2-inch round cookie or biscuit cutter, or a small glass, cut the dough into circles. Place a teaspoon of the filling on one side of each circle. Dip a fingertip in cool water and moisten the dough circle halfway around. Fold the dough over the filling to form a semicircle. Press the edges firmly together to seal. Gather the two corners of the dough and pinch them together. Place the tortelli on the prepared baking sheet. Repeat with the remaining dough and filling.

5 Cover and refrigerate, turning the pieces occasionally, up to 3 hours. (For longer storage, freeze the pasta on the baking sheets. Transfer to heavy-duty plastic bags. Seal tightly and freeze up to one month. Do not thaw before cooking.)

6 When ready to cook the tortelli, bring at least 4 quarts of water to a boil. Bring the sauce to a simmer. Add the pasta to the boiling water with salt to taste. Stir well. Cook over medium heat, stirring frequently, until the pasta is tender yet still firm to the bite.

7 Spoon some of the sauce into a heated serving bowl. Drain the pasta well and add it to the bowl. Top with the remaining sauce and 1/2 cup cheese. Serve immediately.

❧ Fresh Gnocchi

Potato Gnocchi
Gnocchi di Patate con Ragù o al Sugo

MAKES 6 SERVINGS

Roman trattorias often have daily specials. Thursdays are usually their day to serve potato gnocchi, though gnocchi are also made for the big Sunday lunch at mama's house when the whole family gets together.

The important thing to remember in making potato gnocchi is to handle them gently and never overwork the potatoes by putting them in a food processor or mixer. The moisture content of the potatoes will determine how much flour you need.

If you have any doubts about whether you have added enough flour to the dough, try this trick suggested to me by a clever chef. Make a test gnòcco. Pinch off a small piece of dough and cook it in a small saucepan of boiling water until it floats to the surface, then cook it 30 seconds more. Scoop it out of the water and taste it. The dumpling should hold its shape without being mushy or tough. If it is too soft, knead in more flour. If it is tough, it probably has too much flour already. Either start all over again or try cooking the gnocchi a little longer.

4 cups Neapolitan Ragù (page 94) or Fresh Tomato
    Sauce (page 89)

1 1/2 pounds baking potatoes

About 2 cups all-purpose flour

1 large egg yolk, beaten

Salt

1 Prepare the ragù or sauce. Then, place the potatoes in a large pot with cold water to cover. Cover the pot and bring to a simmer. Cook until the potatoes are tender when pierced with a knife, about 20 minutes. Dust two large baking sheets with flour.

2 While the potatoes are still warm, peel them and cut them into chunks. Mash the potatoes, using the smallest holes of a ricer or food mill, or by hand

(continues)

with a potato masher. Add the egg yolk and 2 teaspoons of salt. Stir in one cup of the flour just until blended. The dough will be stiff.

3 Scrape the potatoes onto a floured surface. Knead briefly, adding only enough flour so that the gnocchi will hold their shape when cooked but not so much that they become heavy. The dough should be slightly sticky.

4 Set the dough aside. Scrape the board to remove any dough scraps. Wash and dry your hands, then dust them with flour. Set out one or two large baking pans and dust them with flour.

5 Cut the dough into 8 pieces. Keeping the remaining dough covered, roll one piece into a long rope about 3/4 inch thick. Cut the rope into 1/2 inch-long nuggets.

6 To shape the dough, hold a fork in one hand with the tines pointed down. With the thumb of the other hand, roll each piece of dough over the back of the tines, pressing lightly to make ridges on one side and an indentation from your finger on the other. Let the gnocchi drop onto the prepared pans. The pieces should not touch. Repeat with the remaining dough.

7 Refrigerate the gnocchi until ready to cook. (Gnocchi can also be frozen. Place the baking sheets in the freezer for one hour or until firm. Put the gnocchi in a large heavy-duty plastic bag. Freeze up to one month. Do not thaw before cooking.)

8 Have ready a heated shallow serving bowl. Pour a thin layer of the hot sauce into the bowl.

9 To cook the gnocchi, bring a large pot of water to a boil. Add 2 tablespoons salt. Lower the heat so that the water boils gently. Drop the gnocchi into the water a few pieces at a time. Cook for 30 seconds after the gnocchi rise to the surface. Skim the gnocchi from the pot with a slotted spoon, draining the pieces well. Transfer to the serving bowl. Repeat with remaining gnocchi.

10 Toss the gnocchi with the sauce. Spoon on the remaining sauce; sprinkle with cheese. Serve hot.

Potato Gnocchi with Lamb Ragù
Gnocchi con Ragù di Agnello

MAKES 6 TO 8 SERVINGS

This recipe is from the Abruzzo region of central Italy. The sauce is typically served with pasta alla chitarra—*homemade egg pasta cut with a special device known as a guitar because it is shaped like a frame strung with wires. It also works well in a hearty dish with gnocchi.*

1 pound Potato Gnocchi (page 189–190), through step 7
2 tablespoons olive oil
1 medium onion, finely chopped
1 red bell pepper, seeded and chopped
Pinch of crushed red pepper
2 garlic cloves, finely chopped
1 pound lean ground lamb
1 (28- to 35-ounce) can imported Italian tomatoes with their juice, chopped
1 tablespoon tomato paste
1 bay leaf
Salt to taste
1/2 cup freshly grated Pecorino Romano or Parmigiano-Reggiano

1 Prepare the gnocchi. Then, in a large skillet, cook the olive oil, onion, bell pepper, and red pepper until the vegetables are tender, about 10 minutes. Add the garlic and cook 1 minute more.

2 Stir in the lamb and cook 15 minutes, stirring frequently to break up any lumps, until it is no longer pink. Stir in the tomatoes. Add the tomato paste, bay leaf, and salt.

3 Bring the sauce to a simmer and reduce the heat to low. Cook, stirring occasionally, until the sauce is thickened, about 1 1/2 hours.

4 Bring at least 4 quarts of water to a boil. Lower the heat so that the water boils gently. Drop the gnocchi into the water a few pieces at a time. Cook 30 seconds after the gnocchi rise to the surface.

5 Meanwhile, remove the bay leaf from the sauce. Spoon a thin layer into a large heated serving bowl. Skim the gnocchi from the pot with a slotted spoon, draining the pieces well. Add them to the bowl. Repeat with remaining gnocchi. Top with the remaining sauce and cheese. Serve hot.

Gratinéed Potato Gnocchi
Gnocchi Gratinati

MAKES 6 SERVINGS

In Piedmont, potato gnocchi are topped with cheese and bread crumbs and baked in a heat-proof oval dish known as a gratin. When baked, the cheeses melt and the crumbs become crunchy. The dish can be assembled ahead of time and baked just before you are ready to serve it.

1 recipe Potato Gnocchi (pages 189–190)
2 tablespoons bread crumbs
Salt
6 ounces Fontina Valle d'Aosta
4 tablespoons unsalted butter
Freshly ground black pepper
1/4 cup freshly grated Parmigiano-Reggiano
Pinch of cinnamon

1 Prepare the gnocchi. Then, place a rack in the center of the oven. Preheat the oven to 350°F. Butter a 13 × 9 × 2–inch baking dish. Sprinkle it with the breadcrumbs.

2 Bring a large pot of water to a boil. Add the gnocchi and salt to taste. Cook, stirring occasionally, for 30 seconds after the gnocchi float to the surface. Scoop out the gnocchi with a slotted spoon and make a layer of them in the prepared baking dish. Lay half of the Fontina on top and drizzle with half of the butter. Sprinkle with pepper. Make a second layer of gnocchi, Fontina and butter. Sprinkle with the grated cheese and cinnamon.

3 Bake 20 minutes or until bubbling and lightly golden. Serve hot.

Sorrento-Style Potato Gnocchi
Gnocchi alla Sorrentina

MAKES 8 SERVINGS

In the Naples area, potato gnocchi are often called strangolopreti, *meaning "priest stranglers," the idea being that a greedy priest faced with such delicious home cooking might eat too many and choke. This baked dish is a specialty of Sorrento.*

About 2 cups Marinara Sauce (page 89)
1 recipe Potato Gnocchi (pages 189–190)
Salt
8 ounces fresh mozzarella, thinly sliced
1/4 cup freshly grated Pecorino Romano

1 Prepare the sauce and the gnocchi. Then, place a rack in the center of the oven. Preheat the oven to 400°F. Spread a thin layer of the sauce in a 13 × 9 × 2–inch baking dish.

2 Bring a large pot of water to a boil. Add salt to taste. Lower the heat so that the water boils gently. Drop the gnocchi into the water a few pieces at a time. Cook for 30 seconds after the gnocchi rise to the surface. Skim the gnocchi from the pot with a slotted spoon, draining the pieces well. Spread the gnocchi in the baking dish. Spoon on some of the sauce. Repeat with the remaining gnocchi and sauce. Scatter the mozzarella over the gnocchi. Sprinkle with the grated cheese.

3 Bake 30 minutes or until the sauce is bubbling. Serve hot.

Winter Squash Gnocchi
Gnocchi di Zucca

MAKES 6 SERVINGS

Several varieties of winter squash are grown in Italy, especially in Lombardy, the Veneto, Emilia-Romagna, Puglia, and Campania. The squash are used to make risotto, added to soups, or fried. These gnocchi are typical of Lombardy and the Veneto. The procedure for making them is pretty much the same as for making potato gnocchi, though the squash is baked rather than boiled.

These gnocchi are pale orange and go best with a butter sauce, like Butter and Sage Sauce (page 100).

1 medium butternut squash (about 1 1/2 pounds)
2 to 3 cups all-purpose flour
Salt
Freshly ground nutmeg
8 tablespoon (1 stick) unsalted butter
1/2 cup freshly grated Parmigiano-Reggiano

1 Place a rack in the center of the oven. Preheat the oven to 400°F. Oil a baking pan just large enough to hold the squash. With a large heavy chef's knife, cut the squash in half lengthwise. Scoop out the seeds and fibers. Place the squash cut-side down in the pan. Bake until the squash is tender when pierced in the thickest part with a small sharp knife, about 30 minutes. Let cool slightly. Scrape off the skin. Cut the squash into chunks and pass it through a food mill or puree it in the blender. You should have about 1 1/2 cups of squash.

2 Dust two large baking sheets with flour. In a large bowl, stir together the squash, 1 teaspoon salt, and a big pinch of nutmeg. Stir well. Stir in one cup of the flour just until blended. The dough will be stiff.

3 Scrape the squash onto a floured surface. Knead briefly, adding just as much of the flour as necessary to make a soft dough. It should be slightly sticky. Add just enough flour so that the gnocchi will hold their shape when cooked but not so much that they become heavy.

4 Set the dough aside for a moment. Scrape the board to remove any dough scraps. Wash and dry your hands, then dust them with flour.

5 Cut the dough into 8 pieces. Keeping the remaining dough covered, roll one piece into a long rope about 3/4 inch thick. Cut the rope into 1/2-inch nuggets.

6 To shape the dough, hold a fork in one hand with the tines pointed down. With the thumb of the other hand, roll each piece of dough over the back of the tines, pressing lightly to make ridges on one side and an indentation from your finger on the other. Let the gnocchi drop onto the prepared pans. The pieces should not touch. Repeat with the remaining dough.

7 Refrigerate the gnocchi until ready to cook. (Gnocchi can also be frozen. Place the baking sheets in the freezer for one hour or until firm. Put the gnocchi in a large heavy-duty plastic bag. Freeze up to one month. Do not thaw before cooking.)

8 Have ready a heated shallow serving bowl. Melt the butter in a small saucepan. Pour half the butter into the bowl.

9 To cook the gnocchi, bring a large pot of water to a boil. Add salt to taste. Lower the heat so that the water boils gently. Drop the gnocchi into the water a few pieces at a time. Cook until about 30 seconds after the gnocchi rise to the surface. Skim the gnocchi from the pot with a slotted spoon, draining the pieces well. Transfer to the serving bowl. Repeat with remaining gnocchi. Pour on the remaining butter.

10 Toss the gnocchi gently. Sprinkle with cheese. Serve hot.

Spinach and Potato Gnocchi

Gnocchi di Patate e Spinaci

MAKES 6 SERVINGS

Though it is not often done in Italy, I sometimes like to serve gnocchi with a stew or pot roast. They soak up the sauce nicely and are a nice change from mashed potatoes or polenta. Try these gnocchi (without the sauce and cheese) as an accompaniment to Roman-Style Oxtail Stew (page 326) or Friuli-Style Beef Stew (page 324).

1 1/2 pounds baking potatoes
1 (10-ounce) bag of spinach, trimmed
Salt
2 cups all-purpose flour, plus more for shaping the gnocchi
1 large egg, beaten
1/2 cup Butter and Sage Sauce (page 100)
1 cup freshly grated Parmigiano-Reggiano

1 Place the potatoes in a large pot with cold water to cover. Cover the pot and bring to a simmer. Cook until the potatoes are tender when pierced with a knife, about 20 minutes.

2 Place the spinach in a large pot with 1/2 cup of water and salt to taste. Cover and cook until the spinach is tender, about 2 to 3 minutes. Drain the spinach and let cool. Place the spinach in a towel and squeeze out the liquid. Very finely chop the spinach.

3 While the potatoes are still warm, peel them and cut them into chunks. Mash the potatoes using the smallest holes of a ricer or food mill, or by hand with a potato masher. Add the spinach, egg, and 2 teaspoons of salt. Stir in 1 1/2 cups of the flour just until blended. The dough will be stiff.

4 Scrape the potatoes onto a floured surface. Knead briefly, adding as much of the remaining flour as necessary to make a soft dough, enough so that the gnocchi will hold their shape when cooked but not so much that they become heavy. The dough should be slightly sticky. If you are in doubt, bring a small saucepan of water to a boil and drop in a piece of the dough as a test. Cook until the gnocco rises to the surface. If the dough begins to come apart, add more flour. Otherwise the dough is fine.

5 Set the dough aside for a moment. Scrape the board to remove any dough scraps. Wash and dry your hands, then dust them with flour. Set out one or two large baking pans and dust them with flour.

6 Cut the dough into 8 pieces. Keeping the remaining dough covered, roll one piece into a long rope about 3/4 inch thick. Cut the rope into 1/2-inch nuggets.

7 To shape the dough, hold a fork in one hand with the tines pointed down. With the thumb of the other hand, roll each piece of dough over the back of the tines, pressing lightly to make ridges on one side and an indentation on the other. Let the gnocchi drop onto the prepared pans. The pieces should not touch. Repeat with the remaining dough.

8 Refrigerate the gnocchi until ready to cook. (Gnocchi can also be frozen. Place the baking sheets in the freezer for one hour or until firm. Put the gnocchi in a large heavy-duty plastic bag. Freeze up to one month. Do not thaw before cooking.)

9 Prepare the sauce. To cook the gnocchi, bring a large pot of water to a boil. Add salt to taste. Lower the heat so that the water boils gently. Drop about half of the gnocchi into the water. Cook for about 30 seconds after the gnocchi rise to the surface. Skim the gnocchi from the pot with a slotted spoon, draining the pieces well.

10 Have ready a heated shallow serving bowl. Pour a thin layer of the hot sauce into the bowl. Add the gnocchi and toss gently. Cook the remaining gnocchi in the same way. Spoon on more sauce and sprinkle with cheese. Serve hot.

Seafood Gnocchi with Tomato and Olive Sauce

Gnocchi di Pesce con Salsa di Olive

MAKES 6 SERVINGS

In Sicily, potato gnocchi are sometimes flavored with sole or another delicate fish. I serve them with a slightly spicy tomato sauce, but a butter and herb sauce would also be delicious. Cheese is not needed on this pasta.

1 pound baking potatoes

1/4 cup olive oil

1 small onion, finely chopped

1 garlic clove

12 ounces fillet of sole or other delicate white fish,
    cut into 2-inch pieces

1/2 cup dry white wine

Salt and freshly ground black pepper

1 large egg, beaten

About 2 cups all-purpose flour

SAUCE

1/4 cup olive oil

1 scallion, chopped

2 anchovy fillets

1 tablespoon black olive paste

2 cups peeled, seeded, and chopped fresh tomatoes
    or drained and chopped canned imported Italian
    tomatoes

2 tablespoons chopped fresh flat-leaf parsley

Salt and freshly ground black pepper

1 Place the potatoes in a pot with cold water to cover. Bring to a simmer and cook until very tender when pierced with a knife. Drain and let cool.

2 In a medium skillet, cook the onion and garlic in the olive oil for 5 minutes over medium heat until the onion is tender. Add the fish and cook 1 minute. Add the wine, and salt and pepper to taste. Cook until the fish is tender and the liquid is mostly evaporated, about 5 minutes. Let cool, then scrape the contents of the skillet into a food processor or blender. Puree until smooth.

3 Line large pans with foil or plastic wrap. Pass the potatoes through a ricer or food mill into a large bowl. Add the fish puree and the egg. Gradually add the flour and salt to taste to form a slightly sticky dough. Knead briefly until smooth and well blended.

4 Divide the dough into 6 pieces. Keeping the remaining dough covered, roll one piece into a long rope about 3/4 inch thick. Cut the rope into 1/2-inch long nuggets.

5 To shape the dough, hold a fork in one hand with the tines pointed down. With the thumb of the other hand, roll each piece of dough over the back of the tines, pressing lightly to make ridges on one side and an indentation on the other. Let the gnocchi drop onto the prepared pans. The pieces should not touch. Repeat with the remaining dough.

6 Refrigerate the gnocchi until ready to cook. (Gnocchi can also be frozen. Place the baking sheets in the freezer for one hour or until firm. Put the gnocchi in a large heavy-duty plastic bag. Freeze up to 1 month. Do not thaw before cooking.)

7 For the sauce, combine the oil with the scallion in a large skillet. Add the anchovy fillets and cook until the anchovies are dissolved, about 2 minutes. Stir in the olive paste, tomatoes, and parsley. Add salt and pepper and cook until the tomato juices have thickened slightly, 8 to 10 minutes. Spoon half the sauce into a large warm serving bowl.

8 Prepare the gnocchi: Bring a large pot of water to a boil. Add salt to taste. Lower the heat so that the water boils gently. Drop about half of the gnocchi into the water. Cook for about 30 seconds after the gnocchi rise to the surface. Skim the gnocchi from the pot with a slotted spoon, draining the pieces well. Place the gnocchi in the serving bowl. Cook the remaining gnocchi in the same way. Add the remaining sauce and stir gently. Serve immediately.

Green Gnocchi in Pink Sauce

Gnocchi Verdi in Salsa Rossa

MAKES 6 SERVINGS

I first had these dumplings in Rome, though they are more typical of Emilia-Romagna and Tuscany. They are lighter than potato gnocchi, and the chopped greens give them a surface texture, so there is no need to shape the dumplings on the fork. For a change, try drizzling them with Butter and Sage Sauce (page 100).

3 cups Pink Sauce (page 92)

I pound spinach, stems removed

I pound Swiss chard, stems removed

¼ cup water

Salt

2 tablespoons unsalted butter

¼ cup finely chopped onion

I pound whole or part-skim ricotta

2 large eggs

1½ cups freshly grated Parmigiano-Reggiano

¼ teaspoon ground nutmeg

Freshly ground black pepper

1½ cups all-purpose flour

1 Prepare the sauce. Then, in a large pot, combine the two greens, water, and salt to taste. Cook 5 minutes or until wilted and tender. Drain and let cool. Wrap the greens in a towel and squeeze to extract the liquid. Chop finely.

2 In a medium skillet, melt the butter over medium heat. Add the onion and cook, stirring frequently, until golden, about 10 minutes.

3 In a large bowl, beat together the ricotta, eggs, 1 cup of the Parmigiano-Reggiano, nutmeg, and salt and pepper to taste. Add the onion and chopped greens and mix well. Stir in the flour until well blended. The dough will be soft.

4 Line baking sheets with parchment or wax paper. Dampen your hands with cool water. Scoop up a tablespoonful of the dough. Lightly shape it into a ¾-inch ball. Place the ball on a baking sheet. Repeat with the remaining dough. Cover with plastic wrap and refrigerate until ready to cook.

5 Bring at least 4 quarts of water to a boil. Add salt to taste. Lower the heat slightly. Add half the gnocchi a few at a time. When they rise to the surface, cook 30 seconds longer.

6 Spoon half the hot sauce into a warm serving platter. Remove the gnocchi with a slotted spoon and drain them well. Add them to the platter. Cover and keep warm while you cook the remaining gnocchi in the same way. Spoon on the remaining sauce and cheese. Serve hot.

Gnocchi

The best-known form of gnocchi (prononunced *nee-oh-kee*) is made from potatoes, but these little dumplings can also be made with ricotta, bread, winter squash, or semolina. Gnocchi are made in one form or another in every region of Italy.

Most gnocchi are shaped on the tines of a fork to form ridges that help them cook evenly and capture the sauce. I have a gadget I bought in Italy called a *riga gnocchi*, a small piece of wood with narrow grooves that serves the same purpose as the fork by making ridges in the gnocchi.

Gnocchi means "lumps," and if you have ever had badly made gnocchi, you will know why. But light gnocchi are not difficult to make.

Semolina Gnocchi
Gnocchi alla Romana

MAKES 4 TO 6 SERVINGS

Be sure to fully cook the semolina with the liquid. If it is undercooked, it tends to melt into a mass instead of keeping its shape when baked. But even if that does happen, it will still taste great.

2 cups milk
2 cups water
1 cup fine semolina
2 teaspoons salt
4 tablespoons unsalted butter
²/₃ cup freshly grated Parmigiano-Reggiano
2 egg yolks

1 In a medium saucepan, heat the milk and 1 cup of the water over medium heat until simmering. Stir together the remaining 1 cup water and the semolina. Scrape the mixture into the liquid. Add the salt. Cook, stirring constantly, until the mixture comes to a boil. Reduce the heat to low and cook, stirring well, for 20 minutes, or until the mixture is very thick.

2 Remove the pot from the heat. Stir in 2 tablespoons of the butter and half of the cheese. Rapidly beat in the egg yolks with a whisk.

3 Lightly moisten a baking sheet. Pour the semolina onto the sheet and spread it to a ¹/₂-inch thickness with a metal spatula. Let cool, then cover and chill for one hour or up to 48 hours.

4 Place a rack in the center of the oven. Preheat the oven to 400°F. Butter a 13 × 9 × 2–inch baking dish.

5 Dip a 1¹/₂-inch cookie or biscuit cutter in cool water. Cut out rounds of the semolina and arrange the pieces in the prepared baking dish, overlapping slightly.

6 Melt the remaining 2 tablespoons butter in a small saucepan, and drizzle it over the gnocchi. Sprinkle with remaining cheese. Bake 20 to 30 minutes or until golden brown and bubbling. Let cool 5 minutes before serving.

Abruzzese Bread Dumplings
Polpette di Pane al Sugo

MAKES 6 TO 8 SERVINGS

When I visited the Orlandi Contucci Ponno winery in Abruzzo, I enjoyed a tasting of their outstanding wines, which included both white Trebbiano d'Abruzzo and red Montepulciano d'Abruzzo varieties, as well as several blends. Wines as good as these deserve good food, and our lunch was not disappointing, especially the dumplings made of eggs, cheese, and bread simmered in tomato sauce. Though I had never had them before, a little research showed me that these "meatless meatballs" are also popular in other regions of Italy such as Calabria and Basilicata.

The cook from the winery told me that she made the dumplings with the mollica *of the bread—the inside of the bread with crust removed. I make them with the whole loaf. Since the Italian bread I buy here is not as sturdy as bread in Italy, the crust gives the dumplings added structure.*

If you plan to make these ahead of time, keep the dumplings and sauce separate until just before serving time so that the dumplings do not drink up too much of the sauce.

1 12-ounce loaf Italian or French bread, cut into 1-inch pieces (about 8 cups)
2 cups cool water
3 large eggs
¹/₂ cup grated Pecorino Romano, plus more for serving
¹/₄ cup chopped fresh parsley
1 garlic clove, finely chopped
Vegetable oil for frying

SAUCE

1 medium onion, finely chopped
¹/₂ cup olive oil
2 (28-ounce) cans imported Italian peeled tomatoes with their juice, chopped
1 tiny dried peperoncino, crumbled, or a pinch of crushed red pepper
Salt
6 fresh basil leaves

1 Cut or tear the bread into tiny bits or grind the bread in a food processor into coarse crumbs. Soak the bread in the water for 20 minutes. Squeeze the bread to remove the excess water.

2 In a large bowl, beat the eggs, cheese, parsley, and garlic with a pinch of salt and pepper to taste. Stir in the crumbled bread and mix very well. If the mixture seems dry, stir in another egg. Mix well. Shape the mixture into balls about the size of a golf ball.

3 Pour enough oil to reach a depth of $1/2$ inch into a large heavy skillet. Heat the oil over medium heat until a drop of the bread mixture sizzles when it is placed in the oil.

4 Add the balls to the skillet and cook, turning carefully, until golden brown on all sides, about 10 minutes. Drain the balls on paper towels.

5 To make the sauce, in a large saucepan, cook the onion in the olive oil over medium heat until tender. Add the tomatoes, peperoncino, and salt to taste. Simmer 15 minutes or until slightly thickened.

6 Add the bread balls and baste them with the sauce. Simmer 15 minutes more. Sprinkle with the basil. Serve with additional cheese.

❧ Other Fresh Pasta Dishes

Ricotta-Filled Crepes
Manicotti

MAKES 6 TO 8 SERVINGS

Though many cooks use tubes of pasta to make manicotti, this is my mother's Neapolitan family recipe, made with crepes. The finished manicotti are much lighter than they would be made with pasta, and some cooks find manicotti easier to make with crepes.

3 cups Neapolitan Ragù (page 94)

Crepes
1 cup all-purpose flour
1 cup water
3 eggs
$1/2$ teaspoon salt
Vegetable oil

Filling
2 pounds whole or part-skim ricotta
4 ounces fresh mozzarella, chopped or shredded
$1/2$ cup freshly grated Parmigiano-Reggiano
1 large egg
2 tablespoons chopped fresh flat-leaf parsley
Freshly ground black pepper to taste
Pinch of salt
$1/2$ cup freshly grated Parmigiano-Reggiano

1 Prepare the ragù. Then, in a large bowl, whisk together the crepe ingredients until smooth. Cover and refrigerate 30 minutes or more.

2 Heat a 6-inch nonstick skillet or omelet pan over medium heat. Brush the pan lightly with oil. Holding the pan in one hand, spoon in about $1/3$ cup of the crepe batter. Immediately lift and rotate the pan to completely cover the base with

(continues)

a thin layer of batter. Pour off any excess batter. Cook one minute, or until the edge of the crepe turns brown and begins to lift away from the pan. With your fingers, flip the crepe over and brown lightly on the other side. Cook 30 seconds more or until spotted with brown.

3 Slide the cooked crepe onto a dinner plate. Repeat, making crepes with the remaining batter and stacking them one on top of the other.

4 To make the filling, stir together all of the ingredients in a large bowl until just combined.

5 Spoon a thin layer of the sauce in a 13 × 9 × 2–inch baking dish. To fill the crepes, place about 1/4 cup of the filling lengthwise on one side of a crepe. Roll the crepe into a cylinder and place it in the baking dish seam-side down. Continue filling and rolling the remaining crepes, placing them close together. Spoon on additional sauce. Sprinkle with cheese.

6 Place a rack in the center of the oven. Preheat the oven to 350°F. Bake 30 to 45 minutes or until the sauce is bubbling and the manicotti are heated through. Serve hot.

Abruzzese Crepe and Mushroom Timbale
Timballo di Scrippelle

MAKES 8 SERVINGS

A friend whose grandmother came from Teramo in the Abruzzo region used to reminisce about the delicious casserole of crepes layered with mushrooms and cheese that her grandmother made for holidays. Here is a version of that dish I adapted from the book Ricette di Osterie d'Italia, *by Slow Food Editore. According to the book, the crepes descended from the elaborate crepe preparations introduced by French cooks in the region in the seventeenth Century.*

2 1/2 cups Tuscan Tomato Sauce (pages 90–91)

CREPES
5 large eggs
1 1/2 cups water
1 teaspoon salt
1 1/2 cups all-purpose flour
Vegetable oil for frying

FILLING
1 cup dried mushrooms
1 cup warm water
1/4 cup olive oil
1 pound fresh white mushrooms, rinsed and cut into thick slices
1 garlic clove, finely chopped
2 tablespoons fresh flat-leaf parsley
Salt and freshly ground black pepper
12 ounces fresh mozzarella, sliced and torn into 1-inch pieces
1 cup freshly grated Parmigiano-Reggiano

1 Prepare the tomato sauce. In a large bowl, whisk together the crepe ingredients until smooth. Cover and refrigerate 30 minutes or more.

2 Heat a 6-inch nonstick skillet or omelet pan over medium heat. Brush the pan lightly with oil. Holding the pan in one hand, spoon in about 1/3 cup of the crepe batter. Immediately lift and rotate the pan to completely cover the base with a thin layer of batter. Pour off any excess batter. Cook 1 minute, or until the edge of the crepe turns brown and begins to lift away from the pan. With your fingers, flip the crepe over and brown lightly on the other side. Cook 30 seconds more or until spotted with brown.

3 Slide the cooked crepe onto a dinner plate. Repeat making crepes with the remaining batter, stacking them one on top of the other.

4 To make the filling, soak the dried mushrooms in the water for 30 minutes. Remove the mushrooms and reserve the liquid. Rinse the mushrooms under cold running water to removing any grit, paying special attention to the ends of the stems where soil collects. Chop the mushrooms coarsely.

Strain the mushroom liquid through a paper coffee filter into a bowl.

5 In a large skillet, heat the oil. Add the mushrooms. Cook, stirring often, until the mushrooms are browned, 10 minutes. Add the garlic, parsley, and salt and pepper to taste. Cook until the garlic is golden, about 2 minutes more. Stir in the dried mushrooms and their liquid. Cook 5 minutes or until most of the liquid has evaporated.

6 Place a rack in the center of the oven. Preheat the oven to 375°F. In a 13 × 9 × 2–inch baking dish, spoon a thin layer of tomato sauce. Make a layer of crepes, overlapping them slightly. Follow with a layer of mushrooms, mozzarella, sauce, and cheese. Repeat the layering, ending with the crepes, sauce, and grated cheese.

7 Bake 45 to 60 minutes or until the sauce is bubbling. Let rest 10 minutes before serving. Cut into squares and serve hot.

Tuscan Handmade Spaghetti with Meat Sauce
Pici al Ragù

MAKES 6 SERVINGS

Chewy strands of handmade pasta are popular in Tuscany and parts of Umbria, usually sauced with a meat ragù. The pasta is called either pici *or* pinci, *and it derives from the word* appicciata, *meaning "elongated by hand."*

I learned to make these in Montefollonico at a restaurant called La Chiusa, where the cook comes to each table and gives diners a little demonstration on how to make them. These are very easy to make, though time-consuming.

3 cups unbleached all-purpose flour, plus more for shaping the dough

Salt

1 tablespoon olive oil

About 1 cup water

6 cups Tuscan Meat Sauce (page 95)

1/2 cup freshly grated Parmigiano-Reggiano

1 Place the flour and 1/4 teaspoon salt in a large bowl and stir to mix. Pour the olive oil into the center. Begin stirring the mixture while slowly adding the water, stopping when the dough begins to come together and form a ball. Remove the dough to a lightly floured surface and knead it until smooth and elastic, about 10 minutes.

2 Shape the dough into a ball. Cover with an overturned bowl and let stand 30 minutes.

3 Sprinkle a large baking pan with flour. Divide the dough into quarters. Work with one quarter of the dough at a time while you keep the remainder covered. Pinch off small pieces about the size of a hazelnut.

4 On a lightly floured surface with your hands outstretched, roll out each piece of dough to form thin strands about 1/8 inch thick. Place the strands on the prepared baking sheet with some space between them. Repeat with the remaining dough. Let the pasta dry uncovered about 1 hour.

5 Meanwhile, prepare the sauce. Then, bring 4 quarts of water to a boil in a large pot. Add salt to taste. Add the pici and cook until al dente, tender yet still firm to the bite. Drain and toss the pasta with the sauce in a large warmed bowl. Sprinkle with the cheese and toss again. Serve hot.

Pici with Garlic and Bread Crumbs
Pici con le Briciole

MAKES 4 TO 6 SERVINGS

This dish is from La Fattoria, a quaint lakeside restaurant near the Etruscan town of Chiusi.

1 pound Tuscan Handmade Spaghetti (page 199), steps 1 to 6

1/2 cup olive oil

4 large garlic cloves

1/2 cup fine dry bread crumbs

1/2 cup freshly grated Pecorino Romano

(continues)

1 Prepare the pasta. In a skillet large enough to hold all of the pasta, heat the oil over medium-low heat. Lightly crush the garlic cloves and add them to the pan. Cook until the garlic is golden, about 5 minutes. Do not let it become brown. Remove the garlic from the pan and stir in the bread crumbs. Cook, stirring often, until the crumbs are browned, about 5 minutes.

2 Meanwhile, bring at least 4 quarts of water to a boil. Add the pasta and 2 tablespoons of salt. Stir well. Cook over high heat, stirring frequently, until the pasta is al dente, tender yet firm to the bite. Drain the pasta.

3 Add the pasta to the skillet with the crumbs and toss well over medium heat. Sprinkle with the cheese and toss again. Serve immediately.

Semolina Pasta Dough

MAKES ABOUT 1 POUND

Semolina flour made from hard durum wheat is used to make several types of fresh pasta in southern Italy, especially Puglia, Calabria, and Basilicata. When cooked, these pastas are chewy and work well paired with robust meat and vegetable sauces. The dough is very stiff. It can be kneaded by hand, though it is quite a workout. I prefer to use a food processor or heavy-duty mixer to do the heavy mixing, then knead it briefly by hand to make sure the consistency is just right.

1 1/2 cups fine semolina flour
1 cup all-purpose flour, plus more for dusting
1 teaspoon salt
About 2/3 cup warm water

1 In the bowl of a food processor or heavy-duty stand mixer, stir together the dry ingredients. Gradually add water to make a stiff, nonsticky dough.

2 Turn the dough out onto a lightly floured surface. Knead until smooth, about 2 minutes.

3 Cover the dough with a bowl and let rest 30 minutes. Dust two large baking sheets with flour.

4 Cut the dough into 8 pieces. Work with one piece at a time, keeping the remaining pieces covered with an overturned bowl. On a lightly floured surface, roll one piece of the dough into a long rope about 1/2 inch thick. Shape the dough into cavatelli or orrecchiette, as described in the next recipe.

Cavatelli with Ragù
Cavatelli con Ragù

MAKES 6 TO 8 SERVINGS

Stores and catalogs that specialize in pasta-making equipment often sell a device for making cavatelli. It looks something like an old-fashioned meat grinder. You clamp it to the countertop, insert a rope of dough at one end, turn the crank, and neatly made cavatelli come out the other end. It makes short work of a batch of this dough, but I would not bother with it unless I made cavatelli frequently.

When shaping the cavatelli, work on a wooden or other rough-textured surface. The rough surface will hold the bits of pasta dough, allowing them to be dragged with the knife rather than sliding as they would on a smooth, slick countertop.

Sausage Ragù (page 94) or Sicilian Tomato Sauce (page 90)
1 pound Semolina Pasta Dough (page 200) prepared through step 4
Salt

1 Prepare the ragù or sauce. Have ready 2 baking sheets dusted with flour.

2 Cut the dough into 1/2-inch pieces. Hold a small knife with a dull blade and rounded tip with your index finger pressed against the blade of the knife. Flatten each piece of dough, pressing and dragging it slightly so that the dough curls around the tip of the knife to form a shell shape.

2 Spread the pieces on the prepared pans. Repeat with the remaining dough. (If you are not using the cavatelli within an hour, place the pans in the freezer. When the pieces are firm, scoop them into a plastic bag and seal tightly. Do not thaw before cooking.)

3 To cook, bring four quarts of cold water to a boil over high heat. Add the cavatelli and 2 tablespoons of salt. Cook, stirring occasionally, until the pasta is tender yet still slightly chewy.

4 Drain the cavatelli and pour them into a heated serving bowl. Toss with the sauce. Serve hot.

Cavatelli with Calamari and Saffron
Cavatelli con Sugo di Calamari

MAKES 6 SERVINGS

The slightly chewy texture of calamari complements the chewiness of the cavatelli in this contemporary Sicilian recipe. The sauce gets a smooth, velvety texture from a mixture of flour and olive oil and a lovely yellow color from saffron.

1 teaspoon saffron threads
2 tablespoons warm water
1 medium onion, finely chopped
2 garlic cloves, very finely chopped
5 tablespoons olive oil
1 pound cleaned calamari (squid; see page 276), cut into 1/2-inch rings
1/2 cup dry white wine
Salt and freshly ground black pepper
1 tablespoon flour
1 pound fresh or frozen cavatelli
1/4 cup chopped fresh flat-leaf parsley
Extra-virgin olive oil

1 Crumble the saffron into the warm water and set aside.

2 In a skillet large enough to hold all of the pasta, cook the onion and garlic in 4 tablespoons of the oil over medium heat until the onion is lightly golden, about 10 minutes. Add the calamari and cook, stirring, until the calamari are just opaque, about 2 minutes. Add the wine and salt and pepper to taste. Bring to a simmer and cook 1 minute.

3 Stir together the remaining 1 tablespoon oil and the flour. Stir the mixture into the calamari.

Bring to a simmer. Add the saffron mixture and cook 5 minutes more.

4 Meanwhile, bring at least 4 quarts of water to a boil. Add the pasta and 2 tablespoons of salt. Stir well. Cook over high heat, stirring frequently, until the pasta is tender but slightly underdone. Drain the pasta, reserving some of the cooking water.

5 Stir the pasta into the skillet with the calamari. Add a little of the reserved cooking water if the mixture seems dry. Stir in the parsley and mix well. Remove from the heat and drizzle with a little extra-virgin olive oil. Serve immediately.

Cavatelli with Arugula and Tomato
Cavatelli con Rughetta e Pomodori

MAKES 4 TO 6 SERVINGS

Arugula is best known as a salad green, but in Puglia it is often cooked, or, as in this recipe, stirred into hot soup or pasta dishes at the last minute so that it just wilts. I love the nutty spicy flavor it adds.

1/4 cup olive oil
2 garlic cloves, finely chopped
2 pounds ripe plum tomatoes, peeled, seeded, and chopped, or 1 (28-ounce) can imported Italian peeled tomatoes with their juice
Salt and freshly ground black pepper
1 pound fresh or frozen cavatelli
1/2 cup grated ricotta salata or Pecorino Romano
1 large bunch of arugula, trimmed and torn into bite-size pieces (about 2 cups)

1 In a skillet large enough to hold all of the ingredients, cook the garlic in the oil over medium heat until lightly golden, about 2 minutes. Add the tomatoes and salt and pepper to taste. Bring the sauce to a simmer and cook until thickened, about 20 minutes.

2 Bring at least 4 quarts of water to a boil. Add the pasta and salt to taste. Stir well. Cook over high heat,

(continues)

stirring frequently, until the pasta is tender. Drain the pasta, reserving some of the cooking water.

3 Stir the pasta into the tomato sauce with half of the cheese. Add the arugula and stir well. Add a little of the reserved cooking water if the pasta seems too dry. Sprinkle with the remaining cheese and serve immediately.

Orecchiette with Pork Ragù
Orecchiette con Ragù di Maiale

MAKES 6 TO 8 SERVINGS

My friend Dora Marzovilla comes from Rutigliano, near Bari. She is an expert pasta maker, and I have learned a lot by watching her. Dora has a special wooden pasta board that is used only for pasta making. Though Dora makes many types of fresh pasta, such as gnocchi, cavatelli, ravioli, and maloreddus—Sardinian saffron gnocchi—for her family's New York City restaurant, I Trulli, orecchiette are her specialty.

Making orecchiette is very similar to making cavatelli. The biggest difference is that the pasta shell has a more open dome shape, something like an over-turned Frisbee or, in the fanciful Italian imagination, little ears, which is how they got their name.

1 recipe Semolina Dough (page 200)
3 cups Pork Ragù with Fresh Herbs (see pages 98–99)
1/2 cup freshly grated Pecorino Romano

1 Prepare ragù and dough. Have ready 2 large baking sheets dusted with flour. Cut the dough into 1/2-inch pieces. Hold a small knife with a dull blade and rounded tip with your index finger pressed against the blade of the knife. Flatten each piece of dough with the tip of the knife, pressing and dragging it slightly so that the dough forms a disk. Invert each disk over the tip of your thumb creating a dome shape.

2 Spread the pieces on the prepared pans. Repeat with the remaining dough. (If you are not using the orecchiette within 1 hour, place the pans in the freezer. When the pieces are firm, scoop them into a plastic bag and seal tightly. Do not thaw before cooking.)

3 Bring at least 4 quarts of water to a boil. Add the pasta and salt to taste. Stir well. Cook over high heat, stirring frequently, until the pasta is al dente, tender yet still firm to the bite. Drain the pasta, reserving some of the cooking water.

4 Add the pasta to the ragù. Add the cheese and stir well, adding some of the reserved cooking water, if the sauce seems too thick. Serve immediately.

Orecchiette with Broccoli Rabe
Orecchiette con Cime di Rape

MAKES 4 TO 6 SERVINGS

This is practically the official dish of Puglia, and nowhere will you find it more delicious. It calls for broccoli rabe, sometimes called rapini, *though turnip greens, mustard, kale, or regular broccoli can also be used. Broccoli rabe has long stems and leaves and a pleasantly bitter flavor, though boiling it tames some of the bitterness and makes it tender.*

1 bunch broccoli rabe (about 1 1/2 pounds), cut into 1-inch pieces
Salt
1/3 cup olive oil
4 garlic cloves
8 anchovies fillets
Pinch of crushed red pepper
1 pound fresh orecchiette or cavatelli

1 Bring a large pot of water to a boil. Add the broccoli rabe and salt to taste. Cook the broccoli rabe 5 minutes, then drain it. It should still be firm.

2 Dry the pot. Heat the oil with the garlic over medium-low heat. Add the anchovies and red pepper. When the garlic is golden, add the broccoli rabe. Cook, stirring well to coat the broccoli with the oil, until very tender, about 5 minutes.

3 Bring at least 4 quarts of water to a boil. Add the pasta and salt to taste. Stir well. Cook over high heat, stirring frequently, until the pasta is al dente, tender yet still firm to the bite. Drain the pasta, reserving some of the cooking water.

4 Add the pasta to the broccoli rabe. Cook, stirring, for 1 minute or until the pasta is well blended. Add a little of the cooking water if necessary.

> **Variation:** Eliminate the anchovies. Serve the pasta sprinkled with chopped toasted almonds or grated Pecorino Romano.

> **Variation:** Eliminate the anchovies. Remove the casings from 2 Italian sausages. Chop the meat and cook it with the garlic, hot pepper, and broccoli rabe. Serve sprinkled with Pecorino Romano.

Orecchiette with Cauliflower and Tomatoes
Orecchiette con Cavolfiore e Pomodori

MAKES 4 TO 6 SERVINGS

A Sicilian relative taught me to make this pasta, but it is eaten in Puglia, too. If you prefer, substitute grated cheese for the toasted bread crumbs.

1/3 cup plus 2 tablespoons olive oil

1 garlic clove, finely chopped

3 pounds plum tomatoes, peeled, seeded, and chopped or 1 (28-ounce) can imported Italian peeled tomatoes, with their juice, chopped

1 medium cauliflower, trimmed and cut into florets

Salt and freshly ground black pepper

3 tablespoons plain dry bread crumbs

2 anchovies, chopped (optional)

1 pound fresh orecchiette

1 In a skillet large enough to hold all of the ingredients, cook the garlic in 1/3 cup of the olive oil over medium heat until golden. Add the tomatoes and salt and pepper to taste. Bring to a simmer and cook 10 minutes.

2 Stir in the cauliflower. Cover and cook, stirring occasionally, until the cauliflower is very tender, about 25 minutes. Crush some of the cauliflower with the back of a spoon.

3 In a small skillet, heat the remaining 2 tablespoons of oil over medium heat. Add the bread crumbs and anchovies, if using. Cook, stirring until the crumbs are toasted and the oil is absorbed.

4 Bring at least 4 quarts of water to a boil. Add the pasta and salt to taste. Cook, stirring frequently, until the pasta is al dente, tender yet still firm to the bite. Drain the pasta, reserving a little of the cooking water.

5 Toss the pasta with the tomato and cauliflower sauce. Add a little of the cooking water if needed. Sprinkle with the bread crumbs and serve immediately.

Orecchiette with Sausage and Cabbage
Orecchiette con Salsiccia e Cavolo

MAKES 6 SERVINGS

When my friend Domenica Marzovilla returned from a trip to Tuscany, she described to me this pasta that she had eaten at the home of a friend. It sounded so simple and good, I went home and made it.

2 tablespoons olive oil

8 ounces sweet pork sausages

8 ounces hot pork sausages

2 cups canned imported Italian tomatoes, drained and chopped

Salt

1 pound Savoy cabbage (about 1/2 medium head)

1 pound fresh orecchiette or cavatelli

1 In a medium saucepan, heat the oil over medium heat. Add the sausages and cook until browned on all sides, about 10 minutes.

2 Add the tomatoes and a pinch of salt. Bring to a simmer and cook until the sauce is thickened, about 30 minutes.

(continues)

3 Cut the core from the cabbage. Cut the cabbage into thin strips.

4 Bring a large pot of water to a boil. Add the cabbage and cook until 1 minute after the water returns to the boil. Scoop out the cabbage with a slotted spoon. Drain well. Reserve the cooking water.

5 Remove the sausages to a cutting board, leaving the sauce in the pan. Add the cabbage to the sauce; cook 15 minutes. Slice the sausage thin.

6 Return the water to a boil and cook the pasta with salt to taste. Drain well and toss with the sausage and the sauce. Serve hot.

Orecchiette with Swordfish
Orecchiette con Pesce Spada

MAKES 4 TO 6 SERVINGS

Tuna or shark can be substituted for the swordfish, if you prefer. Salting the eggplant removes some of the bitter juices and improves the texture, though many cooks feel this step is unnecessary. I always salt it, but the choice is up to you. The eggplant can be cooked several hours before the pasta. Simply reheat it on a baking sheet in a 350°F oven for 10 minutes or so before serving. This Sicilian pasta is unusual in Italian cooking in that even though the sauce contains fish, it is finished with cheese, adding to the richness.

1 large or 2 small eggplants (about 1 1/2 pounds)
Coarse salt
Corn or other vegetable oil for frying
3 tablespoons olive oil
1 large garlic clove, very finely chopped
2 green onions, finely chopped
8 ounces swordfish or other meaty fish steak (about 1/2 inch thick), skin removed and cut into 1/2-inch pieces
Freshly ground black pepper to taste
2 tablespoons white wine vinegar
2 cups peeled, seeded, and chopped fresh tomatoes or chopped canned imported Italian tomatoes with their juice
1 teaspoon fresh oregano leaves, chopped, or a pinch of dried oregano
1 pound fresh orecchiette or cavatelli
1/3 cup freshly grated Pecorino Romano

1 Cut the eggplant into 1-inch dice. Place the pieces in a colander set over a plate and sprinkle generously with salt. Let stand 30 minutes to 1 hour. Quickly rinse the eggplant pieces. Place the pieces on paper towels and squeeze until dry.

2 In a large deep skillet over medium heat, heat about 1/2 inch of oil. To test the oil, carefully place a small piece of eggplant in it. If it sizzles and cooks rapidly, add enough eggplant to make a single layer. Do not crowd the pan. Cook, stirring occasionally, until the eggplant is crisp and browned, about 5 minutes. Remove the pieces with a slotted spoon. Drain well on paper towels. Repeat with the remaining eggplant. Set aside.

3 In a medium skillet over medium heat, cook the olive oil with the garlic and green onions for 30 seconds. Add the fish and sprinkle with salt and pepper. Cook, stirring occasionally, until the fish is no longer pink, about 5 minutes. Add the vinegar and cook for 1 minute. Add the tomatoes and oregano. Bring to a simmer and cook for 15 minutes, or until slightly thickened.

4 Meanwhile, bring a large pot of cold water to a boil. Add salt to taste and the pasta. Cook, stirring occasionally, until al dente, tender yet firm to the bite. Drain well.

5 In a large heated serving bowl, combine the pasta, sauce, and eggplant. Toss well. Stir in the cheese. Serve hot.

Rice, Cornmeal, and Other Grains

Rice

White Risotto

Saffron Risotto, Milan Style

Asparagus Risotto

Risotto with Red Pepper

Tomato and Arugula Risotto

Risotto with Red Wine and Radicchio

Risotto with Creamy Cauliflower

Lemon Risotto

Spinach Risotto

Golden Squash Risotto

Venetian Risotto with Peas

Springtime Risotto

Risotto with Tomatoes and Fontina

Shrimp and Celery Risotto

Risotto with "Fruits of the Sea"

"Sea and Mountain" Risotto

Black Risotto

Crisp Risotto Pancake

Stuffed Rice Timbale

Rice and Beans, Veneto Style

Sardinian Sausage Rice

Cornmeal

Polenta

Polenta with Cream

Polenta with Ragù

Polenta Crostini, Three Ways

Polenta Sandwiches

Polenta with Three Cheeses

Polenta with Gorgonzola and Mascarpone

Mushroom Polenta

Buckwheat and Cornmeal Polenta

Baked Polenta with Cheese

Baked Polenta with Sausage Ragù

Polenta "in Chains"

Farro and Barley

Farro Salad

Farro, Amatrice Style

Farro, Tomatoes, and Cheese

Shrimp and Barley Orzotto

Barley and Vegetable Orzotto

Among the many types of grains grown and used throughout Italy, rice and corn-meal are the most common. Farro, cous-cous, and barley are regional favorites, as are wheat berries.

Rice was first brought to Italy from the Middle East. It grows particularly well in northern Italy, especially in the regions of Piedmont and Emilia-Romagna.

Italian cooks are very specific about the type of medium-grain rice they prefer, though the differences between varieties can be subtle. Many cooks will specify one variety for a seafood risotto and another for a risotto made with vegetables. Often, the preferences are regional or simply traditional, though each variety has specific properties. Carnaroli rice holds its shape well and makes a risotto that is slightly more creamy. Vialone Nano cooks faster and has a milder flavor. Arborio is the best known and is widely available, but the flavor is less subtle. It is best for risotto made with strong flavoring ingredients. Any of these three varieties can be used for the risotto recipes in this book.

Corn is a relatively new grain in Italy. It was not until after European exploration of the New World that corn found its way to Spain and spread from there throughout the continent. Corn is easy and inexpensive to grow, so it quickly became widely planted. Most of it is grown for animal feed, but cornmeal, both white and yellow, is typically used for polenta. It is rare to find corn on the cob eaten in Italy, except in Naples, where vendors sometimes sell grilled corn as street food. Romans do sometimes add corn niblets from a can to tossed salads, but it is something of an exotic oddity.

Farro and similar wheatlike grains are most common in central and southern Italy where they are grown. An ancient variety of wheat, farro is regarded as a health food by Italians. It is excellent in soups, salads, and other preparations.

Barley is an ancient grain that grows well in the colder regions of the north. The Romans fed barley and other grains to their armies. It was cooked into a porridge or soup known as *puls*, probably the forerunner of polenta. Today you find barley mostly in the northeast of Italy, near Austria, cooked like risotto or added to soup.

Couscous, made from hard wheat flour rolled into tiny pellets, is typical in western Sicily and is a vestige of the Arab domination of the region centuries ago. It is usually cooked with a soupy seafood or meat stew.

❧ Rice

Rice is grown in northern Italy in the Piedmont and Emilia-Romagna regions, and it is a staple that is often eaten in place of pasta or soup as a first course. The classic method for cooking rice is as risotto, which is my idea of rice in heaven!

If you have never made it before, the risotto technique may seem unusual. No other culture prepares rice in quite the same way as the Italians do, though the technique is similar to making pilaf, where the rice is sautéed and then cooked, and the cooking liquid absorbed. The idea is to cook the rice so that it releases its starch and forms a creamy sauce. The finished rice should be tender, yet still firm to the bite—al dente. The grains will have absorbed the flavors of the other ingredients and be surrounded by a creamy liquid. For best results, risotto needs to be eaten immediately after it is cooked or it may become dry and mushy.

Risotto is at its best when cooked at home. Few restaurants can devote as much time to the cooking of risotto as is needed, though it really isn't very long. In fact, many restaurant kitchens partially precook the rice, then cool it. When someone orders risotto, the rice is reheated, and liquid is added with whatever flavoring ingredients are needed to finish the cooking.

Once you understand the procedure, making risotto is quite simple and can be adapted to many different ingredient combinations. The first step in making risotto is getting the right type of rice. Long-grain rice, such as we commonly find in the United States, is not suitable for making risotto because it does not have the right kind of starch. Medium-grain rice, usually sold as Arborio, Carnaroli, or Vialone Nano varieties, has a kind of starch that releases from the grains when cooked and stirred with broth or another liquid. The starch binds with the liquid and becomes creamy.

Medium-grain rice imported from Italy is widely available in supermarkets. It is also grown in the United States and is now easy to find.

You will also need good chicken, meat, fish, or vegetable broth. Homemade is preferable, but canned (or boxed) broth can be used. I find store-bought broth too strong to use straight out of the container and often dilute it with water. Remember that packaged broth, unless you use a low-sodium variety, contains a lot of salt, so adjust any added salt accordingly. Boullion cubes are very salty and artificial-tasting, so I do not use them.

White Risotto
Risotto in Bianco

MAKES 4 SERVINGS

This plain white risotto is as basic and satisfying as vanilla ice cream. Serve it as is as a first course or as a side dish with braised meats. If you happen to have a fresh truffle, try shaving it over the finished risotto for a luxurious touch. In that case, you should eliminate the cheese.

4 cups Meat Broth (page 62) or Chicken Broth (page 63)
4 tablespoons unsalted butter
1 tablespoon olive oil
1/4 cup minced shallots or onion
1 1/2 cups medium-grain rice, such as Arborio, Carnaroli, or Vialone Nano
1/2 cup dry white wine or sparkling wine
Salt and freshly ground black pepper
1/2 cup freshly grated Parmigiano-Reggiano

1 Prepare the broth, if necessary. Bring the broth to a simmer over medium heat, then lower the heat so that it is just keeping the broth hot. In a wide heavy saucepan, melt 3 tablespoons of the butter with the oil over medium heat. Add the shallots and cook until softened but not browned, about 5 minutes.

2 Add the rice and stir with a wooden spoon until hot, about 2 minutes. Add the wine and cook, stirring, until most of the liquid evaporates.

(continues)

Rice, Cornmeal, and Other Grains   207

Risotto Tips

- Risotto is best eaten immediately after it is cooked, so have the table set and everything ready before you begin.
- Risotto takes about 20 to 25 minutes to cook from start to finish and requires almost constant stirring. Enlist someone to help you, if you like.
- To cut down a little on the cooking time, the first step of sautéeing the onion can be done ahead of time and the ingredients assembled before you begin.
- Use a wide, heavy saucepan—about 10 inches wide and 4 inches deep—so that the liquid evaporates steadily as the rice is simmering.
- Use a wooden spoon for stirring and reach all around the pan to be sure the rice does not stick.
- The broth or water should be heated, but not simmering so that it does not evaporate. Hot broth is absorbed by the rice better than broth that is cold or room-temperature. Add the hot liquid no more than 1/2 cup at a time. Stir until the liquid is absorbed by the rice and the spoon leaves a wide track on the bottom of the pan. If the rice begins to stick, add more liquid, reduce the heat slightly, and stir well.
- Many risotto dishes are made with wine, but more broth or water can be substituted.
- Have some hot water ready to use if you run out of broth. The biggest error novice risotto cooks make is that they cook according to the amount of broth. It may be just the right amount, it may not be enough (and you need the water), or you might actually need less broth, depending on the type of risotto you are making. You cannot predict exactly how much liquid the risotto will require, because there are so many variables, including the type of rice and moisture in other ingredients.
- To tell if the risotto is done, look at the grains and see if they are plump. Taste one or two grains of rice to see if it is al dente; it will feel firm without any trace of graininess. If it is undercooked, the rice will be hard at the core. Add an extra ladleful of liquid to the risotto before serving it. The rice continues to absorb the liquid even after the cooking is finished. The risotto should be moist, creamy, and flow gently; it should not hold a shape or be thick and puddinglike. Add liquid and stir vigorously if it becomes too dry.
- A pat of butter or a drizzle of extra-virgin olive oil is typically stirred into a finished risotto. Do not add cheese to seafood risotto.
- In Italy, risotto is typically served as a first course, not as a side dish, except with osso buco or another long-cooked stew.
- When eaten as a first course, risotto is served in rimmed soup plates and eaten with a fork.

3 Pour 1/2 cup of the broth over the rice. Cook, stirring, until most of the liquid is absorbed. Continue adding broth about 1/2 cup at a time, stirring after each addition. Adjust the heat so that the liquid simmers rapidly but the rice does not stick to the pan. About halfway through the cooking time, add salt and pepper to taste.

4 Use only as much of the broth as needed until the rice becomes tender yet firm to the bite and the risotto is creamy. When you think it may be done, taste a few grains. If not ready, test again in a minute or so. If the broth runs out before the rice is tender, use hot water. Cooking time will be 18 to 20 minutes.

5 Remove the risotto pan from the heat. Stir in the remaining tablespoon of butter and cheese until melted and creamy. Serve immediately.

Saffron Risotto, Milan Style
Risotto Milanese

MAKES 4 TO 6 SERVINGS

Golden risotto flavored with saffron is the classic Milanese accompaniment to Osso Buco (see Veal Shanks, Milan Style, page 347). Adding marrow scooped out of large beef bones to the risotto lends a rich, beefy flavor and is traditional, but the risotto can be made without it.

6 cups Chicken Broth (page 63) or Meat Broth (page 62)
1/2 teaspoon crumbled saffron threads
4 tablespoons unsalted butter
2 tablespoons beef marrow (optional)
2 tablespoons olive oil
1 small onion, very finely chopped
2 cups (about 1 pound) medium-grain rice, such as Arborio, Carnaroli, or Vialone Nano
Salt and freshly ground black pepper
1/2 cup freshly grated Parmigiano-Reggiano

1 Prepare the broth, if necessary. Bring the broth to a simmer over medium heat, then lower the

heat so it is just keeping the broth hot. Remove 1/2 cup broth and put in a small bowl. Add the saffron and allow it to soak.

2 In a wide heavy saucepan, heat 2 tablespoons of the butter, the marrow if using, and the oil over medium heat. When the butter is melted, add the onion and cook, stirring often, until golden, about 10 minutes.

3 Add the rice and cook, stirring with a wooden spoon until hot, about 2 minutes. Add 1/2 cup of the hot broth and stir until the liquid is absorbed. Continue adding the broth 1/2 cup at a time, stirring after each addition. Adjust the heat so that the liquid simmers rapidly but the rice does not stick to the pan. About halfway through the cooking time, stir in the saffron mixture and salt and pepper to taste.

4 Use only as much of the broth as needed until the rice becomes tender yet firm to the bite. When you think it may be done, taste a few grains. If not ready, test again in a minute or so. If the broth runs out before the rice is tender, use hot water. Cooking time will be 18 to 20 minutes.

5 Remove the risotto pan from the heat and stir in the remaining 2 tablespoons of butter and the cheese until melted and creamy. Serve immediately.

Asparagus Risotto
Risotto con Asparagi

MAKES 6 SERVINGS

The Veneto region is famous for its beautiful lavender-tipped white asparagus. To achieve the delicate color, the asparagus are kept covered as they grow so that they are not exposed to sunlight and do not form chlorophyll. White asparagus have a delicate flavor and are more tender than the green variety. White asparagus is ideal for this risotto, but you can make it with the ordinary green variety and the flavor will still be very good.

(continues)

5 cups Chicken Broth (page 63)

1 pound fresh asparagus, trimmed

4 tablespoons unsalted butter

1 small onion, finely chopped

2 cups medium-grain rice, such as Arborio, Carnaroli, or Vialone Nano

1/2 cup dry white wine

Salt and freshly ground black pepper

3/4 cup freshly grated Parmigiano-Reggiano

1 Prepare the broth, if necessary. Bring the broth to a simmer over medium heat, then lower the heat so that it just keeps the broth hot. Cut off the asparagus tips and set them aside. Cut the stems into 1/2-inch slices.

2 Melt 3 tablespoons of the butter in a wide, heavy saucepan. Add the onion and cook over medium heat, stirring occasionally, until very tender and golden, about 10 minutes.

3 Stir in the asparagus stems. Cook, stirring occasionally, 5 minutes.

4 Add the rice and cook, stirring with a wooden spoon until hot, about 2 minutes. Add the wine and cook, stirring constantly, until the liquid evaporates. Pour 1/2 cup of the broth over the rice. Cook, stirring, until most of the liquid is absorbed.

5 Continue adding broth about 1/2 cup at a time, stirring after each addition. Adjust the heat so that the liquid simmers rapidly but the rice does not stick to the pan. After about 10 minutes, stir in the asparagus tips. Season with salt and pepper. Use only as much of the broth as needed until the rice becomes tender yet firm to the bite and the risotto is creamy. When you think it may be done, taste a few grains. If not ready, test again in a minute or so. If the broth runs out before the rice is tender, use hot water. Cooking time will be 18 to 20 minutes.

6 Remove the risotto pan from the heat. Stir in the cheese and the remaining tablespoon butter. Taste for seasoning. Serve immediately.

Risotto with Red Peppers
Risotto con Peperoni Rossi

MAKES 6 SERVINGS

At the height of the season when brilliant red bell peppers are piled high at the greengrocers, I am inspired to use them in many ways. Their sweet, mellow flavor and gorgeous color make everything from omelets to pastas, soups, salads, and stews taste better. This is not a traditional recipe, but one I came up with one day while looking for a new way to use some red peppers. Yellow or orange peppers would be good in this recipe, too.

5 cups Chicken Broth (page 63)

3 tablespoons unsalted butter

1 tablespoon olive oil

1 small onion, finely chopped

2 red bell peppers, seeded and finely chopped

2 cups medium-grain rice, such as Arborio, Carnaroli, or Vialone Nano

Salt and freshly ground black pepper

1/2 cup freshly grated Parmigiano-Reggiano

1 Prepare the broth, if necessary. Bring the broth to a simmer over medium heat, then lower the heat so that it just keeps the broth hot. In a wide heavy saucepan, heat 2 tablespoons of the butter and the oil over medium heat. When the butter is melted, add the onion and cook, stirring often until golden, about 10 minutes. Add the peppers and cook 10 minutes more.

2 Add the rice and stir with a wooden spoon until hot, about 2 minutes. Add 1/2 cup of the hot broth and stir until the liquid is absorbed. Continue adding the broth a 1/2 cup at a time, stirring after each addition. Adjust the heat so that the liquid simmers rapidly but the rice does not stick to the pan. About halfway through the cooking, add salt and pepper to taste.

3 Use only as much of the broth as needed until the rice becomes tender yet firm to the bite and the risotto is creamy. When you think it may be done, taste a few grains. If not ready, test again in a minute or so. If the liquid runs out before the

rice is cooked, finish the cooking with hot water. Cooking time will be 18 to 20 minutes.

4 Remove the risotto pan from the heat. Stir in the remaining tablespoon of butter and the cheese until melted and creamy. Taste for seasoning. Serve immediately.

Tomato and Arugula Risotto
Risotto con Pomodori e Rucola

MAKES 6 SERVINGS

Fresh tomatoes, basil, and arugula make this risotto the essence of summer. I love to serve it with a cool white wine, such as Campania's Furore from producer Matilde Cuomo.

5 cups Chicken Broth (page 63)
I large bunch arugula, trimmed and rinsed
3 tablespoons olive oil
I small onion, finely chopped
2 pounds ripe plum tomatoes, peeled, seeded, and chopped
2 cups medium-grain rice, such as Arborio, Carnaroli, or Vialone Nano
Salt and freshly ground black pepper
1/2 cup freshly grated Parmigiano-Reggiano
2 tablespoons chopped fresh basil
I tablespoon extra-virgin olive oil

1 Prepare the broth, if necessary. Bring the broth to a simmer over medium heat, then lower the heat so that it just keeps the broth hot. Tear the arugula leaves into bite size pieces. You should have about 2 cups.

2 Pour the oil into a wide heavy saucepan. Add the onion and cook over medium heat, stirring occasionally with a wooden spoon, until the onion is very tender and golden, about 10 minutes.

3 Stir in the tomatoes. Cook, stirring occasionally, until most of the juice has evaporated, about 10 minutes.

4 Add the rice and cook, stirring with a wooden spoon until hot, about 2 minutes. Pour 1/2 cup of

the broth over the rice. Cook and stir until most of the liquid is absorbed.

5 Continue adding broth about 1/2 cup at a time, stirring after each addition. Adjust the heat so that the liquid simmers rapidly but the rice does not stick to the pan. Halfway through the cooking, season with salt and pepper. Use only as much of the broth as needed until the rice becomes tender yet firm to the bite and the risotto is creamy. When you think it may be done, taste a few grains. If not ready, test again in a minute or so. If the broth runs out before the rice is tender, use hot water. Cooking time will be 18 to 20 minutes.

6 Remove the risotto pan from the heat. Stir in the cheese, basil, and a tablespoon of extra-virgin olive oil. Taste for seasoning. Stir in the arugula and serve immediately.

Risotto with Red Wine and Radicchio
Risotto al Radicchio

MAKES 6 SERVINGS

Radicchio, a member of the chicory family, is grown in the Veneto. Like endive, to which it is related, radicchio has a slightly bitter-yet-sweet flavor. Though we think of it mostly as a colorful addition to a salad bowl, the Italians often cook radicchio. It can be cut into wedges and grilled, or the leaves can be wrapped around a filling and baked as an appetizer. The vibrant wine-red color turns a dark mahogany brown when it is cooked. I had this risotto at Il Cenacolo, a restaurant in Verona that features traditional recipes.

5 cups Chicken Broth (page 63) or Meat Broth (page 62)
I medium head radicchio (about 12 ounces)
2 tablespoons olive oil
2 tablespoons unsalted butter
I small onion, finely chopped
1/2 cup dry red wine
2 cups medium-grain rice, such as Arborio, Carnaroli, or Vialone Nano
Salt and freshly ground black pepper
1/2 cup freshly grated Parmigiano-Reggiano

(continues)

1 Prepare the broth, if necessary. Bring the broth to a simmer over medium heat, then lower the heat so that it just keeps the broth hot. Trim the radicchio and cut it into 1/2-inch-thick slices. Cut the slices into 1 inch lengths.

2 In a wide heavy saucepan, heat the oil with 1 tablespoon of the butter over medium heat. When the butter is melted, add the onion and cook, stirring occasionally, until the onion is very tender, about 10 minutes.

3 Raise the heat to medium, stir in the radicchio, and cook until wilted, about 10 minutes.

4 Stir in the rice. Add the wine and cook, stirring, until most of the liquid is absorbed. Pour 1/2 cup of the broth over the rice. Cook and stir until most of the liquid is absorbed.

5 Continue adding broth about 1/2 cup at a time, stirring after each addition. Adjust the heat so that the liquid simmers rapidly but the rice does not stick to the pan. Halfway through the cooking, season with salt and pepper. Use only as much of the broth as needed until the rice becomes tender yet firm to the bite and the risotto is creamy. When you think it may be done, taste a few grains. If not ready, test again in a minute or so. If the broth runs out before the rice is tender, use hot water. Cooking time will be 18 to 20 minutes.

6 Remove the saucepan from the heat and stir in the remaining tablespoon of butter and the cheese. Taste for seasoning. Serve immediately.

Risotto with Creamy Cauliflower
Risotto al Cavolfiore

MAKES 6 SERVINGS

In Parma, you might not eat an appetizer or a main course, but you would never want to miss an opportunity to have risotto or pasta; they are always incredibly good. This is my version of a risotto I had there some years ago at La Filoma, an excellent trattoria.

The first time I made this risotto, I happened to have a tube of white truffle paste on hand, and I stirred some in at the end of the cooking time. The flavor was sensational. Try it if you can find truffle paste.

4 cups Chicken Broth (page 63)
4 cups cauliflower, chopped into 1/2-inch florets
1 garlic clove, finely chopped
1 1/2 cups milk
Salt
4 tablespoons unsalted butter
1/4 cup finely chopped onion
2 cups medium-grain rice, such as Arborio, Carnaroli, or Vialone Nano
Freshly ground black pepper
3/4 cup freshly grated Parmigiano-Reggiano

1 Prepare the broth, if necessary. Bring the broth to a simmer over medium heat, then lower the heat so that it just keeps the broth hot. In a medium saucepan, combine the cauliflower, garlic, milk, and a pinch of salt. Bring to a simmer. Cook until most of the liquid is evaporated and the cauliflower is soft, about 10 minutes. Keep the heat very low and stir the mixture occasionally so that it does not scorch.

2 In a wide heavy saucepan, heat the oil with 2 tablespoons of the butter over medium heat. When the butter is melted, add the onion and cook, stirring occasionally, until the onion is very tender and golden, about 10 minutes.

3 Add the rice and cook, stirring with a wooden spoon until hot, about 2 minutes. Pour in about 1/2 cup of the broth. Cook and stir until most of the liquid is absorbed.

4 Continue adding the broth 1/2 cup at a time, stirring constantly, until it is absorbed. Adjust the heat so that the liquid simmers rapidly but the rice does not stick to the pan. About halfway through the cooking, season with salt and pepper.

5 When the rice is almost done, stir in the cauliflower mixture. Use only as much of the broth as needed until the rice becomes tender yet firm to the bite and the risotto is creamy. When you think

it may be done, taste a few grains. If not ready, test again in a minute or so. If the broth runs out before the rice is tender, use hot water. Cooking time will be 18 to 20 minutes.

6 Remove the saucepan from the heat and taste for seasoning. Stir in the remaining 2 tablespoons of butter and the cheese. Serve immediately.

Lemon Risotto
Risotto al Limone

MAKES 6 SERVINGS

The lively flavor of fresh lemon zest and juice brightens up this risotto that I ate in Capri. Though the Italians don't often do it, I like to serve it as a side dish with sautéed scallops or grilled fish.

5 cups Chicken Broth (page 63)
4 tablespoons unsalted butter
1 small onion, finely chopped
2 cups medium-grain rice, such as Arborio, Carnaroli, or Vialone Nano
Salt and freshly ground black pepper
1 tablespoon fresh lemon juice
1 teaspoon grated lemon zest
1/2 cup freshly grated Parmigiano-Reggiano

1 Prepare the broth, if necessary. Bring the broth to a simmer over medium heat, then lower the heat so that it just keeps the broth hot. In a wide heavy saucepan, melt 2 tablespoons of the butter over medium heat. Add the onion and cook, stirring often until golden, about 10 minutes.

2 Add the rice and stir with a wooden spoon until hot, about 2 minutes. Add 1/2 cup of the hot broth and stir until the liquid is absorbed.

3 Continue adding the broth 1/2 cup at a time, stirring after each addition. Adjust the heat so that the liquid simmers rapidly but the rice does not stick to the pan. About halfway through the cooking time, season with salt and pepper.

4 Use only as much of the broth as needed until the rice becomes tender yet firm to the bite and the risotto is creamy. When you think it may be done, taste a few grains. If not ready, test again in a minute or so. If the broth runs out before the rice is tender, use hot water. Cooking time will be 18 to 20 minutes.

5 Remove the risotto pan from the heat. Add the lemon juice and zest, the remaining 2 tablespoons of butter, and the cheese. Stir until the butter and cheese are melted and creamy. Taste for seasoning. Serve immediately.

Spinach Risotto
Risotto agli Spinaci

MAKES 6 SERVINGS

If you have some fresh basil, add that instead of the parsley. Other greens such as Swiss chard or escarole can be used in place of spinach.

5 cups Chicken Broth (page 63)
1 pound fresh spinach, washed and stems removed
1/4 cup water
Salt
4 tablespoons unsalted butter
1 medium onion, finely chopped
2 cups (about 1 pound) medium-grain rice, such as Arborio, Carnaroli, or Vialone Nano
Freshly ground black pepper
1/4 cup chopped fresh flat-leaf parsley
1/2 cup freshly grated Parmigiano-Reggiano

1 Prepare the broth, if necessary. Bring the broth to a simmer over medium heat, then lower the heat so that it just keeps the broth hot. In a large pot, combine the spinach, water, and salt to taste. Cover and bring to a simmer. Cook until the spinach is wilted, about 3 minutes. Drain the spinach and squeeze lightly to extract the juices. Finely chop the spinach.

(continues)

Rice, Cornmeal, and Other Grains   213

2 In a wide heavy saucepan, heat 3 tablespoons of the butter over medium heat. When the butter is melted, add the onion and cook, stirring often, until golden, about 10 minutes

3 Add the rice to the onion and cook, stirring with a wooden spoon, until hot, about 2 minutes. Add 1/2 cup of the hot broth and stir until the liquid is absorbed. Continue adding the broth 1/2 cup at a time, stirring after each addition. Adjust the heat so that the liquid simmers rapidly but the rice does not stick to the pan. Halfway through the cooking, stir in the spinach and salt and pepper to taste.

4 Use only as much of the broth as needed until the rice becomes tender yet firm to the bite and the risotto is creamy. When you think it may be done, taste a few grains. If not ready, test again in a minute or so. If the broth runs out before the rice is tender, use hot water. Cooking time will be 18 to 20 minutes.

5 Remove the risotto pan from the heat. Stir in the remaining butter and the cheese. Serve immediately.

Golden Squash Risotto
Risotto con Zucca d'Oro

MAKES 4 TO 6 SERVINGS

In Italian greenmarkets, cooks can buy wedges of large winter squash to use for risotto. Butternut squash comes closest to the sweet flavor and buttery texture of the Italian varieties. This risotto is a specialty of Mantua in Lombardy.

5 cups Chicken Broth (page 63)
4 tablespoons unsalted butter
1/4 cup finely chopped shallots or onion
2 cups peeled and chopped butternut squash (about 1 pound)
2 cups medium-grain rice, such as Arborio, Carnaroli, or Vialone Nano
1/2 cup dry white wine
Salt and freshly ground black pepper
1/2 cup freshly grated Parmigiano-Reggiano

1 Prepare the broth, if necessary. Bring the broth to a simmer over medium heat, then lower the heat so that it just keeps the broth hot. In a wide heavy saucepan, melt three tablespoons of the butter over medium heat. Add the shallots and cook, stirring often until golden, about 5 minutes.

2 Add the squash and 1/2 cup of the broth. Cook until the broth evaporates.

3 Add the rice and cook, stirring with a wooden spoon until hot, about 2 minutes. Stir in the wine until it evaporates.

4 Add 1/2 cup of the hot broth and stir until the liquid is absorbed. Continue adding the broth 1/2 cup at a time, stirring after each addition. Adjust the heat so that the liquid simmers rapidly but the rice does not stick to the pan. Halfway through the cooking, stir in salt and pepper to taste.

5 Use only as much of the broth as needed until the rice becomes tender yet firm to the bite and the risotto is creamy. When you think it may be done, taste a few grains. If not ready, test again in a minute or so. If the broth runs out before the rice is tender, use hot water. Cooking time will be 18 to 20 minutes.

6 Remove the risotto pan from the heat. Stir in the remaining butter and the cheese. Serve immediately.

Venetian Risotto with Peas
Risi e Bisi

MAKES 6 SERVINGS

In Venice, this risotto is eaten to celebrate the coming of spring and the first of the season's fresh vegetables. Venetians prefer their risotto rather soupy, so add an extra spoonful or so of broth or water to the finished risotto if you're going for authenticity.

6 cups Chicken Broth (page 63)

1 medium yellow onion, finely chopped

4 tablespoons olive oil

2 cups medium-grain rice, such as Arborio, Carnaroli, or Vialone Nano

Salt and freshly ground black pepper

2 cups shelled tender peas, or frozen peas, partially thawed

2 tablespoons finely chopped flat-leaf parsley

1/2 cup freshly grated Parmigiano-Reggiano

2 tablespoons unsalted butter

1 Prepare the broth, if necessary. Bring the broth to a simmer over medium heat, then lower the heat so that it just keeps the broth hot. Pour the oil into a wide heavy saucepan. Add the onion and cook over medium heat until the onion is tender and golden, about 10 minutes.

2 Add the rice and cook, stirring with a wooden spoon, until hot, about 2 minutes. Add about 1/2 cup of the hot broth and stir until it is absorbed. Continue adding broth 1/2 cup at a time, stirring after each addition. Adjust the heat so that the liquid simmers rapidly but the rice does not stick to the pan. Halfway through the cooking, stir in salt and pepper to taste.

3 Add the peas and parsley. Continue adding the liquid and stirring. The rice should be tender yet firm to the bite, and the risotto should have a loose, somewhat soupy, consistency. Use hot water if you run out of broth. Cooking time will be 18 to 20 minutes.

4 When the rice is tender yet still firm, remove the pot from the heat. Add the cheese and butter and stir well. Serve immediately.

Springtime Risotto
Risotto Primavera

MAKES 4 TO 6 SERVINGS

Tiny pieces of colorful vegetables spangle this bright and flavorful risotto. The vegetables are added in stages so that they do not overcook.

6 cups vegetable broth or water

3 tablespoons unsalted butter

1 tablespoon olive oil

1 medium onion, finely chopped

1 small carrot, chopped

1 small tender celery rib, chopped

2 cups medium-grain rice, such as Arborio, Carnaroli, or Vialone Nano

1/2 cup fresh or frozen peas

1 cup sliced mushrooms, any kind

6 asparagus, trimmed and cut into 1/2-inch pieces

Salt and freshly ground black pepper

1 large tomato, seeded and diced

2 tablespoons finely chopped fresh flat-leaf parsley

1/2 cup freshly grated Parmigiano-Reggiano

1 Prepare the broth, if necessary. Bring the broth to a simmer over medium heat, then lower the heat so that it just keeps the broth hot. In a wide heavy saucepan, combine 2 tablespoons of the butter and the oil over medium heat. When the butter has melted, add the onion and cook until it turns golden, about 10 minutes.

2 Add the carrot and celery and cook 2 minutes. Stir in the rice until well coated.

3 Add 1/2 cup of the broth and cook, stirring constantly with a wooden spoon, until the liquid is absorbed. Continue adding broth 1/2 cup at a time, stirring after each addition, for 10 minutes. Adjust the heat so that the liquid simmers rapidly but the rice does not stick to the pan.

4 Stir in the peas, mushrooms, and half of the asparagus. Add salt and pepper to taste. Continue adding broth and stirring 10 minutes more. Stir in the remaining asparagus and tomato. Add broth and stir until the rice is firm yet tender to the bite and the risotto is creamy. When you think it may be done, taste a few grains. If not ready, test again in a minute or so.

5 Remove the risotto pan from the heat. Taste for seasoning. Stir in the parsley and remaining butter. Stir in the cheese. Serve immediately.

Risotto with Tomatoes and Fontina
Risotto con Pomodori e Fontina

MAKES 6 SERVINGS

Genuine Fontina Valle d'Aosta has a pronounced flavor that is nutty, fruity, and earthy, unlike fontina made elsewhere. It is worth seeking out for this risotto from northwestern Italy. This dish would go well with a floral white wine such as Arneis, from the nearby Piedmont region.

5 cups Chicken Broth (page 63)
3 tablespoons unsalted butter
I medium onion, finely chopped
I cup peeled, seeded, and chopped tomatoes
2 cups medium-grain rice, such as Arborio, Carnaroli, or Vialone Nano
1/2 cup dry white wine
Salt and freshly ground black pepper
4 ounces Fontina Valle d'Aosta, shredded
1/2 cup freshly grated Parmigiano-Reggiano

1 Prepare the broth, if necessary. Bring the broth to a simmer over medium heat, then lower the heat so that it just keeps the broth hot. Melt the butter in a wide heavy saucepan over medium heat. Add the onion and cook, stirring occasionally, until the onion is tender and golden, about 10 minutes.

2 Stir in the tomatoes. Cook until most of the liquid has evaporated, about 10 minutes.

3 Add the rice and cook, stirring with a wooden spoon, until hot, about 2 minutes. Pour the wine and 1/2 cup of the broth over the rice. Cook and stir until most of the liquid is absorbed.

4 Continue adding broth about 1/2 cup at a time, stirring after each addition. Adjust the heat so that the liquid simmers rapidly but the rice does not stick to the pan. About halfway through the cooking, season with salt and pepper to taste.

5 Use only as much of the broth as needed until the rice becomes tender yet firm to the bite and the risotto is creamy. When you think it may be done, taste a few grains. If not ready, test again in a minute or so. If the broth runs out before the rice is tender, use hot water. Cooking time is 18 to 20 minutes.

6 Remove the risotto pan from the heat. Stir in the cheeses. Taste for seasoning. Serve immediately.

Shrimp and Celery Risotto
Risotto con Gamberi e Sedano

MAKES 6 SERVINGS

Many Italian recipes are flavored with a soffritto, a combination of either oil or butter, or sometimes both, and aromatic vegetables, which can include but are not limited to onion, celery, carrot, garlic, and sometimes herbs. Sometimes salt pork or pancetta is added to a soffritto for a meaty flavor.

Like most of the Italian cooks I know, I prefer to put the soffritto ingredients into the pot all at once, then turn on the heat so that everything warms up and cooks gently and I can control the results better. I stir the soffritto often, sometimes cooking until the vegetables are just wilted for a mild flavor, or until they are golden brown for greater depth. If, instead, you heat the oil or butter first, the fat can become too hot if the pan is thin, the heat is a little too high, or you are momentarily distracted. Then when the other soffritto flavorings are added, they brown too rapidly and unevenly.

The soffritto for this recipe from Emilia-Romagna is made in two stages. It begins with only the olive oil and onion, because I want the onion to release its flavor to the oil and fade somewhat into the background. The second stage is cooking the celery, parsley, and garlic so that the celery remains a little crunchy and yet releases its flavor and creates another taste layer with the parsley and garlic.

If you buy shrimp with their shells on, save the shells to make a tasty shrimp broth. If you are in a hurry, you can buy shelled shrimp and just use the chicken or fish broth, or even water.

6 cups homemade Chicken Broth (page 63)
   or store-bought fish stock
1 pound medium shrimp
1 small onion, finely chopped
2 tablespoons olive oil
1 cup finely chopped celery
2 garlic cloves, finely chopped
2 tablespoons chopped fresh flat-leaf parsley
2 cups medium-grain rice, such as Arborio, Carnaroli,
   or Vialone Nano
Salt and freshly ground black pepper to taste
1 tablespoon unsalted butter or extra-virgin olive oil

1 Prepare the broth, if necessary. Then, shell and devein the shrimp, reserving the shells. Cut the shrimp into 1/2-inch pieces and set aside. Place the shells in a large saucepan with the broth. Bring to a simmer and cook 10 minutes. Strain the broth and discard the shells. Return the broth to the pan and keep over very low heat.

2 In a wide heavy saucepan, cook the onion in the oil over medium heat, stirring frequently, about 5 minutes. Stir in the celery, garlic, and parsley and cook 5 minutes more.

3 Add the rice to the vegetables and stir thoroughly to combine. Add 1/2 cup of the broth and cook, stirring, until the liquid is absorbed. Continue adding the broth 1/2 cup at a time, stirring after each addition. Adjust the heat so that the liquid simmers rapidly but the rice does not stick to the pan.

4 When the rice is almost done, stir in the shrimp and salt and pepper to taste. Use only as much of the broth as needed until the rice becomes tender yet firm to the bite and the risotto is moist and creamy. When you think it may be done, taste a few grains. If not ready, test again in a minute or so. If the broth runs out before the rice is tender, use hot water. Cooking time is 18 to 20 minutes.

5 Remove the risotto from the heat. Add the butter or oil and stir until blended. Serve immediately.

Risotto with "Fruits of the Sea"
Risotto con Frutti di Mare

MAKES 4 TO 6 SERVINGS

Tiny clams or mussels can be added to this risotto, or even bits of firm fish such as tuna. Cooks in the Veneto, where this recipe originated, prefer the Vialone Nano variety of rice.

6 cups Chicken Broth (page 63) or water
6 tablespoons olive oil
2 tablespoons chopped fresh flat-leaf parsley
2 large garlic cloves, finely chopped
1/2 pound calamari (squid), cut into 1/2-inch rings and
   tentacles halved through the base (see page 276)
1/4 pound shrimp, shelled and deveined and cut into
   1/2-inch pieces
1/4 pound scallops, cut into 1/2-inch pieces
Salt
Pinch of crushed red pepper
1 medium onion, finely chopped
2 cups medium-grain rice, such as Arborio, Carnaroli,
   or Vialone Nano
1/2 cup dry white wine
1 cup peeled, seeded, and chopped tomatoes

1 Prepare the broth, if necessary. Put 3 tablespoons oil with the garlic and parsley into a wide heavy saucepan. Cook over medium heat, stirring occasionally, until the garlic is softened and golden, about 2 minutes. Add all the seafood, salt to taste, and red pepper and cook, stirring until the calamari are just opaque, about 5 minutes.

2 With a slotted spoon, remove the seafood to a plate. Add the chicken broth to the pan and bring to a simmer. Keep the broth over very low heat while cooking the risotto.

3 In a wide heavy saucepan, over medium heat, cook the onion in the remaining 3 tablespoons of the oil until golden, about 10 minutes.

(continues)

4 Add the rice and cook, stirring with a wooden spoon, until hot, about 2 minutes. Stir in the wine. Cook until most of the liquid is absorbed. Add 1/2 cup of the hot broth and stir until the liquid is absorbed. Continue adding the broth 1/2 cup at a time, stirring after each addition. Adjust the heat so that the liquid simmers rapidly but the rice does not stick to the pan. About halfway through the cooking, stir in the tomato, and salt to taste.

5 Use only as much of the broth as needed until the rice becomes tender yet firm to the bite and the risotto is creamy. When you think it may be done, taste a few grains. If not ready, test again in a minute or so. If the broth runs out before the rice is tender, use hot water. Cooking time is 18 to 20 minutes.

6 Add the seafood to the pot and cook 1 minute more. Remove the risotto pan from the heat. Serve immediately.

"Sea and Mountain" Risotto
Risotto Maremonti

MAKES 6 SERVINGS

When you see the term maremonti *on a menu in Italy, you can be sure the dish will contain seafood and mushrooms, representing the sea and the mountains. It is an intriguing combination in this risotto.*

6 cups store-bought vegetable broth or water

3 tablespoons unsalted butter

1/4 cup finely chopped shallots

10 ounces cremini or white mushrooms, thinly sliced

Salt and freshly ground black pepper

2 cups medium-grain rice, such as Arborio, Carnaroli, or Vialone Nano

12 ounces shelled and deveined shrimp, cut into 1/2-inch pieces

1/2 cup freshly grated Parmigiano-Reggiano

1 In a large pot, bring the broth to a simmer over medium heat, then lower the heat so that it just keeps the broth hot. In a wide heavy saucepan, melt 2 tablespoons of the butter over medium heat. Add the shallots and mushrooms. Cook, stirring frequently, until the juices evaporate and the mushrooms begin to turn brown, about 10 minutes. Stir in salt and pepper to taste.

2 Add the rice and cook, stirring with a wooden spoon until hot, about 2 minutes. Add 1/2 cup of the hot broth and stir until the liquid is absorbed. Continue adding the broth 1/2 cup at a time, stirring after each addition. Adjust the heat so that the liquid simmers rapidly but the rice does not stick to the pan. About halfway through the cooking, stir in the shrimp and salt and pepper to taste.

3 Use only as much of the broth as needed until the rice becomes tender yet firm to the bite and the risotto is creamy. When you think it may be done, taste a few grains. If not ready, test again in a minute or so. If the broth runs out before the rice is tender, use hot water. Cooking time is 18 to 20 minutes.

4 Remove the risotto pan from the heat. Stir in the remaining 1 tablespoon butter. Stir in the cheese and serve immediately.

Black Risotto
Risotto alle Seppie

MAKES 4 TO 6 SERVINGS

*In Venice, calamari (squid) or cuttlefish ink tradi-
tionally turns this risotto a caviar-like shade of
black. Most seafood in the United States has the ink
sac removed before you buy it, but you can purchase squid ink in small plastic envelopes at most
seafood stores. The calamari and its ink are so flavorful that I make this risotto with water rather
than broth so that there is nothing to interfere with
their briny flavor.*

6 cups water
4 tablespoons olive oil
I medium onion, finely chopped
I garlic clove, finely chopped
12 ounces calamari (squid), cut into ¹/₂-inch rings and
    tentacles halved through the base (see page 276)
Salt and freshly ground black pepper
I cup dry white wine
2 cups medium-grain rice, such as Arborio, Carnaroli,
    or Vialone Nano
I to 2 teaspoons squid or cuttlefish ink (optional)
I to 2 tablespoons extra-virgin olive oil

I In a medium saucepan, bring the water to a simmer over medium heat, then lower the heat so that
it just keeps the water hot.

2 Pour 4 tablespoons oil in a wide heavy saucepan. Add the onion and cook over medium heat,
stirring frequently, until tender and golden, about
10 minutes. Add the calamari, and salt and pepper to taste. Cover the pan and cook 10 minutes.
Add the wine and cook 1 minute more.

3 Add the rice and cook, stir with a wooden spoon,
until hot, about 2 minutes. Add ¹/₂ cup of the hot
water and stir until the liquid is absorbed. Continue adding the water ¹/₂ cup at a time, stirring
after each addition. Adjust the heat so that the
liquid simmers rapidly but the rice does not stick
to the pan. Halfway through the cooking, stir in
the squid ink, if using, and salt to taste.

4 Use only as much of the water as needed until
the rice becomes tender yet firm to the bite and
the risotto is creamy. When you think it may be
done, taste a few grains. If not ready, test again in
a minute or so. Cooking time is 18 to 20 minutes.

5 Remove risotto pan from the heat. Stir in the
oil until blended. Serve immediately.

Crisp Risotto Pancake
Risotto al Salto

MAKES 2 TO 4 SERVINGS

*This golden risotto pancake is crisp on the outside
and creamy on the inside. In Milan, the pancake is
called* risotto al salto, *meaning "jumping risotto,"
because it is cooked in hot butter, which makes it
seem to jump out of the pan. Though the Milanese
typically prepare the pancake with leftover Saffron
Risotto (page 209), I use all kinds of risotto and sometimes make it from scratch just for this purpose.*

    *You can serve the pancake in many ways—plain,
with a tomato sauce and sprinkled with cheese, or
as the base for a stew. You can cut it into wedges to
accompany a salad or to serve as an appetizer. You
can also make tiny silver-dollar-size pancakes for
individual appetizers or snacks.*

2 cups cold leftover risotto
I large egg, beaten
2 tablespoons unsalted butter

I In a medium bowl, mix together the risotto and
the egg until well blended.

2 In a medium nonstick skillet over medium heat,
melt 1 tablespoon butter. Add the risotto and flatten it out with a spoon. Cook until crusty and golden
brown on the bottom, about 5 minutes.

3 Flip the pancake onto a dinner plate. Melt the
remaining butter and slide the pancake back into
the pan. Flatten it well with the back of the spoon.
Cook until golden, 4 to 5 minutes more.

4 Slide the pancake onto a plate. Cut into wedges
and serve hot.

Stuffed Rice Timbale

Sartù di Riso

MAKES 8 TO 10 SERVINGS

Rice is not a common ingredient in the Neapolitan kitchen, but this dish is one of the classics of that area. It is believed to have its roots in the aristocratic kitchens run by French-trained chefs when Naples was the capital of the Kingdom of the Two Sicilies.

Today, it is made for special occasions, and I have even eaten contemporary versions made in individual-size molds.

This is the kind of spectacular dish that would be ideal for a party. The little meatballs and other ingredients in the filling come tumbling out of the giant rice cake when it is cut. It is not difficult to make, but there are several steps involved. You can make the sauce and filling up to 3 days ahead of assembling the dish.

Sauce

1 ounce dried porcini mushrooms
2 cups warm water
1 medium onion, chopped
2 tablespoons olive oil
1 (28-ounce) can imported Italian peeled tomatoes, passed through a food mill
Salt and freshly ground black pepper

Meatballs and sausages

2 to 3 slices Italian bread, torn into bits (about 1/2 cup)
1/4 cup milk
8 ounces ground veal
1/4 cup freshly grated Parmigiano-Reggiano
1 garlic clove, finely chopped
2 tablespoons chopped fresh flat-leaf parsley, plus more for garnish
1 large egg
Salt and freshly ground black pepper
2 tablespoons olive oil
2 sweet Italian sausages

Assembly

8 ounces fresh mozzarella, chopped
1 cup fresh or frozen peas
2 cups medium-grain rice, such as Arborio, Carnaroli, or Vialone Nano
Salt
1 cup freshly grated Parmigiano-Reggiano
Freshly ground black pepper
2 tablespoons unsalted butter
6 tablespoons plain dry bread crumbs
Chopped fresh flat-leaf parsley for garnish

1 Prepare the sauce: In a medium bowl, soak the mushrooms in the water for 30 minutes. Lift the mushrooms out of the soaking liquid. Strain the liquid through a paper coffee filter or a piece of dampened cheesecloth into a clean bowl and set aside. Rinse the mushrooms under running water, paying special attention to the base where soil collects. Finely chop the mushrooms.

2 Put the onion and oil in a wide heavy saucepan over medium heat. Cook, stirring occasionally until the onion is tender and golden, about 10 minutes. Stir in the chopped mushrooms. Add the tomatoes and the reserved mushroom liquid. Season to taste with salt and pepper. Bring to a simmer. Cook over low heat, stirring occasionally, until thickened, about 30 minutes.

3 Prepare the meatballs: In a medium bowl, soak the bread in the milk for 5 minutes and squeeze dry. In the same bowl, combine the bread, veal, cheese, garlic, parsley, egg, and salt and pepper to taste. Mix well. Shape the mixture into 1-inch meatballs.

4 In a large skillet, heat the oil over medium heat. Add the meatballs and cook, turning them with tongs, until browned on all sides. With a slotted spoon, transfer the meatballs to a plate. Pour off the oil and carefully wipe out the skillet with paper towels.

5 In the same skillet, combine the sausages and enough water to cover them halfway. Cover and cook over medium-low heat until the water evaporates and the sausages begin to brown. Uncover and cook the sausages, turning them occasionally, until cooked through, about 10 minutes. Cut the sausages into slices.

6 In a medium bowl, gently stir together the meatballs, sausage slices, mozzarella, and peas with 2 cups of the tomato and mushroom sauce and set aside.

7 In a large pot, combine the remaining sauce with 4 cups water. Bring the mixture to a boil. Add the rice and 1 teaspoon of salt. Bring the liquid back to the boil and stir once or twice. Cover and cook over low heat until the rice is barely tender, about 15 minutes.

8 Remove the pot from the heat. Let the rice cool slightly. Stir in the Parmigiano. Season to taste with salt and pepper.

9 Butter the inside of a deep 2^1/2-quart casserole dish or ovenproof bowl. Sprinkle it with 4 tablespoons of the bread crumbs. Spoon about two-thirds of the rice into the prepared casserole dish, pressing it against the bottom and sides to make a rice "shell." Spoon the meatball and sausage mixture into the center. Cover with the remaining rice and spread evenly. Sprinkle the top with the remaining crumbs. (If not preparing right away, cover and refrigerate the timbale.)

10 About 2 hours before serving, place a rack in the center of the oven. Preheat the oven to 350°F. Bake the timbale 1^1/2 hours or until the surface is lightly browned and the mixture is hot in the center. (Exact cooking time depends on the size and shape of the casserole. Use an instant-read thermometer to check the temperature in the center. It should be at least 140°F.)

11 Have a cooling rack ready. Let the timbale cool on the rack 10 minutes. Run a knife or a metal spatula around the inside edge of the casserole dish. Place a large platter over the casserole. Holding the dish (with a pot holder) firmly against the platter, invert both to transfer the timbale onto the platter. Sprinkle with parsley. Cut into wedges to serve. Serve hot.

Rice and Beans, Veneto Style
Riso e Fagioli alla Veneta

MAKES 4 SERVINGS

During the summer, rice and beans are served warm, not hot. In the Veneto region, cranberry beans, known in Italian as borlotti, *are the favorite variety. Uncooked cranberry beans are pink with cream-colored markings. When cooked they turn a solid pinkish beige. They look a lot like pinto beans, which can be substituted if you prefer them.*

About 2 cups homemade Meat Broth (page 62) or store-bought beef broth

3 tablespoons oil

I small onion, finely chopped

I medium carrot, finely chopped

I medium celery rib, finely chopped

^{1}/2 cup finely chopped pancetta

2 cups cooked dried cranberry or pinto beans, or I (16-ounce) can beans with their liquid

I cup medium-grain rice, such as Arborio, Carnaroli, or Vialone Nano

Salt and freshly ground black pepper

1 Prepare the broth, if necessary. Then, in a wide heavy saucepan over medium heat, heat the oil with the onion, carrot, celery, and pancetta. Cook, stirring occasionally, until the vegetables are golden, about 20 minutes.

2 Add the beans and 1 cup cold water. Bring to a simmer and cook 20 minutes.

3 Set aside about one-third of the bean mixture. Puree the remainder in a food processor or food mill until smooth. Pour the bean puree and 1 cup of the broth into a large wide saucepan. Bring to a simmer over medium heat. Cook, stirring occasionally, for 5 minutes.

4 Add the rice to the pan, and salt and pepper to taste. Cook 20 minutes, stirring frequently so that the beans do not stick to the bottom of the pan.

(continues)

Add some of the remaining broth a little at a time, until the rice is tender yet still firm. Stir in the reserved bean mixture and turn off the heat.

5 Let rest 5 minutes. Serve hot.

Sardinian Sausage Rice
Riso alla Sarda

MAKES 6 SERVINGS

More like a pilaf than a risotto, this traditional rice dish from Sardinia does not require a lot of stirring.

About 3 cups Meat Broth (page 62)
I medium onion, chopped
2 tablespoons chopped fresh flat-leaf parsley
2 tablespoons olive oil
12 ounces plain Italian pork sausage, casings removed
I cup peeled, seeded, and chopped tomatoes
Salt and freshly ground black pepper
1 1/2 cups medium-grain rice, such as Arborio,
    Carnaroli, or Vialone Nano
1/2 cup freshly grated Pecorino Romano
    or Parmigiano-Reggiano

I Prepare the broth, if necessary. Then, in a wide heavy saucepan over medium heat, cook the onion and parsley in the oil until the onion is softened, about 5 minutes. Add the sausage meat and cook, stirring often, until the sausage is lightly browned, about 15 minutes.

2 Stir in the tomatoes and salt and pepper to taste. Add the broth and bring it to a simmer. Stir in the rice. Cover and cook 10 minutes. Check to see if the mixture is too dry. Add more broth or water if needed. Cover and cook 8 minutes more or until the rice is tender.

3 Remove the pan from the heat. Stir in the cheese. Serve immediately.

❧ Cornmeal

Polenta is the Italian version of cornmeal mush. It is a staple of northern Italy, though it is also eaten in the south. Usually polenta is made from coarsely ground yellow cornmeal, but in the Veneto region white cornmeal is preferred, especially with fish. Venetians say that white polenta has a milder flavor that is better with seafood.

I prefer to use a coarse, stone-ground cornmeal that takes about 40 minutes to cook. Many stores now carry an instant cornmeal that is done in 5 minutes. It is very good and worth seeking out.

Polenta can be cooked an hour or more before serving it. It will stay hot and spoonable in a tightly covered pan placed over a larger pan partially filled with simmering water. Stir in additional hot water if it becomes too thick.

Like molten lava, polenta firms up as it cools. The firm polenta can be sliced, then fried, grilled, or baked. To cut off neat slices, a long piece of sturdy string (unflavored dental floss is perfect) can be slid underneath the polenta, then lifted through it. A dull knife works just as well.

Soft polenta is eaten as a side dish, or topped with a sauce or stew. Families in Italy often have a special round board for serving polenta. I generally pour the polenta onto a platter, press a shallow indentation in the top, then pour on a stew or ragù.

Polenta

MAKES 4 SERVINGS

The traditional way of cooking polenta is to pour the dry cornmeal slowly in a fine stream through the fingers of one hand into a pot of boiling water as you stir it constantly with the other hand. You need a lot of patience to do this correctly; if you go too fast, the cornmeal will form lumps. Meanwhile, your hand is burning from being held over the simmering liquid.

I much prefer the method below for cooking polenta because it is quick and foolproof. Best of all, I have tried this method side by side with the traditional method, and I cannot detect any difference in the end result. Because the cornmeal is first mixed with cold water, lumps, which can easily occur if the dry meal is poured directly into the hot water, do not form.

Be sure to use a pot with a heavy bottom or the polenta may scorch. You can also place the pot on a Flametamer—a metal disk that fits over a stove burner for added pot insulation to control the heat. (Look for it in kitchenware shops.)

You can vary basic polenta by cooking it with broth or using milk in place of some of the water. Stir in some grated cheese at the end of the cooking time, if you wish.

4 cups cold water
**1 cup coarsely ground yellow cornmeal,
    preferably stone-ground**
2 teaspoons salt
2 tablespoons unsalted butter

1 In a 2-quart heavy saucepan, bring 3 cups water to a boil.

2 Meanwhile, in a small bowl, whisk together the cornmeal, salt, and remaining 1 cup water.

3 Pour the mixture into the boiling water and cook, stirring, until the mixture comes to a boil. Reduce the heat to low, cover, and cook, stirring occasionally, until the polenta is thick and creamy, about 30 minutes. If the polenta becomes too thick, stir in a little more water.

4 Stir in the butter. Serve immediately.

Polenta with Cream
Polenta alla Panna

MAKES 4 SERVINGS

On a cold winter day in Milan, I stopped for lunch at a busy trattoria. The menu was limited, but this simple, comforting dish was the day's special. If you have a fresh white or black truffle, shave it over the mascarpone and eliminate the cheese.

To warm a serving bowl or platter, place it in a warm (not hot!) oven for a few minutes or run hot water over it in the sink. Dry the bowl or platter before adding the food.

1 recipe (about 5 cups) hot cooked Polenta (page 223)
1 cup mascarpone or heavy cream
Chunk of Parmigiano-Reggiano

1 Prepare the polenta, if necessary. Then pour the hot cooked polenta onto a warm serving platter.

2 Spoon the mascarpone on top or pour on the cream. With a swivel-blade vegetable peeler, shave the Parmigiano over the top. Serve immediately.

Polenta with Ragù
Polenta al Ragù

MAKES 4 SERVINGS

At one time many northern Italian families had a special copper pot called a paiolo, in which they cooked polenta, and a round board on which they served it. This is delicious comfort food, and quite simple if you have the ragù and the polenta made in advance.

1 recipe (about 3 cups) Ragù Bolognese (page 96)
1 recipe (about 5 cups) hot cooked Polenta (page 223)
1/2 cup freshly grated Parmigiano-Reggiano

1 Prepare the ragù and the polenta, if necessary.

2 Pour the polenta onto a warm platter. Make a shallow indentation in the polenta. Spoon on the sauce. Sprinkle with the cheese and serve immediately.

Polenta Crostini, Three Ways

Slices of crisped polenta can be used in place of bread to make Crostini (pages 26–31). Serve them with a tasty topping (see suggestions that follow) as appetizers, as a side dish with a stew, or as a base for grilled or roasted birds.

1 recipe (about 5 cups) hot cooked Polenta (page 223)

1 Prepare the polenta. As soon as the polenta is cooked, spread it with a rubber spatula to about 1/2-inch thickness on a large baking sheet. Cover and chill until firm, at least 1 hour and up to 3 days, before using.

2 When ready to cook, cut the polenta into squares or another shape with a knife, or cookie or biscuit cutter. The pieces can be baked, broiled, grilled, or fried.

Baked Polenta Crostini: Preheat the oven to 400°F. Oil a baking sheet and arrange the polenta slices on the sheet about 1/2 inch apart. Brush the tops with oil. Bake 30 minutes or until crisp and lightly golden.

Grilled or Broiled Polenta Crostini: Place a barbecue grill or broiler rack about 4 inches away from the heat source. Preheat the grill or broiler. Brush the polenta slices on both sides with olive oil. Place the pieces on the rack. Grill or broil, turning once, until crisp and golden, about 5 minutes. Turn the pieces and grill the other side about 5 minutes more.

Fried Polenta Crostini: Very lightly brush a thin film of corn or olive oil in a nonstick skillet. Heat the skillet over medium heat. Pat the polenta pieces dry. Cook them until golden, about 5 minutes. Turn the pieces and cook until browned on the other side, about 5 minutes more.

Ten Toppings for Hot Polenta Crostini

Crumbled gorgonzola cheese and toasted pine nuts

A spoonful of chopped marinated sun-dried tomatoes and a slice of mozzarella. Heat in the oven until the cheese is softened.

A slice of fontina and thin-sliced mushrooms. Heat in the oven until the cheese is softened.

Green or black olive puree

A slice of soppressata, prosciutto, or smoked salmon

A slice of mozzarella and an anchovy fillet

A spoonful of pesto

Roasted peppers and fresh basil

Soft fresh goat cheese, freshly ground black pepper, and watercress leaves

A spoonful of tomato sauce or ragù and shavings of Parmigiano-Reggiano

Polenta Sandwiches
Panini di Polenta

MAKES 8 SERVINGS

These little sandwiches can be served as appetizers or as a side dish. For a little flair, cut out the polenta with cookie or biscuit cutters.

1 recipe (about 5 cups) Polenta, made without butter (page 223)
4 ounces gorgonzola, thinly sliced
2 tablespoons melted unsalted butter
2 tablespoons Parmigiano-Reggiano

1 Prepare the polenta. As soon as the polenta is cooked, spread it with a rubber spatula to about a ¹/₂-inch thickness on a large baking sheet. Cover and chill until firm, at least 1 hour and up to 3 days, before using.

2 Place a rack in the center of the oven. Preheat the oven to 400°F. Butter a large baking sheet.

3 Cut the polenta into 16 squares. Place half the polenta slices on the cookie sheet. Place the gorgonzola slices on top of them. Top with the remaining polenta, pressing down lightly on the sandwiches.

4 Brush the tops with the butter. Sprinkle with the Parmigiano. Bake 10 to 15 minutes or until the cheese is just melted. Serve hot.

Polenta with Three Cheeses
Polenta con Tre Formaggi

MAKES 4 SERVINGS

The Valle d'Aosta is the region in the far northwestern corner of Italy. It is famed for its Alpine climate and beautiful ski resorts, as well as dairy products, such as Fontina Valle d'Aosta, a semifirm cows' milk cheese.

Milk adds extra richness to this polenta. Butter stands in as an honorary cheese.

2 cups cold water
**1 cup coarsely ground yellow cornmeal,
    preferably stone-ground**
1 teaspoon salt
2 cups cold milk
¹/₂ cup Fontina Valle d'Aosta, chopped
¹/₄ cup freshly grated Parmigiano-Reggiano
2 tablespoons unsalted butter

1 In a 2-quart heavy saucepan, bring the water to a boil.

2 In a small bowl, whisk together the cornmeal, salt, and milk.

3 Pour the cornmeal mixture into the boiling water and cook, stirring, until the mixture comes to a boil. Reduce the heat to low, cover, and cook, stirring occasionally, about 30 minutes or until the polenta is thick and creamy. If the polenta becomes too thick, stir in a little more water.

4 Remove the pan from the heat. Stir in the cheeses and butter until melted. Serve immediately.

Polenta with Gorgonzola and Mascarpone

MAKES 4 TO 6 SERVINGS

Heavenly and rich, this recipe is from Lombardy, where gorgonzola and mascarpone are made.

4 cups cold water
**1 cup coarsely ground yellow cornmeal,
    preferably stone-ground**
¹/₂ teaspoon salt
¹/₂ cup mascarpone
¹/₂ cup gorgonzola, crumbled

1 In a 2-quart heavy saucepan, bring 3 cups water to a boil.

2 In a small bowl, whisk together the cornmeal, salt, and remaining 1 cup of water.

3 Pour the cornmeal mixture into the boiling water and cook, stirring constantly, until the mixture comes to a boil. Reduce the heat to low, cover, and cook, stirring occasionally, about 30 minutes or until the polenta is thick and creamy. If the polenta becomes too thick, stir in a little more water.

4 Remove the polenta from the heat. Stir in the mascarpone and half of the gorgonzola. Pour into a serving bowl and sprinkle with the remaining gorgonzola. Serve hot.

Mushroom Polenta

Polenta con Funghi

MAKES 6 SERVINGS

Pancetta adds rich flavor, but leave it out if you prefer a meatless dish. Leftovers can be cut into slices and fried in a little olive oil or butter as an appetizer or side dish.

2 ounces finely chopped pancetta

I small onion, finely chopped

2 tablespoons olive oil

I (10-ounce) package white mushrooms, trimmed and sliced

2 tablespoons chopped fresh flat-leaf parsley

Salt and freshly ground black pepper

4 cups cold water

I cup coarsely ground yellow cornmeal, preferably stone-ground

1 In a large skillet, combine the pancetta, the onion, and the oil and cook until the pancetta and onion are lightly golden, about 10 minutes. Add the mushrooms and parsley and cook until the mushroom liquid evaporates, about 10 minutes more. Season to taste with salt and pepper.

2 In a 2-quart heavy saucepan, bring 3 cups water to a boil.

3 In a small bowl, whisk together the cornmeal, 1/2 teaspoon salt, and remaining 1 cup cold water.

4 Pour the cornmeal mixture into the boiling water and cook, stirring constantly, until it comes to a boil. Reduce the heat to very low, cover, and cook, stirring occasionally, until the polenta is thick and creamy, about 30 minutes. If the polenta becomes too thick, stir in more water.

5 Stir the contents of the skillet into the polenta saucepan. Pour the mixture onto a warm platter. Serve immediately.

Buckwheat and Cornmeal Polenta

Polenta Taragna

MAKES 4 TO 6 SERVINGS

In Lombardy, this hearty polenta is made with a combination of cornmeal and buckwheat flour. The buckwheat adds an earthy flavor. A local cheese known as bitto *is stirred in at the end of the cooking time. I have never seen* bitto *in the United States, but fontina and Gruyère are good substitutes.*

5 cups cold water

4 tablespoons unsalted butter

I cup coarsely ground yellow cornmeal, preferably stone-ground

1/2 cup buckwheat flour

Salt

4 ounces fontina or Gruyère

1 In a 2-quart heavy saucepan, bring 4 cups of the water and 2 tablespoons of the butter to a boil.

2 In a medium bowl, stir together the cornmeal, buckwheat flour, 1/2 teaspoon salt, and remaining 1 cup water.

3 Whisk the cornmeal mixture into the boiling water. Reduce the heat to very low. Cover and cook, stirring occasionally, about 40 minutes or until the polenta is thick and creamy. If it gets too thick, add a little more water as needed.

4 Remove the polenta from the heat. Stir in the remaining 2 tablespoons butter and the cheese. Serve immediately.

Baked Polenta with Cheese
Polenta Cunsa

MAKES 8 SERVINGS

Assemble up to 24 hours before cooking but, if it is chilled, double the cooking time. Also try it with Gruyère or Asiago.

5 cups cold water

1 cup coarsely ground yellow cornmeal, preferably stone-ground

1 teaspoon salt

3 tablespoons unsalted butter

1 medium onion, chopped

1 cup freshly grated Parmigiano-Reggiano

1/2 cup crumbled gorgonzola

1/2 cup shredded Fontina Valle d'Aosta

1 In a 2-quart heavy saucepan, bring 4 cups water to a boil. In a bowl, whisk together the cornmeal, salt, and the remaining 1 cup water.

2 Pour the mixture into the boiling water and cook, stirring constantly, until the mixture comes to a boil. Reduce the heat to low, cover, and cook, stirring occasionally, about 30 minutes or until the polenta is thick and creamy. If the polenta becomes too thick, stir in a little more water.

3 In a small skillet, melt 2 tablespoons of the butter over medium heat. Add the onion and cook, stirring, until the onion is tender and golden, about 10 minutes. Scrape the onion into the polenta.

4 Place a rack in the center of the oven. Preheat the oven to 375°F. Butter a 9 × 3–inch baking pan.

5 Pour about one third of the polenta into the pan. Set aside 1/4 cup of the Parmigiano for the topping. Scatter half of each of the remaining cheeses onto the polenta layer in the pan. Make a second layer of polenta and the cheese. Pour on the remaining polenta and spread it evenly.

6 Sprinkle the reserved 1/4 cup of Parmigiano over the polenta. Dot with the remaining butter. Bake 30 minutes or until bubbling around the edge. Let rest 10 minutes before serving.

Baked Polenta with Sausage Ragù
Polenta Pasticciato

MAKES 6 SERVINGS

This is something like lasagne, with layers of sliced polenta replacing the pasta.

The name polenta pasticciato *is intriguing. It comes from* pasticciare, *meaning to make a mess of something, but* pasticciato *also indicates a dish made like pasta, with cheese and ragù.*

1 recipe Sausage Ragù (page 94)

8 cups cold water

2 cups coarsely ground yellow cornmeal, preferably stone-ground

1 tablespoon salt

8 ounces fresh mozzarella

1/2 cup freshly grated Parmigiano-Reggiano

1 Prepare the ragù, if necessary. In a large saucepan, bring 6 cups of the water to a boil.

2 In a medium bowl, stir together the cornmeal, salt, and remaining 2 cups of water.

3 Pour the cornmeal mixture into the boiling water, stirring constantly, until the mixture comes to a boil. Reduce the heat to low, cover, and cook, stirring occasionally, about 30 minutes or until the polenta is thick and creamy.

4 Butter a large baking sheet. Pour the polenta into the pan and spread it evenly with a rubber spatula to a 1/2-inch thickness. Let cool until firm, about least 1 hour, or cover and refrigerate overnight.

5 Place a rack in the center of the oven. Preheat the oven to 400°F. Oil a 9-inch square baking dish.

6 Cut the polenta into 9 3-inch squares. Arrange half the polenta in the bottom of the dish. Spoon on half the sauce and top with half the mozzarella and Parmigiano-Reggiano. Make a second layer of the remaining ingredients.

7 Bake 40 minutes or until the polenta is bubbling and the cheese is melted. Let stand 10 minutes before serving.

Polenta "in Chains"
Polenta Incatenata

MAKES 6 SERVINGS

My husband and I once rented an apartment in a villa outside of Lucca in Tuscany. Carlotta was the cheerful housekeeper who took care of the place and kept everything running smoothly. Once in a while, she would surprise us with a home-cooked meal. She told me that this hearty polenta, a local specialty, is said to be "chained" in ribbons of shredded vegetables. Serve this as a vegetarian main dish or a side dish with grilled meat. It is also very good if allowed to cool until it solidifies, then sliced and fried until golden brown.

2 tablespoons olive oil
I garlic clove, finely chopped
2 cups shredded cabbage or kale
4 cups cold water
I cup coarsely ground yellow cornmeal, preferably stone-ground
I¹/₂ teaspoons salt
2 cups cooked or canned cannelini beans
Salt and freshly ground black pepper
¹/₂ cup freshly grated Parmigiano-Reggiano

I In a large saucepan, cook the oil and garlic over medium heat until the garlic is golden, about 2 minutes. Add the cabbage, cover, and cook 10 minutes or until the cabbage is wilted.

2 Add 3 cups of the water and bring it to a simmer.

3 In a small bowl, stir together the cornmeal, salt, and remaining 1 cup of water.

4 Pour the cornmeal mixture into the saucepan. Cook, stirring frequently, until the mixture comes to a simmer. Reduce the heat to low, cover, and cook, stirring occasionally, 20 minutes.

5 Stir in the beans. Cook 10 minutes more or until thick and creamy. Add a little water if the mixture becomes too thick.

6 Remove from the heat. Stir in the cheese and serve immediately.

❧ Farro and Barley

Farro is an ancient grain that is the ancestor of modern wheat. The principal difference between wheat and farro is that with farro the husk adheres to the grain. Farro is often confused with spelt, another grain that looks similar.

Farro can be purchased in natural food stores and gourmet shops, where it is sometimes labeled "pearled" or "semipearled," meaning that it has been all or partially skinned. Both varieties need about the same amount of cooking time, but read the package instructions to be sure. Some cooks say farro should be soaked before cooking like dried beans, but I do not find this necessary.

Farro has become popular in recent years with health food enthusiasts, though it has been eaten for centuries throughout the Mediterranean. In Italy, it is usually eaten in soup or as a first course with a sauce, or in a salad. Ground farro is sometimes mixed with flour to make breads. The people of the Garfagnana region of Tuscany, where a lot of farro is eaten, consider it an aphrodisiac and a secret to longevity.

Farro Salad
Insalata di Farro

MAKES 6 SERVINGS

In Abruzzo, my husband and I had farro salads on several occasions, including this one with crunchy bits of vegetables and refreshing mint.

Salt
I¹/₂ cups farro
I cup finely chopped carrots
I cup finely chopped celery
2 tablespoons finely chopped fresh mint
2 green onions, finely chopped
¹/₃ cup olive oil
I tablespoon fresh lemon juice
Freshly ground black pepper

1 Bring 6 cups of water to a boil. Add salt to taste, then the farro. Reduce the heat to a simmer and cook until the farro is tender yet still chewy, about 15 to 30 minutes. (Cooking time can vary; start tasting after 15 minutes.) Drain well.

2 In a large bowl, combine the farro, carrots, celery, and mint. In a small bowl, mix together the olive oil, lemon juice, and pepper. Pour the dressing over the salad and toss well. Taste and adjust seasoning. Serve warm or at room temperature.

Farro, Amatrice Style
Farro all'Amatriciana

MAKES 8 SERVINGS

Farro is usually used in soups or salads, but in this recipe from the Roman countryside, the grain is simmered with a classic Amatriciana sauce, typically used on pasta.

Salt
2 cups farro
¼ cup olive oil
4 ounces pancetta, chopped
1 medium onion
½ cup dry white wine
1½ cups peeled, seeded, and chopped fresh tomatoes, or drained and chopped canned tomatoes
½ cup freshly grated Pecorino Romano

1 Bring 6 cups of water to a boil. Add salt to taste, then the farro. Reduce the heat to a simmer and cook until the farro is tender, yet still chewy, 15 to 30 minutes. (Cooking time can vary; start tasting after 15 minutes.) Drain well.

2 In a medium skillet, cook the oil, pancetta, and onion over medium heat, stirring often, until the onion is golden, about 10 minutes. Add the wine and bring to a simmer. Add the tomatoes and farro. Bring to a simmer and cook until the farro has absorbed some of the sauce, about 10 minutes. Add a little water if needed to prevent sticking.

3 Remove from the heat. Add the cheese and stir well. Serve immediately.

Farro, Tomatoes, and Cheese
Grano, Pomodori, e Cacio

MAKES 6 SERVINGS

Wheat berries, emmer, kamut, or other similar grains can be cooked this way if you cannot find farro. Don't add too much salt to the grain, as the ricotta salata can be salty. If it is not available, substitute Pecorino Romano. This recipe is from Puglia in the south.

Salt
1½ cups farro
2 tablespoons olive oil
1 small onion, finely chopped
8 ounces chopped tomatoes
4 ounces ricotta salata, coarsely grated

1 Bring 6 cups of water to a boil. Add salt to taste, then the farro. Reduce the heat to a simmer and cook until the farro is tender, 15 to 30 minutes. (Cooking time can vary; start tasting after 15 minutes.) Drain well.

2 Pour the oil into a medium saucepan. Add the onion and cook, stirring frequently, until the onion is golden, about 10 minutes. Add the tomatoes and salt to taste. Cook until slightly thickened, about 10 minutes.

3 Stir the drained farro into the tomato sauce. Add the cheese and stir well. Serve hot.

Shrimp and Barley Orzotto
Orzotto di Gamberi

MAKES 4 SERVINGS

Though most people in the United States think of orzo as a tiny seed-shape pasta, in Italian orzo means "barley." In Friuli–Venezia Giulia in the north, barley is cooked like risotto, and the finished dish is called orzotto.

3 cups **Chicken Broth (page 63), vegetable broth, or water**
2 tablespoons **unsalted butter**
1 tablespoon **olive oil**
1 small **onion, finely chopped**
1 small **carrot, finely chopped**
¹/₂ cup **finely chopped celery**
1 **garlic clove, minced**
6 ounces (²/₃ cup) **pearl barley, rinsed and drained**
Salt and freshly ground black pepper
8 ounces **shrimp, shelled and deveined**
2 tablespoons **chopped fresh flat-leaf parsley**

1 Prepare the broth, if necessary. In a medium saucepan, melt the butter with the oil over medium heat. Add the onion, carrot, celery, and garlic and cook until golden, about 10 minutes.

2 Add the barley to the vegetables in the skillet and stir well. Add the broth, 1 teaspoon salt, and pepper to taste. Bring to a simmer and reduce the heat. Cover and cook, stirring occasionally, 30 to 40 minutes or until the barley is tender. Add a little water if the mixture becomes dry.

3 Meanwhile, chop the shrimp and stir them and the parsley into the barley mixture. Cook until the shrimp are just pink, 2 to 3 minutes. Taste and adjust seasoning. Serve immediately.

Barley and Vegetable Orzotto
Orzotto di Verdure

MAKES 4 SERVINGS

Tiny bits of vegetables are cooked with barley for this orzotto. Serve it as a side dish or first course.

4 cups **Meat Broth (page 62) or Chicken Broth (page 63)**
4 tablespoons **unsalted butter**
1 small **onion, finely chopped**
1 cup **pearl barley, rinsed and drained**
¹/₂ cup **fresh or frozen peas**
¹/₂ cup **chopped mushrooms, any kind**
¹/₄ cup **finely chopped red bell pepper**
¹/₄ cup **finely chopped celery**
Salt and freshly ground black pepper
¹/₄ cup **freshly grated Parmigiano-Reggiano**

1 Prepare the broth, if necessary. In a large saucepan, melt 3 tablespoons of the butter over medium heat. Add the onion and cook, stirring frequently, until golden, about 10 minutes.

2 Add the barley and stir well. Stir in half each of the peas, mushrooms, bell pepper, and celery and cook 2 minutes or until wilted. Add the broth and bring to a simmer. Cover and cook 20 minutes.

3 Stir in the remaining vegetables and salt and pepper to taste. Cook, uncovered, 10 minutes more or until the liquid has evaporated and the barley is tender. Remove from the heat.

4 Stir in the remaining tablespoon of butter and the cheese. Serve immediately.

Eggs

Fried, Poached, and Baked Eggs

Prosciutto and Eggs

Baked Asparagus with Eggs

Eggs in Purgatory

Eggs in Tomato Sauce, Marches Style

Piedmontese-Style Eggs

Eggs Florentine

Baked Eggs with Potatoes and Cheese

Scrambled Eggs

Peppers and Eggs

Potatoes and Eggs

Mushroom and Egg Scramble

Frittatas

Onion and Arugula Frittata

Zucchini and Basil Frittata

Hundred-Herb Frittata

Spinach Frittata

Mushroom and Fontina Frittata

Neapolitan Spaghetti Frittata

Pasta Frittata

Little Omelets

Ricotta and Zucchini Flower Frittata

Omelet Strips in Tomato Sauce

talians are not big breakfast eaters and few eat eggs before lunchtime. In homes, *caffè latte* and crisp packaged toast, known as *fette biscotate,* with butter and jam is the typical way to start the day.

Children typically pick up a slice of fresh-baked focaccia at the bakery on their way to school, while workers stop for coffee and a *pasta* (pastry) at their favorite caffè before work or as a mid-morning break. The pastry is frequently a *cornetto,* the Italian version of a croissant.

Even if they do not typically eat eggs for breakfast, Italians do eat them for lunch and dinner. Eggs are particularly delicious in Italy. The yolks are so bright and richly colored that Italians often refer to the yolk as the "red" of the eggs.

Italian cooks are very creative with eggs. They poach them in broth or tomato sauce, scramble them with vegetables, toss them in salads, roll them inside of meatloaves, or make them into flat omelets called *frittate,* which are eaten hot or at room temperature for lunch or dinner.

Fried, Poached, and Baked Eggs

Prosciutto and Eggs
Uova al Prosciutto

MAKES 2 SERVINGS

A friend with whom I was traveling in Italy was on a high protein diet. She got into the habit of ordering a plate of prosciutto for breakfast. At one little inn in Montepulciano in Tuscany, the host asked if she would like to have some eggs with the prosciutto. My friend said yes, expecting to get a couple of boiled eggs. Instead, a short time later out came the cook with an individual frying pan filled with sizzling prosciutto and sunny-side-up eggs. It looked and smelled so good, soon everyone in the dining room was ordering the same thing, much to the dismay of the harried cook.

This is a perfect way to use up prosciutto that has gotten a little dry around the edges. Serve eggs with prosciutto for brunch with buttered asparagus and roasted tomatoes.

1 tablespoon unsalted butter
4 to 6 thin slices imported Italian prosciutto
4 large eggs
Salt and freshly ground black pepper

1 In a 9-inch nonstick skillet, melt the butter over medium-low heat.

2 Lay the prosciutto slices in the pan, overlapping slightly. Break the eggs into a cup one at a time, then slide the eggs onto the prosciutto. Sprinkle with salt and pepper.

3 Cover and cook over low heat until the eggs are set to taste, about 2 to 3 minutes. Serve hot.

Baked Asparagus with Eggs
Asparagi Milanese

MAKES 2 TO 4 SERVINGS

A journalist once asked me what I eat for dinner when I am cooking for myself. Without giving it much thought I replied asparagus with eggs and Parmigiano— what the Italians call Milanese style. This is so good, yet so simple. It is my idea of comfort food.

1 pound asparagus
Salt
3 tablespoons unsalted butter
Freshly ground black pepper
1/2 cup freshly grated Parmigiano-Reggiano
4 large eggs

1 Trim off the base of the asparagus at the point where the stem turns from white to green. Bring about 2 inches of water to a boil in a large skillet. Add the asparagus and salt to taste. Cook until the asparagus bend slightly when you lift them from the stem end, about 4 to 8 minutes. Cooking time will depend on the thickness of the asparagus. Transfer the asparagus with tongs to a strainer. Drain, then pat them dry.

2 Place a rack in the center of the oven. Preheat the oven to 450°F. Butter a large baking dish.

3 Arrange the asparagus side by side in the baking dish, overlapping them slightly. Dot with 1 tablespoon of the butter, and sprinkle with pepper and the cheese.

4 Bake 15 minutes or until the cheese is melted and golden.

5 In a large nonstick skillet, melt the remaining 2 tablespoons butter over medium heat. When the butter foam subsides, break one egg into a cup, then carefully slide it into the pan. Repeat with the remaining eggs. Sprinkle with salt and cook until the eggs are set to taste, about 2 to 3 minutes.

6 Divide the asparagus among the plates. Place the eggs on top. Spoon the pan juices over the top and serve hot.

Eggs in Purgatory
Uova in Purgatorio

MAKES 4 SERVINGS

When I was growing up, Friday night dinner at our house was always a meatless meal. Our meals were based on Neapolitan cooking. Dinner usually consisted of pasta e fagioli (pasta and beans), tuna salad, or these delicious eggs cooked in a spicy tomato sauce, hence the charming name Eggs in Purgatory. This is a perfect dish for when there is not much in the pantry and you want something hot and quick. Crusty bread is the essential accompaniment.

2 tablespoons olive oil
1/4 cup finely chopped onion
2 cups canned peeled tomatoes, chopped
4 fresh basil leaves, torn into pieces, or a pinch of dried oregano
Pinch of crushed red pepper (*peperoncino*)
Salt
8 large eggs

1 Pour the oil into a medium skillet. Add the onion and cook over medium heat, stirring, until tender and golden, about 10 minutes. Add the tomatoes, basil, red pepper, and salt to taste. Bring to a simmer and cook 15 minutes or until thickened.

2 Break an egg into a small cup. With a spoon, make an indentation in the tomato sauce. Slide the egg into the sauce. Continue with the remaining eggs.

3 Cover the skillet and cook until the eggs are set to taste, 2 to 3 minutes. Serve hot.

Eggs in Tomato Sauce, Marches Style
Uova in Brodetto

MAKES 2 SERVINGS

My uncle Joe, whose family came from the Marche region on the eastern coast of Italy, had a special way of cooking eggs in tomato sauce. His recipe,

though similar to Eggs in Purgatory (page 234), contains a dash of vinegar for a tangy flavor.

1 small onion, very finely chopped
1 tablespoon fresh flat-leaf parsley, very finely chopped
2 tablespoons olive oil
1 1/2 cups peeled, seeded, and chopped fresh tomatoes or drained and chopped canned tomatoes
1 to 2 tablespoons white wine vinegar
Salt and freshly ground black pepper
4 large eggs

1 In a 9-inch nonstick skillet, combine the onion, parsley, and oil and cook over medium heat, stirring occasionally, until the onion is tender and golden, about 10 minutes.

2 Stir in the tomatoes, vinegar, salt, and pepper to taste. Cook 10 minutes or until the sauce is thickened.

3 Break an egg into a small cup. With a spoon, make an indentation in the sauce. Carefully drop in the egg. Repeat with the remaining eggs. Sprinkle with salt and pepper. Cover and cook until the eggs are set to taste, 2 to 3 minutes. Serve hot.

Piedmontese-Style Eggs
Uova al Cirighet

MAKES 4 SERVINGS

Numerous dishes in Piedmont are flavored with garlic and anchovies sharpened with vinegar. Here, eggs get this piquant, flavorful treatment.

4 tablespoons olive oil
4 anchovy fillets, drained and chopped
2 tablespoons chopped fresh flat-leaf parsley
2 tablespoons capers, rinsed and drained
2 garlic cloves, very finely chopped
2 sage leaves, chopped
Pinch of crushed red pepper
1 tablespoon red wine vinegar
1 to 2 teaspoons fresh lemon juice
2 tablespoons unsalted butter
8 large eggs
Salt

1 In a medium skillet, combine the oil, anchovies, parsley, capers, garlic, sage, and crushed red pepper. Cook over medium heat, stirring often, until the anchovies are dissolved, 4 to 5 minutes. Stir in the vinegar and lemon juice. Cook 1 minute more.

2 In a large nonstick skillet, melt the butter over medium heat. When the butter foam subsides, carefully slide the eggs into the pan. Sprinkle with salt and cook 2 to 3 minutes, or until the eggs are set to taste.

3 Spoon the sauce over the eggs. Serve immediately.

Eggs Florentine
Uova alla Fiorentina

MAKES 4 SERVINGS

Eggs Florentine is often made in the United States with butter and a rich hollandaise sauce. This is a version that I had in Florence. Instead of butter, the spinach is cooked with garlic and olive oil, and a light sprinkling of Parmigiano is all that is needed on top of the eggs. It is a much lighter preparation, perfect for a casual brunch.

3 pounds spinach, tough stems removed
Salt
2 tablespoons olive oil
I garlic clove, finely chopped
Freshly ground black pepper
8 eggs
2 tablespoons freshly grated Parmigiano-Reggiano

1 Wash the spinach well in several changes of cold water. Put the spinach, 1/2 cup water, and a pinch of salt into a large pot. Cover the pot and turn on the heat to medium. Cook 5 minutes or until the spinach is wilted and tender. Drain the spinach and press out the excess water.

2 Pour the oil into a large skillet. Add the garlic and cook until golden, about 2 minutes.

3 Stir in the spinach and salt and pepper to taste. Cook, stirring occasionally, until heated through, about 2 minutes.

4 Break an egg into a small cup. With a spoon, make an indentation in the spinach. Slide the egg into the indentation. Repeat with the remaining eggs.

5 Sprinkle the eggs with salt and pepper and the cheese. Cover the skillet and cook 2 to 3 minutes or until the eggs are set to taste. Serve hot.

Baked Eggs with Potatoes and Cheese
Uova al Forno

MAKES 4 SERVINGS

Neapolitan comfort food is the best way to describe this layered casserole of potatoes, cheese, and eggs that my mother often made for me when I was a child.

I pound all-purpose potatoes, such as Yukon gold
Salt
I tablespoon unsalted butter
8 ounces fresh mozzarella, sliced
4 large eggs
Freshly ground black pepper
2 tablespoons Parmigiano-Reggiano

1 Scrub the potatoes and peel them. Cut them into 1/4-inch-thick slices. Place the potatoes in a medium saucepan with cold water to cover and salt to taste. Cover and bring to a simmer. Cook until the potatoes are just tender when pierced with a fork, about 10 minutes. Drain the potatoes and cool slightly.

2 Place a rack in the center of the oven. Preheat the oven to 400°F. Smear the butter around the bottom and sides of a 9-inch square baking dish. Arrange the potato slices in the pan, overlapping them slightly. Place the cheese slices on top of the potatoes. Break the eggs into a small cup, then slide them into the pan on top of the cheese. Sprinkle with salt, pepper, and the grated Parmigiano-Reggiano.

3 Bake until the eggs are set to taste, about 15 minutes. Serve hot.

❧ Scrambled Eggs

Peppers and Eggs
Peperoni e le Uova

MAKES 4 SERVINGS

Sautéed peppers or potatoes finished with scrambled eggs are good for brunch with grilled sausages, or serve them stuffed into wedges of crisp Italian bread for classic hero sandwiches.

1/4 cup olive oil
2 medium red bell peppers, cut into bite-size pieces
1 medium green bell pepper, cut into bite-size pieces
1 small onion, thinly sliced
Salt
8 large eggs
1/4 cup freshly grated Parmigiano-Reggiano
Freshly ground black pepper

1 In a 9-inch nonstick skillet, heat the oil over medium heat. Add the peppers, onion, and salt to taste. Cook, stirring often, until the peppers are browned, about 20 minutes. Cover and cook 5 minutes more or until the peppers are very tender.

2 In a medium bowl, beat the eggs with the cheese and add salt and ground pepper to taste. Pour the eggs over the peppers and let them set briefly. Turn the peppers and eggs with a spatula or spoon to allow the uncooked eggs to reach the surface of the pan. Allow the eggs to set and stir again. Repeat the stirring and cooking until the eggs are set to taste, about 2 to 3 minutes. Serve hot.

Potatoes and Eggs
Patate con le Uova

MAKES 4 SERVINGS

Potatoes scrambled with eggs is a classic combination found all over southern Italy. A small, thinly sliced bell pepper or an onion—or both—can be fried along with the potatoes, if you like. Serve it with sausages for brunch or stuff the potatoes and eggs into Italian bread for a hero sandwich.

1/4 cup olive oil
4 waxy new potatoes, peeled and cut into 1/4-inch slices
Salt
8 large eggs
Freshly ground black pepper

1 In a 9-inch nonstick skillet, heat the oil over medium heat. Pat the potato slices dry, and place them in the skillet. Cook, turning the pieces frequently, until the potatoes are browned and tender, about 10 minutes. Sprinkle with salt.

2 In a medium bowl, beat the eggs with salt and pepper to taste. Pour the eggs into the pan and let them set briefly. Turn the potatoes and eggs with a spatula or spoon to allow the uncooked eggs to reach the surface of the pan. Allow the eggs to set and stir again. Repeat the stirring and cooking until the eggs are set to taste, about 2 to 3 minutes. Serve hot.

Mushroom and Egg Scramble

Uova con Funghi

MAKES 4 SERVINGS

Eggs scrambled with mushrooms are good for a light supper or brunch. White mushrooms are fine, but wild mushrooms add a great earthy flavor.

3 tablespoons unsalted butter
I small onion, finely chopped
2 cups sliced mushrooms
Salt and freshly ground black pepper
8 large eggs

I In a 9-inch nonstick skillet, melt the butter over medium heat. Add the onion, mushrooms, and salt and pepper to taste. Cook, stirring occasionally, until the mushrooms are lightly browned, about 10 minutes.

2 In a medium bowl, beat the eggs with salt and pepper to taste. Pour the eggs over the vegetables and let them set briefly. Turn the mushrooms and eggs with a spatula or spoon to allow the uncooked eggs to reach the surface of the pan. Allow the eggs to set and stir again. Repeat the stirring and cooking until the eggs are set to taste, about 2 to 3 minutes. Serve hot.

❧ Frittatas

A frittata is a flat golden omelet that is one of the mainstays of Italian home cooking. *Frittate* are eaten hot or at room temperature, as appetizers and main dishes, and at lunch or dinner. They are great for picnics, as they are or sliced and stuffed into bread for sandwiches. You can make a frittata with most any kind of vegetable, meat, or cheese, or, best of all, with pasta.

The classic way to cook a frittata is in a skillet on top of the stove. The eggs are cooked on low heat until they are partially set, then the frittata is flipped onto a large plate and slid bottom side up into the pan to finish cooking. This technique is a little bit tricky, especially if you are making a large frittata or using a heavyweight skillet.

To avoid flipping the frittata, there are two alternatives. One is to slide the partially cooked eggs under the broiler to finish cooking. The second is simply to cover the skillet and allow the frittata to cook through over low heat. I have used all of these methods in the recipes that follow.

Once you get the knack of making frittate, the sky's the limit as far as what to put in them. Freshly cooked or leftover vegetables are good, chopped or sliced ham, cooked sausages, or salami can be used, and so can practically any cheese.

Onion and Arugula Frittata

Frittata di Cipolle e Rughetta

MAKES 4 SERVINGS

One day, an old friend of my mother's from Palermo in Sicily came to visit. We knew her as Zia Millie, though she was not really an aunt. She offered to prepare a salad to go with our meal and asked me if I had any mild onions, such as the red or white varieties. I only had the yellow onions that I typically

(continues)

use for cooking, but she said it would be fine. She sliced an onion thin and soaked it in several changes of cold water, which removed the powerful juices. By the time we were ready to eat the salad, the onion was as sweet as any milder variety. I use this method often whenever I want a gentle onion flavor.

This frittata from Puglia is flavored with onion and arugula. Substitute watercress or spinach leaves if you have no arugula.

2 medium onions, thinly sliced
3 tablespoons olive oil
I large bunch of arugula, tough stems removed, torn into bite-size pieces (about 2 cups)
8 large eggs
1/4 cup freshly grated Parmigiano-Reggiano
Salt and freshly ground black pepper

I Place the onions in a bowl with cold water to cover. Let stand 1 hour, changing the water once or twice, until the onions taste sweet. Drain and pat dry.

2 Pour the oil into a 9-inch nonstick skillet. Add the onions. Cook over medium heat, stirring occasionally, until the onions are tender and golden, about 10 minutes. Stir in the arugula until wilted, about 1 minute.

3 In a medium bowl, beat together the eggs, cheese, and salt and pepper to taste. Pour the eggs over the vegetables in the skillet and lower the heat. Cover and cook until the eggs are just set but still moist in the center and the frittata is lightly browned on the bottom, about 5 to 10 minutes.

4 Using a spatula to help, slide the frittata onto a plate. Invert the skillet over the plate and quickly flip both the plate and skillet so that the frittata is back in the pan with the cooked side up. Cook until just set in the center, about 5 minutes more. Or, if you prefer not to flip it, slide the skillet under the broiler 3 to 5 minutes or until the eggs are set to taste.

5 Slide the frittata onto a serving dish and cut into wedges. Serve hot or at room temperature.

Zucchini and Basil Frittata
Frittata di Zucchine

MAKES 4 SERVINGS

My mother used to grow zucchini in our tiny backyard in Brooklyn. At the height of the season, they grew so quickly we could hardly use them fast enough. That is when my mother would make this simple frittata, which we would eat with a fresh tomato salad. No bigger than a hot dog, the homegrown zucchini were mild and flavorful, with tiny seeds and thin skins.

3 tablespoons olive oil
2 to 3 small zucchini (about 1 pound), scrubbed and sliced
8 large eggs
1/4 cup freshly grated Parmigiano-Reggiano
6 fresh basil leaves, stacked and sliced into thin ribbons
Salt and freshly ground black pepper

I In a 9-inch nonstick skillet, heat the oil over medium-high heat. Add the zucchini and cook, turning the pieces occasionally, until the zucchini are nicely browned, about 12 minutes.

2 In a large bowl, beat the eggs, cheese, basil, and salt and pepper to taste. Lower the heat to medium. Pour the mixture over the zucchini. Lift the edges of the frittata as it sets to allow the uncooked egg to reach the surface of the pan. Cook until the eggs are just set but still moist in the center and the frittata is lightly browned on the bottom, about 5 to 10 minutes.

3 Slide the frittata onto a plate, then invert the skillet over the plate. Quickly flip both the plate and skillet so that the frittata is cooked-side up. Cook until just set in the center, about 5 minutes more. Or, if you prefer not to flip it, slide the skillet under the broiler 3 to 5 minutes or until set to taste. Serve hot or at room temperature.

4 Slide the frittata onto a serving dish and cut into wedges. Serve hot or refrigerate and serve cold.

Hundred-Herb Frittata
Frittata con Cento Erbe

MAKES 4 SERVINGS

Though I normally use only five or six herbs in this frittata from Friuli–Venezia Giulia, the name implies that the possibilities are much greater, and you can use whatever fresh herbs you have available. Fresh parsley is essential, but if the only other herbs you have on hand are dried, use just a pinch, or their flavors will be overwhelming.

8 large eggs
1/4 cup freshly grated Parmigiano-Reggiano
2 tablespoons finely chopped fresh flat-leaf parsley
2 tablespoons finely chopped fresh basil
1 tablespoon chopped fresh chives
1 teaspoon chopped fresh tarragon
1 teaspoon finely chopped fresh thyme
Salt and freshly ground black pepper
2 tablespoons olive oil

1 In a large bowl, beat the eggs, cheese, herbs, and salt and pepper to taste until well combined.

2 In a 9-inch non-stick skillet, heat the oil over medium heat. Pour the egg mixture into the pan. Lift the edges of the frittata as it sets to allow the uncooked egg to reach the surface of the pan. Cook until the eggs are just set but still moist in the center and the frittata is lightly browned on the bottom, about 5 to 10 minutes.

3 Slide the frittata onto a plate, then invert the skillet over the plate. Quickly flip both the plate and skillet so that the frittata is cooked-side up. Cook until just set in the center, about 5 minutes more. Or, if you prefer not to flip it, slide the skillet under the broiler 3 to 5 minutes or until set to taste. Serve hot or at room temperature.

Spinach Frittata
Frittata di Spinaci

MAKES 4 SERVINGS

Spinach, escarole, Swiss chard, or other greens can be used in this frittata. Serve it with sautéed mushrooms and sliced tomatoes.

1 pound fresh spinach, trimmed
1/4 cup water
Salt
8 large eggs
1/4 cup heavy cream
1/2 cup freshly grated Parmigiano-Reggiano
2 tablespoons unsalted butter

1 Place the spinach, water, and salt to taste in a large pot. Cover and cook over medium heat until tender and wilted, about 5 minutes. Drain well. Let cool slightly. Place the spinach in a kitchen towel and squeeze it to extract the liquid.

2 In a large bowl, beat the eggs, cream, cheese, and salt and pepper to taste. Stir in the spinach.

3 In a 9-inch non-stick skillet, melt the butter over medium heat. Pour the mixture into the pan. Lift the edges of the frittata as it sets to allow the uncooked egg to reach the surface of the pan. Cook until the eggs are just set but still moist in the center and the frittata is lightly browned on the bottom, about 5 to 10 minutes.

4 Slide the frittata onto a plate, then invert the skillet over the plate. Quickly flip both the plate and skillet so that the frittata is cooked side up. Cook until set in the center, about 5 minutes more. Or, if you prefer not to flip it, slide the skillet under the broiler for 3 to 5 minutes or until set to taste. Serve hot or at room temperature.

Mushroom and Fontina Frittata

Frittata di Funghi e Fontina

MAKES 4 SERVINGS

Genuine Fontina Valle d'Aosta has a woodsy, mushroom aroma and marries well with any mushroom dish. Use wild mushrooms if you prefer them to the white.

3 tablespoons unsalted butter
8 ounces mushrooms, halved or quartered if large
Salt and freshly ground black pepper
8 large eggs
2 tablespoons chopped fresh flat-leaf parsley
4 ounces Fontina Valle d'Aosta, cut into slices

1 In a 9-inch non-stick skillet, melt the butter over medium heat. Add the mushrooms and salt and pepper to taste. Cook, stirring often, until the mushrooms are lightly browned, about 10 minutes.

2 In a large bowl, beat the eggs with the parsley and salt and pepper to taste. Lower the heat to medium. Pour the mixture over the mushrooms. Lift the edges of the frittata as it sets to allow the uncooked egg to reach the surface of the pan. Cover and cook until the eggs are just set but still moist in the center and the frittata is lightly browned on the bottom, about 5 to 10 minutes.

3 Place the slices of cheese on top. Slide the skillet under the broiler and cook 1 to 3 minutes or until the cheese has melted and the eggs are set to taste. Or, if you prefer, cover the pan and cook 3 to 5 minutes, until the cheese is melted and the eggs are set to taste.

4 Slide the frittata onto a serving plate. Serve hot.

Neapolitan Spaghetti Frittata

Frittata di Spaghetti

MAKES 6 SERVINGS

At a family gathering some years ago, a distant relative got to talking about her favorite recipes. She described a flat golden pasta torte filled with meats and cheeses that her children asked for all the time. I wrote down her instructions and tried it at home. It was as good as she said, and I have since learned that it is a traditional Neapolitan recipe. Although you could prepare spaghetti just for this dish, it is traditionally made with leftovers.

8 large eggs
1/2 cup freshly grated Parmigiano-Reggiano
    or Pecorino Romano
Salt and freshly ground black pepper
12 ounces spaghetti or other pasta, cooked and drained
4 ounces sliced salami, imported Italian prosciutto,
    or ham, cut into narrow strips
2 tablespoons olive oil
8 ounces mozzarella, thinly sliced

1 In a large bowl, beat the eggs, cheese, and salt and pepper to taste. Stir in the spaghetti and salami.

2 In a 9-inch nonstick skillet, heat the oil over medium heat. Add half of the spaghetti mixture. Cover with the cheese slices. Pour the remaining pasta mixture over the cheese.

3 Reduce the heat to low. Cook the spaghetti, flattening the surface occasionally, so the pasta sticks together and forms a cake. After about 5 minutes, slide a spatula around the rim of the skillet and lift the cake gently to be sure that it is not sticking. Cook until the eggs are set and the frittata is lightly browned on the bottom, about 15 to 20 minutes.

4 Slide the frittata onto a plate, then invert the skillet over the plate. Quickly flip both the plate and skillet so that the frittata is cooked-side up. Cook until just set in the center, about 5 minutes more. Or, if you prefer not to flip it, slide the skillet under the broiler for 3 to 5 minutes or until set to taste. Serve hot or at room temperature.

Pasta Frittata
Frittata di Pasta

MAKES 4 SERVINGS

Any leftover pasta can be recycled into this delicious frittata. No matter if the pasta is plain or sauced with tomatoes, meat sauce, or vegetables, this frittata always turns out great. Improvise by adding chopped sausages, ham, cheese, or some cut-up cooked vegetables. Quantities are not really important.

6 large eggs
1/2 cup freshly grated Parmigiano-Reggiano
Salt and freshly ground black pepper
8 ounces cooked pasta, with or without a sauce
2 tablespoons olive oil

1 In a large bowl, beat together the eggs, cheese, and salt and pepper to taste. Stir in the cooked pasta.

2 In a 9-inch nonstick skillet, heat the oil over medium heat. Add the pasta mixture and press it flat. Cook until the eggs are just set but still moist in the center and the frittata is lightly browned on the bottom, about 10 minutes.

3 Slide the frittata onto a plate, then invert the skillet over the plate. Quickly flip both the plate and skillet so that the frittata is cooked-side up. Cook until just set in the center, about 5 minutes more. Or, if you prefer not to flip it, slide the skillet under the broiler for 3 to 5 minutes or until set to taste. Serve hot or at room temperature.

Little Omelets
Frittatine

MAKES 6 SERVINGS

Miniature omelets, prepared on a griddle like pancakes, are nice to serve as part of an antipasto assortment or to use as a sandwich filling. This version made with leeks and cabbage is from Piedmont.

About 1/4 cup olive oil
3 cups finely shredded cabbage
1 medium leek, trimmed and thinly sliced
6 large eggs
1/2 cup freshly grated Parmigiano-Reggiano
1/2 teaspoon salt
Freshly ground black pepper

1 In a 9-inch nonstick heavy skillet, heat 3 tablespoons oil over medium-low heat. Stir in the cabbage and leek. Cover the skillet and cook, stirring occasionally, until the cabbage is very tender, about 30 minutes. Let cool.

2 In a medium bowl, beat together the eggs, cheese, and salt and pepper to taste. Stir in the vegetable mixture.

3 Lightly brush a griddle or a large nonstick skillet with oil. Heat over medium heat.

4 Stir the egg mixture and scoop by 1/4 cupful onto the griddle, spacing the omelets about 4 inches apart. Flatten slightly with the back of a spoon. Cook until the eggs are set and the omelets begin to brown on the bottom, about 2 minutes. With a pancake turner, flip the omelets and cook on the other side for about 1 minute more. Transfer the omelets to a plate.

5 Cook the remaining omelets in the same way. Serve hot or at room temperature.

Ricotta and Zucchini Flower Frittata
Frittata di Fiori e Ricotta

MAKES 4 SERVINGS

Zucchini flowers are not only beautiful but also delicious to eat—something Italians know well. My local farmers' market had an abundance of zucchini flowers one Saturday. I bought some to stuff and fry, but I still had plenty leftover, so I made this frittata with the remaining flowers. It was delicate and delicious; I've made it for brunch several times since.

It can also be made just with ricotta if you don't have zucchini flowers.

2 tablespoons unsalted butter
6 zucchini or other squash blossoms, rinsed and dried
6 large eggs, beaten
1/4 cup freshly grated Parmigiano-Reggiano
Salt and freshly ground pepper
1 cup ricotta

1 In a 9-inch nonstick skillet, melt the butter over medium heat. Place the zucchini flowers in the pan in a pinwheel fashion.

2 In a medium bowl, beat together the eggs, Parmigiano, and salt and pepper to taste. Carefully pour the mixture over the flowers without disturbing them. Place spoonfuls of the ricotta around the pan. Lift the edges of the frittata as it sets to allow the uncooked egg to reach the surface of the pan. Cook until the eggs are just set but still moist in the center and the frittata is lightly browned on the bottom, about 5 to 10 minutes.

3 Slide the frittata onto a plate, then invert the skillet over the plate. Quickly flip both the plate and skillet so that the frittata is cooked-side up. Cook until just set in the center, about 5 minutes more. Or, if you prefer not to flip it, slide the skillet under the broiler for 3 to 5 minutes, or until the eggs are set to taste. Serve hot or at room temperature.

Omelet Strips in Tomato Sauce
Fettuccine di Frittata

MAKES 4 SERVINGS

No pasta? No problem. Make a thin frittata and cut it into strips to resemble fettuccine. Though known as fettuccine di frittata throughout Italy, in Rome, this dish is called trippe finte, *meaning false tripe, because the eggs strips resemble innards when cooked this way. Serve it for lunch or dinner with any green vegetable in season, or a green salad.*

2 cups Fresh Tomato Sauce (page 89) or Tuscan Tomato Sauce (pages 90–91)
8 large eggs
1/4 cup freshly grated Parmigiano-Reggiano, plus more for serving
1 tablespoon chopped fresh flat-leaf parsley
1 teaspoon salt
Freshly ground black pepper
2 tablespoons unsalted butter

1 Prepare the tomato sauce, if necessary. Then, place a rack in the center of the oven. Preheat the oven to 400°F. Generously butter a 13 × 9 × 2–inch baking dish.

2 In a medium bowl, beat together the eggs, 1/4 cup of cheese, parsley, salt, and pepper to taste. Pour the egg mixture into the prepared pan. Bake 8 to 10 minutes or until the eggs are just set and a knife inserted in the center comes out clean.

3 Run a knife around the edge of the pan. Invert the eggs onto a cutting board. Cut the omelet into 1/2-inch strips.

4 In a 9-inch nonstick skillet, heat the sauce over low heat until simmering. Slip the egg strips into the sauce. Cook, stirring gently, 2 to 3 minutes. Serve hot with grated cheese.

Fish and Shellfish

Fillets and Steaks

Sea Bass with Olive Crumbs

Sea Bass with Mushrooms

Turbot Fillets with Olive Paste
and Tomatoes

Broiled Cod

Fish in "Crazy Water"

Bluefish with Lemon and Mint

Fillets with Tomato and Balsamic Vinegar

Stuffed Sole

Sole Rolls with Basil and Almonds

Marinated Tuna, Sicilian Style

Skewered Tuna with Orange

Grilled Tuna and Peppers, Molise Style

Grilled Tuna with Lemon and Oregano

Crusty Broiled Tuna Steaks

Seared Tuna with Arugula Pesto

Tuna and Cannellini Bean Stew

Sicilian Swordfish with Onions

Swordfish with Artichokes and Onions

Swordfish, Messina Style

Swordfish Rolls

Roasted Turbot with Vegetables

Pan-Fried Sea Bass with Garlicky Greens

Scrod with Spicy Tomato Sauce

Salmon Carpaccio

Salmon Steaks with Juniper Berries
and Red Onions

Salmon with Spring Vegetables

Fish Steaks in Green Sauce

Halibut Baked in Paper

Whole Fish

Baked Fish with Olives and Potatoes

Citrus Red Snapper

Fish in a Salt Crust

Roasted Fish in White Wine and Lemon

Trout with Prosciutto and Sage

Baked Sardines with Rosemary

Sardines, Venetian Style

Stuffed Sardines, Sicilian Style

Grilled Sardines

Salted and Dried Fish

Fried Salt Cod

Salt Cod, Pizza Style

Salt Cod with Potatoes

(continues)

Shrimp, Lobster, and Scallops

Shrimp and Beans
Shrimp in a Garlic Sauce
Shrimp with Tomatoes, Capers, and Lemon
Shrimp in Anchovy Sauce
Fried Shrimp
Batter-Fried Shrimp and Calamari
Grilled Shrimp Skewers
"Brother Devil" Lobster
Baked Stuffed Lobster
Scallops with Garlic and Parsley
Grilled Scallops and Shrimp

Clams and Mussels

Clams and Mussels Posillipo
Baked Stuffed Clams
Mussels with Black Pepper
Mussels with Garlic and White Wine
Sardinian Mussels with Saffron

Calamari, Octopus, and Conch

Fried Calamari
Venetian-Style Calamari
Calamari with Artichokes and White Wine
Grilled Stuffed Calamari
Calamari Stuffed with Olives and Capers
Stuffed Calamari, Roman Style
Mauro's Grilled Octopus
with Fennel and Orange
Tomato-Braised Octopus
Conch Salad
Conch in Hot Sauce

Mixed Seafood

Seafood Couscous
Mixed Fish Fry
Molise-Style Fish Stew

Italy is a peninsula surrounded by the Ligurian, Mediterranean, Tyrennian, Ionian, and Adriatic Seas. With the country's long coastline, as well as many lakes stocked with freshwater fish, Italians have an amazing variety of seafood to choose from. Some are similar to varieties we find in North America, such as *branzino* (sea bass), *orata* (gilt-head bream), *rana pescatrice* or *coda di rospo* (monkfish), *trota* (trout), and *tonno* (tuna). But Italians also eat many types of seafood that are uncommon in the United States, such as *seppia* (cuttlefish), scampi (prawns), various types of eels and sea snails, whitebait, fresh anchovies, and red mullet. These can, however, sometimes be found in ethnic markets here.

At Italian fishmarkets, seafood is displayed whole, resting on a bed of ice. Big fish like tuna and swordfish are cut into pieces and displayed alongside their heads so shoppers can tell at a glance what type of seafood they are buying and judge whether or not the seafood is fresh.

Whole fish should have bright eyes and irridescent, moist skin. Steaks and fillets should have a moist, slightly pearly sheen with no dryness, browning, or separation of the flesh. Shellfish varieties like mussels and clams should close tightly when tapped, though there are some types, such as razor clams, that are always slightly agape. Scallops in Italy are sold in their shells with the bright, coral red crescent of roe still attached. In this country, scallops usually are shelled and the roe discarded so that the seafood will keep longer. Crustaceans like lobster and crab are sold live, frozen, or already cooked because they spoil rapidly once they are killed. All types of seafood should have a fresh, mild aroma.

At home, keep fish in a plastic bag on top of a bed of ice in the refrigerator. Live varieties like lobsters, clams, and mussels should be taken out of the plastic bag, placed on ice and just lightly covered with a damp cloth. Use all varieties of fish and seafood as soon as possible after purchasing.

Rinse fish and seafood before using, to eliminate loose scales, sand, or bits of shells.

➳ Fillets and Steaks

Sea Bass with Olive Crumbs
Branzino alle Olive

MAKES 4 SERVINGS

Olive trees grow in profusion throughout Tuscany. Most of the olives are pressed to make oil, but cooks still have plenty of flavorful olives at their disposal. Here they flavor the crumbs scattered on top of sea bass fillets.

³/₄ cups plain dry bread crumbs, preferably homemade

¹/₃ cup finely chopped mild black olives

I garlic clove, finely chopped

I tablespoon chopped fresh flat-leaf parsley

I teaspoon grated lemon zest

Salt

Freshly ground black pepper

About ¹/₄ cup olive oil

I¹/₂ pounds sea bass or other firm white fish fillets, skins removed

I Place a rack in the center of the oven. Preheat the oven to 450°F. Oil a large baking pan.

2 Put the bread crumbs, olives, garlic, parsley, lemon zest, a pinch of salt, and black pepper to taste in a bowl. Add the olive oil and stir well.

3 Arrange the fish in the pan in a single layer. Pile the crumbs on top of the fillets.

4 Bake 8 to 10 minutes, depending on the thickness of the fish, or until the crumbs are golden and the fish is just barely opaque when cut in the thickest part. Serve immediately.

When Is Fish "Done"?

Fresh fish does not need a lot of seasoning, but it is important to recognize when fish is done so that it is not undercooked or overcooked. Before cooking, fish is slightly translucent and feels soft when pressed. No matter which cooking method used, a good rule of thumb is to figure about 8 to 10 minutes per inch of thickness of the fish. A sole fillet that is less than a ¹/₂-inch thick will be done in about 4 minutes, while a thick fish steak might take 8 minutes. Of course, this is just a guideline, and there are other cues that will help you to judge when the fish is done. The difficulty is that whole fish and fillets are often uneven in thickness, so getting them cooked just right is a challenge.

Press the fish at the thickest part with your fingertip. It should feel firmer than before it was cooked. If you are still not sure, use a small knife and cut into the thickest part. The fish should be opaque, except for a thin translucent line near the center. For whole fish, cut near the main bone in the center or along the back of the fish. Most varieties should be just slightly translucent to almost opaque. They will finish cooking from residual heat, after you stop the cooking. Some fish, especially steaks cut from tuna, salmon, and swordfish, are best when they are cooked rare to medium-rare. Flakiness is a sign that the fish is overcooked and is to be avoided.

Sea Bass with Mushrooms
Branzino alla Romana

MAKES 4 SERVINGS

Sandwiching a tasty filling between two boneless fish fillets is a good way to get the flavor of stuffed fish without having to deal with bones. Any large fish fillets can be used, such as salmon, grouper, or bluefish. Choose two fillets of similar size and shape.

4 tablespoons olive oil

3 green onions, chopped

1 garlic clove, chopped

8 ounces white mushrooms, trimmed and chopped

2 anchovy fillets, chopped

Salt and freshly ground black pepper

1/2 cup dry white wine

2 tablespoons chopped fresh flat-leaf parsley

2 tablespoons plain bread crumbs

2 sea bass, grouper, or bluefish fillets of similar shape (about 3/4 pounds each), skin removed

1 Place a rack in the center of the oven. Preheat the oven to 400°F. Oil a baking pan large enough to hold the stacked fillets.

2 Pour 3 tablespoons of the oil into a large skillet. Add the green onions and garlic and cook over medium heat until softened, about 5 minutes. Stir in the mushrooms, anchovies, and salt and pepper to taste. Cook 5 minutes, stirring occasionally. Add the wine and simmer 15 minutes or until the liquid is evaporated. Remove from the heat and stir in the parsley and bread crumbs.

3 Lay one fillet skinned-side down in the pan.

4 Spread about two-thirds of the mushroom mixture over the fillet in the pan. Top with the second fillet skinned-side down and spread the remaining mushroom mixture over the top. Drizzle with the remaining tablespoon of oil.

5 Bake 15 to 20 minutes, depending on the thickness, or until the fish is just barely opaque when cut in the thickest part. Serve hot.

Turbot Fillets with Olive Paste and Tomatoes
Rombo con Pasta d'Olive

MAKES 4 SERVINGS

A big jar of black olive paste brought home from Italy and some ripe tomatoes inspired me to come up with this tasty recipe.

1 1/2 pounds turbot, sea bass, or other thick white fish fillets

2 tablespoons black olive paste, or very finely chopped mild black olives

2 medium tomatoes, diced

6 fresh basil leaves, rolled and sliced crosswise into thin ribbons

1 Place a rack in the center of the oven. Preheat the oven to 450°F. Oil a baking pan large enough to hold the fillets in a single layer.

2 Arrange the fillets in the pan in a single layer. Spread the fillets with the olive paste. Scatter the tomatoes and basil over the fish.

3 Bake 8 to 10 minutes, depending on the thickness, until the fish is just barely opaque when cut in the thickest part. Serve immediately.

Broiled Cod
Merluzzo alla Griglia

MAKES 4 SERVINGS

Red snapper, grouper, and mahi-mahi are other good choices for this basic broiled fish. I serve it with Mashed Potatoes with Olives and Parsley (pages 453–454) and Broccoli with Oil and Lemon (see page 411).

1 1/2 pounds fresh cod fillet
3 tablespoons olive oil
2 tablespoons red wine vinegar
2 garlic cloves, thinly sliced
1 teaspoon dried oregano, crumbled
Salt and freshly ground black pepper
2 tablespoons chopped fresh flat-leaf parsley
1 lemon, cut into wedges

1 Preheat the broiler to high. Oil a baking pan large enough to hold the fish in a single layer. Place the fish in the pan.

2 Stir together the oil, vinegar, garlic, oregano, and salt and pepper to taste. Pour the mixture over the fish fillets. Sprinkle with half the parsley.

3 Broil the fish 8 to 10 minutes, depending on the thickness, or until just barely opaque when cut in the thickest part. Sprinkle with the remaining parsley. Serve hot, with lemon wedges.

Fish in "Crazy Water"
Pesce in Acqua Pazza

MAKES 4 SERVINGS

Exactly why this Neapolitan way of cooking fish is called crazy water is not certain, but it is probably a reference to the sea water that fisherman once used to cook their fresh catch. Though this method is usually used to cook whole fish, I find it works well with fillets, too. Use a firm variety that will hold its shape as it simmers.

3 tablespoons olive oil
1 garlic clove, thinly sliced
4 plum tomatoes, halved, seeded, and chopped
1 tablespoon chopped fresh flat-leaf parsley
Pinch of crushed red pepper
1/2 cup water
Salt to taste
1 1/2 pounds firm fish fillets, such as sea bass, turbot, or red snapper

1 Pour the olive oil into a large skillet. Add the garlic and cook over medium heat until golden, about 5 minutes. Add the tomatoes, parsley, red pepper, water, and salt to taste. Bring to a simmer and cook 5 minutes.

2 Add the fish to the skillet and baste it with the sauce. Cover and cook 5 to 10 minutes, or until the fish is just barely opaque when cut in the thickest part. Serve hot.

Bluefish with Lemon and Mint
Pesce Azzurro al Limone

MAKES 4 SERVINGS

Because they have a higher fat content than other varieties, dark-fleshed fish like bluefish have a stronger flavor. Southern Italians cook them in a tasty and refreshing marinade with garlic, mint, and lemon.

2 large garlic cloves, finely chopped
3 tablespoons olive oil
1/4 cup fresh lemon juice
1/2 teaspoon freshly grated lemon zest
Salt and freshly ground black pepper to taste
1/4 cup chopped fresh mint
1 1/2 pounds bluefish or mackerel fillets

1 In a shallow bowl, whisk together the garlic, olive oil, lemon juice, zest, and salt and pepper. Stir in the mint. Add the fish, turning the fillets to coat them on all sides. Cover and marinate 1 hour in the refrigerator.

2 Preheat the broiler. Place the fish in the broiler pan skin-side down. Cook, basting the fillets once with the marinade, 8 to 10 minutes, depending on the thickness of the fish, or until they are lightly browned and just barely opaque in the thickest part. There is no need to turn the fish. Serve hot.

Fillets with Tomato and Balsamic Vinegar
Filleti di Pesce al Balsamico

MAKES 4 SERVINGS

This combination of warm, lightly crispy fish and cool tomato-herb topping is one of my favorites.

I large tomato, peeled, seeded, and finely chopped
2 tablespoons capers, rinsed and drained
2 tablespoons chopped fresh chives
Salt and freshly ground black pepper
I tablespoon balsamic vinegar
1/4 cup flour
1 1/2 pounds grouper, pompano, or other firm fish fillets
4 tablespoons unsalted butter

1 Combine the tomato, capers, chives, and salt and pepper to taste. Stir in the vinegar.

2 Spread the flour on a sheet of wax paper. Sprinkle the fish with salt and pepper. Roll the fillets in the flour, lightly shaking off the excess.

3 In a large skillet, melt the butter over medium heat. Add the fish and cook, turning once, until just barely opaque when cut in the thickest part, about 8 to 10 minutes, depending on the thickness of the fillets.

4 Arrange the fillets on a serving platter. Drain the tomato mixture and spoon it over the fish. Serve hot.

Stuffed Sole
Sogliole Ripiene

MAKES 4 SERVINGS

The presence of raisins, pine nuts, and capers in this tasty stuffing is normally a sign of a Sicilian dish, though this recipe comes from Liguria. Whatever its origins, the stuffing enhances plain white fish fillets. Choose large, thin fillets such as sole or flounder.

1/2 cup plain bread crumbs
2 tablespoons pine nuts
2 tablespoons raisins
2 tablespoons capers, rinsed and drained
I tablespoon chopped fresh flat-leaf parsley
I small garlic clove, finely chopped
3 tablespoons olive oil
2 tablespoons fresh lemon juice
Salt and freshly ground black pepper
4 large sole, flounder, or other thin fillets
    (about 1 1/2 pounds)

1 Place a rack in the center of the oven. Preheat the oven to 400°F. Oil a large baking pan.

2 Mix together the bread crumbs, pine nuts, raisins, capers, parsley, and garlic. Add 2 tablespoons of the oil, the lemon juice, and salt and pepper to taste.

3 Set aside 2 tablespoons of the crumb mixture. Divide the remainder over half of each fillet. Fold the fillets over to enclose the filling. Arrange the fillets in the baking pan. Sprinkle with the reserved crumb mixture. Drizzle with the remaining 1 tablespoon of the oil.

4 Bake 6 to 8 minutes, or until just barely opaque when cut in the thickest part. Serve hot.

Sole Rolls with Basil and Almonds
Sogliola con Basilico e Mandorle

MAKES 4 SERVINGS

Andrea Felluga of the Livio Felluga winery took my husband and me under his wing and showed us around his region of Friuli–Venezia Giulia. One memorable town we visited was Grado, on the Adriatic coast. Situated on an island, Grado was a refuge for Roman citizens of nearby Aquileia fleeing the onslaught of Attila the Hun in the fifth century. Today, it is a beach resort, though few non-Italians seem to visit, instead flocking to nearby Venice. We ate sole prepared this way at Restaurant Colussi, a lively restaurant serving typical regional food.

**4 large sole, flounder, or other thin fillets
    (about 1 1/2 pounds)**
Salt and freshly ground black pepper
6 fresh basil leaves, finely chopped
2 tablespoons unsalted butter, melted
1 tablespoon fresh lemon juice
1/4 cup sliced almonds or pine nuts

1 Place a rack in the center of the oven. Preheat the oven to 350°F. Butter a small baking dish.

2 Cut the sole fillets in half lengthwise. Place the fillets skinned-side up on a flat surface and sprinkle with salt and pepper. Sprinkle with half the basil, butter, and lemon juice. Starting at the wider end, roll up the pieces of fish. Place the rolls seamside down in the baking dish. Drizzle with the remaining lemon juice and butter. Scatter the remaining basil and the nuts over the top.

3 Bake the fish 15 to 20 minutes, or until it is just opaque when cut in the thickest part. Serve hot.

Marinated Tuna, Sicilian Style
Tonno Condito

MAKES 4 SERVINGS

The tuna in this recipe is just gently steamed, then dressed with fresh herbs and seasonings. It would make a cool and refreshing summer meal served on a bed of baby salad greens or arugula with a potato salad.

1 1/4 pounds tuna steaks, about 3/4-inch thick
2 tablespoons red wine vinegar
Salt
3 to 4 tablespoons extra-virgin olive oil
1 garlic clove, finely chopped
2 tablespoons chopped fresh flat-leaf parsley
1 tablespoon chopped fresh mint
1/2 teaspoon crushed red pepper

1 Fill a pot that will fit a steamer rack with 1/2 inch of water. Bring the water to a boil. Meanwhile, cut the tuna into 1/2-inch-thick strips. Spread the fish on the steamer rack. Set the rack in the pot. Cover the pot and allow the tuna to steam for 3 minutes or until slightly pink in the center. Test for doneness by making a small cut in the thickest part of the fish.

2 In a deep dish, beat together the vinegar and salt. Add the oil, garlic, herbs, and crushed red pepper. Stir in the tuna pieces.

3 Let stand about 1 hour before serving.

Skewered Tuna with Orange
Spiedini di Tonno

MAKES 4 SERVINGS

Every spring, Sicilian fishermen gather for la mattanza, *the tuna kill. This ritual fishing marathon involves numerous small boats filled with men that herd the migrating tuna into a series of increasingly smaller nets until they are trapped. Then the huge fish are killed and hauled aboard the boats. The process is laborious, and as the men work they sing special chants that historians date to the Middle Ages or even earlier. Though this practice is disappearing, there are still a few places along the northern and western coasts where* la mattanza *takes place.*

Sicilians have countless ways of cooking tuna. With this one, the aroma of the grilled orange and herbs preludes the enticing flavor of the chunks of firm-fleshed fish.

1 1/2 **pounds fresh tuna, swordfish, or salmon steaks (about I inch thick)**
I navel orange, cut into 16 pieces
I small red onion, cut into 16 pieces
2 tablespoons olive oil
2 tablespoons fresh lemon juice
I tablespoon chopped fresh rosemary
Salt and freshly ground black pepper
6 to 8 bay leaves

1 Cut the tuna into 1 1/2-inch chunks. In a large bowl, toss the tuna, orange, and red onion pieces with the olive oil, lemon juice, rosemary, and salt and pepper to taste.

2 Place the barbecue grill or broiler rack about 5 inches from the heat source. Preheat the grill or broiler.

3 Thread the tuna, orange pieces, onion, and bay leaves alternately on 8 skewers.

4 Broil or grill until the tuna is browned, about 3 to 4 minutes. Turn the skewers and cook until browned on the outside but still pink in the center, about 2 minutes more, or until done to taste. Serve hot.

Grilled Tuna and Peppers, Molise Style
Tonno e Peperoni

MAKES 4 SERVINGS

Peppers and chiles are one of the hallmarks of Molise-style cooking. I first had this dish prepared with sgombri, *which are similar to mackerel, but I often make it with tuna steaks or swordfish.*

4 red or yellow bell peppers
4 tuna steaks (each about 3/4 inch thick)
2 tablespoons olive oil
Salt and freshly ground black pepper
I tablespoon fresh lemon juice
2 tablespoons chopped fresh flat-leaf parsley
I small jalapeno or other fresh chile, finely chopped, or crushed red pepper to taste
I garlic clove, finely chopped

1 Place the grill rack or broiler pan about 5 inches from the source of the heat. Prepare a medium-hot fire in a barbecue grill, or preheat the broiler.

2 Grill or broil the peppers, turning them often, until the skin is blistered and lightly charred, about 15 minutes. Place the peppers in a bowl and cover them with foil or plastic wrap.

3 Brush the tuna steaks with oil and salt and pepper to taste. Grill or broil the fish until browned on one side, about 2 minutes. Turn the fish over with tongs and cook until browned on the other side but still pink in the center, about 2 minutes more, or until done to taste. Test for doneness by making a small cut in the thickest part of the fish.

4 Core, peel, and seed the peppers. Cut the peppers into 1/2-inch strips and place them in a bowl. Season with 2 tablespoons of the oil, the lemon juice, parsley, chile, garlic, and salt to taste. Toss gently.

5 Cut the fish into 1/2-inch slices. Arrange the slices overlapping slightly on a serving plate. Spoon the peppers over the top. Serve warm.

Grilled Tuna with Lemon and Oregano

Tonno alla Griglia

MAKES 4 SERVINGS

The first time I visited Sicily, in 1970, there weren't many restaurants; those that existed all seemed to serve the same menu. I ate either tuna or swordfish steaks prepared this way for practically every lunch and dinner. Fortunately, it was always well prepared. The Sicilians cut the fish steaks only about 1/2-inch thick, but I prefer them about 1-inch thick so that they do not overcook as easily. Tuna is at its best— moist and tender—when cooked until red to pink in the center, while swordfish should be just slightly pink. Because it has cartilage that needs tenderizing, shark can be cooked a little longer.

4 tuna, swordfish, or shark steaks, about 1 inch thick
Olive oil
Salt and freshly ground black pepper
1 tablespoon freshly squeezed lemon juice
1/2 teaspoon dried oregano

1 Place a barbecue grill or broiler rack about 5 inches away from the heat source. Preheat the grill or broiler.

2 Generously brush the steaks with the oil and add salt and pepper to taste.

3 Grill the fish until lightly browned on one side, 2 to 3 minutes. Turn the fish over and cook until lightly browned but still pink inside, about 2 minutes more, or until done to taste. Test for doneness by making a small cut in the thickest part of the fish.

4 In a small bowl, whisk together 3 tablespoons olive oil, the lemon juice, oregano, and salt and pepper to taste. Pour the lemon juice mixture over the tuna steaks and serve immediately.

Crusty Broiled Tuna Steaks

Tonno alla Griglia

MAKES 4 SERVINGS

Bread crumbs make a nice crunchy coating on these fish steaks.

4 (1 inch thick) tuna or swordfish steaks
3/4 cup plain dry bread crumbs
1 tablespoon chopped fresh flat-leaf parsley
1 tablespoon chopped fresh mint or 1 teaspoon dried oregano
Salt and freshly ground black pepper
4 tablespoons olive oil
Lemon wedges

1 Preheat the broiler. Oil the broiler pan. In a bowl, toss together the bread crumbs, parsley, mint, and salt and pepper to taste. Stir in 3 tablespoons of the oil, or enough to moisten the crumbs.

2 Arrange the fish steaks on the broiler pan. Scatter half of the crumbs on top of the fish, patting them in.

3 Broil the steaks about 6 inches from the flame 3 minutes, or until the crumbs are browned. Carefully turn the steaks with a metal spatula and sprinkle with the remaining crumbs. Broil 2 to 3 minutes more or until still pink in the center, or until done to taste. Test for doneness by making a small cut in the thickest part of the fish.

4 Drizzle with the remaining 1 tablespoon of oil. Serve hot, with lemon wedges.

Seared Tuna with Arugula Pesto
Tonno al Pesto

MAKES 4 SERVINGS

The spicy flavor of arugula and bright emerald green color of this sauce is a perfect complement to fresh tuna or swordfish. This dish is also good at a cool room temperature.

4 tuna steaks, about 1 inch thick
Olive oil
Salt and freshly ground black pepper

ARUGULA PESTO
1 bunch arugula, washed and stemmed
    (about 2 cups lightly packed)
1/2 cup lightly packed fresh basil
2 garlic cloves
1/2 cup olive oil
Salt and freshly ground black pepper

1 Rub the fish with a little oil and salt and pepper to taste. Cover and refrigerate until ready to cook.

2 To make the pesto: In a food processor, combine the arugula, basil, and garlic and process until finely chopped. Slowly add the oil and process until smooth. Stir in salt and pepper to taste. Cover and let stand 1 hour at room temperature.

3 In a large nonstick skillet, heat 1 tablespoon oil over medium heat. Add the tuna slices and cook 2 to 3 minutes per side or until browned on the outside but still pink in the center, or until done to taste. Test for doneness by making a small cut in the thickest part of the fish.

4 Serve the tuna hot or at room temperature, drizzled with the arugula pesto.

Tuna and Cannellini Bean Stew
Stufato di Tonno

MAKES 4 SERVINGS

During the winter, I tend to cook more meat than seafood because meat seems more satisfying when the weather is cold. The exception is this stew made with fresh, meaty tuna steaks and beans. It has all the rib-sticking qualities and good flavor of a bean stew but without the meat, making it perfect for people who prefer meatless meals.

2 tablespoons olive oil
1 1/2 pounds fresh tuna (1 inch thick), cut into
    1 1/2-inch pieces
Salt and freshly ground black pepper to taste
1 large red or green bell pepper, cut into bite-size
    pieces
1 cup canned peeled tomatoes, drained and chopped
1 large garlic clove, finely chopped
6 fresh basil leaves, torn into bits
1 (16-ounce) can cannellini beans, rinsed and drained,
    or 2 cups cooked dried beans

1 Heat the oil in a large skillet over medium heat. Pat the tuna pieces dry with paper towels. When the oil is hot, add the tuna pieces without crowding the pan. Cook until the pieces are lightly browned on the outside, about 6 minutes. Transfer the tuna to a plate. Sprinkle with salt and pepper.

2 Add the bell pepper to the skillet and cook, stirring occasionally, until it begins to brown, about 10 minutes. Add the tomato, garlic, basil, and salt and pepper. Bring to a simmer. Add the beans, cover, and reduce the heat to low. Cook for 10 minutes.

3 Stir in the tuna and cook until the tuna is slightly pink in the center, about 2 minutes more, or until done to taste. Test for doneness by making a small cut in the thickest part of the fish. Serve hot.

Sicilian Swordfish with Onions

Pesce Spada a Sfinciuni

MAKES 4 SERVINGS

Sicilian cooks make a mouth-watering pizza called sfinciuni, *a word that derives from the Arabic meaning "light" or "airy." The pizza has a thick yet light crust and is topped with onions, anchovies, and tomato sauce. This traditional swordfish recipe is derived from that pizza.*

3 tablespoons olive oil

I medium onion, thinly sliced

4 anchovy fillets, chopped

I cup peeled, seeded, and chopped fresh tomatoes, or drained and chopped canned tomatoes

Pinch of dried oregano, crumbled

Salt and freshly ground black pepper to taste

4 swordfish steaks, about 3/4 inch thick

2 tablespoons plain dry bread crumbs

I Pour 2 tablespoons of the oil into a medium skillet. Add the onion and cook until softened, about 5 minutes. Stir in the anchovies and cook 5 minutes more or until very tender. Add the tomatoes, oregano, salt, and pepper and simmer 10 minutes.

2 Place a rack in the center of the oven. Preheat the oven to 350°F. Oil a baking pan large enough to hold the fish in a single layer.

3 Pat the swordfish steaks dry. Place them in the prepared pan. Sprinkle with salt and pepper. Spoon on the sauce. Toss the bread crumbs with the remaining 1 tablespoon of the oil. Scatter the crumbs over the sauce.

4 Bake 10 minutes or until the fish is just slightly pink in the center. Test for doneness by making a small cut in the thickest part of the fish. Serve hot.

Swordfish with Artichokes and Onions

Pesce Spada con Carciofi

MAKES 4 SERVINGS

Artichokes are a favorite Sicilian vegetable. They thrive in the hot, arid conditions of Sicily, and people grow them in their home gardens as a decorative plant. The Sicilian variety does not grow as large as the behemoths I sometimes see in markets here, and are much more tender.

2 medium artichokes

2 tablespoons olive oil

4 thick swordfish, tuna, or shark steaks

Salt and freshly ground black pepper

2 medium onions

4 anchovy fillets, chopped

1/4 cup tomato paste

I cup water

1/2 teaspoon dried oregano

I Trim the artichokes down to the central cone of pale green leaves. With a small paring knife, peel the base and stems of the artichokes. Slice off the stem ends. Cut the artichokes in half lengthwise. Scoop out the chokes. Cut the hearts into thin slices.

2 In a large skillet, heat the oil over medium heat. Pat the swordfish dry and cook until browned on both sides, about 5 minutes. Sprinkle with salt and pepper. Remove the fish to a plate.

3 Add the onions and artichokes to the pan. Cook over medium heat, stirring frequently, until the onions are wilted, about 5 minutes. Stir in the anchovies, tomato paste, water, oregano, and salt and pepper to taste. Bring to a simmer and lower the heat. Cook 20 minutes or until the vegetables are tender, stirring occasionally.

4 Push the vegetables to the outside edge of the pan and return the fish to the skillet. Baste the fish with the sauce. Cook 1 to 2 minutes or until the fish is heated through. Serve immediately.

Swordfish, Messina Style

Pesce Spada Messinese

MAKES 4 SERVINGS

Excellent swordfish is caught in the waters around Sicily, and Sicilians have countless ways to prepare it. The fish is eaten raw, sliced paper thin in a kind of carpaccio, or ground into sausages that cook in tomato sauce. Cubes of swordfish are tossed with pasta, roasted like meat, or grilled on a barbecue. This is a classic recipe from Messina, on the east coast of Sicily.

I pound boiling potatoes
2 tablespoons olive oil
I large onion, chopped
¹/₂ cup pitted black olives, coarsely chopped
2 tablespoons capers, rinsed and drained
2 cups peeled, seeded, and chopped tomatoes,
    or drained and chopped canned tomatoes
Salt and freshly ground black pepper
2 tablespoons chopped flat-leaf parsley
4 swordfish steaks, I inch thick

1 Scrub the potatoes and place them in a saucepan with cold water to cover. Bring the water to a boil and cook until the potatoes are tender, about 20 minutes. Drain, let cool a little, then peel the potatoes. Thinly slice them.

2 Pour the oil into a large saucepan. Add the onion and cook, stirring frequently, over medium heat until tender, about 10 minutes. Stir in the olives, capers, and tomatoes. Season to taste with salt and pepper. Cook until thickened slightly, about 15 minutes. Stir in the parsley.

3 Place a rack in the center of the oven. Preheat the oven to 425°F. Spoon half the sauce into a baking pan large enough to hold the fish in a single layer. Arrange the swordfish in the pan and sprinkle it with salt and pepper. Place the potatoes on top, overlapping the slices slightly. Spoon the remaining sauce over all.

4 Bake 10 minutes or until the fish is just slightly pink in the center and the sauce is bubbling. Serve hot.

Swordfish Rolls

Rollatini di Pesce Spada

MAKES 6 SERVINGS

Like veal or chicken cutlets, very thin slices of meaty swordfish are good wrapped around a filling and cooked on a grill or broiler. Vary the filling by adding raisins, chopped olives, or pine nuts.

I¹/₂ pounds swordfish, cut into very thin slices
³/₄ cup plain dry bread crumbs
2 tablespoons capers, rinsed, chopped, and drained
2 tablespoons chopped fresh flat-leaf parsley
I large garlic clove, finely chopped
Salt and freshly ground black pepper
¹/₄ cup olive oil
2 tablespoons fresh lemon juice
I lemon, cut into wedges

1 Place a barbecue grill or broiler rack about 5 inches away from the heat source. Preheat the grill or broiler.

2 Remove the swordfish skin. Place the slices between two sheets of plastic wrap. Gently pound the slices to an even ¹/₄-inch thickness. Cut the fish into 3 × 2–inch pieces.

3 In a medium bowl, combine the bread crumbs, capers, parsley, garlic, and salt and pepper to taste. Add 3 tablespoons of the oil and mix until the crumbs are evenly moistened.

4 Place a tablespoon of the crumb mixture at one end of one piece of fish. Roll up the fish and fasten it closed with a toothpick. Place the rolls on a plate.

5 Whisk together the lemon juice and remaining oil. Brush the mixture over the rolls. Sprinkle the fish with any remaining bread crumb mixture, patting it so that it adheres.

6 Grill the rolls 3 to 4 minutes on each side, or until browned and the rolls feel firm when pressed and are lightly pink in the center. They should be slightly rare. Test for doneness by making a small cut in the thickest part of the fish. Serve hot with lemon wedges.

Roasted Turbot with Vegetables
Rombo al Forno con Verdure

MAKES 4 SERVINGS

Calabria has a long coast along the Mediterranean Sea. In the summer, this region is popular with Italians and other Europeans seeking an inexpensive beach getaway. My husband and I once drove along the coast near Scalea and ate at a local restaurant with a big wood-burning oven. When we arrived, the cook was just removing big pans of vegetables roasted with olive oil and topped with fresh whitefish. The vegetables browned and infused the fish with their delicious flavor. At home, I use turbot when I can find it, but other whitefish steaks would be good too.

1 red pepper, cut into 1-inch pieces
1 medium zucchini, cut into 1-inch pieces
1 medium eggplant, cut into 1-inch pieces
4 medium boiling potatoes, cut into 1-inch pieces
1 medium onion, cut into 1-inch pieces
1 bay leaf
1/4 cup plus 1 tablespoon olive oil
Salt and freshly ground black pepper
4 thick turbot, halibut, or other whitefish steaks
1 tablespoon lemon juice
2 tablespoons chopped fresh flat-leaf parsley

1 Place a rack in the center of the oven. Preheat the oven to 425°F. Choose a baking pan large enough to hold the fish and vegetables in a single layer, or use two smaller pans. In the pan combine the pepper, zucchini, eggplant, potatoes, onion, and bay leaf. Sprinkle with 1/4 cup of the olive oil and salt and pepper to taste. Toss well.

2 Bake the vegetables 40 minutes or until lightly browned and tender.

3 Put the fish steaks on a plate and sprinkle them with the remaining 1 tablespoon oil, lemon juice, parsley, and salt and pepper to taste. Push the vegetables to the outside edge of the pan and add the fish. Bake 8 to 10 minutes more, depending on the thickness of the fish, until it is just barely opaque when cut in the thickest part. Serve hot.

Pan-Fried Sea Bass with Garlicky Greens
Branzino alle Verdure

MAKES 4 SERVINGS

Raisins and garlic flavoring greens such as Swiss chard, spinach, and escarole are a favorite combination from Rome on down through southern Italy. This recipe was inspired by a dish prepared by my friend, chef Mauro Mafrici, who serves the greens with crisp fried fish fillets and roasted potatoes.

1 bunch escarole (about 1 pound)
3 tablespoons olive oil
3 garlic cloves, thinly sliced
Pinch of crushed red pepper
1/4 cup raisins
Salt
1 1/4 pounds Chilean sea bass, cod, or other firm
    skinless fillet, about 1 1/2 inches thick

1 Separate the leaves and wash the escarole in several changes of cool water, paying special attention to the central white ribs where soil collects. Stack the leaves and cut them crosswise into 1-inch strips.

2 Pour 2 tablespoons of the olive oil into a large pot. Add the garlic and red pepper. Cook over medium heat until the garlic is golden, about 2 minutes.

3 Add the escarole, raisins, and a pinch of salt. Cover the pot and cook, stirring occasionally, until the escarole is tender, about 10 minutes. Taste and adjust seasoning.

4 Rinse the fish and pat dry. Sprinkle the pieces with salt and pepper. In a medium nonstick skillet, heat the remaining tablespoon of oil over medium heat. Add the fish pieces skinned-side up. Cook until the fish is golden brown, 4 to 5 minutes. Cover the pan and cook 2 to 3 minutes more, or

until the fish is just barely opaque in the center. Test for doneness by making a small cut in the thickest part of the fish. There is no need to turn the fish.

5 With a slotted spoon, transfer the escarole to 4 serving plates. Top with the fish browned-side up. Serve hot.

Scrod with Spicy Tomato Sauce
Merluzzo in Salsa di Pomodoro

MAKES 4 SERVINGS

We ate this fish at the home of Neapolitan friends, accompanied by Falanghina, a delicious white wine from the region. Couscous goes well with the fish.

2 tablespoons olive oil
1 medium onion, thinly sliced
Pinch of crushed red pepper
2 cups canned tomatoes with their juice, chopped
Pinch of dried oregano, crumbled
Salt
1 1/4 pounds scrod or grouper fillets, cut into
    serving pieces
1/2 teaspoon grated lemon zest

1 Pour the oil into a medium skillet. Add the onion and red pepper. Cook, stirring often, over medium heat, until the onion is tender and golden, about 10 minutes. Add the tomatoes, oregano, and salt and simmer until the sauce is thickened, about 15 minutes.

2 Rinse the fish and pat dry, then sprinkle it with salt. Add the fish to the pan and baste it with the sauce. Cover and cook 8 to 10 minutes, depending on the thickness of the fish, until it is just barely opaque when cut in the thickest part.

3 With a slotted spoon, transfer the fish to a serving platter. If the fish has released a lot of liquid, raise the heat under the pan and cook, stirring frequently, until the sauce is thickened.

4 Remove the sauce from the heat and stir in the lemon zest. Spoon the sauce over the fish and serve immediately.

Salmon Carpaccio
Carpaccio di Salmone

MAKES 4 SERVINGS

Usually, carpaccio refers to paper-thin slices of raw beef served with a creamy pink sauce. The recipe was supposedly created about a hundred years ago by a Venetian restaurateur who wanted to pamper a favorite client whose doctor had advised her to avoid eating cooked food. The restaurateur named the dish after Vittore Carpaccio, a painter whose work was on exhibit at the time.

Today the term carpaccio is applied to thinly sliced foods both raw and cooked. These thin salmon cutlets are cooked on only one side so that they stay moist and keep their shape.

4 cups watercress
3 tablespoons extra-virgin olive oil
1 tablespoon fresh lemon juice
1/2 teaspoon grated lemon zest
Salt and freshly ground black pepper
1 pound salmon fillet, cut into thin slices like cutlets
1 green onion, finely chopped

1 Rinse the watercress in several changes of cool water. Remove the tough stems and dry the leaves thoroughly. Tear into bite-size pieces and place them in a bowl.

2 In a bowl, whisk together 2 tablespoons of oil, lemon juice, zest, and salt and pepper to taste.

3 Heat 1 tablespoon oil in a large nonstick skillet over high heat. Add just enough fish as will fit in a single layer. Cook until lightly browned on the bottom, yet still rare on top, about 1 minute. With a large spatula, remove the salmon from the skillet and turn it browned-side up onto a large serving platter. Sprinkle with salt and pepper to taste and half of the green onion. Cook the remaining salmon in the same way and add it to the platter. Top with the remaining onion.

4 Toss the watercress with the dressing. Pile the salad on top of the salmon. Serve immediately.

Salmon Steaks with Juniper Berries and Red Onions
Salmone al Ginepro

MAKES 4 SERVINGS

Juniper berries are the typical flavoring in gin and are often used to spice up stews made with game. You can find them in many markets that sell gourmet spices. In this salmon dish, which I first ate in Venice, sweet red onions and juniper are cooked until the onions are meltingly soft and become a sauce for the salmon.

3 tablespoons olive oil

4 salmon steaks, about ³/₄ inch thick

Salt and freshly ground black pepper

2 medium red onions, thinly sliced

¹/₂ teaspoon juniper berries

¹/₂ cup dry white wine

1 In a medium skillet, heat the oil over medium heat. Pat the salmon steaks dry and place them in the pan. Cook until browned, about 3 minutes. Turn the salmon steaks and brown on the other side, about 2 minutes more. With a spatula, remove the steaks to a plate. Sprinkle with salt and pepper.

2 Add the onions, juniper berries, and salt to taste to the pan. Add the wine and bring to a simmer. Lower the heat and cover the pan. Cook 20 minutes or until the onions are soft.

3 Return the salmon steaks to the pan and spoon the onions over the fish. Turn the heat to medium. Cover and cook about 2 minutes more or until the fish is just barely opaque when cut in the thickest part. Serve immediately.

Salmon with Spring Vegetables
Salmone Primavera

MAKES 4 SERVINGS

Salmon is not a Mediterranean fish, but a lot of it has been imported to Italy from northern Europe in recent years, and it has become very popular in Italian kitchens. This recipe of roasted salmon with spring vegetables was a special dish at a restaurant in Milan.

Vary the vegetables, but be sure to use a very large pan so that they can be spread out in a shallow layer. If they are too crowded, the vegetables will get soggy instead of browned. I use a 15 × 10 × 1–inch jelly roll pan. If you don't have one large enough, divide the ingredients between two smaller pans.

4 medium red or white waxy potatoes

1 cup peeled and trimmed baby carrots

8 whole shallots or 2 small onions, peeled

3 tablespoons olive oil

Salt and freshly ground black pepper

8 ounces asparagus, cut into 2-inch lengths

4 salmon steaks

2 tablespoons chopped fresh herbs, such as chives, dill, parsley, basil, or a combination

1 Place a rack in the center of the oven. Preheat the oven to 425°F. Cut the potatoes into thick slices and pat them dry. In a large roasting pan, combine the potatoes, carrots, and shallots or onions. Add the oil and salt and pepper to taste. Toss well. Spread the vegetables in the pan and bake for 20 minutes.

2 Stir the vegetables and add the asparagus. Bake 10 minutes more or until the vegetables are lightly browned.

3 Sprinkle the salmon with salt and pepper. Push the vegetables to the sides of the pan. Add the salmon steaks. Bake 7 minutes more or until the salmon is just barely opaque and still moist when cut in the thickest part. Sprinkle with the herbs and serve immediately.

Fish Steaks in Green Sauce
Pesce in Salsa Verde

MAKES 4 SERVINGS

I spent New Year's Eve in Venice with friends one year, and before going to the midnight services at St. Mark's Cathedral, we had dinner at a little trattoria near the Rialto Bridge. We ate grilled prawns, risotto with cuttlefish, and this dish of sautéed fish steaks in a parsley and white wine sauce with peas. After dinner, we walked through the streets, which were filled with good-natured revelers, many wearing fabulous costumes.

1/2 **cup all-purpose flour**

Salt and freshly ground black pepper

4 halibut, tilefish, or other white fish steaks, about 1 inch thick

4 tablespoons olive oil

4 green onions, finely chopped

3/4 **cup dry white wine**

1/4 **cup chopped fresh flat-leaf parsley**

1 cup fresh or frozen baby peas

1 On a piece of wax paper, combine the flour and salt and pepper to taste. Rinse the fish and pat dry, then dredge each steak in the flour mixture to lightly coat both sides. Shake off the excess.

2 In a large skillet, heat 2 tablespoons of the oil over medium heat. Add the fish and brown on one side, about 3 minutes. Turn the fish and brown the other side, about 2 minutes. With a slotted metal spatula, transfer the steaks to a plate. Wipe out the skillet.

3 Pour the remaining 2 tablespoons oil into the skillet. Add the onions. Cook over medium heat until golden, about 10 minutes. Add the wine and bring to a simmer. Cook until most of the liquid is evaporated, about 1 minute. Stir in the parsley.

4 Return the fish to the skillet and baste it with the sauce. Scatter the peas around the fish. Reduce the heat to low. Cover and cook 5 to 7 minutes or until the fish is just barely opaque when cut in the thickest part. Serve immediately.

Halibut Baked in Paper
Pesce in Cartoccio

MAKES 4 SERVINGS

Fish baked in a parchment paper package is a dramatic dish that is actually quite easy to make. The paper holds in all of the flavor of the fish and seasonings and has the added advantage of saving on clean up. Aluminum foil can be substituted for the parchment, but it is not as attractive.

2 medium tomatoes, seeded and chopped

2 green onions, finely chopped

1/4 **teaspoon dried marjoram or thyme**

2 tablespoons fresh lemon juice

2 tablespoons olive oil

Salt and freshly ground black pepper

4 (6-ounce) halibut, salmon, or other fish steaks, about 1-inch thick

1 Place a rack in the center of the oven. Preheat the oven to 400°F. In a medium bowl, mix together all of the ingredients except the fish.

2 Cut 4 sheets of parchment paper into 12-inch squares. Fold each sheet in half. Open the paper and brush the inside with oil. Place a fish steak to one side of the crease. Spoon the tomato mixture over the fish.

3 Fold the paper over the fish. Seal each package by making small folds from one end to the other all along the edges and creasing firmly. Carefully slide the packages onto 2 baking sheets.

4 Bake 12 minutes. To check for doneness, slit one package and cut the fish in the thickest part. It should be just barely opaque.

5 Slide the packages onto serving plates and allow the diners to open their own. Serve hot.

❧ Whole Fish

Baked Fish with Olives and Potatoes
Pesce al Forno

MAKES 4 SERVINGS

Marjoram is an herb that is used often in Liguria, though it is not very well known in the United States. It has a flavor similar to oregano, though it is much less assertive than dried oregano. Thyme is a good substitute.

Start the potatoes ahead of time so that they get a chance to brown and cook thoroughly. Then add the fish so that everything bakes together in perfect harmony. A green salad is all you need to follow.

2 pounds boiling potatoes, peeled and thinly sliced

6 tablespoons olive oil

Salt and freshly ground black pepper to taste

2 tablespoons chopped fresh flat-leaf parsley

1/2 teaspoon dried marjoram or thyme

2 tablespoons fresh lemon juice

1/2 teaspoon freshly grated lemon zest

2 whole fish such as red snapper or sea bass (about 2 pounds each), cleaned with heads and tails intact

1/2 cup mild black olives, such as Gaeta

1 Place a rack in the center of the oven. Preheat the oven to 450°F. In a large bowl, toss the potatoes with 3 tablespoons of the oil and salt and pepper to taste. Spread the potatoes in a large shallow roasting pan. Bake the potatoes 25 to 30 minutes, or until they begin to turn brown.

2 Stir together the remaining 3 tablespoons of the oil, the parsley, marjoram, lemon juice, zest, and salt and pepper to taste. Place half of the mixture inside the cavity of the fish and rub the remainder over the skin.

3 With a large spatula, turn the potatoes and scatter the olives all around. Rinse the fish well and pat dry. Place the fish on top of the potatoes. Bake

about 8 to 10 minutes per inch of thickness at the widest point of the fish, or until the flesh is opaque when cut with a small sharp knife near the bone and the potatoes are tender.

4 Transfer the fish to a warm serving platter. Surround the fish with the potatoes and olives. Serve immediately.

Citrus Red Snapper
Pesce al Agrumi

MAKES 4 SERVINGS

No matter what the weather is outside, you will feel like it is a glorious sunny day when you serve this fish roasted with citrus fruits. The recipe is based on one I tasted in Positano. A crisp, fresh wine such as pinot grigio is the perfect accompaniment.

1 medium orange

1 medium lemon

2 whole fish such as red snapper or sea bass (about 2 pounds each), cleaned with heads and tails intact

2 teaspoons chopped fresh thyme leaves

2 tablespoons olive oil

Salt and freshly ground black pepper

1/2 cup dry white wine

1 orange and 1 lemon, sliced, for garnish

1 With a swivel-blade vegetable peeler, remove half of the zest from the orange and lemon skin. Stack the pieces and cut them into narrow strips. Squeeze the fruits to extract the juice.

2 Place a rack in the center of the oven. Preheat the oven to 400°F. Oil a baking pan large enough to hold the fish in a single layer.

3 Rinse the fish well and pat dry. Place the fish in the pan and stuff the cavity with the thyme and half the zest. Sprinkle inside and out with the oil and salt and pepper to taste. Pour the wine, juice, and remaining zest over the fish.

4 Bake, basting once or twice with the pan juices, about 8 to 10 minutes per inch of thickness at the widest point of the fish, or until the flesh is opaque

when cut with a small sharp knife near the bone. Serve hot, garnished with orange and lemon slices.

Fish in a Salt Crust
Pesce in Sale

MAKES 2 SERVINGS

Fish and seafood baked in salt is a traditional dish in Liguria and along the Tuscan coast. Mixed with egg white, the salt forms a thick hard crust so that the fish inside cooks in its own juices. At Baia Beniamin, a beautiful restaurant right on the water in Ventimiglia near the French border, I watched as the waiter deftly cracked the salt crust with the back of a heavy spoon and lifted it away, removing the skin and salt in one motion. Inside, the fish was cooked to perfection.

6 cups kosher salt

4 large egg whites

1 whole fish such as red snapper or sea bass (about 2 pounds each), cleaned with head and tail intact

1 tablespoon chopped fresh rosemary

2 garlic cloves, finely chopped

1 lemon, cut into wedges

Extra-virgin olive oil

1 Place a rack in the center of the oven. Preheat the oven to 500°F. In a large bowl, stir together the salt and egg whites until the salt is evenly moistened.

2 Oil a baking sheet large enough to hold the fish. Place the fish on the baking sheet. Stuff the cavity with the rosemary and garlic.

3 Mound the salt evenly on the fish, covering it completely. Pat the salt firmly so it will hold.

4 Bake the fish 30 minutes or until the salt is beginning to turn lightly golden around the edges. To test for doneness, insert an instant-read thermometer through the salt into the thickest part of the fish. The fish is done when the temperature reaches 130°F.

5 To serve, crack the salt crust with a large spoon. Lift the salt and skin away from the fish and discard. Carefully lift the flesh away from the bones. Serve hot with the lemon wedges and a drizzle of extra-virgin olive oil.

Roasted Fish in White Wine and Lemon
Pesce al Vino Bianco

MAKES 4 SERVINGS

This is a basic way to cook any medium to small whole fish. I had this in Liguria, where it was accompanied by braised artichokes and potatoes.

2 whole fish such as red snapper or sea bass (about 2 pounds each), cleaned with heads and tails intact

1 tablespoon chopped fresh rosemary

Salt and freshly ground black pepper

1 lemon, thinly sliced

2 tablespoons chopped fresh flat-leaf parsley

1 cup dry white wine

1/4 cup extra-virgin olive oil

1 tablespoon white wine vinegar

1 Place a rack in the center of the oven. Preheat the oven to 400°F. Oil a pan large enough to hold the fish side by side.

2 Rinse the fish and pat dry inside and out. Sprinkle the insides of the fish with the rosemary and salt and pepper to taste. Tuck some of the lemon slices inside the cavity. Place the fish in the pan. Scatter the parsley over the fish and lay the remaining lemon slices on top. Drizzle with the wine, oil, and vinegar.

3 Bake the fish 8 to 10 minutes per inch of thickness at the widest point, or until the flesh is opaque when cut with a small sharp knife near the bone. Serve hot.

Trout with Prosciutto and Sage

Trote al Prosciutto e Salvia

MAKES 4 SERVINGS

Wild trout is very flavorful, though it is rarely found in fish markets. Farm-raised trout is a lot less interesting, but prosciutto and sage enhance the flavor. I had trout prepared this way in Friuli–Venezia Giulia, where it was made with the local prosciutto from the town of San Daniele.

4 small whole trout, cleaned, about 12 ounces each

4 tablespoons olive oil

2 to 3 tablespoons fresh lemon juice

6 fresh sage leaves, finely chopped

Salt and freshly ground black pepper

8 very thin slices imported Italian prosciutto

1 lemon, cut into wedges

1 Oil a baking pan large enough to hold the fish in a single layer.

2 In a small bowl, combine the oil, lemon juice, sage, and salt and pepper to taste. Sprinkle the fish inside and out with the mixture. Marinate the fish in the refrigerator for 1 hour.

3 Place the oven rack in the center of the oven. Preheat the oven to 375°F. Place a slice of prosciutto inside each fish and lay another slice on top. Bake 20 minutes or until the fish is just opaque when cut with a small sharp knife near the bone. Serve hot with lemon wedges.

Baked Sardines with Rosemary

Sarde con Rosamarina

MAKES 4 SERVINGS

Sardines, smelts, and anchovies belong to the family of dark-fleshed fish known in Italy as pesce azzurro. *Other members of this family include mackerel and, of course, bluefish. Rosemary complements them nicely in this recipe from Tuscany.*

1 1/2 pounds fresh sardines, smelts, or anchovies, cleaned (see Note below)

Salt and freshly ground black pepper

1 tablespoon chopped fresh rosemary

1/4 cup olive oil

1/4 cup plain fine dry bread crumbs

1 lemon, cut into wedges

1 Place the rack in the center of the oven. Preheat the oven to 400°F. Oil a baking dish large enough to hold the sardines in a single layer.

2 Place the sardines in the dish and sprinkle inside and out with salt, pepper, and rosemary. Drizzle with the oil and sprinkle with bread crumbs.

3 Bake 15 minutes or until the fish are cooked through. Serve with lemon wedges.

Note: *To clean sardines:* With a large heavy chef's knife or kitchen shears, cut off the heads. Slit the fish open along the belly and remove the innards. Pull out the backbone. Snip off the fins. Rinse and drain.

Sardines, Venetian Style
Sarde in Saor

MAKES 4 SERVINGS

Raisins and vinegar give a delicious sweet-and-sour flavor to fish in this Venetian classic. Be sure to make this recipe at least a day before you plan to serve it so that the flavors can mellow. Small portions are excellent as an appetizer. Whole trout or mackerel can be substituted for the sardines, or try sole fillets. In Venice, sarde in saor is often served with grilled white Polenta (pages 223, 224).

8 tablespoons olive oil
3 onions (about 1 pound), sliced 1/2 inch thick
1 cup dry white wine
1 cup white wine vinegar
2 tablespoons pine nuts
2 tablespoons raisins
2 pounds sardines, cleaned

1 Pour 4 tablespoons of oil into a large heavy skillet. Add the onions and cook over medium-low heat until very tender, about 20 minutes. Stir frequently and watch carefully so that the onions do not brown. Add a tablespoon or two of water if needed to prevent the onions from coloring.

2 Add 1/2 cup of wine, 1/2 cup of vinegar, the raisins, and the pine nuts. Bring to a simmer and cook 1 minute. Remove from the heat.

3 In another skillet, heat the remaining 4 tablespoons oil over medium heat. Add the sardines and cook until just opaque in the center, about 2 to 3 minutes per side. Arrange the sardines in a single layer on a large platter. Pour on the remaining wine and vinegar.

4 Spread the onion mixture over the fish. Cover and refrigerate 1 to 2 days to allow the flavors to mellow. Serve at cool room temperature.

Stuffed Sardines, Sicilian Style
Sarde Beccafico

MAKES 4 SERVINGS

Dr. Joseph Maniscalco, an old family friend who came from Sciacca in Sicily, taught me how to make this typically Sicilian recipe. The Italian name means sardines in the style of a figpecker, a succulent little bird that loves to eat ripe figs.

1 cup plain dry bread crumbs
About 1/4 cup olive oil
4 anchovy fillets, drained and chopped
2 tablespoons chopped fresh flat-leaf parsley
2 tablespoons pine nuts
2 tablespoons raisins
Salt and freshly ground black pepper
2 pounds fresh sardines, cleaned
Bay leaves
Lemon wedges

1 Place a rack in the center of the oven. Preheat the oven to 375°F. Oil a small baking pan.

2 In a large skillet, toast the bread crumbs over medium heat, stirring constantly, until browned. Remove from the heat and stir in just enough oil to moisten them. Add the anchovies, parsley, pine nuts, raisins, and salt and pepper to taste. Mix well.

3 Open the sardines like a book and place them skin side down on a flat surface. Spoon a little of the bread crumb mixture at the head end of each sardine. Roll up the sardines, enclosing the filling, and place them side by side in the pan, separating each with a bay leaf. Sprinkle any remaining crumbs over the top and drizzle with the remaining oil.

4 Bake 20 minutes or until the rolls are just cooked through. Serve hot or at room temperature with lemon wedges.

Grilled Sardines
Sarde alla Griglia

MAKES 4 SERVINGS

Small, tasty fish like sardines, smelts, and anchovies are irresistible when cooked on the grill. At a barbecue dinner at a winery in Abruzzo, the guests arrived to find rows and rows of the little fish cooking over a charcoal fire. Though it looked like there were too many, they soon disappeared, washed down with glasses of chilled white trebbiano wine.

A basket grill does a good job of holding and turning the little fish as they cook. If you are fortunate enough to grow your own lemon or orange trees and they have not been treated with chemicals, use some of the leaves to garnish the serving platter. Otherwise, radicchio or firm lettuce leaves will do.

12 to 16 fresh sardines or smelts, cleaned
2 tablespoons olive oil
Salt and freshly ground black pepper
Untreated lemon leaves or radicchio
2 lemons, cut into wedges

1 Place a barbecue grill or broiler rack about 5 inches away from the heat source. Preheat a barbecue grill or broiler.

2 Pat the sardines dry and brush with the oil. Sprinkle lightly with salt and pepper. Grill or broil the fish until nicely browned, about 3 minutes. Gently turn the fish over and cook until browned on the other side, about 2 to 3 minutes more.

3 Arrange the leaves on a platter. Top with the sardines and garnish with the lemon wedges. Serve hot.

✥ Salted and Dried Fish

Before refrigeration was commonplace, most Italians found it difficult to obtain fresh fish. Because Italy is a Catholic country where the devout were required to eat meatless meals on Fridays and holy days, people came to rely on salted and dried fish. Back then, these preserved fish were inexpensive and widely available. Many recipes evolved to make use of this early convenience food, and today it is part of the culinary tradition of every region of Italy. Baccala and *stoccofisso* (also called *pesce stocco*) are no longer inexpensive but are still often used in Italian cooking. Baccala is salted cod, perch, or a similar whitefish that is typically cut into pieces and salted, and stoccofisso, or stockfish, is left in large fillets that are air-dried until they are hard as wood. Their name comes from the Scandinavian word for stockfish. Markets in Italy sell both types of the fish soaked and ready to cook, so their names are often used interchangeably, and in fact either type of preserved fish can be used in recipes that call for salt and dried fish. The biggest difference between them is the length of time required to reconstitute them. Baccala is usually soft and sufficiently desalinated to use after 24 to 48 hours of soaking, while stoccofisso requires as much as a week to become hydrated. Another difference is that baccala is mild in taste and smell, while stockfish is strong smelling.

Note that fresh fish can be substituted for baccala or stoccofisso in any of the recipes that call for salted and dried fish. Both types of preserved fish are widely available in fish markets and ethnic groceries.

Fried Salt Cod
Baccala Fritta

MAKES 4 SERVINGS

This is a basic recipe for cooking baccala. It can be served plain or topped with tomato sauce. Some cooks like to heat the sauce in a skillet and then add the fried fish, simmering them together briefly.

About 1 cup all-purpose flour

Salt and freshly ground black pepper

1 pound soaked baccala or stockfish, cut into serving pieces

Olive oil

Lemon wedges

1 Spread the flour and salt and pepper to taste on a piece of wax paper.

2 In a large heavy skillet, heat about 1/2 inch of the oil. Quickly dip the fish pieces in the flour mixture, lightly shaking off the excess. Place as many fish pieces in the pan as will fit without crowding.

3 Cook the fish until browned, 2 to 3 minutes. Turn the fish with tongs, then cook until browned and tender, 2 to 3 minutes more. Serve hot with lemon wedges.

Variation: Add lightly crushed whole garlic cloves and/or fresh or dried chile peppers to the frying oil to flavor the fish.

Salt Cod, Pizza Style
Baccala alla Pizzaiola

MAKES 6 TO 8 SERVINGS 8

In Naples, tomatoes, garlic, and oregano are the typical flavors of a classic pizza sauce, so this dish flavored with those ingredients is called pizza-style. For extra flavor, add a handful of olives and a few anchovy fillets to the sauce.

2 pounds soaked salt cod, cut into serving pieces

4 tablespoons olive oil

2 large garlic cloves, very finely chopped

2 tablespoons chopped fresh flat-leaf parsley

Pinch of crushed red pepper

3 cups peeled, seeded, and chopped fresh tomatoes, or 1 (28-ounce) can Italian peeled tomatoes, drained and chopped

2 tablespoons capers, rinsed, drained, and chopped

1 teaspoon dried oregano, crumbled

Salt

1 Bring about 2 inches of water to a simmer in a deep skillet. Add the fish and cook until the fish is tender but does not break apart, about 10 minutes. Remove the fish with a slotted spoon and drain.

2 Pour the oil into a large skillet with the garlic, parsley, and crushed red pepper. Cook until the garlic is lightly golden, about 2 minutes. Add the tomatoes and their juice, the capers, oregano, and a tiny bit of salt. Bring to a simmer and cook until the liquid is slightly thickened, about 15 minutes.

3 Add the drained fish. Baste the fish with the sauce. Cook 10 minutes or until just tender. Serve hot.

How to soak salted and dried fish

When purchasing stockfish, look for pieces of even thickness. Place them in a bowl of cool water and place the bowl in a cool place, preferably where it can be isolated. Change the water several times a day, flexing the fish to help it absorb more water. Stockfish is ready to cook when it is white, puffy, and feels soft.

Baccala comes both with and without skin and bones. The skinless, boneless type is more expensive but well worth it. Soak the fish pieces in cool water for 24 hours, changing the water several times. Keep the bowl in a cool place or in the refrigerator. Taste the water after 24 hours. If it is not salty, the fish is ready to cook. If it tastes of salt, soak the fish 24 hours longer.

Once soaked, both stockfish and baccala can be kept in the refrigerator for at least another day before using. Because both these types of preserved fish look whiter and feel firmer than fresh fish, to determine doneness, check instead for when the fish feels tender when it is cut.

Salt Cod with Potatoes
Baccala Palermitana

MAKES 4 SERVINGS

A stroll through the Vucciria market in Palermo, Sicily, is a fascinating experience for anyone, especially a cook. The market stands line the crowded, winding streets, and shoppers can select from a range of fresh meat, fish, and produce (as well as anything from underwear to batteries). Fishmongers sell baccala and stockfish already soaked and ready to cook. Here in the United States, if you don't have the time to soak the fish, substitute chunks of fresh cod or another firm whitefish for the baccala.

1/4 cup olive oil
I medium onion, sliced
I cup chopped canned tomatoes with their juice
1/2 cup chopped celery
2 medium potatoes, peeled and sliced
1 1/2 pounds baccala, soaked and drained
1/4 cup chopped green olives

1 In a large skillet, heat the oil over medium heat. Add the onion, tomatoes, celery, and potatoes. Bring to a simmer and cook until the potatoes are tender, about 20 minutes.

2 Add the fish and baste the pieces with the sauce. Sprinkle with the olives. Cook until the fish is tender, about 10 minutes. Taste for seasoning and add salt if needed. Serve hot.

❧ Shrimp, Lobster, and Scallops

Most of the shrimp in the United States have been frozen and thawed and are sold with the heads removed. When shopping for shrimp, avoid those with black spots, an indication that the shrimp are beginning to spoil. To shell shrimp, first pull off the feelers. Holding a shrimp between your thumbs and forefingers, pull off the shells in two or three sections. Leave the tail section attached if you like. If there is a dark vein visible along the outer curve of the shrimp, make a shallow cut along the vein. Pull out the vein and discard it. Rinse the shrimp to remove any remaining bits of the vein or shell.

Lobsters are sold live or frozen. When purchasing whole live lobsters, observe them carefully when they are lifted out of the tank. Because they deteriorate rapidly, lobsters that are already dead or nearly dead should be avoided or they may be spoiled by the time they are cooked. Choose lobsters that are lively and that move vigorously when handled. A 1 1/4 pound lobster is about right for a single serving. Except for the head sac, all parts of a lobster are edible, including the green tomalley or liver, and the red coral or roe found in female lobsters. If not cooked right away, place the lobsters on a bed of moist paper towels in a pan in the refrigerator. Use them as soon as possible. Frozen lobster tails are widely available and can be used in any recipe calling for live lobster, though they will not be as flavorful.

Scallops belong to the bivalve family of seafood that has two shells. When most scallops are harvested in North America, the plump white muscle is removed and the coral colored roe is discarded. This lets the muscle stay fresh longer but wastes the more delicate and delicious roe. What we purchase in most markets is the muscle of scallop. The size of the muscle varies with the type of scallop. The largest variety are sea scallops, about 1 1/2 to 2 inches in diameter, followed by medium bay scallops, which are about 1/2 inch in diameter, and calico scallops, about 1/4 inch in diameter. All scallops should be plump and creamy white with no sign of drying or browning. Calico scallops are whiter than other scallops because they are steamed open and therefore partially cooked when sold. When buying scallops, look for so-called "dry" scallops, which have not been soaked in a phosphate solution to keep them fresh. Store scallops in a covered container set over a bowl of ice, and use them as soon as possible after purchasing. I prefer to use sea scallops, but other varieties can be substituted. Just be sure to reduce the cooking time for smaller varieties.

Shrimp and Beans
Gamberi e Fagioli

MAKES 4 SERVINGS

Forte dei Marmi is a beautiful town on the Tuscan coast. It has an old-world elegance, with many Art Deco palazzos, some of which have been converted into hotels. Along the beach you can rent a lounge chair and an umbrella for a day, a week, or a month. My husband and I, with friends Rob and Linda Leahy, had a long discussion about whether to spend a day on the beach or eat at a restaurant called Lorenzo. Linda decided to soak up the sun while the rest of us went to the restaurant, which specializes in simple seafood preparations, like these shrimp. We were glad we did.

16 to 20 large shrimp, peeled and deveined
4 tablespoons olive oil
2 tablespoons finely chopped fresh garlic
2 tablespoons chopped fresh basil
Salt and freshly ground black pepper
3 cups drained cooked or canned cannellini
    or Great Northern beans
2 medium tomatoes, diced
Fresh basil leaves, for garnish

1 In a bowl, drizzle the shrimp with 2 tablespoons of the oil, half the garlic, 1 tablespoon of the basil,

and salt and pepper to taste. Stir well. Cover and refrigerate 1 hour.

2 Place a barbecue grill or broiler rack about 5 inches away from the heat source. Preheat the grill or broiler.

3 In a saucepan, cook the remaining oil, garlic, and basil over medium heat about 1 minute. Stir in the beans. Cover and cook over low heat 5 minutes or until heated through. Remove from the heat. Stir in the tomatoes, and salt and pepper to taste.

4 Broil the shrimp on one side until lightly browned, 1 to 2 minutes. Turn the shrimp and cook until lightly browned and just opaque in the thickest part, about 1 to 2 minutes more.

5 Spoon the beans onto 4 plates. Arrange the shrimp around the beans. Garnish with fresh basil leaves. Serve immediately.

Shrimp in Garlic Sauce
Gamberi al'Aglio

MAKES 4 TO 6 SERVINGS

Shrimp cooked in a garlicky butter sauce is more popular in Italian-American restaurants than it is in Italy. It is often called "shrimp scampi" here, a nonsensical name that is a clue to its non-Italian origins. Scampi is not, as the name implies, a style of cooking but a type of shellfish that looks a lot like a miniature lobster. As for cooking them, scampi are generally grilled with nothing more than a little olive oil, parsley, and lemon.

Whatever you call it, and whatever its origins, shrimp in garlic sauce is delicious. Offer lots of good bread to soak up the sauce.

6 tablespoons unsalted butter
1/4 cup olive oil
4 large garlic cloves, finely chopped
16 to 24 large shrimp, peeled and deveined
Salt
3 tablespoons chopped fresh flat-leaf parsley
2 tablespoons fresh lemon juice

(continues)

1 In a large skillet, melt the butter with the olive oil over medium heat. Stir in the garlic. Cook until the garlic is lightly golden, about 2 minutes.

2 Turn up the heat to medium-high. Add the shrimp, and salt to taste. Cook 1 to 2 minutes, turn the shrimp once, and cook until they are just pink, about 1 to 2 minutes more. Stir in the parsley and lemon juice and cook 1 minute more. Serve hot.

Shrimp with Tomatoes, Capers, and Lemon
Gamberi in Salsa

MAKES 4 SERVINGS

This is one of those quick, adaptable recipes that Italians do so well. Serve it as is for a speedy shrimp main dish, or toss it with pasta and some extra-virgin olive oil for a hearty meal.

2 tablespoons olive oil

I pound medium shrimp, peeled and deveined

I garlic clove, lightly smashed

Salt

I pint grape or cherry tomatoes, halved or quartered if large

2 tablespoons capers, rinsed and drained

2 tablespoons chopped fresh flat-leaf parsley

1/4 teaspoon grated lemon zest

1 In a 10-inch skillet, heat the oil over medium-high heat. Add the shrimp, garlic, and a pinch of salt. Cook until the shrimp turn pink and lightly golden, about 1 to 2 minutes per side. Transfer the shrimp to a plate.

2 Add the tomatoes and capers to the pan. Cook, stirring frequently, until the tomatoes are slightly softened, about 2 minutes. Return the shrimp to the pan and add the parsley and salt to taste. Stir well and cook 2 minutes more.

3 Add the lemon zest. Discard the garlic and serve immediately.

Shrimp in Anchovy Sauce
Gamberi in Salsa di Acciughe

MAKES 4 SERVINGS

One spring, the Gruppo Ristoratori Italiani, an organization of Italian restaurateurs in the United States, asked me to join them and a group of other food writers on a trip to the Marche region of central Italy. We stayed at a hotel on the coast and planned to take trips to explore the surrounding towns. One night, stormy weather made traveling all but impossible, so we ate at a local restaurant called Tre Nodi. The owner was a little eccentric and lectured us on his theories about politics, food, and cooking, but the seafood was wonderful, especially the big red Mediterranean shrimp cooked with anchovies. The shrimp were split nearly in half, then opened flat so that they could be coated thoroughly with the sauce. When we left, the owner gave each of us a small container of sand from the local beach to remind us of our stay.

1 1/2 pounds jumbo shrimp

4 tablespoons unsalted butter

3 tablespoons olive oil

2 tablespoons chopped fresh flat-leaf parsley

2 large garlic cloves, very finely chopped

6 anchovy fillets, chopped

1/3 cup dry white wine

2 tablespoons fresh lemon juice

Salt and freshly ground black pepper

1 Peel the shrimp, leaving the tail sections intact. With a small knife, slit the shrimp lengthwise along the back, cutting almost all the way through to the other side. Remove the dark vein and open the shrimp flat like a book. Rinse the shrimp and pat dry.

2 Place a barbecue grill or broiler rack about 5 inches away from the heat source. Preheat the grill or broiler. In a large broiler-safe skillet, melt the butter with the olive oil over medium heat. When the butter foam subsides, add the parsley, garlic, and anchovies and cook, stirring 1 minute. Add the wine and lemon juice and cook 1 minute more.

4 Remove the skillet from the heat. Add the shrimp cut-sides down. Sprinkle with salt and pepper. Spoon some of the sauce over the shrimp.

5 Run the pan under the broiler and cook about 3 minutes or until the shrimp are just opaque. Serve immediately.

Fried Shrimp
Gamberi Fritti

MAKES 4 TO 6 SERVINGS

A simple flour-and-water batter makes a delicious crispy crust for fried shrimp. Note that this type of batter will not brown much because it has no sugars or protein. For a deeper brown crust, try the beer batter on page 466 (Fried Zucchini, step 2) or one made with eggs, such as in the next recipe. Another trick used by many restaurant chefs is to add a tablespoon of cooking oil left from the previous day's frying to the pot. The reasons are complicated, but if you deep-fry a lot, it is worthwhile to keep some of the cooled leftover oil strained and refrigerated for the next time you fry. It does not keep indefinitely, however, and you should always smell the oil before using it to be sure that it is still fresh.

Serve these shrimp as a main dish or appetizer. If you like, whole green beans, strips of zucchini or peppers, or other vegetables can be fried in the same way. Also good are whole parsley, basil, or sage leaves.

I cup all-purpose flour
I ¹/₂ teaspoons salt
About ³/₄ cup cold water
I ¹/₂ pounds medium shrimp, shelled and deveined
Vegetable oil for frying

I Put the flour and salt in a medium bowl. Gradually add the water, stirring with a wire whisk until smooth. The mixture should be very thick, like sour cream.

2 Rinse the shrimp and pat them dry. Line a tray with paper towels.

3 In a deep heavy saucepan, pour enough oil to reach a depth of 2 inches, or if using an electric deep-fryer, follow the manufacturer's directions. Heat the oil to 370°F. on a frying thermometer or until a drop of the batter placed in the oil sizzles and browns in 1 minute.

4 Place the shrimp in the bowl with the batter and stir to coat. Remove the shrimp one at a time and with tongs carefully place them in the oil. Fry at one time only as many shrimp as will fit without crowding. Cook the shrimp until very lightly golden and crisp, 1 to 2 minutes. Drain on the paper towels. Fry the remaining shrimp in the same way. Serve hot with lemon wedges.

Batter-Fried Shrimp and Calamari
Frutti di Mare in Pastella

MAKES 6 SERVINGS

Wherever you find seafood in Italy, you will find cooks frying it in a crispy batter. This batter is made with eggs and yeast, which gives the crust a light, airy texture, golden color, and good flavor. Though I use olive oil for most cooking purposes, I prefer a tasteless vegetable oil for frying.

I teaspoon active dry yeast or instant yeast
I cup warm water (100 to 110°F)
2 large eggs
I cup all-purpose flour
I teaspoon salt
I pound small shrimp, shelled and deveined
8 ounces cleaned calamari (squid)
Vegetable oil for frying
I lemon, cut into wedges

I In a medium bowl, sprinkle the yeast over the water. Let stand 1 minute or until creamy. Stir to dissolve.

2 Add the eggs to the yeast mixture and beat well. Stir in the flour and salt. Beat with a whisk until smooth.

(continues)

3 Rinse the shrimp and calamari well. Pat dry. Cut the calamari crosswise into 1/2-inch rings. If large, cut the base of each group of tentacles in half.

4 In a deep heavy saucepan, pour enough oil to reach a depth of 2 inches, or if using an electric deep-fryer, follow the manufacturer's directions. Heat the oil to 370°F. on a frying thermometer or until a drop of the batter placed in the oil sizzles and browns in 1 minute.

5 Stir the shrimp and calamari into the batter. Remove the pieces a few at a time, letting the excess batter drip back into the bowl. Very carefully place the pieces in the hot oil. Do not crowd the pan. Fry, stirring once with a slotted spoon, until golden brown, 1 to 2 minutes. Remove the seafood from the pan and drain on paper towels. Fry the remainder in the same way. Serve hot with lemon wedges.

Grilled Shrimp Skewers
Spiedini di Gamberi

MAKES 4 SERVINGS

Though the rich cooking of Parma and Bologna is better known, the cooking of coastal Emilia-Romagna is very good and often very simple. Excellent fruits and vegetables from area farms and wonderful fresh seafood are the mainstays. My husband and I ate these grilled shrimp skewers in the beach town of Milano Marittima. Chunks of firm-fleshed fish can be substituted for the shellfish.

1/2 cup plain bread crumbs
1 tablespoon finely chopped fresh rosemary
1 garlic clove, peeled and finely chopped
Salt and freshly ground black pepper
2 tablespoons olive oil
1 pound medium shrimp, peeled and deveined
1 lemon, cut into wedges

1 Place a barbecue grill or broiler rack about 5 inches away from the heat source. Preheat the grill or broiler.

2 In a medium bowl, combine the bread crumbs, rosemary, garlic, salt and pepper to taste, and oil

and mix well. Add the shrimp and stir to coat well. Thread the shrimp on skewers.

3 Grill or broil until the shrimp are pink and cooked through, about 3 minutes on each side. Serve hot with lemon wedges.

"Brother Devil" Lobster
Aragosta Fra Diavolo

MAKES 2 TO 4 SERVINGS

Though this recipe has many of the characteristics of a classic southern Italian seafood dish, including the tomatoes, garlic, and hot pepper, I have always suspected that it is an Italian-American invention. My friend Arthur Schwartz, host of WOR Radio's Food Talk with Arthur Schwartz, *is an expert on Neapolitan cooking, as well as historical New York City cooking, and he agrees with me. Arthur believes it was probably developed in a New York Italian restaurant some years ago, and it has been popular ever since. The name refers to the spicy tomato sauce in which the lobster is cooked. Serve this with spaghetti or toasted bread rubbed with garlic.*

2 live lobsters, about 1 1/4 pounds each
1/3 cup olive oil
2 large garlic cloves, lightly crushed
Pinch of crushed red pepper
1 cup dry white wine
1 (28-ounce) can peeled tomatoes, drained and chopped
6 fresh basil leaves, torn into bits
Salt

1 Place one of the lobsters on a cutting board with the cavity facing up. Do not remove the bands that keep the claws shut. Protect your hand with a heavy towel or pot holder and hold the lobster above the tail. Plunge the tip of a heavy chef's knife into the body where the tail joins the chest. Cut all the way through, separating the tail from the rest of the body. Use poultry shears to remove the thin shell that covers the tail meat. Pull out and remove the dark vein in the tail, but leave the green tomalley and red coral, if any. Repeat with the second lobster. Cut the tail crosswise into 3 or 4 pieces. Set the tail pieces aside. Cut the lobster bodies and claws at the joints into 1- to 2-inch chunks. Smack the claws with the blunt side of the knife to crack them.

2 In a large heavy saucepan, heat the oil over medium heat. Add all the lobster pieces except the tails and cook, stirring often, for 10 minutes. Scatter the garlic and hot pepper around the pieces. Add the wine and cook 1 minute.

3 Add the tomatoes, basil, and salt. Bring to a simmer. Cook, stirring occasionally, until the tomatoes are thickened, about 25 minutes. Add the lobster tails and cook 5 to 10 minutes more or until the tail meat is firm and opaque. Serve immediately.

Baked Stuffed Lobster
Aragoste Amollicate

MAKES 4 SERVINGS

In Italy, and throughout Europe, the typical lobster variety is the spiny or rock lobster, which lacks the large meaty claws of North American lobsters. Their flavor is very good, though, and they are often sold here as frozen lobster tails. If you don't want to deal with live lobsters, you can make this recipe with frozen tails, reducing the amount of bread crumbs slightly and cooking them without thawing, just until they are opaque in the center. This recipe is typical of Sardinia, though it is eaten all over southern Italy.

4 live lobsters (about 1 1/4 pounds each)
1 cup plain dry bread crumbs
2 tablespoons chopped fresh flat-leaf parsley
1 garlic clove, finely chopped
Salt and freshly ground black pepper
Olive oil
1 lemon, cut into wedges

1 Place one of the lobsters on a cutting board with the cavity facing up. Do not remove the bands that keep the claws shut. Protect your hand with a heavy towel or pot holder and hold the lobster above the tail. Plunge the tip of a heavy chef's knife into

the body where the tail joins the chest. Cut all the way through, separating the tail from the rest of the body. Use poultry shears to remove the thin white shell that covers the underside of the tail and expose the meat. Pull out and remove the dark vein in the tail, but leave the green tomalley and red coral, if any.

2 Place a rack in the center of the oven. Preheat the oven to 450°F. Oil 1 or 2 large roasting pans. Arrange the lobsters on their backs in the baking pans.

3 In a medium bowl, stir together the bread crumbs, parsley, garlic, and salt and pepper to taste. Add 3 tablespoons of oil, or just enough to moisten the crumbs. Scatter the mixture over the lobsters in the pan. Drizzle with a little more oil.

4 Bake the lobsters 12 to 15 minutes, or until the tail meat looks just opaque when cut in the thickest part and feels firm when pressed.

5 Serve immediately with the lemon wedges.

Scallops with Garlic and Parsley
Capesante Aglio e Olio

MAKES 4 SERVINGS

Sweet fresh scallops cook quickly, perfect for a weeknight meal. This recipe comes from Grado on the Adriatic Coast. I like to use large sea scallops, but smaller bay scallops can be substituted.

1/4 cup olive oil
2 garlic cloves, finely chopped
2 tablespoons chopped fresh flat-leaf parsley
1 pound large sea scallops, rinsed and patted dry
Salt and freshly ground black pepper
1 lemon, cut into wedges

1 Pour the oil into a large skillet. Add the garlic, parsley, and hot pepper and cook over medium heat until lightly golden, about 2 minutes.

2 Add the scallops and salt and pepper to taste. Cook, stirring, until the scallops are just barely opaque in the center, about 3 minutes. Serve hot with lemon wedges.

Fish and Shellfish   271

Grilled Scallops and Shrimp
Frutti di Mare alla Griglia

MAKES 4 SERVINGS

A simple lemon sauce dresses grilled shrimp and scallops. Chunks of firm-fleshed fish such as salmon or swordfish can be substituted.

³/₄ pound large sea scallops, rinsed and patted dry
³/₄ pound large shrimp, shelled and deveined
Fresh or dried bay leaves
1 medium red onion, cut into 1 inch pieces
¹/₄ cup olive oil
2 tablespoons fresh lemon juice
1 tablespoon chopped fresh flat-leaf parsley
¹/₂ teaspoon dried oregano, crumbled
Salt and freshly ground black pepper

1 Place a barbecue grill or broiler rack about 5 inches away from the heat source. Preheat the grill or broiler.

2 Thread the scallops and shrimp alternately with the bay leaves and pieces of onion on 8 wood or metal skewers.

3 In a small bowl, whisk together the oil, lemon juice, parsley, oregano, and salt and pepper to taste. Transfer about two-thirds of the sauce mixture to a separate bowl. Reserve. Brush the shellfish with the remaining third of the sauce.

4 Grill or broil until the shrimp are pink and the scallops are lightly browned on one side, about 3 to 4 minutes. Turn over the skewers and cook, until the shrimp are pink and the scallops are lightly browned on the other side, about 3 to 4 minutes more. The shrimp and scallop meat will be just barely opaque in the center. Transfer to a plate and drizzle with the remaining sauce.

❧ Clams and Mussels

Hard-shell clams, such as cherrystone, littlenecks, Manila clams, or cockles can be used for the recipes that follow. When buying clams, make sure they are tightly closed or that they close up readily when tapped, an indication that they are alive. Store them in a bowl in the refrigerator lightly covered with damp cloths. Do not keep them in a sealed plastic bag because they can smother. To clean clams, soak them in cold salted water for 30 minutes. If the shells feel gritty, scrub them with a brush before rinsing and cooking them. Discard any clams with broken shells or that remain open when they are tapped.

Mussels come in many different varieties, but they can be used interchangeably. Farm-raised mussels are generally quite clean and need little preparation. Follow the same purchasing and preparation method as for clams. To remove the "beards"—the small fibers that the shellfish use to attach themselves to rocks—cut or pull them off with kitchen shears or your fingers.

Clams and Mussels Posillipo
Vongole e Cozze in Salsa Piccante

MAKES 4 SERVINGS

Posillipo is the name of a point of land on the Bay of Naples. It also evokes this dish of fresh clams and mussels in a spicy tomato sauce in the minds of many Italian-Americans. Probably named by a homesick restaurateur in the United States, the recipe seems to have gone out of style, though it is so good it deserves a comeback.

Serve these in deep bowls over slices of toasted bread or freselle—*hard, black pepper biscuits available in Italian markets.*

3 dozen small hard-shell clams

2 pounds mussels

1/3 cup olive oil

1 tablespoon finely chopped garlic

Pinch of crushed red pepper

1/2 cup dry white wine

1 (28-ounce) can peeled tomatoes, drained and chopped

1 teaspoon dried oregano, crumbled

Salt and freshly ground black pepper

1/4 cup chopped fresh flat-leaf parsley

Italian bread slices, toasted, or freselle

1 Soak the clams and mussels and clams in cold water 30 minutes. Scrub the clams under cold running water with a stiff brush. Cut or pull off the beards from the mussels. Discard any clams or mussels with cracked shells or that refuse to close tightly when touched.

2 Pour the oil into a large heavy pot. Add the garlic and hot pepper. Cook over medium heat until the garlic is lightly golden, about 2 minutes. Add the wine and cook 1 minute more. Stir in the tomatoes. oregano, and salt and pepper to taste. Bring to a simmer and cook 15 minutes.

3 Add the clams and mussels to the pot and cover tightly. Cook until the shells open, about 5 minutes.

4 Place slices of Italian bread in the bottom of 4 pasta bowls. Spoon on the clams and mussels. Sprinkle with chopped parsley and serve immediately.

Baked Stuffed Clams
Vongole Arraganati

MAKES 4 SERVINGS

Tasty little clams dusted with crunchy seasoned bread crumbs are a favorite all over southern Italy.

I like to make these with small to medium clams. If only larger clams are available, chop up the clam meat before topping them with the crumb mixture.

These can be served as an antipasto, but I often make a whole meal of them.

4 dozen small hard-shell clams

1/2 cup water

1/2 cup plain dry bread crumbs, preferably homemade

1/4 cup freshly grated Parmigiano-Reggiano or Pecorino Romano

1/4 cup chopped fresh flat-leaf parsley

1 garlic clove, finely chopped

Salt and freshly ground black pepper

About 1/3 cup extra-virgin olive oil

1 lemon, cut into wedges

1 Soak the clams in cold water 30 minutes. Scrub with a brush under cold running water. Discard any with cracked shells or that do not close tightly when touched.

2 Place the clams in a large pot with the water. Cover and bring to a simmer. After about 5 minutes, remove the clams as they open and place them in a bowl. Discard clams that don't open.

3 Pour the clam juices into a bowl. Remove the clams from their shells and rinse each one in the liquid to remove any sand. Separate the shell halves. Place half the shells on a large baking sheet. Place a clam in each shell. Strain the clam juice through a paper coffee filter or dampened cheesecloth into a bowl. Spoon a little of the juice on each clam.

4 Preheat the broiler. In a medium bowl, combine the bread crumbs, cheese, parsley, garlic, and salt and pepper to taste. Add enough oil to moisten the crumbs. Spoon a small amount of the crumbs loosely on top of each clam. Do not pack the crumbs down.

5 Broil 4 minutes or until the crumbs are lightly browned. Serve hot with lemon wedges.

Mussels with Black Pepper

Impepata di Cozze

MAKES 4 TO 6 SERVINGS

Inexpensive and widely available, mussels are great in pasta, soups, or stews. The only problem is cleaning them, as wild mussels can require a lot of attention. Farm-raised mussels are the exception. Though they are not as tasty as wild mussels, they are much cleaner and there is less waste from damaged mussels. This recipe has a tangy flavor from the wine, lemon juice, and an unusually large amount of black pepper. It is a classic recipe from Naples.

6 pounds mussels
1/2 cup olive oil
6 garlic cloves, finely chopped
1/2 cup chopped fresh flat-leaf parsley
I tablespoon freshly ground black pepper
I cup dry white wine
I tablespoon fresh lemon juice

1 Soak the mussels in cold water 30 minutes. Cut or pull off the beards. Discard any mussels with cracked shells or that do not close tightly when touched.

2 Pour the oil into a large pot. Add the garlic. Cook over medium heat until golden, about 1 minute. Stir in the parsley and pepper. Add the mussels, wine, and lemon juice to the pot. Cover and cook, shaking the pan occasionally, until the mussels begin to open, about 5 minutes.

3 Transfer the opened mussels to serving bowls. Cook any mussels that remain closed a minute or two longer. Discard any that do not open. Pour the cooking liquid over the mussels. Serve hot.

Mussels with Garlic and White Wine

Cozze agli Aromi

MAKES 4 SERVINGS

Instead of serving them with bread, these mussels can be tossed with hot cooked spaghetti. Small hard-shell clams can be substituted for the mussels.

4 pounds mussels
1/4 cup olive oil
2 garlic cloves, chopped
2 green onions, chopped
2 sprigs fresh thyme
2 tablespoons chopped fresh flat-leaf parsley
I bay leaf
I cup dry white wine
Italian bread slices, toasted

1 Soak the mussels in cold water 30 minutes. Cut or pull off the beards. Discard any mussels with cracked shells or that do not close tightly when touched.

2 Pour the oil into a large saucepan. Add the garlic, green onions, thyme, parsley, and bay leaf. Cook over medium heat until the onions are tender, about 2 minutes.

3 Add the mussels and wine. Cover and cook, shaking the pan occasionally, about 5 minutes or until the mussels begin to open.

4 Transfer the opened mussels to individual serving bowls. Cook any mussels that remain closed a minute or two longer; discard any that do not open. Simmer the liquid 1 minute more and pour it over the mussels. Serve hot with toasted bread.

Sardinian Mussels with Saffron
Cozze allo Zafferano

MAKES 4 SERVINGS

Saffron, a spice made from the stigmas of crocus flowers, adds an exotic flavor and beautiful color to these mussels. Though much of the world's saffron comes from Spain, it is also produced in the Abruzzo region of Italy. When buying saffron, always buy whole threads, which keep their flavor longer. Look for deep red-orange color. The darker color is an indication of better quality.

1 teaspoon saffron threads
1 cup dry white wine
4 pounds mussels
1 medium onion, finely chopped
1/3 cup olive oil
1 cup peeled, seeded, and chopped ripe tomatoes
6 basil leaves, torn into bits
2 tablespoons chopped fresh flat-leaf parsley

1　Soak the saffron in the white wine for 10 minutes. Meanwhile, soak the mussels in cold water for 30 minutes. Cut or pull off the beards. Discard any mussels with cracked shells or that do not close tightly when touched.

2　In a large saucepan, cook the onion in the oil over medium heat until golden, about 10 minutes. Add the saffron, wine, and tomatoes and bring to a simmer. Stir in the basil and parsley.

3　Add the mussels and cover the pan. Cook, shaking the pan occasionally, about 5 minutes or until the mussels begin to open.

4　Transfer the opened mussels to individual serving bowls. Cook any mussels that remain closed a minute or two longer; discard any that do not open. Simmer the liquid 1 minute more and pour it over the mussels. Serve hot.

❧ Calamari, Octopus, and Conch

Calamari (squid) are usually sold cleaned, either fresh, frozen, or thawed. The flesh should be moist and pinkish-white without any sign of browning or dryness. Rinse calamari thoroughly inside and out. For stuffing, buy large calamari, which are easier to handle. Small calamari are fine for stewing or frying. Seppie or cuttlefish are popular in Italy and can occasionally be found in markets here. Handle and cook them just as you would calamari.

Octopus may seem intimidating, but they are very easy to cook and have a sweet, mild flavor. Because they are sold cleaned, they need only a rinse before cooking. Frozen octopus can be thawed in a bowl of cold water overnight.

Scungilli is a Neapolitan dialect name for large sea snails such as conch or whelk. Near the shore, you might be able to find them fresh, but mostly they are sold in ethnic groceries partially cooked and frozen. The meat has a pleasantly briny flavor, like clams, and a dense, meaty texture.

Fried Calamari
Calamari Fritti

MAKES 6 TO 8 SERVINGS

Many people outside of Italy don't really equate calamari with squid, something they may think they don't like. They just know they love "fried calamari," which are as irresistible as potato chips. In Italy, all along the coast, fried calamari are served alone or as part of a mixed fish fry with small shrimp, whitebait, and baby octopus.

In Sicily many years ago, I was served a plateful of tiny whole calamari fried this way. When I stuck my fork into one, I was shocked to find that the ink sac had not been removed and deep purple-black

(continues)

ink spurted all over my plate. It is fine to eat, though it was unexpected. Ink sacs are removed from calamari in the United States because the seafood keeps better without the sacs and can be frozen. (Most calamari sold here has been frozen.)

These calamari are lightly dusted with flour. It makes a thin, sheer coating when fried, and though it is crisp, the color barely changes.

2 pounds cleaned calamari (squid)
I cup all-purpose flour
I teaspoon salt
Freshly ground black pepper
Olive or vegetable oil for frying
I lemon, cut into wedges

I Make a small slit at the pointed end of each calamari. Rinse thoroughly, letting the water run through the body sac. Drain and pat dry. Cut the bodies crosswise into 1/2-inch rings. If large, cut the base of each group of tentacles in half. Pat dry.

2 Spread the flour on a sheet of wax paper and season with salt and pepper. Line a tray with paper towels.

3 Pour oil to a depth of 2 inches in a deep heavy saucepan, or fill a deep-fryer according to the manufacturer's directions. Heat the oil to 370°F on a frying thermometer or until a small piece of the calamari placed in the oil sizzles and browns lightly in 1 minute.

4 When the correct temperature is reached, lightly roll a few pieces of calamari in the flour mixture. Shake off the excess flour. Slip the pieces into the hot oil with tongs without crowding the pan. Cook until the calamari turn lightly golden, about 3 minutes.

5 With a slotted spoon, transfer the calamari to the paper towels. Repeat with the remaining calamari. Sprinkle with salt. Serve hot with lemon wedges.

Cleaning Calamari (Squid)

To clean, hold the body in one hand and the head and tentacles in the other. Gently pull the two apart. Cut off the tentacles just above the eyes. Discard the lower portion. Squeeze the base of the tentacles to extract the hard beak. Pull out the long, clear shell from inside the body. Squeeze out and discard the contents. With your fingers and a small knife, scrape and pull off the skin. Make a small cut in the pointed end. Hold the body under cold running water to flush out the interior.

Most calamari is sold already cleaned, but like precleaned spinach or salad greens, it is a good idea to clean it again at home. There is often a residue of debris inside.

Venetian-Style Calamari
Calamari alla Veneta

MAKES 4 SERVINGS

In Venice, this is made with seppie, cuttlefish and its ink. Because cuttlefish is hard to find, calamari (squid) is a good substitute. Most calamari here is sold with the ink sac removed, though many fish markets sell calamari or cuttlefish ink in little plastic envelopes. If it is available, add some of the ink to the sauce ingredients for a deep rich color and flavor. In Venice, fish is often served with Polenta (page 223) made with white rather than yellow cornmeal.

1/4 olive oil
1/4 cup finely chopped onion
2 whole garlic cloves
2 pounds calamari (squid), cleaned and cut into rings
2 medium tomatoes, peeled, seeded, and chopped, or I cup chopped canned tomatoes
1/2 cup dry white wine
Salt and freshly ground black pepper

1 Pour the oil into a large heavy skillet. Add the onion and garlic and cook over medium heat, stirring frequently, until the onion is golden, about 10 minutes. Discard the garlic.

2 Add the calamari, tomatoes, wine, and salt and pepper to taste. Bring to a simmer and cook until the sauce is thickened and the calamari are tender, about 30 minutes. Serve hot.

Calamari with Artichokes and White Wine
Calamari e Carciofi

MAKES 4 SERVINGS

The sweetness of artichokes complements the flavor of several classic seafood recipes from Liguria. If you don't want to go to the trouble of cleaning fresh artichokes, you can substitute a package of frozen artichoke hearts.

1 1/2 pounds cleaned calamari (squid)
4 medium artichokes
I garlic clove, finely chopped
2 tablespoons chopped fresh flat-leaf parsley
1/4 cup olive oil
I cup dry white wine
Salt and freshly ground black pepper

1 Rinse the calamari thoroughly inside and out. Drain well. Cut the bodies crosswise into 1/2-inch rings. Cut the tentacles in half through the base. Pat dry.

2 Trim the artichokes, removing the stem end and all the outer leaves until you reach the pale green central cone. With a small knife, pare away any dark green patches from the base. Cut the artichokes in half and scrape away the fuzzy inner choke. Cut each half into thin slices.

3 Put the garlic, parsley, and oil in a large skillet over medium heat. Cook until the garlic is golden, about 1 minute. Stir in the calamari and salt to taste. Add the wine and bring to a simmer over low heat. Cover and cook 20 minutes.

4 Stir in the artichokes and 2 tablespoons water. Cook 30 minutes or until tender. Serve hot.

Grilled Stuffed Calamari
Calamari Ripieni

MAKES 4 SERVINGS

Calamari are perfect for stuffing, but buy large calamari or the job will be tedious. Do not fill the body cavities more than half full. They shrink considerably as they cook, so the filling can burst out if they are overstuffed. This recipe is from Puglia in southern Italy.

8 to 12 large calamari (squid), about 6 to 8 inches long, cleaned
I cup plain dry bread crumbs
1/4 cup olive oil
2 tablespoons grated Pecorino Romano or Parmigiano-Reggiano
I garlic clove, finely chopped
I tablespoon chopped fresh flat-leaf parsley
Salt and freshly ground black pepper
I lemon, cut into wedges

1 Make a small slit at the pointed end of each calamari. Rinse thoroughly, letting the water run through the body sac. Drain and pat dry.

2 Stir together the bread crumbs, oil, cheese, garlic, parsley, and salt and pepper to taste. Set aside 1/4 cup of the mixture. Stuff the rest of the mixture loosely into the calamari, filling them only halfway. Tuck the tentacles into the body sac and secure them with wooden picks. Roll the calamari in the remaining bread crumb mixture.

3 Place a barbecue grill or broiler rack about 5 inches from the heat source. Preheat the grill or broiler.

4 Grill or broil the calamari until the bodies are opaque and lightly browned, about 2 minutes per side. Transfer to a platter and serve hot with lemon wedges.

Calamari Stuffed with Olives and Capers
Calamari Ripieni

MAKES 4 SERVINGS

Calamari (squid) toughen quickly when they are heated, but they become tender when cooked in a liquid for at least 30 minutes. For the best texture, cook calamari quickly, grilling or frying them, or stew them slowly until they become tender, as in this recipe.

2 1/2 pounds cleaned large calamari (squid), about 6 to 8 inches long
2 tablespoons olive oil
1 garlic clove, finely chopped
1/2 cup plain bread crumbs
2 tablespoons chopped fresh flat-leaf parsley
2 tablespoons chopped Gaeta or other mild black olives
2 tablespoons chopped, rinsed, and drained capers
1/2 teaspoon dried oregano, crumbled
Salt and freshly ground black pepper

SAUCE

1/4 cup olive oil
1/2 cup dry red wine
2 cups chopped canned peeled tomatoes with their juice
1 large garlic clove, lightly crushed
Pinch of crushed red pepper
Salt

1 Make a small slit at the pointed end of each calamari. Rinse thoroughly, letting the water run through the body sac. Drain and pat dry. Separate the bodies from the tentacles with a knife. Set the bodies aside. Chop the tentacles either with a large knife or in a food processor.

2 Pour the 2 tablespoons oil into a medium skillet. Add the garlic. Cook over medium heat until the garlic begins to turn golden, about 1 minute. Stir in the tentacles. Cook, stirring, for 2 minutes. Add the bread crumbs, parsley, olives, capers, and oregano. Add salt and pepper to taste. Remove from the heat and let cool.

3 With a small spoon, stuff the bread crumb mixture loosely into the calamari bodies, filling them only halfway. Secure the calamari with wooden toothpicks.

4 Choose a skillet large enough to hold all of the calamari in a single layer. Pour in the 1/4 cup oil and heat over medium heat. Add the calamari and cook, turning them with tongs, until they are just opaque, about 2 minutes per side.

5 Add the wine and bring to a simmer. Stir in the tomatoes, garlic, crushed red pepper, and salt to taste. Bring to a simmer. Partially cover the pan and cook, turning the calamari occasionally, until they are very tender, 50 to 60 minutes. Add a little water if the sauce becomes too thick. Serve hot.

Stuffed Calamari, Roman Style
Calamari Ripieni alla Romana

MAKES 4 SERVINGS

When I was studying Italian in Rome many years ago, I frequently had lunch at a family-run trattoria near the school. Every day the place would fill with workers from the nearby shops and office buildings who would pack the dining room clamoring for the home-style dishes they served. The menu was limited, but it was inexpensive and very good. This is my interpretation of their stuffed calamari.

1 1/2 pounds cleaned large calamari (squid), about 6 to 8 inches long
1 cup plain dry bread crumbs
3 garlic cloves, finely chopped
2 tablespoons finely chopped fresh flat-leaf parsley
Salt and freshly ground black pepper
5 tablespoons olive oil
1 large onion, finely chopped
2 cups peeled, seeded, and chopped tomatoes
1/2 cup dry white wine

1 Make a small slit at the pointed end of each calamari. Rinse thoroughly, letting the water run

through the body sac. Drain and pat dry. Finely chop the tentacles.

2 In a bowl, combine the tentacles, bread crumbs, garlic, parsley, and salt and pepper to taste. Add 2 to 3 tablespoons olive oil or enough to moisten the mixture. With a small spoon, stuff the bread crumb mixture loosely into the calamari, filling them only halfway. Secure the calamari with wooden toothpicks.

3 Pour the remaining 3 tablespoons oil into a large skillet. Add the onion. Cook over medium heat, stirring frequently, until tender, about 10 minutes. Stir in the tomatoes, wine, and salt and pepper to taste. Bring to a simmer, then reduce the heat to low. Add the calamari. Cover and cook, stirring occasionally, 50 to 60 minutes, or until the calamari are tender when pierced with a fork. Serve hot.

Mauro's Grilled Octopus with Fennel and Orange
Insalata di Polipo

MAKES 4 SERVINGS

Fennel and orange salad is a classic Sicilian dish. In this creative recipe from my friend Chef Mauro Mafrici, the refreshing salad is topped by crisp grilled octopus. Be sure to slice the fennel as thin as possible, with a sharp knife, a mandoline, or the very fine blade of a food processor.

Octopus may look intimidating, but they need little effort to prepare. When cooked right, they are mild tasting and pleasantly chewy. Octopus is usually sold in supermarket fish departments or fish markets frozen or thawed. If purchased frozen, thaw it in a bowl of cold water, changing the water several times. This recipe is typically made with small octopus weighing about 6 ounces each. One large octopus can be substituted if the small ones are not available.

4 to 8 baby octopus, about 6 ounces each, or 1 large octopus, about 2¹/₂ pounds
5 tablespoons extra-virgin olive oil
1 garlic clove, finely chopped
2 tablespoons coarsely chopped flat-leaf parsley
Salt and freshly ground black pepper
1 medium fennel bulb
1 tablespoon freshly squeezed lemon juice, or to taste
2 or 3 navel oranges, peeled and sectioned
1 cup mild black olives, such as Gaeta

1 Check the base of the octopus to see if the hard, round beak has been removed. Squeeze it out if necessary. Bring a large saucepan of water to a boil. Add the octopus and simmer until tender when pierced with a knife, 30 to 60 minutes. Rinse and dry the octopus. Cut large octopus into 3-inch pieces.

2 In a bowl, combine the octopus with 3 tablespoons of the oil, the garlic, parsley, and a pinch of salt and pepper. Let marinate 1 hour up to overnight in the refrigerator

3 Slice off the base of the fennel and trim off any bruised spots. Remove the green stems, reserving the feathery green leaves, if any, for garnish. Cut the fennel into quarters lengthwise and trim away the core. Slice the quarters crosswise into very thin slices. You should have about 3 cups.

4 In a medium bowl, whisk the remaining 2 tablespoons of the oil, lemon juice, and salt to taste. Add the fennel, orange sections, olives, and fennel leaves, if available, and toss gently.

5 Place a barbecue grill rack or broiler pan about 4 inches from the heat. Preheat the grill or broiler. When ready, grill or broil the octopus, turning once, until browned and crisp, about 3 minutes per side.

6 Arrange the fennel salad on four plates and top with the octopus. Serve immediately.

Tomato-Braised Octopus
Polipetti in Salsa di Pomodoro

MAKES 4

At one time, fishermen used to bash freshly caught octopus against the rocks to tenderize them. But today freezing and thawing them helps to break down the tough fibers. Simmering them in water, a Neopolitan method, ensures that they will be tender. Serve with lots of good bread to soak up the sauce.

4 to 8 baby octopus, about 6 ounces each, or 1 large octopus, about 2¹/₂ pounds

¹/₄ cup olive oil

2 cups chopped canned peeled tomatoes with their juice

4 tablespoons chopped fresh flat-leaf parsley

2 large garlic cloves, finely chopped

Pinch of crushed red pepper

Salt

1 Check the base of the octopus to see if the hard, round beak has been removed. Squeeze it out if necessary. Bring a large saucepan of water to a boil. Add the octopus and simmer until tender when pierced with a knife, 30 to 60 minutes. Drain and dry the octopus, reserving some of the cooking liquid. Cut large octopus into bite-size pieces.

2 In a large heavy saucepan, heat the oil over medium heat. Add the octopus, tomatoes, 3 tablespoons of the parsley, the garlic, red pepper, and salt to taste. Stir to combine. Bring the sauce to a simmer. Cover the pot and cook over very low heat, stirring occasionally, for 30 minutes. Add a little of the reserved liquid if the sauce becomes too dry.

3 Uncover and cook 15 minutes more, or until the sauce is thick. Serve hot.

Conch Salad
Insalata di Scungilli

MAKES 4 SERVINGS

On Christmas Eve, my family's table was always laden with a variety of fish and seafood—served in salads, baked, stuffed, sauced, and fried. My father's favorite was this salad made with conch or whelk—similar types of sea snails—though we always called it by its Neapolitan dialect name of scungilli.

Crunchy celery complements the slightly chewy seafood, though fresh fennel can be substituted.

1 pound fresh or frozen conch or whelk meat (scungilli)

Salt

¹/₃ cup extra-virgin olive oil

2 tender celery ribs

2 tablespoons chopped fresh flat-leaf parsley

1 garlic clove, finely chopped

Pinch of crushed red pepper

2 to 3 tablespoons fresh lemon juice

Radicchio or lettuce leaves

1 If using fresh conch, go to step 2. If the conch are frozen, place them in a bowl with cold water to cover. Put the bowl in the refrigerator at least 3 hours up to overnight, changing the water occasionally.

2 Bring a medium saucepan of water to a boil. Add the conch and 1 teaspoon salt. When the water returns to a simmer, cook the conch until tender when pierced with a fork, about 20 minutes. Drain and pat dry.

3 Begin cutting the conch into ¹/₄-inch slices. When you come to a dark tube filled with a spongy matter, pull or cut it out and discard it, as it can be gritty. There is another tube on the outside of the body that does not need to be removed. Rinse the slices well and pat them dry.

4 In a medium bowl, combine the celery, parsley, garlic, red pepper, 2 tablespoons of the lemon juice, and a pinch of salt. Add the conch and taste for seasoning, adding the remaining lemon juice if needed.

5 Chill up to 1 hour or serve immediately on a bed of radicchio or lettuce leaves.

Conch in Hot Sauce
Scungilli in Salsa Piccante

MAKES 6 TO 8 SERVINGS

When I was a child my family used to go from our home in Brooklyn to Little Italy in downtown Manhattan for seafood. My father and uncles would order this dish, asking the waiter to make theirs extra-spicy. The seafood and sauce was spooned over freselle, *hard biscuits flavored with a lot of black pepper, which made the dish even hotter. My sister and cousins and I would, instead, share a plate of fried seafood or stuffed clams, never imagining we would one day enjoy such spicy food.*

Fresh conch or whelk (known in Italian as scungilli*) is not easy to find in my area, so I use the kind that is partially precooked and frozen. It is available in most fish markets. I also use toasted bread. But if you like,* freselle *can be found in many Italian bakeries. Break them into pieces with your hands and sprinkle them with water to soften them up slightly.*

2 pounds partially cooked fresh or frozen conch
    or whelk meat (scungilli)
1/3 cup olive oil
2 large garlic cloves, finely chopped
Pinch of crushed red pepper, or to taste
2 (28-ounce) cans peeled tomatoes, chopped
1 cup dry white wine
Salt
2 tablespoons chopped fresh flat-leaf parsley
Italian bread slices, toasted

1 If using fresh conch, go to step 2. If the conch are frozen, place them in a bowl with cold water to cover. Put the bowl in the refrigerator several hours or overnight, changing the water occasionally.

2 Begin cutting the conch into 1/4-inch slices. When you come to a dark tube filled with a spongy matter, pull or cut it out and discard it, as it can be gritty. There is another tube on the outside of the body that does not need to be removed. Rinse the slices well and pat them dry.

3 Pour the oil into a large saucepan. Add the garlic and crushed red pepper. Cook over medium heat until the garlic is golden, about 2 minutes. Add the tomatoes and their juice, the wine, and salt to taste. Bring to a simmer. Cook 15 minutes on low heat, stirring occasionally.

4 Add the conch and bring to a simmer. Cook, stirring occasionally, until the conch is tender and the sauce is thickened, about 30 minutes. If the sauce becomes too thick, stir in a little water. Taste for seasoning, adding more pepper, if desired. Stir in the parsley.

5 Place slices of toasted Italian bread in the bottom of 4 pasta bowls. Spoon on the conch and serve immediately.

✤ Mixed Seafood

Seafood Couscous
Cuscusu

MAKES 4 TO 6 SERVINGS

Couscous dates back at least to the ninth century in Sicily, when the Arabs ruled the western portion of the island. At one time it was made by hand-rolling semolina into tiny pellets, but now it is available precooked (instant) in any grocery store. In the seaside town of Trapani, couscous is made with meat, fish, or vegetables. This is my version of the seafood couscous I tasted while visiting that area.

It's usually better to use fish broth with fish dishes, but you can also use chicken broth in a pinch; homemade is always preferred.

2 cups fish or Chicken Broth (page 63)

2 cups water

1 1/2 cups instant couscous

Salt

1/4 cup olive oil

1 large onion, chopped

2 garlic cloves, very finely chopped

1 bay leaf

2 large tomatoes, peeled, seeded, and chopped, or 2 cups chopped canned tomatoes with the juice

4 tablespoons chopped fresh flat-leaf parsley

Pinch of ground cinnamon

Pinch of ground cloves

Pinch of freshly ground nutmeg

Pinch of saffron threads, crumbled

Pinch of ground cayenne

Salt and freshly ground black pepper

2 pounds assorted firm-fleshed fish fillets or steaks, such as swordfish, halibut, monkfish, or sea bass, and shellfish

1 Bring the broth and water to a boil. Place the couscous in a heat-proof bowl and stir in 3 cups of the liquid and salt to taste. Set the remaining liquid aside. Cover the couscous and let stand until the liquid is absorbed, about 10 minutes. Fluff the couscous with a fork.

2 Pour the oil into a pot large enough to hold the fish in a single layer. Add the onion and garlic. Cook over medium-low heat, stirring frequently, until tender, about 10 minutes. Add the bay leaf and cook 1 minute more. Add the tomatoes, 2 tablespoons of the parsley, the cinnamon, cloves, nutmeg, saffron, and cayenne. Cook for 5 minutes. Add 2 cups water and salt and pepper to taste. Bring to a simmer.

3 Meanwhile, remove any skin or bones from the fish. Cut the fish into 2-inch chunks.

4 Add the fish to the pot. Cover and cook 5 to 10 minutes, or until the fish is just barely opaque in the thickest part. With a slotted spoon, transfer the fish to a warm plate. Cover and keep warm.

5 Add the couscous to the pot. Cover and cook 5 minutes, or until hot. Taste and adjust seasoning. Add some of the reserved broth if the couscous seems dry.

6 Spoon the couscous onto a deep serving platter. Top with the fish. Sprinkle with the remaining parsley and serve immediately.

Mixed Fish Fry
Gran Fritto Misto di Pesce

MAKES 4 TO 6 SERVINGS

A thin coating of flour is all that is needed to make a light crust on small fish or cut-up pieces of calamari (squid). You can use this method for one type of fish or seafood, such as calamari, or use several varieties.

4 ounces cleaned calamari (squid)

1 pound very small fresh fish, such as whitebait, fresh (not canned) anchovies, or sardines, cleaned

4 ounces small shrimp, shelled and deveined

1 cup all-purpose flour

1 teaspoon salt

Vegetable oil for frying

1 lemon, cut into wedges

1 Rinse the calamari and drain well. Cut the bodies into 1/2-inch rings. If large, cut each group of tentacles in half through the base. Removing the heads from small whole fish such as anchovies or sardines is optional. Whitebait are always left whole. Rinse the fish thoroughly inside and out. Pat dry.

2 Stir together the flour and salt on a piece of wax paper, then spread it out.

3 Line a tray with paper towels. In a deep heavy saucepan, pour enough oil to reach a depth of 2 inches, or if using an electric deep-fryer, follow the manufacturer's directions. Heat the oil to 370°F on a deep-frying thermometer, or until a 1-inch piece of bread dropped into the oil sizzles and browns in 1 minute.

4 Toss a small handful of the fish and shellfish in the flour mixture. Shake off the excess. Using tongs, carefully slip the fish into the hot oil. Do not crowd the pan. Fry until crisp and lightly golden, about 2 minutes.

5 With a slotted spoon, transfer the fish to the paper towels to drain. Keep warm in a low oven. Cook the remaining seafood in the same way. Serve hot with lemon wedges.

Molise-Style Fish Stew
Zuppa di Pesce alla Marinara

MAKES 6 SERVINGS

Molise-style fish stew differs from that of other regions because of the presence of a large amount of sweet green peppers. Use the long Italian frying peppers or green bell peppers. Ideally you would make this with as wide a variety of fish as possible, but I have made it with only calamari (squid) and monkfish and it was very good. Molise cooks might use lobster, octopus, and rockfish or other firm-fleshed varieties.

1/4 cup olive oil
1 1/2 pounds Italian frying peppers, seeded and chopped
1 onion, chopped
Salt
2 tablespoons red wine vinegar
1/2 pound calamari (squid), cut into rings
1 pound firm whitefish steaks or fillets, cut into 2-inch chunks
1/2 pound medium shrimp, shelled, deveined, and cut into 1/2-inch pieces
2 tablespoons chopped fresh flat-leaf parsley
6 to 12 slices of Italian bread, toasted
Extra-virgin olive oil

1 In a large saucepan, heat the oil over medium heat. Stir in the peppers, onion, and salt to taste. Cover and reduce the heat to low. Cook, stirring occasionally, until very tender, about 40 minutes. Remove from the heat and let cool.

2 Scrape the contents of the pan into a food processor or blender. Process until smooth. Add the vinegar and salt to taste and process again briefly to blend.

3 Scrape the pepper and onion mixture back into the saucepan. Add 1 to 2 cups water or enough to make the liquid as thick as heavy cream. Bring it to a simmer over medium-low heat. Add the calamari and cook until tender when pierced with a fork, about 20 minutes.

4 Add the fish chunks and the shrimp. Cook until the fish is just cooked, about 5 minutes. Stir in the parsley. Serve hot with toasted bread and a drizzle of extra-virgin olive oil.

Poultry

Chicken Cutlets (Scaloppine)

Chicken Cutlets Francese

Chicken Cutlets with Basil and Lemon

Chicken Cutlets with Sage and Peas

Chicken with Gorgonzola and Walnuts

Salad-Topped Chicken Cutlets

Chicken Rolls with Anchovy Sauce

Chicken Rolls in Red Wine

Chicken Parts

"Devil's" Chicken

Crusty Broiled Chicken

Marinated Grilled Chicken

Baked Chicken with Potatoes and Lemon

Country-Style Chicken and Vegetables

Chicken with Lemon and White Wine

Chicken with Sausages and Pickled Peppers

Chicken with Celery, Capers,
and Rosemary

Roman-Style Chicken

Chicken with Vinegar, Garlic,
and Hot Pepper

Tuscan Fried Chicken

Chicken with Prosciutto and Spices

Chicken in the Style of the Hunter's Wife

Chicken with Porcini

Chicken with Olives

Chicken Livers with Vin Santo

Whole Chicken and Capon

Roasted Chicken with Rosemary

Roasted Chicken with Sage and White Wine

Chicken in the Style of Roast Pig

Roasted Chicken with Marsala
and Anchovies

Stuffed Roasted Capon

Stuffed Chicken in Ragù

Roasted Boiled Chicken

Chicken Under a Brick

Lemon Chicken Salad

Chicken Salad with Two Peppers

Piedmont-Style Chicken Salad

Turkey, Duck, and Quail

Rolled Stuffed Turkey Breast

Poached Turkey Meat Loaf

Turkey Rolls in Red Wine Tomato Sauce

Duck Breast with Sweet-and-Sour Figs

Spiced Roasted Duck

Quail in the Pan with Porcini

Grilled Quail

Quail with Tomatoes and Rosemary

Braised Quail

Italian cooks have a wide range of poultry to choose from. In addition to chicken and turkey, capon, pheasant, guinea hen, duck, goose, pigeon, quail, and other birds are readily available.

Until after World War II, chicken was not widely eaten in Italy. Poultry was expensive, and a live chicken could produce eggs for a farm family either to eat or sell. Chickens were killed only when they became too old to lay eggs, when someone in the family was ill and needed extra nourishment, or for special feasts. Many of today's recipes for chicken were once made with wild birds or with rabbit.

For Christmas and other holidays, Italians often serve capon. The flavor of capon is similar to chicken, though deeper and richer. Roasted capon with a meat or bread stuffing is eaten all over Italy. In Emilia-Romagna, capons are roasted and stuffed or boiled to make broth in which to cook tiny hand-formed tortellini. One traditional recipe from the Veneto is capon cut into pieces, seasoned with herbs, and steamed in a pig's bladder to hold in the flavors. In Piedmont, capons are stuffed with truffles and boiled or roasted for holiday meals. A small turkey or large roasting chicken can be substituted for capon, if preferred.

Most of the recipes in this chapter are for chicken and turkey because the supply of those in the United States is reliable and consistent. For good chicken and turkey flavor, I prefer to use free-range poultry raised without antibiotics. Though organic and free-range birds are more expensive, they taste better, have a better texture, and are better for you.

No matter which type of poultry you will be cooking, remove the giblets, liver, and any other parts packed inside the cavity or in the neck area. Rinse the bird well inside and out. Occasionally, you will see still-attached pinfeathers, which should be removed, either with your fingers or with tweezers. Some types of poultry, such as chicken, capon, and duck, have excess fat that can be pulled or cut out of the cavity. If the bird will be cooked whole, bend the wing tips behind the back. Insert any stuffing or flavoring ingredients, then tie the legs together with kitchen string for a neat appearance and more even cooking.

Some chickens, turkeys, and other large birds come with a small thermometer inserted in the breast. These devices are often inaccurate, as they can become clogged with cooking juices. It is best to rely on an instant-read thermometer to check for doneness. Chicken, turkey, and capon are done when the juices run clear when the thigh is pierced with a fork and the temperature in the thickest part of the thigh is 170° to 175°F (for capon, 180°F) on an instant-read thermometer. Be sure that the thermometer does not touch the bone (or the temperature may read higher than that of the meat). Quail, goose, and duck are eaten well done in Italy, with the exception of duck breast. When pan cooked, duck breast is usually served medium rare.

❧ Chicken Cutlets (Scaloppine)

Scaloppine are thin, boneless, skinless slices of meat or poultry, usually called cutlets in English. They can be made from any type of meat and sometimes even firm-fleshed fish, but in the United States veal, chicken, and turkey are the most common. Though not the most flavorful cuts, scaloppine or cutlets are tender, cook rapidly, and take well to a variety of flavorings, so they are a good choice for quick meals.

Veal scaloppine are the most typical of Italian cooking, but good veal is expensive and not always readily available, so many cooks in the United States use chicken or turkey cutlets.

When purchasing chicken cutlets, look for whole, well-trimmed slices. At home, check to see that the slices are thin enough, no more than 1/4 inch is best.

If the meat is thicker or unevenly cut, place the slices between two sheets of wax paper or plastic wrap. Pound them very gently with a smooth object such as a meat mallet. An inexpensive rubber plumber's mallet from the hardware store does a good job. Do not use a mallet with a craggy surface designed to break down fibers and tenderize meat, and do not pound too heavily or you will have finely chopped meat instead of thin, flat cutlets.

Chicken Cutlets Francese
Pollo alla Francese

MAKES 4 SERVINGS

Many Italian-American restaurants used to feature these cutlets in a light, eggy crust with a lemon sauce. I don't know why it is called Francese, *meaning "French-style," but it might be because it was thought to be elegant. It is still a favorite and tastes great with buttery peas or spinach.*

1 1/4 pounds thin-sliced chicken cutlets
Salt and freshly ground black pepper
2 large eggs
1/2 cup all-purpose flour
1/2 cup Chicken Broth (page 63) or store-bought
1/4 cup dry white wine
2 to 3 tablespoons fresh lemon juice
3 tablespoons olive oil
3 tablespoons unsalted butter
1 tablespoon fresh flat-leaf parsley
1 lemon, cut into wedges

1 Place the chicken slices between two sheets of plastic wrap. Gently pound the slices to about 1/4-inch thickness. Sprinkle the chicken with salt and pepper.

2 In a shallow bowl, beat the eggs with salt and pepper until well blended. Spread the flour on a piece of wax paper. Mix together the broth, wine, and lemon juice.

3 In a large skillet, heat the oil with the butter over medium heat until the butter melts. Dip only enough of the cutlets in the flour as will fit in the pan in a single layer. Then dip them in the egg.

4 Arrange the slices in the pan in a single layer. Cook the chicken until golden brown on the bottom, 2 to 3 minutes. Turn the chicken with tongs and brown on the other side, 2 to 3 minutes more. Regulate the heat so that the butter does not burn. Transfer the chicken to a plate. Cover with foil and keep warm. Repeat with the remaining chicken.

5 When all of the chicken is done, add the broth mixture to the pan. Raise the heat and cook, scraping the pan, until the sauce is slightly thickened. Stir in the parsley. Return the chicken pieces to the skillet and turn them once or twice in the sauce. Serve immediately with lemon wedges.

Chicken Cutlets with Basil and Lemon

Scaloppine di Pollo al Basilico e Limone

MAKES 4 SERVINGS

Italians say, "That which grows together, goes together," and that is certainly true of lemons and basil. I had this elegant yet quick and easy dish at the very beautiful Hotel Quisisana on the island of Capri off the coast of Naples. Serve it with buttered spinach or asparagus and a bottle of falanghina, a flavorful white wine from the region of Campania.

1¼ pounds thin-sliced chicken or turkey cutlets
Salt and freshly ground black pepper
3 tablespoons unsalted butter
1 tablespoon olive oil
2 tablespoons fresh lemon juice
12 fresh basil leaves, stacked and cut into thin strips

1 Place the chicken slices between two sheets of plastic wrap. Gently pound the slices to about ¼-inch thickness. Sprinkle the chicken well with salt and pepper.

2 In a large heavy skillet, melt 2 tablespoons of the butter with oil. When the butter is melted, add as many chicken pieces as will fit without touching. Cook the chicken until golden brown, about 4 minutes. Turn the chicken and brown the other side, about 3 minutes more. Transfer the pieces to a plate. Repeat with the remaining chicken, if necessary.

3 Remove the pan from the heat. Add the remaining butter, the lemon juice, and the basil to the skillet and swirl it gently to melt the butter. Return the chicken pieces to the skillet and place it over the heat. Turn the chicken pieces once or twice in the sauce. Serve immediately.

Chicken Cutlets with Sage and Peas

Scaloppine di Pollo al Piselli

MAKES 4 SERVINGS

Here chicken cutlets are married with sage and peas, and it looks as great as it tastes. If you are using frozen peas and don't have time to partially thaw them, just drop the peas into boiling water for 1 minute, or rinse or soak them in very hot water. Drain them well before proceeding.

1¼ pounds thin-sliced chicken cutlets
Salt and freshly ground black pepper
2 tablespoons unsalted butter
2 tablespoons olive oil
12 fresh sage leaves
2 cups shelled fresh peas or partially thawed frozen peas
1 to 2 tablespoons fresh lemon juice

1 Place the chicken slices between two sheets of plastic wrap. Gently pound the slices to about ¼-inch thickness. Sprinkle the chicken well with salt and pepper.

2 In a large skillet, melt the butter with the olive oil over medium heat. Pat the chicken dry. Add the chicken and sage to the pan. Cook the chicken until golden brown, about 4 minutes. Turn the pieces with tongs and brown the other side, about 3 minutes more. Transfer the pieces to a plate.

3 Add the peas and lemon juice to the skillet and stir well. Add salt and pepper to taste. Cover and cook 5 minutes, or until the peas are almost tender.

4 Return the chicken pieces to the skillet and cook, turning them once or twice, until heated through. Serve hot.

Chicken with Gorgonzola and Walnuts

Petti di Pollo con Gorgonzola

MAKES 4 SERVINGS

Gorgonzola is a creamy cow's milk blue cheese from the region of Lombardy. The cheese is creamy-white streaked with blue-green veins of an edible type of penicillin mold. Gorgonzola melts beautifully, and cooks in this region use it to make sauces for pasta and meat. Here it forms a delicious sauce for cutlets. A sprinkling of chopped walnuts gives the dish an added crunch. Serve the chicken with sautéed mushrooms and fresh broccoli.

1 1/4 pounds thin-sliced chicken cutlets
1/2 cup all-purpose flour
Salt and freshly ground black pepper
2 tablespoons unsalted butter
1 tablespoon olive oil
1/4 cup finely chopped shallots
1/2 cup dry white wine
4 ounces gorgonzola, rind removed
2 tablespoons walnuts, coarsely chopped and toasted

1 Place the chicken slices between two sheets of plastic wrap. Gently pound the slices to about 1/4-inch thickness. On a piece of wax paper, combine the flour and salt and pepper, to taste. Dip the chicken cutlets in the mixture. Shake to remove the excess.

2 In a large skillet over medium heat, melt the butter with the oil. Add the chicken and cook until golden brown, about 4 minutes. Turn the pieces with tongs and brown the other side, about 3 minutes more. Remove the chicken to a plate and keep warm.

3 Add the shallots to the skillet and cook for 1 minute. Stir in the wine and cook, scraping the bottom of the pan, until slightly thickened, about 1 minute. Reduce the heat to low. Return the chicken pieces to the skillet and turn them once or twice in the sauce.

4 Cut the cheese into slices and place them on top of the chicken. Cover and cook just until slightly melted, 1 to 2 minutes.

5 Sprinkle with the walnuts and serve immediately.

Salad-Topped Chicken Cutlets

Scaloppine di Pollo a l'Insalata

MAKES 4 SERVINGS

At a favorite restaurant in New York called Dal Barone, large chicken cutlets fried in bread crumbs with a crunchy salad topping were called orecchie di elefante, *"elephant's ears." Though the restaurant closed several years ago, I still make my version of their chicken cutlets. Serve with ripe pears and cheese for dessert.*

1 1/4 pounds thin-sliced chicken cutlets
2 large eggs
1/2 cup freshly grated Parmigiano-Reggiano
2 tablespoons chopped fresh flat-leaf parsley
Salt and freshly ground black pepper
1 to 2 tablespoons all-purpose flour
1/4 cup olive oil

SALAD

2 tablespoons extra-virgin olive oil
1 to 2 tablespoons balsamic vinegar
Salt and freshly ground black pepper
4 cups mixed salad greens, torn into bite-size pieces
1/4 cup thinly sliced red onion
1 medium ripe tomato, diced

1 Place the chicken cutlets between two sheets of plastic wrap. Gently pound the cutlets to a 1/4-inch thickness.

2 In a medium bowl, beat the eggs with the cheese, parsley, and salt and pepper to taste. Beat in enough flour to make a smooth paste just thick enough to coat the chicken. Line a plate or tray with paper towels.

3 In a large skillet over medium heat, heat the 1/4 cup of olive oil until a drop of the egg mixture sizzles when added.

4 Dip the cutlets in the egg mixture until well coated. Place just enough of the cutlets in the pan to fit comfortably in a single layer. Cook until

(continues)

browned, about 4 minutes. Turn the chicken with tongs and brown the other side, about 3 minutes more. Drain on the paper towels. Transfer to a plate, cover with foil, and keep warm. Cook the remaining cutlets in the same way.

5 In a large bowl, whisk the 2 tablespoons olive oil, the vinegar, and salt and pepper to taste. Add the salad ingredients and toss well.

6 Top the cutlets with the salad and serve immediately.

Chicken Rolls with Anchovy Sauce
Involtini con Salsa di Acciughe

MAKES 4 SERVINGS

Anchovies give a zesty flavor to the sauce on these easy chicken rolls. If you don't want to use anchovies, substitute some chopped capers.

¼ cup unsalted butter
4 anchovy fillets, drained and chopped
1 tablespoon chopped fresh flat-leaf parsley
¼ teaspoon freshly grated lemon zest
8 thin-sliced chicken cutlets
Freshly ground black pepper
8 thin slices imported Italian prosciutto

1 Place a rack in the center of the oven. Preheat the oven to 400°F. Butter a small pan.

2 In a small saucepan, melt the butter with the anchovies over medium heat, mashing the anchovies with the back of a spoon. Stir in the parsley and lemon zest. Set the sauce aside.

3 Place the chicken slices between two sheets of plastic wrap. Gently pound the slices to about ¼-inch thickness. Lay the chicken slices on a flat surface. Sprinkle with pepper. Place a piece of prosciutto on each slice. Roll up the slices lengthwise. Place the rolls in the pan seam-side down.

4 Drizzle the sauce over the chicken. Bake 20 to 25 minutes or until the juices run clear when the chicken is cut in the thickest part. Serve hot.

Chicken Rolls in Red Wine
Rollatini di Pollo al Vino Rosso

MAKES 4 SERVINGS

Red wine colors these rolled chicken breasts from Tuscany a deep burgundy and makes a delicious sauce. Garlic, herbs, and thin slices of prosciutto is the typical filling. Though prosciutto from Parma is very good and the best-known variety in the United States, other types from outside the Parma area, such as prosciutto San Daniele, from Friuli, are now available, and though subtly different they are equally good.

The most important thing is to find a good source for prosciutto. The clerks should know how to slice the meat very thinly without shredding it and how to lay the slices out carefully on wax paper so that they do not stick together.

1 tablespoon chopped fresh rosemary
1 tablespoon chopped fresh sage
1 garlic clove, very finely chopped
8 thin-sliced chicken cutlets
Salt and freshly ground black pepper
8 slices imported Italian prosciutto
2 tablespoons olive oil
1 cup dry red wine

1 In a small bowl, combine the rosemary, sage, and garlic.

2 Lay the cutlets out on a flat surface. Sprinkle with the herb mixture and salt and pepper to taste. Place a slice of prosciutto on top. Roll up the cutlets lengthwise and tie them with kitchen string.

3 In a large skillet, heat the oil over medium heat. Add the chicken and cook, turning the pieces frequently with tongs, until browned on all sides, about 10 minutes.

4 Add the wine and cook, turning the pieces occasionally, until the chicken is cooked through and the juices run clear when cut in the thickest part, about 15 minutes.

5 Transfer the chicken rolls to a serving platter. Pour the sauce over them and serve immediately.

❦ Chicken Parts

"Devil's" Chicken
Pollo alla Diavola

MAKES 4 SERVINGS

Tiny hot red chilies are called peperoncini, *"little peppers," in some regions and* diavolicchi, *"little devils," in others. The presence of crushed red pepper accounts for the Tuscan name for this chicken.*

I like to use cut-up chicken pieces for this dish. That way I can cook the legs and thighs a little longer than the more delicate wings and breasts.

I chicken (about 3 pounds), cut into 8 serving pieces
¹/₃ cup freshly squeezed lemon juice
¹/₄ cup olive oil
A generous pinch of crushed red pepper
Salt

I With a chef's knife or poultry shears, remove the wing tips from the chicken.

2 In a large shallow dish, combine the lemon juice, oil, red pepper, and salt to taste. Add the chicken pieces. Cover and marinate at room temperature for 1 hour, turning the pieces occasionally.

3 Arrange a grill rack or broiler pan about 5 inches from the heat source. Preheat the grill or broiler.

4 When ready to cook, remove the chicken from the marinade and pat it dry. Place the chicken with the skin side toward the source of the heat. Grill or broil, basting occasionally with the marinade, until nicely browned, about 10 to 15 minutes. Turn the chicken and cook until the chicken juices run clear when the thigh is pierced with a knife in the thickest part, about 10 to 15 minutes more. Serve hot.

Crusty Broiled Chicken
Pollo Rosolato

MAKES 4 SERVINGS

Chicken in a crisp bread crumb and cheese coating tastes great when just cooked and hot, but it is also good served cold the next day. Plan an Italian picnic with this chicken, Sweet and Sour Potatoes (pages 451–452), Green Bean Salad (pages 430–431), and sliced tomatoes.

I chicken (about 3¹/₂ pounds), cut into serving pieces
Salt and freshly ground black pepper
¹/₂ cup plain dry bread crumbs
2 tablespoons freshly grated Parmigiano-Reggiano
I large garlic clove, finely chopped
¹/₂ teaspoon dried oregano, crumbled
About 2 tablespoons olive oil

I Place a broiler rack about 5 inches away from the heat source. Preheat the broiler.

2 Pat the chicken dry. Sprinkle with salt and pepper. Place the chicken skin-side down on the rack. Broil the chicken until lightly browned, about 10 minutes. Turn the chicken and cook 10 minutes more.

3 While the chicken is cooking, in a medium bowl, combine the bread crumbs, cheese, garlic, oregano, and salt and pepper to taste. Add just enough of the oil to make a thick paste.

4 Remove the broiler pan from the broiler. Set the oven heat to 350°F.

5 Coat the skin side of the chicken with the bread crumb mixture, patting it so that it adheres. Place the pan on the center rack of the oven and bake about 10 to 15 minutes more, until the juices run clear when the chicken is pierced with a knife in the thickest part of the thigh, and the crust is nicely browned. Serve hot or at room temperature.

Marinated Grilled Chicken
Pollo alla Griglia

MAKES 4 SERVINGS

Vinegar, garlic, and herbs—typical ingredients of the Naples area, where my father's family was from— were always included in a marinade for whatever he was barbecuing. Usually the herb was mint, either fresh home-grown or dried, though sometimes he substituted fresh parsley or dried oregano. He used it on chicken, bluefish, and steak, and the results were always delicious.

Because the acid in the vinegar can actually "cook" any protein-rich food it comes in contact with, do not marinate tender fish for more than 30 minutes. Chicken and beef can marinate longer and will pick up more of the marinade flavor as they do.

- $1/2$ cup red wine vinegar
- 2 large garlic cloves, chopped
- 2 tablespoons chopped fresh mint or flat-leaf parsley or 1 teaspoon dried oregano, crumbled
- Salt and freshly ground black pepper
- 1 chicken (about $3 1/2$ pounds), cut into 8 serving pieces

1 In a shallow nonreactive dish, whisk together the vinegar, garlic, herb, and salt and pepper to taste. Add the chicken pieces. Cover and refrigerate for several hours up to overnight.

2 Place a barbecue grill or broiler rack about 5 inches away from the heat source. Preheat the grill or broiler.

3 Remove the chicken from the marinade. Pat the chicken dry. Place the chicken with the skin side toward the source of the heat. Grill or broil 12 to 15 minutes or until nicely browned. Turn the chicken and cook 10 to 15 minutes more, or until the chicken juices run clear when the chicken thigh is pierced with a knife in the thickest part. Serve hot or at room temperature.

Baked Chicken with Potatoes and Lemon
Pollo al Forno con Patate e Limone

MAKES 4 SERVINGS

One of my favorite restaurants on the island of Capri is Da Paolino, set within a lemon grove. One evening my husband and I were enjoying a quiet, candlelit dinner when suddenly a fat ripe lemon from the tree above us crashed down into a glass, splashing water all over the table.

I think of that incident every time I make this lemony chicken. It is a typical home-style dish made all over southern Italy, where citrus is plentiful.

- 2 medium lemons
- 1 tablespoon olive oil
- 1 tablespoon chopped rosemary
- 2 garlic cloves, chopped
- Salt and freshly ground black pepper
- 1 chicken (about $3 1/2$ pounds) cut into 8 serving pieces
- 1 pound all-purpose potatoes, peeled and cut into eighths

1 Place a rack in the center of the oven. Preheat the oven to 450°F. Oil a baking pan large enough to hold all of the ingredients in a single layer.

2 Cut one lemon into thin slices. Squeeze the juice of the remaining lemon into a medium bowl.

3 Add to the bowl the oil, rosemary, garlic, and salt and pepper to taste and whisk until combined.

4 Rinse the chicken pieces and pat dry. Place the chicken in the pan. Pour the lemon juice mixture over the chicken, turning the pieces to coat all sides. Arrange the chicken pieces skin side up. Tuck the potatoes and lemon slices around the chicken.

5 Bake the chicken for 45 minutes. Baste with the pan juices. Continue to bake, basting occasionally, 15 minutes more or until the chicken is browned and the potatoes are tender.

4 Transfer the contents of the pan to a serving platter. Pour the juices over the chicken and serve.

Country-Style Chicken and Vegetables
Pollo alla Paesana

MAKES 4 SERVINGS

Some years ago, I visited Emilia-Romagna to learn about how Parmigiano-Reggiano is produced. I visited a dairy where the owner showed me how cheese was made daily. After a tour and cheesemaking lesson, my host invited me to join his family and coworkers for lunch. As we stepped into the big farmhouse kitchen, his wife was just removing large pans of chicken and vegetables from the oven. We nibbled on homemade salami and the typical crab-shaped white bread of the region known as coppia— *"couple" bread—because it is made in two sections that are joined together. Dessert was as simple as can be, wedges of ripe juicy pears and moist, aged Parmigiano.*

A baking pan large enough to hold all of the chicken and vegetables in a single layer is essential for this dish, or the ingredients will steam and not brown properly. If you don't have one large enough, use two smaller pans, dividing the ingredients evenly between them.

Vary this dish according to the vegetables in season and what you have on hand. Cut-up turnips, squash, or peppers can be added, or try a handful of cherry tomatoes.

1/2 to 1 cup homemade **Chicken Broth** (page 63), or store-bought

4 large garlic cloves, finely chopped

2 tablespoons chopped fresh flat-leaf parsley

2 tablespoons chopped fresh rosemary

1/4 cup olive oil

Salt and freshly ground black pepper

1 (10-ounce) package white mushrooms, halved or quartered if large

6 medium boiling potatoes, peeled and cut into eighths

2 medium carrots, cut into 1-inch chunks

1 medium onion, cut into eighths

1 chicken (about 3 1/2 pounds), cut into 8 serving pieces

1 Prepare the chicken broth, if necessary. Place a rack in the center of the oven. Preheat the oven to 450°F. Choose a baking pan large enough to hold all of the ingredients in a single layer, or use two pans. Oil the pan or pans.

2 Place the garlic, parsley, and rosemary in a small bowl and mix with the oil. Add salt and pepper to taste.

3 Scatter the mushrooms, potatoes, carrots, and onions in the pan. Add half the herb mixture and toss well. Brush the remaining herb mixture over the chicken pieces. Place the chicken skin-side up in the pan, arranging the vegetables around them.

4 Bake for 45 minutes. Baste the chicken with the pan juices. If the chicken seems dry, add a little of the chicken broth. Continue to bake, basting occasionally, 15 minutes more, or until the chicken juices run clear when pierced in the thickest part of the thigh with a knife and the potatoes are tender. If the chicken is not brown enough, run the pans under the broiler for 5 minutes or until the skin is browned and crisp.

5 Transfer the chicken and vegetables to a serving platter. Tip the pan and skim off the fat with a large spoon. Place the pan over medium heat. Add about 1/2 cup of the chicken broth and scrape the bottom of the pan. Bring the juices to a simmer and cook until slightly reduced, about 5 minutes.

6 Pour the juices over the chicken and vegetables and serve immediately.

Chicken with Lemon and White Wine
Pollo allo Scarpariello I

MAKES 4 SERVINGS

Scarpariello means "shoemaker's style," and there are many theories about how the name for this recipe came about. Some say little bits of chopped garlic resemble the nailheads in a shoe, while others say it was a quick dish a busy shoemaker cobbled together. Most likely, it is an Italian-American invention, given an Italian name by a clever restaurateur.

There are many versions of this dish, and every one I have tasted has been delicious. Typically, the chicken is chopped into small chunks, known as spezzatino, from spezzare, "to chop," so that the pieces can absorb more of the tasty sauce. You can do this at home with a cleaver or heavy knife, or have the butcher prepare the chicken for you. If you prefer, you can simply cut the chicken at the joints into serving-size pieces.

I chicken (about 3 1/2 pounds)
Salt and freshly ground black pepper
3 tablespoons olive oil
2 tablespoons unsalted butter
3 large garlic cloves, finely chopped
3 tablespoons fresh lemon juice
3/4 cup dry white wine
1/4 cup chopped fresh flat-leaf parsley

I Trim off the chicken wing tips and tail. Set them aside for another use. With a large heavy knife or cleaver, cut up the chicken at the joints. Cut the breasts, thighs, and legs into 2-inch chunks. Rinse the pieces and pat dry. Sprinkle all over with salt and pepper.

2 Heat the oil in a 12-inch skillet over medium-high heat. Add the chicken pieces in a single layer. Cook, turning the pieces occasionally, until nicely browned, about 15 to 20 minutes.

3 Lower the heat to medium. Spoon off the fat. Place the butter in the pan, and when it is melted, add the garlic. Turn the chicken pieces in the butter and add the lemon juice.

4 Add the wine and bring to a simmer. Cover and cook, turning the pieces occasionally, until the chicken juices run clear when pierced with a knife in the thickest part of the thigh, about 10 minutes.

5 If there is a lot of liquid remaining, remove the chicken to a serving platter and keep warm. Turn the heat to high and boil until the liquid is reduced and slightly thickened. Stir in the parsley and pour over the chicken.

Chicken with Sausages and Pickled Peppers
Pollo allo Scarpariello II

MAKES 6 SERVINGS

Chicken scarpariello probably became popular here before World War II, when many Italian immigrants to this country opened restaurants in big city neighborhoods known as Little Italy. Few were professional cooks, and many of the dishes they served were based on home cooking enhanced by the bounty of ingredients they found in this country.

Here is a second version of shoemaker's-style chicken. With sausage, vinegar, and pickled peppers, it is completely different from the previous recipe. And there are many other versions as well. No matter what its origins, chicken scarpariello is delicious and satisfying.

1/4 cup homemade Chicken Broth (see page 63), or store-bought
I chicken (about 3 1/2 pounds)
I tablespoon olive oil
I pound Italian-style pork sausage, cut into 1-inch chunks
Salt and freshly ground black pepper
6 large garlic cloves, thinly sliced
I cup jarred pickled sweet peppers, cut into bite-size pieces
1/4 cup pickling liquid from the peppers, or white wine vinegar

1 Prepare the chicken broth, if necessary. Trim off the chicken wing tips and tail. Set them aside for another use. With a large heavy knife or cleaver, cut up the chicken at the joints. Cut the breasts, thighs, and legs into 2-inch chunks. Rinse the pieces and dry well.

2 Heat the oil over medium high heat in a skillet large enough to hold all of the ingredients. Add the sausages pieces and brown well on all sides, about 10 minutes. Transfer the pieces to a plate.

3 Place the chicken pieces in the pan. Sprinkle with salt and pepper. Cook, stirring occasionally, until golden, about 15 minutes. Scatter the garlic around the chicken and cook 2 to 3 minutes more.

4 Tip the pan and spoon off most of the fat. Add the sausages, the broth, the peppers, and the pepper liquid or vinegar. Turn the heat to high. Cook, stirring the pieces often and basting them with the liquid, until the liquid is reduced and forms a light glaze, about 15 minutes. Serve immediately.

Chicken with Celery, Capers, and Rosemary
Pollo alla Cacciatora Siciliana

MAKES 4 SERVINGS

This is a Sicilian version of alla cacciatora, *"hunter's wife's" chicken. Celery is a nice touch, giving the sauce a little crunch. Sicilians often make this with rabbit.*

2 tablespoons olive oil
1 chicken (about 3 1/2 pounds), cut into 8 pieces
Salt and freshly ground black pepper
1/3 cup red wine vinegar
1/2 cup chopped celery
1/4 cup capers, rinsed and chopped
1 sprig fresh rosemary

1 Heat the oil in a large skillet over medium heat. Pat the chicken dry with paper towels. Add the chicken pieces and salt and pepper to taste. Cook, turning the pieces occasionally, until golden, about 15 minutes. Tip the pan and spoon off the fat.

2 Pour the vinegar over the chicken and bring to a simmer. Scatter the celery, capers, and rosemary around the chicken.

3 Cover and cook, turning the pieces occasionally, about 20 minutes or until the chicken is tender and most of the vinegar has evaporated. If there is too much liquid left at the end of the cooking, transfer the chicken pieces to a serving dish. Raise the heat and boil the liquid until reduced.

4 Transfer the chicken to a platter. Tip the pan and skim off the fat with a large spoon. Add a little water and scrape the bottom of the pan with a wooden spoon. Pour the juices over the chicken and serve immediately.

Roman-Style Chicken
Pollo alla Romana

MAKES 4 SERVINGS

Marjoram is an herb used frequently in Roman cooking. It tastes something like oregano, though much more delicate. If you don't have marjoram, substitute a pinch of oregano or even thyme. Some Roman cooks embellish this dish by adding sweet peppers sautéed in olive oil to the skillet just before the chicken is done.

2 ounces thickly sliced pancetta, chopped
2 tablespoons olive oil
1 chicken, about 3 1/2 pounds, cut into 8 serving pieces
Salt and freshly ground black pepper
2 garlic cloves, finely chopped
1 teaspoon dried marjoram
1/2 cup dry white wine
2 cups peeled, seeded, and diced tomatoes,
    or chopped canned tomatoes

1 In a large skillet over medium heat, cook the pancetta in the olive oil until golden brown, about 10 minutes.

2 Pat the chicken dry with paper towels. Add the chicken to the skillet and sprinkle with salt and

(continues)

pepper to taste. Cook, turning occasionally, until the pieces are browned on all sides, about 15 minutes.

3 Tip the pan and skim off the excess fat with a large spoon. Sprinkle the chicken with garlic and marjoram. Add the wine and cook 1 minute. Stir in the tomatoes and bring to a simmer. Cook, stirring occasionally, until the juices run clear when the chicken is cut in the thickest part of the thigh, 20 to 30 minutes. Serve hot.

Chicken with Vinegar, Garlic, and Hot Pepper
Spezzatino di Pollo alla Nonna

MAKES 4 SERVINGS

My grandmother taught my mother to make this simple spicy Neapolitan-style chicken, and my mother taught me.

Don't even think of using a sweet vinegar like balsamico for this recipe. A good wine vinegar will give the authentic flavor. It won't be too sharp; cooking mellows the vinegar and all the flavors balance beautifully.

I chicken (about 3 1/2 pounds)
2 tablespoons olive oil
Salt
4 large garlic cloves, finely chopped
1/2 teaspoon crushed red pepper, or to taste
2/3 cup red wine vinegar

1 Trim off the chicken wing tips and tail. With a large heavy knife or cleaver, cut up the chicken at the joints. Cut the breasts, thighs, and legs into 2-inch chunks. Rinse the pieces and dry well.

2 In a skillet large enough to hold all of the chicken in a single layer, heat the oil over medium heat. Add the chicken pieces without crowding. If there is too much chicken to fit comfortably in one pan, divide the chicken between two pans or cook it in batches.

3 Cook until browned, turning occasionally, about 15 minutes. When all of the chicken is browned, tip the pan and spoon out most of the fat. Sprinkle the chicken with salt.

4 Scatter the garlic and crushed red pepper around the chicken pieces. Add the vinegar and stir, scraping up the brown bits on the bottom of the pan with a wooden spoon. Cook, stirring the chicken and basting occasionally, until the chicken is tender and the liquid is thickened and reduced, 15 minutes. If it becomes too dry, add a little warm water.

5 Transfer the chicken to a serving dish and pour the pan juices over all. Serve hot.

Tuscan Fried Chicken
Pollo Fritto alla Toscana

MAKES 4 SERVINGS

In Tuscany, both chicken and rabbit are cut into small chunks coated with a tasty batter, then deep-fried. Often, wedges of artichokes are fried at the same time and served alongside.

Tuscans use a cut-up whole chicken for this recipe, but I sometimes make it with just chicken wings. They cook evenly and everybody loves to eat them.

I chicken (about 3 1/2 pounds), or 8 to 10 chicken wings
3 large eggs
2 tablespoons fresh lemon juice
Salt and freshly ground black pepper
1 1/2 cups all-purpose flour
Vegetable or olive oil for frying
I lemon, cut into wedges

1 Trim off the wing tips and tail if using a whole chicken. With a large heavy knife or cleaver, cut up the chicken at the joints. Cut the breasts, thighs, and legs into 2-inch chunks. Separate the wings at the joints. Rinse the pieces and dry well.

2 In a large bowl, beat the eggs, lemon juice, and salt and pepper to taste. Spread the flour on a sheet of wax paper. Line a tray or trays with paper towels. Preheat oven to 300°F.

3 Stir the chicken pieces into the egg mixture until well coated. Remove the pieces one at a time and roll them in the flour. Tap off the excess. Place the pieces on a rack until ready to cook.

4 Heat about 1 inch of oil in a large deep skillet or wide saucepan over medium heat. Test to see that the oil is hot enough by dropping in some of the egg mixture. When it sizzles and browns in 1 minute, add enough chicken pieces to fit comfortably in the pan without crowding. Fry the pieces, turning occasionally with tongs, until crisp and browned on all sides and the juices run clear when the chicken is pierced in the thickest part, 15 to 20 minutes. As the pieces are done, transfer them to the paper towels to drain. Keep warm in a low oven while frying the remaining chicken.

5 Serve hot with lemon wedges.

Chicken with Prosciutto and Spices
Pollo Speziato

MAKES 4 SERVINGS

I had this sautéed chicken dish when I was in the Marches region. The chicken is not browned first, though it does turn out nicely colored. The spices and herbs give the chicken a lively, complex, and unusual flavor and it is very simple to cook.

I chicken (about 3¹/2 pounds), cut into 8 serving pieces
¹/4 pound imported Italian prosciutto in one piece, cut into narrow strips
6 whole cloves
2 sprigs fresh rosemary
2 fresh sage leaves
2 bay leaves
I garlic clove, thinly sliced
¹/2 teaspoon whole black peppercorns
Salt
¹/2 cup dry white wine

I Arrange the chicken pieces skin-side down in a large heavy skillet. Scatter the prosciutto, cloves, rosemary, sage, bay leaf, garlic, peppercorns, and salt to taste over the chicken. Add the wine and bring it to a simmer over medium heat.

2 Cover the pan and cook 20 minutes. Add a little water if the chicken seems dry. Cook, basting the chicken occasionally with liquid in the pan, 15 minutes more or until the juices run clear when the chicken is pierced with a knife in the thickest part of the thigh.

3 Uncover and cook briefly until the liquid is reduced slightly. Discard the bay leaf. Serve hot.

Chicken in the Style of the Hunter's Wife
Pollo alla Cacciatora

MAKES 4 SERVINGS

I think I could write a whole book of chicken recipes called alla cacciatora. *One explanation for the name is that chicken, until the last 50 years or so, was a special occasion dish in most homes and not eaten every day. But during the hunting season, the hunter's wife would prepare a chicken to fortify her husband for the rigors of the hunt.*

There are so many variations to this dish. Southern Italians make it with tomatoes, garlic, and peppers. In Emilia-Romagna it has onion, carrot, celery, tomatoes, and dry white wine. In Friuli–Venezia Giulia, it is made with mushrooms. The Genoese make it simply with tomatoes and local white wine. This Piedmontese version is a classic.

2 tablespoons olive oil
I chicken (about 3¹/2 pounds), cut into 8 serving pieces
2 medium onions, chopped
I celery rib, chopped
I carrot, chopped
I red bell pepper, thinly sliced
I yellow bell pepper, thinly sliced
¹/2 cup dry white wine
4 ripe tomatoes, peeled, seeded, and chopped, or 2 cups canned tomatoes
6 fresh basil leaves, torn into bits
2 teaspoons chopped fresh rosemary
Salt and freshly ground black pepper

(continues)

1 Heat the oil in a large skillet over medium heat. Rinse and pat the chicken pieces dry. Cook the chicken, turning the pieces frequently until browned on all sides, about 15 minutes. Transfer the chicken to a plate. Tip the pan and skim off all but 2 tablespoons of the fat.

2 Add the onions, celery, carrot, and peppers to the skillet. Cook, stirring occasionally, until the vegetables are lightly browned, about 15 minutes.

3 Return the chicken to the skillet. Add the wine and bring to a simmer. Stir in the tomatoes, basil, rosemary, and salt and pepper to taste. Bring to a simmer and cook, turning the chicken pieces occasionally, until the chicken juices run clear when the thigh is pierced in the thickest part, about 20 minutes. Serve hot.

Chicken with Porcini
Pollo con Funghi Porcini

MAKES 4 SERVINGS

In Piedmont, you will see people selling freshly picked porcini mushrooms from makeshift stands at highway rest stops and in parking lots. Because porcini season is brief, these plump wild mushrooms are often dried to preserve all of their heady flavor and aroma. They are not inexpensive, but a little goes a long way. Packaged dried porcini make great gifts—including for yourself. I buy big bags full, which keep a long time in a sealed container.

^{1}/2 cup dried porcini mushrooms
1 cup warm water
1 tablespoon unsalted butter
2 tablespoons olive oil
1 chicken (about 3^1/2 pounds), cut into 8 serving pieces
Salt and freshly ground black pepper
1 cup dry white wine

1 Soak the mushrooms in the water for 30 minutes. Remove the mushrooms and reserve the liquid. Rinse the mushrooms under cold running water to remove any grit, paying special attention to the ends of the stems where soil collects. Chop the mushrooms coarsely. Strain the mushroom liquid through a paper coffee filter into a bowl.

2 In a large skillet, melt the butter with the oil over medium heat. Pat the chicken dry and place the pieces in the pan. Brown the chicken well on all sides, about 15 minutes. Sprinkle with salt and pepper.

3 Tip the pan and skim off the excess fat with a spoon. Add the wine to the skillet and bring to a simmer. Scatter the mushrooms over the chicken. Pour the mushroom liquid into the pan. Partially cover and cook, turning the pieces occasionally, until the chicken juices run clear when the thigh is pierced in the thickest part, about 20 minutes.

4 Transfer the chicken to a serving platter. If there is a lot of liquid left in the pan, raise the heat and simmer until it is reduced and thickened. Pour the sauce over the chicken and serve immediately.

Chicken with Olives
Pollo al'Olive

Rome is the capital of Italy, and people from all over the country gravitate there because of its importance as the center of government, religion, and (to a lesser extent) business. Many of the city's restaurants are run by non-Romans, and the food is sometimes a reflection of the merging of regional styles. I had this chicken in a trattoria in Trastevere, the bohemian neighborhood across the Tiber from the historic center that is popular with the city's young people. Judging by the amount of garlic in the dish, I suspected that there was a southern hand in the kitchen, but I was not able to find out for sure.

2 tablespoons olive oil

1 chicken (about 3¹/₂ pounds), cut into 8 serving pieces

Salt and freshly ground black pepper

4 garlic cloves, lightly crushed

¹/₂ cup dry white wine

2 tablespoons white wine vinegar

1 cup Gaeta or other mild, flavorful olives, pitted and coarsely chopped

2 anchovy fillets, chopped

1 In a large skillet, heat the oil over medium heat. Pat the chicken pieces dry and place them in the pan. Sprinkle the pieces with salt and pepper. When the chicken is golden brown on one side, after about 10 minutes, turn the pieces, then scatter the garlic all around them. Cook until nicely browned, about 10 minutes more. Remove the garlic if it becomes dark brown.

2 Add the wine and vinegar and bring to a simmer. Scatter the olives and anchovies all around. Partially cover the pan and turn the heat to low. Cook, turning the pieces occasionally, until the chicken is tender and the juices run clear when the thigh is pierced in the thickest part, about 20 minutes.

3 Remove the chicken to a serving platter. Tip the pan and skim off the fat. Spoon the sauce over the chicken. Serve hot.

Chicken Livers with Vin Santo
Fegato di Pollo al Vin Santo

MAKES 4 SERVINGS

Vin santo is a Tuscan dessert wine made by partially drying trebbiano grapes on straw mats before pressing them to make a very concentrated wine. The wine is allowed to age in sealed wood casks until it turns a beautiful amber color and develops an aromatic, nutty flavor and smooth texture. It is a perfect wine to sip after a meal or to accompany nuts, plain cookies, or cake. Vin santo is also used for cooking—in this case, with chicken livers in a delicious buttery sauce.

Marsala can be substituted for the vin santo. Serve these livers over boiled or fried polenta or slices of toasted bread.

1 pound chicken livers

3 tablespoons unsalted butter

Salt and freshly ground black pepper

1 teaspoon chopped fresh sage leaves

4 thin slices imported Italian prosciutto, cut crosswise into slivers

2 tablespoons vin santo or Marsala

2 tablespoons chopped fresh flat-leaf parsley

1 Trim the chicken livers, cutting away the connecting fibers with a sharp knife. Cut each liver into 2 or 3 pieces.

2 In a large skillet, melt 2 tablespoons of the butter over medium heat. Rinse and pat the liver pieces dry and add them to the skillet. Sprinkle with salt and pepper. Add the sage and prosciutto. Cook, turning the liver pieces frequently, until lightly browned yet still pink in the center, about 5 minutes. Transfer the livers to a plate with a slotted spoon.

3 Add the vin santo to the pan and raise the heat. Bring to a simmer and cook 1 minute or until slightly reduced. Remove from the heat and stir in the remaining butter and parsley. Pour the sauce over the liver and serve immediately.

🌿 Whole Chicken and Capon

Roasted Chicken with Rosemary
Pollo Arrosto

MAKES 4 SERVINGS

Before the 1950s, most Italians lived and worked on farms owned by wealthy absentee landowners. At certain times of the year, usually holidays, the farmers would be expected to pay the landowner a portion of their profits, usually in the form of livestock, produce, wheat, wine, or whatever was produced on the farm. In the Veneto, specific items traditionally were associated with certain holidays. Hens were given at Carnevale, which precedes Lent. Chickens were given for the feast of Saint Peter on June 29, geese for All Saints' Day, November 1. Eggs were the gift for Easter and a suckling pig for Saint Martin's Day on November 11. A roasted chicken dinner was a rare feast for the average person, and even today makes a meal seem like an occasion.

Roasting a chicken breast-side down helps to keep the white meat juicy and cooks the bird evenly. For best flavor, use an organically raised chicken.

This is the most elemental of roasted chicken recipes and, in my opinion, the best. The chicken cooks at a low temperature for the entire time. Scatter some potatoes or other root vegetables, like carrots or onions, around the chicken, if you like.

1 chicken (3½ to 4 pounds)
2 garlic cloves, halved
4 tablespoons olive oil
Salt and freshly ground black pepper
2 or 3 sprigs fresh rosemary
1 lemon, halved

1 Place a rack in the center of the oven. Preheat the oven to 350°F. Oil a roasting pan large enough to hold the chicken.

2 Rinse the chicken well and pat it dry. Rub the skin all over with the garlic. Brush with oil and sprinkle inside and out with salt and pepper. Tuck the garlic and rosemary inside the chicken. Squeeze the lemon juice over the chicken. Place the lemon halves inside the chicken cavity. Tie the legs together with kitchen string. Place the chicken breast-side down in the pan.

3 Roast the chicken 30 minutes. Baste the chicken with the accumulated juices. Continue to roast 20 minutes more. Carefully turn the chicken breast-side up and roast, basting occasionally, 30 minutes. The chicken is done when the juices run clear when the thigh is pierced and the temperature in the thickest part of the thigh is 170°F on an instant-read thermometer. If the chicken is not browned enough, turn the heat to 450°F for the last 15 minutes of cooking.

4 Transfer the chicken to a platter. Cover loosely with foil and keep warm for 10 minutes before carving. Serve hot or at room temperature.

Roasted Chicken with Sage and White Wine
Pollo Arrosto alla Salvia

MAKES 4 SERVINGS

The method for this roast chicken is different from the previous recipe. Here the chicken roasts at a higher temperature, which saves some time and gives the skin more color. Wine and lemon juice transform chicken pan juices into a little sauce for the chicken.

1 chicken (3½ to 4 pounds)
4 large garlic cloves
Small branch of fresh sage
Salt and freshly ground black pepper
1 small lemon, thinly sliced
2 tablespoons olive oil
½ cup dry white wine
2 tablespoons fresh lemon juice

1 Place a rack in the center of the oven. Preheat the oven to 450°F. Oil a roasting pan large enough to hold the chicken. Place a roasting rack in the pan.

2 Place the garlic, sage, and lemon slices inside the cavity. Rub the oil over the skin and sprinkle with salt and pepper. Tuck the wingtips behind the back of the chicken. Tie the legs together with kitchen string.

3 Place the chicken on the rack in the pan. Roast 20 minutes. Pour the wine and lemon juice over the chicken. Roast 45 minutes more, basting occasionally with the pan juices. The chicken is done when the juices run clear when the chicken thigh is pierced and the temperature in the thickest part of the thigh is 170°F on an instant-read thermometer.

4 Transfer the chicken to a platter. Cover loosely with foil and keep warm for 10 minutes before carving. Serve hot with the pan juices.

Chicken in the Style of Roast Pig
Pollo alla Porchetta

MAKES 4 TO 6 SERVINGS

In central Italy, porchetta is a whole pig roasted on a spit with fennel, garlic, black pepper, and rosemary. But that is not a dish that is easily made at home, so cooks adapt those same complementary flavors to smaller cuts of pork, rabbit, fish, and poultry. When I first tasted this recipe at the home of winemakers in Umbria, it was made with a guinea fowl, which is similar to a large chicken but with more flavor. A large roasting chicken works just as well. You can use whole fennel seeds in this recipe, or substitute fennel pollen, which is ground up fennel seeds, available at some specialty stores.

2 large garlic cloves, finely chopped
2 tablespoons rosemary leaves, finely chopped
1 tablespoon fennel seeds or fennel pollen
Salt and freshly ground black pepper
2 tablespoons olive oil
1 large chicken (about 5 pounds)

1 Place a rack in the center of the oven. Preheat the oven to 450°F. Oil a roasting pan just large enough to hold the chicken.

2 Very finely chop together the garlic, rosemary, and fennel seeds. Put the seasonings in a small bowl. Add salt and a generous grinding of black pepper. Add 1 tablespoon oil and stir to combine.

3 Rinse the chicken and pat dry. Tuck the wing tips behind the back. With your fingers, loosen the skin around the breast and legs. Insert half the herb mixture evenly under the skin of the chicken. Put the remainder inside the cavity. Tie the legs together with kitchen string. Brush the skin with the remaining oil. Place the chicken breast side up in the pan.

4 Roast for 20 minutes. Reduce the heat to 375°F. Roast 45 to 60 minutes. The chicken is done when the juices run clear when the thigh is pierced and the temperature in the thickest part of the thigh is 170°F on an instant-read thermometer.

5 Transfer the chicken to a platter. Cover loosely with foil and keep warm for 10 minutes before carving. Serve hot or at room temperature.

Roasted Chicken with Marsala and Anchovies

Pollo Arrosto alla Catanzarese

MAKES 4 SERVINGS

Giuseppe, an acquaintance in New York, told me that he was originally from Calabria. When I told him that I was planning to visit Catanzaro in that region, he said that I must be sure to visit a type of rustic restaurant known as a putica *to eat* morzello. *He explained that a* putica *is a humble eatery that often has no sign outside, just a large loaf of ring-shaped bread known as a* pitta *mounted near the door. Inside there are large communal tables, and everyone is served an individual pitta filled with morzello, a stew made from cut-up pieces of tripe and other innards. The name comes from* morsi, *meaning "bites."*

My plans changed, and I never did get to Catanzaro, but I do enjoy making this roast chicken that Giuseppe told me his grandmother used to make for holidays and special occasions. The combination of anchovies, Marsala, and chicken flavors may seem unusual, but the anchovies melt down, adding only a salty richness to the chicken juices, while the Marsala adds a nutty flavor and helps the chicken turn a beautiful golden brown.

I chicken (3¹/₂ to 4 pounds)
Salt and freshly ground black pepper
¹/₂ lemon
2 tablespoons unsalted butter
8 anchovy fillets, chopped
¹/₄ teaspoon freshly ground nutmeg
¹/₂ cup dry Marsala

1 Place a rack in the center of the oven. Preheat the oven to 450°F. Oil a roasting pan just large enough to hold the chicken.

2 Rinse the chicken and pat dry. Tuck the wing tips behind the back. Sprinkle inside and out with salt and pepper. Place the lemon half, butter, anchovies, and nutmeg inside the cavity. Place the chicken in the pan breast-side down.

3 Roast the chicken 20 minutes. Carefully turn the chicken breast-side up and roast 20 minutes more. Pour the Marsala over the chicken. Roast 20 to 30 minutes more, basting 2 or 3 times with the pan juices. The chicken is done when the juices run clear when the thigh is pierced and the temperature in the thickest part of the thigh is 170°F on an instant-read thermometer.

4 Transfer the chicken to a platter. Cover loosely with foil and keep warm for 10 minutes before carving. Serve hot.

Stuffed Roasted Capon

Cappone Ripene al Forno

MAKES 6 TO 8 SERVINGS

For Christmas dinner in the Lombardy region, stuffing for roast capon is traditionally pork sausage and fresh or dried fruit. Mostarda—a variety of fruits, such as figs, tangerines, apricots, cherries, citron, and peaches, jarred in a mustard-flavored syrup—is the typical accompaniment.

Capons, which are castrated roosters weighing 8 to 10 pounds, are generally available fresh around the holidays and frozen the rest of the year. They are meaty and juicy, with a flavor like chicken, only more intense. A large roasting chicken or small turkey can be used for this recipe, but you will need to adjust the cooking time according to weight.

8 ounces day-old Italian or French bread,
    crusts removed and torn into pieces
¹/₂ cup milk
I pound plain pork sausage, casings removed
10 pitted prunes, chopped
2 large eggs, beaten
¹/₄ teaspoon freshly grated nutmeg
Salt and freshly ground black pepper
I capon (about 8 pounds)
2 tablespoons olive oil
2 tablespoons chopped fresh rosemary
¹/₂ cup dry white wine

1 In a large bowl, soak the bread in the milk 15 minutes. Then, remove the bread, discard the milk, and squeeze the bread to drain off the excess liquid. Place it back in the bowl.

2 Add the sausage, prunes, eggs, salt and pepper to taste, and nutmeg and mix well.

3 Place a rack in the center of the oven. Preheat the oven to 350°F. Oil a roasting pan large enough to hold the capon.

4 Rinse the capon and pat dry. Lightly stuff the bird with the sausage mixture. (Any leftover stuffing can be baked at the same time in a buttered baking dish.) Mix together the oil, rosemary, and salt and pepper to taste. Rub the bird all over with the mixture. Place the bird breast-side down in the pan.

5 Roast 30 minutes. Pour the wine into the pan. After another 30 minutes and every half hour thereafter, baste the bird with the accumulated juices. When the bird has roasted 60 minutes, carefully turn the bird breast-side up. Roast a total of 2 hours and 15 minutes, or until an instant-read thermometer inserted in the thickest part of the thigh measures 180°F.

6 Transfer the capon to a platter. Cover lightly with foil for 15 minutes to keep warm.

7 Tip the pan and skim the fat from the pan juices with a large spoon. Carve the capon and serve with the juices and stuffing.

Stuffed Chicken in Ragù

Pollo Ripieno al Ragù

MAKES 6 SERVINGS

My grandmother used to make chicken this way for holidays and special occasions. The stuffing not only flavors the chicken from within, but any that spills out into the sauce gives it extra flavor.

A generous amount of sauce will surround the chicken. You can set it aside to serve with pasta for another meal.

8 ounces spinach, trimmed
8 ounces ground veal
1 large egg, beaten
1/4 cup plain dry bread crumbs
1/4 cup freshly grated Pecorino Romano
Salt and freshly ground black pepper
1 chicken (3 1/2 to 4 pounds)
2 tablespoons olive oil
1 medium onion, chopped
1/2 cup dry white wine
1 (28-ounce) can peeled tomatoes, passed through a food mill
1 bay leaf

1 Put the spinach in a large pot over medium heat with 1/4 cup of water. Cover and cook 2 to 3 minutes or until wilted and tender. Drain and cool. Wrap the spinach in a lint-free cloth and squeeze out as much water as possible. Finely chop the spinach.

2 In a large bowl, combine the chopped spinach, the veal, egg, bread crumbs, cheese, and salt and pepper to taste. Mix well.

3 Rinse the chicken and pat it dry. Sprinkle inside and out with salt and pepper. Fill the chicken cavity loosely with the stuffing.

4 In a large heavy saucepan, heat the oil over medium heat. Add the chicken breast-side down. Cook 10 minutes or until browned. Turn the chicken breast-side up. Scatter the onion around the chicken and brown, about 10 minutes more. Scatter any leftover stuffing around the chicken. Add the wine and simmer 1 minute. Pour the tomatoes, bay leaf, and salt and pepper to taste over the chicken. Lower the heat and partially cover the pan. Cook 30 minutes.

5 Carefully turn the chicken. Cook partially covered 30 minutes more. If the sauce is too thin, uncover the pan. Cook 15 minutes more, or until the chicken comes away from the bone when tested with a fork.

6 Remove the chicken from the sauce. Carve the chicken and arrange it on a platter. Skim the fat from the sauce with a large spoon or with a fat separator. Spoon some of the sauce over the chicken and serve hot.

Roasted Boiled Chicken
Pollo Bollito Arrosto

MAKES 4 SERVINGS

Leona Ancona Cantone, a friend from high school days, told me that her mother, whose family came from Abruzzo, used to make something like this many years ago. I imagine that the recipe came about as a way to get the most out of a chicken, because it provides both broth and roasted meat. The boiling and roasting method makes for a very tender bird.

1 chicken (3¹/₂ to 4 pounds)
1 carrot
1 celery rib
1 onion, peeled
4 or 5 parsley sprigs
Salt
²/₃ cup plain bread crumbs
¹/₃ cup freshly grated Parmigiano-Reggiano
¹/₂ teaspoon dried oregano, crumbled
2 to 3 tablespoons olive oil
2 tablespoons lemon juice
Freshly ground black pepper

1 Tuck the wing tips behind the back. Place the chicken in a large pot and add cold water to cover. Bring the liquid to a simmer and cook 10 minutes. Skim off the foam with a large spoon.

2 Add the carrot, celery, onion, parsley, and salt to taste. Cook over medium-low heat until the chicken is tender when pierced with a fork in the thickest part of the thigh and the juices run clear, about 45 minutes. Remove the chicken from the pot. (You can add more ingredients, such as meat or chicken trimmings, to the broth and cook it for another 60 minutes or so. Strain and refrigerate the broth or freeze for soups or other uses.)

3 Place a rack in the center of the oven. Preheat the oven to 450°F. Oil a large baking pan.

4 On a plate, mix the bread crumbs, cheese, oregano, olive oil, lemon juice, and salt and pepper to taste.

5 With heavy kitchen shears, cut the chicken into serving pieces. Dip the chicken in the crumbs, patting them to adhere. Place the chicken in the prepared baking pan.

6 Bake 30 minutes or until the crust is browned and crisp. Serve hot or at room temperature.

Chicken Under a Brick
Pollo al Mattone

MAKES 2 SERVINGS

Split, flattened chicken cooked under a weight turns out crisp on the outside and juicy within. In Tuscany, you can buy a special heavy terra cotta disk that flattens the chicken and holds it evenly against the surface of the pan. I use a heavy cast-iron skillet, covered on the outside with aluminum foil, as a weight, but ordinary bricks wrapped in foil will work well, too. It is important to use a very small chicken or even a cornish hen with this recipe; otherwise the outside will become dry before the meat near the bone is cooked.

1 small chicken (about 3 pounds)
Salt and freshly ground black pepper
¹/₃ cup olive oil
1 lemon, cut into wedges

1 Pat the chicken dry. With a large chef's knife or poultry shears, split the chicken along the backbone. On a cutting board, open the chicken flat like a book. Cut out the keel bone that separates the breasts. Remove the wing tips and second wing section at the joint. Flatten the chicken by pounding it gently with a rubber mallet or other heavy object. Sprinkle it generously on both sides with salt and pepper.

2 Choose a skillet that will hold the flattened chicken as well as the weight. Choose a second heavy skillet or pan that will be able to press the chicken down evenly. Cover the underside with foil, folding the foil edges over the inside of the pan to secure it. If necessary for weight, fill the foil-covered skillet with bricks.

3 Pour the oil into the cooking skillet and heat over medium heat. Add the chicken skin-side down. Place the weight on top. Cook until the skin is golden brown, 12 to 15 minutes.

4 Slide a thin spatula under the chicken to loosen it from the pan. Carefully turn the chicken skin-side up. Replace the weight and cook the chicken until the juices run clear when the thigh is pierced, about 12 minutes more. Serve hot with lemon wedges.

Lemon Chicken Salad
Insalata di Pollo al Limone

MAKES 6 SERVINGS

One very hot summer day when I was in Bordighera, in Liguria near the French border, I stopped at a cafe for lunch and to get out of the sun. The waiter recommended this freshly made chicken salad, which reminded me of the salade niçoise *I had eaten a few days earlier in France. Canned tuna is typical in Nice, but this Italian version with chicken is good too.*

This is a quick chicken salad so I use chicken breasts, but it can be made with the meat from whole chickens. The chicken can be cooked ahead and marinated in the dressing, but the vegetables taste best if they are not refrigerated after cooking. You can keep them at room temperature for an hour or so until ready to assemble the salad.

**4 cups homemade Chicken Broth (page 63),
    or a mix of store-bought broth and water**

4 to 6 small waxy potatoes, such as Yukon gold

8 ounces green beans, cut into 1-inch pieces

Salt

**2 pounds boneless, skinless chicken breasts,
    trimmed of fat**

DRESSING

¹/₂ cup extra-virgin olive oil

2 tablespoons fresh lemon juice, or to taste

1 tablespoon capers, rinsed, drained, and chopped

¹/₂ teaspoon dried oregano, crumbled

Salt and freshly ground black pepper

2 medium tomatoes, cut into wedges

1 Prepare the broth, if necessary. Place the potatoes in a saucepan. Add cold water to cover. Cover the pan and bring the water to a simmer. Cook until tender when pierced with a knife, about 20 minutes. Drain the potatoes and let cool slightly. Peel off the skins.

2 Bring a medium saucepan of water to a boil. Add the green beans and salt to taste. Cook until the beans are tender, about 10 minutes. Drain the beans and cool under running water. Pat the beans dry.

3 In a large saucepan, bring the broth to a simmer (if it is not just made). Add the chicken breasts and cover the pan. Cook, turning the chicken once, 15 minutes, or until tender and the chicken juices run clear when pierced with a fork. Drain the chicken breasts, reserving the broth for another use. Cut the chicken into crosswise slices and place in a medium bowl.

4 In a small bowl, whisk together the dressing ingredients. Pour half the dressing over the chicken. Toss the pieces well to coat. Taste and adjust seasoning. Mound the chicken in the center of a large platter. Cover and chill up to 2 hours.

5 Arrange the green beans, potatoes, and tomatoes around the chicken. Drizzle with the remaining dressing and serve immediately.

Chicken Salad with Two Peppers

Insalata di Pollo con Peperoni

MAKES 8 TO 10 SERVINGS

Both roasted bell peppers and pickled hot cherry peppers add interest to this salad. If the cherry peppers are not available, substitute another pickled chile, such as jalapeno or peperoncino. Jarred roasted peppers are convenient if you don't have time to roast your own. This recipe makes a lot of chicken, so it is great for a party. If you prefer, the recipe can easily be halved.

2 small chickens (about 3 pounds each)

2 carrots

2 celery ribs

1 onion

A few parsley sprigs

Salt

6 black peppercorns

6 red or yellow bell peppers, roasted, peeled, and cut into thin strips (see page 445)

Sauce

1/2 cup olive oil

3 tablespoons wine vinegar

1/4 cup chopped fresh flat-leaf parsley

2 tablespoons finely chopped pickled hot cherry peppers, or to taste

1 garlic clove, finely chopped

4 to 6 cups mixed baby greens

1 Place the chickens in a large stockpot and add cold water to cover. Bring the liquid to a simmer and cook 10 minutes. With a spoon, skim off and discard the foam that rises to the surface.

2 Add the carrot, celery, onion, parsley, and salt to taste. Cook on medium-low heat until the chicken is tender and the juices run clear, about 45 minutes.

3 Meanwhile, roast the bell peppers, if necessary. When the chicken is cooked, remove it from the pot. Reserve the broth for another use.

4 Let the chicken drain and cool. Remove the meat. Cut the meat into 2-inch chunks and place them in a bowl with the roasted bell peppers.

5 In a medium bowl, whisk together the sauce ingredients. Drizzle half the sauce over the chicken and peppers and toss well. Cover and chill in the refrigerator up to 2 hours.

6 Just before serving, toss the chicken with the remaining sauce. Taste and adjust seasoning, adding more vinegar if needed. Arrange the greens on a serving platter. Top with chicken and peppers. Serve immediately.

Piedmont-Style Chicken Salad

Insalata di Pollo Piemontese

MAKES 6 SERVINGS

In the Piedmont region, restaurant meals typically begin with a long series of antipasti. That is how I first tasted this salad at Belvedere, a classic restaurant of the region. I like to serve it as a main dish for lunch in spring or summer.

For a quick meal, make this salad with a store-bought roasted chicken instead of poached chicken. Roasted turkey would also be good.

1 chicken (3 1/2 to 4 pounds)

2 carrots

2 celery ribs

1 onion

A few parsley sprigs

Salt

6 black peppercorns

8 ounces white mushrooms, thinly sliced

2 celery ribs, thinly sliced

1/4 cup olive oil

1 (2-ounce) can anchovy fillets, drained and chopped

1 teaspoon Dijon mustard

2 tablespoons freshly squeezed lemon juice

Salt and freshly ground black pepper

About 6 cups salad greens, torn into bite-size pieces

A small chunk of Parmigiano-Reggiano

1 Place the chicken in a large pot and add cold water to cover. Bring the liquid to a simmer and cook 10 minutes. With a large spoon, skim off the foam that rises to the surface.

2 Add the carrots, celery, onion, parsley, and salt to taste. Cook on medium-low heat until the chicken is tender and the juices run clear, about 45 minutes. Remove the chicken from the pot. Reserve the broth for another use.

3 Let the chicken drain and cool slightly. Remove the meat from the skin and bones. Cut the meat into 2-inch chunks.

4 In a large bowl, combine the chicken chunks, mushrooms, and thinly sliced celery.

5 In a medium bowl, whisk together the oil, anchovies, mustard, lemon juice, and salt and pepper to taste. Toss the chicken mixture with the dressing. Spread the salad greens on a platter and top with the chicken mixture.

6 With a swivel-blade vegetable peeler, shave the Parmigiano-Reggiano over the salad. Serve immediately.

❧ Turkey, Duck, and Quail

Rolled Stuffed Turkey Breast
Rollata di Tacchino

MAKES 6 SERVINGS

Turkey breast halves are easy to find in most super-markets. In this dish from Emilia-Romagna, after the turkey breast is boned and flattened, the meat is rolled up and roasted with the skin draped over it to keep it moist. Serve the roast hot or cold. It also makes a good sandwich served with lemon mayonnaise.

¹/₂ turkey breast (about 2¹/₂ pounds)
1 garlic clove, finely chopped
1 tablespoon chopped fresh rosemary
Salt and freshly ground black pepper
2 ounces thinly sliced imported Italian prosciutto
2 tablespoons olive oil

1 Place a rack in the center of the oven. Preheat the oven to 350°F. Oil a small roasting pan.

2 With a sharp knife, remove the turkey skin in one piece. Set it aside. Cut the turkey breast meat away from the bone. Place the breast boned-side up on a cutting board. Starting at one long side, cut the turkey breast in half lengthwise, stopping just short of the other long side. Open the turkey breast like a book. Flatten the turkey with a meat mallet to about a ¹/₂-inch thickness.

3 Sprinkle the turkey with the garlic, rosemary, and salt and pepper to taste. Lay the prosciutto on top. Starting at one of the long sides, roll the meat into a cylinder. Drape the turkey skin over the roll. Tie the roll with kitchen string at 2-inch intervals. Place the roll seamside down in the prepared pan. Drizzle with the oil and sprinkle with salt and pepper.

4 Roast the turkey 50 to 60 minutes, or until the internal temperature of the meat is 155°F on an instant-read thermometer. Let stand 15 minutes before slicing. Serve hot or at room temperature.

Poached Turkey Meat Loaf

Polpettone di Tacchino

MAKES 6 SERVINGS

In Italy, turkey is often cut into pieces or ground up rather than roasted whole. This loaf from Piedmont is poached, giving it a texture that is more like a pâté.

This loaf is good hot or cold. Serve with Green Sauce (page 102), or a fresh tomato sauce.

4 or 5 slices Italian bread, crusts removed and
    torn into pieces (about 1 cup)

1/2 cup milk

2 tablespoons chopped fresh flat-leaf parsley

1 large garlic clove

4 ounces pancetta, chopped

1/2 cup freshly grated Parmigiano-Reggiano

Salt and freshly ground black pepper

1 pound ground turkey

2 large eggs

1/4 cup pistachios, skinned and coarsely chopped

1 Soak the bread in the cold milk for 5 minutes or until soft. Gently squeeze the bread and place it in a food processor fitted with a steel blade. Discard the milk.

2 Add the parsley, garlic, pancetta, cheese, and salt and pepper to taste. Process until finely chopped. Add the turkey and eggs and blend until smooth. Stir in the pistachios with a spatula.

3 Lay a 14 × 12–inch piece of dampened cheese-cloth out on a flat surface. Shape the turkey mixture into an 8 × 3–inch loaf and center it on the cloth. Wrap the cloth around the turkey, enclosing it completely. With kitchen string, tie the loaf up at 2-inch intervals as though tying a roast.

4 Fill a large pot with 3 quarts of cold water. Bring the liquid to a simmer.

5 Add the loaf and poach, partly covered, 45 minutes or until the juices run clear when the loaf is pierced in the center with a fork.

6 Remove the loaf from the liquid and let cool 10 minutes. Unwrap and cut into slices to serve.

Turkey Rolls in Red Wine Tomato Sauce

Rollatini in Salsa Rosa al Vino

MAKES 4 SERVINGS

When I was first married, a neighbor gave me this recipe from her family's region of origin, Puglia. I have tinkered with it over the years, and though she used veal cutlets, I prefer to make it with turkey. The rolls can be prepared in advance and stored in the refrigerator. They reheat nicely a day or two later.

4 ounces ground veal or turkey

2 ounces pancetta, finely chopped

1/4 cup chopped fresh flat-leaf parsley

1 small garlic clove, finely chopped

1/4 cup plain dry bread crumbs

Salt and freshly ground black pepper

1 1/4 pound thin-sliced turkey cutlets, cut into 12 pieces

2 tablespoons olive oil

1/2 cup dry red wine

2 cups peeled, seeded, and chopped fresh tomatoes,
    or drained and chopped canned tomatoes

Pinch of crushed red pepper

1 In a large bowl, combine the veal, pancetta, parsley, garlic, bread crumbs, and salt and pepper to taste. Shape the mixture into 12 small sausage shapes about 3 inches long. Place one sausage at the end of a turkey cutlet. Roll up the meat to enclose the sausage. With a toothpick, pin the roll closed in the center, parallel to the roll. Repeat with the remaining sausages and cutlets.

2 In a medium skillet, heat the olive oil over medium heat. Add the rolls and brown on all sides, about 10 minutes. Add the wine and bring it to a simmer. Cook 1 minute, turning the rolls.

3 Add the tomatoes, salt to taste, and a pinch of crushed red pepper. Reduce the heat to low. Partially cover the pan. Cook, adding a little warm water

as needed to prevent the sauce from becoming too dry, for 20 minutes or until the rolls are tender when pierced with a fork.

4 Transfer the rolls to a platter. Remove the toothpicks and spoon the sauce over the top. Serve hot.

Duck Breast with Sweet-and-Sour Figs
Petto di Anatra con Agrodolce di Fichi

MAKES 4 SERVINGS

This contemporary recipe from Piedmont for duck breasts sautéed with figs and balsamic vinegar is perfect for a special dinner party. Duck breast is at its best when cooked to medium-rare and still pink in the thickest part. Serve with buttered spinach and a potato gratin.

2 boneless duck breasts (about 2 pounds each)
Salt and freshly ground black pepper
8 fresh ripe green or black figs, or dried figs
I tablespoon sugar
1/4 cup aged balsamic vinegar
I tablespoon unsalted butter
I tablespoon chopped fresh flat-leaf parsley

1 Remove the duck breasts from the refrigerator 30 minutes before cooking. Rinse the duck breasts and pat dry. Cut 2 or 3 diagonal slashes in the skin of the duck breasts without cutting through to the meat. Sprinkle generously with salt and pepper.

2 Meanwhile, cut the fresh figs in half or quarters if large. If using dried figs, soak them in warm water until plump, 15 to 30 minutes. Drain, then cut into quarters.

3 Place a rack in the center of the oven. Preheat the oven to 350°F. Have ready a small baking pan.

4 Heat a large non-stick skillet over medium-high heat. Add the duck breasts skin-side down. Cook the duck without turning it until nicely browned on the skin side, 4 to 5 minutes.

5 Brush the baking pan with some of the duck fat from the skillet. Place the duck breasts skin-side up in the pan and roast 5 to 6 minutes, or until the meat is a rosy pink color when cut in the thickest part.

6 While the duck is in the oven, pour off the fat from the skillet but don't wipe it clean. Add the figs, sugar, and balsamic vinegar. Cook, swirling the pan, until the liquid is slightly thickened, about 2 minutes. Remove from the heat and swirl in the butter.

7 When done, place the duck breasts on a cutting board. Cut the breasts into 3/4-inch diagonal slices. Fan the slices on 4 warm serving plates. Spoon on the fig sauce. Sprinkle with parsley and serve immediately.

Spiced Roasted Duck
Anatra allo Spezie

MAKES 2 TO 4 SERVINGS

In Piedmont, wild ducks are braised with red wine, vinegar, and spices. Because the Peking variety of domesticated ducks that are available in the United States are very fatty, I have adapted this recipe for roasting. There is not a lot of meat on a duck, so expect to get only two large or four small servings. Poultry shears are a big help in cutting the duck into serving pieces.

I duck (about 5 pounds)
2 garlic cloves, chopped
2 medium onions, thinly sliced
I tablespoon chopped fresh rosemary
3 whole cloves
1/2 teaspoon ground cinnamon
1/4 cup dry red wine
2 tablespoons red wine vinegar

1 With a fork, prick the skin all over to allow the fat to escape when cooked. Be careful to prick only the surface of the skin and avoid puncturing the meat.

(continues)

2 In a medium bowl, mix together the garlic, onions, rosemary, cloves, and cinnamon. Scatter about a third of the mixture in a medium roasting pan. Place the duck in the pan and stuff some of the mixture inside. Pile the remaining mixture on top of the duck. Cover and refrigerate overnight.

3 Place a rack in the center of the oven. Preheat the oven to 325°F. Scrape the marinade ingredients off the duck into the pan. Roast the duck, breast-side down, for 30 minutes.

4 Turn the duck breast-side up and pour on the wine and vinegar. Roast 1 hour, basting every 15 minutes with the liquid in the pan. Raise the oven temperature to 400°F. Roast 30 minutes more, or until the duck is nicely browned and the temperature in the thigh registers 175°F on an instant-read thermometer.

5 Transfer the duck to a cutting board. Cover with foil and let rest 15 minutes. Strain the pan juices and skim the fat with a spoon. Reheat the pan juices if necessary.

6 Cut the duck into serving pieces and serve hot with the juices.

Quail in the Pan with Porcini

Quaglie in Tegame con Funghi Porcini

MAKES 4 TO 8 SERVINGS

In Buttrio, in Friuli–Venezia Giulia, my husband and I ate at Trattoria Al Parco, a restaurant that has been in business since the 1920s. The heart of the restaurant is the fogolar, *an enormous open fireplace typical of homes in this region. People in Friuli often recount fondly childhood memories of nights spent around the fogolar, cooking and telling stories. The fogolar at Al Parco is lit every night and used for grilling meats and mushrooms. The night that we were there, little birds in a rich mushroom sauce were the specialty.*

1 ounce dried porcini mushrooms (about ³/₄ cup)
2 cups hot water
8 quail, prepared as directed at far right
8 sage leaves
4 slices pancetta
Salt and freshly ground black pepper
2 tablespoons unsalted butter
1 tablespoon olive oil
1 small onion, finely chopped
1 carrot, finely chopped
1 tender celery rib, finely chopped
¹/₂ cup dry white wine
2 teaspoons tomato paste

1 Soak the mushrooms in the water for at least 30 minutes. Lift the mushrooms out of the water, reserving the liquid. Rinse the mushrooms under cool running water, paying special attention to the stem ends where soil collects. Strain the reserved mushroom liquid through a cloth napkin or paper coffee filter into a bowl. Chop the mushrooms coarsely. Set aside.

2 Rinse the quail inside and out and pat them thoroughly dry. Look them over for any pinfeathers and remove them. Place a piece of pancetta, a sage leaf, and a pinch of salt and pepper inside.

3 In a large skillet, heat the butter and oil over medium heat. Add the quail and cook, turning them occasionally, until nicely browned on all sides, about 15 minutes. Transfer the quail to a plate. Add the onion, carrot, and celery to the pan. Cook, stirring frequently, 5 minutes or until softened.

4 Add the wine and simmer 1 minute. Stir in the mushrooms, tomato paste, and mushroom liquid. Return the quail to the pan. Sprinkle with salt and pepper.

5 Bring the liquid to a simmer. Reduce heat to low. Cover and cook, turning and basting the quail occasionally, about 1 hour or until the birds are very tender when pierced with a fork.

6 If there is too much liquid in the pan, remove the quail to a serving platter and cover with foil to keep them warm. Turn the heat to high and boil the liquid until it is reduced. Spoon the sauce over the quail and serve immediately.

Grilled Quail
Qualie alla Griglia

SERVES 2 TO 4

The restaurant at La Badia in Orvieto specializes in meats cooked on a wood-fired rotisserie. Sausages, small birds, and large roasts slowly turn over the flames, filling the restaurant with mouthwatering aromas. These quail, cooked on a barbecue grill or in the broiler, are inspired by those I ate in Umbria. The birds turn out crisp on the outside and juicy on the inside.

4 quail, thawed if frozen
I large garlic clove, finely chopped
I tablespoon fresh rosemary, chopped
¹/4 cup olive oil
Salt and freshly ground black pepper
I lemon, cut into wedges

I Rinse the quail inside and out and pat them thoroughly dry. Look them over for any pinfeathers and remove them. With poultry shears, cut the quail in half through the back and breastbone. Gently pound the quail halves with a meat or rubber mallet to flatten them slightly.

2 In a large bowl, combine the garlic, rosemary, oil, and salt and pepper to taste. Add the quail to the bowl, stirring to coat. Cover and refrigerate 1 hour up to overnight.

3 Place a barbecue grill or broiler rack about 5 inches away from the heat source. Preheat the grill or broiler.

4 Grill or broil the quail halves until nicely browned on both sides, about 10 minutes. Serve hot with lemon wedges.

Quail

Italians love to cook and eat quail. If you haven't tried eating these tiny tender birds, you should; they are widely available in the United States, too. I usually buy them frozen. Because they are small, buy two per person for a main course.

To prepare them, thaw the frozen birds in the refrigerator overnight, then rinse them thoroughly in cool water. Drain the birds and pat them dry inside and out. Look them over for any tiny pinfeathers and pull them out with your fingers or tweezers.

Either tuck the wing tips behind the backs of the quail or trim them off at the first joint with kitchen shears. Stuff the birds if called for in the recipe. Tie the legs together with a bit of kitchen string.

When grilling quail, I cook the meat just until it is browned on the outside and rosy and juicy on the inside. When preparing quail in a stew or braised dish, I cook it longer—until the meat is tender enough to pull right off with a fork.

Quail with Tomatoes and Rosemary
Quaglie in Salsa

MAKES 4 TO 8 SERVINGS

Molise, located on the Adriatic coast in southern Italy, is one of the least-known regions of the country. It is largely agricultural, with few facilities for tourists, and until the 1960s was actually part of the combined region of Abruzzo and Molise. My husband and I went there to visit Majo di Norante, a wine estate and agriturismo (a working farm or winery that also operates as a hostelry) that produces some of the best wines of the region.

We ate quail prepared in a light tomato sauce flavored with rosemary at the Vecchia Trattoria da Tonino in Campobasso. Try it with a Majo di Norante wine, such as a sangiovese.

1 small onion, chopped

2 ounces pancetta, chopped

2 tablespoons olive oil

8 fresh or thawed frozen quail

1 tablespoon chopped fresh rosemary

Salt and freshly ground black pepper

3 tablespoons tomato paste

1 cup dry white wine

1 In a large skillet with a tight-fitting lid, cook the onion and pancetta in the olive oil over medium heat until the onion is golden, about 10 minutes. Push the ingredients to the sides of the pan.

2 Rinse the quail inside and out and pat them thoroughly dry. Look them over for any pinfeathers and remove them. Add the quail to the pan and brown them on all sides, about 15 minutes. Sprinkle with the rosemary, and salt and pepper to taste.

3 In a small bowl, stir together the tomato paste and wine. Pour the mixture over the quail and stir well. Reduce the heat to low. Cover and cook, turning the quail occasionally, about 50 minutes or until they are very tender when pierced with a fork. Serve hot.

Braised Quail
Quaglie Stufate

MAKES 4 SERVINGS

Gianni Cosetti is the chef and owner of the Restaurant Roma in Tolmezzo, in the mountainous Carnia region of Friuli–Venezia Giulia. He is famous for his modern interpretations of traditional recipes and local ingredients. When I ate there, he told me that this recipe is traditionally prepared with becacce, small game birds that were hunted as they passed through the region on their annual migration. Today, Gianni uses only fresh game birds and wraps them in a jacket of pancetta so that they stay moist and tender as they cook He recommended serving them with a schioppetino, a red wine from Friuli.

8 quail

16 juniper berries

About 16 fresh sage leaves

4 garlic cloves, thinly sliced

Salt and freshly ground black pepper

8 thin slices pancetta

2 tablespoons unsalted butter

2 tablespoons olive oil

1 cup dry white wine

1 Rinse the quail inside and out and pat them thoroughly dry. Look them over for any pinfeathers and remove them. Stuff each quail with 2 juniper berries, one sage leaf, and some of the garlic slices. Sprinkle the birds with salt and pepper. Place a sage leaf on top of each quail. Unroll the pancetta and wrap a slice around each quail. Tie a piece of kitchen string around the pancetta to hold it in place.

2 In a large skillet with a tight fitting lid, melt the butter with the oil over medium heat. Add the quail and brown the birds on all sides, about 15 minutes.

3 Add the wine and bring to a simmer. Cover the pan, lower the heat, and cook, turning and basting the quail with the liquid several times, 45 to 50 minutes or until the quail are very tender. Add a little water if the pan becomes too dry. Serve hot.

Meat

Steaks

Grilled Steak, Florentine Style

Steak with Balsamic Glaze

Shell Steak with Shallots, Pancetta,
and Red Wine

Sliced Steak with Arugula

Tenderloin Steak with Gorgonzola

Beef Stews and Braises

Stuffed Beef Rolls in Tomato Sauce

Beef and Beer

Beef and Onion Stew

Peppery Beef Stew

Friuli-Style Beef Stew

Mixed Meat Stew, Hunter's Style

Beef Goulash

Oxtail Stew, Roman Style

Braised Beef Shank

Meatballs and Ground Beef Dishes

Beef-Stuffed Eggplant

Neapolitan Meatballs

Meatballs with Pine Nuts and Raisins

Meatballs with Cabbage and Tomatoes

Meatballs, Bologna Style

Meatballs in Marsala

Meatloaf, Old Naples Style

Beef Roasts

Pot Roast with Red Wine

Pot Roast with Onion Sauce and Pasta

Sicilian Stuffed Beef Roll

Roast Tenderloin with Olive Sauce

Mixed Boiled Meats

Sardinian Saffron Meat Pies

(continues)

Veal Cutlets (Scaloppine)

Veal Cutlets with Prosciutto and Sage

Veal Cutlets with Truffles

Veal with Marsala and Mushrooms

Veal Rolls in White Wine

Veal Rolls with Anchovies

Veal Rolls with Spinach

Veal Rolls with Prosciutto and Cheese

Grilled Veal Rolls with Mozarella
and Bread Crumbs

Veal Chops

Skillet Veal Chops

Veal Chops with Rosemary and White Wine

Roasted Veal Chops

Veal Chops with Sweet Peppers

Stuffed Veal Chops with Ham and Fontina

Veal Chops, Milan Style

Braised Veal Chops

Veal Stews

Veal, Potato, and Green Bean Stew

Veal Stew with Rosemary and Peas

Veal and Pepper Stew

Veal Stew with Red Wine

Veal Goulash with Cream

Veal, Sausage, and Mushroom Skewers

Veal Shanks

Veal Shanks, Milan Style

Veal Shanks with Barbera

Veal Shanks with Porcini

Roasted Veal Shanks

Veal Roast, Grandmother's Style

Veal Roasts

Veal Roast with Pancetta

Veal in Tuna Sauce

Braised Veal Shoulder

Other Veal Dishes

Veal-Stuffed Cabbage

Veal and Tuna Loaf

Venetian Liver and Onions

Stuffed Breast of Veal

Pork Sausages

Sausage and Pepper Skillet

Roasted Sausages and Potatoes

Umbrian Sausage and Lentil Stew

Sausages with Grapes

Sausages with Olives and White Wine

Sausages with Mushrooms

Sausages with Broccoli Rabe

Sausages with Lentils

Pork Ribs and Chops

Pork Ribs and Cabbage

Grilled Spareribs

Grilled Marinated Pork Chops

Spareribs, Friuli Style

Spareribs with Tomato Sauce

Spiced Ribs, Tuscan Style

Spareribs and Beans

Spicy Pork Chops with Pickled Peppers

Pork Chops with Rosemary and Apples

Pork Chops with Mushroom-Tomato Sauce

Pork Chops with Porcini and Red Wine

Pork Chops with Cabbage

Pork Chops with Fennel and White Wine

Pork Chops, Pizzamaker's Style

Pork Chops, Molise Style

Pork Tenderloins and Roasts

Balsamic-Glazed Pork Tenderloin
with Arugula and Parmigiano

Herbed Pork Tenderloin

Calabrian-Style Pork Tenderloin
with Honey and Chile

Roast Pork with Potatoes and Rosemary

Pork Loin with Lemon

Pork Loin with Apples and Grappa

Roast Pork with Hazelnuts and Cream

Tuscan Pork Loin

Roast Pork Shoulder with Fennel

Roast Suckling Pig

Boneless Spiced Pork Loin Roast

Braised Pork Shoulder in Milk

Braised Pork Shoulder with Grapes

Beer-Braised Pork Shoulder

Lamb Chops

Lamb Chops with White Wine

Lamb Chops with Capers, Lemon, and Sage

Lamb Chops in Crispy Coating

Lamb Chops with Artichokes and Olives

Lamb Chops with Tomato, Caper,
and Anchovy Sauce

"Burn-the-Fingers" Lamb Chops

Grilled Lamb, Basilicata Style

Grilled Lamb Skewers

(continues)

Lamb Stews and Braises

Lamb Stew with Rosemary, Mint,
and White Wine

Umbrian Lamb Stew with Chickpea Puree

Hunter's-Style Lamb

Lamb, Potato, and Tomato Stew

Lamb and Pepper Stew

Lamb Casserole with Eggs

Lamb or Kid with Potatoes, Sicilian Style

Apulian Lamb and Potato Casserole

Lamb Shanks

Lamb Shanks with Chickpeas

Lamb Shanks with Peppers and Prosciutto

Lamb Shanks with Capers and Olives

Lamb Shanks in Tomato Sauce

Lamb Roasts

Lamb Pot Roast with Cloves, Roman Style

Braised Stuffed Lamb Shoulder

Roast Leg of Lamb with Potatoes,
Garlic, and Rosemary

Leg of Lamb with Lemon,
Herbs, and Garlic

Braised Lamb–Stuffed Zucchini

Rabbit

Rabbit with White Wine and Herbs

Rabbit with Olives

Rabbit, Porchetta Style

Rabbit with Tomatoes

Sweet-and-Sour Braised Rabbit

Roasted Rabbit with Potatoes

Italians eat a much more diversified range of meats than Americans do. Pork, veal, and lamb are the most common, but Italians also eat a lot of game, especially venison and wild boar. Kid, or baby goat, is popular in the south; the flavor is very much like lamb. In some regions, such as the Veneto and Puglia, horsemeat is eaten, and I was once offered stewed donkey in Piedmont.

Italy does not have a lot of flat open land for large grazing animals like cattle, so it does not have a strong culinary tradition involving beef. The exception is Tuscany and parts of Umbria, where a variety of cattle known as Chianina is raised. This all-white breed is renowned for its flavorful meat, especially the *bistecca fiorentina*, a thick cut of porterhouse steak that is grilled over charcoal and served drizzled with the region's fine extra-virgin olive oil.

Aside from the Chianina beef, and prime cuts like the tenderloin, beef in Italy tends to be chewy. It is best pot roasted, stewed, or braised, cooked in ragù, or ground up for meatballs, loaves, or stuffings. Piedmont cooks are proud of their beef in Barolo, a large cut of meat marinated and slowly cooked in the region's most famous red wine. Neapolitans cook small beef steaks *alla pizzaiola,* braising the meat in a tomato sauce flavored with garlic and oregano. In Sicily, large thin slices of beef are stuffed, rolled, and cooked like a roast for *farsumagru,* meaning "false lean," because its plain appearance hides the filling inside.

More commonly eaten in Italy than beef is veal, the meat of young male calves, usually no more than eight to sixteen weeks old. The best is milk-fed, meaning that the animal is so young that it has never eaten grass or animal feed. The meat of milk-fed veal has a pale pink color and is very tender. Veal from older animals that feed on grain is darker red, more strongly flavored, and chewier, though it can be very good.

Juicy sausages, tender roasts, and crisp ribs are just a few of the flavorful pork preparations eaten in Italy. A favorite sight in central Italy is the *porchetta* truck—a specially outfitted van that houses a whole roasted pig highly seasoned with garlic, fennel, herbs, and black pepper. The vans can be found at fairs and markets and parked on roadsides near beaches and parks. Everyone has her or his preferred source of porchetta, and you can order a few slices to take away for dinner or a sandwich to enjoy on the spot. Those in the know ask for extra *sale,* meaning not just salt but the whole mixture of seasonings that flavors the meat.

When we visited the Majo di Norante winery in Abruzzo, we feasted on roast suckling pig cooked outdoors in a wood-burning oven. The skin was crisp and golden, and the pig was served with a lemon in its mouth and a wreath of rosemary branches around its neck.

In Friuli–Venezia Giulia, we ate at Ristorante Blasut, where the owner told us all about his annual *maialata.* The hogs that have been fattening up all summer and fall are slaughtered, and a day-long festival ensues. The event takes place in January when the weather is cold, so that there is less chance of contamination. Every bit of the pig is used. In fact, many of Italy's flavorful cold cuts, including prosciutto, pancetta, salame, and mortadella, evolved as a way to preserve meat and make use of all of the scraps.

When people ask me why the food in Italy tastes so different from the same foods prepared here, I always think of pork as an example. In Italy the meat is juicy and full of flavor because it is fatty, but in the United States pork has been bred to be very, very low in fat. With the reduction in fat, the meat also suffers from a lack of flavor and is very difficult to cook without it becoming dry and tough.

In Italy, lamb is still mostly a seasonal dish, enjoyed in the spring when lambs are very young and the meat is extremely tender. Italians associate lamb with the end of winter and the rebirth and renewal that comes with Easter. It is an essential part of holiday celebrations.

Most of Italy's lamb is raised in the central and southern regions, because the land there is hilly and rocky, better suited to grazing sheep than cattle. If you visit Tuscany, Umbria, Abruzzo, and the Marches, you will see flocks of sheep grazing on the hillsides. From a distance they look like fluffy white cotton balls strewn over the grass. In the fall, the sheep are herded toward the south and Puglia. They return to central Italy in the spring in an annual rite called the *trasumanza*. This way, the animals can feed on the natural herbs and grasses that grow in those regions at different times of the year.

Many of these sheep are raised for their milk, and central and southern Italy produce a wide variety of sheep's milk cheeses. Goats are raised for both their milk and meat, and there are numerous recipes that call for kid. Lamb and kid have a very similar flavor and texture, and either can be used in these recipes.

Rabbit is a popular meat in Italy, and you will find recipes for preparing it in every region. I would guess that it is more popular than chicken, and certainly more highly regarded. Rabbit meat is mild-tasting and lends itself to many different preparations.

Supermarket meat quality varies widely. Often, only a limited range of meats is available. Try to find a knowledgeable butcher who will cut meat to your specifications and advise you on the right cut of meat for your purpose.

When you get the meat home, store it in the refrigerator and cook it, preferably, within 24 to 48 hours. For longer storage, wrap the meat tightly and freeze it. Thaw frozen meats overnight in the refrigerator.

Rinse and pat the meat dry with paper towels just before cooking it. Moisture on the surface of the meat inhibits browning and creates steam that can toughen the meat.

❧ Steaks

Grilled Steak, Florentine Style
Bistecca Fiorentina

MAKES 6 TO 8 SERVINGS

The best-quality beef in Italy comes from the large, pure white breed of cattle known as Chianina. This breed, named for the Chiana Valley in Tuscany, is believed to be one of the oldest types of domestic cattle. Originally they were kept as draft animals and bred to be very large and docile. Because machines have taken over their work on modern farms, Chianina cattle are now raised for their high-quality meat.

Porterhouse steaks, which are a cross-section cut of the short loin and tenderloin separated by a T-shaped bone, are cut from Chianina beef and cooked this way in Tuscany. Although Chianina beef is not available in the United States, you can still turn out delicious steaks with this recipe. Buy the best-quality meat you can.

**2 porterhouse steaks, 1 1/2 inches thick
   (about 2 pounds each)**
Salt and freshly ground black pepper
Extra-virgin olive oil
Lemon wedges

1 Place a barbecue grill or broiler rack about 4 inches away from the heat source. Preheat the grill or broiler.

2 Sprinkle the steaks with salt and pepper. Grill or broil the meat 4 to 5 minutes. Turn the meat over with tongs and cook about 4 minutes more for rare, or 5 to 6 minutes for medium rare, depending on the thickness of the steaks. To check for doneness, make a small cut in the thickest part. For longer cooking, move the steaks to a cooler part of the grill.

3 Let the steaks rest 5 minutes before cutting crosswise into thin slices. Sprinkle with more salt and pepper. Drizzle with oil. Serve hot with lemon wedges.

Choosing Beef Cuts

Choosing the right cut of beef for your purpose is essential. Naturally tender cuts like the tenderloin, ribs, and sirloin are the best choices for grilling, broiling, sautéeing, and roasting. These milder-tasting cuts come from the sections of the animal that move the least, so the muscles are not as developed and have more fat.

The rump, chuck, and shoulder are tougher, though tastier, because they come from the areas that get the most exercise. They have a lot of connective tissue that needs long, slow cooking to break down, so they are best for braising and stewing. When purchasing beef, look for deep red color with creamy white fat. Steaks should be evenly speckled with fat and have a minimum of connective tissue. Expensive cuts like porterhouse and tenderloin are best when cooked no more than medium-rare, or they will become tough and dry. For pot roasts and stews, look for chuck or bottom-round rump cuts. With long, slow cooking, these meats become tender, juicy, and full of flavor.

Steak with Balsamic Glaze

Bistecca al Balsamico

MAKES 6 SERVINGS

Lean, boneless flank steak tastes great when bathed in balsamic vinegar and olive oil before grilling or broiling. Balsamic vinegar contains natural sugars, so when it is brushed on meats before grilling, roasting, or broiling, it helps to form a nice brown crust that seals in the meat juices and adds a mellow flavor. Use the best balsamic vinegar you can find.

**2 tablespoons extra-virgin olive oil, plus more
    for drizzling
2 tablespoons balsamic vinegar
1 garlic clove, finely chopped
1 flank steak, about 1 1/2 pounds
Salt and freshly ground black pepper**

1 In a shallow dish just large enough to hold the steak, combine the oil, vinegar, and garlic. Add the steak, turning it to coat it with the marinade. Cover and refrigerate up to 1 hour, turning the steak occasionally.

2 Place a barbecue grill or broiler rack about 4 inches from the heat source. Preheat the grill or broiler. Remove the steak from the marinade and pat dry. Grill or broil the steak 3 to 4 minutes. Turn the meat over with tongs and cook about 3 minutes more for rare, or 4 minutes for medium rare, depending on the thickness of the steak. To check for doneness, make a small cut in the thickest part. For longer cooking, move the steak to a cooler part of the grill.

3 Sprinkle the steak with salt and pepper. Let rest 5 minutes before cutting the meat across the grain into thin slices. Drizzle with a little extra-virgin olive oil.

Shell Steaks with Shallots, Pancetta, and Red Wine

Bistecca al Vino Rosso

MAKES 4 SERVINGS

Tender shell steaks get a flavor boost from pancetta, shallots, and red wine.

**2 tablespoons unsalted butter
1 thick slice of pancetta (about 1 ounce), finely chopped
2 boneless shell steaks, about 1 inch thick
Salt and freshly ground black pepper
1/4 cup chopped shallots
1/2 cup dry red wine
1/2 cup homemade Meat Broth (page 62)
    or store-bought beef broth
2 tablespoons balsamic vinegar**

1 Preheat the oven to 200°F. In a large skillet, melt 1 tablespoon of the butter over medium heat. Add the pancetta. Cook until the pancetta is golden, about 5 minutes. Remove the pancetta with a slotted spoon and pour out the fat.

2 Pat the steaks dry. Melt the remaining tablespoon of the butter in the same skillet over medium heat. When the butter foam subsides, place the steaks in the skillet and cook until nicely browned, 4 to 5 minutes. Sprinkle with salt and pepper. Turn the meat over with tongs and cook 4 minutes on the other side for rare, or 5 to 6 minutes for medium rare. To check for doneness, make a small cut in the thickest part. Transfer the steaks to a heatproof plate and keep warm in the oven.

3 Add the shallots to the pan and cook, stirring, for 1 minute. Add the wine, broth, and balsamic vinegar. Bring to a simmer and cook until the liquid is thick and syrupy, about 3 minutes.

4 Stir the pancetta into the pan juices. Spoon the sauce over the steaks and serve immediately.

Sliced Steak with Arugula
Straccetti di Manzo

MAKES 4 SERVINGS

Straccetti *means "little rags," which these narrow strips of meat resemble. Before preparing this dish, place the beef in the freezer until it is just firm enough to slice thin. Have all the ingredients ready, but don't dress the salad until just before cooking the meat.*

2 bunches arugula
4 tablespoons extra-virgin olive oil
I tablespoon balsamic vinegar
I tablespoon chopped shallots
Salt and freshly ground black pepper
1¼ pounds lean boneless sirloin or other tender beefsteak
I teaspoon chopped fresh rosemary

1 Trim the arugula, discarding the stems and any leaves that are bruised. Wash them in several changes of cool water. Dry very well. Tear the arugula into bite-size pieces.

2 In a large bowl, whisk 2 tablespoons of the oil, the vinegar, shallots, and salt and pepper to taste.

3 With a sharp slicing knife, cut the steak cross-wise into very thin slices. Heat a large heavy frying pan over medium heat. When it is very hot, add the remaining 2 tablespoons olive oil. Place the beef slices in the pan in a single layer, in batches if necessary, and cook until browned, about 2 minutes. Turn the meat over with tongs and sprinkle with salt and pepper. Cook until very lightly browned, about 1 minute, for rare.

4 Toss the arugula with the dressing and arrange it on a platter. Arrange the beef slices on top of the arugula and sprinkle with the rosemary. Serve immediately.

Tenderloin Steaks with Gorgonzola
Filetto di Manzo al Gorgonzola

MAKES 4 SERVINGS

Tenderloin steaks are mild tasting, but this luxurious sauce gives them a lot of character. Have the butcher cut the steaks no more than 1¼ inch thick for easy cooking, and tie each steak with kitchen string so that they hold their shape. Be sure to measure out and line up all of the ingredients before you begin cooking, as it goes very quickly.

4 beef tenderloin steaks, about I inch thick
Extra-virgin olive oil
Salt and freshly ground black pepper
3 tablespoons unsalted butter
I small shallot, finely chopped
¼ cup dry white wine
I tablespoon Dijon mustard
About 4 ounces gorgonzola cheese, rind removed and cut into pieces

1 Rub the steaks with olive oil and sprinkle them with salt and pepper. Cover and refrigerate. Remove the steaks from the refrigerator about 1 hour before cooking.

2 Preheat the oven to 200°F. Melt 2 tablespoons of the butter in a large skillet over medium heat. When the butter foam subsides, pat the steaks dry. Place them in the skillet and cook until nicely browned, 4 to 5 minutes. Turn the meat over with tongs and cook on the other side, 4 minutes for rare, or 5 to 6 minutes for medium-rare. To check for doneness, make a small cut in the thickest part. Transfer the steaks to a heatproof plate and keep them warm in the oven.

3 Add the shallot to the pan and cook, stirring, for 1 minute. Stir in the wine and mustard. Turn the heat to low and add the gorgonzola. Stir in any juices that have collected around the steaks. Remove from the heat and whisk in the remaining 1 tablespoon butter.

4 Spoon the sauce over the steaks and serve.

❧ Beef Stews and Braises

Stuffed Beef Rolls in Tomato Sauce
Braciole al Pomodoro

MAKES 4 SERVINGS

Thin slices of beef round are perfect for braciole—*commonly pronounced* bra-zholl—*a flavorful, slow-cooked favorite. Look for large slices of beef without a lot of connective tissue so that they will hold their shape well.*

Braciole can be cooked as part of Neapolitan Ragù (page 94). Some cooks stuff braciole with a hard-cooked egg, while others add raisins and pine nuts to the basic filling.

4 thin slices boneless beef round, about I pound

3 garlic cloves, finely chopped

2 tablespoons grated Pecorino Romano cheese

2 tablespoons chopped fresh flat-leaf parsley

Salt and freshly ground black pepper

2 tablespoons olive oil

I cup dry red wine

2 cups canned imported Italian tomatoes with their juice, passed through a food mill

4 fresh basil leaves, torn into small pieces

I Place the beef between 2 pieces of plastic wrap and pound gently with the flat side of a meat pounder or a rubber mallet to an even ⅛-inch thickness. Discard the top piece of plastic.

2 Set aside 1 chopped garlic clove for the sauce. Sprinkle the meat with the remaining garlic, the cheese, parsley, and salt and pepper to taste. Roll up each piece like a sausage and tie it like a small roast with cotton kitchen string.

3 Heat the oil in a large pot. Add the braciole. Cook, turning the meat occasionally, until it is browned on all sides, about 10 minutes. Scatter the remaining garlic around the meat and cook 1 minute . Add the wine and simmer for 2 minutes. Stir in the tomatoes and basil.

4 Cover and cook over low heat, turning the meat occasionally, until it is tender when pierced with a fork, about 2 hours. Add a little water if the sauce becomes too thick. Serve hot.

Beef and Beer
Carbonata di Bue

MAKES 6 SERVINGS

Beef, beer, and onions is a winning combination in this stew from the Alto Adige. It is similar to the French carbonnade of beef, from just across the border.

Boneless beef chuck is a good choice for stew. It has just enough marbling to remain moist through the long cooking.

4 tablespoons unsalted butter

2 tablespoons olive oil

3 medium onions (about I pound), thinly sliced

3 pounds boneless beef stew, cut into I½-inch pieces

½ cup all-purpose flour

12 ounces beer, any kind

2 cups peeled, seeded, and chopped fresh tomatoes or canned tomato puree

Salt and freshly ground black pepper

I Melt 2 tablespoons of the butter with 1 tablespoon of the oil in a large skillet over medium-low heat. Add the onions and cook, stirring frequently, until the onions are lightly golden, about 20 minutes.

2 In a large Dutch oven or other deep, heavy pot with a tight-fitting lid, melt the remaining butter with the oil over medium heat. Dredge half the beef in the flour and shake off the excess. Brown the pieces well on all sides, about 10 minutes. Transfer the meat to a plate. Repeat with the remaining meat.

3 Pour off the fat from the casserole dish. Add the beer and bring to a simmer, scraping the bottom of the casserole dish to blend the browned bits with the beer. Cook 1 minute.

4 Place a rack in the center of the oven. Preheat the oven to 375°F. Return all the meat to the casserole dish. Add the onions, tomatoes, and salt and pepper to taste. Bring the liquid to a simmer.

5 Cover the casserole dish and bake in the oven, stirring occasionally, for 2 hours or until the meat is tender when pierced with a knife. Serve hot.

Beef and Onion Stew
Carbonade

MAKES 6 SERVINGS

In Trentino–Alto Adige, this stew with a name similar to the previous one is made with red wine and spices. Venison or other game is sometimes substituted for the beef. Soft, buttery polenta is the classic accompaniment to this hearty stew, but I also like it with Cauliflower Puree (page 414).

3 tablespoons unsalted butter

3 tablespoons olive oil

2 medium onions, quartered and thinly sliced

1/2 cup all-purpose flour

3 pounds boneless beef chuck, cut into 2-inch pieces

I cup dry red wine

1/8 teaspoon ground cinnamon

1/8 teaspoon ground cloves

1/8 teaspoon ground nutmeg

I cup beef broth

Salt and freshly ground black pepper

1 In a large skillet, melt 1 tablespoon of the butter with 1 tablespoon of the oil over medium-low heat. Add the onions and cook, stirring occasionally, until very tender, about 15 minutes.

2 In a large Dutch oven or other deep, heavy pot with a tight-fitting lid, melt the remaining butter with the oil over medium heat. Spread the flour on a sheet of wax paper. Roll the meat in the flour, shaking off the excess. Add only enough pieces to the pan as will fit comfortably without crowding. As the meat is browned, transfer it to a plate, then fry the remaining meat in the same way.

3 When all of the meat is browned and removed, add the wine to the pan and bring to a simmer,

scraping the bottom of the pan to blend the browned bits with the wine. Simmer 1 minute.

4 Return the meat to the pan. Add the onions, spices, and broth. Season with salt and pepper. Bring to a simmer and cover the pan. Cook, stirring occasionally, for 3 hours, or until the meat is very tender when pierced with a fork. Add a little water if the liquid becomes too thick. Serve hot.

Peppery Beef Stew
Peposo

MAKES 6 SERVINGS

Tuscans make this peppery stew with veal or beef shanks, but I prefer to use boneless beef chuck. According to Giovanni Righi Parenti, author of La Grande Cucina Toscana, *when pepper was prohibitively expensive long ago, cooks would save up the peppercorns from slices of salame until there were enough to make* peposo.

My friend Marco Bartolini Baldelli, who owns the Fattoria di Bagnolo winery, told me that this stew was a favorite of the Tuscan brick makers in the town of Impruneta, who would cook it in their kilns. A bottle of Fattoria di Bagnolo Chianti Colli Fiorentini Riserva would be an ideal accompaniment.

2 tablespoons olive oil

3 pounds beef chuck, cut into 2-inch pieces

Salt and freshly ground black pepper

2 garlic cloves, finely chopped

2 cups dry red wine

1 1/2 cups peeled, seeded, and chopped tomatoes

I teaspoon freshly ground black pepper, or to taste

1 In a large Dutch oven or other deep, heavy pot with a tight-fitting lid, heat the oil over medium heat. Pat the beef dry and brown it on all sides, in batches, without crowding the pan, about 10 minutes per batch. Sprinkle with salt and pepper. Transfer the meat to a plate.

2 Stir the garlic into the fat in the pan. Add the red wine, salt and pepper to taste, and the tomatoes.

(continues)

Bring to a simmer and return the meat to the pan. Add just enough cold water to cover the meat. Cover the pot. Turn the heat to low and cook, stirring occasionally, for 2 hours.

3 Add the wine and cook 1 hour more, or until the beef is very tender when pierced with a fork. Taste and adjust seasoning. Serve hot.

Friuli-Style Beef Stew
Manzo in Squazet

MAKES 6 SERVINGS

Chicken, beef, and duck are just a few of the different types of meat that are cooked in squazet, *meaning "stewed" in the dialect of Friuli–Venezia Giulia.*

1/2 **cup dried porcini mushrooms**

I cup warm water

1/4 **cup olive oil**

3 pounds beef chuck, cut into 2-inch pieces

2 large onions, finely chopped

2 tablespoons tomato paste

I cup dry red wine

2 bay leaves

Pinch of ground cloves

Salt and freshly ground black pepper

**2 cups homemade Meat Broth (page 62)
    or store-bought beef broth**

I Soak the mushrooms in the water for 30 minutes. Remove the mushrooms and reserve the liquid. Rinse the mushrooms under cold running water to removing any grit, paying special attention to the ends of the stems where soil collects. Chop the mushrooms coarsely. Strain the mushroom liquid through a paper coffee filter into a bowl.

2 In a large skillet, heat the oil over medium heat. Pat the beef dry. Add the beef and brown well on all sides, about 10 minutes, transfering the pieces to a plate as they brown.

3 Add the onions to the pot and cook until softened, about 5 minutes. Stir in the tomato paste. Add the wine and bring the liquid to a simmer.

4 Return the meat to the pan. Add the mushrooms and their liquid, the bay leaves, cloves, and salt and pepper to taste. Add the broth. Cover and simmer, stirring occasionally, until the meat is tender and the liquid is reduced, 2 1/2 to 3 hours. If there is too much liquid, uncover the pot for the last 30 minutes. Remove the bay leaves. Serve hot.

Mixed Meat Stew, Hunter's Style
Scottiglia

MAKES 8 TO 10 SERVINGS

In Tuscany, when meat was scarce, several hunters would get together and contribute small bits of whatever meat they had to create this complex stew. Anything from beef, chicken, lamb, or pork to pheasant, rabbit, or guinea fowl can be added or substituted. The larger the variety of meats, the richer the stew will taste.

1/4 **cup olive oil**

I chicken, cut into 8 serving pieces

I pound boneless veal stew, cut into 2-inch chunks

I pound lamb shoulder, cut into 2-inch chunks

I pound pork shoulder, cut into 2-inch chunks

I large red onion, finely chopped

2 tender celery ribs, chopped

2 large carrots, finely chopped

2 garlic cloves, finely chopped

I cup dry red wine

Salt

1/2 **teaspoon crushed red pepper**

2 cups chopped tomatoes, fresh or canned

I tablespoon chopped fresh rosemary

**2 cups homemade Chicken Broth (page 63),
    Meat Broth (page 62), or store-bought
    chicken or beef broth**

GARNISH

8 slices Italian or French bread

2 large garlic cloves, peeled

1 In a Dutch oven large enough to hold all of the ingredients, or another deep, heavy pot with a tight-fitting lid, heat the oil over medium heat. Pat the meat dry. Add only as many pieces as will fit comfortably in a single layer. Brown the pieces well on all sides, about 10 minutes per batch, then transfer to a plate. Continue until all of the meat is browned.

2 Add the onion, celery, carrots, and garlic to the pan. Cook, stirring frequently, until tender, about 10 minutes.

3 Return the meat to the pan and add the wine, salt to taste, and crushed red pepper. Bring the liquid to a simmer. Add the tomatoes, rosemary, and broth. Lower the heat so that the liquid is barely bubbling. Cook, stirring occasionally, until all of the meats are tender, about 90 minutes. (Add a little water if the sauce becomes too dry.)

4 Toast the bread slices and rub them with the peeled garlic. Arrange the meat and sauce on a large platter. Place the bread slices all around. Serve hot.

Beef Goulash

Gulasch di Manzo

MAKES 8 SERVINGS

The northern part of Trentino–Alto Adige was once part of Austria; it was annexed by Italy after World War I. As a result, the food is Austrian, but with an Italian accent.

Dried spices such as paprika are good for only about six months after the container is opened. After that, the flavor fades. It is worth buying a new jar when preparing this stew. Be sure to use paprika imported from Hungary. You can use all sweet paprika or a combination of sweet and hot to your taste.

3 tablespoons lard, bacon drippings, or vegetable oil
2 pounds boneless beef chuck, cut into 2-inch pieces
Salt and freshly ground black pepper
3 large onions, thinly sliced
2 garlic cloves, chopped
2 cups dry red wine
1/4 cup sweet Hungarian paprika, or a combination of sweet and hot paprika
1 bay leaf
2-inch strip lemon zest
1 tablespoon double-concentrated tomato paste
1 teaspoon ground cumin
1/2 teaspoon dried marjoram
Fresh lemon juice

1 In a large Dutch oven or other deep, heavy pot with a tight-fitting lid, heat the lard or drippings over medium heat. Pat the meat dry and add to the pan only as many pieces as will fit comfortably in a single layer. Brown the pieces well on all sides, about 10 minutes per batch. Transfer the meat to a plate and sprinkle with salt and pepper.

2 Add the onions to the pan and cook, stirring frequently, until they are tender and golden, about 15 minutes. Stir in the garlic. Add the wine and scrape the bottom of the pan. Return the meat to the pan. Bring the liquid to a simmer.

3 Stir in the paprika, bay leaf, lemon zest, tomato paste, cumin, and marjoram. Add enough water to barely cover the meat.

4 Cover the pot and cook 2 1/2 to 3 hours, or until the meat is fork-tender. Stir in the lemon juice. Remove the bay leaf and lemon zest. Taste and adjust seasoning. Serve hot.

Oxtail Stew, Roman Style
Coda alla Vaccinara

MAKES 4 TO 6 SERVINGS

Though oxtails don't have much meat on them, what is there is very tasty and tender when slowly simmered the Roman way. Leftover sauce is good on rigatoni or another thick-cut pasta.

1/4 cup olive oil

3 pounds oxtail, cut into 1 1/2-inch chunks

1 large onion, chopped

2 garlic cloves, finely chopped

1 cup dry red wine

2 1/2 cups peeled, seeded, and chopped fresh tomatoes, or drained and chopped canned tomatoes

1/4 teaspoon ground cloves

Salt and freshly ground black pepper

2 cups water

6 tender celery ribs, chopped

1 tablespoon chopped bittersweet chocolate

3 tablespoons pine nuts

3 tablespoons raisins

1 In a large Dutch oven or other deep, heavy pot with a tight-fitting lid, heat the olive oil. Pat the oxtail dry and add to the pan only as many pieces as will fit comfortably in a single layer. Brown the pieces well on all sides, about 10 minutes per batch. Transfer the pieces to a plate.

2 Add the onion and cook, stirring occasionally, until golden. Stir in the garlic and cook 1 minute more. Stir in the wine, scraping the bottom of the pan.

3 Return the oxtail to the pan. Add the tomatoes, cloves, salt and pepper to taste, and water. Cover the pan and bring the liquid to a simmer. Reduce the heat and cook, stirring occasionally, until the meat is tender and coming away from the bones, about 3 hours.

4 Meanwhile, bring a large saucepan of water to a boil. Add the celery and cook 1 minute. Drain well.

5 Stir the chocolate into the pan with the oxtails. Add the celery, pine nuts, and raisins. Bring to a simmer. Serve hot.

Braised Beef Shank
Garretto al Vino

MAKES 6 SERVINGS

In this richly flavored, slow-cooked dish, thick slices of beef shanks are stewed with vegetables and red wine. The cooked vegetables that accompany it are pureed with the cooking juices to make a delicious sauce for the meat. Serve it with a side dish of potatoes or polenta, or spoon some of the sauce over Potato Gnocchi (pages 189–190).

2 tablespoons unsalted butter

1 tablespoon olive oil

3 (1 1/2-inch-thick) slices beef shank (about 3 pounds), well trimmed

Salt and freshly ground black pepper

4 carrots, chopped

3 celery ribs, chopped

1 large onion, chopped

2 cups dry red wine

1 bay leaf

1 In a large Dutch oven or other deep, heavy pot with a tight-fitting lid, melt the butter with the oil. Pat the meat dry and brown it well on all sides, about 10 minutes. Sprinkle with salt and pepper. Transfer the meat to a plate.

2 Add the vegetables and cook, stirring often, until nicely browned, about 10 minutes.

3 Add the wine and cook, scraping the bottom of the pan with a wooden spoon. Simmer the wine for 1 minute. Return the beef to the pot and add the bay leaf.

4 Cover the pan and reduce the heat to low. If the liquid evaporates too much, add some warm water. Cook 2 1/2 to 3 hours, turning the meat occasionally, until tender when pierced with a knife.

5 Remove the meat to a platter and cover to keep warm. Discard the bay leaf. Pass the vegetables through a food mill or puree them in a blender. Taste and adjust seasoning. Reheat if necessary. Spoon the vegetable sauce over the beef. Serve immediately.

🌿 Meatballs and Ground Beef Dishes

Beef-Stuffed Eggplant
Melanzane Ripiene

MAKES 4 TO 6 SERVINGS

Small eggplants about three inches in length are ideal for stuffing. These are good hot or at room temperature.

2¹/2 cups any Tomato Sauce (pages 89–92)
8 baby eggplants
Salt
12 ounces ground beef chuck
2 ounces chopped salami or imported Italian prosciutto
1 large egg
1 garlic clove, finely chopped
¹/3 cup plain dry bread crumbs
¹/4 cup grated Pecorino Romano or Parmigiano-Reggiano
2 tablespoons chopped fresh flat-leaf parsley
Salt and freshly ground black pepper

1 Prepare the tomato sauce, if necessary. Then, place a rack in the center of the oven. Preheat the oven to 375°F. Oil a 12 × 9 × 2–inch baking dish.

2 Bring a large pot of water to a boil. Trim the tops off the eggplants and cut the eggplants in half lengthwise. Add the eggplants to the water with salt to taste. Simmer until the eggplants are softened, 4 to 5 minutes. Place the eggplants in a colander to drain and cool.

3 With a small spoon, scoop out the pulp of each eggplant, leaving a ¹/4-inch-thick shell. Chop the pulp and place it in a large bowl. Arrange the shells in the baking dish skin-side down.

4 To the eggplant pulp, add the beef, salami, egg, garlic, bread crumbs, cheese, parsley, and salt and pepper to taste. Spoon the mixture into the eggplant shells, smoothing the tops. Spoon the tomato sauce over the eggplants.

5 Bake until the filling is cooked through, about 20 minutes. Serve hot or at room temperature.

Neapolitan Meatballs
Polpette

MAKES 6 SERVINGS

My mother made a batch of these meatballs once a week to add to a big pot of ragù. Whenever she wasn't looking, someone would snatch one out of the pot to eat as a snack. Of course she knew, so she often made a double batch.

3 cups Neapolitan Ragù (page 94) or Marinara Sauce (page 89)
1 pound ground beef chuck
2 large eggs, beaten
1 large garlic clove, finely chopped
¹/2 cup freshly grated Pecorino Romano
¹/2 cup plain bread crumbs
2 tablespoons finely chopped fresh flat-leaf parsley
1 teaspoon salt
Freshly ground black pepper
¹/4 cup olive oil

1 Prepare the ragù or sauce, if necessary. Then, in a large bowl, combine the beef, eggs, garlic, cheese, bread crumbs, parsley, and salt and pepper to taste. With your hands, thoroughly mix together all of the ingredients.

2 Rinse your hands with cool water to prevent sticking, then lightly shape the mixture into 2-inch balls. (If you are making meatballs to use in lasagne or baked ziti, shape the meat into tiny balls the size of a small grape.)

3 Heat the oil in a large heavy skillet over medium heat. Add the meatballs and fry them until nicely browned on all sides, about 15 minutes. (Turn them carefully with tongs.) Transfer the meatballs to a plate.

4 Transfer the meatballs to the pan of ragù or tomato sauce. Simmer until cooked through, about 30 minutes. Serve hot.

Meatballs with Pine Nuts and Raisins

Polpette con Pinoli e Uve Secche

MAKES 20 2-INCH MEATBALLS

The secret to a good juicy meatball or meat loaf is adding bread or bread crumbs to the mixture. The bread absorbs the meat juices and holds them as the meat cooks. For an extra-crusty exterior, these meatballs are also rolled in dry bread crumbs before cooking. This recipe was given to me by my friend Kevin Benvenuti who owns a gourmet shop in Westin, Florida. The recipe was his grandmother Carolina's.

Some cooks like to skip the frying step and add the meatballs directly to the sauce. The meatballs turn out softer. I prefer the firmer texture and better flavor you get by frying.

3 cups Neapolitan Ragù (page 94) or another tomato
    sauce (see pages 89–92)
I cup plain dry bread crumbs
4 slices Italian bread, crusts removed and torn into
    small pieces (about 2 cups)
1/2 cup milk
2 pounds mixed ground beef, veal, and pork
4 large eggs, lightly beaten
2 garlic cloves, finely chopped
2 tablespoons finely chopped fresh flat-leaf parsley
1/2 cup raisins
1/2 cup pine nuts
1/2 cup grated Pecorino Romano or Parmigiano-Reggiano
I 1/2 teaspoons salt
1/4 teaspoon freshly ground nutmeg
Freshly ground black pepper
1/4 cup olive oil

1 Prepare the ragù or sauce, if necessary. Place the bread crumbs in a shallow bowl. Then, soak the bread in the milk for 10 minutes. Drain the bread and squeeze out the excess liquid.

2 In a large bowl, combine the meats, bread, eggs, garlic, parsley, raisins, pine nuts, cheese, salt, nutmeg, and pepper to taste. With your hands, thoroughly mix together all of the ingredients.

3 Rinse your hands in cool water to prevent sticking, then lightly shape the mixture into 2-inch balls. Roll the meatballs lightly in the bread crumbs.

4 Heat the oil in a large heavy skillet over medium heat. Add the meatballs and fry until nicely browned on all sides, about 15 minutes. (Turn them carefully with tongs.)

5 Place the meatballs in the ragù or sauce. Simmer until cooked through, about 30 minutes. Serve hot.

Meatballs with Cabbage and Tomatoes

Polpettine Stufato con Cavolo

MAKES 4 SERVINGS

Meatballs are one of those soul-satisfying dishes that are made almost everywhere, certainly in every region of Italy. Italians never serve meatballs with spaghetti, though. They feel that the heaviness of the meat would overwhelm the delicate strands of pasta. Also, pasta is a first course, and any meat larger than bite-size is served as a second course. In this recipe from Friuli–Venezia Giulia, the meatballs are served with slow-cooked cabbage. It is a hearty dish to serve on a cold night.

2 garlic cloves, finely chopped
2 tablespoons olive oil
I small head cabbage, shredded
I 1/2 cups drained canned whole tomatoes, chopped
Salt

MEATBALLS

I cup torn crustless Italian or French bread
1/2 cup milk
I pound ground beef chuck
I large egg, beaten
1/2 cup freshly grated Parmigiano-Reggiano
I large garlic clove, chopped
2 tablespoons chopped fresh flat-leaf parsley
Salt and freshly ground black pepper
1/4 cup olive oil

1 In a large pot, cook the garlic in the olive oil over medium heat until lightly golden, about 2 minutes. Add the cabbage and stir well. Add the tomatoes and salt to taste. Cover and cook over low heat, stirring occasionally, for 45 minutes.

2 In a medium bowl, combine the bread and milk. Let stand 10 minutes, then squeeze out the excess milk.

3 In a large bowl, combine the beef, bread, egg, cheese, garlic, parsley, and salt and pepper to taste. With your hands, thoroughly mix together all of the ingredients.

4 Rinse your hands in cool water to prevent sticking, then lightly shape the meat mixture into 2-inch balls. Heat the oil in a large heavy skillet over medium heat. Fry the meatballs until nicely browned on all sides. (Turn them carefully with tongs.) Transfer the meatballs to a plate.

5 If there is a lot of liquid in the pot with the cabbage, leave the cover off and cook until reduced. Add the meatballs and cover them with the cabbage. Cook 10 minutes more. Serve hot.

Meatballs, Bologna Style
Polpette alla Bolognese

MAKES 6 SERVINGS

This recipe is my adaptation of a dish at Trattoria Gigina in Bologna. Though it is as homespun as any meatball recipe, the mortadella in the meat mixture and cream in the tomato sauce make it seem a little more sophisticated.

SAUCE
I small onion, finely chopped
I medium carrot, finely chopped
I small tender celery rib, finely chopped
2 tablespoons olive oil
1 1/2 cups tomato puree
1/2 cup heavy cream
Salt and freshly ground black pepper

MEATBALLS
I pound lean ground beef
8 ounces mortadella
1/2 cup freshly grated Parmigiano-Reggiano
2 large eggs, beaten
1/2 cup plain dry bread crumbs
I teaspoon kosher or sea salt
1/4 teaspoon ground nutmeg
Freshly ground black pepper

1 Prepare the sauce: In a large saucepan or deep heavy skillet, cook the onion, carrot, and celery in the olive oil over medium heat until golden and tender, about 10 minutes. Add the tomato, cream, and salt and pepper to taste. Bring to a simmer.

2 Prepare the meatballs: Place the meatball ingredients in a large bowl. With your hands, thoroughly mix together all of the ingredients. Rinse your hands in cool water to prevent sticking, then lightly shape the mixture into 2-inch balls.

3 Transfer the meatballs into the simmering sauce. Cover and cook, turning the meatballs occasionally, until cooked through, about 20 minutes. Serve hot.

Meatballs in Marsala
Polpette al Marsala

MAKES 4 SERVINGS

My friend Arthur Schwartz, an authority on the cooking of Naples, described this recipe to me, which he says is very popular in Naples.

1 cup crustless Italian bread, torn into bits
1/4 cup milk
About 1/2 cup all-purpose flour
1 pound ground beef round
2 large eggs, beaten
1/2 cup freshly grated Parmigiano-Reggiano
1/4 cup chopped ham
2 tablespoons chopped fresh flat-leaf parsley
Salt and freshly ground pepper
3 tablespoons unsalted butter
1/2 cup dry Marsala
1/2 cup homemade Meat Broth (page 62)
  or store-bought beef broth

1 In a small bowl, soak the bread in the milk for 10 minutes. Squeeze out the liquid. Place the flour in a shallow bowl.

2 In a large bowl, place the bread, beef, eggs, cheese, ham, parsley, and salt and pepper. With your hands, thoroughly mix together all of the ingredients. Rinse your hands in cool water to prevent sticking, then lightly shape the mixture into eight 2-inch balls. Roll the balls in flour.

3 In a skillet large enough to hold all of the meatballs, melt the butter over medium-low heat. Add the meatballs and cook, turning them carefully with tongs, until nicely browned, about15 minutes. Add the Marsala and the broth. Cook until the liquid is reduced and the meatballs are cooked through, 4 to 5 minutes. Serve hot.

Meat Loaf, Old Naples Style
Polpettone di Santa Chiara

MAKES 4 TO 6 SERVINGS

This recipe calls for oven baking, though originally the loaf would have been browned all over in a skillet, then cooked with a little wine in a covered pan. The hard-cooked eggs in the center create a bull's-eye effect when the loaf is sliced. Though this recipe calls for all beef, a mix of ground meats works well.

2/3 cup crustless day-old Italian bread
1/3 cup milk
1 pound ground beef round
2 large eggs, beaten
Salt and freshly ground black pepper
4 ounces unsmoked ham, chopped
1/2 cup chopped Pecorino Romano or provolone cheese
4 tablespoons plain dry bread crumbs
2 hard-cooked eggs

1 Place a rack in the center of the oven. Preheat the oven to 350°F. Oil a 9-inch square baking pan.

2 Soak the bread in the milk for 10 minutes. Squeeze the bread to remove the excess liquid.

3 In a large bowl, mix together the beef, bread, eggs, and salt and pepper to taste. Stir in the ham and cheese.

4 On a large sheet of wax paper, scatter half the bread crumbs on a piece of wax paper. Spread half the meat mixture on the paper in a rectangle 8 × 4 inches. Place the two hard-cooked eggs lengthwise in a row down the center. Pile the remaining meat mixture on top, pressing the meat together to form a neat loaf about 8 inches long. Place the loaf in the prepared pan. Sprinkle the top and sides with the remaining crumbs.

5 Bake the loaf about 1 hour or until the internal temperature reaches 155°F on an instant-read thermometer. Let cool 10 minutes before slicing. Serve hot.

sauce and adjust for seasoning. Slice the beef and serve it hot with the sauce.

✍ Beef Roasts

Pot Roast with Red Wine
Brasato al Barolo

MAKES 6 TO 8 SERVINGS

Piedmontese cooks simmer large cuts of beef in the Barolo wine of the region, but another hearty dry red wine would work well, too.

3 tablespoons olive oil
I boneless beef chuck or bottom round roast
    (about 3¹/₂ pounds)
2 ounces pancetta, chopped
I medium onion, chopped
2 garlic cloves, finely chopped
I cup dry red wine, such as Barolo
2 cups peeled, seeded, and chopped tomatoes
2 cups homemade Meat Broth (page 62)
    or store-bought beef broth
2 carrots, sliced
I celery rib, sliced
2 tablespoons chopped fresh flat-leaf parsley
Salt and freshly ground black pepper

I In a large Dutch oven or other deep, heavy pot with a tight-fitting lid, heat the oil over medium heat. Add the beef and brown it well on all sides, about 20 minutes. Season to taste with salt and pepper. Transfer to a plate.

2 Spoon off all but two tablespoons of the fat. Add the pancetta, onion, and garlic to the pot. Cook, stirring frequently, until tender, about 10 minutes. Add the wine and bring it to a simmer.

3 Add the tomatoes, broth, carrots, celery, and parsley. Cover the pan and bring the liquid to a simmer. Cook at a simmer, turning the meat occasionally, 2¹/₂ to 3 hours, or until it is tender when pierced with a fork.

4 Transfer the meat to a plate. Cover and keep warm. If the liquid in the pot seems too thin, raise the heat and boil until slightly reduced. Taste the

Pot Roast with Onion Sauce and Pasta
La Genovese

MAKES 8 SERVINGS

Onions, carrots, prosciutto, and salami are the primary flavoring ingredients for this tender pot roast. This is an old Neapolitan recipe that, unlike most dishes from the area, does not contain tomatoes. Historians explain that centuries ago, sailors who traveled between the ports of Genoa and Naples brought this dish home with them.

    La Genovese *was a specialty of my grandmother, who would serve the onion sauce over* mafalde, *long pasta ribbons with a wavy edge, or with long fusilli. The sliced meat was then eaten with the remaining sauce as a second course.*

2 tablespoons olive oil
I boneless beef chuck or bottom round roast
    (about 3¹/₂ pounds)
Salt and freshly ground black pepper
6 to 8 medium onions (about 3 pounds), thinly sliced
6 medium carrots, thinly sliced
2 ounces Genoa salami, cut into thin strips
2 ounces imported Italian prosciutto, cut into thin strips
I pound mafalde or fusilli
Freshly grated Parmigiano-Reggiano or Pecorino
    Romano

I Place a rack in the center of the oven. Preheat the oven to 325°F. In a large Dutch oven or other deep, heavy pot with a tight-fitting lid, heat the oil over medium heat. Add the meat and brown it well on all sides, about 20 minutes. Sprinkle it with salt and pepper. When the meat is completely browned, transfer it to a plate and drain the fat from the pot.

2 Pour 1 cup water into the pot and scrape the bottom with a wooden spoon to loosen any browned

(continues)

bits. Add the onions, carrots, salami, and prosciutto to the pot. Return the roast to the pot. Cover and bring the liquid to a simmer.

3 Transfer the pot to the oven. Cook, turning the meat occasionally, 2¹/2 to 3 hours. or until it is very tender when pierced with a fork.

4 About 20 minutes before the meat is done, bring a large pot of water to a boil. Add 2 tablespoons of salt, then the pasta, gently pushing it down until it is completely covered with water. Cook until al dente, just tender yet firm to the bite.

5 When done, transfer the meat to a platter. Cover and keep warm. Let the sauce cool slightly. Puree the contents of the pot by passing it through a food mill or blending it in a food processor or blender. Taste and adjust seasoning. Return the sauce to the pot with the meat. Reheat gently.

6 Serve some of the sauce over the pasta. Sprinkle with the cheese. Reheat the sauce and meat if necessary. Slice the meat and serve it as a second course with the remaining sauce.

Sicilian Stuffed Beef Roll
Farsumagru

MAKES 6 SERVINGS

Farsumagru, *in Sicilian dialect, or* falsomagro, *in standard Italian, means "falsely lean." The name is probably a reference to the rich stuffing packed inside the thin slice of meat. There are many variations on this dish. Some cooks use a slice of veal instead of beef for the outer roll and ground veal or beef in the stuffing instead of pork sausage. Ham, salami, or pancetta is sometimes used in place of the prosciutto. Other cooks add vegetables such as potatoes or peas to the simmering sauce.*

The most difficult thing about this recipe is getting a single slice of beef about 8 × 6 × 1/2 inches that can be pounded to a 1/4-inch thickness. Ask your butcher to cut it for you.

12 ounces plain Italian pork sausage, casings removed
1 egg, beaten
¹/2 cup freshly grated Pecorino Romano
¹/4 cup fine dry bread crumbs
2 tablespoons chopped fresh flat-leaf parsley
1 garlic clove, finely chopped
Salt and freshly ground black pepper
1 pound ¹/2-inch-thick boneless beef round steak
2 ounces thinly sliced imported Italian prosciutto
2 hard-cooked eggs, peeled
3 tablespoons olive oil
1 onion, finely chopped
¹/2 cup dry white wine
1 (28-ounce) can crushed tomatoes
1 cup water

1 In a large bowl, mix together the pork, egg, cheese, bread crumbs, parsley, garlic, and salt and pepper to taste.

2 Lay a large piece of plastic wrap on a flat surface and place the beef on top. Place a second sheet of plastic over the beef and pound gently to flatten the meat to about a 1/4-inch thickness.

3 Discard the top sheet of plastic. Arrange the prosciutto slices over the beef. Spread the meat mixture over the prosciutto, leaving a 1/2-inch border all around. Place the hard-cooked eggs in a row on one long side of the meat. Fold the meat lengthwise over the eggs and filling and roll up like a jelly roll, using the bottom sheet of plastic wrap to help you roll. With cotton kitchen string, tie the roll at 1-inch intervals like a roast.

4 Heat the oil over medium heat in a large Dutch oven or other deep, heavy pot with a tight-fitting lid. Add the beef roll and brown well on one side, about 10 minutes. Turn the meat with tongs and scatter the onion all around. Brown the meat on the other side, about 10 minutes.

5 Add the wine and bring it to a simmer. Stir in the crushed tomatoes and water. Cover the pan and cook, turning the meat occasionally, about 1¹/2 hours, or until the beef is tender when pierced with a fork.

6 Transfer the meat to a plate. Let the meat cool 10 minutes. Remove the strings and cut the roll into 1/2-inch slices. Arrange the slices on a warm platter. Reheat the sauce if needed. Spoon the sauce over the meat and serve.

Roast Tenderloin with Olive Sauce
Filetto alle Olive

MAKES 8 TO 10 SERVINGS

A tender filet roast is suitable for an elegant dinner party. Serve it hot or at room temperature with a luscious olive sauce or substitute Sun-Dried Tomato Sauce (page 103). Never cook this cut of meat to more than medium-rare, or it will be dry.

Olive Sauce (page 104)
3 tablespoons olive oil
2 tablespoons balsamic vinegar
1 teaspoon salt
Freshly ground black pepper
1 beef tenderloin, trimmed and tied (about 4 pounds)
1 tablespoon chopped fresh rosemary

1 Prepare the sauce, if necessary. Whisk together the oil, vinegar, salt, and a generous grinding of pepper. Place the beef in a large roasting pan and pour on the marinade, turning the meat to coat on all sides. Cover the pan with foil and marinate 1 hour at room temperature or up to 24 hours in the refrigerator.

2 Place a rack in the center of the oven. Preheat the oven to 425°F. Roast the beef 30 minutes or until the temperature in the thickest part reaches 125°F for medium-rare on an instant-read thermometer. Transfer the roast from the oven to a platter.

3 Let stand 15 minutes before carving. Cut the meat into 1/2-inch slices and serve hot or at room temperature with the sauce.

Mixed Boiled Meats
Bollito Misto

MAKES 8 TO 10 SERVINGS

Bollito misto, *meaning "mixed boil," is a combination of meats and vegetables slow-cooked together in a simmering liquid. In northern Italy, pasta is added to the broth to make a first course. The meat is sliced and served afterward with a variety of sauces. Bollito misto is very festive and makes an impressive dinner for a crowd.*

Every region has its own way of making it. The Piedmontese insist it should be made with seven kinds of meat and served with a tomato and bell pepper sauce. Green sauce is probably the most traditional, while in Emilia-Romagna and Lombardy mostarda—fruits preserved in sweet mustard syrup—is typical. Mostarda can be purchased in many Italian markets and gourmet shops.

Though bollito misto is not difficult to make, it does require long cooking. Calculate about four hours from the time you turn on the heat. When all of the meats are cooked, they can be kept warm in the pot for another hour. A separate pot is needed to cook the cotechino or other large sausage, because the fat that it releases would make the broth greasy.

In addition to the sauces, I like to serve the meats with steamed vegetables, such as carrots, zucchini, and potatoes.

1 large ripe tomato, halved and seeded
4 parsley sprigs with stems
2 celery ribs with leaves, coarsely chopped
2 large carrots, coarsely chopped
1 large onion, coarsely chopped
1 garlic clove
1 boneless beef chuck roast, about 3 pounds
Salt
Green Sauce (page 101) or Red Pepper and Tomato Sauce (page 103)
1 boneless veal shoulder roast, rolled and tied, about 3 pounds
1 cotechino or other large garlic sausage, about 1 pound
1 whole chicken, about 3 1/2 pounds

(continues)

1 In a 5-gallon stockpot or two smaller pots of the same capacity, combine the vegetables and 3 quarts of water. Bring to a simmer over medium heat.

2 Add the beef and 2 teaspoons salt. Cook for 1 hour after the liquid returns to the simmer. Meanwhile, prepare the sauce, if necessary.

3 Add the veal to the stockpot; after the liquid returns to the simmer, cook 1 hour. If necessary, add more water so that the meats remain covered.

4 In a separate pot, combine the cotechino with water to cover by 1 inch. Cover and bring to a simmer. Cook 1 hour.

5 Add the chicken to the pot with veal and beef. Bring to a simmer and cook, turning the chicken once or twice, for 1 hour, or until all of the meats are tender when pierced with a fork.

6 With a large spoon, skim the fat from the surface of the broth. Taste and adjust for salt. (If serving the broth as a first course, strain some of the broth into a pot, leaving the meats with the remaining broth in the stockpot to stay warm. Bring the broth to a simmer and cook the pasta in it. Serve hot with grated Parmigiano-Reggiano.)

7 Have ready a large warmed platter. Slice the meats and arrange on the platter. Drizzle with a little of the broth. Serve the sliced meat immediately with the sauces of your choice.

Sardinian Saffron Meat Pies

Impanadas

MAKES 8

These little pastries filled with ground meats, olives, and dried tomatoes are fun for parties, picnics, and away-from-home meals. If they seem more Spanish than Italian, it is because Sardinia was controlled by Spain for more than four centuries. Both the language and cooking reflect that influence.

The pastries are made like stuffed pasta—with a filling between two pieces of dough. If you prefer

smaller pastries, you can make these as turnovers, placing less filling within one disk of dough, then folding the disk in half over the filling.

Traditionally, lard is used for best flavor, but olive oil will also work.

PASTRY

3¹/₂ cups unbleached all-purpose flour
1 teaspoon salt
¹/₄ cup melted lard or olive oil
About 1 cup warm water

FILLING

¹/₂ teaspoon saffron threads
¹/₄ cup warm water
1 pound ground round
¹/₄ pound Italian-style pork sausage, casings removed
2 large eggs, beaten
¹/₂ cup plain dry bread crumbs
¹/₂ cup dried tomatoes, finely chopped
¹/₂ cup pitted and chopped green olives
¹/₄ cup chopped fresh flat-leaf parsley
2 garlic cloves, finely chopped
1 teaspoon salt
Freshly ground black pepper

1 Prepare the pastry dough: In a large bowl, stir together the flour and salt. Add the lard or oil and water. Stir until the mixture comes together and forms a soft dough. Add a little more water if needed. Transfer the dough to a lightly floured surface. Knead it briefly until the dough is smooth. Shape the dough into a ball. Let rest, covered with a bowl, for 20 minutes to 1 hour.

2 Prepare the filling: In a small cup, soak the saffron in the warm water for 10 minutes.

3 In a large bowl, stir together all of the remaining filling ingredients. Add the saffron water and mix well.

4 Cut the dough into 16 pieces. (Cut the dough into quarters. Cut each quarter in half, then each eighth in half.) Cover all but 1 piece with an overturned bowl. On a lightly floured surface, shape the piece into a ball. With a rolling pin, roll out the dough to a 4-inch circle. Roll out the remaining dough circles in the same way.

5 Preheat the oven to 400°F. Grease two large baking sheets. Set a small bowl of water near your work surface.

6 Divide the filling into 8 portions. Place a portion of the filling in the center of one circle of dough, leaving a narrow border all around. Dip your finger in a little water and moisten the border of the dough. Place a second circle of dough on top, forming the dough around the filling and gently pressing out the air. With a fork, firmly press the edges of the dough together to seal.

7 Place the little pie on the prepared baking sheet. With a small knife, poke several holes in the top to allow steam to escape. Repeat with the remaining dough and filling, placing the meat pies about 1 inch apart.

8 Bake 25 minutes, or until the pies are golden brown and the meat juices are bubbling.

9 Transfer the pies to racks to cool. Serve warm or at room temperature.

❧ Veal Cutlets (Scaloppine)

Veal cutlets, or *scaloppine*, are the first thing that comes to mind when I think of Italian veal recipes; there are many great dishes made with this cut. They can be grilled or fried, stuffed, sautéed, or braised. The important thing is to get cutlets that have been cut from the leg in one piece. This way they will have no connective tissue to toughen as the meat cooks. Good veal cutlets are expensive, though, so you can always substitute cutlets made from pork, chicken, or turkey, if you prefer.

No matter which kind of meat you use, cutlets should be no more than 1/4 inch thick. If the meat is slightly thicker or uneven, place the veal between two pieces of plastic wrap and pound it gently with a rolling pin or similar object until it is about 1/8 inch thick. Do not pound too hard or use a mallet with a rough surface, as this will break up the meat instead of flattening it.

Veal Cutlets with Prosciutto and Sage
Saltimbocca

MAKES 4 SERVINGS

Little squares of veal topped with prosciutto and sage are called saltimbocca, *or "jump in the mouth," in Rome, because they are so quick to make and eat. Serve them with tender spring peas and asparagus.*

1 pound veal cutlets, pounded thin and cut into 8 pieces
Salt and freshly ground black pepper
8 fresh sage leaves
4 thin slices imported Italian prosciutto, cut in half crosswise
2 tablespoons butter
1 tablespoon olive oil
1/3 cup dry white wine

1 Sprinkle both sides of the veal with salt and pepper. Place 1 sage leaf on each piece. Top with the

(continues)

prosciutto slices. With toothpicks, pin the meats and sage together.

2 In a large heavy skillet, melt 1 tablespoon of the butter with the oil over medium-high heat. Add half the veal pieces and cook until browned on one side, 3 to 4 minutes. Turn the veal and cook until browned, about 3 minutes. Transfer the meat to a serving dish and keep warm. Repeat with the remaining veal.

3 Add the wine and cook over high heat, scraping the pan until the liquid is slightly syrupy. Remove from the heat and swirl in the remaining 1 tablespoon butter. Pour the sauce over the veal and serve immediately.

Veal Cutlets with Truffles
Vitello alla Petroniana

MAKES 4 SERVINGS

Many years ago, my husband and I discovered a fine little trattoria near our home in New York's Westchester County. It was run by a family from Emilia-Romagna, and every day the mother of the family would make the most delicate handmade pastas. As far as I can recall, I always ordered the same thing: tortellini alla panna (tortellini with cream sauce) and this dish of veal scaloppine in a light Marsala sauce with truffles. After we had moved away from the area, I thought about the veal dish for many years, and one day, to my surprise, I came across a version of the recipe in an old cookbook my mother had given me. I have adapted this to suit my memory.

Truffles add a luxurious touch, but the veal is still very good without them.

1/2 cup all-purpose flour

Salt and freshly ground black pepper

2 tablespoons unsalted butter

1 tablespoon vegetable oil

1 pound veal cutlets, pounded thin

1/2 cup dry Marsala

2 tablespoons freshly grated Parmigiano-Reggiano

Fresh or canned black truffles, very thinly sliced
(optional)

1 On a piece of wax paper, stir together the flour and salt and pepper to taste.

2 In a large skillet, melt the butter with the oil over medium heat. Quickly dip the veal in the flour and shake off the excess. Place half the veal slices in the pan and cook until browned on one side, 3 to 4 minutes. Turn the veal and cook until browned, about 3 minutes. Transfer the meat to a serving dish; keep warm. Repeat with the remaining veal.

3 Add the Marsala and cook 1 minute, scraping the bottom of the pan. Turn the heat to low. Return the veal slices to the pan and baste them with the juices. Sprinkle the veal with the cheese and arrange the truffle slices on top, if using. Cover the pan and cook 1 minute more. Serve immediately.

Veal with Marsala and Mushrooms
Scaloppine alla Marsala

MAKES 4 SERVINGS

An English wine merchant named John Woodhouse was the first to produce the Marsala wine we know today. In 1773, Woodhouse, in search of a way to stabilize wines from Sicily so that they would survive a long sea voyage back to Britain, found he could add spirits to the wine, in a process similar to that used to make port, sherry, and Madeira. The fortified wine was a huge success in Britain. Though less popular for drinking today, Marsala is often used in Italian cooking. Both dry and sweet varieties of Marsala are available. Dry Marsalas, especially the aged vergine and soleras versions, are high-quality wines and can be drunk like sherry as an aperitif. Use dry Marsala for cooking savory dishes such as this classic one and sweet Marsala for desserts like zabaglione.

3 tablespoons unsalted butter

2 tablespoons olive oil

12 ounces mushrooms, any kind, thinly sliced

Salt and freshly ground black pepper

1/2 cup all-purpose flour

1 pound veal cutlets, pounded thin

3/4 cup dry Marsala

1 In a large skillet, melt 2 tablespoon of the butter with 1 tablespoon of the oil over medium heat. Add the mushrooms and salt and pepper to taste. Cook, stirring often, until the mushrooms are tender and browned, about 15 minutes. Transfer the mushrooms to a plate.

2 On a piece of wax paper, stir together the flour and salt and pepper to taste. To the skillet, add the remaining 1 tablespoon each of butter and oil. When the butter is melted, quickly dip the cutlets in the flour and shake off the excess. Add half the veal pieces to the pan and cook until browned on one side, 3 to 4 minutes. Turn the veal with tongs and cook until browned, about 3 minutes. Transfer the meat to a serving dish and keep warm. Repeat with the remaining veal.

3 Add the Marsala to the skillet. Cook, stirring with a wooden spoon, until the sauce is slightly syrupy, about 2 minutes.

4 Return the veal and mushrooms to the pan. Cook, turning the veal in the sauce to coat, until heated through, about 1 minute. Serve immediately.

Veal Rolls in White Wine
Rollatini di Vitello al Vino Bianco

MAKES 4 SERVINGS

Throughout Italy, rolling and stuffing is a common method for making the most of a small amount of veal cutlets. Cured or ground meats, cheese, or vegetables can be used for the stuffing. This recipe is popular in many Italian restaurants in the United States.

1 pound veal cutlets, pounded thin
Salt and freshly ground black pepper
4 very thin slices imported Italian prosciutto,
     cut in half crosswise
2 tablespoons grated Parmigiano-Reggiano
2 teaspoons chopped fresh flat-leaf parsley
2 tablespoons unsalted butter
1 tablespoon olive oil
1/4 cup dry white wine
1/4 cup chicken broth

1 Sprinkle the veal on both sides with salt and pepper. Lay a slice of prosciutto on each piece of veal. Sprinkle with the cheese, then with the parsley. Roll up the cutlets and pin them closed with a toothpick.

2 In a medium skillet, melt 1 tablespoon of the butter with the oil over medium heat. Add the rolls and cook, turning the pieces until browned on all sides, about 10 minutes. Transfer the rolls to a plate and keep warm.

3 Add the wine and chicken broth to the skillet and cook over high heat, scraping the pan, until the liquid is slightly syrupy, about 2 minutes. Remove from the heat and swirl in the remaining 1 tablespoon butter. Pour the sauce over the veal and serve immediately.

Rollatini or Involtini

Thin veal cutlets rolled around a filling, then pan cooked, are known as either *rollatini* or *involtini*, meaning little rolls or little stuffed things. The rolls can also be threaded on a skewer and grilled or broiled, in which case they are called *spiedini*.

For easy stuffing and rolling, the veal pieces should be no more than 1/8 inch thick and about 4 × 3 inches in size. I use sturdy round toothpicks and pin the veal closed in the center parallel to the roll. The rolls stay closed with only one toothpick, and they are easy to turn in the pan. If you are making spiedini, there is no need to use toothpicks: hold the roll closed, then thread the skewer through the open edge to secure it.

Veal Rolls with Anchovies
Rollatini alla Napolitana

MAKES 4 SERVINGS

Neapolitans use anchovies in their veal roll filling to add a zesty flavor to the mild taste of meat and mozzarella.

1 pound veal cutlets, pounded thin, cut into 8 pieces
4 ounces fresh mozzarella, cut into 8 (2-inch) sticks
8 anchovy fillets, drained and patted dry
Freshly ground black pepper
3 tablespoons unsalted butter
1/2 cup dry white wine
2 tablespoons chopped fresh flat-leaf parsley

1 Place a piece of cheese and an anchovy at one short end of each piece of veal. Sprinkle with pepper. Roll up the veal slices and pin each one closed with a toothpick.

2 In a large skillet, melt 2 tablespoons of the butter over medium heat. Add the rolls and cook until the veal feels firm to the touch and is nicely browned, about 10 minutes. Transfer the rolls to a serving dish and keep warm.

3 Turn the heat to high and add the wine to the skillet. Cook, scraping the pan, until the liquid is slightly thickened, about 2 minutes. Remove from the heat and swirl in the remaining 1 tablespoon butter and the parsley. Pour the sauce over the veal and serve immediately.

Veal Rolls with Spinach
Rollatini di Vitello con Spinaci

MAKES 4 SERVINGS

You can assemble these veal rolls well in advance of cooking them. Keep them covered in the refrigerator until serving time. Don't be concerned if some of the spinach leaks out. It adds color to the creamy sauce.

8 ounces fresh spinach
4 tablespoons unsalted butter
1/4 cup very finely chopped shallot or onion
Pinch of freshly grated nutmeg
Salt and freshly ground black pepper
1 pound veal cutlet, cut into 8 pieces, pounded thin
4 slices imported Italian prosciutto, cut in half crosswise
1/2 cup dry white wine
1/2 cup heavy cream

1 Put the spinach in a large pot over medium heat with 1/4 cup of water. Cover and cook 2 to 3 minutes, or until wilted and tender. Drain and cool. Wrap the spinach in a lint-free cloth and squeeze out as much water as possible. Finely chop the spinach.

2 In a large skillet, melt two tablespoons of the butter over medium heat. Add the shallot or onion and cook until very tender, about 5 minutes. Stir in the spinach, nutmeg, and salt and pepper to taste. Remove from the heat.

3 Lay the veal cutlets out on a flat surface. Sprinkle with salt and pepper. Spread with some of the spinach. Place half of a prosciutto slice on each. Roll up the cutlets from the short end and pin each one closed with a toothpick.

4 Melt the remaining butter in a large skillet. Add the veal rolls and brown on all sides, about 10 minutes. Add the wine and bring to a simmer. Cook 10 minutes, turning the rolls occasionally.

5 Add the cream and stir well. Simmer, turning the rolls often, until the sauce is thickened and coats the rolls, 4 to 5 minutes. Remove the toothpicks before serving. Serve hot.

Veal Rolls with Prosciutto and Cheese
Spiedini di Vitello al Prosciutto

MAKES 4 SERVINGS

Anna Tasca Lanza operates a cooking school called The World of Regaleali at her family's farm and winery in Vallelunga in Sicily. Anna taught me an excellent trick for preparing veal rolls and other foods to prevent them from rotating on the skewer during broiling or grilling. Instead of just one skewer, use two, holding the skewers side by side about an inch apart like the tines of a large meat fork. Spear the rolls on both skewers at once. This holds the pieces securely and makes turning them easier.

1 pound veal cutlets, pounded thin, cut into 8 pieces

Salt and freshly ground black pepper

4 thin slices imported Italian prosciutto, cut in half crosswise

4 ounces fontina or mozzarella, cut into 8 (2-inch) sticks

About 12 large fresh sage leaves

2 tablespoons extra-virgin olive oil

1 Place the veal cutlets on a flat surface. Sprinkle lightly with freshly ground pepper.

2 Lay a piece of prosciutto on each veal cutlet, trimming it to fit as needed. Place a piece of cheese on one end of each. Roll up the cutlets from the short end, tucking in the sides to form neat rolls.

3 Place a barbecue grill or broiler rack about 5 inches from the heat source. Preheat the grill or broiler. Hold two metal skewers side by side about 1 inch apart like the tines of a large meat fork. Alternate the rolls on the skewers with the sage leaves, beginning and ending with the leaves.

4 Brush the rolls with the olive oil. Grill or broil until the meat is lightly browned, about 5 minutes on each side. Serve hot.

Grilled Veal Rolls with Mozzarella and Bread Crumbs
Spiedini di Vitello alla Mamma

MAKES 6 SERVINGS

For summer barbecues, my mother would make big batches of these veal rolls in assembly-line fashion. First she would lay out the meat slices, then top each piece with a dab of homemade lard, an ingredient often used in Neapolitan cooking. Next my sister and I would follow along with the remaining filling ingredients. Rolled and skewered, the meat could be prepared and refrigerated up to several hours before it was cooked. Though I still like to make these rolls, I eliminate the lard in a concession to modern tastes.

1 1/2 pounds veal cutlets pounded thin, cut into 12 pieces

Salt and freshly ground black pepper

8 ounces fresh mozzarella, cut into 12 (1/2-thick) sticks

3 tablespoons chopped fresh flat-leaf parsley

2 garlic cloves, finely chopped

3/4 cup plain bread crumbs

3 tablespoons olive oil

1 Lay the veal out on a flat surface. Sprinkle the pieces with salt and pepper. Place a piece of cheese at one end of each veal cutlet. Sprinkle with the parsley and garlic. Roll up the veal from the short end.

2 Place a barbecue grill or broiler rack about 5 inches from the heat source. Preheat the grill or broiler. Hold two metal or bamboo skewers parallel, about 1 inch apart. Spear one of the rolls on the skewers as if they were the tines of a large meat fork. Thread the remaining rolls on the skewers in the same way.

3 In a small bowl, blend the bread crumbs with salt and freshly ground pepper. Brush the rolls with olive oil and sprinkle them with the crumbs, patting them to adhere.

4 Grill or broil the skewers, turning once, just until the meat feels firm when pressed and the cheese is slightly melted, about 10 minutes. Serve hot.

❧ Veal Chops

Veal chops can be from the loin, rib, or shoulder. The first two are much more expensive but very good for grilling, broiling, or pan frying. Shoulder chops can be cooked in the same ways, but they need to be well trimmed. Shoulder chops can also be braised or cut up for stew.

Skillet Veal Chops
Lombatine in Padella

MAKES 4 SERVINGS

At one time, the finest veal came from very young calves that were fed only their mother's milk. Today most animals are fed on formula and raised in pens that restrict their movement. This results in pale white, very tender meat that is quite lean. Choice cuts like loin or rib chops can be expensive. To make the most of them they should be carefully cooked just until medium-rare and pink in the center, otherwise they will be chewy and tasteless.

This recipe and the one that follows are two basic ways to cook veal chops on the stove top that are used throughout Italy.

4 veal loin chops, about 1 inch thick
Salt and freshly ground black pepper
2 tablespoons unsalted butter
1 tablespoon olive oil
8 large fresh sage leaves, torn into pieces

1 Pat the chops dry with paper towels. Sprinkle the chops on both sides with salt and pepper.

2 In a skillet large enough to hold the chops in a single layer, melt the butter with the oil over medium-high heat. Add the chops to the pan. Scatter the sage around the chops. Cook 3 minutes on one side, or until nicely browned. Turn the meat over with tongs and brown the other side until just pink in the center, about 2 minutes more. Serve immediately.

Veal Chops with Rosemary and White Wine
Lombatine di Vitello al Vino Bianco

MAKES 4 SERVINGS

A light coating of flour before cooking helps these chops to brown nicely. The flour also lightly thickens the pan sauce. These chops lend themselves to a number of variations.

2 tablespoons olive oil
4 veal loin chops, about 1 inch thick
1/2 cup all-purpose flour
2-inch sprig rosemary
Salt and freshly ground black pepper
1/2 cup dry white wine
1 tablespoon unsalted butter

1 In a skillet large enough to hold the chops in a single layer, heat the oil over medium-high heat. Quickly roll the chops in the flour and shake off the excess. Place the chops in the pan with the rosemary. Cook 3 minutes on one side, or until nicely browned. Turn the meat over with tongs and brown the other side about 2 minutes more, or until just pink in the center. Transfer the chops to a plate and sprinkle with salt and pepper.

2 Pour off the oil. Add the wine to the skillet and simmer, scraping the bottom of the pan to blend in the browned bits, until the liquid is reduced and slightly thickened. Remove from the heat and swirl in the butter.

3 Return the chops and any accumulated juices to the pan. Cook over low heat 1 minute to heat through. Transfer the chops to a plate and serve hot.

Variations: Use sage or thyme instead of the rosemary. Add a lightly crushed garlic clove to the pan. Or try substituting dry Marsala for the white wine.

Roasted Veal Chops

Lombatine al Forno

MAKES 4 SERVINGS

Thick-cut chops take well to this method, a combination of stove-top and oven cooking. Just be sure not to overcook the chops, or they will be dry.

1/4 cup olive oil
4 veal chops, about 2 inches thick
Salt and freshly ground black pepper
1 tablespoon unsalted butter
3 garlic cloves, finely chopped
2 sprigs fresh rosemary
6 fresh sage leaves
1/2 cup dry white wine
1 cup beef or chicken broth

1 Place a rack in the center of the oven. Preheat the oven to 400°F.

2 Pat the chops dry with paper towels. In an oven-proof skillet large enough to hold the chops in a single layer, heat the oil over medium heat. Sprinkle the chops on both sides with salt and pepper. Place the chops in the pan and cook until nicely browned, about 4 minutes. Turn the meat over with tongs and brown the other side 3 to 4 minutes more.

3 Transfer the pan to the center rack of the oven and cook until medium-rare, about 10 minutes. To check for doneness, cut one chop in the thickest part near the bone. The meat should be just pink. Place the chops on a platter. Cover and keep warm.

4 Pour the oil out of the skillet. Place the skillet over medium heat. Add the butter, garlic, rosemary, and sage. Cook 1 minute, scraping the pan. Add the wine and bring to a simmer. Cook 1 minute. Add the broth and cook until the liquid is reduced and slightly thickened, about 3 minutes. Season to taste with salt and pepper. Strain the sauce over the chops. Serve hot.

Veal Chops with Sweet Peppers

Vitello con Peperoni

MAKES 4 SERVINGS

This is a simple weeknight dish that can be varied many ways. Try adding a few anchovies along with the garlic if you like them.

4 tablespoons olive oil
3 to 4 large red or yellow bell peppers, stemmed, cored, and thinly sliced
2 garlic cloves, finely chopped
8 fresh sage leaves
Salt and freshly ground black pepper to taste
4 veal loin or rib chops, about 1 inch thick
1/2 cup dry white wine

1 In a skillet large enough to hold the chops in a single layer, heat 3 tablespoons of the oil over medium heat. Add the peppers and cook, stirring occasionally, for 5 minutes. Stir in the garlic, sage, and salt and pepper top taste and cook until the peppers are tender and lightly browned, about 10 minutes more. Transfer the peppers to a plate and wipe out the skillet.

2 Heat the remaining 1 tablespoon oil over medium high heat. Pat the chops dry and sprinkle them on both sides with salt and pepper. Add the veal to the skillet and cook until nicely browned, 4 to 5 minutes. Turn the chops over with tongs and cook until browned, about 4 minutes. Spoon off the excess fat.

3 Add the wine and bring to a simmer. Cover and cook until the chops are done to taste, about 2 minutes for medium-rare. To check for doneness, cut one chop in the thickest part near the bone. The meat should be just pink. Transfer the chops to a serving platter. Cover and keep warm.

4 Raise the heat and reduce the liquid in the pan until it is slightly thickened, about 2 minutes. Add the peppers and cook 1 minute or until heated through.

5 Spoon the peppers over the veal and serve hot.

Stuffed Veal Chops with Ham and Fontina

Costolette alla Valdostana

MAKES 4 SERVINGS

Rib chops are the best choice for this recipe, because the bone is on the outside and it is easy to cut a slit in the meat for stuffing.

1/2 cup all-purpose flour
2 large eggs, beaten
Salt and freshly ground black pepper
1 cup plain dry bread crumbs
4 veal rib chops, about 1 inch thick
4 slices boiled ham
2 ounces Fontina Valle d'Aosta, cut into 4 slices
4 tablespoons unsalted butter

1 Spread the flour on a piece of wax paper. In a shallow bowl, beat the eggs with the salt and pepper to taste and place it next to the wax paper. Put the bread crumbs in a shallow plate and place it next to the eggs, so all three ingredients are in a row.

2 Place a cooling rack over a tray. Place the chops on a cutting board. Trim off the fat around the edge of the chops. Holding a sharp knife parallel to the cutting board, make a slit like a pocket in each of the chops. Tuck a piece each of the ham and the cheese in each chop. Pat the chops dry. Dip the chops in the flour, then in the eggs, then in the bread crumbs, patting to coat the chops completely. Place the chops on the rack to dry 15 minutes.

3 In a skillet large enough to hold the chops in a single layer, melt the butter over medium heat. Add the chops and cook until golden brown and crisp, about 5 minutes. Turn the chops over with tongs and brown on the other side, about 4 minutes. To check for doneness, cut one chop in the thickest part near the bone. The meat should be just pink. Serve immediately.

Veal Chops, Milan Style

Costolette alla Milanese

MAKES 4 SERVINGS

Though often made with veal cutlets in this country, in Milan veal Milanese is made with veal chops pounded thin. The coating for these chops is just eggs and bread crumbs, and the resulting crust is thinner and more delicate than in the previous recipe. These chops are often served with a chopped tomato salad.

4 veal rib chops, about 3/4 inch thick
1 cup plain dry bread crumbs, preferably homemade
2 large eggs
1 teaspoon salt
4 tablespoons unsalted butter
1 lemon, cut into wedges

1. Trim off the fat around the edge of the chops. Place the chops between two sheets of plastic wrap. Gently pound the meat to a 1/4-inch thickness.

2 Spread the bread crumbs on a piece of wax paper. In a shallow plate, beat the eggs with the salt and place it next to the wax paper. Dip the chops in the egg mixture, then in the bread crumbs, patting to coat the chops completely. Place the chops on a rack to dry for 10 minutes.

3 In a skillet large enough to hold the chops in a single layer, melt the butter over medium heat. When the butter foam subsides, add the chops and cook until browned and crisp, 3 to 4 minutes. Turn the chops over with tongs and brown the other side about 3 minutes.

4 Serve hot with lemon wedges.

Braised Veal Chops
Rustin Negaa

MAKES 4 SERVINGS

Milan can be cold and damp in winter, so hearty braised meat dishes are popular home cooking. These braised chops are a typical meal on a bone-chilling day. Serve them with mashed potatoes.

¼ cup all-purpose flour
Salt and freshly ground black pepper
2 tablespoons unsalted butter
1 medium onion, finely chopped
1 carrot, finely chopped
2 tablespoons chopped pancetta
2 sage leaves, chopped
1 2-inch sprig rosemary
4 veal shoulder chops, about 1 inch thick, trimmed
½ cup dry white wine
½ cup chicken broth

1 On a piece of wax paper, mix together the flour and salt and pepper to taste.

2 In a skillet large enough to hold all of the chops in a single layer, melt the butter over medium heat. Pat the chops dry. Dip the chops in the flour and shake off the excess. Add the chops to the skillet and brown them about 3 minutes. Turn the chops over with tongs and brown on the other side, about 2 minutes.

3 Scatter the onion, carrot, pancetta, sage, and rosemary around the chops. Cook until the vegetables are softened, about 5 minutes.

4 Add the wine and broth and bring to a simmer. Reduce the heat to low. Cover and cook 1 hour, turning the chops occasionally, until the veal is very tender when pierced with a fork. Add a little water if the sauce becomes too thick. Serve hot.

❧ Veal Stews

Veal, Potato, and Green Bean Stew
Spezzatino di Vitello

MAKES 4 SERVINGS

Every Italian cook has a recipe like this one in his or her repertoire. It lends itself to any number of variations, such as adding fresh or frozen peas or lima beans instead of the green beans, or wedges of turnips or carrots for the potatoes. Because the onion is cooked in the pot first, the veal never takes on more than a light-brown color.

2 medium onions, chopped
2 tablespoons olive oil
2 pounds boneless veal shoulder, trimmed and cut into 2-inch chunks
Salt and freshly ground black pepper
2 teaspoons fresh rosemary
1 garlic clove, finely chopped
2 tablespoons tomato paste
½ cup dry white wine
3 medium potatoes, peeled and cut into wedges
12 ounces green beans, trimmed and cut into 1-inch lengths

1 In a large pot, cook the onions in the oil over medium heat, stirring frequently, until tender and golden, about 10 minutes. Add the veal pieces to the pot. Cook until lightly browned, about 15 minutes.

2 Sprinkle with salt and pepper. Add the rosemary and garlic. Stir in the tomato paste. Add the wine and simmer until most of the liquid evaporates, about 3 minutes.

3 Add the potatoes to the pot. Sprinkle with salt and pepper to taste. Add 2 cups water and bring the mixture to a simmer.

4 Lower the heat. Cover the pot and cook, stirring occasionally, 1 hour or until the veal is tender when pierced with a fork.

(continues)

5 Add the green beans to the pot and simmer 10 minutes more or until all of the meat and vegetables are tender. Taste and adjust seasoning. Serve hot.

Veal Stew with Rosemary and Peas
Stufato di Vitello

MAKES 4 SERVINGS

Veal shoulder seems to be the most readily available cut for stewing, but chuck is good too, or you can substitute bone-in cuts like the breast or shanks. Bone-in cuts will take much longer to cook, though the bones add a lot of flavor to the stew, as well as collagen, which adds texture and richness to the cooking liquid. I had this stew at La Campana, a favorite trattoria in Rome.

2 tablespoons olive oil

1 1/2 pounds boneless veal shoulder, trimmed and
    cut into 2-inch chunks

1 medium onion, chopped

3 large garlic cloves, finely chopped

2 teaspoons chopped rosemary

Salt and freshly ground black pepper

1/2 cup dry white wine

1/2 cup **Chicken Broth (page 63)** or **Meat Broth (page 62)**

2 cups fresh peas or 1 (10-ounce) package frozen
    peas, partially thawed

1 In a large Dutch oven or other deep, heavy pot with a tight-fitting lid, heat the oil over medium-high heat. Add just enough of the veal pieces as will fit comfortably in the pot in a single layer. Cook, turning frequently, until browned on all sides, about 15 minutes. Transfer the browned pieces to a dish. Repeat with the remaining veal. When browned, return the meat to the pot.

2 Stir in the onion, garlic, and rosemary. Sprinkle with salt and pepper to taste. Add the wine and bring to a simmer. Add the broth. Cover the pan and lower the heat. Simmer the veal, stirring occasionally, over low heat for 1 hour or until the meat is tender when pierced with a fork. Add a little water if the stew seems dry.

3 Stir in the peas. Cover and cook 10 minutes more. Taste and adjust seasoning. Serve hot.

Veal and Pepper Stew
Stufato di Vitello e Peperoni

MAKES 6 SERVINGS

In southern Italian regions, stews such as this one are made from whatever meat is on hand, and sometimes a mixture is used. The peppers and tomatoes add zesty flavor to mild-tasting veal, but the stew can also be made with lamb or pork. Sometimes I add a pinch of crushed red pepper or some fresh rosemary to the ingredients. Soft polenta is the perfect accompaniment to this simple stew.

1/4 cup olive oil

2 pounds boneless veal shoulder, trimmed and
    cut into 2-inch chunks

2 medium onions, sliced

3 large red, green, or yellow bell peppers,
    cut into 1/2-inch strips

1 pound ripe tomatoes, peeled, seeded, and chopped,
    or 2 cups chopped canned tomatoes

Salt and freshly ground black pepper

1 In a large saucepan, heat the olive oil over medium heat. Add only enough of the veal pieces to the pan as will fit comfortably in a single layer without crowding. Cook, turning the pieces often, until browned, about 15 minutes. Transfer the browned pieces to a dish and repeat with the remaining veal.

2 Put the onions and peppers in the pan. Cook, stirring often, until the vegetables are wilted, about 5 minutes.

3 Add the veal, tomatoes, and salt and pepper to taste. Reduce the heat to low. Cover and cook 1 hour, stirring occasionally, or until the veal is tender when pierced with a fork. Taste and adjust seasoning. Serve hot.

Veal Stew with Red Wine
Vitello al Vino Rosso

MAKES 6 SERVINGS

I had this veal stew in Piedmont at the home of winemaker friends. They recommend using barbera, a red wine of the region.

Barbera is made from the barbera grape, native to Piedmont. It has the distinction of being the only Italian grape variety that is considered feminine, so it is called la barbera, *taking the feminine article. Because it is high in acid, barbera is a good wine to go with many foods and is the everyday drinking wine of the Piedmontese. Substitute another hearty red wine if you cannot find barbera.*

1/4 cup all-purpose flour
3 pounds boneless veal shoulder, cut into 2-inch chunks
2 tablespoons unsalted butter
2 tablespoons olive oil
I medium onion, finely chopped
2 tablespoons tomato paste
2 cups dry red wine, such as barbera or Chianti
I cup chicken or beef broth
I large garlic clove, finely chopped
I bay leaf
Pinch of dried thyme
Salt and freshly ground black pepper

1 Place the flour on a sheet of wax paper. Pat the veal dry, then toss the veal with the flour. Shake off the excess.

2 In a large Dutch oven or other deep, heavy pot with a tight-fitting lid, melt the butter with the oil over medium heat. Add just enough of the veal pieces to fit comfortably in a single layer without crowding. Cook, turning the pieces often, until browned on all sides, about 15 minutes. Transfer the veal to a dish. Cook the remaining veal in the same way.

3 Add the onion to the pot and cook until softened, about 5 minutes. Stir in the tomato paste. Add the wine and cook, scraping the bottom of the pot with a wooden spoon, until the wine comes to a simmer. Return the meat to the pan and add the broth, garlic, herbs, and salt and pepper. Partially cover the pan and reduce the heat to low.

4 Cook 1 1/2 hours, stirring occasionally, until the meat is tender when pierced with a fork. Add a little more broth or water if the sauce becomes too thick. Taste and adjust seasoning. Serve hot.

Veal Goulash with Cream
Gulasch di Vitello

MAKES 4 TO 6 SERVINGS

A hint of lemon flavors this elegant stew from Alto Adige. The technique is slightly different from other stews in that the flour is added to the flavoring ingredients rather than coating the meat, making the stew seem lighter.

The herbs are tied together in a small bouquet so that they can easily be removed before serving.

This stew goes well with boiled potatoes, gnocchi, or rice.

2 tablespoons unsalted butter
2 1/2 pounds boneless veal stew, trimmed and
    cut into 1 1/2-inch pieces
Salt and freshly ground black pepper
I medium onion, finely chopped
2 tablespoons all-purpose flour
2 cups chicken or beef broth
I bay leaf
3 sprigs fresh parsley
A few sprigs fresh thyme
2-inch strip lemon zest
1/4 cup heavy cream

1 In a large Dutch oven or other deep, heavy pot with a tight-fitting lid, melt the butter over medium heat. Add just enough of the veal pieces to fit comfortably in a single layer. Cook until browned on all sides, about 15 minutes. Transfer the browned meat to a dish. Repeat with the remaining veal. Sprinkle with salt and pepper.

(continues)

2 Add the onion and cook 5 minutes more. Sprinkle with the flour. Raise the heat to medium-high and cook, stirring constantly, for 2 minutes or until the flour is browned.

3 Stir in the broth, scraping and blending in the browned bits at the bottom of the pan with a wooden spoon. Tie together the bay leaf, parsley, thyme, and lemon zest with kitchen string and add it to the liquid. Bring the liquid to a simmer and reduce the heat to low. Cover the pan and cook, stirring occasionally, until the meat is tender when pierced with a fork, about 1 1/2 hours.

4 Remove the herb bouquet. Stir in the cream. Simmer uncovered until thickened, about 5 minutes. Taste and adjust seasoning. Serve hot.

Veal, Sausage, and Mushroom Skewers
Spiedini di Vitello

MAKES 4 SERVINGS

If you want to find something different to serve at your next barbecue, look no further. Small pieces of veal, sausages, and mushrooms are a winning combination, especially when grilled over a wood fire as I had them at Trattoria La Piazza in Tuscany. They are also good cooked indoors under the broiler.

1 pound boneless veal shoulder, trimmed and cut into 1 1/2-inch chunks

2 tablespoons olive oil

2 tablespoons fresh lemon juice

Salt and freshly ground black pepper

1 medium red onion, cut into wedges and separated into layers

16 white mushrooms, rinsed

1 pound Italian pork sausages, cut into 1 1/2-inch chunks

Fresh sage leaves

Lemon wedges

1 In a large bowl, combine the veal, oil, lemon juice, and salt and pepper to taste. Cover and marinate at least 1 hour and up to 3 hours.

2 Place a barbecue grill or broiler rack about 5 inches from the heat source. Preheat the grill or broiler.

3 Thread the veal, onion, mushrooms, sausage, and sage leaves alternately on 8 short skewers.

4 Grill or broil the skewers, turning them frequently, for 6 minutes or until browned on all sides and the sausages are cooked through. Serve hot with lemon wedges.

❧ Veal Shanks

In Friuli–Venezia Giulia, veal shanks are often cooked whole as a roast, while in Lombardy they are typically cut into thick slices for osso buco.

Veal Shanks, Milan Style
Osso Buco alla Milanese

MAKES 4 SERVINGS

In Milan, osso buco is a classic and beloved dish. Tender slices of braised veal shanks are served sprinkled with very finely chopped garlic, lemon zest, and anchovy to give a final lift to the sauce. Serve osso buco (literally, "bone with a hole") with small spoons to scoop out the tasty bone marrow. Serious marrow lovers can find long thin marrow spoons to remove every last bit. Saffron Risotto (page 209) is the perfect accompaniment.

¹/₄ cup all-purpose flour

4 (1¹/₂-inch-thick) meaty slices veal shank

2 tablespoons unsalted butter

1 tablespoon olive oil

Salt and freshly ground black pepper

1 small onion, finely chopped

¹/₂ cup dry white wine

1 cup peeled, seeded, and chopped fresh tomatoes or chopped canned tomatoes

1 cup chicken or beef broth

2 garlic cloves, finely chopped

2 tablespoons finely chopped flat-leaf parsley

2 anchovy fillets (optional)

1 teaspoon grated lemon zest

1 Spread the flour on a piece of wax paper. Dredge the veal in the flour, shaking off the excess.

2 In a Dutch oven or other deep, heavy pot with a tight-fitting lid, melt the butter with the oil over medium heat. Add the veal and sprinkle it with salt and pepper. Cook until browned, about 10 minutes. Turn the slices over with tongs and sprinkle with salt and pepper. Scatter the onion around the meat. Cook until the onion is tender and the meat is browned, about 10 minutes more.

3 Add the wine and cook, scraping up and blending in the browned bits at the bottom of the pan with a wooden spoon. Stir in the tomatoes and broth and bring to a simmer. Turn the heat to low and partially cover the pan.

4 Cook, basting the meat occasionally with the sauce, until the veal is tender and coming away from the bone when tested with a fork, 1¹/₂ to 2 hours. If there is too much liquid, remove the cover and allow it to evaporate.

5 About 5 minutes before serving, mix together the garlic, parsley, anchovy (if using), and the lemon zest. Stir the mixture into the sauce in the pan and baste the meat. Serve immediately.

Veal Shanks with Barbera
Osso Buco al Vino Rosso

MAKES 4 SERVINGS

Though the Milanese version of osso buco is the best known, the dish is made in other regions as well. This is a Piedmontese recipe.

When purchasing veal shank for osso buco, try to get slices cut from the hind legs. They are meatier than those cut from the foreshank. Look for bones with plenty of marrow.

2 tablespoons unsalted butter

1 tablespoon olive oil

4 (1¹/₂-inch-thick) meaty slices veal shank

Salt and freshly ground black pepper

2 carrots, chopped

1 medium onion, chopped

1 celery rib, chopped

1 cup dry red wine such as Italian barbera or chianti

1 cup chopped fresh or canned tomatoes

2 teaspoons chopped fresh thyme, or ¹/₂ teaspoon dried

1 cup beef broth (Meat Broth, page 62)

1 In a large Dutch oven or other deep, heavy pot with a tight-fitting lid, melt the butter with the oil

(continues)

over medium heat. Pat the veal dry. Add the veal to the pot and sprinkle it with salt and pepper. Cook, turning the shanks occasionally, until browned, about 10 minutes. Transfer the veal to a plate.

2 Add the carrots, onion, and celery to the pot. Cook, stirring often, until tender and golden, about 10 minutes.

3 Add the wine and cook, scraping the pan with a wooden spoon. Stir in the tomatoes, thyme, and broth and bring to a simmer. Return the meat to the pot.

4 When the liquid is simmering, partially cover the pot. Turn the heat to low. Cook 1 1/2 to 2 hours, turning the meat occasionally and basting with the sauce until the meat is very tender and coming away from the bone when tested with a fork. If the sauce seems dry, add a little water or more broth to the pot.

5 Transfer the veal to a serving platter. If the sauce is thin, cover the veal and set it aside. Place the pot over high heat. Cook, stirring frequently, until the liquid is reduced and slightly syrupy. Spoon the sauce over the meat and serve immediately.

Veal Shanks with Porcini
Stinco di Vitello al Porcini

MAKES 6 TO 8 SERVINGS

Though veal shanks are more often sawed crosswise into slices for individual servings in the United States, in the Friuli–Venezia Giulia and Veneto regions of Italy, the shank is often left whole for braising or roasting.

The whole shank is a great-looking cut of meat. The bone serves as a handle to make slicing easier, and the meat, sliced parallel to the bone, is flavorful, tender, and moist. The butcher will probably have to trim the shanks, so be sure to order them in advance. Ask to have the excess bone cut off above and below the meat.

I ounce dried porcini mushrooms
2 whole veal shanks, trimmed as for a roast (about 2 1/2 pounds) and tied
1/4 cup olive oil
I tablespoon unsalted butter
Salt and freshly ground black pepper
2 carrots, finely chopped
I celery rib, finely chopped
I medium onion, finely chopped
2 garlic cloves, chopped
I cup dry white wine
I tablespoon tomato paste
I (2-inch) sprig fresh rosemary
4 fresh sage leaves
I bay leaf

1 Place the mushrooms in a bowl with 1 cup warm water. Let stand 30 minutes. Lift the mushrooms out of the liquid and rinse them well under running water, paying special attention to the base of the stems where soil collects. Drain and chop fine. Strain the mushroom liquid through a paper coffee filter into a bowl. Reserve the liquid.

2 In a Dutch oven large enough to hold the veal shanks side by side, or another deep, heavy pot with a tight-fitting lid, heat the olive oil with the butter over medium heat. Add the veal and cook, turning the shanks occasionally, until browned, about 20 minutes. Sprinkle with salt and pepper.

3 Scatter the mushrooms, carrots, celery, onion, and garlic around the shanks and cook until the vegetables are tender, about 10 minutes. Add the white wine and let simmer for 1 minute. Stir in the tomato paste, mushroom liquid, and herbs. Bring to a simmer and cook over low heat, turning the meat occasionally, until it is very tender and comes away from the bone when tested with a fork, about 2 hours. (Add a little water if the liquid evaporates too quickly.)

4 Transfer the meat to a platter and cover to keep warm. Tip the pot and skim the fat from the juices. Discard the herbs. Boil the juices until slightly thickened.

5 Remove the strings from the veal shanks. Holding each shank by the bone, carve the meat lengthwise. Arrange the slices on a platter and spoon the juices over all. Serve immediately.

Roasted Veal Shanks
Stinco al Forno

MAKES 6 TO 8 SERVINGS

In Friuli–Venezia Giulia, whole veal shanks braised with herbs and white wine are served frequently. Accompany the shanks with roasted potatoes and brussels sprouts.

2 tablespoons unsalted butter

I tablespoon olive oil

2 whole veal shanks, trimmed as for a roast (about 2¹/2 pounds) and tied

Salt and freshly ground black pepper

¹/4 cup chopped shallot

6 fresh sage leaves

I 2-inch sprig of rosemary

¹/2 cup dry white wine

I Place a rack in the center of the oven. Preheat the oven to 400°F. In a Dutch oven large enough to hold the meat in a single layer, or another deep, heavy pot with a tight-fitting lid, melt the butter with the oil over medium heat. Pat the veal dry. Add the veal shanks to the pan. Cook, turning the meat with tongs, until browned on all sides, about 20 minutes. Sprinkle with salt and pepper.

2 Scatter the shallots and herbs around the meat. Cook 1 minute. Add the wine and simmer 1 minute.

3 Cover the pot and put it in the oven. Cook, turning the meat occasionally, 2 hours or until it is very tender and coming away from the bone. (Add a little water if the liquid evaporates too quickly.)

4 Transfer the meat to a platter. Remove the strings. Holding each shank by the bone, carve the meat lengthwise. Arrange the slices on a platter and spoon the juices over all. Serve immediately.

Veal Shanks, Grandmother's Style
Brasato di Stinco di Vitello alla Nonna

MAKES 6 TO 8 SERVINGS

My friend Maria Colombo's family came from Friuli and settled in Toronto, where there is a large Friulan population. This recipe was a specialty of her grandmother Ada.

2 whole veal shanks, trimmed as for a roast (about 2¹/2 pounds)

2 tablespoons unsalted butter

2 tablespoons olive oil

Salt and freshly ground black pepper

2 medium carrots, finely chopped

I medium onion, finely chopped

2 garlic cloves, chopped

Sprig of fresh rosemary

I cup dry white wine

I cup peeled seeded and chopped tomatoes

2 cups beef broth (Meat Broth, page 62)

I Place a rack in the center of the oven. Preheat the oven to 350°F. In a Dutch oven large enough to hold the veal shanks, or another deep, heavy pot with a tight-fitting lid, melt the butter with the olive oil over medium heat. Pat the meat dry and place it in the pot. Brown the meat on all sides, about 20 minutes. Sprinkle with the salt and pepper.

2 Scatter the carrots, onion, garlic, and rosemary around the meat. Cook until the vegetables are softened, about 10 minutes more.

3 Add the wine to the pot and simmer 1 minute. Add the tomatoes and broth.

4 Cover the pot and place it in the oven. Cook, turning the meat occasionally, 2 hours or until it is very tender and coming away from the bone. Transfer the meat to a platter. (If the sauce is too thin, simmer the liquid until slightly reduced.)

5 Holding each shank by the bone, carve the meat lengthwise. Arrange the slices on a warm platter. Drizzle with some of the sauce. Serve immediately, with the remaining sauce on the side.

❧ Veal Roasts

Veal Roast with Pancetta
Vitello Arrosto

MAKES 8 SERVINGS

The pancetta wrapping gets crisp as it moistens and flavors this Roman-style veal roast.

4 carrots, cut into quarters

2 onions, cut into quarters

2 tablespoons olive oil

Salt and freshly ground black pepper

3 pounds boneless veal shoulder or rib roast, tied

3 or 4 sprigs of rosemary

4 slices pancetta

^{1}/$_2$ cup homemade Meat Broth (page 62)
    or store-bought beef broth

1 Place a rack in the center of the oven. Preheat the oven to 350°F.

2 In a roasting pan, toss together the carrots, onions, olive oil, and salt and pepper to taste.

3 Sprinkle the veal with salt and pepper. Tuck the rosemary sprigs under the strings holding the roast. Uncoil the pancetta and drape the slices lengthwise or crosswise over the veal. Place the veal on top of the vegetables in the pan.

4 Roast the veal 1^1/$_2$ hours, or until the internal temperature reaches 140°F when measured with an instant-read thermometer. Transfer the veal from the pan to a cutting board and the vegetables to a platter. Cover loosely with foil and let rest 15 minutes.

5 Add the broth to the pan. Cook, scraping the bottom of the pan with a wooden spoon. Boil for 1 minute.

6 Remove the strings and slice the veal. Transfer the slices to a platter, add the vegetables, and pour the juice over all. Serve hot.

Veal in Tuna Sauce
Vitello Tonnato

MAKES 6 SERVINGS

Veal blanketed in a rich tuna sauce is a classic summer dish in northern Italy. Substitute pork loin or turkey or chicken breasts for the veal, if you prefer. Plan to make it at least 24 hours before serving.

Vitello tonnato is sometimes served as a first course, but I prefer it as a main course with green beans and a rice salad.

2 quarts water

2 onions

2 celery ribs, cut up

2 carrots, cut up

6 peppercorns

1 teaspoon salt

2 pounds boneless veal shoulder or round roast, trimmed and tied

SAUCE

2 large eggs

1 teaspoon Dijon mustard

1 tablespoon lemon juice

Salt

1 cup extra-virgin olive oil

1 can Italian tuna in olive oil, drained

2 anchovy fillets

1 tablespoon capers, rinsed and drained, plus more for garnish

Parsley and lemon wedges, for garnish

1 In a large pot, combine the water, onions, carrots, and peppercorns. Add the salt. Bring the water to a simmer. Add the veal. Partly cover the pan and simmer 2 hours, or until the veal is tender when pierced with a knife. Let the meat cool in its broth.

2 Prepare the sauce: In a small saucepan, cook the eggs with cold water to cover 12 minutes. Drain the eggs, let them cool, then peel them. Place the yolks in a food processor or blender. Set the whites aside for another use.

3 Add the mustard, lemon juice, and a pinch of salt. Process until smooth. With the processor running, add the oil in a slow stream.

4 When all of the oil has been added, blend in the tuna, anchovies, and capers until smooth. Taste for seasoning, adding more lemon juice or salt if needed.

5 To serve: Cut the veal into very thin slices. Spread some of the sauce on a serving platter. Make a layer of veal on the platter without overlapping the slices. Spread with more of the sauce. Repeat the layering, spreading the remaining sauce over the top. Cover with plastic wrap and refrigerate at least 3 hours or up to overnight.

6 Just before serving, sprinkle with parsley and capers. Garnish with lemon wedges.

Braised Veal Shoulder
Spalla di Vitello Brasato

MAKES 6 SERVINGS

This old-fashioned veal pot roast is an ideal centerpiece for a memorable Sunday dinner. Start the meal with Creamy Cauliflower Soup (page 75) and accompany the veal with Roast Potatoes with Mushrooms (page 455) and Steamed Tomatoes (page 459). Finish the meal with Amaretto Baked Apples (page 504).

3 pounds boneless veal shoulder roast, tied
3 tablespoons olive oil
2 garlic cloves
I (2-inch) sprig rosemary
Salt and freshly ground black pepper
I cup dry white wine
I cup homemade Meat Broth (page 62),
    or store-bought beef broth

1 Set the oven rack at the middle level of the oven. Preheat the oven to 350°F.

2 In a Dutch oven or other deep, heavy pot with a tight-fitting lid, heat the olive oil over medium heat. Place the roast in the pot. Brown the meat well on all sides, about 20 minutes.

3 Scatter the garlic and rosemary around the veal. Sprinkle the meat with salt and pepper. Add the wine and bring it to a simmer, about 1 minute. Add the broth and cover the pan. Transfer it to the oven.

4 Cook the meat 1 1/2 hours, or until the meat is very tender when pierced with a fork.

5 Transfer the meat to a cutting board. Cover it and let it rest for 10 minutes. If there is too much liquid left in the pot, place the pot on top of the stove and boil it down until it is reduced. Season to taste with salt and pepper.

6 Remove the strings and slice the meat and arrange it on a warm platter. Spoon on the sauce and serve hot.

Other Veal Dishes

Veal-Stuffed Cabbage
Involtini di Verza

MAKES 8 SERVINGS

Milanese cooks serve veal-stuffed cabbage rolls with a simple rice pilaf or mashed potatoes. The veal should be very finely ground for this recipe, so I grind it myself in the food processor. Wrinkly-leafed Savoy cabbage is milder and sweeter than smooth-leaf cabbage, but either can be used in this recipe.

16 large leaves of Savoy cabbage

1 1/2 pounds boneless veal shoulder, cut into 2-inch pieces and well trimmed

1/2 red or yellow bell pepper, chopped

2 large eggs

3/4 cup freshly grated Parmigiano-Reggiano

2 tablespoons chopped fresh flat-leaf parsley

1/4 teaspoon freshly ground nutmeg

1 1/2 teaspoons salt

Freshly ground black pepper

1/2 cup all-purpose flour

2 tablespoons unsalted butter

2 tablespoons vegetable oil

1 cup peeled, seeded, and chopped fresh tomatoes or chopped canned tomatoes

2 cups homemade Chicken Broth (page 63) or Meat Broth (page 62), or store-bought chicken or beef broth

1 Bring a large pot of water to a boil. Add the cabbage leaves and cook until they are soft and flexible, about 2 minutes. Drain the cabbage and cool under running water. Pat the leaves dry and arrange them on a flat surface.

2 In a food processor, finely chop the veal. Add the bell pepper, eggs, cheese, parsley, nutmeg, and salt and pepper. Process until very fine.

3 Scoop 1/4 cup of the meat mixture into the center of each cabbage leaf. Fold the sides over the meat, then fold over the top and bottom to form a neat package. Seal lengthwise with a toothpick.

4 Place the flour in a shallow bowl. In a large skillet, melt the butter with the oil over medium heat. Roll the cabbage packages a few at a time in the flour, then place them in the pan. (Add just enough rolls to fit comfortably in the pan.) Brown on all sides about 10 minutes. Transfer them to a plate. Brown the remainder in the same way.

5 When all the rolls have been transferred to the plate, add the tomatoes and broth to the pan. Season with salt and pepper. Return the cabbage rolls to the pan. Partially cover and cook 40 minutes, turning the rolls once, after 20 minutes.

6 Transfer the rolls to a serving platter. (If the sauce is too thin, boil the sauce until thickened.) Spoon the sauce over the rolls and serve hot.

Veal and Tuna Loaf
Polpettone di Vitello e Tonno

MAKES 8 SERVINGS

This stove-top loaf from the Piedmont region combines the flavors of vitello tonnato (Veal in Tuna Sauce, pages 350–351)—cold poached veal in a tuna sauce—in a meat loaf. It is great for a party because you can make it ahead of time and serve it at cool room temperature. Serve it on a bed of lettuce with small pickles and tomato wedges alongside. The light caper and lemon sauce here is the usual accompaniment, but you could substitute Green Sauce (page 102) or Lemon Mayonnaise (page 104).

1 cup torn crustless Italian or French bread

1/2 cup milk

1 (6 1/2 ounce) can Italian tuna in olive oil, drained

6 anchovy fillets, drained

2 garlic cloves, finely chopped

1 1/4 pounds ground veal

2 large eggs, beaten

2 tablespoons chopped fresh flat-leaf parsley

Salt and freshly ground black pepper

DRESSING

½ cup extra-virgin olive oil

2 tablespoons fresh lemon juice

2 tablespoons capers, rinsed, drained, and chopped

1 tablespoon chopped fresh flat-leaf parsley

1 Soak the bread in the milk until soft, about 5 minutes. Squeeze out the excess liquid and place the bread in a large bowl.

2 Finely chop together the tuna, anchovies, and garlic. Scrape the mixture into the bowl and add the veal, eggs, parsley, and salt and pepper to taste. Mix very well.

3 Lightly dampen a 14 × 12–inch piece of cheesecloth with water. Lay it on a flat surface. Shape the meat mixture into a 9-inch loaf and center it on the cloth. Wrap the cloth around the loaf, folding in like a package and enclosing it completely. With kitchen string, tie the loaf at 2-inch intervals like a roast.

4 Fill a pot large enough to contain the meat loaf with water and bring it to a simmer. Add the meat loaf, cover the pot partway, and cook 45 minutes, turning the loaf over once or twice. Turn off the heat and let stand 15 minutes.

5 Remove the meat loaf from the liquid and place it on a rack to drain and cool slightly. If you're not ready to serve it, remove the cheesecloth, wrap the loaf in plastic wrap, and refrigerate.

6 When ready to serve, whisk together the dressing ingredients in a small bowl. Unwrap the meat loaf and cut into slices. Arrange the slices on a platter and drizzle with the sauce. Serve immediately.

Venetian Liver and Onions
Fegato alla Veneziana

MAKES 4 SERVINGS

In this classic dish of the Veneto, calf's liver is sliced into very thin strips and sautéed with thinly sliced onions. If you can, have the butcher trim and slice the veal for you. Serve the liver and onions with hot Polenta (page 223) made from white cornmeal.

3 tablespoons olive oil

3 large onions, thinly sliced

1½ pounds calf's liver, trimmed and cut into very thin strips

Salt and freshly ground black pepper

1 tablespoon white wine vinegar

1 tablespoon chopped fresh flat-leaf parsley

1 In a large skillet, heat 2 tablespoons of the oil over medium heat. Add the onions and cook, stirring often, until the onions are very tender and golden, about 15 minutes. Add a little water if necessary to prevent them from browning.

2 Scrape the onions onto a plate. Add the remaining oil to the skillet and heat over medium heat. Add the liver and salt and pepper to taste. Raise the heat to high and cook, stirring often, until the liver just loses its pink color, about 5 minutes.

3 Return the onions to the pan and add the vinegar. Stir until the onions are heated through, about 3 minutes. Sprinkle with the parsley and serve immediately.

Stuffed Breast of Veal

Cima alla Genovese

MAKES 10 TO 12 SERVINGS

A boneless breast of veal stuffed with ground meat, vegetables, and cheese is an important part of Christmas dinner in many homes in Genoa, though it is also eaten throughout the year. The veal is cut into thin slices and served plain or with Green Sauce (page 102). Order the veal from the butcher, and ask him or her to remove as much fat as possible and to make a deep pocket. Stuffing the veal is a bit of work, but it can be cooked several days ahead of time, so it is great for a party.

You will need a pot large enough to hold the veal, such as a 4- to 5-gallon stockpot or a large turkey roaster. Either of these can be purchased inexpensively, or you can arrange to borrow one from a friend. You'll also need a sturdy needle and unflavored dental floss to sew the stuffing inside the breast.

4 quarts cold water

2 carrots

1 celery rib

2 medium onions

2 garlic cloves

A few parsley sprigs

1 tablespoon salt

FILLING

3 slices Italian or French bread, crusts removed and torn into bits (about ¹/₂ cup)

¹/₄ cup milk

1 pound ground veal

4 large eggs, beaten

1 cup freshly grated Parmigiano-Reggiano

2 garlic cloves, finely chopped

¹/₄ cup chopped fresh flat-leaf parsley

Salt and freshly ground black pepper

2 cups of fresh peas or 1 (10-ounce) package frozen peas, partially thawed

4 ounces ham in one piece, cut into small dice

¹/₄ cup pine nuts

About 5 pounds boneless breast of veal with a pocket, well trimmed

Radicchio, cherry tomatoes, olives, or pickled vegetables for garnish

1 In a pot large enough to hold the stuffed veal breast, combine the cold water, carrots, celery, onion, garlic, parsley, and salt. Over medium heat, bring the water to a simmer. Cook at a simmer 20 minutes.

2 Meanwhile, prepare the filling: In a small bowl, combine the bread and milk. Let stand 5 minutes. Gently squeeze the bread to drain it.

3 In a large bowl, combine the bread, ground veal, eggs, cheese, garlic, parsley, and salt and pepper to taste. Mix well. Gently stir in the peas, ham, and pine nuts.

4 Rinse the veal breast and pat dry with paper towels. Stuff the mixture into the veal pocket, filling it evenly to eliminate air bubbles. (Do not fill the pocket more than two-thirds full, or the filling may burst out as it cooks.) Sew up the opening using a large needle and unflavored dental floss for thread. Check the sides, and if there are any openings that threaten to allow the filling to leak out, sew them closed also.

5 Lay the veal breast on a 12 × 16–inch piece of cheesecloth. Wrap the cloth around the veal to form a package. Tie up the meat roll with kitchen string in 2-inch sections, like a roast.

6 Carefully lower the veal into the simmering liquid. Place a small pot lid or other object on top of the veal to keep it submerged. Add more water if needed, so that it is completely covered.

7 Bring the liquid back to a simmer. Regulate the heat so that the water continues to simmer. Cover and cook 1 hour. Uncover and cook 1 to 1¹/₂ hours more, or until the veal is tender when pierced with a small knife. (Insert it through the cheesecloth.)

8 Have a large roasting pan ready. Transfer the meat roll to the pan. Cover the wrapped meat with a baking pan or cookie sheet. Lay a heavy weight, such as a cutting board and large cans, on top. Chill in the refrigerator overnight or up to 2 days.

9 When ready to serve, unwrap the veal. Place the veal on a cutting board.

10 Cut the veal into thin slices and place them on a platter. Decorate with radicchio or garnish of your choice. Serve at cool room temperature.

❧ Pork Sausages

Summer Sundays when I was growing up meant an early morning trip to Manhattan Beach in Brooklyn—we had to get there very early to get one of the few picnic spots available. Other family members would arrive soon after, until there were 15 or 20 adults and children assembled, often feeling rather chilled in the stiff morning breeze. We wrapped ourselves in beach towels and drank cups of hot coffee. The barbecue would be lit, and soon we would be eating scrambled eggs and grilled Italian-style sausages for breakfast.

These were not just any sausages. My mother, like her mother before her, had only one or two pork butchers that she trusted in our Brooklyn neighborhood. She knew she could rely on them because the butcher made the sausages while she watched, adding only fresh chunks of pork, trimmed of connective tissue. She would never dream of buying sausages anywhere else.

Juicy, plump pork sausage links called *salsicce* are a specialty of central and southern Italian cooking. The sausages should be pink and meaty, with just enough fat to make them moist and tasty. Though there are variations, most Italians do not care for sausages flavored with anything more exotic than salt and black pepper. Exceptions include sweet sausage with fennel seed and hot sausages with a dose of ground red chile. One Neapolitan specialty is the long thin sausage flavored with flat parsley and grated Pecorino Romano that is coiled into a large wheel held together with wooden pegs. These are not used as an ingredient in a stew or a ragù, but they are great on the barbecue.

Northern Italians prefer *luganega*, a mild pork sausage that is stuffed into a long casing and either tied into long narrow links or coiled into a tight spiral. Sometimes Parmigiano-Reggiano cheese or nutmeg is added.

If you can't get freshly made pork sausages from a butcher, just use the best you can find, avoiding those flavored with pesto, sun-dried tomatoes, or other nontypical flavorings.

Sausage and Pepper Skillet
Salsicce in Padella

MAKES 4 SERVINGS

I can always tell when there is a street fair in my New York neighborhood. The aroma of the sausages, onions, and peppers cooking on the grill fills the air long before the fair comes into view. This same combination cooked in a skillet makes a quick one-dish meal. Serve it with a rustic red wine and Italian bread.

2 tablespoons olive oil
1 pound Italian-style pork sausages, cut into 1-inch chunks
1 medium onion, cut into 1-inch pieces
3 medium all-purpose potatoes, peeled and cut into 1-inch chunks
1 green bell pepper, seeded and cut into 1-inch pieces
1 red bell pepper, seeded and cut into 1-inch pieces
Salt and freshly ground black pepper

1 Heat the oil in a large skillet over medium heat. Add the sausages and brown well on all sides. Spoon off the excess fat.

2 Add the remaining ingredients to the skillet. Cover and cook over low heat, stirring occasionally, until the potatoes are tender and the sausages are cooked through, about 20 minutes. Serve hot.

Roasted Sausages and Potatoes

Salsicce e Patate al Forno

MAKES 4 SERVINGS

The potatoes absorb the spicy sausage flavor as they roast in the same pan. Add some sliced bell peppers or mushrooms for a variation.

4 medium all-purpose potatoes, peeled and
    cut into wedges
I medium onion, halved and thinly sliced
4 tablespoons olive oil
Salt and freshly ground black pepper
I pound sweet or hot Italian-style sausage,
    cut into 2 or 3 chunks

1 Place a rack in the center of the oven. Preheat the oven to 450°F.

2 In a roasting pan large enough to hold all of the ingredients without crowding, toss the potatoes with the onion, olive oil, and salt and pepper to taste.

3 Bake 30 minutes. Remove the pan from the oven. Turn the potatoes and onions. Tuck the sausage pieces among the vegetables. Return the pan to the oven and bake 20 to 30 minutes more, or until the sausages are browned and the potatoes are tender. Serve hot.

Umbrian Sausage and Lentil Stew

Salsicce in Umido

MAKES 6 SERVINGS

Sausage and lentils is a classic dish from Umbria. The lentils used there are a tiny, brown variety called lenticchie di Castelluccio. *These tasty little legumes are paired with another Umbrian specialty, pork sausages made from the highly prized local pigs, which are crumbled and cooked with the lentils in a stew. Even without the Umbrian specialties, this is still a delicious, satisfying dish.*

2 ounces pancetta, chopped
I medium onion, chopped
I celery rib, chopped
I carrot, chopped
6 fresh sage leaves
Pinch of crushed red pepper
2 tablespoons olive oil
2 cups lentils, picked over, rinsed, and drained
I cup chopped fresh or drained canned tomatoes
Salt
I pound plain Italian-style pork sausage, casings removed

1 In a large pot, cook the pancetta, onion, celery, carrot, sage, and red pepper with the oil over medium heat. When the pancetta is lightly browned, after about 15 minutes, stir in the lentils, tomatoes, and 1 teaspoon salt. Add cold water to cover by one inch. Bring to a simmer. Simmer the lentils 45 minutes.

2 Meanwhile, chop the sausage and place it in a medium skillet. Cook over medium heat, stirring occasionally, until the sausage meat is nicely browned, about 10 minutes.

3 When the lentils are almost tender, stir in the sausage and cook 15 minutes more. Taste and adjust seasoning. Serve hot.

Sausages with Grapes

Salsicce con l'Uva

MAKES 4 SERVINGS

Grapes are a sweet counterpoint to rich, tasty pork sausages. Add some lightly mashed garlic cloves, if you like.

I tablespoon olive oil
I pound Italian-style sweet pork sausages
2 cups seedless red or green grapes

1 In a medium skillet, heat the oil over medium heat. Add the sausages and brown well on all sides, about 10 minutes. Spoon off the excess fat.

2 Scatter the grapes around the sausages and cook until the sausages are cooked through, 5 to 10 minutes more. Serve hot.

Sausages with Olives and White Wine

Salsicce con Olive

MAKES 4 SERVINGS

This Roman dish goes well with Peppers with Balsamic Vinegar (page 446).

1 tablespoon olive oil
1 pound Italian-style sweet pork sausages
1/2 cup oil-cured black olives, such as Gaeta
1 garlic clove, thinly sliced
1/2 cup dry white wine
2 tablespoons chopped fresh flat-leaf parsley

1 Heat the oil in a medium skillet over medium heat. Add the sausages and brown on all sides, about 10 minutes.

2 Add the olives, garlic, and wine. Lower the heat. Simmer until the liquid is reduced and the sausages are cooked through, about 10 minutes. Sprinkle with the parsley and serve immediately.

Sausages with Mushrooms

Salsicce con Funghi

MAKES 4 SERVINGS

Basilicata is one of Italy's smallest regions and historically one of its poorest. But the forests in the center of the region yield many types of wild mushrooms. The finest are the porcini—boletus edulis—often called by their French name, cèpes. Though I had sausages cooked with fresh porcini there, the dish is also delicious when made with dried mushrooms. Serve these sausages with polenta or mashed potatoes.

1 ounce dried porcini mushrooms
2 cups warm water
2 tablespoons olive oil
1 pound Italian-style sweet sausages
1 medium onion, finely chopped
1 garlic clove, finely chopped
1/4 cup tomato paste
Salt and freshly ground black pepper

1 Soak the mushrooms in the water for 30 minutes. Remove the mushrooms and reserve the liquid. Rinse the mushrooms under cold running water to remove any grit, paying special attention to the ends of the stems where soil collects. Chop the mushrooms coarsely. Pour the mushroom liquid through a paper coffee filter–lined strainer into a bowl.

2 In a medium skillet, heat the oil over medium heat. Cook the sausages until browned on all sides, about 10 minutes. Add the onion and garlic and cook 5 minutes more.

3 Stir in the mushrooms and tomato paste. Add the mushroom liquid and salt and pepper to taste. Bring to a simmer. Cook over low heat, stirring occasionally, until the sauce is thick, about 20 minutes. Serve hot.

Sausages with Broccoli Rabe

Salsicce con Cima di Rape

MAKES 6 SERVINGS

I like to make this with a combination of sweet and hot Italian-style pork sausages, but either one can be used alone. This makes a good filling for a hero sandwich.

3 tablespoons olive oil
2 pounds hot and/or sweet Italian-style sausages, cut into 1 1/2-inch pieces
3 large garlic cloves, lightly crushed
1 1/2 pounds broccoli rabe, cut into 1-inch pieces.
1/4 cup water
Salt

1 In a large skillet, heat the oil over medium heat. Add the sausages and garlic cloves to the skillet. Cook 10 minutes, turning the sausages until browned on all sides. (Discard the garlic if it begins to turn more than a golden brown.)

2 Add the broccoli rabe and water. Sprinkle with salt. Cover the pan and cook 5 minutes or until the broccoli is tender. Serve hot.

Sausages with Lentils
Cotechino con Lenticchie

MAKES 8 SERVINGS

Cotechino is a large pork sausage about 8 inches long and 2 1/2 inches wide. The meat is subtly flavored with sweet spices and wrapped in pork skin, or cotica, so that it stays very moist and tender as it cooks. In Emilia-Romagna and Lombardy, cotechino is typically served with lentils or beans for New Year's Day. The legumes, which symbolize coins, are said to bring good luck for the whole year.

Zampone, a large pork sausage stuffed into a pig's foot, is also served this way. If you can't find either of these sausages, substitute another large sausage, such as French garlic sausage.

1 onion, finely chopped
1 carrot, finely chopped
1 celery rib, finely chopped
3 tablespoons olive oil
1 garlic clove, finely chopped
Pinch of crushed red pepper
1 pound lentils, picked over, rinsed, and drained
1 cup chopped fresh or canned tomatoes
5 to 6 cups water
Salt
2 cotechini or other large pork sausages, about 1 pound

1 In a large pot, cook the onion, carrot, and celery over medium heat with the olive oil until the vegetables are wilted, about 5 minutes.

2 Stir in the garlic and red pepper and cook 2 minutes more. Stir in the lentils, tomato, water, and salt to taste. Bring to a simmer. Lower the heat, and cook about 45 minutes, or until the lentils are tender. (Add more water if the lentils seem dry.)

3 While the lentils are cooking, put the sausages into a large pot with water to cover. Partially cover the pan and bring to a simmer. Cook 45 minutes or as recommended by the manufacturer.

4 Transfer the sausage to a cutting board. Cut the sausages into thick slices. Spoon the lentils onto a warm serving platter. Arrange the sausage slices on top. Serve immediately.

❧ Pork Ribs and Chops

Pork cuts like chops are easy to test for doneness by touch and sight. Lightly press the meat with your fingertip. If it is soft, it is underdone, but if it is firm and unmoving, it is overdone. What you are looking for is meat that springs back when it is poked. If in doubt, make a small cut near the bone with a sharp knife. It should be pink and juicy, not white or gray. Residual heat will continue to cook the pork, and the juices will become clear as the meat cools slightly before it gets to the table.

Pork Ribs and Cabbage
Spuntature di Maiale e Cavolo

MAKES 4 SERVINGS

In Friuli–Venezia Giulia, pork ribs and cabbage, cooked slowly until the meat is falling off the bone and the vegetable practically melting, are flavored with tasty sausages. Serve with buttery polenta or mashed potatoes for a hearty winter meal.

2 tablespoons olive oil
1 1/2 pounds meaty pork ribs, well trimmed
2 Italian-style sweet pork sausages, cut into 1-inch pieces
1 large onion, chopped
1/2 cup dry white wine
1/2 head shredded cabbage (about 8 cups)
Salt

1 In a large Dutch oven or other deep, heavy pot with a tight-fitting lid, cook the pork ribs and the sausages in the oil over medium heat until browned on one side, about 8 minutes.

2 Turn the meats with tongs and scatter the onion around the pieces. Cook, stirring occasionally, until the onion is tender and golden, about 10 minutes.

3 Add the wine and bring to a simmer. Stir in the cabbage. Sprinkle with salt. Cover the pot and reduce the heat to low. Cook, stirring occasionally, about 1 hour and 30 minutes, or until the rib meat is very tender and coming away from the bone. Transfer to a serving platter and serve hot.

Grilled Spareribs
Spuntatura alla Griglia

MAKES 4 TO 6 SERVINGS

Grilling or broiling is a great way to cook spareribs quickly. Set the grilling rack or broiler pan far enough away from the heat source that the ribs don't burn. Turn them often so that they cook evenly.

3 garlic cloves, finely chopped
$1/4$ cup olive oil
I tablespoon finely chopped fresh rosemary
Pinch of crushed red pepper
Salt
4 pounds spareribs, cut into individual ribs

I In a shallow dish, combine the garlic, oil, rosemary, red pepper, and salt to taste. Add the ribs and stir them to coat with the marinade. Cover and refrigerate 3 hours up to overnight.

2 Place a barbecue grill or broiler pan about 6 inches away from the heat source. Preheat the grill or broiler. Grill or broil the ribs, turning them frequently with tongs, until browned and cooked through, about 20 minutes. Serve hot.

Grilled Marinated Pork Chops
Braciole di Maiale ai Ferri

MAKES 6 SERVINGS

This is a great recipe for quick summer dinners. To test pork chops for doneness, make a small cut near the bone. The meat should still be slightly pink.

I cup dry white wine
$1/4$ cup olive oil
I small onion, thinly sliced
I garlic clove, finely chopped
I tablespoon chopped fresh rosemary
I tablespoon chopped fresh sage
6 center-cut pork loin chops, about $3/4$ inch thick
Lemon wedges, for garnish

I Combine the wine, oil, onion, garlic, and herbs in a baking dish large enough to hold the chops in a single layer. Add the chops, cover, and refrigerate for at least 1 hour.

2 Place a barbecue grill or broiler rack about 5 inches from the heat source. Preheat the grill or broiler. Pat the chops dry with paper towels.

3 Grill the meat 5 to 8 minutes, or until nicely browned. Turn the chops over with tongs and cook on the other side for 6 minutes, or until browned and just slightly pink when cut near the bone. Serve hot, garnished with lemon wedges.

Spareribs, Friuli Style
Spuntature di Maiale alla Friulana

MAKES 4 TO 6 SERVINGS

In Fruili, spareribs are simmered slowly until the meat is tender and falling away from the bone. Serve them with mashed potatoes or a plain risotto.

2 cups homemade Meat Broth (page 62)
    or store-bought beef broth
3 pounds pork spareribs, cut into individual ribs
3/4 cup all-purpose flour
Salt and freshly ground black pepper
3 tablespoons olive oil
I large onion, chopped
2 medium carrots, chopped
1/2 cup dry white wine

1 Prepare the broth, if necessary. Pat the ribs dry with paper towels.

2 On a piece of wax paper, combine the flour and salt and pepper to taste. Roll the ribs in the flour, then shake them to remove the excess.

3 In a wide heavy saucepan, heat the oil over medium heat. Add as many ribs as will fit comfortably in a single layer and brown them well on all sides, about 15 minutes. Transfer the ribs to a plate. Repeat until all of the ribs are browned. Drain off all but 2 tablespoons of the fat.

4 Add the onion and carrots to the pan. Cook, stirring occasionally, until lightly browned, about 10 minutes. Add the wine and cook 1 minute, scraping up and blending in the browned bits at the bottom of the pan with a wooden spoon. Return the ribs to the pan and add the broth. Bring the liquid to a simmer. Reduce the heat to low, cover, and cook, stirring occasionally, about 1 1/2 hours, or until the meat is very tender and coming away from the bones. (Add water if the meat becomes too dry.)

5 Transfer the ribs to a warm serving platter and serve immediately.

Spareribs with Tomato Sauce
Spuntature al Pomodoro

MAKES 4 TO 6 SERVINGS

My husband and I had spareribs like these at a favorite osteria, *a casual family-style restaurant in Rome called Enoteca Corsi. It is only open for lunch, and the menu is very limited. But every day it is packed with hordes of workers from nearby offices attracted by its very fair prices and delicious homestyle food.*

2 tablespoons olive oil
3 pounds pork spareribs, cut into individual ribs
Salt and freshly ground black pepper
I medium onion, finely chopped
I medium carrot, finely chopped
I tender celery rib, finely chopped
2 garlic cloves, finely chopped
4 sage leaves, chopped
1/2 cup dry white wine
2 cups canned crushed tomatoes

1 In a Dutch oven or wide, heavy saucepan, heat the oil over medium heat. Add just enough of the ribs to fit comfortably in the pan. Brown them well on all sides, about 15 minutes. Transfer the ribs to a plate. Sprinkle with salt and pepper. Continue with the remaining ribs. When all are done, spoon off all but 2 tablespoons of the fat.

2 Add the onion, carrot, celery, garlic, and sage, and cook until wilted, about 5 minutes. Stir in the wine and bring to a simmer 1 minute, stirring with a wooden spoon and scraping up and blending in the browned bits at the bottom of the pan.

3 Return the ribs to the pan. Add the tomatoes, and salt and pepper to taste. Cook 1 to 1 1/2 hours, or until the ribs are very tender and the meat is coming away from the bones.

4 Transfer ribs and tomato sauce to a serving plate and serve immediately.

Spiced Ribs, Tuscan Style
Spuntature alla Toscana

MAKES 4 TO 6 SERVINGS

With friends from the Lucini olive oil company, I visited the home of olive growers in the Chianti region of Tuscany. Our group of journalists ate lunch in a grove of olive trees. After various bruschette *and* salami, *we were served steak, sausages, ribs, and vegetables, all grilled over grapevine cuttings. The pork ribs marinated in a tasty rub of olive oil and crushed spices were my favorite, and we all tried to guess what was in the mix. Cinnamon and fennel were easy, but we were all surprised to learn another spice was star anise. I like to use little baby-back ribs for this recipe, but spareribs would be fine, too.*

2 star anise
I tablespoon fennel seeds
6 juniper berries, lightly crushed with the side of a heavy knife
I tablespoon kosher or fine sea salt
I teaspoon cinnamon
I teaspoon finely ground black pepper
Pinch of crushed red pepper
4 tablespoons olive oil
4 pounds baby-back ribs, cut into individual ribs

1 In a spice grinder or blender, combine the star anise, fennel, juniper, and salt. Grind until fine, about 1 minute.

2 In a large shallow bowl, combine the contents of the spice grinder with the cinnamon and black and red pepper. Add the oil and stir well. Rub the mixture all over the ribs. Place the ribs in the bowl. Cover with plastic wrap and refrigerate 24 hours, stirring occasionally.

3 Place a barbecue grill or broiler rack about 6 inches from the heat source. Preheat the grill or broiler. Pat the ribs dry, then grill or broil the ribs, turning them frequently, until browned and cooked through, about 20 minutes. Serve hot.

Spareribs and Beans
Puntini e Fagioli

MAKES 6 SERVINGS

When I know I have a busy week ahead, I like to make up stews like this one. They only improve when made in advance, and need just a quick reheating to make a satisfying dinner. Serve these with cooked greens like spinach or escarole, or a green salad.

2 tablespoons olive oil
3 pounds country-style pork spareribs, cut into individual ribs
I onion, chopped
I carrot, chopped
I garlic clove, finely chopped
2¹/₂ pounds fresh tomatoes, peeled, seeded, and chopped, or I (28-ounce) can peeled tomatoes, chopped
I (3-inch) sprig rosemary
I cup water
Salt and freshly ground black pepper
3 cups cooked or canned cannellini or cranberry beans, drained

1 In a large Dutch oven or other deep, heavy pot with a tight-fitting lid, heat the oil over medium heat. Add just enough of the ribs to fit comfortably in the pan. Brown them well on all sides, about 15 minutes. Transfer the ribs to a plate. Sprinkle with salt and pepper. Continue with the remaining ribs. When all are done, pour off all but 2 tablespoons of the fat.

2 Add the onion, carrot, and garlic to the pot. Cook, stirring frequently, until the vegetables are tender, about 10 minutes. Add the ribs, then the tomatoes, rosemary, water, and salt and pepper to taste. Bring to a simmer over low heat and cook 1 hour.

3 Add the beans, cover, and cook 30 minutes or until the meat is very tender and coming away from the bone. Taste and adjust seasoning. Serve hot.

Spicy Pork Chops with Pickled Peppers
Braciole di Maiale con Peperoncini

MAKES 4 SERVINGS

Pickled hot chiles and sweet pickled peppers are a fine topping for juicy pork chops. Adjust the proportions of the chiles and sweet peppers to suit your taste. Serve these with fried potatoes.

2 tablespoons olive oil

4 center-cut pork loin chops, each about 1 inch thick

Salt and freshly ground black pepper

4 garlic cloves, thinly sliced

1 1/2 cups sliced pickled sweet peppers

1/4 cup sliced pickled hot peppers, such as peperoncini or jalapeños, or more of the sweet peppers

2 tablespoons pickling juice or white wine vinegar

2 tablespoons chopped fresh flat-leaf parsley

1 In a large heavy skillet, heat the oil over medium-high heat. Pat the chops dry with paper towels then sprinkle them with salt and pepper. Cook the chops until browned, about 2 minutes, then turn them over with tongs and brown on the other side, about 2 minutes more.

2 Reduce the heat to medium. Scatter the garlic slices around the chops. Cover the pan and cook 5 to 8 minutes or until the chops are tender and just slightly pink when cut near the bone. Regulate the heat so that the garlic does not become dark brown. Transfer the chops to a serving platter and cover to keep warm.

3 Add the sweet and hot peppers and pickling juice or vinegar to the skillet. Cook, stirring, for 2 minutes or until the peppers are heated through and the juices are syrupy.

4 Stir in the parsley. Spoon the contents of the pan over the chops and serve immediately.

Pork Chops with Rosemary and Apples
Braciole al Mele

MAKES 4 SERVINGS

The sweet-tart flavor of apples is a perfect complement to pork chops. This recipe is from Friuli–Venezia Giulia.

4 center-cut pork chops, each about 1 inch thick

Salt and freshly ground black pepper

1 tablespoon chopped fresh rosemary

1 tablespoon unsalted butter

4 golden delicious apples, peeled and cut into 1/2-inch pieces

1/2 cup Chicken Broth (page 63)

1 Pat the meat dry with paper towels. Sprinkle the chops on both sides with the salt, pepper, and rosemary.

2 In a large heavy skillet, melt the butter over medium heat. Add the chops and cook until they are nicely browned on one side, about 2 minutes. Turn the chops over with tongs and brown on the other side, about 2 minutes more.

3 Scatter the apples around the chops and pour in the broth. Cover the skillet and turn the heat to low. Cook about 5 to 10 minutes, turning the chops once, until they are tender and just slightly pink when cut near the bone. Serve immediately.

Pork Chops with Mushroom-Tomato Sauce
Costolette di Maiale con Funghi

MAKES 4 SERVINGS

When buying pork chops, look for chops of similar size and thickness so that they will cook evenly. White button mushrooms, wine, and tomatoes are the sauce for these pork chops. This same treatment is also good on veal chops.

4 tablespoons olive oil

4 center-cut pork loin chops, each about 1 inch thick

Salt and freshly ground black pepper

1/2 cup dry white wine

1 cup chopped fresh or canned tomatoes

1 tablespoon chopped fresh rosemary

1 (12-ounce) package white mushrooms, lightly rinsed, stemmed, and halved or quartered if large

1 In a large heavy skillet, heat 2 tablespoons of the oil over medium heat. Sprinkle the chops with salt and pepper. Place the chops in the pan in a single layer. Cook until they are nicely browned on one side, about 2 minutes. Turn the chops over with tongs and brown on the other side, about 1 to 2 minutes more. Transfer the chops to a plate.

2 Add the wine to the skillet and bring to a simmer. Add the tomatoes, rosemary, and salt and pepper to taste. Cover and cook 10 minutes.

3 Meanwhile, in a medium skillet, heat the remaining 2 tablespoons of oil over medium heat. Add the mushrooms, and salt and pepper to taste. Cook, stirring frequently, until the liquid evaporates and the mushrooms are browned, about 10 minutes.

4 Return the pork chops to the skillet with the tomato sauce. Stir in the mushrooms. Cover and cook 5 to 10 minutes more or until the pork is just cooked through and the sauce is slightly thickened. Serve immediately.

Pork Chops with Porcini and Red Wine
Costolette con Funghi e Vino

MAKES 4 SERVINGS

Browning chops or other cuts of meat adds flavor and improves their appearance. Always pat the chops dry just before browning them, as surface moisture will cause the meat to steam and not brown. After browning, these chops are simmered with dried porcini and red wine. A touch of heavy cream gives the sauce a smooth texture and rich flavor.

1 ounce dried porcini mushrooms

1 1/2 cups warm water

2 tablespoons olive oil

4 center-cut pork loin chops, about 1 inch thick

Salt and freshly ground black pepper

1/2 cup dry red wine

1/4 cup heavy cream

1 Place the mushrooms in a bowl with the water. Let stand 30 minutes. Lift the mushrooms out of the liquid and rinse them well under running water, paying special attention to the base of the stems where soil collects. Drain, then chop fine. Pour the soaking liquid through a paper coffee filter–lined strainer into a bowl.

2 In a large skillet, heat the oil over medium heat. Pat the chops dry. Place the chops in the pan in a single layer. Cook until they are nicely browned, about 2 minutes. Turn the chops over with tongs and brown on the other side, about 1 to 2 minutes more. Sprinkle with salt and pepper. Transfer the chops to a plate.

3 Add the wine to the skillet and simmer 1 minute. Add the porcini and their soaking liquid. Reduce the heat to low. Simmer 5 to 10 minutes, or until the liquid is reduced. Stir in the cream and cook 5 minutes more.

4 Return the chops to the pan. Cook 5 minutes more, or until the chops are just cooked through and the sauce is thickened. Serve immediately.

Pork Chops
with Cabbage
Costolette di Maiale con Cavolo Rosso

MAKES 4 SERVINGS

Balsamic vinegar adds color and sweetness to red cabbage and offers a nice balance to the pork. It is not necessary to use an aged balsamic vinegar for this recipe. Save it to use as a condiment for cheese or cooked meat.

2 tablespoons olive oil

4 center-cut pork loin chops, about 1 inch thick

Salt and freshly ground black pepper

1 large onion, chopped

2 large garlic cloves, finely chopped

2 pounds red cabbage, cut into thin strips

1/4 cup balsamic vinegar

2 tablespoons water

1 In a large skillet, heat the oil over medium heat. Pat the chops dry with paper towels. Add the chops to the pan. Cook until nicely browned, about 2 minutes. Turn the meat over with tongs and brown on the other side, about 1 to 2 minutes more. Sprinkle with salt and pepper. Transfer the chops to a plate.

2 Add the onion to the skillet and cook 5 minutes. Stir in the garlic and cook 1 minute more.

3 Add the cabbage, balsamic vinegar, water, and salt to taste. Cover and cook, stirring occasionally, until the cabbage is tender, about 45 minutes.

4 Add the chops to the pan and cook, turning the chops once or twice in the sauce, until the meat is just cooked through and slightly pink when cut near the bone, about 5 minutes more. Serve immediately.

Pork Chops with Fennel
and White Wine
Braciole di Maiale al Vino

MAKES 4 SERVINGS

There is not a lot of sauce left in the pan when these chops are done, just a tablespoon or two of concentrated glaze to moisten the meat. If you prefer not to use fennel seeds, try substituting a tablespoon of fresh rosemary.

2 tablespoons olive oil

4 center-cut pork loin chops, about 1 inch thick

1 garlic clove, lightly crushed

Salt and freshly ground black pepper

2 teaspoons fennel seeds

1 cup dry white wine

1 In a large skillet, heat the oil over medium-high heat. Pat the pork chops dry. Add the pork chops and garlic to the pan. Cook until the chops are browned, about 2 minutes. Sprinkle with the fennel seeds and the salt and pepper. Turn the chops over with tongs and brown on the second side, about 1 to 2 minutes more.

2 Add the wine and bring to a simmer. Cover and cook 3 to 5 minutes or until the chops are cooked through and just pink when cut near the bone.

3 Transfer the chops to a plate and discard the garlic. Cook the pan juices until reduced and syrupy. Pour the juices over the chops and serve immediately.

Pork Chops, Pizzamaker's Style
Braciole alla Pizzaiola

MAKES 4 SERVINGS

In Naples, pork chops and small steaks, too, can be prepared alla pizzaiola, *in the style of the pizzamaker. The sauce is typically served over spaghetti as a first course. The chops are served as a second course with a green salad. There should be just enough sauce for a half-pound of spaghetti, with a spoonful or so left to serve with the chops.*

2 tablespoons olive oil

4 pork rib chops, about 1 inch thick

Salt and freshly ground black pepper

2 large garlic cloves, finely chopped

1 (28-ounce) can peeled tomatoes, drained and chopped

1 teaspoon dried oregano

Pinch crushed red pepper

2 tablespoons chopped fresh flat-leaf parsley

1 In a large skillet, heat the oil over medium heat. Pat the chops dry and sprinkle with salt and pepper. Add the chops to the pan. Cook until the chops are browned, about 2 minutes. Turn the chops over with tongs and brown on the other side, about 2 minutes more. Transfer the chops to a plate.

2 Add the garlic to the pan and cook 1 minute. Add the tomatoes, oregano, red pepper, and salt to taste. Bring the sauce to a simmer. Cook, stirring occasionally, 20 minutes or until the sauce is thickened.

3 Return the chops to the sauce. Cook 5 minutes, turning the chops once or twice, until they are just cooked through and slightly pink when cut near the bone. Sprinkle with parsley. Serve immediately, or if using the sauce for spaghetti, cover the chops with foil to keep warm.

Pork Chops, Molise Style
Pampanella Sammartinese

MAKES 4 SERVINGS

These chops are spicy and unusual. At one time cooks in Molise would dry their own sweet red peppers in the sun to make paprika. Today, commercially made sweet paprika is used in Italy. In the United States, use paprika imported from Hungary for best flavor.

Grilling pork chops is tricky because they can dry out so easily. Watch them carefully and cook them only until the meat is just slightly pink near the bone.

1/4 cup sweet paprika

2 garlic cloves, chopped

1 teaspoon salt

Crushed red pepper

2 tablespoons white wine vinegar

4 center-cut pork loin chops, about 1 inch thick

1 In a small bowl, mix together the paprika, garlic, salt, and a generous pinch of crushed red pepper. Add the vinegar and stir until smooth. Place the chops on a plate and brush them on all sides with the paste. Cover and refrigerate 1 hour up to overnight.

2 Place a barbecue grill or broiler rack about 6 inches from the heat source. Preheat the grill or broiler. Cook pork chops until browned on one side, about 6 minutes, then turn the meat over with tongs and brown the other side, about 5 minutes more. Cut into the chops near the bone; the meat should be slightly pink. Serve immediately.

❧ Pork Tenderloins and Roasts

The most important matter in cooking pork well is not to overcook. Many old cookbooks recommend cooking roasts to an internal temperature of 180°F. It was important that pork be very well done at a time when the meat was marbled with fat and carried the danger of trichinosis. But today's pork is extremely lean, and bacteria are eradicated at 140°F, so lean pork cuts such as the loin and tenderloin will be rosy pink, juicy, and safe to eat at 150°F. Pork shoulder, butt, and leg, which are fattier and have more connective tissue, can be cooked longer to reach a temperature of 165°F, as can suckling pig. An instant-read thermometer inserted in the thickest part of the meat away from the bone can be used to test the internal temperature of large cuts of meat. Let roasts rest about 10 minutes after cooking them and the temperature will rise another 5 degrees or so.

I have adapted many traditional recipes to accommodate the type of lean pork and the cuts now available in the United States. Pork loin today is usually sold boneless, with the tenderloin removed and sold separately. For a bone-in pork loin, you will most likely have to place a special order with the butcher. The tenderloin is excellent for roasting, grilling, and broiling. For braising, I suggest pork butt, which is fattier and has more connective tissue, so it is better able to withstand long, slow cooking.

Brining or soaking the meat in a salt-water solution is another method used by some cooks today to ensure moist pork, but it is time-consuming, and I prefer not to add all that salt.

Balsamic-Glazed Pork Tenderloin with Arugula and Parmigiano
Maiale al Balsamico con Insalata

MAKES 6 SERVINGS

Pork tenderloins are quick-cooking and low in fat. Here, the glazed pork slices are paired with a crisp arugula salad. If you cannot find arugula, substitute watercress.

2 pork tenderloins (about 1 pound each)
1 garlic clove, finely chopped
1 tablespoon balsamic vinegar
1 teaspoon honey
Salt and freshly ground black pepper

Salad

2 tablespoons olive oil
1 tablespoon balsamic vinegar
Salt and freshly ground black pepper
6 cups trimmed arugula, rinsed and dried
A piece of Parmigiano-Reggiano

1 Place a rack in the center of the oven. Preheat the oven to 450°F. Oil a baking pan just large enough to hold the pork.

2 Pat the pork dry with paper towels. Fold the thin ends under to make it an even thickness. Place the tenderloins about an inch apart in the pan.

3 In a small bowl, stir together the garlic, vinegar, honey, and salt and pepper to taste.

4 Brush the mixture over the meat. Place the pork in the oven and roast 15 minutes. Pour 1/2 cup of water around the meat. Roast 10 to 20 minutes more or until browned and tender. (Pork is done when the internal temperature reaches 150°F on an instant-read thermometer.) Remove the pork from the oven. Leave it in the pan and let it rest at least 10 minutes.

5 In a large bowl, whisk together the oil, vinegar, and salt and pepper to taste. Add the arugula and toss with the dressing. Pile the arugula in the center of a large platter or individual dinner plates.

6 Thinly slice the pork and arrange it around the greens. Drizzle with the pan juices. With a swivel-blade vegetable peeler, shave thin slices of Parmigiano-Reggiano over the arugula. Serve immediately.

Herbed Pork Tenderloin
Filetto di Maiale alle Erbe

MAKES 6 SERVINGS

Pork tenderloins are now readily available, usually packed two to a package. They are lean and tender, if not overcooked, though the flavor is very mild. Grilling gives them added flavor, and they can be served hot or at room temperature.

2 pork tenderloins (about 1 pound each)
2 tablespoons olive oil
2 tablespoons chopped fresh sage
2 tablespoons chopped fresh basil
2 tablespoons chopped fresh rosemary
1 garlic clove, finely chopped
Salt and freshly ground black pepper

1 Pat the meat dry with paper towels. Place the pork tenderloins on a plate.

2 In a small bowl, mix together the oil, herbs, garlic, and salt and pepper to taste. Rub the mixture over the tenderloins. Cover and refrigerate at least 1 hour or up to overnight.

3 Preheat the grill or broiler. Grill the tenderloins 7 to 10 minutes, or until browned. Turn the meat over with tongs and cook 7 minutes more, or until an instant-read thermometer inserted in the center reads 150°F. Sprinkle with salt. Let the meat rest 10 minutes before slicing. Serve hot or at room temperature.

Calabrian-Style Pork Tenderloin with Honey and Chile
Carne 'ncantarata

MAKES 6 SERVINGS

More than any other region in Italy, cooks in Calabria incorporate chile peppers into their cooking. Chiles are used fresh, dried, ground, or crushed into flakes or powder—as paprika or cayenne.

In Castrovillari, my husband and I ate at the Locanda di Alia, an elegant country restaurant and inn. The region's most famous restaurant is run by the Alia brothers. Gaetano is the chef, while Pinuccio manages the front of the house. Their specialty is pork marinated with fennel and chiles in a honey and chile sauce. Pinuccio explained that the recipe, which is at least two hundered years old, was made with preserved pork that had been salted and cured for several months. This is a more streamlined way of making it.

Fennel pollen can be found at many shops specializing in herbs and spices. (See Sources on pages 625–626.) Crushed fennel seeds can be used if the pollen is not available.

2 pork tenderloins (about 1 pound each)
2 tablespoons honey
1 teaspoon salt
1 teaspoon fennel pollen or crushed fennel seeds
Pinch of crushed red pepper
1/2 cup orange juice
2 tablespoons paprika

1 Place a rack in the center of the oven. Preheat the oven to 425°F. Oil a baking pan just large enough to hold the pork.

2 Fold the thin ends of the tenderloins under to make an even thickness. Place the tenderloins about an inch apart in the pan.

3 In a small bowl, stir together the honey, salt, fennel pollen, and crushed red pepper. Brush the

(continues)

mixture over the meat. Place the pork in the oven and roast 15 minutes.

4 Pour the orange juice around the meat. Roast 10 to 20 minutes more, or until browned and tender. (Pork is done when the internal temperature reaches 150°F on an instant-read thermometer.) Transfer the pork to a cutting board. Cover with foil and keep warm while preparing the sauce.

5 Place the baking pan over medium heat. Stir in the paprika and cook, scraping the bottom of the pan, for 2 minutes.

6 Slice the pork and serve it with the sauce.

Roast Pork with Potatoes and Rosemary
Arista di Maiale con Patate

MAKES 6 TO 8 SERVINGS

Everybody loves this pork roast—it's easy to make, and the potatoes absorb the flavors of the pork as they cook together in the same pan. Irresistible.

1 center-cut boneless pork loin roast (about 3 pounds)
2 tablespoons chopped fresh rosemary
2 tablespoons chopped fresh garlic
4 tablespoons olive oil
Salt and freshly ground black pepper
2 pounds new potatoes, halved, or quartered if large

1 Place a rack in the center of the oven. Preheat the oven to 425°F. Oil a roasting pan large enough to hold the pork and potatoes without crowding.

2 In a small bowl, make a paste with the rosemary, garlic, 2 tablespoons of the oil, and a generous amount of salt and pepper. Toss the potatoes in the pan with the remaining 2 tablespoons of oil and half of the garlic paste. Push the potatoes aside and place the meat fat-side up in the center of the pan. Rub or spread the remaining paste all over the meat.

3 Roast 20 minutes. Turn the potatoes. Reduce the heat to 350°F. Roast 1 hour more, turning the potatoes every 20 minutes. The meat is done when

the internal temperature of the pork reaches 150°F on an instant-read thermometer.

4 Transfer the meat to a cutting board. Cover loosely with foil and let rest 10 minutes. The potatoes should be browned and tender. If necessary, turn up the heat and cook them a little more.

5 Slice the meat and arrange it on a warm serving platter surrounded by the potatoes. Serve hot.

Pork Loin with Lemon
Maiale con Limone

MAKES 6 TO 8 SERVINGS

Pork loin roasted with lemon zest makes a fine Sunday dinner. I serve it with slow-cooked cannellini beans and a green vegetable like broccoli or brussels sprouts.

Butterflying the loin is easy enough to do yourself if you follow the instructions; otherwise have the butcher handle it.

1 center-cut boneless pork loin roast (about 3 pounds)
1 teaspoon grated lemon zest
2 garlic cloves, finely chopped
2 tablespoons chopped fresh flat-leaf parsley
2 tablespoons olive oil
Salt and freshly ground black pepper
1/2 cup dry white wine

1 Place a rack in the center of the oven. Preheat the oven to 425°F. Oil a roasting pan just large enough to hold the meat.

2 In a small bowl, mix together the lemon zest, garlic, parsley, oil, and salt and pepper to taste.

3 Pat the meat dry with paper towels. To butterfly the pork, place it on a cutting board. With a long sharp knife such as a boning knife or chef's knife, cut the pork almost in half lengthwise, stopping about 3/4 inch from one long side. Open the meat like a book. Spread the lemon and garlic mixture over the side of the meat. Roll up the pork from one long side to the other like a sausage and tie it with kitchen string at 2-inch intervals. Sprinkle the outside with salt and pepper.

4 Place the meat fat-side up in the prepared pan. Roast 20 minutes. Reduce the heat to 350°F. Roast 40 minutes more. Add the wine and roast 15 to 30 minutes longer, or until the temperature on an instant-read thermometer reaches 150°F.

5 Transfer the roast to a cutting board. Cover the meat loosely with foil. Let rest 10 minutes before slicing. Place the pan on the stove over medium heat and reduce the pan juices slightly. Slice the pork and transfer it to a serving platter. Pour the juices over the meat. Serve hot.

Pork Loin with Apples and Grappa
Maiale con Mele

MAKES 6 TO 8 SERVINGS

Apples and onions teamed with grappa and rosemary flavor this tasty roast pork loin from Friuli–Venezia Giulia.

I center-cut boneless pork loin roast (about 3 pounds)

I tablespoon chopped fresh rosemary, plus more for garnish

Salt and freshly ground black pepper

2 tablespoons olive oil

2 Granny Smith or other tart apples, peeled and thinly sliced

I small onion, thinly sliced

¼ cup grappa or brandy

½ cup dry white wine

1 Place a rack in the center of the oven. Preheat the oven to 350°F. Lightly oil a roasting pan large enough to hold the meat.

2 Rub the pork with the rosemary, salt and pepper to taste, and olive oil. Place the meat fat-side up in the pan and surround it with the apple and onion slices.

3 Pour the grappa and wine over the meat. Roast for 1 hour and 15 minutes, or until an instant-read thermometer inserted in the center reads 150°F. Transfer the meat to a cutting board and cover with foil to keep warm.

4 The apples and onions should be soft. If not, return the pan to the oven and roast 15 minutes more.

5 When they are tender, scrape the apples and onions into a food processor or blender. Puree until smooth. (Add a tablespoon or two of warm water to thin the mixture if needed.)

6 Slice the meat and arrange it on a heated platter. Spoon the apple-onion puree to one side. Garnish with fresh rosemary. Serve hot.

Roast Pork with Hazelnuts and Cream
Arrosto di Maiale alle Nocciole

MAKES 6 TO 8 SERVINGS

This is a variation on a Piedmontese roast pork recipe that first appeared in my book Italian Holiday Cooking. *Here cream, along with hazelnuts, enriches the sauce.*

I center-cut boneless pork loin roast (about 3 pounds)

2 tablespoons chopped fresh rosemary

2 large garlic cloves, finely chopped

2 tablespoons olive oil

Salt and freshly ground black pepper

I cup dry white wine

½ cup hazelnuts, toasted, skinned, and coarsely chopped (see page 559)

I cup homemade Meat Broth (page 62) or Chicken Broth (page 63), or store-bought beef or chicken broth

½ cup heavy cream

1 Place a rack in the center of the oven. Preheat the oven to 425°F. Oil a roasting pan just large enough to hold the meat.

2 In a small bowl, mix together the rosemary, garlic, oil, and salt and pepper to taste. Place the meat fat-side up in the pan. Rub the garlic mixture all over the pork. Roast the meat 15 minutes.

3 Pour the wine over the meat. Cook 45 to 60 minutes more, or until the temperature of the pork reaches 150°F on an instant-read thermometer and

(continues)

the meat is tender when pierced with a fork. Meanwhile, prepare the hazelnuts, if necessary.

4 Transfer the meat to a cutting board. Cover with foil to keep warm.

5 Place the pan over medium heat on the top of the stove and bring the juices to a simmer. Add the broth and simmer 5 minutes, scraping up and blending in the browned bits on the bottom of the pan with a wooden spoon. Add the cream and simmer until slightly thickened, about 2 minutes more. Stir in the chopped nuts and remove from the heat.

6 Slice the meat and arrange the slices on a warm serving platter. Spoon the sauce over the pork and serve hot.

Tuscan Pork Loin
Arista di Maiale

MAKES 6 TO 8 SERVINGS

Here is a classic Tuscan-style pork roast. Cooking the meat with the bone makes it much more flavorful, and the bones are also great to gnaw on.

3 large garlic cloves
2 tablespoons fresh rosemary
Salt and freshly ground black pepper
2 tablespoons olive oil
I bone-in center-cut rib roast, about 4 pounds
I cup dry white wine

I Place a rack in the center of the oven. Preheat the oven to 325°F. Oil a roasting pan just large enough to hold the roast.

2 Very finely chop the garlic and rosemary together, then place them in a small bowl. Add the salt and pepper to taste and mix well to form a paste. Place the roast fat-side up in the pan. With a small knife, make deep slits all over the surface of the pork, then insert the mixture into the slits. Rub the roast all over with the olive oil.

3 Roast 1 hour 15 minutes or until the meat reaches an internal temperature of 150°F on an instant-read thermometer. Transfer the meat to a

cutting board. Cover with foil to keep warm. Let rest 10 minutes.

4 Place the pan over low heat on the top of the stove. Add the wine and cook, scraping up and blending in the browned bits at the bottom of the pan with a wooden spoon until slightly reduced, about 2 minutes. Pour the juices through a strainer into a bowl and skim off the fat. Reheat if necessary.

5 Slice the meat and arrange it on a warm serving platter. Serve it hot with the pan juices.

Roast Pork Shoulder with Fennel
Porchetta

MAKES 12 SERVINGS

This is my version of the fabulous roast pig known as porchetta, sold all around central Italy, including Lazio, Umbria, and Abruzzo. Slices of the pork are sold from special trucks, and you can order it on a sandwich or wrapped in paper to take home. Though the meat is luscious, the crackling pork skin is the best part.

The roast is cooked for a long time and to a high temperature because it is very dense. The high fat content keeps the meat moist, and the skin gets brown and crunchy. A fresh ham can be substituted for the pork shoulder.

I (7-pound) pork shoulder roast
8 to 12 garlic cloves
2 tablespoons chopped fresh rosemary
I tablespoon fennel seeds
I tablespoon salt
I teaspoon freshly ground black pepper
1/4 cup olive oil

I About 1 hour before you begin roasting the meat, remove it from the refrigerator.

2 Very finely chop together the garlic, rosemary, fennel, and salt, then place the seasonings in a small bowl. Stir in the pepper and oil to form a smooth paste.

3 With a small knife, cut deep slits into the surface of the pork. Insert the paste into the slits.

4 Place a rack in the lower third of the oven. Preheat the oven to 350°F. When ready, place the roast in the oven and cook 3 hours. Spoon off the excess fat. Roast the meat 1 to 1¹/₂ hours longer, or until the temperature reaches 160°F on an instant-read thermometer. When the meat is done, the fat will be crisp and a deep nutty brown.

5 Transfer the meat to a cutting board. Cover with foil to keep warm and let stand 20 minutes. Carve and serve hot or at room temperature.

Roast Suckling Pig
Maialino Arrosto

MAKES 8 TO 10 SERVINGS

A suckling pig is one that has not been allowed to eat adult pig food. In the United States, suckling pigs typically weigh between 15 and 20 pounds, though in Italy they are half that size. Even at the higher weight, there really is not much meat on a suckling pig, so don't plan to serve more than eight to ten guests. Also, be sure you have a very large baking pan to accommodate a whole piglet, which will be about 30 inches long, and be sure your oven will accommodate the pan. Any good butcher should be able to obtain a fresh piglet for you, but make inquiries before planning on it.

Sardinian cooks are famous for their suckling pig, but I have eaten it in many places in Italy. The one I remember best was part of a memorable luncheon enjoyed at the Majo di Norante winery in Abruzzo.

1 suckling pig, about 15 pounds
4 garlic cloves
2 tablespoons chopped fresh flat-leaf parsley
1 tablespoon chopped fresh rosemary
1 tablespoon chopped fresh sage
1 teaspoon juniper berries, chopped
Salt and freshly ground black pepper
6 tablespoons olive oil
2 bay leaves
1 cup dry white wine
Apple, orange, or other fruit for garnish (optional)

1 Place a rack in the lower third of the oven. Preheat the oven to 425°F. Oil a baking pan large enough to hold the pig.

2 Rinse the pig well inside and out and pat dry with paper towels.

3 Chop together the garlic, parsley, rosemary, sage, and juniper berries, then place the seasonings in a small bowl. Add a generous amount of salt and freshly ground pepper. Stir in two tablespoons of the oil.

4 Place the pig on its side on a large roasting rack in the prepared pan and spread the herb mixture inside the body cavity. Add the bay leaves. Cut slashes about ¹/₂ inch deep along both sides of the backbone. Rub the remaining oil all over the surface of the pig. Cover the ears and tail with aluminum foil. (If you want to serve the pig whole with an apple or other fruit in its mouth, prop the mouth open with a ball of aluminum foil about the size of the fruit.) Sprinkle the outside with salt and pepper.

5 Roast the pig 30 minutes. Reduce the heat to 350°F. Baste with the wine. Roast 2 to 2¹/₂ hours more, or until an instant-read thermometer inserted in the meaty part of the hindquarter registers 170°F. Baste every 20 minutes with the pan juices.

6 Transfer the pig to a large cutting board. Cover with foil and let rest 30 minutes. Remove the foil covering and the ball of foil from the mouth, if using. Replace the foil ball with the fruit, if using. Transfer to a serving platter and serve hot.

7 Skim the fat from the pan juices and reheat them over low heat. Pour the juices over the meat. Serve immediately.

Boneless Spiced Pork Loin Roast
Maiale in Porchetta

MAKES 6 TO 8 SERVINGS

Boneless pork loin is roasted with the same spices used for porchetta (baby pig roasted on a spit) in many parts of central Italy. After a brief period of cooking at high heat, the oven temperature is turned down low, which keeps the meat tender and juicy.

4 garlic cloves
1 tablespoon fresh rosemary
6 fresh sage leaves
6 juniper berries
1 teaspoon salt
1/2 teaspoon freshly ground black pepper
1 boneless center-cut pork loin roast, about 3 pounds
Extra-virgin olive oil
1 cup dry white wine

1 Place a rack in the center of the oven. Preheat the oven to 450°F. Oil a roasting pan just large enough to hold the pork.

2 Very finely chop together the garlic, rosemary, sage, and juniper berries. Stir together the herb mixture, the salt, and the pepper.

3 With a large, sharp knife, cut the meat lengthwise down the center, leaving it attached on one side. Open the meat like a book and spread two-thirds of the spice mixture over the meat. Close the meat and tie it with string at 2-inch intervals. Rub the remaining spice mixture over the outside. Place the meat in the pan. Drizzle with olive oil.

4 Roast the pork 10 minutes. Reduce the heat to 300°F and roast 60 minutes more, or until the internal temperature of the pork reaches 150°F.

5 Remove the roast to a serving platter and cover with foil. Let rest 10 minutes.

6 Add the wine to the pan and place it over medium heat on the top of the stove. Cook, scraping up any brown bits in the pan with a wooden spoon, until the juices are reduced and syrupy. Slice the pork and spoon on the pan juices. Serve hot.

Braised Pork Shoulder in Milk
Maiale al Latte

MAKES 6 TO 8 SERVINGS

In Lombardy and the Veneto, veal, pork, and chicken are sometimes cooked in milk. This keeps the meat tender, and when it is done the milk makes a creamy brown sauce to serve with the meat.

Vegetables, pancetta, and wine add flavor. I use a boneless shoulder or butt roast for this dish because it takes well to slow, moist cooking. The meat is cooked on the stove, so you don't need to turn on your oven.

1 boneless pork shoulder or butt roast (about 3 pounds)
4 ounces finely diced pancetta
1 carrot, finely chopped
1 small tender celery rib
1 medium onion, finely chopped
1 quart milk
Salt and freshly ground black pepper
1/2 cup dry white wine

1 In a large Dutch oven or other deep, heavy pot with a tight-fitting lid, combine the pork, pancetta, carrot, celery, onion, milk, and salt and pepper to taste. Bring the liquid to a simmer over medium heat.

2 Partially cover the pot and cook over medium heat, turning occasionally, about 2 hours or until the meat is tender when pierced with a fork.

3 Transfer the meat to a cutting board. Cover with foil to keep warm. Raise the heat under the pot and cook until the liquid is reduced and lightly browned. Pour the juices through a strainer into a bowl, then pour the liquid back into the pot

4 Pour the wine into the pot and bring to a simmer, scraping up and blending in any browned bits with a wooden spoon. Slice the pork and arrange it on a warm serving platter. Pour the cooking liquid over the top. Serve hot.

Braised Pork Shoulder with Grapes
Maiale all' Uva

MAKES 6 TO 8 SERVINGS

Pork shoulder or butt is particularly good for brais-
ing. It stays nice and moist despite the long simmer-
ing. I used to make this Sicilian recipe with pork
loin, but I now find that the loin is too lean and
shoulder has more flavor.

1 pound pearl onions

3 pounds boneless pork shoulder or butt, rolled and tied

2 tablespoons olive oil

Salt and freshly ground black pepper

1/4 cup white wine vinegar

1 pound seedless green grapes, stemmed (about 3 cups)

1 Bring a large pot of water to a boil. Add the
onions and cook for 30 seconds. Drain and cool
under cold running water.

2 With a sharp paring knife, shave off the tip of the
root ends. Do not slice off the ends too deeply or
the onions will fall apart during cooking. Remove
the skins.

3 In a Dutch oven just large enough to hold the
meat or another deep, heavy pot with a tight-fitting
lid, heat the oil over medium-high heat. Pat the
pork dry with paper towels. Place the pork in the
pot and brown well on all sides, about 20 minutes.
Tip the pot and spoon off the fat. Sprinkle the
pork with salt and pepper.

4 Add the vinegar and bring it to a simmer, scraping up the browned bits at the bottom of the pot
with a wooden spoon. Add the onions and 1 cup
water. Reduce the heat to low and simmer 1 hour.

5 Add the grapes. Cook 30 minutes more or until
the meat is very tender when pierced with a fork.
Transfer the meat to a cutting board. Cover with
foil to keep warm and let sit 15 minutes.

6 Slice the pork and arrange it on a warm serving
platter. Spoon on the grape and onion sauce and
serve immediately.

Beer-Braised Pork Shoulder
Maiale alla Birra

MAKES 8 SERVINGS

Fresh pork shanks are cooked this way in Trentino–
Alto Adige, but since that cut is not widely available
in the United States, I use the same flavorings to
cook a bone-in shoulder roast. There will be a lot of
fat at the end of the cooking time, but this can eas-
ily be skimmed off the surface of the cooking liquid.
Better yet, cook the pork a day ahead of serving
and chill the meat and cooking juices separately. The
fat will harden and can easily be removed. Reheat
the pork in the cooking liquid before serving.

5 to 7 pounds bone-in pork shoulder
    (picnic or Boston butt)

Salt and freshly ground black pepper

2 tablespoons olive oil

1 medium onion, finely chopped

2 garlic cloves, finely chopped

2 sprigs fresh rosemary

2 bay leaves

12 ounces beer

1 Pat the pork dry with paper towels. Sprinkle
the meat all over with salt and pepper.

2 In a large Dutch oven or other deep, heavy pot
with a tight-fitting lid, heat the oil over medium
heat. Place the pork in the pot and brown it well
on all sides, about 20 minutes Spoon off all but
1 or 2 tablespoons of the fat.

3 Scatter the onion, garlic, rosemary, and bay
leaves all around the meat and cook 5 minutes.
Add the beer and bring to a simmer.

4 Cover the pot and cook, turning the meat occasionally, for 2 1/2 to 3 hours, or until the meat is
tender when pierced with a knife.

5 Strain the pan juices and skim off the fat. Slice
the pork and serve it with the pan juices. Serve hot.

❧ Lamb Chops

Lamb meat sold in Italy comes from animals that are much younger than those brought to market in the United States. The flavor is delicate, and the texture is very tender. Lamb chops, ground lamb, and braised or roasted lamb are all popular in Italy. Loin or rib chops are best for grilling, broiling, or quick sautéeing, though a whole rack can be roasted. Shoulder chops are fattier and chewier, but with a little trimming can be used in the same way. Shoulder chunks and shank cuts have more connective tissue, so they are excellent for slow moist-heat cooking methods like stewing and braising. Whole leg of lamb is perfect for roasting, but when boned and butterflied it is tender enough for grilling or broiling.

There is one major difference between the Italian and non-Italian way of cooking lamb. The meat in Italy is always cooked to well-done, whether it is a leg of lamb or tiny lamb chops. I prefer to cook lamb chops and legs to medium-rare. When Italian friends visit, they always express surprise, then enjoyment at this way of cooking lamb, though they return to cooking it well-done in Italy.

Lamb Chops with White Wine
Braciole di Agnello al Vino Bianco

MAKES 4 SERVINGS

Here is a basic way of preparing lamb chops that can be made with either tender loin or rib cuts or chewier, but much less expensive, shoulder chops. For best flavor, trim the meat of excess fat and cook the chops just until pink in the center.

2 tablespoons olive oil
8 loin or rib lamb chops, 1 inch thick, trimmed
4 garlic cloves, lightly crushed
3 or 4 (2-inch) rosemary sprigs
Salt and freshly ground black pepper
1 cup dry white wine

1 In a skillet large enough to hold the chops comfortably in a single layer, heat the oil over medium-high heat. When the oil is hot, pat the chops dry. Sprinkle the chops with salt and pepper, then place them in the pan. Cook until the chops are browned, about 4 minutes. Scatter the garlic and rosemary around the meat. Using tongs, turn the chops and brown on the other side, about 3 minutes. Transfer the chops to a plate.

2 Add the wine to the skillet and bring to a simmer. Cook, scraping up and blending in the browned bits in the bottom of the pan, until the wine is reduced and slightly thickened, about 2 minutes.

3 Return the chops to the pan and cook them 2 minutes more, turning them in the sauce once or twice until rosy pink when cut near the bone. Transfer the chops to a platter, pour the pan juices over the chops, and serve immediately.

Lamb Chops with Capers, Lemon, and Sage
Braciole di Agnello con Capperi

MAKES 4 SERVINGS

Vecchia Roma is one of my favorite Roman restaurants. On the fringe of the old ghetto, it has a beautiful outdoor garden for eating when the weather is warm and sunny, but I also enjoy the cozy inside dining rooms when it is cold or rainy. This lamb is inspired by a dish I tasted there made with tiny nuggets of baby lamb. I have adapted it to tender chops instead, because they are widely available here.

1 tablespoon olive oil
8 loin or rib lamb chops, 1 inch thick, trimmed
Salt and freshly ground black pepper
1/2 cup dry white wine
3 tablespoons fresh lemon juice
3 tablespoons capers, rinsed and chopped
6 fresh sage leaves

1 In a large skillet, heat the oil over medium-high heat. Pat the chops dry. When the oil is hot, sprinkle

them with salt and pepper, then place chops in the pan. Cook until the chops are browned, about 4 minutes. Using tongs, turn the chops and brown on the other side, about 3 minutes. Transfer the chops to a plate.

2 Pour the fat out of the pan. Reduce the heat to low. Stir the wine, the lemon juice, capers, and sage into the pan. Bring to a simmer and cook 2 minutes or until slightly syrupy.

3 Return the chops to the pan and turn them once or twice until heated through and just pink when cut near the bone. Serve immediately.

Lamb Chops in Crispy Coating
Braciolette Croccante

MAKES 4 SERVINGS

In Milan, I ate goat meat chops prepared this way, accompanied by artichoke hearts fried in the same crispy coating. Romans use tiny lamb chops instead of goat and leave out the cheese. Either way, a crisp mixed salad is the perfect accompaniment.

8 to 12 rib lamb chops, about 3/4 inch thick, well trimmed
2 large eggs
Salt and freshly ground black pepper
1 1/4 cups plain dry bread crumbs
1/2 cup freshly grated Parmigiano-Reggiano
Olive oil for frying

1 Place the chops on a cutting board and gently pound the meat to about a 1/2-inch thickness.

2 In a shallow plate, beat the eggs with salt and pepper to taste. Toss the bread crumbs with the cheese on a sheet of wax paper.

3 Dip the chops one at a time in the eggs, then roll them in the bread crumbs, patting the crumbs in well.

4 Turn the oven on to the lowest setting. Pour about 1/2 inch of the oil into a deep skillet. Heat the oil over medium-high heat until a little of the egg

mixture cooks quickly when dropped in the oil. With tongs, carefully place a few of the chops in the oil without crowding the pan. Cook until browned and crisp, 3 to 4 minutes. Turn the chops with tongs and brown, 3 minutes. Drain the chops on paper towels. Keep the fried chops warm in the oven while frying the remainder. Serve hot.

Lamb Chops with Artichokes and Olives
Costolette di Agnello ai Carciofi e Olive

MAKES 4 SERVINGS

All of the ingredients of this dish cook in the same skillet so that the complementary flavors of the lamb, artichokes, and olives blend smoothly. A bright vegetable like carrots or baked tomatoes would be a good accompaniment.

2 tablespoons olive oil
8 rib or loin lamb chops, about 1 inch thick, trimmed
Salt and freshly ground black pepper to taste
2 tablespoons olive oil
3/4 cup dry white wine
8 small or 4 medium artichokes, trimmed and cut into eighths
1 garlic clove, finely chopped
1/2 cup small mild black olives, such as Gaeta
1 tablespoon chopped fresh flat-leaf parsley

1 In a skillet large enough to hold the chops in a single layer, heat the oil over medium heat. Pat the lamb dry. When the oil is hot, sprinkle the chops with salt and pepper, then place them in the pan. Cook until the chops are browned, 3 to 4 minutes. Using tongs, turn the chops to brown on the other side, about 3 minutes. Transfer the chops to a plate.

2 Turn the heat to medium-low. Add the wine and bring to a simmer. Cook 1 minute. Add the artichokes, garlic, and salt and pepper to taste.

(continues)

Cover the pan and cook 20 minutes or until the artichokes are tender.

3 Stir in the olives and parsley and cook 1 minute more. Return the chops to the pan and cook, turning the lamb once or twice until heated through. Serve immediately.

Lamb Chops with Tomato, Caper, and Anchovy Sauce
Costelette d'Agnello in Salsa

MAKES 4 SERVINGS

A spicy tomato sauce flavors these Calabrese-style chops. Pork chops can also be cooked this way.

2 tablespoons olive oil
8 rib or loin lamb chops, about ³/₄ inch thick, trimmed
6 to 8 plum tomatoes, peeled, seeded, and chopped
4 anchovy fillets, chopped
1 tablespoon capers, rinsed and chopped
2 tablespoons chopped fresh flat-leaf parsley

1 In a skillet large enough to hold the chops comfortably in a single layer, heat the oil over medium heat. When the oil is hot, pat the chops dry. Sprinkle the chops with salt and pepper, then add the chops to the pan. Cook until the chops are browned, about 4 minutes. Using tongs, turn the chops and brown on the other side, about 3 minutes. Transfer the chops to a plate.

2 Add the tomatoes, anchovies, and capers to the pan. Add a pinch of salt and pepper to taste. Cook 5 minutes or until slightly thickened.

3 Return the chops to the pan and cook, turning them once or twice in the sauce until heated through and pink when cut near the bone. Sprinkle with parsley and serve immediately.

"Burn-the-Fingers" Lamb Chops
Agnello a Scottadito

MAKES 4 SERVINGS

In the recipe that inspired this dish, from an old cookbook on Umbrian cuisine, finely chopped prosciutto fat flavors the lamb. Most cooks today substitute olive oil. Lamb riblets are also good this way.

Presumably the name comes from the idea that the chops are so delicious you can't help but eat them right away—hot, right off the grill or out of the pan.

¹/₄ cup olive oil
2 garlic cloves, finely chopped
1 tablespoon chopped fresh rosemary
1 teaspoon chopped fresh thyme
8 rib lamb chops, about 1 inch thick, trimmed
Salt and freshly ground black pepper

1 In a small bowl, stir together the oil, garlic, herbs, and salt and pepper to taste. Brush the mixture over the lamb. Cover and refrigerate 1 hour.

2 Place a grill or broiler rack about 5 inches away from the heat source. Preheat the grill or broiler.

3 Scrape off some of the marinade. Grill or broil the chops until browned and crisp, about 5 minutes. With tongs, turn the chops over and cook until browned and just pink in the center, about 5 minutes more. Serve hot.

Grilled Lamb, Basilicata Style

Agnello allo Spiedo

MAKES 4 SERVINGS

Basilicata may be best known by its portrayal in Carlo Levi's Christ Stopped at Eboli. *The author painted a bleak portrait of the region before World War II, when many political prisoners were sent there in exile. Today Basilicata, though still sparsely populated, is thriving, with many tourists venturing there for the beautiful beaches near Maratea.*

Pork and lamb are typical meats in this region, and the two are combined in this recipe. The pancetta wrapping around the lamb cubes gets crisp and tasty. It keeps the lamb moist and adds flavor as it grills.

1 1/2 pounds boneless leg of lamb, cut into 2-inch chunks
2 garlic cloves, finely chopped
1 tablespoon chopped fresh rosemary
Salt and freshly ground black pepper
4 ounces thinly sliced pancetta
1/4 cup olive oil
2 tablespoons red wine vinegar

1 Place a barbecue grill or broiler rack about 5 inches away from the heat source. Preheat the grill or broiler.

2 In a large bowl, toss the lamb with the garlic, rosemary, and salt and pepper to taste.

3 Unroll the pancetta slices. Wrap a slice of pancetta around each chunk of lamb.

4 Thread the lamb on wooden skewers, securing the pancetta in place with the skewer. Place the pieces close together without crowding. In a small bowl, whisk together the oil and vinegar. Brush the mixture over the lamb.

5 Grill or broil the skewers, turning them occasionally, until done to taste—5 to 6 minutes for medium-rare. Serve hot.

Grilled Lamb Skewers

Arrosticini

MAKES 4 SERVINGS

In Abruzzo, small bites of lamb are marinated, threaded on wooden skewers, and grilled over a hot fire. The cooked skewers are served standing in a tall cup or jug, and everyone helps themselves, eating the lamb right off the sticks. They are great for a buffet, served with roasted or sautéed peppers.

2 garlic cloves
Salt
1 pound lamb from the leg, trimmed and cut into 3/4-inch chunks
3 tablesoons extra-virgin olive oil
2 tablespoons chopped fresh mint
1 teaspoon chopped fresh thyme
Freshly ground black pepper

1 Chop the garlic very fine. Sprinkle the garlic with a pinch of salt and mash it with the side of a large heavy chef's knife into a fine paste.

2 In a large bowl, toss the lamb with the garlic paste, oil, herbs, and salt and pepper to taste. Cover and marinate at room temperature for 1 hour or in the refrigerator for several hours or overnight.

3 Place a barbecue grill or broiler rack about 5 inches from the heat source. Preheat the grill or broiler.

4 Thread the meat on the skewers. Place the pieces close together without crowding. Grill or broil the lamb 3 minutes or until browned. Turn the meat over with tongs and cook 2 to 3 minutes more or until browned on the outside but still pink in the center. Serve hot.

❧ Lamb Stews and Braises

Lamb Stew with Rosemary, Mint, and White Wine
Agnello in Umido

MAKES 4 SERVINGS

Lamb shoulder is ideal for stewing. The meat has enough moisture to stand up to long, slow cooking, and though tough if cooked rare, it turns out fork-tender in a stew. If only bone-in lamb shoulder is available, it can be adapted to stewing recipes. Figure on an extra pound or two of bone-in meat, depending on just how bony it is. Cook bone-in lamb about 30 minutes longer than boneless, or until the meat is coming away from the bones.

2¹/₂ pounds boneless lamb shoulder, cut into
    2-inch chunks
¹/₄ cup olive oil
Salt and freshly ground black pepper to taste
I large onion, chopped
4 garlic cloves, chopped
2 tablespoons chopped fresh rosemary
2 tablespoons chopped fresh flat-leaf parsley
I tablespoon chopped fresh mint
¹/₂ cup dry white wine
About ¹/₂ cup beef broth (Meat Broth, page 62) or water
2 tablespoons tomato paste

I In a large Dutch oven or other deep, heavy pot with a tight-fitting lid, heat the oil over medium heat. Dry the lamb with paper towels. Put just as many lamb pieces as will fit comfortably in a single layer into the pot. Cook, stirring frequently, until browned on all sides, about 20 minutes. Transfer the browned lamb to a plate. Sprinkle with salt and pepper. Cook the remaining lamb in the same way.

2 When all the meat is browned, spoon off the excess fat. Add the onion, garlic, and herbs and stir well. Cook until the onion has wilted, about 5 minutes.

3 Add the wine and bring to a simmer, scraping up and blending in the browned bits on the bottom of the pot. Cook 1 minute.

4 Add the broth and tomato paste. Reduce heat to low. Cover and cook 1 hour, stirring occasionally, or until the lamb is tender. Add a little water if the sauce becomes too dry. Serve hot.

Umbrian Lamb Stew with Chickpea Puree
Agnello del Colle

MAKES 6 SERVINGS

Polenta and mashed potatoes are frequent accompaniments to stews in Italy, so I was surprised when this stew was served with mashed chickpeas in Umbria. Canned chickpeas work just fine, or you can cook dried chickpeas in advance.

2 tablespoons olive oil
3 pounds boneless lamb shoulder, cut into
    2-inch chunks
Salt and freshly ground black pepper
2 garlic cloves, finely chopped
I cup dry white wine
I¹/₂ cups chopped fresh or canned tomatoes
I(10-ounce) package white mushrooms, sliced
2 (16-ounce) cans chickpeas or 5 cups cooked chickpeas
Extra-virgin olive oil

I In a large Dutch oven or other deep, heavy pot with a tight-fitting lid, heat the oil over medium heat. Put just enough lamb pieces in the pot as will fit comfortably in a single layer. Cook, stirring occasionally, until browned on all sides, about 20 minutes. Transfer the browned lamb to a plate. Sprinkle with salt and pepper. Cook the remaining lamb in the same way.

2 When all of the meat is browned, spoon the excess fat from the pan. Scatter the garlic in the pan and cook 1 minute. Add the wine. With a wooden spoon, scrape up and blend in to the browned bits in the bottom of the pan. Bring to a simmer and cook 1 minute.

3 Return the lamb to the pot. Add the tomatoes and mushrooms and bring to a simmer. Reduce heat to low. Cover and cook, stirring occasionally, 1½ hours or until the lamb is tender and the sauce is reduced. If there is too much liquid, remove the cover for the last 15 minutes.

4 Just before serving, heat the chickpeas and their liquid in a medium saucepan. Then transfer them to a food processor to puree or mash them with a potato masher. Stir in a little extra-virgin olive oil and black pepper to taste. Reheat if necessary.

5 To serve, scoop some of the chickpeas onto each plate. Surround the puree with the lamb stew. Serve hot.

Hunter's-Style Lamb
Agnello alla Cacciatora

MAKES 6 TO 8 SERVINGS

Romans make this lamb stew with abbacchio, *lamb so young that it has never eaten grass. I think the flavor of mature lamb is a better match for the zesty chopped rosemary, vinegar, garlic, and anchovy that finish the sauce.*

**4 pounds bone-in lamb shoulder, cut into
    2-inch chunks**
Salt and freshly ground black pepper
2 tablespoons olive oil
4 garlic cloves, chopped
4 fresh sage leaves
2 (2-inch) sprigs fresh rosemary
I cup dry white wine
6 anchovy fillets
I teaspoon finely chopped fresh rosemary leaves
2 to 3 tablespoons wine vinegar

I Pat the pieces dry with paper towels. Sprinkle them with salt and pepper.

2 In a large Dutch oven or other deep, heavy pot with a tight-fitting lid, heat the oil over medium heat. Add just enough lamb as will fit comfortably in one layer. Cook, stirring, to brown well on all sides. Transfer the browned meat to a plate. Continue with the remaining lamb.

3 When all the lamb has been browned, spoon off most of the fat from the pan. Add half the garlic, the sage, and the rosemary, and stir. Add the wine and cook 1 minute, scraping up and blending in the browned bits on the bottom of the pan with a wooden spoon.

4 Return the lamb pieces to the pan. Reduce the heat to low. Cover and cook, stirring occasionally, for 2 hours or until the lamb is tender and coming away from the bones. Add a little water if the liquid evaporates too rapidly.

5 To make the pesto: Chop the anchovies, rosemary, and remaining garlic together. Place them in a small bowl. Stir in just enough of the vinegar to form a paste.

6 Stir the pesto into the stew and simmer 5 minutes. Serve hot.

Lamb, Potato, and Tomato Stew

Stufato di Agnello e Verdure

MAKES 4 TO 6 SERVINGS

Though I usually use lamb shoulder for stew, I sometimes use trimmings left over from the leg or shank. The texture of these cuts is slightly chewier, but they require less cooking and still make a good stew. Notice that in this recipe from southern Italy, the meat is put into the pot all at once, so it is only lightly browned before the other ingredients are added.

I large onion, chopped

2 tablespoons olive oil

2 pounds boneless leg or shank of lamb, cut into
    I-inch chunks

Salt and freshly ground black pepper, to taste

1/2 cup dry white wine

3 cups drained and chopped canned tomatoes

I tablespoon chopped fresh rosemary

I pound waxy boiling potatoes, cut into I-inch pieces

2 carrots, cut into 1/2-inch-thick slices

I cup fresh peas or frozen peas, partially thawed

2 tablespoons chopped fresh flat-leaf parsley

I In a large Dutch oven or other deep, heavy pot with a tight-fitting lid, cook the onion in the olive oil over medium heat until softened, about 5 minutes. Add the lamb. Cook, stirring frequently, until the pieces are lightly browned. Sprinkle with salt and pepper. Add the wine and bring it to a simmer.

2 Stir in the tomatoes and rosemary. Reduce the heat to low. Cover and cook 30 minutes.

3 Add the potatoes, carrots, and salt and pepper to taste. Simmer 30 minutes more, stirring occasionally, until the lamb and potatoes are tender. Add the peas and cook 10 minutes more. Sprinkle with parsley and serve immediately.

Lamb and Pepper Stew

Spezzato d'Agnello con Peperone

MAKES 4 SERVINGS

The piquancy and sweetness of peppers and the richness of lamb make them two foods perfectly suited for each other. In this recipe, once the meat is browned, there is little to do except stir it occasionally.

1/4 cup olive oil

2 pounds boneless lamb shoulder, cut into
    1 1/2-inch pieces

Salt and freshly ground black pepper, to taste

1/2 cup dry white wine

2 medium onions, sliced

I large red bell pepper

I large green bell pepper

6 plum tomatoes, peeled, seeded, and chopped

I In a large casserole dish or Dutch oven, heat the oil over medium heat. Pat the lamb dry. Add just enough lamb to the pan as will fit comfortably in a single layer. Cook, stirring, until browned on all sides, about 20 minutes. Transfer the browned lamb to a plate. Continue cooking the remaining lamb in the same way. Sprinkle the meat all over with the salt and pepper.

2 When all the meat has been browned, spoon off excess fat. Add the wine to the pot and stir well, scraping up the browned bits. Bring to a simmer.

3 Return the lamb to the pot. Stir in the onions, peppers, and tomatoes. Reduce heat to low. Cover the pot and cook for 1 1/2 hours or until the meat is very tender. Serve hot.

Lamb Casserole with Eggs
Agnello Cacio e Uova

MAKES 6 SERVINGS

Because eggs and lamb are both associated with springtime, it is only natural to pair them in recipes. In this dish, popular in one form or another throughout central and southern Italy, eggs and cheese form a light custardy topping on a lamb stew. It's a typical Easter recipe, so if you want to make it for the holiday meal, transfer the cooked stew to a pretty bake-and-serve casserole dish before adding the topping. A combination of lamb meat from the leg and shoulder makes for a more interesting texture.

2 tablespoons olive oil

2 medium onions

3 pounds boneless lamb leg and shoulder, trimmed and cut into 2-inch chunks

Salt and freshly ground black pepper to taste

1 tablespoon finely chopped rosemary

1 1/2 cups homemade Meat Broth (page 62) or Chicken Broth (page 63), or store-bought beef or chicken broth

2 cups shelled fresh peas or 1 (10-ounce) package frozen peas, partially thawed

3 large eggs

1 tablespoon chopped fresh flat-leaf parsley

1/2 cup freshly grated Pecorino Romano

1 Place a rack in the center of the oven. Preheat the oven to 425°F. In a Dutch oven or other deep, heavy pot with a tight-fitting lid, heat the oil over medium heat. Add the onion and lamb. Cook, stirring occasionally, until the lamb is lightly browned on all sides, about 20 minutes. Sprinkle with salt and pepper.

2 Add the rosemary and the broth. Stir well. Cover and bake, stirring occasionally, 60 minutes or until the meat is just tender. Add a little warm water if necessary to prevent the lamb from drying out. Stir in the peas and cook 5 minutes more.

3 In a medium bowl, beat the eggs, parsley, cheese, and salt and pepper to taste, until well blended. Pour the mixture evenly over the lamb.

4 Bake uncovered 5 minutes or until the eggs are just set. Serve immediately.

Lamb or Kid with Potatoes, Sicilian Style
Capretto o Agnello al Forno

MAKES 4 TO 6 SERVINGS

Baglio Elena, near Trapani in Sicily, is a working farm that produces olives, olive oil, and other foods. It is also an inn where visitors can stop for a meal in a charming, rustic dining room or stay for a vacation. When I visited, I was served a multicourse dinner of Sicilian specialties that included several types of olives prepared in different ways, excellent salame made on the premises, a variety of vegetables, and this simple stew. The meat and potatoes cook in no liquid other than a small amount of wine and the juices from the meat and vegetables, creating a symphony of flavors.

Kid is available in many ethnic butcher shops, including Haitian, Middle Eastern, and Italian. It is so similar to lamb that it can be hard to tell the difference.

3 pounds bone-in kid (young goat) or lamb shoulder, cut into 2-inch chunks

2 tablespoons olive oil

Salt and freshly ground black pepper

2 onions, thinly sliced

1/2 cup dry white wine

1/4 teaspoon ground cloves

2 (2-inch) sprigs rosemary

1 bay leaf

4 medium all-purpose potatoes, cut into 1-inch pieces

2 cups cherry tomatoes, halved

2 tablespoons chopped fresh flat-leaf parsley

1 Place a rack in the center of the oven. Preheat the oven to 350°F. In a large Dutch oven or other deep, heavy pot with a tight-fitting lid, heat the oil over medium heat. Pat the lamb dry with paper towels. Add just enough meat to fit in the pot comfortably without crowding. Cook, turning the pieces with tongs until browned on all sides,

(continues)

about 15 minutes. Transfer the pieces to a plate. Continue cooking the remaining meat in the same way. Sprinkle with salt and pepper.

2 When all the meat has been browned, pour off most of the fat from the pan. Add the onion and cook, stirring occasionally, until the onion has wilted, about 5 minutes.

3 Return the meat to the pot. Add the wine and bring it to a simmer. Cook 1 minute, stirring with a wooden spoon. Add the cloves, rosemary, bay leaf, and salt and pepper to taste. Cover the pot and transfer it to the oven. Cook 45 minutes.

4 Stir in the potatoes and tomatoes. Cover and cook 45 minutes more or until the meat and potatoes are tender when pierced with a fork. Sprinkle with parsley and serve hot.

Apulian Lamb and Potato Casserole
Tiella di Agnello

MAKES 6 SERVINGS

Layered casseroles baked in the oven are an Apulian specialty. They can be made with meat, fish, or vegetables, alternating with potatoes, rice, or bread crumbs. Tiella is a name given to both this method of cooking and the type of dish the casserole is cooked in. The classic tiella is a round deep dish made of terra cotta, though nowadays metal pans often are used.

The cooking method is most unusual. None of the ingredients is browned or precooked. Everything is simply layered and baked until tender. The meat will be well done, but still moist and delicious because the pieces are surrounded by the potatoes. The bottom layer of potatoes is meltingly soft and tender and full of the meat and tomato juices, while the top layer comes out as crisp as potato chips, though much more flavorful.

For the meat, use well-trimmed chunks of leg of lamb. I buy half of a butterflied leg of lamb at the supermarket, then I cut it at home into 2- to 3-inch chunks, trimming away the fat. It is just right for this recipe.

4 tablespoons olive oil

2 pounds baking potatoes, peeled and thinly sliced

1/2 cup plain dry bread crumbs

1/2 cup freshly grated Pecorino Romano or Parmigiano-Reggiano

1 garlic clove, finely chopped

1/2 cup chopped fresh flat-leaf parsley

1 tablespoon chopped fresh rosemary, or 1 teaspoon dried

1/2 teaspoon dried oregano

Salt and freshly ground black pepper

2 1/2 pounds boneless lamb, trimmed and cut into 2- to 3-inch pieces

1 cup drained canned tomatoes, chopped

1 cup dry white wine

1/2 cup water

1 Place a rack in the center of the oven. Preheat the oven to 400°F. Spread 2 tablespoons of the oil in a 13 × 9 × 2–inch baking pan. Pat the potatoes dry and spread about half of them, overlapping slightly, on the bottom of the pan.

2 In a medium bowl, stir together the bread crumbs, cheese, garlic, herbs, and salt and pepper to taste. Scatter half of the crumb mixture over the potatoes. Arrange the meat on top of the crumbs. Season the meat with salt and pepper. Spread the tomatoes over the meat. Arrange the remaining potatoes on top. Pour in the wine and water. Scatter the remaining crumb mixture over all. Drizzle with the remaining 2 tablespoons olive oil.

3 Bake 1 1/2 to 1 3/4 hours or until the meat and potatoes are tender when pierced with a fork and everything is nicely browned. Serve hot.

❧ Lamb Shanks

Lamb Shanks with Chickpeas
Stinco di Agnello con Ceci

MAKES 4 SERVINGS

Shanks need long, slow cooking, but when they are done, the meat is moist and just about melts in your mouth. If you purchase lamb shanks in the super-market, the meat may need some extra trimming. With a small boning knife, cut away as much of the fat as possible, but leave intact the thin, pearly-looking covering on the meat known as the silver skin. It helps the meat to keep its shape as it cooks. I use shanks for a number of recipes that Italians would make with their smaller leg of lamb.

2 tablespoons olive oil

4 small lamb shanks, well trimmed

Salt and freshly ground black pepper

I small onion, chopped

2 cups beef broth (Meat Broth, page 62)

I cup peeled, seeded, and chopped tomatoes

¹/₂ teaspoon dried marjoram or thyme

4 carrots, peeled and cut into I-inch pieces

2 tender celery ribs, cut into I-inch chunks

3 cups cooked or 2 (16-ounce) cans chickpeas, drained

I In a Dutch oven large enough to hold the shanks in a single layer, or another deep, heavy pot with a tight-fitting lid, heat the oil over medium heat. Pat the lamb shanks dry and brown them well on all sides, about 15 minutes. Tip the pan and spoon off the excess fat. Sprinkle with salt and pepper. Add the onion and cook 5 minutes more.

2 Add the broth, tomatoes, and marjoram and bring to a simmer. Reduce heat to low. Cover and cook 1 hour, turning the shanks occasionally.

3 Add the carrots, celery, and chickpeas. Cook 30 minutes more or until the meat is tender when pierced with a small knife. Serve hot.

Lamb Shanks with Peppers and Prosciutto
Brasato di Stinco di Agnello con Peperoni e Prosciutto

MAKES 6 SERVINGS

In Senagalia, on the Adriatic coast in the Marches, I ate at the Osteria del Tempo Perso, in the historic center of this lovely old town. For a first course, I had cappelletti, stuffed "little hats" of fresh pasta with a sausage and vegetable sauce, followed by a lamb stew topped with bright-colored bell peppers and strips of prosciutto. I have adapted the flavors of the stew to lamb shanks in this recipe.

4 tablespoons olive oil

6 small lamb shanks, well trimmed

Salt and freshly ground black pepper

¹/₂ cup dry white wine

2-inch sprig fresh rosemary, or ¹/₂ teaspoon dried

I¹/₂ cups Meat Broth (page 62)

2 red bell peppers, cut into ¹/₂-inch strips

I yellow bell pepper, cut into ¹/₂-inch strips

I tablespoon unsalted butter

2 ounces sliced imported Italian prosciutto, cut into thin strips

2 tablespoons chopped fresh flat-leaf parsley

I In a Dutch oven just large enough to hold the lamb shanks in a single layer, or another deep, heavy pot with a tight-fitting lid, heat the oil over medium heat. Pat the lamb shanks dry. Brown them well on all sides, turning the pieces with tongs, about 15 minutes. Tip the pan and spoon off the excess fat. Sprinkle with salt and pepper.

2 Add the wine and cook, scraping up and blending in the browned bits at the bottom of the pan with a wooden spoon. Bring to a simmer and cook 1 minute.

3 Add the rosemary and broth and bring the liquid to a simmer.

4 Partially cover the pan. Reduce heat to low. Cook, turning the meat occasionally, until the lamb is

(continues)

very tender when pierced with a fork, about 1 1/4 to 1 1/2 hours.

5 While the lamb is cooking, in a medium saucepan, combine the peppers, butter, and 2 tablespoons of water over medium heat. Cover and cook 10 minutes, or until the vegetables are almost tender.

6 Add the softened peppers and the prosciutto to the lamb along with the parsley. Cook uncovered over medium heat until the peppers are tender, about 5 minutes.

7 With a slotted spoon, transfer the shanks and peppers to the warmed platter. Cover and keep warm. If the liquid left in the pan is too thin, raise the heat to high and boil until reduced and slightly thickened. Taste and adjust the seasoning. Pour the sauce over the lamb and serve immediately.

Lamb Shanks with Capers and Olives
Stinchi di Agnello con Capperi e Olive

MAKES 4 SERVINGS

In Sardinia, goat meat is typically used for this dish. The flavors of lamb and goat are very similar, so lamb shanks are a good substitute and are a lot easier to find.

2 tablespoons olive oil

4 small lamb shanks, well trimmed

Salt and freshly ground black pepper

1 medium onion, chopped

3/4 cup dry white wine

1 cup peeled, seeded, and chopped fresh
    or canned tomatoes

1/2 cup chopped pitted black olives, such as Gaeta

2 garlic cloves, finely chopped

2 tablespoons capers, rinsed and chopped

2 tablespoons chopped fresh flat-leaf parsley

1 In a Dutch oven large enough to hold the shanks in a single layer, or another deep, heavy pot with a tight-fitting lid, heat the oil over medium heat. Pat

the lamb dry and brown it well on all sides. Spoon off the excess fat. Sprinkle with salt and pepper.

2 Scatter the onion around the lamb and cook until the onion is wilted, about 5 minutes. Add the wine and cook 1 minute. Stir in the tomatoes and bring to a simmer. Reduce the heat to low and cover the pan. Cook 1 to 1 1/2 hours, turning the shanks occasionally, until the meat is very tender when pierced with a knife.

3 Add the olives, garlic, capers, and parsley and cook 5 minutes more, turning the meat to coat with the sauce. Serve hot.

Lamb Shanks in Tomato Sauce
Stinco di Agnello al Pomodoro

MAKES 6 SERVINGS

If the only lamb shanks you can find are on the large side, you can either have the butcher split them for you, or you can cook fewer shanks, leaving them whole, then carve the meat off the bone at serving time.

6 small lamb shanks, well trimmed

2 tablespoons olive oil

2 garlic cloves, thinly sliced

1 tablespoon chopped fresh rosemary

1/2 cup dry white wine

1 cup chopped peeled tomatoes

1 1/2 cups beef broth (Meat Broth, page 62)

2 tablespoons chopped fresh flat-leaf parsley

1 In a Dutch oven large enough to hold the shanks in a single layer, or another deep, heavy pot with a tight-fitting lid, heat the oil. Brown the meat on all sides, about 15 minutes. Spoon off the excess fat. Sprinkle the shanks with salt and pepper.

2 Add the garlic and rosemary to the pan and cook 1 minute. Add the wine and bring to a simmer. Add the tomatoes and broth. Reduce the heat to low, cover the pan, and cook the shanks, turning them occasionally, about 1 1/2 hours or until the meat is fork tender and comes away easily from the bone.

3 Sprinkle with parsley and serve hot.

Lamb Pot Roast with Cloves, Roman Style

Garofolato di Agnello

MAKES 6 SERVINGS

Cloves, called chiodi di garofalo *in Italian, add a distinctive flavor to this lamb pot roast from the Roman countryside. The Romans use boned and rolled lamb shoulder, but if you can't find that cut, you can substitute leg of lamb with good results.*

5 whole cloves

3¹/₂ pounds boneless lamb shoulder roast, rolled and tied

Salt and freshly ground black pepper

2 tablespoons olive oil

1 medium onion, finely chopped

1 tender celery rib, finely chopped

1 carrot, chopped

¹/₄ cup chopped fresh flat-leaf parsley

A pinch of crushed red pepper

1 cup dry white wine

2 cups tomato puree

1 cup homemade Meat Broth (page 62) or canned beef broth

1 Stick the cloves into the lamb. Sprinkle the meat all over with salt and pepper.

2 In a large casserole dish or Dutch oven, heat the oil over medium heat. Add the lamb and cook, turning it with tongs, until browned on all sides, about 20 minutes.

3 Scatter the onion, celery, carrot, parsley, and red pepper around the meat. Add the wine and cook until it evaporates, about 2 minutes. Add the tomato puree and broth. Reduce the heat to low.

4 Cover and cook, turning the meat occasionally, for 2¹/₂ to 3 hours or until tender when pierced with a fork.

5 Transfer the meat to a cutting board. Cover and keep it warm. Skim the fat from the pan juices. Pour the vegetables and pan juices into a food processor or blender and puree until smooth. Taste and adjust seasoning. Pour the sauce into a medium saucepan and reheat it over low heat. If it is too thin, simmer it until reduced. Slice the lamb and serve hot with the sauce.

Braised Stuffed Lamb Shoulder

Cosciotto di Agnello Farcito

MAKES 8 SERVINGS

The sausage, veal, and pistachio stuffing elevates this lamb shoulder pot roast to dinner-party fare. Marsala gives the sauce a special flavor.

2 slices crustless Italian or French bread, torn into bits (about ¹/₂ cup)

¹/₂ cup water

1 boneless lamb shoulder (about 3¹/₂ pounds)

8 ounces pork sausage meat

4 ounces ground veal

¹/₄ cup coarsely chopped pistachios

2 teaspoons chopped fresh rosemary

1 garlic clove, finely chopped

2 large eggs

Salt and freshly ground black pepper

¹/₄ cup olive oil

1 onion, chopped

1 celery rib, chopped

2 carrots, chopped

1 cup dry Marsala

About 2 cups beef broth (Meat Broth, page 62)

1 Soak the bread in the water for 5 minutes. Squeeze out the water.

2 In a large bowl, combine the soaked bread, sausage, veal, pistachios, rosemary, and garlic. Stir in the eggs and salt and pepper to taste.

(continues)

3 Place a long piece of plastic wrap on a flat surface. Lay the lamb on the plastic, boned-side up. Cover the lamb with another sheet of plastic wrap. Pound the lamb gently with the flat side of a mallet to a 1-inch thickness; make it as even as possible. Remove the top sheet of plastic. Sprinkle the lamb with salt and pepper.

4 Spread the meat mixture over the lamb, leaving a 1-inch border all around. Beginning at a longer end, roll the lamb lengthwise into a cylinder or sausage shape. Wrap kitchen string around the length of the lamb roll, thread the string under and back along the length of the roll, and knot the string on the other side to secure it.

5 In a large Dutch oven or other deep, heavy pot with a tight-fitting lid, heat the olive oil over medium heat. Add the lamb roll and brown well on all sides, turning the meat with tongs, about 20 minutes. Scatter the onion, celery, and carrot around the meat. Cook until the onion has wilted, about 5 minutes.

6 Add the Marsala and bring to a boil. Add one cup of the broth and bring to a simmer. Reduce the heat to low, then cover and cook 3 hours, turning the meat occasionally. Add more of the broth if needed.

7 When the meat is tender when pierced with a fork, transfer it to a cutting board and cover with foil to keep it warm. Skim the fat from the pan juices. Pour the contents of the pot into a food processor or blender to puree. Taste and adjust seasoning.

8 Return the sauce to the pot and reheat gently. Slice the meat and serve it hot with the sauce.

Roast Leg of Lamb with Potatoes, Garlic, and Rosemary
Agnello al Forno

MAKES 6 SERVINGS

Italians would serve this lamb well done, but I think it tastes best when medium-rare, which is about 130°F on an instant-read thermometer. Let the lamb rest after roasting it so that the juices have a chance to retreat to the center of the meat.

6 all-purpose potatoes, peeled and cut into 1-inch chunks
3 tablespoons olive oil
Salt and freshly ground black pepper
1 bone-in leg of lamb, trimmed (about 5 1/2 pounds)
6 garlic cloves, finely chopped
2 tablespoons chopped fresh rosemary

1 Place a rack in the middle of the oven. Preheat oven to 350°F. Place the potatoes in a roasting pan large enough to hold the meat and potatoes without crowding. Toss with the oil, and salt and pepper to taste.

2 Make shallow slits all over the lamb with a small knife. Poke some of the garlic and rosemary into the slits, reserving a little for the potatoes. Sprinkle the meat generously with salt and pepper. Push the potatoes aside and add the meat fat-side up.

3 Place the pan in the oven and cook 30 minutes. Turn the potatoes. Roast 30 to 45 minutes longer or until the internal temperature measures 130°F on an instant-read thermometer placed in the thickest part of the meat, away from the bone. Remove the pan from the oven and transfer the lamb to a cutting board. Cover the meat with foil. Let rest at least 15 minutes before slicing.

4 Test the potatoes for doneness by piercing them with a sharp knife. If they need further cooking, turn the oven up to 400°F., return the pan to the oven, and cook until tender.

5 Slice the lamb and serve hot with the potatoes.

Leg of Lamb with Lemon, Herbs, and Garlic

Agnello Steccato

MAKES 6 SERVINGS

Basil, mint, garlic, and lemon perfume this lamb roast. Once it is in the oven, there is not much else to do. It is the perfect dish for a small dinner party or a Sunday dinner. Add some potatoes, carrots, turnips, or other root vegetables to the roasting pan, if you like.

I shank-end leg of lamb, well trimmed (about 3 pounds)

2 garlic cloves

2 tablespoons chopped fresh basil

I tablespoon chopped fresh mint

1/4 cup freshly grated Pecorino Romano or Parmigiano-Reggiano

I teaspoon grated lemon zest

1/2 teaspoon dried oregano

Salt and freshly ground black pepper

2 tablespoons olive oil

I Place a rack in the center of the oven. Preheat the oven to 425°F.

2 Very finely chop the garlic, basil, and mint. In a small bowl, stir the mixture together with the cheese, lemon zest, and oregano. Stir in 1 teaspoon salt and freshly ground pepper to taste. With a small knife, make slits about 3/4-inch deep all over the meat. Stuff a little of the herb mixture into each slit. Rub the oil all over the meat. Roast for 15 minutes.

3 Turn the heat down to 350°F. Roast 1 hour more or until the meat is medium-rare and the internal temperature reaches 130°F on an instant-read thermometer placed in the thickest part but not touching the bone.

4 Remove the lamb from the oven and transfer to a cutting board. Cover the lamb with foil and let rest 15 minutes before carving. Serve hot.

Braised Lamb–Stuffed Zucchini

Zucchine Ripiene

MAKES 6 SERVINGS

A leg of lamb feeds a crowd, but after a small dinner party, I often have leftovers. That's when I make these tasty stuffed zucchini. Other types of cooked meat or even poultry can be substituted.

2 to 3 (1/2-inch thick) slices Italian bread

1/4 cup milk

I pound cooked lamb

2 large eggs

2 tablespoons chopped fresh flat-leaf parsley

2 garlic cloves, finely chopped

1/2 cup freshly grated Pecorino Romano or Parmigiano-Reggiano

Salt and freshly ground black pepper

6 medium zucchini, scrubbed and trimmed

2 cups tomato sauce, such as Marinara Sauce (page 89)

I Place a rack in the center of the oven. Preheat the oven to 425°F. Oil a 13 × 9 × 2–inch baking pan.

2 Remove the bread crust and tear the bread into pieces. (You should have about 1 cup.) Place the pieces into a medium bowl, pour on the milk, and let soak.

3 In a food processor, chop the meat very fine. Transfer to a large bowl. Add the eggs, parsley, garlic, soaked bread, 1/4 cup of the cheese, and salt and pepper to taste. Mix well.

4 Cut the zucchini in half lengthwise. Scoop out the seeds. Stuff the zucchini with the meat mixture. Place the zucchini side by side in the pan. Spoon on the sauce and sprinkle with the remaining cheese.

5 Bake 35 to 40 minutes or until the stuffing is cooked through and the zucchini are tender. Serve hot or at room temperature.

⤳ Rabbit

Most supermarkets carry fresh or frozen rabbit, and you can order the meat from any good butcher. Look for rabbits weighing 3 pounds or less. Larger rabbits can be tough. If possible, have the butcher cut the rabbit into serving pieces. Otherwise, you can do it yourself with a large heavy knife or cleaver. Typically, a rabbit is cut into eight pieces to serve four people. The pieces include the two front legs, the two loin or saddle sections, which are halved crosswise to make four pieces, and the two hind legs.

Rabbit has a flavor similar to chicken, though it is very low in fat. As a result, rabbit meat can become dry if overcooked, so watch it carefully and cook it just until the meat is tender when pierced with a fork. This is especially important for rabbits that have been frozen, which may cook faster and release a lot of their juices as they thaw and cook.

Rabbit with White Wine and Herbs
Coniglio al Vino Bianco

MAKES 4 SERVINGS

This is a basic rabbit recipe from Liguria that can be varied by adding black or green olives or other herbs. Cooks in this region prepare rabbit in many different ways, including with pine nuts, mushrooms, or artichokes.

1 rabbit (2¹/₂ to 3 pounds), cut into 8 pieces
Salt and freshly ground black pepper
3 tablespoons olive oil
1 small onion, finely chopped
¹/₂ cup finely chopped carrot
¹/₂ cup finely chopped celery
1 tablespoon chopped fresh rosemary leaves
1 teaspoon chopped fresh thyme
1 bay leaf
¹/₂ cup dry white wine
1 cup chicken broth

1 Rinse the rabbit pieces and pat dry with paper towels. Sprinkle with salt and pepper.

2 In a large skillet, heat the oil over medium heat. Add the rabbit and brown lightly on all sides, about 15 minutes.

3 Scatter the onion, carrot, celery, and herbs around the rabbit pieces and cook until the onion is softened, about 5 minutes.

4 Add the wine and bring it to a simmer. Cook until most of the liquid is evaporated, about 2 minutes. Add the broth and bring it to a simmer. Reduce the heat to low. Cover the pan and cook, turning the rabbit occasionally with tongs, until tender when pierced with a fork, about 30 minutes.

5 Transfer the rabbit to a serving platter. Cover and keep warm. Increase the heat and boil the contents of the skillet until reduced and syrupy, about 2 minutes. Discard the bay leaf.

6 Pour the contents of the pan over the rabbit and serve immediately.

Rabbit with Olives
Coniglio alla Stimperata

MAKES 4 SERVINGS

Red pepper, green olives, and capers flavor this Sicilian-style rabbit dish. The term alla stimperata is given to a number of Sicilian recipes, though its meaning is not clear. It may stem from stemperare, *meaning "to dissolve, dilute, or mix" and referring to the addition of water to the pot as the rabbit cooks.*

1 rabbit (2¹/₂ to 3 pounds), cut into 8 pieces
¹/₄ cup olive oil
3 garlic cloves, chopped
1 cup pitted green olives, rinsed and drained
2 red bell peppers, cut into thin strips
1 tablespoon capers, rinsed
Pinch of oregano
Salt and freshly ground black pepper
2 tablespoons white wine vinegar
¹/₂ cup water

1 Rinse the rabbit pieces and pat dry with paper towels.

2 In a large skillet, heat the oil over medium heat. Add the rabbit and brown the pieces well on all sides, about 15 minutes. Transfer the rabbit pieces to a plate.

3 Add the garlic to the skillet and cook 1 minute. Add the olives, pepper, capers, and oregano. Cook, stirring 2 minutes.

4 Return the rabbit to the pan. Season with salt and pepper to taste. Add the vinegar and water and bring to a simmer. Reduce the heat to low. Cover and cook, turning the rabbit occasionally, until the rabbit is tender when pierced with a fork, about 30 minutes. Add a little water if the liquid evaporates. Transfer to a serving platter and serve hot.

Rabbit, Porchetta Style
Coniglio in Porchetta

MAKES 4 SERVINGS

The combination of seasonings used to make roast pork is so delicious that cooks have adapted it to other meats that are more convenient to cook. Wild fennel is used in the Marches region, but dried fennel seed can be substituted.

I rabbit (2¹/₂ to 3 pounds), cut into 8 pieces
Salt and freshly ground black pepper
2 tablespoons olive oil
2 ounces pancetta
3 garlic cloves, finely chopped
2 tablespoons chopped fresh rosemary
I tablespoon fennel seeds
2 or 3 sage leaves
I bay leaf
I cup dry white wine
1/2 cup water

1 Rinse the rabbit pieces and pat them dry with paper towels. Sprinkle with salt and pepper.

2 In a skillet large enough to hold the rabbit pieces in a single layer, heat the oil over medium heat. Place the pieces in the pan. Scatter the pancetta all around. Cook until the rabbit is browned on one side, about 8 minutes.

3 Turn the rabbit and scatter the garlic, rosemary, fennel, sage, and bay leaf all around. When the rabbit is browned on the second side, after about 7 minutes, add the wine and stir, scraping the bottom of the pan. Simmer the wine for 1 minute.

4 Cook uncovered, turning the meat occasionally, until the rabbit is very tender and coming away from the bone, about 30 minutes. (Add a little water if the pan becomes too dry.)

5 Discard the bay leaf. Transfer the rabbit to a serving platter and serve hot with the pan juices.

Rabbit with Tomatoes
Coniglio alla Ciociara

MAKES 4 SERVINGS

In the Ciociara region outside Rome, known for its delicious cooking, rabbit is braised in tomato sauce and white wine.

I rabbit (2¹/₂ to 3 pounds), cut into 8 pieces
2 tablespoons olive oil
2 ounces pancetta, thickly sliced and chopped
2 tablespoons chopped fresh flat-leaf parsley
I garlic clove, lightly smashed
Salt and freshly ground black pepper
I cup dry white wine
2 cups peeled, seeded, and chopped plum tomatoes

1 Rinse the rabbit pieces, then pat dry with paper towels. Heat the oil in a large skillet over medium heat. Place the rabbit in the pan, then add the pancetta, parsley, and garlic. Cook until the rabbit is nicely browned on all sides, about 15 minutes. Sprinkle with salt and pepper.

2 Remove the garlic from the pan and discard it. Stir in the wine and simmer 1 minute.

3 Reduce the heat to low. Stir in the tomatoes, then cook until the rabbit is tender and coming away from the bone, about 30 minutes.

4 Transfer the rabbit to a serving platter and serve hot with the sauce.

Sweet-and-Sour Braised Rabbit

Coniglio in Agrodolce

MAKES 4 SERVINGS

Sicilians are known for their sweet tooth, a legacy of the Arab domination of the island that lasted at least two hundred years. Raisins, sugar, and vinegar give this rabbit a mildly sweet-and-sour flavor.

1 rabbit (2½ to 3 pounds), cut into 8 pieces
2 tablespoons olive oil
2 ounces thickly sliced pancetta, chopped
1 medium onion, finely chopped
Salt and freshly ground black pepper
1 cup dry white wine
2 whole cloves
1 bay leaf
1 cup beef or chicken broth
1 tablespoon sugar
¼ cup white wine vinegar
2 tablespoons raisins
2 tablespoons pine nuts
2 tablespoons chopped fresh flat-leaf parsley

1 Rinse the rabbit pieces, then pat dry with paper towels. In a large skillet, heat the oil and pancetta over medium heat for 5 minutes. Add the rabbit and cook on one side until browned, about 8 minutes. Turn the rabbit pieces with tongs and scatter the onion all around. Sprinkle with salt and pepper.

2 Add the wine, cloves, and bay leaf. Bring the liquid to a simmer and cook until most of the wine has evaporated, about 2 minutes. Add the broth and cover the pan. Reduce the heat to low and cook until the rabbit is tender, 30 to 45 minutes.

3 Transfer the rabbit pieces to a plate. (If there is a lot of liquid left, boil it over high heat until reduced.) Stir in the sugar, vinegar, raisins, and pine nuts. Stir until the sugar dissolves, about 1 minute.

4 Return the rabbit to the pan and cook, turning the pieces in the sauce, until they seem well coated, about 5 minutes. Stir in the parsley and serve hot with the pan juices.

Roasted Rabbit with Potatoes

Coniglio Arrosto

MAKES 4 SERVINGS

At my friend Dora Marzovilla's home, a Sunday dinner or special occasion meal often begins with an assortment of tender, crisp fried vegetables, such as artichoke hearts or asparagus, followed by steaming bowls of homemade orecchiette or cavatelli tossed with a delicious ragù made with tiny meatballs. Dora, who comes from Rutigliano in Puglia, is a wonderful cook, and this rabbit dish, which she serves as the main course, is one of her specialties.

1 rabbit (2½ to 3 pounds), cut into 8 pieces
¼ cup olive oil
1 medium onion, finely chopped
2 tablespoons chopped fresh flat-leaf parsley
½ cup dry with wine
Salt and freshly ground black pepper
4 medium all-purpose potatoes, peeled and cut into 1-inch wedges
½ cup water
½ teaspoon oregano

1 Rinse the rabbit pieces and pat dry with paper towels. In a large skillet, heat two tablespoons of the oil over medium heat. Add the rabbit, onion and parsley. Cook, turning the pieces occasionally, until lightly browned, about 15 minutes. Add the wine and cook 5 minutes more. Sprinkle with salt and pepper.

2 Place a rack in the center of the oven. Preheat the oven to 425°F. Oil a roasting pan large enough to hold all of the ingredients in a single layer.

3 Scatter the potatoes in the pan and toss them with the remaining 2 tablespoons oil. Add the contents of the skillet to the pan, tucking the rabbit pieces around the potatoes. Add the water. Sprinkle with the oregano and salt and pepper. Cover the pan with aluminum foil. Roast 30 minutes. Uncover and cook 20 minutes more or until the potatoes are tender.

4 Transfer to a serving platter. Serve hot.

Vegetables

Artichokes

Marinated Artichokes
Roman-Style Artichokes
Braised Artichokes
Artichokes, Jewish Style
Roman Spring Vegetable Stew
Crispy Artichoke Hearts
Stuffed Artichokes
Sicilian-Style Stuffed Artichokes

Asparagus

Asparagus "In the Pan"
Asparagus with Oil and Vinegar
Asparagus with Lemon Butter
Asparagus with Various Sauces
Asparagus with Caper-Egg Dressing
Asparagus with Parmesan and Butter
Asparagus and Prosciutto Bundles
Roasted Asparagus
Asparagus in Zabaglione
Asparagus with Taleggio and Pine Nuts
Asparagus Timbales

Beans

Country-Style Beans
Tuscan Beans
Bean Salad
Beans and Cabbage
Beans in Tomato-Sage Sauce
Chickpea Stew
Fava Beans with Bitter Greens
Fresh Fava Beans, Roman Style
Fresh Fava Beans, Umbrian Style

Broccoli, Broccoli Rabe, and Cauliflower

Broccoli with Oil and Lemon
Broccoli, Parma Style
Broccoli Rabe with Garlic and Hot Pepper
Broccoli with Prosciutto
Bread Bites with Broccoli Rabe
Broccoli Rabe with Pancetta and Tomatoes
Little Vegetable Cakes
Fried Cauliflower
Cauliflower Puree

(continues)

Roasted Cauliflower

Smothered Cauliflower

Cauliflower with Parsley and Onion

Cauliflower in Tomato Sauce

Cauliflower Torte

Brussels Sprouts and Cabbage

Brussels Sprouts with Butter

Roasted Brussels Sprouts

Brussels Sprouts with Pancetta

Browned Cabbage with Garlic

Shredded Cabbage with Capers and Olives

Cabbage with Smoked Pancetta

Cardoons

Fried Cardoons

Cardoons with Parmigiano-Reggiano

Cardoons in Cream

Carrots

Carrots and Turnips with Marsala

Roasted Carrots with Garlic and Olives

Carrots in Cream

Sweet-and-Sour Carrots

Eggplant

Marinated Eggplant with Garlic and Mint

Grilled Eggplant with Fresh Tomato Salsa

Eggplant and Mozzarella "Sandwiches"

Eggplant with Garlic and Herbs

Neapolitan-Style Eggplant Sticks with Tomatoes

Eggplant Stuffed with Prosciutto and Cheese

Eggplant Stuffed with Anchovies, Capers, and Olives

Eggplant with Vinegar and Herbs

Fried Eggplant Cutlets

Eggplant with Spicy Tomato Sauce

Eggplant Parmigiana

Fennel

Roasted Fennel

Fennel with Parmesan Cheese

Fennel with Anchovy Sauce

Green and Wax Beans

Green Beans with Parsley and Garlic

Green Beans with Hazelnuts

Green Beans with Green Sauce

Green Bean Salad

Green Beans in Tomato-Basil Sauce

Green Beans with Pancetta and Onion
Green Beans in Tomato and Pancetta Sauce
Green Beans with Parmigiano
Wax Beans with Olives

Leafy Greens

Spinach with Lemon
Spinach or Other Greens with Butter and Garlic
Spinach with Raisins and Pine Nuts
Spinach with Anchovies, Piedmont Style
Escarole with Garlic
Dandelion with Potatoes

Mushrooms

Mushrooms with Garlic and Parsley
Mushrooms, Genoa Style
Roasted Mushrooms
Creamed Mushrooms
Creamy Baked Stuffed Mushrooms
Mushrooms with Tomato and Herbs
Mushrooms in Marsala
Grilled Mushrooms
Fried Mushrooms
Mushroom Gratin
Oyster Mushrooms with Sausage

Onions

Baked Onions
Onions with Balsamic Vinegar
Red Onion Confit
Roasted Onion and Beet Salad
Pearl Onions with Honey and Orange

Peas

Peas with Onions
Peas with Prosciutto and Green Onions
Sweet Peas with Lettuce and Mint
Easter Pea Salad

Peppers

Roasted Peppers
Roasted Pepper Salad
Roasted Peppers with Onions and Herbs
Baked Peppers with Tomatoes
Peppers with Balsamic Vinegar
Pickled Peppers
Peppers with Almonds
Peppers with Tomatoes and Onions
Stuffed Frying Peppers
Neapolitan-Style Stuffed Peppers
Stuffed Peppers, Ada Boni's Style
Fried Peppers
Sautéed Peppers with Zucchini and Mint
Roasted Pepper and Eggplant Terrine

(continues)

Potatoes

Sweet-and-Sour Potatoes

Potatoes with Balsamic Vinegar

Venetian-Style Potatoes

"Jumped" Potatoes

Potato-Pepper Sauté

Mashed Potatoes with Parsley and Garlic

Herbed New Potatoes with Pancetta

Potatoes with Tomatoes and Onions

Roasted Potatoes with Garlic and Rosemary

Roasted Potatoes with Mushrooms

Potatoes and Cauliflower, Basilicata Style

Potatoes and Cabbage in the Pan

Potato and Spinach Torte

Neapolitan Potato Croquettes

Dad's Neapolitan Potato Pie

Tomatoes

Skillet Tomatoes

Steamed Tomatoes

Baked Tomatoes

Tomatoes Stuffed with Farro

Roman Stuffed Tomatoes

Roasted Tomatoes with Balsamic Vinegar

Zucchini and Winter Squash

Zucchini Carpaccio

Zucchini with Garlic and Mint

Sautéed Zucchini

Zucchini with Prosciutto

Zucchini with Parmesan Crumbs

Zucchini Gratin

Zucchini with Tomatoes and Anchovies

Zucchini Stew

Zucchini Stuffed with Amaretti

Zucchini Stuffed with Porcini Mushrooms

Tuna-Stuffed Zucchini

Fried Zucchini

Zucchini Flans

Sweet-and-Sour Winter Squash

Mixed Vegetables

Grilled Vegetables

Roasted Winter Root Vegetables

Summer Vegetable Stew

Layered Vegetable Casserole

ew, if any, cuisines have as many creative ways of cooking vegetables as Italy's. It just scratches the surface to cite the popular preparations for tomatoes, eggplants, peppers, and squash in southern Italy or for cabbage, asparagus, and potatoes in the north. Many different varieties of vegetables are cooked in every conceivable way.

Of the vegetables included in this chapter, artichokes and cardoons may be among the least familiar in the United States. They are members of the same vegetable family and have a similar flavor, which is a combination of bitter, sweet, and buttery. Unfortunately, they are not as widely distributed here as some vegetables, and they often are not handled properly, so those that are available may not be the best. But once you have enjoyed fresh artichokes stuffed the southern Italian way with bread crumbs, garlic, and herbs, or cardoons baked with butter and cheese, you will appreciate how good they can be.

Few need to be convinced of the great flavor and versatility of vegetables like potatoes, peppers, and tomatoes. These three are native to the Western Hemisphere, but made their way to Italy after European explorers returned from the New World. The number of ways they can be cooked either separately or combined could fill a whole cookbook.

Tuscans are called *mangia fagioli*—"bean eaters"—by the rest of Italy because of their devotion to all kinds of beans, both fresh and dried. Whenever I travel in Tuscany, I look for some of the unusual varieties grown there, such as small, round *pigna* beans or enormous, meaty corona beans. They add interest beyond the typical assortment I find in supermarkets at home.

If the Tuscans are *mangia fagioli*, then the Campanians are *mangia foglie*, leaf eaters, because they eat a lot of leafy greens such as escarole, broccoli, and lettuces. Most of these are best when simply cooked with garlic, olive oil, and hot pepper, though they are also good with pasta and in soups.

Mushrooms, cabbage, cauliflower, and asparagus are just a few of the other kinds of vegetables you will find in this chapter. Enjoying vegetables is easy when they are prepared the Italian way.

❧ Artichokes

Artichokes may seem mysterious, but they are not difficult to prepare once you know how. When buying artichokes, make sure that they look fresh and green. Touches of purple are natural, but avoid those that look dried out or have dark brown or black spots. Look at the stems to see that there are no holes from insects.

I like to buy medium artichokes. Behemoth artichokes are usually too much for one person to eat, and they can cook unevenly, with the outer leaves soft before the hearts are done. For braising, small artichokes are best.

Artichokes darken when they are cooked, so I don't see the point in rubbing them with a cut lemon or putting them in a bath of ice water with a squeezed lemon as is often recommended. But there is no harm in it either, so the choice is up to you. Avoid cooking artichokes in cast-iron or aluminum pots, which can react with the artichokes and discolor them.

To prepare whole artichokes

With a serrated knife or very sharp chef's knife, trim off the top 3/4 to 1 inch of the artichoke leaves. With scissors, trim the pointed tops off the remaining leaves. Cut off the stems so that the artichokes can stand upright. With a vegetable peeler or sharp paring knife, remove the tough outer skin of the stems and set the stems aside. The stems can be chopped and added to stuffings, or just steamed along with the artichokes. Bend back and snap off the small leaves around the base and one or two rows of darker green leaves all around the artichoke.

Gently spread the leaves open. Rinse well in cool water. If removing the choke, before rinsing, use a small knife with a rounded tip to scrape out the fuzzy leaves in the center.

To prepare artichoke hearts

With a serrated knife or very sharp chef's knife, cut off the top 3/4 to 1 inch of the artichoke leaves. With scissors, trim the pointed tops off the remaining leaves. Rinse the artichokes under cold water, spreading the leaves open. Bend back and snap off all of the dark green leaves until you reach the pale yellowish cone of tender leaves at the center of the artichoke. With a vegetable peeler or sharp paring knife, peel off the tough outer skin around the base and stems. Leave the stems attached to the base. Trim off the ends of the stems. Cut the artichokes in half lengthwise and scoop out the fuzzy chokes. Cut the artichokes into quarters, wedges, or lengthwise slices according to the recipe.

Marinated Artichokes
Carciofi Marinati

MAKES 6 TO 8 SERVINGS

These artichokes are excellent in salads, with cold cuts, or as part of an antipasto assortment. The artichokes will last at least two weeks in the refrigerator.

If baby artichokes are not available, substitute medium artichokes, cut into eight wedges.

I cup white wine vinegar
2 cups water
I bay leaf
I whole garlic clove
8 to 12 baby artichokes, trimmed and quartered (to prepare whole artichokes, see at left)
Pinch of crushed red pepper
Salt
Extra-virgin olive oil

1 In a large saucepan, combine the vinegar, water, bay leaf, and garlic. Bring the liquid to a simmer.

2 Add the artichokes, crushed red pepper, and salt to taste. Cook until tender when pierced with a knife, 7 to 10 minutes. Remove from the heat. Pour the contents of the pan through a fine-mesh strainer into a bowl. Reserve the liquid.

3 Pack the artichokes into sterilized glass jars. Pour in the cooking liquid to cover. Let cool completely. Cover and refrigerate at least 24 hours or up to 2 weeks.

4 To serve, drain the artichokes and toss them with oil.

Roman-Style Artichokes
Carciofi alla Romana

MAKES 8 SERVINGS

Small farms all around Rome produce loads of fresh artichokes during the spring and fall artichoke seasons. Little trucks bring them to the street-corner markets, where they are sold right off the back of the truck. The artichokes have long stems and leaves still attached, because the stems, once peeled, are good to eat. Romans cook artichokes with the stem side up. They look very appealing when laid out on a serving platter.

2 large garlic cloves, finely chopped

2 tablespoons chopped fresh flat-leaf parsley

1 tablespoon chopped fresh mint or
   1/2 teaspoon dried marjoram

Salt and freshly ground black pepper

1/4 cup olive oil

8 medium artichokes, prepared for stuffing
   (to prepare whole artichokes, page 396)

1/2 cup dry white wine

1 In a small bowl, stir together the garlic, parsley, and mint or marjoram. Add salt and pepper to taste. Stir in 1 tablespoon of the oil.

2 Gently spread the leaves of the artichokes and push some of the garlic mixture down into the center. Squeezing the artichokes slightly to hold in the filling, place them stem-side up in a pan just large enough to hold them upright. Pour the wine around the artichokes. Add water to a depth of 3/4 inch. Drizzle the artichokes with the remaining oil.

3 Cover the pan and bring the liquid to a simmer over medium heat. Cook 45 minutes or until the artichokes are tender when pierced with a knife. Serve hot or at room temperature.

Braised Artichokes
Carciofi Stufati

MAKES 8 SERVINGS

Artichokes are members of the thistle family, and they grow on low bushy plants. They are found wild in many places in southern Italy, and many people cultivate them in their home gardens. An artichoke is actually an unopened flower. Very large artichokes grow at the top of the bush, while small ones sprout near the base. The small artichokes, often called baby artichokes, are great for braising. Prepare them for cooking as you would a larger artichoke. Their buttery sweet flavor and texture is especially good with fish.

1 small onion, finely chopped

1/4 cup olive oil

1 garlic clove, finely chopped

2 tablespoons chopped fresh flat-leaf parsley

2 pounds baby artichokes, trimmed and cut into
   quarters (page 396)

1/2 cup water

Salt and freshly ground black pepper

1 In a large saucepan, cook the onion in the oil over medium heat until tender, about 10 minutes. Stir in the garlic and parsley.

2 Place the artichokes in the pan and stir well. Add the water and salt and pepper to taste. Cover and cook over low heat until the artichokes are tender when pierced with a knife, about 15 minutes. Serve warm or at room temperature.

Variation: In Step 2, add 3 medium potatoes, peeled and cut into 1-inch cubes, with the onion.

Artichokes, Jewish Style
Carciofi alla Giudia

MAKES 4 SERVINGS

Jewish people first arrived in Rome in the first century B.C. They settled near the Tiber River and in 1556 were confined to a walled ghetto by Pope Paul IV. Many were poor, and they made do with whatever simple, inexpensive foods were available, such as salt cod, zucchini, and artichokes. By the time the ghetto walls came down in the mid-1800s, the Jews of Rome had developed their own style of cooking, which later became fashionable with other Romans. Today, Jewish dishes such as fried stuffed zucchini blossoms, Semolina Gnocchi (page 196), and these artichokes are considered Roman classics.

The Jewish Quarter of Rome still exists, and there are several good restaurants where you can sample this style of cooking. At Piperno and Da Giggetto, two favorite trattorias, these fried artichokes are served hot with plenty of salt. The leaves are as crisp as potato chips. The artichokes spatter as they cook, so stand back from the stove and protect your hands.

4 medium artichokes, prepared as for stuffing (page 396)
Olive oil
Salt

1 Pat the artichokes dry. Place an artichoke with the bottom up on a flat surface. With the heel of your hand, press down on the artichoke to flatten it and spread the leaves open. Repeat with the remaining artichokes. Turn them so the leaf tips face up.

2 In a large deep skillet or wide heavy saucepan, heat about 2 inches of the olive oil over medium heat until an artichoke leaf slipped into the oil sizzles and browns quickly. Protect your hand with an oven mitt, as the oil can spit and spatter if the artichokes are moist. Add the artichokes with leaf tips down. Cook, pressing the artichokes down

into the oil with a slotted spoon until browned on one side, about 10 minutes. With tongs, carefully turn the artichokes and cook until browned, about 10 minutes more.

3 Drain on paper towels. Sprinkle with salt and serve immediately.

Roman Spring Vegetable Stew
La Vignarola

MAKES 4 TO 6 SERVINGS

Italians are very much in tune with the seasons, and the arrival of the first spring artichokes indicates that winter is over and warm weather will soon be returning. To celebrate, Romans eat bowls of this fresh spring vegetable stew, featuring artichokes, as a main course.

4 ounces sliced pancetta, chopped
1/4 cup olive oil
1 medium onion, chopped
4 medium artichokes, trimmed and quartered (page 396)
1 pound fresh fava beans, shelled, or substitute 1 cup frozen fava or lima beans
1/2 cup Chicken Broth (page 63)
Salt and freshly ground black pepper
1 pound fresh peas, shelled (about 1 cup)
2 tablespoons chopped fresh flat-leaf parsley

1 In a large frying pan, cook the pancetta in the oil over medium heat. Stir frequently until the pancetta begins to brown, 5 minutes. Add the onion and cook until golden, about 10 minutes more.

2 Add the artichokes, fava beans, broth, and salt and pepper to taste. Lower the heat. Cover and cook 10 minutes or until the artichokes are almost tender when pierced with a knife. Add the peas and parsley and cook 5 minutes more. Serve hot or at room temperature.

Crispy Artichoke Hearts
Carciofini Fritti

MAKES 6 TO 8 SERVINGS

In the United States, artichokes are grown primarily in California, where they were first planted in the early twentieth century by Italian immigrants. The varieties are different from those in Italy, and they are often very mature when picked, so that they are sometimes tough and woody. Frozen artichoke hearts can be very good and save a lot of time. I sometimes use them for this recipe. Fried artichoke hearts are delicious with lamb chops or as an appetizer.

12 baby artichokes, trimmed and quartered
    (page 396), or 2 (10-ounce) packages frozen
    artichoke hearts, slightly undercooked according
    to package directions
3 large eggs, beaten
Salt
2 cups plain dry bread crumbs
Oil for frying
Lemon wedges

1 Pat the fresh or cooked artichokes dry. In a medium shallow bowl, beat the eggs with salt to taste. Spread the bread crumbs on a sheet of wax paper.

2 Place a wire cooling rack over a baking sheet. Dip the artichokes in the egg mixture, then roll them in the crumbs. Place the artichokes on the rack to dry at least 15 minutes before cooking.

3 Line a tray with paper towels. Pour oil to a depth of 1 inch in a large heavy skillet. Heat the oil until a drop of the egg mixture sizzles. Add just enough of the artichokes to fit comfortably in the pan without crowding. Cook, turning the pieces with tongs, until golden brown, about 4 minutes. Drain on the paper towels and keep warm while frying the remaining artichokes, in batches if necessary.

4 Sprinkle with salt and serve hot with the lemon wedges.

Stuffed Artichokes
Carciofi Ripieni

MAKES 8 SERVINGS

This is the way my mother always made artichokes — it's a classic preparation all over southern Italy. There is only enough stuffing to season the artichokes and enhance their flavor. Too much stuffing gets soggy and makes the artichokes heavy, so don't increase the amount of bread crumbs, and of course use crumbs from good-quality bread. The artichokes can be made ahead of time and served at room temperature or eaten hot and freshly made.

8 medium artichokes, prepared for stuffing (page 396)
3/4 cup plain dry bread crumbs
1/4 cup chopped fresh flat-leaf parsley
1/4 cup freshly grated Pecorino Romano or
    Parmigiano-Reggiano
1 garlic clove, very finely chopped
Salt and freshly ground black pepper
Olive oil

1 With a large chef's knife, finely chop the artichoke stems. Mix the stems in a large bowl with the bread crumbs, parsley, cheese, garlic, and salt and pepper to taste. Add a little oil and toss to moisten the crumbs evenly. Taste and adjust the seasoning.

2 Gently spread the leaves apart. Lightly stuff the center of the artichokes with the bread crumb mixture, also adding a little stuffing between the leaves. Do not pack the stuffing in.

3 Stand the artichokes in a pot just wide enough to hold them upright. Add water to a depth of 3/4 inch around the artichokes. Drizzle the artichokes with 3 tablespoons olive oil.

4 Cover the pot and place it over medium heat. When the water comes to a simmer, reduce the heat to low. Cook about 40 to 50 minutes (depending on the size of the artichokes) or until the artichoke bottoms are tender when pierced with a knife and a leaf pulls out easily. Add additional warm water if needed to prevent scorching. Serve warm or at room temperature.

Sicilian-Style Stuffed Artichokes

Carciofi alla Siciliana

MAKES 4 SERVINGS

The hot dry climate of Sicily is perfect for growing artichokes. The plants, which have jagged, silvery leaves, are quite beautiful, and many people use them as decorative shrubs in their home gardens. At the end of the season, artichokes left on the plant open all the way, exposing the fully matured choke at the center, which is purple and brushy.

This is the Sicilian way of stuffing artichokes, which is more complex than the previous recipe. Serve as a first course before roasted fish or a leg of lamb.

4 medium artichokes, prepared for stuffing
   (see page 396)

1/2 cup plain bread crumbs

4 anchovy fillets, finely chopped

2 tablespoons chopped drained capers

2 tablespoons pine nuts, toasted

2 tablespoons golden raisins

2 tablespoons chopped fresh flat-leaf parsley

1 large garlic clove, finely chopped

Salt and freshly ground black pepper

4 tablespoons olive oil

1/2 cup dry white wine

Water

1 In a medium bowl, combine the bread crumbs, anchovies, capers, pine nuts, raisins, parsley, garlic, and salt and pepper to taste. Stir in two tablespoons of the oil.

2 Gently spread the leaves apart. Stuff the artichokes loosely with the bread crumb mixture, also adding a little stuffing between the leaves. Do not pack the stuffing in.

3 Stand the artichokes in a pot just large enough to hold them upright. Add water to a depth of 3/4 inch around the artichokes. Drizzle with the remaining 2 tablespoons oil. Pour the wine around the artichokes.

4 Cover the pot and place it over medium heat. When the water comes to a simmer, reduce the heat to low. Cook 40 to 50 minutes (depending on the size of the artichokes) or until the artichoke bottoms are tender when pierced with a knife and a leaf pulls out easily. Add additional warm water if needed to prevent scorching. Serve warm or at room temperature.

❧ Asparagus

When asparagus are in season, Italians eat them every which way—from simply boiled to baked or fried, and in soup, pasta, and risotto. Both green and white varieties are eaten, with white more delicately flavored and tender. These pale stalks are kept covered from the sun's rays as they grow, blocking chlorophyll development, which would turn them green.

I like both thick and pencil-thin asparagus. I use the thick ones in recipes where the asparagus need to withstand cooking for long temperatures or at high heat, such as in baked and fried dishes. Thin asparagus are good in salads and with pasta.

Soak asparagus in cold water before trimming and cooking. The tips can be sandy. If you like, peel asparagus with a swivel-blade vegetable peeler. Snap off the bases first, then peel them.

Asparagus "In the Pan"
Asparagi in Padella

MAKES 4 TO 6 SERVINGS

These asparagus are quickly stir-fried. Add chopped garlic or fresh herbs, if you like.

3 tablespoons olive oil
I pound asparagus
Salt and freshly ground black pepper
2 tablespoons chopped fresh flat-leaf parsley

I Trim off the base of the asparagus at the point where the stem turns from white to green. Cut the asparagus into 2-inch lengths.

2 In a large skillet, heat the oil over medium heat. Add the asparagus and salt and pepper to taste. Cook 5 minutes, stirring often, or until the asparagus are lightly browned.

3 Cover the pan and cook 2 minutes more or until the asparagus are just tender. Stir in the parsley and serve immediately.

Asparagus with Oil and Vinegar
Insalata di Asparagi

MAKES 4 TO 6 SERVINGS

As soon as the first locally grown spears appear in the spring, I prepare them this way and eat a big batch to satisfy the craving that has developed through the long winter. Turn the asparagus in the dressing while they are still warm so that they absorb the flavor.

I pound asparagus
Salt
¼ cup extra-virgin olive oil
I to 2 tablespoons red wine vinegar
Freshly ground black pepper

I Trim off the base of the asparagus at the point where the stem turns from white to green. Bring about 2 inches of water to a boil in a large skillet. Add the asparagus and salt to taste. Cook until the asparagus bend slightly when you lift them from the stem end, 4 to 8 minutes. Cooking time will depend on the thickness of the asparagus. Remove the asparagus with tongs. Drain on paper towels and pat them dry.

2 In a large shallow dish, combine the oil, vinegar, a pinch of salt, and a generous grind of pepper. Whisk with a fork until blended. Add the asparagus and turn them gently until coated. Serve warm or at room temperature.

Asparagus with Lemon Butter

Asparagi al Burro

MAKES 4 TO 6 SERVINGS

Asparagus cooked this basic way goes with practically everything, from eggs to fish to meat. Add chopped fresh chives, parsley, or basil to the butter as a variation.

1 pound asparagus
Salt
2 tablespoons unsalted butter, melted
1 tablespoon fresh lemon juice
Freshly ground black pepper

1 Trim off the base of the asparagus at the point where the stem turns from white to green. Bring about 2 inches of water to a boil in a large skillet. Add the asparagus and salt to taste. Cook until the asparagus bend slightly when you lift them from the stem end, 4 to 8 minutes. Cooking time will depend on the thickness of the asparagus. Remove the asparagus with tongs. Drain them on paper towels and pat them dry.

2 Wipe out the skillet. Add the butter and cook over medium heat until melted, about 1 minute. Stir in the lemon juice. Return the asparagus to the pan. Sprinkle them with pepper and turn them gently to coat with the sauce. Serve immediately.

Asparagus with Various Sauces

MAKES 4 TO 6 SERVINGS

Plain boiled asparagus are wonderful served at room temperature with different sauces. They are great for a dinner party because they can be made ahead. It doesn't matter whether they are thick or thin, but try to get asparagus that are all pretty much the same size, so that they cook evenly.

Olive Oil Mayonnaise (page 104), Orange Mayonnaise (page 105), or Green Sauce (page 102)
1 pound asparagus
Salt

1 Prepare the sauce or sauces, if necessary. Then, trim off the base of the asparagus at the point where the stem turns from white to green.

2 Bring about 2 inches of water to a boil in a large skillet. Add the asparagus and salt to taste. Cook until the asparagus bend slightly when you lift them from the stem end, 4 to 8 minutes. Cooking time will depend on the thickness of the asparagus.

3 Remove the asparagus with tongs. Drain them on paper towels and pat them dry. Serve the asparagus at room temperature with one or more of the sauces.

Asparagus with Caper-Egg Dressing

Asparagi con Caperi e Uove

MAKES 4 TO 6 SERVINGS

In Trentino–Alto Adige and the Veneto, thick white asparagus are a rite of spring. They are fried and boiled, added to risottos, soups, and salads. An egg dressing is a typical condiment, such as this one with lemon juice, parsley, and capers.

1 pound asparagus
Salt
1/4 cup olive oil
1 teaspoon fresh lemon juice
Freshly ground pepper
1 hard cooked egg, diced
2 tablespoons chopped fresh flat-leaf parsley
1 tablespoon capers, rinsed and drained

1 Trim off the base of the asparagus at the point where the stem turns from white to green. Bring about 2 inches of water to a boil in a large skillet.

Add the asparagus and salt to taste. Cook until the asparagus bend slightly when you lift them from the stem end, 4 to 8 minutes. Cooking time will depend on the thickness of the asparagus. Remove the asparagus with tongs. Drain them on paper towels and pat them dry.

2 In a small bowl, whisk together the oil, lemon juice, and a pinch of salt and pepper. Stir in the egg, parsley, and capers.

3 Place the asparagus on a serving platter and spoon on the sauce. Serve immediately.

Asparagus with Parmesan and Butter
Asparagi alla Parmigiana

MAKES 4 TO 6 SERVINGS

This is sometimes called asparagi alla Milanese—*asparagus, Milan style—though it is eaten in many different regions. If you can find white asparagus, they take particularly well to this treatment.*

I pound thick asparagus
Salt
2 tablespoons unsalted butter
Freshly ground black pepper
1/2 cup freshly grated Parmigiano-Reggiano

I Trim off the base of the asparagus at the point where the stem turns from white to green. Bring about 2 inches of water to a boil in a large skillet. Add the asparagus and salt to taste. Cook until the asparagus bend slightly when you lift them from the stem end, 4 to 8 minutes. Cooking time will depend on the thickness of the asparagus. Remove the asparagus with tongs. Drain them on paper towels and pat them dry.

2 Place a rack in the center of the oven. Preheat the oven to 450°F. Butter a large baking dish.

3 Arrange the asparagus side by side in the baking dish, overlapping them slightly. Dot with butter and sprinkle with pepper and the cheese.

4 Bake 15 minutes or until the cheese is melted and golden. Serve immediately.

Asparagus and Prosciutto Bundles
Fagottini di Asparagi

MAKES 4 SERVINGS

For a more substantial dish, I sometimes top each bundle with slices of Fontina Valle d'Aosta, mozzarella, or another cheese that will melt well.

I pound asparagus
Salt and freshly ground pepper
4 slices imported Italian prosciutto
2 tablespoons butter
1/4 cup freshly grated Parmigiano-Reggiano

I Trim off the base of the asparagus at the point where the stem turns from white to green. Bring about 2 inches of water to a boil in a large skillet. Add the asparagus and salt to taste. Cook until the asparagus bend slightly when you lift them from the stem end, 4 to 8 minutes. Cooking time will depend on the thickness of the asparagus. Remove the asparagus with tongs. Drain on paper towels and pat them dry.

2 Place a rack in the center of the oven. Preheat the oven to 350°F. Butter a large baking dish.

3 Melt the butter in a large skillet. Add the asparagus and sprinkle them with salt and pepper. Using two spatulas, turn the asparagus carefully in the butter to coat them well.

4 Divide the asparagus into 4 groups. Place each group in the center of a slice of prosciutto. Wrap the ends of the prosciutto around the asparagus. Place the bundles in the baking dish. Sprinkle with the Parmigiano.

5 Bake the asparagus 15 minutes or until the cheese is melted and forms a crust. Serve hot.

Roasted Asparagus
Asparagi al Forno

MAKES 4 TO 6 SERVINGS

Roasting browns the asparagus and brings out their natural sweetness. These are perfect when you are roasting meat. You can remove the cooked meat from the oven, and while it rests, bake the asparagus. Use thick asparagus for this recipe.

I pound asparagus
¼ cup olive oil
Salt

I Place a rack in the center of the oven. Preheat the oven to 450°F. Trim off the base of the asparagus at the point where the stem turns from white to green.

2 Place the asparagus in a baking pan large enough to hold them in a single layer. Drizzle with oil and salt. Roll the asparagus from side to side to coat them with the oil.

3 Bake 8 to 10 minutes or until the asparagus are just tender.

Asparagus in Zabaglione
Asparagi allo Zabaione

MAKES 6 SERVINGS

Zabaglione is a fluffy egg custard that is usually served sweetened for dessert. In this case, the eggs are beaten with white wine and no sugar and served over asparagus. This makes an elegant first course for a spring meal. Peeling the asparagus is optional but ensures that the asparagus will be tender from tip to stem.

I ½ pounds asparagus
2 large egg yolks
¼ cup dry white wine
Pinch of salt
I tablespoon unsalted butter

I Trim off the base of the asparagus at the point where the stem turns from white to green. To peel the asparagus, start below the tip and, using a swivel-blade peeler, strip away the dark green peel down to the stem end.

2 Bring about 2 inches of water to a boil in a large skillet. Add the asparagus and salt to taste. Cook until the asparagus bend slightly when you lift them from the stem end, 4 to 8 minutes. Cooking time will depend on the thickness of the asparagus. Remove the asparagus with tongs. Drain on paper towels and pat them dry.

3 Bring about an inch of water to a simmer in the bottom half of a double boiler or saucepan. Place the egg yolks, wine, and salt in the top of the double boiler, or in a heatproof bowl that fits comfortably over the saucepan without touching the water.

4 Beat the egg mixture until blended, then place the pan or bowl over the simmering water. Beat with a hand-held electric mixer or with a wire whisk until the mixture is pale-colored and holds a soft shape when the beaters are lifted, about 5 minutes. Beat in the butter just until blended.

5 Spoon the warm sauce over the asparagus and serve immediately.

Asparagus with Taleggio and Pine Nuts

Asparagi con Taleggio e Pinoli

MAKES 6 TO 8 SERVINGS

Not far from Peck's, the famous gastronomia (gourmet food store) in Milan, is the Trattoria Milanese. It is a great place to try simple, classic Lombardian dishes, such as these asparagus topped with taleggio— *a buttery, semisoft and aromatic cow's milk cheese that is made locally and is one of Italy's finest cheeses. Fontina or Bel Paese can be substituted if taleggio is not available.*

2 pounds asparagus
Salt
2 tablespoons unsalted butter, melted
6 ounces taleggio, Fontina Valle d'Aosta or Bel Paese, cut into bite-size pieces
1/4 cup chopped pine nuts or sliced almonds
1 tablespoon plain bread crumbs

1 Place a rack in the center of the oven. Preheat the oven to 450°F. Butter a 13 × 9 × 2–inch baking dish.

2 Trim off the base of the asparagus at the point where the stem turns from white to green. To peel the asparagus, start below the tip and, using a swivel-blade peeler, strip away the dark green peel down to the stem end.

3 Bring about 2 inches of water to a boil in a large skillet. Add the asparagus and salt to taste. Cook until the asparagus bend slightly when you lift them by the stem end, 4 to 8 minutes. Cooking time will depend on the thickness of the asparagus. Remove the asparagus with tongs. Drain them on paper towels and pat them dry.

4 Arrange the asparagus in the baking dish. Drizzle with the butter. Scatter the cheese over the asparagus. Sprinkle with the nuts and bread crumbs.

5 Bake until the cheese is melted and the nuts are browned, about 15 minutes. Serve hot.

Asparagus Timbales

Sformatini di Asparagi

MAKES 6 SERVINGS

Silky smooth custards like these are an old-fashioned preparation, but one that continues to be popular in many Italian restaurants, essentially because it is very delicious. Practically any vegetable can be made this way, and these little molds are good for a side dish, first course, or vegetarian main dish. Sformatini, literally "little unmolded things," can be served plain, topped with a tomato or cheese sauce, or surrounded with buttery sautéed vegetables.

1 cup Béchamel Sauce (page 101)
1 1/2 pounds asparagus, trimmed
3 large eggs
1/4 cup freshly grated Parmigiano-Reggiano
Salt and freshly ground black pepper

1 Prepare the béchamel, if necessary. Bring about 2 inches of water to a boil in a large skillet. Add the asparagus and salt to taste. Cook until the asparagus bend slightly when you lift them by the stem end, 4 to 8 minutes. Cooking time will depend on the thickness of the asparagus. Remove the asparagus with tongs. Drain them on paper towels and pat them dry. Cut off and set aside 6 of the tips.

2 Place the asparagus in a food processor and process until smooth. Blend in the eggs, béchamel, cheese, 1 teaspoon salt, and pepper to taste.

3 Place a rack in the center of the oven. Preheat the oven to 350°F. Generously butter six 6-ounce ramekins or custard cups. Pour the asparagus mixture into the cups. Place the cups in a large roasting pan and pour boiling water into the pan to reach halfway up the sides of the cups.

4 Bake 50 to 60 minutes or until a knife inserted in the center comes out clean. Remove the molds from the pan and run a small knife around the edge. Invert the molds onto serving dishes. Top with the reserved asparagus tips and serve hot.

❧ Beans

Dried legumes *(fagioli secchi)*, including beans, peas, and lentils, are a staple of Italian cooking. They are mostly eaten in soups, pasta dishes, and salads, though in Tuscany and Umbria they appear as a side dish with everything from steak to sausages. One of my fondest food memories of traveling in Tuscany is the sight in many homes of enormous green jars of *fagioli al fiasco* simmering on the hearth. A large, round old-fashioned wine bottle with a narrow neck (like a flask) called a *fiasco* is partially filled with beans, water, herbs, and olive oil. The narrow opening keeps the liquid from evaporating too quickly as the beans slowly simmer and swell up with the liquid. They turn tender, but keep their shape and never get mushy. The beans are then poured out and drizzled with dark green extra-virgin olive oil and freshly ground black pepper. They are so good that little else is needed.

As with most other foods, each region of Italy seems to have a favorite variety of legume. Borlotti, or cranberry beans, are preferred in the Veneto region and are usually used in soup. Tuscans prefer cannellini beans and black-eyed peas, while in Puglia they eat a lot of chickpeas, both the black and the white varieties, and *cicerchie,* an ancient variety of legume that looks like a flattened chickpea. Lentils are a specialty of Umbria.

It takes patience to cook beans well, though not a lot of skill. Most Italian cooks buy the beans dried, soak them in water, then simmer them with aromatic vegetables and herbs. One of the biggest mistakes that novice bean cookers make is not soaking or cooking the beans long enough so that they turn out tender, creamy, and full of flavor. Cooking beans to perfection takes time, but most of the cooking is unattended. It is difficult to give exact cooking times for beans, because a lot depends on the variety and how old they are. Be sure to allow extra time when cooking beans.

They can always be reheated if they are done ahead of schedule.

The conventional wisdom about salting beans is that the salt toughens the skins as they cook, so it is best to add the salt at the end of the cooking time. I have experimented with salting before and after cooking and really don't see any difference, but to be safe I generally salt them at the end of the cooking.

Once they are cooked, legumes keep perfectly in the refrigerator for up to a week, or they can be frozen for longer storage. Canned beans can easily be substituted for home-cooked beans and are very convenient for quick meals. Some canned beans are mushy, so try several brands to find one that you like.

Country-Style Beans
Fagioli alla Paesana

MAKES ABOUT 6 CUPS OF BEANS, SERVING 10 TO 12

This is a basic cooking method for all types of beans. The soaking beans can ferment if left at room temperature, so I place them in the refrigerator. Once they are cooked, serve them as is with a drizzle of extra-virgin olive oil, or add them to soups or salads.

I pound cranberry, cannellini, or other dried beans
I carrot, trimmed
I celery rib with leaves
I onion
2 garlic cloves
2 tablespoons olive oil
Salt

I Rinse the beans and pick them over to remove any broken beans or small stones.

2 Place the beans in a large bowl with cold water to cover by 2 inches. Refrigerate 4 hours up to overnight.

3 Drain the beans and place them in a large pot with fresh cold water to cover by 1 inch. Bring the water to a simmer over medium heat. Reduce the heat to low and skim off the foam that rises to the surface. When the foam stops rising, add the vegetables and olive oil.

4 Cover the pot and simmer 1 1/2 to 2 hours, adding more water if needed, until the beans are very tender and creamy. Add salt to taste and let stand about 10 minutes. Discard the vegetables. Serve hot or at room temperature.

Tuscan Beans
Fagioli Stufati

MAKES 6 SERVINGS

Tuscans are the masters of bean cookery. They slowly simmer the dried legumes with herbs in barely bubbling liquid. Long, slow cooking yields tender, creamy beans that keep their shape as they cook.

Always test several beans to determine doneness, because not all of them will be cooked at the same moment. I let the beans sit awhile on the turned-off stove after cooking to be sure that they are done evenly. They are good when lukewarm, and they reheat perfectly.

Beans are good as a side dish or in soups, or try them spooned over warm toasted Italian bread that has been rubbed with garlic and drizzled with oil.

8 ounces dried cannellini, cranberry, or other beans

I large garlic clove, slightly crushed

6 fresh sage leaves, or a small branch of rosemary, or 3 sprigs of fresh thyme

Salt

Extra-virgin olive oil

Freshly ground black pepper

I Rinse the beans and pick them over to remove any broken beans or small stones. Place the beans in a large bowl with cold water to cover by 2 inches. Refrigerate 4 hours up to overnight.

 2 Preheat the oven to 300°F. Drain the beans and place them in a Dutch oven or other deep,

heavy pot with a tight-fitting lid. Add fresh water to cover by 1 inch. Add the garlic and sage. Bring to a simmer over low heat.

3 Cover the pot and place it on the center rack of the oven. Cook until the beans are very tender, about 1 hour and 15 minutes or more, depending on the type and age of the beans. Check occasionally to see if more water is needed to keep the beans covered. Some beans may require 30 minutes more cooking time.

4 Taste the beans. When they are completely tender, add salt to taste. Let the beans stand for 10 minutes. Serve warm with a drizzle of olive oil and a sprinkle of black pepper.

Bean Salad
Insalata di Fagioli

MAKES 4 SERVINGS

Dressing the beans while they are warm helps them to absorb the flavors.

2 tablespoons extra-virgin olive oil

2 tablespoons fresh lemon juice

Salt and freshly ground black pepper

2 cups warm cooked or canned beans, such as cannellini or cranberry beans

I small yellow bell pepper, diced

I cup cherry tomatoes, halved or quartered

2 green onions, cut into 1/2-inch pieces

I bunch arugula, trimmed

I In a medium bowl, whisk together the oil, lemon juice, and salt and pepper to taste. Drain the beans and add them to the dressing. Stir well. Let stand 30 minutes.

2 Add the pepper, tomatoes, and onions and toss together. Taste and adjust seasoning.

3 Arrange the arugula on a platter and top with the salad. Serve immediately.

Beans and Cabbage
Fagioli e Cavolo

MAKES 6 SERVINGS

Serve this as a first course in place of pasta or soup, or as a side dish with roast pork or chicken.

2 ounces pancetta (4 thick slices), cut into ¹/₂-inch strips
2 tablespoons olive oil
I small onion, chopped
2 large garlic cloves
¹/₄ teaspoon crushed red pepper
4 cups shredded cabbage
I cup chopped fresh or canned tomatoes
Salt
3 cups drained cooked or canned cannellini
    or cranberry beans

I In a large skillet, cook the pancetta in the olive oil for 5 minutes. Stir in the onion, garlic, and hot pepper and cook until the onion is softened, about 10 minutes.

2 Add the cabbage, tomatoes, and salt to taste. Reduce the heat to low and cover the pan. Cook 20 minutes or until the cabbage is tender. Stir in the beans and cook 5 minutes more. Serve hot.

Beans in Tomato-Sage Sauce
Fagioli all'Uccelletto

MAKES 8 SERVINGS

These Tuscan beans are cooked in the manner of little game birds, with sage and tomato, hence their Italian name.

I pound dried cannellini or Great Northern beans,
    rinsed and picked over
Salt
2 sprigs fresh sage
3 large garlic cloves
¹/₄ cup olive oil
3 large tomatoes, peeled, seeded, and chopped,
    or 2 cups canned tomatoes

I Place the beans in a large bowl with cold water to cover by 2 inches. Place them in the refrigerator to soak 4 hours up to overnight.

2 Drain the beans and place them in a large pot with cold water to cover by 1 inch. Bring the liquid to a simmer. Cover and cook until the beans are tender, 1¹/₂ to 2 hours. Add salt to taste and let stand 10 minutes.

3 In a large saucepan, cook the sage and garlic in the oil over medium heat, flattening the garlic with the back of a spoon, until the garlic is golden, about 5 minutes. Stir in the tomatoes.

4 Drain the beans, reserving the liquid. Add the beans to the sauce. Cook 10 minutes, adding some of the reserved liquid if the beans become dry. Serve warm or at room temperature.

Chickpea Stew
Ceci in Zimino

MAKES 4 TO 6 SERVINGS

This hearty stew is good on its own, or you can add some cooked small pasta or rice and water or broth to turn it into a soup.

I medium onion, chopped
I garlic clove, finely chopped
4 tablespoons olive oil
I pound Swiss chard or spinach, trimmed and chopped
Salt and freshly ground black pepper
3¹/₂ cups drained cooked or canned chickpeas
Extra-virgin olive oil

I In a medium saucepan, cook the onion and garlic in the oil over medium heat until golden, 10 minutes. Add the Swiss chard and salt to taste. Cover and cook 15 minutes.

2 Add the chickpeas with some of their cooking liquid or water and salt and pepper to taste. Cover and cook 30 minutes more. Stir occasionally and mash some of the chickpeas with the back of a spoon. Add a little more liquid if the mixture becomes too dry.

3 Let cool slightly before serving. Drizzle with a little extra-virgin olive oil if desired

Fava Beans with Bitter Greens
Fave e Cicoria

MAKES 4 TO 6 SERVINGS

Dried fava beans have an earthy, slightly bitter flavor. When buying them, look for the peeled variety. They are slightly more expensive, but are worth it to avoid the tough skins. They also cook more quickly than skin-on favas. You can find dried peeled fava beans in ethnic markets and those specializing in natural foods.

This recipe is from Puglia, where it is practically the national dish. Any kind of bitter greens can be used, such as chicory, broccoli rabe, turnip greens, or dandelion. I like to add a pinch of crushed red pepper to the vegetables as they cook, but that is not traditional.

8 ounces peeled dried fava beans, rinsed and drained
I medium boiling potato, peeled and cut into I-inch pieces
Salt
I pound chicory or dandelion greens, trimmed
¼ cup extra-virgin olive oil
I garlic clove, finely chopped
Pinch of crushed red pepper

I Place the beans and potato in a large pot. Add cold water to cover by ½ inch. Bring to a simmer and cook until the beans are very soft and falling apart and all the water is absorbed.

2 Add salt to taste. Mash the beans with the back of a spoon or a potato masher. Stir in the oil.

3 Bring a large pot of water to a boil. Add the greens and salt to taste. Cook until tender, depending on the variety of greens, 5 to 10 minutes. Drain well.

4 Dry the pot. Add the oil, garlic, and crushed red pepper. Cook over medium heat until the garlic is golden, about 2 minutes. Add the drained greens and salt to taste. Toss well.

5 Spread the bean puree on a serving platter. Pile the greens on top. Drizzle with more oil if desired. Serve hot or warm.

Fresh Fava Beans, Roman Style
Fave alla Romana

MAKES 4 SERVINGS

Fresh fava beans in their pods are an important spring vegetable throughout central and southern Italy. The Romans like to pop them out of the shells and eat them raw as an accompaniment to young pecorino cheese. The beans are also stewed with other spring vegetables such as peas and artichokes.

If the fava beans are very young and tender, it is not necessary to peel off the thin skin that covers each bean. Try eating one with the peel and another without it to decide if they are tender.

The flavor and texture of fresh favas is completely different from dried favas, so do not substitute one for the other. If you can't find fresh favas, look for the frozen beans sold in many Italian and Middle Eastern markets. Fresh or frozen lima beans also work well in this dish.

I small onion, finely chopped
4 ounces pancetta, diced
2 tablespoons olive oil
4 pounds fresh fava beans, shelled (about 3 cups)
Salt and freshly ground black pepper
¼ cup water

I In a medium skillet, cook the onion and pancetta in the olive oil over medium heat for 10 minutes or until golden.

2 Stir in the fava beans and salt and pepper to taste. Add the water and lower the heat. Cover the pan and cook 5 minutes or until the beans are almost tender.

3 Uncover the pan and cook until the beans and pancetta are lightly browned, about 5 minutes. Serve hot.

Fresh Fava Beans, Umbrian Style

Scafata

MAKES 6 SERVINGS

Fava bean pods should be firm and crisp, not wrinkled or soft, which indicates that they are too old. The smaller the pod, the more tender the beans. Figure about 1 pound of fresh favas in the pod for 1 cup shelled favas.

2¹/₂ pounds fresh fava beans, shelled, or 2 cups frozen favas

1 pound Swiss chard, trimmed and cut in ¹/₂-inch strips

1 onion, chopped

1 medium carrot, chopped

1 celery rib, chopped

¹/₄ cup olive oil

1 teaspoon salt

Freshly ground black pepper

1 medium ripe tomato, peeled, seeded, and chopped

1 In a medium saucepan, stir together all of the ingredients except the tomato. Cover and cook over low heat, stirring occasionally, for 15 minutes or until the beans are tender. Add a little water if the vegetables begin to stick.

2 Stir in the tomato and cook uncovered for 5 minutes. Serve hot.

❧ Broccoli, Broccoli Rabe, and Cauliflower

These three vegetables are all members of the *Brassica* genus. Though available year round, they are at their best in the late summer and fall.

When buying broccoli, look for dark green bunches without any trace of yellowing. The stalks and any leaves should be crisp. Occasionally, I see purple broccoli in the market. The flavor is about the same as the green variety, and it should be purchased and cooked the same way. *Romanesco* broccoli is a bright chartreuse color with a beautiful pointed shape that resembles a seashell. It is slightly milder in taste than regular broccoli.

Broccoli rabe, sometimes called broccoli raab or rape (pronounced rah-peh), is more widely available now than it was a few years ago. It resembles a leggy version of broccoli, with smaller heads and narrow stems. It too should be crisp and green. Sometimes broccoli rabe has a few yellow flowers, which are edible, but there should be no more than a few open flowers or the broccoli may be too mature. Broccoli rabe has a pleasant bitter flavor that I find addictive.

Cauliflower ranges in color from creamy white to orange and purple. The heads should be firm and unbruised. Broccoflower is a combination of broccoli and cauliflower with a mild flavor.

Wash broccoli, brcoccoli rabe, and cauliflower in cool water and trim off and discard any bruised portions.

Broccoli with Oil and Lemon
Broccoli al Agro

MAKES 6 SERVINGS

This is the basic way of serving many types of cooked green vegetables in southern Italy. They are always served at room temperature.

1 1/2 pounds broccoli
Salt
1/4 cup extra-virgin olive oil
1 to 2 tablespoons fresh lemon juice
Lemon wedges, for garnish

1 Cut the broccoli into large florets. Trim off the ends of the stems. Peel off the tough skin with a swivel-blade vegetable peeler. Cut thick stems crosswise into 1/4-inch slices.

2 Bring a large pot of water to a boil. Add the broccoli and salt to taste. Cook until the broccoli is tender, 5 to 7 minutes. Drain and cool slightly under cold running water.

3 Drizzle the broccoli with the oil and lemon juice. Garnish with the lemon wedges. Serve at room temperature.

Broccoli, Parma Style
Broccoli alla Parmigiana

MAKES 4 SERVINGS

For variety, make this dish with a combination of cauliflower and broccoli.

1 1/2 pounds broccoli
Salt
3 tablespoons unsalted butter
Freshly ground black pepper
1/2 cup freshly grated Parmigiano-Reggiano

1 Cut the broccoli into large florets. Trim off the ends of the stems. Peel off the tough skin with a swivel-blade vegetable peeler. Cut thick stems crosswise into 1/4-inch slices.

2 Bring a large pot of water to a boil. Add the broccoli and salt to taste. Cook until the broccoli is partially done, about 5 minutes. Drain and cool under cold water.

3 Place a rack in the center of the oven. Preheat the oven to 375°F. Butter a baking dish large enough to hold the broccoli.

3 Arrange the spears in the prepared dish, overlapping them slightly. Dot with the butter and sprinkle with pepper. Sprinkle the cheese on top.

4 Bake 10 minutes or until the cheese is melted and slightly browned. Serve hot.

Broccoli Rabe with Garlic and Hot Pepper
Cime di Rape col Peperoncino

MAKES 4 SERVINGS

It doesn't get much better than this recipe when it comes to seasoning broccoli rabe. This dish can also be made with regular broccoli or cauliflower. Some versions include a few anchovies sautéed with the garlic and oil, or try adding a handful of olives for a salty tang. This also makes a great topping for pasta.

1 1/2 pounds broccoli rabe
Salt
3 tablespoons olive oil
2 large garlic cloves, thinly sliced
Pinch of crushed red pepper

1 Separate the broccoli rabe into florets. Trim off the base of the stems. Peeling the stems is optional. Cut each floret crosswise into 2 or 3 pieces.

2 Bring a large pot of water to a boil. Add the broccoli rabe and salt to taste. Cook until the broccoli is almost tender, about 5 minutes. Drain.

3 Dry the pot and add the oil, garlic, and red pepper. Cook over medium heat until the garlic is lightly golden, about 2 minutes. Add the broccoli and a sprinkle of salt. Stir well. Cover and cook until tender, 3 minutes more. Serve hot or at room temperature.

Broccoli with Prosciutto
Brasato di Broccoli

MAKES 4 SERVINGS

The broccoli in this recipe is cooked until it is soft enough to mash with a fork. Serve it as a side dish or spread it on toasted Italian bread for crostini.

1 1/2 pounds broccoli
Salt
1/4 cup olive oil
1 medium onion, chopped
1 garlic clove, finely chopped
4 thin slices imported Italian prosciutto, cut crosswise
    into thin strips

1 Cut the broccoli into large florets. Trim off the ends of the stems. Peel off the tough skin with a swivel-blade vegetable peeler. Cut thick stems crosswise into 1/4-inch slices.

2 Bring a large pot of water to a boil. Add the broccoli and salt to taste. Cook until the broccoli is partially done, about 5 minutes. Drain and cool under cold water.

3 Dry the pot and add the oil, onion, and garlic. Cook over medium heat until golden, about 10 minutes. Stir in the broccoli. Cover and turn the heat to low. Cook until the broccoli is soft, about 15 minutes.

4 Coarsely mash the broccoli with a potato masher or a fork. Stir in the prosciutto. Season to taste with salt and pepper. Serve hot.

Bread Bites with Broccoli Rabe
Morsi con Cime di Rape

MAKES 4 SERVINGS

A minestra can be a thick soup made with pasta or rice, or a hearty vegetable dish, such as this one from Puglia containing cubes of bread. Though it was probably invented by a thrifty housewife with

leftover bread and many mouths to fill, it is tasty enough for a first course or as a side dish with pork ribs or chops.

1 1/2 pounds broccoli rabe
3 garlic cloves, thinly sliced
Pinch of crushed red pepper
1/3 cup olive oil
4 to 6 (1/2-inch-thick) slices Italian or French bread,
    cut into bite-size pieces

1 Separate the broccoli rabe into florets. Trim off the base of the stems. Peeling the stems is optional. Cut each floret crosswise into 1-inch pieces.

2 Bring a large pot of water to a boil. Add the broccoli rabe and salt to taste. Cook until the broccoli is almost tender, about 5 minutes. Drain.

3 In a large skillet, cook the garlic and red pepper in the oil for 1 minute. Stir in the bread cubes and cook, stirring often until the bread is lightly toasted, about 3 minutes.

4 Stir in the broccoli rabe and a pinch of salt. Cook, stirring, 5 minutes more. Serve hot.

Broccoli Rabe with Pancetta and Tomatoes
Cime di Rape al Pomodori

MAKES 4 SERVINGS

In this recipe, the meaty flavor of pancetta, onion, and tomato complements the bold flavor of the broccoli rabe. This is another one of those dishes that would be great tossed with some hot cooked pasta.

1 1/2 pounds broccoli rabe
Salt
2 tablespoons olive oil
2 thick slices pancetta, chopped
1 medium onion, chopped
Pinch of crushed red pepper
1 cup chopped canned tomatoes
2 tablespoons dry white wine or water

1 Separate the broccoli rabe into florets. Trim off the base of the stems. Peeling the stems is optional. Cut each floret crosswise into 1-inch pieces.

2 Bring a large pot of water to a boil. Add the broccoli rabe and salt to taste. Cook until the broccoli is almost tender, about 5 minutes. Drain.

3 Pour the oil into a large skillet. Add the pancetta, onion, and red pepper and cook over medium heat until the onion is translucent, about 5 minutes. Add the tomatoes, wine, and a pinch of salt. Cook 10 minutes more or until thickened.

4 Stir in the broccoli rabe and cook until heated, about 2 minutes. Serve hot.

Little Vegetable Cakes
Frittelle di Erbe di Campo

MAKES 8 SERVINGS

In Sicily, these little vegetable pancakes are made with bitter wild greens. You can use broccoli rabe, mustard greens, borage, or chicory. These little cakes are traditionally eaten at Easter time as an appetizer or side dish. They are good hot or at room temperature.

1¹/₂ **pounds broccoli rabe**
Salt
4 large eggs
2 tablespoons grated caciocavallo or Pecorino Romano
Salt and freshly ground black pepper
2 tablespoons olive oil

1 Separate the broccoli rabe into florets. Trim off the base of the stems. Peeling the stems is optional. Cut each floret crosswise into 1-inch pieces.

2 Bring a large pot of water to a boil. Add the broccoli rabe and salt to taste. Cook until the broccoli is almost tender, about 5 minutes. Drain. Let cool slightly, then press out the water. Chop broccoli rabe.

3 In a large bowl, whisk the eggs, cheese, and salt and pepper to taste. Stir in the greens.

4 Heat the oil in a large skillet over medium heat. Scoop up a heaping tablespoonful of the mixture and place it in the pan. Flatten the mixture with a spoon into a small pancake. Repeat with the remaining mixture. Cook 1 side of the cakes until lightly browned, about 2 minutes, then turn them over with a spatula and cook the other side until browned and cooked through. Serve hot or at room temperature.

Fried Cauliflower
Cavolfiore Fritte

MAKES 4 SERVINGS

Try serving cauliflower prepared this way to someone who does not normally like this versatile vegetable, and you are sure to make a convert. The crisp, cheese-flavored coating provides an excellent contrast to the tender cauliflower. These can be passed as party appetizers or served as a side dish with grilled chops. For best texture, serve them immediately after cooking.

1 small cauliflower (about 1 pound)
Salt
1 cup plain dry bread crumbs
3 large eggs
¹/₂ **cup freshly grated Parmigiano-Reggiano**
Freshly ground black pepper
Vegetable oil
Lemon wedges

1 Cut the cauliflower into 2-inch florets. Trim off the ends of the stems. Cut thick stems crosswise into ¹/₄-inch slices.

2 Bring a large pot of water to a boil. Add the cauliflower and salt to taste. Cook until the cauliflower is almost tender, about 5 minutes. Drain and cool under cold water.

3 Put the bread crumbs in a shallow plate. In a small bowl, whisk the eggs, cheese, and salt and pepper to taste. Dip the cauliflower pieces in the

(continues)

egg, then roll them in the bread crumbs. Let dry on a rack for 15 minutes.

4 Pour the oil into a large deep skillet to a depth of $1/2$ inch. Heat over medium heat until a bit of the egg mixture dropped into the pan sizzles and cooks rapidly. Meanwhile, line a tray with paper towels.

5 Place only enough pieces of cauliflower in the pan as will fit comfortably without touching. Fry the pieces, turning them with tongs, until golden brown and crisp all over, about 6 minutes. Drain the cauliflower on the paper towels. Repeat with the remaining cauliflower.

6 Serve the cauliflower hot, with lemon wedges.

Cauliflower Puree
Purèa di Cavolfiore

MAKES 4 SERVINGS

Though it looks like ordinary mashed potatoes, this puree of cauliflower and potatoes is much lighter and more flavorful. It is a nice change from mashed potatoes and could even be served with a hearty stew, such as Braised Beef Shank (page 326).

1 small cauliflower (about 1 pound)
3 medium boiling potatoes, peeled and quartered
Salt
1 tablespoon unsalted butter
2 tablespoons grated Parmigiano-Reggiano
Freshly ground black pepper

1 Cut the cauliflower into 2-inch florets. Trim off the ends of the stems. Cut thick stems crosswise into $1/4$-inch slices.

2 In a pot large enough to hold all the vegetables, combine the potatoes with 3 quarts cold water and salt to taste. Bring to a simmer and cook 5 minutes.

3 Add the cauliflower and cook until the vegetables are very tender, about 10 minutes. Drain the cauliflower and potatoes. Blend them until smooth with an electric mixer or hand-held blender. Do not overbeat them or the potatoes will become gluey.

4 Stir in the butter, cheese, and salt and pepper to taste. Serve hot.

Roasted Cauliflower
Cavolfiore al Forno

MAKES 4 TO 6 SERVINGS

Cauliflower goes from bland to delicious when it is roasted until lightly browned. For variation, toss the cooked cauliflower with a little balsamic vinegar.

1 medium cauliflower (about $1 1/2$ pounds)
$1/4$ cup olive oil
Salt and freshly ground black pepper

1 Cut the cauliflower into 2-inch florets. Trim off the ends of the stems. Cut thick stems crosswise into $1/4$-inch slices.

2 Place a rack in the center of the oven. Preheat the oven to 350°F. Spread the cauliflower in a roasting pan just large enough to hold it in single layer. Toss with the oil and a generous sprinkle of salt and pepper.

3 Bake, stirring occasionally, for 45 minutes or until the cauliflower is tender and lightly browned. Serve warm.

Smothered Cauliflower
Cavolfiore Stufato

MAKES 4 TO 6 SERVINGS

Some people say that cauliflower is bland, but I say that its mild flavor and creamy texture is a perfect backdrop for flavorful ingredients.

1 medium cauliflower (about $1 1/2$ pounds)
3 tablespoons olive oil
$1/4$ cup water
2 garlic cloves, thinly sliced
Salt
$1/2$ cup mild black olives, such as Gaeta, pitted and sliced
4 anchovies, chopped (optional)
2 tablespoons chopped fresh flat-leaf parsley

1 Cut the cauliflower into 2-inch florets. Trim off the ends of the stems. Cut thick stems crosswise into 1/4-inch slices.

2 Pour the oil into a large skillet and add the cauliflower. Cook over medium heat until the cauliflower begins to brown. Add the water, garlic, and a pinch of salt. Cover and cook over low heat until the cauliflower is tender when pierced with a knife and the water has evaporated, about 10 minutes.

3 Add the olives, anchovies, and parsley and toss well. Cook uncovered 2 minutes more, stirring occasionally. Serve hot.

Cauliflower with Parsley and Onion
Cavolfiore Trifolato

MAKES 4 TO 6 SERVINGS

The onion, garlic, and parsley infuse this cauliflower with flavor as they all steam together gently in the pan.

1 medium cauliflower (about 1 1/2 pounds)
2 tablespoons olive oil
1 medium onion, thinly sliced
2 garlic cloves, finely chopped
2 tablespoons water
1/4 cup chopped fresh flat-leaf parsley
Salt and freshly ground black pepper

1 Cut the cauliflower into 2-inch florets. Trim off the ends of the stems. Peel off the tough skin with a swivel-blade vegetable peeler. Cut thick stems crosswise into 1/4-inch slices.

2 In a large skillet, cook the onion and garlic in the olive oil and cook 5 minutes, stirring occasionally.

3 Add the cauliflower, water, parsley, and salt and pepper to taste. Toss well. Cover the pan and cook 15 minutes more or until the cauliflower is tender. Serve hot.

Cauliflower in Tomato Sauce
Cavolfiore in Salsa

MAKES 6 TO 8 SERVINGS

If you like, add a handful of drained capers to the sauce for this dish. It is also good served as a pasta sauce, topped with a sprinkle of toasted bread crumbs.

1 medium cauliflower (about 1 1/2 pounds)
1 medium onion, chopped
2 garlic cloves, finely chopped
Pinch of crushed red pepper
2 tablespoons olive oil
1 (28-ounce) can peeled tomatoes, chopped
Salt
2 tablespoons chopped fresh basil or flat-leaf parsley

1 Cut the cauliflower into 2-inch florets. Trim off the ends of the stems. Cut thick stems crosswise into 1/4-inch slices.

2 In a large saucepan, cook the onion, garlic, and crushed red pepper in the oil over medium heat, stirring occasionally, until the onion is tender, about 10 minutes. Stir in the tomatoes. Bring to a simmer. Cook 10 minutes.

3 Stir in the cauliflower and basil or parsley, and salt to taste. Cover and cook 15 minutes, stirring occasionally. Uncover and cook 5 minutes more.

Cauliflower Torte
Tortino di Cavolfiore

MAKES 6 SERVINGS

Enormous, creamy white heads of cauliflower are piled high at my local farmer's market each fall. They remind me to make this excellent dish, which I first had in Tuscany. When baked, it looks like a golden cake and cuts neatly into squares.

I large cauliflower (about 2 pounds)
Salt
1/4 cup olive oil
2 large garlic cloves, finely chopped
3 tablespoons plain dry bread crumbs
4 large eggs
1/2 cup freshly grated Parmigiano-Reggiano
Freshly ground black pepper

1 Cut the cauliflower into 2-inch florets. Trim off the ends of the stems. Cut thick stems crosswise into 1/4-inch slices.

2 Bring a large pot of water to a boil. Add the cauliflower and salt to taste. Cook until the cauliflower is soft, about 15 minutes. Drain well. Place the cauliflower in a large bowl and mash it with a potato masher or the back of a spoon. It should not be perfectly smooth.

3 Pour the oil into a small skillet. Add the garlic and cook over medium heat until golden, about 2 minutes. Scrape the garlic and oil into the cauliflower and stir well.

4 Place a rack in the center of the oven. Preheat the oven to 400°F. Oil a 9-inch square baking pan. Sprinkle the pan with one tablespoon of the crumbs. Beat together the eggs, cheese, and salt and pepper to taste. Stir the egg mixture into the cauliflower. Scrape the mixture into the pan and smooth the top. Sprinkle with the remaining crumbs.

5 Bake 30 to 35 minutes or until a knife inserted in the center comes out clean and the top is lightly browned. Let cool 10 minutes. Cut into squares and serve hot or at room temperature.

❦ Brussels Sprouts and Cabbage

Brussels sprouts look like miniature cabbages, and in fact the two vegetables belong to the same species. Brussels sprouts are at their best from late summer through early spring. When buying them, avoid those that are dry or yellowed. The sprouts should be bright green with tightly packed leaves.

Cabbage is available year round, and there are several different varieties. Italians use both ordinary white cabbage, called *cavolo cappuccio*, and Savoy cabbage, which is called *verza*. Savoy cabbage has soft, pale green, crinkled leaves and is slightly milder.

Whichever cabbage you use, avoid any with yellowed or limp leaves.

Brussels Sprouts with Butter
Cavolini di Bruxelles al Burro

MAKES 4 TO 6 SERVINGS

When boiling brussels sprouts, it is important not to overcook them, as their flavor and odor will become overpowering. Add lemon juice, herbs, garlic, or mustard to the butter if you like. You can also sprinkle the buttered sprouts with Parmigiano-Reggiano and leave them covered for a minute until the cheese melts.

I pound brussels sprouts
Salt
2 tablespoons unsalted butter
Freshly ground black pepper

1 With a small knife, shave a thin slice off the base of the brussels sprouts. Cut them in half through the base.

2 Bring a large pot of water to a boil. Add the brussels sprouts and salt to taste. Cook until the sprouts are tender when pierced with a knife, 6 to 8 minutes.

3 Melt the butter in a large skillet over medium heat. Add the sprouts and salt and pepper to taste. Cook 2 to 3 minutes, shaking the pan occasionally. Serve hot.

Roasted Brussels Sprouts
Cavolini al Forno

MAKES 4 TO 6 SERVINGS

If you have never tried roasted brussels sprouts, you will be amazed at how good they taste. I roast them until they are nice and brown. The outer leaves get crisp while the insides remain soft. These are great with roast pork.

1 pound brussels sprouts
1/3 cup olive oil
Salt
3 garlic cloves, sliced

1 With a small knife, shave a thin slice off the base of the brussels sprouts. Cut them in half through the base.

2 Preheat the oven to 375°F. Pour the oil into a roasting pan large enough to hold the sprouts in a single layer. Add the sprouts, salt, and garlic. Toss well and turn the sprouts cut-side down.

3 Roast the sprouts, stirring once, 30 to 40 minutes, or until browned and tender. Serve hot.

Brussels Sprouts with Pancetta
Cavolini di Bruxelles al Pancetta

MAKES 4 TO 6 SERVINGS

Garlic and pancetta flavor these sprouts. Substitute bacon for the pancetta for a hint of smoky flavor.

1 pound brussels sprouts
Salt to taste
2 tablespoons olive oil
2 thick slices of pancetta (2 ounces), cut into matchstick strips
4 large garlic cloves, thinly sliced
Pinch of crushed red pepper

1 With a small knife, shave a thin slice off the base of the brussels sprouts.

2 Bring a large pot of water to a boil. Add the sprouts and salt to taste. Cook until the sprouts are almost tender, about 5 minutes.

3 In a large skillet, cook the pancetta in the oil until lightly golden, about 5 minutes. Add the garlic and crushed red pepper and cook until the garlic is golden, about 2 minutes more.

4 Add the brussels sprouts, 2 tablespoons of water, and a sprinkle of salt. Cook, stirring occasionally, until the sprouts are tender and beginning to brown, about 5 minutes. Serve hot.

Browned Cabbage with Garlic
Cavolo al'Aglio

MAKES 4 SERVINGS

Cabbage cooked this way tastes nothing like the bland and soggy vegetable we all love to hate. I always thought that overcooking ruined cabbage, but in this case, like the roasted brussels sprouts above, long, slow cooking browns the cabbage and gives it a rich, sweet flavor. I first tasted it at Manducatis, a restaurant in Long Island City whose owners come from Montecassino in Italy.

1 medium head of cabbage (about 1 1/2 pounds)
3 large garlic cloves, finely chopped
Crushed red pepper
1/4 cup olive oil
Salt

1 Trim off the outer leaves of the cabbage. With a large heavy chef's knife, cut the cabbage into quarters. Cut out the core. Cut the cabbage into bite-size pieces.

2 In a large pot, cook the garlic and red pepper in the olive oil over medium-low heat until the garlic is golden, about 2 minutes.

(continues)

3 Add the cabbage and salt. Stir well. Cover and cook, stirring often, for 20 minutes, or until the cabbage is lightly browned and tender. Add a little water if the cabbage begins to stick. Serve hot.

Shredded Cabbage with Capers and Olives
Cavolo al Capperi

MAKES 4 SERVINGS

Olives and capers dress up shredded cabbage. If you don't want to buy a whole cabbage, try making this using a bag of undressed coleslaw from the produce section of the supermarket. The brand I buy is a combination of white cabbage, a little red cabbage, and carrots. It works perfectly in this recipe.

4 tablespoons olive oil
I small head of cabbage (about I pound)
About 3 tablespoons water
I to 2 tablespoons white wine vinegar
Salt
¹/₂ cup chopped green olives
I tablespoon chopped capers

1 Trim off the outer leaves of the cabbage. With a large heavy chef's knife, cut the cabbage into quarters. Cut out the core. Cut the quarters crosswise into narrow strips.

2 In a large pot, heat the oil over medium heat. Add the cabbage, water, vinegar, and a small amount of salt. Stir well.

3 Cover the pot and turn the heat to low. Cook until the cabbage is almost tender, about 15 minutes.

4 Stir in the olives and capers. Cook until the cabbage is very tender, about 5 minutes more. If there is a lot of liquid left in the pan, uncover and cook until it evaporates. Serve hot.

Cabbage with Smoked Pancetta
Verze con Pancetta Affumicata

MAKES 6 SERVINGS

Here is another traditional Friulian recipe inspired by chef Gianni Cosetti. Gianni uses smoked pancetta for this recipe, but you can substitute bacon or smoked ham.

2 tablespoons olive oil
I medium onion, chopped
2 ounces chopped smoked pancetta, bacon, or ham
¹/₂ medium head of cabbage, thinly sliced
Salt and freshly ground black pepper

1 In a large pot, cook the oil, onion, and pancetta for 10 minutes or until golden.

2 Stir in the cabbage and salt and pepper to taste. Lower the heat. Cover and cook 30 minutes or until very soft. Serve hot.

✣ Cardoons
Cardoni

Cardoons are a member of the thistle genus that includes artichokes. In fact, the name *cardoon* is derived from the Latin word for thistle.

Cardoons grow wild in many places and are easily gathered if you know what to look for. Many Italian produce markets sell them in the fall and winter. They grow in bunches resembling grayish green celery, though they have a dull, almost fuzzy texture. They are typically sold with the top leaves cut off, because they grow rather large and take up a lot of space.

Italians eat cardoons a variety of ways. In Piedmont they even eat tender cardoons raw with the hot oil bath called Bagna Cauda (Piedmontese Hot Bath, pages 24–25), though the cardoons sold in the United States are too tough and bitter for that. They need to be cooked before using, and the exact cooking time will depend on how mature they are. Once cooked, they can be dressed with a variety of sauces, coated with batter and fried, added to salads or soups, or used in any recipe that calls for artichoke hearts.

Fried Cardoons
Cardoni Fritti

MAKES 6 SERVINGS

Here is a basic recipe for cardoons: they are boiled, coated with bread crumbs, and fried until crisp. These are good as part of an antipasto assortment or as a side dish with lamb or fish.

1 lemon, cut in half
2 pounds cardoons
3 large eggs
2 tablespoons freshly grated Parmigiano-Reggiano
Salt and freshly ground black pepper
2 cups plain bread crumbs
Vegetable oil for frying
Lemon wedges

1 Squeeze the lemon into a large bowl of cold water. Trim the ends of the cardoons and separate the stalk into ribs. With a paring knife, peel each rib to remove the long tough strings and any leaves. Cut each rib into 3-inch lengths. Place the pieces in the lemon water.

2 Bring a large saucepan of water to a boil. Drain the cardoons and add them to the pan. Boil until tender when pierced with a knife, about 20 to 30 minutes. Drain well and cool under running water. Pat the pieces dry.

3 Line a tray with paper towels. In a shallow bowl, beat the eggs with the cheese, salt, and pepper to taste. Spread the bread crumbs on a sheet of wax paper. Dip the cardoons in the egg, then roll them in the bread crumbs.

4 In a large deep skillet, heat about 1/2 inch of oil over medium heat until a small drop of the egg sizzles and cooks rapidly when dropped into the pan. Add just enough of the cardoons to fit in one layer without crowding. Cook, turning the pieces with tongs, until browned and crisp on all sides, about 3 to 4 minutes. Drain on the paper towels. Keep them warm in a low oven while frying the remainder. Serve hot with lemon wedges.

Cardoons with Parmigiano-Reggiano
Cardoni alla Parmigiana

MAKES 6 SERVINGS

Cardoons taste delicious baked with butter and Parmigiano.

1 lemon, cut in half
About 2 pounds cardoons
Salt and freshly ground pepper
3 tablespoons unsalted butter
1/2 cup freshly grated Parmigiano-Reggiano

1 Prepare the cardoons as in Fried Cardoons (see above) through step 2.

(continues)

2 Place a rack in the center of the oven. Preheat the oven to 450°F. Generously butter a 13 × 9 × 2–inch baking pan.

3 Arrange the cardoon pieces in the pan. Dot with the butter and sprinkle with salt and pepper. Scatter the cheese over the top.

4 Bake 10 to 15 minutes, or until the cheese is slightly melted. Serve hot.

Cardoons in Cream
Cardoni alla Panna

MAKES 6 SERVINGS

These cardoons are simmered in a skillet with a little cream. Parmigiano-Reggiano provides the finishing touch.

I lemon, cut in half
About 2 pounds cardoons
2 tablespoons unsalted butter
Salt and freshly ground black pepper
¹/₂ cup heavy cream
¹/₂ cup freshly grated Parmigiano-Reggiano

I Prepare the cardoons as in Fried Cardoons (page 419) through step 2.

2 In a large skillet, melt the butter over medium heat. Add the cardoons and salt and pepper to taste. Stir until coated with the butter, about 1 minute.

3 Add the cream and bring to a simmer. Cook until the cream is slightly thickened, about 1 minute. Sprinkle with cheese and serve hot.

❧ Carrots

Even ordinary carrots take on a new personality when cooked the Italian way. Their appealing color and sweet flavor complement many meals.

Buy small to medium-size carrots. The oversized ones taste woody. Packaged "baby" carrots are convenient, but I often find that they are waterlogged and lacking in flavor. I don't recommend them in roasting recipes or when you want the carrots to brown. The excess water makes them resistant to browning.

Carrots and Turnips with Marsala
Misto di Rape e Carote

MAKES 4 SERVINGS

Sweet, nutty-tasting Marsala enhances the flavor of root vegetables like carrots and turnips.

4 medium carrots
2 medium turnips, or I large rutabaga
2 tablespoons unsalted butter
Salt
¹/₄ cup dry Marsala
I tablespoon chopped fresh flat-leaf parsley

I Peel the carrots and turnips and cut them into 1-inch pieces.

2 In a large skillet, melt the butter over medium heat. Add the vegetables and salt to taste. Cook for 5 minutes, stirring occasionally.

3 Add the Marsala. Cover and cook 5 minutes more or until the wine evaporates and the vegetables are tender. Sprinkle with parsley and serve immediately.

Roasted Carrots with Garlic and Olives
Carote al Forno

MAKES 4 SERVINGS

Carrots, garlic, and olives are a surprisingly good combination, with the saltiness of the olives playing off the sweetness of the carrots. I had these in Liguria, near the border with France.

8 medium carrots, peeled and cut diagonally into ¹/₂-inch-thick slices
2 tablespoons olive oil
3 garlic cloves, sliced
Salt and freshly ground black pepper
¹/₂ cup pitted imported mild black olives, such as Gaeta

1 Place a rack in the center of the oven. Preheat the oven to 425°F. In a large baking pan, toss the carrots with the oil, garlic, and salt and pepper to taste.
2 Roast 15 minutes. Stir in the olives and cook until the carrots are tender, about 5 minutes more, Serve hot.

Carrots in Cream
Carote alla Panna

MAKES 4 SERVINGS

Carrots are so often eaten raw, we forget how good they can be when cooked. In this recipe, heavy cream complements their sweet flavor.

8 medium carrots
2 tablespoons unsalted butter
Salt
¹/₂ cup heavy cream
Pinch of grated nutmeg

1 Peel the carrots. Cut them into ¹/4-inch thick slices.
2 In a medium saucepan over medium heat, melt the butter. Add the carrots and salt to taste. Cover and cook, stirring occasionally, until the carrots are softened, about 5 minutes.
3 Stir in the cream and nutmeg. Cook until the cream is thickened and the carrots are tender, 4 to 5 minutes more. Serve immediately.

Sweet-and-Sour Carrots
Carote in Agrodolce

MAKES 4 SERVINGS

I like to serve these carrots with roast pork or chicken. If you have some parsley, mint, or basil on hand, chop the herb and toss it with the carrots just before serving.

8 medium carrots
1 tablespoon unsalted butter
3 tablespoons white wine vinegar
2 tablespoons sugar
Salt

1 Peel the carrots. Cut them into ¹/4-inch-thick slices.
2 In a medium saucepan, melt the butter over medium heat. Add the vinegar and sugar and stir until the sugar is dissolved. Stir in the carrots and salt to taste. Cover the pot and cook until the carrots are softened, about 5 minutes.
3 Uncover the pan and cook the carrots, stirring frequently, until tender, about 5 minutes more. Taste for seasoning. Serve hot or at room temperature.

❧ Eggplant

Eggplants come in a variety of sizes, shapes, and colors. The most familiar are the large, dark-purple kind, but there are also miniature eggplants, long skinny Japanese eggplants, round white eggplants, lavender-striped eggplants, and so on. Apart from their color, size, and shape, all eggplants are interchangeable. Baby eggplants are good for stuffing.

A ripe eggplant should be firm, with a fresh green cap at the stem end and no soft spots or brownish bruises. An old wives' tale claims that there is a difference between male and female eggplants, but it is not true. Avoid eggplants that are oversized for their variety. The very large ones tend to be overgrown, with tough seeds.

Unless you are sure the eggplants are very fresh, it is best to salt them before cooking to draw out the bitter juices. If I buy eggplants from the farmer's market, I skip the salting step.

Peeling eggplant is optional. The skin is attractive and helps the eggplant hold its shape as it cooks, but it can be tough. Sometimes, if I think the eggplant skin may be tough, I peel off half of the skin in strips at one-inch intervals.

Marinated Eggplant with Garlic and Mint
Melanzane Marinate

MAKES 4 TO 6 SERVINGS

This is excellent as a side dish with grilled chicken or as part of an antipasto assortment. Zucchini and carrots can also be prepared this way.

2 medium eggplants (about 1 pound each)
Salt
Olive oil
3 tablespoons red wine vinegar
2 garlic cloves, finely chopped
¼ cup chopped fresh mint
Freshly ground black pepper

1 Trim the tops and bottoms of the eggplants. Cut the eggplants crosswise into ¹/₂-inch-thick slices. Arrange the slices in a colander, sprinkling each layer with salt. Place the eggplant over a plate to drain for at least 30 minutes. Rinse off the salt with cool water and dry the slices with paper towels.

2 Preheat the oven to 450°F. Brush the eggplant slices with the oil and arrange them oiled-side down in a single layer on cookie sheets. Brush the tops with oil. Bake the slices for 10 minutes. Turn and bake until browned and tender, about 10 minutes more.

3 In a shallow plastic container with a tight-fitting lid, make a layer of the eggplant slices, overlapping them slightly. Sprinkle with vinegar, garlic, mint, and pepper. Repeat the layering until all of the ingredients are used.

4 Cover and refrigerate for at least 24 hours before serving. These keep well for several days.

Grilled Eggplant with Fresh Tomato Salsa
Melanzane alla Griglia con Salsa

MAKES 4 SERVINGS

Here, eggplant slices are grilled, then topped with a fresh tomato salsa. Serve with burgers, steaks, or chops. I had eggplant prepared this way in Abruzzo, where fresh green chiles are often used. Substitute crushed red pepper from a jar if you prefer.

1 medium eggplant (about 1 pound)
Salt
3 tablespoons olive oil
1 medium ripe tomato
2 tablespoons chopped fresh flat-leaf parsley
1 tablespoon finely chopped fresh chile (or to taste)
1 teaspoon fresh lemon juice

1 Trim the tops and bottoms of the eggplants. Cut the eggplant crosswise into ¹/₂-inch-thick slices. Arrange the slices in a colander, sprinkling each layer with salt. Place the eggplant over a plate to

drain for at least 30 minutes. Rinse off the salt with cool water and dry the slices with paper towels.

2 Place a barbecue grill or broiler rack about 5 inches away from the heat source. Preheat the grill or broiler Brush the eggplant slices with olive oil on one side and place them with the oiled side toward the source of the heat. Cook until lightly browned, about 5 minutes. Turn the slices and brush them with oil. Cook until browned and tender, about 4 minutes.

3 Arrange the slices on a platter, overlapping slightly.

4 Cut the tomato in half and squeeze out the seeds and juice. Chop the tomato. In a medium bowl, toss the tomato with the parsley, chile, lemon juice, and salt to taste. Spoon the tomato mixture over the eggplant. Serve at room temperature.

Eggplant and Mozzarella "Sandwiches"

Panini di Mozzarella

MAKES 6 SERVINGS

I sometimes add a folded slice of prosciutto to these "sandwiches" and serve them as an antipasto. Spoon on a little tomato sauce if you have some, and sprinkle with grated Parmigiano if you like.

2 medium eggplants (about 1 pound each)
Salt
Olive oil
Freshly ground black pepper
1 tablespoon chopped fresh thyme or flat-leaf parsley
8 ounces fresh mozzarella, thinly sliced

1 Trim the tops and bottoms of the eggplants. With a swivel-blade peeler, remove strips of skin lengthwise at about 1-inch intervals. Cut the eggplants crosswise into an even number of 1/2-inch thick slices. Arrange the slices in a colander, sprinkling each layer with salt. Place the colander over a plate to drain for at least 30 minutes. Rinse off the salt with cool water and dry the slices with paper towels.

2 Preheat the oven to 450°F. Brush the eggplant slices with olive oil and arrange them oiled-side down in a single layer on cookie sheets. Brush the tops with additional oil. Sprinkle with pepper and the herbs. Bake 10 minutes. Turn the slices and bake about 10 minutes more, or until lightly browned and tender.

4 Remove the the eggplants from the oven, but leave the oven turned on.

5 Top half of the eggplant slices with mozzarella. Place the remaining eggplant slices on top. Return the pans to the oven for 1 minute or until the cheese begins to melt. Serve hot.

Eggplant with Garlic and Herbs

Melanzane al Forno

MAKES 6 TO 8 SERVINGS

I like to use long, slim Japanese eggplants when I see them at my farmer's market during the summer months. They are very good for summer meals simply roasted with garlic and herbs.

3 tablespoons olive oil
8 small Japanese eggplants (all about the same size)
1 garlic clove, very finely chopped
2 tablespoons chopped fresh basil
Salt and freshly ground black pepper

1 Place a rack in the center of the oven. Preheat the oven to 400°F. Oil a large baking pan.

2 Trim the stem ends from the eggplants and cut them in half lengthwise. Cut several shallow slits in the cut surfaces. Arrange the eggplants cut-sides up in the baking pan.

3 In a small bowl, mix together the oil, garlic, basil, and salt and pepper to taste. Spread the mixture over the eggplants, pushing a little into the slits.

4 Bake 25 to 30 minutes or until the eggplants are tender. Serve hot or at room temperature.

Neapolitan-Style Eggplant Sticks with Tomatoes

Bastoncini di Melanzane

MAKES 4 SERVINGS

At Restaurant Dante and Beatrice in Naples, meals begin with a series of small appetizers. Sticks of small eggplants in a fresh tomato and basil sauce are one of the dishes my husband and I enjoyed there. Japanese eggplants are milder than the large globe variety, but either kind can be used for this recipe.

6 small Japanese eggplants (about 1 1/2 pounds)
Vegetable oil for frying
Salt
2 garlic cloves, peeled and lightly smashed
Pinch of crushed red pepper
3 tablespoons olive oil
4 plum tomatoes, peeled, seeded, and chopped
1/4 cup basil leaves, stacked and cut into thin strips

1 Trim the tops and bottoms of the eggplants and cut them into 6 wedges lengthwise. Cut crosswise into 3 pieces. Pat the pieces dry with paper towels.

2 Line a tray with paper towels. Pour about 1/2 inch of the oil into a medium skillet. Heat over medium heat until a small piece of eggplant sizzles when added to the pan. Carefully add just as many eggplants as will fit comfortably in the pan in a single layer. Cook, stirring occasionally, until lightly browned around the edges, about 5 minutes. Remove the eggplants with a slotted spoon or skimmer and drain on the paper towels. Repeat with the remaining eggplant. Sprinkle with salt.

3 In a large skillet, cook the garlic with the red pepper in the olive oil until the garlic is deep golden, about 4 minutes. Remove and discard the garlic. Add the tomatoes and cook 5 minutes or until thickened.

4 Stir in the eggplants and basil and cook 2 minutes more. Season with salt to taste. Serve hot or at room temperature

Eggplant Stuffed with Prosciutto and Cheese

Melanzane Ripiene

MAKES 6 SERVINGS

Cousins and uncles and aunts came from all over the region the first time my husband Charles and I went to visit his relatives, who live near the famous Valley of the Temples in Agrigento in Sicily. Each family unit wanted us to visit their home, have a meal, and stay overnight. We wanted to spend time with everyone, but we also wanted to see some of the local historical sites that we had always heard so much about, and we only had a few days. Fortunately, my husband's cousin Angela took charge and made sure that we were well taken care of. When I told her I was interested in the local cooking, she taught me how to make this delicious eggplant dish.

6 small eggplants (about 1 1/2 pounds)
Salt
1/4 cup olive oil
1 medium onion, chopped
1 medium tomato
2 eggs, beaten
1/2 cup grated caciocavallo, provolone,
    or Parmigiano-Reggiano
1/4 cup finely chopped fresh basil
2 ounces imported Italian prosciutto, finely chopped
1/2 cup plus 1 tablespoon unflavored bread crumbs
Salt and freshly ground black pepper

1 Trim off the tops of the eggplants and cut them in half lengthwise. With a small sharp knife and a spoon, scoop out the pulp of the eggplants, leaving the shells about 1/4 inch thick. Chop the eggplant pulp.

2 Place the chopped eggplant in a colander. Sprinkle generously with salt and let drain over a plate at least 30 minutes. Sprinkle the eggplant shells with salt and place them cut-sides down on a plate to drain.

3 Rinse off the salt with cool water and dry the eggplant with paper towels. Squeeze the pulp to extract the water.

4 In a medium skillet, heat the oil over medium heat. Add the onion and chopped eggplant and cook, stirring frequently, until tender, about 15 minutes. Scrape the mixture into a bowl.

5 Cut the tomato in half and squeeze out the seeds and juice. Chop the tomato and add it to the bowl. Stir in the eggs, cheese, basil, prosciutto, 1/2 cup bread crumbs, and salt and pepper to taste. Mix well.

6 Place a rack in the center of the oven. Preheat the oven to 400°F. Oil a baking pan just large enough to hold the eggplant shells in a single layer.

7 Fill the shells with the eggplant mixture, rounding the surface. Place them in the pan. Sprinkle with the 1 tablespoon bread crumbs. Pour 1/4 cup of water around the eggplants. Bake 45 to 50 minutes or until the shells are tender when pierced. Serve hot or at room temperature.

Eggplant Stuffed with Anchovies, Capers, and Olives
Melanzane Ripiene

MAKES 4 SERVINGS

There seems to be no limit to the Sicilian ways to cook eggplant. This one combines the classic flavors of anchovies, olives, and capers.

2 medium eggplants (about 1 pound each)
Salt
1/4 cup plus 1 tablespoon olive oil
1 large garlic clove, finely chopped
2 medium tomatoes, peeled, seeded, and chopped
6 anchovy fillets
1/2 cup chopped Gaeta or other mild black olives
2 tablespoons capers, rinsed and drained
1/2 teaspoon dried oregano
1/3 cup plain dry bread crumbs

1 Trim off the tops of the eggplants. Cut the eggplants in half lengthwise. With a small sharp knife and a spoon, scoop out the eggplant pulp, leaving a shell about 1/2 inch thick. Coarsely chop the pulp and place it in a colander. Sprinkle generously with salt and set over a plate to drain. Sprinkle the insides of the eggplant shells with salt and place them upside down on paper towels. Let drain for 30 minutes.

2 Rinse off the salt with cool water and dry the eggplant with paper towels. Squeeze the pulp to extract the water.

3 Heat the oil in a large skillet over medium-high heat until a small piece of eggplant sizzles when added to the pan. Add the eggplant pulp and cook, stirring frequently, until it begins to brown, 15 to 20 minutes. Stir in the garlic and cook 1 minute. Add the tomatoes, anchovies, olives, capers, oregano, and salt and pepper to taste. Cook until thickened, about 5 minutes more.

4 Place a rack in the center of the oven. Preheat the oven to 400°F. Oil a baking pan just large enough to hold the eggplant shells in a single layer.

5 Fill the shells with the eggplant mixture. Place them in the pan. Toss the bread crumbs with the remaining oil and sprinkle them over the shells. Bake 45 minutes or until the shells are tender when pierced. Let cool slightly. Serve warm or at room temperature.

Eggplant with Vinegar and Herbs

Melanzane alle Erbe

MAKES 6 TO 8 SERVINGS

Plan to make this at least an hour before serving. Letting it sit will give the vinegar a chance to mellow. I like to serve this with grilled tuna or swordfish as part of a summer barbecue.

2 medium eggplants (about 1 pound each) cut into
    1-inch pieces
Salt
1/2 cup olive oil
1/2 cup red wine vinegar
1/4 cup sugar
2 tablespoons chopped fresh flat-leaf parsley
2 tablespoons chopped fresh mint

1 Trim the tops and bottoms of the eggplants. Cut the eggplants into 1-inch pieces. Place the pieces in a colander, sprinkling each layer with salt. Place the colander over a plate to drain for at least 30 minutes. Rinse off the salt with cool water and pat the pieces dry with paper towels.

2 Line a tray with paper towels. Heat 1/4 cup of the oil in a large skillet over medium heat. Add half the eggplant pieces and cook, stirring frequently, until browned, about 15 minutes. With a slotted spoon, transfer the eggplant to the paper towels to drain. Add the remaining oil to the skillet and fry the remaining eggplant in the same way.

3 Remove the skillet from the heat and carefully pour off any remaining oil. Carefully wipe out the skillet with paper towels.

4 Place the skillet over medium heat and add the vinegar and sugar. Stir until the sugar is dissolved. Return all of the eggplant to the skillet and cook, stirring, until the liquid is absorbed, about 5 minutes.

5 Transfer the eggplant to a serving dish and sprinkle with the parsley and mint. Let cool. Serve at room temperature.

Fried Eggplant Cutlets

Melanzane Fritte

MAKES 4 TO 6 SERVINGS

The only difficulty with these cutlets is that it's hard to stop eating them. They are so good when hot and freshly made. Serve them in sandwiches or as a side dish.

1 medium eggplant (about 1 pound)
Salt
2 large eggs
1/4 cup freshly grated Parmigiano-Reggiano
Freshly ground black pepper
1/2 cup all-purpose flour
1 1/2 cups plain dry bread crumbs
Vegetable oil for frying

1 Trim the tops and bottoms of the eggplants. Cut the eggplant crosswise into 1/4-inch-thick slices. Arrange the slices in a colander, sprinkling each layer with salt. Place the colander over a plate to drain for at least 30 minutes. Rinse off the salt with cool water and dry the slices with paper towels.

2 Put the flour in a shallow bowl. In another shallow bowl, beat together the eggs, cheese, and salt and pepper to taste. Dip the eggplant slices into the flour, then in the egg mixture, then in the bread crumbs, patting to coat well. Let the slices dry on a rack for 15 minutes.

3 Line a tray with paper towels. Turn the oven on to the lowest setting. In a large heavy skillet, heat 1/2 inch of oil until a small drop of the egg mixture sizzles when it touches the oil. Add just enough of the eggplant slices to fit in a single layer without crowding. Fry until golden brown on one side, about 3 minutes, then turn them over and brown on the other side, about 2 to 3 minutes more. Drain the eggplant slices on the paper towels. Keep them warm in a low oven while frying the remainder in the same way. Serve hot.

Eggplant with Spicy Tomato Sauce

Melanzane in Salsa

MAKES 6 TO 8 SERVINGS

This layered dish is similar to eggplant parmigiana— without the Parmigiano. Because there is no cheese, it is lighter and fresher—nice for summer meals.

2 medium eggplants (about 1 pound each)
Salt
Olive oil
2 garlic cloves, crushed
2 cups tomato puree
$1/2$ teaspoon crushed red pepper
$1/2$ cup torn fresh basil leaves

1 Trim the tops and bottoms of the eggplants. Cut the eggplants crosswise into $1/2$-inch-thick slices. Arrange the slices in a colander, sprinkling each layer with salt. Place the colander over a plate to drain for at least 30 minutes. Rinse off the salt with cool water and dry the slices with paper towels.

2 Place a rack in the center of the oven. Preheat the oven to 450°F. Brush two large jelly roll pans with oil. Arrange the eggplant slices in a single layer. Brush with oil. Bake until lightly browned, about 10 minutes. Turn the slices with a metal spatula and bake until the second side is browned and the slices are tender when pierced, about 10 minutes more.

3 In a medium saucepan, cook the garlic in $1/4$ cup olive oil over medium heat until golden, about 2 minutes. Add the tomato puree, red pepper, and salt to taste. Simmer for 15 minutes or until thick. Discard the garlic.

4 In a shallow dish, arrange half the eggplant in a single layer. Spread with half the sauce and basil. Repeat with the remaining ingredients. Serve at room temperature.

Eggplant Parmigiana

Melanzane alla Parmigiana

MAKES 6 TO 8 SERVINGS

This is one of those dishes I never tire of. If you prefer not to fry the eggplant, try making this with grilled or baked slices.

$2^{1}/2$ cups Marinara Sauce (page 89) or other plain tomato sauce
2 medium eggplants (about 1 pound each)
Salt
Olive oil or vegetable oil for frying
8 ounces fresh mozzarella, sliced
$1/2$ cup freshly grated Parmigiano-Reggiano or Pecorino Romano

1 Prepare the sauce, if necessary. Then, trim the tops and bottoms off the eggplants. Cut the eggplants crosswise into $1/2$-inch-thick slices. Arrange the slices in a colander, sprinkling each layer with salt. Place the colander over a plate to drain for at least 30 minutes. Rinse off the salt with cool water and dry the slices with paper towels.

2 Line a tray with paper towels. Heat about $1/2$ inch of the oil in a large skillet over medium heat until a small piece of eggplant sizzles when added to the pan. Add just enough of the eggplant slices to fit in a single layer without crowding. Fry until golden brown on one side, about 3 minutes, then turn them over and brown on the other side, about 2 to 3 minutes more. Drain the slices on the paper towels. Cook the remaining eggplant slices in the same way.

3 Place a rack in the center of the oven. Preheat the oven to 350°F. Spread a thin layer of tomato sauce in a $13 \times 9 \times 2$–inch baking dish. Make a layer of eggplant slices, overlapping them slightly. Top with a layer of mozzarella, another layer of sauce, and a sprinkle of grated cheese. Repeat the layering, ending with eggplant, sauce, and grated cheese.

4 Bake for 45 minutes, or until the sauce is bubbling. Let stand 10 minutes before serving.

❧ Fennel

Crisp green-and-white fennel is crunchy like celery, but it has a mild licorice or anise flavor. It is often mislabeled as anise.

In Italy, fennel is usually eaten raw as part of a fruit selection after a meal and is believed to have qualities that help digestion. It is also good in salads and cooked.

Buy fennel without brown spots or bruises. The leafy fronds are typically removed before the fennel is sold, but if they are left intact, they can be used for garnishing. To prepare fennel for eating or cooking, trim off the base and the green stems. Cut the fennel into wedges and cut out the core.

Roasted Fennel
Finocchio al Forno

MAKES 4 SERVINGS

When I was growing up, we never ate fennel cooked. It was always served raw, adding a refreshing crunchiness to salads or served in wedges after a meal, especially big holiday feasts. But baking tames some of the flavor and changes the texture, so that it becomes soft and tender.

2 medium fennel bulbs (about 1 pound)
1/4 cup olive oil
Salt

1 Place a rack in the center of the oven. Preheat the oven to 425°F. Trim off the green stalks of the fennel down to the rounded bulb. Pare away any bruises with a small knife or vegetable peeler. Slice off a thin layer from the root end. Cut the fennel in half lengthwise. Cut each half lengthwise into 1/2-inch-thick slices.

2 Pour the oil into a 13 × 9 × 2–inch baking pan. Add the fennel slices and turn them to coat with oil. Arrange the slices in a single layer. Sprinkle with salt.

3 Cover the pan with foil. Bake 20 minutes. Uncover and bake 15 to 20 minutes more or until the fennel is tender when pierced with a knife. Serve hot or at room temperature.

Fennel with Parmesan Cheese
Finocchio alla Parmigiano

MAKES 6 SERVINGS

This fennel is simmered in water first to make it extra tender. Then it is topped with grated Parmigiano and baked. Serve this with roast veal or pork.

2 small fennel bulbs (about 1 pound)
Salt
2 tablespoons unsalted butter
Freshly ground black pepper
1/4 cup grated Parmigiano-Reggiano

1 Place a rack in the center of the oven. Preheat the oven to 450°F. Generously butter a 13 × 9 × 2–inch baking dish.

2 Trim off the green stalks of the fennel down to the rounded bulb. Pare away any bruises with a small knife or vegetable peeler. Slice off a thin layer from the root end. Cut the bulbs lengthwise through the core into 1/4-inch-thick slices.

3 In a large pot, bring 2 quarts of water to a boil. Add the fennel and 1 teaspoon salt. Reduce the heat and simmer uncovered, until the fennel is crisp-tender, 8 to 10 minutes. Drain well and pat dry.

4 Arrange the fennel slices in a single layer in the baking dish. Dot with the butter and sprinkle with salt and pepper to taste. Top with the cheese. Bake 10 minutes, or until the cheese is lightly browned. Serve hot or at room temperature.

Fennel with Anchovy Sauce
Finocchio con Salsa di Acciughe

MAKES 4 SERVINGS

Instead of tenderizing the fennel by boiling it, in this recipe you cover and bake it, allowing it to steam in its own juices. The flavor remains intact, and the fennel turns out slightly crunchy yet still tender. If you prefer fennel softer, boil it as in the recipe for Fennel with Parmesan Cheese (page 428).

Because fennel cooked this way is so tasty, I like to serve it with unadorned grilled chicken or pork chops. This also makes a good antipasto dish at room temperature.

2 medium fennel bulbs (about one pound)
4 anchovy fillets, drained and chopped
2 tablespoons chopped fresh flat-leaf parsley
2 tablespoons capers, rinsed and drained
Freshly ground black pepper
Salt (optional)
1/4 cup olive oil

1 Place a rack in the center of the oven. Preheat the oven to 375°F. Oil a 13 × 9 × 2–inch baking dish.

2 Trim off the green stalks of the fennel down to the rounded bulb. Pare away any bruises with a small knife or vegetable peeler. Slice off a thin layer from the root end. Cut the bulbs lengthwise through the core into 1/4-inch-thick slices.

3 Arrange the fennel in a single layer in the pan, overlapping the slices slightly. Scatter the anchovies, parsley, capers, and pepper over the top. Add salt, if desired. Drizzle with the oil.

4 Cover the pan with aluminum foil. Bake 40 minutes or until the fennel is tender. Carefully remove the foil and bake 5 minutes more, or until the fennel is just tender when pierced, but not soft. Let cool slightly before serving.

Green and Wax Beans

Green beans and wax beans are known as *fagiolini* in Italian. They are good in salads, with sauces, and in sautées. They can be substituted for one another in recipes, for convenience or for a change.

Try to buy beans of the same size so that they cook evenly. Avoid beans that are bruised or limp. Green and wax beans need little trimming or preparation. I just snap off the stem end, leaving the pointed tip intact. Italians tend to cook beans until they are on the softer side of tender. The slightly longer cooking brings out more of their flavor.

If you are boiling green beans ahead of time for a dish, wrap the cooked beans in a towel and keep them at room temperature up to three hours. Their flavor changes when they are refrigerated.

Green Beans with Parsley and Garlic
Fagiolini al Aglio

MAKES 4 SERVINGS

Fresh parsley is essential in the Italian kitchen. I always keep a bunch in my refrigerator. When I bring it home from the store, I trim the ends and stick the stems in a jar of water. Covered with a plastic bag, parsley stays fresh at least a week in the refrigerator, especially if I am careful about changing the water in the jar. Wash parsley before using it to eliminate any grit, and pinch the leaves off the stems. Chop the parsley on a board with a large chef's knife, or if you prefer, just tear it into bits. Fresh chopped parsley adds color and freshness to many foods.

As a variation, give these beans a final toss in the skillet with some grated lemon zest before serving.

1 pound green beans
Salt
3 tablespoons olive oil
1 garlic clove, finely chopped
2 tablespoons chopped fresh flat-leaf parsley
Freshly ground black pepper

(continues)

1 Snap off the stem ends of the green beans. Bring about 2 quarts of water to a boil in a large saucepan. Add the beans and salt to taste. Cook uncovered until the beans are crisp-tender, 4 to 5 minutes.

2 Drain the beans and pat them dry. (If you are not using them immediately, cool them under cold running water. Wrap the beans in a kitchen towel and leave at room temperature up to 3 hours.)

3 Just before serving, heat the oil with the garlic and parsley in a large pan over medium heat. Add the beans and a sprinkle of pepper. Toss gently 2 minutes until just hot. Serve hot.

Green Beans with Hazelnuts
Fagiolini al Nocciole

MAKES 4 SERVINGS

Walnuts and almonds are good with these beans too, if you prefer.

I pound green beans
Salt
3 tablespoons unsalted butter
1/3 cup chopped hazelnuts

1 Snap off the stem ends of the green beans. Bring about 2 quarts of water to a boil in a large saucepan. Add the beans and salt to taste. Cook uncovered until the beans are crisp-tender, 4 to 5 minutes.

2 Drain the beans well and pat them dry. (If you are not using them immediately, cool them under cold running water. Wrap the beans in a kitchen towel and leave at room temperature up to 3 hours.)

3 Just before serving, heat the butter in a large pan. Add the hazelnuts and cook, stirring often, until the nuts are lightly toasted and the butter is lightly browned, about 3 minutes.

4 Add the beans and a pinch of salt. Cook, stirring often, until heated, 2 to 3 minutes. Serve immediately.

Green Beans with Green Sauce
Fagiolini al Pesto

MAKES 4 SERVINGS

Add some boiled new potatoes to these green beans, if you like. Serve them with grilled salmon steaks or tuna.

1/4 cup Green Sauce (page 101)
I pound green beans
Salt

1 Prepare the green sauce, if necessary. Then, snap off the stem ends of the green beans. Bring about 2 quarts of water to a boil in a large saucepan. Add the beans and salt to taste. Cook uncovered until the beans are tender, 5 to 6 minutes.

2 Drain the beans well and pat them dry. Toss with the sauce. Serve warm or at room temperature.

Green Bean Salad
Fagiolini in Insalata

MAKES 6 SERVINGS

Anchovies and fresh herbs add zest to this green bean salad. If you like, add some strips of roasted red bell peppers.

1 1/2 pounds green beans
4 anchovy fillets
2 garlic cloves, finely chopped
2 tablespoons chopped fresh flat-leaf parsley
I tablespoon chopped fresh mint
1/4 cup olive oil
2 tablespoons red wine vinegar
Salt and freshly ground black pepper

1 Snap off the stem ends of the green beans. Bring about 2 quarts of water to a boil in a large saucepan. Add the beans and salt to taste. Cook uncovered until the beans are tender, 5 to 6 minutes.

2 Rinse the beans under cold water and drain well. Pat dry.

3 In a medium bowl, combine the anchovies, garlic, parsley, mint, and salt and pepper to taste. Whisk in the oil and vinegar.

4 Toss the green beans with the dressing and serve.

Green Beans in Tomato-Basil Sauce
Fagiolini in Salsa di Pomodoro

MAKES 6 SERVINGS

These go well with grilled sausages or ribs.

1 ¹/₂ pounds green beans
Salt
2 tablespoons unsalted butter
1 small onion, finely chopped
2 cups peeled, seeded, and chopped fresh tomatoes
Freshly ground black pepper
6 fresh basil leaves, torn into bits

1 Snap off the stem ends of the green beans. Bring about 2 quarts of water to a boil in a large saucepan. Add the beans and salt to taste. Cook uncovered until the beans are crisp-tender, 4 to 5 minutes. Rinse the beans under cold water and drain well. Pat dry.

2 In a medium saucepan, melt the butter over medium heat. Add the onion and cook, stirring frequently, until golden, about 10 minutes. Add the tomatoes and salt and pepper to taste. Bring to a simmer and cook 10 minutes.

3 Stir in the green beans and basil. Cook until heated through, about 5 minutes more.

Green Beans with Pancetta and Onion
Fagiolini alla Pancetta

MAKES 6 SERVINGS

Green beans are more flavorful and have a better texture when cooked until tender. Exact cooking time depends on the size, freshness, and maturity of the beans. I usually taste one or two to be sure. I like them when they no longer snap but are not soft or mushy. This recipe is from Friuli–Venezia Giulia.

1 pound green beans
Salt
¹/₂ cup chopped pancetta (about 2 ounces)
1 small onion, chopped
2 garlic cloves, finely chopped
2 tablespoons chopped fresh flat-leaf parsley
2 fresh sage leaves
2 tablespoons olive oil

1 Snap off the stem ends of the green beans. Bring about 2 quarts of water to a boil in a large saucepan. Add the beans and salt to taste. Cook uncovered until the beans are crisp-tender, 4 to 5 minutes. Rinse the beans under cold water and drain well. Pat dry. Cut the beans into bite-size pieces.

2 In a large skillet, cook the pancetta, onion, garlic, parsley, and sage in the oil over medium heat until the onion is golden, about 10 minutes. Add the green beans and a pinch of salt. Cook until heated through, about 5 minutes more. Serve hot.

Green Beans with Tomato and Pancetta Sauce
Fagiolini con Salsa di Pomodori e Pancetta

MAKES 4 SERVINGS

These beans make a great meal with a frittata or omelet.

1 pound green beans
Salt
1/4 cup chopped pancetta (about 1 ounce)
1 garlic clove, finely chopped
2 tablespoons olive oil
2 large ripe tomatoes, peeled, seeded, and chopped
2 sprigs fresh rosemary
Freshly ground black pepper

1 Prepare the beans as described in step 1 of the previous recipe, but do not cut them into pieces.

2 In a medium saucepan, cook the pancetta and garlic in the oil over medium heat until golden, about 5 minutes. Stir in the tomatoes, rosemary, and salt and pepper to taste. Bring to a simmer and cook 10 minutes.

3 Stir the beans into the sauce and cook until heated through, about 5 minutes. Remove the rosemary. Serve hot.

Green Beans with Parmigiano
Fagiolini alla Parmigiana

MAKES 4 SERVINGS

Lemon zest, nutmeg, and cheese flavor these green beans. Use fresh ingredients for best results.

1 pound green beans, trimmed
2 tablespoons butter
1 small onion, chopped
1/2 teaspoon grated fresh lemon zest
Pinch of freshly ground nutmeg
Salt and freshly ground black pepper
1/4 cup freshly grated Parmigiano-Reggiano

1 Snap off the stem ends of the green beans. Bring about 2 quarts of water to a boil in a large saucepan. Add the beans and salt to taste. Cook uncovered until the beans are crisp-tender, 4 to 5 minutes. Rinse the beans under cold water and drain well. Pat dry.

2 In a medium skillet, melt the butter over medium heat. Add the onion and cook until golden, about 10 minutes. Stir in the beans, lemon zest, nutmeg, and salt and pepper to taste. Sprinkle with the cheese and remove from the heat. Let the cheese melt a little and serve hot.

Wax Beans with Olives
Fagiolini Giallo con Olive

MAKES 4 SERVINGS

Shiny black olives and green parsley offer a vibrant color contrast for pale yellow wax beans; green beans taste good prepared this way, too. To serve these beans at room temperature, substitute olive oil for the butter, which would firm up as it cooled.

1 pound yellow wax or green beans
Salt
3 tablespoons unsalted butter
1 small onion, chopped
1 garlic clove, finely chopped
1/2 cup mild black olives, such as Gaeta, pitted and chopped
2 tablespoons chopped fresh flat-leaf parsley

1 Snap off the stem ends of the green beans. Bring about 2 quarts of water to a boil in a large saucepan. Add the beans and salt to taste. Cook uncovered until the beans are crisp-tender, 4 to 5 minutes. Rinse the beans under cold water and drain well. Pat dry. Cut the beans into 1-inch pieces.

2 In a skillet large enough to hold all of the beans, melt the butter over medium heat. Add the onion and garlic and cook until tender and golden, about 10 minutes.

3 Stir in the beans, olives, and parsley until heated through, about 2 minutes. Serve hot.

❧ Leafy Greens

Hunting for wild greens is an old tradition in Italy. Especially in the springtime when the greens are young and tender, you will see people foraging in fields all over the country, packing the wild greens into shopping bags. Tender leaves are eaten in salads, while more mature greens are cooked. One green that is especially prized is nettles. They have a slightly bitter, grassy flavor. Collecting nettles is particularly challenging because the leaf edges are pointed and can sting. Heavy rubber gloves are worn when handling them.

Swiss chard, spinach, escarole, dandelion, chicory, beet greens, and kale are among the many cultivated greens eaten in Italy. Whether wild or cultivated, leafy greens are treated in similar ways in Italian kitchens, so feel free to adapt the recipes in this chapter to whichever vegetables you can find. Typically the greens are boiled, drained, and served warm or at room temperature with lemon and olive oil, or cooked with other flavorings. Cooking time is the biggest variable, so be sure to adjust it according to the variety of greens, their freshness, and their maturity.

Greens can be sandy. Even if they are sold prewashed, they should be rinsed again before cooking. Even a small amount of grit can ruin a dish.

Spinach with Lemon
Spinaci al Limone

MAKES 4 SERVINGS

A drizzle of good olive oil and a few drops of fresh lemon juice perk up the flavor of cooked spinach or other leafy greens.

2 pounds fresh spinach, tough stems removed
¼ cup water
Salt
Extra-virgin olive oil
Lemon wedges

1 Wash the spinach well in several changes of cold water. Put the spinach, water, and a pinch of salt in a large pot. Cover the pot and turn on the heat to medium. Cook 5 minutes or until the spinach is wilted and tender. Drain the spinach and press out the excess water.

2 In a serving bowl, toss the spinach with olive oil to taste.

3 Serve, hot or at room temperature, garnished with lemon wedges.

Spinach or Other Greens with Butter and Garlic
Verdura al Burro

MAKES 6 SERVINGS

The mellowness of butter and garlic goes particularly well with the slight bitterness of greens such as spinach or Swiss chard.

2 pounds spinach, tough stems removed
¼ cup water
Salt
2 tablespoons unsalted butter
1 garlic clove, finely chopped
Freshly ground black pepper

1 Wash the spinach well in several changes of cold water. Put the spinach, water, and a pinch of salt in a large pot. Cover the pot and turn on the heat to medium. Cook 5 minutes or until the spinach is wilted and tender. Drain the spinach and press out the excess water.

2 In a medium skillet, melt the butter over medium heat. Add the garlic and cook until golden, about 2 minutes.

3 Stir in the spinach and salt and pepper to taste. Cook, stirring occasionally, until heated through, about 2 minutes. Serve hot.

Spinach with Raisins and Pine Nuts

Spinaci con Uva e Pinoli

MAKES 4 SERVINGS

Raisins and pine nuts are used to flavor many dishes in southern Italy and throughout the Mediterranean. Swiss chard or beet greens can also be prepared this way.

2 pounds fresh spinach, tough stems removed
1/4 cup water
Salt
2 tablespoons unsalted butter
Freshly ground black pepper
2 tablespoons raisins
2 tablespoons pine nuts, toasted

1 Wash the spinach well in several changes of cold water. Put the spinach, water, and a pinch of salt in a large pot. Cover the pot and turn on the heat to medium. Cook 5 minutes or until the spinach is wilted and tender. Drain the spinach and press out the excess water.

2 Wipe out the pot. Melt the butter in the pot, then add the spinach and raisins. Stir once or twice and cook 5 minutes until the raisins are plump. Sprinkle with the pine nuts and serve immediately.

Spinach with Anchovies, Piedmont Style

Spinaci alla Piemontesa

MAKES 6 SERVINGS

In Piedmont, this savory spinach is often served on slices of bread fried in butter, but it is also good on its own. Another variation is to top the spinach with fried or poached eggs.

2 pounds fresh spinach, tough stems removed
1/4 cup water
Salt
1/4 cup unsalted butter
4 anchovy fillets
1 garlic clove, finely chopped

1 Wash the spinach well in several changes of cold water. Put the spinach, water, and a pinch of salt in a large pot. Cover the pot and turn on the heat to medium. Cook 5 minutes or until the spinach is wilted and tender. Drain the spinach and press out the excess water.

2 Wipe out the pot. Melt the butter in the pot. Add the anchovies and garlic and cook, stirring, until the anchovies dissolve, about 2 minutes. Stir in the spinach and cook, stirring constantly, until heated through, 2 to 3 minutes. Serve hot.

Escarole with Garlic

Scarola al'Aglio

MAKES 4 SERVINGS

Escarole is a member of the large and varied chicory family, which includes endive, frisée, dandelion, and radicchio. Escarole is very popular in Neapolitan kitchens. Small heads of escarole are stuffed and braised, tender inner leaves are eaten raw in salads, and escarole is also cooked in soup. Vary this dish by leaving out the red pepper and adding 1/4 cup of raisins.

1 head escarole (about 1 pound)
3 tablespoons olive oil
3 garlic cloves, thinly sliced
Pinch of crushed red pepper (optional)
Salt

1 Trim the escarole and discard any bruised leaves. Cut off the stem ends. Separate the leaves and wash well in cool water, especially in the center of the leaves where soil collects. Stack the leaves and cut them into bite-size pieces.

2 In a large pot, cook the garlic and red pepper, if using, in the olive oil over medium heat until the garlic is golden, about 2 minutes. Add the escarole and salt to taste. Stir well. Cover the pot and cook until the escarole is tender, about 12 to 15 minutes. Serve hot.

Dandelion with Potatoes
Dente di Leone con Patate

MAKES 4 SERVINGS

Kale or chard can be substituted for the dandelion greens—you need a vegetable firm enough to cook at the same time as the potatoes. A bit of wine vinegar sparks up the flavor of these garlicky greens and potatoes.

I bunch dandelion greens (about I pound)
6 small waxy potatoes, peeled and sliced
Salt
3 garlic cloves, chopped
3 tablespoons olive oil
I tablespoon white wine vinegar

I Trim the dandelion and discard any bruised leaves. Cut off the stem ends. Separate the leaves and wash well in cool water, especially in the center of the leaves where soil collects. Cut the leaves crosswise into bite-size pieces.

2 Bring about 4 quarts of water to a boil. Add the potato slices, dandelion, and salt to taste. Bring the water back to the boil and cook until the vegetables are tender, about 10 minutes. Drain well.

3 In a large skillet, cook the garlic in the oil until golden, about 2 minutes. Add the vegetables, vinegar, and a pinch of salt. Cook, stirring well, until heated through, about 2 minutes. Serve hot.

❧ Mushrooms

In the fall, when wild mushrooms are abundant, Italians eat them prepared every possible way, from simple to extravagant. Hunters go to their favorite secret spots to gather them by the basketful. Orange and white *ovoli* and creamy white porcini are especially highly regarded, but Italians eat plenty of cultivated white button mushrooms too.

Truffles are members of the same family of fungi but are very rare and extremely expensive, especially in years that have endured a very hot and dry summer and fall. White truffles are typically shaved over hot foods like pasta or risotto so that the heat can release their aroma. Black truffles and summer truffles, which are black outside and creamy beige inside, are less expensive and often used in cooked dishes.

Mushrooms should look fresh and moist, with no bruises. White or button mushrooms should be very white, and the caps should be tightly closed. To prepare mushrooms for cooking, trim the ends of the stems if they seem dry. Either wipe the mushrooms clean with a damp cloth or quickly swish them in a bowl of cool water and pat them dry. Do not soak mushrooms, or they will become waterlogged.

Mushrooms with Garlic and Parsley
Funghi Trifolati

MAKES 4 SERVINGS

This is probably the most popular way to prepare mushrooms in Italy. Try adding some exotic mushroom varieties for more flavor.

1 (10- to 12-ounce) package white mushrooms
¼ cup olive oil
2 tablespoons chopped fresh flat-leaf parsley
2 large garlic cloves, thinly sliced
Salt and freshly ground black pepper

1 Place the mushrooms in a colander and rinse them quickly under cold running water. Drain the mushrooms and pat them dry. Cut the mushrooms into halves or quarters if large. Trim off the ends if they look dry.

2 In a large skillet, heat the oil over medium heat. Add the mushrooms. Cook, stirring often, until the mushrooms are browned, 8 to 10 minutes. Add the parsley, garlic, salt, and pepper. Cook until the garlic is golden, about 2 minutes more. Serve hot.

Mushrooms, Genoa Style
Funghi alle Erbe

MAKES 6 SERVINGS

The hillsides around Genoa are full of wild mushrooms and herbs, so naturally cooks there use them in many ways. Porcini mushrooms are typically used for this dish, though any large cultivated mushroom can be substituted. Because porcini are not often available in the United States, I substitute meaty and flavorful portobello mushrooms. I sometimes serve them as the centerpiece for a meatless meal.

6 large portobello mushrooms
4 tablespoons olive oil
Salt and freshly ground black pepper
2 garlic cloves, finely chopped
3 tablespoons finely chopped fresh flat-leaf parsley
1 teaspoon chopped fresh rosemary
½ teaspoon dried marjoram

1 Place a rack in the center of the oven. Preheat the oven to 425°F. Oil a baking pan large enough to hold the mushroom caps in a single layer.

2 Wipe the mushrooms clean with damp paper towels. Snap off the stems of the mushrooms and trim the ends where soil collects. Thinly slice the stems. Place the mushroom stems in a bowl and toss them with 2 tablespoons of the oil.

3 Place the mushroom caps open-side up in the pan. Sprinkle with salt and pepper.

4 In a small bowl, stir together the garlic, parsley, rosemary, marjoram, and salt and pepper to taste. Toss with the remaining 2 tablespoons oil. Place a pinch of the herb mixture on each mushroom cap. Top with the stems.

5 Bake 15 minutes. Check the mushrooms to see if the pan is too dry. Add a little warm water if needed. Bake 15 minutes more or until tender. Serve hot or at room temperature.

Roasted Mushrooms
Funghi al Forno

MAKES 4 TO 6 SERVINGS

In the spring and fall, when they are most plentiful, porcini mushrooms are roasted in olive oil until lightly browned around the edges yet tender and meaty inside. Porcini are rare and expensive in the United States, but you can apply the same treatment to other thick, fleshy mushroom varieties, such as cremini, portobello, or white mushrooms, with good results. Don't crowd the pan, though, as some varieties give off a lot of water and the mushrooms will steam instead of turning brown.

1 pound mushrooms, such as white, cremini,
    or portobello
4 large garlic cloves, thinly sliced
1/4 cup extra-virgin olive oil
Salt and freshly ground black pepper

1 Place a rack in the center of the oven. Preheat the oven to 400°F. Wipe the mushrooms clean with damp paper towels. Snap off the stems of the mushrooms and trim the ends where soil collects. Cut the mushrooms into quarters, or eighths if large. In a roasting pan large enough to hold the ingredients in a single layer, toss the mushrooms, garlic, and oil with salt and pepper to taste. Spread them evenly in the pan.

2 Roast 30 minutes, stirring once or twice, until the mushrooms are tender and browned. Serve hot.

Creamed Mushrooms
Funghi alla Panna

MAKES 4 SERVINGS

These creamy mushrooms are heavenly as a side dish with steak, or they can be an appetizer, served over thin slices of toast.

1 (10- to 12-ounce) package white mushrooms
2 tablespoons unsalted butter
1/4 cup chopped shallot
Salt and freshly ground black pepper
1/2 cup heavy cream

1 Wipe the mushrooms clean with damp paper towels. Snap off the stems of the mushrooms and trim the ends where soil collects. Cut the mushrooms into thick slices.

2 In a large skillet, melt the butter over medium heat. Add the shallot and cook until softened, about 3 minutes. Add the mushrooms and salt and pepper to taste. Cook, stirring often, until the mushrooms are lightly browned, about 10 minutes.

3 Stir in the cream and bring to a simmer. Cook until the cream is thickened, about 2 minutes. Serve hot or warm.

Creamy Baked Stuffed Mushrooms
Funghi al Gratin

MAKES 4 SERVINGS

I like to serve these as a side dish with a simple grilled steak or roast beef, but smaller mushrooms prepared this way are good as an appetizer.

12 large white or cremini mushrooms
4 tablespoons unsalted butter
1/4 cup chopped shallot or onion
1 teaspoon chopped fresh thyme or a pinch of
    dried thyme
Salt and freshly ground black pepper
1/4 cup heavy or whipping cream
2 tablespoons plain dry bread crumbs

1 Wipe the mushrooms clean with damp paper towels. Snap off the stems of the mushrooms and trim the ends where soil collects. Chop the stems.

2 In a medium skillet, melt 2 tablespoons of the butter. Add the mushroom stems, shallot, and thyme. Season with salt and pepper to taste. Cook, stirring often, until the mushroom stems are lightly browned, about 10 minutes.

3 Stir in the cream and simmer until thickened, about 2 minutes. Remove from the heat.

4 Place a rack in the center of the oven. Preheat the oven to 375°F. Butter a baking dish large enough to hold the mushroom caps in a single layer.

5 Spoon the cream mixture into the caps. Place the caps in the prepared pan. Sprinkle with the bread crumbs. Dot with the remaining 2 tablespoons butter.

6 Bake the mushrooms 15 minutes or until the crumbs are golden and the caps are tender. Serve hot.

Mushrooms with Tomato and Herbs
Funghi al Pomodoro

MAKES 4 SERVINGS

These mushrooms are cooked with garlic, tomato, and rosemary. Spoon them over pork chops or steak.

1 pound white mushrooms
¼ cup olive oil
1 garlic clove, finely chopped
1 teaspoon chopped fresh rosemary
1 large tomato, peeled, seeded, and chopped
Salt and freshly ground black pepper
2 tablespoons chopped fresh flat-leaf parsley

1 Wipe the mushrooms clean with damp paper towels. Snap off the stems of the mushrooms and trim the ends where soil collects. Cut the mushrooms into halves or quarters. In a large skillet, heat the oil over medium heat. Add the mushrooms, garlic, and rosemary. Cook, stirring frequently, until the mushrooms are browned, about 10 minutes.

2 Add the tomato and salt and pepper to taste. Cook until the juices evaporate, about 5 minutes more. Stir in the parsley and serve immediately.

Mushrooms in Marsala
Funghi al Marsala

MAKES 4 SERVINGS

Mushrooms and Marsala are meant for each other. Serve these with chicken or veal.

1 (10- to 12-ounce) package white mushrooms
¼ cup unsalted butter
1 tablespoon olive oil
1 medium onion, chopped
Salt and freshly ground black pepper
2 tablespoons dry Marsala
2 tablespoons chopped fresh flat-leaf parsley

1 Wipe the mushrooms clean with damp paper towels. Snap off the stems of the mushrooms and trim the ends where soil collects. Cut the mushrooms into halves or quarters, if large. In a large skillet, melt the butter with the oil over medium heat. Add the onion and cook until softened, 5 minutes.

2 Stir in the mushrooms, salt and pepper to taste, and the Marsala. Cook, stirring frequently, until most of the liquid evaporates and the mushrooms are lightly browned, about 10 minutes. Stir in the parsley and remove from the heat. Serve hot.

Grilled Mushrooms
Funghi alla Griglia

MAKES 4 SERVINGS

Large mushrooms such as portobello, shiitake, and best of all, porcini are wonderful cooked on the grill. Their texture and flavor are meaty and juicy enhanced by the smoky flavors of the grill. The stems of shiitake are too woody to eat. Discard them and cook only the caps.

4 large fresh mushrooms, such as shiitake, portobello, or porcini
3 to 4 tablespoons olive oil
2 to 3 large garlic cloves
2 tablespoons chopped fresh flat-leaf parsley
Salt and freshly ground black pepper

1 Place a barbecue grill or broiler rack about 5 inches away from the heat source. Preheat the grill or broiler.

2 Wipe the mushrooms clean with damp paper towels. Snap off the stems of the mushrooms and trim the ends where soil collects. Cut the stems of portobello or porcini mushrooms into thick slices. Discard the stems of shiitake mushrooms. Brush the mushrooms with oil. Arrange the caps and stems on the grill with the rounded tops of the caps toward the source of the heat. Grill until slightly browned, about 5 minutes.

3 In a small bowl, stir together 2 tablespoons of the oil, the garlic, parsley, and salt and pepper to taste. Turn the mushroom pieces and brush with the oil mixture.

4 Cook until the mushrooms are tender, 2 to 3 minutes more. Serve hot.

Fried Mushrooms
Funghi Fritti

MAKES 6 SERVINGS

A crisp bread-crumb crust coats these mushrooms. They are good as appetizers.

1 cup plain dry bread crumbs
1/4 cup freshly grated Parmigiano-Reggiano
2 large eggs, beaten
Salt and freshly ground black pepper
1 pound fresh white mushrooms
Vegetable oil for frying
Lemon wedges

1 On a piece of wax paper, toss the bread crumbs with the cheese and spread the mixture on a sheet of wax paper.

2 In a small bowl, beat the eggs with salt and pepper to taste.

3 Quickly rinse the mushrooms under cold water. Pat them dry. Cut them in half or into quarters if large. Dip the mushrooms in the egg mixture and roll them in the bread crumbs, coating them completely. Let the coating dry about 10 minutes.

4 Line a tray with paper towels. In a deep wide saucepan, heat the oil until a small drop of the egg sizzles and cooks quickly. Add just enough mushrooms to the pan as will fit in a single layer without crowding. Fry the mushrooms until crisp and brown, about 4 minutes. Transfer to the paper towels to drain. Fry the remaining mushrooms in the same way.

5 Serve the mushrooms hot with lemon wedges.

Mushroom Gratin
Tiella di Funghi

MAKES 4 SERVINGS

Large white mushrooms can be used in this layered casserole from Puglia, or substitute another fleshy variety such as shiitake, portobello, or cremini. This is good hot or at room temperature.

1 pound portabello, cremini, or large white
   mushrooms, thickly sliced
1/2 cup plain dry bread crumbs
1/2 cup freshly grated Pecorino Romano
2 tablespoons chopped fresh flat-leaf parsley
4 tablespoons olive oil
Salt and freshly ground black pepper
2 medium onions, thinly sliced
2 medium tomatoes, peeled, seeded and chopped

1 Wipe the mushrooms clean with damp paper towels. Snap off the stems of the mushrooms and trim the ends where soil collects. Slice the mushrooms at least 1/4 inch thick. Place a rack in the center of the oven. Preheat the oven to 350°F. Oil a 13 × 9 × 2–inch baking pan.

2 In a medium bowl, stir together the bread crumbs, cheese, and parsley. Add 2 tablespoons of the oil and salt and pepper to taste.

3 In the baking pan, make a layer of half the mushrooms, overlapping the slices slightly. Place a layer of half of the onions and tomatoes over the mushrooms. Sprinkle with salt and pepper. Spread with half of the crumb mixture. Repeat with the remaining ingredients. Drizzle with the remaining 2 tablespoons oil.

4 Bake 45 minutes or until the mushrooms are tender when pierced with a knife. Serve hot.

Oyster Mushrooms with Sausage
Funghi al Salsiccie

MAKES 4 SERVINGS

My friend Phil Cicconi has many fond memories of his father, Guido, who came from Ascoli Piceno in the Marches. He settled in West Philadelphia, where there was an enclave of people from the region, and he taught Phil to forage for wild mushrooms and broccoli rabe in the fields near their home. Now Phil carries on this tradition with his three daughters. Oyster mushrooms, which grow on certain maple trees, are particularly prized. Phil's mother, Anna Maria, who came from Abruzzo, would prepare the mushrooms this way. They ate it as a side dish with crusty Italian bread.

Cultivated oyster mushrooms can be used in this recipe, or substitute sliced white mushooms.

1 pound oyster mushrooms
2 tablespoons olive oil
2 garlic cloves, finely chopped
2 shallots, finely chopped
8 ounces Italian sweet pork sausages, casings removed
Salt
Pinch of crushed red pepper
1 cup peeled, seeded, and chopped fresh tomatoes

1 Wipe the mushrooms with dampened paper towels. Tear the mushrooms into thin strips along the gills.

2 Pour the oil into a large skillet. Add the garlic and shallots and cook until softened, about 2 minutes. Stir in the sausage and cook, stirring frequently, until browned.

3 Add mushrooms, salt to taste, and crushed red pepper and stir well. Add the tomatoes and 1/4 cup of water. Bring to a simmer.

4 Turn the heat to low and cover the pan. Cook, stirring occasionally, 30 minutes or until the sausage is tender and the sauce is thickened. Serve hot.

❧ Onions

Though most of us have onions on hand at all times, seldom do we think of onions in anything more than a supporting role with other ingredients. However, large onions are wonderful roasted whole, and small onions are good simmered in a sauce, as they are in Pearl Onions with Honey and Orange (page 442).

When buying onions, try smelling them. Onions that are bruised or turning bad will have a strong odor, while fresh onions smell very mild.

Baked Onions
Cipolle al Forno

MAKES 4 TO 8 SERVINGS

These onions turn smooth and sweet when cooked; try them with roast beef.

4 medium white or red onions, peeled
1/2 cup plain dry bread crumbs
1/4 cup freshly grated Parmigiano-Reggiano
    or Pecorino Romano
2 tablespoons olive oil
Salt and freshly ground black pepper

1 Bring a medium saucepan of water to a boil. Add the onions and reduce the heat so that the water just simmers. Cook 5 minutes. Let the onions cool in the water in the pan. Drain the onions and cut them in half crosswise.

2 Place a rack in the center of the oven. Preheat the oven to 350°F. Oil a baking pan just large enough to hold the onions in a single layer. Place the onions in the pan cut-side up. In a small bowl, mix together the bread crumbs, cheese, olive oil, and salt and pepper to taste. Spoon the bread crumbs on top of the onions.

3 Bake 1 hour or until the onions are golden and tender when pierced with a knife. Serve hot or at room temperature.

Onions with Balsamic Vinegar
Cipolle al Balsamico

MAKES 6 SERVINGS

Balsamic vinegar complements the sweet flavor and color of red onions. These go well with roast pork or pork chops.

6 medium red onions
6 tablespoons extra-virgin olive oil
3 tablespoons balsamic vinegar
Salt and freshly ground black pepper

1 Place a rack in the center of the oven. Preheat the oven to 375°F. Line a baking pan with foil.

2 Wash the onions, but do not peel them. Place the onions in the prepared pan. Bake the onions 1 hour to 1½ hours, until tender when pierced with a knife.

3 Trim off the root ends of the onions and peel off the skin. Cut the onions into quarters and place them in a bowl. Add the oil, vinegar, and salt and pepper to taste, and toss to combine. Serve hot or at room temperature.

Red Onion Confit
Confettura di Cipolle Rosse

MAKES ABOUT 1 PINT

Tropea, on the Calabrian coast, is known for its sweet red onions. Though the red onions in the United States are more pungent, you can still make this delicious jam that we ate at Locanda di Alia in Castrovillari. The jam was served with golden fried sardines, but it is also good with pork chops or grilled chicken. I also like it as a condiment with a sharp cheese, such as aged pecorino.

A variation of the jam includes some chopped fresh mint. Be sure to use a heavy-bottomed saucepan and keep the heat very low to prevent the onions from sticking. Add a little water if they dry out too quickly.

1¼ pounds red onions, very finely chopped
1 cup dry red wine
1 teaspoon salt
2 tablespons unsalted butter
1 tablespoon balsamic vinegar
1 or 2 tablespoons honey
About 1 tablespoon sugar

1 In a medium heavy saucepan, combine the onions, red wine, and salt over medium heat. Bring to a simmer and turn the heat to low. Cover and cook, stirring often, for 1 hour 15 minutes or until the onions are very tender. The onions will be slightly translucent.

2 Stir in the butter, balsamic vinegar, and 1 tablespoon each of the honey and sugar. Cook uncovered, stirring often, until all of the liquid has evaporated and the mixture is very thick.

3 Let cool slightly. Serve at room temperature or slightly warm. This keeps in the refrigerator for up to a month. To reheat, place the confit in a small bowl set over a pan of simmering water, or warm it in a microwave.

Roasted Onion and Beet Salad

Insalata di Cipolla e Barbabietola

MAKES 6 SERVINGS

If you have never had fresh beets in season, you really should try them. When they are young and tender, they are remarkably sweet and flavorful. Buy them in the summer and fall, when they are at their best. As they age they become woody and tasteless.

6 beets, trimmed and scrubbed
2 large onions, peeled
6 tablespoons olive oil
2 tablespoons red wine vinegar
Salt and freshly ground black pepper
6 fresh basil leaves

1 Place a rack in the center of the oven. Preheat the oven to 400°F. Scrub the beets and wrap them in a large sheet of aluminum foil, sealing tightly. Place the package on a baking sheet.

2 Cut the onions into bite-size pieces. Place them in a baking pan and toss with 2 tablespoons of the olive oil.

3 Place the package of beets and the pan of onions side by side in the oven. Bake 1 hour or until the beets are tender when pierced with a knife and the onions are browned.

4 Let the beets cool. Peel off the skins and cut the beets into wedges.

5 In a large bowl, toss the beets and onions with 1/4 cup olive oil, the vinegar, and salt and pepper to taste. Sprinkle with the basil and serve immediately.

Pearl Onions with Honey and Orange

Cipolline Profumate all'Arancia

MAKES 8 SERVINGS

Sweet and tart pearl onions flavored with honey, orange, and vinegar are good with a holiday turkey or capon, roast pork, or as an appetizer with sliced salumi. You can make them ahead, but they should be reheated gently before serving.

2 pounds pearl onions
1 navel orange
2 tablespoons unsalted butter
1/4 cup honey
1/4 cup white wine vinegar
Salt and freshly ground black pepper

1 Bring a large pot of water to a boil. Add the onions and cook for 3 minutes. Drain and cool them under running water. With a sharp paring knife, shave off the tip of the root ends. Do not slice off the ends too deeply or the onions will fall apart during cooking. Slip off the skins.

2 With a swivel-blade vegetable peeler, remove the orange zest. Stack the strips of zest and cut them into thin matchsticks. Squeeze the juice from the orange. Set aside.

3 In a large skillet, melt the butter over medium heat. Add the onions and cook 30 minutes or until lightly browned, shaking the pan occasionally so that they do not stick.

4 Add the orange juice, zest, honey, vinegar, and salt and pepper to taste. Turn the heat to low and cook 10 minutes, turning the onions frequently, until the onions are tender when pierced with a knfe and glazed with the sauce. Let cool slightly. Serve warm.

❧ Peas

The fresh pea season is very brief, so Italians try to make the most of it. The best peas are those you grow yourself. If that is not possible, buy them directly from a farm. Peas, like corn, lose their sweetness and become starchy if they are not eaten soon after they are picked.

When buying peas in the pod, do not buy them if they are large, as they are probably overgrown. Avoid soft, flabby pods. Frozen peas are often a lot better than fresh because they are picked when ripe and then quickly frozen, which preserves their flavor.

Peas with Onions
Piselli con Cipolle

MAKES 4 SERVINGS

A little water added to the pan helps the onion to mellow and soften without browning. The sweetness of the onion enhances the flavor of the peas.

2 tablespoons olive oil
1 medium onion, finely chopped
4 tablespoons water
2 cups fresh shelled peas or 1 (10-ounce) package frozen peas
Pinch of dried oregano
Salt

1 Pour the oil into a medium saucepan. Add the onion and 2 tablespoons of the water. Cook, stirring frequently, until the onion is very tender, about 15 minutes.

2 Stir in the peas, the remaining 2 tablespoons of water, the oregano, and the salt. Cover and cook until the peas are tender, 5 to 10 minutes.

Peas with Prosciutto and Green Onions
Piselli al Prosciutto

MAKES 4 SERVINGS

These peas are good with lamb chops or roast lamb.

3 tablespoons unsalted butter
4 green onions, trimmed and thinly sliced
2 cups fresh shelled peas or 1 (10-ounce) package frozen peas
1 teaspoon sugar
Salt
4 thin slices imported Italian prosciutto, cut crosswise into thin strips

1 Melt 2 tablespoons of the butter in a medium skillet. Add the green onions and cook 1 minute.

2 Add the peas, sugar, and salt to taste. Stir in 2 tablespoons water and cover the pan. Cook over low heat until the peas are tender, 5 to 10 minutes.

3 Stir in the prosciutto and remaining 1 tablespoon of butter. Cook 1 minute more and serve hot.

Sweet Peas with Lettuce and Mint
Piselli alla Menta

MAKES 4 SERVINGS

Even frozen peas taste like fresh-picked when they are prepared this way. The lettuce adds a slight crunch and the mint a bright, fresh flavor.

2 tablespoons unsalted butter
1/4 cup onion, very finely chopped
2 cups fresh shelled peas or 1 (10-ounce) package frozen peas
1 cup shredded lettuce leaves
12 mint leaves, torn into bits
Salt and freshly ground black pepper

1 In a medium saucepan, melt the butter over medium heat. Add the onion and cook until tender and golden, about 10 minutes. *(continues)*

2 Add the peas, lettuce, mint leaves, and salt and pepper to taste. Stir in 2 tablespoons water and cover the pan. Cook 5 to 10 minutes or until the peas are tender. Serve hot.

Easter Pea Salad

Insalata di Pasqua

MAKES 4 SERVINGS

In the 1950s Romeo Salta was considered one of the best Italian restaurants in New York City. It stood out because it was very elegant and served northern Italian food at a time when most people were only familiar with family-style restaurants serving the red sauced dishes of the south. The owner, Romeo Salta, had learned the restaurant business by working on luxury cruise liners—at that time, the finest training ground for restaurant personnel. This salad would appear on the menu around Easter, when fresh peas became abundant. The original recipe also contained anchovies, though I prefer the salad without them. Sometimes I add chopped Swiss or a similar cheese along with the prosciutto.

2¹/₂ cups fresh shelled peas or 1 (10-ounce) package frozen peas

Salt

1 hard-cooked egg yolk

¹/₄ cup olive oil

¹/₄ cup lemon juice

Freshly ground black pepper

2 ounces sliced imported Italian prosciutto, cut crosswise into narrow strips

1 For either fresh or frozen peas, bring a medium saucepan of water to boiling. Add the peas and salt to taste. Cook until the peas are barely tender, about 3 minutes. Drain the peas. Cool them under cold running water. Blot the peas dry.

2 In a serving bowl, mash the egg yolk with a fork. Whisk in the oil, lemon juice, and salt and pepper to taste. Add the peas and toss gently. Add the prosciutto strips and serve immediately.

❧ Peppers

Bell peppers and chile peppers grow in amazing variety in Italy. Most bell peppers are sweet and mild, but when I first visited Tuscany in the 1980s I was surprised to taste big, bright orange-yellow peppers that looked like the bell variety but were hot. The Piedmontese are justly proud of their very large, square bell peppers, which are meaty and sweet. Neapolitans have finger-shaped mild green peppers called *papacelli* that they serve fried or pickled. In Abruzzo, chile peppers are eaten both fresh and dried. At meals, people pass around these long skinny green chiles and a knife, slicing the hot pepper to taste over soup or pasta. And Italians eat not only the flesh of the chile, but also the seeds, which contain a lot of the heat.

When buying peppers, either sweet or hot, look for firm, bright flesh without soft spots. The stem should be bright green.

To quickly seed bell peppers, stand them on a cutting board with the stem up. Holding the stem in one hand, place the cutting edge of a large heavy chef's knife just beyond the edge of the cap. Cut straight down. Turn the pepper and cut straight down again. Repeat all around. Discard the core, seeds, and stem, which will be in one piece.

Red chiles are hotter than green chiles, but the degree of heat depends on the variety and where it is grown. Always wear gloves when handling fresh chiles, as the the oils can burn if they come in contact with your skin, eyes, or nose.

Tiny dried chiles, about the size of your pinky nail, are called *diavolilli* in Italy, meaning "little devils," because they are so hot. They can be substituted for fresh chiles, or you can use the crushed red pepper available in jars.

Roasted Peppers

Peperoni Arrostiti

MAKES 8 SERVINGS

Roasted peppers are good in salads, omelets, and sandwiches. They freeze well, too, so you can make a batch in the summer when peppers are plentiful and keep them for winter meals.

8 large red, yellow, or green bell peppers

1 Cover the broiler pan with foil. Place the broiler pan about 3 inches away from the heat source. Place the whole peppers on the pan. Turn on the broiler to high. Broil the peppers, turning them frequently with tongs, about 15 minutes or until the skin blisters and they are charred all over. Put the peppers in a bowl. Cover with foil and let cool.

3 Cut the peppers in half, draining the juices into a bowl. Peel off the skins and discard the seeds and stems.

4 Cut the peppers lengthwise into 1-inch strips and place them in a serving bowl. Strain the juices over the peppers.

5 Serve at room temperature or store in the refrigerator and serve chilled. The peppers keep 3 days in the refrigerator or 3 months in the freezer.

Roasted Pepper Salad

Insalata di Peperoni Arrostiti

MAKES 8 SERVINGS

Serve these peppers as part of an antipasto assortment, as a side dish with grilled tuna or pork, or as an antipasto with sliced fresh mozzarella.

1 recipe (8 peppers) Roasted Peppers (recipe above)
1/3 cup extra-virgin olive oil
4 basil leaves, torn into bits
2 garlic cloves, thinly sliced
Salt and freshly ground black pepper

Prepare the peppers, if necessary. Toss the peppers with the oil, basil, garlic, and salt and pepper to taste. Let stand 1 hour before serving.

Roasted Peppers with Onions and Herbs

Peperoni Arrostiti con Cipolle

MAKES 4 SERVINGS

Serve these peppers hot or at room temperature. They also make a good topping for crostini.

1/2 recipe Roasted Peppers (page 445);
    use red or yellow bell peppers
1 medium onion, halved and thinly sliced
Pinch of crushed red pepper
2 tablespoons olive oil
Salt
1/2 teaspoon dried oregano, crumbled
2 tablespoons chopped fresh flat-leaf parsley

1 Prepare the peppers through step 3, if necessary. Then, drain the peppers and cut them lengthwise into 1/2-inch strips.

2 In a medium skillet, cook the onion with the crushed red pepper in the oil over medium heat until the onion is tender and golden, about 10 minutes. Add the peppers, oregano, and salt to taste. Cook, stirring occasionally, until heated through, about 5 minutes. Stir in the parsley and cook 1 minute more. Serve hot or at room temperature.

Baked Peppers with Tomatoes
Peperoni al Forno

MAKES 4 SERVINGS

In this recipe from Abruzzo, a fresh, not-too-hot chile seasons the bell peppers. Crushed red pepper or a small dried chile pepper can be substituted. These peppers are good in a sandwich.

2 large red bell peppers
2 large yellow bell peppers
I chile, such as jalapeño, seeded and chopped
3 tablespoons olive oil
Salt
2 garlic cloves, chopped
2 medium tomatoes, peeled, seeded, and chopped

I Place a rack in the center of the oven. Preheat the oven to 400°F. Oil a large baking pan. Stand the peppers on a cutting board. Holding the stem in one hand, place the cutting edge of a large heavy chef's knife just beyond the edge of the cap. Cut straight down. Turn the pepper 90° and cut straight down again. Repeat, turning and cutting the remaining two sides. Discard the core, seeds, and stem, which will be in one piece. Cut away any membranes and scrape out any seeds.

2 Cut the peppers lengthwise into 1-inch strips. Add the chile to the pan. Add the oil and salt to taste and toss well. Spread the peppers out in the pan.

3 Bake the peppers 25 minutes. Add the garlic and tomatoes and stir well. Bake 20 minutes more or until the peppers are tender when pierced with a knife. Serve hot.

Peppers with Balsamic Vinegar
Peperoni al Balsamico

MAKES 6 SERVINGS

The sweetness of balsamic vinegar complements the sweetness of peppers. Serve these hot with pork or lamb chops or at room temperature with cold chicken or roast pork.

6 large red bell peppers
1/4 cup olive oil
Salt and freshly ground black pepper
2 tablespoons balsamic vinegar

I Place a rack in the center of the oven. Preheat the oven to 400°F. Stand the peppers on a cutting board. Holding the stem in one hand, place the cutting edge of a large heavy chef's knife just beyond the edge of the cap. Cut straight down. Turn the pepper 90° and cut straight down again. Repeat, turning and cutting the remaining two sides. Discard the core, seeds, and stem, which will be in one piece. Cut away any membranes and scrape out any seeds.

2 Cut the peppers into 1-inch strips. Place them in a large shallow roasting pan with the oil and salt and pepper. Toss well. Bake the peppers 30 minutes.

3 Stir in the vinegar. Bake the peppers 20 minutes more or until tender. Serve hot or at room temperature.

Pickled Peppers
Peperoni Sott'Aceto

MAKES 2 PINTS

Colorful peppers packed in vinegar are delicious in sandwiches or with cold meats. These can be used to make the Molise-Style Pepper Sauce on page 104.

2 large red bell peppers
2 large yellow bell peppers
Salt
2 cups white wine vinegar
2 cups water
Pinch of crushed red pepper

1 Stand the peppers on a cutting board. Holding the stem in one hand, place the cutting edge of a large heavy chef's knife just beyond the edge of the cap. Cut straight down. Turn the pepper 90° and cut straight down again. Repeat, turning and cutting the remaining two sides. Discard the core, seeds, and stem, which will be in one piece. Cut away any membranes and scrape out any seeds. Cut the peppers lengthwise into 1-inch strips. Place the peppers in a colander set over a plate and sprinkle with salt. Let stand 1 hour to drain.

2 In a nonreactive saucepan, combine the vinegar, water, and crushed red pepper. Bring to a simmer. Remove from the heat and let cool slightly.

3 Rinse the bell peppers under cold water and pat them dry. Pack the peppers in 2 sterilized pint jars. Pour on the cooled vinegar mixture and seal. Let stand in a cool, dark place 1 week before using.

Peppers with Almonds
Peperoni alle Mandorle

MAKES 4 SERVINGS

An old friend of my mother's whose family came from Ischia, a small island in the bay of Naples, gave her this recipe. She liked to serve it for lunch over slices of Italian bread fried in olive oil until golden.

2 red and 2 yellow bell peppers
1 garlic clove, lightly crushed
3 tablespoons olive oil
2 medium tomatoes, peeled, seeded, and chopped
1/4 cup water
2 tablespoons capers
4 anchovy fillets, chopped
4 ounces toasted almonds, coarsely chopped

1 Stand the peppers on a cutting board. Holding the stem in one hand, place the cutting edge of a large heavy chef's knife just beyond the edge of the cap. Cut straight down. Turn the pepper 90° and cut straight down again. Repeat, turning and cutting the remaining two sides. Discard the core, seeds, and stem, which will be in one piece. Cut away any membranes and scrape out any seeds.

2 In a large skillet, cook the garlic with the oil over medium heat, pressing the garlic once or twice with the back of a spoon. As soon as it is lightly browned, about 4 minutes, discard the garlic.

3 Add the peppers to the pan. Cook, stirring often, until softened, about 15 minutes.

4 Add the tomatoes and water. Cook until the sauce is thickened, about 15 minutes more.

5 Stir in the capers, anchovies, and almonds. Taste for salt. Cook 2 minutes more. Let cool slightly before serving.

Peppers with Tomatoes and Onions

Peperonata

MAKES 4 SERVINGS

Every region seems to have its version of peperonata. Some add capers, olives, herbs, or anchovies. Serve this as a side dish or as a sauce for roast pork or grilled fish.

4 red or yellow bell peppers (or a mix)

2 medium onions, thinly sliced

3 tablespoons olive oil

3 large tomatoes, peeled, seeded, and coarsely chopped

1 garlic clove, finely chopped

Salt

1 Stand the peppers on a cutting board. Holding the stem in one hand, place the cutting edge of a large heavy chef's knife just beyond the edge of the cap. Cut straight down. Turn the pepper 90° and cut straight down again. Repeat, turning and cutting the remaining two sides. Discard the core, seeds, and stem, which will be in one piece. Cut away any membranes and scrape out any seeds. Cut the peppers into 1/4-inch strips.

2 In a large skillet over medium heat, cook the onions in the olive oil until tender and golden, about 10 minutes. Add the pepper strips and cook 10 minutes more.

3 Stir in the tomatoes, garlic, and salt to taste. Cover and cook 20 minutes or until the peppers are tender when pierced with a knife. If there is a lot of liquid remaining, uncover and cook until the sauce is thickened and reduced. Serve hot or at room temperature.

Stuffed Frying Peppers

Peperoni Ripieni

MAKES 4 TO 8 SERVINGS

My grandmother always made these peppers in the summertime. She would cook them in a big black skillet in the morning, and by lunchtime they were just the right temperature for serving with sliced bread.

1 1/4 cups plain dry bread crumbs made from Italian or French bread

1/3 cup freshly grated Pecorino Romano or Parmigiano-Reggiano

1/4 cup chopped fresh flat-leaf parsley

1 garlic clove, finely chopped

Salt and freshly ground black pepper

About 1/2 cup olive oil

8 long light-green Italian frying peppers

3 cups peeled, seeded, and chopped fresh tomatoes or 1 (28-ounce) can crushed tomatoes

6 fresh basil leaves, torn into bits

1 In a bowl, mix together the bread crumbs, cheese, parsley, garlic, and salt and pepper to taste. Stir in 3 tablespoons of the oil, or enough to moisten the crumbs evenly.

2 Cut off the tops of the peppers and scoop out the seeds. Spoon the bread crumb mixture into the peppers, leaving about 1 inch of clearance at the top. Do not overstuff the peppers, or the filling will spill out as the peppers cook.

3 In a large skillet, heat 1/4 cup of oil over medium heat until a piece of pepper sizzles in the pan. With tongs, add the peppers carefully. Cook, turning occasionally with tongs, until browned on all sides, about 20 minutes.

4 Pour the tomatoes, basil, and salt and pepper to taste around the peppers. Bring to a simmer. Cover and cook, turning the peppers once or twice, until very tender, about 15 minutes. If the sauce is too dry, add a little water. Uncover and cook until the sauce is thick, about 5 minutes more. Serve warm or at room temperature.

Neapolitan-Style Stuffed Peppers
Peperoni alla Nonna

MAKES 6 SERVINGS

If Sicilians have countless ways to cook eggplants, Neapolitans have the same creativity with peppers. This is another typical Neapolitan recipe that my grandmother used to make.

2 medium eggplants (about 1 pound each)
6 large red, yellow, or green bell peppers, cut into
  $^{1}/_{2}$-inch strips
$^{1}/_{2}$ cup plus 3 tablespoons olive oil
3 medium tomatoes, peeled, seeded, and chopped
$^{3}/_{4}$ cup pitted and chopped mild, oil-cured black olives,
  such as Gaeta
6 anchovy fillets, finely chopped
3 tablespoons capers, rinsed and drained
1 large garlic clove, peeled and finely chopped
3 tablespoons chopped fresh flat-leaf parsley
Freshly ground black pepper
$^{1}/_{2}$ cup plus 1 tablespoon plain bread crumbs

1 Trim the eggplants and cut them into $^{3}/_{4}$-inch cubes. Layer the pieces in a colander, sprinkling each layer with salt. Place the colander over a plate and let drain for 1 hour. Rinse the eggplant and pat dry with paper towels.

2 In a large skillet, heat the $^{1}/_{2}$ cup of oil over medium heat. Add the eggplant and cook, stirring occasionally, until tender, about 10 minutes.

3 Stir in the tomatoes, olives, anchovies, capers, garlic, parsley, and pepper to taste. Bring to a simmer, then cook 5 minutes more. Stir in the $^{1}/_{2}$ cup of bread crumbs and remove from the heat.

4 Place a rack in the center of the oven. Preheat the oven to 450°F. Oil a baking pan just large enough to hold the peppers upright.

5 Cut off the stems of the peppers and remove the seeds and white membranes. Stuff the eggplant mixture into the peppers. Stand the peppers in the prepared pan. Sprinkle with the remaining 1 tablespoon

bread crumbs and drizzle with the remaining 3 tablespoons oil.

6 Pour 1 cup water around the peppers. Bake 1 hour 15 minutes or until the peppers are very tender and lightly browned. Serve hot or at room temperature.

Stuffed Peppers, Ada Boni's Style
Peperoni Ripieni alla Ada Boni

MAKES 4 TO 8 SERVINGS

Ada Boni was a famous Italian food writer and the author of numerous cookbooks. Her Italian Regional Cooking *is a classic, and one of the first books on the subject translated into English. This recipe is adapted from the Sicily chapter.*

4 medium red or yellow bell peppers
1 cup toasted plain bread crumbs
4 tablespoons raisins
$^{1}/_{2}$ cup chopped pitted mild black olives
6 anchovy fillets, chopped
2 tablespoons chopped fresh basil
2 tablespoons capers, rinsed, drained, and chopped
$^{1}/_{4}$ cup plus 2 tablespoons olive oil
1 cup Sicilian Tomato Sauce (see page 90)

1 Place a rack in the center of the oven. Preheat the oven to 375°F. Oil a 13 × 9 × 2–inch baking dish.

2 With a large heavy chef's knife, cut the peppers in half lengthwise. Cut out the stems, seeds, and white membranes.

3 In a large bowl, mix together the bread crumbs, raisins, olives, anchovies, basil, capers, and $^{1}/_{4}$ cup of the oil. Taste and adjust seasoning. (Salt will probably be unnecessary.)

4 Spoon the mixture into the pepper halves. Top with the sauce. Bake 50 minutes or until the peppers are very tender when pierced with a knife. Serve hot or at room temperature.

Fried Peppers
Peperoni Fritti

MAKES 6 TO 8 SERVINGS

Crisp and sweet, these are hard to resist. Serve them with an omelet or with any cooked meat.

4 large red or yellow bell peppers
1/2 cup all-purpose flour
Salt

1 Stand the peppers on a cutting board. Holding the stem in one hand, place the cutting edge of a large heavy chef's knife just beyond the edge of the cap. Cut straight down. Turn the pepper 90° and cut straight down again. Repeat, turning and cutting the remaining two sides. Discard the core, seeds, and stem, which will be in one piece. Cut away any membranes and scrape out any seeds. Cut the peppers into 1/4-inch strips.

2 Heat about 2 inches of oil in a deep heavy saucepan until the temperature reaches 375°F on a frying thermometer.

3 Line a tray with paper towels. Put the flour in a shallow bowl. Roll the pepper strips in the flour, shaking off the excess.

4 Add the peppers strips to the hot oil a few at a time. Fry until golden and tender, about 4 minutes. Drain on the paper towels. Fry the remainder in batches, in the same way. Sprinkle with salt and serve immediately.

Sautéed Peppers with Zucchini and Mint
Peperoni e Zucchini in Padella

MAKES 6 SERVINGS

The longer this sits, the better it tastes, so make it early in the day to serve for a later meal.

1 red bell pepper
1 yellow bell pepper
2 tablespoons olive oil
4 small zucchini, cut into 1/4-inch slices
Salt
2 tablespoons white wine vinegar
2 garlic cloves, very finely chopped
2 tablespoons chopped fresh mint
1/2 teaspoon dried oregano
Pinch of crushed red pepper

1 Stand the peppers on a cutting board. Holding the stem in one hand, place the cutting edge of a large heavy chef's knife just beyond the edge of the cap. Cut straight down. Turn the pepper 90° and cut straight down again. Repeat, turning and cutting the remaining two sides. Discard the core, seeds, and stem, which will be in one piece. Cut away any membranes and scrape out any seeds. Cut the peppers into 1-inch strips.

2 In a large skillet, heat the oil over medium heat. Add the peppers and cook, stirring, for 10 minutes.

3 Add the zucchini and salt to taste. Cook, stirring often, until the zucchini are tender, about 15 minutes.

4 While the vegetables are cooking, in a medium bowl, whisk together the vinegar, garlic, herbs, red pepper, and salt to taste.

5 Stir in the peppers and zucchini. Let stand until the vegetables are at room temperature. Taste and adjust seasoning.

Roasted Pepper and Eggplant Terrine
Sformato di Peperoni e Melanzane

MAKES 8 TO 12 SERVINGS

This is an unusual and beautiful terrine of layered peppers, eggplant, and flavorings. The pepper juices gel slightly after chilling and hold the terrine together. Serve it as a first course or as a side dish with grilled meats.

4 large red bell peppers, roasted and peeled
(see page 445)
2 large eggplants (about 1 1/2 pounds each)
Salt
Olive oil
1/2 cup torn fresh basil leaves
4 large garlic cloves, peeled, seeded,
and finely chopped
1/4 cup red wine vinegar
Freshly ground black pepper

1 Prepare the peppers, if necessary. Trim the eggplants and cut them lengthwise into 1/4-inch-thick slices. Layer the slices in a colander, sprinkling each layer with salt. Let stand at least 30 minutes.

2 Preheat the oven to 450°F. Brush two large jelly roll pans with oil.

3 Rinse the eggplant slices in cool water and pat dry with paper towels. Arrange the eggplant in the pans in a single layer. Brush with oil. Bake the eggplant about 10 minutes, until lightly browned on top. Turn the pieces with tongs and bake about 10 minutes more or until tender and lightly browned.

4 Drain the peppers and cut them into 1-inch strips.

5 Line an 8 × 4 × 3–inch loaf pan with plastic wrap. Place a layer of eggplant slices in the bottom of the pan, overlapping them slightly. Make a layer of the roasted peppers over the eggplant. Sprinkle with some of the basil, garlic, vinegar, oil, and salt and pepper to taste. Continue layering, pressing each layer down firmly, until all of the ingredients are used. Cover with plastic wrap and weight the contents with a second loaf pan filled with heavy cans. Refrigerate for at least 24 hours or up to 3 days.

6 To serve, uncover the terrine and invert it onto a serving place. Carefully remove the plastic wrap. Cut the terrine into thick slices. Serve cold or at room temperature.

～ Potatoes

Idaho-type bakers are not available in Italy. But the varieties that are grown there are very flavorful. Some are yellow and some are white. Italians use them for frying, baking, roasting, and mashing, as well as for soups and pasta. Italians don't put potatoes in the starch category with rice and pasta as we do in the United States. They are served as any other vegetable would be.

Potatoes should be dry, firm, and smooth, with no cuts or bruises. Sprouted potatoes should be avoided, as should those that are greenish. Peeling is optional. Very fresh new potatoes don't need peeling, but I generally peel older potatoes, or when I want them to look less rustic.

My favorite all-purpose potatoes are Yukon gold. They have good flavor and warm color, and they keep their shape well for salads and when roasted.

Sweet-and-Sour Potatoes
Patate in Agrodolce

MAKES 6 TO 8 SERVINGS

This is a Sicilian-style potato salad to serve at room temperature with grilled pork ribs, chicken, or sausages.

2 pounds all-purpose potatoes, such as Yukon gold
1 onion
2 tablespoons olive oil
1 cup pitted mild black olives, such as Gaeta
2 tablespoons capers
Salt and freshly ground black pepper
2 tablespoons white wine vinegar
2 tablespoons sugar

(continues)

1 Scrub the potatoes with a brush under cold running water. Peel them if desired. Cut the potatoes into halves or quarters if large. In a large skillet, cook the onion in the oil until tender and golden, about 10 minutes.

2 Stir in the potatoes, olives, capers, and salt and pepper to taste. Add 1 cup of water and bring to a simmer. Cook 15 minutes.

3 In a small bowl, stir together the vinegar and sugar, and add it to the skillet. Continue to cook until the potatoes are tender, about 5 minutes. Remove from the heat and let cool completely. Serve at room temperature.

Potatoes with Balsamic Vinegar
Patate al Balsamico

MAKES 6 SERVINGS

Red onion and balsamic vinegar flavor these potatoes. They are good at room temperature, too.

2 pounds all-purpose potatoes, such as Yukon gold
2 tablespoons olive oil
I large red onion, chopped
2 tablespoons water
Salt and freshly ground black pepper
2 tablespoons balsamic vinegar

1 Scrub the potatoes with a brush under cold running water. Peel them if desired. Cut the potatoes into halves or quarters if large.

2 Heat the oil in a medium saucepan over medium heat. Add the potatoes, onion, water, and salt and pepper to taste. Cover the pan and reduce the heat to low. Cook 20 minutes or until the potatoes are tender.

3 Uncover the pan and stir in the vinegar. Cook until most of the liquid evaporates, about 5 minutes. Serve hot or at room temperature.

Venetian-Style Potatoes
Patate alla Veneziana

MAKES 4 SERVINGS

Though I use Yukon gold potatoes for most cooking, there are many other good varieties available, especially at farmer's markets, and they add variety to potato dishes. Yellow Finn potatoes are good for roasting and baking, and Red Russians are excellent in salads. Though odd looking, blue potatoes can be very good too.

I 1/4 pounds all-purpose potatoes, such as Yukon gold
2 tablespoons unsalted butter
I tablespoon olive oil
I medium onion, chopped
Salt and freshly ground black pepper
2 tablespoons chopped fresh flat-leaf parsley

1 Scrub the potatoes with a brush under cold running water. Peel them if desired. Cut the potatoes into halves or quarters if large. In a large skillet, melt the butter with the oil over medium heat. Add the onion and cook until softened, about 5 minutes.

2 Add the potatoes and salt and pepper to taste. Cover the pan and cook, stirring occasionally, about 20 minutes, or until the potatoes are tender.

3 Add the parsley and stir well. Serve hot.

"Jumped" Potatoes
Patate al Salto

MAKES 4 SERVINGS

When you order fried potatoes in an Italian restaurant, this is what you get. The potatoes become lightly crusty on the outside and soft and creamy inside. They are called "jumped" potatoes because they need frequent stirring or tossing in the pan.

1 1/4 pounds all-purpose potatoes, such as Yukon gold
1/4 cup olive oil
Salt and freshly ground black pepper

1 Scrub the potatoes with a brush under cold running water. Peel the potatoes. Cut them into 1-inch pieces.

2 Pour the oil into a 9-inch skillet. Place the pan over medium-high heat until the oil is very hot and a piece of potato sizzles when added.

3 Dry the potatoes well with paper towels. Add the potatoes to the hot oil and let cook 2 minutes. Turn the potatoes and cook 2 minutes more. Continue cooking and turning the potatoes every 2 minutes or until lightly browned on all sides, about 10 minutes in all.

4 Add salt and pepper to taste. Cover the pan and cook, turning occasionally, until the potatoes are tender when pierced with a knife, about 5 minutes. Serve immediately.

Variation: Potatoes with Garlic and Herbs: In step 4 add 2 garlic cloves, chopped, and a tablespoon of chopped fresh rosemary or sage.

Potato-Pepper Sauté
Patate e Peperoni in Padella

MAKES 6 SERVINGS

Peppers, garlic, and hot red pepper flavor this tasty sauté.

1 1/4 pounds all-purpose potatoes, such as Yukon gold
4 tablespoons olive oil
2 large red or yellow bell peppers, cut into 1-inch pieces
Salt
1/4 cup chopped fresh flat-leaf parsley
2 large garlic cloves
Pinch of crushed red pepper

1 Scrub the potatoes with a brush under cold running water. Peel the potatoes and cut them into 1-inch pieces.

2 In a large skillet, heat 2 tablespoons of the oil over medium heat. Dry the potatoes well with paper towels and place them in the pan. Cook, stirring the potatoes from time to time, until they begin to turn brown, about 10 minutes. Sprinkle with salt. Cover the pan and cook 10 minutes.

3 While the potatoes cook, in another skillet, heat the remaining 2 tablespoons oil over medium heat. Add the bell peppers and salt to taste. Cook, stirring occasionally, until the peppers are almost tender, about 10 minutes.

4 Stir the potatoes, then add the peppers. Stir in the parsley, garlic, and crushed red pepper. Cook until the potatoes are tender, about 5 minutes. Serve hot.

Mashed Potatoes with Parsley and Garlic
Patate Schiacciate all'Aglio e Prezzemolo

MAKES 4 SERVINGS

Mashed potatoes get an Italian treatment with parsley, garlic, and olive oil. If you like your potatoes spicy, stir in a big pinch of crushed red pepper.

1 1/4 pounds all-purpose potatoes, such as Yukon gold
Salt
1/4 **cup olive oil**
1 large garlic clove, finely chopped
1 tablespoon chopped fresh flat-leaf parsley
Freshly ground black pepper

1 Scrub the potatoes with a brush under cold running water. Peel the potatoes and cut them into quarters. Place the potatoes in a medium saucepan with cold water to cover and salt to taste. Cover and bring to a simmer. Cook 15 minutes or until the potatoes are tender when pierced with a knife. Drain the potatoes, reserving some of the water.

2 Dry the pan in which the potatoes were cooked. Add 2 tablespoons of the oil and the garlic and

(continues)

cook over medium heat until the garlic is just fragrant, about 1 minute. Add the potatoes and parsley to the pan. Mash the potatoes with a masher or a fork, stirring them well to blend them with the garlic and parsley. Add the remaining oil, and salt and pepper to taste. Add a little of the cooking water if needed. Serve immediately.

Variation: Mashed Potatoes with Olives: Stir in 2 tablespoons chopped black or green olives just before serving.

Herbed New Potatoes with Pancetta
Patatine alle Erbe Aromatiche

MAKES 4 SERVINGS

Little new potatoes are delicious cooked this way. (New potatoes are not a variety. Any freshly dug potato with thin skin can be called a new potato.) Use an all-purpose potato if new potatoes are not available.

1 1/4 pounds small new potatoes
2 ounces sliced pancetta, diced
I medium onion, chopped
2 tablespoons olive oil
I garlic clove, finely chopped
6 fresh basil leaves, torn into bits
I teaspoon chopped fresh rosemary
I bay leaf
Salt and freshly ground black pepper

1 Scrub the potatoes with a brush under cold running water. Peel them if desired. Cut the potatoes into 1-inch pieces.

2 Combine the pancetta, onion, and olive oil in a large skillet. Cook over medium heat until softened, about 5 minutes.

3 Add the potatoes and cook, stirring occasionally, for 10 minutes.

4 Stir in the garlic, basil, rosemary, bay leaf, and salt and pepper to taste. Cover the pan and cook

for 20 minutes more, stirring occasionally, until the potatoes are tender when pierced with a fork. Add a little water if the potatoes begin to brown too rapidly.

5 Remove the bay leaf and serve hot.

Potatoes with Tomatoes and Onions
Patate alla Pizzaiola

MAKES 6 TO 8 SERVINGS.

Potatoes roasted with pizza flavors are typical in Naples and elsewhere in the south.

2 pounds all-purpose potatoes, such as Yukon gold
2 large tomatoes, peeled, seeded, and chopped
2 medium onions, sliced
I garlic clove, finely chopped
1/2 teaspoon dried oregano
1/4 cup olive oil
Salt and freshly ground black pepper

1 Preheat the oven to 450°F. Scrub the potatoes with a brush under cold running water. Peel them if desired. Cut the potatoes into 1-inch pieces. In a baking pan large enough to hold the ingredients in a single layer, toss together the potatoes, tomatoes, onions, garlic, oregano, oil, and salt and pepper to taste. Spread the ingredients out evenly in the pan.

2 Place a rack in the center of the oven. Roast the vegetables, stirring 2 or 3 times, for 1 hour or until the potatoes are cooked through. Serve hot.

Roasted Potatoes with Garlic and Rosemary
Patate Arrosto

MAKES 4 SERVINGS

I can never make enough of these crusty brown potatoes. No one can resist them. The trick to making them is to use a pan large enough so that the potato pieces are barely touching and not piled on top of one another. If your roasting pan is not large enough, use a 15 × 10 × 1–inch jelly roll pan, or use two smaller pans.

2 pounds all-purpose potatoes, such as Yukon gold
¼ cup olive oil
1 tablespoon chopped fresh rosemary
Salt and freshly ground black pepper
2 garlic cloves, finely chopped

1 Place a rack in the center of the oven. Preheat the oven to 400°F. Scrub the potatoes with a brush under cold running water. Peel them if desired. Cut the potatoes into 1-inch pieces. Dry the potatoes with paper towels. Put them in a roasting pan large enough to hold the potatoes in a single layer. Drizzle with the oil and toss with the rosemary and salt and pepper to taste. Spread the potatoes out evenly.

2 Roast the potatoes, stirring every 15 minutes, for 45 minutes. Stir in the garlic and cook 15 minutes more or until the potatoes are tender. Serve hot.

Roasted Potatoes with Mushrooms
Patate e Funghi al Forno

MAKES 6 SERVINGS

The potatoes pick up some of the mushroom and garlic aromas as they roast in the same pan.

1½ pounds all-purpose potatoes, such as Yukon gold
1 pound mushrooms, any kind, halved or quartered if large
¼ cup olive oil
2 to 3 garlic cloves, thinly sliced
Salt and freshly ground black pepper
2 tablespoons chopped fresh flat-leaf parsley

1 Place a rack in the center of the oven. Preheat the oven to 400°F. Scrub the potatoes with a brush under cold running water. Peel them if desired. Cut the potatoes into 1-inch pieces. Place the potatoes and mushrooms in a large roasting pan. Toss the vegetables with the oil, garlic, and a generous sprinkle of salt and pepper.

2 Roast the vegetables 15 minutes. Toss them well. Bake 30 minutes more, stirring occasionally, or until the potatoes are tender. Sprinkle with chopped parsley and serve hot.

Potatoes and Cauliflower, Basilicata Style
Patate e Cavolfiore al Forno

MAKES 4 TO 6

Put a pan of potatoes and cauliflower in the oven alongside a roast pork or chicken for a fine Sunday dinner. The vegetables should be crisp and brown around the edges, their flavors enhanced by the perfume of the oregano.

1 small cauliflower
¼ cup olive oil
3 medium all-purpose potatoes, such as Yukon gold quartered
½ teaspoon dried oregano, crumbled
Salt and freshly ground black pepper

1 Cut the cauliflower into 2-inch florets. Trim off the ends of the stems. Cut thick stems crosswise into ¼-inch slices.

2 Place a rack in the center of the oven. Preheat the oven to 400°F. Pour the oil into a 13 × 9 × 2–inch roasting pan. Add the vegetables and toss well. Sprinkle with the oregano and salt and pepper to taste. Toss again.

3 Bake 45 minutes or until the vegetables are tender and browned. Serve hot.

Potatoes and Cabbage in the Pan
Patate e Cavolo in Tegame

MAKES 4 TO 6 SERVINGS

Versions of this dish exist all over Italy. In Friuli, smoked pancetta is added to the skillet with the onion. I like this simple version from Basilicata. The pale pink of the onion complements the creamy white potatoes and green cabbage. The potatoes become so soft that they are like mashed potatoes by the time the cabbage is tender.

3 tablespoons olive oil
I medium red onion, chopped
1/2 head medium cabbage, thinly sliced (about 4 cups)
3 medium all-purpose potatoes, such as Yukon gold, peeled and cut into bite-size pieces
1/2 cup water
Salt and freshly ground black pepper

I Pour the oil into a large skillet. Add the onion and cook over medium heat, stirring frequently, until softened, about 5 minutes.

2 Stir in the cabbage, potatoes, water, and salt and pepper to taste. Cover and cook, stirring occasionally, 30 minutes or until the vegetables are soft. Add a little more water if the vegetables begin to stick. Serve hot.

Potato and Spinach Torte
Torta di Patate e Spinaci

MAKES 8 SERVINGS

When I had this layered vegetable torte in Rome, it was made with chicory instead of spinach. Roman chicory looks something like young dandelion or mature arugula. Spinach is a good stand-in for the chicory. For best flavor, be sure to let this dish cool slightly before serving it.

2 pounds all-purpose potatoes, such as Yukon gold
Salt
4 tablespoons unsalted butter
I small onion, very finely chopped
1 1/2 pounds spinach, chicory, dandelion, or Swiss chard, trimmed
1/2 cup water
1/2 cup hot milk
I cup freshly grated Parmigiano-Reggiano
Freshly ground black pepper
I tablespoon plain bread crumbs

I Scrub the potatoes with a brush under cold running water. Peel the potatoes and place them in a medium pot with cold water to cover. Add salt and cover the pot. Bring to a boil and cook about 20 minutes, or until the potatoes are tender.

2 In a small skillet, melt 2 tablespoons of the butter over medium heat. Add the onion and cook, stirring often, until the onion is tender and golden.

3 Place the spinach in a large pot with the 1/2 cup of water and salt to taste. Cover and cook until tender, about 5 minutes. Drain well and squeeze out the excess liquid. Chop the spinach on a board.

4 Add the spinach to the skillet and stir it together with the onion.

5 When the potatoes are tender, drain them and mash them until smooth. Stir in the remaining 2 tablespoons of butter and the milk. Add 3/4 cup of the cheese and mix well. Season to taste with salt and pepper.

6 Place a rack in the center of the oven. Preheat the oven to 375°F.

7 Generously butter a 9-inch baking dish. Spread half the potatoes in the dish. Make a second layer of all of the spinach. Top with the remaining potatoes. Sprinkle with the remaining 1/4 cup of cheese and the bread crumbs.

8 Bake 45 to 50 minutes or until the top is golden. Let rest 15 minutes before serving.

Neapolitan Potato Croquettes

Panzerotti or Crocche

MAKES ABOUT 24

In Naples, pizzerias set up sidewalk stands to sell these tasty logs of mashed potatoes in a crisp bread-crumb jacket, making them easy for passersby to eat for lunch or a snack. This, however, is my grandmother's recipe. We ate potato croquettes for holidays and festive occasions all year round, usually as a side dish with roast beef.

2¹/2 pounds all-purpose potatoes, such as Yukon gold
3 large eggs
I cup freshly grated Pecorino Romano
     or Parmigiano-Reggiano
2 tablespoons chopped fresh flat-leaf parsley
¹/4 cup finely chopped salame (about 2 ounces)
Salt and freshly ground black pepper
2 cups plain dry bread crumbs
Vegetable oil for frying

1 Scrub the potatoes with a brush under cold running water. Place the potatoes in a large saucepan with cold water to cover. Cover the pan and bring the water to a boil. Cook over medium heat until the potatoes are tender when pierced with a fork, about 20 minutes. Drain the potatoes, then let them cool slightly. Peel the potatoes. Put them in a large bowl and mash them with a masher or fork until smooth.

2 Separate the eggs, putting the yolks in a small bowl and setting the whites aside in a shallow dish. Spread the bread crumbs on a sheet of wax paper.

3 Stir the egg yolks, cheese, parsley, and salame into the mashed potatoes. Add salt and pepper to taste.

4 Using about ¹/4 cup of the potato mixture, form a sausage shape about 1 inch wide and 2¹/2 inches long. Repeat with the remaining potatoes.

5 Beat the egg whites with a whisk or a fork until frothy. Dip the potato logs into the whites, then roll them in the crumbs, coating them completely. Place the logs on a wire rack and let dry 15 to 30 minutes.

6 Pour about ¹/2 inch of the oil into a large heavy skillet. Heat over medium heat until a bit of the egg white sizzles when dropped in the oil. Carefully place some of the logs in the pan, leaving a little space between them. Fry them, turning occasionally with tongs, until evenly browned, about 10 minutes. Transfer the browned croquettes to paper towels to drain.

7 Serve immediately or keep the croquettes warm in a low oven while frying the remainder.

Dad's Neapolitan Potato Pie

Gatto'

MAKES 6 TO 8 SERVINGS

Gatto' comes from the French gateau, *meaning "cake." The derivation leads me to think this recipe was made popular by the French-trained* monzu—*chefs who cooked for the aristocrats at the court of Naples.*

In our house, we called this potato pie, and if we weren't having potato croquettes with our Sunday dinner, we had this potato dish, which was my father's specialty.

2¹/2 pounds all-purpose potatoes, such as Yukon gold
Salt
¹/4 cup plain dry bread crumbs
4 tablespoons (¹/2 stick) unsalted butter, softened
I cup warm milk
I cup plus 2 tablespoons freshly grated
     Parmigiano-Reggiano
I large egg, beaten
¹/4 teaspoon freshly grated nutmeg
Salt and freshly ground black pepper
8 ounces fresh mozzarella, chopped
4 ounces salame or imported Italian prosciutto,
     chopped

(continues)

1 Scrub the potatoes with a brush under cold running water. Place the potatoes in a large saucepan with cold water to cover. Add salt to taste. Cover the pan and bring the water to a boil. Cook over medium heat until the potatoes are tender when pierced with a fork, about 20 minutes. Drain and let cool slightly.

2 Place a rack in the center of the oven. Preheat the oven to 400°F. Butter a 2-quart baking dish. Sprinkle with the bread crumbs.

3 Peel the potatoes, put them in a large bowl, and mash them with a masher or fork until smooth. Stir in 3 tablespoons of the butter, the milk, 1 cup of the Parmigiano, the egg, nutmeg, and salt and pepper to taste. Fold in the mozzarella and salame.

4 Spread the mixture evenly in the prepared dish. Sprinkle with the remaining Parmigiano. Dot with the remaining 1 tablespoon butter.

5 Bake 35 to 45 minutes or until the top is browned. Let stand briefly at room temperature before serving.

Tomatoes

A perfectly ripe tomato needs no more enhancement than a bit of salt. Sadly, though, the season for ripe tomatoes is a brief one. And when they are in season, there are often so many around that you can't eat them fast enough.

Cooking helps to bring out the flavor of tomatoes that are less than perfect and extends the tomato season. In the winter, when tomatoes are out of season, do not make recipes that rely on fresh tomatoes. Despite the efforts of chemists to bring us ripe tomatoes year round, the winter ones, though they may be pretty and round and unblemished, are overpriced and disappointing in flavor. The only possible exception is the grape tomato, a relatively new cultivar that is very sweet and tasty.

Looks may be deceiving with tomatoes. A uniform bright red color and globe shape does not always signify the best-tasting tomato. The most delicious tomatoes I have eaten are heirloom varieties that were streaked with green or yellow and unevenly shaped. In Liguria recently, I had a variety called Cuore di Bue ("beef heart") that was extraordinary. I hope these catch on and are as good in the United States as they were in Italy. Good tomatoes should be heavy for their size and free of soft spots.

Skillet Tomatoes
Pomodori in Padella

MAKES 6 TO 8 SERVINGS

Serve these as a side dish with grilled or roasted meats, or at room temperature, mashed onto toasted country bread as an appetizer.

8 plum tomatoes
¹/₄ cup olive oil
2 garlic cloves, finely chopped
2 tablespoons chopped fresh basil
Salt and freshly ground black pepper

1 Rinse the tomatoes and pat dry. With a small knife, cut around the stem end of each tomato and remove it. Cut the tomatoes in half lengthwise.

2 In a large skillet, heat the oil with the garlic and basil over medium heat. Add the tomato halves cut-side down. Sprinkle with salt and pepper. Cook until the tomatoes are browned and tender, about 10 minutes. Serve hot or at room temperature.

Steamed Tomatoes
Pomodori al Vapore

MAKES 4 SERVINGS

Here, sweet little tomatoes are cooked in their own juices. Serve them as a side dish with meat or fish, or spoon them over a frittata. If the tomatoes are not quite sweet enough, add a pinch of sugar as they cook.

1 pint cherry or grape tomatoes
2 tablespoons extra-virgin olive oil
Salt
6 basil leaves, stacked and cut into narrow strips

1 Rinse the tomatoes and pat dry. Cut them in half through the stem end. In a small saucepan, combine the tomatoes, oil, and salt. Cover the pan and place on low heat. Cook 10 minutes or until the tomatoes are just softened but still hold their shape.

2 Add the basil. Serve hot or at room temperature.

Baked Tomatoes
Pomodori al Forno

MAKES 8 SERVINGS

A bread-crumb topping seasons these tomatoes. They are good with roasted fish and most egg dishes.

8 plum tomatoes
1 cup bread crumbs
4 anchovy fillets, finely chopped
2 tablespoons capers, rinsed and drained
¹/₂ cup freshly grated Pecorino Romano
¹/₂ teaspoon dried oregano
3 tablespoons olive oil
Salt and freshly ground black pepper

1 Rinse and dry the tomatoes. Cut the tomatoes in half lengthwise. With a small spoon, scoop out the seeds into a fine-mesh strainer set over a bowl to collect the juices. In a large skillet, toast the bread crumbs over medium heat, stirring often, until they are just fragrant, not browned, about 5 minutes. Remove from the heat and let cool slightly.

2 Place a rack in the center of the oven. Preheat the oven to 400°F. Oil a large baking pan. Arrange the tomato shells cut-side up in the pan.

3 To the bowl with the tomato juice, add the bread crumbs, anchovies, capers, cheese, oregano, and salt and pepper. Stir in 2 tablespoons of the olive oil. Stuff the mixture into the tomato shells. Drizzle with the remaining tablespoon of oil.

4 Bake 40 minutes or until the tomatoes are tender and the crumbs are golden. Serve hot.

Tomatoes Stuffed with Farro
Pomodori Ripieni

MAKES 4 SERVINGS

Farro, an ancient grain that is popular in Italy, makes a great stuffing for tomatoes when mixed with cheese and onion. I had something like this at L'Angolo Divino, a wine bar in Rome.

1 cup semipearled farro (or substitute wheat
    berries or bulgur)
Salt
4 large round tomatoes
1 small onion, finely chopped
2 tablespoons olive oil
¼ cup grated Pecorino Romano or
    Parmigiano-Reggiano
Freshly ground black pepper

1 In a medium saucepan, bring 4 cups of water to a boil. Add the farro and salt to taste. Cook until the farro is tender but still chewy, about 30 minutes. Drain the farro and place it in a bowl.

2 In a small saucepan, cook the onion in the oil over medium heat until golden, about 10 minutes.

3 Place a rack in the center of the oven. Preheat the oven to 350°F. Oil a small baking pan just large enough to hold the tomatoes.

4 Rinse and dry the tomatoes. Cut a slice ½ inch thick from the top of each tomato and reserve. With a small spoon, scoop out the insides of the tomatoes and place the pulp in a fine-mesh strainer set over a bowl. Arrange the tomato shells in the baking dish.

5 To the bowl with the farro, add the strained tomato liquid, sautéed onion, cheese, and salt and pepper to taste. Spoon the mixture into the tomato shells. Cover the tomatoes with the reserved tops.

6 Bake 20 minutes or until the tomatoes are tender. Serve hot or at room temperature.

Roman Stuffed Tomatoes
Pomodori Ripieni alla Romana

MAKES 6 SERVINGS

This is a classic Roman dish, typically eaten at room temperature as a first course.

¾ cup medium-grain rice, such as Arborio, Carnaroli,
    or Vialone Nano
Salt
6 large round tomatoes
4 tablespoons olive oil
3 anchovy fillets, finely chopped
1 small garlic clove, finely chopped
¼ cup chopped fresh basil
¼ cup freshly grated Parmigiano-Reggiano

1 Bring 1 quart of water to a boil over high heat. Add the rice and 1 teaspoon salt. Reduce the heat to low and simmer for 10 minutes or until the rice is partially cooked but still very firm. Drain well. Put the rice in a large bowl.

2 Place a rack in the center of the oven. Preheat the oven to 350°F. Oil a baking pan just large enough to hold the tomatoes.

3 Cut a ½-inch slice from the top of the tomatoes and reserve. With a small spoon, scoop out the insides of the tomatoes and place the pulp in a fine-mesh strainer set over a bowl. Place the tomato shells in the pan.

4 To the bowl with the rice, add the strained tomato liquid and the oil, anchovies, garlic, basil, cheese, and salt to taste. Stir well. Spoon the mixture into the tomato shells. Cover the tomatoes with the reserved tops.

5 Bake 20 minutes or until the rice is tender. Serve hot or at room temperature.

Roasted Tomatoes with Balsamic Vinegar
Pomodori al Balsamico

MAKES 6 SERVINGS

Balsamic vinegar has a nearly magical way of enhancing the flavor of vegetables. Try this simple dish and serve it as an appetizer or with meats.

8 plum tomatoes
2 tablespoons olive oil
I tablespoon balsamic vinegar
Salt and freshly ground black pepper

I Place a rack in the center of the oven. Preheat the oven to 375°F. Oil a baking dish large enough to hold the tomatoes in a single layer.

2 Rinse the tomatoes and pat dry. Cut the tomatoes in half lengthwise. Scoop out the tomato seeds. Place the tomato halves cut-sides up in the pan. Drizzle with the oil and vinegar and sprinkle with salt and pepper.

3 Bake the tomatoes 45 minutes or until tender. Serve at room temperature.

❧ Zucchini and Winter Squash

Practically every part of the zucchini plant is edible. Sicilians make soup out of the green leaves and vines, known as *tenerumi*. Zucchini and other large squash flowers are stuffed with meat or cheese and fried or poached. The zucchini themselves are used in countless preparations.

Occasionally, I find pale green *romanesco* zucchini in my farmer's market. These are more flavorful than the familiar dark green variety and less watery. The most important thing about zucchini is to choose the smallest ones you can find. They have fewer and more tender seeds and more flavor. The gigantic zucchini generous gardeners are always trying to foist on unsuspecting friends are watery and all but useless.

Winter squashes are sold by the slice in Italy. The varieties used there are often very large, but their texture is similar to the hard squashes found in the United States. Most of the time I rely on butternut squash, which are sweet and buttery, though acorn, Hubbard, or pumpkin can also be used.

Zucchini Carpaccio
Carpaccio in Giallo e Verde

MAKES 4 SERVINGS

I first ate a simpler version of this refreshing salad at the home of winemaker friends in Tuscany. Over the years, I have embellished it by using a combination of yellow and green zucchini and adding fresh mint.

2 or 3 small zucchini, preferably a mix of yellow and green
3 tablespoons fresh lemon juice
1/3 cup extra-virgin olive oil
Salt and freshly ground black pepper
2 tablespoons finely chopped fresh mint
About 2 ounces Parmigiano-Reggiano, in I piece

(continues)

1 Scrub the zucchini with a brush under cold running water. Trim off the ends.

2 In a food processor or on a mandoline slicer, cut the zucchini into very thin slices. Place the slices in a medium bowl.

3 In a small bowl, whisk together the lemon juice, olive oil, and salt and pepper to taste until blended. Stir in the mint. Drizzle over the zucchini and toss well. Spread the slices out on a shallow platter.

4 With a vegetable peeler, shave the Parmigiano into thin slices. Scatter the slices over the zucchini. Serve immediately.

Zucchini with Garlic and Mint
Zucchine a Scapece

MAKES 8 SERVINGS

Zucchini or other squash, eggplant, and carrots can be prepared a scapece, "in the style of Apicius," an early Roman who wrote about food. The vegetables are fried, flavored, and then chilled. Be sure to make this at least 24 hours before serving for best flavor.

2 pounds small zucchini
Vegetable oil for frying
3 tablespoons red wine vinegar
2 large garlic cloves, finely chopped
1/4 cup chopped fresh mint or basil
Salt and freshly ground black pepper

1 Scrub the zucchini with a brush under cold running water. Trim off the ends. Cut the zucchini into 1/4-inch slices.

2 Pour 1 inch of oil into a deep heavy skillet or wide saucepan. Heat the oil over medium heat until a small piece of vegetable dropped into the oil sizzles.

3 Pat the zucchini slices dry with paper towels. Carefully slip about one-fourth of the zucchini into the hot oil. Cook until lightly browned around the edges, about 3 minutes. With a slotted spoon, transfer the zucchini to paper towels to drain. Fry the remainder in the same way.

4 Layer the zucchini in a dish, sprinkling each layer with some of the vinegar, garlic, mint, and salt and pepper to taste. Cover and refrigerate at least 24 hours before serving.

Sautéed Zucchini
Zucchine in Padella

MAKES 6 SERVINGS

This is a quick way to make a tasty side dish with zucchini, onions, and parsley.

1 pound small zucchini
2 tablespoons unsalted butter
1 small onion, very finely chopped
Salt and freshly ground black pepper
3 tablespoons chopped flat-leaf parsley

1 Scrub the zucchini with a brush under cold running water. Trim off the ends. Cut into 1/8-inch slices.

2 In a medium skillet over medium-low heat, melt the butter. Add the onion and cook until softened, about 5 minutes.

3 Add the zucchini and toss to coat with the butter. Cover and cook 5 minutes, or until the zucchini is just tender when pierced with a fork.

4 Add the salt and pepper to taste and parsley and toss well. Serve immediately.

Zucchini with Prosciutto
Zucchine al Prosciutto

MAKES 4 SERVINGS

These zucchini are good as a side dish with chicken, but also as a sauce for hot cooked penne or another pasta.

1 1/2 pounds small zucchini
1 medium onion, chopped
2 tablespoons olive oil
1 garlic clove, chopped
1/2 teaspoon dried marjoram or thyme
Salt and freshly ground black pepper
3 thin slices imported Italian prosciutto, cut crosswise into narrow strips

1 Scrub the zucchini with a brush under cold running water. Trim off the ends. Cut the zucchini into $1/8$-inch slices.

2 In a large skillet, cook the onion in the oil over medium heat. Cook, stirring, until the onion is tender and golden, about 10 minutes. Add the garlic and marjoram and cook 1 minute more.

3 Stir in the zucchini slices and salt and pepper to taste. Cook 5 minutes.

4 Add the prosciutto and cook until the zucchini are tender, about 2 minutes more. Serve hot.

Zucchini with Parmesan Crumbs
Zucchine alla Parmigiana

MAKES 4 SERVINGS

Buttery, cheesy bread crumbs flavor this zucchini gratin.

1 pound small zucchini
2 tablespoons unsalted butter, melted and cooled
2 tablespoons bread crumbs, preferably homemade
$1/4$ cup grated Parmigiano-Reggiano
Salt and freshly ground pepper

1 Scrub the zucchini with a brush under cold running water. Trim off the ends.

2 Place a rack in the center of the oven. Preheat oven to 425°F. Butter a $13 \times 9 \times 2$–inch baking dish.

3 Spread the zucchini slices in the baking dish, overlapping slightly. In a medium bowl, mix together the butter, crumbs, cheese, and salt and pepper to taste. Sprinkle the crumb mixture over the zucchini.

4 Bake 30 minutes or until the crumbs are golden and the zucchini are tender. Serve hot.

Zucchini Gratin
Zucchine Gratinate

MAKES 4 TO 6 SERVINGS

When I think of this gratin, I imagine serving it as part of a summer picnic buffet, with grilled meat or fish and several salads. It is good hot or cold.

2 medium yellow onions, chopped
2 garlic cloves, finely chopped
4 tablespoons olive oil
Salt and freshly ground black pepper
1 tablespoon chopped fresh thyme, basil, or oregano
4 small zucchini, cut into $1/8$-inch slices
3 medium round tomatoes, cut into thin slices
$1/2$ cup grated Parmigiano-Reggiano

1 In a medium skillet, cook the onions and garlic in 2 tablespoons of the olive oil over medium-low heat until golden, about 10 minutes. Season with salt and pepper to taste.

2 Place a rack in the center of the oven. Preheat the oven to 375°F. Oil a $13 \times 9 \times 2$–inch baking dish.

3 Spread the onion mixture evenly in the baking dish. Scatter one-third of the thyme over the onions. Arrange the zucchini and tomatoes in overlapping slices over the onions. Sprinkle with the remaining thyme, and salt and pepper to taste. Drizzle with the remaining olive oil.

4 Bake 40 to 45 minutes or until the vegetables are tender and the juices are sizzling. Sprinkle with the cheese and bake until slighly melted, about 5 minutes more. Let rest 10 minutes before serving.

Zucchini with Tomatoes and Anchovies

Zucchine al Forno

MAKES 4 SERVINGS

This southern-style gratin is flavored with anchovies and garlic.

1 pound small zucchini
4 plum tomatoes, thinly sliced
1/4 cup plain dry bread crumbs
3 anchovy fillets, chopped
2 tablespoons olive oil
1 small garlic clove, finely chopped
Salt and freshly ground black pepper

1 Scrub the zucchini with a brush under cold running water. Trim off the ends. Cut into 1/8-inch slices.

2 Place a rack in the center of the oven. Preheat the oven to 375°F. Oil a 13 × 9 × 2–inch baking pan. Arrange the zucchini and tomatoes in overlapping rows in the pan.

3 In a medium bowl, stir together the bread crumbs, anchovies, oil, garlic, and salt and pepper to taste. Scatter the mixture over the vegetables.

4 Bake 30 minutes, or until the vegetables are tender. Let rest 10 minutes before serving.

Zucchini Stew

Ciambotta di Zucchine

MAKES 4 TO 6 SERVINGS

Here is another member of the southern Italian ciambotta family of vegetable stews, one that my mom used to make again and again in the summer when I was growing up. Though I wasn't fond of it as a child, because we had it so often, I enjoy it—once in a while—now.

3 small to medium zucchini
2 medium onions, chopped
3 tablespoons olive oil
1 garlic clove, very finely chopped
4 plum tomatoes, cut into bite-size pieces
2 medium potatoes, peeled and cut into bite-size pieces
Salt and freshly ground black pepper
2 tablespoons chopped fresh basil

1 Scrub the zucchini with a brush under cold running water. Trim off the ends. Cut the zucchini into bite-size pieces.

2 In a large saucepan, cook the onions in the oil over medium heat until softened, about 5 minutes. Stir in the garlic and cook 1 minute more.

3 Add the tomatoes, zucchini, potatoes, and salt and pepper to taste. Cover and cook, stirring occasionally, 30 minutes or until the potatoes are very tender. Add a little water if the mixture seems dry.

4 When the ciambotta is done, remove from the heat and stir in the basil. Serve hot or at room temperature.

Zucchini Stuffed with Amaretti

Zucchine Ripiene Dolci

MAKES 6 SERVINGS

Amaretti cookies add a surprising sweet note and nutty flavor to these stuffed zucchini. I had them in Cremona in Lombardy. Serve this with roast turkey or chicken.

6 small zucchini
Salt
2 amaretti cookies, crumbled
2 tablespoons bread crumbs
1 large egg, beaten
2 tablespoons unsalted butter, melted
1 teaspoon sugar

1 Scrub the zucchini with a brush under cold running water. Trim off the ends. Bring a medium pot of water to a boil. Add the zucchini and salt to taste. Simmer until softened, about 5 minutes. Drain the zucchini and cool under running water.

2 Place a rack in the center of the oven. Preheat the oven to 400°F. Butter a small baking pan.

3 Cut the zucchini in half lengthwise. With a small spoon, scoop out the pulp, leaving a 1/4-inch shell, and set the pulp aside. Place the shells cut-side up in the prepared pan.

4 Chop the zucchini pulp and place it in a bowl with the amaretti, bread crumbs, egg, butter, and 1/4 teaspoon salt. Stir well.

5 Spoon the mixture into the zucchini shells. Sprinkle with the sugar. Bake 30 minutes or until the zucchini are browned and tender when pierced with a knife. Serve hot.

Zucchini Stuffed with Porcini Mushrooms
Zucchine al Porcini

SERVES 6

The woodsy flavor of dried porcini enhances the flavor of these baked stuffed zucchini.

1/2 cup dried porcini mushrooms

2 cups warm water

6 medium zucchini

I large egg, beaten

1/2 cup plain bread crumbs

1/4 cup plus 2 tablespoons freshly grated
     Parmigiano-Reggiano

I garlic clove, finely chopped

I tablespoon chopped fresh flat-leaf parsley

Pinch of freshly grated nutmeg

Salt and freshly ground black pepper

1 Soak the mushrooms in the water for 30 minutes. Remove the mushrooms and reserve the liquid. Rinse the mushrooms under cold running water

to remove any grit, paying special attention to the ends of the stems where soil collects. Chop the mushrooms finely. Strain the mushroom liquid through a paper coffee filter into a clean bowl. Reserve the liquid for another use.

2 Scrub the zucchini with a brush under cold running water. Trim off the ends.

3 Place a rack in the center of the oven. Preheat the oven to 400°F. Oil a 13 × 9 × 2–inch roasting pan.

4 Cut the zucchini in half lengthwise. With a small spoon, scoop out the pulp, leaving a 1/4-inch shell, and set the pulp aside. Arrange the zucchini shells cut-side up in the prepared pan.

5 Chop the zucchini pulp and place it in a bowl with the mushrooms, egg, bread crumbs, cheese, garlic, parsley, nutmeg, and salt and pepper to taste. Spoon the mixture into the zucchini shells. Sprinkle with the remaining 2 tablespoons cheese.

6 Bake 30 minutes or until the zucchini are tender when pierced with a knife and the filling is golden. Serve hot or at room temperature.

Tuna-Stuffed Zucchini
Zucchine al Tonno

MAKES 6 SERVINGS

I had these as an appetizer at a countryside restaurant in Tuscany. I often serve them as a main dish with a green salad.

2 slices day-old Italian or French bread,
     crust removed (about 1/3 cup bread)

1/2 cup milk

6 small zucchini, trimmed

I (6 1/2-ounce) can tuna packed in olive oil

1/4 cup freshly grated Parmigiano-Reggiano
     plus 2 tablespoons

I garlic clove, finely chopped

2 tablespoons finely chopped fresh flat-leaf parsley

Freshly grated nutmeg

Salt and freshly ground black pepper

I large egg, lightly beaten

(continues)

1 Place a rack in the center of the oven. Preheat the oven to 425°F. Oil a baking pan just large enough to hold the zucchini halves in a single layer.

2 Sprinkle the bread with the milk and let soak until softened. Scrub the zucchini with a brush under cold running water. Trim off the ends.

3 Cut the zucchini in half lengthwise. With a small spoon, scoop out the pulp, leaving a 1/4-inch shell, and set the pulp aside. Arrange the zucchini shells cut-side up in the prepared pan. Chop the zucchini pulp and place it in a bowl.

4 Drain the tuna, reserving the oil. Mash the tuna in a large bowl. Squeeze out the bread and add it to the tuna along with the chopped zucchini pulp, 1/4 cup of cheese, garlic, parsley, nutmeg, and salt and pepper to taste. Mix well. Stir in the egg.

5 Spoon the mixture into the zucchini shells. Arrange the zucchini in the baking pan. Drizzle with a little of the reserved tuna oil. Sprinkle with the remaining cheese. Pour 1/2 cup of water around the zucchini.

6 Bake 30 to 40 minutes or until the zucchini are browned and tender when pierced with a knife. Serve warm or at room temperature.

Fried Zucchini
Zucchine Fritte

MAKES 6 SERVINGS

Beer gives this batter good flavor and color, while the bubbles make it light. The batter is also good for frying fish, onion rings, and other vegetables.

6 small zucchini
1 cup all-purpose flour
2 large eggs
1/4 cup beer
Vegetable oil for frying
Salt

1 Scrub the zucchini with a brush under cold running water. Trim off the ends. Cut the zucchini into 2 × 1/4 × 1/4–inch strips.

2 Spread the flour on a sheet of wax paper. In a medium shallow bowl, beat the eggs until foamy. Beat in the beer until well blended.

3 Pour about 2 inches of the oil into a deep heavy saucepan or into a deep-fryer following the manufacturer's instructions. Heat the oil over medium heat until a drop of egg mixture sizzles when added to the pan and the temperature reaches 370°F on a frying thermometer.

4 Dredge about one-quarter of the zucchini strips in flour, then dip them in the egg mixture.

5 Holding the zucchini with tongs, let the excess batter drip off, then place the zucchini in the oil one piece at a time. Add only as many as will fit without crowding. Fry the zucchini until crisp and golden brown, about 2 minutes. Remove the zucchini with a slotted spoon. Drain on paper towels. Keep warm in a low oven while frying the remainder.

6 Sprinkle with salt and serve hot.

Zucchini Flans
Sformato di Zucchine

MAKES 6 SERVINGS

You will need six little ramekins or ovenproof cups to make these delicate flans. Serve them as a side dish with roasts or with ham for a spring brunch. I usually let them rest a minute or two and then unmold them, but if you serve them straight from the oven while they are still puffed, they make a fine first course soufflé. Hurry, though; they sink fast.

You can substitute broccoli, asparagus, carrots, or other vegetables for the zucchini.

1 tablespoon unsalted butter, melted
3 medium zucchini, cut into thick slices
4 large eggs, separated
1/2 cup grated Parmigiano-Reggiano
Pinch of salt
Pinch of ground nutmeg

1 Scrub the zucchini with a brush under cold running water. Trim off the ends.

2 Place a rack in the center of the oven. Preheat the oven to 350°F. Generously brush six 4-ounce ramekins or ovenproof custard cups with the melted butter.

3 Bring a large pot of water to a boil. Add the zucchini and bring to a simmer. Cook 1 minute. Drain the zucchini well. Pat the pieces dry with paper towels. Pass the zucchini through a food mill or blend in a processor until smooth. Transfer the zucchini puree to a large bowl.

4 Add the egg yolks, Parmigiano, salt, and nutmeg to the zucchini and stir well.

5 In a large bowl, with an electric mixer, beat the egg whites until they hold soft peaks when the beater is lifted. With a rubber spatula, gently fold the whites into the zucchini mixture.

6 Pour the mixture into the cups. Bake 15 to 20 minutes or until the tops are lightly spotted with brown and a knife inserted near the center comes out clean. Remove the cups from the oven. Let rest 2 minutes, then run a small knife around the inside of the cups and invert the flans onto a plate.

Sweet-and-Sour Winter Squash
Fegato dei Sette Cannoli

The Sicilian name for this squash is "liver of the seven cannons." The Seven Cannons district of Palermo, named for a famous fountain and monument, was once so poor that its residents could not afford meat. They substituted squash in this recipe, which is typically prepared with liver. It can also be made with zucchini, carrot, or eggplant slices.

Plan to make this at least one day before serving it, because the flavor improves as it stands. It keeps well for several days.

Though Sicilians typically fry the squash, I prefer to bake it. This is also good as an antipasto.

1 small butternut, acorn, or other winter squash
    or pumpkin, cut into ¹/₄-inch-thick slices
Olive oil
¹/₃ cup red wine vinegar
1 tablespoon sugar
Salt
2 garlic cloves, very finely chopped
¹/₃ cup chopped fresh flat-leaf parsley or mint

1 Rinse the squash and pat dry. Cut off the ends with a large heavy chef's knife. Peel off the skin with a vegetable peeler. Cut the squash in half and scoop out the seeds. Cut the squash into ¹/₄-inch thick slices. Preheat the oven to 400°F.

2 Generously brush the squash slices on both sides with the oil. Arrange the slices on baking sheets in a single layer. Bake 20 minutes or until softened. Turn the slices and bake 15 to 20 minutes more, or until the squash is tender when pierced with a knife and lightly browned.

3 Meanwhile, heat the vinegar, sugar, and salt to taste in a small saucepan. Stir until the sugar and salt are dissolved.

4 On a platter or in a shallow bowl, arrange some of the squash slices in a single layer, overlapping slightly. Sprinkle with some of the garlic and parsley. Repeat the layering until all of the squash, garlic, and parsley are used. Pour the vinegar mixture over all. Cover and refrigerate at least 24 hours before serving.

❧ Mixed Vegetables

Grilled Vegetables
Verdure alla Griglia

MAKES 8 SERVINGS

Grilling is one of the best ways to cook vegetables. The grill gives them a smoky flavor, and the grill marks add visual appeal. Cut the vegetables into thick slices or large pieces so that they do not fall through the grill rack into the flames. If you like, these can be dressed with an oil and vinegar dressing before serving.

1 medium eggplant (about 1 pound) cut into
⅟₂-inch-thick slices
Salt
1 large red or Spanish onion, cut into ⅟₂-inch-thick
slices
4 large mushrooms, such as portabello, stems removed
4 medium tomatoes, cored and cut in half crosswise
2 large red or yellow bell peppers, cored, seeded,
and cut into quarters
Olive oil
Freshly ground black pepper
6 fresh basil leaves, torn into bits

1 Trim the tops and bottoms of the eggplants. Cut the eggplant crosswise into ⅟₂-inch-thick slices. Sprinkle the eggplant slices generously with salt. Place the slices in a colander and let stand over a plate to drain 30 minutes. Rinse off the salt with cool water and dry the slices with paper towels.

2 Place a barbecue grill or broiler rack about 5 inches away from the heat source. Preheat the grill or broiler.

3 Brush the vegetable slices with olive oil and place them with the oiled side toward the source of the heat. Cook until lightly browned, about 5 minutes. Turn the slices and brush them with oil. Cook until browned and tender, about 4 minutes. Sprinkle the vegetables with salt and pepper.

4 Arrange the vegetables on a platter. Drizzle with additional oil and sprinkle with the basil. Serve hot or at room temperature.

Roasted Winter Root Vegetables
Verdure al Forno

MAKES 6 SERVINGS

This was inspired by the beautifully browned, savory vegetables that often accompany roast meats in northern Italy. If your pan is not big enough to hold the vegetables in a single layer, use two pans.

2 medium turnips, peeled and quartered
2 medium carrots, peeled and cut into 1-inch lengths
2 medium parsnips, peeled and cut into 1-inch lengths
2 medium all-purpose potatoes, cut into quarters
2 medium onions, cut into quarters
4 garlic cloves, peeled
⅓ cup olive oil
Salt and freshly ground black pepper

1 Place a rack in the center of the oven. Preheat the oven to 450°F. Combine the cut-up vegetables and garlic cloves in a large roasting pan. The vegetables should be only one layer deep. Use two pans, if necessary, so that the vegetables are not crowded. Toss the vegetables with the oil and salt and pepper to taste.

2 Roast the vegetables about 1 hour 10 minutes, turning them every 15 minutes or so until they are tender and browned.

3 Transfer the vegetables to a serving dish. Serve hot.

Summer Vegetable Stew
Ciambotta

SERVES 4 TO 6

In the summertime, I go to our local farmer's market several times a week. I love to talk to the farmers and try the many unusual products they sell. If it weren't for the market, I am sure I would never have tasted things like red dandelion, purslane, lamb's quarters, and so many other vegetables that you can't find in supermarkets. Unfortunately, I often buy too much. That's when I make ciambotta, *a southern Italian vegetable stew.*

This particular ciambotta is the classic one, a combination of eggplant, peppers, potatoes, and tomatoes. It is wonderful as a side dish or topped with grated cheese as a meatless main dish. You can also eat it cold spread on toasted bread for crostini and warm as a sandwich filling with sliced mozzarella.

I medium onion

4 plum tomatoes

2 all-purpose potatoes, peeled

I medium eggplant

I medium red bell pepper

I medium yellow bell pepper

Salt and freshly ground black pepper

3 tablespoons olive oil

1/2 cup torn fresh basil leaves or freshly grated
    Parmigiano-Reggiano or Pecorino Romano
    (optional)

1 Trim the vegetables and cut them into bite-size pieces. In a large skillet, cook the onion in the oil over medium-low heat until tender, about 5 to 8 minutes.

2 Add the tomatoes, potatoes, eggplant, and peppers. Add salt and pepper to taste. Cover and cook, stirring occasionally, about 40 minutes, or until all the vegetables are tender and most of the liquid has evaporated. If the mixture becomes too dry, add a couple of tablespoons of water. If there is too much liquid, uncover and cook 5 minutes more.

3 Serve warm or at room temperature, plain or garnished with basil or cheese.

Variation: Ciambotta with Eggs: When the vegetables are ready, beat 4 to 6 eggs with salt until blended. Pour the eggs over the vegetables. Do not stir. Cover the pan. Cook until the eggs are set, about 3 minutes. Serve warm or at room temperature.

Layered Vegetable Casserole
Teglia di Verdure

SERVES 6 TO 8

Use an attractive bake-and-serve dish for this casserole, and serve the vegetables out of the dish. It goes well with frittatas, chicken, and many other dishes.

I medium eggplant (about I pound), peeled and
    thinly sliced

Salt

3 medium all-purpose potatoes (about I pound),
    peeled and thinly sliced

Freshly ground black pepper

2 medium onions

I red and I green bell pepper, cored and thinly sliced

3 medium tomatoes, chopped

6 basil leaves, torn into bits

1/3 cup olive oil

1 Peel the eggplant and cut it into thin crosswise slices. Layer the slices in a colander, sprinkling each one generously with salt. Place the colander over a plate and let stand 30 to 60 minutes to drain. Rinse the eggplant slices and pat them dry.

2 Place a rack in the center of the oven. Preheat the oven to 375°F. Generously oil a 13 × 9 × 2– inch baking dish.

3 Make a layer of overlapping potato slices on the bottom of the dish. Sprinkle with salt and pepper. Cover the potatoes with a layer of eggplant and sprinkle with salt. Add layers of onions, peppers, and tomatoes. Sprinkle with salt and pepper. Scatter the basil over the top. Drizzle with the olive oil.

4 Cover with foil. Bake 45 minutes. Carefully remove the foil. Cook 30 minutes more or until browned and the vegetables are tender when pierced with a knife. Serve warm or at room temperature.

Breads, Pizzas, Savory Pies, and Sandwiches

Breads

Homestyle Bread

Herb Bread

Marches-Style Cheese Bread

Golden Corn Rolls

Black Olive Bread

Stromboli Bread

Walnut Cheese Bread

Tomato Rolls

Country Brioche

Flatbreads and Breadsticks

Sardinian Music-Paper Bread

Red Onion Flatbread

White Wine Flatbread

Sun-Dried Tomato Flatbread

Roman Potato Flatbread

Griddle Breads from Emilia-Romagna

Breadsticks

Fennel Rings

Almond and Black Pepper Rings

Pizzas and Turnovers

Homestyle Pizza

Neapolitan-Style Pizza Dough

Mozzarella, Tomato, and Basil Pizza

Tomato, Garlic, and Oregano Pizza

Pizza with Wild Mushrooms

Calzoni

Anchovy Fritters

Tomato and Cheese Turnovers

Savory Pies

Easter Pie

Sicilian Swordfish Torte

Green Onion Pie

Escarole Pie

Savory Pie Pastry

Spinach Ricotta Tart

Leek Tart

Italian Sandwiches (Panini)

Mozzarella, Basil, and
Roasted Pepper Sandwiches

Spinach and Robiola Sandwiches

Riviera Sandwich

Tuna and Roasted Pepper
Triangle Sandwiches

Prosciutto and Fig Triangle Sandwiches

Buono come il pane, "good as bread," is an old Italian way of describing someone or something very special. It also illustrates how important is bread. Every Italian knows that bread is the ultimate, the best, and nothing could be better than bread. Whether it is the *rosetta*, a sectioned round roll that is all crust and little crumb, or the *scaletta*, ladder-shaped, golden, hard-wheat loaves from Sicily baked in ovens fired with almond shells, Italian breads have wonderful character and flavor. Every region has a distinctive style. Tuscan and Umbrian bread is made without salt, which takes some getting used to. The bread from Altamura in Puglia is pale golden and practically a national treasure. People in Rome and places to the north pay premium prices to get it. Roman bread is moist inside and full of holes, with a crunchy, toasty brown crust.

Then there are the flatbreads: pizza, focaccia, *piadina*, and all the other delicious variations. Every region has its favorite. Naples is proud of its reputation as the birthplace of the modern pizza, while the Genovese take credit for focaccia. Instead of having the flavoring on top, in southern Italy, savory pies made from two layers of bread or pizza dough baked around a filling of vegetables, meats, or cheese are popular, eaten as a snack or a full meal.

The recipes that follow are just a few of the many possibilities. Few Italians bake bread at home, because every neighborhood has a local *forno* ("oven"), as the bread bakery is called, where fresh bread is baked several times a day. The breads are made with slowly risen doughs that create complex flavors and good texture and chewiness. Because they are baked in ovens that reach temperatures higher than those in home kitchens, they have crisp crunchy crusts.

The recipes in this chapter work well without a lot of special equipment. However, if you enjoy making yeast breads, it would be worthwhile to invest in a baking stone or unglazed baking tiles. A heavy-duty mixer equipped with a dough hook or a large capacity food processor makes short work of mixing a heavy, sticky dough. A bread machine can also be used to mix and raise the dough, but is not appropriate for baking these types of breads.

I have also included recipes for savory tarts made with cheese and vegetables. These are good for a first course or with a salad for a whole meal.

Sandwiches are popular for snacks and light meals all over Italy. The Milanese have invented the *paninoteca,* a sandwich shop where you can order your heart's desire of combinations on all sorts of bread, to be served toasted or not. The paninoteca is especially popular with younger people, who stop by for sandwiches and beer.

In other parts of the country, you can eat a panino made with white bread, focaccia, or rolls. The Romans love the thin, crustless *tramezzino* (triangle-cut) sandwich, while in Bologna the sandwiches are made on rosette, the local crusty rolls. On my way home from Italy, I always leave time for a stop at the airport *caffè* for a prosciutto and arugula sandwich *portare via*, "to take away," and enjoy it on the plane home.

❧ Breads

Homestyle Bread
Pane di Casa

MAKES 2 LOAVES

Here's a basic Italian-style bread that turns out nice and crusty in a home oven. Because the dough is very sticky, it is best to make this bread in either a heavy-duty mixer or food processor. Don't be tempted to add more flour to the dough. It should be very moist to get the right results, with large holes in the crumb and a crunchy crust.

1 teaspoon active dry yeast
2 cups warm water (100° to 110°F)
4 1/2 cups bread flour
2 teaspoons salt
2 tablespoons fine semolina

1 Pour the water into a heavy-duty mixer bowl. Sprinkle with the yeast. Let stand until the yeast is creamy, about 2 minutes. Stir until the yeast dissolves.

2 Add the flour and salt. Stir well until a soft dough forms. The dough should be very sticky. Beat the dough until it is smooth and elastic, about 5 minutes.

3 Oil the inside of a large bowl. Scrape the dough into the bowl, turning it over to oil the top. Cover with plastic wrap and let rise in a warm, draft-free place until doubled in bulk, about 1 1/2 hours.

4 Flatten the dough and divide it in half. Shape each piece into a ball. Scatter the semolina on a large baking sheet. Place the balls of dough several inches apart on the baking sheet. Cover with plastic wrap and let rise in a warm, draft-free place until doubled, about 1 hour.

5 Place the rack in the center of the oven. Preheat the oven to 450°F. With a razor blade or very sharp knife, cut an X into the top of each loaf. Transfer the dough to the baking stone. Bake until the loaves are golden brown and sound hollow when tapped on the bottom, 40 minutes.

6 Slide the loaves onto racks to cool completely. Store wrapped in foil up to 24 hours at room temperature or in the freezer up to one month.

Bread-Making Tips

- Test the temperature of the water or milk for dissolving the yeast with an instant-read thermometer.
- Baking bread on a stone or quarry tiles makes the crust golden brown and crunchy. Place the stone or tiles in the oven to heat at least 30 minutes before adding the bread dough. Place the dough on a floured pizza peel or rimless baking sheet. Slide the dough onto the stone or tiles and bake as directed.

Herb Bread
Pane alle Erbe

MAKES ONE 12-INCH LOAF

In the town of Forlimpopoli, in Emilia-Romagna, I ate at a restaurant that a young couple had opened in a seventeenth-century villa. Before the meal, they brought out a delicious herb bread. When I inquired about it, the cook gladly shared the recipe, advising me that for best results I should go out to the garden at dawn to pick the herbs while they were still wet with the morning dew. But you will still get good results with herbs picked fresh from the supermarket.

I envelope (2¹/₂ teaspoons) active dry yeast
      or 2 teaspoons instant yeast
I cup warm water (100° to 110°F)
2 tablespoons unsalted butter, melted and cooled
About 2¹/₂ cups unbleached all-purpose flour
I tablespoon sugar
I teaspoon salt
I tablespoon chopped fresh flat-leaf parsley
I tablespoon chopped fresh mint
I tablespoon chopped fresh thyme
I tablespoon snipped fresh chives
I egg yolk plus I tablespoon water

1 Pour the water into a large bowl. Sprinkle with the yeast. Let stand until the yeast is creamy, about 2 minutes. Stir until the yeast dissolves.

2 Add the butter and 2 cups flour, the sugar, and the salt and stir until a soft dough forms. Turn the dough out onto a lightly floured surface. Sprinkle with the herbs and knead until smooth and elastic, about 10 minutes, adding more flour as necessary to make a moist but not sticky dough. (Or make the dough in a heavy-duty mixer, food processor, or bread machine following the manufacturer's directions.)

3 Oil the inside of a large bowl. Put the dough in the bowl, turning it once to oil the top. Cover with plastic wrap and let rise in a warm spot until doubled in volume, about 1 hour.

4 Oil a large baking sheet. Place the dough on a lightly floured surface and flatten it with your hands to eliminate the air bubbles. Roll the dough between your hands to form a rope about 12 inches long. Lay the dough on the baking sheet. Cover with plastic wrap and let rise until doubled, about 1 hour.

5 Place the rack in the center of the oven. Preheat the oven to 400°F. Brush the dough with the egg yolk mixture. With a razor or very sharp knife, cut 4 slashes across the top. Bake until the loaf is golden brown and sounds hollow when tapped on the bottom, about 30 minutes.

6 Slide the bread onto a wire rack to cool completely. Wrap in foil and store at room temperature up to 24 hours, or freeze up to 1 month.

Marches-Style Cheese Bread
Ciaccia

MAKES ONE 9-INCH ROUND LOAF

The Marches region in central Italy may not be well known as far as food is concerned, but it does have a lot to offer. Along the coast there is excellent seafood, while inland, where there are rugged mountains, the cooking is hearty and features game and truffles. One local specialty is ciauscolo, *a soft sausage made with very finely ground pork flavored with garlic and spices that can be spread on bread. This flavorful bread made with two kinds of cheese is served for snacks or as an appetizer with a glass of wine. It is great for a picnic, with hard-cooked eggs, salami, and a salad.*

I envelope (2¹/₂ teaspoons) active dry yeast
      or 2 teaspoons instant yeast
I cup warm milk (100° to 110°F)
2 large eggs, beaten
2 tablespoons olive oil
¹/₂ cup freshly grated Pecorino Romano
¹/₂ cup freshly grated Parmigiano-Reggiano
About 3 cups unbleached all-purpose flour
¹/₂ teaspoon salt
¹/₂ teaspoon freshly ground black pepper

1 In a large bowl, sprinkle the yeast over the milk. Let stand until the yeast is creamy, about 2 minutes. Stir until the yeast dissolves.

2 Add the eggs, oil, and cheeses and beat well. With a wooden spoon, stir in the flour, salt, and pepper until a soft dough forms. Turn the dough out onto a lightly floured surface. Knead until smooth and elastic, about 10 minutes, adding more flour as necessary to make a moist but not sticky dough. (Or make the dough in a heavy-duty mixer, food processor, or bread machine following the manufacturer's directions.) Shape the dough into a ball.

3 Oil the inside of a large bowl. Place the dough in the bowl, turning it once to oil the top. Cover with plastic and let rise 1 1/2 hours or until doubled in bulk.

4 Press the dough down to eliminate the air bubbles. Shape the dough into a ball.

5 Oil a 9-inch springform pan. Add the dough, cover, and let rise again until doubled, about 45 minutes.

6 Place the rack in the center of the oven. Preheat the oven to 375°F. Brush the top of the dough with the egg yolk. Bake until golden brown, about 35 minutes.

7 Let cool 10 minutes in the pan. Remove the sides of the pan, then slide the bread onto a rack to cool completely. Wrap in foil and store at room temperature up to 24 hours, or freeze up to 1 month.

Golden Corn Rolls
Panini d'Oro

MAKES 8 TO 10 SERVINGS

Little round rolls topped with a half cherry tomato get their golden color from cornmeal. The dough is shaped into balls, which merge into one loaf as they bake. The rolls can be served as a whole loaf, with everyone tearing off his or her own. These are especially good for a soup supper or with cheese.

I envelope (2 1/2 teaspoons) active dry yeast
  or 2 teaspoons instant yeast
1/2 cup warm water (100° to 110°F)
1/2 cup milk
1/4 cup olive oil
About 2 cups unbleached all-purpose flour
1/2 cup fine yellow cornmeal
I teaspoon salt
10 cherry tomatoes, halved

1 In a large bowl, sprinkle the yeast over the water. Let stand until the yeast is creamy, about 2 minutes. Stir until the yeast dissolves. Stir in the milk and 2 tablespoons of the oil.

2 In a large bowl, mix together the flour, cornmeal, and salt.

3 Add the dry ingredients to the liquid and stir until a dough forms. Turn the dough out onto a lightly floured surface. Knead until smooth and elastic, about 10 minutes, adding more flour as necessary to make a moist, slightly sticky dough. (Or make the dough in a heavy-duty mixer, food processor, or bread machine following the manufacturer's directions.) Shape the dough into a ball.

4 Oil the inside of a large bowl. Add the dough, turning once to oil the top. Cover with plastic wrap and let rise 1 1/2 hours in a warm, draft-free place.

5 Oil a 10-inch springform pan. Press the dough down to eliminate the air bubbles. Cut the dough into quarters. Cut each quarter into 5 even pieces. Roll each piece into a ball. Arrange the pieces in the pan. Press a tomato half cut-side down in the center of each piece of dough. Cover with plastic wrap and let rise in a warm place 45 minutes or until doubled.

6 Place the rack in the center of the oven. Preheat the oven to 400°F. Drizzle the dough with the remaining 2 tablespoons olive oil. Bake 30 minutes or until golden brown.

7 Remove the sides of the pan. Slide the rolls onto a rack to cool. Wrap in foil and store at room temperature up to 24 hours, or freeze up to 1 month.

Black Olive Bread
Pane di Olive

MAKES TWO 12-INCH LOAVES

This bread is made with a starter, a mixture of flour, water, and yeast. The starter rises separately and is added to the dough to give extra flavor to the bread. Plan to make the starter at least 1 hour or up to one day ahead of time.

Though I generally use flavorful Italian black olives for this recipe, green olives can be used, too. Or try a mixture of several different types of olives. This bread is popular in the Veneto region.

1 envelope (2 1/2 teaspoons) active dry yeast
    or 2 teaspoons instant yeast

2 cups warm water (100° to 110°F)

About 4 1/2 cups unbleached all-purpose flour

1/2 cup whole wheat flour

2 teaspoons salt

2 tablespoons olive oil

1 1/2 cups flavorful black olives, such as Gaeta,
    pitted and coarsely chopped

1 In a medium bowl, sprinkle the yeast over 1 cup of the water. Let stand until the yeast is creamy, about 2 minutes. Stir until the yeast dissolves. Stir in 1 cup of the all-purpose flour. Cover with plastic wrap and let stand in a cool place until bubbly, about 1 hour or overnight. (If the weather is hot, place the starter in the refrigerator. Remove it about 1 hour before making the dough.)

2 In a large bowl, stir together the remaining 3 1/2 cups of all-purpose flour, the whole wheat flour, and the salt. Add the starter, the remaining 1 cup of warm water, and the oil. With a wooden spoon, stir until a soft dough forms.

3 Turn the dough out onto a lightly floured surface and knead until smooth and elastic, about 10 minutes, adding more flour as necessary to make a moist and slightly sticky dough. (Or make the dough in a heavy-duty mixer, food processor, or bread machine following the manufacturer's directions.) Shape the dough into a ball.

4 Oil the inside of a large bowl. Add the dough, turning it once to oil the top. Cover with plastic wrap and let rise in a warm place until doubled in bulk, about 1 1/2 hours.

5 Oil a large baking sheet. Flatten the dough to remove the air bubbles. Briefly knead in the olives. Divide the dough in two and shape each piece into a loaf about 12 inches long. Place the loaves several inches apart on the prepared baking sheet. Cover with plastic wrap and let rise until doubled in bulk, about 1 hour.

6 Place the rack in the center of the oven. Preheat the oven to 400°F. Using a single-edge razor blade or sharp knife, make 3 or 4 diagonal slashes on the surface of each loaf. Bake 40 to 45 minutes or until golden brown.

7 Slide the loaves onto a rack to cool. Wrap in foil and store at room temperature up to 24 hours, or freeze up to 1 month.

Stromboli Bread
Rotolo di Pane

MAKES TWO 10-INCH LOAVES

As far as I can tell, this bread filled with cheese and cured meats is an Italian-American creation, possibly inspired by the Sicilian bonata, *bread dough wrapped around a filling and baked into a loaf. Stromboli is a famous Sicilian volcano, so the name is probably a reference to the fact that the filling oozes out of the steam vents, resembling molten lava. Serve the bread as an appetizer or snack.*

1 teaspoon active dry yeast or 2 teaspoons
    instant yeast

3/4 cup warm water (100° to 110°F)

About 2 cups unbleached all-purpose flour

1 teaspoon salt

4 ounces sliced mild provolone or Swiss cheese

2 ounces thin-sliced salami

4 ounces sliced ham

1 egg yolk beaten with 2 tablespoons water

1 In a large bowl, sprinkle the yeast over the water. Let stand until the yeast is creamy, about 2 minutes. Stir until the yeast dissolves.

2 Add the flour and salt. With a wooden spoon, stir until a soft dough forms. Turn the dough out onto a lightly floured surface and knead until smooth and elastic, about 10 minutes, adding more flour as necessary to make a moist but not sticky dough. (Or make the dough in a heavy-duty mixer, food processor, or bread machine following the manufacturer's directions.)

3 Oil the inside of a large bowl. Add the dough to the bowl, turning it once to oil the top. Cover with plastic wrap. Place in a warm, draft-free place and let rise until doubled, about 1 1/2 hours.

4 Remove the dough from the bowl and flatten it gently to remove the air bubbles. Cut the dough in half and shape it into two balls. Place the balls on a floured surface and cover each with a bowl. Let rise 1 hour or until doubled.

5 Place an oven rack in the center of the oven. Preheat the oven to 400°F. Oil a large baking sheet.

6 On a lightly floured surface with a rolling pin, flatten one piece of the dough into a 12-inch circle. Arrange half the cheese slices over the dough. Top with half of the ham and salami. Tightly roll up the dough and filling into a cylinder. Pinch the seam to seal. Place the roll seam-side down on the baking sheet. Fold the ends of the dough under the roll. Repeat with the remaining ingredients.

7 Brush the rolls with the egg yolk mixture. With a knife, cut 4 shallow slashes evenly spaced in the top of the dough. Bake 30 to 35 minutes or until golden brown.

8 Transfer to wire racks to cool slightly. Serve warm, cut into diagonal slices. Wrap in foil and store at room temperature up to 24 hours, or freeze up to 1 month.

Walnut Cheese Bread
Pan Nociato

MAKES TWO 8-INCH ROUND LOAVES

With salame, olives, and a bottle of red wine, this Umbrian bread makes a fine meal. This version is savory, but in Todi, one of the region's most beautiful medieval cities, I had a sweet version that was made with red wine, spices, and raisins, and baked in grape leaves.

1 envelope (2 1/2 teaspoons) active dry yeast
 or 2 teaspoons instant yeast
2 cups warm water (100° to 110°F)
About 4 1/2 cups unbleached all-purpose flour
1/2 cup whole wheat flour
2 teaspoons salt
2 tablespoons olive oil
1 cup shredded Pecorino Toscano
1 cup chopped walnuts, toasted

1 In a medium bowl, sprinkle the yeast over 1 cup of the water. Let stand until the yeast is creamy, about 2 minutes. Stir until the yeast dissolves.

2 In a large bowl, stir together 4 cups of the all-purpose flour, the whole wheat flour, and the salt. Add the yeast mixture, the remaining 1 cup warm water, and the oil. Stir with a wooden spoon until a soft dough forms. Turn the dough out onto a lightly floured surface and knead until smooth and elastic, about 10 minutes, adding more flour as necessary to make a moist, slightly sticky dough. (Or make the dough in a heavy-duty mixer, food processor, or bread machine following the manufacturer's directions.)

3 Oil the inside of a large bowl. Add the dough, turning it once to oil the top. Cover with plastic wrap and let rise in a warm place until doubled in bulk, about 1 1/2 hours.

4 Oil a large baking sheet. Flatten the dough to remove the air bubbles. Scatter the cheese and nuts

(continues)

on top and knead just to distribute the ingredients. Divide the dough in two and shape each piece into a round loaf. Place the loaves several inches apart on the prepared baking sheet. Cover with plastic wrap and let rise until doubled in bulk, about 1 hour.

5 Place the oven rack in the center of the oven. Preheat the oven to 400°F. Using a single-edge razor blade or sharp knife, make 3 or 4 diagonal slashes on the surface of each loaf. Bake until golden brown and the loaves sound hollow when tapped on the bottom, about 40 to 45 minutes.

6 Slide the loaves onto a rack to cool completely. Serve at room temperature. Wrap in foil and store at room temperature up to 24 hours or freeze up to 1 month.

Tomato Rolls
Panini al Pomodoro

MAKES 8 ROLLS

Tomato paste tints these rolls a nice orangey red and adds a hint of tomato flavor. I like to use the double-concentrated tomato paste sold in tubes like toothpaste. It has good sweet tomato flavor, and because most recipes require just a tablespoon or two of the paste, you can use just as much as you need, then close the tube and store it in the refrigerator, unlike canned tomato paste.

Though I don't often think of the Veneto when I think of tomatoes, these rolls are popular there.

I envelope (2¹/₂ teaspoons) active dry yeast
    or 2 teaspoons instant yeast
¹/₂ cup plus ³/₄ cup warm water (100° to 110°F)
¹/₄ cup tomato paste
2 tablespoons olive oil
About 2³/₄ cups unbleached all-purpose flour
2 teaspoons salt
I teaspoon dried oregano, crumbled

1 In a medium bowl, sprinkle the yeast over ¹/₂ cup of the water. Let stand until the yeast is creamy,

about 2 minutes. Stir until the yeast dissolves. Add the tomato paste and the rest of the water and stir until smooth. Stir in the olive oil.

2 In a large mixing bowl, stir together the flour, salt, and oregano.

3 Pour the liquid into the dry ingredients. With a wooden spoon, stir until a soft dough forms. Turn the dough out onto a lightly floured surface and knead until smooth and elastic, about 10 minutes, adding more flour as necessary to make a moist, slightly sticky dough. (Or make the dough in a heavy-duty mixer, food processor, or bread machine following the manufacturer's directions.)

5 Oil the inside of a large bowl. Add the dough, turning it once to oil the top. Cover with plastic wrap and let rise 1¹/₂ hours or until doubled.

6 Oil a large baking sheet. Flatten the dough to eliminate air bubbles. Cut the dough into 8 even pieces. Shape each piece into a ball. Arrange the balls several inches apart on the baking sheet. Cover with plastic wrap and let rise until doubled, about 1 hour.

7 Place the rack in the center of the oven. Preheat the oven to 400°F. Bake until the rolls are golden brown and sound hollow when tapped on the bottom, about 20 minutes.

8 Slide the rolls onto a wire rack to cool completely Serve at room temperature. Store wrapped in foil up to 24 hours, or freeze up to 1 month.

Country Brioche
Brioche Rustica

MAKES 8 SERVINGS

Butter- and egg-rich brioche dough, probably introduced by French cooks in Naples around 1700, is enhanced with chopped prosciutto and cheese. This tasty bread makes a fine antipasto, or serve it with a salad course before or after a meal. Note that this dough is beaten until smooth and not kneaded.

1/2 cup warm milk (100° to 110°F)

1 envelope (2 1/2 teaspoons) active dry yeast
     or 2 teaspoons instant yeast

4 tablespoons (1/2 stick) unsalted butter, at room
     temperature

1 tablespoon sugar

1 teaspoon salt

2 large eggs, at room temperature

About 2 1/2 cups unbleached all-purpose flour

1/2 cup chopped fresh mozzarella, blotted dry if moist

1/2 cup chopped provolone

1/2 cup chopped prosciutto

1 Pour the milk into a small bowl and sprinkle the yeast in. Let stand until the yeast is creamy, about 2 minutes. Stir until the yeast dissolves.

2 In a large heavy-duty mixer bowl or a food processor, beat the butter, sugar, and salt until blended. Beat in the eggs. With a wooden spoon, stir in the milk mixture. Add the flour and beat until smooth. The dough will be sticky.

3 On a lightly floured surface, shape the dough into a ball. Cover with an inverted bowl and let rest 30 minutes.

4 Butter and flour a 10-inch tube or Bundt pan.

5 Lightly flour a rolling pin. Roll out the dough to a rectangle 22 × 8 inches. Scatter the cheese and meat over the dough, leaving a 1-inch border on the long sides. Starting at one long side, tightly roll up the dough to form a cylinder. Pinch the seam to seal. Place the roll seam-side down in the prepared pan. Pinch the ends together to seal. Cover the pan with plastic wrap. Let the dough rise in a warm, draft-free place until doubled, about 1 1/2 hours.

6 Place the oven rack in the center of the oven. Preheat the oven to 350°F. Bake until the loaves are golden brown and sound hollow when tapped on the bottom, about 35 minutes.

7 Slide the loaves onto a wire rack to cool completely. Serve at room temperature. Wrap in foil and store at room temperature up to 24 hours, or freeze up to 1 month.

❧ Flatbreads and Breadsticks

Sardinian Music-Paper Bread
Carta da Musica

MAKES 8 TO 12 SERVINGS

Big sheets of paper-thin bread are called "music paper" in Sardinia, because at one time bread, like the paper, was rolled up for easier storage. Sardinians snap the sheets into smaller pieces to eat them with meals or as a snack with soft goat or sheep's cheese, or soak them in soup, or layer them with sauces like pasta. Semolina flour can be found in many specialty stores or in catalogs such as the King Arthur Flour Baker's Catalogue (Sources, page 626).

About 1 1/4 cups unbleached all-purpose or bread flour

1 1/4 cups fine semolina flour

1 teaspoon salt

1 cup warm water

1 In a large bowl, combine the all-purpose or bread flour, the semolina flour, and the salt. With a wooden spoon, stir in the water until the mixture forms a soft dough.

2 Scrape the dough onto a lightly floured surface. Knead the dough, adding additional flour as necessary, to form a stiff dough that is smooth and elastic, about 5 minutes. Shape the dough into a ball. Cover with an inverted bowl and let rest at room temperature for 1 hour.

3 Place the rack in the center of the oven. Preheat the oven to 450°F.

4 Divide the dough into six pieces. With a rolling pin on a lightly floured surface, roll out one piece of dough to a 12-inch circle, thin enough so that you can see your hand through it when the dough

(continues)

is held up to the light. Drape the dough over the rolling pin to lift it. Lay the dough on an ungreased baking sheet, being careful to straighten out any wrinkles.

5 Bake about 2 minutes or until the top of the bread is just firm. Protect one hand with a potholder, and holding a large metal spatula in the other hand, turn the dough over. Bake about 2 minutes more or until lightly browned.

6 Transfer the bread to a wire rack to cool completely. Repeat with the remaining dough.

7 To serve, break each sheet into 2 or 4 pieces. Store leftovers in a dry place in a tightly sealed plastic bag.

Variation: To serve as an appetizer, reheat the bread on a baking sheet in a low oven for 5 minutes or until warm. On a plate, stack the pieces, drizzling each layer with extra-virgin olive oil and coarse salt or chopped fresh rosemary. Serve warm.

Red Onion Flatbread
Focaccia alle Cipolle Rosso

MAKES 8 TO 10 SERVINGS

The dough for this focaccia is very moist and sticky, so it is mixed entirely in a bowl without any kneading. Mix it by hand with a wooden spoon, or use a heavy-duty electric mixer, food processor, or bread machine. A long, slow rise gives this bread a delicious flavor and light cakey texture. Though most focaccias taste best warm, this one is so moist that it holds up even at room temperature.

I envelope (2¹/₂ teaspoons) active dry yeast or instant yeast
¹/₂ cup warm water (100° to 110°F)
1¹/₂ cups milk, at room temperature
6 tablespoons olive oil
About 5 cups unbleached all-purpose flour
2 tablespoons finely chopped fresh rosemary
2 teaspoons salt
¹/₂ cup coarsely chopped red onion

1 In a medium bowl, sprinkle the yeast over the warm water. Let stand until the yeast is creamy, about 2 minutes. Stir until the yeast dissolves. Add the milk and 4 tablespoons of the oil and stir to combine.

2 In a large heavy-duty mixer bowl or a food processor, stir together the flour, rosemary, and salt. Add the yeast mixture and stir until a soft dough forms. Knead until smooth and elastic, about 3 to 5 minutes. The dough will be sticky.

3 Oil a large bowl. Scrape the dough into the bowl and cover it with plastic wrap. Let rise in a warm, draft-free place until doubled, about 1¹/₂ hours.

4 Oil a 13 × 9 × 2–inch baking pan. Scrape the dough into the pan, spreading it out evenly. Cover with plastic wrap and let rise 1 hour or until doubled in bulk.

5 Place the oven rack in the center of the oven. Preheat the oven to 450°F.

6 With your fingertips, press down firmly into the dough to make dimples about 1 inch apart and ¹/₂ inch deep. Drizzle the surface with the remaining 2 tablespoons olive oil and scatter the onion slices on top. Sprinkle with coarse salt. Bake until crisp and golden brown, about 25 to 30 minutes.

7 Slide the focaccia onto a wire rack to cool. Cut into squares. Serve warm or at room temperature. Store at room temperature wrapped in foil up to 24 hours.

White Wine Flatbread
Focaccia al Vino

MAKES 8 TO 10 SERVINGS

White wine gives this Genoa-style focaccia a unique flavor. It is usually topped with crystals of coarse sea salt, but you can substitute fresh sage or rosemary if you prefer. In Genoa, it is eaten at every meal, including breakfast, and schoolchildren pick up a slice at the bakery to eat for their midmorning snack. The dough for this focaccia is very moist and sticky, so it is best to make it in a heavy-duty mixer or food processor.

This focaccia is made with a starter—a combination of yeast, flour, and water that gives many breads extra flavor and good texture. The starter can be made as little as 1 hour or as much as 24 hours before making the bread, so plan accordingly.

1 envelope (2¹/2 teaspoons) active dry yeast
    or 2 teaspoons instant yeast
1 cup warm water (100° to 110°F)
About 4 cups unbleached all-purpose flour
2 teaspoons salt
¹/2 cup dry white wine
¹/4 cup olive oil

TOPPING

3 tablespoons extra-virgin olive oil
1 teaspoon coarse sea salt

1 To make the starter, sprinkle the yeast over the water. Let stand until the yeast is creamy, about 2 minutes. Stir until the yeast dissolves. Whisk in 1 cup of the flour until smooth. Cover with plastic wrap and leave at room temperature for about 1 hour or up to 24 hours. (If the weather is hot, place the starter in the refrigerator. Remove it about 1 hour before making the dough.)

2 In a heavy-duty mixer or food processor, combine 3 cups of the flour and the salt. Add the starter, wine, and oil. Stir the dough until smooth and elastic, about 3 to 5 minutes. It will be very sticky, but do not add more flour.

3 Oil the inside of a large bowl. Add the dough. Cover with plastic wrap and let rise in a warm, draft-free place until doubled in bulk, about 1¹/2 hours.

4 Oil a large baking sheet or a 15 × 10 × 1–inch jelly roll pan. Flatten the dough. Place it in the pan, patting and stretching it out with your hands to fit. Cover with plastic wrap and let rise until doubled, about 1 hour.

5 Place the rack in the center of the oven. Preheat the oven to 425°F. Press the dough firmly with your fingertips to make dimples about 1 inch apart all over the surface. Drizzle with the 3 tablespoons

oil. Sprinkle with sea salt. Bake 25 to 30 minutes or until crisp and golden brown.

6 Slide the focaccia onto a rack to cool slightly. Cut into squares or rectangles and serve warm.

Sun-Dried Tomato Flatbread
Focaccia di Pomodori Secchi

MAKES 8 TO 10 SERVINGS

Moist, marinated sun-dried tomatoes are the kind to use for this free-form focaccia. If you only have the dried tomatoes that are not reconstituted, simply soak them in warm water for a few minutes until plumped.

1 teaspoon active dry yeast
1 cup warm water (100° to 110°F)
About 3 cups unbleached all-purpose flour
1 teaspoon salt
4 tablespoons extra-virgin olive oil
8 to 10 pieces marinated sun-dried tomatoes,
    drained and cut into quarters
Pinch of dried oregano, crumbled

1 Sprinkle the yeast over the water. Let stand until the yeast is creamy, about 2 minutes. Stir until the yeast dissolves. Add 2 tablespoons of the oil.

2 In a large bowl, stir together the flour and salt. Add the yeast mixture and stir with a wooden spoon until a soft dough forms.

3 Turn the dough out onto a lightly floured surface. Knead until smooth and elastic, about 10 minutes, adding more flour as necessary to make a moist, slightly sticky dough. (Or make the dough in a heavy-duty mixer, food processor, or bread machine following the manufacturer's directions.) Shape the dough into a ball.

4 Oil the inside of a large bowl. Add the dough, turning once to oil the top. Cover with plastic wrap and let rise in a warm, draft-free place until doubled in bulk, about 1¹/2 hours.

(continues)

5 Oil a large baking sheet or a 12-inch round pizza pan. Place the dough on the pan. Oil your hands and flatten the dough out to a 12-inch circle. Cover with plastic wrap and let rise until doubled, about 45 minutes.

6 Place the oven rack in the center of the oven. Preheat the oven to 450°F. With your fingertips, make dimples in the dough about 1 inch apart. Press a bit of tomato in each dimple. Drizzle with the remaining 2 tablespoons olive oil, spreading it with your fingers. Sprinkle with the oregano. Bake 25 minutes or until the golden brown.

7 Slide the focaccia onto a cutting board and cut into squares. Serve warm.

Roman Potato Flatbread
Pizza di Patate

MAKES 8 TO 10 SERVINGS

While Romans eat a lot of pizza with the typical toppings, their first love is pizza bianca, *"white pizza," a long rectangular flatbread similar to the Genoa-style focaccia, only crisper and bumpier. Pizza bianca is usually topped only with salt and olive oil, though this variation with thin-sliced crispy potatoes is popular too.*

**1 envelope (2¹/₂ teaspoons) active dry yeast
   or 2 teaspoons instant yeast**
1 cup warm water (100° to 110°F)
About 3 cups unbleached all-purpose flour
1 teaspoon salt plus more for the potatoes
6 tablespoons olive oil
**1 pound yellow-flesh potatoes, such as Yukon gold,
   peeled and very thinly sliced**
Freshly ground black pepper

1 Sprinkle the yeast over the water. Let stand until the yeast is creamy, about 2 minutes. Stir until the yeast dissolves.

2 In a large bowl, combine 3 cups flour and 1 teaspoon of the salt. Add the yeast mixture and 2 tablespoons of the oil. With a wooden spoon,

stir until a soft dough forms. Turn the dough out onto a lightly floured surface and knead until smooth and elastic, about 10 minutes, adding more flour as necessary to make a moist but not sticky dough. (Or make the dough in a heavy-duty mixer, food processor, or bread machine following the manufacturer's directions.)

3 Oil the inside of a large bowl. Add the dough and turn it once to oil the top. Cover with plastic wrap. Let rise in a warm, draft-free place until doubled in bulk, about 1¹/₂ hours.

4 Oil a 15 ×10 × 1–inch pan. Gently flatten the dough and place it in the pan. Stretch and pat the dough out to fit the pan. Cover with plastic wrap and let rise until doubled, about 45 minutes.

5 Place the rack in the center of the oven. Preheat the oven to 425°F. In a bowl, toss the potatoes with the remaining 4 tablespoons olive oil and salt and pepper to taste. Arrange the slices on top of the dough, overlapping them slightly.

6 Bake 30 minutes. Raise the heat to 450°F. Bake 10 minutes more or until the potatoes are tender and browned. Slide the pizza onto a board and cut into squares. Serve hot.

Griddle Breads from Emilia-Romagna
Piadine

MAKES 8 BREADS

Piadina *is a round flatbread baked on a griddle or stone that is popular in Emilia-Romagna. At the beach towns along the Adriatic Coast, colorful striped canvas booths appear on street corners during the summer. Around lunchtime, the booths open for business and the uniform-clad operators roll and bake piadine to order on flat griddles. About nine inches in diameter, the hot piadine are folded in half, then filled with cheese, sliced prosciutto, salami, or sautéed greens (such as* Escarole with Garlic, *pages 434–435), and eaten like sandwiches.*

Though piadine are usually made with lard, I substitute olive oil, as fresh lard is not always available. For an antipasto or snack, cut piadine into wedges.

3¹/2 cups unbleached all-purpose flour
1 teaspoon salt
1 teaspoon baking powder
1 cup warm water
¹/4 cup fresh lard, melted and cooled, or olive oil
Cooked greens, sliced meats, or cheeses

1 In a large bowl, stir together the flour, salt, and baking powder. Add the water and lard or oil. With a wooden spoon, stir until a soft dough forms. Scrape the dough onto a lightly floured surface and knead the dough briefly until it is smooth. Shape the dough into a ball. Cover with an inverted bowl and let rest 30 minutes to 1 hour.

2 Cut the dough into 8 even pieces. Leaving the remaining pieces covered, roll out one piece of the dough into an 8-inch circle. Repeat with the remaining dough, stacking the circles with a piece of wax paper between each one.

3 Preheat the oven to 250°F. Over medium heat, heat a large nonstick skillet or pancake griddle until it is very hot and a drop of water sizzles and disappears quickly when it touches the surface. Place a circle of dough on the surface and cook 30 to 60 seconds, or until the piadina begins to firm up and turns golden brown. Turn the dough and cook for 30 to 60 seconds more, or until nicely browned on the other side.

4 Wrap the piadina in foil and keep warm in the oven while cooking the remaining dough circles in the same way.

5 To serve, place greens or slices of prosciutto, salami, or cheese to one side of a piadina. Fold the piadina over the filling and eat it like a sandwich.

Breadsticks
Grissini

MAKES ABOUT 6 DOZEN BREADSTICKS

A pasta machine fitted with the fettuccine cutter can also make long, thin breadsticks called grissini. *(I also provide instructions if you want or need to cut the breadstick dough by hand.) Vary the flavor by adding ground black pepper or dried herbs such as chopped rosemary, thyme, or oregano to the dough.*

1 envelope (2¹/2 teaspoons) active dry yeast
**   or 2 teaspoons instant yeast**
1 cup warm water (100° to 110°F)
2 tablespoons extra-virgin olive oil
About 2¹/2 cups unbleached all-purpose flour
**   or bread flour**
1 teaspoon salt
2 tablespoons yellow cornmeal

1 In a large bowl, sprinkle the yeast over the water. Let stand until the yeast is creamy, about 2 minutes. Stir until the yeast dissolves.

2 Stir in the olive oil. Add 2¹/2 cups of the flour and the salt. Stir until a soft dough forms.

3 On a lightly floured surface, knead the dough until firm and elastic, about 10 minutes, adding additional flour as needed to make a nonsticky dough. (Or make the dough in a heavy-duty mixer, food processor, or bread machine following the manufacturer's directions.)

4 Oil the inside of a large bowl. Place the dough in the bowl, turning it once to oil the top. Cover with plastic wrap and let rise in a warm, draft-free place until doubled in bulk, about 1¹/2 hours.

5 Place two racks in the center of the oven. Preheat the oven to 350°F. Sprinkle two large baking sheets with cornmeal.

6 Knead the dough briefly to eliminate air bubbles. Divide the dough into 6 pieces. Flatten one piece of dough into a 5 × 4 × ¹/4–inch oval. Dust it with additional flour so that it is not sticky. Keep the remaining dough covered.   *(continues)*

7 Insert a short end of the dough into the fettuccine cutter on a pasta machine and cut the dough into 1/4-inch strips. To cut the dough by hand, flatten it with a rolling pin on a cutting board. Cut into 1/4-inch strips with a large heavy knife dipped in flour.

8 Arrange the strips 1/2 inch apart on one of the prepared baking sheets. Repeat with the remaining dough. Bake 20 to 25 minutes or until lightly browned, rotating the pans about halfway throughe.

9 Cool in pans on wire racks. Store in an airtight container up to 1 month.

Fennel Rings
Taralli al Finocchio

MAKES 3 DOZEN RINGS

Taralli are crisp, ring-shaped bread sticks. They can be flavored simply with olive oil or with crushed red pepper, black pepper, oregano, or other herbs, and are popular all over southern Italy. There are also sweet taralli, which are good for dunking in wine or with coffee. Taralli can be as small as a nickel or several inches in size, but they are always hard and crunchy. I like to serve them with wine and cheese.

I envelope (2¹/₂ tablespoons) active dry yeast
    or 2 teaspoons instant yeast
¹/₄ cup warm water (100° to 110°F)
I cup unbleached all-purpose flour
I cup semolina flour
I tablespoon fennel seeds
I teaspoon salt
¹/₃ cup dry white wine
¹/₄ cup olive oil

1 In a measuring cup, sprinkle the yeast over the water. Let stand until the yeast is creamy, about 2 minutes. Stir until the yeast dissolves.

2 In a large bowl, stir together the two flours, the fennel, and the salt. Add the yeast mixture, wine, and oil. Stir until a soft dough forms, about 2 minutes. Scrape the dough onto a lightly floured surface

and knead until smooth and elastic, about 10 minutes. Shape the dough into a ball.

3 Oil the inside of a large bowl. Place the dough in the bowl, turning it once to oil the top. Cover and let rise in a warm, draft-free place until doubled in bulk, about 1 hour.

4 Divide the dough into thirds, then each third in half to make 6 even pieces. Keeping the remainder covered with an overturned bowl, cut one piece into 6 even pieces. Roll out the pieces into 4-inch lengths. Shape each into a ring, pinching the ends together to seal. Repeat with the remaining dough.

5 Lay out several lint-free kitchen towels. Fill a large skillet half-full with water. Bring the water to a boil. Add the dough rings a few at a time. (Do not crowd them.) Boil 1 minute or until the rings rise to the surface. Remove the rings with a slotted spoon and place them on the kitchen towels to drain. Repeat with the remaining dough.

6 Place two racks in the center of the oven. Preheat the oven to 350°F. Arrange the dough rings an inch apart on 2 large ungreased baking sheets. Bake until golden brown, about 45 minutes, rotating the pans about halfway through. Turn off the oven and open the door slightly. Let the rings cool in the oven for 10 minutes.

7 Transfer the rings to wire racks to cool. Store in an airtight container up to 1 month.

Almond and Black Pepper Rings
Taralli con le Mandorle

MAKES 32 RINGS

Whenever I go to Naples, one of my first stops is the bakery to buy a big bag of these crunchy bread rings. They are more flavorful than pretzels or other snacks and perfect for munching before or with meals. The Neapolitans make them with pork lard, which gives them a marvelous flavor and melt-in-the-mouth texture, but they are also excellent made with olive oil. These keep well and are nice to have on hand for company.

1 envelope (2¹/₂ tablespoons) active dry yeast
    or 2 teaspoons instant yeast
1 cup warm water (100° to 110°F)
¹/₂ cup pork lard, melted and cooled, or olive oil
3¹/₂ cups unbleached all-purpose flour
2 teaspoons salt
2 teaspoons freshly ground black pepper
1 cup almonds, finely chopped

1 Sprinkle the yeast over the water. Let stand until the yeast is creamy, about 2 minutes. Stir until the yeast dissolves.

2 In a large bowl, combine the flour, salt, and pepper. Stir in the yeast mixture and the lard. Stir until a soft dough forms. Turn the dough out onto a lightly floured surface and knead until smooth and elastic, about 10 minutes. Knead in the almonds.

3 Shape the dough into a ball. Cover the dough with an overturned bowl and let rise in a warm place until doubled, about 1 hour.

4 Place 2 racks in the center of the oven. Preheat the oven to 350°F. Press the dough down to eliminate the air bubbles. Cut the dough in half, then cut each half in half again, then each quarter in half to make 8 even pieces. Keeping the remaining dough covered, divide 1 piece into 4 even pieces. Roll each piece into a 6-inch rope. Twist each rope 3 times, then shape it into a ring, pinching the ends to seal. Place the rings 1 inch apart on two ungreased baking sheets. Repeat with the remaining dough.

5 Bake the rings for 1 hour or until browned and crisp, rotating the pans about halfway through. Turn off the heat and let the rings cool and dry out in the oven for 1 hour.

6 Remove from the oven and transfer to wire racks to cool completely. Store in an airtight container up to 1 month.

➽ Pizzas and Turnovers

Homestyle Pizza
Pizza di Casa

MAKES 6 TO 8 SERVINGS

If you visit a home in southern Italy, this is the type of pizza you will be served. It is quite different from the round, pizzeria-type pie.

A homemade pizza is about ³/₄ of an inch thick when baked in a large pan. Because the pan is oiled, the bottom gets crunchy. It is baked with just a light sprinkling of grated cheese rather than mozzarella, which would become too chewy if the pizza was served at room temperature, as it often is. This type of pizza will stand up well to reheating.

Try this pie with a sausage or mushroom sauce and add mozzarella or another melting cheese if you plan to eat it as soon as it is baked.

DOUGH

1 envelope (2¹/₂ tablespoons) active dry yeast
    or 2 teaspoons instant yeast
1¹/₄ cups warm water (100° to 110°F)
About 3¹/₂ cups unbleached all-purpose flour
2 teaspoons salt
2 tablespoons olive oil

TOPPING

1 recipe (about 3 cups) Pizzaiola Sauce (page 91)
¹/₂ cup freshly grated Pecorino Romano
Olive oil

1 Prepare the dough: Sprinkle the yeast over the water. Let stand until the yeast is creamy, about 2 minutes. Stir until the yeast dissolves.

2 In a large bowl, combine 3¹/₂ cups of the flour and the salt. Add the yeast mixture and the olive oil. Stir with a wooden spoon until a soft dough forms. Turn the dough out onto a lightly floured surface and knead until smooth and elastic, adding

(continues)

more flour if necessary to make a moist but not sticky dough, about 10 minutes. (Or make the dough in a heavy-duty mixer, food processor, or bread machine following the manufacturer's directions).

3 Lightly coat a large bowl with oil. Place the dough in the bowl, turning it once to oil the top. Cover with plastic wrap. Place in a warm, draft-free spot and let rise until doubled, about 1¹/₂ hours.

4 Place a rack in the center of the oven. Oil a 15 × 10 × 1–inch jelly roll pan. Gently flatten the dough. Place the dough in the center of the pan and stretch and pat it out to fit. Cover it with plastic wrap and let it rise about 45 minutes, or until puffy and nearly doubled in bulk.

5 While the dough rises in the pan, prepare the sauce. Preheat the oven to 450°F. With your fingertips, firmly press the dough to make dimples at 1-inch intervals all over the surface. Spread the sauce over the dough, leaving a ¹/₂-inch border all the way around. Bake 20 minutes.

6 Sprinkle with the cheese. Drizzle with oil. Return the pizza to the oven and bake 5 minutes, or until the cheese is melted and the crust is browned. Cut into squares and serve hot or at room temperature.

Neapolitan-Style Pizza Dough

MAKES ENOUGH FOR FOUR 9-INCH PIZZAS

In Naples, where pizza making is an art form, the ideal pizza crust is chewy and only slightly crisp, flexible enough that it can be folded without the crust cracking. Neapolitan pizzas are neither thick and cakey nor thin and crunchy.

To achieve the right balance with the type of flour available in the United States, a combination of soft, low-gluten cake flour and harder, higher gluten all-purpose flour is needed. For a crisper crust, increase the amount of all-purpose flour and proportionally decrease the amount of cake flour.

Bread flour, which is very high in gluten, would make the pizza crust too hard.

Pizza dough can be mixed and kneaded in a heavy-duty electric mixer or food processor or even in a bread machine. For real pizza-shop texture, bake the pies directly on a baking stone or unglazed quarry tiles, available in cookware stores.

This recipe makes enough for four pizzas. In Naples, everyone gets his or her own pizza, but because it is difficult to bake more than one pie at a time in a home oven, I cut each pie into wedges for serving.

1 teaspoon active dry yeast or instant yeast
1 cup warm water (100 to 110°F)
1 cup plain cake flour (not self-rising)
About 3 cups unbleached all-purpose flour
2 teaspoons salt

1 Sprinkle the yeast over the water. Let stand until the yeast is creamy, about 2 minutes. Stir until the yeast dissolves.

2 In a large bowl, combine the two flours and the salt. Add the yeast mixture and stir until a soft dough forms. Turn the dough out onto a lightly floured surface and knead until smooth and elastic, adding more flour as necessary to make a moist but not sticky dough, about 10 minutes. (Or make the dough in a heavy-duty mixer, food processor, or bread machine following the manufacturer's directions.)

3 Shape the dough into a ball. Place it on a floured surface and cover it with an overturned bowl. Let rise about 1¹/₂ hours at room temperature or until doubled.

4 Uncover the dough and press out the air bubbles. Cut the dough in half or in quarters, depending on the size of the pizzas you will be making. Shape each piece into a ball. Place the balls several inches apart on a floured surface and cover with a towel or plastic wrap. Let rise 1 hour or until doubled.

5 Lightly dust your work surface with flour. Pat and stretch one piece of dough out into a 9- to

12-inch circle, about 1/4 inch thick. Leave the border of the dough slightly thicker.

6 Dust a pizza peel or a rimless baking sheet generously with flour. Carefully place the circle of dough on the peel. Shake the peel to be sure that the dough is not sticking. If it is, lift the dough and add more flour to the peel. The dough is ready to be topped and baked per your recipe.

Mozzarella, Tomato, and Basil Pizza
Pizza Margherita

MAKES FOUR 9-INCH PIZZAS OR TWO 12-INCH PIZZAS

Neapolitans call this classic pizza—made with mozzarella, plain tomato sauce, and basil—pizza Margherita in honor of a beautiful queen who enjoyed pizza back in the nineteenth century.

1 recipe Neapolitan Pizza Dough (above), prepared through step 6
2¹/₂ cups Marinara Sauce (page 89), at room temperature
12 ounces fresh mozzarella, thinly sliced
Freshly grated Parmigiano-Reggiano, optional
Extra-virgin olive oil
8 fresh basil leaves

1 Prepare the dough and sauce, if necessary. Then, 30 to 60 minutes before baking, place a pizza stone or unglazed quarry tiles or a baking sheet on a rack in the lowest level of the oven. Turn on the oven to the maximum—500° or 550°F.

2 Spread the dough with a thin layer of the sauce, leaving a ¹/₂-inch border all the way around. Arrange the mozzarella on top and sprinkle with the grated cheese, if using.

3 Open the oven and gently slide the dough off the peel by tilting it slightly toward the back of the stone and shaking it gently forward and then back. Bake the pizza 6 to 7 minutes or until the crust is crisp and browned.

4 Transfer to a cutting board and drizzle with a little extra-virgin olive oil. Tear 2 basil leaves into pieces and scatter them over the pizza. Cut into wedges and serve immediately. Make more pizzas in the same way with the remaining ingredients.

Variation: Top the baked pizza with chopped fresh arugula and sliced prosciutto.

Tomato, Garlic, and Oregano Pizza
Pizza Marinara

MAKES FOUR 9-INCH OR TWO 12-INCH PIZZAS

Though they consume many different types of pizza in Naples, the official Neapolitan pizzamakers' association sanctions only two types of pizza as autentico, meaning the real thing. Pizza Margherita (above), named for a beloved queen, is one, and the other is pizza marinara, which despite its name (marinara meaning "of the mariner") is made without seafood. However, if you order this type of pizza in Rome instead of Naples, it will likely have anchovies on it.

Neapolitan-Style Pizza Dough (pages 486–487), prepared though step 6
2¹/₂ cups Marinara Sauce (page 89), at room temperature
1 can of anchovies, drained (optional)
Dried oregano, crumbled
3 garlic cloves, thinly sliced
Extra-virgin olive oil

1 Prepare the dough and sauce, if necessary. Then, 30 to 60 minutes before baking, place a pizza stone, unglazed quarry tiles, or a baking sheet on a rack in the lowest level of the oven. Turn on the oven to the maximum—500° or 550°F.

2 Spread the dough with a thin layer of the sauce, leaving a ¹/₂-inch border all the way around. Arrange the anchovies on top. Sprinkle with the oregano and scatter the garlic on top.

(continues)

3 Open the oven and gently slide the dough off the peel by tilting it toward the back of the stone and shaking it gently forward and then back. Bake the pizza 6 to 7 minutes or until the crust is crisp and browned.

4 Transfer to a cutting board and drizzle with a little extra-virgin olive oil. Cut into wedges and serve immediately. Make more pizzas with the remaining ingredients.

Variation: Before baking, top this pizza with thinly sliced pepperoni and drained pickled hot peppers.

Pizza with Wild Mushrooms
Pizza alla Boscaiola

MAKES FOUR 9-INCH PIZZAS

In Piedmont, winemaker friends took my husband and me to a pizzeria opened by a man from Naples. He made us a pizza topped with two local ingredients, Fontina Valle d'Aosta, a velvety cow's milk cheese, and fresh porcini mushrooms. The cheese melted beautifully and complemented the woodsy flavor of the mushrooms. Though fresh porcini are hard to come by in the United States, this pizza is still good made with other types of mushrooms.

Neapolitan-Style Pizza Dough (pages 486–487), prepared though step 6

3 tablespoons extra-virgin olive oil

1 garlic clove, thinly sliced

1 pound assorted mushrooms, such as white, shiitake, and oyster mushrooms (or use just white mushrooms), trimmed and sliced

1/2 teaspoon chopped fresh thyme or a pinch of dried thyme, crumbled

Salt and freshly ground black pepper

2 tablespoons chopped fresh flat-leaf parsley

8 ounces Fontina Valle d'Aosta, Asiago, or mozzarella, thinly sliced

1 Prepare the dough, if necessary. Then, 30 to 60 minutes before baking, place a pizza stone, unglazed quarry tiles, or a baking sheet on a rack in the lowest level of the oven. Turn on the oven to the maximum—500° or 550°F.

2 In a large skillet, heat the oil with the garlic over medium heat. Add the mushrooms, thyme, and salt and pepper to taste and cook, stirring frequently, until the mushroom juices evaporate and the mushrooms are browned, about 15 minutes. Stir in the parsley and remove from the heat.

3 Spread the cheese slices over the dough, leaving a 1-inch border all around. Top with the mushrooms.

4 Open the oven and gently slide the dough off the peel by tilting it toward the stone and shaking it gently forward and then back. Bake the pizza 6 to 7 minutes or until the crust is crisp and browned. Drizzle with a little extra-virgin olive oil.

5 Transfer to a cutting board and drizzle with a little extra-virgin olive oil. Cut into wedges and serve immediately. Make more pizzas with the remaining ingredients.

Pizza Variations

Once you have the dough, it is easy to vary the pizza toppings. Here are some classic combinations:

- Drained chopped fresh tomatoes, olive oil, basil, and fresh mozzarella
- Mozzarella, grated Parmigiano-Reggiano, and cherry tomatoes
- Marinara sauce, grated Parmigiano-Reggiano, and cooked sausage
- Mozzarella and broccoli or broccoli rabe cooked with garlic
- Thin-sliced salami, red onions, and strips of roasted peppers
- Marinated artichoke hearts
- Marinara sauce with squid, small shrimp, and clams, capers, and oregano

Calzoni

MAKES 4 CALZONI

In the streets of Spaccanapoli, the old part of Naples, you might be lucky enough to come upon a street vendor making calzoni. *The word means "big sock," an apt description of this filled pastry. A calzone is made with a circle of pizza dough folded like a turnover around filling. Street vendors fry them in big pots of boiling oil set over portable stoves. In pizzerias, calzoni are usually baked.*

1 envelope (2¹/₂ teaspoons) active dry yeast
    or 2 teaspoons instant yeast
1¹/₃ cups warm water (100° to 110°F)
About 3¹/₂ cups unbleached all-purpose flour
2 teaspoons salt
2 tablespoons olive oil, plus more for brushing the tops

FILLING

1 pound whole or part-skim milk ricotta
8 ounces fresh mozzarella, chopped
4 ounces prosciutto, salami, or ham, chopped
¹/₂ cup freshly grated Parmigiano-Reggiano

1 In a large bowl, sprinkle the yeast over the water. Let stand until the yeast is creamy, about 2 minutes. Stir until the yeast dissolves.

2 Add 3¹/₂ cups of flour, the salt, and the 2 tablespoons olive oil. Stir with a wooden spoon until a soft dough forms. Turn the dough out onto a lightly floured surface and knead, adding more flour if necessary, until smooth and elastic, about 10 minutes.

3 Lightly coat a large bowl with oil. Place the dough in the bowl, turning it to oil the top. Cover with plastic wrap. Place in a warm, draft-free place and let rise until doubled in bulk, about 1¹/₂ hours.

4 Flatten the dough with your fist. Cut the dough into 4 pieces. Shape each piece into a ball. Place the balls several inches apart on a lightly floured surface. Cover loosely with plastic wrap and let rise until doubled in bulk, about 1 hour.

5 Meanwhile, stir together the filling ingredients until well blended.

6 Place two racks in the center of the oven. Preheat the oven to 425°F. Oil 2 large baking sheets.

7 On a lightly floured surface with a rolling pin, roll out one piece of dough to a 9-inch circle. Spoon one quarter of the filling on half of the circle, leaving a ¹/₂-inch border for sealing. Fold the dough over to enclose the filling, pressing out the air. Pinch the edges firmly together to seal. Then fold the border over and seal again. Place the calzone on one of the baking sheets. Repeat with the remaining dough and filling, placing the calzoni several inches apart.

8 Cut a small slit in the top of each calzone to allow steam to escape. Brush the top with olive oil.

9 Bake 35 to 40 minutes or until crisp and browned, rotating the pans about halfway through. Slide onto a rack to cool 5 minutes. Serve hot.

Variations: Fill the calzoni with a combination of ricotta, goat cheese, garlic, and basil, or serve calzoni topped with tomato sauce.

Anchovy Fritters
Crispeddi di Alici

MAKES 12

These little rolls stuffed with anchovies are a favorite all over southern Italy. Crispeddi *is a Calabrian name; Sicilians call them* fanfarichi *or simply* pasta fritta, *"fried dough." My husband's Sicilian family always ate them on New Year's Eve, while other families enjoy them during Lent.*

1 envelope (2¹/₂ teaspoons) active dry yeast
    or 2 teaspoons instant yeast
1¹/₃ cups warm water (100° to 110°F)
About 3¹/₂ cups unbleached all-purpose flour
2 teaspoons salt
1 (2-ounce) can flat anchovy fillets, drained and
    patted dry
About 4 ounces mozzarella, cut into ¹/₂-inch thick strips
Vegetable oil for frying

(continues)

1 Sprinkle the yeast over the water. Let stand until the yeast is creamy, about 2 minutes. Stir until the yeast dissolves.

2 In a large bowl, combine 3 1/2 cups of flour and the salt. Add the yeast mixture and stir until a soft dough forms. Turn the dough out onto a lightly floured surface and knead, adding more flour if necessary, until smooth and elastic, about 10 minutes.

3 Oil a large bowl. Place the dough in the bowl, turning it once to oil the top. Cover with plastic wrap. Place in a warm, draft-free place and let rise until doubled in bulk, about 1 hour.

4 Flatten the dough to eliminate the air bubbles. Cut the dough into 12 pieces. Place 1 piece on a lightly floured surface, keeping the remaining pieces covered.

5 Roll out the dough to a circle about 5 inches in diameter. Place a piece of anchovy and a piece of mozzarella in the center of the circle. Lift the edges of the dough and press them together around the filling, forming a point like a purse. Flatten the point, pressing out the air. Pinch the seam to seal it tightly. Repeat with the remaining ingredients.

6 Line a tray with paper towels. Pour enough oil to reach 1/2 inch in depth in a large heavy skillet. Heat the oil over medium heat. Add a few rolls at a time, placing them seam-side down. Fry the rolls, flattening them with the back of a spatula, until golden brown, about 2 minutes on each side. Drain on the paper towels. Sprinkle with salt.

7 Fry the remaining rolls in the same way. Let cool slightly before serving.

Note: Be careful when you bite into them; the inside remains very hot while the outside cools.

Tomato and Cheese Turnovers
Panzerotti Pugliese

MAKES 16 TURNOVERS

Little turnovers similar to the anchovy fritters above are a specialty of Dora Marzovilla, who comes from Puglia. She makes them every day for her family's restaurant, I Trulli, in New York City. These can be made with or without anchovies.

1 recipe fritter dough (from Anchovy Fritters, pages 489–490)
3 plum tomatoes, seeded and chopped
Salt
4 ounces fresh mozzarella, cut into 16 pieces
Vegetable oil for frying

1 Prepare the dough. Then, cut the tomatoes in half and squeeze out the juice and seeds. Chop the tomatoes and season them with salt and pepper.

2 Cut the dough into quarters. Cut each quarter into 4 pieces. Keeping the remaining dough covered, roll out one piece to a 4-inch circle. Place 1 teaspoon of the tomatoes and a piece of mozzarella to one side of the circle. Fold the other half of the dough over the filling to form a half-moon. Press out the air and pinch the edges together to seal. Crimp the edges firmly with a fork.

3 Line a tray with paper towels. In a deep heavy saucepan or a deep-fryer, heat at least 1 inch of oil to 375°F on a frying thermometer, or until a 1-inch piece of bread browns in 1 minute. Carefully place the turnovers a few at a time into the hot oil. Leave enough room between them so that they do not touch. Turn the turnovers once or twice and cook until golden brown, about 2 minutes per side.

4 Transfer the turnovers to the paper towels to drain. Sprinkle with salt. Serve hot.

Note: Be careful when you bite into them; the inside remains very hot while the outside cools.

❧ Savory Pies

Easter Pie
Pizza Rustica or Pizza Chiene

MAKES 12 SERVINGS

Most southern Italians make one version or another of this very rich, savory pie for Easter. Some of the pies are made with a yeast dough, and others use a sweetened pie dough. Hard-cooked eggs are often added to the filling, and every cook has her or his own favorite combination of cheeses and cured meats. This is the way my grandmother made Easter pie.

Pizza rustica is also known as pizza chiene (pronounced "pizza gheen"), a dialect form of pizza ripiene, meaning "stuffed" or "full" pie. It is typically eaten at the Easter Monday picnic that families plan to celebrate the coming of spring. Because it is so rich, a small slice goes a long way.

CRUST

4 cups unbleached all-purpose flour

1 1/2 teaspoons salt

1/2 cup solid vegetable shortening

1/2 cup (1 stick) unsalted butter, chilled and cut into pieces

2 large eggs, beaten

3 to 4 tablespoons ice water

FILLING

8 ounces sweet Italian sausage, casings removed

3 large eggs, lightly beaten

1 cup freshly grated Parmigiano-Reggiano or Pecorino Romano

2 pounds whole or part-skim ricotta, drained overnight (page 577)

8 ounces fresh mozzarella, cut into small dice

4 ounces prosciutto, cut into small dice

4 ounces cooked ham, cut into small dice

4 ounces sopressata, cut into small dice

GLAZE

1 egg, lightly beaten

1 Prepare the crust: Combine the flour and salt in a bowl. Cut in the shortening and butter with a pastry blender or fork until the mixture resembles large crumbs. Add the eggs and stir until a soft dough forms. Scoop up some of the mixture with your hand and rapidly squeeze it until it holds together. Repeat with the rest of the dough until the ingredients hold together and can be formed into a smooth ball. If the mixture seems too dry and crumbly, add a little ice water. Gather the dough into two disks, one three times as large as the other. Wrap each disk in plastic wrap. Refrigerate 1 hour up to overnight.

2 To make the filling, cook the sausage meat in a small skillet over medium heat, stirring occasionally, until no longer pink, about 10 minutes. Remove the meat with a slotted spoon. Chop the meat on a board.

3 In a large bowl, beat the eggs and Parmigiano until well blended. Stir in the ricotta, sausage meat, mozzarella, and diced meats.

4 Place the oven rack in the lower third of the oven. Preheat the oven to 375°F. On a lightly floured surface with a floured rolling pin, roll out the large piece of dough to form a 14-inch circle. Drape the dough over the rolling pin. Transfer the dough to a 9-inch springform pan, pressing it smoothly against the bottom and up the sides of the pan. Scrape the filling into the pan.

5 Roll out the remaining piece of dough into a 9-inch circle. With a fluted pastry wheel, cut the dough into 1/2-inch strips. Place half the strips 1 inch apart over the filling. Turn the pan a quarter of the way around and place the remaining strips on top, forming a lattice pattern. Pinch the edges of the top and bottom layers of dough together to seal. Brush the dough with the egg glaze.

6 Bake the pie 1 to 1 1/4 hours or until the crust is golden and the filling is puffed. Cool the pie in the pan on a wire rack for 10 minutes. Remove the sides of the pan and let cool completely. Serve warm or at room temperature. Cover tightly and store in the refrigerator up to 3 days.

Sicilian Swordfish Torte
Impanata di Pesce Spada

MAKES 8 TO 10 SERVINGS

Sicilians make this savory pie with either swordfish or tuna, and eggplant or zucchini. It is a spectacular dish, and whenever I make it, I think of Giuseppe de Lampedusa's description of the banquet table in his novel The Leopard, *about the declining Sicilian aristocracy. It is a bit of a production but well worth the effort.*

DOUGH

4 cups unbleached all-purpose flour

2 tablespoons sugar

1 teaspoon salt

1/2 cup (4 ounces) cold vegetable shortening

1/2 cup (1 stick) cold unsalted butter, cut into 1/4-inch-thick slices

1 teaspoon grated orange zest

2 large eggs, beaten

About 3 to 4 tablespoons cold dry white wine

FILLING

Olive oil

1 medium eggplant (about 1 pound) cut into 1/4-inch-thick slices

Salt

1 medium onion, chopped

1 tender celery rib, finely chopped

5 ripe tomatoes, peeled, seeded, and chopped, or 2 1/2 cups chopped drained canned tomatoes

1/2 cup pitted green olives, chopped

2 tablespoons chopped capers, rinsed and drained

2 tablespoons raisins

2 tablespoons pine nuts

1 pound thin sliced swordfish

Salt and freshly ground black pepper

1 Prepare the dough: Put the flour, sugar, and salt in a large bowl. With a pastry blender or fork, cut in the shortening, butter, and orange zest until the mixture resembles coarse crumbs. Stir in the eggs and just enough wine so that the dry ingredients begin to come together and form a dough. Scoop up some of the mixture with your hand and rapidly squeeze it until it holds together. Repeat with the rest of the dough until it holds together and can be formed into a ball. If the mixture seems too dry and crumbly, add a teaspoon or so of cold water. Gather the dough into two disks, one twice as large as the other. Wrap each disk in plastic wrap. Refrigerate 1 hour up to overnight.

2 Prepare the filling: Heat 1/4 cup of olive oil in a large skillet. Blot the eggplant slices dry and fry them a single layer at a time until nicely browned. Sprinkle with salt.

3 In another large skillet, combine 1/4 cup of olive oil, the onion, and the celery over medium heat. Cook, stirring frequently, until the vegetables are softened, about 10 minutes. Stir in the tomatoes, capers, olives, raisins, and pine nuts. Cook until the juices evaporate and the sauce is thick. Add the swordfish, then salt and pepper to taste. Baste the fish with the sauce. Cover and cook 5 to 8 minutes or until the fish is just pink in the thickest part. If there is too much liquid in the pan, remove the fish to a plate and reduce the liquid over medium heat. Let cool.

4 Place the oven rack in the center of the oven. Preheat the oven to 375°F.

5 If the dough has been refrigerated overnight, let it stand at room temperature 20 to 30 minutes before rolling it out. Roll out the larger piece of dough to a 14-inch circle. Loosely wrap the dough around the rolling pin to transfer the dough to a 9-inch springform pan. Gently press the dough into the base of the pan and along the sides. Spoon half of the swordfish mixture across the dough. Cover with the eggplant. Top with the remaining swordfish and sauce.

6 Roll out the smaller piece of dough to a 10-inch circle. Center the dough on top of the pie. Trim off all but a 1/2-inch border of dough. Fold the dough over, pinching the edges to seal.

7 With a small knife, cut several slits in the top of the dough to allow steam to escape. Bake 50 to 60 minutes or until the top is golden brown and the juices visible in the slits are bubbling.

8 Cool 10 minutes on a wire rack. Remove the sides of the pan. Let cool 15 minutes more. Serve hot or at room temperature.

Green Onion Pie
Pizza di Cippollotti

MAKES 8 SERVINGS

In Puglia, this pie's filling is made with tender leeks or green onions. I use green onions more often because they are a little easier to work with, but try using leeks, if you like. Serve it with sheep's milk cheese and primitivo, a robust red wine from this region, or a zinfandel.

DOUGH

1 envelope (2¹/₂ teaspoons) active dry yeast
³/₄ cup warm water (100° to 110°F)
3 tablespoons extra-virgin olive oil
About 2¹/₂ cups unbleached all-purpose flour
1 teaspoon salt

FILLING

3 bunches green onions (about 12 ounces)
3 tablespoons extra-virgin olive oil
1 cup large green olives, pitted and coarsely chopped

1 In a large bowl, sprinkle the yeast over the water. Let stand until the yeast is creamy, about 2 minutes. Stir until the yeast dissolves.

2 Add the olive oil, 2¹/₂ cups of flour, and the salt. Stir the mixture until a soft dough forms. Turn the dough out onto a lightly floured surface. Knead until smooth and elastic, about 10 minutes, adding more flour if needed. The dough should feel moist but not sticky. Shape the dough into a ball.

3 Oil a large bowl and place the dough in it, turning it once to oil the top. Cover with plastic wrap and let rise in a warm, draft-free place until doubled in bulk, about 1¹/₂ hours.

4 Meanwhile, prepare the filling: Trim the onions, removing the root end and any bruised outer leaves. Trim about 1 inch from the tops. Cut the onions in half lengthwise, then crosswise into ¹/₂-inch pieces.

5 In a large skillet, heat the oil over medium-low heat. Stir in the onions. Cover the pan and cook, stirring occasionally, until the onions are tender but not browned, about 10 minutes. Remove from the heat. Stir in the olives and let cool.

6 Place a rack in the center of the oven. Preheat oven to 400°F. Flatten the dough to eliminate air bubbles. Divide the dough into 2 pieces, one about twice as large as the other.

7 On a lightly floured surface, roll out the larger piece of dough to a 12-inch circle. Loosely wrap the dough around the rolling pin and transfer it to a 9-inch springform pan. Center the dough in the pan and press evenly to fit. Spread the filling evenly over the dough leaving a 1-inch border all around.

8 Roll out the remaining dough to a 9-inch circle. Place the circle over the filling. Pinch the edges of the dough together to seal. With a small, sharp knife, cut eight ¹/₂-inch slits in the top of the dough.

9 Bake 40 minutes or until browned. Cool 10 minutes on a wire rack. Remove the sides of the pan. Let cool 15 minutes more. Serve hot or at room temperature.

Escarole Pie

Pizza di Scarola

MAKES 8 TO 10 SERVINGS

Christmas Eve dinner was always a special, meatless meal in our home. My mother would make this Neapolitan-style pie as an appetizer preceding an array of seafood and fish dishes.

Some cooks add raisins and pine nuts to the escarole mixture. Others use this filling to stuff Calzoni (page 489).

DOUGH

1 envelope (2¹/₂ teaspoons) active dry or instant yeast

1¹/₃ cups warm water (100° to 110°F)

About 3¹/₂ cups unbleached all-purpose flour

2 teaspoons salt

2 teaspoons freshly ground black pepper

2 tablespoons olive oil

FILLING

2 pounds escarole, cleaned and cut into ¹/₂-inch strips

Salt

¹/₄ cup olive oil

3 large garlic cloves, finely chopped

Pinch of crushed red pepper

1 (2-ounce) can anchovy fillets, drained

3 tablespoons capers, rinsed and drained

1 Prepare the dough: Sprinkle the yeast over the water. Let stand until the yeast is creamy, about 2 minutes. Stir until the yeast dissolves.

2 In a large bowl, combine 3¹/₂ cups flour, the salt, and the pepper. Add the yeast mixture and oil and stir with a wooden spoon until a soft dough forms. Turn the dough out onto a lightly floured surface and knead, until smooth and elastic, about 10 minutes, adding more flour if necessary to make a moist but not sticky dough. (Or make the dough in a heavy-duty mixer, food processor, or bread machine, following the manufacturer's directions.) Shape the dough into a ball.

3 Oil a large bowl. Add the dough, turning it once to oil the top. Cover and let rise at room temperature until doubled in bulk, about 1¹/₂ hours.

4 Press the air bubbles out of the dough. Divide the dough into two pieces. Shape the pieces into balls. Dust the tops with flour. Place the balls on a floured surface at least 6 inches apart. Cover with plastic wrap and let rise until doubled, about 1¹/₂ hours.

5 While the dough is rising, prepare the filling: Bring a large pot of water to a boil. Add the escarole and salt to taste. Cover and cook over medium heat until tender, about 15 minutes. Drain well and let cool. Wrap the escarole in a lint-free towel to squeeze out the remaining liquid.

6 In a large skillet, heat the oil over medium heat. Add the garlic, red pepper, anchovies, and capers, mashing the anchovies with the back of a spoon. Add the escarole and stir well. Reduce the heat to low and cook 10 minutes. Let cool.

7 Place a rack in the center of the oven. Preheat the oven to 425°F. Oil a 12-inch pizza pan.

8 On a lightly floured surface with a rolling pin, roll out 1 piece of the dough to a 12-inch circle. Drape the dough over the pin and transfer the dough to the pan. Spread the filling over the dough, leaving a ¹/₂-inch border all around.

9 Roll out the remaining dough to a 12-inch circle. Center the dough over the filling, pressing the edges of the top and bottom dough together firmly to seal. With a small sharp knife, cut six ¹/₂-inch slits in the top of the dough.

10 Bake 35 to 40 minutes or until the top is browned and crisp. Cut into wedges and serve hot, or slide the pie onto a cooling rack and serve at room temperature.

Savory Pie Pastry
Pasta Frolla Salata

MAKES ONE 9- TO 10-INCH PIE SHELL

A savory pie similar to a quiche can be made with cheese, eggs, and vegetables. These pies are good at room temperature or hot, and can be served as a piatto unico—one-dish meal—or as an appetizer. This pastry is good for all types of savory pies.

I roll out this dough between two sheets of plastic wrap. It prevents the dough from sticking to the board and rolling pin, so it is not necessary to add more flour, which can toughen the dough. To ensure that the crust is crisp on the bottom, I partially prebake the shell before adding the filling.

1 ½ cups all-purpose flour
1 teaspoon salt
½ cup (1 stick) unsalted butter, at room temperature
1 egg yolk
3 to 4 tablespoons ice water

1 Prepare the dough: Combine the flour and salt in a large bowl. With a pastry blender or a fork, cut in the butter until the mixture resembles coarse crumbs.

2 Beat the egg yolk together with 2 tablespoons of the water. Sprinkle the mixture over the flour. Mix together lightly until the dough is evenly moistened and comes together without being sticky. Add the remaining water if needed.

3 Shape the dough into a disk. Wrap in plastic wrap. Refrigerate 30 minutes or overnight.

4 If the dough has been refrigerated overnight, let it stand at room temperature 20 to 30 minutes before rolling it out. Place the dough between two sheets of plastic wrap and roll it out to a 12-inch circle, turning the dough and rearranging the plastic wrap with each turn. Remove the top sheet of plastic wrap. Using the remaining sheet to lift the dough, center the dough with the plastic up in a 9- to 10-inch tart pan with a removable base. Peel off the plastic wrap. Gently press the dough into the base and along the sides.

5 Roll the rolling pin over the top of the pan and trim off the overhanging dough. Press the dough against the side of the pan to create a rim higher than the edge of the pan. Chill the pastry shell in the refrigerator 30 minutes.

6 Place the oven rack in the lower third of the oven. Preheat the oven to 450°F. With a fork, prick the bottom of the tart shell at 1-inch intervals. Bake for 5 minutes, then prick the dough again. Bake until just set, 10 minutes more. Remove the shell from the oven. Cool on a rack 10 minutes.

Spinach Ricotta Tart
Crostata di Spinaci

MAKES 8 SERVINGS

I had a tart like this at Ferrara, a favorite restaurant in Rome. Something like a quiche, it is made with ricotta for extra creaminess. It is great for a lunch or brunch dish, served with a salad and chilled pinot grigio wine.

I recipe Savory Pie Pastry (page 495)

FILLING

I pound spinach, trimmed and rinsed
1/4 cup water
1 1/2 cups whole or part-skim ricotta
1/2 cup heavy cream
3/4 cup freshly grated Parmigiano-Reggiano
2 large eggs, beaten
1/4 teaspoon freshly grated nutmeg
Salt and freshly ground black pepper

I Prepare and partially bake the crust. Reduce the oven temperature to 375°F.

2 Meanwhile, prepare the filling. Put the spinach in a large pot over medium heat with the water. Cover and cook 2 to 3 minutes or until wilted and tender. Drain and cool. Wrap the spinach in a lint-free cloth and squeeze out as much water as possible. Finely chop the spinach.

3 In a large bowl, beat together the spinach, ricotta, cream, cheese, eggs, nutmeg, and salt and pepper to taste. Scrape the mixture into the prepared tart shell.

4 Bake 35 to 40 minutes or until the filling is set and lightly browned.

5 Cool the tart in the pan 10 minutes. Remove the outer rim and place the tart on a serving dish. Serve warm or at room temperature.

Leek Tart
Crostata di Porri

MAKES 6 TO 8 SERVINGS

I had this tart at an enoteca, *or wine bar, in Bologna. The nutty flavor of the Parmigiano and the cream enhance the sweet flavor of the leeks. It can also be made with sautéed mushrooms or peppers instead of the leeks.*

I recipe Savory Pie Pastry (page 495)

FILLING

4 medium leeks, about 1 1/4 pounds
3 tablespoons unsalted butter
Salt
2 large eggs
3/4 cup heavy cream
1/3 cup freshly grated Parmigiano-Reggiano
Freshly grated nutmeg
Freshly ground black pepper

I Prepare and partially bake the crust. Reduce the oven temperature to 375°F.

2 Prepare the filling: Trim off the roots and most of the green tops of the leeks. Cut them in half lengthwise and rinse them very well between each layer under cold running water. Cut the leeks into thin crosswise slices.

3 In a large skillet, melt the butter over medium heat. Add the leeks and a pinch of salt. Cook, stirring often, until the leeks are tender when pierced with a knife, about 20 minutes. Remove the pan from the heat and let cool.

4 In a medium bowl, beat together the eggs, cream, cheese, and a pinch of nutmeg. Stir in the leeks and pepper to taste.

5 Scrape the mixture into the partially baked tart shell. Bake 35 to 40 minutes or until the filling is set. Serve warm or at room temperature.

❧ Italian Sandwiches (Panini)

In Italy, *panini* can refer either to bread rolls or the sandwiches made on rolls. In the United States, the word has come to mean any kind of sandwich filled with Italian ingredients, often pressed and toasted. The bread used in the United States is often a roll, though some panini are made with chewy sliced bread. You can buy a special sandwich press to make panini or improvise one easily by placing the sandwich on a grill pan and weighting it with heavy cans or a pot.

Of course, panini can be made with a wide variety of fillings, but they are only as good as the ingredients that go into them. Use imported Italian cheeses and good bread for authentic flavor. If using rolls for the bread, pull out the soft crumb in the center so that there will not be too much bread. Don't overstuff panini. Sandwiches in Italy are thin, with a moderate amount of filling—some would even say a scant amount—in proportion to the bread. It works, though, because the ingredients are of such good quality and are full of flavor.

Mozzarella, Basil, and Roasted Pepper Sandwiches
Panini di Mozzarella

MAKES 2 SERVINGS

I sometimes make this sandwich substituting arugula for the basil and prosciutto for the red peppers.

4 ounces fresh mozzarella cheese, cut into 8 slices
4 slices country bread
4 fresh basil leaves
1/4 cup roasted red or yellow bell peppers, cut into thin strips

1 Trim the mozzarella slices to fit the bread. If the mozzarella is juicy, pat it dry. Lay half the cheese in a single layer on two slices of bread.

2 Arrange the basil leaves and peppers on the cheese and top with the remaining mozzarella. Place the remaining bread on top and press down firmly with your hands.

3 Preheat a sandwich press or stove-top grill pan. Place the sandwiches in the press and cook until toasted, about 4 to 5 minutes. If using a grill pan, place a heavy weight such as a frying pan on top. Turn the sandwiches when browned on one side, cover with the weight, and toast on the second side. Serve hot.

Spinach and Robiola Sandwiches
Panino di Spinaci e Robiola

MAKES 2 SERVINGS

Focaccia adds nice flavor and texture to pressed panini. Other greens can be substituted for the spinach, or use leftover vegetables. For the cheese, I like to use robiola, a soft creamy cheese made from cow's, goat's, or sheep's milk, or a combination, from Piedmont and Lombardy. Other possibilities are fresh goat cheese or even whipped cream cheese. Add a drop or two of truffle oil to the filling for an earthy flavor and a touch of luxury.

1 (10-ounce) package fresh spinach
4 ounces fresh robiola, or substitute goat cheese
Truffle oil (optional)
2 serving-size squares or wedges of fresh focaccia

1 Put the spinach in a large pot over medium heat with 1/4 cup of water. Cover and cook 2 to 3 minutes or until wilted and tender. Drain and cool. Wrap the spinach in a lint-free cloth and squeeze out as much water as possible.

2 Finely chop the spinach and place it in a medium bowl. Add the cheese and mash the spinach into the cheese. Add a drop or two of truffle oil, if you like.

3 With a long serrated knife, carefully cut the focaccia in half horizontally. Spread the mixture on the inside of the bottom halves of the focaccia. Place the tops on the sandwiches and flatten gently.

4 Preheat a sandwich press or stove-top grill pan. If using a press, place the sandwiches in the press and cook until toasted, about 4 to 5 minutes. If using a grill pan, place the sandwiches on the pan, then a heavy weight, such as a frying pan, on top.

5 When browned on one side, turn the sandwiches, cover with the weight, and toast on the second side. Serve hot.

Riviera Sandwich
Panino della Riviera

MAKES 4 SERVINGS

The geographic border dividing Italy and France does not also signify a distinction in the food eaten on either side. With their similar climate and geography, people living along the Italian and French coasts share very similar food customs. A case in point is the French pan bagnat *and Italian* pane bagnato, *meaning "bathed bread," which is sometimes called a Riviera sandwich in Italy. This hearty sandwich, bathed in a lively vinaigrette dressing, is stuffed with tuna and roasted peppers in France. On the Italian side of the border, mozzarella stands in for the tuna, and anchovies are added, but the rest is pretty much the same. This is the perfect sandwich to take on a picnic, because the flavors marry well, and it only gets better as it stands.*

1 loaf Italian bread, about 12 inches long

DRESSING
1 garlic clove, very finely chopped
1/4 cup olive oil
2 tablespoons vinegar
1/2 teaspoon dried oregano, crumbled
Salt and freshly ground black pepper

2 ripe tomatoes, sliced
1 (2-ounce) can anchovies
8 ounces sliced mozzarella
2 peeled and seeded roasted peppers with their juice
12 oil-cured olives, pitted and chopped

1 Cut the bread loaf in half lengthwise and remove the soft bread inside.

2 In a small bowl, whisk together the dressing ingredients and pour half the dressing over the cut sides of the bread. Layer the bottom half of the bread with the tomatoes, anchovies, mozzarella, roasted peppers, and olives, drizzling each layer with some of the dressing.

3 Place the top on the sandwich and press it together. Wrap in foil and cover with a board or heavy pan. Let stand at room temperature up to 2 hours or store in the refrigerator overnight.

4 Slice into 3-inch-wide sandwiches. Serve at room temperature.

Tuna and Roasted Pepper Triangle Sandwiches
Tramezzini al Tonno e Peperoni

MAKES 3 SANDWICHES

Some of the same flavors of the hearty Riviera sand-wich find their way into this delicate triangle sand-wich I tasted at a favorite Roman café. The tuna was seasoned with fennel seeds, but I like to substi-tute fennel pollen, which is nothing more than ground-up fennel seeds, but has more flavor. A lot of chefs are using it these days, and it can be found in gourmet shops specializing in dried herbs as well as on Internet sites. If you can't find fennel pollen, substitute fennel seeds, which you can grind yourself in a spice grinder or chop with a knife.

I small roasted red pepper, drained and cut into
   thin strips
Extra-virgin olive oil
Salt
I (3¹/₂-ounce) can Italian tuna packed in olive oil
2 tablespoons mayonnaise
I to 2 teaspoons fresh lemon juice
I tablespoon chopped green onion
I teaspoon fennel pollen
4 slices good-quality white sandwich bread

1 Toss the roasted pepper with a little oil and salt.

2 Drain the tuna and place it in a bowl. Mash the tuna well with a fork. Blend in the mayonnaise, lemon juice to taste, and green onion.

3 Spread the tuna on two of the bread slices. Top with the pepper strips. Cover with the remaining bread, pressing down slightly.

4 With a large chef's knife, trim off the bread crusts. Cut the sandwiches in half diagonally to form two triangles. Serve immediately or cover tightly with plastic wrap and refrigerate until ready to serve.

Tramezzini

Among the many delights of Roman caffès are *tramezzini*. These triangular sandwiches made on crustless bread became popular in the post–World War II era, when the occupying American forces introduced Italians to our typical loaves of white sandwich bread, known in Italy as *pane a cassetta*. With crusts re-moved, the large slices of white bread are cut diagonally in half and filled with soft fillings like tuna, chicken or meat salads, eggs, or vegetables—usually bound with mayonnaise—soft cheese, or a creamy dressing. The freshly made sandwiches are arranged by the color of the filling and stacked up in glass cases, each one separated from the next by a spot-less cloth napkin so that they are ready to be sold as snacks or as a quick lunch. The sand-wiches are thin and elegant, never overstuffed or sloppy. The bread and fillings must be very fresh and the finished sandwiches must be beautiful to qualify as real Italian tramezzini.

If you make tramezzini in advance, cover the plate with a slightly damp cloth so that the bread stays moist and fresh. Use a good-quality white sandwich bread, nothing too soft or spongy. I sometimes moisten my hands slightly while making tramezzini to keep the bread from drying out as I assemble the sandwiches.

Prosciutto and Fig Triangle Sandwiches

Tramezzini di Prosciutto e Fichi

MAKES 2 SANDWICHES

The saltiness of the prosciutto and sweetness of the fig jam offer a pleasant contrast in this sandwich. It is very good as an appetizer if you cut it into quarters. Serve it with sparkling Prosecco.

Unsalted butter, at room temperature
4 slices good-quality white sandwich bread
About 2 tablespoons fig jam
4 thin slices imported Italian prosciutto

1 Spread a little butter on one side of each slice of bread. Spread about 2 teaspoons fig jam over the butter on each slice.

2 Arrange two slices of prosciutto on half of the slices. Place the remaining slices of bread jam-side-down on the prosciutto.

3 With a large chef's knife, trim off the bread crusts. Cut the sandwiches in half diagonally to form two triangles. Serve immediately or cover with plastic wrap and refrigerate.

Tramezzini Fillings

- Tuna packed in olive oil, with mayonnaise, thin-sliced tomato, and shredded lettuce
- Cooked spinach and taleggio or fontina cheese
- Sliced hard-cooked eggs, anchovies, mayonnaise, and lettuce
- Gorgonzola mashed with mascarpone, ricotta, or cream cheese, topped with shredded radicchio
- Bresaola (air-dried beef) and soft fresh goat cheese
- Butter, prosciutto, and arugula
- Toasted walnuts and cream cheese
- Sliced fresh mozzarella with egg salad
- Very thin vegetable frittatas
- Nutella, a sweet chocolate hazelnut spread, which is as popular in Italy as peanut butter is in the United States

Fruit, Ice Cream, and Spoon Desserts

Fruit Desserts

Amaretto Baked Apples

Livia's Apple Cake

Apricots in Lemon Syrup

Berries with Lemon and Sugar

Strawberries with Balsamic Vinegar

Raspberries with Mascarpone
and Balsamic Vinegar

Cherries in Barolo

Hot Roasted Chestnuts

Fig Preserves

Chocolate-Dipped Figs

Figs in Wine Syrup

Dora's Baked Figs

Honeydew in Mint Syrup

Oranges in Orange Syrup

Oranges Gratinéed with Zabaglione

White Peaches in Asti Spumante

Peaches in Red Wine

Amaretti-Stuffed Peaches

Pears in Orange Sauce

Pears with Marsala and Cream

Pears with Warm Chocolate Sauce

Rum-Spiced Pears

Spiced Pears with Pecorino

Poached Pears with Gorgonzola

Pear or Apple Pudding Cake

Warm Fruit Compote

Venetian Caramelized Fruit

Fruit with Honey and Grappa

Winter Fruit Salad

Grilled Summer Fruit

"Eat-and-Drink" Dessert

Spoon Desserts

Warm Ricotta with Honey

Coffee Ricotta

Mascarpone and Peaches

Chocolate Foam with Raspberries

Tiramisù

Strawberry Tiramisù

Italian Trifle

(continues)

Zabaglione
Chocolate Zabaglione
Chilled Zabaglione with Berries
Lemon Gelatin
Orange Rum Gelatin
Espresso Gelatin
Panna Cotta
Crème Brûlée
Mascarpone and Coffee Cups
Chestnut "Mountain"
Chocolate Pudding
Chocolate Chip Rice Pudding
Coffee Caramel Custard
Chocolate Crème Caramel
Amaretti Caramel Custard

Italian Ices

Simple Syrup for Granita
Lemon Granita
Watermelon Granita
Tangerine Granita
Strawberry Wine Granita
Coffee Granita
Citrus and Campari Granita
White Peach and Prosecco Granita
Chocolate Sorbet
Prosecco Lemon Slush
Pink Prosecco Slush

Ice Cream (Gelato)

"Cream" Ice Cream
Lemon Ice Cream
Ricotta Ice Cream
Mascarpone Ice Cream
Cinnamon Ice Cream
Espresso Ice Cream
Walnut Caramel Ice Cream
Honey Ice Cream with Nougat
Amaretti Gelato
"Drowned" Ice Cream
Ice Cream with Balsamic Vinegar
Ice Cream Truffles
Almond Cream Cups
Orange Spumone
Almond Semifreddo
Florentine Frozen Dome Cake

Dessert Sauces

Honeyed Mascarpone Sauce
Fresh Strawberry Sauce
Warm Berry Sauce
Year-Round Raspberry Sauce
Warm Chocolate Sauce

Italian meals typically end with seasonal fruit. In the fall, there might be persimmons, pomegranates, apples, and grapes, while winter brings clementines and all kinds of roasted nuts. The first fresh fruit to ripen in the spring is the *nespola,* a medlar fruit about the size and color of an apricot, with tart-sweet flesh. Then come the fresh berries, including my favorite, *fragoline di bosco,* tiny Alpine strawberries with an intensely perfumed aroma, plus raspberries, blackberries, and currants. Summer fruits include a variety of cherries, yellow- and white-fleshed peaches, figs, and all kinds of melons. Italians indulge in fresh fruit plain or with simple sauces or ice cream, and they typically eat them with a knife and fork or spoon.

Though Italians normally purchase pastries, cakes, tarts, and cookies at a bakery, many custards, creams, and other soft desserts, known as *dolci di cucchiaio,* or "spoon desserts," are prepared at home. This chapter includes recipes for gelatins made with fresh fruit juices or espresso, sophisticated egg custards like zabaglione, and other kinds of creamy desserts that are easy to make at home and always welcome at the table.

Frozen desserts like ice cream and ices are also very popular, though they are typically eaten after the fruit course. In Sicily, where summers are very hot, ice cream and granita are eaten in the morning and throughout the day. The ice cream is usually tucked into a *brioscia,* a sweet roll, and eaten like a sandwich. In Rome, frozen coffee granita replaces hot coffee in the summer. In the afternoon and evening, Italians like to go for a *passaggiata,* a stroll, and stop at a favorite cafe for an ice-cream cone. This is also a social event, when adults discuss the day's events with friends and neighbors and young people gather to talk and flirt.

A fruit or chocolate sauce can dress up many kinds of desserts, from ice cream to homemade or store-bought cake. I have included several variations on the theme.

❧ Fruit Desserts

It seems strange when I think about it, but I never order whole fresh fruit in a restaurant in the United States. The only exception might be a bowl of fresh strawberries or raspberries. Whole fruits, such as peaches, apricots, an apple, or even a bunch of grapes, are simply not offered in American restaurants.

Restaurants in Italy, however, always have fresh ripe fruit available. One of my favorite dinner rituals in Italy is to order *frutta fresca* for dessert. It usually comes with a bowl of cold water so that you can dip and refresh the fruits. The assortment will vary with the season, but you can expect apples, pears, and citrus in the cold months and peaches, grapes, plums, apricots, and cherries in the warm months. The fruit bowl dessert is unlimited, so you can eat as much as you like. Berries are ordered separately. They are most often served either doused with lemon and sugar or topped with a scoop of ice cream or lemon sorbet. Zabaglione (page 521), a rich and creamy Marsala-infused custard, is also very good on fresh berries, but I have seen it more in the United States than in Italy. Very large fruits like pineapple (although not native to Italy) and melons are served cut into wedges.

Italians eat a lot of fruit salads and cooked fruit desserts, too. The fruits are excellent, because they are in season and locally grown. Instead of having to endure long trips over thousands of miles in refrigerator trucks, fruits are picked ripe and quickly brought from the fields to nearby markets.

Amaretto Baked Apples
Mele al'Amaretto

MAKES 6 SERVINGS

Amaretto is a sweet liqueur; amaretti are crisp cookies. Both of these Italian products are flavored with two kinds of almonds—the familiar variety, plus a slightly bitter almond that is not eaten on its own, though it is frequently used in Italy to flavor desserts. Amaro means "bitter," and both the liqueur and the cookies take their name from these almonds. Both are widely available—the cookies in specialty shops and by mail order and the liqueur in many liquor stores.

The most familiar brand of amaretti cookies is packaged in distinctive red tins or boxes. The cookies are wrapped in pairs in pastel tissue paper. There are other brands of amaretti that pack the cookies loose in bags. I always have amaretti in the house. They keep a long time and are nice with a cup of tea, or as an ingredient in a number of sweet and savory dishes.

Golden delicious are the apples I prefer for baking. The locally grown ones are sweet and crisp, yet they hold their shape nicely when baked.

6 baking apples, such as golden delicious
6 amaretti cookies
6 tablespoons sugar
2 tablespoons unsalted butter
6 tablespoons amaretto or rum

1 Place a rack in the center of the oven. Preheat the oven to 375°F. Butter a baking dish just large enough to hold the apples standing upright.

2 Remove the apple cores and peel the apples about two-thirds of the way down from the stem end.

3 Place the amaretti cookies in a plastic bag and crush them gently with a heavy object, such as a rolling pin. In a medium bowl, blend the crumbs with the sugar and butter.

4 Stuff a little of the mixture into the center of each apple. Spoon the amaretto over the apples. Pour 1 cup water around the apples.

5 Bake 45 minutes or until the apples are tender when pierced with a knife. Serve warm or at room temperature.

Livia's Apple Cake
Torta di Mele alla Livia

MAKES 8 SERVINGS

My friend Livia Colantonio lives in Umbria on a farm called Podernovo. The farm raises Chianina cattle, grows a variety of wine grapes, and bottles wine under the Castello delle Regine label.

Guests can stay in one of the beautifully restored guesthouses at Podernovo, which is just 45 minutes from Rome, and enjoy a restful vacation. Livia makes this simple but sensational "cake" that is always good after a fall or winter meal. It isn't a cake in the traditional sense, because it is made almost entirely of apples, with just a few cookie crumbs between the layers to hold some of the fruit juices. Serve it with a dollop of whipped cream or rum-raisin ice cream.

You will need a round pan or baking dish 9 inches wide by 3 inches deep. Use a cake pan, or a casserole or soufflé dish, but do not use a springform pan because the apple juices will leak out.

12 amaretti cookies

3 pounds golden delicious, Granny Smith, or other firm apples (about 6 large)

1/2 cup sugar

1 Place the amaretti cookies in a plastic bag and crush them gently with a heavy object, such as a rolling pin. You should have about 3/4 cup of crumbs.

2 Peel the apples and cut them into quarters lengthwise. Cut the quarters into 1/8-inch-thick slices.

3 Place a rack in the center of the oven. Preheat the oven to 350°F. Generously butter a 9 × 3–inch round baking pan or a tube pan. Line the bottom of the pan with a circle of parchment paper. Butter the paper.

4 Make a layer of apples overlapping slightly in the bottom of the pan. Sprinkle with a little of the crumbs and sugar. Alternate layers of the remaining apple slices in the pan with the remaining crumbs and sugar. The apple slices do not have to

be arranged neatly. Place a sheet of foil over the top, molding it over the rim of the pan.

5 Bake the apples 1 1/2 hours. Uncover and bake 30 minutes more or until the apples are tender when pierced with a knife and diminished in volume. Transfer the pan to a wire rack. Let cool at least 15 minutes. Run a knife around the edge of the pan. Holding the pan with a pot holder in one hand, place a flat serving plate over the top of the pan. Invert them both, so the apples transfer onto the plate.

6 Serve at room temperature, cut into wedges. Cover with an inverted bowl and store in the refrigerator up to 3 days.

Apricots in Lemon Syrup
Albicocche al Limone

MAKES 6 SERVINGS

Perfectly ripe apricots really need no enhancement, but if you have some that are less than perfect, try cooking them in a simple lemon syrup. Serve the poached apricots chilled, possibly with amaretto-flavored whipped cream.

1 cup cold water

1/4 cup sugar, or to taste

2 (2-inch) strips lemon zest

2 tablespoons fresh lemon juice

1 pound apricots (about 8)

1 In a saucepan or skillet large enough to hold the apricot halves in a single layer, combine the water, sugar, zest, and juice. Bring to a simmer over medium-low heat and cook, swirling the pan once or twice, for 10 minutes.

2 Following the line on the apricots, cut them in half and remove the pits. Place the halves in the simmering syrup. Cook, turning once, until the fruit is tender, about 5 minutes.

3 Let the apricots cool briefly in the syrup, then cover and store in the refrigerator. Serve chilled.

Berries with Lemon and Sugar
Frutti di Bosco al Limone

MAKES 4 SERVINGS

Fresh lemon juice and sugar bring out all the flavor of berries. Try this with just one berry variety or a combination. Top the dressed berries with a scoop of lemon ice or sorbet if you like.

One of my favorite berries, the tiny wild strawberry (fragoline del bosco), is common in Italy but not widely available here. Wild strawberries have a mouthwatering strawberry aroma and are easy to grow in a flowerpot. Seeds are available from many catalog companies, and you can buy the plants at many nurseries here in the United States.

I cup sliced strawberries
I cup blackberries
I cup blueberries
I cup raspberries
Freshly squeezed lemon juice (about 2 tablespoons)
Sugar (about I tablespoon)

1 In a large bowl, gently toss the berries together. Drizzle with the lemon juice and sugar to taste. Taste and adjust seasoning.

2 Place the berries in shallow serving dishes. Serve immediately.

Strawberries with Balsamic Vinegar
Fragole al Balsamico

MAKES 2 SERVINGS

If you can find the little wild strawberries known in Italian as fragoline del bosco, use them in this dessert. But ordinary fresh strawberries, too, will benefit from a quick marinate in aged balsamic vinegar. Like a sprinkle of fresh lemon juice on a piece of fish, or salt on a steak, the intense sweet-and-tangy flavor of balsamic vinegar enhances many

foods. Think of it as a condiment rather than as a vinegar.

You probably will have to buy aged balsamic vinegar at a specialty store. In the New York area, one of my favorite sources is Di Palo Fine Foods on Grand Street in Little Italy (see Sources on page 626). Louis Di Palo is a walking encyclopedia on balsamic vinegar, as well as just about any other food product imported from Italy. The first time I asked for balsamico, he brought out several bottles and offered everyone in the shop samples as he explained each one.

The best balsamico is made in the provinces of Modena and Reggio in Emilia-Romagna. Smooth, complex, and syrupy, it tastes more like a rich liqueur than a harsh vinegar, and it is often drunk as a cordial. Look for the words Aceto Balsamico Tradizionale on the label. Though it is expensive, a little bit goes a long way.

I pint wild or cultivated strawberries, sliced if large
2 tablespoons best-quality aged balsamic vinegar, or to taste
2 tablespoons sugar

In a medium bowl, toss the strawberries with the vinegar and sugar. Let stand 15 minutes before serving.

Raspberries with Mascarpone and Balsamic Vinegar
Lampone con Mascarpone e Balsamico

MAKES 4 SERVINGS

Always rinse delicate raspberries just before you are ready to use them—if you rinse them earlier, the moisture could cause them to spoil more quickly. Before serving them, look them over and discard those that show any signs of mold. Store berries in an uncovered shallow container in the refrigerator, *but use them as soon as possible after purchasing them, as they deteriorate rapidly.*

Mascarpone is a thick, smooth cream that is called a cheese, though it has only the slightest cheesy tang. It has a texture similar to sour cream, or slightly thicker. If you prefer, crème fraîche, ricotta, or sour cream can be substituted.

1 1/2 cups mascarpone
About 1/4 cup sugar
1 to 2 tablespoons best-quality aged balsamic vinegar
2 cups raspberries, lightly rinsed and dried

1 In a small bowl, whisk the mascarpone and sugar until well blended. Stir in the balsamic vinegar to taste. Let stand 15 minutes and stir again.

2 Divide the raspberries among 4 goblets or serving bowls. Top with the mascarpone and serve immediately.

Cherries in Barolo
Ciliege al Barolo

MAKES 4 SERVINGS

Here, sweet, ripe cherries are simmered Piedmont style in Barolo or another full-bodied red wine.

3/4 cup sugar
1 cup Barolo or other dry red wine
1 pound ripe sweet cherries, pitted
1 cup heavy or whipping cream, well chilled

1 At least 20 minutes before you are ready to whip the cream, place a large bowl and the beaters of an electric mixer in the refrigerator.

2 In a large saucepan, combine the sugar and wine. Bring to a simmer and cook 5 minutes.

3 Add the cherries. After the liquid returns to a simmer, cook until the cherries are tender when pierced with a knife, about 10 minutes more. Let cool.

4 Just before serving, remove the bowl and beaters from the refrigerator. Pour the cream into the bowl and whip the cream at high speed until it holds its shape softly when the beaters are lifted, about 4 minutes.

5 Spoon the cherries into serving bowls. Serve at room temperature or slightly chilled with whipped cream.

Hot Roasted Chestnuts
Caldarroste

MAKES 8 SERVINGS

St. Martin's Day, November 11, is celebrated all over Italy with hot roasted chestnuts and newly made red wine. The celebration marks not only the feast day of a beloved saint who was known for his kindness to the poor, but also the end of the growing season, the day the earth goes into repose for winter.

Roasted chestnuts are also a classic finishing touch to winter holiday meals throughout Italy. I put them in the oven to cook when we sit down to dinner, and by the time we are finished with our main course, they are ready to eat.

1 pound fresh chestnuts

1 Place a rack in the center of the oven. Preheat the oven to 425°F. Rinse the chestnuts and pat them dry. Place the chestnuts flat-side down on a cutting board. Carefully cut an X on the top of each with the tip of a small sharp knife.

2 Place the chestnuts on a large sheet of heavy-duty aluminum foil. Fold one end over the other to enclose the chestnuts. Fold the ends over to seal. Place the package in a baking pan. Roast the chestnuts until tender when pierced with a small knife, about 45 to 60 minutes.

3 Transfer the foil package to a cooling rack. Leave the chestnuts wrapped in the foil for 10 minutes. Serve hot.

Fig Preserves
Marmellata di Fichi

MAKES 1½ PINTS

Fig trees, both domesticated and wild, grow all over Italy, except in the northernmost regions where it is too cold. Because they are so sweet and widely available, figs are used in many desserts, especially in southern Italy. Ripe figs do not keep well, so when they are abundant in late summer they are preserved in several different ways. In Puglia, the figs are cooked with water to make thick, sweet syrup that is used for desserts. Figs are also dried in the sun or turned into fig preserves.

A small batch of fig preserves is easy to make and can be stored for a month in the refrigerator. For longer storage, the jam should be canned (following safe canning methods) or frozen. Serve it as a complement to a cheese course or for breakfast on buttered walnut bread.

1½ pounds fresh ripe figs, rinsed and dried
2 cups sugar
2 strips lemon zest

1 Peel the figs and cut them into quarters. Place them in a medium bowl with sugar and lemon zest. Stir well. Cover and refrigerate overnight.

2 The next day, transfer the contents of the bowl to a large heavy saucepan. Bring to a simmer over medium heat. Cook, stirring occasionally, until the mixture thickens slightly, about 5 minutes. To test if the mixture is thick enough, place a drop of the slightly cooled liquid between your thumb and index finger. If the mixture forms a thread when the thumb and finger are slightly separated, the preserves are ready.

3 Spoon into sterilized jars and store in the refrigerator up to 30 days.

Chocolate-Dipped Figs
Fichi al Cioccolato

MAKES 8 TO 10 SERVINGS

Moist dried figs stuffed with nuts and dipped in chocolate are nice as a little after-dinner treat.

I like to buy candied orange peel at Kalustyan's, a shop in New York City that specializes in spices, dried fruits, and nuts. Because they sell a lot of it, it is always fresh and full of flavor. Many other specialty shops sell good candied orange peel. You can also order it by mail (see Sources, page 626). Supermarket candied orange peel and other fruits are chopped into small bits and usually dry and tasteless.

18 moist dried figs (about 1 pound)
18 toasted almonds
½ cup candied orange peel
4 ounces bittersweet chocolate, chopped or broken into small pieces
2 tablespoons unsalted butter

1 Line a tray with wax paper and set a wire cooling rack on top. Make a small slit in the base of each fig. Insert an almond and a piece of orange peel into the figs. Pinch the slit closed.

2 In the top half of a double boiler set over simmering water, melt the chocolate and butter, about 5 minutes. Remove from the heat and stir until smooth. Let stand 5 minutes.

3 Dip each fig in the melted chocolate and place on the wire rack. When all of the figs have been dipped, place the tray in the refrigerator to set the chocolate, about 1 hour.

4 Place the figs in an airtight container, separating each layer with wax paper. Store in the refrigerator up to 30 days.

Figs in Wine Syrup
Fichi alla Contadina

MAKES 8 SERVINGS

Dried calimyrna and mission figs from California are moist and plump. Either variety can be used for this recipe. After poaching, they are good as is, or served with ice cream or whipped cream. They also go well with gorgonzola cheese.

1 cup vin santo, Marsala, or dry red wine
2 tablespoons honey
2 (2-inch) strips lemon zest
18 moist dried figs (about 1 pound)

1 In a medium saucepan, combine the vin santo, honey, and lemon zest. Bring to a simmer over low heat and cook 1 minute.

2 Add the figs and cold water to cover. Bring the liquid to a simmer over low heat and cover the pot. Cook until the figs are tender, about 10 minutes.

3 With a slotted spoon, transfer the figs from the pot to a bowl. Cook the liquid, uncovered, until reduced and slightly thickened, about 5 minutes. Pour the syrup over the figs and let cool. Refrigerate at least 1 hour and up to 3 days. Serve slightly chilled.

Dora's Baked Figs
Fichi al Forno

MAKES 2 DOZEN

Dried figs stuffed with nuts are a Pugliese specialty. This recipe is from my friend Dora Marzovilla, who serves them as an after-dinner treat at her family's New York restaurant, I Trulli. Serve the figs with a glass of dessert wine, such as Moscato di Pantelleria.

24 moist dried figs (about 1½ pounds), stem ends removed
24 toasted almonds
1 tablespoon fennel seeds
¼ cup bay leaves

1 Place a rack in the center of the oven. Preheat the oven to 350°F. Remove the hard stem ends from each fig. With a small knife, cut a slit in the base of the figs. Insert an almond in the figs and pinch the slit closed.

2 Arrange the figs on a baking sheet and bake 15 to 20 minutes or until lightly browned. Let cool on a wire rack.

3 Make a layer of the figs in a 1-quart airtight plastic or glass container. Sprinkle with some of the fennel seeds. Top with a layer of bay leaves. Repeat the layering until all of the ingredients are used. Cover and store in a cool place (but not the refrigerator) at least 1 week before serving.

Honeydew in Mint Syrup
Melone alla Menta

MAKES 4 SERVINGS

After a big fish dinner at a seaside restaurant in Sicily, we were served this cool combination of honeydew melon bathed in a fresh mint syrup.

1 cup cold water
½ cup sugar
½ cup packed fresh spearmint leaves, plus more for garnish
8 to 12 slices peeled ripe honeydew melon

1 In a saucepan, combine the water, sugar, and mint leaves. Bring to a simmer and cook 1 minute or until the leaves are wilted. Remove from the heat. Let cool, then pass the syrup through a fine-mesh strainer into a bowl to strain out the mint leaves.

2 Place the melon on a serving platter and pour the syrup over the melon. Chill in the refrigerator briefly. Serve garnished with mint leaves.

Oranges in Orange Syrup
Arancia Marinate

MAKES 8 SERVINGS

Juicy oranges in a sweet syrup are a perfect dessert after a rich meal. I especially like to serve these in winter when fresh oranges are at their best. Arranged on a platter, the oranges look very pretty with their topping of orange zest strips and glistening syrup. As a variation, cut the oranges into wedges and combine them with sliced ripe pineapple. Serve the orange sauce over all.

8 large navel oranges

1 1/4 cups sugar

2 tablespoons orange brandy or liqueur

1 Scrub the oranges with a brush. Trim off the ends. With a vegetable peeler, peel off the colored part of the orange skin (the zest) in wide strips. Avoid digging into the bitter white pith. Stack the zest strips and cut them into narrow matchstick pieces.

2 Remove the white pith from the oranges. Place the oranges on a serving platter.

3 Bring a small saucepan of water to a boil. Add the orange zest and bring to a simmer. Cook 1 minute. Drain the zest and rinse under cool water. Repeat. (This will help to remove some of the bitterness from the zest.)

4 Place the sugar and 1/4 cup of water in another small saucepan over medium heat. Bring the mixture to a boil. Cook until the sugar is melted and the syrup thickens, about 3 minutes. Stir in the orange zest and cook 3 minutes more. Let cool.

5 Add the orange brandy to the contents of the pot. With a fork, remove the orange zest from the syrup and pile it on top of the oranges. Spoon on the syrup. Cover and chill up to 3 hours until ready to serve.

Oranges Gratinéed with Zabaglione
Arancia allo Zabaglione

MAKES 4 SERVINGS

Gratiné is a French word meaning to brown the surface of a dish. Usually it applies to savory foods that are sprinkled with bread crumbs or cheese to help them brown.

Zabaglione is typically served plain or as a sauce for fruit or cake. Here it is spooned over oranges and broiled briefly until it browns slightly and forms a creamy topping. Bananas, kiwis, berries, or other soft fruits can also be prepared this way.

6 navel oranges, peeled and thinly sliced

ZABAGLIONE

1 large egg

2 large egg yolks

1/3 cup sugar

1/3 cup dry or sweet Marsala

1 Preheat the broiler. Arrange the orange slices in a flameproof baking dish, overlapping slightly.

2 Prepare the zabaglione: Fill a small saucepan or the bottom of a double boiler with 2 inches of water. Bring it to a simmer over low heat. In a bowl larger than the rim of the pan or the top of the double boiler, combine the egg, yolks, sugar, and Marsala. Beat with a hand-held electric beater until foamy. Place over the pan of simmering water. Beat until the mixture is pale-colored and holds a soft shape when the beaters are lifted, about 5 minutes.

3 Spread the zabaglione over the oranges. Put the dish under the broiler 1 to 2 minutes or until the zabaglione is browned in spots. Serve immediately.

White Peaches in Asti Spumante
Pesche Bianche in Asti Spumante

MAKES 4 SERVINGS

Asti Spumante is a sweet, sparkling dessert wine from Piedmont in northwestern Italy. It has a delicate orange-blossom flavor and aroma that comes from muscat grapes. If you can't find white peaches, yellow peaches will work well or substitute another summer fruit, such as nectarines, plums, or apricots.

4 large ripe white peaches
1 tablespoon sugar
8 ounces chilled Asti Spumante

1 Peel and pit the peaches. Cut them into thin slices.

2 Toss the peaches with the sugar and let stand 10 minutes.

3 Spoon the peaches into goblets or parfait glasses. Pour on the Asti Spumante and serve immediately.

Peaches in Red Wine
Pesche al Vino Rosso

MAKES 4 SERVINGS

I remember watching my grandfather cutting up his homegrown white peaches to soak in a pitcher of red wine. The sweet peach juices tamed any roughness in the wine. White peaches are my favorite, but yellow peaches or nectarines are good too.

1/3 cup sugar, or to taste
2 cups fruity red wine
4 ripe peaches

1 In a medium bowl, combine the sugar and wine.

2 Cut the peaches in half and remove the pits. Cut the peaches into bite-size pieces. Stir them into the wine. Cover and refrigerate 2 to 3 hours.

3 Spoon the peaches and wine into goblets and serve.

Amaretti-Stuffed Peaches
Pesche al Forno

MAKES 4 SERVINGS

This is a favorite dessert from Piedmont. Serve it drizzled with heavy cream or topped with a scoop of ice cream.

8 medium peaches, not too ripe
8 amaretti cookies
2 tablespoons softened unsalted butter
2 tablespoons sugar
1 large egg

1 Place a rack in the center of the oven. Preheat the oven to 375°F. Butter a baking dish large enough to hold the peach halves in a single layer.

2 Place the amaretti cookies in a plastic bag and crush them gently with a heavy object, such as a rolling pin. You should have about 1/2 cup. In a medium bowl, mix together the butter and sugar and stir in the crumbs.

3 Following the line around the peaches, cut them in half and remove the pits. With a grapefruit spoon or a melon baller, scoop out a little of the peach flesh from the center to widen the opening and add it to the crumb mixture. Stir the egg into the mixture.

4 Arrange the peach halves cut sides up in the dish. Spoon some of the crumb mixture into each peach half.

5 Bake 1 hour or until the peaches are tender. Serve hot or at room temperature.

Pears in Orange Sauce
Pere all' Arancia

MAKES 4 SERVINGS

When I visited Anna Tasca Lanza at Regaleali, her family's wine estate in Sicily, she gave me some of her excellent mandarin orange marmalade to take home. Anna uses the marmalade both as a spread and as a dessert sauce, and inspired me to stir some into the poaching liquid of some pears I was cooking. The pears had a beautiful golden glaze, and everyone loved the result. Now I make this dessert often. Because I quickly used up the supply of marmalade Anna gave me, I use quality store-bought orange marmalade.

1/2 cup sugar
1 cup dry white wine
4 firm ripe pears, such as Anjou, Bartlett, or Bosc
1/3 cup orange marmalade
2 tablespoons orange liqueur or rum

1 In a saucepan just large enough to hold the pears upright, combine the sugar and wine. Over medium heat, bring to a simmer and cook until the sugar is dissolved.

2 Add the pears. Cover the pan and cook about 30 minutes or until the pears are tender when pierced with a knife.

3 With a slotted spoon, transfer the pears to a serving platter. Add the marmalade to the liquid in the saucepan. Bring to a simmer and cook 1 minute. Remove from the heat and stir in the liqueur. Spoon the sauce over and around the pears. Cover and chill in the refrigerator at least 1 hour before serving.

Pears with Marsala and Cream
Pere al Marsala

MAKES 4 SERVINGS

I had pears prepared this way at a trattoria in Bologna. If you prepare them just before eating dinner, they will be at the right serving temperature when you are ready for dessert.

You can find both dry and sweet Marsala imported from Sicily, though the dry is of better quality. Either can be used for making desserts.

4 large Anjou, Bartlett, or Bosc pears, not too ripe
1/4 cup sugar
1/2 cup water
1/2 cup dry or sweet Marsala
1/4 cup heavy cream

1 Peel the pears and cut them in half lengthwise.

2 In a skillet large enough to hold the pear halves in a single layer, bring the sugar and water to a simmer over medium heat. Stir to dissolve the sugar. Add the pears and cover the skillet. Cook 5 to 10 minutes or until the pears are almost tender when pierced with a fork.

3 With a slotted spoon, transfer the pears to a plate. Add the Marsala to the skillet and bring to a simmer. Cook until the syrup is slightly thickened, about 5 minutes. Stir in the cream and simmer 2 minutes more.

4 Return the pears to the skillet and baste them with the sauce. Transfer the pears to serving dishes and spoon the sauce over the top. Let cool to room temperature before serving.

Pears with Warm Chocolate Sauce

Pere Affogato al Cioccolato

MAKES 6 SERVINGS

Sweet fresh pears bathed in a bittersweet chocolate sauce is a classic European dessert. I had this in Bologna, where the chocolate sauce was made with Majani chocolate, a locally made brand that unfortunately does not travel far from its hometown. Use a good-quality bittersweet chocolate. One brand that I like, Scharffen Berger, is made in California.

6 Anjou, Bartlett, or Bosc pears, not too ripe
2 cups water
3/4 cup sugar
4 (2 × 1/2–inch) strips orange zest, cut into matchsticks
1 1/2 cups Warm Chocolate Sauce (page 544)

1 Peel the pears, leaving the stems intact. With a melon baller or small spoon, scoop out the core and seeds, working from the bottom of the pears.

2 In a saucepan large enough to hold all the pears upright, bring the water, sugar, and orange zest to a simmer over medium heat. Stir until the sugar is dissolved.

3 Add the pears and reduce the heat to low. Cover the pan and cook, turning the pears once, for 20 minutes or until tender when pierced with a small knife. Let the pears cool in the syrup.

4 When ready to serve, prepare the chocolate sauce.

5 With a slotted spoon, transfer the pears to serving dishes. (Cover and refrigerate the syrup for another use, such as tossing with cut-up fruits for a salad.) Drizzle with warm chocolate sauce. Serve immediately.

Rum-Spiced Pears

Pere al Rhum

MAKES 6 SERVINGS

The sweet, mild, almost floral taste of ripe pears lends itself to many other complementary flavors. Fruits such as oranges, lemons, and berries and many cheeses go well with them, and Marsala and dry wines are often used to poach pears. In Piedmont I was pleasantly surprised to be served these pears simmered in a spiced rum syrup accompanying a simple hazelnut cake.

6 Anjou, Bartlett, or Bosc pears, not too ripe
1/4 cup brown sugar
1/4 cup dark rum
1/4 cup water
4 whole cloves

1 Peel the pears, leaving the stems intact. With a melon baller or small spoon, scoop out the core and seeds, working from the bottom of the pears.

2 In a saucepan just large enough to hold the pears, stir together the sugar, rum, and water over medium heat until the sugar is melted, about 5 minutes. Add the pears. Scatter the cloves around the fruit.

3 Cover the pan and bring the liquid to a simmer. Cook over medium-low heat 15 to 20 minutes or until the pears are tender when pierced with a knife. With a slotted spoon, transfer the pears to a serving dish.

4 Simmer the liquid uncovered until reduced and syrupy. Strain the liquid over the pears. Let cool.

5 Serve at room temperature or cover and chill in the refrigerator.

Spiced Pears
with Pecorino
Pere allo Spezie e Pecorino

MAKES 6 SERVINGS

Tuscans are rightly proud of their excellent sheep's milk cheese. Every town has its own version, and each tastes slightly different from the others, depending on how it is aged and where the milk comes from. Usually the cheeses are eaten when they are quite young and still semifirm. When eaten for dessert, the cheese is sometimes drizzled with a little honey or served with pears. I like this sophisticated presentation that I had in Montalcino— pecorino served with pears cooked in the local red wine and spices, accompanied by fresh walnuts.

Of course, the pears are also good served plain or with a large spoonful of whipped cream.

6 medium Anjou, Bartlett, or Bosc pears, not too ripe

1 cup dry red wine

1/2 cup sugar

1 (3-inch) piece cinnamon stick

4 whole cloves

8 ounces Pecorino Toscano, Asiago, or Parmigiano-
    Reggiano cheese, cut into 6 pieces

12 walnut halves, toasted

1 Place a rack in the center of the oven. Preheat the oven to 450°F. Arrange the pears in a baking dish just large enough to hold them upright.

2 Stir together the wine and sugar until the sugar softens. Pour the mixture over the pears. Scatter the cinnamon and cloves around the pears.

3 Bake the pears, basting them occasionally with the wine, 45 to 60 minutes or until they are tender when pierced with a knife. If the liquid begins to dry up before the pears are done, add a little warm water to the pan.

4 Let the pears cool in the dish, basting them occasionally with the pan juices. (As the juices cool, they thicken and coat the pears with a rich red glaze.) Remove the spices.

5 Serve the pears with the syrup at room temperature or slightly chilled. Place them on serving dishes with two walnut halves and a piece of the cheese.

Poached Pears
with Gorgonzola
Pere al Gorgonzola

MAKES 4 SERVINGS

The spicy flavor of gorgonzola cheese blended to a smooth cream is a savory complement to these pears poached in a lemony white-wine syrup. A sprinkling of pistachios adds a bright touch of color. Anjou, Bartlett, and Bosc pears are my favorite varieties for poaching, because their slender shape allows them to cook through evenly. Poached pears hold their shape better when the fruit are not too ripe.

2 cups dry white wine

2 tablespoons fresh lemon juice

3/4 cup sugar

2 (2-inch) strips lemon zest

4 pears, such as Anjou, Bartlett, or Bosc

4 ounces gorgonzola

2 tablespoons ricotta, mascarpone, or heavy cream

2 tablespoons chopped pistachios

1 In a medium saucepan, combine the wine, lemon juice, sugar, and lemon zest. Bring to a simmer and cook for 10 minutes.

2 Meanwhile, peel the pears and cut them in half lengthwise. Remove the cores.

3 Slip the pears into the wine syrup and cook until tender when pierced with a knife, about 10 minutes. Let cool.

4 With a slotted spoon, transfer two pear halves to each serving dish, cored-side up. Drizzle the syrup around the pears.

5 In a small bowl, mash the gorgonzola with the ricotta to make a smooth paste. Scoop some of the cheese mixture into the cored space of each pear half. Sprinkle with the pistachios. Serve immediately.

Pear or Apple Pudding Cake

Budino di Pere o Mele

MAKES 6 SERVINGS

Not quite a cake or a pudding, this dessert consists of fruit cooked until tender, then baked with a slightly cakelike topping. It is good with apples or pears or even peaches or plums.

I like to use dark rum for flavoring this dessert, but light rum, cognac, or even grappa can be substituted.

³/4 **cup raisins**
¹/2 **cup dark rum, cognac, or grappa**
2 **tablespoons unsalted butter**
8 **firm ripe pears or apples, peeled and cut into**
    ¹/2**-inch slices**
¹/3 **cup sugar**

Topping

6 **tablespoons unsalted butter, melted and cooled**
¹/3 **cup sugar**
¹/2 **cup all-purpose flour**
3 **large eggs, separated**
²/3 **cup whole milk**
2 **tablespoons dark rum, cognac, or grappa**
1 **teaspoon pure vanilla extract**
Pinch of salt
Confectioner's sugar

1 In a small bowl, toss together the raisins and rum. Let stand for 30 minutes.

2 Melt the butter in a large skillet over medium heat. Add the fruit and sugar. Cook, stirring occasionally, until the fruit is almost tender, about 7 minutes. Add the raisins and rum. Cook 2 minutes more. Remove from the heat.

3 Place a rack in the center of the oven. Preheat the oven to 350°F. Grease a 13 × 9 × 2–inch baking dish. Spoon the fruit mixture into the baking dish.

4 Prepare the topping: In a large bowl, with an electric mixer, beat the butter and sugar until blended, about 3 minutes. Stir in the flour, just to combine.

5 In a medium bowl, whisk together the egg yolks, milk, rum, and vanilla. Stir the egg mixture into the flour mixture until blended.

6 In another large bowl, with clean beaters beat the egg whites with the salt on low speed until foamy. Increase the speed and beat until soft peaks form, about 4 minutes. Gently fold the whites into the rest of the batter. Pour the batter over the fruit in the baking dish and bake 25 minutes or until the top is golden and firm to the touch.

7 Serve warm or at room temperature, sprinkled with confectioner's sugar.

Warm Fruit Compote

Composta di Frutta Calda

MAKES 6 TO 8 SERVINGS

Rum is often used to flavor desserts in Italy. Dark rum has a deeper flavor than light rum. Substitute another liqueur or a sweet wine such as Marsala for the rum in this recipe if you like. Or make a non-alcoholic version with orange or apple juice.

2 **firm ripe pears, peeled and cored**
1 **golden delicious or Granny Smith apple,**
    peeled and cored
1 **cup pitted prunes**
1 **cup dried figs, stem ends removed**
¹/2 **cup dried pitted apricots**
¹/2 **cup dark raisins**
¹/4 **cup sugar**
2 **(2-inch) strips lemon zest**
1 **cup water**
¹/2 **cup dark rum**

1 Cut the pears and apple into 8 wedges. Cut the wedges into bite-size pieces.

2 Combine all of the ingredients in a large saucepan. Cover and bring to a simmer over medium-low heat. Cook until the fresh fruits are tender and the dried fruits are plump, about 20 minutes. Add a little more water if they seem dry.

3 Let cool slightly before serving or cover and refrigerate up to 3 days.

Venetian Caramelized Fruit

Golosezzi Veneziani

MAKES 8 SERVINGS

The caramel coating on these Venetian skewered fruits hardens, with a result something like a candy apple. Pat the fruits thoroughly dry and make these fruit skewers on a dry day. If the weather is humid, the caramel will not harden properly.

1 tangerine or clementine, peeled, divided into sections
8 small strawberries, hulled
8 seedless grapes
8 pitted dates
1 cup sugar
1/2 cup light corn syrup
1/4 cup water

1 Thread the fruit pieces alternately on each of eight 6-inch wood skewers. Set a wire cooling rack on top of a tray.

2 In a skillet large enough to fit the skewers into lengthwise, combine the sugar, corn syrup, and water. Cook over medium heat, stirring occasionally until the sugar is completely dissolved, about 3 minutes. When the mixture begins to boil, stop stirring and cook until the syrup starts to brown around the edges. Then gently swirl the pan over the heat until the syrup is an even golden brown, about 2 minutes more.

3 Remove the pan from the heat. Using tongs, quickly dip each skewer in the syrup, turning to coat the fruit lightly but thoroughly. Let the excess syrup drain back into the pan. Place the skewers on the rack to cool. (If the syrup in the pan hardens before all of the skewers have been dipped, reheat it gently.) Serve at room temperature within 2 hours.

Fruit with Honey and Grappa

Composta di Frutta alla Grappa

MAKES 6 SERVINGS

Grappa is a kind of brandy made from vinaccia, the skins and seeds that are left after grapes are pressed to make wine. At one time, grappa was a coarse beverage mostly drunk in northern Italy by farm-hands and laborers for warmth on cold winter days. Today, grappa is a very refined drink, sold in designer bottles with ornate stoppers. Some grappas are fla-vored with fruit or herbs, while others are aged in wood casks. Use a simple, unflavored grappa for this fruit salad and for other cooking purposes.

1/3 cup honey
1/3 cup grappa, brandy, or fruit liqueur
1 tablespoon fresh lemon juice
2 kiwis, peeled and sliced
2 navel oranges, peeled and cut into wedges
1 pint strawberries, sliced
1 cup halved seedless green grapes
2 medium bananas, sliced

1 In a large serving bowl, mix together the honey, grappa, and lemon juice.

2 Stir in the kiwis, oranges, strawberries, and grapes. Chill for at least 1 hour or up to 4 hours. Stir in the bananas just before serving.

Winter Fruit Salad
Macedonia del' Inverno

MAKES 6 SERVINGS

In Italy, a fruit salad is called Macedonia, because that country was once divided up into many little sections that were brought together to make a whole, just as the salad is made up of bite-size pieces of different fruits. In the winter, when fruit choices are limited, Italians make salads like this one dressed with honey and lemon juice. As a variation, substitute apricot jam or orange marmalade for the honey.

3 tablespoons honey
3 tablespoons orange juice
I tablespoon fresh lemon juice
2 grapefruits, peeled and separated into wedges
2 kiwis, peeled and sliced
2 ripe pears
2 cups seedless green grapes, halved lengthwise

I In a large bowl, mix together the honey, orange juice, and lemon juice.

2 Add the fruits to the bowl and toss well. Chill for at least 1 hour or up to 4 hours before serving.

Grilled Summer Fruit
Spiedini alla Frutta

MAKES 6 SERVINGS

Grilled summer fruits are great for a barbecue. Serve them plain or with slices of sponge cake and ice cream.

If using wood skewers, soak them in cold water at least 30 minutes to prevent burning.

2 nectarines, cut into I-inch chunks
2 plums, cut into I-inch chunks
2 pears, cut into I-inch chunks
2 apricots, cut into quarters
2 bananas, cut into I-inch chunks
Fresh mint leaves
About 2 tablespoons sugar

I Place a barbecue grill or broiler rack about 5 inches away from the heat source. Preheat the grill or broiler.

2 Alternate pieces of the fruits with the mint leaves on 6 skewers. Sprinkle with the sugar.

3 Grill or broil the fruit 3 minutes on one side. Turn the skewers and grill or broil until lightly browned, about 2 minutes more. Serve hot.

"Eat-and-Drink" Dessert
Mangia e Bevi

MAKES 6 SERVINGS

Fruit salads are popular all year round in Italy, but come summertime, the Florentines like to top theirs with a scoop of gelato. As the ice cream melts, it blends with the fruit juices, giving the dessert its name. A tablespoon or two of orange or apricot brandy is a nice addition. This is a great way to get non–fruit eaters to enjoy fruit.

I pint Lemon Ice Cream (page 535), Orange Spumone (page 541), or vanilla ice cream, softened
I ripe peach, cut into bite-size pieces
I large banana, sliced
I cup sliced strawberries
2 kiwis, peeled and sliced
1/4 cup fresh orange juice or apple juice
2 tablespoons sugar (optional)

I Prepare the gelato or spumone, if necessary. Then, in a large bowl, toss together the fruits, juice, and sugar, if using any.

2 Spoon the fruit salad into serving dishes. Top with scoops of gelato, spumone, or ice cream. Serve immediately.

❧ Spoon Desserts

Dolci di cucchiaio, meaning "spoon sweets," is a collective term for puddings, gelatins, custards, flans, and most other desserts eaten with a spoon. One exception is frozen desserts like gelati, sorbets, and ices, which make up a separate category. Spoon desserts are rather loosely defined; I think of them as comfort desserts.

Some of the simplest desserts in this chapter are those made with mascarpone and ricotta. If you are fortunate enough to have a source for these cheeses freshly made, you know how good they can be right out of the container. In Sicily, at Regaleali, a winery and working farm in Vallelunga, we ate sheep's milk ricotta so fresh it was still warm. Many Italians eat fresh ricotta sprinkled with sugar or honey for breakfast. Though both ricotta and mascarpone are used as ingredients in cheesecakes and pastry fillings, they can also make simple and delicious desserts with the addition of a few flavorings.

Panna cotta, a Piedmontese dessert made with thickened cream and sugar, may be replacing tiramisù as the most overdone dessert around the world, but there is a good reason for it's popularity—it's delicious! I have also included a variety of caramelized desserts, such as *bunet*, a Piedmontese baked chocolate custard, as well as my version of the Roman way with crème brûlée.

Zabaglione is probably the most classic of the spoon desserts. It is a foamy custard made by whipping eggs with sweet or dry Marsala and sugar. Zabaglione lovers will also enjoy the chocolate and chilled variations.

Warm Ricotta with Honey
Ricotta al Miele

MAKES 2 TO 3 SERVINGS

The success of this dessert depends on the quality of the ricotta, so buy the freshest available. While part-skimmed-milk ricotta is fine, the fat-free is very grainy and tasteless, so don't use it. If you like, add some fresh fruit, or try raisins and a pinch of cinnamon.

I cup whole-milk ricotta
2 tablespoons honey

I Place the ricotta in a small bowl set over a smaller pan of simmering water. Heat until warm, about 10 minutes. Stir well.

2 Scoop the ricotta into serving dishes. Drizzle with the honey. Serve immediately.

Coffee Ricotta
Ricotta all' Caffè

MAKES 2 TO 3 SERVINGS

Here is a quick dessert that lends itself to a multitude of variations. Serve it with some plain butter cookies.

If you can't buy finely ground espresso, be sure to run the grounds through your coffee grinder or food processor. If the grounds are too large, the dessert won't blend right, leaving it with a gritty texture.

I cup (8 ounces) whole or part-skim ricotta
I tablespoon finely ground (espresso) coffee
I tablespoon sugar
Chocolate shavings

In a medium bowl, whisk together the ricotta, espresso, and sugar until the mixture is smooth and the sugar is dissolved. (For a creamier texture, mix the ingredients in a food processor.) Spoon into parfait glasses or goblets and top with chocolate shavings. Serve immediately.

Variation: For chocolate ricotta, substitute I tablespoon unsweetened cocoa for the coffee.

Mascarpone and Peaches
Mascarpone al Pesche

MAKES 6 SERVINGS

Smooth, creamy mascarpone and peaches with crunchy amaretti look beautiful in parfait or wine glasses. Serve this dessert at a dinner party. No one will guess how easy it is to make.

1 cup (8 ounces) mascarpone
1/4 cup sugar
1 tablespoon fresh lemon juice
1 cup very cold whipping cream
3 peaches or nectarines, peeled and cut into
   bite-size pieces
1/3 cup orange liqueur, amaretto, or rum
8 amaretti cookies, crushed into crumbs
   (about 1/2 cup)
2 tablespoons toasted sliced almonds

1 At least 20 minutes before you are ready to make the dessert, place a large bowl and the beaters of an electric mixer in the refrigerator.

2 When ready, in a medium bowl, whisk together the mascarpone, sugar, and lemon juice. Remove the bowl and beaters from the refrigerator. Pour the cream into the chilled bowl and whip the cream at high speed until it holds its shape softly when the beaters are lifted, about 4 minutes. With a spatula, gently fold the whipped cream into the mascarpone mixture.

3 In a medium bowl, toss together the peaches and liqueur.

4 Spoon half of the mascarpone cream into six parfait glasses or wine goblets. Make a layer of the peaches, then sprinkle with the amaretti crumbs. Top with the remaining cream. Cover and chill in the refrigerator up to 2 hours.

5 Sprinkle with the almonds before serving.

Chocolate Foam with Raspberries
Spuma di Cioccolato al Lampone

MAKES 8 SERVINGS

Whipped cream folded into mascarpone and chocolate is like an instant chocolate mousse. The raspberries are a sweet and tangy complement.

1 pint raspberries
1 to 2 tablespoons sugar
2 tablespoons raspberry, cherry, or orange liqueur
3 ounces bittersweet or semisweet chocolate
1/2 cup (4 ounces) mascarpone, at room temperature
2 cups chilled heavy or whipping cream
Chocolate shavings, for garnish

1 At least 20 minutes before you are ready to make the dessert, place a large bowl and the beaters of an electric mixer in the refrigerator.

2 When ready, toss the raspberries with the sugar and liqueur in a medium bowl. Set aside.

2 Fill a small pot with an inch of water. Bring it to a simmer over low heat. Place the chocolate in a bowl larger than the rim of the pot and set the bowl over the simmering water. Let stand until the chocolate is melted. Remove from the heat and stir the chocolate until smooth. Let cool slightly, about 15 minutes. With a rubber spatula, fold in the mascarpone.

3 Remove the chilled bowl and beaters from the refrigerator. Pour the cream into the bowl and whip the cream at high speed until it holds its shape softly when the beaters are lifted, about 4 minutes.

4 With a spatula, gently fold half of the cream into the chocolate mixture, reserving the second half for the topping.

5 Spoon half of the chocolate cream into eight parfait glasses. Layer with the raspberries. Spoon on the remaining chocolate cream. Top with the whipped cream. Garnish with the chocolate shavings. Serve immediately.

Tiramisù

Tiramisù

MAKES 8 TO 10 SERVINGS

No one is quite sure why this dessert is called "pick me up" in Italian, but it is assumed the name comes from the jolt of caffeine it provides from the coffee and chocolate. While the classic version contains raw egg yolks mixed in with the mascarpone, my version is eggless because I do not like the flavor of raw eggs and find they make the dessert heavier than it needs to be.

Savoiardi—crisp ladyfingers imported from Italy—are widely available, but ordinary lady fingers or slices of plain cake can be substituted. If you like, add a couple of tablespoons of rum or cognac to the coffee.

1 cup chilled heavy or whipping cream
1 pound mascarpone
1/3 cup sugar
24 savoiardi (imported Italian ladyfingers)
1 cup brewed espresso coffee at room temperature
2 tablespoons unsweetened cocoa powder

1 At least 20 minutes before you are ready to make the dessert, place a large bowl and the beaters of an electric mixer in the refrigerator.

2 When ready, remove the bowl and beaters from the refrigerator. Pour the cream into the bowl and whip the cream at high speed until it holds its shape softly when the beaters are lifted, about 4 minutes.

3 In a large bowl, whisk together the mascarpone and sugar until smooth. Take about one third of the whipped cream, and with a flexible spatula, gently fold it into the mascarpone mixture to lighten it. Carefully fold in the remaining cream.

4 Lightly and quickly dip half of the savoiardi in the coffee. (Do not saturate them or they will fall apart.) Arrange the cookies in a single layer in a 9 × 2–inch square or round serving dish. Spoon on half of the mascarpone cream.

5 Dip the remaining savoiardi in the coffee and arrange them in a layer over the mascarpone. Top with the remaining mascarpone mixture and spread it smooth with the spatula. Place the cocoa in a fine-mesh strainer and shake it over the top of the dessert. Cover with foil or plastic wrap and refrigerate 3 to 4 hours or overnight so that the flavors can meld. It will keep well in the refrigerator up to 24 hours.

Strawberry Tiramisù

Tiramisù alle Fragole

MAKES 8 SERVINGS

Here is a strawberry version of tiramisù that I came across in an Italian cooking magazine. I like it even better than the coffee version, but then I favor fruit-based desserts of all kinds.

Maraschino is a clear, slightly bitter Italian cherry liqueur named for the marasche variety of cherries. Maraschino is available here, but you can substitute another fruit liqueur if you prefer.

3 pints strawberries, washed and hulled
1/2 cup orange juice
1/4 cup maraschino, crème di cassis, or orange liqueur
1/4 cup sugar
1 cup chilled heavy or whipping cream
8 ounces mascarpone
24 savoiardi (Italian lady fingers)

1 Set aside 2 cups of the best-looking strawberries for garnish. Chop the remainder. In a large bowl, combine the strawberries with the orange juice, liqueur, and sugar. Let stand at room temperature 1 hour.

2 Meanwhile, place a large bowl and the beaters of an electric mixer in the refrigerator. When ready, remove the bowl and beaters from the refrigerator. Pour the cream into the bowl and whip the cream at high speed until it holds its shape softly when the beaters are lifted, about 4 minutes. With a flexible spatula, gently fold in the mascarpone.

3 Make a layer of ladyfingers in a 9 × 2–inch square or round serving dish. Spoon on half of the strawberries and their juice. Spread half of the mascarpone cream over the berries.

4 Repeat with a second layer of ladyfingers, strawberries, and cream, spreading the cream smooth with a spatula. Cover and refrigerate 3 to 4 hours or overnight so that the flavors can meld.

5 Just before serving, slice the remaining strawberries and arrange them in rows on top.

Italian Trifle
Zuppa Inglese

MAKES 10 TO 12 SERVINGS

"English soup" is the whimsical name for this lush dessert. It is believed that Italian cooks borrowed the idea from English trifle and added Italian touches.

1 Sponge Cake (page 570) or 1 (12-ounce) store-bought pound cake, cut into slices, 1/4 inch thick
1/2 cup sour cherry or raspberrry jam
1/2 cup dark rum or orange liqueur
2 1/2 cups each Chocolate and Vanilla Pastry Cream (pages 608–609)
1 cup heavy or whipping cream
Fresh raspberries, for garnish
Chocolate shavings, for garnish

1 Prepare the sponge cake and pastry creams, if necessary. Then, in a small bowl, stir together the jam and rum.

2 Spoon half of the vanilla pastry cream into the bottom of a 3-quart serving bowl. Place 1/4 of the cake slices on top and brush with 1/4 of the jam mixture. Spoon half of the chocolate pastry cream on top.

3 Make another layer of 1/4 of the cake and jam mixture. Repeat with the remaining vanilla cream, 1/4 of the remaining cake and jam mixture, chocolate cream, and the rest of the cake and jam mixture. Cover tightly with plastic and refrigerate at least 3 hours and up to 24 hours.

4 At least 20 minutes before serving, place a large bowl and the beaters of an electric mixer in the refrigerator. Just before serving, remove the bowl and beaters from the refrigerator. Pour the cream into the bowl and whip at high speed until it holds its shape softly when the beaters are lifted, about 4 minutes.

5 Spoon the cream on top of the trifle. Garnish with raspberries and chocolate shavings.

Zabaglione

MAKES 2 SERVINGS

In Italy, zabaglione (pronounced tsah-bahl-yo-neh; the g is silent) is a sweet, creamy, egg-based dessert, often served as a strength-building tonic for someone suffering from a cold or other ailment. Illness or no illness, it is a delicious dessert on its own or as a sauce for fruit or cake.

Zabaglione should be eaten as soon as it is made, or it can collapse. To make zabaglione ahead of time, see the recipe for chilled zabaglione that follows.

3 large egg yolks
3 tablespoons sugar
3 tablespoons dry or sweet Marsala or vin santo

1 In the bottom half of a double boiler or in a medium saucepan, bring about 2 inches of water to a simmer.

2 In the top half of the double boiler or in a heatproof bowl that fits comfortably over the saucepan, beat the egg yolks and sugar with a hand-held electric mixer on medium speed until light, about 2 minutes. Blend in the Marsala. Place the mixture over the simmering water. (Do not allow the water to boil, or the eggs will scramble.)

3 While it warms over the simmering water, continue to beat the egg mixture until it is pale yellow and very fluffy and holds a soft shape when dropped from the beaters, 3 to 5 minutes.

4 Spoon into tall goblets and serve immediately.

Chocolate Zabaglione
Zabaglione al Cioccolato

MAKES 4 SERVINGS

This variation on zabaglione is like a rich chocolate mousse. Serve it warm with cool whipped cream.

3 ounces bittersweet or semisweet chocolate, chopped
1/4 cup heavy cream
4 large egg yolks
1/4 cup sugar
2 tablespoons rum or amaretto liqueur

1 In the bottom half of a double boiler or in a medium saucepan, bring about 2 inches of water to a simmer. Combine the chocolate and cream in a small heatproof bowl set over the simmering water. Let stand until the chocolate is melted. Stir with a flexible spatula until smooth. Remove from the heat.

2 In the top of the double boiler or in another heatproof bowl that fits over the saucepan, beat the egg yolks and sugar with a hand-held electric mixer until light, about 2 minutes. Blend in the rum. Place the mixture over the simmering water. (Do not allow the water to boil, or the eggs will scramble.)

3 Beat the yolk mixture until it is pale and fluffy and holds a soft shape when dropped from the beaters, 3 to 5 minutes. Remove from the heat.

4 With a rubber spatula, gently fold in the chocolate mixture. Serve immediately.

Chilled Zabaglione with Berries
Zabaglione Freddo con Frutti di Bosco

MAKES 6 SERVINGS

If you don't want to make zabaglione right before serving, this cold version is a good alternative. The zabaglione is cooled in an ice-water bath, then folded into whipped cream. It can be made up to 24 hours ahead. I like to serve it over fresh berries or ripe figs.

1 recipe (about 1 1/2 cups) Zabaglione (page 521)
3/4 cup chilled heavy or whipping cream
2 tablespoons confectioner's sugar
1 tablespoon orange liqueur
1 1/2 cups blueberries, raspberries, or a combination, rinsed and patted dry

1 At least 20 minutes before you are ready to make the zabaglione, place a large bowl and the beaters of an electric mixer in the refrigerator. Fill another large bowl with ice and water.

2 Prepare the zabaglione through step 3. As soon as the zabaglione is finished, remove it from the simmering water and set the bowl over the ice water. With a wire whisk, beat the zabaglione until it is cold, about 3 minutes.

3 Remove the chilled bowl and beaters from the refrigerator. Pour the cream into the bowl and whip the cream at high speed until it begins to hold a soft shape, about 2 minutes. Add the confectioner's sugar and orange liqueur. Whip the cream until it holds a soft shape when the beaters are lifted, about 2 minutes more. With a flexible spatula, gently fold in the chilled zabaglione. Cover and chill in the refrigerator at least 1 hour until ready to serve.

4 Divide the berries among 6 serving dishes. Top with the chilled zabaglione cream and serve immediately.

Lemon Gelatin
Gelatina di Limone

MAKES 6 SERVINGS

Lemon juice and zest make this dessert light and refreshing.

2 envelopes unflavored gelatin
1 cup sugar
2¹/₂ cups cold water
2 (2-inch) strips lemon zest
²/₃ cup fresh lemon juice
Lemon slices and mint sprigs, for garnish

1 In a medium saucepan, stir together the gelatin and sugar. Add the water and lemon zest. Cook over medium heat, stirring constantly, until the gelatin is completely dissolved, about 3 minutes. (Do not allow the mixture to boil.)

2 Remove from the heat and stir in the lemon juice. Pour the mixture through a fine-mesh strainer into a 5-cup mold or bowl. Cover and chill until set, 4 hours up to overnight.

3 When ready to serve, fill a bowl with warm water and dip the mold into the water for 30 seconds. Run a small knife around the sides. Lay a plate over the mold, and holding them together, invert them both so that the gelatin transfers to the plate. Garnish with lemon slices and mint sprigs.

Orange Rum Gelatin
Gelatina di Arancia al Rhum

MAKES 4 SERVINGS

Rum-scented whipped cream is a nice accompaniment. Blood orange juice works best here.

2 envelopes unflavored gelatin
¹/₂ cup sugar
¹/₂ cup cold water
3 cups fresh orange juice
2 tablespoons dark rum
Orange slices, for garnish

1 In a medium saucepan, stir together the gelatin and sugar. Add the water and cook over medium heat, stirring constantly, until the gelatin is completely dissolved, about 3 minutes. (Do not allow the mixture to boil.)

2 Remove from the heat and stir in orange juice and rum. Pour mixture into a 5-cup mold or bowl. Cover and chill until set, 4 hours up to overnight.

3 When ready to serve, fill a bowl with warm water and dip the mold into the water for 30 seconds. Run a small knife around the sides. Lay a plate over the mold, and holding them together, invert them both so that the gelatin transfers to the plate. Garnish with the orange slices.

Espresso Gelatin
Gelatina di Caffè

MAKES 4 SERVINGS

When I first tasted this coffee gelatin in Milan, it was served with both whipped cream and Chilled Zabaglione (page 522), a dazzling combination. This is also refreshing, light, and delicious on its own.

2 envelopes unflavored gelatin
1 cup sugar
2¹/₂ cup cold water
2 tablespoons instant espresso powder

1 In a medium saucepan, stir together the gelatin and sugar. Add the water and cook over medium heat, stirring constantly, until the gelatin is completely dissolved, about 3 minutes. Do not allow the mixture to boil.

2 Remove from the heat. Stir in the instant coffee. Pour the mixture into a 1-quart mold. Cover and chill until set, 4 hours up to overnight.

3 When ready to serve, fill a bowl with warm water and dip the mold into the water for 30 seconds. Run a small knife around the sides. Lay a plate over the mold, and holding them together, invert them so the gelatin transfers to the plate.

Panna Cotta

MAKES 6 SERVINGS

The best version of this dessert I have had was in Piedmont at the Giardino da Felicin, a favorite restaurant in Monforte d'Alba. It had just been made and was barely gelled. When I touched it with my spoon, its shape yielded smoothly. The dessert melted in my mouth and tasted of nothing but the finest sweet, fresh cream.

The name of this Piedmontese dessert means "cooked cream," though there is practically no cooking involved. A fresh berry sauce or warm chocolate sauce goes well with it, or just some fresh fruit.

I envelope unflavored gelatin
1¹/₂ cups whole milk
1¹/₂ cups heavy or whipping cream
I vanilla bean or 2 teaspoons pure vanilla extract
I (2-inch) strip lemon zest
¹/₄ cup sugar
Fresh Strawberry Sauce (page 543)

1 Sprinkle the gelatin over the milk and let stand 2 minutes until the gelatin absorbs some of the liquid and softens.

2 In a medium saucepan, combine the cream, vanilla bean (if using vanilla extract, reserve until later), lemon zest, and sugar. Bring to a simmer over medium heat. Add the gelatin mixture and cook, stirring frequently, until the gelatin is completely dissolved, about 3 minutes.

3 Remove the vanilla bean and lemon zest with a slotted spoon. Slit the vanilla bean lengthwise with a small sharp knife and scrape the seeds out. Stir the seeds into the cream mixture. (Or add the vanilla extract, if using.)

4 Pour the cream into a large bowl. Fill a larger bowl with ice and set the bowl with the cream in the ice. Let the cream cool, stirring frequently, until it begins to set, about 10 minutes. Pour the cream into 6 individual custard cups. Cover and chill until set, 4 hours up to overnight.

5 Prepare the strawberry sauce, if necessary. When ready to serve, briefly dip the bottom of the cups in a bowl filled with warm water to loosen. Run a small knife around the inside of the cups. Invert the cups onto serving plates. Spoon the sauce over each and serve.

Crème Brûlée
Crema Bruciata

MAKES 4 SERVINGS

At Il Matriciano Restaurant in Rome, the crème brûlée is baked in big roasting pans. The custard base is thick and rich with egg yolks and cream, and the caramel topping is hard, clear, and crunchy like candy. This is my interpretation of their version.

2 cups heavy cream
3 tablespoons sugar
4 large egg yolks
I teaspoon pure vanilla extract

Topping

¹/₂ cup sugar
3 tablespoons water

1 Place a rack in the center of the oven. Preheat oven to 300°F. Have ready a 4-cup shallow baking dish and a wire cooling rack.

2 In a medium saucepan, combine the cream and sugar. Bring to a simmer over medium heat, stirring to dissolve the sugar.

3 In a large bowl, beat the egg yolks and vanilla. Whisking constantly, pour in the hot cream. Pour the mixture into the baking dish.

4 Place the baking dish in a larger roasting pan. Place the pan in the oven. Carefully pour hot water into the larger pan until it comes to a depth of 1 inch up the side of the baking dish. Bake 45 to 50 minutes, just until set but still slightly soft in the center. Transfer the baking dish to the rack to cool for 30 minutes. Cover and refrigerate.

5 Up to 12 hours before serving, combine the sugar and water in a small heavy saucepan. Cook over medium heat, stirring occasionally, until the sugar is completely dissolved, about 3 minutes. When the mixture begins to boil, stop stirring and cook until the syrup starts to brown around the edges. Then gently swirl the pan over the heat until the syrup is an even golden brown, about 2 minutes more.

6 With a paper towel, blot the surface of the chilled cream mixture in the baking dish. Carefully pour the hot syrup over the top. Return the dish to the refrigerator for 10 minutes until the caramel is firm.

7 To serve, crack the caramel with the side of a spoon. Scoop the cream and caramel into serving dishes.

Mascarpone and Coffee Cups
Coppa di Mascarpone al Caffè

MAKES 6 SERVINGS

Though mascarpone is typically made in Lombardy, it is often used in Venetian desserts. This one blends coffee and flavorings into mascarpone and cream, with chopped chocolate for texture. It is similar to tiramisù, which is also from the Veneto, though it does not contain cookies.

You don't need any fancy equipment to make espresso for this dessert or any of the others in this book. An ordinary drip coffee maker can be used, or even instant espresso.

¹/₃ cup hot strong brewed espresso

¹/₄ cup sugar

¹/₄ cup cognac or rum

4 ounces (¹/₂ cup) mascarpone, at room temperature

1 cup heavy or whipping cream

¹/₂ cup chopped semisweet chocolate (about 2 ounces)

1 At least 20 minutes before you are ready to make the dessert, place a medium bowl and the beaters of an electric mixer in the refrigerator. Combine the espresso and sugar. Stir until the sugar is

dissolved. Stir in the cognac. Let cool to room temperature.

2 In a large bowl, whisk the mascarpone and coffee together until smooth. Remove the bowl and beaters from the refrigerator. Pour the cream into the bowl and whip the cream at high speed until it holds its shape softly when the beaters are lifted, about 4 minutes.

3 With a flexible spatula, gently fold the cream into the mascarpone mixture. Set aside 2 tablespoons of the chocolate for garnish, and fold the remaining chocolate into the mascarpone.

4 Spoon the mixture into six goblets. Sprinkle with the reserved chocolate. Cover and chill 1 hour up to overnight.

Chestnut "Mountain"
Monte Bianco

MAKES 6 SERVINGS

This mountain of chestnut puree, whipped cream, and chocolate shavings is named for Mont Blanc, Monte Bianco in Italian, one of the Alps that separate France and Italy in the region of Valle d'Aosta.

Fresh chestnuts in their shell are cooked, then peeled and flavored with rum and chocolate to make this festive dessert. You can avoid the boiling and peeling steps by substituting vacuum-packed cooked chestnuts, either whole or in pieces, sold in jars or cans. You can make most of the recipe several hours in advance of serving.

1 pound fresh chestnuts, or substitute 1 pound vacuum-packed cooked unsweetened chestnuts

1 teaspoon salt

2 cups whole milk

¹/₂ cup sugar

3 ounces bittersweet chocolate, melted

2 tablespoons dark or light rum or brandy

1 cup heavy or whipping cream

¹/₂ teaspoon pure vanilla extract

Shaved bittersweet chocolate, for garnish

(continues)

1 If using fresh chestnuts, place the nuts flat side down on a cutting board. With a small sharp knife, make a slit in the shell without cutting through to the chestnut itself. Place the chestnuts in a saucepan with cold water to cover by two inches and the salt. Bring to a boil and cook until tender when pierced with a knife, about 15 minutes. Let cool slightly in the water. Remove the chestnuts from the water one at a time and peel them while they are still warm, removing both the outer shell and inner skin.

2 Place the peeled chestnuts, or vacuum-packed chestnuts, in a medium saucepan. Add the milk and sugar and bring to a simmer over low heat. Cover and cook, stirring occasionally, until the chestnuts are tender but still hold their shape, about 10 minutes for the vacuum-packed or 20 minutes for the fresh-peeled.

3 Place the chestnuts and cooking liquid in a food processor with the rum. Process until smooth, about 3 minutes. Stir in the melted chocolate. Let cool to room temperature.

4 Scrape the mixture into a food mill fitted with the large-hole blade, or into a potato ricer. Holding the food mill over a serving plate, pass the chestnut mixture through the blade, forming a cone or "mountain" shape. (Can be made ahead up to 3 hours. Cover with plastic wrap and keep at cool room temperature.)

5 At least 20 minutes before serving, place a large bowl and the beaters of an electric mixer in the refrigerator. Remove the bowl and beaters from the refrigerator. Pour the cream into the bowl and whip the cream at high speed until it holds its shape softly when the beaters are lifted, about 4 minutes.

6 Spoon the cream over the chestnut "mountain," letting it drift down softly from the peak like snow. Garnish with the shaved chocolate.

Chocolate Pudding
Crema di Cioccolato

MAKES 8 SERVINGS

Cocoa, chocolate, and heavy cream make this dessert rich, creamy, and flavorful. Serve it in small portions topped with whipped cream and shaved chocolate.

2/3 cup sugar
1/4 cup cornstarch
3 tablespoons unsweetened cocoa powder
1/4 teaspoon salt
2 cups whole milk
1 cup heavy cream
4 ounces bittersweet or semisweet chocolate, chopped, plus more for garnish (optional)

1 In a large bowl, sift together 1/3 cup of the sugar, the cornstarch, cocoa, and salt. Stir in 1/4 cup of the milk until smooth and well blended.

2 In a large saucepan, combine the remaining 1/3 cup sugar, 1 3/4 cups milk, and the heavy cream. Cook over medium heat, stirring frequently, until the sugar is dissolved and the mixture comes to a simmer, about 3 minutes.

3 With a whisk, beat the cocoa mixture into the hot milk mixture. Cook, stirring, until the mixture comes to a simmer. Turn the heat to low and cook until thickened and smooth, 1 minute more.

4 Pour the contents of the saucepan into a large bowl. Add the chocolate and stir until melted and smooth. Cover securely with a piece of plastic wrap, fitting the wrap closely to the pudding surface to prevent a skin from forming. Refrigerate until cold, 3 hours up to overnight.

5 To serve, spoon the pudding into dessert bowls. Garnish with a little chopped chocolate, if desired, and serve.

Chocolate Chip Rice Pudding
Budino di Riso al Cioccolato

MAKES 6 SERVINGS

I had this creamy rice pudding in Bologna, where tarts and puddings made with rice are very popular. It wasn't until I tasted it that I discovered that what appeared to be raisins were actually small chunks of bittersweet chocolate. Whipped cream lightens this rich pudding, made with Italian medium-grain rice. Serve it plain or with Year-Round Raspberry Sauce (page 544) or Warm Chocolate Sauce (page 544).

6 cups whole milk

3/4 cup medium-grain rice, such as Arborio, Carnaroli or Vialone Nano

1/2 teaspoon salt

3/4 cup sugar

2 tablespoons dark rum or cognac

I teaspoon pure vanilla extract

I cup heavy or whipping cream

3 ounces bittersweet chocolate, chopped

1 In a large saucepan, combine the milk, rice, and salt. Bring the milk to a simmer and cook, stirring frequently, until the rice is very tender and the milk is absorbed, about 35 minutes.

2 Transfer the cooked rice to a large bowl. Stir in the sugar and let cool to room temperature. Stir in the rum and vanilla.

3 At least 20 minutes before you are ready to make the dessert, place a large bowl and the beaters of an electric mixer in the refrigerator.

4 When chilled, remove the bowl and beaters from the refrigerator. Pour the cream into the bowl and whip the cream at high speed until it holds its shape softly when the beaters are lifted, about 4 minutes.

5 With a flexible spatula, fold the whipped cream and chopped chocolate into the rice mixture. Serve immediately or cover and chill in the refrigerator.

Coffee Caramel Custard
Pan di Caffè

MAKES 6 SERVINGS

This old Tuscan recipe is like a crème caramel in texture, but it contains no milk or cream. The custard is rich, dark, and dense, though not as heavy as it would be if made with cream. The Italian name shows that at one time it was baked in a loaf shape like bread—pane in Italian.

2 cups hot strong brewed espresso

1 1/2 cups sugar

2 tablespoons water

5 large eggs

I tablespoon rum or cognac

1 Place a rack in the center of the oven. Preheat the oven to 350°F. Have ready 6 heatproof custard cups.

2 In a large bowl, whisk the espresso with 3/4 cup of the sugar until the sugar is dissolved. Let stand until the coffee is at room temperature, about 30 minutes.

3 In a small heavy saucepan, combine the remaining 3/4 cup of sugar and the water. Cook over medium heat, stirring occasionally, until the sugar is completely dissolved, about 3 minutes. When the mixture begins to boil, stop stirring and cook until the syrup starts to brown around the edges. Then gently swirl the pan over the heat until the syrup is an even golden brown, about 2 minutes more. Protecting your hand with an oven mitt, immediately pour the hot caramel into the custard cups.

4 In a large bowl, beat the eggs until blended. Stir in the cooled coffee and the rum. Pour the mixture through a fine-mesh strainer into a bowl, then add it to the custard cups.

5 Place the cups in a large roasting pan. Place the pan in the center of the oven, then pour hot water into the pan to a depth of 1 inch. Bake 30 minutes or until a knife inserted 1/2 inch from the center of

(continues)

the custards comes out clean. Transfer the cups from the pan to the rack to cool. Cover and chill at least 3 hours or overnight.

6 To serve, run a small knife around the inside of each custard cup. Invert onto serving plates and serve immediately.

Chocolate Crème Caramel
Crème Caramel al Cioccolato

MAKES 6 SERVINGS

Crème caramel is a silky smooth baked custard. I like this version, flavored with chocolate, that I had in Rome.

CARAMEL

3/4 cups sugar

2 tablespoons water

CREAM

2 cups whole milk

4 ounces bittersweet or semisweet chocolate, chopped

3/4 cup sugar

4 large eggs

2 large egg yolks

1 Place a rack in the center of the oven. Preheat the oven to 350°F. Have ready 6 heatproof custard cups.

2 Prepare the caramel: In a small heavy saucepan, combine the sugar and the water. Cook over medium heat, stirring occasionally, until the sugar is completely dissolved, about 3 minutes. When the mixture begins to boil, stop stirring and cook until the syrup starts to brown around the edges. Then gently swirl the pan over the heat until the syrup is an even golden brown, about 2 minutes more. Protecting your hand with an oven mitt, immediately pour the hot caramel into the custard cups.

3 Prepare the cream: In a small saucepan, heat the milk over low heat until small bubbles form around the edges. Remove from the heat. Add the chocolate and remaining 3/4 cup sugar and let stand until the chocolate is melted. Stir until blended.

4 In a large bowl, beat the eggs and yolks until blended. Stir in the chocolate milk. Pour the mixture through a fine-mesh strainer into a bowl, then add it to the custard cups.

5 Place the cups in a large roasting pan. Place in the center of the oven. Carefully pour hot water into the pan to a depth of 1 inch. Bake 20 to 25 minutes or until a knife inserted 1/2 inch from the center of the custards comes out clean. Transfer the cups from the pan to the rack to cool. Cover and chill at least 3 hours or overnight.

6 To serve, run a small knife around the inside of each custard cup. Invert onto serving plates and serve immediately.

Amaretti Caramel Custard
Bonet

MAKES 8 SERVINGS

Custards are usually smooth, but this version from Piedmont is pleasantly grainy because it is made with crushed amaretti cookies. It is often baked in a bowl, and the name comes from a dialect word for the crown of a hat. I prefer to bake it in a layer cake pan (not a springform pan), because it is easier to cut and serve in that shape.

CARAMEL

2/3 cup sugar

1/4 cup water

CUSTARD

3 cups whole milk

4 large eggs

1 cup sugar

1 cup Dutch-process unsweetened cocoa powder

3/4 cup finely crushed imported Italian amaretti cookies (about 12)

2 tablespoons dark rum

1 teaspoon pure vanilla extract

1 Prepare the caramel: In a small heavy saucepan, combine the sugar and water. Cook over medium heat, stirring occasionally, until the sugar is completely dissolved, about 3 minutes. When the mixture begins to boil, stop stirring and cook until the syrup starts to brown around the edges. Then gently swirl the pan over the heat until the syrup is an even golden brown, about 2 minutes more. Protecting your hand with an oven mitt, immediately pour the caramel into an 8- or 9-inch layer cake pan. Tilt the pan to coat the bottom and part of the sides with the caramel.

2 Place a rack in the center of the oven. Preheat the oven to 325°F. Place a roasting pan large enough to hold the cake pan in the center of the oven.

3 Prepare the custard: In a large heavy saucepan, heat the milk over low heat until small bubbles form around the edge.

4 Meanwhile, in a large bowl, whisk the eggs with the sugar just until blended. Stir in the cocoa, cookie crumbs, rum, and vanilla. Gradually stir in the hot milk.

5 Pour the custard mixture through a fine-mesh strainer into the prepared pan. Place the pan in the center of the roasting pan. Carefully pour very hot water into the roasting pan to a depth of 1 inch.

6 Bake 1 hour and 10 minutes or until the top is set, but the center is still slightly jiggly. (Protecting your hand with an oven mitt, shake the pan gently.) Have a wire cooling rack ready. Transfer the pan to the rack to cool for 15 minutes. Cover and refrigerate 3 hours up to overnight.

7 To unmold, run a small knife around the inside edge of the pan. Invert the custard onto a serving plate. Cut into slices to serve immediately.

❧ Italian Ices

Frozen ices, granita, are a favorite way to beat the heat during a hot summer. Romans skip their afternoon caffè in favor of a *granita di caffè*, often capped with a cloud of unsweetened whipped cream. Lemon granita rules in southern Italy, where there are plenty of big juicy lemons. Sicilians plop a scoop of lemon granita into their iced tea and other cold drinks. They also like exotically flavored granitas, such as jasmine and cinnamon.

Granitas should be made fresh, as they tend to get as hard as a rock if frozen too long. Ices are especially easy to make at home because no special equipment is required. Just mix up the flavoring ingredients and water, then freeze them in a pan in the freezer. If you like the grainy, crystalline texture that gives the granita its name, stir the mixture from time to time until it is completely frozen. For a smoother texture, the mixture can be cranked in an ice-cream maker, or frozen solid in a pan, then broken into chunks and pureed in a heavy-duty mixer or food processor.

Simple Syrup for Granita

MAKES 1 1/4 CUP

If you like to make granitas on a moment's notice, double or triple this recipe and keep it in a sealed jar in the refrigerator for up to two weeks.

1 cup cold water
1 cup sugar

1 In a small saucepan, combine the water and sugar. Bring to a simmer over medium heat and cook, stirring occasionally, until the sugar is dissolved, about 3 minutes.

2 Let the syrup cool slightly. Pour it into a container, cover, and refrigerate until ready to use.

Lemon Granita
Granita di Limone

MAKES 6 SERVINGS

The ultimate summer refresher—serve as is with a lemon slice and a sprig of mint, or stir it into summer cocktails. Lemon granita is also good affogato, meaning "drowned," with a spoonful of grappa or limoncello, *the delicious lemon liqueur from Capri.*

1 cup water
2/3 cup sugar
2 1/2 cups ice cubes
1 teaspoon grated lemon zest
1/2 cup freshly squeezed lemon juice

1 In a small saucepan, combine the water and sugar. Bring to a simmer over medium heat and cook, stirring occasionally, until the sugar is dissolved, about 3 minutes. Let cool slightly. Place the ice cubes in a large bowl and pour the syrup over the ice cubes. Stir until the ice is melted. Refrigerate until chilled, about 1 hour.

2 Chill a 13 × 9 × 2–inch metal pan in the freezer. In a medium bowl, combine the sugar syrup, lemon zest, and lemon juice. Remove the pan from the freezer, then pour the mixture into it. Freeze 30 minutes or until a 1-inch border of ice crystals forms around the edges.

3 Stir the ice crystals into the center of the mixture. Return the pan to the freezer and continue freezing, stirring every 30 minutes, until all of the liquid is frozen, about 2 to 2 1/2 hours. Serve immediately, or scrape the mixture into a plastic container, cover, and store in the freezer up to 24 hours.

4 Remove from the freezer to soften about 15 minutes before serving, if necessary.

Tips on Making Granitas

- Have everything very cold before making the granita. Make the syrup in advance, and chill it well, either in the refrigerator or by placing the syrup bowl over a bowl of ice water. (You can make and store the syrup in the refrigerator up to two weeks.)
- Place the pan and spoon you will use to stir the ice in the freezer before beginning.
- If making the granita in a food processor or mixer, chill the blade or beaters.
- If the granita turns solid from sitting in the freezer too long, simply allow it to soften slightly at room temperature. Break it into small chunks and beat it in an electric mixer until smooth. This can be messy at first, as the chunks tend to fly out of the bowl, so start at a slow speed. Work quickly so that the ice does not melt too much. Refreeze to the desired consistency.

Watermelon Granita

Granita di Cocomero

MAKES 6 SERVINGS

The flavor in this granita is so concentrated and the coolness so refreshing, it may even be better than fresh watermelon. It is a favorite in Sicily, where summers can be extremely hot.

1 cup water
1/2 cup sugar
4 cups watermelon chunks, seeds removed
2 tablespoons fresh lemon juice, or to taste

1 In a small saucepan, combine the water with the sugar. Bring to a simmer over medium heat, then cook, stirring occasionally, until the sugar dissolves, about 3 minutes. Let cool slightly, then refrigerate until cold, about 1 hour.

2 Chill a 13 × 9 × 2–inch metal pan in the freezer. Put the watermelon chunks in a blender or food processor and blend until smooth. Pour through a fine-mesh strainer into a bowl to eliminate any pieces of seeds. You should have about 2 cups juice.

3 In a large bowl, stir together the juice and the syrup. Add lemon juice to taste.

4 Remove the pan from the freezer, then pour the mixture into it. Freeze 30 minutes or until a 1-inch border of ice crystals forms around the edges. Stir the ice crystals into the center of the mixture. Return the pan to the freezer and continue freezing, stirring every 30 minutes, until all of the liquid is frozen, about 2 to 2 1/2 hours. Serve immediately, or scrape the mixture into a plastic container, cover, and store in the freezer up to 24 hours.

5 Remove from the freezer to soften about 15 minutes before serving, if necessary.

Tangerine Granita

Granita di Mandarino

MAKES 4 SERVINGS

Southern Italy abounds in all kinds of citrus fruits. I had this granita in Taranto in Puglia. Tangerine, tangelo, clementine, or mandarin juice can be prepared this way.

Don't be tempted to add more liqueur to this mixture, or the alcohol may prevent it from freezing.

1 cup chilled Simple Syrup (page 529)
1 cup fresh tangerine juice (from about 4 medium tangerines)
1 teaspoon freshly grated tangerine zest
2 tablespoons mandarin or orange liqueur

1 Prepare the simple syrup, if necessary, and chill it. Then, place a 13 × 9 × 2–inch metal pan in the freezer.

2 In a large bowl, stir together the juice, zest, syrup, and liqueur until well blended. Remove the chilled pan from the freezer and pour the liquid into the pan.

3 Place the pan in the freezer for 30 minutes or until a 1-inch border of ice crystals forms around the edges. Stir the ice crystals into the center of the mixture. Return the pan to the freezer and continue freezing, stirring every 30 minutes, until all of the liquid is frozen, about 2 to 2 1/2 hours. Serve immediately, or scrape the mixture into a plastic container, cover, and store in the freezer up to 24 hours.

4 Remove from the freezer to soften about 15 minutes before serving, if necessary.

Strawberry Wine Granita
Granita di Fragola al Vino

MAKES 6 TO 8 SERVINGS

With fresh ripe strawberries, this is delicious, but even so-so strawberries taste great in this granita.

2 pints strawberries, rinsed and hulled
1/2 cup sugar, or to taste
1 cup dry white wine
2 to 3 tablespoons fresh lemon juice

1 Place a 13 × 9 × 2–inch pan in the freezer to chill. Cut the strawberries in half or, if large, in quarters. In a large saucepan, combine the strawberries, sugar, and wine. Bring to a simmer and cook 5 minutes, stirring occasionally, until the sugar is dissolved. Remove from the heat and let cool. Refrigerate until cold, at least 1 hour.

2 Pour the mixture into a food processor or blender. Puree until smooth. Stir in the lemon juice to taste.

3 Remove the chilled pan from the freezer and pour the mixture into the pan. Place the pan in the freezer for 30 minutes or until a 1-inch border of ice crystals forms around the edges. Stir the ice crystals into the center of the mixture. Return the pan to the freezer and continue freezing, stirring every 30 minutes, until all of the liquid is frozen, about 2 to 2 1/2 hours. Serve immediately, or scrape the mixture into a plastic container, cover, and store in the freezer up to 24 hours.

4 Remove from the freezer to soften about 15 minutes before serving, if necessary.

Coffee Granita
Granita di Caffè

MAKES 8 SERVINGS

Caffè Tazza d'Oro near the Pantheon in Rome makes some of the city's best coffee. In summer tourists and natives alike switch to their granita di caffè, espresso coffee ices, served with or without a dollop of freshly whipped cream. It is easy to make and refreshing after a summer meal.

4 cups water
5 heaping teaspoons instant espresso powder
2 to 4 tablespoons sugar
Whipped cream (optional)

1 Place a 13 × 9 × 2–inch pan in the freezer to chill. Bring the water to a boil. Remove from the heat. Stir in the instant espresso powder and sugar to taste. Let cool slightly, then cover. Refrigerate until chilled, about 1 hour.

2 Remove the chilled pan from the freezer and pour the coffee into the pan. Freeze until a 1-inch border of ice crystals forms around the edges. Stir the ice crystals into the center of the mixture. Return the pan to the freezer and continue freezing, stirring every 30 minutes, until all of the liquid is frozen, about 2 to 2 1/2 hours.

3 Serve immediately, topped with the cream, if using, or scrape the mixture into a plastic container, cover, and store in the freezer up to 24 hours.

4 Remove from the freezer to soften about 15 minutes before serving, if necessary.

Citrus and Campari Granita
Granita di Agrumi e Campari

MAKES 6 SERVINGS

Campari, a bright red aperitif, is usually drunk over ice or mixed with soda before a meal. For this granita, it is combined with citrus juice. The Campari has a pleasantly bitter edge that is very refreshing, and the granita has a beautiful rosy color.

1 cup water
1/2 cup sugar
2 cups freshly squeezed grapefruit juice
1 cup freshly squeezed orange juice
1 teaspoon grated orange zest
3/4 cup Campari

1 Place a 13 × 9 × 2–inch pan in the freezer to chill at least 15 minutes. Combine the water and sugar in a small saucepan. Bring to a simmer over medium heat, then cook, stirring occasionally, until the sugar dissolves. Stir well. Remove from the heat and let cool. Chill the syrup.

2 Stir together the chilled syrup, juices, Campari, and orange zest.

3 Remove the chilled pan from the freezer and pour the mixture into the pan. Place the pan in the freezer for 30 minutes or until a 1-inch border of ice crystals forms around the edges. Stir the ice crystals into the center of the mixture. Return the pan to the freezer and continue freezing, stirring every 30 minutes, until all of the liquid is frozen, about 2 to 2¹/2 hours. Serve immediately, or scrape the mixture into a plastic container, cover, and store in the freezer up to 24 hours.

4 Remove from the freezer to soften about 15 minutes before serving, if necessary.

White Peach and Prosecco Granita
Granita di Pesche e Prosecco

MAKES 6 SERVINGS

This granita is inspired by the Bellini, a delicious cocktail made famous by Harry's Bar in Venice. A Bellini is made with the juice of white peaches and prosecco, a sparkling white wine from the Veneto region.

Superfine sugar blends more easily than granulated sugar, but if you can't find it, use some chilled Simple Syrup (page 529) to taste.

5 medium ripe white peaches, peeled and cut into chunks
¹/2 cup superfine sugar
2 tablespoons fresh lemon juice, or to taste
1 cup prosecco or other dry sparkling white wine

1 Place a 13 × 9 × 2–inch pan in the freezer to chill at least 15 minutes. In a blender or food processor, combine the peaches, superfine sugar, and lemon juice. Blend or process until the sugar is completely dissolved. Stir in the wine.

2 Remove the chilled pan from the freezer and pour the mixture into the pan. Place the pan in the freezer for 30 minutes or until a 1-inch border of ice crystals forms around the edges. Stir the ice crystals into the center of the mixture. Return the pan to the freezer and continue freezing, stirring every 30 minutes, until all of the liquid is frozen, about 2 to 2¹/2 hours. Serve immediately, or scrape the mixture into a plastic container, cover, and store in the freezer up to 24 hours.

3 Remove from the freezer to soften about 15 minutes before serving, if necessary.

Chocolate Sorbet
Sorbetto di Cioccolato

MAKES 6 SERVINGS

A sorbet is a smooth-textured frozen dessert that contains milk or egg white for creaminess. This is my version of the sorbet I had at Caffè Florian, a historic coffee bar and tea room in Venice's Piazza San Marco.

¹/2 cup sugar
3 ounces bittersweet chocolate, broken up
1 cup water
1 cup whole milk

1 In a small saucepan, combine all of the ingredients. Bring to a simmer over medium heat. Cook, stirring constantly with a whisk, until blended and smooth, about 5 minutes.

2 Pour the mixture into a medium bowl. Cover and refrigerate until chilled.

3 Follow the manufacturer's instructions on your ice cream freezer, or freeze in shallow pans until firm but not hard, about 2 hours. Scrape the mixture into a mixer bowl and beat until smooth. Pack into a plastic container, cover, and store in the freezer. Serve within 24 hours.

Prosecco Lemon Slush

Sgroppino

MAKES 4 SERVINGS

Venetians like to finish their meals with a sgroppino, a sophisticated creamy slush of lemon sorbet whipped with prosecco, a dry sparkling white wine. It must be made at the last minute, and it is a fun dessert to prepare at the table. I like to serve it in martini glasses. Use a good-quality store-bought lemon sorbet or sherbet. It is not traditional, but orange would be good too.

1 cup lemon sorbet
1 cup very cold prosecco or other dry sparkling wine
Mint sprigs

1 Several hours before you plan to serve the dessert, chill 4 large goblets or parfait glasses in the refrigerator.

2 Just before serving, remove the sorbet from the freezer. Let stand at room temperature until soft enough to scoop, about 10 minutes. Spoon the sorbet into a medium bowl. Beat until soft and smooth.

3 Slowly add the prosecco and beat briefly with a whisk until creamy and smooth. Quickly pour the slush into the chilled wine goblets or martini glasses. Garnish with mint. Serve immediately.

Pink Prosecco Slush

Sgroppino alle Fragole

MAKES 6 SERVINGS

If the fresh strawberries in your market are not ripe and fragrant, try using frozen strawberries for this easy dessert.

1 cup sliced strawberries
1 to 2 tablespoons sugar
1 cup lemon sorbet
1 cup prosecco or other dry sparkling wine
Small fresh strawberries or lemon slices, for garnish

1 Several hours before you plan to serve the dessert, chill 6 large goblets or parfait glasses in the refrigerator.

2 Put the strawberries and 1 tablespoon sugar in a food processor or blender. Puree the berries until smooth. Taste for sweetness. Add more sugar, if needed.

3 Just before serving, remove the sorbet from the freezer. Let stand at room temperature until soft enough to scoop, about 10 minutes. Spoon the sorbet into a medium bowl. Beat until soft and smooth. Beat in the strawberry puree. Quickly whisk in the wine and beat until the mixture is creamy and smooth. Pour into the chilled glasses. Garnish with strawberries or lemon slices and serve immediately.

❧ Ice Cream (Gelato)

Gelato, or Italian-style ice cream, is made with more milk than cream. Because the fat content is lower, you can really taste the fruits, nuts, or whatever flavoring ingredients you are putting in. Gelato melts readily on the tongue, so it seems lighter and fresher than other ice creams. Because it does not have stabilizers like store-bought brands, homemade gelato should be eaten soon after it is made, preferably within 24 hours.

An ice-cream maker is essential for making gelato. The kind that you put in the freezer compartment is inexpensive and works fine, except that I never have enough room in my freezer to hold it. The type that I prefer is an electric model that works with ice and salt. It is noisy, but I put it in another room and close the door while it is cranking the ice cream. There are several excellent ice-cream makers available for home cooks that require no ice. They do a terrific job of making gelato in a minimum amout of time. The down side is that they are expensive and take up a lot of space. They are worth getting, though, if you like to make a lot of gelato.

"Cream" Ice Cream
Gelato di Crema

MAKES 6 TO 8 SERVINGS

A hint of lemon flavors this light, fresh-tasting gelato. I love to make it when local strawberries are in season and serve them together.

3 cups whole milk
4 egg yolks
2/3 cup sugar
1 teaspoon pure vanilla extract
1 teaspoon grated lemon zest

1 In a medium saucepan, heat the milk over medium heat until small bubbles form around the edge of the pan. Do not boil the milk. Remove from the heat.

2 In a heatproof mixing bowl, whisk the egg yolks, and sugar until thick and well blended. Add the hot milk, slowly at first, and whisk constantly until all of the milk has been blended in. Stir in the lemon zest.

3 Pour the mixture back into the saucepan. Place the saucepan over medium heat. Cook, stirring constantly with a wooden spoon, until steam begins to rise from the pot and the cream thickens slightly, about 5 minutes.

4 Pour the cream through a mesh strainer into a bowl. Add the vanilla. Let cool slightly, then cover and refrigerate until completely chilled, about 1 hour.

5 Freeze in an ice-cream maker according to the manufacturer's instructions. Pack the ice cream into a plastic container, cover, and freeze up to 24 hours.

Lemon Ice Cream
Gelato al Limone

MAKES ABOUT 3 TO 4 SERVINGS

You will need two or three large lemons to get enough juice and zest for this simple and delicious gelato.

1/3 cup freshly squeezed lemon juice
1 tablespoon freshly grated lemon zest
1 cup sugar
1 pint half-and-half

1 In a medium bowl, combine the lemon juice, zest, and sugar and stir well. Let stand 30 minutes.

2 Add the half-and-half and stir well. Pour the mixture into the container of an ice-cream maker and follow the manufacturer's directions for freezing.

3 Pack the ice cream into a plastic container, cover, and freeze up to 24 hours.

Ricotta Ice Cream
Gelato di Ricotta

MAKES 6 TO 8 SERVINGS

Ricotta ice cream is a favorite flavor at Giolitti, one of several excellent Roman gelaterias. Every night in the summer, large crowds gather to buy cones packed with their delicious ice creams.

A couple of tablespoons of chopped chocolate or pistachios can be added to the ice-cream mixture. Serve this rich ice cream in small portions, drizzled with a little orange liqueur or rum, if you like.

Both candied orange zest and citron are available in Italian and Middle Eastern specialty stores or from mail order sources (pages 625–626).

16 ounces fresh whole or part-skim ricotta
1/2 cup sugar
2 tablespoons sweet or dry Marsala
1 teaspoon pure vanilla extract
1/2 cup chilled heavy or whipping cream
2 tablespoons chopped citron
2 tablespoons chopped candied orange zest

1 At least 20 minutes before you are ready to make the dessert, place a large bowl and the beaters of an electric mixer in the refrigerator. Place the ricotta in a fine-mesh strainer set over a bowl. With a rubber spatula, push the ricotta through the strainer into the bowl. Whisk in the sugar, Marsala, and vanilla.

2 Remove the bowl and beaters from the refrigerator. Pour the cream into the bowl and whip the cream at high speed until it holds its shape softly when the beaters are lifted, about 4 minutes.

3 With a flexible spatula, fold the cream, citron, and zest into the ricotta mixture. Scrape the mixture into the container of an ice-cream maker and freeze according to the manufacturer's instructions.

4 Pack the ice cream into a plastic container, cover, and freeze up to 24 hours.

Mascarpone Ice Cream
Gelato di Mascarpone

MAKES 4 SERVINGS

Mascarpone makes this richer than the usual gelato.

1 cup whole milk
1 cup sugar
1/2 cup mascarpone
1/2 cup freshly squeezed lemon juice
1 teaspoon grated lemon zest

1 In a small saucepan, combine the milk and sugar. Cook over low heat, stirring frequently, until the sugar is dissolved, about 3 minutes. Let cool slightly.

2 Whisk in the mascarpone and beat until smooth. Add the lemon juice and zest.

3 Freeze in an ice-cream maker according to the manufacturer's instructions.

4 Pack the ice cream into a plastic container, cover, and freeze up to 24 hours.

Cinnamon Ice Cream
Gelato di Cannela

MAKLES 6 SERVINGS

One summer in Italy a few years ago, this ice cream was all the rage served with Warm Berry Sauce (page 544), and I happily ate it over and over. The ice cream is delicious on its own, or try it with Mocha Sauce (page 544).

2 cups whole milk
1 cup heavy cream
1 (2-inch) strip of lemon zest
1/2 teaspoon ground cinnamon
4 large egg yolks
1/2 cup sugar

1 In a medium saucepan, combine the milk, cream, lemon zest, and cinnamon. Heat over low heat until small bubbles form around the edges. Remove from the heat.

2 In a large heatproof bowl, whisk the egg yolks and sugar until foamy. Gradually pour the warm milk into the egg yolk mixture, whisking until blended.

3 Pour the mixture back into the saucepan. Place the saucepan over medium heat. Cook, stirring constantly with a wooden spoon, until steam begins to rise from the pot and the custard thickens slightly, about 5 minutes.

4 Pour the custard through a mesh strainer into a bowl. Let cool. Cover and chill in the refrigerator at least 1 hour or overnight. (To cool the custard mixture rapidly, pour it into a bowl set within a larger bowl filled with ice water. Stir the mixture frequently.)

5 Freeze the mixture in an ice-cream freezer according to the manufacturer's instructions. Pack the ice cream into a plastic container, cover, and freeze up to 24 hours.

Espresso Ice Cream
Gelato di Caffè

MAKES 6 TO 8 SERVINGS

At home, most Italians make coffee in a specially designed pot on top of the stove. It forces hot steam, not hot water, through the coffee, and that is what makes a classic espresso.

But you can make good coffee with espresso-type beans in an ordinary drip pot. Just be sure to use good-quality espresso and make it strong, especially for this ice cream. It is heavenly topped with Warm Chocolate Sauce (page 544).

2 cups whole milk
²/₃ cup sugar
3 large egg yolks
I cup strong brewed espresso

I In a small saucepan, heat the milk with the sugar until small bubbles form around the edges, about 3 minutes. Stir until the sugar is dissolved.

2 In a large heatproof bowl, beat the egg yolks until pale yellow. Gradually whisk in the hot milk. Pour the mixture into the saucepan. Cook over low heat, stirring constantly with a wooden spoon, until wisps of steam rise from the surface and the mixture is slightly thickened Immediately pour the mixture through a fine-mesh strainer into a bowl. Stir in the brewed coffee. Cover and chill at least 1 hour.

3 Freeze the mixture in an ice-cream freezer according to the manufacturer's instructions. Pack the ice cream into a plastic container, cover, and freeze up to 24 hours.

Walnut Caramel Ice Cream
Gelato di Noci

MAKES 6 SERVINGS

Drizzle a little rum or cognac over this ice cream before serving it.

I ¹/₄ cups sugar
¹/₄ cup water
I cup heavy cream
2 cups whole milk
5 large egg yolks
I teaspoon pure vanilla extract
³/₄ cup walnuts

I In a small heavy saucepan, combine the sugar and water. Cook over medium heat, stirring occasionally until the sugar is completely dissolved, about 3 minutes. When the mixture begins to boil, stop stirring and cook until the syrup starts to brown around the edges. Then gently swirl the pan over the heat until the syrup is an even golden brown, about 2 minutes more.

2 Remove the pan from the heat. When the bubbling stops, carefully pour in the cream. Be careful, as the caramel may bubble up. When all of the cream has been added, the caramel will harden.

(continues)

Place the pan back on the heat. Cook, stirring constantly, until the caramel is liquid and smooth. Pour the mixture into a large bowl.

3 In the same saucepan, heat the milk until small bubbles form around the edge of the pan, about 3 minutes.

4 In a medium heatproof bowl, whisk the egg yolks with the remaining 1/4 cup of the sugar until well blended. Gradually beat in the hot milk. Pour the mixture into the saucepan and cook over low heat, stirring constantly, until wisps of steam rise from the surface and the mixture is slightly thickened.

5 Immediately pour the egg yolk mixture through a fine-mesh strainer into the bowl with the caramel. Add the vanilla and stir until smooth. Cover and chill in the refrigerator at least 1 hour.

6 Place a rack in the center of the oven. Preheat the oven to 350°F. Spread the walnuts in a small pan. Bake, stirring once or twice, for 10 minutes or until lightly toasted. Rub the walnut pieces in a towel to remove some of the skin. Let cool. Chop coarsely.

7 Freeze the mixture in an ice-cream freezer according to the manufacturer's instructions.

8 When the gelato is ready, stir in the nuts. Pack the ice cream into a plastic container, cover, and freeze up to 24 hours.

Honey Ice Cream with Nougat
Gelato di Miele al Torrone

MAKES 6 SERVINGS

Italians are wild about honey, especially if it is made by bees that pollinate aromatic flowers and trees such as lavender and chestnut. Honey is spread on toast, drizzled over cheese, and used in cooking. This gelato takes on the flavor of the kind of honey used, so find one with an interesting flavor.

There are two types of torrone in Italy. One is a softer nougat candy, made with honey, egg whites, and nuts. The other type, which is easy to make at home (see Almond Brittle, page 568), is a hard praline, made with sugar, water, and nuts. Both types of torrone are also sold in a bar shape and can be found in Italian groceries and pastry shops, especially around Christmas.

The torrone topping is optional, but very good. Either the soft or the hard kind can be used.

2 cups whole milk
4 large egg yolks
1/2 cup honey
1 cup heavy cream
About 6 tablespoons rum or cognac
1/2 cup finely chopped torrone (optional)

1 In a medium saucepan, heat the milk over low heat until small bubbles form around the edge of the pan, about 3 minutes.

2 In a large heatproof bowl, whisk the egg yolks and honey until smooth. Gradually whisk in the hot milk. Pour the mixture into the saucepan and cook over low heat, stirring constantly, until wisps of steam rise from the surface and the mixture thickens slightly.

3 Immediately pour the mixture through a fine-mesh strainer into a bowl. Stir in the cream. Cover and refrigerate until chilled, about 1 hour.

4 Freeze the mixture in an ice-cream freezer according to the manufacturer's instructions. Pack the ice cream into a plastic container. Cover and freeze up to 24 hours. Serve each portion topped with a tablespoon of rum or cognac and a sprinkle of crushed torrone.

Amaretti Gelato
Gelato di Amaretti

MAKES 6 TO 8 SERVINGS

Italians love amaretti—light, crunchy almond cookies—alone or in their desserts. Crisp nuggets of amaretti cookies stud this gelato. Serve it with a splash of amaretto liqueur.

2 cups whole milk
4 large egg yolks
1/2 cup sugar
I cup heavy cream
I teaspoon pure vanilla extract
I cup coarsely crushed amaretti cookies

1 Heat the milk in a large saucepan over low heat until small bubbles form around the edges, about 3 minutes.

2 In a large heatproof bowl, whisk the egg yolks and sugar until well blended. Gradually add the hot milk, whisking constantly. When all the milk has been added, pour the mixture into the saucepan. Cook over medium heat, stirring constantly, until wisps of steam rise from the surface and the mixture thickens slightly.

3 Immediately pour the mixture through a fine-mesh strainer into a bowl. Add the cream and vanilla. Cover and refrigerate until chilled, about 1 hour.

4 Freeze the gelato in an ice-cream freezer, following the manufacturer's directions. When frozen, stir in the crumbs. Pack the ice cream into a plastic container, cover, and freeze up to 24 hours.

"Drowned" Ice Cream
Gelato Affogato

MAKES 4 SERVINGS

Any flavor of ice cream can be "drowned" in hot espresso, but walnut caramel and cream are two of my favorites. The ice cream melts slightly, creating a creamy sauce. You can leave out the liqueur, if you like.

4 scoops Walnut Caramel (pages 537–538) or "Cream" Ice Cream (page 535)
1/2 cup hot brewed espresso
2 tablespoons orange or amaretto liqueur (optional)

1 Prepare the ice cream, if necessary. Scoop the ice cream into two serving bowls.

2 If using the liqueur, in a small bowl, mix together the espresso and liqueur, then pour the mixture over the ice cream. Serve immediately.

Ice Cream with Balsamic Vinegar
Gelato al Balsamico

MAKES 4 SERVINGS

Ice cream and vinegar may sound like a strange combination, and it would be if it were made with an ordinary balsamic vinegar. For this unique dessert, popular in Parma, only the finest aged balsamico should be used as a mellow, slightly astringent sauce over the sweet ice cream. The supermarket variety would be too sharp.

4 scoops premium vanilla ice cream or frozen yogurt, or "Cream" Ice Cream (page 535), softened
2 to 3 teaspoons well-aged balsamic vinegar

Prepare the ice cream, if necessary. Scoop the ice cream into serving dishes. Drizzle with the balsamic vinegar. Serve immediately.

Ice Cream Truffles

Tartufi

MAKES 6 SERVINGS

Ever since my first trip to Italy in 1970, I cannot go to Rome without a quick stop at Tre Scalini in Piazza Navona for a tartufo. This popular caffè has been known for years for its luscious ice cream truffles, balls of ice cream rolled in good chocolate flakes surrounding a sour cherry heart. Ice cream truffles are easy to make at home and make a festive dessert. Just be sure to keep everything well chilled and work quickly. A large ice cream scoop with a spring-operated lever to release the ice cream is the best tool for this.

4 ounces semisweet chocolate chips

6 Italian sour cherries in syrup (Amarena cherries, available in jars) or maraschino cherries tossed with a little brandy

2 tablespoons slivered almonds

1 pint vanilla ice cream

1 pint chocolate ice cream

1 Line a small metal baking pan with wax paper and place it in the freezer. Line a baking sheet with aluminum foil.

2 In the bottom half of a double boiler or in a medium saucepan, bring 2 inches of water to a simmer. Place the chocolate chips in the top half of the double boiler or in a bowl that will sit comfortably over the saucepan. Let the chocolate stand until softened, about 5 minutes. Stir until smooth. Scrape the melted chocolate onto the foil-lined sheet. Spread the chocolate evenly and thinly over the foil. Chill in the refrigerator until firm, about 1 hour.

3 When the chocolate is hardened, lift the foil from the pan and break the chocolate sheet into 1/2-inch flakes with a spatula or your fingers. Scatter the flakes over the baking sheet.

4 Remove the chilled pan from the freezer. Dip a large ice cream scoop into the vanilla ice cream,

filling the scoop halfway. Dip the scoop into the chocolate ice cream, filling it completely. Holding the ice cream in the scoop, poke a hole in the center and insert one of the cherries and a few almonds. Mold the ice cream over the filling. Drop the ice cream scoop onto the chocolate flakes and roll the ice cream around quickly, pressing the chocolate into the surface. Using a metal spatula to lift it, transfer the coated ice cream to the chilled pan. Return the pan to the freezer.

5 Make 5 more ice cream truffles in the same way. Cover the truffles and the pan with plastic wrap before returning the pan to the freezer. Freeze at least 1 hour or up to 24 hours before serving.

Almond Cream Cups

Biscuit Tortoni

MAKES 8 SERVINGS

When I was growing up, this was the standard Italian restaurant dessert, something like tiramisù has been for the last 15 years or so. Though it may be out of fashion, it is still delicious and easy to make.

If you want a more elegant-looking dessert, spoon the mixture into parfait glasses or ramekins. The maraschino cherries add a touch of color, but you can leave them out if you prefer.

2 cups chilled heavy or whipping cream

1/2 cup confectioners' sugar

2 teaspoons pure vanilla extract

1/2 teaspoon almond extract

2 egg whites, at room temperature

Pinch of salt

8 maraschino cherries, drained and chopped (optional)

2 tablespoons finely chopped toasted almonds

12 to 16 imported Italian amaretti cookies, finely crushed (about 1 cup crumbs)

1 At least 20 minutes before you are ready to whip the cream, place a large bowl and the beaters of

an electric mixer in the refrigerator. Line a muffin tin with 8 pleated paper or foil cupcake liners.

2 Remove the bowl and beaters from the refrigerator. Pour the cream, sugar, and extracts into the bowl and whip the mixture at high speed until it holds its shape softly when the beaters are lifted, about 4 minutes. Refrigerate the whipped cream.

3 In a large clean bowl with clean beaters, whip the egg whites with the salt on low speed until foamy. Gradually increase the speed and beat until the whites hold soft peaks when the beaters are lifted. With a flexible spatula, gently fold the whites into the whipped cream.

4 Set aside 2 tablespoons of the amaretti crumbs. Fold the remaining crumbs, the cherries, and the almonds into the cream mixture. Spoon into the prepared muffin cups. Sprinkle with the reserved amaretti crumbs.

5 Cover with foil and freeze at least 4 hours or up to overnight. Remove from the refrigerator 15 minutes before serving.

Orange Spumone
Spumone di Arancia

MAKES 6 SERVINGS

Spumone comes from spuma, *meaning "foam." It has a creamier texture than regular gelato because the egg yolks are cooked with the hot sugar syrup to make a thick custard. Though it is rich with egg yolks, it is light and airy from the egg foam and whipped cream.*

3 navel oranges
1 cup water
3/4 cup sugar
6 large egg yolks
1 cup chilled heavy or whipping cream

1 Grate the zest from the oranges and squeeze the juice. (There should be 3 tablespoons of the zest and 2/3 cup of juice.)

2 In a medium saucepan, combine the water and sugar. Bring to a simmer over medium heat, then cook, stirring occasionally, until the sugar dissolves.

3 In a large heatproof bowl, whisk the egg yolks until blended. Slowly add the hot sugar syrup in a thin stream, whisking constantly. Pour the mixture into the saucepan and cook over low heat, stirring with a wooden spoon, until slightly thickened and the mixture lightly coats the spoon.

4 Pour the mixture through a fine-mesh strainer into a bowl. Stir in the orange juice and zest. Let cool, then cover and refrigerate until chilled, at least 1 hour. Place a large bowl and the beaters of an electric mixer in the refrigerator.

5 Just before serving, remove the bowl and beaters from the refrigerator. Pour the cream into the bowl and whip the cream at high speed until it holds its shape softly when the beaters are lifted, about 4 minutes. With a flexible spatula, gently fold the cream into orange mixture.

6 Freeze in an ice-cream freezer according to the manufacturer's instructions. Pack into a container, cover, and freeze. Serve within 24 hours.

Fruit, Ice Cream, and Spoon Desserts   541

Almond Semifreddo
Semifreddo alle Mandorle

MAKES 8 SERVINGS

Semifreddo means "half-cold." This dessert got its name because though it is frozen, its texture stays soft and creamy. It melts easily, so have everything very cold while you make it. Warm Chocolate Sauce (page 544) is a good accompaniment.

¾ cup chilled heavy or whipping cream
1 teaspoon pure vanilla extract
¾ cup sugar
¼ cup water
4 large eggs, at room temperature
6 amaretti cookies, finely crushed
2 tablespoons toasted almonds, finely chopped
2 tablespoons sliced almonds

1 Line a 9 × 5 × 3–inch metal loaf pan with plastic wrap, leaving a 2-inch overhang on the ends. Chill the pan in the freezer. At least 20 minutes before you are ready to whip the cream, place a large bowl and the beaters of an electric mixer in the refrigerator.

2 When ready, remove the bowl and beaters from the refrigerator. Pour the cream and vanilla into the bowl and whip the cream at high speed until it holds its shape softly when the beaters are lifted, about 4 minutes. Return the bowl to the refrigerator.

3 In a small saucepan, combine the sugar and water. Bring to a simmer over medium heat, then cook, stirring occasionally, until the sugar is completely dissolved, about 2 minutes.

4 In a large mixer bowl, beat the eggs with the mixer on medium speed until foamy, about 1 minute. Slowly beat the hot sugar syrup into the eggs in a thin stream. Continue beating until the mixture is very light and fluffy and feels cool to the touch, 8 to 10 minutes.

5 With a flexible spatula, gently fold the whipped cream into the egg mixture. Gently fold in the cookie crumbs and chopped almonds.

6 Scrape the mixture into the prepared loaf pan. Cover securely with the plastic wrap and freeze 4 hours up to overnight.

7 Unwrap the pan. Invert a serving plate on top of the pan. Holding the plate and pan together, invert them both. Lift off the pan and carefully remove the plastic wrap. Sprinkle with the sliced almonds.

8 Cut into slices and serve immediately.

Florentine Frozen Dome Cake
Zuccotto

MAKES 8 SERVINGS

Inspired by the dome of the beautiful Duomo, the cathedral in the heart of Florence, this impressive dessert is actually quite easy to make, partly because it uses prepared cake.

1 (12-ounce) pound cake
2 tablespoons rum
2 tablespoons orange liqueur

FILLING

1 pint heavy or whipping cream
¼ cup confectioner's sugar, plus more for garnish
1 teaspoon pure vanilla extract
4 ounces semisweet chocolate, finely chopped
2 tablespoons sliced almonds, toasted and cooled
Fresh berries (optional)

1 At least 20 minutes before you are ready to whip the cream, place a large bowl and the beaters of an electric mixer in the refrigerator. Line a 2-quart round bowl or mold with plastic wrap. Cut the cake into slices no more than ¼-inch

thick. Cut each slice in half diagonally, forming two triangular pieces, and lay them all on a platter.

2 In a small bowl, mix together the rum and liqueur, and sprinkle the mixture over the cake. Place as many cake pieces as needed side by side—pointed-side down—in the bowl to form one layer. Cover the remaining inside surface of the bowl with the remaining cake, cutting the pieces to fit as needed. Fill in any gaps with cut-up pieces of cake. Set aside the remaining cake for the top.

3 Prepare the filling: Remove the bowl and beaters from the refrigerator. Pour the cream into the bowl. Add the confectioners' sugar and vanilla. Whip at high speed until the cream holds its shape softly when the beaters are lifted, about 4 minutes. Gently fold in the chocolate and almonds.

4 Spoon the cream mixture into the mold, being careful not to disturb the cake. Place the remaining cake slices in a layer on top. Cover securely with plastic wrap and freeze the mold 4 hours up to overnight.

5 To serve, remove the plastic wrap and invert a serving plate on top of the bowl. Holding the plate and bowl together, invert them both. Lift off the bowl. Remove the plastic wrap and sprinkle with confectioner's sugar. Place the berries around the cake. Cut into wedges to serve.

❧ Dessert Sauces

Honeyed Mascarpone Sauce
Salsina di Mascarpone

MAKES 2 CUPS

Serve this on fresh berries or on Marsala Walnut Cake (page 586).

1/2 cup mascarpone
3 tablespoons honey
1/2 teaspoon grated lemon zest
I cup chilled heavy cream, whipped

In a large bowl, whisk the mascarpone, honey, and lemon zest until smooth. Fold in the whipped cream. Serve immediately.

Fresh Strawberry Sauce
Salsina di Fragole

MAKES I 1/2 CUPS

Raspberries can also be prepared this way. If you do use raspberries, strain the sauce to eliminate the seeds.

I pint fresh strawberries, rinsed and hulled
3 tablespoons sugar, or to taste
1/4 cup fresh orange juice
2 tablespoons orange liqueur, cassis, or light rum

In a food processor or blender, combine all of the ingredients. Puree until smooth. Serve or transfer to an airtight container and store in the refrigerator up to 24 hours.

Warm Berry Sauce

Salsina Calda di Frutti di Bosco

MAKES ABOUT 2¹/₂ CUPS

This sauce is excellent on lemon, mascarpone, cinnamon, or "cream" ice cream or plain cake.

4 cups mixed fresh berries, such as blueberries, strawberries, raspberries, and blackberries
¹/₄ cup water
¹/₄ cup sugar or more

1 Rinse the berries and remove the hulls or stems. Cut the strawberries into halves or quarters if they are large.

2 In a medium saucepan, combine the berries, water, and sugar. Bring to a simmer over medium heat. Cook, stirring occasionally, until the berries are soft and the juices are slightly thickened, about 5 minutes. Taste and add more sugar, if necessary. Remove from the heat and let cool slightly. Serve or transfer to an airtight container and store in the refrigerator up to 24 hours.

Year-Round Raspberry Sauce

Salsa di Lampone

MAKES ABOUT 2 CUPS

Even when berries are not in season, you can still make a delicious fresh-tasting sauce. The raspberry flavor and color goes especially well with almond- and chocolate-flavored desserts and cakes. For a simple but beautiful dessert, pour this sauce, and a few fresh berries, too, over thin slices of cantaloupe.

The sauce can also be made with frozen blueberries or strawberries or a combination of berries. If you can't find berries in syrup, use unsweetened fruit and add sugar to taste.

2 (10-ounce) packages frozen raspberries in syrup, partially thawed
1 teaspoon cornstarch mixed with 2 tablespoons water
About 1 teaspoon fresh lemon juice

1 Pass the berries through a food mill fitted with a fine blade, or puree them in a food processor and press them through a fine-mesh strainer.

2 Bring the puree to a simmer in a small saucepan. Stir in the cornstarch mixture and cook, stirring frequently, until slightly thickened, about 1 minute. Stir in the lemon juice. Let cool slightly. Serve or transfer to an airtight container and store in the refrigerator up to 3 days.

Warm Chocolate Sauce

Salsa Calda al Cioccolato

MAKES ABOUT 1¹/₂ CUPS

Espresso intensifies the chocolate flavor of this delicious sauce, but you can leave it out if you prefer. Serve with ice cream, semifreddo, or plain cakes; it goes with a wide variety of desserts.

8 ounces bittersweet or semisweet chocolate, chopped
1 cup heavy cream

Place the chocolate and cream in the top of a double boiler or in a heatproof bowl set over a pan of simmering water. Let stand until the chocolate is softened. Stir until smooth. Serve warm or transfer to an airtight container and store in the refrigerator up to 3 days. Reheat gently.

Warm Mocha Sauce: Stir in 1 teaspoon instant espresso powder with the chocolate.

Cookies, Cakes, Tarts, and Pastries

Basic Cookies

Ladyfingers
Semolina Cookies
Vin Santo Rings
Marsala Cookies
Sesame Wine Biscuits
Sesame Cookies
Anisette Toast
"S" Cookies
Butter Rings
Lemon Knots
Spice Cookies
Wafer Cookies
Sweet Ravioli
"Ugly-but-Good" Cookies

Chocolate Cookies

Jam Spots
Double-Chocolate Nut Biscotti
Chocolate Kisses
No-Bake Chocolate "Salame"

Nut Cookies

Prato Biscuits
Umbrian Fruit and Nut Biscotti
Lemon Nut Biscotti
Walnut Biscotti
Almond Macaroons
Pine Nut Macaroons
Hazelnut Bars
Walnut Butter Cookies
Rainbow Cookies
Christmas Fig Cookies
Almond Brittle
Sicilian Nut Rolls

(continues)

545

Plain Cakes

Sponge Cake

Citrus Sponge Cake

Lemon Olive-Oil Cake

Marble Cake

Rum Cake

Grandmother's Cake

Cakes with Fruit

Apricot Almond Cake

Summer Fruit Torte

Autumn Fruit Torte

Polenta and Pear Cake

Cakes with Ricotta

Ricotta Cheesecake

Sicilian Ricotta Cake

Ricotta Crumb Cake

Easter Wheat-Berry Cake

Chocolate Cakes

Chocolate Hazelnut Cake

Chocolate Almond Cake

Chocolate Orange Torte

Chocolate Rum Raisin Cake

Cakes with Dried Fruit and Nuts

Abruzzo-Style Almond Cake
with Chocolate Frosting

Rum and Currant Loaf Cakes

Warm Amaretti Cakes

Marsala Walnut Cake

Crunchy Walnut Cake

Piedmontese Hazelnut Cake

Mantua Cake

Christmas Sweet Bread (Panettone)

Bread Puddings

Chocolate-Raisin Bread Pudding
Panettone Bread Pudding
Biscotti Bread Pudding
Pear and Apple Cake

Tarts

Single-Crust Pastry
Double-Crust Pastry
Berry Mascarpone Tart
Summer Fruit Tart
Blueberry Crostata
Raspberry Cream Tart
Sour-Cherry Jam Tart
Apple Marzipan Tart
Fig and Walnut Crostata
Dried Fig Tart
Lemon Almond Tart
Almond and Peach Tart
Pine Nut Tart
Winter Fruit and Nut Crostata
Ricotta Lattice Tart

Roman Ricotta Tart
Ricotta Jam Tart
Chocolate Tart
Rice Pudding Tart
Cornmeal Berry Tart
Spice and Nut Tart
Cinnamon Plum Torte

Pastries

Cannoli Cream
Chocolate Cannoli Cream
Pastry Cream
Cream Puffs
St. Joseph's Fritters
Honey Balls
Feast Day Puffs
Ricotta Fritters
Bow Ties
Honey Pinwheels
Ricotta Pockets
Crisp Ricotta Pastries
Cannoli

Walk by any *pasticceria,* or pastry shop, in Italy and just try to resist the tempting window display of cookies, cakes, tarts, and pastries. These desserts are beloved by Italians, and rightly so. Not only beautiful, they are also delicious. Most pastry shops in Italy double as coffee bars, so it is easy to sample whatever is on display, accompanied by your favorite beverage.

Biscotti, or cookies, are the most beloved and most often eaten sweet in Italy. They range from hard, slightly sweet biscuitlike cookies eaten with the morning cappucino to more elaborate confections filled with fruit and nuts enjoyed on holidays and feast days. *Biscotti* means "biscuits." It derives from *bis* and *cotti,* literally "cooked again" or "cooked twice." Though all cookies are called biscotti in Italy, not all biscotti are actually baked twice.

The cookies that actually are baked twice are the crunchy slices that are typical in Tuscany, Umbria, the Marches, and other regions of central Italy. The dough is formed into a long log and partially baked until it is just set, but slightly soft in the center. Then the log is cut into crosswise slices and baked again briefly until cooked through and toasted.

Twice-baked biscotti are hard and crunchy. Do not confuse them with the kind of soft, buttery rich cookie you may find at your local coffee shop in the United States. Italians make biscotti very hard and dry because they want to dunk them in wine or coffee. The liquid is absorbed and provides all the softening the cookies need. To get this consistency, Italian cooks leave out most of the sugar and butter that would typically be used in this country. In fact, many Italian biscotti recipes have no butter or shortening at all. The hard, dry cookies are meant to be kept around for a while, and butter or other fats would hasten their becoming stale.

Aside from the twice-cooked variety, Italians make a great variety of cookies. Hazelnut cookies are popular in northern Italy, while almond macaroons (amaretti) are made in various forms throughout southern Italy, where both bitter and sweet almond trees grow. Butter cookies and chocolate cookies are more prevalent in the north.

In this chapter you will also find variations on Italian cookies that are made in the United States. These include biscotti rich in butter and sugar that are not quite as crunchy as the Italian kind.

Though they often serve delicious cakes at teatime or for special occasion meals, most of my Italian friends who are home cooks do not bake. Because there is always a pastry shop nearby with a delicious specialty, even the best cooks in Italy leave fancy cake making to the professionals. On major holidays like Christmas and Easter, you will see crowds of customers filling the bakeries and pastry shops to purchase artistically prepared cakes. In Sicily, the holiday specialty might be a beautiful *cassata,* layers of cake and sweetened ricotta elaborately garnished with candied fruits and tinted almond paste. In Turin, look for *torta gianduja*, a rich dense cake made with chocolate and hazelnuts. Milanese bakers are reknowned for their *panettone*, a yeast cake with candied fruits and nuts.

Homemade cakes in Italy are usually quite simple, whether sponge cakes or rustic cakes made with fruits and nuts. I find them delicious and uncomplicated to make. If a more elaborate dessert is desired, you can always dress them up with a special sauce or ice cream. This chapter includes a selection of basic and elaborate cakes that are well within the range of anyone who enjoys baking.

Crostate and *torte* (tarts and cakes) always have pride of place in pastry shops in Italy. According to the season and region, they may be filled with gemlike glazed fruit, creamy cheese, nuts, or chocolate, and they are always appealing.

Torte usually have a thicker cake layer as a base, while crostate are thin-crusted like a tart. Don't be surprised if the distinction between the two is blurred, however. And sometimes, a thin tartlike pastry is also called a *pizza dolce*. No matter what they are called, these are my favorite baked desserts. The crusts are buttery, the fruit and nut toppings intensely flavored, and the pastry cream and cheese fillings are smooth and light.

Special occasions, particularly in southern Italy, are a time for feasting, and no feast would be complete without pastries, which may be either baked or fried. At one time, many of these special sweets were prepared in bakeries operated by cloistered nuns. There are still a few of those bakeries left, and a visit to one is a glimpse into the past. Most special-occasion sweets today are made in pastry shops. Sundays and holidays all year round, there are lines out the door of famous pastry shops like Scaturchio in Naples or Stancampiano in Palermo, as customers wait to buy their *sfogliatelle,* cannoli, and other treats.

For those who can't satisfy their cravings in Italy, I give you the recipes to make these delicious pastries at home.

⌘ Basic Cookies

Ladyfingers
Savoiardi

MAKES 4 DOZEN

These crisp, light cookies, called Savoiardi, are named for the royal house of Savoy that ruled the region of Piedmont from the fifteenth century and all of Italy from 1861 up until World War II. They are perfect tea cookies and are excellent with ice cream or fruit, but they can also be used in composed desserts like tiramisù.

Potato starch is used to make the cookies crisp and light. You can find potato starch in many supermarkets, or you can substitute cornstarch.

4 large eggs, at room temperature
2/3 cup sugar
2 teaspoons pure vanilla extract
1/2 cup all-purpose flour
1/4 cup potato starch
Pinch of salt

I Preheat the oven to 400°F. Grease and flour 3 large baking sheets.

2 Separate the eggs. In a large bowl, using an electric mixer at medium speed, beat the egg yolks with 1/3 cup of the sugar and the vanilla until thick and pale yellow, about 7 minutes.

3 In a large clean bowl with clean beaters, beat the egg whites with a pinch of salt on low speed until foamy. Increase the speed to high and gradually add the remaining 1/3 cup sugar. Beat until the egg whites hold soft peaks when the beaters are lifted, about 5 minutes.

4 With a rubber spatula, fold about 1/3 of the egg whites into the egg yolks to lighten them. Gradually fold in the remaining whites.

5 Place the flour and starch in a small fine-mesh strainer. Shake the strainer over the eggs and fold in the dry ingredients gently but thoroughly.

6 Scoop the batter into a large pastry bag fitted with a 1/2-inch tip or into a heavy-duty plastic bag with a corner cut off. (Do not fill the bag more than halfway.) Pipe the batter onto the baking sheets, forming 3 × 1–inch logs about 1 inch apart.

7 Have several wire cooling racks ready. Bake the cookies 10 to 12 minutes, or until they are golden brown and feel firm when touched lightly in the center.

8 Transfer the baking sheets to the cooling racks. Cool the cookies 2 minutes on the baking sheets, then transfer them to the racks to cool completely. Store in an airtight container at room temperature up to 2 weeks.

Semolina Cookies
Canestrelli

MAKES 36

Canistrelli means "little baskets." Crisp and buttery, these Ligurian cookies are made with semolina, which gives them a creamy color and slightly gritty texture.

Semolina is pale gold, hard durum wheat that has been ground so that it has a sandlike texture. Semolina can be fine or coarse. Fine semolina is often labeled semolina flour or pasta flour. It is typically used to make bread, especially in Sicily, and certain types of pasta and gnocchi, such as the

Roman Semolina Gnocchi on page 196. Semolina can be purchased in many supermarkets, natural food stores, and ethnic markets or from mail order sources (see pages 625–626).

1²/₃ cups all-purpose flour
¹/₂ cup fine semolina
¹/₂ teaspoon salt
1 cup (2 sticks) unsalted butter, at room temperature
¹/₂ cup confectioner's sugar
1 large egg

1 In a large bowl, sift together the flour, semolina, and salt.

2 In a large bowl with an electric mixer, beat the butter on medium speed until light and fluffy, about 2 minutes. Add the sugar and beat until well blended, about 1 minute more. Beat in the egg until blended.

3 Add the dry ingredients and stir on low speed until just blended. (Do not overmix.) Gather the dough into a ball and wrap in plastic wrap. Refrigerate 1 hour up to overnight.

4 Preheat the oven to 350°F. Grease 2 large baking sheets.

5 On a lightly floured surface, with a rolling pin, roll out the dough to a 9-inch circle about ¹/₄ inch thick. With a cookie or biscuit cutter, cut the dough into 2-inch circles. Place on the prepared baking sheets about 1 inch apart.

6 Have ready 2 wire cooling racks. Bake 13 minutes or until the cookies are lightly golden around the edge.

7 Transfer the baking sheets to the cooling racks. Let the cookies cool 5 minutes on the baking sheets, then transfer them to the wire racks to cool completely. Store in an airtight container up to 2 weeks.

Cookie-Making Tips

- Very lightly dampen your hands with cool water when shaping sticky biscotti dough.
- Make all the cookies the same size so that they will bake evenly. For drop cookies, use a small spring-operated scoop to measure out even amounts.
- Bring eggs, flour, butter, and other chilled ingredients to room temperature before using so that they will blend better.
- Remember that every oven is a little different, so check to see how quickly the cookies are baking several minutes before the recipe recommends. Adjust the cooking time accordingly.
- If baking more than one pan of cookies at a time, reverse the positions of the pans halfway through the baking time.
- Always use the best ingredients, such as fresh butter, high-quality bittersweet chocolate, freshly squeezed lemon juice, high-quality flavoring extracts, and fresh nuts.
- Store nuts and seeds in tightly closed containers in the refrigerator or freezer. Because they have a lot of fat in them, they can easily pick up unwanted flavors from other foods in the refrigerator. At room temperature, they will quickly go rancid, so use them as soon as possible.

Vin Santo Rings
Ciambelline al Vin Santo

MAKES ABOUT 4 DOZEN

Vin santo is a Tuscan dry dessert wine. It is usually served as an accompaniment to dipping cookies, but here it is the principal flavoring ingredient in ring-shaped biscuits. They are made with olive oil and do not have any eggs or butter. The vin santo gives the cookies a subtle wine flavor, while the texture is tender and crumbly. The recipe was given to me by the cook at the Selvapiana winery in Tuscany.

2¹/2 cups all-purpose flour
¹/2 cup sugar
¹/2 cup extra-virgin olive oil
¹/2 cup vin santo

1 Preheat the oven to 350°F. Have ready 2 large ungreased baking sheets.

2 In a large bowl, with a wooden spoon, combine the flour and sugar. Add the oil and wine and stir until smooth and well blended. Shape the dough into a ball.

3 Divide the dough into 6 sections. Cut one section into 8 pieces. Roll each piece between your palms into a 4 × ¹/2–inch log. Shape the log into a ring, pinching the edges together to seal. Repeat with the remaining dough, placing the rings 1 inch apart on the baking sheets.

4 Have ready 2 wire cooling racks. Bake the rings 20 minutes or until golden brown.

5 Transfer the baking sheets to the racks. Let the cookies cool 5 minutes on the baking sheets, then transfer them to the wire racks to cool completely. Store in an airtight container up to 2 weeks.

Marsala Cookies
Biscotti al Marsala

MAKES 4 DOZEN

The warm, sunny flavor of Marsala enhances these Sicilian cookies. Either dry or sweet Marsala can be used. Be sure to serve these with a glass of the same wine. They are similar to the Vin Santo Rings at left, though the texture is lighter and crisper because of the eggs and baking powder, and they are glazed with sugar.

2¹/2 cups all-purpose flour
2 teaspoons baking powder
1 teaspoon salt
1 cup sugar
¹/2 cup dry or sweet Marsala
2 large eggs
¹/4 cup extra-virgin olive oil
1 teaspoon pure vanilla extract

1 Preheat the oven to 375°F. Grease 2 large baking sheets.

2 In a large bowl, sift together the flour, baking powder, and salt. Pour ¹/2 cup of the sugar into a small bowl and ¹/4 cup of the Marsala into another.

3 In a large bowl, whisk the eggs and the remaining ¹/2 cup of sugar until well blended. Beat in the remaining ¹/4 cup of Marsala, the oil, and the vanilla extract. With a wooden spoon, stir in the dry ingredients. Knead briefly until well blended and shape the dough into a ball.

4 Divide the dough into 6 sections. Cut one section into 8 pieces. Roll each piece between your palms into a 4 × ¹/2–inch log. Shape the log into a ring, pinching the edges together to seal. Repeat with the remaining dough.

5 Dip the top or bottom of each ring first in the wine, then in the sugar. Place the rings sugar-side up and 1 inch apart on the prepared baking sheets. Bake 18 to 20 minutes, or until golden brown. Have ready 2 wire cooling racks.

6 Transfer the baking sheets to the racks. Let the cookies cool 5 minutes on the baking sheets, then transfer them to the wire racks to cool completely. Store in an airtight container up to 2 weeks.

Sesame Wine Biscuits
Biscotti di Vino

MAKES 2 DOZEN

Only slightly sweet, with a spicy spike from black pepper, these Neapolitan biscuits are good for snacking with a glass of wine and some cheese.

2¹/₂ cups all-purpose flour
¹/₂ cup sugar
1¹/₂ teaspoons baking powder
1 teaspoon salt
1 teaspoon freshly ground black pepper
¹/₂ cup dry red wine
¹/₂ cup olive oil
1 egg white, beaten until foamy
2 tablespoons sesame seeds

1 Preheat the oven to 350°F. Have ready 2 large ungreased baking sheets.

2 In a large bowl, stir together the flour, sugar, baking powder, salt, and pepper. Add the wine and olive oil and stir until well blended.

3 Shape the dough into a ball. Divide the dough into 4 pieces. Shape each piece into a 10-inch log. Flatten the logs slightly. Brush with the egg white and sprinkle with the sesame seeds.

4 Cut the logs into ³/4-inch pieces. Place the pieces 1 inch apart on the baking sheets. Bake for 25 minutes, or until lightly browned.

5 Have ready 2 large cooling racks. Transfer the baking sheets to the racks. Let the cookies cool 5 minutes on the baking sheets, then transfer them to the racks to cool completely. Store in an airtight container up to 2 weeks.

Sesame Cookies
Biscotti Regina

MAKES 48

Sicilians call these regina, or "queen," cookies because they are so highly esteemed. Though they are rather plain looking, their toasty sesame flavor is addictive. One invariably leads to another.

Look for fresh, unhulled sesame seeds in ethnic markets and natural food stores. These cookies were originally made with lard. Sicilian cooks today often use margarine, but I prefer a combination of butter for flavor and vegetable shortening for tenderness.

4 cups all-purpose flour
1 cup sugar
1 tablespoon baking powder
1 teaspoon salt
¹/₂ cup (1 stick) unsalted butter, at room temperature
¹/₂ cup solid vegetable shortening
2 large eggs, at room temperature
1 teaspoon pure vanilla extract
1 teaspoon grated lemon zest
2 cups unhulled sesame seeds
¹/₂ cup milk

1 Preheat the oven to 375°F. Grease and flour two large baking sheets or line them with parchment.

2 In a large electric mixer bowl, stir together the flour, sugar, baking powder, and salt. On low speed, stir in the butter and shortening a little at a time until the mixture resembles coarse crumbs.

3 In a medium bowl, whisk the eggs, vanilla, and lemon zest. Stir the egg mixture into the dry ingredients until smooth and well blended, about 2 minutes. Cover the dough with plastic wrap and refrigerate 1 hour.

4 Spread the sesame seeds on a piece of wax paper. Put the milk in a small bowl next to the sesame seeds.

5 Take the dough out of the refrigerator. Scoop out a portion of the dough the size of a golf ball

(continues)

and shape it into a log 2¹/₂ inches long and ³/₄ inch wide. Dip the log in the milk, then roll it in the sesame seeds. Place the log on the baking sheet and flatten slightly with your fingers. Continue with the remaining dough, placing the logs 1 inch apart.

6 Bake 25 to 30 minutes or until well browned. Have ready 2 large cooling racks.

7 Transfer the baking sheets to the racks. Let the cookies cool 5 minutes on the baking sheets, then transfer them to the racks to cool completely. Store in an airtight container up to 2 weeks.

Anisette Toast
Biscotti di Anice

MAKES ABOUT 3 DOZEN

Anise, a member of the same family of plants as fennel, caraway, and dill, is considered an aid to digestion. In southern Italy, anise seeds are used to flavor after-dinner liqueurs such as Sambuca and anisette, which gives these cookies their distinctive licorice flavor. For a more pronounced flavor, add a teaspoon of anise seeds to the batter before baking.

2 large eggs, at room temperature
1 tablespoon anisette liqueur or anise extract
¹/₂ cup sugar
1 cup all-purpose flour
2 tablespoons cornstarch
1 teaspoon baking powder

1 Place a rack in the center of the oven. Preheat the oven to 350°F. Grease a 9-inch square baking pan. Line the bottom of the pan with wax paper. Grease and flour the paper. Tap out the excess flour.

2 In a large electric mixer bowl, combine the eggs, liqueur, and sugar. Begin beating the eggs on low speed, gradually increasing the speed to high. Continue to beat the eggs until they are very light and foamy and tripled in volume, about 5 minutes.

3 Place the flour, cornstarch, and baking powder in a fine-mesh strainer. Shake the strainer over the egg mixture, gradually folding in the dry ingredients with a rubber spatula. Be careful not to deflate the eggs.

4 Scrape the batter into the prepared pan and smooth the top. Bake 20 to 25 minutes, or until firm when touched lightly in the center and golden brown. Have ready a large baking sheet and a large cooling rack.

5 Remove the pan from the oven, but leave the oven turned on. Run a small knife around the edges of the pan. Invert the cake onto a cutting board.

6 Raise the oven temperature to 375°F. With a long serrated knife, cut the cake into 3-inch strips. Cut each strip crosswise into ³/₄-inch- thick slices. Place the slices in a single layer on a large baking sheet. Bake the slices 7 minutes or until toasted and golden.

7 Remove the cookies from the oven and transfer to wire racks to cool. Store in a tightly covered container up to 2 weeks.

"S" Cookies

Biscotti Esse

MAKES 4 DOZEN

My husband and I had these lovely butter and spice cookies in Milan, where I spent ten days researching an article for the Wine Spectator *magazine on the city's best restaurants.*

3 cups all-purpose flour

I tablespoon baking powder

$1/2$ teaspoon salt

$1/2$ teaspoon ground cinnamon

$1/4$ teaspoon ground cloves

$1/4$ teaspoon ground allspice

$1/2$ cup (I stick) unsalted butter, at room temperature

I cup sugar

3 large eggs, beaten

2 teaspoons pure vanilla extract

1 Sift together the flour, baking powder, salt, and spices onto a piece of wax paper.

2 In a large electric mixer bowl, beat the butter with the sugar on medium speed until light and fluffy, about 2 minutes. Beat in the eggs one at a time. Add the vanilla and beat until well blended, about 1 minute more

3 Stir in the dry ingredients. Shape the dough into a ball. Wrap in plastic and chill in the refrigerator 1 hour.

4 Preheat the oven to 400°F. Grease 2 large baking sheets.

5 Divide the dough into 2 pieces. Cut each piece into 8. Roll each piece into a $1/2$-inch-thick rope. Cut the ropes into 4-inch lengths. Place the lengths in an S shape 1 inch apart on baking sheets.

6 Bake 13 to 16 minutes or until lightly browned. Have ready 2 wire cooling racks.

7 Transfer the baking sheets to the racks. Let the cookies cool 5 minutes on the baking sheets, then transfer them to the wire racks to cool completely. Store in an airtight container up to 2 weeks.

Butter Rings

Bussolai

MAKES 36

These Venetian cookies are simple to make and a pleasure to have around the house for a midday snack or whenever guests stop in.

I cup sugar

$1/2$ cup (I stick) unsalted butter, at room temperature

3 large egg yolks

I teaspoon grated lemon zest

I teaspoon grated orange zest

I teaspoon pure vanilla extract

2 cups all-purpose flour

$1/2$ teaspoon salt

I egg white, beaten until foamy

1 Set aside $1/3$ cup of the sugar.

2 In the large bowl of an electric mixer, beat the butter with the remaining $2/3$ cup of sugar at medium speed until light and fluffy, about 2 minutes. Beat in the egg yolks one at a time. Add the lemon and orange zests and vanilla extract and beat, scraping the sides of the bowl, until smooth, about 2 minutes more.

3 Stir in the flour and salt until well blended. Shape the dough into a ball. Wrap in plastic wrap and refrigerate 1 hour up to overnight.

4 Preheat the oven to 325°F. Grease 2 large baking sheets. Cut the dough into 6 pieces. Divide each piece again into 6 pieces. Roll each piece into a 4-inch rope, shape into a ring, and pinch the ends together to seal. Place the rings 1 inch apart on the prepared baking sheets. Brush lightly with the egg white and sprinkle with the reserved $1/3$ cup of sugar.

5 Bake 15 minutes or until lightly browned. Have ready 2 wire cooling racks.

6 Transfer the baking sheets to the racks. Let the cookies cool 5 minutes on the baking sheets, then transfer them to the wire racks to cool completely. Store in an airtight container up to 2 weeks.

Lemon Knots

Tarralucci

MAKES 40

Every Italian bakery in Brooklyn, New York, made these refreshing Sicilian lemon cookies when I was growing up. I like to serve them with iced tea.

If the weather is hot and humid, the icing may refuse to firm up at room temperature. In that case, store the cookies in the refrigerator.

4 cups all-purpose flour
4 teaspoons baking powder
I cup sugar
1/2 cup solid vegetable shortening
3 large eggs
1/2 cup milk
2 tablespoons lemon juice
2 teaspoons grated lemon zest

ICING

1 1/2 cups confectioner's sugar
I tablespoon freshly squeezed lemon juice
2 teaspoons grated lemon zest
Milk

I Sift together the flour and baking powder onto a piece of wax paper.

2 In a large bowl, with an electric mixer at medium speed, beat the sugar and shortening until light and fluffy, about 2 minutes. Beat in the eggs one at a time until well blended. Stir in the milk, lemon juice, and zest. Scrape the sides of the bowl. Stir in the dry ingredients until smooth, about 2 minutes. Cover with plastic wrap and refrigerate at least 1 hour.

3 Preheat the oven to 350°F. Have ready 2 large baking sheets. Pinch off a piece of dough the size of a golf ball. Lightly roll the dough into a 6-inch rope. Tie the rope into a knot. Place the knot on an ungreased baking sheet. Continue making the knots and placing them about 1 inch apart on the sheets.

4 Bake the cookies 12 minutes or until firm when pressed on top but not browned. Have ready 2 wire cooling racks.

5 Transfer the baking sheets to the racks. Let the cookies cool 5 minutes on the baking sheets, then transfer them to the wire racks to cool completely.

6 Combine the confectioner's sugar, lemon juice, and zest in a large bowl. Add milk 1 teaspoon at a time and stir until the mixture forms a thin icing with the consistency of heavy cream.

7 Dip the tops of the cookies in the icing. Place them on a rack until the icing is hardened. Store in airtight containers up to 3 days.

Spice Cookies

Bicciolani

MAKES 75

In caffès in Turin you can order barbajada, *a combination of half coffee and half hot chocolate. It would be perfect with these thin, buttery spice cookies.*

I cup (2 sticks) unsalted butter, at room temperature
I cup sugar
I egg yolk
2 cups all-purpose flour
1/2 teaspoon salt
I teaspoon ground cinnamon
1/8 teaspoon freshly grated nutmeg
1/8 teaspoon ground cloves

I Preheat the oven to 350°F. Grease a 15 × 10 × 1–inch jelly roll pan.

2 In a bowl, stir together the flour, salt, and spices.

3 In a large electric mixer bowl, beat the butter, sugar, and egg yolk on medium speed until light and fluffy, about 2 minutes. Reduce the speed to low and stir in the dry ingredients until thoroughly blended, about 2 minutes more.

4 Crumble the dough into the prepared pan. With your hands, firmly press the dough out into an even layer. With the back of a fork, make shallow ridges in the top of the dough.

5 Bake 25 to 30 minutes or until lightly browned. Transfer the pan to a wire cooling rack. Cool 10 minutes. Then cut the dough into 2 × 1–inch cookies.

6 Cool completely in the pan. Store at room temperature in an airtight container up to 2 weeks.

Wafer Cookies
Pizzelle

MAKES ABOUT 2 DOZEN

Many families in central and southern Italy are proud of their pizzelle irons, beautifully crafted forms traditionally used to make these pretty wafers. Some irons are embossed with the original owner's initials, while others have silhouettes such as a couple toasting each other with a glass of wine. They were once a typical wedding gift.

Though charming, these old fashioned irons are heavy and unwieldy on today's stoves. An electric pizzelle press, similar to a waffle iron, does an efficient and quick job of turning out these cookies.

When they are freshly made, pizzelle are pliable and can be molded into cone, tube, or cup shapes. They can be filled with whipped cream, ice cream, cannoli cream, or fruit. They cool and crisp in no time, so you must work quickly and carefully to shape them. Of course, they are good flat as well.

1³/4 cups unbleached all-purpose flour
1 teaspoon baking powder
Pinch of salt
3 large eggs
²/3 cup sugar
1 tablespoon pure vanilla extract
1 stick (¹/2 cup) unsalted butter, melted and cooled

1 Preheat the pizzelle maker according to the manufacturer's directions. In a bowl, stir together the flour, baking powder, and salt.

2 In a large bowl, beat the eggs, sugar, and vanilla with an electric mixer on medium speed until thick and light, about 4 minutes. Beat in the butter. Stir in the dry ingredients until just blended, about 1 minute.

3 Place about 1 tablespoon of the batter in the center of each pizzelle mold. (The exact amount will depend on the design of the mold.) Close the cover and bake until lightly golden. This will depend on the maker and how long the mold has been heating. Check it carefully after 30 seconds.

4 When the pizzelle are golden, slide them off the molds with a wooden or plastic spatula. Let cool flat on a wire rack. Or, to make cookie cups, bend each pizzelle into the curve of a wide coffee or dessert cup. To make cannoli shells, shape them around cannoli tubes or a wooden dowel.

5 When the pizzelle are cool and crisp, store them in an airtight container until ready to use. These last for several weeks.

Flavor Variations: *Anise:* Substitute 1 tablespoon anise extract and 1 tablespoon anise seeds for the vanilla. *Orange or Lemon:* Add 1 tablespoon grated fresh orange or lemon zest to the egg mixture. *Rum or Almond:* Stir in 1 tablespoon rum or almond extract instead of the vanilla. *Nut:* Stir in ¹/4 cup of nuts ground to a very fine powder along with the flour.

Sweet Ravioli
Ravioli Dolci

MAKES 2 DOZEN

Jam fills these crisp dessert ravioli. Any flavor will do, as long as it has a thick consistency so that it will stay in place and not ooze out of the dough as it bakes. This was a favorite recipe of my father, who perfected it from his memories of the cookies his mother used to make.

1³/₄ cup all-purpose flour
¹/₂ cup potato or corn starch
¹/₂ teaspoon salt
¹/₂ cup (1 stick) unsalted butter, at room temperature
¹/₂ cup sugar
1 large egg
2 tablespoons rum or brandy
1 teaspoon grated lemon zest
1 teaspoon pure vanilla extract
1 cup thick sour cherry, raspberry, or apricot jam

1 In a large bowl, sift together the flour, starch, and salt.

2 In a large bowl with an electric mixer, beat the butter with the sugar until light and fluffy, about 2 minutes. Beat in the egg, rum, zest, and vanilla. On low speed, stir in the dry ingredients.

3 Divide the dough in half. Shape each half into a disk. Wrap each separately in plastic and refrigerate 1 hour up to overnight.

4 Preheat the oven to 350°F. Grease 2 large baking sheets.

5 Roll out the dough to a ¹/₈-inch thickness. With a fluted pastry or pasta cutter, cut the dough into 2-inch squares. Arrange the squares about 1 inch apart on the prepared baking sheets. Place ¹/₂ teaspoon of the jam in the center of each square. (Do not use more jam, or the filling will leak out as it bakes.)

6 Roll out the remaining dough to a ¹/₈-inch thickness. Cut the dough into 2-inch squares.

7 Cover the jam with the dough squares. Press the edges all around with a fork to seal in the filling.

8 Bake 16 to 18 minutes, or until lightly browned. Have ready 2 wire cooling racks.

9 Transfer the baking sheets to the racks. Let the cookies cool 5 minutes on the baking sheets, then transfer them to the wire racks to cool completely. Sprinkle with confectioner's sugar. Store in an airtight container up to 1 week.

"Ugly-but-Good" Cookies
Brutti ma Buoni

MAKES 2 DOZEN

"Ugly but good" is the meaning of the name of these Piedmontese cookies. The name is only half-true: The cookies are not ugly, but they are good. The technique for making these is unusual. The cookie batter is cooked in a saucepan before it is baked.

3 large egg whites, at room temperature
Pinch of salt
1¹/₂ cups sugar
1 cup unsweetened cocoa powder
1¹/₄ cups hazelnuts, toasted, peeled, and coarsely chopped (page 559)

1 Preheat the oven to 300°F. Grease 2 large baking sheets.

2 In a large bowl, with an electric mixer at medium speed, beat the egg whites and salt until foamy. Increase the speed to high and gradually add the sugar. Beat until soft peaks form when the beaters are lifted.

3 On low speed, mix in the cocoa. Stir in the hazelnuts.

4 Scrape the mixture into a large heavy saucepan. Cook over medium heat, stirring constantly with a wooden spoon, until the mixture is shiny and smooth, about 5 minutes. Be careful that it does not scorch.

5 Immediately drop the hot batter by tablespoonfuls onto the prepared baking sheets. Bake 30 minutes or until firm and slightly cracked on the surface.

6 While the cookies are still hot, transfer them to a rack to cool, using a thin-blade metal spatula. Store in an airtight container up to 2 weeks.

How To Toast and Skin Nuts

Toasting brings out the flavor and crunchiness of nuts. Almonds are sold in a variety of ways: whole, with their skins intact; blanched, meaning the skins have been removed; sliced into thin flakes; and slivered. Sometimes you can find them already toasted, but if not, they can be baked for 5 to 10 minutes in a 300° F oven until they smell toasted and are lightly browned.

I usually do not skin almonds because the skins add flavor and color to most recipes, and they are thin enough not to be intrusive. The exception is when making delicate cookies such as macaroons. In that case, I buy blanched almonds, which are always available.

For hazelnuts and walnuts, toasting not only adds flavor but also helps to remove the skins, which can be tough and bitter. You can toast and skin the nuts yourself or buy them already toasted and skinned at natural foods and ethnic markets that sell them in bulk.

To toast hazelnuts or walnuts, place them in a shallow pan in a 300°F oven. Stir the nuts every 3 minutes and toast until the skins begin to crack and loosen and the nuts are lightly browned, about 5 to 8 minutes. Watch them carefully, as they quickly go from toasted to burned. Setting a timer helps.

While they are still hot, place the nuts on a clean towel. Rub the nuts in the towel to remove the skins. Let cool before using.

❧ Chocolate Cookies

Jam Spots
Biscotti di Marmellata

MAKES 40

Chocolate, nuts, and jam are a winning combination in these tasty cookies. They are always a hit on Christmas cookie trays.

³/₄ cup (1¹/₂ sticks) unsalted butter, at room temperature
¹/₂ cup sugar
¹/₂ teaspoon salt
3 ounces bittersweet chocolate, melted and cooled
2 cups all-purpose flour
³/₄ cup finely chopped almonds
¹/₂ cup thick seedless raspberry jam

1 Preheat the oven to 350°F. Grease 2 large baking sheets.

2 In a large bowl, with an electric mixer on medium speed, beat the butter, sugar, and salt until light and fluffy, about 2 minutes. Add the melted chocolate and beat until well blended, scraping the sides of the bowl. Stir in the flour until smooth.

3 Place the nuts in a shallow bowl. Shape the dough into 1-inch balls. Roll the balls in the nuts, pressing lightly so they will adhere. Place the balls about 1¹/₂ inches apart on the prepared baking sheets.

4 With the handle end of a wooden spoon, poke a deep hole in each ball of dough, molding the dough around the handle to maintain the round shape. Place about ¹/₄ teaspoon jam in each cookie. (Do not add more jam, as it may melt and leak out when the cookies bake.)

5 Bake the cookies 18 to 20 minutes, or until the jam is bubbling and the cookies are lightly browned. Have ready 2 wire cooling racks.

6 Transfer the baking sheets to the racks. Let the cookies cool 5 minutes on the baking sheets, then transfer them to the wire racks to cool completely. Store in an airtight container up to 2 weeks.

Double-Chocolate Nut Biscotti

Biscotti al Cioccolato

MAKES 4 DOZEN

These rich biscotti have chocolate in the dough, both melted and in chunks. I have never seen them in Italy, but they are similar to what I have tasted in coffee bars here.

2¹/₂ cups all-purpose flour

2 teaspoons baking powder

¹/₂ teaspoon salt

3 large eggs, at room temperature

1 cup sugar

1 teaspoon pure vanilla extract

6 ounces bittersweet chocolate, melted and cooled

6 tablespoons (¹/₂ stick plus 2 tablespoons) unsalted butter, melted and cooled

1 cup walnuts, coarsely chopped

1 cup chocolate chips

1 Place a rack in the center of the oven. Preheat the oven to 300°F. Grease and flour 2 large baking sheets.

2 In a large bowl, sift together the flour, baking powder, and salt.

3 In a large bowl, with an electric mixer at medium speed, beat the eggs, sugar, and vanilla until foamy and light, about 2 minutes. Stir in the chocolate and butter until blended. Add the flour mixture and stir until smooth, about 1 minute more. Stir in the nuts and chocolate chips.

4 Divide the dough in half. With moistened hands, shape each piece into a 12 × 3–inch log on the prepared baking sheet. Bake for 35 minutes or until the logs are firm when pressed in the center. Remove the pan from the oven, but do not turn off the heat. Let cool 10 minutes.

5 Slide the logs onto a cutting board. Cut the logs into ¹/₂-inch-thick slices. Lay the slices on the baking sheet. Bake for 10 minutes or until the cookies are lightly toasted.

6 Have ready 2 large cooling racks. Transfer the baking sheets to the racks. Let the cookies cool 5 minutes on the baking sheets, then transfer them to the racks to cool completely. Store in an airtight container up to 2 weeks.

Chocolate Kisses

Baci di Cioccolato

MAKES 3 DOZEN

Chocolate and vanilla "kisses" are a favorite in Verona, home of Romeo and Juliet, where they are made in a variety of combinations.

1²/₃ cups all-purpose flour

¹/₃ cup unsweetened Dutch-process cocoa powder, sifted

¹/₄ teaspoon salt

1 cup (2 sticks) unsalted butter, at room temperature

¹/₂ cup confectioner's sugar

1 teaspoon pure vanilla extract

¹/₂ cup finely chopped toasted almonds (see page 559)

FILLING

2 ounces semisweet or bittersweet chocolate, chopped

2 tablespoons unsalted butter

¹/₃ cup almonds, toasted and finely chopped

1 In a large bowl, sift together the flour, cocoa, and salt.

2 In a large bowl, with an electric mixer at medium speed, beat the butter and sugar until light and fluffy, about 2 minutes. Beat in the vanilla. Stir in the dry ingredients and the almonds until blended, about 1 minute more. Cover with plastic and chill in the refrigerator 1 hour up to overnight.

3 Preheat the oven to 350°F. Have ready 2 ungreased baking sheets. Roll teaspoonfuls of the dough into ³/₄-inch balls. Place the balls 1 inch apart on the baking sheets. With your fingers, press the balls to flatten them slightly. Bake the cookies until firm but not browned, 10 to 12 minutes. Have ready 2 large cooling racks.

4 Transfer the baking sheets to the racks. Let the cookies cool 5 minutes on the baking sheets, then transfer them to the racks to cool completely.

5 Bring about 2 inches of water to a simmer in the bottom half of a double boiler or a small saucepan. Place the chocolate and the butter in the top half of the double boiler or in a small heatproof bowl that fits comfortably over the saucepan. Place the bowl over the simmering water. Let stand uncovered until the chocolate is softened. Stir until smooth. Stir in the almonds.

6 Spread a small amount of the filling mixture on the bottom of one cookie. Place a second cookie bottom-side down on the filling and press together lightly. Place the cookies on a wire rack until the filling is set. Repeat with the remaining cookies and filling. Store in an airtight container in the refrigerator up to 1 week.

How To Melt Chocolate

Bring about 2 inches of water to a simmer in the bottom half of a double boiler or a small saucepan. Break up the chocolate and place it in the top half of the double boiler or in a small heatproof bowl that fits comfortably over the saucepan. Let stand uncovered until the chocolate is softened. Stir until smooth. Be careful not to let the chocolate get wet, or it may seize, causing its texture to get hard and grainy. If it does, add a little vegetable shortening to the chocolate, allow it to melt, and stir until smooth.

No-Bake Chocolate "Salame"

Salame del Cioccolato

MAKES 32 COOKIES

Crunchy chocolate nut slices that require no baking are a specialty of Piedmont. Other cookies can be substituted for the amaretti, if you prefer, such as vanilla or chocolate wafers, graham crackers, or shortbread. These are best made a few days ahead, to allow the flavors to blend. If you prefer not use the liqueur, substitute a spoonful of orange juice.

18 amaretti cookies
$1/3$ cup sugar
$1/3$ cup unsweetened cocoa powder
$1/2$ cup (1 stick) unsalted butter, softened
1 tablespoon grappa or rum
$1/3$ cup chopped walnuts

1 Place the cookies in a plastic bag. Crush the cookies with a rolling pin or heavy object. There should be about $3/4$ cup of crumbs.

2 Place the crumbs in a large bowl. With a wooden spoon, stir in the sugar and cocoa. Add the butter and grappa. Stir until the dry ingredients are moistened and blended. Stir in the walnuts.

3 Place a 14-inch sheet of plastic wrap on a flat surface. Pour the dough mixture onto the plastic wrap. Shape the dough into an $8 \times 2^1/2$–inch log. Roll the log in the plastic wrap, folding the ends over to enclose it completely. Refrigerate the log at least 24 hours and up to 3 days.

4 Cut the log into $1/4$-inch-thick slices. Serve chilled. Store the cookies in an airtight plastic container in the refrigerator up to 2 weeks.

❧ Nut Cookies

Prato Biscuits
Biscotti di Prato

MAKES ABOUT 4½ DOZEN

In the town of Prato in Tuscany, these are the classic biscotti to dip in vin santo, the great dessert wine of the region. Eaten plain, they are rather dry, so do provide a beverage for dunking them.

2½ cups all-purpose flour
1½ teaspoons baking powder
1 teaspoon salt
4 large eggs
¾ cup sugar
1 teaspoon grated lemon zest
1 teaspoon grated orange zest
1 teaspoon pure vanilla extract
1 cup toasted almonds (see page 559)

1 Place a rack in the center of the oven. Preheat the oven to 325°F. Grease and flour a large baking sheet.

2 In a medium bowl, sift together the flour, baking powder, and salt.

3 In a large bowl with an electric mixer, beat the eggs and sugar on medium speed until light and foamy, about 3 minutes. Beat in the lemon and orange zests and vanilla. On low speed, stir in the dry ingredients, then stir in the almonds.

4 Lightly dampen your hands. Shape the dough into two 14 × 2–inch logs. Place the logs on the prepared baking sheet several inches apart. Bake for 30 minutes or until firm and golden.

5 Remove the baking sheet from the oven and reduce the oven heat to 300°F. Let the logs cool on the baking sheet for 20 minutes.

6 Slide the logs onto a cutting board. With a large heavy chef's knife, cut the logs on the diagonal into ½-inch-thick slices. Lay the slices on the baking sheet. Bake 20 minutes or until lightly golden.

7 Transfer the cookies to wire racks to cool. Store in an airtight container.

Umbrian Fruit and Nut Biscotti
Tozzetti

MAKES 80

Made without fat, these cookies keep a long time in an airtight container. The flavor actually improves, so plan to make them several days before serving them.

3 cups all-purpose flour
½ cup cornstarch
2 teaspoons baking powder
3 large eggs
3 egg yolks
2 tablespoons Marsala, vin santo, or sherry
1 cup sugar
1 cup raisins
1 cup almonds
¼ cup chopped candied orange peel
¼ cup chopped candied citron
1 teaspoon anise seeds

1 Preheat the oven to 350°F. Grease 2 large baking sheets.

2 In a medium bowl, sift together the flour, cornstarch, and baking powder.

3 In a large bowl with an electric mixer, beat together the eggs, yolks, and Marsala. Add the sugar and beat until well blended, about 3 minutes. Stir in the dry ingredients, the raisins, almonds, peel, citron and anise seeds until blended. The dough will be stiff. If necessary, turn the dough out onto a countertop and knead it until blended.

4 Divide the dough into quarters. Dampen your hands with cool water and shape each quarter into a 10-inch log. Place the logs 2 inches apart on the prepared baking sheets.

5 Bake the logs 20 minutes or until they feel firm when pressed in the center and are golden brown around the edges. Remove the logs from the oven but leave the oven on. Let the logs cool 5 minutes on the baking sheets.

6 Slide the logs onto a cutting board. With a large chef's knife, cut them into 1/2-inch-thick slices. Place the slices on the baking sheets and bake 10 minutes or until lightly toasted.

7 Have ready 2 large cooling racks. Transfer the cookies to the racks. Let cool completely. Store in an airtight container up to 2 weeks.

Lemon Nut Biscotti
Biscotti al Limone

MAKES 48

Lemon and almonds flavor these biscotti.

1 1/2 cups all-purpose flour
1 teaspoon baking powder
1/4 teaspoon salt
1/2 cup (1 stick) unsalted butter, at room temperature
1/2 cup sugar
2 large eggs, at room temperature
2 teaspoons freshly grated lemon zest
1 cup toasted almonds, coarsely chopped

1 Place a rack in the center of the oven. Preheat the oven to 350°F. Grease and flour a large baking sheet.

2 In a bowl, sift together the flour, baking powder, and salt.

3 In a large bowl with an electric mixer, beat the butter and sugar until light and fluffy, about 2 minutes. Beat in the eggs one at a time. Add the lemon zest, scraping the inside of the bowl with a rubber spatula. Gradually stir in the flour mixture and the nuts until blended.

4 Divide the dough in half. With moistened hands, shape each piece into a 12 × 2–inch log on the prepared baking sheet. Bake for 20 minutes or

until the logs are lightly browned and firm when pressed in the center. Remove the pan from the oven, but do not turn off the heat. Let the logs cool 10 minutes on the baking sheet.

5 Slide the logs onto a cutting board. Cut the logs into 1/2-inch-thick slices. Place the slices on the baking sheet. Bake for 10 minutes or until the cookies are lightly toasted.

6 Have ready 2 large cooling racks. Transfer the cookies to the racks. Let cool completely. Store in an airtight container up to 2 weeks.

Walnut Biscotti
Biscotti di Noce

MAKES ABOUT 80

Olive oil can be used for baking in a wide range of recipes. Use a mild-flavored extra-virgin olive oil. It complements many types of nuts and citrus fruits. Here is a biscotti recipe I developed for an article in the Washington Post *about baking with olive oil.*

2 cups all-purpose flour
1 teaspoon baking powder
1 teaspoon salt
2 large eggs, at room temperature
2/3 cup sugar
1/2 cup extra-virgin olive oil
1/2 teaspoon grated lemon zest
2 cups toasted walnuts (see page 559)

1 Preheat the oven to 325°F. Grease 2 large baking sheets.

2 In a large bowl, combine the flour, baking powder, and salt.

3 In another large bowl, whisk the eggs, sugar, oil, and lemon zest until well blended. With a wooden spoon, stir in the dry ingredients just until blended. Stir in the walnuts.

4 Divide the dough into four pieces. Shape the pieces into 12 × 1 1/2–inch logs, placing them several

(continues)

inches apart on the prepared baking sheets. Bake for 20 to 25 minutes or until lightly browned. Remove from the oven, but do not turn it off. Let the cookies cool on the baking sheets 10 minutes.

5 Slide the logs onto a cutting board. With a large heavy knife, cut the logs diagonally into 1/2-inch slices. Lay the slices on the baking sheets and return the sheets to the oven. Bake 10 minutes or until toasted and golden.

6 Have ready 2 large cooling racks. Transfer the cookies to the racks. Let cool completely. Store in an airtight container up to 2 weeks.

Almond Macaroons
Amaretti

MAKES 3 DOZEN

In southern Italy, these are made by grinding up both sweet and bitter almonds. Bitter almonds, which come from a particular variety of almond tree, are not sold in the United States. They have a flavor component similar to cyanide, a lethal poison, so they are not approved for commercial use. The closest we can come to the correct flavor is commercial almond paste and a little almond extract. Do not confuse almond paste with marzipan, which is similar, but has a higher sugar content. Buy the almond paste sold in cans for best flavor. If you can't find it, ask at your local bakery to see if they will sell you some.

These cookies stick, so I bake them on nonstick baking mats known as Silpat. The mats never need greasing, are easy to clean, and reusable. You can find them at good kitchen supply stores. If you don't have the mats, the baking pans can be lined with parchment paper or aluminum foil.

1 (8-ounce) can almond paste, crumbled
1 cup sugar
2 large egg whites, at room temperature
1/4 teaspoon almond extract
36 candied cherries or whole almonds

1 Preheat the oven to 350°F. Line 2 large baking sheets with parchment paper or aluminum foil.

2 Crumble the almond paste into a large bowl. With an electric mixer on low speed, beat in the sugar until blended. Add the egg whites and almond extract. Increase the speed to medium and beat until very smooth, about 3 minutes.

3 Scoop up 1 tablespoon of the batter and lightly roll it into a ball. Dampen your fingertips with cool water if necessary to prevent sticking. Place the balls about one inch apart on the prepared baking sheet. Press a cherry or almond into the top of the dough.

4 Bake 18 to 20 minutes or until the cookies are lightly browned. Let cool briefly on the baking sheet.

5 With a thin metal spatula, transfer the cookies to wire racks to cool completely. Store the cookies in airtight containers. (If you want to keep these cookies for more than a day or two, freeze them to maintain their soft texture. They can be eaten directly from the freezer.)

Pine Nut Macaroons
Biscotti di Pinoli

MAKES 40

I have made many variations of these cookies over the years. This version is my favorite because it is made with both almond paste and ground almonds for both flavor and texture and has the added rich flavor of toasted pine nuts (pignoli).

1 (8-ounce) can almond paste
1/3 cup finely ground blanched almonds
2 large egg whites
1 cup confectioner's sugar, plus more for decorating
2 cups pine nuts or slivered almonds

1 Place a rack in the center of the oven. Preheat the oven to 350°F. Grease a large baking sheet.

2 In a large bowl, crumble the almond paste. With an electric mixer on medium speed, beat in the almonds, egg whites, and 1 cup of confectioner's sugar until smooth.

3 Scoop up a tablespoon of the batter. Roll the batter in the pine nuts, covering it completely and forming a ball. Place the ball on the prepared baking sheet. Repeat with the remaining ingredients, placing the balls about 1 inch apart.

4 Bake 18 to 20 minutes or until lightly browned. Place the baking sheet on a cooling rack. Let the cookies cool 2 minutes on the baking sheet.

5 Transfer the cookies to racks to cool completely. Dust with confectioner's sugar. Store in an airtight container in the refrigerator up to 1 week.

Hazelnut Bars
Nocciolate

MAKES 6 DOZEN

These tender, crumbly bars are packed with nuts. They barely hold together and melt in the mouth. Serve them with chocolate ice cream.

2¹/₃ cups all-purpose flour
1¹/₂ cups peeled, toasted hazelnuts, finely chopped
    (see page 559)
1¹/₂ cups sugar
¹/₂ teaspoon salt
1 cup (2 sticks) unsalted butter, melted and cooled
1 large egg plus 1 egg yolk, beaten

1 Place a rack in the center of the oven. Preheat the oven to 350°F. Grease a 15 × 10 × 1–inch jelly roll pan.

2 In a large bowl with a wooden spoon, stir together the flour, nuts, sugar, and salt. Add the butter and stir until evenly moistened. Add the eggs. Stir until well blended and the mixture holds together.

3 Pour the mixture into the prepared pan. Firmly pat it out into an even layer.

4 Bake 30 minutes or until golden brown. While still hot, cut into 2 × 1–inch rectangles.

5 Let cool 10 minutes in the pan. Transfer the cookies to large racks to cool completely.

Walnut Butter Cookies
Biscotti di Noce

MAKES 5 DOZEN

Nutty and buttery, these crescent-shaped cookies from Piedmont are perfect for Christmas. Though they are often made with hazelnuts, I like to use walnuts. Almonds can also be substituted.

These cookies can be made entirely in the food processor. If you don't have one, grind the nuts and sugar in a blender or nut grinder, then stir in the remaining ingredients by hand.

1 cup walnut pieces
¹/₃ cup sugar plus 1 cup more for rolling the cookies
2 cups all-purpose flour
1 cup (2 sticks) unsalted butter, at room temperature

1 Preheat oven to 350°F. Grease and flour 2 large baking sheets.

2 In a food processor, combine the walnuts and sugar. Process until the nuts are finely chopped. Add the flour and process until blended.

3 Add the butter a little at a time and pulse to blend. Remove the dough from the container and squeeze it together with your hands.

4 Pour the remaining 1 cup of sugar into a shallow bowl. Pinch off a piece of dough the size of a walnut and form it into a ball. Shape the ball into a crescent, tapering the ends. Gently roll the crescent in sugar. Place the crescent on a prepared baking sheet. Repeat with the remaining dough and sugar, placing each cookie about 1 inch apart.

5 Bake 15 minutes or until lightly browned. Place the baking sheets on wire racks to cool 5 minutes.

6 Transfer the cookies to the racks to cool completely. Store in an airtight container up to 2 weeks.

Cookies, Cakes, Tarts, and Pastries   565

Rainbow Cookies

Biscotti Tricolori

MAKES ABOUT 4 DOZEN

Though I have never seen them in Italy, these "rainbow," or tricolored, cookies with a chocolate glaze are a favorite at Italian and other bakeries in the United States. Unfortunately, they are often colored garishly and can be dry and tasteless.

Try this recipe and you will see how good these cookies can be. They are a bit fussy to make, but the results are very pretty and delicious. If you prefer not to use food coloring, the cookies will still be attractive. For convenience, it is best to have three identical baking pans. But you can still make the cookies with only one pan if you bake one batch of dough at a time. The finished cookies keep well in the refrigerator.

8 ounces almond paste

1¹/₂ cups (3 sticks) unsalted butter

1 cup sugar

4 large eggs, separated

¹/₄ teaspoon salt

2 cups unbleached all-purpose flour

10 drops red food coloring, or to taste (optional)

10 drops green food coloring, or to taste (optional)

¹/₂ cup apricot preserves

¹/₂ cup seedless raspberry jam

1 (6-ounce) package semisweet chocolate chips

1 Preheat the oven to 350°F. Grease three 13×9×2–inch identical baking pans. Line the pans with wax paper and grease the paper.

2 Crumble the almond paste into a large mixer bowl. Add the butter, ¹/₂ cup of the sugar, the egg yolks, and salt. Beat until light and fluffy. Stir in the flour just until blended.

3 In another large bowl, with clean beaters, beat the egg whites on medium speed until foamy. Gradually beat in the remaining sugar. Increase the speed to high. Continue beating until the egg whites form soft peaks when the beaters are lifted.

4 With a rubber spatula, fold ¹/₃ of the whites into the yolk mixture to lighten it. Gradually fold in the remaining whites.

5 Scoop ¹/₃ of the batter into one bowl, and another ¹/₃ into another bowl. If using the food coloring, fold the red into one bowl and the green into the other.

6 Spread each bowl of batter into a separate prepared pan, smoothing it out evenly with a spatula. Bake the layers 10 to 12 minutes, until the cake is just set and very lightly colored around the edges. Let cool in the pan for 5 minutes, then lift the layers onto cooling racks, leaving the wax paper attached. Let cool completely.

7 Using the paper to lift one layer, invert the cake and place it paper-side up on a large tray. Carefully peel off the paper. Spread with a thin layer of the raspberry jam.

8 Set a second layer paper-side up on top of the first. Remove the paper and spread the cake with the apricot jam.

9 Place the remaining layer paper-side up on top. Peel off the paper. With a large heavy knife and a ruler as a guide, trim the edges of the cake to make the layers straight and even all around.

10 Bring about 2 inches of water to a simmer in the bottom half of a double boiler or a small saucepan. Place the chocolate chips in the top half of the double boiler or in a small heatproof bowl that fits comfortably over the saucepan. Place the bowl over the simmering water. Let stand uncovered until the chocolate is softened. Stir until smooth. Pour the melted chocolate on top of the cake layers and spread it smooth with a spatula. Refrigerate until the chocolate is just beginning to set, about 30 minutes. (Don't let it get too hard, or it will crack when you cut it.)

11 Remove the cake from the refrigerator. Using a ruler or other straight edge as a guide, cut the cake lengthwise into 6 strips by first cutting it into thirds, then cutting each third in half. Cut crosswise into 5 strips. Chill the cut cake in the pan in the refrigerator until the chocolate is firm. Serve or transfer the cookies to an airtight container and store in the refrigerator. These keep well for several weeks.

Christmas Fig Cookies
Cuccidati

MAKES 18 LARGE COOKIES

I can't imagine Christmas without these cookies. For many Sicilians, making them is a family project. The women mix and roll the dough, while the men chop and grind the filling ingredients. The children decorate the filled cookies. They are traditionally cut into many fanciful shapes resembling birds, leaves, or flowers. Some families make dozens of them to give away to friends and neighbors.

DOUGH

2¹/₂ cups all-purpose flour

¹/₃ cup sugar

2 teaspoons baking powder

¹/₂ teaspoon salt

6 tablespoons unsalted butter

2 large eggs, at room temperature

1 teaspoon pure vanilla extract

FILLING

2 cups moist dried figs, stems removed

¹/₂ cup raisins

1 cup walnuts, toasted and chopped

¹/₂ cup chopped semisweet chocolate (about 2 ounces)

¹/₃ cup honey

¹/₄ cup orange juice

1 teaspoon orange zest

1 teaspoon ground cinnamon

¹/₈ teaspoon ground cloves

ASSEMBLY

1 egg yolk beaten with 1 teaspoon water

Colored candy sprinkles

1 Prepare the dough: In a large bowl, combine the flour, sugar, baking powder, and salt. Cut in the butter, using an electric mixer or pastry blender, until the mixture resembles coarse crumbs.

2 In a bowl, whisk the eggs and vanilla. Add the eggs to the dry ingredients, stirring with a wooden spoon until the dough is evenly moistened. If the dough is too dry, blend in a little cold water a few drops at a time.

3 Gather the dough into a ball and place it on a sheet of plastic wrap. Flatten it into a disk and wrap well. Refrigerate at least 1 hour or overnight.

4 Prepare the filling: In a food processor or meat grinder, grind the figs, raisins, and nuts until coarsely chopped. Stir in the remaining ingredients. Cover and refrigerate if not using within the hour.

5 To assemble the pastries, preheat the oven to 375°F. Grease two large baking sheets.

6 Cut the dough into 6 pieces. On a lightly floured surface, roll each piece into a log about 4 inches long.

7 With a floured rolling pin, roll one log into a 9 × 5-inch rectangle. Trim the edges.

8 Spoon a ³/₄-inch strip of the filling lengthwise slightly to one side of the center of the rolled out dough. Fold one long side of the dough over to the other and press the edges together to seal. Cut the filled dough crosswise into 3 even pieces.

9 With a sharp knife, cut slits ³/₄-inch long at ¹/₂-inch intervals through the filling and dough. Curving them slightly to open the slits and reveal the fig filling, place the pastries one inch apart on the baking sheets.

10 Brush the pastry with the egg wash. Drizzle with candy sprinkles if desired. Repeat with the remaining ingredients.

11 Bake the cookies 20 to 25 minutes or until golden brown.

12 Cool the cookies on wire racks. Store in an airtight container in the refrigerator up to 1 month.

Almond Brittle

Croccante or Torrone

MAKES 10 TO 12 SERVINGS

Sicilians make these sweets with pine nuts, pistachios, or sesame seeds in place of the almonds. A lemon is perfect to smooth out the hot syrup.

Vegetable oil

2 cups sugar

1/4 cup honey

2 cups almonds (10 ounces)

1 whole lemon, washed and dried

1 Brush a marble surface or a metal baking sheet with neutral-flavored vegetable oil.

2 In a medium saucepan, combine the sugar and honey. Cook over medium-low heat, stirring occasionally, until the sugar begins to melt, about 20 minutes. Bring to a simmer and cook without stirring 5 minutes more or until the syrup is clear.

3 Add the nuts and cook until the syrup is amber-colored, about 3 minutes. Carefully pour the hot syrup onto the prepared surface, using the lemon to smooth the nuts to a single layer. Let cool completely. When the brittle is cool and hard, after about 30 minutes, slide a thin metal spatula underneath it. Lift the brittle and break it into 1 1/2-inch pieces. Store in airtight containers at room temperature.

Sicilian Nut Rolls

Mostaccioli

MAKES 64 COOKIES

At one time these cookies were made with mosto cotto, concentrated wine grape juice. Today's cooks use honey.

DOUGH

3 cups all-purpose flour

1/2 cup sugar

1 teaspoon salt

1/2 cup shortening

4 tablespoons (1/2 stick) unsalted butter, at room temperature

2 large eggs

2 to 3 tablespoons cold milk

FILLING

1 cup toasted almonds

1 cup toasted walnuts

1/2 cup toasted and skinned hazelnuts

1/4 cup sugar

1/4 cup honey

2 teaspoons orange zest

1/4 teaspoon ground cinnamon

Confectioner's sugar

1 In a large bowl, combine the flour, sugar, and salt. Cut in the shortening and butter until the mixture resembles coarse crumbs.

2 In a small bowl, whisk the eggs with two tablespoons of the milk. Add the mixture to the dry ingredients, stirring until the dough is evenly moistened. If needed, blend in a little more milk.

3 Gather the dough into a ball and place it on a sheet of plastic wrap. Flatten it into a disk and wrap well. Refrigerate 1 hour up to overnight.

4 Process the nuts and sugar in a food processor. Process until fine. Add the honey, zest, and cinnamon, and process until blended. Preheat the oven to 350°F. Grease 2 large baking sheets.

5 Divide the dough into 4 pieces. Roll out one piece between two sheets of plastic wrap to form a square slightly larger than 8 inches. Trim the edges and cut the dough into 2-inch squares. Place a heaping teaspoon of the filling along one side of each square. Roll up the dough to enclose the filling completely. Place seam-side down on the baking pan. Repeat with the remaining dough and filling, placing the cookies 1 inch apart.

6 Bake 18 minutes or until the cookies are lightly browned. Transfer the cookies to wire racks to cool. Store in a tightly sealed container up to 2 weeks. Sprinkle with confectioner's sugar before serving.

Tips on Making Cakes

- Measure all ingredients carefully, using dry measuring cups for dry ingredients and liquid measures for liquids. A seemingly small amount of variation in the amount of an ingredient can make a big difference in the outcome of a cake.

- Measure flour and other dry ingredients by spooning them into a heap in a dry measuring cup, then sweeping off the excess with a knife. Never pack dry ingredients down.

- Overbeating makes cakes tough and causes them to collapse, because it overworks the protein in the flour, known as gluten. Always fold or stir batter just until the mixture is blended.

- To beat egg whites to maximum volume, start with eggs at room temperature. You can warm them up quickly by placing them in a bowl of warm water for 10 minutes. Separate the eggs, placing the whites in a large bowl. Be careful not to get any of the egg yolk into the whites, and make sure the bowl and beaters are squeaky clean. Any trace of fat from the yolk or other ingredients can prevent the whites from whipping.

- Begin beating the whites in a large bowl with an electric mixer at medium speed. Beat the egg whites until foamy, about 1 minute. Increase the speed to high and gradually add the sugar. Beat until the whites are shiny and thick and soft peaks form, then bend over gently, when the beaters are lifted, about 4 minutes more. Do not overbeat the whites or they may become dry and break down.

- Folding is an important technique in baking cakes and desserts. When folded correctly, a batter is blended in such a way as not to deflate it. To fold egg whites into a batter, begin by scooping up a small amount of the beaten egg whites with a rubber spatula. Place the egg whites on top of the batter. Holding the spatula with the curved side of the blade toward the bottom of the bowl, cut down through the center of the batter and scoop up some of the mixture over the whites. Rotate the bowl a quarter-turn and repeat, cutting down with the spatula and scooping the batter over the whites. Repeat, turning and scooping, and occasionally scraping the side of the bowl, until all of the ingredients are blended and there are no streaks.

- When blending whipped cream into desserts or adding nuts or other solid ingredients into a cake batter, you should fold the ingredients carefully together to maintain the texture of the batter.

- Before preheating the oven, position the oven rack so that the cake will cook evenly. For big, deep cakes, place the rack about 1/3 of the way up from the bottom of the oven. For layer and other shallow cakes, place the rack in the center of the oven.

- Unless they contain creamy fillings, most cakes stay fresher longer at room temperature. Rather than covering them with plastic wrap that may allow moisture to form and make the cake sticky, I cover most cakes with an inverted bowl. Just be sure that air cannot get in. The bowl protects the appearance of the cake better, too.

❧ Plain Cakes

Sponge Cake
Pan di Spagna

MAKES TWO 8- OR 9-INCH LAYERS

This classic and versatile Italian sponge cake works well with fillings such as fruit preserves, whipped cream, pastry cream, ice cream, or ricotta cream. The cake also freezes well, so it is convenient to have on hand for quick desserts.

Butter for the pan
6 large eggs, at room temperature
²/₃ cup sugar
1¹/₂ teaspoons pure vanilla extract
1 cup sifted all-purpose flour

1 Place the rack in the center of the oven. Preheat the oven to 375°F. Butter two 8- or 9-inch layer cake pans. Line the bottom of the pans with circles of waxed paper or parchment paper. Butter the paper. Dust the pans with flour and tap out the excess.

2 In a large bowl with an electric mixer, begin beating the eggs on low speed. Slowly add the sugar, gradually increasing the mixer speed to high. Add the vanilla. Beat the eggs until thick and pale yellow, about 7 minutes.

3 Place the flour in a fine-mesh strainer. Shake about one-third of the flour over the egg mixture. Gradually and very gently fold in the flour with a rubber spatula. Repeat, adding the flour in 2 additions and folding it in until there are no streaks.

4 Spread the batter evenly in the prepared pans. Bake 20 to 25 minutes or until the cakes spring back when pressed lightly in the center and the top is lightly browned. Have ready 2 cooling racks. Cool the cakes 10 minutes in the pans on the wire racks.

5 Invert the cakes onto the racks and remove the pans. Carefully peel off the paper. Let cool completely. Serve immediately or cover with an inverted bowl and store at room temperature up to 2 days.

Citrus Sponge Cake
Torta di Agrumi

SERVES 10 TO 12

Olive oil gives this cake a distinctive flavor and texture. Use a mild olive oil or the flavor could be intrusive. Because it does not contain butter, milk, or other dairy products, this cake is good for people who cannot eat those foods.

This is a big cake, though it is very light and airy. To bake it, you will need a 10-inch tube pan with a removable bottom—the kind used for angel cakes.

A little bit of cream of tartar, available in the spice section of most supermarkets, helps to stabilize the egg whites in this large cake.

2¹/₄ cups plain cake flour (not self-rising)
1 tablespoon baking powder
1 teaspoon salt
6 large eggs, separated, at room temperature
1¹/₄ cups sugar
1¹/₂ teaspoons orange zest
1¹/₂ teaspoons grated lemon zest
³/₄ cup freshly squeezed orange juice
1/₂ cup extra-virgin olive oil
1 teaspoon pure vanilla extract
1/₄ teaspoon cream of tartar

1 Place the oven rack in the lower third of the oven. Preheat the oven to 325°F. In a large bowl, sift together the flour, baking powder, and salt.

2 In a large bowl with an electric mixer, beat the egg yolks, 1 cup of the sugar, the orange and lemon zests, the orange juice, oil, and vanilla extract until smooth, about 5 minutes. With a rubber spatula, fold the liquid into the dry ingredients.

3 In another large bowl with clean beaters, beat the egg whites on medium speed until foamy. Gradually add the remaining 1/4 cup of sugar and the cream of tartar. Increase the speed to high. Beat until soft peaks form when the beaters are lifted, about 5 minutes. Fold the whites into the batter.

4 Scrape the batter into an ungreased 10-inch tube pan with a removable bottom. Bake 55 minutes or until the cake is golden brown and a toothpick inserted in the center comes out clean.

5 Place the pan upside down on a cooling rack and let the cake cool completely. Run a thin-blade knife around the inside of the pan to loosen the cake. Lift out the cake and the bottom of the pan. Slide the knife under the cake and remove the pan bottom. Serve immediately, or cover with an overturned bowl and store at room temperature up to 2 days.

About Cake Flour

Cake flour has a lower protein content than all-purpose flour, so it makes cakes that are more tender. Be careful when purchasing cake flour, because there are two kinds: plain and self-rising. I only use the plain cake flour, because self-rising contains salt and baking powder, and I prefer to add my own.

Lemon Olive-Oil Cake
Torta di Limone

MAKES 8 SERVINGS

A light, lemony cake from Puglia that is always a pleasure to have on hand.

1 1/2 cups plain cake flour (not self-rising)
1 1/2 teaspoons baking powder
1/2 teaspoon salt
3 large eggs, at room temperature
1 cup sugar
1/3 cup olive oil
1 teaspoon pure vanilla extract
1 teaspoon grated lemon zest
1/4 cup freshly squeezed lemon juice

1 Place the rack in the lowest third of the oven. Preheat oven to 350°F. Grease a 9-inch springform pan.

2 In a large bowl, sift together the flour, baking powder, and salt.

3 Break the eggs into a large electric mixer bowl. Beat on medium speed until thick and pale yellow, about 5 minutes. Slowly add in the sugar and beat 3 minutes more. Slowly add the oil. Beat one minute more. Add the vanilla and lemon zest.

4 With a rubber spatula, fold in the dry ingredients in three additions, alternating with the lemon juice in two additions.

5 Scrape the batter into the prepared pan. Bake 35 to 40 minutes or until the cake is golden brown and springs back when pressed in the center.

6 Turn the pan upside down on a wire rack. Let cool completely. Run a knife around the outside rim and remove it. Serve immediately, or cover with an overturned bowl and store at room temperature up to 2 days.

Marble Cake
Torta Marmorata

MAKES 8 TO 10 SERVINGS

Breakfast is not given a lot of attention in Italy. Eggs and cereal are rarely eaten, and most Italians get by on coffee with toast or perhaps a plain cookie or two. Hotel breakfasts often overcompensate for foreign tastes with a lavish variety of cold meats, cheeses, fruit, eggs, yogurt, bread, and pastries. At one hotel in Venice, I spotted a magnificent marble cake, one of my personal favorite cakes, proudly displayed on a cake stand. It was heavenly with a cup of cappuccino, and I would have enjoyed it equally at teatime. The waiter told me the cake was delivered fresh daily from a local bakery where it was a specialty. This is my version, inspired by the one in Venice.

1 1/2 cups plain cake flour (not self-rising)
1 1/2 teaspoons baking powder
1/2 teaspoon salt
3 large eggs, at room temperature
1 cup sugar
1/3 cup vegetable oil
1 teaspoon pure vanilla extract
1/4 teaspoon almond extract
1/2 cup milk
2 ounces bittersweet or semisweet chocolate,
    melted and cooled

1 Place the oven rack in the lowest third of the oven. Preheat the oven to 325°F. Grease and flour a 10-inch tube pan and tap out the excess flour.

2 In a large bowl, sift together the flour, baking powder, and salt.

3 In another large bowl, with an electric mixer, beat the eggs on medium speed until thick and pale yellow, about 5 minutes. Slowly beat in the sugar a tablespoon at a time. Continue beating 2 minutes more.

4 Gradually beat in the oil and extracts. Fold in the flour in 3 additions, alternately adding the milk in two additions.

5 Remove about 1 1/2 cups of the batter and place it in a small bowl. Set aside. Scrape the remaining batter into the prepared pan.

6 Fold the melted chocolate into the reserved batter. Place large spoonfuls of the chocolate batter on top of the batter in the pan. To swirl the batter, hold a table knife with the tip down. Insert the knife blade down through batter, running it gently all around the pan at least 2 times.

7 Bake 40 minutes or until the cake is golden brown and a toothpick comes out clean when inserted in the center. Let cool on a rack 10 minutes.

8 Invert the cake onto the rack and remove the pan. Turn the cake right-side up on another rack. Let cool completely. Serve immediately, or cover with an inverted bowl and store at room temperature up to 2 days.

Rum Cake
Baba au Rhum

MAKES 8 TO 10 SERVINGS

According to a popular story, this cake was invented by a Polish king who found his babka, *a Polish yeast cake, too dry and poured a glass of rum on it. His creation was named* baba, *after Ali Baba of the Arabian Nights. How it became popular in Naples is not certain, but it has been for some time.*

Because it is leavened with yeast rather than baking powder, baba has a spongy texture, perfect for absorbing the rum syrup. Some versions are baked in miniature muffin pans, while others have a pastry cream filling. I like to serve this with strawberries and whipped cream on the side—not typical, but delicious, and makes a lovely presentation.

1 package (2½ teaspoons) active dry yeast
    or instant yeast
¼ cup warm milk (100° to 110°F)
6 large eggs
2⅔ cups all-purpose flour
3 tablespoons sugar
½ teaspoon salt
¾ cup (1½ sticks) unsalted butter, at room
    temperature

SYRUP

2 cups sugar
2 cups water
2 (2-inch) strips lemon zest
¼ cup rum

1 Grease a 10-inch tube pan.

2 Sprinkle the yeast over the warm milk. Let stand until creamy, about 1 minute, then stir until dissolved.

3 In a large mixing bowl, with an electric mixer on medium speed, beat the eggs until foamy, about 1 minute. Beat in the flour, sugar, and salt. Add the yeast and butter and beat until well blended, about 2 minutes

4 Scrape the dough into the prepared pan. Cover with plastic wrap and let stand in a warm place 1 hour or until the dough has doubled in volume.

5 Place a rack in the center of the oven. Preheat the oven to 400°F. Bake the cake 30 minutes or until it is golden and a toothpick inserted in the center comes out clean.

6 Invert the cake onto a cooling rack. Remove the pan and let cool for 10 minutes.

7 To make the syrup, combine the sugar, water, and lemon zest in a medium saucepan. Bring the mixture to a boil and stir until the sugar is dissolved, about 2 minutes. Remove the lemon zest. Stir in the rum. Set aside ¼ cup of the syrup.

8 Return the cake to the pan. With a fork, poke holes all over the surface. Slowly spoon the syrup over the cake while both are still hot. Let cool completely in the pan.

9 Just before serving, invert the cake onto a serving plate Drizzle with the remaining syrup. Serve immediately. Store covered with an overturned bowl at room temperature up to 2 days.

Grandmother's Cake
Torta della Nonna

MAKES 8 SERVINGS

I couldn't decide whether to include this recipe— called torta della nonna—*with the tarts or with the cakes; however, because Tuscans call it a torta, I include it with the cakes. It consists of two layers of pastry filled with a thick pastry cream. I don't know whose grandmother invented it, but everyone loves her cake. There are many variations, some including lemon flavoring.*

1 cup milk
3 large egg yolks
⅓ cup sugar
1½ teaspoons pure vanilla extract
2 tablespoons all-purpose flour
2 tablespoons orange liqueur or rum

DOUGH

1⅔ cup all-purpose flour
½ cup sugar
1 teaspoon baking powder
½ teaspoon salt
½ cup (1 stick) unsalted butter, at room temperature
1 large egg, lightly beaten
1 teaspoon pure vanilla extract
1 egg yolk beaten with 1 teaspoon water, for egg wash
2 tablespoons pine nuts
Confectioner's sugar

1 In a medium saucepan, heat the milk over low heat until bubbles form around the edges. Remove from the heat.

(continues)

2 In a medium bowl, whisk the egg yolks, sugar, and vanilla until pale yellow, about 5 minutes. Whisk in the flour. Gradually add the hot milk, whisking constantly. Transfer the mixture to the saucepan and cook over medium heat, stirring constantly, until boiling. Reduce the heat and simmer for 1 minute. Scrape the mixture into a bowl. Stir in the liqueur. Place a piece of plastic wrap directly on the surface of the custard to prevent a skin from forming. Refrigerate 1 hour up to overnight.

3 Place the rack in the center of the oven. Preheat the oven to 350°F. Grease a 9 × 2–inch round cake pan.

4 Prepare the dough: In a large bowl, stir together the flour, sugar, baking powder, and salt. With a pastry blender, cut in the butter until the mixture resembles coarse crumbs. Add the egg and vanilla and stir until a dough forms. Divide the dough in half.

5 Scatter half of the dough evenly in the bottom of the prepared pan. Press the dough into the bottom of the pan and 1/2 inch up the sides. Spread the chilled custard over the center of the dough, leaving a 1-inch border around the edge.

6 On a lightly floured surface, roll out the remaining dough to a 9¹/₂-inch circle. Place the dough over the filling. Press the edges of the dough together to seal. Brush the egg wash over the top of the cake. Sprinkle with the pine nuts. With a small knife, make several slits in the top to allow steam to escape.

7 Bake 35 to 40 minutes, or until golden brown on top. Let cool in the pan on a rack for 10 minutes.

8 Invert the cake onto the rack, then invert onto another rack to cool completely. Sprinkle with confectioner's sugar before serving. Serve immediately, or wrap the cake in plastic wrap and refrigerate up to 8 hours. Wrap and store in the refrigerator.

☙ Cakes with Fruit

Apricot Almond Cake
Torta di Albicocche e Mandorle

MAKES 8 SERVINGS

Apricots and almonds are very compatible flavors. If you can't find fresh apricots, substitute peaches or nectarines.

TOPPING

²/₃ cup sugar

¹/₄ cup water

12 to 14 apricots or 6 to 8 peaches, halved, pitted, and cut into ¹/₄-inch-thick slices

CAKE

1 cup all-purpose flour

1 teaspoon baking powder

¹/₂ teaspoon salt

¹/₂ cup almond paste

2 tablespoons unsalted butter

²/₃ cup sugar

¹/₂ teaspoon pure vanilla extract

2 large eggs

²/₃ cup milk

1 Prepare the topping: Place the sugar and water in a small heavy saucepan. Cook over medium heat, stirring occasionally, until the sugar is completely dissolved, about 3 minutes. When the mixture begins to boil, stop stirring and cook until the syrup starts to brown around the edges. Then gently swirl the pan over the heat until the syrup is an even golden brown, about 2 minutes more.

2 Protecting your hand with a pot holder, immediately pour the caramel into a 9 × 2–inch round cake pan. Tilt the pan to coat the bottom evenly. Let the caramel cool until set, about 5 minutes.

3 Place the oven rack in the center of the oven. Preheat the oven to 350°F. Arrange the sliced fruit, overlapping them slightly, in circles on top of the caramel.

4 Combine the flour, baking powder, and salt in a fine-mesh strainer set over a piece of wax paper. Sift the dry ingredients onto the paper.

5 In a large electric mixer bowl, beat the almond paste, butter, sugar, and vanilla until fluffy, about 4 minutes. Beat in the eggs one at a time, scraping the side of the bowl. Continue beating until smooth and well blended, about 4 minutes more.

6 With the mixer on low speed, stir in $1/3$ of the flour mixture. Add $1/3$ of the milk. Add the remaining flour mixture and milk in two more additions in the same way, ending with the flour. Stir just until smooth.

7 Pour the batter over the fruit. Bake 40 to 45 minutes or until the cake is golden and a toothpick inserted in the center comes out clean.

8 Let the cake cool in the pan on a wire rack 10 minutes. Run a thin metal spatula around the inside of the pan. Invert the cake onto a serving plate (the fruit will be on top) and let cool completely before serving. Serve immediately, or cover with an inverted bowl and store at room temperature up to 24 hours.

Summer Fruit Torte
Torta dell'Estate

MAKES 8 SERVINGS

Soft stone fruits such as plums, apricots, peaches, and nectarines are ideal for this torte. Try making it with a combination of fruits.

12 to 16 prune plums or apricots, or 6 medium
    peaches or nectarines, halved, pitted, and
    cut into $1/2$-inch slices
1 cup all-purpose flour
1 teaspoon baking powder
$1/2$ teaspoon salt
$1/2$ cup (1 stick) unsalted butter, at room temperature
$2/3$ cup plus 2 tablespoons sugar
1 large egg
1 teaspoon grated lemon zest
1 teaspoon pure vanilla extract
Confectioner's sugar

1 Place the rack in the center of the oven. Preheat the oven to 350°F. Grease a 9-inch springform pan.

2 In a large bowl, mix together the flour, baking powder, and salt.

3 In another large bowl, beat the butter with $2/3$ cup of the sugar until light and fluffy, about 3 minutes. Beat in the egg, lemon zest, and vanilla until smooth. Add the dry ingredients and stir just until blended, about 1 minute more.

4 Scrape the batter into the prepared pan. Arrange the fruit, overlapping it slightly, on top in concentric circles. Sprinkle with the remaining 2 tablespoons of sugar.

5 Bake 45 to 50 minutes or until the cake is golden brown and a toothpick inserted in the center comes out clean.

6 Let the cake cool in the pan on a wire rack 10 minutes, then remove the rim of the pan. Let the cake cool completely. Sprinkle with confectioner's sugar before serving. Serve immediately, or cover with an overturned bowl and store at room temperature up to 24 hours.

Autumn Fruit Torte
Torta del Autunno

MAKES 8 SERVINGS

Apples, pears, figs, or plums are good in this simple cake. The batter forms a top layer that does not quite cover the fruit, allowing it to peek through the surface of the cake. I like to serve it slightly warm.

1 1/2 cups all-purpose flour
1 teaspoon baking powder
1/2 teaspoon salt
2 large eggs
1 cup sugar
1 teaspoon pure vanilla extract
4 tablespoons unsalted butter, melted and cooled
2 medium apples or pears, peeled, cored, and sliced into thin wedges
Confectioner's sugar

1 Place the rack in the center of the oven. Preheat the oven to 350°F. Grease and flour a 9-inch springform cake pan. Tap out the excess flour.

2 In a bowl, stir together the flour, baking powder, and salt.

3 In a large bowl, beat the eggs with the sugar and vanilla until blended, about 2 minutes. Beat in the butter. Stir in the flour mixture until just blended, about 1 minute more.

4 Spread half of the batter in the prepared pan. Cover with the fruits. Drop the remaining batter on top by spoonfuls. Spread the batter evenly over the fruits. The layer will be thin. Don't be concerned if the fruit is not completely covered.

5 Bake 30 to 35 minutes or until the cake is golden brown and a toothpick inserted in the center comes out clean.

6 Let the cake cool 10 minutes in the pan on a wire rack. Remove the rim of the pan. Cool the cake completely on the rack. Serve warm or at room temperature with a sprinkle of confectioner's sugar. Store covered with a large inverted bowl at room temperature up to 24 hours.

Polenta and Pear Cake
Dolce di Polenta

MAKES 8 SERVINGS

Yellow cornmeal adds a pleasant texture and warm golden color to this rustic cake from the Veneto.

1 cup all-purpose flour
1/3 cup finely ground yellow cornmeal
1 teaspoon baking powder
1/2 teaspoon salt
3/4 cup (1 1/2 sticks) unsalted butter, softened
3/4 cup plus 2 tablespoons sugar
1 teaspoon pure vanilla extract
1/2 teaspoon grated lemon zest
2 large eggs
1/3 cup milk
1 large ripe pear, cored and thinly sliced

1 Place a rack in the center of the oven. Preheat the oven to 350°F. Grease and flour a 9-inch springform pan. Tap out the excess flour.

2 In a large bowl, sift together the flour, cornmeal, baking powder, and salt.

3 In a large bowl with an electric mixer, beat the butter, gradually adding 3/4 cup of the sugar until light and fluffy, about 3 minutes. Beat in the vanilla and lemon zest. Beat in the eggs one at time, scraping the sides of the bowl. On low speed, stir in half of the dry ingredients. Add the milk. Stir in the remaining dry ingredients just until smooth, about 1 minute.

4 Spread the batter in the prepared pan. Arrange the pear slices on top, overlapping them slightly. Sprinkle the pear with the remaining 2 tablespoons of sugar.

5 Bake 45 minutes or until the cake is golden brown and a toothpick inserted in the center comes out clean.

6 Cool the cake in the pan 10 minutes on a wire rack. Remove the pan rim and cool the cake completely on the rack. Serve immediately, or cover with a large inverted bowl and store at room temperature up to 24 hours.

❧ Cakes with Ricotta

Ricotta Cheesecake
Torta di Ricotta

MAKES 12 SERVINGS

I like to think of this as an American-style Italian cheesecake. It is a large cake, though the flavor is delicate, with lemon zest and cinnamon. This cake is baked in a water bath so that it cooks evenly. The base of the pan is wrapped in foil to prevent the water from seeping into the pan.

1¼ cups sugar
⅓ cup all-purpose flour
½ teaspoon ground cinnamon
3 pounds whole or part-skim ricotta
8 large eggs
2 teaspoons pure vanilla extract
2 teaspoons grated lemon zest

1 Place a rack in the center of the oven. Preheat the oven to 350°F. Grease and flour a 9-inch spring-form pan. Tap out the excess flour. Place the pan on a 12-inch square of heavy-duty aluminum foil. Mold the foil tightly around the base and about 2 inches up the sides of the pan so that water cannot seep in.

2 In a medium bowl, stir together the sugar, flour, and cinnamon.

3 In a large mixing bowl, whisk the ricotta until smooth. Beat in the eggs, vanilla, and lemon zest until well blended. (For a smoother texture, beat the ingredients with an electric mixer or process them in a food processor.) Whisk in the dry ingredients just until blended.

4 Pour the batter into the prepared pan. Set the pan in a large roasting pan and place it in the oven. Carefully pour hot water to a depth of 1 inch in the roasting pan. Bake 1½ hours or until the top of the cake is golden and a toothpick inserted 2 inches from the center comes out clean.

5 Turn off the oven and prop the door open slightly. Let the cake cool in the turned off oven 30 minutes. Remove the cake from the oven and remove the foil wrapping. Cool to room temperature in the pan on a wire rack.

6 Serve at room temperature or refrigerate and serve slightly chilled. Store covered with an inverted bowl in the refrigerator up to 3 days.

To Drain Ricotta

Depending on the brand, the moisture content of ricotta can vary, and excess moisture can make cakes and pastries heavy and soggy. To eliminate excess moisture, the ricotta can be drained. Line a fine-mesh strainer with cheesecloth. Place the strainer over a bowl. Add the ricotta to the strainer. Cover the ricotta with plastic wrap and place a heavy object such as a small plate on top of the ricotta. Place the strainer and bowl in the refrigerator and let stand 8 hours up to overnight. When ready to use, discard the liquid in the bowl. Use the ricotta according to the recipe directions.

Sicilian Ricotta Cake

Cassata

MAKES 10 TO 12 SERVINGS

Cassata is the glory of Sicilian desserts. It consists of two layers of pan di Spagna *(Sponge Cake, page 570) filled with sweetened, flavored ricotta. The whole cake is frosted with two icings, one of tinted almond paste and the other flavored with lemon. Sicilians decorate the cake with glistening candied fruits and almond paste cutouts so that it looks like something out of a fairy tale.*

Originally served only at Easter time, cassata is now found at celebrations throughout the year.

2 Sponge Cake layers (page 570)

1 pound whole or part-skim ricotta

1/2 cup confectioner's sugar

1 teaspoon pure vanilla extract

1/4 teaspoon ground cinnamon

1/2 cup chopped semisweet chocolate

2 tablespoons chopped candied orange peel

Icing

4 ounces almond paste

2 or 3 drops green food coloring

2 egg whites

1/4 teaspoon grated lemon zest

1 tablespoon fresh lemon juice

2 cups confectioner's sugar

Candied or dried fruits, such as cherries, pineapple, or citron

1 Prepare the sponge cake, if necessary. Then, in a large bowl with a wire whisk, beat the ricotta, sugar, vanilla, and cinnamon until smooth and creamy. Fold in the chocolate and orange peel.

2 Place one cake layer on a serving plate. Spread the ricotta mixture on top. Place the second cake layer over the filling.

3 For the decoration, crumble the almond paste into a food processor fitted with the steel blade. Add one drop of the food coloring. Process until evenly tinted a light green, adding more color if needed. Remove the almond paste and shape it into a short thick log.

4 Cut the almond paste into 4 lengthwise slices. Place one slice between two sheets of wax paper. With a rolling pin, flatten it into a narrow ribbon 3 inches long and 1/8-inch thick. Unwrap and trim off any rough edges, reserving the scraps. Repeat with the remaining almond paste. The ribbons should be about the same width as the height of the cake. Wrap the almond paste ribbons end to end all around the sides of the cake, overlapping the ends slightly.

5 Gather the scraps of almond paste and reroll them. Cut into decorative shapes, such as stars, flowers, or leaves, with cookie cutters.

6 Prepare the icing: Whisk the egg whites, lemon zest, and juice. Add the confectioner's sugar and stir until smooth.

7 Spread the icing evenly over the top of the cake. Decorate the cake with the almond paste cutouts and the candied fruits. Cover with a large overturned bowl and refrigerate until serving time, up to 8 hours. Store leftovers covered in the refrigerator up to 2 days.

Ricotta Crumb Cake

Sbriciolata di Ricotta

MAKES 8 SERVINGS

Brunch, a very American meal, is fashionable right now in Milan and other cities in northern Italy. This is my version of the ricotta-filled crumb cake I ate at brunch at a caffè not far from the Piazza del Duomo in the heart of Milan.

2¹/2 cups all-purpose flour
¹/2 teaspoon salt
¹/2 teaspoon ground cinnamon
³/4 cup (1 ¹/2 sticks) unsalted butter
²/3 cup sugar
1 large egg

FILLING

1 pound whole or part-skim ricotta
¹/4 cup sugar
1 teaspoon grated lemon zest
1 large egg, beaten
¹/4 cup raisins
Confectioner's sugar

1 Place a rack in the center of the oven. Preheat the oven to 350°F. Grease and flour a 9-inch spring-form pan. Tap out the excess flour.

2 In a large bowl, stir together the flour, salt, and cinnamon.

3 In a large bowl, with an electric mixer at medium speed, beat together the butter and sugar until light and fluffy, about 3 minutes. Beat in the egg. On low speed, stir in the dry ingredients until the mixture is blended and forms a firm dough, about 1 minute more.

4 Prepare the filling: Stir together the ricotta, sugar, and lemon zest until blended. Add the egg and stir well. Stir in the raisins.

5 Crumble ²/3 of the dough into the prepared pan. Pat the crumbs firmly to form the bottom crust. Spread with the ricotta mixture, leaving a ¹/2-inch border all around. Crumble the remaining dough over the top, scattering the crumbs evenly.

6 Bake 40 to 45 minutes or until the cake is golden brown and a toothpick inserted in the center comes out clean. Let cool in the pan on a rack 10 minutes.

7 Run a thin metal spatula around the inside of the pan. Remove the pan rim and cool the cake completely. Sprinkle with confectioner's sugar before serving. Store covered with a large inverted bowl in the refrigerator up to 2 days.

Easter Wheat-Berry Cake
La Pastiera

Wheat berries add a slightly chewy texture to this traditional Neapolitan Easter cake. This was my father's mother's recipe, which she brought with her from Procida, an island off the coast of Naples. Neapolitans love this dessert, and you will find it in bakeries and restaurants in the area all year round. Both the crust and the filling are flavored with cinnamon and orange-flower water, a delicate essence made from orange blossoms that is frequently used in southern Italian desserts. It can be found in many gourmet stores, spice shops, and ethnic markets. Substitute fresh orange juice if you cannot find it. Hulled wheat is often found in Italian markets and natural food stores, or try the mail order sources on pages 625–626.

DOUGH

3 cups all-purpose flour
¹/2 teaspoon ground cinnamon
¹/2 teaspoon salt
³/4 cup (1 ¹/2 sticks) unsalted butter, softened
1 cup confectioner's sugar
1 large egg
2 large egg yolks
2 teaspoons orange-flower water

FILLING

4 ounces hulled wheat (about ¹/2 cup)
¹/2 teaspoon salt
¹/2 cup (1 stick) unsalted butter, softened
1 teaspoon grated orange zest
1 pound (2 cups) whole or part-skim ricotta
4 large eggs, at room temperature
²/3 cup sugar
3 tablespoons orange-flower water
1 teaspoon ground cinnamon
¹/2 cup very finely chopped candied citron
¹/2 cup very finely chopped candied orange peel
Confectioner's sugar

(continues)

1 Prepare the dough: In a large bowl, stir together the flour, cinnamon, and salt.

2 In a large bowl with an electric mixer on medium speed, beat the butter and confectioner's sugar until light and fluffy, about 3 minutes. Add the egg and yolks and beat until smooth. Beat in the orange-flower water. Add the dry ingredients and stir just until blended, about 1 minute more.

3 Shape 1/4 of the dough into a disk. Make a second disk with the remaining dough. Wrap each piece in plastic wrap and chill 1 hour up to overnight.

4 Prepare the filling: Place the wheat in a large bowl, add cold water to cover, and let soak overnight in the refrigerator. Drain the wheat.

5 Place the soaked wheat in a medium saucepan with cold water to cover. Add the salt and bring to a simmer over medium heat. Cook, stirring occasionally, until the wheat is tender, 20 to 30 minutes. Drain, and place in a large bowl. Stir in the butter and orange zest. Let cool.

6 Place the rack in the lower third of the oven. Preheat the oven to 350°F. Grease and flour a 9 × 3–inch springform pan. In a large bowl, whisk together the ricotta, eggs, sugar, orange-flower water, and cinnamon. Beat until blended. Stir in the wheat mixture, citron, and candied orange peel.

7 Roll out the larger piece of dough to a 16-inch circle. Drape the dough over the rolling pin. Using the pin to lift it, fit the dough into the pan, flattening out any wrinkles against the inside of the pan. Scrape the filling onto the dough and smooth the top.

8 Roll out the smaller piece of dough to a 10-inch circle. With a fluted pastry cutter, cut the dough into 1/2-inch-wide strips. Lay the strips across the filling in a lattice pattern. Press the ends of the strips against the dough on the sides of the pan. Trim the dough, leaving 1/2 inch of excess all around the rim, and fold the edge of the crust over the ends of the lattice strips. Press firmly to seal.

9 Bake 1 hour 10 minutes or until the cake is golden brown on top and a toothpick inserted in the center comes out clean.

10 Let the cake cool in the pan on a rack 15 minutes. Remove the rim of the pan and let the cake cool completely on a wire rack. Just before serving, sprinkle with confectioner's sugar. Store covered with an inverted bowl in the refrigerator up to 3 days.

❧ Chocolate Cakes

Chocolate Hazelnut Cake
Torta Gianduja

MAKES 8 TO 10 SERVINGS

Chocolate and hazelnut, a favorite combination in Piedmont, is known as gianduja *(pronounced gyan-doo-ya). You will find many candies made or filled with gianduja, gelato flavored with gianduja, and the most famous gianduja of all, Nutella, a creamy jarred chocolate hazelnut spread that Italian kids prefer to peanut butter. Gianduja is also the name of the stock character in commedia dell'arte who represents Turin, the capital city of Piedmont.*

This Piedmontese cake is dark, dense, and extremely rich.

6 ounces semisweet or bittersweet chocolate
1²/₃ cups hazelnuts, toasted and skinned (page 559)
¹/₂ cup (1 stick) unsalted butter, at room temperature
1 cup sugar
5 large eggs, separated
Pinch of salt

GLAZE
6 ounces semisweet or bittersweet chocolate, chopped
2 tablespoons unsalted butter

1 In the bottom half of a double boiler or in a medium saucepan, bring 2 inches of water to a simmer. Place the chocolate in the top half of the double boiler or in a bowl that will sit comfortably over the saucepan. Let the chocolate stand until softened, about 5 minutes. Stir until smooth. Let cool slightly.

2 Place the oven rack in the center of the oven. Preheat the oven to 350°F. Grease a 9 × 2–inch round cake pan.

3 In a food processor or blender, finely chop the hazelnuts. Set aside 2 tablespoons.

4 In a large bowl, with an electric mixer at medium speed, beat the butter with the sugar until light and fluffy, about 3 minutes. Add the egg yolks and beat until smooth. With a rubber spatula, stir in the chocolate and hazelnuts.

5 In a large clean bowl with clean beaters, whip the egg whites and salt on medium speed until foamy, about 1 minute. Increase the speed to high and beat until soft peaks form, about 5 minutes. With a rubber spatula, gently fold a large spoonful of the whites into the chocolate mixture to lighten it. Then gradually fold in the remainder. Scrape the batter into the prepared pan and smooth the surface. Bake 55 to 60 minutes, or until the cake is firm around the edge but slightly moist in the center.

6 Let cool in the pan for 15 minutes on a wire rack. Then unmold the cake onto a rack, invert onto another rack, and let cool completely right-side up.

7 Prepare the glaze: Bring about 2 inches of water to a simmer in the bottom half of a double boiler or a small saucepan. Place the chocolate and the butter in the top half of the double boiler or in a small heatproof bowl that fits comfortably over the saucepan. Place the bowl over the simmering water. Let stand uncovered until the chocolate is softened. Stir until smooth.

8 Place the cake on a cake rack set over a large piece of wax paper. Pour the glaze over the cake and spread it evenly over the sides and top with a long metal spatula.

9 Sprinkle the remaining 2 tablespoons of chopped nuts around the edge of the cake. Let stand in a cool place until the glaze is set.

10 Serve at room temperature. Store covered with a large inverted bowl in the refrigerator up to 3 days.

Chocolate Almond Cake
Torta Caprese

MAKES 8 SERVINGS

I am not sure how this delicate cake became a specialty of Capri, but for me it is a great memento of my visits there. Serve it with whipped cream.

8 ounces semisweet or bittersweet chocolate
1 cup (2 sticks) unsalted butter, at room temperature
1 cup sugar
6 large eggs, separated, at room temperature
1 1/2 cups almonds, very finely ground
Pinch of salt
Unsweetened cocoa powder

1 In the bottom half of a double boiler or in a medium saucepan, bring 2 inches of water to a simmer. Place the chocolate in the top half of the double boiler or in a heatproof bowl that will sit comfortably over the saucepan. Let the chocolate stand until softened, about 5 minutes. Stir until smooth. Let cool slightly.

2 Place the oven rack in the center of the oven. Preheat the oven to 350°F. Grease and flour a 9-inch round cake pan. Tap out the excess flour.

3 In a large bowl with an electric mixer at medium speed, beat the butter with 3/4 cup of the sugar until light and fluffy, about 3 minutes. Add the egg yolks one at a time, beating well after each addition. With a rubber spatula, stir in the chocolate and the almonds.

4 In a large clean bowl with clean beaters, beat the egg whites with the salt on medium speed until foamy. Increase the speed to high and beat in the remaining 1/4 cup of sugar. Continue to beat until the egg whites are glossy and hold soft peaks when the beaters are lifted, about 5 minutes.

5 Fold about 1/4 of the whites into the chocolate mixture to lighten it. Gradually fold in the remaining whites.

6 Scrape the batter into the prepared pan. Bake 45 minutes or until the cake is set around the edge but soft and moist in the center and a toothpick inserted in the center comes out covered with chocolate. Let cool in the pan on a rack 10 minutes.

7 Run a thin metal spatula around the inside of the pan. Invert the cake onto a plate. Turn it right-side up onto a cooling rack. Let cool completely, then dust with cocoa powder. Serve at room temperature. Store covered with a large inverted bowl in the refrigerator up to 3 days.

Chocolate Orange Torte
Torta di Cioccolatta all' Arancia

MAKES 8 SERVINGS

Chocolate and orange make an excellent combination in this unusual cake from Liguria. Be sure to use moist, flavorful candied orange peel for this cake.

6 ounces bittersweet or semisweet chocolate
6 large eggs, at room temperature, separated
2/3 cup sugar
2 tablespoons orange liqueur
1 2/3 cup walnuts, toasted and very finely chopped (see page 559)
1/3 cup finely chopped candied orange peel
Confectioner's sugar

1 Place the rack in the lower third of the oven. Preheat the oven to 350°F. Grease and flour a 9-inch springform pan, tapping out the excess flour.

2 In the bottom half of a double boiler or in a medium saucepan, bring 2 inches of water to a simmer. Place the chocolate in the top half of the double boiler or in a bowl that will sit comfortably over the saucepan. Let the chocolate stand until softened, about 5 minutes. Stir until smooth.

3 In a large bowl, with an electric mixer at medium speed, beat the egg yolks and 1/3 cup of the sugar until thick and pale yellow, about 5 minutes. Beat in the orange liqueur. Stir in the chocolate, nuts, and orange peel.

4 In a large clean mixer bowl, beat the egg whites on medium speed until foamy. Gradually beat in the remaining 1/3 cup of sugar. Increase the speed and beat until the whites are glossy and soft peaks form, about 5 minutes. With a rubber spatula, fold 1/3 of the beaten whites into the chocolate mixture to lighten it. Gradually fold in the remainder.

5 Scrape the batter into the prepared pan. Bake 45 minutes or until the cake is set around the edge but still slightly moist when a toothpick is inserted in the center.

6 Cool the cake completely in the pan on a wire rack. Run a thin metal spatula around the inside of the pan to release it. Remove the rim and place the cake on a serving plate. Just before serving, sprinkle the cake with confectioner's sugar. Serve at room temperature. Store covered with a large inverted bowl in the refrigerator up to 3 days.

Chocolate Rum Raisin Cake

Torta di Cioccolata al Rhum

MAKES 8 SERVINGS

Dark Jamaican rum flavors many Piedmontese desserts. This cake is inspired by one I ate in Novara a number of years ago when visiting my friends Carla and Bud Simons. Carla is a native of that city and knew just where to go for the best pastries. Serve it with vanilla or rum raisin ice cream.

9 ounces bittersweet or semisweet chocolate, coarsely chopped

1/2 cup (1 stick) unsalted butter

6 large eggs, separated

1/3 cup sugar

1/3 cup dark rum

1 teaspoon pure vanilla extract

1/2 cup dark raisins

3/4 cup plus 1 tablespoon all-purpose flour

Pinch of salt

Confectioner's sugar

1 Place the rack in the center of the oven. Preheat the oven to 350°F. Grease and flour a 9-inch springform pan. Tap out the excess flour.

2 In the bottom half of a double boiler or in a medium saucepan, bring 2 inches of water to a simmer. Place the chocolate and butter in the top half of the double boiler or in a bowl that will sit comfortably over the saucepan. Let stand until the chocolate is softened, about 5 minutes. Stir until smooth. Let cool slightly.

3 In a large bowl, whisk the egg yolks, sugar, rum, and vanilla until thick and well blended, about 5 minutes. Gradually stir in the chocolate mixture

4 Toss the raisins with 1 tablespoon of the flour. Stir the remaining 3/4 cup of flour into the chocolate mixture. Stir in the raisins.

5 In a large clean bowl with clean beaters, beat the egg whites and salt with an electric mixer on medium speed until the whites are glossy and soft peaks form, about 5 minutes. Fold 1/3 of the whites into the chocolate mixture to lighten it. Gently fold in the remaining whites.

6 Scrape the mixture into the prepared pan. Bake 45 to 50 minutes or until the cake is puffed and slight cracks appear on the surface. The cake should be slightly moist when a toothpick is inserted in the center.

7 Let the cake cool in the pan on a wire rack 10 minutes. Remove the rim of the pan and place the cake on a wire rack to cool completely. Sprinkle with confectioner's sugar. Serve at room temperature. Store covered with a large inverted bowl in the refrigerator up to 3 days.

Cakes with Dried Fruit and Nuts

Abruzzo-Style Almond Cake with Chocolate Frosting

Parozzo

MAKES 8 SERVINGS

Parozzo *is an Abbruzzese dialect word meaning "rough bread," though nowadays it also indicates this lovely almond cake. I have sampled versions baked in everything from long loaf shapes to small cupcake pans.*

1 cup all-purpose flour
1 teaspoon baking powder
1/2 teaspoon salt
1 cup blanched almonds
1 cup sugar
1/2 cup plus 2 tablespoons unsalted butter
3 large eggs
1 teaspoon pure vanilla extract
1/4 teaspoon almond extract
4 ounces bittersweet or semisweet chocolate, chopped
1 tablespoon slivered almonds, toasted and cooled

1 Place the rack in the center of the oven. Preheat the oven to 375°F. Grease and flour a 9 × 2–inch round cake pan. Tap out the excess flour.

2 In a large bowl, sift together the flour, baking powder, and salt.

3 In a food processor, grind the almonds with 1/4 cup of the sugar until very fine.

4 In a large bowl, with an electric mixer at medium speed, beat 1/2 cup of the butter with the remaining 3/4 cup of sugar until light and fluffy. Beat in the eggs and extracts until blended. Add the ground almond mixture and stir until smooth.

5 Scrape the batter into the prepared pan. Bake 30 minutes or until the cake is golden brown and a toothpick inserted in the center comes out clean.

6 Cool the cake in the pan on a wire rack 10 minutes. Invert the cake onto the rack. Turn it right side up onto another rack and let cool completely.

7 Bring about 2 inches of water to a simmer in the bottom half of a double boiler or a small saucepan. Place the chocolate and the remaining 2 tablespoons of butter in the top half of the double boiler or in a small heatproof bowl that fits comfortably over the saucepan. Place the bowl over the simmering water. Let stand uncovered until the chocolate is softened. Stir until smooth.

8 Pour half the chocolate over the cake, allowing some to drip over the sides. Smooth the sides and top. Spread the remaining glaze over the cake swirling it with a spatula. Sprinkle with the slivered almonds. Let set at room temperature at least 30 minutes before serving. Cover with a large inverted bowl and store in the refrigerator up to 3 days.

Rum and Currant Loaf Cakes

Plumcake

MAKES TWO 8 × 4–INCH LOAF CAKES

Currants and rum are the main flavoring in this Italian-style tea cake, known as plumcake, even though it contains no plums. The cake is probably an adaptation of an English recipe and has retained its English name.

The combination of cake flour and potato starch makes it feather light. The recipe makes two loaves, so you can freeze one or give it away.

1 cup currants or dark raisins
1 cup plain cake flour
1/2 cup potato starch or cornstarch
1 teaspoon baking powder
1/2 pound (2 sticks) unsalted butter, at room temperature
1 cup sugar
4 large eggs, at room temperature
1/3 cup dark rum or brandy

1 Place a rack in the center of the oven. Preheat the oven to 325°F. Butter and flour two 8 × 4–inch loaf pans. Tap out the excess flour.

2 Toss the currants with 2 tablespoons of the flour. Set aside.

3 Place the remaining flour in a fine-mesh strainer with the potato starch and baking powder. Sift the mixture over a sheet of wax paper.

4 In a large bowl, with an electric mixer at medium speed, beat the butter with the sugar until light and fluffy, about 3 minutes. Beat in the eggs one at a time. On low speed, stir in half of the dry ingredients. Add the rum and beat until blended. Add the remaining dry ingredients and stir just until blended. With a rubber spatula, fold in the currants.

5 Scrape the mixture into the prepared pans. Bake 1 hour or until the cakes are golden brown and a toothpick inserted in the center comes out clean.

6 Cool the cakes 10 minutes in the pans on wire racks. Invert the cakes onto the racks. Turn the cakes right side up on the racks. Let cool completely. Serve at room temperature. Store covered with foil at room temperature up to 3 days.

Warm Amaretti Cakes
Tartine di Amaretti

MAKES 6 SERVINGS

Sauris in Friuli–Venezia Giulia is a town best known for its smoked meats, such as prosciutto and speck, smoked cured ham. I will always remember it for the wonderful meal I enjoyed at Ristorante alla Pace. The dessert consisted of these warm little cakes. Serve with whipped cream or ice cream.

22 amaretti cookies
15 vanilla wafers
2 large egg yolks
1/3 cup heavy or whipping cream
4 large egg whites, at room temperature
Pinch of salt
Confectioner's sugar
Whipped cream or vanilla ice cream, optional

1 Place the rack to the center of the oven. Preheat the oven to 350°F.

2 Generously butter six 6-ounce timbales, ramekins, or custard cups. Place a folded kitchen towel inside a roasting pan large enough to hold the ramekins. Place the pan in the oven. Pour hot water into the pan to a depth of 1/2 inch.

3 Place the amaretti cookies in a large heavy plastic bag. Seal the bag and lightly crush the cookies with a rolling pin or other heavy object. You should have about 1 cup minus 2 tablespoons of crumbs. Repeat with the vanilla wafers in another bag. There should be 1/2 cup of these crumbs.

4 In a large bowl, stir together the egg yolks and cream. Add the crumbs and stir until moistened.

5 In a large bowl with an electric mixer, beat the egg whites on medium speed with a pinch of salt until foamy, about 1 minute. Increase the speed to high and continue beating until the whites are glossy and form soft peaks when the beaters are lifted. With a rubber spatula, gently fold a spoonful of the whites into the crumb mixture to lighten it. Fold in the remaining whites.

6 Scrape the batter into the prepared cups. Carefully place the cups on the folded towel in the pan in the oven, leaving an inch or two of space between them.

7 Bake 50 minutes or until the cakes are golden brown and a toothpick inserted in the center comes out clean.

8 Remove the cups from the pan and cool 10 minutes on a wire rack. Run a thin metal spatula around the cakes and unmold them onto serving plates. Sprinkle with confectioner's sugar. Serve warm.

Marsala Walnut Cake

Torta di Noci al Marsala

MAKES 8 TO 10 SERVINGS

Marsala wine gives a distinctive flavor to this cake. I like to serve it with softly whipped cream.

1 1/4 cups all-purpose flour
2 teaspoons baking powder
Pinch of salt
3 large eggs
1 cup sugar
1/3 cup olive oil
1/3 cup dry Marsala
1 cup walnut pieces, toasted and finely chopped
    (see page 559)

1 Place the rack in the center of the oven. Preheat the oven to 350°F. Grease a 9 × 2–inch round baking pan.

2 In a bowl, stir together the flour, baking powder, and salt.

3 In a large bowl, with an electric mixer on medium speed, beat the eggs until foamy, about 1 minute. Gradually add the sugar and continue beating until thick and pale yellow. Beat in the oil and Marsala. Fold in the dry ingredients until blended. Stir in the walnuts.

4 Scrape the batter into the prepared pan. Bake 40 minutes or until the cake is golden brown and a toothpick inserted in the center comes out clean.

5 Cool the cake in the pan on a wire rack 10 minutes. Invert the cake onto a cooling rack and let cool completely. Sprinkle with confectioner's sugar before serving. Store covered with an inverted bowl at room temperature up to 3 days.

Crunchy Walnut Cake

Torta Croccante

MAKES 8 SERVINGS

This simple cake is like a giant shortbread cookie. It is crumbly, so don't try to cut it with a knife before serving. Just break it into pieces at the table.

3/4 cup sugar
1 cup chopped walnuts
1 cup (2 sticks) unsalted butter, at room
    temperature
1 teaspoon salt
2 cups all-purpose flour

1 Place the rack in the center of the oven. Preheat the oven to 350°F. Line the bottom and sides of a 9-inch round cake pan with aluminum foil. Grease the foil.

2 Sprinkle 1/4 cup of the sugar and 1/2 cup of the walnuts over the bottom of the prepared pan.

3 In a large bowl, with an electric mixer on medium speed, beat the butter, the remaining 1/2 cup of sugar, and the salt until light and fluffy. On low speed, stir in the flour just until blended.

4 Crumble the dough and scatter half of the dough over the walnuts in the prepared pan. Press it into an even layer. Sprinkle with the remaining nuts. Scatter the remaining dough over the walnuts and press it into an even layer.

5 Bake for 45 minutes or until the top of the cake is firm when pressed and lightly browned.

6 Let cool for 10 minutes in the pan. Invert the cake onto a rack and carefully lift off the foil. Let cool completely. Store covered with an inverted bowl at room temperature up to 3 days.

Piedmontese Hazelnut Cake

Torta di Nocciole

MAKES 8 SERVINGS

This cake is practically all nuts and butter. I like to serve it as they do in Piedmont, with a generous spoonful of warm zabaglione, but it is also good plain or with chocolate sauce and ice cream.

1½ cups toasted and skinned hazelnuts (see page 559)
½ cup all-purpose flour
½ teaspoon baking powder
½ teaspoon salt
½ cup (1 stick) unsalted butter
⅔ cup sugar
3 large eggs, at room temperature
Confectioner's sugar

1 Place the rack in the center of the oven. Preheat the oven to 350°F. Grease a 9 × 2–inch round baking pan.

2 In a food processor or blender, finely chop the nuts. Add the flour, baking powder, and salt and pulse just to blend.

3 In a large bowl, with an electric mixer on medium speed, beat the butter until softened. Gradually add the sugar and beat until light and fluffy, about 3 minutes. Scrape the sides of the bowl. Add the eggs one at a time, beating well after each addition. Stir in the nut mixture just until blended.

4 Spread the batter in the prepared pan. Bake 30 minutes or until the cake golden brown and a toothpick inserted in the center comes out clean.

5 Let cool 5 minutes in the pan. Invert the cake onto a cooling rack. Turn the cake right-side up onto another rack and cool completely.

6 Sprinkle with confectioner's sugar. Store covered with an inverted bowl at room temperature up to 3 days.

Mantua Cake

Torta Sbricciolona

MAKES 12 SERVINGS

From Mantua, Rigoletto's hometown, comes this crumbly cake made with nuts and corn meal. It has the texture of a large crumbly cookie and should be broken rather than cut.

1 cup (2 sticks) unsalted butter, at room temperature
1 cup sugar
½ teaspoon salt
1 large egg
2 teaspoons grated lemon zest
1 teaspoon pure vanilla extract
2 cups all-purpose flour
½ cup fine yellow cornmeal
1½ cups almonds, finely chopped
Confectioner's sugar

1 Place a rack in the center of the oven. Preheat the oven to 350°F. Grease a 12 × 1–inch round pizza pan or a large baking sheet.

2 In a large bowl, beat the butter with the sugar and salt until light and fluffy. Beat in the egg, lemon zest, and vanilla. Stir in the flour, cornmeal, and nuts just until blended.

3 Scatter the dough in the prepared pan. Pat the dough out into a 12-inch circle. Bake for 30 minutes or until the center feels firm when touched and the cake is golden brown.

4 Cool 5 minutes in the pan on a wire rack. Slide a metal spatula under the cake and transfer it to a rack to cool completely

5 Sprinkle with confectioner's sugar before serving. Store covered with foil at room temperature up to 3 days.

Christmas Sweet Bread

Panettone

MAKES 8 TO 10 SERVINGS

At one time a specialty of northern Italy, panettone is now eaten all over Italy throughout the Christmas season, from morning breakfast with coffee to dessert with a glass of sweet wine. Visitors often bring this tall, fragrant, raisin- and candied-fruit-studded bread as a gift, so there is always plenty of it around. Leftover panettone is good toasted and spread with butter or mascarpone, or it can be mixed with other ingredients to make Panettone Bread Pudding (page 589).

1/2 cup milk

1/2 cup sugar

6 tablespoons unsalted butter

2 packages (5 teaspoons) active dry yeast or
    instant yeast

1/2 cup warm water (100° to 110°F.)

2 large eggs

2 large egg yolks

3/4 cup finely chopped candied citron

1/2 cup currants or raisins

1/2 cup finely chopped candied orange peel

I teaspoon grated lemon zest

5 1/2 cups all-purpose flour

1 In a small saucepan, heat the milk until small bubbles form around the edges of the pan. Remove from the heat. Add the sugar and butter and let stand, stirring occasionally, until the sugar is dissolved and the mixture has cooled to lukewarm.

2 In a large electric mixer bowl, sprinkle the yeast over the warm water. Let stand until creamy, about 1 minute, then stir until the yeast is dissolved. Add the milk mixture, eggs, and yolks and beat at low speed until blended. Stir in the citron, raisins, orange peel, and lemon zest. Add the flour and beat until a stiff dough forms, about 2 minutes.

3 Scrape the dough into a large buttered bowl and turn it once to grease the top. Cover with a towel and let rise in a warm place until doubled in bulk, about 1 1/2 hours.

4 Grease a 9 × 4–inch springform pan. (If your pan is less than 4 inches deep, make a collar for the pan: Tear off a 3-foot length of aluminum foil, and fold it in half lengthwise. Grease one side of the foil, and wrap it around the outside of the pan, greased side in. The foil will be 6 inches high. Tie kitchen string around the pan to secure the foil.)

5 Press the dough down to eliminate air bubbles. Place the dough in the prepared pan, cover with a towel, and let rise until doubled, about 1 hour.

6 Place the oven rack in the lower third of the oven. Preheat the oven to 350°F.

7 With a sharp knife, slash a cross in the top of the dough. Bake 1 hour, or until the cake is golden brown on top and a toothpick inserted in the center comes out clean.

8 Cool the cake in the pan on a rack 10 minutes. Invert the cake onto the rack, then turn it right-side up onto another rack. Let cool completely. Store covered with an inverted bowl at room temperature up to 3 days.

❧ Bread Puddings

Chocolate-Raisin Bread Pudding
Torta di Pane Raffermo

MAKES 8 SERVINGS

Italian cooks never waste bread. Leftover pieces are toasted and used as croutons or ground into crumbs. They are added to soups, torn up for meat loaves and meat balls, and even used in desserts. Bread puddings like this one are popular with home cooks. Serve it with warm Zabaglione (page 521) or Warm Chocolate Sauce (page 544).

1 1/2 cups dark raisins

1/3 cup dark rum or cognac

4 cups cubed Italian or French bread

1/2 cup sugar

1 quart milk

3 large eggs

1/2 cup unsweetened cocoa powder

1/3 cup chocolate or vanilla cookie crumbs

3 ounces semisweet or bittersweet chocolate, coarsely chopped

1 In a small bowl, soak the raisins in the rum for 1 hour.

2 Combine the bread, sugar, and milk in a large bowl. Let stand for 1 hour until the bread is very soft.

3 Place a rack in the center of the oven. Preheat the oven to 400°F. Grease a 13 × 9 × 2–inch baking dish.

4 In a large bowl, beat the eggs and cocoa. Stir the mixture into the soaked bread along with the cookie crumbs and half the chocolate.

5 Scrape the mixture into the prepared pan. Smooth the top and sprinkle with the remaining chocolate. Bake 40 minutes or until a knife inserted 1 inch from the edge of the pudding comes out clean.

6 Serve warm. Store covered with plastic wrap in the refrigerator up to 3 days.

Panettone Bread Pudding
Torta di Panettone

MAKES 8 SERVINGS

Leftover sweet bread such as panettone or stollen is the traditional base for this bread pudding, but brioche or white bread can also be used.

2 cups milk

3/4 cup sugar

1 cup heavy cream

1/4 cup orange liqueur

1/4 cup rum

3 large eggs

2 teaspoons grated orange zest

1/2 teaspoon ground cinnamon

8 to 12 (1/2-inch-thick) slices leftover homemade or store-bought panettone

2/3 cup raisins

1 Bring the milk and sugar to a simmer in a small saucepan. Stir until the sugar is dissolved, about 1 minute. Remove from the heat. Stir in the cream, orange liqueur, and rum.

2 Whisk together the eggs, zest, and cinnamon. Stir in the milk mixture.

3 Grease a 13 × 9 × 2–inch baking dish. Layer half the bread slices in the pan. Scatter the raisins on top. Arrange the remaining bread slices in the pan. Carefully pour the milk mixture over the bread slices, pressing the bread down to keep it submerged. Let stand 10 minutes until the liquid is absorbed.

4 Place a rack in the center of the oven. Preheat the oven to 375°F. Bake the pudding 40 minutes or until a knife inserted near the center comes out clean and the top is golden.

5 Cool on a wire rack. Serve warm or cool, sprinkled with confectioner's sugar. Store covered with plastic wrap in the refrigerator up to 3 days.

Biscotti Bread Pudding

Miascia

MAKES 8 TO 10 SERVINGS

Dry cookie and cake crumbs can be put to good use in this dessert, created by a thrifty housewife. It is so good no one will guess it was made from leftovers. Serve it slightly warm or at room temperature. Dress it up with a fruit sauce, whipped cream, or ice cream.

6 cups cubed Italian or French bread or brioche

3 cups coarsely chopped or crushed biscotti
    or other cookies

6 cups milk

4 large eggs

I cup sugar

3/4 cup raisins

4 ounces bittersweet or semisweet chocolate,
    chopped or chocolate chips

2 tablespoons slivered almonds

Confectioner's sugar

I In a large bowl, combine the bread, cookie crumbs, and milk. Let stand for 1 hour or until the milk is absorbed.

2 Place a rack in the center of the oven. Preheat the oven to 375°F. Grease a 13 × 9 × 2–inch baking dish.

3 Beat together the eggs and sugar. Stir the egg mixture, raisins, and chocolate into the soaked bread. Spread the mixture in the prepared pan. Scatter the almonds over the top. Bake 1 hour or until the top is golden brown and a knife inserted 2 inches from the edge of the dish comes out clean.

4 Serve warm or cool, sprinkled with confectioner's sugar. Store covered with plastic wrap in the refrigerator up to 3 days.

Pear and Apple Cake

Torta di Pere e Mele

MAKES 8 SERVINGS

More like a moist bread pudding than a cake, this is the perfect dessert after a winter meal. Serve it warm or chilled with whipped cream or ice cream, or with a glass of dessert wine.

Half of a small Italian or French bread loaf,
    cut into I-inch cubes (about 2 cups)

2 cups milk

4 tablespoons unsalted butter

2 medium pears, such as Bartlett or Anjou, peeled,
    cored, and thinly sliced

2 medium apples, such as golden delicious or mutsu,
    peeled, cored, and thinly sliced

I cup sugar

3 large eggs

I teaspoon grated lemon zest

1/2 teaspoon ground cinnamon

1/2 cup golden raisins

I In a large bowl, combine the bread and milk. Let stand until the liquid is absorbed.

2 Melt the butter in a medium saucepan over medium heat. Add the pears, apples, and sugar. Cover and cook, stirring occasionally, for 10 minutes. If there is a lot of liquid in the pan, uncover it. Cook until the fruit is very soft and the juices are thickened, about 10 to 15 minutes more.

3 Place a rack in the center of the oven. Preheat the oven to 400°F. Butter a 9-inch square baking dish.

4 Beat the eggs, lemon zest, and cinnamon. Stir the mixture into the soaked bread. Add the cooked fruits and raisins and stir well. Pour the mixture into the prepared pan and smooth the top. Bake 40 to 45 minutes or until the top is golden brown and a toothpick inserted in the center comes out clean.

5 Serve warm or at room temperature. Store covered with plastic wrap in the refrigerator up to 3 days.

❧ Tarts

Single-Crust Pastry
Pasta Frolla

MAKES ONE 9- TO 10-INCH TART SHELL

A teaspoon of freshly grated lemon or orange zest is commonly added to this pastry for extra flavor.

1 1/2 cups all-purpose flour
1/4 cup sugar
1/2 teaspoon salt
8 tablespoons (1 stick) cold unsalted butter, cut into bits
2 tablespoons cold vegetable shortening
1 large egg yolk
1 teaspoon pure vanilla extract
3 to 4 tablespoons ice water

1 In a large bowl, stir together the flour, sugar, and salt.

2 Cut the butter into small pieces. Add the butter and shortening to the flour mixture. With a pastry blender or fork, blend the butter and shortening into the flour until the mixture resembles small crumbs.

3 In a small bowl, beat together the egg yolk, vanilla, and 3 tablespoons of the water. Pour the mixture over the flour and stir with a fork. Scoop up some of the mixture with your hand and rapidly squeeze it until it holds together. Repeat with the rest of the dough until the ingredients hold together and can be formed into a ball. If the mixture seems too dry and crumbly, add a teaspoon or so of cold water. Gather the dough into a disk. Wrap it in plastic wrap. Refrigerate 1 hour up to overnight.

Double-Crust Pastry
Pasta Frolla

MAKES ENOUGH DOUGH FOR 1 DOUBLE-CRUST OR LATTICE-TOP 9- TO 10-INCH TART

2 1/2 cups all-purpose flour
1/3 cup sugar
1/2 teaspoon salt
12 tablespoons (1 1/2 sticks) cold unsalted butter, cut into bits
2 tablespoons cold vegetable shortening
1 large egg yolk
1 teaspoon pure vanilla extract
3 to 4 tablespoons ice water

1 In a large bowl, stir together the flour, sugar, and salt.

2 Add the butter and shortening to the flour mixture. With a pastry blender or fork, blend the butter and shortening into the flour until the mixture resembles small crumbs.

3 In a small bowl, beat together the egg yolk, vanilla, and 3 tablespoons of the water. Pour the mixture over the flour and stir with a fork. Scoop up some of the mixture with your hand and rapidly squeeze it until it holds together. Repeat with the rest of the dough until the ingredients hold together and can be formed into a ball. If the mixture seems too dry and crumbly, add a teaspoon or so of cold water. Gather the dough into two disks, one twice as large as the other. Wrap each disk in plastic wrap. Refrigerate 1 hour up to overnight.

Tips on Making Pastry Dough

Pasta frolla, the Italian name for pie crust dough, means "soft and tender pastry."

With a high proportion of butter and sugar, pasta frolla resembles cookie dough. In fact, the same dough is rolled out slightly thicker than for a pie shell and cut into shapes, decorated, and baked as butter cookies. Here are things to know before making the dough:

- Have all of the ingredients well chilled. If the kitchen is warm, it helps to work on a marble surface and chill the tools as well. Work quickly so that the ingredients don't get too warm. If they do, put everything in the refrigerator until the dough firms up. Do not overwork the dough. Handle the dough as little as possible. If using an electric mixer or food processor, just barely combine the ingredients. Handling the dough causes the formation of gluten, a protein that makes the dough tough and hard to work with. A food processor also throws off a lot of heat, which can soften the dough excessively.

- Do not add more water or flour than is absolutely necessary. Excess flour or water can make the dough tough.

- After chilling it, you may find the dough is too firm to roll out. Let it sit at room temperature a few minutes to warm slightly. If the edge cracks as you roll the dough out, it is probably still too cold.

- Pastry dough can be refrigerated up to overnight or frozen up to one month before using.

- Roll the dough out between two pieces of plastic wrap. Place the rolling pin in the center of the disk and gently push it away from you. Rotate the plastic-covered disk of dough a quarter-turn, center the pin on the dough, and again roll it away from you. Continue rolling and turning the dough until you make one full circle. Gently lift the plastic off the dough and replace it. Turn the dough over and repeat the rolling, lifting, and turning until the dough is circular and about 1/8- to 1/4-inch thick. If the dough becomes too soft and difficult to handle at any time, place it in the refrigerator to cool.

- Use dough scraps from the edge to patch the dough if needed.

- Handle tart pans with a removable rim carefully—and by the rim only. If you lift the bottom while the crust is unbaked and soft, it may pinch the crust and make a hole in it.

- Most tarts are best when eaten within 2 or 3 hours of baking. Tarts with moist fillings like pastry cream or ricotta are the most fragile, because they will become soggy as they stand. Those with jam, and most cooked or dried fruits, will stay crisp longer, up to 24 hours.

- I like to cover fruit tarts with a large inverted bowl rather than plastic wrap, to protect the surface of the tart. If you do not have a large enough bowl, cover the tart with foil, leaving a space between the surface of the tart and the wrapping.

Berry Mascarpone Tart

Crostata di Frutti di Bosco

MAKES 8 SERVINGS

Thick, rich mascarpone makes an easy filling for fruit tarts. It varies in density, so whisk in a little cream to make it light and spreadable. Pile an assortment of your favorite fresh berries on top of the cream.

1 recipe Single-Crust Pastry (page 591)
8 ounces (1 cup) mascarpone
2 tablespoons sugar
1/2 teaspoon grated lemon zest
About 1/4 cup heavy cream
1 pint raspberries
1/2 pint blackberries

Glaze

1/2 cup seedless raspberry or red current jam
2 tablespoons sugar

1 Prepare the pastry, if necessary. Then, let the dough soften briefly at room temperature. Place the dough between 2 sheets of plastic wrap and roll it out to form a 12-inch circle, about 1/8-inch thick.

2 When the dough is ready, remove the top sheet of plastic wrap. Using the remaining sheet to lift the dough, center the dough in a 9- to 10- inch tart pan, with the plastic-covered side up. Peel off the plastic wrap. Gently press the dough into the base of the pan and along the sides. Roll the rolling pin over the top of the pan and trim off the overhanging dough. Press the dough against the sides of the pan to create a rim higher than the edge of the pan. Refrigerate the pastry shell 30 minutes.

3 Place the oven rack in the lower third of the oven. Preheat the oven to 400°F. With a fork, prick the bottom of the tart shell at 1-inch intervals. Bake 5 minutes, then prick the dough again. Bake 20 minutes more or until lightly browned and crisp.

4 Place the tart shell on a rack to cool completely. Remove the pan rim and place the tart on a serving dish.

5 In a medium bowl, combine the mascarpone, sugar, lemon zest, and enough cream to make the mixture spreadable. Spoon the mixture into the baked tart shell and spread it evenly. Pile the berries on top.

6 Prepare the glaze: In a small saucepan, combine the jam and the sugar and bring to a simmer over medium heat. Cook until slightly thickened, 3 to 5 minutes. Brush the glaze over the berries. Serve the tart within 2 hours.

Summer Fruit Tart

Crostata di Albicocche

MAKES 8 SERVINGS

Apricots, peaches, nectarines, plums, or figs can be used for this simple tart, which is perfect with ice cream or whipped cream.

1 recipe Single-Crust Pastry (page 591)
10 to 12 ripe apricots
1/4 cup plus 2 tablespoons sugar
1/4 cup apricot jam
1 tablespoon rum or orange juice
Confectioner's sugar

1 Prepare the pastry, if necessary. Then, let the dough soften briefly at room temperature. Place the dough between two sheets of plastic wrap and roll it out to form a 12-inch circle, about 1/8 inch thick.

2 When the dough is ready, remove the top sheet of plastic wrap. Using the remaining sheet to lift the dough, center the dough in a 9- to 10-inch tart pan, with the plastic-covered side up. Peel off the plastic wrap. Gently press the dough into the base of the pan and along the sides. Roll the rolling pin

(continues)

over the top of the pan and trim off the overhanging dough. Gently press the dough against the sides of the pan to create a rim higher than the edge of the pan. Refrigerate the pastry shell 30 minutes.

3 Place the oven rack in the lower third of the oven. Preheat the oven to 400°F.

4 Following the line around the apricots, cut them in half. Discard the pits and cut the halves into quarters. Place the quartered apricots in the pastry shell cut-side up, in concentric circles. Sprinkle with 1/4 cup of sugar. Bake 40 to 45 minutes or until the apricots are tender and the pastry is golden brown.

5 Cool the tart in the pan on a wire cooling rack 10 minutes. Remove the pan rim and let the tart cool completely

6 In a small saucepan, heat the jam, the remaining 2 tablespoons sugar, and the rum over medium heat. Cook, stirring, until the jam is melted. Brush the glaze over the apricots. Serve within 2 hours. Just before serving, sprinkle with confectioner's sugar.

Blueberry Crostata
Crostata di Mirtille

MAKES 8 SERVINGS

Blueberries are not as common as other berries in Italy. Because my husband loves blueberries, and fruit crostate, I came up with this recipe, which combines fresh and cooked berries.

1 recipe Single-Crust Pastry for a 9- or 10-inch
    tart pan (page 591)
5 cups blueberries, rinsed and dried
1/3 cup sugar
1 tablespoon lemon juice
2 tablespoons cornstarch
2 tablespoons water
Confectioner's sugar

1 Prepare the pastry, if necessary. Let the dough soften briefly at room temperature. Place the dough between two sheets of plastic wrap and roll it out to form a 12-inch circle, about 1/8-inch thick.

2 When the dough is ready, remove the top sheet of plastic wrap. Using the remaining sheet to lift the dough, center the dough in a 9- to 10-inch tart pan with the plastic-covered side up. Peel off the plastic wrap. Gently press the dough into the base of the pan and along the sides. Roll the rolling pin over the top of the pan and trim off the overhanging dough. Gently press the dough against the sides of the pan to create a rim higher than the edge of the pan. Refrigerate the pastry shell 30 minutes.

3 Place the rack in the lowest third of the oven. Preheat the oven to 400°F. With a fork, prick the bottom of the tart shell at 1-inch intervals. Bake 5 minutes, then prick the dough again. Bake 20 minutes more or until the tart shell is lightly browned and crisp.

4 Place the tart shell in the pan on a rack and cool 10 minutes. Remove the pan rim and cool completely. Place the tart shell on a serving dish.

5 To make the filling, in a medium saucepan, stir together 2 cups of the blueberries, the sugar, and the lemon juice. Bring to a simmer over very low heat. Cook until the blueberries release their juices. In a small bowl, mix together the cornstarch and 2 tablespoons of water. Pour the mixture into the simmering blueberries and cook, stirring constantly, until the mixture is thick and the juices are clear, about 1 minute. Remove from the heat and stir in 1 cup of the remaining blueberries. (If using frozen berries, stir the remaining 3 cups into the cooked berries.)

6 Spread the blueberry mixture in the prepared tart shell. Top with the remaining fresh berries. Let cool completely. Just before serving, sprinkle with confectioner's sugar. Serve within 2 hours.

Raspberry Cream Tart
Crostata di Lampone

MAKES 8 SERVINGS

This is a more elaborate tart than the Berry Mascarpone Tart (page 593). It consists of a crust that is prebaked, a creamy custard filling, and a fresh raspberry topping with a brilliant raspberry glaze. The crust can be baked and the filling made and chilled up to a day ahead. Assemble the tart up to 2 hours before serving. Store it in the refrigerator until ready to serve.

1 recipe Single-Crust Pastry (page 591)
2 large egg yolks
1/2 cup sugar
3 tablespoons all-purpose flour
1/4 teaspoon salt
1 cup milk
2 tablespoons orange liqueur
1 teaspoon pure vanilla extract
1 pint raspberries

GLAZE
1/3 cup red currant jam
2 tablespoons sugar

1 Prepare the pastry, if necessary. Let the dough soften briefly at room temperature. Place the dough between two sheets of plastic wrap and roll it out to form a 12-inch circle, about 1/8 inch thick.

2 When the dough is ready, remove the top sheet of plastic wrap. Using the remaining sheet to lift the dough, center the dough in a 9- to 10-inch tart pan with the plastic-covered side up. Peel off the plastic wrap. Gently press the dough into the base of the pan and along the sides. Roll the rolling pin over the top of the pan and trim off the overhang. Press the dough against the sides of the pan to create a rim higher than the edge of the pan. Refrigerate the pastry shell 30 minutes.

(continues)

3 Place the rack in the lower third of the oven. Preheat the oven to 400°F. With a fork, prick the bottom of the tart shell at 1-inch intervals. Bake 5 minutes, then prick the dough again. Bake 20 minutes more or until the tart shell is lightly browned and crisp.

4 Let the tart shell cool completely. Remove the pan rim and place the tart shell on a serving dish.

5 To make the filling, whisk the egg yolks and sugar in a large bowl until blended. Beat in the flour and salt just until smooth.

6 In a medium saucepan, heat the milk until small bubbles form around the edges. Gradually whisk the hot milk into the egg yolks. Pour the mixture into the saucepan and cook over low heat, stirring constantly, until it comes to a boil. Lower the heat and cook 2 minutes more.

7 Pour the mixture into a bowl and stir in the orange liqueur and vanilla. Place a piece of plastic wrap directly on the surface to prevent a skin from forming. Refrigerate until chilled, at least 1 hour.

8 Pour the mixture into the pastry shell. Arrange the berries on top.

9 Prepare the glaze: Combine the jam and sugar in a small saucepan. Bring to a simmer over medium heat. Cook until thickened, about 4 minutes. Brush the glaze over the berries. Chill the tart and serve within 2 hours.

Sour-Cherry Jam Tart
Crostata di Marmellata

MAKES 8 SERVINGS

Romans make this lattice-top tart with tangy sour-cherry jam. Other flavors can be used, and I have even judiciously combined a few half-empty jars of preserves with great success.

I recipe Double-Crust Pastry (page 591)
1¹/₂ cups sour-cherry jam
I egg yolk beaten with I teaspoon water
Confectioner's sugar

I Prepare the pastry, if necessary. Then, let the dough soften briefly at room temperature. Place the larger disk of dough between two sheets of plastic wrap and roll it out to form a 12-inch circle, about ¹/₈ inch thick.

2 When the dough is ready, remove the top sheet of plastic wrap. Using the remaining sheet to lift the dough, center the dough in a 9- to 10-inch tart pan, with the plastic-covered side up. Peel off the plastic wrap. Gently press the dough into the base of the pan and along the sides. Roll the rolling pin over the top of the pan and trim off the overhang. Press the dough against the sides of the pan to create a rim higher than the edge of the pan. Refrigerate the pastry shell 30 minutes.

3 Place the rack in the lower third of the oven. Preheat the oven to 400°F.

4 Spread the jam in the bottom of the prepared shell. Roll out the remaining dough to a 10-inch circle about ¹/₈ inch thick. With a fluted pastry cutter, cut the dough into ¹/₂-inch-wide strips. Arrange the strips about 1 inch apart across the jam. Rotate the tart a quarter-turn and place the remaining strips across the top, forming a lattice pattern. Press the ends of the strips against the sides of the tart to seal, and trim off the overhang. Brush the dough with the egg yolk.

5 Bake 35 to 40 minutes or until the pastry is golden brown. Let cool on a wire rack 10 minutes. Remove the pan rim and let the tart cool completely. Sprinkle with confectioner's sugar before serving. Store covered with a large inverted bowl at room temperature up to 24 hours.

Apple Marzipan Tart
Crostata di Mele

MAKES 8 SERVINGS

I like to use golden delicious apples to make this beautiful tart, because they are sweet and hold their shape when baked. Another firm baking apple can be substituted.

The lattice topping on this crostata is unusual. It is made with almond paste that is piped on top of the apples. If you don't have a pastry bag, a heavy-duty plastic bag can be used.

I recipe **Single-Crust Pastry (page 591)**

TOPPING

8 ounces almond paste

I tablespoon unsalted butter, softened

I large egg

I teaspoon pure vanilla extract

I teaspoon grated lemon zest

1/4 cup all-purpose flour

FILLING

3 large golden delicious apples (about 1 1/2 pounds), peeled and cut into thin slices

I cup sugar

1/2 cup golden raisins

3 tablespoons amaretti cookie crumbs or plain dry bread crumbs

I teaspoon ground cinnamon

2 tablespoons fresh lemon juice or to taste

I large egg yolk beaten with I teaspoon water

Confectioner's sugar

1 Prepare the pastry, if necessary. Let the dough soften briefly at room temperature. Place the dough between two sheets of plastic wrap and roll it out to form a 12-inch circle, about 1/8 inch thick.

2 When the dough is ready, remove the top sheet of plastic wrap. Using the remaining sheet to lift the dough, center the dough in a 9- to 10-inch tart pan, with the plastic-covered side up. Peel off the plastic wrap. Gently press the dough into the base of the pan and along the sides. Roll the rolling pin over the top of the pan and trim off the overhanging dough. Gently press the dough against the sides of the pan to create a rim higher than the edge of the pan. Refrigerate the pastry shell 30 minutes.

3 Prepare the topping: Crumble the almond paste into a food processor or electric mixer bowl. Add the butter, egg, vanilla, and lemon zest and blend or beat until smooth. Add the flour and stir just until blended. Scoop the almond paste mixture into a pastry bag fitted with a 1/2-inch tip.

4 Place the oven rack in the center of the oven. Preheat the oven to 400°F.

5 Combine all of the apple filling ingredients in a large bowl and stir well. Scrape the apple mixture into the prepared tart shell, packing it down lightly.

6 Pipe a circle of almond paste mixture just inside the rim of the pastry shell, being careful not to let it touch the pan, or it will stick. Pipe the remainder in a lattice pattern over the filling. Brush the egg yolk mixture over the lattice topping.

7 Place a baking sheet on the rack below the tart to catch drips. Bake the tart 1 hour 15 minutes, or until the topping is browned and the apple juices are bubbling. If the topping browns too rapidly, cover loosely with foil.

8 Cool the tart on a rack 10 minutes. Remove the pan rim and let the tart cool completely. Serve at room temperature sprinkled with confectioner's sugar. Store covered with a large inverted bowl at room temperature up to 24 hours.

Fig and Walnut Crostata
Crostata di Fichi e Noci

MAKES 8 SERVINGS

For this Piedmontese crostata, fresh figs in a creamy custard are baked in a walnut crust.

Because figs do not ripen once they are picked, look for fully matured fruits. The best are soft, with a honeylike drop of nectar visible in the small opening at the base. If ripe figs are not available, try this tart with halved apricots or sliced peaches.

Because this pastry is slightly softer than some other doughs, I like to bake the tart shell lined with buttered aluminum foil to help it hold its shape as it is baking.

(continues)

1 1/3 cups all-purpose flour

1/3 cup sugar

1/3 cup walnuts, toasted and finely ground

1/2 teaspoon salt

1/2 cup (1 stick) unsalted butter, cut into small bits

1 large egg, lightly beaten

1/2 teaspoon pure vanilla extract

FILLING

3 tablespoons sugar

1 tablespoon flour

1/2 cup heavy cream

1 large egg, lightly beaten

1/2 teaspoon pure vanilla extract

12 to 15 ripe figs

Confectioner's sugar

1 In a large bowl, stir together the flour, sugar, walnuts, and salt. With a pastry blender or a fork, blend in the butter until the mixture resembles coarse meal. In a small bowl, beat together the egg and vanilla. Pour the egg mixture over the dry ingredients and stir with a fork. Scoop up some of the mixture with your hand and rapidly squeeze it until it holds together. Repeat with the rest of the mixture until it can be formed into a ball. If the mixture seems too dry and crumbly, add a teaspoon or so of cold water. Gather the dough into a disk. Wrap it in plastic wrap. Refrigerate 1 hour up to overnight.

2 Let the dough soften briefly at room temperature. Place the dough between two sheets of plastic wrap and roll it out to form a 12-inch circle, about 1/8 inch thick.

3 When the dough is ready, remove the top sheet of plastic wrap. Using the remaining sheet to lift the dough, center the dough in a 9- to 10-inch tart pan, with the plastic-covered side up. Peel off the plastic wrap. Gently press the dough into the base of the pan and along the sides. Roll the rolling pin over the top of the pan and trim off the overhanging dough. Gently press the dough against the sides of the pan to create a rim higher than the edge of the pan. Refrigerate the pastry shell 30 minutes.

4 Place the rack in the lowest third of the oven. Preheat the oven to 450°F. Butter a sheet of aluminum foil. Fit the foil buttered-side down against the pastry. Bake the shell on the lowest rack of the oven 20 to 25 minutes or until lightly golden.

5 While the shell is baking, prepare the filling. In a large bowl, mix together the sugar and flour. Stir in the cream, egg, and vanilla until smooth.

6 Remove the stems of the figs and cut them in half from stem end to blossom end.

7 Remove the tart shell from the oven and place it on a cooling rack. Reduce the oven heat to 375°F. Remove the foil. If the pastry has puffed up, flatten it gently with spoon. Arrange the fig halves cutside up in the shell. Whisk the cream filling again and drizzle it over the figs.

8 Place the tart in the oven and bake 50 minutes or until the cream is set.

9 Cool the tart on a wire rack 10 minutes Remove the pan rim and let cool completely. Dust with confectioner's sugar before serving. Store covered with a large inverted bowl at room temperature up to 24 hours.

Dried Fig Tart
Crostata di Fichi

MAKES 8 SERVINGS

The fresh fig season is short, but sweet dried figs are available all year. For this tart, the figs are cooked into a thick, jamlike puree and sandwiched between two layers of tender pastry.

1 recipe Double-Crust Pastry dough (page 591)

1 pound dried figs, stemmed and coarsely chopped

1/4 cup sugar

1/2 cup fresh orange juice

3/4 cup water

1/2 teaspoon grated orange zest

1 egg yolk beaten with 1 teaspoon water, for glaze

Confectioner's sugar

1 Prepare the pastry, if necessary. Let the larger piece of dough soften briefly at room temperature. Place the dough between two sheets of plastic wrap and roll it out to form a 12-inch circle, about 1/8 inch thick.

2 When the dough is ready, remove the top sheet of plastic wrap. Using the remaining sheet to lift the dough, center the dough in a 9- to 10-inch tart pan, with the plastic-covered side up. Peel off the plastic wrap. Gently press the dough into the base of the pan and along the sides. Roll the rolling pin over the top of the pan and trim off the overhanging dough. Gently press the dough against the sides of the pan to create a rim higher than the edge of the pan. Refrigerate the pastry shell 30 minutes.

3 In a medium saucepan, combine the figs, sugar, juice, and water. Bring to a simmer over medium heat. Cook, stirring occasionally, until thick, about 10 minutes. Let cool 30 minutes. Stir in the zest.

4 Place the oven rack on the lowest level. Preheat the oven to 350°F. Spread the fig mixture in the bottom of the prepared shell.

5 Roll out the remaining dough to a 10-inch circle about 1/8 inch thick. With a fluted pastry wheel, cut the dough into 1/2-inch-wide strips. Arrange the strips about 1 inch apart across the jam. Rotate the tart a quarter-turn and place the remaining strips across the top, forming a lattice pattern. Press the ends of the strips against the sides of the tart to seal. Brush the dough with the egg yolk.

6 Bake 35 to 40 minutes or until the pastry is golden brown.

7 Let the tart cool in the pan on a wire rack 10 minutes. Remove the pan rim and let the tart cool completely. Sprinkle with confectioner's sugar. Store covered with a large inverted bowl at room temperature up to 24 hours.

Lemon Almond Tart
Crostata di Limone e Mandorle

MAKES 8 SERVINGS

This Pugliese-style tart has an almond crust and a lemon creamy filling.

PASTRY

1/3 cup almonds

3 tablespoons sugar

1 cup all-purpose flour

1/2 teaspoon salt

6 tablespoons unsalted butter

About 3 tablespoons ice water

1/2 teaspoon pure vanilla extract

FILLING

3 large eggs

1 cup sugar

1/2 cup fresh lemon juice

1 tablespoon grated lemon zest

4 tablespoons unsalted butter, melted and cooled

1 Prepare the pastry: Place the almonds and sugar in a food processor or blender. Process or blend until the nuts are very finely chopped.

2 Transfer the almond mixture to a large bowl. Stir in the flour and salt. With a pastry blender, cut in the butter until the mixture resembles coarse crumbs. Drizzle with 3 tablespoons of the water and toss until the dough begins to hold together and form a dough. Add a little more water if necessary. Transfer the dough to a sheet of plastic wrap and press it together to form a disk. Wrap and refrigerate 1 hour up to overnight.

3 Let the dough soften briefly at room temperature. Place the dough between two sheets of plastic wrap and roll it out to form a 12-inch circle, about 1/8 inch thick.

4 When the dough is ready, remove the top sheet of plastic wrap. Using the remaining sheet to lift the dough, center the dough in a 9- to 10-inch tart

(continues)

pan, with the plastic-covered side up. Peel off the plastic wrap. Gently press the dough into the base of the pan and along the sides. Roll the rolling pin over the top of the pan and trim off the overhanging dough. Gently press the dough against the sides of the pan to create a rim higher than the edge of the pan. Refrigerate the pastry shell 30 minutes.

5 Place the oven rack in the lowest third of the oven. Preheat the oven to 425°F. With a fork, prick the bottom of the tart shell at 1-inch intervals. Bake the pastry 5 minutes. Prick the shell again. Bake 20 minutes more or until the tart shell is lightly browned and crisp. Remove the tart shell from the oven and place it on a wire rack. Reduce the heat to 325°F.

6 Prepare the filling: Whisk the eggs, sugar, lemon juice, and zest in a large bowl. Whisk in the butter.

7 Pour the filling into the crust. Bake the tart 20 minutes or until the filling is set but still slightly soft in the center.

8 Cool the tart 10 minutes in the pan on a wire rack. Remove the rim of the pan and let the tart cool completely on the rack. Transfer the tart to a serving platter. Serve at room temperature. Store covered with a large inverted bowl in the refrigerator up to 24 hours.

Almond and Peach Tart
Crostata di Mandorle

MAKES 8 SERVINGS

Almond paste and thick peach preserves make a memorable filling combination in this rich tart.

1 recipe Single-Crust Pastry (page 591)
3 large eggs, at room temperature
¼ cup sugar
8 ounces almond paste
½ cup all-purpose flour
¾ cup peach or apricot jam
½ cup sliced almonds
Confectioner's sugar

1 Prepare the pastry, if necessary. Let the dough soften briefly at room temperature. Place the dough between two sheets of plastic wrap and roll it out to form a 12-inch circle, about ⅛ inch thick.

2 When the dough is ready, remove the top sheet of plastic wrap. Using the remaining sheet to lift the dough, center the dough in a 9- to 10-inch tart pan, with the plastic-covered side up. Peel off the plastic wrap. Gently press the dough into the base of a 9- to 10-inch tart pan and along the sides. Roll the rolling pin over the top of the pan and trim off the overhanging dough. Gently press the dough against the sides of the pan to create a rim higher than the edge of the pan. Refrigerate the pastry shell 30 minutes.

3 Place an oven rack on the lowest level. Preheat the oven to 350°F.

4 In a large bowl, with an electric mixer, beat the eggs until foamy. Gradually beat in the sugar. Crumble the almond paste into the egg mixture and beat until smooth, about 4 minutes. Fold in the flour.

5 Spread the jam over the bottom of the prepared shell. Spread the almond paste mixture over the jam. Sprinkle with the sliced almonds.

6 Bake 30 to 35 minutes, or until the filling is puffed and golden.

7 Let the tart cool in the pan on a wire rack 10 minutes. Remove the pan rim and let the tart cool completely. Just before serving, sprinkle with confectioner's sugar. Serve at room temperature. Store covered with an inverted bowl in the refrigerator up to 24 hours.

Pine Nut Tart
Crostata di Pinoli

MAKES 8 SERVINGS

Pine nuts, tender seeds extracted from pinecones, are used in many desserts and savory dishes throughout Italy. Buy them in bulk at health food stores or ethnic markets rather than in those expensive little jars at the supermarket. If you prefer, slivered almonds can be substituted for the pine nuts.

I recipe **Single-Crust Pastry (page 591)**
1/2 cup apricot or peach jam
2 large eggs, separated
1/2 cup sugar
I teaspoon pure vanilla extract
Pinch of salt
I cup toasted pine nuts
Confectioner's sugar

1 Prepare the pastry, if necessary. Let the dough soften briefly at room temperature. Place the dough between two sheets of plastic wrap and roll it out to form a 12-inch circle, about 1/8 inch thick.

2 When the dough is ready, remove the top sheet of plastic wrap. Using the remaining sheet to lift the dough, center the dough in a 9- to 10-inch tart pan, with the plastic-covered side up. Peel off the plastic wrap. Gently press the dough into the base of the pan and along the sides. Roll the rolling pin over the top of the pan and trim off the overhanging dough. Gently press the dough against the sides of the pan to create a rim higher than the edge of the pan. Refrigerate the pastry shell 30 minutes.

3 Place an oven rack on the lowest level. Preheat the oven to 350°F.

4 Spread the jam over the bottom of the prepared pastry.

5 In a large bowl, with an electric mixer on medium speed, whisk the egg yolks, sugar, and vanilla until fluffy and pale yellow, about 4 minutes.

6 In a large clean bowl with clean beaters, beat the egg whites with the salt on low speed until foamy. Increase the speed to high and beat until the egg whites hold soft peaks when the beaters are lifted, about 4 minutes. Fold the whites into the yolk mixture. Gently fold in the pine nuts. Scrape the mixture into the tart shell.

7 Bake 35 to 40 minutes or until the tart is puffed and golden.

8 Let the tart cool in the pan on a wire rack 10 minutes. Remove the pan rim and let the tart cool completely. Sprinkle with confectioner's sugar before serving. Store covered with an inverted bowl in the refrigerator up to 24 hours.

Winter Fruit and Nut Crostata
Crostata di Inverno

MAKES 8 SERVINGS

Dried fruits and nuts have a rich flavor that is a welcome complement to winter meals.

I recipe **Double-Crust Pastry (page 591)**
I (12-ounce) box pitted dried plums (prunes)
I cup dark raisins
I cup water
I teaspoon grated orange zest
1/4 cup orange liqueur or rum
2 tablespoons honey
1/2 teaspoon ground cinnamon
I cup toasted walnuts, chopped (see page 559)
I egg yolk beaten with I teaspoon water
Confectioner's sugar

1 Prepare the pastry, if necessary. Let the dough soften briefly at room temperature. Place the larger disk of dough between two sheets of plastic wrap and roll it out to form a 12-inch circle, about 1/8 inch thick.

2 When the dough is ready, remove the top sheet of plastic wrap. Using the remaining sheet to lift the dough, center the dough in a 9- to 10-inch tart pan, with the plastic-covered side up. Peel off the plastic wrap. Gently press the dough into the base of the pan and along the sides. Roll the rolling pin over the top of the pan and trim off the overhanging dough. Gently press the dough against the sides of the pan to create a rim higher than the edge of the pan. Refrigerate the pastry shell 30 minutes.

(continues)

Cookies, Cakes, Tarts, and Pastries 601

3 In a medium saucepan, combine the prunes, raisins, and water. Cook over low heat until soft, about 10 minutes. Let cool. In a food processor or blender, puree the fruit mixture with the orange zest. Add the liqueur, honey, and cinnamon and process until smooth. With a spatula, stir in the walnuts.

4 Spread the fruit and nut mixture in the prepared tart shell.

5 Place an oven rack in the lower third of the oven. Preheat the oven to 350°F.

6 Roll out the remaining dough to a 10-inch circle. With a fluted pastry wheel, cut the dough into 1/2-inch-wide strips. Arrange the strips about 1 inch apart across the tart pan. Rotate the tart a quarter-turn and place the remaining strips across the top, forming a lattice pattern. Press the ends of the strips against the sides of the tart to seal. Brush the dough with the egg yolk mixture.

7 Bake 35 to 40 minutes, or until the pastry is golden brown.

8 Let the tart cool in the pan on a wire rack 10 minutes. Remove the pan rim and let the tart cool completely. Sprinkle with confectioner's sugar. Store covered with a large inverted bowl at room temperature up to 24 hours.

Ricotta Lattice Tart
Crostata di Ricotta

MAKES 8 SERVINGS

Tarts and cakes made with ricotta are popular all over southern Italy. There are infinite variations.

I recipe Double-Crust Pastry Dough (page 591)

1/2 cup dark raisins

2 tablespoons orange liqueur or rum

16 ounces whole or part-skim ricotta

2 large eggs

1/2 cup sugar

I teaspoon pure vanilla extract

I egg yolk beaten with I teaspoon water

Confectioner's sugar

I Prepare the pastry, if necessary. Let the dough soften briefly at room temperature. Place the larger piece of dough between two sheets of plastic wrap and roll it out to form a 12-inch circle, about 1/8 inch thick.

2 When the dough is ready, remove the top sheet of plastic wrap. Using the remaining sheet to lift the dough, center the dough in a 9- to 10-inch tart pan, with the plastic-covered side up. Peel off the plastic wrap. Gently press the dough into the base of the pan and along the sides. Roll the rolling pin over the top of the pan and trim off the overhanging dough. Gently press the dough against the sides of the pan to create a rim higher than the edge of the pan. Refrigerate the pastry shell 30 minutes.

3 In a small bowl, toss the raisins with the liqueur. Let stand 30 minutes.

4 In a large bowl, beat together the ricotta, eggs, sugar, and vanilla until well blended. Stir in the raisins and liqueur. Scrape the filling into the prepared pastry shell.

5 Place the oven rack in the lowest third of the oven. Preheat the oven to 350°F. Roll out the remaining piece of pastry to a 10-inch circle about 1/8 inch thick. With a fluted pastry wheel, cut the dough into 1/2-inch-wide strips. Arrange half the strips about 1 inch apart over the filling. Rotate the tart a quarter-turn and arrange the remaining strips over the tart, forming a lattice pattern. Press the ends of the strips against the sides of the tart shell to seal. Lightly brush the dough strips with the egg wash.

6 Bake 50 minutes, or until the filling is puffed and the pastry is golden brown.

7 Let cool in the pan on a wire rack 10 minutes. Remove the rim of the pan and transfer the tart to a serving platter. Store covered with a large inverted bowl in the refrigerator up to 24 hours.

Roman Ricotta Tart
Pizza Dolce di Ricotta

MAKES 8 SERVINGS

Almost as flat as a pizza, this ricotta tart is my version of one from the popular Forno, a bakery in Rome's Campo dei Fiori. Customers line up for slices of fresh-baked pizza bianca, olive bread, and simple sweets like this tart. Though they are always busy, the good-natured staff makes sure that everyone's cravings are satisfied.

This tart is a little more rustic than the others and is made with a dough that is patted out, rather than rolled. The dough is made with baking powder, so it puffs up slightly as it bakes.

PASTRY

1 1/2 cups all-purpose flour

1/3 cup sugar

1/2 teaspoon salt

1/2 teaspoon baking powder

6 tablespoons (3/4 stick) chilled unsalted butter, cut into bits

2 tablespoons solid vegetable shortening

1 large egg, lightly beaten

FILLING

1 (3-ounce) package cream cheese, softened

1/4 cup sugar

1 tablespoon dark rum

1 large egg yolk

1 cup (8 ounces) whole or part-skim ricotta

1 Prepare the pastry: In a large bowl, combine the flour, sugar, salt, and baking powder.

2 Add the butter and shortening to the flour mixture. With a pastry blender or a fork, cut in the butter until the mixture resembles small crumbs. Stir in the egg until a soft dough forms. Scoop up some of the mixture with your hand and rapidly squeeze it until it holds together. Repeat with the rest of the dough until it can be formed into a ball. If the mixture seems too dry and crumbly, add a teaspoon or so of cold water. Pat the dough

into the bottom and against the sides of a 9- to 10-inch tart pan with a removable bottom. Refrigerate 30 minutes.

3 Place the oven rack in the lower third of the oven. Preheat the oven to 350°F. Prepare the filling: In a large bowl, beat together the cream cheese, sugar, and rum. Beat in the egg yolk until well blended. Add the ricotta and beat until smooth.

4 Spread the mixture in the prepared tart shell. Bake 45 minutes or until puffed and golden brown.

5 Cool the tart in the pan on a wire rack 10 minutes. Remove the pan rim and let the tart cool completely. Serve at room temperature or refrigerate about 1 hour and serve slightly chilled. Store covered with an inverted bowl in the refrigerator up to 24 hours.

Ricotta Jam Tart
Crostata di Ricotta e Marmellata

MAKES 8 SERVINGS

I like to use apricot jam for this tart, but fruit flavors such as raspberry or orange marmalade would be good too.

1 recipe Single-Crust Pastry (page 591)

FILLING

1 1/2 cups (12 ounces) whole or part-skim ricotta

2 large eggs

1/4 cup sugar

1 teaspoon pure vanilla extract

1 cup best-quality apricot jam

1 Prepare the pastry, if necessary. Let the dough soften briefly at room temperature. Place the dough between two sheets of plastic wrap and roll it out to form a 12-inch circle, about 1/8 inch thick.

2 When the dough is ready, remove the top sheet of plastic wrap. Using the remaining sheet to lift the dough, center the dough in a 9- to 10-inch tart pan, with the plastic-covered side up. Peel off the

(continues)

plastic wrap. Gently press the dough into the base of the pan and along the sides. Roll the rolling pin over the top of the pan and trim off the overhanging dough. Gently press the dough against the sides of the pan to create a rim higher than the edge of the pan. Refrigerate the pastry shell 30 minutes.

3 Place an oven rack in the lowest third of the oven. Preheat the oven to 350°F.

4 Prepare the filling: In a large bowl, whisk together the ricotta, eggs, sugar, and vanilla until well blended.

5 Spread the jam in the prepared tart shell. Pour the ricotta mixture over the jam and spread it evenly.

6 Bake 55 to 60 minutes or until puffed and golden.

7 Let the tart cool in the pan on a wire rack 10 minutes. Remove the pan rim and let the tart cool completely. Serve at room temperature or refrigerate about 1 hour and serve slightly chilled. Store covered with an inverted bowl in the refrigerator up to 24 hours.

Chocolate Tart
Crostata di Cioccolata

MAKES 8 SERVINGS

Trieste is a cosmopolitan city that has at different times belonged to both Austria and Italy. True to its Austrian roots, it has many old-world coffee houses serving a range of pastries that you will not find anywhere else in Italy. At one, I had a memorable tart filled with lush chocolate cream, like the inside of a truffle. This is my version of that rich tart.

1 recipe Single-Crust Pastry (page 591)

FILLING
1 cup heavy cream
8 ounces bittersweet chocolate, broken into small pieces
1/2 teaspoon instant espresso powder

1 Prepare the pastry, if necessary. Let the dough soften briefly at room temperature. Place the dough between two sheets of plastic wrap and roll it out to form a 12-inch circle, about 1/8-inch thick.

2 When the dough is ready, remove the top sheet of plastic wrap. Using the remaining sheet to lift the dough, center the dough a 9- to 10-inch tart pan, with the plastic-covered side up. Peel off the plastic wrap. Gently press the dough into the base of the pan and along the sides. Roll the rolling pin over the top of the pan and trim off the overhanging dough. Gently press the dough against the side of the pan to create a rim higher than the edge of the pan. Refrigerate the pastry shell 30 minutes.

4 Place an oven rack in the lowest third of the oven. Preheat the oven to 450°F. With a fork, prick the bottom of the tart shell at 1-inch intervals. Bake 5 minutes, then prick the dough again. Bake 20 minutes more or until lightly browned and crisp.

5 Place the tart shell on a rack to cool. Remove the pan rim and place the tart on a serving dish.

6 To make the filling, place the cream in a small heavy saucepan. Bring the cream to a simmer and remove from the heat. Add the chocolate and espresso powder. Let stand several minutes or until the chocolate is softened. Stir the filling until smooth.

7 Pour the chocolate into the cooled tart shell. Refrigerate 4 hours up to overnight. Serve chilled.

Rice Pudding Tart
Crostata di Riso

MAKES 8 SERVINGS

In Parma, miniature versions of this comforting tart are served with midmorning coffee. I like it best when it is still slightly warm.

3 cups whole milk
1/4 cup medium-grain rice, such as Arborio, Carnaroli, or Vialone Nano
1/2 cup sugar
2 tablespoons unsalted butter
1 recipe Single-Crust Pastry (page 591)
2 large eggs
1 teaspoon grated lemon zest
2 tablespoons finely chopped candied orange peel or citron
2 tablespoons golden raisins

1 In a medium saucepan, bring the milk to a simmer. Add the rice, sugar, and butter and cook over low heat, stirring occasionally, until the rice is very tender, about 30 minutes. Transfer to a bowl and let cool about 30 minutes, stirring occasionally.

2 Prepare the pastry, if necessary. Let the dough soften briefly at room temperature. Place the dough between two sheets of plastic wrap and roll it out to form a 12-inch circle, about 1/8 inch thick.

3 When the dough is ready, remove the top sheet of plastic wrap. Using the remaining sheet to lift the dough, center the dough in a 9- to 10- inch tart pan, with the plastic-covered side up. Peel off the plastic wrap. Gently press the dough into the base of the pan and along the sides. Roll the rolling pin over the top of the pan and trim off the overhanging dough. Gently press the dough against the sides of the pan to create a rim higher than the edge of the pan. Refrigerate the pastry shell 30 minutes.

4 Place an oven rack on the lowest level. Preheat the oven to 350° F.

5 In a medium bowl, beat the eggs and lemon zest. Stir into the cooled rice mixture. Stir in the orange peel and raisins. Scrape the mixture into the prepared shell.

6 Bake 40 to 45 minutes or until the filling is just set.

7 Let the tart cool in the pan on a wire rack 10 minutes. Remove the pan rim and let the tart cool 1 hour. Store covered with an inverted bowl in the refrigerator up to 24 hours.

Cornmeal Berry Tart
Crostata di Mirtilli e Lampone

MAKES 8 SERVINGS

Cornmeal adds a pleasant crunch and golden color to the crust for this tart I had in Tuscany. The dough is crumbly, so it is easier to pat it into the pan than to roll it out. The lattice topping is made by rolling pieces of the dough into long ropes. The filling is a tart-sweet mix of fresh berries—I like to use blueberries and raspberries, but others can be substituted.

FILLING

2 cups blueberries
I cup raspberries
I cup sugar
1/8 teaspoon ground cinnamon

PASTRY

2 cups all-purpose flour
1/3 cup yellow cornmeal
1/2 cup sugar
I teaspoon baking powder
I teaspoon grated lemon zest
1/2 teaspoon salt
3/4 cup (1 1/2 sticks) chilled unsalted butter, cut into bits
3 large egg yolks
3 to 4 tablespoons ice water
Confectioner's sugar

1 Prepare the filling: In a medium saucepan, combine the berries, sugar, and cinnamon. Cover and bring to a simmer over medium heat. Uncover and cook, stirring occasionally, until the mixture has thickened, about 20 minutes. Transfer to a bowl and let cool, then cover and chill in the refrigerator 1 hour up to overnight. The mixture will thicken further as it cools.

2 Prepare the crust: In a large bowl, combine the flour, cornmeal, sugar, lemon zest, baking powder, and salt. With a pastry blender or a fork, cut in the butter until the mixture resembles coarse crumbs. Beat 2 of the egg yolks together with 3 tablespoons of the water. Drizzle the mixture over the dough and stir lightly into the flour mixture until it begins to form a dough.

3 Scoop up a handful of the dough and squeeze it together. Continue squeezing the dough by handfuls until the dough can be formed into a ball. Add the remaining 1 tablespoon of water if needed.

(continues)

4 Place the oven rack in the lowest third of the oven. Preheat the oven to 350°F. Scatter about two-thirds of the crust mixture over the bottom of a 9-inch tart pan with a removable bottom. Press the crumbs evenly over the bottom and up the sides of the pan to form a pastry shell. Spoon the chilled blueberry mixture into the shell and smooth the top.

5 On a lightly floured surface, roll the remaining crust mixture with your hands into 1/2-inch-thick ropes. Arrange the ropes 1 inch apart across the filling. Rotate the tart a quarter-turn and place the remaining strips across the top, forming a lattice pattern. Press the ends of the strips against the sides of the tart to seal, and trim off the overhang. Brush the dough with the remaining egg yolk.

6 Bake the tart 45 to 50 minutes, or until golden brown.

7 Let the tart cool in the pan on a wire rack 10 minutes. Remove the rim of the pan and let the tart cool completely. Just before serving, sprinkle with confectioner's sugar. Store covered with an inverted bowl at room temperature up to 24 hours.

Spice and Nut Tart
Crostata allo Spezie

MAKES 8 SERVINGS

This tart from the Alto Adige area is something like a Linzer tart. Serve it in small slices at teatime.

2¹/2 cups all-purpose flour
I teaspoon baking powder
I teaspoon ground cinnamon
¹/2 teaspoon ground cloves
¹/2 teaspoon salt
I cup ground toasted walnuts (see page 559)
¹/2 cup (I stick) cold unsalted butter, cut into bits
I cup sugar
2 large eggs
I teaspoon grated lemon zest
I cup blackberry or raspberry jam
Confectioner's sugar

I In a large bowl, stir together the flour, baking powder, cinnamon, cloves, and salt. Stir in the walnuts.

2 In another large bowl, using an electric mixer, beat the butter with the sugar until light and fluffy, about 2 minutes. Add the eggs one at a time, beating well after each addition. Beat in the lemon zest. Add the dry ingredients and stir on low speed until blended, about 2 minutes more. Divide the dough into 2 disks, one twice as large as the other. Wrap each disk in plastic wrap and refrigerate 1 hour up to overnight.

3 Let the dough soften briefly at room temperature. Place the largest ball of dough between two sheets of plastic wrap and roll it out to form a 12-inch circle, about 1/8 inch thick.

4 When the dough is ready, remove the top sheet of plastic wrap. Using the remaining sheet to lift the dough, center the dough in a 9- to 10-inch tart pan, with the plastic-covered side up. Peel off the plastic wrap. Gently press the dough into the base of the pan and along the sides. Roll the rolling pin over the top of the pan and trim off the overhanging dough. Gently press the dough against the sides of the pan to create a rim higher than the edge of the pan. Refrigerate the pastry shell 30 minutes.

5 Place the oven rack in the lowest third of the oven. Preheat the oven to 375°F.

6 Spread the jam evenly in the tart shell. Roll out the remaining dough to a 10-inch circle. Cut the dough into 1/2-inch-wide strips. Arrange half the strips 1 inch apart across the filling. Press the ends against the sides of the tart shell to seal. Rotate the tart pan a quarter-turn and arrange the remaining strips of dough 1 inch apart across the tart to form a lattice pattern. Press the ends against the sides to seal. Trim off the excess dough.

7 Bake the tart 40 minutes or until the crust is golden brown.

8 Cool the tart in the pan on a rack 10 minutes. Remove the pan rim. Let the tart cool completely.

Just before serving, sprinkle with confectioner's sugar. Store at room temperature covered with a large inverted bowl up to 24 hours.

Cinnamon Plum Torte
Torta di Susine

MAKES 8 SERVINGS

Deeper than a tart, this fruit-filled torte is baked in a springform pan.

3 cups all-purpose flour

3/4 cup sugar

2 teaspoons baking powder

1/2 teaspoon ground cinnamon

I teaspoon salt

3/4 cup (1 1/2 sticks) unsalted butter, at room
    temperature

I large egg

I large egg yolk

I teaspoon grated lemon zest

I teaspoon pure vanilla extract

FILLING

2 1/2 pounds firm ripe prune plums, thinly sliced

1/2 cup sugar

1/2 teaspoon ground cinnamon

I tablespoon fresh lemon juice

I tablespoon unsalted butter, cut into bits

I large egg yolk, lightly beaten

Confectioner's sugar

1 In a large bowl, stir together the flour, sugar, baking powder, cinnamon, and salt. Cut the butter into small pieces. With a pastry blender, cut in the butter until the mixture resembles coarse crumbs. In a small bowl, beat the whole egg, egg yolk, lemon zest, and vanilla. Stir into the flour mixture until a dough forms. Add a little ice water if the dough seems dry.

2 Divide the dough into two pieces, one twice as large as the other. Shape each piece into a flat disk. Wrap each one in plastic wrap and chill for at least 1 hour or overnight.

3 Let the dough soften briefly at room temperature. Place the larger portion of dough between two sheets of plastic wrap and roll it out to form a 12-inch circle, about 1/8 inch thick.

4 When the dough is ready, remove the top sheet of plastic wrap. Using the remaining sheet to lift the dough, center the dough in a 9- to 10-inch tart pan, with the plastic-covered side up. Peel off the plastic wrap. Gently press the dough into the base of the pan and along the sides. Roll the rolling pin over the top of the pan and trim off the overhanging dough. Gently press the dough against the sides of the pan to create a rim higher than the edge of the pan. Refrigerate the pastry shell 30 minutes.

5 Place the oven rack in the lowest third of the oven. Preheat the oven to 350°F.

6 Prepare the filling: In a large bowl, toss together the plums, sugar, cinnamon, and lemon juice. Spread the filling in the prepared pastry shell. Dot with the butter.

7 Roll out the remaining dough to a 10-inch circle. With a pastry cutter, cut the dough into 1/2-inch-wide strips. Arrange half the strips 1 inch apart across the filling. Press the ends against the sides of the tart shell to seal. Rotate the tart pan a quarter-turn and place the remaining strips of dough 1 inch apart across the tart to form a lattice pattern. Press the ends against the sides to seal. Trim off the excess dough.

8 Brush the top with the egg yolk. Bake 1 hour or until the pastry is golden brown and the juices are bubbling.

9 Transfer the pan to a cooling rack and let cool 10 minutes. Remove the rim of the pan and let the tart cool completely. Sprinkle with confectioner's sugar. Store covered with a large inverted bowl at room temperature up to 24 hours.

❧ Pastries

Cannoli Cream
Ricotta Cream

MAKES ABOUT 4 CUPS

This cream is good not just as a filling for cannoli shells or cream puffs but also layered with fresh fruit as a spoon dessert. It can be made up to 24 hours before using.

2 pounds whole or part-skim milk ricotta, drained, if necessary (page 577)

1 1/2 cups confectioner's sugar

1 teaspoon pure vanilla extract

1/2 teaspoon ground cinnamon

2 ounces semisweet chocolate, chopped (optional)

2 tablespoons chopped candied orange peel or citron (optional)

1 Put the ricotta in a food processor and blend it until creamy. Add the sugar, vanilla, and cinnamon and blend until smooth. Scrape the mixture into a bowl.

2 With a spoon or spatula, stir in the chocolate and candied fruit, if using. Cover and refrigerate until ready to use.

Chocolate Cannoli Cream

MAKES ABOUT 4 CUPS

To make black-and-white cannoli, fill one side of the cannoli tube with the vanilla filling above, and the other side with this chocolate filling. This is also good as a filling for layer cake or cream puff shells.

2 pounds whole or part-skim ricotta, drained if necessary (page 577)

1 1/2 cups confectioner's sugar

1/2 cup unsweetened cocoa powder

1 teaspoon pure vanilla extract

In an electric mixer or food processor, combine the ricotta, sugar, cocoa, and vanilla. Mix until smooth and well blended.

Pastry Cream
Crema Pasticciera

MAKES ABOUT 5 CUPS

This cream is the foundation for many Italian desserts, including Italian Trifle (Zuppa Inglese, page 521). Flavor the cream with lemon or orange zest or dried or candied fruits. Use it as a filling for Cream Puffs (page 609) and napoleons, serve it like pudding, or spoon it over fruit or cake. This recipe can easily be halved.

1 quart milk

1/2 cup sugar

6 large egg yolks

1/2 cup all-purpose flour

2 teaspoons pure vanilla extract

1 In a heavy saucepan, bring 3 cups of the milk and the sugar to a simmer over medium heat, stirring to dissolve the sugar. Remove from the heat.

2 In a large heatproof bowl, whisk the egg yolks and the remaining 1 cup milk until blended. Place the flour in a fine-mesh strainer. Shake it over the egg yolks. Whisk until smooth. Beat in the hot milk a little at a time.

3 When all of the milk has been added, transfer the mixture to the saucepan and return it to the heat. Cook over medium heat, stirring constantly with a wooden spoon, until the mixture begins to boil. Reduce the heat and cook 30 seconds more. Remove the pan from the heat and stir in the vanilla.

4 Transfer to a bowl. Cover with plastic wrap, pressing the plastic against the surface of the cream. Chill up to 24 hours.

Variation: *Chocolate and Vanilla Pastry Creams*: Make Pastry Cream through step 3. Divide the cream between two bowls. Add 4 ounces chopped semi-sweet chocolate to one bowl and let stand 1 minute until softened. Stir well. Cover both creams with plastic wrap, pressing the plastic against the surface of the cream, and chill.

Cream Puffs

Bignè

MAKES 12

Though made all over Italy, bignè, or cream puffs, are a Neapolitan specialty. When I was growing up, my mother made them for every holiday. At Gambrinus, a favorite cafe near the Naples opera house, my husband and I indulged in jumbo cream puffs filled with whipped cream, the inspiration for this recipe.

The typical fillings are pastry cream and ricotta cream, but ice cream is also good. Tuscans fill small cream puffs with vanilla pastry cream, pile them on a platter, and drizzle them with chocolate sauce. They call them bongo bongo. *The puffs can be baked ahead and frozen until needed. If they have been frozen, place them in a 350°F oven to crisp. Let them cool before filling them.*

¹/₂ cup (1 stick) unsalted butter

1 cup water

¹/₂ teaspoon salt

1 cup all-purpose flour

4 large eggs, at room temperature

2 cups chilled heavy or whipping cream

1 teaspoon pure vanilla extract

2 tablespoons confectioner's sugar, plus more
    for dusting the tops

1 Place a rack in the center of the oven. Preheat the oven to 400°F. Butter and flour a large baking sheet.

2 In a medium saucepan over medium-low heat, bring the butter, water, and salt to a rapid boil. Remove from the heat. Add the flour all at once and stir well with a wooden spoon until the flour is completely incorporated and a dough has formed.

3 Return the saucepan to the stove over medium heat. Cook, stirring constantly and turning the dough often, until the dough begins to leave a thin film on the bottom of the saucepan, about 3 minutes. (This dries the dough so the cream puffs will be crisp.) With a rubber spatula, scrape the dough into a large bowl.

4 With a wooden spoon, beat in the eggs one at a time until they are thoroughly incorporated. Continue to beat until smooth and shiny, about 2 minutes.

5 Scoop up a rounded tablespoon of the dough. Use a second spoon to push the dough off the spoon onto the prepared baking sheet. Form 12 mounds, spaced about 3 inches apart. With moistened fingertips, pat the tops to round the shape.

6 Bake the cream puffs 40 to 45 minutes, until golden brown. Turn off the oven and remove the puffs. With a small knife, make a small hole in the side of each puff to allow the steam to escape. Return the puffs to the oven for 10 minutes to dry.

7 Using a serrated knife, cut the puffs partway in half horizontally. Open like a book and scoop out the soft dough from the inside. Transfer to a wire rack and let cool completely.

8 At least 20 minutes before you are ready to fill the cream puffs, place a large bowl and the beaters of an electric mixer in the refrigerator.

9 Remove the bowl and beaters. Pour the cream into the bowl. Add the vanilla and the 2 tablespoons confectioner's sugar. With the mixer, whip the cream until it holds soft peaks, about 4 minutes. Spoon the cream into the puffs. Dust with additional confectioner's sugar and serve immediately.

St. Joseph's Fritters
Sfinci di San Giuseppe

MAKES 8 SERVINGS

St. Joseph is the patron saint of fathers in Sicily, and these pastries are eaten on his feast day, March 19. Though they are usually filled with ricotta cream, you can also make them with Pastry Cream (pages 608–609).

¹/₂ recipe Cannoli Cream (page 608)

DOUGH

1 cup water
¹/₄ cup unsalted butter
1 teaspoon salt
1 cup all-purpose flour
4 large eggs
Vegetable oil for frying
Candied orange peel and candied cherries, for garnish
Confectioner's sugar

1 Prepare the cream, if necessary. In a medium saucepan over medium-low heat, heat the water, butter, and salt until the butter melts and the mixture reaches a boil. Remove from the heat. Add the flour all at once and stir well with a wooden spoon until the flour is completely incorporated and a dough has formed.

2 Return the saucepan to the stove over medium heat. Cook, stirring constantly and turning the dough often, until the dough begins to leave a thin film on the bottom of the saucepan, about 3 minutes. (This dries the dough so the fritters will be crisp.) With a rubber spatula, scrape the dough into a large bowl.

3 With a wooden spoon, beat in the eggs one at a time until thoroughly incorporated. Continue to beat until smooth and shiny, about 2 minutes.

4 Line a tray with paper towels. In a deep heavy saucepan or deep-fryer, heat 3 inches of oil to 370° F

on a frying thermometer, or until a small bit of the dough dropped into the oil sizzles and swims rapidly around the pan and turns brown in 1 minute. Scoop up about 1 rounded tablespoon of the batter. With another spoon, push the batter into the oil, being careful not to splash it.

5 Add just enough spoonfuls of batter to the pan to fit without crowding. The batter will puff up and double or triple in size. Cook, turning the fritters often, about 4 minutes. (When they are almost done, the fritters will break open.) Continue to cook 1 to 2 minutes more or until the fritters are crisp and golden brown. Remove the fritters with a slotted spoon or skimmer. Place them on the paper towels to drain. Repeat with the remaining batter.

6 When all of the fritters have been fried, let them cool about 10 minutes. With a small knife, split the fritters partially open like a book. Fill with the cannoli cream. Garnish the cream with strips of candied orange peel and candied cherries.

7 Sprinkle with confectioner's sugar and serve warm. These are best eaten soon after they are made.

Honey Balls
Struffoli

MAKES 8 SERVINGS

Struffoli are an important part of Christmas celebrations in Neapolitan homes. The crisp little fritters are drenched in honey and piled into heaps or shaped into rings that are garnished like wreaths with candied fruits and nuts. My mother made mountains of struffoli every year, some to keep and some to give away to relatives and friends.

These keep well up to three days. Store them covered with a large inverted bowl or plastic wrap at room temperature.

1 cup all-purpose flour plus more for kneading
    the dough
1/4 teaspoon salt
2 large eggs, beaten
1/2 teaspoon grated lemon or orange zest
Vegetable oil for frying
1 cup honey
Possible garnishes: multicolored sprinkles, chopped
    candied orange peel, citron or cherries, toasted
    sliced almonds

1 In a large bowl, combine 1 cup flour and the salt. Add the eggs and lemon zest and stir until well blended.

2 Turn the dough out onto a lightly floured board and knead until smooth, about 5 minutes. Add a little more flour if the dough seems sticky. Shape the dough into a ball. Cover the dough with an overturned bowl. Let the dough rest 30 minutes.

3 Cut the dough into 1/2-inch-thick slices. Roll one slice between your palms into a 1/2-inch-thick rope. Cut the rope into 1/2-inch nuggets. If the dough feels sticky, use a tiny bit of flour to dust the board or your hands. (Excess flour will cause the oil to foam up when you fry the struffoli.)

4 Line a tray with paper towels. Pour about 2 inches of oil into a wide heavy saucepan. Heat the oil to 370°F on a frying thermometer, or until a small bit of the dough dropped into the oil sizzles and turns brown in 1 minute.

5 Being careful not to splash the oil, slip just enough struffoli into the pan to fit without crowding. Cook, stirring once or twice with a slotted spoon, until the struffoli are crisp and evenly golden brown, 1 to 2 minutes. Remove the struffoli with a slotted spoon or skimmer and drain on paper towels. Repeat with the remaining dough.

6 When all of the struffoli are fried, gently heat the honey just to a simmer in a large shallow saucepan. Remove from the heat. Add the drained struffoli and toss well. Pile the struffoli onto a serving plate. Decorate with the multicolored sprinkles, candied fruits, or nuts.

7 To serve, break off a portion of the struffoli with two large spoons or a salad server. Store covered with an overturned bowl at room temperature up to 3 days.

Feast Day Puffs
Zeppole

MAKES 8 SERVINGS

Zeppole are the fried dough puffs that are commonly seen at street fairs in Italian neighborhoods—and devoured quickly, right out of the paper bag, usually with the confectioner's sugar coating settling onto clothes and shoes.

In my home, zeppole were a frequent treat. On Sunday nights, we ate them hot with a special sprinkling of cinnamon sugar. They are also good dipped in warm honey.

This recipe is from my friend Donatella Arpaia, whose family comes from Naples and Apulia. Donatella is an excellent cook and the owner of the New York restaurant Bellini. She sometimes serves these with hot chocolate sauce.

1 teaspoon active dry yeast or instant yeast
2 teaspoons sugar
3/4 cup warm water (100° to 110°F)
1 1/2 cups all-purpose flour
1 teaspoon salt
Vegetable oil for frying
Confectioner's sugar

1 In a small bowl, sprinkle the yeast and sugar over the water. Let stand until creamy, about 2 minutes. Stir until the yeast dissolves.

2 In a large mixing bowl, combine the flour and salt. Add the yeast mixture and stir until well blended. Cover with plastic wrap. Let rise in a warm place for 1 1/2 hours.

3 In a deep heavy saucepan, pour enough oil to reach a depth of 2 inches, or if using an electric deep-fryer, follow the manufacturer's directions.

(continues)

Heat the oil to 370°F on a frying thermometer, or until a drop of the dough slipped into the oil sizzles and browns in 1 minute. Have ready a tray lined with paper towels.

4 Scoop up a rounded tablespoon of the dough. Use a second spoon to slip the dough off the spoon into the oil. Do not crowd the pan. Cook the zeppole until golden brown and puffed, about 3 minutes.

5 Remove the zeppole with a slotted spoon or skimmer and drain on paper towels. Fry the remainder in the same way. Dust generously with confectioner's sugar. Serve hot.

Ricotta Fritters
Frittelle

MAKES 4 TO 6 SERVINGS

For an elegant dessert, pile these on serving plates, surround them with strawberry sauce, and sprinkle them with confectioner's sugar.

2 large eggs
2 tablespoons sugar
I teaspoon pure vanilla extract
I cup (8 ounces) whole or part-skim ricotta
¹/₂ teaspoon grated orange or lemon zest
¹/₂ cup all-purpose flour
2 teaspoons baking powder
Pinch of salt
Vegetable oil for deep frying
Confectioner's sugar

I In a large bowl, whisk the eggs, sugar, and vanilla until frothy. Beat in the ricotta and citrus zest.

2 Combine the flour, baking powder, and salt. Stir the mixture into the ricotta.

3 In a deep heavy saucepan, pour enough oil to reach a depth of 2 inches, or if using an electric deep-fryer, follow the manufacturer's directions.

Heat the oil to 370°F on a frying thermometer or until a drop of the batter placed in the oil sizzles and browns in 1 minute. Have ready a tray lined with paper towels.

4 Scoop up a rounded tablespoon of the dough. Use a second spoon to slip the dough off the spoon into the oil. Do not crowd the pan. Cook the fritters until golden brown and puffed, about 3 minutes.

5 Remove the frittelle with a slotted spoon or skimmer and drain on paper towels. Fry the remainder in the same way. Dust generously with confectioner's sugar. Serve hot.

Bow Ties
Chiacchiere, Frittelle, Wandi, or Cenci

MAKES ABOUT 3 DOZEN

The various Italian names I have given for these fried pastry strips are an indication of how popular they are and how readily they cross regional lines. Southern Italians call them chiacchiere, *meaning "gossip," because the trail of confectioner's sugar the pastries leave behind tells the tale of what you have been eating.* Frittelle *is another southern Italian name for a small fried thing.* Wandi, *according to Nancy Verde Barr, author of* We Called It Macaroni, *is a corruption of* guanti, *meaning "gloves." It is a term used mostly by Italian-Americans from Rhode Island, originally, it is said, because the strips of dough wave like fingers as they fry.* Cenci *is the pastry's Tuscan name. Just as the names are different, the recipes for bow ties vary slightly from one region to another.*

Originally made from strips of leftover pasta dough, these pastries are traditionally eaten during Carnevale. They may be looped and knotted into bows, as indicated here, shaped into bow ties, or left as strips. Either olive or vegetable oil can be used for frying them.

2 large eggs
I tablespoon sugar
I teaspoon olive oil
I teaspoon pure vanilla extract
About 2 cups all-purpose flour
Vegetable or olive oil for deep frying
Confectioner's sugar

1 In a large bowl, beat the eggs, sugar, olive oil, and vanilla until well blended.

2 Gradually add 2 cups flour, stirring until the mixture is smooth and forms a soft dough. If the dough is sticky, add an additional spoonful of flour.

3 Shape the dough into a ball and cut it in half. Keep one half covered while working with the other.

4 On a lightly floured surface, roll out the dough to a 1/8-inch thickness. With a fluted pastry wheel, cut the dough into 6 × 1–inch strips. Tie each strip into a loose knot. Place the knots on a tray or baking sheet. Repeat with the remaining dough.

5 In a deep heavy saucepan, pour enough oil to reach a depth of 2 inches, or if using an electric deep-fryer, follow the manufacturer's directions. Heat the oil to 370°F on a frying thermometer, or until a bit of the dough placed in the oil sizzles and browns in 1 minute. Have ready a tray lined with paper towels.

6 Add as many of the dough pieces to the pan as will fit without crowding. Cook, turning once, until golden brown, about 3 minutes.

7 Remove the bows with a slotted spoon or skimmer and drain on paper towels. Fry the remainder in the same way. Dust generously with confectioner's sugar. These are best when eaten soon after they are made.

Honey Pinwheels
Cartellate

MAKES 32

Dora Marzovilla, whose family owns I Trulli Restaurant in New York City, makes these pretty, crisp pastry flowers. Dora uses a pasta machine to flatten the dough into long strips. Once they are fried, she drizzles the pinwheels with either home-made fig syrup or warm honey.

About 2 cups flour
1/2 teaspoon salt
1/2 cup water
2 tablespoons extra-virgin olive oil
Vegetable oil for deep frying
2 cups honey

1 Oil 2 large baking sheets. In a large electric mixer bowl, combine 2 cups flour and the salt. Stir in the water and olive oil until a soft dough forms. Turn the dough out onto a lightly floured surface and knead until smooth, about 4 minutes. Shape the dough into a ball. Wrap it in plastic and let it rest at room temperature 1 hour.

2 Divide the dough into four pieces. Keeping the other pieces covered with an overturned bowl, flatten one piece of dough slightly. Dust it with flour and pass it through a pasta machine set at the widest opening. Continue to stretch the dough, passing it through the pasta machine on a higher setting and flouring it each time.

3 When the dough reaches the highest setting, remove it from the machine. With a wavy-edge pastry cutter, cut it into strips 11/4 inches wide and 10 inches long.

4 Brush off any excess flour. Lightly fold each strip in half lengthwise. Do not press it down. With the wavy edge up, wind each strip into a loose, flat spiral about two inches wide. Pinch the ends to seal. Repeat with remaining dough.

(continues)

Cookies, Cakes, Tarts, and Pastries   613

5 Place the spirals on the prepared baking sheets. Let dry at room temperature 2 hours.

6 In a deep heavy saucepan, pour enough oil to reach a depth of 2 inches, or if using an electric deep-fryer, follow the manufacturer's directions. Heat the oil to 370°F on a frying thermometer, or until a drop bit of the dough placed in the oil sizzles and browns in 1 minute. Have ready a tray lined with paper towels.

7 Add as many of the spirals to the pan as will fit without crowding. Cook, turning once, until golden brown, about 3 minutes.

8 Remove the pinwheels with a slotted spoon or skimmer and drain on paper towels. Fry the remainder in the same way.

9 Heat the honey in a medium saucepan until thinned. Arrange the pinwheels in a single layer on a platter. Drizzle with the warm honey. Serve warm or at room temperature. Store at room temperature covered loosely with foil up to 2 days.

Ricotta Pockets
Cassatedde di Santa Ninfa

MAKES 24

Versions of these ricotta-filled turnovers are made all over southern Italy. This recipe was given to me by a food writer friend, Marie Bianco, who learned how to make cassatedde *from a friend of hers who lives in the Sicilian town of Santa Ninfa. There the pastries are made with goat's milk ricotta rather than the cow's milk variety, and they are fried in dark green oil pressed from luscious Sicilian olives.*

These are at their best when they are freshly fried and still warm, but they do reheat well in a 325°F oven. The recipe makes a lot, so plan to make them for a crowd.

2¹/₂ cups all-purpose flour
¹/₂ cup (1 stick) butter, melted and cooled
1 large egg, plus 1 egg yolk, lightly beaten
¹/₂ cup sweet or dry Marsala

FILLING

1¹/₂ pounds whole or part-skim ricotta, drained overnight (page 577)
¹/₂ cup sugar
2 ounces semisweet chocolate, finely chopped
1 teaspoon grated lemon zest
2 tablespoons butter, melted and cooled
Olive oil for frying
About 1 cup sugar

1 Place the flour in a large mixing bowl. Add the butter and stir until it is absorbed. Gradually stir in the eggs and Marsala to form a soft dough. Turn the dough out on a countertop and knead until smooth, about 10 minutes. The dough should be stiff. If it is too dry, work in 1 to 2 tablespoons of water. Wrap the dough in plastic and refrigerate 30 minutes up to overnight.

2 Pass the ricotta through a fine-mesh strainer or blend it in a food processor until smooth. Stir in the sugar, chocolate, and lemon zest.

3 Cut the dough into quarters. Keep the remaining pieces covered with an inverted bowl while you work. On a lightly floured surface, roll out one piece into a 12 × 12–inch square. Brush with 1 tablespoon of the butter. Tightly roll up the dough into a 12-inch rope. Cut the rope crosswise into 12 pieces. Place the pieces on a plate. Cover and refrigerate while you prepare the remaining dough in the same way. You should have 48 pieces of dough.

4 Have ready a small bowl of cold water. Dip both cut sides of one piece of dough lightly in flour. Roll out the piece into a 5- to 6-inch circle. Place about 2 tablespoons of the ricotta filling to one side of the circle. Dip a finger in the water and lightly moisten the edge. Fold in half and seal by pressing the edge firmly with your fingertips. Repeat with the remaining dough and filling.

5 In a deep heavy saucepan, pour enough oil to reach a depth of 2 inches, or if using an electric deep-fryer, follow the manufacturer's directions. Heat the oil to 370°F on a frying thermometer, or until a drop of the batter placed in the oil sizzles and browns in 1 minute.

6 Add as much of the dough pieces to the pan as will fit without crowding. Cook, turning once, until golden brown, about 3 minutes.

7 Remove the pastries with a slotted spoon or skimmer and drain on paper towels. Fry the remainder in the same way.

8 While still warm, roll the turnovers in granulated sugar. Serve warm or at room temperature.

Crisp Ricotta Pastries
Sfogliatelle

MAKES 12

Neapolitans are as proud of these crisp pastries as Sicilians are of cannoli. For sfogliatelle, layers of thin pastry are baked around an unusual ricotta filling flavored with orange and cinnamon. They are shaped like a clam, and the technique for making them is a little tricky, so read the recipe thoroughly and be sure you understand it before beginning. These pastries are at their best served warm.

DOUGH

3 cups unbleached all-purpose flour
I teaspoon salt
¼ cup solid vegetable shortening, at room temperature
¼ cup (½ stick) unsalted butter, at room temperature
I tablespoon honey
About ⅔ cup water

FILLING

I cup water
¼ cup sugar
¼ cup fine semolina or cream of wheat cereal
I cup whole or part-skim ricotta
I teaspoon grated orange zest
¼ teaspoon ground cinnamon
I large egg, beaten
I teaspoon pure vanilla extract
¼ cup very finely chopped candied citron or orange peel

ASSEMBLY

½ cup solid vegetable shortening
¼ cup (½ stick) unsalted butter
Confectioner's sugar

I In a large bowl with an electric mixer, combine the flour and the salt. Add the shortening and butter and mix on low speed until the mixture resembles coarse crumbs. With the machine running, add the honey and about ½ cup of the water. Add more water a spoonful at a time until the dough begins to come together and form a ball. On a lightly floured surface, knead the dough 1 minute or until smooth. Flatten the dough into a disk and wrap it in plastic. Refrigerate 1 hour up to overnight.

2 Prepare the filling: In a medium saucepan, stir together the water, sugar, and semolina. Cook over medium heat, stirring constantly, until the mixture comes to a simmer. Cook until the mixture is thick, about 2 minutes. Remove from the heat. Stir in the ricotta, zest, and cinnamon. Add the egg and vanilla. Mix in the citron or orange peel. Cover and refrigerate 1 hour up to 24 hours.

3 To shape the sfogliatelle, melt the remaining ½ cup of shortening and ¼ cup of butter together. Divide the dough into 4 pieces. Place one piece on a lightly floured surface. Keep the remaining dough covered with an overturned bowl while you work. With a rolling pin, roll the dough out into a rectangle, at least 24 inches long by 6 inches wide. Set the strip of dough aside while you roll out the remaining pieces in the same way.

4 Lightly brush one strip of dough with the melted shortening and butter. Place a second strip on top and repeat the brushing. Stack and brush the remaining pieces in the same way.

5 Beginning at one of the narrow ends, tightly roll up the stack of dough into a log. Wrap in plastic wrap and refrigerate at least 1 hour or until firm. Cover the remaining shortening mixture and refrigerate until ready to proceed.

(continues)

6 Preheat the oven to 400°F. Cover two large baking sheets with foil.

7 Trim the ends of the rolled up dough to make them even. Cut the dough crosswise into twelve ¹/₂-inch slices. Place one slice cut-side down on a lightly floured surface. Center a rolling pin on the slice and roll first to the left, then to the right to flatten the dough into an oval shape about 6-inches long. Place about two tablespoons of the filling to one side of the center. Fold the other half of the dough over and press it lightly around the edges to seal. Place the sfogliatelle on a prepared baking sheet. Continue making the remaining sfogliatelle in the same way.

8 In a small saucepan, melt the reserved shortening mixture. Brush the mixture over the pastries. Bake 15 minutes. Brush again with the shortening. Bake another 10 minutes, and brush again with the shortening. Bake 10 to 15 minutes more or until the pastries are golden and crisp.

9 Transfer the sfogliatelle onto a rack to cool slightly. Sprinkle with confectioner's sugar. Serve warm or at room temperature.

Cannoli

MAKES 16

At one time, cooks used lengths of cane or broom handles to make the molds to shape cannoli pastry shells. Now, inexpensive metal cannoli tubes are available at kitchenware shops, generally in sets of four. You can reuse them, but it is easier if you have at least eight to work with. Making the dough with a pasta machine ensures that the pastry shells will be thin and crisp.

1 recipe Chocolate or Vanilla Cannoli Cream (page 608)

Shells

2 cups all-purpose flour
1 tablespoon sugar
1 teaspoon unsweetened cocoa powder
¹/₂ teaspoon ground cinnamon
¹/₂ teaspoon salt
3 tablespoons vegetable oil
1 tablespoon white wine vinegar
¹/₄ cup Marsala or dry white wine
1 egg white, beaten

Vegetable oil for frying
¹/₄ cup chopped pistachios or candied cherries, for garnish
Confectioner's sugar

1 Prepare the cream, if necessary.

2 Prepare the shells: In the large bowl of an electric mixer, combine the flour, sugar, cocoa, cinnamon, and salt. Stir in the oil, vinegar, and enough of the wine to make a soft dough. Turn the dough out onto a lightly floured surface and knead until smooth and well blended, about 2 minutes. Shape the dough into a ball. Cover with plastic wrap and let rest at room temperature at least 30 minutes.

3 Cut the dough into four pieces. Keep the remaining dough covered while you work. Starting at the middle setting, run one of the pieces of dough through the rollers of a pasta machine. Lightly dust the dough with flour as needed to keep it from sticking. Pass the dough through the machine repeatedly, until you reach the highest or second-highest setting. The dough should be about 4 inches wide and thin enough to see your hand through. (The dough can be rolled on a board with a rolling pin, but be sure to roll it very thin.) Cut the strip of dough into pieces about 1 inch shorter than your cannoli tubes.

4 Continue rolling out the remaining dough. If you do not have enough cannoli tubes for all of the dough, lay the pieces of dough on sheets of plastic wrap and keep them covered until you are ready to use them.

5 Oil the outside of the cannoli tubes. Place a cannoli tube crosswise from corner to corner on top of one piece of dough. Fold the two remaining corners of the dough around the tube, being careful not to stretch or pull it. Dab a little egg white on the dough where the edges overlap. (Avoid getting egg white on the tube, or the pastry will stick to it.) Press to seal. Set aside.

6 In a deep heavy saucepan, pour enough oil to reach a depth of 2 inches, or if using an electric deep-fryer, follow the manufacturer's directions. Heat the oil to 370°F on a frying thermometer, or until a small piece of the dough placed in the oil sizzles and browns in 1 minute. Have ready a tray lined with paper towels.

7 Carefully lower a few of the cannoli tubes into the hot oil. Do not crowd the pan. Fry the shells until golden, about 2 minutes, turning them so that they brown evenly.

8 With tongs grasp a cannoli tube at one end. Very carefully remove the cannoli tube with the open sides straight up and down so that the oil flows back into the pan. Place the tube on paper towels to drain. Repeat with the remaining tubes. While they are still hot, grasp the tubes with a potholder and pull the cannoli shells off the tubes with a pair of tongs, or with your hand protected by an oven mitt or towel. Let the shells cool completely on the paper towels.

9 Repeat making and frying the shells with the remaining dough. If you are reusing the cannoli tubes, let them cool before wrapping them in the dough.

10 To assemble the cannoli: Fill a pastry bag fitted with a 1/2-inch plain tip, or a heavy-duty plastic storage bag, with the ricotta cream. If using a plastic bag, cut about 1/2 inch off one corner. Insert the tip in the cannoli shell and squeeze gently until the shell is half filled. Turn the shell and fill the other side.

11 Sprinkle the ends with pistachios, or press a candied cherry into the cream. Serve within 3 hours.

Italian Wines

Italian wines are recognized as some of the world's finest and are widely available in the United States. I have always found that they are the best complement to Italian food.

Choosing wine need not be complicated. The best way to discover wines that you like is to find a wine store with a large selection and a knowledgeable staff. Tell the staff what you plan to eat and ask for recommendations.

Probably the most important thing you can to do is keep a notebook, recording the wines you have tried, what you served them with, and how you liked them. It is all too easy to forget the name of a wine, no matter how much you liked it. Telling the sales clerk you want the red wine with the green label may or may not be helpful the next time you want to buy a bottle. Many high-quality stores keep computerized records of customers' purchases, and for this service they are worth patronizing.

Generally speaking, light- to medium-bodied wines go well with lighter foods, and richer, heavier dishes are complemented by more complex and more flavorful wines. White wines are usually the best choice with fish, while red wines go with meats. Dry wines are typically a better choice with savory foods, while sweet wines are best for dessert. But there are exceptions to these guidelines, so don't hesitate to experiment if you are so inclined. Your personal taste should be the deciding factor and is really all that matters.

The temperature of the wine is important. Icy cold can mask a white wine's flavor, while too high a temperature may make reds seem heavy and dull. White wine should be chilled to about 45°F, while reds are best at cool room temperature, about 65°F. Dessert wines that are not sparkling are usually drunk at about the same temperature as red wines, or slightly chilled, while both sweet and dry sparkling wines should be served cold, at about 45°F.

Many of the recipes in this book call for dry red or white wine. Wine that is dry is not sweet, though it may have pleasant floral or fruit flavors, depending on the type of grapes used and how they are vinified. Dry wines are often sold as table wines, because they are meant to accompany meals, as opposed to sweet or dessert wines, which are served after a meal.

Wine is often drunk with meals in Italian homes, and it is a simple matter to use some of the same wine for cooking. Wines are made in every region of Italy, and most Italians prefer to drink wines from their region on a day-to-day basis. While I would not use my finest aged wines for cooking, because their flavors may be too delicate—and because they may be very expensive—neither would I use a wine that I do not enjoy drinking. Any of the light- to medium-bodied table wines listed here would be ideal for cooking and drinking. Medium- to full-bodied wines are more flavorful and can be used in spicier, heartier preparations.

Marsala, a dark brownish red wine with a rich, nutlike flavor, is often used in cooking. Both dry and sweet varieties are available. Typically, sweet Marsala is used for desserts and dry for savory dishes, though I have sometimes substituted one for the other without any problem.

Below are some of the Italian wines that I enjoy from some of the country's most reliable producers. I have categorized these wines according to their body, or weight. Keep in mind that each producer has his or her own style and that many will have several styles of the same wine. Regional differences, vintage (the year the wine was made), and age will influence the wine too.

Sparkling Wines
SERVE AT 45°F.

Serve dry sparkling wines before a meal with appetizers or throughout the meal. They should be served chilled.

Name	Region	Producer
Prosecco	Veneto	Nino Franco, Aneri, Capene Malvolti
Spumante	Trentino, Lombardy	Ferrari, Bellavista, Berlucchi, Ca' del Bosco

White Wines
SERVE AT 45°F.

Light- to Medium-Bodied White Wines

Serve these wines as aperitifs instead of cocktails, or with delicate dishes such as scallops and other seafood and white fish.

Name	Region	Producer
Albana di Romagna	Emilia-Romagna	Fattoria Paradiso, Uberto Cesari Tre Monti
Arneis	Piedmont	Vietti, Bruno Giacosa, Ceretto
Frascati	Lazio	Fontana Candida, Villa Simone, Castel de Paolis
Orvieto	Umbria	Tenuta Le Velette, Bigi
Pinot Bianco	Trentino–Alto Adige	De Tarczal, Peter Zimmer, Josef Brigl
Pinot Grigio	Friuli–Venezia Giulia	Livio Felluga, Schiopetto, Vincentini Orgnani
Verdicchio	Le Marche	Gioacchino Garofoli, Filli Bucci, Fazi Battaglia

(continues)

Medium- to Full-Bodied White Wines

Serve these wines with fish in rich butter or cream sauces, pasta with fish or vegetables, and goat cheeses.

Name	Region	Producer
Fiano di Avellino	Campania	Mastroberardino, Terra Dora di Paola, Cantina Caputo
Gavi	Piedmont	La Scolca, Banfi, La Zerba
Greco di Tufo	Campania	Feudi di San Gregorio, Mastroberardino, Cantina Caputo
Sauvignon Blanc	Friuli–Venezia Giulia	Ascevi, St. Michael–Eppan, Puiatti Alto Adige
Soave	Veneto	Pieropan, Guerreri Rizzardi, Inama
Tocai	Friuli–Venezia Giulia	Mario Schiopetto, Ronco di Tassi, Venica & Venica
Trebbiano	Abruzzo	Edoardo Valentini, Dino Illuminati, Gianni Masciarelli
Vermentino	Sardinia	Tenuta Sella & Mosca, Cantina di Dolianova, Antonio Argiolas
Vernaccia	Tuscany	Teruzzi & Puthod, Famiglia Cecchi

Red Wines
SERVE AT 65°F.

Light- to Medium-Bodied Red Wines

Serve these with chicken, veal, grilled beef, and some dark meaty fish like tuna or swordfish.

Name	Region	Producer
Barbera	Piedmont	Vietti, Carlo Benotto, Cascina Castlet
Bardolino	Veneto	Bolla
Chianti	Tuscany	Monsanto, Vitticio, Ruffino, Travignoli, Antinori, Buondonno
Dolcetto	Piedmont	Vietti, Poderi Marcarini, Renato Ratti
Rubesco	Umbria	Lungarotti
Valpolicella	Veneto	Allegrini, Masi, Bertani

Medium- to Full-Bodied Red Wines

These go well with stews and roasts, game, pork, and lamb.

Name	Region	Producer
Aglianico del Vulture	Basilicata	Paternoster, D'Angelo, Sasso
Amarone	Veneto	Tommasi, Masi, Allegrini

Name	Region	Producer
Barbaresco	Piedmont	Pio Cesare, Produttori del Barbaresco, Marchesi di Gresy
Barolo	Piedmont	Vietti, Borgogno, Poderi Marcarini, Giuseppe Mascarello & Figlio
Brunello	Tuscany	Castello Banfi, Castelgiocondo, Mastrojanni, Poggio Antico
Carmignano	Tuscany	Capezzano, Fattoria Ambra, Artimino
Colle Picchioni	Lazio	Paola di Mauro, Vigna del Vassallo
Merlot	Umbria, Sicily, Tuscany	Castello delle Regine, Planeta, Avignonesi
Montepulciano d'Abruzzo	Abruzzo	Edoardo Valentini, Dino Illuminati, Bruno Nicodemi, Tenuta Cataldi Madonna
Nero d'Avola	Sicily	Morgante, Planeta, Benanti
Primitivo di Manduria	Puglia	Savese, Coppi, Cantina Sociale Locorotondo
Salice Salentino	Puglia	Agricole Vallone, Cosimo Taurino, Conti Zecca
Sagrantino	Umbria	Terre di Trinci, Rocco di Fabbri, Antonelli–San Marco
Sangiovese	Umbria, Tuscany, Emilia-Romagna	Castello delle Regine, Carobbio, Fattoria Paradiso
Taurasi	Campania	Mastroberardino, Feudi di San Gregorio, Terredora di Paolo
Vino Nobile di Montepulciano	Tuscany	Avignonesi, Salcheto, Poliziano, Tenuta Il Faggeto

Dessert Wines

Sparkling Dessert Wines

These are low in alcohol and should be served well chilled, about 45°F.
Serve with fruit, creamy desserts, or pastry.

Name	Region	Producer
Asti Spumante	Piedmont	Fontanafredda, Contratto, Cinzano
Moscato d'Asti	Piedmont	Vietti, Cascina Castlet, Santo Stefano

Rich Dessert Wines

Serve with biscotti, plain fruit and nut cakes, with cheese, or as dessert by themselves. Serve at 65°F.

Name	Region	Producer
Marsala	Sicily	Florio, Rallo, De Bartoli
Picolit	Friuli–Venezia Giulia	Livio Felluga, Furlan, Dorigo
Vin Santo	Tuscany, Umbria	Antinori, Lungarotti, Travignoli, Avignonesi

Glossary

alla pizzaiola: anything cooked with tomatoes, garlic, and oregano

amaretti: crisp Italian macaroons made with bitter almond

amaretto: almond-flavored liqueur

arancini: fried rice balls with meat or other filling

Arborio: a variety of medium-grain rice from Piedmont used for making risotto

baccalà: salted cod

balsamico or balsamic vinegar: Italian vinegar made from cooked trebbiano grape must; the best labelled *tradizionale* and aged many years in barrels made with various types of wood

biscotti: literally "twice cooked," though it refers to all kinds of cookies

bistecca fiorentina: thick-cut grilled porterhouse steak prepared in the Florentine style

bollito misto: mixed boiled meats served with various sauces, a specialty of northern Italy

bottarga: preserved roe of tuna or mullet that is either pressed and sealed in wax or dried and sold ground or in flakes; the best being pressed bottarga from Sardinia

braciola: thin slice of meat, usually stuffed, rolled, and cooked in tomato sauce

branzino: sea bass

brodo: broth

bruschetta: grilled or toasted bread rubbed with garlic and brushed with olive oil or topped with tomato salad

caciocavallo: Sicilian cow's milk cheese similar to provolone

calzone: literally "big sock"; pizza dough folded around a filling and baked or fried

capers: the tiny unopened buds of the caper flower, a wild plant that grows all over the Mediterranean, typically sold in salt or in vinegar

caprino: Italian goat cheese

Carnaroli: a medium-grain rice preferred by many cooks for making risotto

carpaccio: thin slices of raw veal or beef, served cold with a pink sauce; also, by association, thin slices of vegetables and fresh or smoked fish, served cold with a dressing

cassata: Sicilian cake layered with ricotta cream

crespelle: crepes

cotechino: a large, preserved sausage, often served with lentils or mashed potatoes

crostata: a sweet or savory tart

crostini: toasted bread topped with cheese, vegetables, pâté, etc., usually served as an appetizer

diavolicchi, also known as **diavolilli:** literally "little devils"; tiny dried hot chilies

dolci di cucchiaio: desserts such as custards, puddings, etc., that are eaten with a spoon

enoteca: a bar or store with a large selection of wines

fagioli secchi: dried beans

fagiolini: green beans

farro: an ancient grain similar to wheat, spelt, and emmer, eaten whole in salads or soups or ground into flour

fennel pollen: ground dried fennel used to season pork and other meats in Tuscany

fettuccine: narrow ribbons of fresh or dried egg pasta

fettuccine di frittata: "noodles" made from cooked eggs

finocchiona: Tuscan salame flavored with fennel seeds

focaccia: flatbread seasoned with olive oil and salt; can also be baked with herbs, olives, onions, tomatoes, etc.

Fontina Valle d'Aosta: creamy, semifirm cow's milk cheese that melts beautifully; good for cooking and eating

forno: oven

fragoline del bosco: tiny Alpine strawberries

freselle: hard black pepper-flavored biscuits to soak and serve as a base for stews or salad

frittata: flat omelet

fruttivendolo: produce vendor

giardiniera: mixed pickled vegetables often sold in jars

gorgonzola: blue-veined cheese from Lombardy used for cooking and eating

gnocchi: dumplings eaten with a sauce or in broth, most often made with potatoes, but also with bread, squash, or other ingredients

grana: a crumbly cheese suitable for grating

granita di caffè: coffee ice dessert

Grana Padano: a type of cow's milk grana cheese

grappa: spirits made from distilled grape seeds, skins, and pulp left after the juice has been pressed out for wine

grissini: breadsticks

involtini: small stuffed meat rolls

lenticchie di Castelluccio: tiny, flavorful lentils from Umbria

luganega: long, thin, fresh sausages

manicotti: baked crepes or pasta tubes with a cheese filling

mascarpone: creamy, soft, and mild cheese from Lombardy used for pasta and desserts

minestra: soup

montasio : cow's milk cheese from Friuli–Venezia Giulia, mild when young and sharp when aged

mortadella : large cured pork sausage made with finely ground spiced meat

mostarda: fruits preserved in mustard syrup

mosto cotto: grape juice cooked to form a thick dark syrup, used to flavor desserts

mozzarella: semifirm cheese from Campania made with either cow's milk or water-buffalo's milk

Nutella: a popular jarred chocolate hazelnut spread, which is the equivalent of peanut butter for Italian children

orata: gilt head bream

orzo: barley in Italy, though a small, seed-shaped pasta in the United States

orzotto: barley cooked like risotto

osteria: an informal Italian restaurant

ovoli: a type of wild mushroom

pancetta: unsmoked Italian bacon made from pork belly seasoned with salt, pepper, and sometimes spices, tightly rolled and cured in salt

pan di Spagna: sponge cake

pane a cassetta: sliced white bread

panettone: a yeast risen cake with dried fruits originally from Milan, but now eaten all over Italy especially at Christmas

paninoteca: an informal restaurant that features sandwiches

panino: either a round roll or a sandwich made on such a roll

panna cotta: literally "cooked cream"; gelled heavy cream usually served with a fruit or chocolate sauce

Parmigiano-Reggiano: a partially skimmed cow's milk cheese made exclusively around the cities of Reggio-Emilia and Parma, aged about 18 months, used for both cooking and eating

pasta: literally "paste"; it can refer to any type of dough or foods made from dough, including noodles, dumplings, and pastries

pasta frolla: pastry dough

pasticceria: pastry shop

pecorino: any cheese made from sheep's milk, typically from Tuscany, Umbria, or southern Italy, excellent for eating when young and semifirm; used for grating when older.

Pecorino Romano: firm aged sheep's milk cheese made around Rome and in Sardinia

peperoncino: any type of small fresh or dried chile

pesce azzurro: any type of dark-fleshed fish

pesto: any type of sauce made with mashed ingredients; basil pesto is the best known

piadina: a flatbread from Emilia-Romagna

pizza bianca: pizza dough baked with olive oil, cheese, or other toppings, but no tomatoes

pizza dolce: cake or sweet bread

pizzelle: lacy wafer cookie

polenta: white or yellow corn meal mush, served soft like mashed potatoes or sliced, then grilled or fried

porchetta: whole roast pig cooked with herbs and garlic

porcini: meaty wild mushrooms

prosciutto: cured unsmoked Italian ham

provolone: piquant firm cow's milk cheese originally from Sicily

puntarella: pale green and white shoots of Catalan chicory, a favorite Roman salad green in springtime, served with anchovy and garlic dressing

ragù: meat sauce for pasta

rana pescatrice: monkfish

rapini: one of several names for broccoli rabe

ribollita: Tuscan bread and vegetable soup

ricotta: soft fresh cheese made from sheep's or cow's milk, used for pasta and desserts

risotto: rice cooked and stirred with broth and flavorings until creamy

risotto al salto: crisp risotto pancake

robiola: a soft fresh cheese from Piedmont usually made from cow's milk, though sometimes blended with sheep's or goat's milk

rollatini: small stuffed meat rolls, usually cooked in a sauce

rughetta: Italian arugula

salame: ground meat cured with salt and spices shaped like a sausage

salsa balsamella: white sauce made from milk, flour, and butter

salsicce: sausages

salumi: collective name for salame, prosciutto, mortadella, and other cured meats

scaloppine: a small, thin slice of meat. A cutlet

seppia: cuttlefish

sfinciuni: Sicilian onion and anchovy thick-crust pizza

sfogliatelle: Neapolitan pastry filled with ricotta, semolina, and orange zest

soffritto: a flavoring base, usually made with onions, celery, peppers, and meat sautéed in oil

sopressata: a type of salame

spiedini: anything cooked on a skewer

stoccofisso: dried salt cod

tagliarini: very thin fresh egg pasta ribbons

tagliatelle: fresh pasta ribbons similar to fettuccine

taleggio: an aromatic, flavorful soft cow's milk cheese from Lombardy

taralli: round sweet or savory biscuits from southern Italy

tonno: tuna fish

torrone: either nougat or hard caramel candy made with nuts or sesame seeds

torta: a sweet or savory layered cake or other dessert

tramezzino: thin Roman sandwich made on white bread with crusts removed

trota: trout

tartufi: truffles, black or white varieties of a mushroom family, rare and very expensive, that grow underground near tree roots, especially in Piedmont and Umbria, and are located for harvesting by specially trained dogs

ventresca di tonno: tuna belly preserved in olive oil

Vialone Nano: a variety of medium-grain rice used for making risotto

vongole: small hard-shell clams

zabaglione: whipped egg custard flavored with sugar and wine, served as a dessert or sauce

zampone: sausage stuffed pig's foot

zeppole: yeast raised donuts

zucca: squash

zuppa: soup

Sources

For cheeses, salumi, fresh and dried pasta, anchovies, capers, olive oil, vinegars, preserves, dried mushrooms and tomatoes, canned tomatoes and tuna, herbs and spices, flour, polenta, farro, rice, beans, nuts, dried and candied fruits, amaretti, and wine, try the following suppliers.

A. G. Ferrari
various California locations
www.agferrari.com
Oil, vinegar, pasta, and tomatoes

Agata & Valentina
1505 First Avenue
New York, NY 10021
212-452-0690
Fresh produce, cheese, and pasta

Buon Italia
75 Ninth Avenue
New York, NY 10011
212-633-9090
www.buonitalia.com
Canned tomatoes, tuna, oil, salumi, and pasta

Citarella
various New York locations
212-874-0383
www.citarella.com
Fresh meat and fish, produce, oil, vinegar, and honey

Coluccio's
1214 60th Street
Brooklyn, New York 11219
718-436-6700
Southern Italian specialties including pasta, cheese, salumi, olives, oil, and tuna

Convito Italiano
1515 Sheridan Road
Wilmette, IL 60091
847-251-3654
www.convitoitaliano.com
Cheese, polenta, prosciutto, and other salumi

Corti Brothers
5810 Folsom Boulevard
Sacramento, CA 95819-4693
800-509-3663
Oil, vinegar, wine, and pasta

Dean & Deluca
various locations in the United States and Japan
www.deandeluca.com
Cheese, groceries, and selected kitchen equipment

(continues)

De Palo Fine Foods
200 Grand Street
New York, NY 10013
212-226-1033
Balsamic vinegar, cheese, and salumi

www.Gustiamo.com
online Italian food store
Canned tuna, panettone, and olive oil

Formaggio Kitchen
244 Huron Avenue
Cambridge, MA 02138
617-354-3224
www.formaggiokitchen.com
Extensive selection of cheeses

Kalustyan's
123 Lexington Avenue
New York, NY 10016
212-685-3451
www.kalustyans.com
Global foods, especially spices, grains, candied
fruit, nuts, specialty flours, and beans

King Arthur Flour Baker's Catalogue
PO Box 876
Norwich, VT 05055
800-827-6836
www.bakerscatalogue.com
Grains, flour, and baking supplies

Manicaretti Italian Food Imports
5332 College Avenue
Oakland, CA 94618
800-799-9830
www.manicaretti.com
Farro and other grains, dried mushrooms, and
artisan pasta

The Mozzarella Company
2944 Elm Street
Dallas, TX 75226
800-798-2954
www.mozzco.com
Fresh mozzarella and other cheeses

Todaro Brothers
557 Second Avenue
New York, NY 10016
877-472-2767
www.todarobros.com
Cheese, pasta, rice, salumi, and olives

Vino
Italian Wines and Spirits
121 East 27 Street
New York, NY 10016
212-725-6516
www.vinosite.com
Italian wine, grappa, and spirits, and wine books

Zingerman's
422 Detroit Street
Ann Arbor, MI 48104
888-636-8162
www.zingermans.com
Cheese, pasta, and other groceries

Bibliography

The following are some of my favorite cookbooks.

Artusi, Pellegrino. *La Scienza in Cucina e l'Arte di Mangiar Bene*. Milan: Einaudi Editore, 1991.

Boni, Ada. *Italian Regional Cooking*. New York: Bonanza Books, 1969.

Castello, Antonio. *Sapori e Piaceri d'Italia*. Rome: Editrice Sallustiana, 1996.

Cavalcanti, Ottavio. *Il Libro d'Oro della Cucina e dei Vini di Calabria e Basilicata*. Milan: Mursia Editore, 1979.

Della Salda, Anna Gosetti. *Le Ricette Regionali Italiane*. Milan: Casa Editrice Solares, 1980.

Di Leo, Maria Adele. *La Cucina Siciliana*. Rome: Newton & Compton Editori, 1998.

Dolcino, Esther and Michelangelo. *Le Ricette Liguri per Tutte le Occasioni*. Genoa: Nuova Editrice Genovese, 1990.

Francesconi, Jeanne Carola. *La Cucina Napoletana*. Rome: Newton Compton Editori, 1992.

Lanza, Anna Tasca. *The Heart of Sicily*. New York: Clarkson Potter, 1993.

———. *The Flavors of Sicily*. Danbury, Conn.: Ici La Press, 2001.

Parenti, Giovanni Righi. *La Grande Cucina Toscana*, volumes I and II. Milan: SugarCo, 1986.

Pradelli, Alessandro Molinari. *La Cucina Piemontese*. Rome: Newton & Compton Editori, 1996.

———. *La Cucina Sarda*. Rome: Newton & Compton Editori, l997.

Ricette di Osterie d'Italia. Bra, Italy: Slow Food Editore, 2001.

Ristoranti Trattorie e Cose Buone d'Italia. Milan: Editoriale Giorgio Mondadori, S.P.A., 1997.

Sada, Luigi. *La Cucina Pugliese*. Rome: Newton Compton Editori, 1994.

Schwartz, Arthur. *Naples at Table*. New York: HarperCollins, 1998.

Serra, Anna e Piero. *La Cucina della Campania*. Naples: Franco di Mauro Editore, s.r.l., 1983.

Simeti, Mary Taylor. *Pomp and Sustenance: Twenty-Five Centuries of Sicilian Food*. New York: Knopf, 1989.

Valli, Emilia. *La Cucina Friulana*. Padua: Franco Muzzio, 1992.

Index

About the Author

Michele Scicolone is a writer and teacher. After her first visit to Italy in 1970, she became passionate about the country and its people: their customs, history, food, and wine. Since then, she has spent a portion of each year in Italy with her husband, Charles Scicolone, an authority on Italian wine, travelling and learning, tasks made possible by the generosity and enthusiasm of the Italian people.

Michele is the author of ten cookbooks, including *The Sopranos Family Cookbook*, coauthored with Allen Rucker; *Pizza: Anyway You Slice It!*, coauthored with Charles Scicolone; *Italian Holiday Cooking; Savoring Italy; A Fresh Taste of Italy; La Dolce Vita;* and *The Antipasto Table*. Several have been nominated by the James Beard Foundation and the International Association of Culinary Professionals for awards for best cookbook in their categories.

Michele's articles have appeared in *Wine Spectator, Gourmet, Family Circle, Food & Wine, Prevention, Simply Perfect Italian* (Better Homes & Gardens Family Food Collection), the *Washington Post, New York Times, Los Angeles Times,* and many other publications. She teaches cooking at schools around the United States. She has been a guest on numerous national and local television and radio shows. Michele has been a spokesperson for the Italian Trade Commission and has lectured on Italian culture and cuisine at the Smithsonian Institution, Hofstra University, and Henderson State University.

An active member of many food and wine professional organizations, Michele has served on the boards of the New York Women's Culinary Alliance, Les Dames d'Escoffier, the National Organization of Italian American Women, and the New York Association of Cooking Teachers.

She and her husband, who is wine and beverage director for New York's I Trulli restaurant and Enoteca and Vino, an Italian wine and spirits store, live in New York City, where they enjoy sharing great Italian meals and wines with friends.